Course	Intermediate Accounting Ninth Edition Volume 1
ourse Number	**with Connect**
	VIRGINIA TECH
	ACIS 3115

http://create.mheducation.com

ISBN-10: 1309090440 ISBN-13: 9781309090442

Contents

Credits

Online Supplements

About the Authors

DAVID SPICELAND

David Spiceland is professor of accounting at the University of Memphis, where he teaches intermediate accounting and other financial accounting courses at the undergraduate and master's levels. He received his BS degree in finance from the University of Tennessee, his MBA from Southern Illinois University, and his PhD in accounting from the University of Arkansas.

Professor Spiceland's primary research interests are in earnings management and educational research. He has published articles in a variety of journals, including *The Accounting Review, Accounting and Business Research, Journal of Financial Research,* and *Journal of Accounting Education,* and is an author of McGraw-Hill's *Financial Accounting* with Wayne Thomas and Don Herrmann. Professor Spiceland has received university and college awards and recognition for his teaching, research, and technological innovations in the classroom.

MARK NELSON

Mark Nelson is the Anne and Elmer Lindseth Dean and Professor of Accounting at Cornell University's S. C. Johnson Graduate School of Management. He received his BBA degree from Iowa State University and his MA and PhD degrees from The Ohio State University. Professor Nelson has won ten teaching awards, including an inaugural Cook Prize from the American Accounting Association.

Professor Nelson's research focuses on decision making in financial accounting and auditing. His research has been published in the *Accounting Review;* the *Journal of Accounting Research; Contemporary Accounting Research; Accounting, Organizations and Society;* and several other journals. He has received the American Accounting Association's Notable Contribution to Accounting Literature Award, as well as the AAA's Wildman Medal for work judged to make a significant contribution to practice.

Professor Nelson served three terms as an area editor of *The Accounting Review* and is a member of the editorial boards of several journals. He also served for four years on the FASB's Financial Accounting Standards Advisory Council.

WAYNE THOMAS

Wayne Thomas is the John T. Steed Chair and Professor of Accounting at the University of Oklahoma's Price College of Business. He received his BS degree from Southwestern Oklahoma State University and his MS and PhD from Oklahoma State University. He has received teaching awards at the university, college, and departmental levels, and has received the Outstanding Educator Award from the Oklahoma Society of CPAs. He is an author of McGraw-Hill's *Financial Accounting* with David Spiceland and Don Herrmann.

His research focuses on various financial reporting issues and has been published in *The Accounting Review, Journal of Accounting Research, Journal of Accounting and Economics, Contemporary Accounting Research, Review of Accounting Studies, Accounting Organizations and Society,* and others. He has served as an editor for *The Accounting Review* and has won the American Accounting Association's Competitive Manuscript Award and Outstanding International Accounting Dissertation.

Professor Thomas enjoys various activities such as tennis, basketball, golf, and crossword puzzles, and most of all, he enjoys spending time with his wife and kids.

Intermediate Accounting Ninth Edition:

Welcome to the fastest-growing learning program in intermediate accounting! Instructors recognize the "Spiceland advantage" in content that's intensive and thorough, as well as in writing that's fluid and precise—together, these combine to form a resource that's rigorous yet readable. By blending a comprehensive approach, clear conversational tone, current updates on key standards, and the market-leading technological innovations of Connect®, the Spiceland team delivers an unrivaled experience. As a result of Spiceland's rigorous yet readable learning system, students develop a deeper and more complete understanding of intermediate accounting topics.

> "The chapters are well written in a style that makes difficult materials approachable for students."
>
> **—Kathy Hsiao Yu Hsu, *University of Louisiana–Lafayette***

The *Intermediate Accounting* learning system is built around four key attributes: current, comprehensive, clear, and Connect®

Current: Few disciplines see the rapid changes that accounting experiences. The Spiceland team is committed to keeping instructors' courses up to date. The ninth edition fully integrates the latest FASB updates, including:

- **NEW** Chapter 15, covering the latest standard on leases (ASU No. 2016–02, Leases (Topic 842)).
- ASU No. 2016–01, Financial Instruments—Overall (Subtopic 825–10): Recognition and Measurement of Financial Assets and Financial Liabilities
- ASU No. 2016–013, Financial Instruments—Credit Losses (Topic 326) on "Current Expected Credit Loss" (CECL) model for accounting for credit losses, as well as current GAAP requirements for recognizing impairments of investments.
- ASU No. 2015–17, Income Taxes (Topic 740): Balance Sheet Classification of Deferred Taxes
- ASU No. 2015–03, Interest—Imputation of Interest (Subtopic 835–30)
- ASU No. 2016–10, Revenue from Contracts with Customers: Identifying Performance Obligations and Licensing (Topic 606)
- ASU No. 2016–09, Improvements to Employee Share-Based Payment Accounting, which amends ASC Topic 718, Compensation—Stock Compensation.

Current events regularly focus public attention on the key role of accounting in providing information useful to financial decision makers. The CPA exam, too, has changed to emphasize the professional skills needed to critically evaluate accounting method alternatives. *Intermediate Accounting* provides a **decision makers' perspective,** highlighting the professional judgment and critical thinking skills required of accountants in today's business environment.

> "The *Spiceland Intermediate Accounting* provides a truly up to date view of financial reporting. The authors explain complex topics in a very relevant, engaging, easy to follow approach for students with excellent examples and illustrations."
>
> **— Celina Jozsi, *Florida Southern University***

Comprehensive: The Spiceland team ensures comprehensive coverage and quality throughout the learning system by building content and assets with a unified methodology that meets rigorous standards. Students are challenged through diverse examples and carefully crafted problem sets which promote in-depth understanding and drive development of critical-thinking skills.

The author team is committed to providing a learning experience that fully prepares students for the future by solidifying core comprehension and enabling confident application of key concepts. Students can feel confident that the conceptual underpinnings and practical skills conveyed in the ninth edition will prepare them for a wide range of real world scenarios.

Rigorous yet readable

Clear: Reviewers, instructors, and students have all hailed *Intermediate Accounting's* ability to explain both simple and complex topics in language that is coherent and approachable. The author team's highly acclaimed conversational writing style establishes a friendly dialogue—establishing the impression of a conversation with students, as opposed to lecturing at them.

This tone remains consistent throughout the learning system, as authors Spiceland, Nelson, and Thomas write not only the primary content, but also every major supplement: study guide, instructor's resource manual, solutions manual, and test bank. All end-of-chapter material, too, is written by the author team and tested in their classrooms. *Intermediate Accounting* is written to be the most complete, coherent, and student-oriented resource on the market.

"This textbook is written in a way that is easy to read, provides clear examples, includes thorough coverage of necessary topics, and provides ample opportunity for practice and mastery of the material through end of chapter problems."

—Terra Brown, *University of Texas–Arlington*

Connect: Today's accounting students expect to learn in multiple modalities. As a result, the ninth edition of Spiceland's learning system features the following: Connect, SmartBook's adaptive learning and reading experience, **NEW** Concept Overview Videos, Guided Examples, **NEW** Excel® simulations, and General Ledger problems.

Quality assessment continues to be a focus of Connect, with over **2,500 questions** available for assignment, including more than 1,125 algorithmic questions.

McGraw-Hill Education is continually updating and improving our digital resources. To that end, we have a new partnership with Roger CPA, providing multiple choice practice questions directly within our Connect banks, as well as links to the Roger CPA site for complementary selected simulations.

"Connect is a great resource for any course, but the new updates to the General Ledger and Excel Simulations allow this package to go above and beyond; students will exit the intermediate series with a strong foundation in Excel and the accounting cycle."

—Joshua Neil, *University of Colorado–Boulder*

Spiceland's Financial Accounting Series

Intermediate Accounting forms a complete learning system when paired with *Financial Accounting* by authors David Spiceland, Wayne Thomas, and Don Herrmann. Now in its fourth edition, *Financial Accounting* uses the same proven approach that has made *Intermediate Accounting* a success—a conversational writing style with real-world focus and author-prepared supplements, combined with Connect's market leading technology solutions and assessment.

"If you like Spiceland's intermediate text, you will be thrilled with the financial accounting text. It is written in the same conversational style, addresses topics directly and clearly, and the illustrations are terrific too."

—Nancy Snow, *University of Toledo*

What Keeps SPICELAND Users Coming Back?

Where We're Headed

These boxes describe the potential financial reporting effects of many of the FASB and IASB joint projects intended to further align U.S. GAAP and IFRS, as well as other projects the Boards are pursuing separately. Where We're Headed boxes allow instructors to deal with ongoing projects to the extent they desire.

Where We're Headed 

In 2004, the FASB and IASB began working together on a project, Financial Statement Presentation, to establish a common standard for presenting information in the financial statements, including classifying and displaying line items and aggregating line items into subtotals and totals. This project could have a dramatic impact on the format of financial statements. An important part of the proposal involves the organization of elements of the balance sheet (statement of financial position), statement of comprehensive income (including the inc classifications.

Progress was concentrate on FASB's agenda. all of the financi FASB issued an

"Where We're Headed boxes allow the students to be updated with the most current accounting changes without inundating them with needless technical specifications. A perfect balance!"

—Cheryl Bartlett, *Indiana University—South Bend*

Financial Reporting Cases

Each chapter opens with a Financial Reporting Case that places the student in the role of the decision maker, engaging the student in an interesting situation related to the accounting issues to come. Then, the cases pose questions for the student in the role of decision maker. Marginal notations throughout the chapter point out locations where each question is addressed. The case questions are answered at the end of the chapter.

Financial Reporting Case Solution

© goodluz/123RF

1. **What purpose do adjusting entries serve?** *(p. 63)* Adjusting entries help ensure that all revenues are recognized in the period goods or services are transferred to customers, regardless of when cash is received. In this instance, for example, $13,000 cash has been received for services that haven't yet been performed. Also, adjusting entries enable a company to recognize all expenses incurred during a period, regardless of when cash is paid. Without depreciation, the friends' cost of using the equipment is not taken into account. Conversely, without adjustment, the cost of rent is overstated by $3,000 paid in advance for part of next year's rent.

With adjustments, we get an accrual measure of a company's operating perfo operating cash flows. Similarly, the bal of assets and liabilities as sources of fut

"The case at the beginning of each chapter is very captivating. After I read the case, I wanted to get paper and pencil and answer the questions."

—Carol Shaver, *Louisiana Tech University*

Decision Makers' Perspective

These sections appear throughout the text to illustrate how accounting information is put to work in today's firms. With the CPA exam placing greater focus on application of skills in realistic work settings, these discussions help your students gain an edge that will remain with them as they enter the workplace.

Decision Makers' Perspective

Cash often is referred to as a *nonearning* asset because it earns no interest. For this reason, managers invest idle cash in either cash equivalents or short-term investments, both of which provide a return. Management's goal is to hold the minimum amount of cash necessary to conduct normal business operations, meet its obligations, and take advantage of opportunities. Too much cash reduces profits through lost returns, while too little cash increases risk. This trade-off between risk and return is an ongoing choice made by management (internal decision makers). Whether the choice m by investors and creditors (external decis

A company must have cash available previous section as well as for planned di and financing cash flows. However, becau amounts, a company needs an additional events. The size of the cushion depends o

"This is an excellent feature of the book. It is so important to know why and how information is used and not just memorizing the 'right' answers."

—Jeff Mankin, *Lipscomb University*

In talking with so many intermediate accounting faculty, we heard more than how to improve the book—there was much, much more that both users and nonusers insisted we not change. Here are some of the features that have made Spiceland such a phenomenal success in its previous editions.

Additional Consideration

Discounts in Contracts with Multiple Performance Obligations. Note that Illustration 5–7 shows that Tri-Box systems are sold at a discount—TrueTech sells the system for a transaction price ($250) that's less than the $300 sum of the stand-alone selling prices of the Tri-Box module ($240) and the subscription to Tri-Net ($60). Because there is no evidence that the discount relates to only one of the performance obligations, it is spread between them in the allocation process. If TrueTech had clear evidence from sales of those goods and services that the discount related to only one of them, the entire discount would be allocated to that good or service.

"This is a good technique that I actually use in my class and it's good to see it in a book!"

—Ramesh Narasimhan, *Montclair State University*

Ethical Dilemma 

You recently have been employed by a large retail chain that sells sporting goods. One of your tasks is to help prepare periodic financial statements for external distribution. The chain's largest creditor, National Savings & Loan, requires quarterly financial statements, and you are currently working on the statements for the three-month period ending June 30, 2018.

During the months of May an
TV advertising campaign. The $
as well as the radio and TV time
charged to advertising expense
to prepare a June 30 adjusting
set up an asset called *prepaid a*
that "This advertising campaign
will continue to bring in custome
an asset, we can match the cost
we expense the advertising in M

"Having ethical dilemma boxes in every chapter is much more significant than having a separate chapter devoted to ethics. Students can relate to the importance of being ethical in every aspect of business dealings."

—Gloria Worthy, *Southwest Tennessee Community College*

Broaden Your Perspective

Apply your critical-thinking ability to the knowledge you've gained. These cases will provide you an opportunity to develop your research, analysis, judgment, and communication skills. You also will work with other students, integrate what you've learned, apply it in real-world situations, and consider its global and ethical ramifications. This practice will broaden your knowledge and further develop your decision-making abilities.

Judgment Case 4–1
Earnings quality
● LO4–2, LO4–3

The financial community in the United States has become increasingly concerned with the quality of reported company earnings.

Required:
1. Define the term
2. Explain the dis

"I think students would benefit tremendously from the cases."

—Joyce Njoroge, *Drake University*

Additional Consideration Boxes

These are "on the spot" considerations of important, but incidental or infrequent, aspects of the primary topics to which they relate. Their parenthetical nature, highlighted by enclosure in Additional Consideration boxes, helps maintain an appropriate level of rigor of topic coverage without sacrificing clarity of explanation.

Ethical Dilemmas

Because ethical ramifications of business decisions impact so many individuals as well as the core of our economy, Ethical Dilemmas are incorporated within the context of accounting issues as they are discussed. These features lend themselves very well to impromptu class discussions and debates.

Broaden Your Perspective Cases

Finish each chapter with these powerful and effective cases, a great way to reinforce and expand concepts learned in the chapter.

Star Problems 

In each chapter, particularly challenging problems, designated by a ★, require students to combine multiple concepts or require significant use of judgment.

Required=Results

McGraw-Hill Connect®
Learn Without Limits

Connect is a teaching and learning platform that is proven to deliver better results for students and instructors.

Connect empowers students by continually adapting to deliver precisely what they need, when they need it, and how they need it, so your class time is more engaging and effective.

Connect's Impact on Retention Rates, Pass Rates, and Average Exam Scores

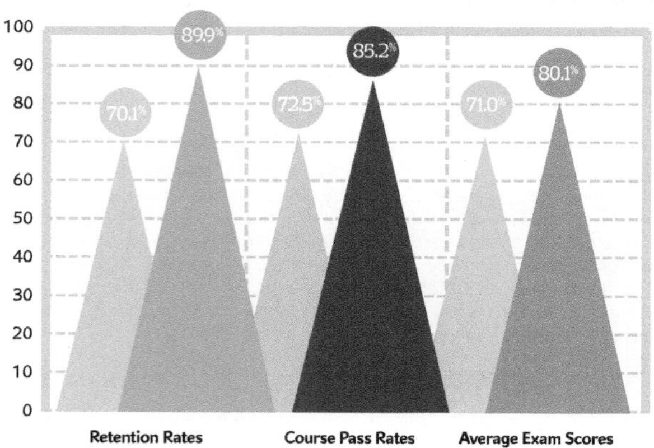

without Connect
with Connect

Using **Connect** improves retention rates by **19.8%**, passing rates by **12.7%**, and exam scores by **9.1%**.

73% of instructors who use **Connect** require it; instructor satisfaction **increases** by 28% when **Connect** is required.

Analytics

Connect Insight®

Connect Insight is Connect's new one-of-a-kind visual analytics dashboard that provides at-a-glance information regarding student performance, which is immediately actionable. By presenting assignment, assessment, and topical performance results together with a time metric that is easily visible for aggregate or individual results, Connect Insight gives the user the ability to take a just-in-time approach to teaching and learning, which was never before available. Connect Insight presents data that helps instructors improve class performance in a way that is efficient and effective.

Impact on Final Course Grade Distribution

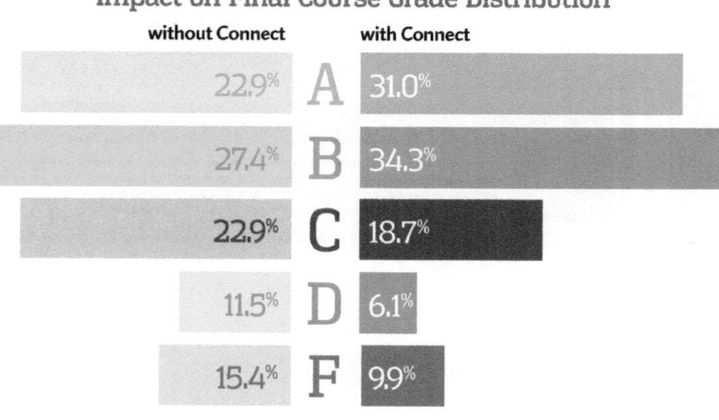

ONLINE ASSIGNMENTS

Connect helps students learn more efficiently by providing feedback and practice material when they need it, where they need it. Connect grades homework automatically and gives immediate feedback on any questions students may have missed. The extensive assignable, gradable end-of-chapter content includes a general journal application that looks and feels more like what you would find in a general ledger software package. Also, select questions have been redesigned to test students' knowledge more fully. They now include tables for students to work through rather than requiring that all calculations be done offline.

End-of-chapter questions in Connect include:

- Brief Exercises
- Exercises
- Problems

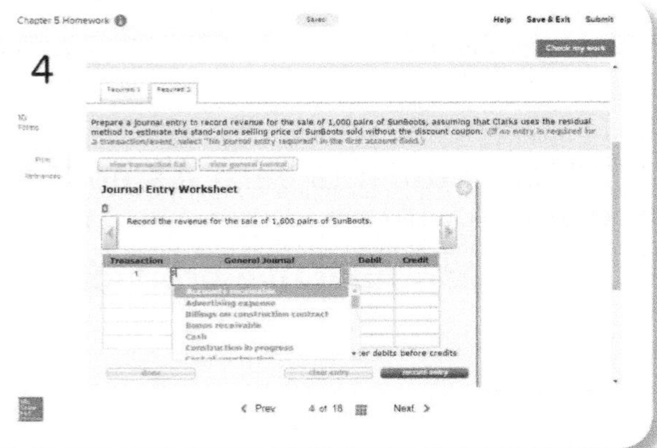

> "The textbook's General Ledger, Concept Overview Videos, and Excel Simulations are outstanding."
>
> **—Professor Kaye Sheridan, *Troy University***

NEW! GENERAL LEDGER PROBLEMS

New **General Ledger Problems** provide a much-improved student experience when working with accounting cycle questions, offering improved navigation and less scrolling. Students can audit their mistakes by easily linking back to their original entries and can see how the numbers flow through the various financial statements. Many General Ledger Problems include an analysis tab that allows students to demonstrate their critical thinking skills and a deeper understanding of accounting concepts.

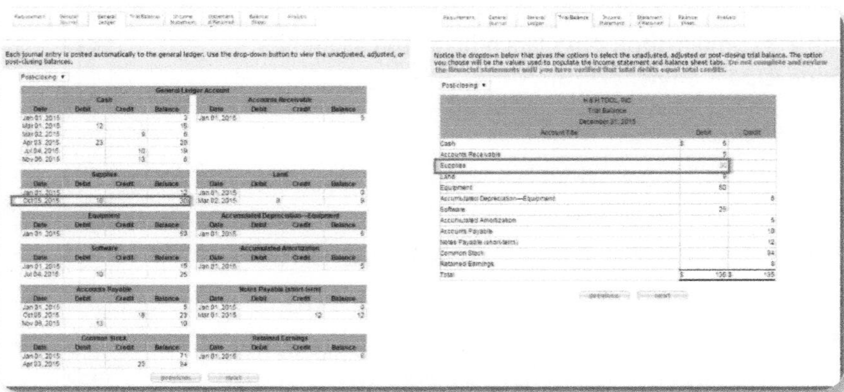

NEW! CONCEPT OVERVIEW VIDEOS

The **Concept Overview Videos** provide engaging narratives of key topics in an assignable and interactive online format. They follow the structure of the text and are organized to match the specific learning objectives within each chapter of *Intermediate Accounting*. The Concept Overview Videos provide additional explanation and enhancement of material from the text chapter, allowing students to learn, study, and practice with instant feedback, at their own pace.

NEW! EXCEL SIMULATIONS

Simulated Excel Questions, assignable within Connect, allow students to practice their Excel skills—such as basic formulas and formatting—within the content of financial accounting. These questions feature animated, narrated Help and Show Me tutorials (when enabled), as well as automatic feedback and grading for both students and professors.

GUIDED EXAMPLES

The **Guided Examples** in Connect provide a narrated, animated, step-by-step walk-through of select exercises similar to those assigned. These short presentations can be turned on or off by instructors and provide reinforcement when students need it most.

"As a student I need to interact with course material in order to retain it, and **Connect** offers a perfect platform for this kind of learning. Rather than just reading through textbooks, **Connect** has given me the tools to feel engaged in the learning process."

—Jennah Epstein Kraus, student, *Bunker Hill Community College*

CPA SIMULATIONS

McGraw-Hill Education has partnered with Roger CPA Review, a global leader in CPA Exam preparation, to provide students a smooth transition from the accounting classroom to successful completion of the CPA Exam. While many aspiring accountants wait until they have completed their academic studies to begin preparing for the CPA Exam, research shows that those who become familiar with exam content earlier in the process have a stronger chance of successfully passing the CPA Exam. Accordingly, students using these McGraw-Hill materials will have access to sample CPA Exam Multiple-Choice questions and Task-based Simulations from Roger CPA Review, with expert-written explanations and solutions. All questions are either directly from the AICPA or are modeled on AICPA questions that appear in the exam. Task-based Simulations are delivered via the Roger CPA Review platform, which mirrors the look, feel and functionality of the actual exam. McGraw-Hill Education and Roger CPA Review are dedicated to supporting every accounting student along their journey, ultimately helping them achieve career success in the accounting profession. For more information about the full Roger CPA Review program, exam requirements and exam content, visit www.rogercpareview.com.

> "*Intermediate Accounting* is current, complete, well written, and highly detailed. It belongs in the library of anyone who is preparing for the CPA exam."
>
> **—Barbara K. Parks, *American Intercontinental University—Online***

Other Student Supplements

Study Guide

Volume 1: ISBN-13: 9781260030259 (MHID: 1260030253)

Volume 2: ISBN-13: 9781260030266 (MHID: 1260030261)

The Study Guide, written by the text authors, provides chapter summaries, detailed illustrations, and a wide variety of self-study questions, exercises, and multiple-choice problems (with solutions).

ALEKS®

ALEKS ACCOUNTING CYCLE

ALEKS Accounting Cycle is a web-based program that provides targeted coverage of prerequisite and introductory material necessary for student success in Intermediate Accounting. ALEKS uses artificial intelligence and adaptive questioning to assess precisely a student's preparedness and deliver personalized instruction on the exact topics the student is **most ready to learn.** Through comprehensive explanations, practice, and immediate feedback, ALEKS enables students to quickly fill individual knowledge gaps in order to build a strong foundation of critical accounting skills. Better prepared students saves you valuable time at the beginning of your course!

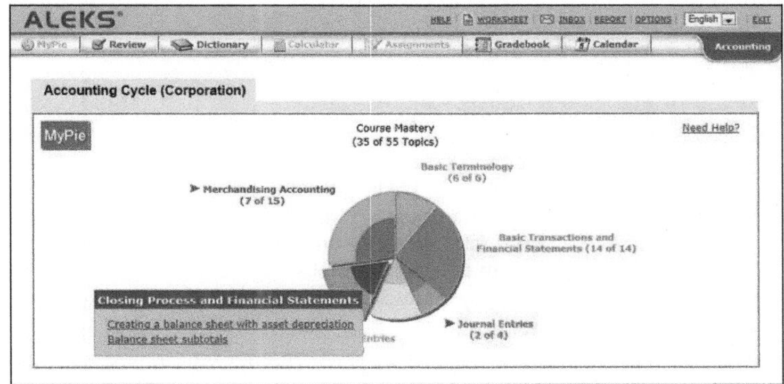

Use ALEKS Accounting Cycle as a pre-course assignment or during the first three weeks of the term to see improved student confidence and performance, as well as fewer drops.

ALEKS Accounting Cycle Features:

- **Artificial Intelligence:** Targets Gaps in Prerequisite Knowledge
- **Individualized Learning and Assessment:** Ensure Student Preparedness
- **Open-Response Environment:** Avoids Multiple-Choice and Ensures Mastery
- **Dynamic, Automated Reports:** Easily Identify Struggling Students

For more information, please visit: www.aleks.com/highered/business.

Read ALEKS Success Stories: www.aleks.com/highered/business/success_stories.

"With ALEKS, the issues that our finance majors were having with *Intermediate Accounting* have practically disappeared."

—Eric Kelley, *University of Arizona*

INSTRUCTOR LIBRARY

The Connect Instructor Library is a repository for additional resources to improve student engagement in and out of class. You can select and use any asset that enhances your lecture. The Connect Instructor Library includes:

- Presentation slides
- Animated PowerPoint® exercises
- Solutions manual
- Test bank available in Connect and TestGen
    - TestGen is a complete, state-of-the-art test generator and editing application software that allows instructors to quickly and easily select test items from McGraw Hill's test bank content. The instructors can then organize, edit, and customize questions and answers to rapidly generate tests for paper **or online administration.** Questions can include stylized text, symbols, graphics, and equations that are inserted directly into questions using built-in mathematical templates. TestGen's random generator provides the option to display different text or calculated number values each time questions are used. With both quick-and-simple test creation and flexible and robust editing tools, TestGen is a complete test generator system for today's educators.
- Instructor's resource manual
- Instructor Excel templates. Solutions to the student Excel Templates used to solve selected end-of-chapter exercises and problems. These assignments are designated by the Excel icon.

MCGRAW-HILL EDUCATION CUSTOMER EXPERIENCE GROUP CONTACT INFORMATION

At McGraw-Hill Education, we understand that getting the most from new technology can be challenging. That's why our services don't stop after you purchase our products. You can contact our Product Specialists 24 hours a day to get product training online. Or you can search the knowledge bank of Frequently Asked Questions on our support website. For Customer Support, call **800-331-5094,** or visit www.mhhe.com/support. One of our Technical Support Analysts will be able to assist you in a timely fashion.

ASSURANCE OF LEARNING READY

Many educational institutions today are focused on the notion of *assurance of learning,* an important element of some accreditation standards. *Intermediate Accounting* is designed specifically to support your assurance of learning initiatives with a simple, yet powerful solution.

Each test bank question for *Intermediate Accounting* maps to a specific chapter learning objective listed in the text. You can use Connect to easily query for learning outcomes/objectives that directly relate to the learning objectives for your course. You can then use the reporting features of Connect to aggregate student results in a similar fashion, making the collection and presentation of assurance of learning data simple and easy.

AACSB STATEMENT

AACSB INTERNATIONAL

McGraw-Hill Education is a proud corporate member of AACSB International. Understanding the importance and value of AACSB accreditation, *Intermediate Accounting* recognizes the curricula guidelines detailed in the AACSB standards for business accreditation by connecting selected questions in the test bank to the eight general knowledge and skill guidelines in the AACSB standards.

The statements contained in *Intermediate Accounting* are provided only as a guide for the users of this textbook. The AACSB leaves content coverage and assessment within the purview of individual schools, the mission of the school, and the faculty. While *Intermediate Accounting* and the teaching package make no claim of any specific AACSB qualification or evaluation, within the Test Bank to accompany *Intermediate Accounting* we have labeled selected questions according to the eight general knowledge and skill areas.

What's New in the Ninth Edition?

Revising a program as successful as *Intermediate Accounting* takes careful consideration and a strong vision for how the print and digital content work together to provide a robust learning solution. The Spiceland team only implements changes that constitute real improvements as identified through extensive research with users. The result is a program that never loses its original strengths, continuing to gain usefulness and flexibility with each revision.

Pervasive changes throughout the program include the following:

- **Updated content to reflect the latest GAAP and Accounting Standards Updates including:**
    - **Leases**
    - **Coverage of financial instruments**
    - **Revenue recognition**
- **New partnership with Roger CPA Review,** with new assignable multiple-choice CPA Exam Review questions in Connect and access to CPA simulations.
- Updated and revised all real-world illustrations, amounts, and discussions.
- **Revised** Air France–KLM IFRS case to reflect financial statements for the year ended December 31, 2015.
- Added a **new Continuing Case featuring Target Corporation** and a variety of characteristics of financial statements prepared using U.S. GAAP. A comprehensive version of the case is available in Appendix B.
- Reviewed, updated, and introduced new end-of-chapter material in each chapter to support new topics and learning objectives.
- Incorporated the latest technology, including a **new Connect interface for students,** along with **Connect Insight for students,** an updated SmartBook, and **new Connect problem formats** include **General Ledger Problems** that auto-post from journal entries to T-accounts to trial balances, **Excel Simulations,** and **Concept Overview Videos.**

Chapter 1

ENVIRONMENT AND THEORETICAL STRUCTURE OF FINANCIAL ACCOUNTING

- Changed opening case to introduce Target, and featured Target throughout the chapter.
- Added Pathways visualization "THIS is accounting!" and related discussion.
- Improved discussion of cash basis vs. accrual basis accounting.
- Enhanced description of IFRS organizational structure and convergence process.
- Added a Where We're Headed box regarding the FASB's materiality exposure draft.

Chapter 2

REVIEW OF THE ACCOUNTING PROCESS

- Replaced all CPA Exam Questions with current ones from Roger CPA Review.
- Added a Target case.
- Added an Air France case.

Chapter 3

THE BALANCE SHEET AND FINANCIAL DISCLOSURES

- Revised introduction to include reference to SEC's EDGAR filing system.
- Added reference to the accounting equation in Illustration 3–1.
- Updated discussion of assets, liabilities, and shareholders' equity to include those of Nike.
- Updated discussion of operating cycle to include distinction between merchandising and manufacturing company.
- Revised discussion of categories of long-term assets, including consideration of management intent.
- Added discussion and key term for accumulated other comprehensive income component of shareholders' equity.
- Revised discussion of auditors' report to clearly distinguish the different report types.
- Moved discussion of management compensation to be included with other management-related disclosures.

Chapter 4

THE INCOME STATEMENT, COMPREHENSIVE INCOME, AND THE STATEMENT OF CASH FLOWS

- Revised introduction to make clear the difference in reporting perspective for the balance sheet (point in time) versus the income statement and statement of cash flows (interval of time).
- Revised discussion of earnings quality, income smoothing, and classification shifting.
- Revised section on "Operating Income and Earnings Quality" to include analysis of The Hershey Company.
- Created separate section on non-GAAP earnings, discussing HP.
- Clarified discussion of what constitutes of a discontinued operation.
- Clarified discussion and added new Additional Consideration box on presentation of discontinued operations.
- Added discussion of the modified retrospective approach for accounting changes.
- Revised introduction to the discussion of earnings per share.
- Provided additional discussion of comprehensive income.
- Moved discussion of profitability analysis from chapter 5 to chapter 4, including all related end-of-chapter material.

Chapter 5

REVENUE RECOGNITION

- Added learning objective regarding differences between U.S. GAAP and IFRS, IFRS boxes that meet the objective, and related end-of-chapter material.
- Changed discussion of identifying separate performance obligations to incorporate ASU 2016–10.
- Added Additional Consideration for shipping costs to incorporate ASU 2016–10.
- Changed discussion of licenses to incorporate ASU 2016–10.
- Added IFRS box discussing differences in licensing criteria.

- Moved discussion of Profitability Analysis and related end-of-chapter material to Chapter 4 to focus Chapter 5 more tightly on revenue recognition.
- Added significant new end-of-chapter material to incorporate ASU 2016–10 and various IFRS differences.

Chapter 6

TIME VALUE OF MONEY CONCEPTS

- Replaced all CPA Exam Questions with current ones from Roger CPA Review.
- Added a Target case.
- Added an Air France case.

Chapter 7

CASH AND RECEIVABLES

- Added new opening case: Community Health Systems.
- Completely revised coverage of initial and subsequent valuation of accounts receivable, including discussions of time value of money, discounts, sales returns, accounting for bad debts, and accounting for notes receivable, to tie coverage more tightly to revenue recognition and impairment recognition criteria and practice.
- In chapter, as well as Appendix 7B, included coverage of ASU 2016–013's CECL model for accounting for credit losses, as well as current GAAP requirements for recognizing impairments of receivables.
- Revised Illustration 7–24 and related discussion of analysis of accounts receivable.
- Added or updated cases relevant to Microsoft, Nike, Avon Products, Tyson Foods, and Pilgrim's Pride Corp.

Chapter 8

INVENTORIES: MEASUREMENT

- Changed feature story to Kroger Company.
- Revised discussion of goods in transit.
- Revised discussion of accounting for transactions that affect net purchases related to freight-in, returns, and discounts, including revisions to Illustration 8–6.
- Incorporated beginning inventory into Illustration 8–7 to clarify calculation of goods available for sale and to better link to Illustrations 8–7B through 8–7H.
- Revised discussion of the LIFO reserve adjustment.
- Clarified discussion and added calculation to demonstrate dollar-value LIFO.

Chapter 9

INVENTORIES: ADDITIONAL ISSUES

- Revised section on subsequent measurement of inventory to include both lower of cost or market (LCM) and lower of cost or net realizable value (LCNRV).
- Clarified discussion of which companies are required to use LCNRV versus LCM.
- Added new end-of-chapter material for LCM – BE 9–3, BE 9–4, E 9–4, E 9–5, E 9–6, E 9–7, P 9–3, and P 9–4.

Chapter 10

PROPERTY, PLANT, AND EQUIPMENT AND INTANGIBLE ASSETS: ACQUISITION

- Moved discussion of asset dispositions and related end-of-chapter material to chapter 11.
- Moved discussion of noncash acquisitions (deferred payments, stock issuances, and donations) to Part B with nonmonetary exchanges.
- Added Illustration 10–16 to summarize effects of different types of nonmonetary exchanges.
- Provided additional discussion to clarify accounting for software development costs.
- Reorganized section on R&D to include more real-world examples and clarification of which R&D-type costs are capitalized.
- Added end-of-chapter material for fixed asset turnover (BE 10–9), software development costs (BE 10–17), various types of research and development costs (BE 10–18), and start-up costs (BE 10–19 and E 10–33).

Chapter 11

PROPERTY, PLANT, AND EQUIPMENT AND INTANGIBLE ASSETS: UTILIZATION AND DISPOSITION

- Revised discussion of the conceptual meaning of cost allocation.
- Added Illustration 11–3A and related discussion of depreciation expense versus accumulated depreciation.
- Added discussion and illustrations of asset dispositions, as well as related end-of-chapter material from chapter 10.
- Added a Decision Maker's Perspective box to explain in more detail the interpretation of gains and losses on the sale of depreciable assets.
- Modified Illustration 11–12 to include disposal of an intangible asset.
- Revised discussion of intangible assets not subject to amortization.
- Revised discussion of two-step process for goodwill impairment.
- Added a Where We're Headed box to explain the FASB's current proposal to simplify measurement of goodwill impairment.

Chapter 12

INVESTMENTS

- Reorganized Chapter to include Part A (Accounting for Debt Investments) and Part B (Accounting for Equity Investments).
- Revised coverage of debt investments, including improved treatment of trading securities and available-for-sale investments to enhance student understanding and better reflect practice and the ASC.
- Revised coverage of equity investments to incorporate ASU 2016–01 (prohibiting AFS treatment and requiring "fair value through net income" treatment of most insignificant-influence investments).
- Revised coverage of the equity method to enhance and clarify examples.
- Revised IFRS boxes for differences between IFRS and U.S. GAAP.
- In chapter, as well as Appendix 12B, included coverage of ASU 2016–013's CECL model for accounting for credit losses, as well as current GAAP requirements for recognizing impairments of investments.
- Revised end-of-chapter material to incorporate ASU 2016–013's CECL model for accounting for credit losses.

Chapter 13

CURRENT LIABILITIES AND CONTINGENCIES

- Updated General Mills example used in Illustration 13–1 and throughout the chapter.
- Added Additional Consideration box regarding escheatment laws relevant to gift cards.
- Updated contingent liability examples.
- Added new Trueblood cases.

Chapter 14

BONDS AND LONG-TERM NOTES

- Revised discussion of debt issue costs to conform with Accounting Standards Update 2015–03, *Interest—Imputation of Interest* (Subtopic 835–30).
- Added and revised end-of-chapter material pertaining to debt issue costs.

Chapter 15

LEASES

- Rewrote the entire chapter to conform to Accounting Standards Update 2016–02, *Leases* (Topic 842).
- Created a Chapter Supplement—Leases: GAAP in Effect Prior to ASU No. 2016–02.
- Developed all-new ancillaries (Connect, Test bank, Instructors' resource manual, Solutions manual, PowerPoint presentations, and videos) to conform to the new Leases standard.

Chapter 16

ACCOUNTING FOR INCOME TAXES

- Added new version of Real World "Shoe Carnival" case covering linkage between tax expense journal entry and changes in deferred tax assets, liabilities, and the valuation allowance.
- Revised coverage of balance sheet presentation of deferred tax accounts to incorporate ASU 2015–17.
- Added or modified end-of-chapter material to incorporate ASU 2015–17.

Chapter 17

PENSIONS AND OTHER POSTRETIREMENT BENEFIT PLANS

- Added a Real World Case involving Microsoft's pension plan.
- Added discussion of new FASB requirement to report service cost separate from other components of pension expense.

Chapter 18

SHAREHOLDERS' EQUITY

- Replaced all CPA Exam Questions and Simulation with current ones from Roger CPA Review.
- Revised Research Case involving Cisco's accumulated other comprehensive income in its balance sheet as a component of shareholders' equity.

Chapter 19

SHARE-BASED COMPENSATION AND EARNINGS PER SHARE

- Revised discussion and illustration of graded vesting stock options.
- Revised discussion of forfeitures of stock options and restricted stock to conform with Accounting Standards Update No. 2016–09, Compensation—Stock Compensation (Topic 718): Improvements to Employee Share-Based Payment Accounting.
- Added and revised end-of-chapter material pertaining to forfeitures of stock options and restricted stock.
- Revised discussion of tax issues related to share-based compensation to conform with Accounting Standards Update No. 2016–09—Compensation—Stock Compensation (Topic 718): Improvements to Employee Share-Based Payment Accounting.
- Revised end-of-chapter material pertaining to tax issues related to share-based compensation.

Chapter 20

ACCOUNTING CHANGES AND ERROR CORRECTIONS

- Revised discussion of approaches to account for accounting changes to include the modified retrospective approach.

Chapter 21

STATEMENT OF CASH FLOWS REVISITED

- Revised a CVS Caremark Corp illustration of presenting cash flows from operating activities by the direct method.
- Added an enhanced Additional Consideration box on reporting bad debt expense in the SCF.
- Added a Toys "R" Us illustration of presenting cash flows from operating activities by the indirect method.
- Revised a Research Case related to FedEx's investing and financing activities.
- Added a Real World Case on Staples reporting of its SCF.

Appendix A

DERIVATIVES

- Revised a Real World Case related to the Chicago Mercantile Exchange.
- Revised a Johnson & Johnson Real World Case on hedging transactions.

Acknowledgments

Intermediate Accounting is the work not just of its talented authors, but of the more than 750 faculty reviewers who shared their insights, experience, and insights with us. Our reviewers helped us to build *Intermediate Accounting* into the very best learning system available. A blend of Spiceland users and nonusers, these reviewers explained how they use texts and technology in their teaching, and many answered detailed questions about every one of Spiceland's 21 chapters. The work of improving *Intermediate Accounting* is ongoing—even now, we're scheduling new symposia and reviewers' conferences to collect even more opinions from faculty.

We would like to acknowledge and highlight the Special Reviewer role that Ilene Leopold Persoff of Long Island University (LIU Post) took on the ninth edition. Utilizing her accounting and reviewing expertise, Ilene verified the accuracy of the manuscript and promoted our efforts toward quality and consistency. Her deep subject-matter knowledge, keen eye for detail, and professional excellence in all aspects were instrumental in ensuring a current, comprehensive, and clear edition. Her contributions are deeply appreciated.

In addition, we want to recognize the valuable input of all those who helped guide our developmental decisions for the ninth edition.

Noel Addy, *Mississippi State University*
Naser Albarghouthi, *Hudson County Community College*
Elizabeth Almer, *Portland State University*
Matthew Anderson, *Michigan State University*
Ryan Anthony, *University of Washington*
Sidney Askew, *Borough of Manhattan Community College*
Lynn Bible, *Fayetteville State University*
John Borke, *University of Wisconsin, Platteville*
Salem Boumediene, *Montana State University–Billings*
Brian Bratten, *University of Kentucky, Lexington*
Alisa Brink, *Virginia Commonwealth University*
Kevin Brown, *Wright State University*
Esther Bunn, *Stephen F. Austin State University*
Linda Carrington-Duvall, *Sam Houston State University*
Mary Ellen Carter, *Boston College*
Meghann Cefaratti, *Northern Illinois University*
Kam Chan, *Pace University*
Nandini Chandar, *Rider University*
Shannon Charles, *University of Utah*
Cheryl Corke, *Genesee Community College*
Marc Cussatt, *Washington State University*
Judy Daulton, *Piedmont Technical College*
Denise De La Rosa, *Grand Valley State University*
David Deboskey, *San Diego State University–San Diego*
Marcus Doxey, *University of Alabama*
Amie Dragoo, *Edgewood College*
Barbara Durham, *University of Central Florida*
Kathryn Easterday, *Wright State University*
David Emerson, *Salisbury University*
James Emig, *Villanova University*
Denise English, *Boise State University*
Caroline Falconetti, *Nassau Community College*
Dov Fischer, *Brooklyn College*
Mitchell Franklin, *Lemoyne College*
Laurel Franzen, *Loyola Marymount University*
Lori Fuller, *West Chester University*
Gregory Gaynor, *University of Baltimore*
Hubert Glover, *Drexel University*
Sunita Goel, *Siena College*
Ying Guo, *California State University–East Bay*
Joohyung Ha, *University of San Francisco*
Lizhong Hao, *California State University–Fresno*
Don Herrmann, *Oklahoma State University*
Dana Hollie, *Louisiana State University–Baton Rouge*
Pei Hui Hsu, *California State University–East Bay*
Kathy Hsiao Yu Hsu, *University of Louisiana–Lafayette*
Xuerong Huang, *Ball State University*
Ying Huang, *University of Louisville*

Stacie Hughes, *Athens University*
Paul Hutchison, *University of North Texas*
Mark Jackson, *University of Nevada, Reno*
John Jiang, *Michigan State University*
Kevin Jones, *University of California–Santa Cruz*
Robert L. Kachur, *Richard Stockton College of New Jersey*
Julia Karcher, *University of Louisville*
Sergey Komissarov, *University of Wisconsin–La Crosse*
Lisa Kutcher, *Colorado State University*
Richard Lahijani, *Queens College*
Marco Lam, *Western Carolina University*
Melissa Larson, *Brigham Young University*
Charles Leflar, *University of Arkansas–Fayetteville*
Charles Lewis, *Houston Community College*
Shu Lin, *California State University–Fresno*
Lin Liu, *California State University–Dominguez Hills*
Ricki Livingston, *University of Connecticut*
Ming Lu, *Santa Monica College*
Mostafa Maksy, *Kutztown University of Pennsylvania*
Nancy Mangold, *California State University–East Bay*
Christina Manzo, *Queensborough Community College*
Joshua Neil, *University of Colorado–Boulder*
Kelly Noe, *Stephen F. Austin State University*
Shailendra Pandit, *University of Illinois–Chicago*
Veronica Paz, *Pennsylvania State University*
Aimee Pernsteiner, *University of Wisconsin–Eau Claire*
Mikhail Pevzner, *University of Baltimore*
Eric Press, *Temple University*
Dirk Pruis, *Calvin College*
K.K. Raman, *University of Texas–San Antonio*
K. Ramesh, *Rice University*
Arundhati Rao, *Towson University*
Barbara Reider, *University of Montana*
Douglas Smith, *Dalton State College*
Kevin Smith, *Utah Valley University*
Sheldon Smith, *Utah Valley University*
Dennis Stovall, *Grand Valley State University*
Joel Strong, *Saint Cloud State University*
C. Daniel Stubbs, *Rutgers University–Newark*
Ronald Stunda, *Valdosta State University*
Amy Sun, *University of Houston*
Jenny Teruya, *University of Hawaii–Manoa*
Paula B. Thomas, *Middle Tennessee State University*
Robin Thomas, *North Carolina State University–Raleigh*
John Trussel, *University of Tennessee–Chattanooga*
Ingrid Ulstad, *University of Wisconsin–Eau Claire*
Huishan Wan, *University of Nebraska*
Barbara White, *University of West Florida*
Jan Williams, *University of Baltimore*
Donald Wygal, *Rider University*
Yan Xiong, *California State University–Sacramento*
Jing-Wen Yang, *California State University–East Bay*
Jian Zhang, *San Jose State University*

We Are Grateful

The authors and McGraw-Hill's *Intermediate Accounting* team are deeply indebted to Jim Sepe of the Accounting Department, Leavey School of Business, Santa Clara University, for his invaluable role in the creation and development of the book from its inception through its eighth edition. Jim's passion for transforming challenging financial reporting topics into accessible and engaging presentations remains quite evident in each component of the learning system. We wish him the very best as he turns a new page in his life!

We would like to acknowledge and thank the following individuals for their contributions in developing, reviewing. and shaping the extensive ancillary package: Kim Fatten, *Capital College;* Jeannie Folk, *College of DuPage;* Burch Kealey, *University of Nebraska–Omaha;* Mark McCarthy, *East Carolina University;* Barbara Muller, *Arizona State University;* Helen Roybark, *Radford University;* Kevin Smith, *Utah Valley University;* Emily Vera, *University of Colorado–Denver;* Beth Woods of Accuracy Counts; and Teri Zuccaro, *Clarke University,* who contributed new content and accuracy checks of Connect and LearnSmart. We greatly appreciate everyone's hard work on these products!

We are most grateful for the talented assistance and support from the many people at McGraw-Hill Education. We would particularly like to thank Tim Vertovec, managing director; Natalie King, marketing director; Rebecca Olson, executive brand manager; Rebecca Mann, senior product developer; Randall Edwards, product developer; Zach Rudin, marketing manager; Peggy Hussey, director of digital content; Xin Lin, digital product analyst; Daryl Horrocks, program manager; Pat Frederickson, lead content project manager; Angela Norris, senior content project manager; Laura Fuller, buyer; Matt Diamond, senior designer; and Melissa Homer and Lori Slattery, content licensing specialists.

Finally, we extend our thanks to Roger CPA Review for their assistance developing simulations for inclusion in the end-of-chapter material, as well as Target and Air France–KLM for allowing us to use their Annual Reports throughout the text. We also acknowledge permission from the AICPA to adapt material from the Uniform CPA Examination, and the IMA for permission to adapt material from the CMA Examination.

David Spiceland *Mark Nelson* *Wayne Thomas*

The Role of Accounting as an Information System

CHAPTER

1 Environment and Theoretical Structure of Financial Accounting

OVERVIEW

The primary function of financial accounting is to provide useful financial information to users who are external to the business enterprise, particularly investors and creditors. These users make critical resource allocation decisions that affect the global economy. The primary means of conveying financial information to external users is through financial statements and related notes.

In this chapter you explore such important topics as the reason why financial accounting is useful, the process by which accounting standards are produced, and the conceptual framework that underlies financial accounting. The perspective you gain in this chapter serves as a foundation for more detailed study of financial accounting.

LEARNING OBJECTIVES

After studying this chapter, you should be able to:

- **LO1–1** Describe the function and primary focus of financial accounting. *(p. 3)*
- **LO1–2** Explain the difference between cash and accrual accounting. *(p. 7)*
- **LO1–3** Define generally accepted accounting principles (GAAP) and discuss the historical development of accounting standards, including convergence between U.S. and international standards. *(p. 9)*
- **LO1–4** Explain why establishing accounting standards is characterized as a political process. *(p. 13)*
- **LO1–5** Explain factors that encourage high-quality financial reporting. *(p. 15)*
- **LO1–6** Explain the purpose of the conceptual framework. *(p. 19)*
- **LO1–7** Identify the objective and qualitative characteristics of financial reporting information and the elements of financial statements. *(p. 21)*
- **LO1–8** Describe the four basic assumptions underlying GAAP. *(p. 24)*
- **LO1–9** Describe the recognition, measurement, and disclosure concepts that guide accounting practice. *(p. 26)*
- **LO1–10** Contrast a revenue/expense approach and an asset/liability approach to accounting standard setting. *(p. 33)*
- **LO1–11** Discuss the primary differences between U.S. GAAP and IFRS with respect to the development of accounting standards and the conceptual framework underlying accounting standards. *(p. 14* and *20)*

© Lev Dolgachov/Syda Productions/age fotostock

FINANCIAL REPORTING CASE

Misguided Marketing Major

During a class break in your investments class, a marketing major tells the following story to you and some friends:

The chief financial officer (CFO) of a large company is interviewing three candidates for the top accounting position with his firm. He asks each the same question:

CFO:	What is two plus two?
First candidate:	Four.
CFO:	What is two plus two?
Second candidate:	Four.
CFO:	What is two plus two?
Third candidate:	What would you like it to be?
CFO:	You're hired.

After you take some good-natured ribbing from the non-accounting majors, your friend says, "Seriously, though, there must be ways the accounting profession prevents that kind of behavior. Aren't there some laws, or rules, or something? Is accounting based on some sort of theory, or is it just arbitrary?"

By the time you finish this chapter, you should be able to respond appropriately to the questions posed in this case. Compare your response to the solution provided at the end of the chapter.

QUESTIONS

1. What should you tell your friend about the presence of accounting standards in the United States and the rest of the world? Who has the authority for standard setting? Who has the responsibility? (*p. 8*)
2. What is the economic and political environment in which standard setting occurs? (*p. 13*)
3. What is the relationship among management, auditors, investors, and creditors that tends to preclude the "What would you like it to be?" attitude? (*p. 15*)
4. In general, what is the conceptual framework that underlies accounting principles? (*p. 20*)

Financial Accounting Environment

PART A

● LO1–1

In 1902, George Dayton took ownership of the Dayton Dry Goods Company, the fourth largest department store in Minneapolis, Minnesota. Successive generations of Daytons were innovative managers, flying in inventory to prevent shortages (1920), committing to giving five percent of profits back to the community (1946), and creating the nation's first enclosed shopping mall (1956). In 1962, George's grandchildren transformed Dayton's, by then a regional department store chain, into the Target Corporation, promising "a quality store with quality merchandise at discount prices".[1] Today Target has grown to be the second largest general merchandise retailer in America, with over 1,800 stores, almost 350,000 employees, and www.target.com reaching the online market. However, Target still stands by its "Expect More, Pay Less" motto, and still donates five percent of profits back to the community (giving more than $4 million per week, mostly in support of education).

[1]"Target Through the Years" at https://corporate.target.com/about/history/Target-through-the-years.

Many factors contributed to Target's success. The Daytons were visionary in their move into the upscale discount retail market. The company's commitment to quality products, customer service, and community support also played an important role. But the ability to raise money from investors and lenders at various times also was critical to Target's evolution. Target used proceeds from its 1967 initial public stock offering to expand nationally. Creditors (lenders) also supplied needed capital at various times. In fact, without access to capital, the Target Corporation we know today likely would not exist.

Investors and creditors use many different kinds of information before supplying capital to businesses like Target. They use the information to predict the future risk and potential return of their prospective investments or loans.[2] For example, information about the enterprise's products and its management is key to this assessment. Investors and creditors also rely on various kinds of accounting information.

Think of accounting as a special "language" that companies like Target use to communicate financial information to help people inside and outside of the business to make decisions. The Pathways Commission of the American Accounting Association developed an illustration to help visualize this important role of accounting.[3] As shown in Illustration 1-1, accounting provides useful information about economic activity to help produce good decisions and foster a prosperous society. Economic activity is complex, and decisions have real consequences, so critical thinking and many judgments are needed to produce the most useful accounting information possible.

The primary focus of *financial accounting* is on the information needs of investors and creditors.

This book focuses on **financial accounting**, which is chiefly concerned with providing financial information to various *external* users.[4] The chart in Illustration 1–2 lists a number of groups that provide financial information as well as several external user groups.

Illustration 1–1

Pathways Commission visualization: "THIS is accounting!"

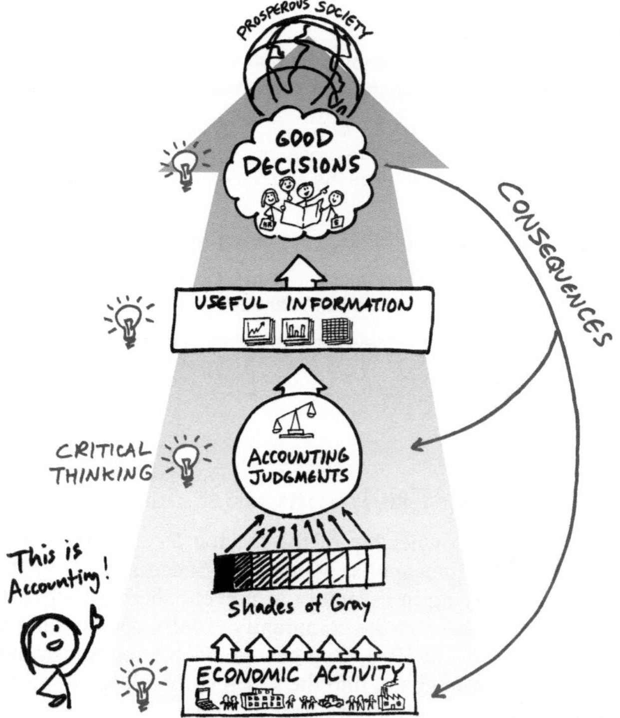

[2]Risk refers to the variability of possible outcomes from an investment. Return is the amount received over and above the investment.

[3]Reprinted with permission from the American Accounting Association. This work is by The Pathways Commission and is licensed under a Creative Commons Attribution-NoDerivs 3.0 Unported License.

[4]In contrast, *managerial* accounting deals with the concepts and methods used to provide information to an organization's *internal users,* that is, its managers. You study managerial accounting elsewhere in your curriculum.

PROVIDERS OF FINANCIAL INFORMATION		USERS OF FINANCIAL INFORMATION
• Profit-oriented companies • Not-for-profit entities (e.g., government entities, charitable organizations, schools) • Households	→	• Investors • Creditors (banks, bondholders, other lenders) • Employees • Labor unions • Customers • Suppliers • Government regulatory agencies (e.g., Internal Revenue Service, Securities and Exchange Commission) • Financial intermediaries (e.g., financial analysts, stockbrokers, mutual fund managers, credit-rating organizations)

Illustration 1–2

Financial Information Providers and External User Groups

For these groups, the primary focus of financial accounting is on the financial information provided by *profit-oriented companies to their present and potential investors and creditors.* One external user group, often referred to as *financial intermediaries,* includes financial analysts, stockbrokers, mutual fund managers, and credit rating organizations. These users provide advice to investors and creditors and/or make investment-credit decisions on their behalf.

The primary means of conveying financial information to investors, creditors, and other external users is through financial statements and related disclosure notes. The financial statements most frequently provided are (1) the balance sheet, also called the statement of financial position, (2) the income statement, also called the statement of operations, (3) the statement of cash flows, and (4) the statement of shareholders' equity. Also, companies must either provide a statement of other comprehensive income immediately following the income statement, or present a combined statement of comprehensive income that includes the information normally contained in both the income statement and the statement of other comprehensive income.[5] As you progress through this book, you will review and expand your knowledge of the information in these financial statements, the way the elements in these statements are measured, and the concepts underlying these measurements and related disclosures. We use the term **financial reporting** to refer to the process of providing this information to external users. Keep in mind, though, that external users receive important financial information in a variety of other formats as well, including news releases and management forecasts, prospectuses, and reports filed with regulatory agencies.

Target's financial statements for the fiscal year ended January 30, 2016, and related disclosure notes are provided in Connect. You also can access these statements and notes under the Investor Relations link at the company's website (Target.com). A Target case is included among the Real-Word Cases that accompany each chapter, so you can see how each chapter's topics relate to a single familiar company.

The Economic Environment and Financial Reporting

In the United States, we have a highly developed free-enterprise economy with the majority of productive resources privately owned rather than government owned. For the economy to operate efficiently, these resources should be allocated to private enterprises that will use

[5]FASB ASC 220-45: Comprehensive Income-Other Presentation Matters (originally "Presentation of Comprehensive Income," *Accounting Standards Update No. 2011-05* (Norwalk, CT: FASB, June 2011)).

The *capital markets* provide a mechanism to help our economy allocate resources efficiently.

them best to provide the goods and services desired by society, and not to enterprises that will waste them. The mechanisms that foster this efficient allocation of resources are the **capital markets**. We can think of the capital markets simply as a composite of all investors and creditors.

Businesses go to the capital markets to get the cash necessary for them to function. The three primary forms of business organization are the sole proprietorship, the partnership, and the corporation. In the United States, sole proprietorships and partnerships outnumber corporations. However, the dominant form of business organization, in terms of the ownership of productive resources, is the **corporation**. Investors provide resources, usually cash, to a corporation in exchange for an ownership interest, that is, shares of stock. Creditors lend cash to the corporation, either by making individual loans or by purchasing publicly traded debt such as bonds.

Corporations acquire capital from investors in exchange for ownership interest and from creditors by borrowing.

Stocks and bonds usually are traded on organized security markets such as the New York Stock Exchange and the NASDAQ. New cash is provided by **initial market transactions** in which the corporation sells shares of stock or bonds to individuals or other entities that want to invest in it. For example, **Target** first "went public" in 1967, selling shares to finance its expansion. Subsequent transfers of these stocks and bonds between investors and creditors are referred to as **secondary market transactions**. Corporations receive no new cash from secondary market transactions. Nevertheless, secondary market transactions are very important to the efficient allocation of resources in our economy. These transactions help establish market prices for additional shares and for bonds that corporations may wish to issue in the future to acquire additional capital. Also, many investors and creditors might be unwilling to buy stocks and bonds if they thought they couldn't eventually sell those securities to others in the future.

Initial market transactions involve issuance of stocks and bonds by the corporation.

Secondary market transactions involve the transfer of stocks and bonds between individuals and institutions.

What information do investors and creditors need when determining which companies will receive capital? We explore that question next.

The Investment-Credit Decision—A Cash Flow Perspective

While the decisions made by investors and by creditors are somewhat different, they are similar in at least one important way. Investors and creditors are willing to provide capital to a corporation (buy stocks or bonds) only if they expect to receive more cash in return at some time in the future. A corporation's shareholders will receive cash from their investment through the ultimate sale of the ownership shares of stock. In addition, many corporations distribute cash to their shareholders in the form of periodic dividends. For example, if an investor provides a company with \$10,000 cash by purchasing stock at the end of 2017, receives \$400 in dividends from the company during 2018, and sells the ownership interest (shares) at the end of 2018 for \$10,600, the investment would have generated a **rate of return** of 10% for 2018, calculated as follows:

The expected rate of return and the uncertainty, or risk, of that return are key variables in the investment decision.

$$\frac{\$400 \text{ dividends} + \$600 \text{ share price appreciation}}{\$10{,}000 \text{ initial investment}} = 10\%$$

All else equal, investors and creditors would like to invest in stocks or bonds that provide the highest expected rate of return. However, there are many variables to consider before making an investment decision. For example, the *uncertainty*, or *risk*, of that expected return also is important. To illustrate, consider the following two investment options:

1. Invest \$10,000 in a savings account insured by the U.S. government that will generate a 5% rate of return.
2. Invest \$10,000 in a profit-oriented company.

While the rate of return from option 1 is known with virtual certainty, the return from option 2 is uncertain. The amount and timing of the cash to be received in the future from option 2 are unknown. The company in option 2 will be able to provide investors with a return only if it can generate a profit. That is, it must be able to use the resources provided by investors and creditors to generate cash receipts from selling a product or service that exceed the cash disbursements necessary to provide that product or service. Therefore, potential investors require

A company will be able to provide a positive return to investors and creditors only if it can generate a profit from selling its products or services.

information about the company that will help them estimate the potential for future profits, as well as the return they can expect on their investment and the risk that is associated with it. If the potential return is high enough, investors will prefer to invest in the profit-oriented company, even if that return has more risk associated with it.

In summary, the primary objective of financial accounting is to provide investors and creditors with information that will help them make investment and credit decisions. That information should help investors and creditors evaluate the *amounts, timing,* and *uncertainty* of the enterprise's future cash receipts and disbursements. The better this information is, the more efficient will be investor and creditor resource allocation decisions. But financial accounting doesn't only benefit companies and their investors and creditors. By providing key information to capital market participants, financial accounting plays a vital role that helps direct society's resources to the companies that will utilize those resources most effectively.

The objective of financial accounting is to provide investors and creditors with useful information for decision making.

Cash versus Accrual Accounting

● LO1–2

Even though predicting future cash flows is the primary goal of many users of financial reporting, the model best able to achieve that goal is the accrual accounting model. A competing model is cash basis accounting. Each model produces a periodic measure of performance that could be used by investors and creditors for predicting future cash flows.

CASH BASIS ACCOUNTING. Cash basis accounting produces a measure called net operating cash flow. This measure is the difference between cash receipts and cash payments from transactions related to providing goods and services to customers during a reporting period.

Net operating cash flow **is the difference between cash receipts and cash disbursements from providing goods and services.**

Over the life of a company, net operating cash flow definitely is the measure of concern. However, over short periods of time, operating cash flows may not be indicative of the company's long-run cash-generating ability. Sometimes a company pays or receives cash in one period that relates to performance in multiple periods. For example, in one period a company receives cash that relates to prior period sales, or makes advance payments for costs related to future periods.

To see this more clearly, consider Carter Company's net operating cash flows during its first three years of operations, shown in Illustration 1–3. Carter's operations for these three years included the following:

1. Credit sales to customers were $100,000 each year ($300,000 total), while cash collections were $50,000, $125,000 and $125,000. Carter's customers owe Carter nothing at the end of Year 3.
2. At the beginning of Year 1, Carter prepaid $60,000 for three years' rent ($20,000 per year).
3. Employee salaries of $50,000 were paid in full each year.
4. Utilities cost was $10,000 each year, but $5,000 of the cost in Year 1 was not paid until Year 2.
5. In total, Carter generated positive net operating cash flow of $60,000.

Illustration 1–3
Cash Basis Accounting

	Year 1	Year 2	Year 3	Total
Sales (on credit)	$100,000	$100,000	$100,000	$300,000
Net Operating Cash Flows				
Cash receipts from customers	$ 50,000	$125,000	$125,000	$300,000
Cash disbursements:				
Prepayment of three years' rent	(60,000)	–0–	–0–	(60,000)
Salaries to employees	(50,000)	(50,000)	(50,000)	(150,000)
Utilities	(5,000)	(15,000)	(10,000)	(30,000)
Net operating cash flow	$ (65,000)	$ 60,000	$ 65,000	$ 60,000

Over short periods of time, operating cash flow may not be an accurate predictor of future operating cash flows.

Is the three-year pattern of net operating cash flows indicative of the company's year-by-year performance? No. Sales to customers and costs of operating the company (rent, salaries, and utilities) occurred evenly over the three years, but net operating cash flows occurred at an uneven rate. Net operating cash flows varied each year because Carter (a) didn't collect cash from customers in the same pattern that sales occurred and (b) didn't pay for rent and utilities in the same years in which those resources were actually consumed. This illustration also shows why operating cash flows may not predict the company's long-run cash-generating ability. Net operating cash flow in Year 1 (negative $65,000)[6] is not an accurate predictor of Carter's future cash-generating ability in Year 2 (positive $60,000) or Year 3 (positive $65,000).

Net income is the difference between *revenues and expenses.*

ACCRUAL ACCOUNTING. If we measure Carter's activities by the accrual accounting model, we get a more accurate prediction of future operating cash flows and a more reasonable portrayal of the periodic operating performance of the company. The accrual accounting model doesn't focus only on cash flows. Instead, it also reflects other resources provided and consumed by operations during a period. The accrual accounting model's measure of resources provided by business operations is called *revenues,* and the measure of resources sacrificed to produce revenues is called *expenses.* The difference between revenues and expenses is net income, or net loss if expenses are greater than revenues.[7]

Illustration 1–4 shows how we would measure revenues and expenses in this very simple situation.

Net income is considered a better indicator of future operating cash flows than is current net operating cash flow.

Revenue for year 1 is the $100,000 sales. Given that sales eventually are collected in cash, the year 1 revenue of $100,000 is a better measure of the inflow of resources from company operations than is the $50,000 cash collected from customers. Also, net income of $20,000 for year 1 appears to be a reasonable predictor of the company's cash-generating ability, as total net operating cash flow for the three-year period is a positive $60,000. Comparing the three-year pattern of net operating cash flows in Illustration 1–3 to the three-year pattern of net income in Illustration 1–4, the net income pattern is more representative of Carter Company's steady operating performance over the three-year period.[8]

While this example is somewhat simplistic, it allows us to see the motivation for using the accrual accounting model. Accrual income attempts to measure the resource inflows and outflows generated by operations during the reporting period, which may not correspond to cash inflows and outflows. Does this mean that information about cash flows from operating activities is not useful? No. Indeed, one of the basic financial statements—the statement of cash flows—reports information about cash flows from operating, investing and financing activities, and provides important information to investors and creditors.[9] Focusing on

Illustration 1–4
Accrual Accounting

CARTER COMPANY
Income Statements

	Year 1	Year 2	Year 3	Total
Revenues	$100,000	$100,000	$100,000	$300,000
Expenses:				
Rent	20,000	20,000	20,000	60,000
Salaries	50,000	50,000	50,000	150,000
Utilities	10,000	10,000	10,000	30,000
Total expenses	80,000	80,000	80,000	240,000
Net Income	$ 20,000	$ 20,000	$ 20,000	$ 60,000

[6]If cash flow from operating the company is negative, the company can continue to operate by using cash obtained from investors or creditors to make up the difference.

[7]Net income also includes gains and losses, which are discussed later in the chapter.

[8]Empirical evidence that accrual accounting provides a better measure of short-term performance than cash flows is provided by Patricia Dechow, "Accounting Earnings and Cash Flows as Measures of Firm Performance: The Role of Accrual Accounting," *Journal of Accounting and Economics* 18 (1994), pp. 3–42.

[9]The statement of cash flows is discussed in detail in Chapters 4 and 21.

accrual accounting as well as cash flows provides a more complete view of a company and its operations.

The Development of Financial Accounting and Reporting Standards

● LO1–3

Accrual accounting is the financial reporting model used by the majority of profit-oriented companies and by many not-for-profit companies. The fact that companies use the same model is important to investors and creditors, allowing them to *compare* financial information among companies. To facilitate these comparisons, financial accounting employs a body of standards known as generally accepted accounting principles, often abbreviated as GAAP (and pronounced *gap*). GAAP is a dynamic set of both broad and specific guidelines that companies should follow when measuring and reporting the information in their financial statements and related notes. The more important concepts underlying GAAP are discussed in a subsequent section of this chapter and revisited throughout this book in the context of particular accounting topics.

FINANCIAL Reporting Case

Q1, p. 3

Historical Perspective and Standards

Pressures on the accounting profession to establish uniform accounting standards began after the stock market crash of 1929. Some felt that insufficient and misleading financial statement information led to inflated stock prices and that this contributed to the stock market crash and the subsequent depression.

The 1933 Securities Act and the 1934 Securities Exchange Act were designed to restore investor confidence. The 1933 Act sets forth accounting and disclosure requirements for initial offerings of securities (stocks and bonds). The 1934 Act applies to secondary market transactions and mandates reporting requirements for companies whose securities are publicly traded on either organized stock exchanges or in over-the-counter markets.[10]

The 1934 Act also created the Securities and Exchange Commission (SEC). Congress gave the SEC the authority to set accounting and reporting standards for companies whose securities are publicly traded. However, the SEC, a government appointed body, has *delegated* the task of setting accounting standards to the private sector. It is important to understand that the power still lies with the SEC. If the SEC does not agree with a particular standard issued by the private sector, it can force a change in the standard. In fact, it has done so in the past.[11]

The Securities and Exchange Commission (SEC) has the authority to set accounting standards for companies, but it relies on the private sector to do so.

EARLY U.S. STANDARD SETTING. The first private sector body to assume the task of setting accounting standards was the Committee on Accounting Procedure (CAP). The CAP was a committee of the American Institute of Accountants (AIA). The AIA was renamed the American Institute of Certified Public Accountants (AICPA) in 1957, which is the national professional organization for certified professional public accountants.

From 1938 to 1959, the CAP issued 51 *Accounting Research Bulletins (ARBs)* which dealt with specific accounting and reporting problems. No theoretical framework for financial accounting was established. This piecemeal approach of dealing with individual issues without a framework led to criticism.

In 1959 the Accounting Principles Board (APB) replaced the CAP. The APB operated from 1959 through 1973 and issued 31 *Accounting Principles Board Opinions (APBOs),* various *Interpretations,* and four *Statements.* The *Opinions* also dealt with specific accounting and reporting problems. Many *ARBs* and *APBOs* still represent authoritative GAAP.

The APB suffered from a variety of problems. It was never able to establish a conceptual framework for financial accounting and reporting that was broadly accepted. Also, members

[10]Reporting requirements for SEC registrants include Form 10-K, the annual report form, and Form 10-Q, the report that must be filed for the first three quarters of each fiscal year.

[11]The SEC issues *Financial Reporting Releases (FRRs),* which regulate what information companies must report to it. The SEC staff also issues *Staff Accounting Bulletins* that provide the SEC's interpretation of standards previously issued by the private sector. To learn more about the SEC, consult its Internet site at www.sec.gov.

served on the APB on a voluntary, part-time basis, so the APB was not able to act quickly enough to keep up with financial reporting issues as they developed. Perhaps the most important flaw of the APB was a perceived lack of independence. Because the APB was composed almost entirely of certified public accountants and supported by the AICPA, critics charged that the clients of the represented public accounting firms exerted self-interested pressure on the board and inappropriately influenced decisions. A related complaint was that other interest groups lacked an ability to provide input to the standard-setting process.

The *FASB* was established to set U.S. accounting standards.

THE FASB. Criticism of the APB led to the creation in 1973 of the Financial Accounting Standards Board (FASB) and its supporting structure. There are seven full-time members of the FASB. FASB members represent various constituencies concerned with accounting standards, and have included representatives from the auditing profession, profit-oriented companies, accounting educators, financial analysts, and government. The FASB is supported by its parent organization, the Financial Accounting Foundation (FAF), which is responsible for selecting the members of the FASB and its Financial Accounting Standards Advisory Council (FASAC), ensuring adequate funding of FASB activities and exercising general oversight of the FASB's activities.[12,13]

In 1984, the FASB's Emerging Issues Task Force (EITF) was formed to improve financial reporting by resolving narrowly defined financial accounting issues within the framework of existing GAAP. The EITF primarily addresses implementation issues, thereby speeding up the standard-setting process and allowing the FASB to focus on pervasive long-term problems. EITF rulings are ratified by the FASB and are considered part of GAAP.

Illustration 1–5 summarizes this discussion on accounting standards. The graphic shows the hierarchy of accounting standard setting in order of authority.

CODIFICATION. Present-day GAAP includes a huge amount of guidance. The FASB has developed a conceptual framework (discussed in Part B of this chapter) that is not authoritative GAAP but provides an underlying structure for the development of accounting standards. The FASB also has issued many accounting standards, currently called *Accounting*

Illustration 1–5

Accounting Standard Setting

HIERARCHY OF STANDARD-SETTING AUTHORITY

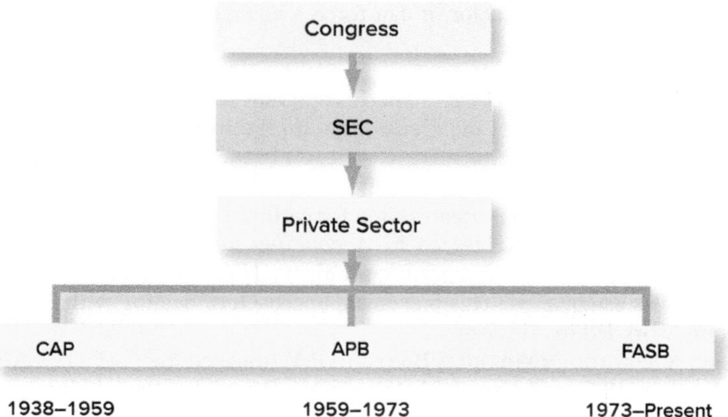

[12]The FAF's primary sources of funding are fees assessed against issuers of securities under the *Public Company Accounting Reform and Investor Protection Act of 2002,* commonly referred to as the *Sarbanes-Oxley Act.* The FAF is governed by trustees, the majority of whom are appointed from the membership of eight sponsoring organizations. These organizations represent important constituencies involved with the financial reporting process. For example, one of the founding organizations is the CFA Institute which represents financial information users, and another is the Financial Executives International which represents financial information preparers. The FAF also raises funds to support the activities of the Governmental Accounting Standards Board (GASB).

[13]The major responsibility of the FASAC is to advise the FASB on the priorities of its projects, including the suitability of new projects that might be added to its agenda. FASAC includes approximately 35 representatives from auditing firms, private companies, various user groups, and academia.

Standards Updates (*ASUs*) and previously called *Statements of Financial Accounting Standards* (*SFASs*), as well as numerous FASB *Interpretations, Staff Positions, Technical Bulletins,* and *EITF Issue Consensuses.* The SEC also has issued various important pronouncements. Determining the appropriate accounting treatment for a particular event or transaction might require an accountant to research several of these sources.

To simplify the task of researching an accounting topic, in 2009 the FASB implemented its *FASB Accounting Standards Codification.* The Codification integrates and topically organizes all relevant accounting pronouncements comprising GAAP in a searchable, online database. It represents the single source of authoritative nongovernmental U.S. GAAP, and also includes portions of SEC accounting guidance that are relevant to financial reports filed with the SEC. When the FASB issues a new ASU, it becomes authoritative when it is entered into the Codification. The Codification is organized into nine main topics and approximately 90 subtopics. The main topics and related numbering system are presented in Illustration 1–6.[14] The Codification can be located at www.fasb.org.

The *FASB Accounting Standards Codification* is the only source of authoritative U.S. GAAP, other than rules and interpretive releases of the SEC.

Throughout this book, we use the Accounting Standards Codification System (ASC) in footnotes when referencing generally accepted accounting principles (FASB ASC followed by the appropriate number). Each footnote also includes a reference to the original accounting standard that is codified in the ASC.

INTERNATIONAL STANDARD SETTING. Most industrialized countries have organizations responsible for determining accounting and reporting standards. In some countries, the United Kingdom, for instance, the responsible organization is a private sector body similar to the FASB in the United States. In other countries, the organization is a governmental body. Historically, these different organizations often produced different accounting

Illustration 1–6
FASB Accounting Standards Codification Topics

FASB Accounting Standards Codification Topics

Topic	Numbered
General Principles	100–199
Presentation	200–299
Assets	300–399
Liabilities	400–499
Equity	500–599
Revenues	600–699
Expenses	700–799
Broad Transactions	800–899
Industry	900–999

Additional Consideration

Accounting standards and the standard-setting process discussed above relate to profit-oriented organizations and nongovernmental not-for-profit entities. In 1984, the Governmental Accounting Standards Board (GASB) was created to develop accounting standards for governmental units such as states and cities. The FAF oversees and funds the GASB, and the Governmental Accounting Standards Advisory Council (GASAC) provides input to it.

[14]FASB ASC 105–10: Generally Accepted Accounting Principles–Overall (previously "The FASB Accounting Standards Codification® and the Hierarchy of Generally Accepted Accounting Principles—a replacement of FASB Statement No. 162," *Statement of Financial Accounting Standards No. 168* (Norwalk, Conn.: FASB: 2009)).

standards, which complicated accounting by multinational companies, reduced comparability between companies using different standards, and potentially made it harder for companies to raise capital in international markets.

The ***International Accounting Standards Board (IASB)*** is dedicated to developing a single set of global accounting standards.

In response to these problems, the **International Accounting Standards Committee (IASC)** was formed in 1973 to develop global accounting standards. The IASC reorganized itself in 2001 and created a new standard-setting body called the **International Accounting Standards Board (IASB)**. The IASB's main objective is to develop a single set of high-quality, understandable, and enforceable global accounting standards to help participants in the world's capital markets and other users make economic decisions.[15]

As shown in Illustration 1–7, the way international standard setting is structured is similar in many respects to the way standard setting is structured in the U.S.

International Financial Reporting Standards are issued by the IASB.

The IASC issued 41 International Accounting Standards (IASs), and the IASB endorsed these standards when it was formed in 2001. Since then, the IASB has revised many IASs and has issued new standards of its own, called **International Financial Reporting Standards (IFRS)**. More and more countries are basing their national accounting standards on IFRS. By 2016, approximately 120 jurisdictions, including Hong Kong, Egypt, Canada, Australia, and the countries in the European Union (EU), require or permit the use of IFRS or a local variant of IFRS.[16]

EFFORTS TO CONVERGE U.S. AND INTERNATIONAL STANDARDS. Should the U.S. also adopt IFRS? Many argue that a single set of global standards will improve comparability of financial reporting and facilitate access to capital. However, others argue that U.S. standards should remain customized to fit the stringent legal and regulatory requirements of the U.S. business environment. There also is concern that differences in implementation and enforcement from country to country will make accounting under IFRS appear more uniform and comparable than actually is the case. Another argument is that competition between alternative standard-setting regimes is healthy and can lead to improved standards.[17]

The FASB and IASB have been working for many years to converge to one global set of accounting standards. Here are some important steps along the way:

- **October 2002:** The FASB and IASB sign the Norwalk Agreement, pledging to remove existing differences between their standards and to coordinate their future standard-setting agendas so that major issues are worked on together.

Illustration 1–7

Comparison of Organizations of U.S. and International Standard Setters

	U.S. GAAP	IFRS
Regulatory oversight provided by:	Securities Exchange Commission (SEC)	Monitoring Board
Foundation providing oversight, appointing members, raising funds:	Financial Accounting Foundation (FAF): 20 trustees	IFRS Foundation: 22 trustees
Standard-setting board:	Financial Accounting Standards Board (FASB): 7 members	International Accounting Standards Board (IASB): 14 members
Advisory council providing input on agenda and projects:	Financial Accounting Standards Advisory Council (FASAC): 30–40 members	IFRS Advisory Council: 30–40 members
Group to deal with emerging issues:	Emerging Issues Task Force (EITF): 15 members	IFRS Interpretations Committee: 14 members

[15]www.ifrs.org.

[16]See http://www.ifrs.com/ifrs_faqs.html.

[17]For a comprehensive analysis of the pros and cons of U.S. adoption of IFRS, see L. Hail, C. Leuz and P. Wysocki, "Global Accounting Convergence and the Potential Adoption of IFRS in the US (Part 1): An Analysis of Economic and Policy Factors," *Accounting Horizons 24* (No 3.), September 2010, pp. 355–394, and ". . . (Part 2): Political Factors and Future Scenarios for U.S. Accounting Standards," *Accounting Horizons* 24 (No. 4), December 2010, pp. 567–588.

- **November 2007:** The SEC signals its view that IFRS are of high quality by eliminating the requirement for foreign companies that issue stock in the United States to include in their financial statements a reconciliation of IFRS to U.S. GAAP. As a consequence, hundreds of foreign companies have access to U.S. capital markets with IFRS-based financial statements.
- **April 2008:** The FASB and IASB agrees to accelerate the convergence process and focus on a subset of key convergence projects. Already-converged standards that you will encounter later in this book deal with such topics as revenue recognition, earnings per share, share-based compensation, nonmonetary exchanges, inventory costs, and the calculation of fair value. Where We're Headed boxes throughout the book describe additional projects that are ongoing.
- **November 2008:** The SEC issues a *Roadmap* that listed necessary conditions (called "milestones") that must be achieved before the U.S. will shift to requiring use of IFRS by public companies. Milestones include completion of key convergence projects, improving the structure and funding of the IASB, and updating the education and licensing of U.S. accountants.
- **November 2011:** The SEC issues two studies comparing U.S. GAAP and IFRS and analyzing how IFRS are applied globally. In these studies, the SEC identifies key differences between U.S. GAAP and IFRS, and notes that U.S. GAAP provides significantly more guidance about particular transactions or industries. The SEC also notes some diversity in the application of IFRS that suggests the potential for non-comparability of financial statements across countries and industries.
- **July 2012:** The SEC staff issues its Final Staff Report in which it concludes that it is not feasible for the U.S. to simply adopt IFRS, given (1) a need for the U.S. to have strong influence on the standard-setting process and ensure that standards meet U.S. needs, (2) the high costs to companies of converting to IFRS, and (3) the fact that many laws, regulations, and private contracts reference U.S. GAAP.[18]

At the time this book is being written, recent events suggest that full convergence will not be achieved in the foreseeable future. For example, as discussed further in Chapter 12, the FASB and IASB eventually concluded that full convergence was not possible with respect to accounting for financial instruments. While it appears likely that the FASB and IASB will continue to work together to converge where possible, some differences between IFRS and U.S. GAAP will remain.

Nonetheless, you should be aware of important differences that exist between U.S. GAAP and IFRS. Therefore, International Financial Reporting Standards boxes are included throughout the book to highlight circumstances in which IFRS differs from U.S. GAAP. Throughout this book, and also in the end-of-chapter questions, exercises, problems, and cases, IFRS-related material is marked with the globe icon that you see beside this paragraph. And, similar to the Target case, an Air France–KLM (AF) case is included among the Real-World Cases that accompany each chapter, so you can see how each chapter's IFRS material relates to a single, familiar company.

The Standard-Setting Process

● LO1–4

FINANCIAL Reporting Case

Q2, p. 3

DUE PROCESS. When developing accounting standards, a standard setter must understand the nuances of the economic transactions the standards address and the views of key constituents concerning how accounting would best capture that economic reality. Therefore, the FASB undertakes a series of elaborate information-gathering steps before issuing an Accounting Standards Update. These steps include open hearings, deliberations, and requests for written comments from interested parties. Illustration 1–8 outlines the FASB's standard-setting process.[19]

[18] "Work Plan for the Consideration of Incorporating International Financial Reporting Standards into the Financial Reporting System for U.S. Issuers: Final Staff Report," Office of the Chief Accountant, United States Securities and Exchange Commission, July 13, 2012, available at www.sec.gov.

[19] www.FASB.org.

Illustration 1–8
The FASB's Standard-Setting Process

Step	Explanation
1.	The Board identifies financial reporting issues based on requests/recommendations from stakeholders or through other means.
2.	The Board decides whether to add a project to the technical agenda based on a staff-prepared analysis of the issues.
3.	The Board deliberates at one or more public meetings the various issues identified and analyzed by the staff.
4.	The Board issues an Exposure Draft. (In some projects, a Discussion Paper may be issued to obtain input at an early stage that is used to develop an Exposure Draft.)
5.	The Board holds a public roundtable meeting on the Exposure Draft, if necessary.
6.	The staff analyzes comment letters, public roundtable discussion, and any other information. The Board redeliberates the proposed provisions at public meetings.
7.	The Board issues an Accounting Standards Update describing amendments to the Accounting Standards Codification.

The FASB undertakes a series of information gathering steps before issuing an Accounting Standards Update.

These steps help the FASB acquire information to determine the preferred method of accounting. However, as a practical matter this information gathering also exposes the FASB to much political pressure by various interest groups who want an accounting treatment that serves their economic best interest. As you will see later in this chapter, the FASB's concepts statements indicate that standards should present information in a neutral manner, rather than being designed to favor particular economic consequences, but sometimes politics intrudes on the standard-setting process.

POLITICS IN STANDARD SETTING. A change in accounting standards can result in a substantial redistribution of wealth within our economy. Therefore, it is no surprise that the FASB has had to deal with intense political pressure over controversial accounting standards, and sometimes has changed standards in response to that pressure.

One example of the effect of politics on standard setting occurred in the mid-1990's with respect to accounting for employee stock options. The accounting standards in place at that time typically did not recognize compensation expense if a company paid their employees with stock options rather than cash. Yet, the company was sacrificing something of value to compensate its employees. Therefore, the FASB proposed that companies recognize compensation expense in an amount equal to the fair value of the options, with some of the expense recognized in each of the periods in which the employee earned the options. Numerous companies (particularly in California's Silicon Valley, where high-tech companies had been compensating employees with stock options to a great extent) applied intense political pressure against this proposal, and eventually the FASB backed down and required only disclosure of options-related compensation expense in the notes to the financial statements. Nearly a decade later, this contentious issue resurfaced in a more amenable political climate, and the FASB issued a standard requiring expense recognition as originally proposed. This issue is discussed at greater length in Chapter 19.

● LO1–11

Another example of the political process at work in standard setting is the controversy surrounding the implementation of the fair value accounting standard issued in 2007. Many financial assets and liabilities are reported at fair value in the balance sheet, and many types of fair value changes are included in net income. Some have argued that fair values were estimated in a manner that exacerbated the financial crisis of 2008–2009 by forcing financial institutions to take larger than necessary write-downs of financial assets in the illiquid markets that existed at that time. As discussed further in Chapter 12, pressure from lobbyists and politicians influenced the FASB to revise its guidance on recognizing investment losses in these situations, and ongoing pressure remains to reduce the extent to which fair value changes are included in the determination of net income.

International Financial Reporting Standards

Politics in International Standard Setting. Political pressures on the IASB's standard-setting process are severe. Politicians from countries that use IFRS lobby for the standards they prefer. The European Union (EU) is a particularly important adopter of IFRS and utilizes a formal evaluation process for determining whether an IFRS standard will be endorsed for use in EU countries. Economic consequences for EU member nations are an important consideration in that process.

For example, in 2003 and 2004 French banks lobbied against some aspects of accounting for financial instruments stridently enough that the EU eventually "carved out" two key provisions before endorsing the relevant accounting standard (IAS 39).[20] Similarly, in 2008 the EU successfully pressured the IASB to suspend its due process and immediately allow reclassification of investments so that EU banks could avoid recognizing huge losses during a financial crisis.[21] Commenting on standards setting at that time, Charlie McCreevy, European Commissioner for Internal Markets and Service, stated that "Accounting is now far too important to be left to . . . accountants!"[22]

Additional Consideration

Private Company Council (PCC). Are the complex, comprehensive standards that are necessary to reflect the activities of a huge multinational conglomerate like General Electric also appropriate for a private company that, say, just needs to provide financial statements to its bank to get a loan? Private companies might be able to avoid much of that complexity. They don't sell securities like stocks and bonds to the general public, and they usually can identify the information needs of the specific users who rely on their financial statements and provide direct access to management to answer questions. Private companies typically also have a smaller accounting staff than do public companies. For those reasons, private companies have long sought a version of GAAP that is less costly to apply and better meets the information needs of the users of their financial statements.

In 2012, the Financial Accounting Foundation responded to this concern by establishing the Private Company Council (PCC). The ten-member PCC determines whether changes to existing GAAP are necessary to meet the needs of users of private company financial statements. But, a proposed exception or modification for private companies must be endorsed by the FASB before being issued as an Accounting Standards Update and added to the Codification. The PCC also advises the FASB about its current projects that affect private companies.

Encouraging High-Quality Financial Reporting

● LO1–5

Numerous factors affect the quality of financial reporting. In this section, we discuss the role of the auditor, recent reforms in financial reporting, and the debate about whether accounting standards should emphasize rules or underlying principles.

FINANCIAL Reporting Case

Q3, p. 3

The Role of the Auditor

It is the responsibility of management to apply GAAP appropriately. Another group, **auditors**, serves as an independent intermediary to help ensure that management has in fact appropriately applied GAAP in preparing the company's financial statements. Auditors

***Auditors* express an opinion on the compliance of financial statements with GAAP.**

[20]Stephen A. Zeff, "IFRS Developments in the USA and EU, and Some Implications for Australia," *Australian Accounting Review* 18 (2008), pp. 275–282.

[21]Sarah Deans and Dane Mott, "Lowering Standards," www.morganmarkets.com, 10/14/2008.

[22]Charlie McCreevy, Keynote Address, "Financial Reporting in a Changing World" Conference, Brussels, 5/7/2009.

examine (audit) financial statements to express a professional, independent opinion about whether the statements fairly present the company's financial position, its results of operations, and its cash flows in compliance with GAAP. Audits add credibility to the financial statements, increasing the confidence of those who rely on the information. Auditors, therefore, play an important role in the capital markets.

Most companies receive what's called an unmodified audit report. For example, Apple Inc.'s 2015 audit report by Ernst & Young LLP states, "In our opinion, the financial statements referred to above present fairly, in all material respects, the consolidated financial position of Apple Inc. at September 26, 2015 and September 27, 2014, and the consolidated results of its operations and its cash flow for each of the three years in the period ended September 26, 2015, in conformity with U.S. generally accepted accounting principles." This is known as a clean opinion. Had there been any material departures from GAAP or other problems that caused the auditors to question the fairness of the statements, the report would have been modified to inform readers. Normally, companies correct any material misstatements that auditors identify in the course of an audit, so companies usually receive clean opinions. The audit report for public companies also provides the auditors' opinion on the effectiveness of the company's internal control over financial reporting.

Certified public accountants (CPAs) **are licensed by states to provide audit services.**

In most states, only individuals licensed as certified public accountants (CPAs) can represent that the financial statements have been audited in accordance with generally accepted auditing standards. Requirements to be licensed as a CPA vary from state to state, but all states specify education, testing, and experience requirements. The testing requirement is to pass the Uniform CPA Examination.

Financial Reporting Reform

The dramatic collapse of Enron in 2001 and the dismantling of the international public accounting firm of Arthur Andersen in 2002 severely shook U.S. capital markets. The credibility of the accounting profession itself as well as of corporate America was called into question. Public outrage over accounting scandals at high-profile companies like WorldCom, Xerox, Merck, Adelphia Communications, and others increased the pressure on lawmakers to pass measures that would restore credibility and investor confidence in the financial reporting process.

Driven by these pressures, Congress acted swiftly and passed the *Public Company Accounting Reform and Investor Protection Act of 2002,* commonly referred to as the *Sarbanes-Oxley Act* or *SOX* for the two congressmen who sponsored the bill. SOX applies to public securities-issuing entities. It provides for the regulation of auditors and the types of services they furnish to clients, increases accountability of corporate executives, addresses conflicts of interest for securities analysts, and provides for stiff criminal penalties for violators. Illustration 1–9 outlines key provisions of the Act.

Section 404 is perhaps the most controversial provision of SOX. It requires that company management document internal controls and report on their adequacy. Auditors also must express an opinion on whether the company has maintained effective control over financial reporting.

No one argues the importance of adequate internal controls, but many argued that the benefits of Section 404 did not justify the costs of complying with it. Research provides evidence that 404 reports affect investors' risk assessments and companies' stock prices, indicating these reports are seen as useful by investors.[23] Unfortunately, it is not possible to quantify the more important benefit of potentially avoiding business failures like Enron by focusing attention on the implementation and maintenance of adequate internal controls.

The costs of 404 compliance initially were quite steep. For example, one survey of Fortune 1,000 companies estimated that large companies spent, on average, approximately $8.5 million and $4.8 million (including internal costs and auditor fees) during the first two years of the act to comply with 404 reporting requirements.[24] As expected, the costs dropped

[23]Hollis Ashbaugh Skaife, Daniel W. Collins, William R. Kinney, Jr., and Ryan LaFond, "The Effect of SOX Internal Control Deficiencies on Firm Risk and Cost of Equity," *Journal of Accounting Research* 47 (2009), pp. 1–43.

[24]"Sarbanes-Oxley 404 Costs and Implementation Issues: Spring 2006 Survey Update," CRA International (April 17, 2006).

Illustration 1–9

Public Company Accounting Reform and Investor Protection Act of 2002 (Sarbanes-Oxley)

Key Provisions of the Sarbanes-Oxley Act:

- **Oversight board.** The five-member (two accountants) Public Company Accounting Oversight Board has the authority to establish standards dealing with auditing, quality control, ethics, independence and other activities relating to the preparation of audit reports, or can choose to delegate these responsibilities to the AICPA. Prior to the act, the AICPA set auditing standards. The SEC has oversight and enforcement authority.
- **Corporate executive accountability.** Corporate executives must personally certify the financial statements and company disclosures with severe financial penalties and the possibility of imprisonment for fraudulent misstatement.
- **Nonaudit services.** The law makes it unlawful for the auditors of public companies to perform a variety of nonaudit services for audit clients. Prohibited services include bookkeeping, internal audit outsourcing, appraisal or valuation services, and various other consulting services. Other nonaudit services, including tax services, require pre-approval by the audit committee of the company being audited.
- **Retention of work papers.** Auditors of public companies must retain all audit or review work papers for seven years or face the threat of a prison term for willful violations.
- **Auditor rotation.** Lead audit partners are required to rotate every five years. Mandatory rotation of audit firms came under consideration.
- **Conflicts of interest.** Audit firms are not allowed to audit public companies whose chief executives worked for the audit firm and participated in that company's audit during the preceding year.
- **Hiring of auditor.** Audit firms are hired by the audit committee of the board of directors of the company, not by company management.
- **Internal control.** Section 404 of the act requires that company management document and assess the effectiveness of all internal control processes that could affect financial reporting. The PCAOB's *Auditing Standard No. 2* (since replaced by *Auditing Standard No. 5*) requires that the company auditors express an opinion on whether the company has maintained effective internal control over financial reporting.

significantly in the second year, and continued to drop as the efficiency of internal control audits increased. Many companies now perceive that the benefits of these internal control reports exceed their costs.[25]

We revisit Section 404 in Chapter 7 in the context of an introduction to internal controls.

A Move Away from Rules-Based Standards?

The accounting scandals at Enron and other companies involved managers using elaborately structured transactions to try to circumvent specific rules in accounting standards. One consequence of those scandals was a rekindled debate over **principles-based**, or more recently termed **objectives-oriented**, versus **rules-based accounting standards**. In fact, a provision of the Sarbanes-Oxley Act required the SEC to study the issue and provide a report to Congress on its findings. That report, issued in July 2003, recommended that accounting standards be developed using an objectives-oriented approach.[26]

A ***principles-based***, or ***objectives-oriented***, **approach to standard-setting stresses professional judgment, as opposed to following a list of rules.**

An objectives-oriented approach to standard setting emphasizes using professional judgment, as opposed to following a list of rules, when choosing how to account for a transaction. Proponents of an objectives-oriented approach argue that a focus on professional judgment means that there are few rules to sidestep, and we are more likely to arrive at an appropriate accounting treatment. Detractors, on the other hand, argue that the absence of detailed rules opens the door to even more abuse, because management can use the latitude provided by objectives to justify their preferred accounting approach. Even in the absence

[25] Protiviti, Inc., *2011 Sarbanes-Oxley Compliance Survey* (June, 2011).

[26] "Study Pursuant to Section 108 (d) of the Sarbanes-Oxley Act of 2002 on the Adoption by the United States Financial Reporting System of a Principles-Based Accounting System," Securities and Exchange Commission (July 2003).

of intentional misuse, reliance on professional judgment might result in different interpretations for similar transactions, raising concerns about comparability. Also, detailed rules help auditors withstand pressure from clients who want a more favorable accounting treatment, and help companies ensure that they are complying with GAAP and avoid litigation or SEC inquiry. For these reasons, it's challenging to avoid providing detailed rules in the U.S. reporting environment.

Regardless of whether accounting standards are based more on rules or on objectives, prior research highlights that there is some potential for abuse, either by structuring transactions around precise rules or opportunistically interpreting underlying principles.[27] The key is whether management is dedicated to high-quality financial reporting. It appears that poor ethical values on the part of management are at the heart of accounting abuses and scandals, so we now turn to a discussion of ethics in the accounting profession.

Ethics in Accounting

Ethics deals with the ability to distinguish right from wrong.

Ethics is a term that refers to a code or moral system that provides criteria for evaluating right and wrong. An ethical dilemma is a situation in which an individual or group is faced with a decision that tests this code. Many of these dilemmas are simple to recognize and resolve. For example, have you ever been tempted to call your professor and ask for an extension on the due date of an assignment by claiming a pretended illness? Temptation like this will test your personal ethics.

Accountants, like others in the business world, are faced with many ethical dilemmas, some of which are complex and difficult to resolve. For instance, the capital markets' focus on near-term profits may tempt a company's management to bend or even break accounting rules to inflate reported net income. In these situations, technical competence is not enough to resolve the dilemma.

ETHICS AND PROFESSIONALISM. One characteristic that distinguishes a profession from other occupations is the acceptance by its members of a responsibility for the interests of those it serves. Ethical behavior is expected of those engaged in a profession. That expectation often is articulated in a code of ethics. For example, law and medicine are professions that have their own codes of professional ethics. These codes provide guidance and rules to members in the performance of their professional responsibilities.

Public accounting has achieved widespread recognition as a profession. The AICPA, the national organization of certified public accountants, has its own Code of Professional Conduct that prescribes the ethical conduct members should strive to achieve. Similarly, the Institute of Management Accountants (IMA)—the primary national organization of accountants working in industry and government—has its own code of ethics, as does the Institute of Internal Auditors—the national organization of accountants providing internal auditing services for their own organizations.

ANALYTICAL MODEL FOR ETHICAL DECISIONS. Ethical codes are informative and helpful, but the motivation to behave ethically must come from within oneself and not just from the fear of penalties for violating professional codes. Presented below is a sequence of steps that provide a framework for analyzing ethical issues. These steps can help you apply your own sense of right and wrong to ethical dilemmas:[28]

Step 1. Determine the facts of the situation. This involves determining the who, what, where, when, and how.

Step 2. Identify the ethical issue and the stakeholders. Stakeholders may include shareholders, creditors, management, employees, and the community.

[27]Mark W. Nelson, John A. Elliott, and Robin L. Tarpley, "Evidence From Auditors About Manager' and Auditors Earnings Management Decisions," *The Accounting Review* 77 (2002), pp. 175–202.

[28]Adapted from Harold Q. Langenderfer and Joanne W. Rockness, "Integrating Ethics into the Accounting Curriculum: Issues, Problems, and Solutions," *Issues in Accounting Education* (Spring 1989). These steps are consistent with those provided by the American Accounting Association's Advisory Committee on Professionalism and Ethics in their publication *Ethics in the Accounting Curriculum: Cases and Readings, 1990.*

Ethical Dilemma

You recently have been employed by a large retail chain that sells sporting goods. One of your tasks is to help prepare periodic financial statements for external distribution. The chain's largest creditor, National Savings & Loan, requires quarterly financial statements, and you are currently working on the statements for the three-month period ending June 30, 2018.

During the months of May and June, the company spent $1,200,000 on a hefty radio and TV advertising campaign. The $1,200,000 included the costs of producing the commercials as well as the radio and TV time purchased to air the commercials. All of the costs were charged to advertising expense. The company's chief financial officer (CFO) has asked you to prepare a June 30 adjusting entry to remove the costs from advertising expense and to set up an asset called *prepaid advertising* that will be expensed in July. The CFO explained that "This advertising campaign has led to significant sales in May and June and I think it will continue to bring in customers through the month of July. By recording the ad costs as an asset, we can match the cost of the advertising with the additional July sales. Besides, if we expense the advertising in May and June, we will show an operating loss on our income statement for the quarter. The bank requires that we continue to show quarterly profits in order to maintain our loan in good standing."

Step 3. Identify the values related to the situation. For example, in some situations confidentiality may be an important value that might conflict with the right to know.

Step 4. Specify the alternative courses of action.

Step 5. Evaluate the courses of action specified in step 4 in terms of their consistency with the values identified in step 3. This step may or may not lead to a suggested course of action.

Step 6. Identify the consequences of each possible course of action. If step 5 does not provide a course of action, assess the consequences of each possible course of action for all of the stakeholders involved.

Step 7. Make your decision and take any indicated action.

Ethical dilemmas are presented throughout this book. The analytical steps outlined above provide a framework you can use to evaluate these situations.

The Conceptual Framework

PART B

● LO1–6

FINANCIAL Reporting Case

Q4, p. 3

Sturdy buildings are built on sound foundations. The U.S. Constitution is the foundation for the laws of our land. The **conceptual framework** has been described as an "Accounting Constitution" because it provides the underlying foundation for U.S. accounting standards. The conceptual framework provides structure and direction to financial accounting and reporting but does not directly prescribe GAAP. It is a coherent system of interrelated objectives and fundamentals that is intended to lead to consistent standards and that prescribes the nature, function, and limits of financial accounting and reporting. The fundamentals are the underlying concepts of accounting that guide the selection of events to be accounted for, the measurement of those events, and the means of summarizing and communicating them to interested parties.[29]

The *conceptual framework* does not prescribe GAAP. It provides an underlying foundation for accounting standards.

The FASB disseminates this framework through *Statements of Financial Accounting Concepts (SFACs)*. *SFAC 8* discusses the objective of financial reporting and the qualitative characteristics of useful financial information. *SFAC 7* describes how cash flows and present values are used when making accounting measurements. *SFAC 6* defines the accounts

[29] "Conceptual Framework for Financial Accounting and Reporting: Elements of Financial Statements and Their Measurement," *Discussion Memorandum* (Stamford, Conn.: FASB, 1976), p. 2.

Illustration 1–10
The Conceptual Framework

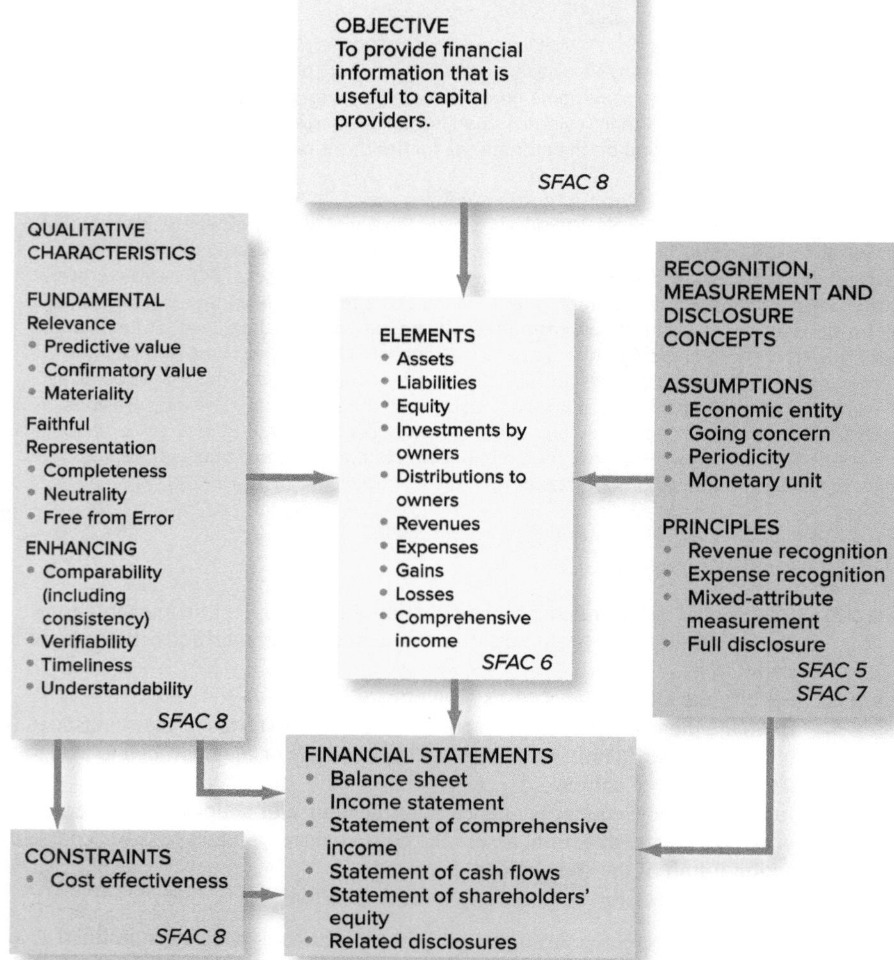

and accrual accounting concepts that appear in financial statements, and *SFAC 5* discusses recognition and measurement concepts. Earlier *SFAC*s either have been superseded or involve nonbusiness organizations that aren't considered in this book.

OBJECTIVE
To provide financial information that is useful to capital providers.
SFAC 8
QUALITATIVE CHARACTERISTICS
FUNDAMENTAL
Relevance
• Predictive value
• Confirmatory value
• Materiality
Faithful Representation
• Completeness
• Neutrality
• Free from Error
ENHANCING
• Comparability (including consistency)
• Verifiability
• Timeliness
• Understandability
SFAC 8
ELEMENTS
• Assets
• Liabilities
• Equity
• Investments by owners
• Distributions to owners
• Revenues
• Expenses
• Gains
• Losses
• Comprehensive income
SFAC 6
RECOGNITION, MEASUREMENT AND DISCLOSURE CONCEPTS
ASSUMPTIONS
• Economic entity
• Going concern
• Periodicity
• Monetary unit
PRINCIPLES
• Revenue recognition
• Expense recognition
• Mixed-attribute measurement
• Full disclosure
SFAC 5
SFAC 7
FINANCIAL STATEMENTS
• Balance sheet
• Income statement
• Statement of comprehensive income
• Statement of cash flows
• Statement of shareholders' equity
• Related disclosures
CONSTRAINTS
• Cost effectiveness
SFAC 8

In the remainder of this section we discuss the components of the conceptual framework, as depicted in Illustration 1–10.

International Financial Reporting Standards

● LO1–11

Role of the conceptual framework. The conceptual frameworks in U.S. GAAP and IFRS are very similar, and are converging even more with ongoing efforts by the FASB and IASB. However, in U.S. GAAP, the conceptual framework primarily provides guidance to standard setters to help them develop high-quality standards. In IFRS the conceptual framework guides standard setting, but in addition it provides a basis for practitioners to make accounting judgments when another IFRS standard does not apply. Also, IFRS emphasizes the overarching concept of the financial statements providing a "fair presentation" of the company. U.S. GAAP does not include a similar requirement, but U.S. auditing standards require this consideration.

Objective of Financial Reporting

● LO1–7

As indicated in Part A of this chapter, the objective of general purpose financial reporting is to provide financial information about companies that is useful to capital providers in making decisions. For example, investors decide whether to buy, sell, or hold equity or debt securities, and creditors decide whether to provide or settle loans. Information that is useful to capital providers may also be useful to other users of financial reporting information, such as regulators or taxing authorities.

Investors and creditors are interested in the amount, timing, and uncertainty of a company's future cash flows. Information about a company's economic resources (assets) and claims against resources (liabilities) also is useful. Not only does this information about resources and claims provide insight into future cash flows, it also helps decision makers identify the company's financial strengths and weaknesses and assess liquidity and solvency.

Qualitative Characteristics of Financial Reporting Information

What characteristics should information have to best meet the objective of financial reporting? Illustration 1–11 indicates the desirable qualitative characteristics of financial reporting information, presented in the form of a hierarchy of their perceived importance. Notice that these characteristics are intended to enhance the decision usefulness of information.

Decision usefulness requires that information possess the qualities of *relevance* and *faithful representation.*

Fundamental Qualitative Characteristics

For financial information to be useful, it should possess the fundamental decision-specific qualities of relevance and faithful representation. Both are critical. Information is of little value if it's not relevant. And even if information is relevant, it is not as useful if it doesn't faithfully represent the economic phenomenon it purports to represent. Let's look closer at each of these two qualitative characteristics, including the components that make those characteristics desirable. We also consider other characteristics that enhance usefulness.

Relevance requires that information have predictive and confirmatory value.

RELEVANCE. Obviously, to make a difference in the decision process, information must be relevant to the decision. Relevance in the context of financial reporting means that information must possess predictive value and/or confirmatory value, typically both.

Illustration 1–11

Hierarchy of Qualitative Characteristics of Financial Information

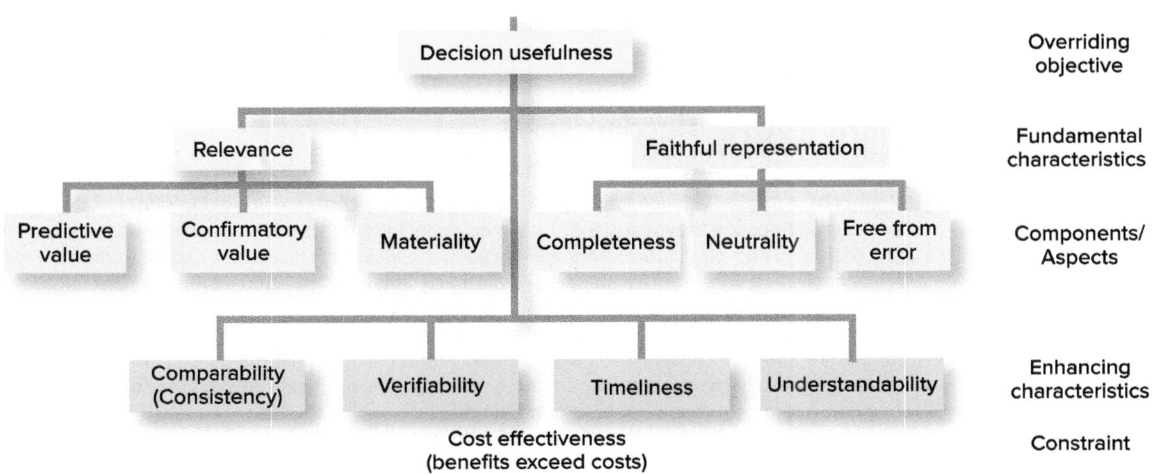

For example, current-period net income has predictive value if it helps users predict a company's future cash flows, and it has confirmatory value if it helps investors confirm or change their prior assessments regarding a company's cash-flow generating ability. Predictive and confirmatory value are central to the concept of "earnings quality," the ability of reported earnings (income) to predict a company's future earnings.

Information is *material* if it has an effect on decisions.

Financial information is material if omitting it or misstating it could affect users' decisions. Materiality is an aspect of relevance that depends on a company's particular situation and is based on the nature or magnitude of the item that is being reported. Recall that Apple Inc.'s audit report discussed earlier only expressed an opinion about material items. If information is immaterial, it's not relevant.

The threshold for materiality often depends on the *relative* dollar amount of the transaction. For example, $10,000 in total anticipated bad debts for a multibillion dollar company would not be considered material. This same $10,000 amount, however, might easily be material for a neighborhood pizza parlor. Because of the context-specific nature of materiality, the FASB has been reluctant to establish any quantitative materiality guidelines. The threshold for materiality has been left to the subjective judgment of the company preparing the financial statements and its auditors.

Professional judgment determines what amount is material in each situation.

Materiality often relates to the nature of the item as well. It depends on qualitative as well as quantitative considerations. For example, an illegal payment of a $10,000 bribe to an official of a foreign government to secure a valuable contract probably would be considered material qualitatively even if the amount is small relative to the size of the company. Similarly, a small dollar amount that changes a net loss to a net income for the reporting period could be viewed as material to financial statement users for qualitative reasons.

Faithful representation means agreement between a measure and a real-world phenomenon that the measure is supposed to represent.

FAITHFUL REPRESENTATION. Faithful representation exists when there is agreement between a measure or description and the phenomenon it purports to represent. For example, the term *inventory* in the balance sheet of a retail company is understood by external users to represent items that are intended for sale in the ordinary course of business. If inventory includes, say, accounts receivable, it lacks faithful representation.

A depiction is *complete* if it includes all information necessary for faithful representation.

To break it down further, faithful representation requires that information be *complete, neutral,* and *free from error.* A depiction of an economic phenomenon is complete if it includes all the information necessary for faithful representation of the economic phenomenon that it purports to represent. Omitting a portion of that information can cause it to be false or misleading.

Neutral implies freedom from bias.

A financial accounting standard, and the standard-setting process, is neutral if it is free from bias. You learned earlier that changes in accounting standards can lead to adverse economic consequences for certain companies and that political pressure is sometimes brought to bear on the standard-setting process in hopes of achieving particular outcomes. Accounting standards should be established with the goal of providing high-quality information, and should try not to achieve particular social outcomes or favor particular groups or companies.

Where We're Headed 

A concern with existing materiality guidance is that many companies include unnecessary disclosures because they worry that their materiality judgments will be second guessed. As part of its ongoing disclosure framework project, the FASB has issued an exposure draft, titled "Assessing Whether Disclosures are Material" that is intended to clarify the concept of materiality. The exposure draft indicates that materiality is a legal concept that is applied to quantitative and qualitative disclosures individually and in combination in the context of the company's financial statements. It also clarifies that omitting immaterial information is not an accounting error. The changes proposed in the exposure draft are controversial because they could reduce the amount of information that companies disclose. The FASB has committed to seek more input before moving forward with this proposal.

The FASB faces a difficult task in maintaining neutrality in the face of economic consequences and resulting political pressures.

Representational faithfulness also is enhanced if information is **free from error**, meaning that there are no errors or omissions in the description of the amount or the process used to report the amount. Uncertainty is a fact of life when we measure many items of financial information included in financial statements. Estimates are common, and some inaccuracy is likely. An estimate is represented faithfully if it is described clearly and accurately as being an estimate, and financial statement users are given enough information to understand the potential for inaccuracy that exists.

Information is *free from error* if it contains no errors or omissions.

Many accountants have recommended that we deal with the potential for error by employing **conservatism**. Conservatism means that accountants require greater verification before recognizing good news than bad news. The result is that losses are reflected in net income more quickly than are gains, and net assets tend to be biased downwards.

Conservatism requires greater verification for good news than for bad news.

SFAC 8 explicitly rejects conservatism as a desirable characteristic of accounting information, stating that conservatism undermines representational faithfulness by being inconsistent with neutrality. Nevertheless, some accounting practices appear to be generated by a desire to be conservative. For example, companies are required to recognize losses for declines in the value of inventory, buildings and equipment, but aren't allowed to recognize gains for increases in those values. One justification for these practices is that investors and creditors who lose money on their investments are less likely to sue the company if bad news has been exaggerated and good news underestimated. Another justification is that conservative accounting can trigger debt covenants that allow creditors to protect themselves from bad management. So, despite the lack of support for conservatism in the conceptual framework, it is likely to persist as an important consideration in accounting practice and in the application of some accounting standards.

Enhancing Qualitative Characteristics

Illustration 1–11 identifies four *enhancing* qualitative characteristics, *comparability (*including *consistency), verifiability, timeliness,* and *understandability.*

Comparability helps users see similarities and differences between events and conditions. We already have discussed the importance of investors and creditors being able to compare information *among companies* to make their resource allocation decisions. Closely related to comparability is the notion that **consistency** of accounting practices over time permits valid comparisons *among different reporting periods.* The predictive and confirmatory value of information is enhanced if users can compare the performance of a company over time.[30] Companies typically include as Note 1 to the financial statements a Summary of significant accounting policies, and provide full disclosure of any changes in those policies to alert users to the potential for diminished consistency.

Information is *comparable* if similar items are treated the same way and different items are treated differently.

Information is *consistent* if it is measured and reported the same way in each time period.

Verifiability implies that different knowledgeable and independent measurers would reach consensus regarding whether information is a faithful representation of what it is intended to depict. Direct verification involves observing the item being depicted. For example, the historical cost of a parcel of land to be reported in a company's balance sheet usually is highly verifiable. The cost can be traced to an exchange transaction, the purchase of the land. On the other hand, the fair value of that land is much more difficult to verify. Appraisers could differ in their assessment of fair value. Verification of their estimates would be indirect, involving examination of their valuation models and assessments of the reasonableness of model inputs. The term *objectivity* often is linked to verifiability. The historical cost of the land is objective and easy to verify, but the land's fair value is subjective, and may be influenced by the measurer's past experience and biases. A measurement that is subjective is more difficult to verify, which may make users doubt its representational faithfulness.

Information is *verifiable* if different measurers would reach consensus about whether it is representationally faithful.

Timeliness also is important for information to be useful. Information is timely when it's available to users early enough to allow them to use it in their decision process. To enhance

Information is *timely* if it is available to users before a decision is made.

[30]Companies occasionally do change their accounting practices, which makes it difficult for users to make comparisons among different reporting periods. Chapter 4 and Chapter 20 describe the disclosures that a company makes in this situation to restore consistency among periods.

timeliness, the SEC requires its registrants to submit financial statement information on a quarterly as well as on an annual basis for each fiscal year.

Information is *understandable* if users can comprehend it.

Understandability means that users must be able to comprehend the information within the context of the decision being made. This is a user-specific quality because users will differ in their ability to comprehend any set of information. The overriding objective of financial reporting is to provide comprehensible information to those who have a *reasonable understanding* of business and economic activities and are diligent in studying the information.

Key Constraint: Cost Effectiveness

Information is *cost effective* if the benefit of increased *decision usefulness* exceeds the costs of providing that information.

Most of us learn early in life that we can't get everything we want. The latest electronic gadget may have all the qualitative characteristics that current technology can provide, but limited resources may lead us to buy a model with fewer bells and whistles. **Cost effectiveness** constrains the accounting choices we make. The benefits of endowing financial information with all the qualitative characteristics we've discussed must exceed the costs of doing so.

The costs of providing financial information include any possible adverse economic consequences of accounting standards.

The costs of providing financial information include those of gathering, processing, and disseminating information. There also are costs to users when interpreting information. In addition, costs include possible adverse economic consequences of implementing accounting standards. For example, consider the requirement that companies having more than one operating segment must disclose certain disaggregated financial information.[31] In addition to the costs of information gathering, processing, and communicating that information, many companies feel that this reporting requirement imposes what could be called *competitive disadvantage costs.* These companies are concerned that their competitors will gain some advantage from having access to the disaggregated data.

The perceived benefit from this or any accounting standard is increased *decision usefulness* of the information provided, which, ideally, improves the resource allocation process. It is inherently impossible to quantify this benefit. The elaborate information-gathering process undertaken by the FASB in setting accounting standards is an attempt to assess both costs and benefits of a proposed accounting standard, even if in a subjective, nonquantifiable manner.

Elements of Financial Statements

The 10 elements of financial statements defined in *SFAC 6* describe financial position and periodic performance.

SFAC 6 defines 10 elements of financial statements. These elements are "the building blocks with which financial statements are constructed—the classes of items that financial statements comprise."[32] They focus directly on items related to reporting financial position and measuring performance. The *accrual accounting* model is embodied in the element definitions. For now, we list and define the elements in Illustration 1–12. You will learn much more about these elements in subsequent chapters.

Underlying Assumptions

● LO1–8

Though not emphasized in the FASB's concepts statements, four basic assumptions underlie GAAP: (1) the economic entity assumption, (2) the going concern assumption, (3) the periodicity assumption, and (4) the monetary unit assumption. These assumptions identify the entity that is being reported on, the assumption that the entity will continue to exist, and the frequency and denomination in which reports occur.

Illustration 1–13 summarizes the four assumptions underlying GAAP.

Economic Entity Assumption

The *economic entity assumption* presumes that economic events can be identified with a particular economic entity.

The **economic entity assumption** presumes that all economic events can be identified with a particular **economic entity**. Investors desire information about an economic entity that

[31]FASB ASC 280: Segment Reporting (previously "Disclosures about Segments of an Enterprise and Related Information," *Statement of Financial Accounting Standards No. 131* (Norwalk, Conn.: FASB, 1997)).

[32]"Elements of Financial Statements," *Statement of Financial Accounting Concepts No. 6* (Stamford, Conn.: FASB, 1985), par. 5.

Illustration 1–12

Elements of Financial Statements

	Elements of Financial Statements
Assets	Probable future economic benefits obtained or controlled by a particular entity as a result of past transactions or events.
Liabilities	Probable future sacrifices of economic benefits arising from present obligations of a particular entity to transfer assets or provide services to other entities in the future as a result of past transactions or events.
Equity (or net assets)	Called shareholders' equity or stockholders' equity for a corporation, it is the residual interest in the assets of an entity that remains after deducting its liabilities.
Investments by owners	Increases in equity of a particular business enterprise resulting from transfers to it from other entities of something of value to obtain or increase ownership interests in it.
Distributions to owners	Decreases in equity of a particular enterprise resulting from transfers to owners.
Comprehensive income	The change in equity of a business enterprise during a period from transactions and other events and circumstances from nonowner sources. It includes all changes in equity during a period except those resulting from investments by owners and distributions to owners.
Revenues	Inflows or other enhancements of assets of an entity or settlements of its liabilities during a period from delivering or producing goods, rendering services, or other activities that constitute the entity's ongoing major or central operations.
Expenses	Outflows or other using up of assets or incurrences of liabilities during a period from delivering or producing goods, rendering services, or other activities that constitute the entity's ongoing major or central operations.
Gains	Increases in equity from peripheral or incidental transactions of an entity.
Losses	Represent decreases in equity arising from peripheral or incidental transactions of an entity.

Illustration 1–13

Summary of Assumptions Underlying GAAP

Assumptions	**Description**
Economic entity	All economic events can be identified with a particular economic entity.
Going concern	In the absence of information to the contrary, it is anticipated that a business entity will continue to operate indefinitely.
Periodicity	The life of a company can be divided into artificial time periods to provide timely information to external users.
Monetary unit	In the United States, financial statement elements should be measured in terms of the U.S. dollar.

corresponds to their ownership interest. For example, if you were considering buying some ownership stock in Google, you would want information on the various operating units that constitute Google. You would need information not only about its United States operations but also about its European and other international operations. The financial information for the various companies (subsidiaries) in which Google owns a controlling interest (greater than 50% ownership of voting stock) should be combined with that of Google (the parent) to provide a complete picture. The parent and its subsidiaries are separate *legal* entities but one *accounting* entity.

Another key aspect of this assumption is the distinction between the economic activities of owners and those of the company. For example, the economic activities of a sole proprietorship, Uncle Jim's Restaurant, should be separated from the activities of its owner, Uncle Jim. Uncle Jim's personal residence, for instance, is not an asset of the business.

Going Concern Assumption

The *going concern* assumption presumes that a business will operate indefinitely.

Another necessary assumption is that, in the absence of information to the contrary, we anticipate that a business entity will continue to operate indefinitely. Accountants realize that the going concern assumption does not always hold since there certainly are many business failures. However, this assumption is critical to many broad and specific accounting principles. For example, the assumption provides justification for measuring many assets based on their historical costs. If it were known that an enterprise would cease operations in the near future, assets and liabilities would be measured at their current liquidation values. Similarly, when we depreciate a building over an estimated life of 40 years, we assume the business will operate that long.

Periodicity Assumption

The *periodicity assumption* allows the life of a company to be divided into artificial time periods to provide timely information.

The periodicity assumption relates to the qualitative characteristic of *timeliness*. External users need *periodic* information to make decisions. This need for periodic information requires that the economic life of a company (presumed to be indefinite) be divided into artificial time periods for financial reporting. Corporations whose securities are publicly traded are required to provide financial information to the SEC on a quarterly and annual basis.[33] Financial statements often are prepared on a monthly basis for banks and others that might need more timely information.

For many companies, the annual time period (the fiscal year) is the calendar year. However, other companies have chosen a fiscal year that does not correspond to the calendar year. The accounting profession and the SEC advocate that companies adopt a fiscal year that corresponds to their natural business year. A natural business year is the 12-month period that ends when the business activities of a company reach their lowest point in the annual cycle. For example, many retailers, Walmart for example, have adopted a fiscal year ending on January 31. Business activity in January generally is quite slow following the very busy Christmas period. The Campbell Soup Company's fiscal year ends in July; Clorox's in June; and Monsanto's in August.

Monetary Unit Assumption

The *monetary unit assumption* states that financial statement elements should be measured in a particular monetary unit (in the United States, the U.S. dollar).

The monetary unit assumption requires that financial statement elements be measured in nominal units of money, without any adjustment for changes in purchasing power. In the United States, the U.S. dollar is the monetary unit used in financial statements. In the EU, the euro is the monetary unit. Other countries use other currencies as their monetary units.

One problem with use of a monetary unit like the dollar or the euro is that it is presumed to be stable over time. That is, the value of the dollar, in terms of its ability to purchase certain goods and services, is assumed to be constant over time. This assumption obviously does not strictly hold. The U.S. economy has experienced periods of rapidly changing prices. To the extent that prices are unstable, and machines, trucks, and buildings were purchased at different times, the monetary unit used to measure them is not the same. The effect of changing prices on financial information generally is discussed elsewhere in your accounting curriculum, often in an advanced accounting course.

Recognition, Measurement, and Disclosure Concepts

● LO1–9

Now that we have identified the various elements and underlying assumptions of the financial statements, we discuss *when* the elements should be recognized (recorded) and how they should be *measured* and *disclosed*. For example, an asset was previously defined as a probable future economic benefit obtained or controlled by a company as a result of past transactions or events. But *when* should the asset be recorded, at *what* amount, and what other important information about the asset should be provided in the financial statements? *SFAC 5* addresses these issues. Recognition refers to the process of admitting information into the financial statements. Measurement is the process of associating numerical amounts

[33]The report that must be filed for the first three quarters of each fiscal year is Form 10-Q and the annual report is Form 10-K.

with the elements. Disclosure refers to including pertinent information in the financial statements and accompanying notes.

Recognition

Recognition criteria determine whether items should be included in the financial statements.

GENERAL RECOGNITION CRITERIA. According to *SFAC 5,* an item should be recognized in the basic financial statements when it meets the following four criteria, subject to a cost effectiveness constraint and materiality threshold:

1. *Definition.* The item meets the definition of an element of financial statements.
2. *Measurability.* The item has a relevant attribute measurable with sufficient reliability.
3. *Relevance.* The information about it is capable of making a difference in user decisions.
4. *Reliability.* The information is representationally faithful, verifiable, and neutral.[34]

SFAC 5 provides further guidance with respect to revenue and expense recognition, and you will learn about more specific guidelines throughout this book.

Revenues are inflows of assets or settlements of liabilities as a result of providing goods or services to customers.

REVENUE RECOGNITION. Revenues are inflows of assets or settlements of liabilities resulting from providing a product or service to a customer. An income statement should report the results of these activities only for the time period specified in the financial statements. Therefore, the *timing* of revenue recognition is a key element of earnings measurement. Not adhering to revenue recognition criteria could result in overstating revenue and hence net income in one reporting period and, consequently, understating revenue and net income in another period.

Until recently, revenue recognition was guided by the *realization principle,* which requires that two criteria be satisfied before revenue can be recognized:

1. The earnings process is judged to be complete or virtually complete.
2. There is reasonable certainty as to the collectibility of the asset to be received (usually cash).

As discussed further in Chapter 5, the FASB recently issued *ASU No. 2014-09,* which changes how we determine the timing and measurement of revenue.[35] That standard requires that companies recognize revenue when goods or services are transferred to customers for the amount the company expects to be entitled to receive in exchange for those goods or services. Revenue is recognized at a point in time or over a period of time, depending on when goods or services are transferred to customers. For example, revenue for the sale of most goods is recognized upon delivery, but revenue for services like renting apartments or lending money is recognized over time as those services are provided. No revenue is recognized if it isn't probable that the seller will collect the amounts it's entitled to receive. While that standard doesn't rely on the realization principle, you can see that aspects of the realization principle remain—we still focus on the seller fulfilling its obligations to its customers, and before revenue can be recognized we still require a relatively high likelihood that the seller will be paid.

Notice that these criteria help implement the accrual accounting model. Revenue is recognized when the seller transfers goods or services to a customer, which isn't necessarily at the same time the seller is paid by the customer.

The timing of revenue recognition also affects the timing of asset recognition. When revenue is recognized by crediting a revenue account, the corresponding debit typically increases some asset, usually cash or an account receivable.

Expenses are outflows or other using up of assets or incurrences of liabilities from providing goods and services.

EXPENSE RECOGNITION. Expenses are outflows or other using up of assets or incurrences of liabilities from providing goods or services. When are expenses recognized? In practice, expense recognition often matches revenues and expenses that arise from the same

[34] "Recognition and Measurement in Financial Statements," *Statement of Financial Accounting Concepts No. 5* (Stamford, Conn.: FASB, 1984), par. 63. *SFAC 8* has replaced reliability with faithful representation as the second primary qualitative characteristic of financial information.

[35] "Revenue from Contracts with Customers (Topic 606)," *Accounting Standards Update 2014–09* (Norwalk, Conn: FASB, 2014).

transactions or other events.[36] There is a cause-and-effect relationship between revenue and expense recognition implicit in this approach. The net result is a measure—net income—that identifies the amount of profit or loss for the period provided by operations.

Although these concepts are straightforward, their implementation can be difficult, because many expenses are not incurred *directly* to produce a particular amount of revenue. Instead, the association between revenue and many expenses is indirect. Therefore, expense recognition is implemented by one of four different approaches, depending on the nature of the specific expense:[37]

- **Based on an exact cause-and-effect relationship.** This approach is appropriate for *cost of goods sold,* as one example. There is a definite cause-and-effect relationship between PetSmart's revenue from selling dog food and its costs to purchase that dog food from suppliers. Commissions paid to salespersons for obtaining revenues also is an example of an expense recognized based on this approach.
- **By associating an expense with the revenues recognized in a specific time period.** Many expenses can be related only to periods of time during which revenue is earned. For example, the monthly salary paid to an office worker is not directly related to any specific revenue event. Instead, the employee provides benefits to the company for that one month that *indirectly* relate to the revenue recognized in that same period.
- **By a systematic and rational allocation to specific time periods.** Some costs are incurred to acquire assets that provide benefits to the company for more than one reporting period, so we recognize expenses over those time periods. For example, straight-line depreciation is a "systematical and rational" way to allocate the cost of equipment to the periods in which that equipment is used to produce revenue.
- **In the period incurred, without regard to related revenues.** Sometimes costs are incurred, but it is impossible to determine in which period or periods, if any, related revenues will occur. For example, let's say Google spends $1 million for a series of television commercials. It's difficult to determine when, how much, or even whether additional revenues occur as a result of that particular series of ads. As a result, we recognize advertising expenditures as expenses in the period incurred.

The timing of expense recognition also affects the timing of asset and liability recognition and de-recognition. When we debit an expense, the corresponding credit usually either decreases an asset (for example, decreasing cash because it was used to pay an employee's salary) or increases a liability (for example, increasing salaries payable to accrue wages that will be paid at a later date).

Measurement

If an amount is to be recognized, it also must be measured. As indicated in *SFAC 5,* GAAP currently employs a "mixed attribute" measurement model. If you look at a balance sheet, for instance, you might see land measured at historical cost, accounts receivable at net realizable value, a liability at the present value of future cash payments, and an investment at fair value. The attribute chosen to measure a particular item should be the one that maximizes the combination of relevance and representational faithfulness. *SFAC 5* lists five measurement attributes employed in GAAP:

1. Historical cost
2. Net realizable value
3. Current cost

[36]The term *matching principle* is sometimes used to refer to the practice of first recognizing revenue and then recognizing all expenses that were incurred to generate that revenue. However, the conceptual framework does not include that term. Rather, *SFACs 5* and *6* discuss matching as a result of recognizing expenses and revenues that arise from the same underlying transactions or events. Standard setters are reluctant to apply matching more broadly, because they are concerned that doing so could result in inappropriately recognizing as assets some amounts that do not provide "probable future economic benefits," and therefore don't meet the definition of an asset. We discuss this topic more in the "Evolving GAAP" section at the end of this chapter.

[37]"Elements of Financial Statements–a replacement of FASB Concepts Statement No. 3 (incorporating an amendment of FASB Concepts Statement No. 2)," *Statement of Financial Accounting Concepts No. 6* (Norwalk, Conn.: FASB, 1985).

4. Present (or discounted) value of future cash flows
5. Fair value

These different measurement attributes often indicate the same amount, particularly when the amount is initially recognized. However, sometimes they differ in important ways.

HISTORICAL COST. We often measure assets and liabilities based on their *original transaction value,* that is, their historical cost. Some accountants refer to this practice as applying the *historical cost principle.* For an asset, historical cost equals the value of what is given in exchange (usually cash) for the asset at its initial acquisition. For liabilities, it is the current cash equivalent received in exchange for assuming the liability. Historical cost for long-lived, revenue-producing assets such as equipment typically is adjusted subsequent to its initial measurement by recognizing depreciation or amortization.

Historical cost bases measurements on the amount given or received in the original exchange transaction.

Why base measurement on historical costs? First, historical cost provides important cash flow information as it represents the cash or cash equivalent paid for an asset or received in exchange for the assumption of a liability. Second, because historical cost valuation is the result of an exchange transaction between two independent parties, the agreed-upon exchange value is objective and highly verifiable.

NET REALIZABLE VALUE. Some assets are measured at their net realizable value, which is defined by the FASB as the estimated selling price in the ordinary course of business, less reasonably predictable costs of completion, disposal, and transportation. Intuitively, net realizable value is the amount of cash into which an asset is expected to be converted in the ordinary course of business. For example, if inventory could be sold for $10,000, and the company would incur additional costs of $2,000 to complete it and transport it to a customer, the inventory's net realizable value is $8,000. Departures from historical cost measurement such as this provide useful information to aid in the prediction of future cash flows.

Net realizable value bases measurements on the amount of cash into which the asset or liability will be converted in the ordinary course of business.

CURRENT COST. Companies sometimes report current costs, particularly if they operate in inflationary economies. The current cost of an asset is the cost that would be incurred to purchase or reproduce the asset.

Current cost is the cost that would be incurred to purchase or reproduce an asset.

PRESENT VALUE. Because of its importance to many accounting measurements, present value is the focus of a FASB concept statement, *SFAC 7,* which provides a framework for using future cash flows as the basis for accounting measurement and also indicates that the objective in valuing an asset or liability using present value is to approximate its fair value.[38] We explore the topic of present value in depth in Chapter 6 and the application of present value in accounting measurement in subsequent chapters.

Present value bases measurement on future cash flows discounted for the time value of money.

FAIR VALUE. We measure many financial assets and liabilities at fair value (called *current market value* originally in *SFAC 5*). Also, we use fair values when determining whether the value of nonfinancial assets like property, plant, equipment and intangible assets has been impaired. Given the complexity and growing importance of this measurement attribute, we discuss it in some detail.

Fair value bases measurements on the price that would be received to sell assets or transfer liabilities in an orderly market transaction.

Fair value is defined as the price that would be received to sell assets or paid to transfer a liability in an orderly transaction between market participants at the measurement date. A key aspect of this definition is its focus on the perspective of *market participants.* For instance, if a company buys a competitor's patent, not intending to use it but merely to keep the competitor from using it, the company still will have to assign a value to the asset because a market participant would find value in using the patent.

The FASB has provided a framework for measuring fair value whenever fair value is called for in applying generally accepted accounting principles.[39] The IASB recently

[38] "Using Cash Flow Information and Present Value in Accounting Measurements," *Statement of Financial Accounting Concepts No. 7* (Norwalk, Conn.: FASB, 2000).

[39] FASB ASC 820: Fair Value Measurements and Disclosures (previously "Fair Value Measurements," *Statement of Financial Accounting Standards No. 157* (Norwalk, Conn.: FASB, 2006)).

Fair value can be measured using:
1. **Market approaches.**
2. **Income approaches.**
3. **Cost approaches.**

converged to use the same framework.[40] In the framework, three types of valuation techniques can be used to measure fair value. *Market approaches* base valuation on market information. For example, the value of a share of a company's stock that's not traded actively could be estimated by multiplying the earnings of that company by the P/E (price of shares/ earnings) multiples of similar companies. *Income approaches* estimate fair value by first estimating future amounts (for example, earnings or cash flows) and then mathematically converting those amounts to a single present value. You will see how to apply such techniques in Chapter 6 when we discuss time value of money concepts. *Cost approaches* determine value by estimating the amount that would be required to buy or construct an asset of similar quality and condition. A firm can use one or more of these valuation approaches, depending on availability of information, and should try to use them consistently unless changes in circumstances require a change in approach.

To increase consistency and comparability in applying this definition, the framework provides a "hierarchy" that prioritizes the inputs companies should use when determining fair value. The priority is based on three broad preference levels. The higher the level (Level 1 is the highest), the more preferable the input. The framework encourages companies to strive to obtain the highest level input available for each situation. Illustration 1–14 describes the type of inputs and provides an example for each level.

Companies also must provide detailed disclosures about their use of fair value measurements. The disclosures include a description of the inputs used to measure fair value. For recurring fair value measurements that rely on significant *unobservable* inputs (within Level 3 of the fair value hierarchy), companies should disclose the effect of the measurements on earnings (or changes in net assets) for the period.

Illustration 1–14

Fair Value Hierarchy

Fair Value Hierarchy

Level	Inputs	Example
1 **Most Desirable**	Quoted market prices in active markets for identical assets or liabilities.	In Chapter 12 you will learn that certain investments in marketable securities are reported at their *fair values*. Fair value in this case would be measured using the quoted market price from the NYSE, NASDAQ, or other exchange on which the security is traded.
2	Inputs other than quoted prices that are *observable* for the asset or liability. These inputs include quoted prices for *similar* assets or liabilities in active or inactive markets and inputs that are derived principally from or corroborated by observable related market data.	In Chapter 10 we discuss how companies sometimes acquire assets with consideration other than cash. In any noncash transaction, each element of the transaction is recorded at its *fair value*. If one of the assets in the exchange is a building, for instance, then quoted market prices for similar buildings recently sold could be used to value the building or, if there were no similar buildings recently exchanged from which to obtain a comparable market price, valuation could be based on the price per square foot derived from observable market data.
3 **Least Desirable**	*Unobservable* inputs that reflect the entity's own assumptions about the assumptions market participants would use in pricing the asset or liability developed based on the best information available in the circumstances.	Asset retirement obligations (AROs), discussed in Chapter 10, are measured at *fair value*. Neither Level 1 nor Level 2 inputs would be possible in most ARO valuation situations. Fair value would be estimated using Level 3 inputs to include the present value of expected cash flows estimated using the entity's own data if there is no information indicating that market participants would use different assumptions.

[40] "Fair Value Measurement," *International Financial Reporting Standard No. 13* (London, UK: IASCF, 2011).

The use of the fair value measurement attribute is increasing, both under U.S. GAAP and IFRS. This trend, though, is controversial. Proponents of fair value cite its relevance and are convinced that historical cost information may not be useful for many types of decisions. Opponents of fair value counter that estimates of fair value may lack representational faithfulness, particularly when based on inputs from Level 3 in the fair value hierarchy, and that managers might be tempted to exploit the unverifiability of such inputs to manipulate earnings. They argue that accounting should emphasize verifiability by recognizing only those gains and other increases in fair value that actually have been realized in transactions or are virtually certain to exist.

FAIR VALUE OPTION. Usually the measurement attribute we use for a particular financial statement item is not subject to choice. However, GAAP allows a **fair value option** in some circumstances which permits companies to choose whether to report *financial* assets and liabilities at fair value.[41] For example, in Chapter 14 you will learn that a company normally would report bonds payable at historical cost (adjusted for unamortized premium or discount), but the fair value option allows that company to choose instead to report the bonds payable at fair value. If a company chooses the fair value option, future changes in fair value are reported as gains and losses in the income statement.

The *fair value option* lets companies choose whether to value some financial assets and liabilities at fair value.

Why allow the fair value option for financial assets and liabilities, and not for, say, buildings or land? Financial assets and liabilities are cash and other assets and liabilities that convert directly into known amounts of cash. These include investments in stocks and bonds of other entities, notes receivable and payable, bonds payable, and derivative securities.[42] Some of these financial assets and liabilities currently are *required* under GAAP to be reported at fair value, and others are not, leading to some potential inconsistencies in how similar or related items are treated. The fair value option provides companies a way to reduce volatility in reported earnings without having to comply with complex hedge accounting standards. It also helps in the convergence with international accounting standards we discussed earlier in the chapter as the IASB also has adopted a fair value option for financial instruments.

Disclosure

Remember, the purpose of accounting is to provide information that is useful to decision makers. So, naturally, if there is accounting information not included in the primary financial statements that would benefit users, that information should be provided too. The **full-disclosure principle** means that the financial reports should include any information that could affect the decisions made by external users. Of course, the benefits of that information should exceed the costs of providing the information. Such information is disclosed in a variety of ways, including:

The *full-disclosure principle* requires that any information useful to decision makers be provided in the financial statements, subject to the cost effectiveness constraint.

1. **Parenthetical comments** or **modifying comments** placed on the face of the financial statements.
2. **Disclosure notes** conveying additional insights about company operations, accounting principles, contractual agreements, and pending litigation.
3. **Supplemental schedules and tables** that report more detailed information than is shown in the primary financial statements.

We discuss and illustrate disclosure requirements as they relate to specific financial statement elements in later chapters as those elements are discussed.

Illustration 1–15 provides an overview of key recognition, measurement and disclosure concepts.

[41]FASB ASC 825–10–25–1: Financial Instruments–Overall–Recognition–Fair Value Option (previously "The Fair Value Option for Financial Assets and Financial Liabilities," *Statement of Financial Accounting Standards No. 159* (Norwalk, Conn.: FASB, 2007)).

[42]The fair value option does not apply to certain specified financial instruments, including pension obligations and assets or liabilities arising from leases.

Illustration 1–15
Summary of Recognition, Measurement, and Disclosure Concepts

Concept	Description
Recognition	General criteria: 1. Meets the definition of an element 2. Has a measurement attribute 3. Is relevant 4. Is reliable (representationally faithful) Examples of recognition timing: 1. Revenues 2. Expenses
Measurement	Mixed attribute model in which the attribute used to measure an item is chosen to maximize relevance and representational faithfulness. These attributes include: 1. Historical cost 2. Net realizable value 3. Current cost 4. Present (or discounted) value of future cash flows 5. Fair value
Disclosure	Financial reports should include all information that could affect the decisions made by external users. Examples of disclosures: 1. Parenthetical amounts 2. Notes to the financial statements 3. Supplemental schedules and tables

Where We're Headed

"Disclosure overload" is a frequent complaint by companies and investors alike. The notes to the financial statements can be very useful, but they are costly for companies to prepare and difficult for many users to sift through and understand. In response to that concern, the FASB has been developing a framework intended to make disclosures more effective and less redundant.

As part of that project, in March 2014 the FASB issued an exposure draft of a proposed addition to Concepts Statement No. 8, titled *Chapter 8: Notes to Financial Statements.*[43] The exposure draft describes three types of information that should be included in the notes to financial statements:

1. General information about the nature of the company, its activities, and any special advantages it enjoys or restrictions it faces.
2. Additional information that explains or amplifies financial statement line items.
3. Information about past events and current circumstances that might affect the company's future cash flows but don't yet appear in the financial statements.

The exposure draft also suggests a series of questions that the FASB and its staff should consider when determining what notes should be required by new standards. A separate part of the project will develop further guidance to help companies apply judgment when meeting disclosure requirements. The next step is for the FASB to deliberate on the comments received in response to its exposure draft.

[43] *Proposed Statement of Financial Accounting Concepts: Chapter 8: Notes to Financial Statements* (Norwalk, Conn.: FASB, March 4, 2014).

Evolving GAAP

● LO1–10

Earlier in this chapter you learned that the convergence of accounting standards with international standards is having a profound effect on financial reporting in the United States. More broadly, U.S. and international GAAP have been evolving over time from an emphasis on revenues and expenses to an emphasis on assets and liabilities. Of course, you know from introductory accounting that the balance sheet and income statement are intertwined and must reconcile with each other. For example, the revenues reported in the income statement depict inflows of assets whose balances at a particular point in time are reported in the balance sheet. But which comes first, identifying revenues and expenses, or identifying assets and liabilities? That emphasis can affect accounting standards in important ways. To help you understand the changes taking place, we start by discussing the revenue/expense approach and then discuss the asset/liability approach.

Under the **revenue/expense approach**, we emphasize principles for recognizing revenues and expenses, with some assets and liabilities recognized as necessary to make the balance sheet reconcile with the income statement. For example, when accounting for a sales transaction our focus would be on whether revenue has been earned, and if we determine that to be the case, we would record an asset (usually cash or accounts receivable) that is associated with the revenue.[44] We would identify the expenses necessary to earn that revenue, and then would adjust assets and liabilities accordingly.

With the *revenue/expense approach*, recognition and measurement of revenues and expenses are emphasized.

Under the **asset/liability approach**, on the other hand, we first recognize and measure the assets and liabilities that exist at a balance sheet date and, secondly, recognize and measure the revenues, expenses, gains and losses needed to account for the changes in these assets and liabilities from the previous measurement date. Proponents of this approach point out that, since revenues and expenses are defined in terms of inflows and outflows of assets and liabilities, the fundamental concepts underlying accounting are assets and liabilities. Therefore, we should try to recognize and measure assets and liabilities appropriately, and as a result will also capture their inflows and outflows in a manner that provides relevant and representationally faithful information about revenues and expenses.

With the *asset/liability approach*, recognition and measurement of assets and liabilities drives revenue and expense recognition.

For example, when accounting for a sales transaction, our focus would be on whether a potential accounts receivable meets the definition of an asset (a probable future economic benefit). We would consider such factors as whether the receivable is supported by an enforceable contract and whether the seller has performed its obligations enough to be able to expect receipt of cash flows. The key would be determining if the seller has an asset, and then recognizing whatever amount of revenue is implied by the inflow of that asset. Also, we would not attempt to match expenses to revenues. Rather, we would determine those net assets that had decreased as part of operations during the period, and recognize those decreases as expenses.

In subsequent chapters you will see that recent standards involving accounting for revenue, investments, and income taxes follow this asset/liability approach. These changes are controversial. It may seem like it shouldn't matter whether standard setters use the revenue/expense or asset/liability approach, given that both approaches affect both the income statement and balance sheet, and it is true that these approaches often will result in the same accounting outcomes. For example, whether matching is a principle used to determine when expenses are recognized, or a result of recognizing that assets were consumed as part of the economic activity that occurred in a particular period in which revenue was also recognized, we typically still will see expenses recognized in the periods in which they are incurred to produce revenues. However, the particular approach used by a standard setter can affect recognition and measurement in important ways. In particular, the asset/liability approach encourages us to focus on accurately measuring assets and liabilities. It perhaps is not surprising, then, that a focus on assets and liabilities has led standard setters to lean more and more toward fair value measurement. The future changes to the conceptual framework discussed in the following Where We're Headed box are likely to continue this emphasis on the asset/liability approach.

[44]Some assets and liabilities aren't related to revenue or expense. For example, issuance of shares of stock increases cash as well as shareholders' equity. The treatment of these sorts of transactions is not affected by whether GAAP emphasizes revenues and expenses or assets and liabilities.

Where We're Headed

Since 2010, the FASB and IASB worked separately on their conceptual frameworks. The FASB has worked on relatively narrow projects, such as the definition of materiality and a more general disclosure framework. The IASB, in contrast, has moved forward with a more comprehensive overhaul of its conceptual framework. The IASB's 2015 exposure draft of its concepts statement addressed a range of issues, including the objective and qualitative characteristics of financial reporting, the definitions of key financial-statement elements, when to recognize and de-recognize assets and liabilities, when to use various measurement approaches, the distinction between net income and other comprehensive income, and what constitutes a reporting entity. The IASB anticipates issuing a concepts statement sometime in 2016.

Financial Reporting Case Solution

© Lev Dolgachov/Syda Productions/ age fotostock

1. **What should you tell your friend about the presence of accounting standards in the United States? Who has the authority for standard setting? Who has the responsibility?** *(p. 8)* In the United States we have a set of standards known as generally accepted accounting principles (GAAP). GAAP is a dynamic set of both broad and specific guidelines that companies should follow when measuring and reporting the information in their financial statements and related notes. The Securities and Exchange Commission has the authority to set accounting standards for companies whose securities are publicly traded but it relies on the private sector to accomplish that task. At present, the Financial Accounting Standards Board is the private sector body responsible for standard setting.
2. **What is the economic and political environment in which standard setting occurs?** *(p. 13)* The setting of accounting and reporting standards often has been characterized as a *political process.* Standards, particularly changes in standards, can have significant differential effects on companies, investors and creditors, and other interest groups. A change in an accounting standard or the introduction of a new standard can result in a substantial redistribution of wealth within our economy. The FASB's due process is designed to obtain information from all interested parties to help determine the appropriate accounting approach, but standards are supposed to be neutral with respect to the interests of various parties. Nonetheless, both the FASB and IASB sometimes come under political pressure that sways the results of the standard-setting process.
3. **What is the relationship among management, auditors, investors, and creditors that tends to preclude the "What would you like it to be?" attitude?** *(p. 15)* It is the responsibility of management to apply accounting standards when communicating with investors and creditors through financial statements. Auditors serve as independent intermediaries to help ensure that the management-prepared statements are presented fairly in accordance with GAAP. In providing this assurance, the auditor precludes the "What would you like it to be?" attitude.
4. **In general, what is the conceptual framework that underlies accounting principles?** *(p. 20)* The conceptual framework is a coherent system of interrelated objectives and fundamentals that can lead to consistent standards and that prescribe the nature, function, and limits of financial accounting and reporting. The fundamentals are the underlying concepts of accounting, concepts that guide the selection of events to be accounted for, the measurement of those events, and the means of summarizing and communicating them to interested parties. ●

The Bottom Line

- **LO1–1** Financial accounting is concerned with providing relevant financial information to various external users. However, the primary focus is on the financial information provided by profit-oriented companies to their present and potential investors and creditors. *(p. 3)*
- **LO1–2** Cash basis accounting provides a measure of periodic performance called *net operating cash flow,* which is the difference between cash receipts and cash disbursements from transactions related to providing goods and services to customers. Accrual accounting provides a measure of performance called *net income,* which is the difference between revenues and expenses. Periodic net income is considered a better indicator of future operating cash flows than is current net operating cash flows. *(p. 7)*
- **LO1–3** Generally accepted accounting principles (GAAP) comprise a dynamic set of both broad and specific guidelines that companies follow when measuring and reporting the information in their financial statements and related notes. The Securities and Exchange Commission (SEC) has the authority to set accounting standards in the United States. However, the SEC has always delegated the task to a private sector body, at this time the Financial Accounting Standards Board (FASB). The International Accounting Standards Board (IASB) sets global accounting standards and works with national accounting standard setters to achieve convergence in accounting standards around the world. *(p. 9)*
- **LO1–4** Accounting standards can have significant differential effects on companies, investors, creditors, and other interest groups. Various interested parties sometimes lobby standard setters for their preferred outcomes. For this reason, the setting of accounting standards often has been characterized as a political process. *(p. 13)*
- **LO1–5** Factors encouraging high-quality financial reporting include conceptually based financial accounting standards, external auditors, financial reporting reforms (such as the Sarbanes-Oxley Act), ethical management, and professional accounting organizations that prescribe ethical conduct and license practitioners. *(p. 15)*
- **LO1–6** The FASB's conceptual framework is a set of cohesive objectives and fundamental concepts on which financial accounting and reporting standards can be based. *(p. 19)*
- **LO1–7** The objective of financial reporting is to provide useful financial information to capital providers. The primary decision-specific qualities that make financial information useful are relevance and faithful representation. To be relevant, information must possess predictive value and/or confirmatory value, and all material information should be included. Completeness, neutrality, and freedom from error enhance faithful representation. The 10 elements of financial statements are assets, liabilities, equity, investments by owners, distributions to owners, revenues, expenses, gains, losses, and comprehensive income. *(p. 21)*
- **LO1–8** The four basic assumptions underlying GAAP are (1) the economic entity assumption, (2) the going concern assumption, (3) the periodicity assumption, and (4) the monetary unit assumption. *(p. 24)*
- **LO1–9** Recognition determines whether an item is reflected in the financial statements, and measurement determines the amount of the item. Measurement involves choice of a monetary unit and choice of a measurement attribute. In the United States, the monetary unit is the dollar. Various measurement attributes are used in GAAP, including historical cost, net realizable value, current cost, present value, and fair value. *(p. 26)*
- **LO1–10** A revenue/expense approach to financial reporting emphasizes recognition and measurement of revenues and expenses, while an asset/liability approach emphasizes recognition and measurement of assets and liabilities. *(p. 33)*
- **LO1–11** IFRS and U.S. GAAP are similar in the organizations that support standard setting and in the presence of ongoing political pressures on the standard-setting process. U.S. GAAP and IFRS also have similar conceptual frameworks, although the role of the conceptual framework in IFRS is to provide guidance to preparers as well as to standard setters, while the role of the conceptual framework in U.S. GAAP is more to provide guidance to standard setters. *(pp. 14 and 20)*

Questions For Review of Key Topics

Q 1–1 What is the function and primary focus of financial accounting?

Q 1–2 What is meant by the phrase *efficient allocation of resources?* What mechanism fosters the efficient allocation of resources in the United States?

Q 1–3 Identify two important variables to be considered when making an investment decision.

Q 1–4 What must a company do in the long run to be able to provide a return to investors and creditors?

Q 1–5 What is the primary objective of financial accounting?

Q 1–6 Define net operating cash flows. Briefly explain why periodic net operating cash flows may not be a good indicator of future operating cash flows.

Q 1–7 What is meant by GAAP? Why should all companies follow GAAP in reporting to external users?

Q 1–8 Explain the roles of the SEC and the FASB in the setting of accounting standards.

Q 1–9 Explain the role of the auditor in the financial reporting process.

Q 1–10 List three key provisions of the Sarbanes-Oxley Act of 2002. Order your list from most important to least important in terms of the likely long-term impact on the accounting profession and financial reporting.

Q 1–11 Explain what is meant by *adverse economic consequences* of new or changed accounting standards.

Q 1–12 Why does the FASB undertake a series of elaborate information-gathering steps before issuing a substantive accounting standard?

Q 1–13 What is the purpose of the FASB's conceptual framework?

Q 1–14 Discuss the terms *relevance* and *faithful representation* as they relate to financial accounting information.

Q 1–15 What are the components of relevant information? What are the components of faithful representation?

Q 1–16 Explain what is meant by: The benefits of accounting information must exceed the costs.

Q 1–17 What is meant by the term *materiality* in financial reporting?

Q 1–18 Briefly define the financial accounting elements: (1) assets, (2) liabilities, (3) equity, (4) investments by owners, (5) distributions to owners, (6) revenues, (7) expenses, (8) gains, (9) losses, and (10) comprehensive income.

Q 1–19 What are the four basic assumptions underlying GAAP?

Q 1–20 What is the going concern assumption?

Q 1–21 Explain the periodicity assumption.

Q 1–22 What are four key accounting practices that often are referred to as principles in current GAAP?

Q 1–23 What are two advantages to basing the valuation of assets and liabilities on their historical cost?

Q 1–24 Describe how revenue recognition relates to transferring goods or services.

Q 1–25 What are the four different approaches to implementing expense recognition? Give an example of an expense that is recognized under each approach.

Q 1–26 In addition to the financial statement elements arrayed in the basic financial statements, what are some other ways to disclose financial information to external users?

Q 1–27 Briefly describe the inputs that companies should use when determining fair value. Organize your answer according to preference levels, from highest to lowest priority.

Q 1–28 What measurement attributes are commonly used in financial reporting?

Q 1–29 Distinguish between the revenue/expense and the asset/liability approaches to setting financial reporting standards.

IFRS **Q 1–30** What are the functions of the conceptual framework under IFRS?

IFRS **Q 1–31** What is the standard-setting body responsible for determining IFRS? How does it obtain its funding?

IFRS **Q 1–32** In its Final Staff Report (issued in 2012), what type of convergence between U.S. GAAP and IFRS did the SEC staff argue was not feasible? What reasons did the SEC staff give for that conclusion?

Brief Exercises

BE 1–1
Accrual accounting
● LO1–2

Cash flows during the first year of operations for the Harman-Kardon Consulting Company were as follows: Cash collected from customers, $340,000; Cash paid for rent, $40,000; Cash paid to employees for services rendered during the year, $120,000; Cash paid for utilities, $50,000.

In addition, you determine that customers owed the company $60,000 at the end of the year and no bad debts were anticipated. Also, the company owed the gas and electric company $2,000 at year-end, and the rent payment was for a two-year period. Calculate accrual net income for the year.

BE 1–2
Financial statement elements
● LO1–7

For each of the following items, identify the appropriate financial statement element or elements: (1) probable future sacrifices of economic benefits; (2) probable future economic benefits owned by the company; (3) inflows of assets from ongoing, major activities; (4) decrease in equity from peripheral or incidental transactions.

BE 1–3
Basic assumptions and principles
● LO1–7 through LO1–9

Listed below are several statements that relate to financial accounting and reporting. Identify the accounting concept that applies to each statement.

1. SiriusXM Radio Inc. files its annual and quarterly financial statements with the SEC.
2. The president of Applebee's International, Inc., travels on the corporate jet for business purposes only and does not use the jet for personal use.
3. Jackson Manufacturing does not recognize revenue for unshipped merchandise even though the merchandise has been manufactured according to customer specifications.
4. Lady Jane Cosmetics depreciates the cost of equipment over their useful lives.

BE 1–4
Basic assumptions and principles
● LO1–7 through LO1–9

Identify the accounting concept that was violated in each of the following situations.

1. Astro Turf Company recognizes an expense, cost of goods sold, in the period the product is manufactured.
2. McCloud Drug Company owns a patent that it purchased three years ago for $2 million. The controller recently revalued the patent to its approximate market value of $8 million.
3. Philips Company pays the monthly mortgage on the home of its president, Larry Crosswhite, and charges the expenditure to miscellaneous expense.

BE 1–5
Basic assumptions and principles
● LO1–7 through LO1–9

For each of the following situations, (1) indicate whether you agree or disagree with the financial reporting practice employed and (2) state the accounting concept that is applied (if you agree), or violated (if you disagree).

1. Winderl Corporation did not disclose that it was the defendant in a material lawsuit because the trial was still in progress.
2. Alliant Semiconductor Corporation files quarterly and annual financial statements with the SEC.
3. Reliant Pharmaceutical paid rent on its office building for the next two years and charged the entire expenditure to rent expense.
4. Rockville Engineering records revenue only after products have been shipped, even though customers pay Rockville 50% of the sales price in advance.

BE 1–6
IFRS
● LO1–11

IFRS

Indicate the organization related to IFRS that performs each of the following functions:

1. Obtains funding for the IFRS standard-setting process.
2. Determines IFRS.
3. Oversees the IFRS Foundation.
4. Provides input about the standard-setting agenda.
5. Provides implementation guidance about relatively narrow issues.

Exercises

E 1–1
Accrual accounting
● LO1–2

Listed below are several transactions that took place during the first two years of operations for the law firm of Pete, Pete, and Roy.

	Year 1	Year 2
Amounts billed to clients for services rendered	$170,000	$220,000
Cash collected from clients	160,000	190,000
Cash disbursements		
Salaries paid to employees for services rendered during the year	90,000	100,000
Utilities	30,000	40,000
Purchase of insurance policy	60,000	–0–

In addition, you learn that the firm incurred utility costs of $35,000 in year 1, that there were no liabilities at the end of year 2, no anticipated bad debts on receivables, and that the insurance policy covers a three-year period.

Required:

1. Calculate the net operating cash flow for years 1 and 2.
2. Prepare an income statement for each year similar to Illustration 1–4 according to the accrual accounting model.
3. Determine the amount of receivables from clients that the firm would show in its year 1 and year 2 balance sheets prepared according to the accrual accounting model.

E 1–2
Accrual accounting
● LO1–2

Listed below are several transactions that took place during the second and third years of operations for the RPG Company.

	Year 2	Year 3
Amounts billed to customers for services rendered	$350,000	$450,000
Cash collected from credit customers	260,000	400,000
Cash disbursements:		
Payment of rent	80,000	–0–
Salaries paid to employees for services rendered during the year	140,000	160,000
Travel and entertainment	30,000	40,000
Advertising	15,000	35,000

In addition, you learn that the company incurred advertising costs of $25,000 in year 2, owed the advertising agency $5,000 at the end of year 1, and there were no liabilities at the end of year 3. Also, there were no anticipated bad debts on receivables, and the rent payment was for a two-year period, year 2 and year 3.

Required:

1. Calculate accrual net income for both years.
2. Determine the amount due the advertising agency that would be shown as a liability on RPG's balance sheet at the end of year 2.

E 1–3
FASB codification research
● LO1–3

Access the *FASB Accounting Standards Codification* at the FASB website (www.fasb.org).

Required:

1. Identify the Codification topic number that provides guidance on fair value measurements.
2. What is the specific citation that lists the disclosures required in the notes to the financial statements for each major category of assets and liabilities measured at fair value?
3. List the disclosure requirements.

E 1–4
FASB codification research
● LO1–3

Access the *FASB Accounting Standards Codification* at the FASB website (www.fasb.org). Determine the specific citation for each of the following items:

1. The topic number for business combinations
2. The topic number for related party disclosures
3. The topic, subtopic, and section number for the initial measurement of internal-use software
4. The topic, subtopic, and section number for the subsequent measurement of asset retirement obligations
5. The topic, subtopic, and section number for the recognition of stock compensation

E 1–5
Participants in establishing GAAP
● LO1–3

Three groups that participate in the process of establishing GAAP are users, preparers, and auditors. These groups are represented by various organizations. For each organization listed below, indicate which of these groups it primarily represents.

1. Securities and Exchange Commission
2. Financial Executives International
3. American Institute of Certified Public Accountants
4. Institute of Management Accountants
5. Association of Investment Management and Research

E 1–6
Financial statement elements
● LO1–7

For each of the items listed below, identify the appropriate financial statement element or elements.

1. Obligation to transfer cash or other resources as a result of a past transaction
2. Dividends paid by a corporation to its shareholders
3. Inflow of an asset from providing a good or service
4. The financial position of a company
5. Increase in equity during a period from nonowner transactions
6. Increase in equity from peripheral or incidental transaction
7. Sale of an asset used in the operations of a business for less than the asset's book value

8. The owners' residual interest in the assets of a company
9. An item owned by the company representing probable future benefits
10. Revenues plus gains less expenses and losses
11. An owner's contribution of cash to a corporation in exchange for ownership shares of stock
12. Outflow of an asset related to the production of revenue

E 1–7
Concepts; terminology; conceptual framework
● LO1–7

Listed below are several terms and phrases associated with the FASB's conceptual framework. Pair each item from List A (by letter) with the item from List B that is most appropriately associated with it.

List A	List B
______ 1. Predictive value	a. Decreases in equity resulting from transfers to owners.
______ 2. Relevance	b. Requires consideration of the costs and value of information.
______ 3. Timeliness	c. Important for making interfirm comparisons.
______ 4. Distribution to owners	d. Applying the same accounting practices over time.
______ 5. Confirmatory value	e. Users understand the information in the context of the decision being made.
______ 6. Understandability	f. Agreement between a measure and the phenomenon it purports to represent.
______ 7. Gain	g. Information is available prior to the decision.
______ 8. Faithful representation	h. Pertinent to the decision at hand.
______ 9. Comprehensive income	i. Implies consensus among different measurers.
______ 10. Materiality	j. Information confirms expectations.
______ 11. Comparability	k. The change in equity from nonowner transactions.
______ 12. Neutrality	l. The process of admitting information into financial statements.
______ 13. Recognition	m. The absence of bias.
______ 14. Consistency	n. Increases in equity from peripheral or incidental transactions of an entity.
______ 15. Cost effectiveness	o. Information is useful in predicting the future.
______ 16. Verifiability	p. Concerns the relative size of an item and its effect on decisions.

E 1–8
Qualitative characteristics
● LO1–7

The conceptual framework indicates the desired fundamental and enhancing qualitative characteristics of accounting information. Several constraints impede achieving these desired characteristics. Answer each of the following questions related to these characteristics and constraints.

1. Which component would allow a large company to record the purchase of a $120 printer as an expense rather than capitalizing the printer as an asset?
2. Donald Kirk, former chairman of the FASB, once noted that "... there must be public confidence that the standard-setting system is credible, that selection of board members is based on merit and not the influence of special interests ..." Which characteristic is implicit in Mr. Kirk's statement?
3. Allied Appliances, Inc., changed its revenue recognition policies. Which characteristic is jeopardized by this change?
4. National Bancorp, a publicly traded company, files quarterly and annual financial statements with the SEC. Which characteristic is relevant to the timing of these periodic filings?
5. In general, relevant information possesses which qualities?
6. When there is agreement between a measure or description and the phenomenon it purports to represent, information possesses which characteristic?
7. Jeff Brown is evaluating two companies for future investment potential. Jeff's task is made easier because both companies use the same accounting methods when preparing their financial statements. Which characteristic does the information Jeff will be using possess?
8. A company should disclose information only if the perceived benefits of the disclosure exceed the costs of providing the information. Which constraint does this statement describe?

E 1–9
Basic assumptions, principles, and constraints
● LO1–7 through LO1–9

Listed below are several terms and phrases associated with the accounting concepts. Pair each item from List A (by letter) with the item from List B that is most appropriately associated with it.

List A	List B
______ 1. Expense recognition	a. The enterprise is separate from its owners and other entities.
______ 2. Periodicity	b. A common denominator is the dollar.
______ 3. Historical cost principle	c. The entity will continue indefinitely.
______ 4. Materiality	d. Record expenses in the period the related revenue is recognized.
______ 5. Revenue recognition	e. The original transaction value upon acquisition.
______ 6. Going concern assumption	f. All information that could affect decisions should be reported.
______ 7. Monetary unit assumption	g. The life of an enterprise can be divided into artificial time periods.
______ 8. Economic entity assumption	h. Criteria usually satisfied for products at point of sale.
______ 9. Full-disclosure principle	i. Concerns the relative size of an item and its effect on decisions.

E 1–10
Basic assumptions and principles
● LO1–7 through LO1–9

Listed below are several statements that relate to financial accounting and reporting. Identify the accounting concept that applies to each statement.

1. Jim Marley is the sole owner of Marley's Appliances. Jim borrowed $100,000 to buy a new home to be used as his personal residence. This liability was not recorded in the records of Marley's Appliances.
2. Apple Inc. distributes an annual report to its shareholders.
3. Hewlett-Packard Corporation depreciates machinery and equipment over their useful lives.
4. Crosby Company lists land on its balance sheet at $120,000, its original purchase price, even though the land has a current fair value of $200,000.
5. Honeywell International Inc. records revenue when products are delivered to customers, even though the cash has not yet been received.
6. Liquidation values are not normally reported in financial statements even though many companies do go out of business.
7. IBM Corporation, a multibillion dollar company, purchased some small tools at a cost of $800. Even though the tools will be used for a number of years, the company recorded the purchase as an expense.

E 1–11
Basic assumptions and principles
● LO1–8, LO1–9

Identify the accounting concept that was violated in each of the following situations.

1. Pastel Paint Company purchased land two years ago at a price of $250,000. Because the value of the land has appreciated to $400,000, the company has valued the land at $400,000 in its most recent balance sheet.
2. Atwell Corporation has not prepared financial statements for external users for over three years.
3. The Klingon Company sells farm machinery. Revenue from a large order of machinery from a new buyer was recorded the day the order was received.
4. Don Smith is the sole owner of a company called Hardware City. The company recently paid a $150 utility bill for Smith's personal residence and recorded a $150 expense.
5. Golden Book Company purchased a large printing machine for $1,000,000 (a material amount) and recorded the purchase as an expense.
6. Ace Appliance Company is involved in a major lawsuit involving injuries sustained by some of its employees in the manufacturing plant. The company is being sued for $2,000,000, a material amount, and is not insured. The suit was not disclosed in the most recent financial statements because no settlement had been reached.

E 1–12
Basic assumptions and principles
● LO1–7 through LO1–9

For each of the following situations, indicate whether you agree or disagree with the financial reporting practice employed and state the accounting concept that is applied (if you agree) or violated (if you disagree).

1. Wagner Corporation adjusted the valuation of all assets and liabilities to reflect changes in the purchasing power of the dollar.
2. Spooner Oil Company changed its method of accounting for oil and gas exploration costs from successful efforts to full cost. No mention of the change was included in the financial statements. The change had a material effect on Spooner's financial statements.
3. Cypress Manufacturing Company purchased machinery having a five-year life. The cost of the machinery is being expensed over the life of the machinery.
4. Rudeen Corporation purchased equipment for $180,000 at a liquidation sale of a competitor. Because the equipment was worth $230,000, Rudeen valued the equipment in its subsequent balance sheet at $230,000.
5. Davis Bicycle Company received a large order for the sale of 1,000 bicycles at $100 each. The customer paid Davis the entire amount of $100,000 on March 15. However, Davis did not record any revenue until April 17, the date the bicycles were delivered to the customer.
6. Gigantic Corporation purchased two small calculators at a cost of $32.00. The cost of the calculators was expensed even though they had a three-year estimated useful life.
7. Esquire Company provides financial statements to external users every three years.

E 1–13
Basic assumptions and principles
● LO1–7 through LO1–9

For each of the following situations, state whether you agree or disagree with the financial reporting practice employed, and briefly explain the reason for your answer.

1. The controller of the Dumars Corporation increased the carrying value of land from its original cost of $2 million to its recently appraised value of $3.5 million.
2. The president of Vosburgh Industries asked the company controller to charge miscellaneous expense for the purchase of an automobile to be used solely for personal use.
3. At the end of its 2018 fiscal year, Dower, Inc., received an order from a customer for $45,350. The merchandise will ship early in 2019. Because the sale was made to a long-time customer, the controller recorded the sale in 2018.
4. At the beginning of its 2018 fiscal year, Rossi Imports paid $48,000 for a two-year lease on warehouse space. Rossi recorded the expenditure as an asset to be expensed equally over the two-year period of the lease.

5. The Reliable Tire Company included a note in its financial statements that described a pending lawsuit against the company.
6. The Hughes Corporation, a company whose securities are publicly traded, prepares monthly, quarterly, and annual financial statements for internal use but disseminates to external users only the annual financial statements.

E 1–14
Basic assumptions and principles
● LO1–7 through LO1–9

Listed below are accounting concepts discussed in this chapter.

a. Economic entity assumption
b. Going concern assumption
c. Periodicity assumption
d. Monetary unit assumption
e. Historical cost principle
f. Conservatism
g. Matching
h. Full-disclosure principle
i. Cost effectiveness
j. Materiality

Identify by letter the accounting concept that relates to each statement or phrase below.

______ 1. Inflation causes a violation of this assumption.
______ 2. Information that could affect decision making should be reported.
______ 3. Recognizing expenses in the period they were incurred to produce revenue.
______ 4. The basis for measurement of many assets and liabilities.
______ 5. Relates to the qualitative characteristic of timeliness.
______ 6. All economic events can be identified with a particular entity.
______ 7. The benefits of providing accounting information should exceed the cost of doing so.
______ 8. A consequence is that GAAP need not be followed in all situations.
______ 9. Not a qualitative characteristic, but a practical justification for some accounting choices.
______ 10. Assumes the entity will continue indefinitely.

E 1–15
Multiple choice; concept statements, basic assumptions, principles
● LO1–6 through LO1–9

Determine the response that best completes the following statements or questions.

1. The primary objective of financial reporting is to provide information
   a. About a firm's management team
   b. Useful to capital providers
   c. Concerning the changes in financial position resulting from the income-producing efforts of the entity
   d. About a firm's financing and investing activities
2. *Statements of Financial Accounting Concepts* issued by the FASB
   a. Represent GAAP
   b. Have been superseded by *SFAS*s
   c. Are subject to approval of the SEC
   d. Identify the conceptual framework within which accounting standards are developed
3. In general, revenue is recognized when
   a. The sales price has been collected
   b. A purchase order has been received
   c. A good or service has been delivered to a customer
   d. A contract has been signed
4. In depreciating the cost of an asset, accountants are most concerned with
   a. Conservatism
   b. Recognizing revenue in the appropriate period
   c. Full disclosure
   d. Recognizing expense in the appropriate period
5. The primary objective of the matching principle is to
   a. Provide full disclosure
   b. Record expenses in the period that related revenues are recognized
   c. Provide timely information to decision makers
   d. Promote comparability between financial statements of different periods
6. The separate entity assumption states that, in the absence of contrary evidence, all entities will survive indefinitely.
   a. True
   b. False

Broaden Your Perspective

Apply your critical-thinking ability to the knowledge you've gained. These cases will provide you an opportunity to develop your research, analysis, judgment, and communication skills. You will also work with other students, integrate what you've learned, apply it in real-world situations, and consider its global and ethical ramifications. This practice will broaden your knowledge and further develop your decision-making abilities.

Judgment Case 1–1
The development of accounting standards
● LO1–3

In 1934, Congress created the Securities and Exchange Commission (SEC) and gave the commission both the power and responsibility for setting accounting and reporting standards in the United States.

Required:

1. Explain the relationship between the SEC and the various private sector standard-setting bodies that have, over time, been relied upon to set accounting standards.
2. Can you think of any reasons why the SEC relies on private sector bodies to set accounting standards, rather than undertaking the task itself?

Research Case 1–2
Accessing SEC information through the Internet
● LO1–3

Internet access to the World Wide Web has provided a wealth of information accessible with our personal computers. Many chapters in this book contain Real World Cases that require you to access the web to research an accounting issue. The purpose of this case is to introduce you to the Internet home page of the Securities and Exchange Commission (SEC) and its EDGAR database.

Required:

1. Access the SEC home page on the Internet. The web address is www.sec.gov.
2. Choose the subaddress "About the SEC." What are the two basic objectives of the 1933 Securities Act?
3. Return to the SEC home page and access EDGAR. Describe the contents of the database.

Research Case 1–3
Accessing FASB information through the Internet
● LO1–4

The purpose of this case is to introduce you to the information available on the website of the Financial Accounting Standards Board (FASB).

Required:

Access the FASB home page on the Internet. The web address is www.fasb.org. Answer the following questions.

1. Describe the mission of the FASB.
2. Who are the current Board members of the FASB? Briefly describe their backgrounds.
3. How are topics added to the FASB's technical agenda?

Research Case 1–4
Accessing IASB information through the Internet
● LO1–3

The purpose of this case is to introduce you to the information available on the website of the International Accounting Standards Board (IASB).

Required:

Access the IASB home page on the Internet. The web address is www.iasb.org. Answer the following questions.

1. Describe the mission of the IASB.
2. The IASB has how many board members?
3. Who is the current chairman of the IASB?
4. Where is the IASB located?

Research Case 1–5
Accounting standards in China
● LO1–3, LO1–4

Economic reforms in the People's Republic of China are moving that nation toward a market-driven economy. China's accounting practices must also change to accommodate the needs of potential investors. In an article entitled "Institutional Factors Influencing China's Accounting Reforms and Standards," Professor Bing Xiang analyzes the changes in the accounting environment of China during the recent economic reforms and their implications for the development of accounting reforms.

Required:

1. In your library or from some other source, locate the indicated article in *Accounting Horizons,* June 1998.
2. Briefly describe the economic reforms that led to the need for increased external financial reporting in China.
3. Conformity with International Accounting Standards was specified as an overriding objective in formulating China's accounting standards. What is the author's opinion of this objective?

Communication Case 1–6
Relevance and reliability
● LO1–7

Some theorists contend that companies that create pollution should report the social cost of that pollution in income statements. They argue that such companies are indirectly subsidized as the cost of pollution is borne by society while only production costs (and perhaps minimal pollution fines) are shown in the income statement. Thus, the product sells for less than would be necessary if all costs were included.

Assume that the FASB is considering a standard to include the social costs of pollution in the income statement. The process would require considering both relevance and faithful representation of the information produced by the new standard. Your instructor will divide the class into two to six groups depending on the size of the class. The mission of your group is to explain how the concepts of relevance and faithful representation relate to this issue.

Required:

Each group member should consider the question independently and draft a tentative answer prior to the class session for which the case is assigned.

In class, each group will meet for 10 to 15 minutes in different areas of the classroom. During that meeting, group members will take turns sharing their suggestions for the purpose of arriving at a single group treatment.

After the allotted time, a spokesperson for each group (selected during the group meetings) will share the group's solution with the class. The goal of the class is to incorporate the views of each group into a consensus answer to the question.

Communication Case 1–7
Accounting standard setting
● LO1–4

One of your friends is a financial analyst for a major stock brokerage firm. Recently she indicated to you that she had read an article in a weekly business magazine that alluded to the political process of establishing accounting standards. She had always assumed that accounting standards were established by determining the approach that conceptually best reflected the economics of a transaction.

Required:

Write a one to two-page article for a business journal explaining what is meant by the political process for establishing accounting standards. Be sure to include in your article a discussion of the need for the FASB to balance accounting considerations and economic consequences.

Ethics Case 1–8
The auditors' responsibility
● LO1–4

It is the responsibility of management to apply accounting standards when communicating with investors and creditors through financial statements. Another group, auditors, serves as an independent intermediary to help ensure that management has in fact appropriately applied GAAP in preparing the company's financial statements. Auditors examine (audit) financial statements to express a professional, independent opinion. The opinion reflects the auditors' assessment of the statements' fairness, which is determined by the extent to which they are prepared in compliance with GAAP.

Some feel that it is impossible for an auditor to give an independent opinion on a company's financial statements because the auditors' fees for performing the audit are paid by the company. In addition to the audit fee, quite often the auditor performs other services for the company such as preparing the company's income tax returns.

Required:

How might an auditor's ethics be challenged while performing an audit?

Judgment Case 1–9
Qualitative characteristics
● LO1–7

Generally accepted accounting principles do not require companies to disclose forecasts of any financial variables to external users. A friend, who is a finance major, is puzzled by this and asks you to explain why such relevant information is not provided to investors and creditors to help them predict future cash flows.

Required:

Explain to your friend why this information is not routinely provided to investors and creditors.

Judgment Case 1–10
GAAP, comparability, and the role of the auditor
● LO1–4, LO1–7

Mary McQuire is trying to decide how to invest her money. A friend recommended that she buy the stock of one of two corporations and suggested that she should compare the financial statements of the two companies before making a decision.

Required:

1. Do you agree that Mary will be able to compare the financial statements of the two companies?
2. What role does the auditor play in ensuring comparability of financial statements between companies?

Judgment Case 1–11
Cost effectiveness
● LO1–7

Concepts Statement 8 includes a discussion of the cost effectiveness constraint. Assume that the FASB is considering revising an important accounting standard.

Required:

1. What is the desired benefit from revising an accounting standard?
2. What are some of the possible costs that could result from a revision of an accounting standard?
3. What does the FASB do in order to assess possible benefits and costs of a proposed revision of an accounting standard?

Judgment Case 1–12
Revenue recognition
● LO1–9

A new client, the Wolf Company, asks your advice concerning the point in time that the company should recognize revenue from the rental of its office buildings. Renters usually pay rent on a quarterly basis at the beginning of the quarter. The owners contend that the critical event that motivates revenue recognition should be the date the cash is received from renters. After all, the money is in hand and is very seldom returned.

Required:

Do you agree or disagree with the position of the owners of Wolf Company? Support your answer.

Analysis Case 1–13
Expense recognition
● LO1–9

Revenues measure the accomplishments of a company during the period. Expenses are then matched with revenues to produce a periodic measure of performance called *net income.*

Required:

1. Explain what is meant by the phrase *matched with revenues.*
2. Describe the four approaches used to implement expense recognition and label them 1 through 4.
3. For each of the following, identify which expense recognition approach should be used to recognize the cost as expense.
   a. The cost of producing a product
   b. The cost of advertising
   c. The cost of monthly rent on the office building
   d. The salary of an office employee
   e. Depreciation on an office building

Judgment Case 1–14
Capitalize or expense?
● LO1–9

When a company makes an expenditure that is neither a payment to a creditor nor a distribution to an owner, management must decide if the expenditure should be capitalized (recorded as an increase in an asset) or expensed (recorded as an expense thereby decreasing owners' equity).

Required:

1. Which factor or factors should the company consider when making this decision?
2. Are there any constraints that could cause the company to alter its decision?

Real World Case 1–15
Elements; disclosures; The Gap, Inc.
● LO1–7, LO1–9

Real World Financials

Access the financial statements for the year ended January 30, 2016 for The Gap, Inc. by downloading them from www.gapinc.com, and use them to answer the following questions.

Required:

1. What amounts did The Gap report for the following items for the fiscal year ended January 30, 2016?
   a. Total net revenues
   b. Total operating expenses
   c. Net income (earnings)
   d. Total assets
   e. Total stockholders' equity
2. How many shares of common stock did The Gap have issued on January 30, 2016?
3. Why do you think The Gap reports more than one year of data in its financial statements?

Judgment Case 1–16
Convergence
● LO1–11

IFRS

Consider the question of whether the United States should converge accounting standards with IFRS.

Required:

1. Make a list of arguments that favor convergence.
2. Make a list of arguments that favor nonconvergence.
3. Indicate your own conclusion regarding whether the United States should converge with IFRS, and indicate the primary considerations that determined your conclusion.

Continuing Cases

Target Case
● LO1-9

Target Corporation prepares its financial statements according to U.S. GAAP. Target's financial statements and disclosure notes for the year ended January 30, 2016, are available in the Connect. This material also is available under the Investor Relations link at the company's website (www.target.com).

Required:

1. What amounts did Target report for the following items for the year ended January 30, 2016?
   a. Total Revenues
   b. Income from current operations
   c. Net income or net loss
   d. Total assets
   e. Total equity
2. What was Target's basic earnings per share for the year ended January 30, 2016?
3. Why do you think Target has chosen to have its fiscal year end on January 30, as opposed to December 31?
4. Regarding Target's audit report:
   a. Who is Target's auditor?
   b. Did Target receive a "clean" (unmodified) audit opinion?

Air France–KLM Case

● LO1-11

Air France–KLM (AF), a Franco-Dutch company, prepares its financial statements according to International Financial Reporting Standards. AF's financial statements and disclosure notes for the year ended December 31, 2015, are available in Connect. This material is also available under the Finance link at the company's website (www.airfranceklm.com).

Required:

1. What amounts did AF report for the following items for the year ended December 31, 2015?
   a. Total revenues
   b. Income from current operations
   c. Net income or net loss (AF equity holders)
   d. Total assets
   e. Total equity
2. What was AF's basic earnings or loss per share for the year ended December 31, 2015?
3. Examine Note 4.1.1 of AF's annual report. What accounting principles were used to prepare AF's financial statements? Under those accounting principles, could AF's financial information differ from that of a company that exactly followed IFRS as published by the IASB? Explain.

CPA Exam Questions and Simulations

Sample CPA Exam questions from Roger CPA Review are available in Connect as support for the topics in this chapter. These Multiple Choice Questions and Task-Based Simulations include expert-written explanations and solutions, and provide a starting point for students to become familiar with the content and functionality of the actual CPA Exam.

CHAPTER

2 Review of the Accounting Process

OVERVIEW

Chapter 1 explained that the primary means of conveying financial information to investors, creditors, and other external users is through financial statements and related notes. The purpose of this chapter is to review the fundamental accounting process used to produce the financial statements. This review establishes a framework for the study of the concepts covered in intermediate accounting.

Actual accounting systems differ significantly from company to company. This chapter focuses on the many features that tend to be common to any accounting system.

LEARNING OBJECTIVES

After studying this chapter, you should be able to:

- **LO2–1** Analyze routine economic events—transactions—and record their effects on a company's financial position using the accounting equation format. *(p. 48)*
- **LO2–2** Record transactions using the general journal format. *(p. 52)*
- **LO2–3** Post the effects of journal entries to general ledger accounts and prepare an unadjusted trial balance. *(p. 59)*
- **LO2–4** Identify and describe the different types of adjusting journal entries. *(p. 62)*
- **LO2–5** Record adjusting journal entries in general journal format, post entries, and prepare an adjusted trial balance. *(p. 63)*
- **LO2–6** Describe the four basic financial statements. *(p. 71)*
- **LO2–7** Explain the closing process. *(p. 75)*
- **LO2–8** Convert from cash basis net income to accrual basis net income. *(p. 79)*

© goodluz/123RF

FINANCIAL REPORTING CASE

Engineering Profits

After graduating from college last year, two of your engineering-major friends started an Internet consulting practice. They began operations on July 1 and felt they did quite well during their first year. Now they would like to borrow $20,000 from a local bank to buy new computing equipment and office furniture. To support their loan application, the friends presented the bank with the following income statement for their first year of operations ending June 30:

Consulting revenue		$96,000
Operating expenses:		
Salaries	$32,000	
Rent	9,000	
Supplies	4,800	
Utilities	3,000	
Advertising	1,200	(50,000)
Net income		$46,000

The bank officer noticed that there was no depreciation expense in the income statement and has asked your friends to revise the statement after making year-end adjustments. After agreeing to help, you discover the following information:

a. The friends paid $80,000 for equipment when they began operations. They think the equipment will be useful for five years.

b. They pay $500 a month to rent office space. In January, they paid a full year's rent in advance. This is included in the $9,000 rent expense.

c. Included in consulting revenue is $13,000 they received from a customer in June as a deposit for work to be performed in August.

QUESTIONS

By the time you finish this chapter, you should be able to respond appropriately to the questions posed in this case. Compare your response to the solution provided at the end of the chapter.

1. What purpose do adjusting entries serve? *(p. 63)*

2. What year-end adjustments are needed to revise the income statement? Did your friends do as well their first year as they thought? *(p. 63)*

A solid foundation is vital to a sound understanding of intermediate accounting. So, we review the fundamental accounting process here to serve as a framework for the new concepts you will learn in this course.

Chapter 1 introduced the theoretical structure of financial accounting and the environment within which it operates. The primary function of financial accounting—to provide financial information to external users that possesses the fundamental decision-specific qualities of relevance and faithful representation—is accomplished by periodically disseminating financial statements and related notes. In this chapter we review the process used to identify, analyze, record, summarize, and then report the economic events affecting a company's financial position.

Keep in mind as you study this chapter that the accounting information systems businesses actually use are quite different from company to company. Larger companies generally use more complex systems than smaller companies use. The types of economic events affecting companies also cause differences in systems. We focus on the many features that tend to be common to all accounting systems.

Computers are used to process accounting information. In this chapter we provide an overview of the basic model that underlies computer software programs.

It's important to understand that this chapter and its appendices are not intended to describe actual accounting systems. In most business enterprises, the sheer volume of data that must be processed precludes a manual accounting system. Fortunately, the computer provides a solution. *We describe and illustrate a manual accounting information system to provide an overview of the basic model that underlies the computer software programs actually used to process accounting information.*

Electronic data processing is fast, accurate, and affordable. Many large and medium-sized companies own or rent their own mainframe computers and company-specific data processing systems. Smaller companies can take advantage of technology with relatively inexpensive desktop and laptop computers and generalized data software packages such as QuickBooks and Peachtree Accounting Software. Enterprise Resource Planning (ERP) systems are now being installed in companies of all sizes. The objective of ERP is to create a customized software program that integrates all departments and functions across a company onto a single computer system that can serve the information needs of those different departments, including the accounting department.

The Basic Model

Economic events cause changes in the financial position of the company.

The first objective of any accounting system is to identify the **economic events** that can be expressed in financial terms by the system.[1] An economic event for accounting purposes is any event that *directly* affects the financial position of the company. Recall from Chapter 1 that financial position comprises assets, liabilities, and owners' equity. Broad and specific accounting principles determine which events should be recorded, when the events should be recorded, and the dollar amount at which they should be measured.

External events involve an exchange between the company and another entity.

Economic events can be classified as either external events or internal events. **External events** involve an exchange between the company and a separate economic entity. Examples are purchasing merchandise inventory for cash, borrowing cash from a bank, and paying salaries to employees. In each instance, the company receives something (merchandise, cash, and services) in exchange for something else (cash, assumption of a liability, or both).

Internal events do not involve an exchange transaction but do affect the company's financial position.

On the other hand, **internal events** directly affect the financial position of the company but don't involve an exchange transaction with another entity. Examples are the depreciation of equipment and the use of supplies. As we will see later in the chapter, these events must be recorded to properly reflect a company's financial position and results of operations in accordance with the accrual accounting model.

The Accounting Equation

● LO2–1

The **accounting equation** underlies the process used to capture the effect of economic events.

$$\text{Assets} = \text{Liabilities} + \text{Owners' Equity}$$

This general expression portrays the equality between the total economic resources of an entity (its assets)—shown on the left side of the equation—and the total claims against the entity (liabilities and equity)—shown on the right side. In other words, the resources of an enterprise are provided by creditors and owners.

Each event, or *transaction,* has a dual effect on the accounting equation.

The equation also implies that each economic event affecting this equation will have a dual effect because resources always must equal claims. For illustration, consider the events (we refer to these throughout the text as **transactions**) in Illustration 2–1.

[1]There are many economic events that affect a company *indirectly* and are not recorded. For example, when the Federal Reserve changes its discount rate, it is an important economic event that can affect the company in many ways, but it is not recorded by the company.

Illustration 2–1
Transaction analysis

1. **An attorney invested $50,000 to open a law office.**
An investment by the owner causes both assets and owners' equity to increase.

Assets	=	Liabilities	+	Owners' Equity
+$50,000 (cash)				+$50,000 (investment by owner)

2. **$40,000 was borrowed from a bank and a note payable was signed.**
This transaction causes assets and liabilities to increase. A bank loan increases cash and creates an obligation to repay it.

Assets	=	Liabilities	+	Owners' Equity
+$40,000 (cash)		+$40,000 (note payable)		

3. **Supplies costing $3,000 were purchased on account.**
Buying supplies on credit also increases both assets and liabilities.

Assets	=	Liabilities	+	Owners' Equity
+$3,000 (supplies)		+$3,000 (accounts payable)		

Transactions 4, 5, and 6 are revenue and expense transactions. Revenues and expenses (and gains and losses) are events that cause owners' equity to change. Revenues and gains describe inflows of assets, causing owners' equity to increase. Expenses and losses describe outflows of assets (or increases in liabilities), causing owners' equity to decrease.

4. **Services were performed on account for $10,000.**

Assets	=	Liabilities	+	Owners' Equity
+$10,000 (accounts receivable)				+$10,000 (revenue)

5. **Salaries of $5,000 were paid to employees.**

Assets	=	Liabilities	+	Owners' Equity
−$5,000 (cash)				−$5,000 (expense)

6. **$500 of supplies were used.**

Assets	=	Liabilities	+	Owners' Equity
−$500 (supplies)				−$500 (expense)

7. **$1,000 was paid on account to the supplies vendor.**
This transaction causes assets and liabilities to decrease.

Assets	=	Liabilities	+	Owners' Equity
−$1,000 (cash)		−$1,000 (accounts payable)		

Each transaction is analyzed to determine its effect on the equation and on the specific financial position elements.

The accounting equation can be expanded to include a column for each type of asset and liability and for each type of change in owners' equity.

As discussed in Chapter 1, owners of a corporation are its shareholders, so owners' equity for a corporation is referred to as shareholders' equity. Shareholders' equity for a corporation arises primarily from two sources: (1) amounts *invested* by shareholders in the corporation and (2) amounts *earned* by the corporation (on behalf of its shareholders). These are reported as (1) **paid-in capital** and (2) **retained earnings**. Retained earnings equals net income less distributions to shareholders (primarily dividends) since the inception of the corporation. Illustration 2–2 shows the basic accounting equation for a corporation with shareholders' equity expanded to highlight its composition. We use the corporate format throughout the remainder of the chapter.

Owners' equity for a corporation, called *shareholders' equity*, is classified by source as either *paid-in capital* or *retained earnings*.

The *double-entry system* is used to process transactions.

Illustration 2–2
Accounting Equation for a Corporation

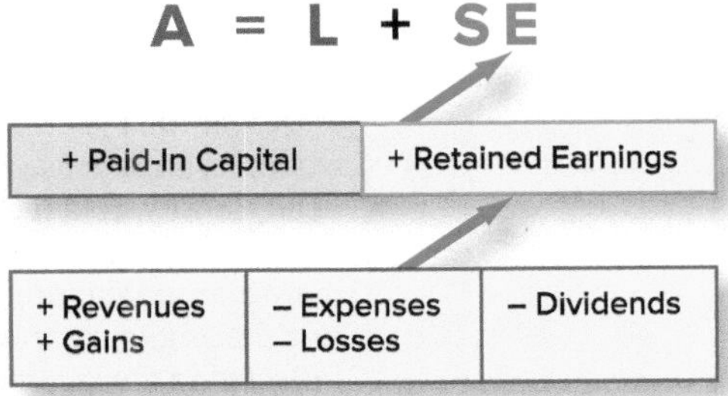

Account Relationships

All transactions could be recorded in columnar fashion as increases or decreases to elements of the accounting equation. However, even for a very small company with few transactions, this would become cumbersome. So, most companies use a process called the **double-entry system**. The term *double-entry* refers to the dual effect that each transaction has on the accounting equation.

A general ledger is a collection of storage areas, called *accounts*, used to keep track of increases and decreases in financial position elements.

Elements of the accounting equation are represented by **accounts** which are contained in a **general ledger**. Increases and decreases in each element of a company's financial position are recorded in these accounts. A separate account is maintained for individual assets and liabilities, retained earnings, and paid-in capital. Also, to accumulate information needed for the income statement, we use separate accounts to keep track of the changes in retained earnings caused by revenues, expenses, gains, and losses. The number of accounts depends on the complexity of the company's operations.

An account includes the account title, an account number to aid the processing task, and columns or fields for increases, decreases, the cumulative balance, and the date. For instructional purposes we use **T-accounts** instead of formal ledger accounts. A T-account has space at the top for the account title and two sides for recording increases and decreases.

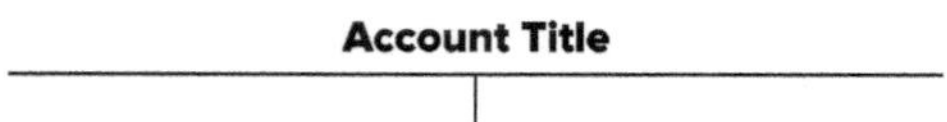

In the double-entry system, *debit* means *left* side of an account and *credit* means *right* side of an account.

For centuries, accountants have effectively used a system of **debits** and **credits** to increase and decrease account balances in the ledger. Debits merely represent the *left* side of the account and credits the *right* side, as shown below.

Asset *increases* are entered on the *debit* side of accounts and *decreases* are entered on the *credit* side. Liability and equity account *increases* are *credits* and *decreases* are *debits*.

Account Title	
Debit side	Credit side

Whether a debit or a credit represents an increase or a decrease depends on the type of account. Accounts on the left side of the accounting equation (assets) are *increased* (+) by *debit* entries and *decreased* (−) by *credit* entries. Accounts on the right side of the accounting equation (liabilities and shareholders' equity) are *increased* (+) by *credit* entries and *decreased* (−) by *debit* entries. This arbitrary, but effective, procedure ensures that for each transaction the net impact on the left sides of accounts always equals the net impact on the right sides of accounts.

For example, consider the bank loan in our earlier illustration. An asset, cash, increased by $40,000. Increases in assets are *debits*. Liabilities also increased by $40,000. Increases in liabilities are *credits*.

Assets		=	Liabilities		+	Owners' Equity
Cash			Note Payable			
Debit	Credit		Debit	Credit		
+ 40,000				40,000 +		

The debits equal the credits in every transaction (dual effect), so both before and after a transaction the accounting equation is in balance.

Prior exposure to the terms debit and credit probably comes from your experience with a bank account. For example, when a bank debits your checking account for service charges, it decreases your account balance. When you make a deposit, the bank credits your account, increasing your account balance. You must remember that from the bank's perspective, your bank account balance is a liability—it represents the amount that the bank owes you. Therefore, when the bank debits your account, it is decreasing its liability. When the bank credits your account, its liability increases.

Illustration 2–3 demonstrates the relationship among the accounting equation, debits and credits, and the increases and decreases in financial position elements.

Notice that increases and decreases in retained earnings are recorded *indirectly*. For example, an expense represents a decrease in retained earnings, which requires a debit. That debit, however, is recorded in an appropriate expense account rather than in retained earnings itself. This allows the company to maintain a separate record of expenses incurred during an accounting period. The debit to retained earnings for the expense is recorded in a closing entry (reviewed later) at the end of the period, only after the expense total is reflected in the income statement. Similarly, an increase in retained earnings due to revenue

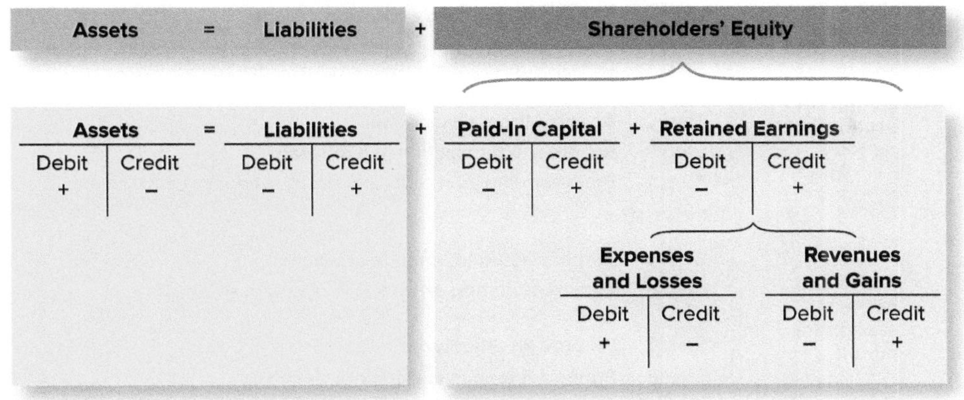

Illustration 2–3
Accounting Equation, Debits and Credits, Increases and Decreases

is recorded indirectly with a credit to a revenue account, which is later reflected as a credit to retained earnings.

The general ledger accounts serve as control accounts. Subsidiary accounts associated with a particular general ledger control account are maintained in separate subsidiary ledgers. For example, a subsidiary ledger for accounts receivable contains individual account receivable accounts for each of the company's credit customers and the total of all subsidiary accounts would equal the amount in the control account. Subsidiary ledgers are discussed in more detail in Appendix 2C.

Each general ledger account can be classified as either *permanent* or *temporary.* **Permanent accounts** represent assets, liabilities, and shareholders' equity at a point in time. **Temporary accounts** represent changes in the retained earnings component of shareholders' equity for a corporation caused by revenue, expense, gain, and loss transactions. It would be cumbersome to record each revenue/expense, gain/loss transaction directly into the retained earnings account. The different types of events affecting retained earnings should be kept separate to facilitate the preparation of the financial statements. The balances in these temporary accounts are periodically, usually once a year, closed (zeroed out), and the net effect is recorded in the permanent retained earnings account. The temporary accounts need to be zeroed out to measure income on an annual basis. This closing process is discussed in a later section of this chapter.

Permanent accounts represent the basic financial position elements of the accounting equation.

Temporary accounts keep track of the changes in the retained earnings component of shareholders' equity.

The Accounting Processing Cycle

Now that we've reviewed the basics of the double-entry system, let's look closer at the process used to identify, analyze, record, and summarize transactions and prepare financial statements. This section deals only with *external transactions,* those that involve an exchange transaction with another entity. Internal transactions are discussed in a later section.

The 10 steps in the accounting processing cycle are listed in Illustration 2–4. Steps 1–4 take place during the accounting period while steps 5–8 occur at the end of the accounting period. Steps 9 and 10 are required only at the end of the year.

We now discuss these steps in order.

STEP 1
Obtain information about transactions from source documents.

The first step in the process is to *identify* external transactions affecting the accounting equation. An accountant usually does not directly witness business transactions. A mechanism is needed to relay the essential information about each transaction to the accountant. **Source documents** such as sales invoices, bills from suppliers, and cash register tapes serve this need.

STEP 2
Analyze the transaction.

These source documents usually identify the date and nature of each transaction, the participating parties, and the monetary terms. For example, a sales invoice identifies the date of sale, the customer, the specific goods sold, the dollar amount of the sale, and the payment terms. With this information, the second step in the processing cycle, **transaction analysis**, can be accomplished. Transaction analysis is the process of reviewing the source documents to determine the dual effect on the accounting equation and the specific elements involved.

Illustration 2–4

The Accounting Processing Cycle

The Steps of the Accounting Processing Cycle

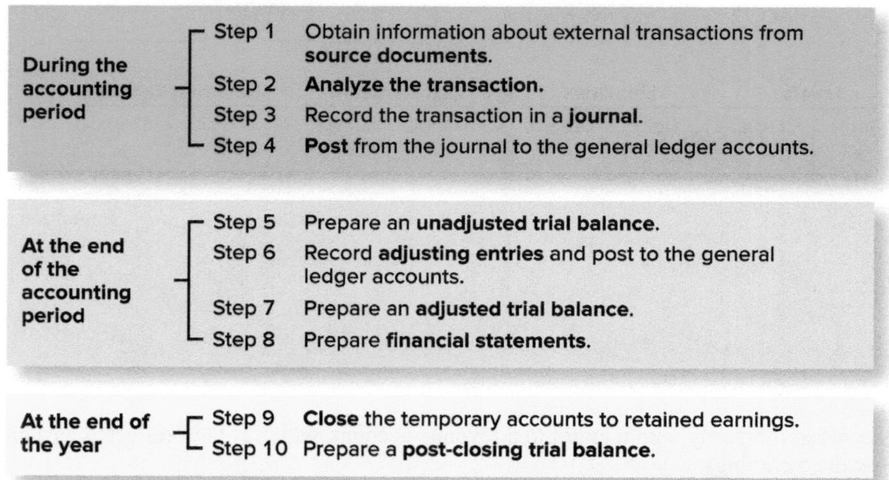

During the accounting period
Step 1 Obtain information about external transactions from source documents.
Step 2 Analyze the transaction.
Step 3 Record the transaction in a journal.
Step 4 Post from the journal to the general ledger accounts.
At the end of the accounting period
Step 5 Prepare an unadjusted trial balance.
Step 6 Record adjusting entries and post to the general ledger accounts.
Step 7 Prepare an adjusted trial balance.
Step 8 Prepare financial statements.
At the end of the year
Step 9 Close the temporary accounts to retained earnings.
Step 10 Prepare a post-closing trial balance.

This process is summarized in Illustration 2–5 for the seven transactions described previously in Illustration 2–1. The item in each T-account is numbered to show the related transaction. We don't use dollar signs next to numbers in the accounting records (journal entries, journals, ledgers, trial balances)—only in the actual financial statements.

STEP 3

Record the transaction in a *journal.*

The third step in the process is to record the transaction in a journal. A journal provides a chronological record of all economic events affecting a firm. Each journal entry is expressed in terms of equal debits and credits to accounts affected by the transaction being recorded. Debits and credits represent increases or decreases to specific accounts, depending on the type of account, as explained earlier. For example, for credit sales, we record a debit to accounts receivable and a credit to sales revenue in a sales journal.

A sales journal is an example of a special journal used to record a repetitive type of transaction. In Appendix 2C we discuss the use of special journals in more depth. In this chapter and throughout the text, we use the general journal format to record all transactions.

● LO2–2

Any type of transaction can be recorded in a general journal. It has a place for the date of the transaction, a place for account titles, account numbers, and supporting explanations, as well as a place for debit entries, and a place for credit entries. A simplified journal entry is used throughout the text that lists the account titles to be debited and credited and the dollar amounts. A common convention is to list the debited accounts first, indent the credited accounts, and use the first of two columns for the debit amounts and the second column for the credit amounts. An explanation is entered for each journal entry (for ease in this example the explanation is located in the margin). For example, the journal entry for the bank loan in Illustration 2–1, which requires a debit to cash and a credit to note payable, is recorded as follows:

To record the borrowing of cash and the signing of a note payable.

Cash	40,000	
Note payable		40,000

STEP 4

Post from the journal to the general ledger accounts.

Step 4 is to periodically transfer or *post* the debit and credit information from the journal to individual ledger accounts. Recall that a ledger is simply a collection of all of the company's various accounts. Each account provides a summary of the effects of all events and transactions on that individual account. This process is called posting. Posting involves transferring debits and credits recorded in individual journal entries to the specific accounts affected. As discussed earlier in the chapter, most accounting systems today are computerized. For these systems, the journal input information creates a stored journal and simultaneously posts each entry to the ledger accounts.

Illustration 2–5 Transaction Analysis, the Accounting Equation, and Debits and Credits

Transaction	Transaction Analysis	Assets	=	Liabilities	+	Owners' Equity	Account Entry	
		Accounting Equation						
1. An attorney invested $50,000 to open a law office.	Assets (cash) and owners' equity each increased by $50,000.	**+50,000**				**+50,000**	**Cash** 1. 50,000 |	**Owners' Equity** | 50,000 1.
	Cumulative balances	50,000	=			50,000		
2. $40,000 was borrowed from a bank and a note payable was signed.	Assets (cash) and liabilities (note payable) each increased by $40,000.	**+40,000**		**+40,000**			**Cash** 1. 50,000 | 2. 40,000 |	**Note Payable** | 40,000 2.
	Cumulative balances	90,000	=	40,000	+	50,000		
3. Supplies costing $3,000 were purchased on account.	Assets (supplies) and liabilities (accounts payable) each increased by $3,000.	**+3,000**		**+3,000**			**Supplies** 3. 3,000 |	**Accounts Payable** | 3,000 3.
	Cumulative balances	93,000	=	43,000	+	50,000		
4. Services were performed on account for $10,000.	Assets (accounts receivable) and owners' equity (revenue) each increased by $10,000.	**+10,000**				**+10,000**	**Accounts Receivable** 4. 10,000 |	**Owners' Equity (Revenue)** | 10,000 4.
	Cumulative balances	103,000	=	43,000	+	60,000		
5. Salaries of $5,000 were paid to employees.	Assets (cash) decreased and owners' equity decreased (salaries expense increased) by $5,000.	**−5,000**				**−5,000**	**Cash** 1. 50,000 | 5,000 5. 2. 40,000 |	**Owners' Equity (Salaries Expense)** 5. 5,000 |
	Cumulative balances	98,000	=	43,000	+	55,000		
6. $500 of supplies were used.	Assets (supplies) decreased and owners' equity decreased (supplies expense increased) by $500.	**−500**				**−500**	**Supplies** 3. 3,000 | 500 6.	**Owners' Equity (Supplies Expense)** 6. 500 |
	Cumulative balances	97,500	=	43,000	+	54,500		
7. $1,000 was paid on account to the supplies vendor.	Assets (cash) and liabilities (accounts payable) each decreased by $1,000.	**−1,000**		**−1,000**			**Cash** 1. 50,000 | 5,000 5. 2. 40,000 | 1,000 7.	**Accounts Payable** 7. 1,000 | 3,000 3.
	Cumulative balances	96,500	=	42,000	+	54,500		

These first four steps in the processing cycle are illustrated using the external transactions in Illustration 2–6 which occurred during the month of July 2018, the first month of operations for Dress Right Clothing Corporation. The company operates a retail store that sells men's and women's clothing. Dress Right is organized as a corporation so owners' equity is classified by source as either paid-in capital or retained earnings.

Illustration 2–6
External Transactions for July 2018

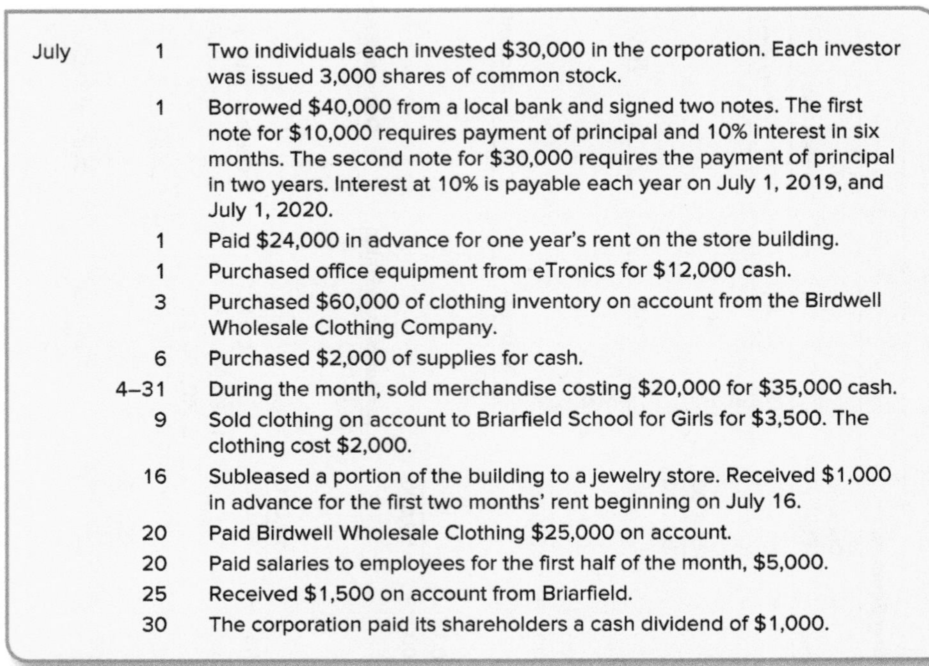

July		
	1	Two individuals each invested $30,000 in the corporation. Each investor was issued 3,000 shares of common stock.
	1	Borrowed $40,000 from a local bank and signed two notes. The first note for $10,000 requires payment of principal and 10% interest in six months. The second note for $30,000 requires the payment of principal in two years. Interest at 10% is payable each year on July 1, 2019, and July 1, 2020.
	1	Paid $24,000 in advance for one year's rent on the store building.
	1	Purchased office equipment from eTronics for $12,000 cash.
	3	Purchased $60,000 of clothing inventory on account from the Birdwell Wholesale Clothing Company.
	6	Purchased $2,000 of supplies for cash.
	4–31	During the month, sold merchandise costing $20,000 for $35,000 cash.
	9	Sold clothing on account to Briarfield School for Girls for $3,500. The clothing cost $2,000.
	16	Subleased a portion of the building to a jewelry store. Received $1,000 in advance for the first two months' rent beginning on July 16.
	20	Paid Birdwell Wholesale Clothing $25,000 on account.
	20	Paid salaries to employees for the first half of the month, $5,000.
	25	Received $1,500 on account from Briarfield.
	30	The corporation paid its shareholders a cash dividend of $1,000.

The local bank requires that Dress Right furnish financial statements on a monthly basis. The transactions listed in the illustration are used to demonstrate the accounting processing cycle for the month of July 2018.

For each transaction, a source document provides the necessary information to complete steps two and three in the processing cycle: transaction analysis and recording the appropriate journal entry. Each transaction listed in Illustration 2–6 is analyzed below, preceded by the necessary journal entry.

To record the issuance of common stock.

July 1		
Cash	60,000	
Common stock		60,000

This first transaction is an investment by owners that increases an asset, cash, and also increases shareholders' equity. Increases in assets are recorded as debits and increases in shareholders' equity are recorded as credits. We use the paid-in capital account called common stock because stock was issued in exchange for cash paid in.[2]

To record the borrowing of cash and the signing of a notes payable.

July 1		
Cash	40,000	
Notes payable		40,000

This transaction causes increases in both cash and the liability, notes payable. Increases in assets are debits and increases in liabilities are credits. The notes require payment of

[2]The different types of stock are discussed in Chapter 18.

\$40,000 in principal and \$6,500 [(\$10,000 × 10% × $\frac{6}{12}$ = \$500) + (\$30,000 × 10% × 2 years = \$6,000)] in interest. However, at this point we are concerned only with the external transaction that occurs when the cash is borrowed and the notes are signed. Later we discuss how the interest is recorded.

July 1		
Prepaid rent	24,000	
Cash		24,000

To record the payment of one year's rent in advance.

This transaction increased an asset called prepaid rent, which is debited, and decreased the asset cash (a credit). Dress Right acquired the right to use the building for one full year. This is an asset because it represents a future benefit to the company. As we will see later, this asset expires over the one-year rental period.

July 1		
Office equipment	12,000	
Cash		12,000

To record the purchase of office equipment.

This transaction increases one asset, office equipment, and decreases another, cash.

July 3		
Inventory	60,000	
Accounts payable		60,000

To record the purchase of merchandise inventory.

This purchase of merchandise on account is recorded by a debit to inventory, an asset, and a credit to accounts payable, a liability. Increases in assets are debits. Increases in liabilities are credits.

The Dress Right Clothing Company uses the *perpetual inventory system* to keep track of its merchandise inventory. This system requires that the cost of merchandise purchased be recorded in inventory, an asset account. When inventory is sold, the inventory account is decreased by the cost of the item sold. An alternative method, the *periodic system,* is briefly discussed later in this chapter. We explore the topic of inventory in depth in Chapters 8 and 9.

July 6		
Supplies	2,000	
Cash		2,000

To record the purchase of supplies.

We record the acquisition of supplies as a debit to the asset account supplies (an increase) and as a credit to the asset cash (a decrease). Supplies are an asset because they represent future benefits.

July 4–31		
Cash	35,000	
Sales revenue		35,000
Cost of goods sold (expense)	20,000	
Inventory		20,000

To record the month's cash sales and the cost of those sales.

During the month of July, cash sales to customers totaled \$35,000. The company's assets (cash) increase by this amount as does shareholders' equity. This increase in equity is recorded by a credit to the temporary account sales revenue.

At the same time, an asset, inventory, decreases and retained earnings decreases. Recall that expenses are outflows or using up of assets from providing goods and services. Dress Right incurred an expense equal to the cost of the inventory sold. The temporary account cost of goods sold increases. However, this increase in an expense represents a *decrease* in shareholders' equity—retained earnings—and accordingly the account is debited. Both of these transactions are *summary* transactions. Normally each sale made during the month requires a separate and similar entry in a special journal, which we discuss in Appendix 2C.

To record a credit sale and the cost of that sale.

July 9

Accounts receivable	3,500	
Sales revenue		3,500
Cost of goods sold	2,000	
Inventory		2,000

This transaction is similar to the cash sale shown earlier. The only difference is that the asset acquired in exchange for merchandise is accounts receivable rather than cash.

Additional Consideration

Periodic Inventory System

The principal alternative to the perpetual inventory system is the periodic system. By this approach, we record the cost of merchandise purchased in a temporary account called *purchases*. When inventory is sold, the inventory account is not decreased and cost of goods sold is not recorded. Instead, we determine the balance in the inventory account only at the end of a reporting period (periodically), and then we can determine the cost of good sold for the period.

For example, the purchase of $60,000 of merchandise on account by Dress Right Clothing is recorded as follows:

Purchases	60,000	
Accounts payable		60,000

No cost of goods sold entry is recorded when sales are made in the periodic system.

At the end of July, the amount of ending inventory is determined (either by means of a physical count of goods on hand or by estimation) to be $38,000 and cost of goods sold for the month is determined as follows:

Beginning inventory	$ –0–
Plus: Purchases	60,000
Less: Ending inventory	(38,000)
Cost of goods sold	$22,000

We record the cost of goods sold for the period and adjust the inventory account to the actual amount on hand (in this case from zero to $38,000) this way:

Cost of goods sold	22,000	
Inventory	38,000	
Purchases		60,000

We discuss inventory in depth in Chapters 8 and 9.

To record the receipt of rent in advance.

July 16

Cash	1,000	
Deferred rent revenue (liability)		1,000

Cash increases by $1,000 so we debit the cash account. At this point, Dress Right does not recognize revenue yet even though cash has been received. Instead, revenue is recorded only after Dress Right has provided the jewelry store with the use of facilities; that is, as the rental period expires. On receipt of the cash, a liability called *deferred rent revenue* increases and is credited. This liability represents Dress Right's obligation to provide the use of facilities to the jewelry store.

July 20		
Accounts payable	25,000	
Cash		25,000

To record the payment of accounts payable.

This transaction decreases both an asset (cash) and a liability (accounts payable). A debit decreases the liability, and a credit decreases the asset.

July 20		
Salaries expense	5,000	
Cash		5,000

To record the payment of salaries for the first half of the month.

Employees were paid for services rendered during the first half of the month. The cash expenditure did not create an asset since no future benefits resulted. Cash decreases and is credited; shareholders' equity decreases and is debited. The reduction in shareholders' equity is recorded in the temporary account, salaries expense.

July 25		
Cash	1,500	
Accounts receivable		1,500

To record receipt of cash on account.

This transaction is an exchange of one asset, accounts receivable, for another asset, cash.

July 30		
Retained earnings	1,000	
Cash		1,000

To record the payment of a cash dividend.

The payment of a cash dividend is a distribution to owners that reduces both cash and retained earnings.

Additional Consideration

An alternative method of recording a cash dividend is to debit a temporary account called dividends. In that case, the dividends account is later closed (transferred) to retained earnings along with the other temporary accounts at the end of the fiscal year. The journal entry to record the dividend using this approach is as follows:

Dividends	1,000	
Cash		1,000

We discuss and illustrate the closing process later in the chapter.

Illustration 2–7 summarizes each of the transactions we just discussed as they would appear in a general journal. In addition to the date, account titles, and debit and credit columns, the journal also has a column titled Post Ref. (Posting Reference). In this column we enter the number assigned to the general ledger account that is being debited or credited. For purposes of this illustration, all asset accounts have been assigned numbers in the 100s, all liabilities are 200s, permanent shareholders' equity accounts are 300s, revenues are 400s, and expenses are 500s.

Illustration 2–7

The General Journal

General Journal				Page 1
Date 2018	**Account Title and Explanation**	**Post Ref.**	**Debit**	**Credit**
July 1	Cash	100	60,000	
	Common stock	300		60,000
	To record the issuance of common stock.			
1	Cash	100	40,000	
	Notes payable	220		40,000
	To record the borrowing of cash and the signing of notes payable.			
1	Prepaid rent	130	24,000	
	Cash	100		24,000
	To record the payment of one year's rent in advance.			
1	Office equipment	150	12,000	
	Cash	100		12,000
	To record the purchase of office equipment.			
3	Inventory	140	60,000	
	Accounts payable	210		60,000
	To record the purchase of merchandise inventory.			
6	Supplies	125	2,000	
	Cash	100		2,000
	To record the purchase of supplies.			
4–31	Cash	100	35,000	
	Sales revenue	400		35,000
	To record cash sales for the month.			
4–31	Cost of goods sold	500	20,000	
	Inventory	140		20,000
	To record the cost of cash sales.			
9	Accounts receivable	110	3,500	
	Sales revenue	400		3,500
	To record credit sale.			
9	Cost of goods sold	500	2,000	
	Inventory	140		2,000
	To record the cost of a credit sale.			
16	Cash	100	1,000	
	Deferred rent revenue	230		1,000
	To record the receipt of rent in advance.			
20	Accounts payable	210	25,000	
	Cash	100		25,000
	To record the payment of accounts payable.			
20	Salaries expense	510	5,000	
	Cash	100		5,000
	To record the payment of salaries for the first half of the month.			
25	Cash	100	1,500	
	Accounts receivable	110		1,500
	To record the receipt of cash on account.			
30	Retained earnings	310	1,000	
	Cash	100		1,000
	To record the payment of a cash dividend.			

The ledger accounts also contain a posting reference, usually the page number of the journal in which the journal entry was recorded. This allows for easy cross-referencing between the journal and the ledger.

Step 4 in the processing cycle is to transfer (post) the debit/credit information from the journal to the general ledger accounts. Illustration 2–8 contains the ledger accounts (in T-account form) for Dress Right *after* all the general journal transactions have been posted. The reference GJ1 next to each of the posted amounts indicates that the source of the entry is page 1 of the general journal. An alternative is to number each of the entries in chronological order and reference them by number. Note that each account shows the balance that we call a *normal balance*—that is, the balance is the debit or credit side used to increase the account.

● LO2–3

Illustration 2–8

General Ledger Accounts

Balance Sheet Accounts

Cash 100

Debit		Credit	
July 1 GJ1	60,000	24,000	July 1 GJ1
1 GJ1	40,000	12,000	1 GJ1
4–31 GJ1	35,000	2,000	6 GJ1
16 GJ1	1,000	25,000	20 GJ1
25 GJ1	1,500	5,000	20 GJ1
		1,000	30 GJ1
July 31 Bal.	**68,500**		

Prepaid Rent 130

Debit		Credit	
July 1 GJ1	24,000		
July 31 Bal.	**24,000**		

Accounts Receivable 110

Debit		Credit	
July 9 GJ1	3,500	1,500	July 25 GJ1
July 31 Bal.	**2,000**		

Inventory 140

Debit		Credit	
July 3 GJ1	60,000	20,000	July 4–31
		2,000	9 GJ1
July 31 Bal.	**38,000**		

Supplies 125

Debit		Credit	
July 6 GJ1	2,000		
July 31 Bal.	**2,000**		

Office equipment 150

Debit		Credit	
July 1 GJ1	12,000		
July 31 Bal.	**12,000**		

Accounts Payable 210

Debit		Credit	
July 20 GJ1	25,000	60,000	July 3 GJ1
		35,000	**July 31 Bal.**

Notes Payable 220

Debit		Credit	
		40,000	July 1 GJ1
		40,000	**July 31 Bal.**

Deferred Rent Revenue 230

Debit		Credit	
		1,000	July 16 GJ1
		1,000	**July 31 Bal.**

Common Stock 300

Debit		Credit	
		60,000	July 1 GJ1
		60,000	**July 31 Bal.**

Retained Earnings 310

Debit		Credit	
July 30 GJ1	1,000		
July 31 Bal.	**1,000**		

Income Statement Accounts

Sales Revenue 400

Debit		Credit	
		35,000	July 4–31 GJ1
		3,500	9 GJ1
		38,500	**July 31 Bal.**

Cost of Goods Sold 500

Debit		Credit	
July 4–31 GJ1	20,000		
9 GJ1	2,000		
July 31 Bal.	**22,000**		

Salaries Expense 510

Debit		Credit	
July 20 GJ1	5,000		
July 31 Bal.	**5,000**		

STEP 5

Prepare an *unadjusted trial balance.*

Before preparing financial statements and adjusting entries (internal transactions) at the end of an accounting period, we prepare an **unadjusted trial balance**—Step 5. A trial balance is simply a list of the general ledger accounts along with their balances at a particular date, listed in the order that they appear in the ledger. The purpose of the trial balance is to allow us to check for completeness and to verify that the sum of the accounts with debit balances equals the sum of the accounts with credit balances. The fact that the debits and credits are equal, though, does not necessarily ensure that the equal balances are correct. The trial balance could contain offsetting errors. As we will see later in the chapter, this trial balance also helps with preparing adjusting entries.

The unadjusted trial balance at July 31, 2018, for Dress Right appears in Illustration 2–9. Notice that retained earnings has a debit balance of $1,000. This reflects the payment of the cash dividend to shareholders. We record increases and decreases in retained earnings from revenue, expense, gain and loss transactions *indirectly* in temporary accounts. Before the start of the next year, we transfer these increases and decreases to the retained earnings account.

Illustration 2–9

Unadjusted Trial Balance

DRESS RIGHT CLOTHING CORPORATION
Unadjusted Trial Balance
July 31, 2018

Account Title	Debits	Credits
Cash	68,500	
Accounts receivable	2,000	
Supplies	2,000	
Prepaid rent	24,000	
Inventory	38,000	
Office equipment	12,000	
Accounts payable		35,000
Notes payable		40,000
Deferred rent revenue		1,000
Common stock		60,000
Retained earnings	1,000	
Sales revenue		38,500
Cost of goods sold	22,000	
Salaries expense	5,000	
Totals	174,500	174,500

At any time, the total of all debit balances should equal the total of all credit balances.

Concept Review Exercise

JOURNAL ENTRIES FOR EXTERNAL TRANSACTIONS

The Wyndham Wholesale Company began operations on August 1, 2018. The following transactions occur during the month of August.

a. Owners invest $50,000 cash in the corporation in exchange for 5,000 shares of common stock.
b. Equipment is purchased for $20,000 cash.
c. On the first day of August, $6,000 rent on a building is paid for the months of August and September.
d. Merchandise inventory costing $38,000 is purchased on account. The company uses the perpetual inventory system.
e. $30,000 is borrowed from a local bank, and a note payable is signed.
f. Credit sales for the month are $40,000. The cost of merchandise sold is $22,000.
g. $15,000 is collected on account from customers.
h. $20,000 is paid on account to suppliers of merchandise.
i. Salaries of $7,000 are paid to employees for August.

j. A bill for $2,000 is received from the local utility company for the month of August.
k. $20,000 cash is loaned to another company, evidenced by a note receivable.
l. The corporation pays its shareholders a cash dividend of $1,000.

Required:

1. Prepare a journal entry for each transaction.
2. Prepare an unadjusted trial balance as of August 31, 2018.

Solution:

1. Prepare a journal entry for each transaction.
   a. The issuance of common stock for cash increases both cash and shareholders' equity (common stock).

Cash	50,000	
Common stock		50,000

b. The purchase of equipment increases equipment and decreases cash.

Equipment	20,000	
Cash		20,000

c. The payment of rent in advance increases prepaid rent and decreases cash.

Prepaid rent	6,000	
Cash		6,000

d. The purchase of merchandise on account increases both inventory and accounts payable.

Inventory	38,000	
Accounts payable		38,000

e. Borrowing cash and signing a note increases both cash and note payable.

Cash	30,000	
Note payable		30,000

f. The sale of merchandise on account increases both accounts receivable and sales revenue. Also, cost of goods sold increases and inventory decreases.

Accounts receivable	40,000	
Sales revenue		40,000
Cost of goods sold	22,000	
Inventory		22,000

g. The collection of cash on account increases cash and decreases accounts receivable.

Cash	15,000	
Accounts receivable		15,000

h. The payment to suppliers on account decreases both accounts payable and cash.

Accounts payable	20,000	
Cash		20,000

i. The payment of salaries for the period increases salaries expense (decreases retained earnings) and decreases cash.

Salaries expense	7,000	
Cash		7,000

j. The receipt of a bill for services rendered increases both an expense (utilities expense) and accounts payable. The expense decreases retained earnings.

Utilities expense	2,000	
Accounts payable		2,000

k. The lending of cash to another entity and the signing of a note increases note receivable and decreases cash.

Note receivable	20,000	
Cash		20,000

l. Cash dividends paid to shareholders reduce both retained earnings and cash.

Retained earnings[3]	1,000	
Cash		1,000

2. Prepare an unadjusted trial balance as of August 31, 2018.

Account Title	**Debits**	**Credits**
Cash	21,000	
Accounts receivable	25,000	
Prepaid rent	6,000	
Inventory	16,000	
Note receivable	20,000	
Equipment	20,000	
Accounts payable		20,000
Note payable		30,000
Common stock		50,000
Retained earnings	1,000	
Sales revenue		40,000
Cost of goods sold	22,000	
Salaries expense	7,000	
Utilities expense	2,000	
Totals	140,000	140,000

● LO2–4

STEP 6

Record *adjusting entries* and post to the ledger accounts.

Adjusting Entries

Step 6 in the processing cycle is to record in the general journal and post to the ledger accounts the effect of *internal events* on the accounting equation. These transactions do not involve an exchange transaction with another entity and, therefore, are not initiated by a source document. They are recorded *at the end of any period when financial statements are prepared.* These transactions are commonly referred to as **adjusting entries**.

Even when all transactions and events are analyzed, corrected, journalized, and posted to appropriate ledger accounts, some account balances will require updating. Adjusting entries

[3]An alternative is to debit a temporary account–dividends–that is closed to retained earnings at the end of the fiscal year along with the other temporary accounts.

are required to implement the *accrual accounting model.* More specifically, these entries help ensure that all revenues are recognized in the period goods or services are transferred to customers, regardless of when the cash is received. Also, they enable a company to recognize all expenses incurred during a period, regardless of when cash payment is made. As a result, a period's income statement provides a more complete measure of a company's operating performance and a better measure for predicting future operating cash flows. The balance sheet also provides a more complete assessment of assets and liabilities as sources of future cash receipts and disbursements. You might think of adjusting entries as a method of bringing the company's financial information up to date before preparing the financial statements.

FINANCIAL Reporting Case

Q1, p. 47

Adjusting entries are necessary for three situations:

1. Prepayments, sometimes referred to as *deferrals*
2. Accruals
3. Estimates

FINANCIAL Reporting Case

Q2, p. 47

Prepayments

Prepayments occur when the cash flow *precedes* either expense or revenue recognition. For example, a company may buy supplies in one period but use them in a later period. The cash outflow creates an asset (supplies) which then must be expensed in a future period as the asset is used up. Similarly, a company may receive cash from a customer in one period but provide the customer with a good or service in a future period. For instance, magazine publishers usually receive cash in advance for magazine subscriptions. The cash inflow creates a liability (deferred revenue) that is recognized as revenue in a future period when the goods or services are transferred to customers.

Prepayments are transactions in which the cash flow *precedes* expense or revenue recognition.

PREPAID EXPENSES. Prepaid expenses are the costs of assets acquired in one period and expensed in a future period. Whenever cash is paid, and it is not to (1) satisfy a liability or (2) pay a dividend or return capital to owners, it must be determined whether or not the payment creates future benefits or whether the payment benefits only the current period. The purchase of buildings, equipment, or supplies or the payment of rent in advance are examples of payments that create future benefits and should be recorded as assets. The benefits provided by these assets expire in future periods and their cost is expensed in future periods as related revenues are recognized.

Prepaid expenses represent assets recorded when a cash disbursement creates benefits beyond the current reporting period.

To illustrate this concept, assume that a company paid a radio station $2,000 in July for advertising. If that $2,000 were for advertising provided by the radio station during the month of July, the entire $2,000 would be expensed in the same period as the cash disbursement. If, however, the $2,000 was a payment for advertising to be provided in a future period, say the month of August, then the cash disbursement creates an asset called *prepaid advertising.* Then, an adjusting entry is required at the end of August to increase advertising expense (decrease shareholders' equity) and to decrease the asset, prepaid advertising, by $2,000. So, the adjusting entry for a prepaid expense is a *debit to an expense* and a *credit to an asset.*

The adjusting entry required for a prepaid expense is a *debit to an expense* and a *credit to an asset.*

The unadjusted trial balance can provide a starting point for determining which adjusting entries are required for a period, particularly for prepayments. Review the July 31, 2018, unadjusted trial balance for the Dress Right Clothing Corporation in Illustration 2–9 and try to anticipate the required adjusting entries for prepaid expenses.

The first asset that requires adjustment is supplies, $2,000 of which were purchased during July. This transaction created an asset as the supplies will be used in future periods. The company could either track the supplies used or simply count the supplies at the end of the period and determine the dollar amount of supplies remaining. Assume that Dress Right determines that at the end of July, $1,200 of supplies remain. The following adjusting journal entry is required.

● LO2–5

Supplies		
Beg. bal.	0	
	2,000	800
End bal.	1,200	

Supplies Expense		
Beg. bal.	0	
	800	
End bal.	800	

July 31		
Supplies expense	800	
Supplies		800

To record the cost of supplies used during the month of July.

The next prepaid expense requiring adjustment is rent. Recall that at the beginning of July, the company paid $24,000 to its landlord representing one year's rent in advance. As it is reasonable to assume that the rent services provided each period are equal, the monthly rent is $2,000. At the end of July 2018, one month's prepaid rent has expired and must be recognized as expense.

To record the cost of expired rent for the month of July.

July 31		
Rent expense ($24,000 ÷ 12)	2,000	
Prepaid rent		2,000

Rent Expense

	Debit	Credit
Beg. bal.	0	
	2,000	
End bal.	2,000	

Prepaid Rent

	Debit	Credit
Beg. bal.	0	
	24,000	2,000
End bal.	22,000	

After this entry is recorded and posted to the ledger accounts, the prepaid rent account will have a debit balance of $22,000, representing 11 remaining months at $2,000 per month, and the rent expense account will have a $2,000 debit balance.

The final prepayment involves the asset represented by office equipment that was purchased for $12,000. This asset has a long life but nevertheless will expire over time. For the previous two adjusting entries, it was fairly straightforward to determine the amount of the asset that expired during the period.

However, it is difficult, if not impossible, to determine how much of the benefits from using the office equipment expired during any particular period. Recall from Chapter 1 that one approach is to recognize an expense "by a systematic and rational allocation to specific time periods."

Assume that the office equipment has a useful life of five years (60 months) and will be worthless at the end of that period, and that we choose to allocate the cost equally over the period of use. The amount of monthly expense, called *depreciation expense,* is $200 ($12,000 ÷ 60 months = $200), and the following adjusting entry is recorded.

To record depreciation of office equipment for the month of July.

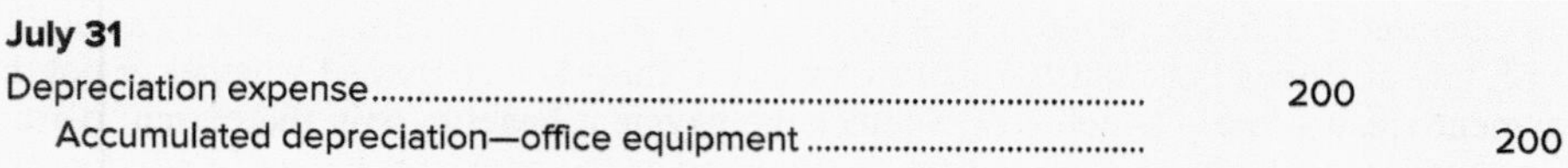

July 31		
Depreciation expense	200	
Accumulated depreciation—office equipment		200

The entry reduces an asset, office equipment, by $200. However, the asset account is not reduced directly. Instead, the credit is to an account called *accumulated depreciation.* This is a contra account to office equipment. The normal balance in a contra asset account will be a credit, that is, "contra," or opposite, to the normal debit balance in an asset account. The purpose of the contra account is to keep the original cost of the asset intact while reducing it indirectly. In the balance sheet, office equipment is reported net of accumulated depreciation. This topic is covered in depth in Chapter 11.

After this entry is recorded and posted to the ledger accounts, the accumulated depreciation account will have a credit balance of $200 and the depreciation expense account will have a $200 debit balance. If a required adjusting entry for a prepaid expense is not recorded, net income, assets, and shareholders' equity (retained earnings) will be overstated.

Deferred revenues represent liabilities recorded when cash is received from customers in advance of providing a good or service.

DEFERRED REVENUES. Deferred revenues are created when a company receives cash from a customer in one period for goods or services that are to be provided in a future period. The cash receipt, an external transaction, is recorded as a debit to cash and a credit to a liability. This liability reflects the company's obligation to provide goods or services in the future.

To illustrate a deferred revenue transaction, assume that during the month of June a magazine publisher received $24 in cash for a 24-month subscription to a monthly magazine. The subscription begins in July. On receipt of the cash, the publisher records a liability, deferred subscription revenue, of $24. Subsequently, revenue of $1 is recognized as each monthly magazine is published and mailed to the customer. An adjusting entry is required each month to increase shareholders' equity (revenue) to recognize the $1 in revenue and to decrease the liability. Assuming that the cash receipt entry included a credit to a liability, the adjusting entry for deferred revenues, therefore, is a *debit to a liability,* in this case deferred subscription revenue, and a *credit to revenue.*

The adjusting entry required when deferred revenues are recognized is a *debit to a liability* and a *credit to revenue.*

Once again, the unadjusted trial balance provides information concerning deferred revenues. For Dress Right Clothing Corporation, the only deferred revenue in the trial balance is deferred rent revenue. Recall that the company subleased a portion of its building to a jewelry store for $500 per month. On July 16, the jewelry store paid Dress Right $1,000 in advance for the first two months' rent. The transaction was recorded as a debit to cash and a credit to deferred rent revenue.

At the end of July, how much of the $1,000 must be recognized? Approximately one-half of one month's rent service has been provided, or $250, requiring the following adjusting entry.

July 31		
Deferred rent revenue	250	
Rent revenue		250

To record previously deferred rent revenue recognized during July.

Deferred Rent Revenue

Debit	Credit
	0 Beg. bal.
250	1,000
	750 End bal.

Rent Revenue

Debit	Credit
	0 Beg. bal.
	250
	250 End bal.

After this entry is recorded and posted to the ledger accounts, the deferred rent revenue account is reduced to a credit balance of $750 for the remaining one and one-half months' rent, and the rent revenue account will have a $250 credit balance. If this entry is not recorded, net income and shareholders' equity (retained earnings) will be understated, and liabilities will be overstated.

ALTERNATIVE APPROACH TO RECORD PREPAYMENTS. The same end result can be achieved for prepayments by recording the external transaction directly into an expense or revenue account. In fact, many companies prefer this approach. For simplicity, bookkeeping instructions might require all cash payments for expenses to be debited to the appropriate expense accounts and all cash payments for revenues to be credited to the appropriate revenue accounts. In the adjusting entry, then, the *unexpired* prepaid expense (asset) or *deferred* revenue (liability) as of the end of the period are recorded.

For example, on July 1, 2018, Dress Right paid $24,000 in cash for one year's rent on its building. The entry included a debit to prepaid rent. The company could have debited rent expense instead of prepaid rent.

Alternative Approach		
July 1		
Rent expense	24,000	
Cash		24,000

Rent Expense

Debit	Credit
Beg. bal. 0	
24,000	22,000
End bal. 2,000	

The adjusting entry then records the amount of prepaid rent as of the end of July, $22,000, and reduces rent expense to $2,000, the cost of rent for the month of July.

Alternative Approach		
July 31		
Prepaid rent	22,000	
Rent expense		22,000

Prepaid Rent

Debit	Credit
Beg. bal. 0	
22,000	
End bal. 22,000	

The net effect of handling the transactions in this manner is the same as the previous treatment. Either way, the prepaid rent account will have a debit balance at the end of July of $22,000 to represent 11 months remaining prepaid rent, and the rent expense account will have a debit balance of $2,000 to represent the one month of rent used in the period of this income statement being prepared. What's important is that an adjusting entry is recorded to ensure the appropriate amounts are reflected in both the expense and asset *before financial statements are prepared.*

Similarly, the July 16 cash receipt from the jewelry store representing an advance for two months' rent initially could have been recorded by Dress Right as a credit to rent revenue instead of deferred rent revenue (a liability).

Rent Revenue

	0 Beg. bal.
750	1,000
	250 End bal.

Alternative Approach
July 16

Cash	1,000	
Rent revenue		1,000

If Dress Right records the entire $1,000 as rent revenue in this way, it would then use the adjusting entry to record the amount of deferred revenue as of the end of July, $750 to represent the one and one-half month of rent revenue remaining as collected in advance, and the rent revenue account will have a credit balance of $250, which is for the one-half month of July that has passed in the current period.

Deferred Rent Revenue

	0 Beg. bal.
	750
	750 End bal.

Alternative Approach
July 31

Rent revenue	750	
Deferred rent revenue		750

Accruals

Accruals involve transactions where the cash outflow or inflow takes place in a period subsequent to expense or revenue recognition.

Accruals occur when the cash flow comes *after* either expense or revenue recognition. For example, a company often uses the services of another entity in one period and pays for them in a subsequent period. An expense must be recognized in the period incurred and an accrued liability recorded. Also, goods and services often are provided to customers on credit. In such instances, a revenue is recognized in the period goods or services are transferred to customers and an asset, a receivable, is recorded.

Many accruals involve external transactions that automatically are recorded from a source document. For example, a sales invoice for a credit sale provides all the information necessary to record the debit to accounts receivable and the credit to sales revenue. However, there are some accruals that involve internal transactions and thus require adjusting entries. Because accruals involve recognition of expense or revenue before cash flow, the unadjusted trial balance will not be as helpful in identifying required adjusting entries as with prepayments.

Accrued liabilities represent liabilities recorded when an expense has been incurred prior to cash payment.

The adjusting entry required to record an accrued liability is a *debit to an expense* and a *credit to a liability.*

ACCRUED LIABILITIES. For accrued liabilities, we are concerned with expenses incurred but not yet paid. Dress Right Clothing Corporation requires two adjusting entries for accrued liabilities at July 31, 2018.

The first entry is for employee salaries for the second half of July. Recall that on July 20 the company paid employees $5,000 for salaries for the first half of the month. Salaries for the second half of July probably will be paid in early August. Nevertheless, an expense is incurred in July for services rendered to the company by its employees. The accrual income statement for July must reflect these services for the entire month regardless of when the cash payment is made.

Therefore, an obligation exists at the end of July to pay the salaries earned by employees for the last half of that month. An adjusting entry is required to increase salaries expense (decrease shareholders' equity) and to increase liabilities for the salaries payable. The adjusting entry for an accrued liability always includes a *debit to an expense,* and a *credit to a liability.* Assuming that salaries for the second half of July are $5,500, the following adjusting entry is recorded.

To record accrued salaries at the end of July.

Salaries Payable

	0 Beg. bal.
	5,500
	5,500 End bal.

Salaries Expense

Beg. bal. 0	
July 20 5,000	
5,500	
End bal. 10,500	

July 31

Salaries expense	5,500	
Salaries payable		5,500

After this entry is recorded and posted to the general ledger, the salaries expense account will have a debit balance of $10,500 ($5,000 + 5,500), and the salaries payable account will have a credit balance of $5,500.

The unadjusted trial balance does provide information about the second required accrued liability entry. In the trial balance we can see a balance in the notes payable account of $40,000. The company borrowed this amount on July 1, 2018, evidenced by two notes, each requiring the payment of 10% interest. Whenever the trial balance reveals interest-bearing debt, and interest is not paid on the last day of the period, an adjusting entry is required for the amount of interest that has built up (accrued) since the last payment date or the last date interest was accrued. In this case, we calculate interest as follows:

$$\text{Principal} \times \text{Interest rate} \times \text{Time} = \text{Interest}$$
$$\$40{,}000 \times 10\% \times 1/12 = \$333 \text{ (rounded)}$$

Interest rates always are stated as the annual rate. Therefore, the above calculation uses this annual rate multiplied by the principal amount multiplied by the amount of time outstanding, in this case one month or one-twelfth of a year.

To accrue interest expense for July on notes payable.

July 31		
Interest expense	333	
Interest payable		333

After this entry is recorded and posted to the ledger accounts, the interest expense account will have a debit balance of $333, and the interest payable account will have a credit balance of $333. Failure to record a required adjusting entry for an accrued liability will cause net income and shareholders' equity (retained earnings) to be overstated, and liabilities to be understated.[4]

ACCRUED RECEIVABLES. Accrued receivables involve the recognition of revenue for goods or services transferred to customers *before* cash is received. An example of an internal accrued revenue event is the recognition of interest earned on a loan to another entity. For example, assume that Dress Right loaned another corporation $30,000 at the beginning of August, evidenced by a note receivable. Terms of the note call for the payment of principal, $30,000, and interest at 8% in three months. An external transaction records the cash disbursement—a debit to note receivable and a credit to cash of $30,000.

Accrued receivables involve situations when the revenue is recognized in a period prior to the cash receipt.

What adjusting entry would be required at the end of August? Dress Right needs to record the interest revenue earned but not yet received along with the corresponding receivable. Interest receivable increases and interest revenue (shareholders' equity) also increases. The adjusting entry for accrued receivables always includes a *debit to an asset,* a receivable, and a *credit to revenue.* In this case, at the end of August Dress Right recognizes $200 in interest revenue ($30,000 × 8% × 1/12) and makes the following adjusting entry. If this entry is not recorded, net income, assets, and shareholders' equity (retained earnings) will be understated.

The adjusting entry required to record an accrued revenue is a *debit to an asset,* a receivable, and a credit to revenue.

To accrue interest revenue earned in August on note receivable.

August 31		
Interest receivable	200	
Interest revenue		200

There are no accrued revenue adjusting entries required for Dress Right at the end of July.

The required adjusting entries for prepayments and accruals are recapped with the aid of T-accounts in Illustration 2–10. In each case an expense or revenue is recognized in a period that differs from the period in which cash was paid or received. These adjusting entries are necessary to properly measure operating performance and financial position on an accrual basis.

[4]Dress Right Clothing is a corporation. Corporations are income-tax-paying entities. Income taxes–federal, state, and local–are assessed on an annual basis and payments are made throughout the year. An additional adjusting entry would be required for Dress Right to accrue the amount of estimated income taxes payable that are applicable to the month of July. Accounting for income taxes is introduced in Chapter 4 and covered in depth in Chapter 16.

Illustration 2–10
Adjusting Entries

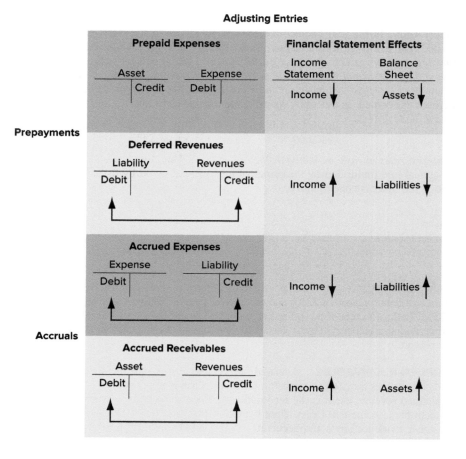

Adjusting Entries

	Adjusting Entry		Financial Statement Effects: Income Statement	Financial Statement Effects: Balance Sheet
Prepayments	**Prepaid Expenses**			
	Asset: Credit	Expense: Debit	Income ↓	Assets ↓
	Deferred Revenues			
	Liability: Debit ↑	Revenues: Credit ↑	Income ↑	Liabilities ↓
Accruals	**Accrued Expenses**			
	Expense: Debit ↑	Liability: Credit ↑	Income ↓	Liabilities ↑
	Accrued Receivables			
	Asset: Debit ↑	Revenues: Credit ↑	Income ↑	Assets ↑

Estimates

Accountants often must make *estimates* in order to comply with the accrual accounting model.

A third classification of adjusting entries is **estimates**. Accountants often must make estimates of future events to comply with the accrual accounting model. For example, the calculation of depreciation expense requires an estimate of expected useful life of the asset being depreciated as well as its expected residual value. We discussed the adjusting entries for depreciation expense in the context of its being a prepayment, but it also could be thought of as an estimate.

One adjusting-entry situation involving an estimate that does not fit neatly into either the prepayment or accrual classification is bad debts. Accounting for bad debts requires a company to estimate the amount of accounts receivable that ultimately will prove to be uncollectible and to reduce accounts receivable by that estimated amount. This is neither a prepayment nor an accrual because it does not involve the payment of cash either before or after income is reduced. We explore accounts receivable and bad debts in depth in Chapter 7.

Illustration 2–11 recaps the July 31, 2018, adjusting entries for Dress Right Clothing Corporation as they would appear in a general journal. The journal entries are numbered (1) to (6) corresponding to the number used in the worksheet illustrated in Appendix 2A.

After the adjusting entries are posted to the general ledger accounts, the next step—Step 7—in the processing cycle is to prepare an **adjusted trial balance**. The term adjusted refers to the fact that adjusting entries have now been posted to the accounts. Recall that the column titled Post. Ref. (Posting Reference) is the number assigned to the general ledger account that is being debited or credited. Illustration 2–12 shows the July 31, 2018, adjusted trial balance for Dress Right Clothing Corporation.

Illustration 2–11
The General Journal—Adjusting Entries

DRESS RIGHT CLOTHING CORPORATION
General Journal **Page 2**

Date 2018		Account Title and Explanation	Post. Ref.	Debit	Credit
July (1)	31	Supplies expense	520	800	
		Supplies	125		800
		To record the cost of supplies used during the month of July.			
(2)	31	Rent expense	530	2,000	
		Prepaid rent	130		2,000
		To record the cost of expired rent for the month of July.			
(3)	31	Depreciation expense	540	200	
		Accumulated depreciation—office equipment	155		200
		To record depreciation of office equipment *for the month of July.*			
(4)	31	Deferred rent revenue	230	250	
		Rent revenue	410		250
		To record previously deferred rent revenue recognized during July.			
(5)	31	Salaries expense	510	5,500	
		Salaries payable	230		5,500
		To record accrued salaries at the end of July.			
(6)	31	Interest expense	550	333	
		Interest payable	240		333
		To accrue interest expense for July on notes payable.			

Illustration 2–12
Adjusted Trial Balance

STEP 7
Prepare an *adjusted trial balance.*

DRESS RIGHT CLOTHING CORPORATION
Adjusted Trial Balance
July 31, 2018

Account Title	Debits	Credits
Cash	68,500	
Accounts receivable	2,000	
Supplies	1,200	
Prepaid rent	22,000	
Inventory	38,000	
Office equipment	12,000	
Accumulated depreciation—office equipment		200
Accounts payable		35,000
Notes payable		40,000
Deferred rent revenue		750
Salaries payable		5,500
Interest payable		333
Common stock		60,000
Retained earnings	1,000	
Sales revenue		38,500
Rent revenue		250
Cost of goods sold	22,000	
Salaries expense	10,500	
Supplies expense	800	
Rent expense	2,000	
Depreciation expense	200	
Interest expense	333	
Totals	180,533	180,533

Concept Review Exercise

ADJUSTING ENTRIES

The Wyndham Wholesale Company needs to prepare financial statements at the end of August 2018 for presentation to its bank. An unadjusted trial balance as of August 31, 2018, was presented in a previous concept review exercise.

The following information also is available:

a. The note payable requires the entire $30,000 in principal plus interest at 10% to be paid on July 31, 2019. The date of the loan is August 1, 2018.
b. Depreciation on the equipment for the month of August is $500.
c. The note receivable is dated August 16, 2018. The note requires the entire $20,000 in principal plus interest at 12% to be repaid in four months (the loan was outstanding for one-half month during August).
d. The prepaid rent of $6,000 represents rent for the months of August and September.

Required:

1. Prepare any necessary adjusting entries at August 31, 2018.
2. Prepare an adjusted trial balance as of August 31, 2018.
3. What is the total net effect on income (overstated or understated) if the adjusting entries are not recorded?

Solution:

1. Prepare any necessary adjusting entries at August 31, 2018.
   a. An adjusting entry is required to accrue the interest expense on the note payable for the month of August. Accrued interest is calculated as follows:

$$\$30,000 \times 10\% \times 1/12 = \$250$$

Interest expense	250	
Interest payable		250

   b. Depreciation expense on the equipment must be recorded.

Depreciation expense	500	
Accumulated depreciation—equipment		500

   c. An adjusting entry is required for the one-half month of accrued interest revenue earned on the note receivable. Accrued interest is calculated as follows:

$$\$20,000 \times 12\% \times 1/12 \times 1/2 = \$100$$

Interest receivable	100	
Interest revenue		100

   d. An adjusting entry is required to recognize the amount of prepaid rent that expired during August.

Rent expense	3,000	
Prepaid rent		3,000

2. Prepare an adjusted trial balance as of August 31, 2018.

Account Title	Debits	Credits
Cash	21,000	
Accounts receivable	25,000	
Prepaid rent	3,000	
Inventory	16,000	
Interest receivable	100	
Note receivable	20,000	
Equipment	20,000	
Accumulated depreciation—equipment		500
Accounts payable		20,000
Interest payable		250
Note payable		30,000
Common stock		50,000
Retained earnings	1,000	
Sales revenue		40,000
Interest revenue		100
Cost of goods sold	22,000	
Salaries expense	7,000	
Utilities expense	2,000	
Interest expense	250	
Depreciation expense	500	
Rent expense	3,000	
Totals	140,850	140,850

3. What is the effect on income (overstated or understated), if the adjusting entries are not recorded?

Adjusting Entry	Income overstated (understated)
Interest expense	$ 250
Depreciation expense	500
Interest revenue	(100)
Rent expense	3,000
Net effect, income overstated by	$3,650

We now turn our attention to the preparation of financial statements.

Preparing the Financial Statements

The purpose of each of the steps in the processing cycle to this point is to provide information for Step 8—preparation of the financial statements. The adjusted trial balance contains the necessary information. After all, the financial statements are the primary means of communicating financial information to external parties.

● LO2–6

STEP 8

Preparation of *financial statements.*

The Income Statement and the Statement of Comprehensive Income

The purpose of the income statement is to summarize the profit-generating activities of a company that occurred during a particular period of time. It is a *change* statement in that it reports the changes in shareholders' equity (retained earnings) that occurred during the period as a result of revenues, expenses, gains, and losses. Illustration 2–13 shows the income statement for Dress Right Clothing Corporation for the month of July 2018.

The *income statement* is a *change* statement that summarizes the profit-generating transactions that caused shareholders' equity (retained earnings) to change during the period.

The income statement indicates a profit for the month of July of $2,917. During the month, the company was able to increase its net assets (equity) from activities related to selling its product. Dress Right is a corporation and subject to the payment of income tax on its profits. We ignore this required accrual here and address income taxes in a later chapter.

The components of the income statement usually are classified, that is, grouped according to common characteristics. A common classification scheme is to separate operating items from nonoperating items, as we do in Dress Right's income statement. Operating items

Illustration 2–13
Income Statement

DRESS RIGHT CLOTHING CORPORATION Income Statement For the Month of July 2018		
Sales revenue		$38,500
Cost of goods sold		22,000
Gross profit		16,500
Operating expenses:		
Salaries	$10,500	
Supplies	800	
Rent	2,000	
Depreciation	200	
Total operating expenses		13,500
Operating income		3,000
Other income (expense):		
Rent revenue	250	
Interest expense	(333)	(83)
Net income		$ 2,917

include revenues and expenses directly related to the principal revenue-generating activities of the company. For example, operating items for a manufacturing company include sales revenues from the sale of products and all expenses related to this activity. Companies that sell products like Dress Right often report a subtotal within operating income, sales less cost of goods sold, called *gross profit.* Nonoperating items include certain gains and losses and revenues and expenses from peripheral activities. For Dress Right Clothing, rent revenue and interest expense are nonoperating items because they do not relate to the principal revenue-generating activity of the company, selling clothes. In Chapter 4 we discuss the format and content of the income statement in more depth.

The **statement of comprehensive income** extends the income statement by reporting all changes in shareholders' equity during the period that were not a result of transactions with owners. A few types of gains and losses, called **other comprehensive income (OCI) or loss** items, are excluded from the determination of net income and the income statement, but are included in the broader concept of **comprehensive income**. Comprehensive income can be reported in one of two ways: (1) in a single, continuous statement of comprehensive income, or (2) in two separate, but consecutive statements.[5]

In the single statement approach, net income is a subtotal within the statement followed by these OCI items, culminating in a final total of comprehensive income. In the two statement approach, a company presents an income statement immediately followed by a statement of comprehensive income. The statement of comprehensive income begins with net income as the first component followed by OCI items to arrive at comprehensive income. Obviously, the approaches are quite similar; in the separate statement approach, we separate the continuous statement into two parts, but the content is the same.

Dress Right Clothing has no OCI items so the company presents only an income statement in Illustration 2–13. An entity that has no OCI items is not required to report OCI or comprehensive income. We discuss comprehensive income and the alternative approaches to its presentation in more depth in Chapter 4.

The Balance Sheet

The purpose of the **balance sheet** is to present the financial position of the company on a particular date. Unlike the income statement, which is a change statement reporting events that occurred *during a period of time,* the balance sheet is a statement that presents an

The *balance sheet* presents an organized list of assets, liabilities and equity at a particular point in time.

[5]FASB ASC 220–10-45–1: Comprehensive Income–Overall–Other Presentation Matters (*Accounting Standards Update No. 2011–05* (Norwalk, Conn.: FASB, June 2011)).

organized list of assets, liabilities, and shareholders' equity *at a point in time.* To provide a quick overview, Illustration 2–14 shows the balance sheet for Dress Right at July 31, 2018.

Illustration 2–14
Balance Sheet

DRESS RIGHT CLOTHING CORPORATION
Balance Sheet
At July 31, 2018

Assets		
Current assets:		
Cash		$ 68,500
Accounts receivable		2,000
Supplies		1,200
Inventory		38,000
Prepaid rent		22,000
Total current assets		131,700
Property and equipment:		
Office equipment	$12,000	
Less: Accumulated depreciation	200	11,800
Total assets		$143,500
Liabilities and Shareholders' Equity		
Current liabilities:		
Accounts payable		$ 35,000
Salaries payable		5,500
Deferred rent revenue		750
Interest payable		333
Note payable		10,000
Total current liabilities		51,583
Long-term liabilities:		
Note payable		30,000
Shareholders' equity:		
Common stock, 6,000 shares issued and outstanding	$60,000	
Retained earnings	1,917*	
Total shareholders' equity		61,917
Total liabilities and shareholders' equity		$143,500

*Beginning retained earnings + Net income − Dividends
$0 + 2,917 − 1,000 = $1,917

Balance sheet items usually are classified (grouped) according to common characteristics.

As we do in the income statement, we group the balance sheet elements into meaningful categories. For example, most balance sheets include the classifications of current assets and current liabilities. Current assets are those assets that are cash, will be converted into cash, or will be used up within one year or the operating cycle, whichever is longer. Current liabilities are those liabilities that will be satisfied within one year or the operating cycle, whichever is longer. For a manufacturing company, the operating cycle refers to the period of time necessary to convert cash to raw materials, raw materials to a finished product, the finished product to receivables, and then finally receivables back to cash. For most companies, this period is less than a year.

Examples of assets not classified as current include property and equipment and long-term receivables and investments. The only noncurrent asset that Dress Right has at July 31, 2018, is office equipment, which is classified under the property and equipment category.

All liabilities not classified as current are listed as long term. Dress Right's liabilities at July 31, 2018, include the $30,000 note payable due to be paid in 23 months. This liability is classified as long term.

Shareholders' equity lists the *paid-in capital* portion of equity—common stock—and *retained earnings.* Notice that the income statement we looked at in Illustration 2–13 ties in to the balance sheet through retained earnings. Specifically, the revenue, expense, gain, and loss transactions that make up net income in the income statement ($2,917) become the major components of retained earnings. Later in the chapter we discuss the closing process we use to transfer, or close, these *temporary* income statement accounts to the *permanent* retained earnings account.

During the month, retained earnings, which increased by the amount of net income, also decreased by the amount of the cash dividend paid to shareholders, $1,000. The net effect of these two changes is an increase in retained earnings from zero at the beginning of the period to $1,917 ($2,917 − 1,000) at the end of the period and also is reported in the statement of shareholders' equity in Illustration 2–16.

The Statement of Cash Flows

The purpose of the *statement of cash flows* is to report the events that caused cash to change during the period.

Similar to the income statement, the statement of cash flows also is a change statement. The purpose of the statement is to report the events that caused cash to change during the period. The statement classifies all transactions affecting cash into one of three categories: (1) operating activities, (2) investing activities, and (3) financing activities. Operating activities are inflows and outflows of cash related to transactions entering into the determination of net income. Investing activities involve the acquisition and sale of (1) long-term assets used in the business and (2) nonoperating investment assets. Financing activities involve cash inflows and outflows from transactions with creditors and owners.

The statement of cash flows for Dress Right for the month of July 2018 is shown in Illustration 2–15. As this is the first period of operations for Dress Right, the cash balance at the beginning of the period is zero. The net increase in cash of $68,500, therefore, equals the ending balance of cash disclosed in the balance sheet.

Illustration 2–15

Statement of Cash Flows

DRESS RIGHT CLOTHING CORPORATION
Statement of Cash Flows
For the Month of July 2018

Cash Flows from Operating Activities		
Cash inflows:		
From customers	$36,500	
From rent	1,000	
Cash outflows:		
For rent	(24,000)	
For supplies	(2,000)	
To suppliers of merchandise	(25,000)	
To employees	(5,000)	
Net cash flows from operating activities		$(18,500)
Cash Flows from Investing Activities		
Purchase of office equipment		(12,000)
Cash Flows from Financing Activities		
Issue of common stock	$60,000	
Increase in notes payable	40,000	
Payment of cash dividend	(1,000)	
Net cash flows from financing activities		99,000
Net increase in cash		$ 68,500

There are two generally accepted formats that can be used to report operating activities, the direct method and the indirect method. In Illustration 2–15 we use the direct method. These two methods are discussed and illustrated in subsequent chapters.

The Statement of Shareholders' Equity

The final statement, the statement of shareholders' equity, also is a change statement. Its purpose is to disclose the sources of the changes in the various permanent shareholders' equity accounts that occurred during the period from investments by owners, distributions to owners, net income, and other comprehensive income. Illustration 2–16 shows the statement of shareholders' equity for Dress Right for the month of July 2018.[6]

***The statement of shareholders' equity* discloses the sources of changes in the permanent shareholders' equity accounts.**

Illustration 2–16

Statement of Shareholders' Equity

DRESS RIGHT CLOTHING CORPORATION
Statement of Shareholders' Equity
For the Month of July 2018

	Common Stock	Retained Earnings	Total Shareholders' Equity
Balance at July 1, 2018	$ –0–	$ –0–	$ –0–
Issue of common stock	60,000		60,000
Net income for July 2018		2,917	2,917
Less: Dividends		(1,000)	(1,000)
Balance at July 31, 2018	$60,000	$1,917	$61,917

The individual profit-generating transactions causing retained earnings to change are summarized in the income statement. Therefore, the statement of shareholders' equity only shows the net effect of these transactions on retained earnings, in this case an increase of $2,917. In addition, the company paid its shareholders a cash dividend that reduced retained earnings.

The Closing Process

STEP 9

Close the temporary accounts to retained earnings (at year-end only).

At the end of any interim reporting period, the accounting processing cycle is now complete. An interim reporting period is any period when financial statements are produced other than at the end of the fiscal year. However, at the end of the fiscal year, two final steps are necessary, closing the temporary accounts—Step 9—and preparing a post-closing trial balance—Step 10.

● LO2–7

The closing process serves a *dual purpose:* (1) the temporary accounts (revenues, expenses, gains and losses) are reduced to *zero balances,* ready to measure activity in the upcoming accounting period, and (2) these temporary account balances are *closed (transferred) to retained earnings* to reflect the changes that have occurred in that account during the period. Often, an intermediate step is to close revenues and expenses to income summary, and then income summary is closed to retained earnings. The use of the income summary account is just a bookkeeping convenience that provides a check that all temporary accounts have been properly closed (that is, the balance equals net income or loss).

To illustrate the closing process, assume that the fiscal year-end for Dress Right Clothing Corporation is July 31. Using the adjusted trial balance in Illustration 2–12, we can prepare the following closing entries.

To close the revenue accounts to income summary.

July 31		
Sales revenue	38,500	
Rent revenue	250	
Income summary		38,750

[6]Some companies choose to disclose the changes in the retained earnings component of shareholders' equity in a separate statement or in a combined statement of income and retained earnings.

The first closing entry transfers the revenue account balances to income summary. Because revenue accounts have credit balances, they are debited to bring them to zero. After this entry is posted to the accounts, both revenue accounts have a zero balance.

To close the expense accounts to income summary.

July 31		
Income summary	35,833	
Cost of goods sold		22,000
Salaries expense		10,500
Supplies expense		800
Rent expense		2,000
Depreciation expense		200
Interest expense		333

The second closing entry transfers the expense account balances to income summary. As expense accounts have debit balances, they are credited to bring them to zero. After this entry is posted to the accounts, the expense accounts have a zero balance and the income summary account has a credit balance equal to net income for the period, in this case $2,917.

Income Summary

Expenses	35,833	38,750	Revenues
		2,917	Net income

The third entry closes the income summary account to retained earnings.

To close the income summary account to retained earnings.

July 31		
Income summary	2,917	
Retained earnings		2,917

After this entry is posted to the accounts, the temporary accounts have zero balances and retained earnings has increased by the amount of the net income. It is important to remember that the temporary accounts are closed only at year-end and not at the end of any interim period. Closing the temporary accounts during the year would make it difficult to prepare the annual income statement.

Additional Consideration

A previous additional consideration indicated that an alternative method of recording a cash dividend is to debit a temporary account called dividends, rather than debiting retained earnings. If this approach is used, an additional closing entry is required to close the dividend account to retained earnings, as follows:

Retained earnings	1,000	
Dividends		1,000

As you can see, the net result of a cash dividend is the same—a reduction in retained earnings and a reduction in cash.

STEP 10

Prepare a *post-closing trial balance* (at year-end only).

After the closing entries are posted to the ledger accounts, a **post-closing trial balance** is prepared. The purpose of this trial balance is to verify that the closing entries were prepared and posted correctly and that the accounts are now ready for next year's transactions. Illustration 2–17 shows the post-closing trial balance for Dress Right at July 31, 2018, assuming a July 31 fiscal year-end.

DRESS RIGHT CLOTHING CORPORATION
Post-Closing Trial Balance
July 31, 2018

Account Title	Debits	Credits
Cash	68,500	
Accounts receivable	2,000	
Supplies	1,200	
Prepaid rent	22,000	
Inventory	38,000	
Office equipment	12,000	
Accumulated depreciation—office equipment		200
Accounts payable		35,000
Notes payable		40,000
Deferred rent revenue		750
Salaries payable		5,500
Interest payable		333
Common stock		60,000
Retained earnings		1,917
Totals	143,700	143,700

Illustration 2–17

Post-Closing Trial Balance

Concept Review Exercise

FINANCIAL STATEMENT PREPARATION AND CLOSING

Refer to the August 31, 2018, adjusted trial balance of the Wyndham Wholesale Company presented in a previous concept review exercise.

Required:

1. Prepare an income statement and a statement of shareholders' equity for the month ended August 31, 2018, and a classified balance sheet as of August 31, 2018.
2. Assume that August 31 is the company's fiscal year-end. Prepare the necessary closing entries and a post-closing trial balance.

Solution:

1. Prepare an income statement and a statement of shareholders' equity for the month ended August 31, 2018, and a classified balance sheet as of August 31, 2018.

WYNDHAM WHOLESALE COMPANY
Income Statement
For the Month of August 2018

Sales revenue		$40,000
Cost of goods sold		22,000
Gross profit		18,000
Operating expenses:		
Salaries	$7,000	
Utilities	2,000	
Depreciation	500	
Rent	3,000	
Total operating expenses		12,500
Operating income		5,500
Other income (expense):		
Interest revenue	100	
Interest expense	(250)	(150)
Net income		$ 5,350

WYNDHAM WHOLESALE COMPANY
Statement of Shareholders' Equity
For the Month of August 2018

	Common Stock	Retained Earnings	Total Shareholders' Equity
Balance at August 1, 2018	$ –0–	$ –0–	$ –0–
Issue of common stock	50,000		50,000
Net income for August 2018		5,350	5,350
Less: Dividends		(1,000)	(1,000)
Balance at August 31, 2018	$50,000	$4,350	$54,350

WYNDHAM WHOLESALE COMPANY
Balance Sheet
At August 31, 2018
Assets

Current assets:		
Cash		$ 21,000
Accounts receivable		25,000
Inventory		16,000
Interest receivable		100
Note receivable		20,000
Prepaid rent		3,000
Total current assets		85,100
Property and equipment:		
Equipment	$20,000	
Less: Accumulated depreciation	500	19,500
Total assets		$104,600
Liabilities and Shareholders' Equity		
Current liabilities:		
Accounts payable		$ 20,000
Interest payable		250
Note payable		30,000
Total current liabilities		50,250
Shareholders' equity:		
Common stock, 5,000 shares issued and outstanding	$50,000	
Retained earnings	4,350	
Total shareholders' equity		54,350
Total liabilities and shareholders' equity		$104,600

2. Assume that August 31 is the company's fiscal year-end. Prepare the necessary closing entries and a post-closing trial balance.

To close the revenue accounts to income summary.	**August 31**		
	Sales revenue	40,000	
	Interest revenue	100	
	Income summary		40,100
To close the expense accounts to income summary.	**August 31**		
	Income summary	34,750	
	Cost of goods sold		22,000
	Salaries expense		7,000
	Utilities expense		2,000
	Depreciation expense		500
	Rent expense		3,000
	Interest expense		250
To close the income summary account to retained earnings.	**August 31**		
	Income summary	5,350	
	Retained earnings		5,350

Post-Closing Trial Balance

Account Title	Debits	Credits
Cash	21,000	
Accounts receivable	25,000	
Prepaid rent	3,000	
Inventory	16,000	
Interest receivable	100	
Note receivable	20,000	
Equipment	20,000	
Accumulated depreciation—equipment		500
Accounts payable		20,000
Interest payable		250
Note payable		30,000
Common stock		50,000
Retained earnings		4,350
Totals	105,100	105,100

Conversion from Cash Basis to Accrual Basis

LO2–8

In Chapter 1, we discussed and illustrated the differences between cash and accrual accounting. Cash basis accounting produces a measure called *net operating cash flow.* This measure is the difference between cash receipts and cash disbursements during a reporting period from transactions related to providing goods and services to customers. On the other hand, the accrual accounting model measures an entity's accomplishments and resource sacrifices during the period, regardless of when cash is received or paid. At this point, you might wish to review the material in Chapter 1 to reinforce your understanding of the motivation for using the accrual accounting model.

Adjusting entries, for the most part, are conversions from cash basis to accrual basis. Prepayments and accruals occur when cash flow precedes or follows expense or revenue recognition.

Accountants sometimes are called upon to convert cash basis financial statements to accrual basis financial statements, particularly for small businesses. You now have all of the tools you need to make this conversion. For example, if a company paid $20,000 cash for insurance during the fiscal year and you determine that there was $5,000 in prepaid insurance at the beginning of the year and $3,000 at the end of the year, then you can determine (accrual basis) *insurance expense* for the year. Prepaid insurance decreased by $2,000 during the year, so insurance expense must be $22,000 ($20,000 in cash paid *plus* the decrease in prepaid insurance). You can visualize as follows:

	Prepaid Insurance
Balance, beginning of year	$ 5,000
Plus: Cash paid	20,000
Less: Insurance expense	?
Balance, end of year	$ 3,000

Insurance expense of $22,000 completes the explanation of the change in the balance of prepaid insurance. Prepaid insurance of $3,000 is reported as an asset in an accrual basis balance sheet.

Suppose a company paid $150,000 for salaries to employees during the year and you determine that there were $12,000 and $18,000 in salaries payable at the beginning and end of the year, respectively. What was salaries expense for the year?

	Salaries Payable
Balance, beginning of year	$ 12,000
Plus: Salaries expense	?
Less: Cash paid	150,000
Balance, end of year	$ 18,000

Salaries payable increased by $6,000 during the year, so *salaries expense* must be $156,000 ($150,000 in cash paid *plus* the increase in salaries payable). Salaries payable of $18,000 is reported as a liability in an accrual basis balance sheet.

Using T-accounts is a convenient approach for converting from cash to accrual accounting.

Salaries Payable

		12,000	Beg. balance
Cash paid	150,000		
		?	Salaries expense
		18,000	End. balance

Salaries Expense

?	

The debit to salaries expense and credit to salaries payable must have been $156,000 to balance the salaries payable account.

For another example using T-accounts, assume that the amount of cash collected from customers during the year was $220,000, and you know that accounts receivable at the beginning of the year was $45,000 and $33,000 at the end of the year. You can use T-accounts to determine that *sales revenue* for the year must have been $208,000, the necessary debit to accounts receivable and credit to sales revenue to balance the accounts receivable account.

Accounts Receivable

Beg. balance	45,000		
Credit sales	?		
		220,000	Cash collections
End. balance	33,000		

Sales Revenue

	?	Credit sales

Now suppose that, on occasion, customers pay in advance of receiving a product or service. Recall from our previous discussion of adjusting entries that this event creates a liability called deferred revenue. Assume the same facts in the previous example except you also determine that deferred revenues were $10,000 and $7,000 at the beginning and end of the year, respectively. A $3,000 decrease in deferred revenues means that the company recognized an additional $3,000 in sales revenue for which the cash had been collected in a previous year. So, *sales revenue* for the year must have been $211,000, the $208,000 determined in the previous example *plus* the $3,000 decrease in deferred revenue.

Illustration 2–18 provides another example of converting from cash basis net income to accrual basis net income.

Notice a pattern in the adjustments to cash net income. When converting from cash to accrual income, we add increases and deduct decreases in assets. For example, an increase in accounts receivable means that the company recognized more revenue than cash collected, requiring the addition to cash basis income. Conversely, we add decreases and deduct increases in accrued liabilities. For example, a decrease in interest payable means that the company incurred less interest expense than the cash interest it paid, requiring the addition to cash basis income. These adjustments are summarized in Illustration 2–19.

Most companies must convert from an accrual basis to a cash basis when preparing the statement of cash flows.

Most companies keep their books on an accrual basis.[7] A more important conversion for these companies is from the accrual basis to the cash basis. This conversion, essential for the preparation of the statement of cash flows, is discussed and illustrated in Chapters 4

[7]Generally accepted accounting principles require the use of the accrual basis. Some small, nonpublic companies might use the cash basis in preparing their financial statements as another comprehensive basis of accounting.

Illustration 2–18

Cash to Accrual

The Krinard Cleaning Services Company maintains its records on the cash basis, with one exception. The company reports equipment as an asset and records depreciation expense on the equipment. During 2018, Krinard collected $165,000 from customers, paid $92,000 in operating expenses, and recorded $10,000 in depreciation expense, resulting in net income of $63,000. The owner has asked you to convert this $63,000 in net income to full accrual net income. You are able to determine the following information about accounts receivable, prepaid expenses, accrued liabilities, and deferred revenues:

	January 1, 2018	December 31, 2018
Accounts receivable	$16,000	$25,000
Prepaid expenses	7,000	4,000
Accrued liabilities (for operating expenses)	2,100	1,400
Deferred revenues	3,000	4,200

Accrual net income is $68,500, determined as follows:

Cash basis net income	$63,000
Add: Increase in accounts receivable	9,000
Deduct: Decrease in prepaid expenses	(3,000)
Add: Decrease in accrued liabilities	700
Deduct: Increase in deferred revenues	(1,200)
Accrual basis net income	$68,500

Illustration 2–19

Converting Cash Basis to Accrual Basis Income

Converting Cash Basis Income to Accrual Basis Income

	Increases	Decreases
Assets	Add	Deduct
Liabilities	Deduct	Add

and 21. The lessons learned here, though, will help you with that conversion. For example, if sales revenue for the period is $120,000 and beginning and ending accounts receivable are $20,000 and $24,000, respectively, how much cash did the company collect from its customers during the period? The answer is $116,000. An increase in accounts receivable of $4,000 means that the company collected $4,000 less from customers than accrual sales revenue, and cash basis income is $4,000 less than accrual basis income.

Financial Reporting Case Solution

© goodluz/123RF

1. **What purpose do adjusting entries serve?** *(p. 63)* Adjusting entries help ensure that all revenues are recognized in the period goods or services are transferred to customers, regardless of when cash is received. In this instance, for example, $13,000 cash has been received for services that haven't yet been performed. Also, adjusting entries enable a company to recognize all expenses incurred during a period, regardless of when cash is paid. Without depreciation, the friends' cost of using the equipment is not taken into account. Conversely, without adjustment, the cost of rent is overstated by $3,000 paid in advance for part of next year's rent.

   With adjustments, we get an accrual income statement that provides a more complete measure of a company's operating performance and a better measure for predicting future operating cash flows. Similarly, the balance sheet provides a more complete assessment of assets and liabilities as sources of future cash receipts and disbursements.

2. What year-end adjustments are needed to revise the income statement? Did your friends do as well their first year as they thought? *(p. 63)* Three year-end adjusting entries are needed:

1. Depreciation expense ($80,000 ÷ 5 years)	16,000	
Accumulated depreciation—equipment		16,000
2. Prepaid rent [$500 × 6 months (July–Dec.)]	3,000	
Rent expense		3,000
3. Consulting revenue	13,000	
Deferred consulting revenue		13,000

No, your friends did not fare as well as their cash based statement would have indicated. With appropriate adjustments, their net income is actually only $20,000:

Consulting revenue ($96,000 − 13,000)		$83,000
Operating expenses:		
Salaries	$32,000	
Rent ($9,000 − 3,000)	6,000	
Supplies	4,800	
Utilities	3,000	
Advertising	1,200	
Depreciation	16,000	63,000
Net income		$20,000

The Bottom Line

- **LO2–1** The accounting equation underlies the process used to capture the effect of economic events. The equation (Assets = Liabilities + Owners' Equity) implies an equality between the total economic resources of an entity (its assets) and the total claims against the entity (liabilities and equity). It also implies that each economic event affecting this equation will have a dual effect because resources always must equal claims. *(p. 48)*
- **LO2–2** After determining the dual effect of external events on the accounting equation, the transaction is recorded in a journal. A journal is a chronological list of transactions in debit/credit form. *(p. 52)*
- **LO2–3** The next step in the processing cycle is to periodically transfer, or *post,* the debit and credit information from the journal to individual general ledger accounts. A general ledger is simply a collection of all of the company's various accounts. Each account provides a summary of the effects of all events and transactions on that individual account. The process of entering items from the journal to the general ledger is called *posting.* An unadjusted trial balance is then prepared. *(p. 59)*
- **LO2–4** The next step in the processing cycle is to record the effect of *internal events* on the accounting equation. These transactions are commonly referred to as *adjusting entries.* Adjusting entries can be classified into three types: (1) prepayments, (2) accruals, and (3) estimates. Prepayments are transactions in which the cash flow *precedes* expense or revenue recognition. Accruals involve transactions where the cash outflow or inflow takes place in a period *subsequent* to expense or revenue recognition. Estimates for items such as future bad debts on receivables often are required to comply with the accrual accounting model. *(p. 62)*
- **LO2–5** Adjusting entries are recorded in the general journal and posted to the ledger accounts at the end of any period when financial statements must be prepared for external use. After these entries are posted to the general ledger accounts, an adjusted trial balance is prepared. *(p. 63)*
- **LO2–6** The adjusted trial balance is used to prepare the financial statements. The basic financial statements are: (1) the income statement, (2) the statement of comprehensive income, (3) the balance sheet, (4) the statement of cash flows, and (5) the statement of shareholders' equity. The purpose of the income statement is to summarize the profit-generating activities of the company that occurred during a particular period of time. A company also must report its other comprehensive income (OCI) or loss items either in a single, continuous statement or in a separate statement of comprehensive income. In the single statement approach, net income is a subtotal within the statement followed by these OCI items, culminating in a final total of comprehensive income. In the two statement approach, a company presents an income statement

immediately followed by a statement of comprehensive income. The statement of comprehensive income begins with net income as the first component followed by OCI items to arrive at comprehensive income. The balance sheet presents the financial position of the company on a particular date. The statement of cash flows discloses the events that caused cash to change during the reporting period. The statement of shareholders' equity discloses the sources of the changes in the various permanent shareholders' equity accounts that occurred during the period. (*p. 71*)

● **LO2–7** At the end of the fiscal year, a final step in the accounting processing cycle, closing, is required. The closing process serves a *dual purpose:* (1) the temporary accounts (revenues and expenses) are reduced to *zero balances,* ready to measure activity in the upcoming accounting period, and (2) these temporary account balances are *closed (transferred) to retained earnings* to reflect the changes that have occurred in that account during the period. Often, an intermediate step is to close revenues and expenses to *income summary;* then *income summary* is closed to *retained earnings.* (*p. 75*)

● **LO2–8** Cash basis accounting produces a measure called *net operating cash flow.* This measure is the difference between cash receipts and cash disbursements during a reporting period from transactions related to providing goods and services to customers. On the other hand, the accrual accounting model measures an entity's accomplishments and resource sacrifices during the period, regardless of when cash is received or paid. Accountants sometimes are called upon to convert cash basis financial statements to accrual basis financial statements, particularly for small businesses. (*p. 79*) ●

APPENDIX 2A

Use of a Worksheet

A **worksheet** often is used to organize the accounting information needed to prepare adjusting and closing entries and the financial statements. It is an informal tool only and is not part of the accounting system. There are many different ways to design and use worksheets. We will illustrate a representative method using the financial information for the Dress Right Clothing Corporation presented in the chapter. Software such Excel facilitates the use of worksheets.

A *worksheet* can be used as a tool to facilitate the preparation of adjusting and closing entries and the financial statements.

Illustration 2A–1 presents the completed worksheet. The worksheet is utilized in conjunction with Step 5 in the processing cycle, preparation of an unadjusted trial balance.

Illustration 2A–1 Worksheet, Dress Right Clothing Corporation, July 31, 2018

	A	B	C	D	E	F	G	H	I	J	K	L	M
1	Worksheet, Dress Right Clothing Corporation, July 31, 2018												
2		Unadjusted Trial Balance		Adjusting Entries				Adjusted Trial Balance		Income Statement		Balance Sheet	
3	Account Title	Dr.	Cr.	Dr.		Cr.		Dr.	Cr.	Dr.	Cr.	Dr.	Cr.
4													
5	Cash	68,500						68,500				68,500	
6	Accounts receivable	2,000						2,000				2,000	
7	Supplies	2,000				(1)	800	1,200				1,200	
8	Prepaid rent	24,000				(2)	2,000	22,000				22,000	
9	Inventory	38,000						38,000				38,000	
10	office equipment	12,000						12,000				12,000	
11	Accumulated depreciation -												
12	office equipment		0			(3)	200		200				200
13	Accounts payable		35,000						35,000				35,000
14	Note payable		40,000						40,000				40,000
15	Deferred rent revenue		1,000	(4)	250				750				750
16	Salaries payable		0			(5)	5,500		5,500				5,500
17	Interest payable		0			(6)	333		333				333
18	Common stock		60,000						60,000				60,000
19	Retained earnings	1,000						1,000				1,000	
20	Sales revenue		38,500						38,500		38,500		
21	Rent revenue		0			(4)	250		250		250		
22	Cost of goods sold	22,000						22,000		22,000			
23	Salaries expense	5,000		(5)	5,500			10,500		10,500			
24	Supplies expense	0		(1)	800			800		800			
25	Rent expense	0		(2)	2,000			2,000		2,000			
26	Depreciation expense	0		(3)	200			200		200			
27	Interest expense	0		(6)	333			333		333			
28	Totals	174,500	174,500		9,083		9,083	180,533	180,533				
29													
30	Net income									2,917			2,917
31	Totals									38,750	38,750	144,700	144,700
32													

Sheet1 Sheet2 Sheet3

The first step is to enter account titles in column A and the unadjusted account balances in columns B and C.

Step 1. The account titles as they appear in the general ledger are entered in column A and the balances of these accounts are copied onto columns B and C, entitled Unadjusted Trial Balance. The accounts are copied in the same order as they appear in the general ledger, which usually is assets, liabilities, shareholders' equity permanent accounts, revenues, and expenses. The debit and credit columns are totaled to make sure that they balance. This procedure is repeated for each set of columns in the worksheet to check for accuracy.

The second step is to determine end-of-period adjusting entries and enter them in columns E and G.

Step 2. The end-of-period adjusting entries are determined and entered directly on the worksheet in columns E and G, entitled Adjusting Entries. The adjusting entries for Dress Right Clothing Corporation were discussed in detail in the chapter and exhibited in general journal form in Illustration 2–11. You should refer back to this illustration and trace each of the entries to the worksheet. For worksheet purposes, the entries have been numbered from (1) to (6) for easy referencing.

For example, entry (1) records the cost of supplies used during the month of July with a debit to supplies expense and a credit to supplies for $800. A (1) is placed next to the $800 in the debit column in the supplies expense row as well as next to the $800 in the credit column in the supplies row. This allows us to more easily reconstruct the entry for general journal purposes and locate errors if the debit and credit columns do not balance.

The third step adds or deducts the effects of the adjusting entries on the account balances.

Step 3. The effects of the adjusting entries are added to or deducted from the account balances listed in the Unadjusted Trial Balance columns and copied across to columns H and I, entitled Adjusted Trial Balance. For example, supplies had an unadjusted balance of $2,000. Adjusting entry (1) credited this account by $800, reducing the balance to $1,200.

The fourth step is to transfer the temporary retained earnings account balances to columns J and K.

Step 4. The balances in the temporary retained earnings accounts, revenues and expenses, are transferred to columns J and K, entitled Income Statement. The difference between the total debits and credits in these columns is equal to net income or net loss. In this case, because credits (revenues) exceed debits (expenses), a net income of $2,917 results. To balance the debits and credits in this set of columns, a $2,917 debit entry is made in the line labeled Net income.

The fifth step is to transfer the balances in the permanent accounts to columns L and M.

Step 5. The balances in the permanent accounts are transferred to columns L and M, entitled Balance Sheet. To keep the debits and credits equal in the worksheet, a $2,917 credit must be recorded to offset the $2,917 debit recorded in Step 4 and labeled as net income. This credit represents the fact that when the temporary accounts are closed out to retained earnings, a $2,917 credit to retained earnings will result. The credit in column M, therefore, represents an increase in retained earnings for the period, that is, net income.

After the worksheet is completed, the financial statements can be prepared directly from columns J–M. The financial statements for Dress Right Clothing Corporation are shown in Illustrations 2–13 through 2–16. The accountant must remember to then record the adjusting entries in the general journal and post them to the general ledger accounts. An adjusted trial balance should then be prepared, which should be identical to the one in the worksheet. At fiscal year-end, the income statement columns can then be used to prepare closing entries. ●

APPENDIX 2B Reversing Entries

Accountants sometimes use reversing entries at the beginning of a reporting period. These optional entries remove the effects of some of the adjusting entries recorded at the end of the previous reporting period for the sole purpose of simplifying journal entries recorded during the new period. If the accountant does use reversing entries, these entries are recorded in the general journal and posted to the general ledger accounts on the first day of the new period.

Reversing entries are used most often with accruals. For example, the following adjusting entry for accrued salaries was recorded at the end of July 2018 for the Dress Right Clothing Corporation in the chapter:

To record accrued salaries at the end of July.

July 31		
Salaries expense	5,500	
Salaries payable		5,500

If reversing entries are not used, when the salaries actually are paid in August, the accountant needs to remember to debit salaries payable and not salaries expense.

The account balances before and after salary payment can be seen below with the use of T-accounts.

Salaries Expense			Salaries Payable		
Bal. July 31	10,500			5,500	Bal. July 31
			(Cash Payment) 5,500		
				–0–	Balance

If the accountant for Dress Right employs reversing entries, the following entry is recorded on August 1, 2018:

August 1		
Salaries payable	5,500	
Salaries expense		5,500

To reverse accrued salaries expense recorded at the end of July.

This entry reduces the salaries payable account to zero and reduces the salary expense account by $5,500. When salaries actually are paid in August, the debit is to salaries expense, thus increasing the account by $5,500.

Salaries Expense				Salaries Payable		
Bal. July 31	10,500				5,500	Bal. July 31
		5,500	(Reversing entry)	5,500		
(Cash payment)	5,500					
Balance	10,500				–0–	Balance

We can see that balances in the accounts after cash payment is made are identical. The use of reversing entries for accruals, which is optional, simply allows cash payments or cash receipts to be entered directly into the temporary expense or revenue accounts without regard to the accruals recorded at the end of the previous period.

Reversing entries also can be used with prepayments and deferred revenues. For example, earlier in the chapter Dress Right Clothing Corporation used the following entry to record the purchase of supplies on July 6:

July 6		
Supplies	2,000	
Cash		2,000

To record the purchase of supplies.

If reversing entries are not used, an adjusting entry is needed at the end of July to record the amount of supplies consumed during the period. In the illustration, Dress Right recorded this adjusting entry at the end of July:

July 31		
Supplies expense	800	
Supplies		800

To record the cost of supplies used during the month of July.

T-accounts help us visualize the account balances before and after the adjusting entry.

Supplies				Supplies Expense	
(Cash payment)	2,000				
		800	(Adjusting entry)	800	
Bal. July 31	1,200		Bal. July 31	800	

If the accountant for Dress Right employs *reversing entries,* the purchase of supplies is recorded as follows:

To record the purchase of supplies.

July 6		
Supplies expense	2,000	
Cash		2,000

The adjusting entry then is used to establish the balance in the supplies account at $1,200 (amount of supplies still on hand at the end of the month) and reduce the supplies expense account from the amount purchased to the amount used.

To record the cost of supplies on hand at the end of July.

July 31		
Supplies (balance on hand)	1,200	
Supplies expense ($2,000 – 800)		1,200

T-accounts make the process easier to see before and after the adjusting entry.

Supplies

	Debit	Credit
	1,200	
Bal. July 31	1,200	

Supplies Expense

	Debit	Credit
(Cash payment)	2,000	
(Adjusting entry)		1,200
Bal. July 31	800	

Notice that the ending balances in both accounts are the same as when reversing entries are not used. Up to this point, this approach is the alternate approach to recording prepayments discussed in a previous section of this chapter. The next step is an optional expediency.

On August 1, the following reversing entry can be recorded:

To reverse the July adjusting entry for supplies on hand.

August 1		
Supplies expense	1,200	
Supplies		1,200

This entry reduces the supplies account to zero and increases the supplies expense account to $2,000. Subsequent purchases would then be entered into the supplies expense account and future adjusting entries would record the amount of supplies still on hand at the end of the period. At the end of the fiscal year, the supplies expense account, along with all other temporary accounts, is closed to retained earnings.

Using reversing entries for prepayments, which is optional, simply allows cash payments to be entered directly into the temporary expense accounts without regard to whether only the current, or both the current and future periods, are benefitted by the expenditure. Adjustments are then recorded at the end of the period to reflect the amount of the unexpired benefit (asset). ●

APPENDIX 2C Subsidiary Ledgers and Special Journals

Subsidiary Ledgers

Accounting systems employ a ***subsidiary ledger,*** which contains a group of subsidiary accounts associated with particular general ledger control accounts.

The general ledger contains what are referred to as *control accounts.* In addition to the general ledger, a **subsidiary ledger** contains a group of subsidiary accounts associated with a particular general ledger control account. For example, there will be a subsidiary ledger for accounts receivable that keeps track of the increases and decreases in the account receivable balance for each of the company's customers purchasing goods or services on credit. After all of the postings are made from the appropriate journals, the balance in the accounts receivable control account should equal the sum of the balances in the accounts receivable subsidiary ledger accounts. Subsidiary ledgers also are used for accounts payable, property and equipment, investments, and other accounts.

Special Journals

An actual accounting system employs many different types of journals. The purpose of each journal is to record, in chronological order, the dual effect of a transaction in debit/credit form. The chapter used the general journal format to record each transaction. However, even for small companies with relatively few transactions, the general journal is used to record only a few types of transactions.[8]

For most external transactions, *special journals* are used to capture the dual effect of the transaction in debit/credit form.

The majority of transactions are recorded in special journals. These journals capture the dual effect of *repetitive* types of transactions. For example, cash receipts are recorded in a cash receipts journal, cash disbursements in a cash disbursements journal, credit sales in a sales journal, and the purchase of merchandise on account in a purchases journal.

Special journals simplify the recording process in the following ways:

1. Journalizing the effects of a particular transaction is made more efficient through the use of specifically designed formats.
2. Individual transactions are not posted to the general ledger accounts but are accumulated in the special journals and a summary posting is made on a periodic basis.
3. The responsibility for recording journal entries for the repetitive types of transactions is placed on individuals who have specialized training in handling them.

The concepts of subsidiary ledgers and special journals are illustrated using the *sales journal* and the *cash receipts journal.*

Sales Journal

The purpose of the sales journal is to record all credit sales. Cash sales are recorded in the cash receipts journal. Every entry in the sales journal has exactly the same effect on the accounts; the sales revenue account is credited and the accounts receivable control account is debited. Therefore, there is only one column needed to record the debit/credit effect of these transactions. Other columns are needed to capture information for updating the accounts receivable subsidiary ledger. Illustration 2C–1 presents the sales journal for Dress Right Clothing Corporation for the month of August 2018.

All credit sales are recorded in the sales journal.

Illustration 2C–1

Sales Journal, Dress Right Clothing Corporation, August 2018

				Page 1
Date	**Accounts Receivable Subsidiary Account No.**	**Customer Name**	**Sales Invoice No.**	**Cr. Sales Revenue (400) Dr. Accounts Receivable (110)**
2018				
Aug. 5	801	Leland High School	10-221	1,500
9	812	Mr. John Smith	10-222	200
18	813	Greystone School	10-223	825
22	803	Ms. Barbara Jones	10-224	120
29	805	Hart Middle School	10-225	650
				3,295

During the month of August, the company made five credit sales, totaling $3,295. This amount is posted as a debit to the accounts receivable control account, account number 110, and a credit to the sales revenue account, account number 400. The T-accounts for accounts receivable and sales revenue appear below. The reference SJ1 refers to page 1 of the sales journal.

General Ledger

Accounts Receivable	110
July 31 Balance 2,000	
Aug. 31 SJ1 3,295	

Sales Revenue	400
	3,295 Aug. 31 SJ1

[8]For example, end-of-period adjusting entries would be recorded in the general journal.

In a computerized accounting system, as each transaction is recorded in the sales journal, the subsidiary ledger accounts for the customer involved will automatically be updated. For example, the first credit sale of the month is to Leland High School for $1,500. The sales invoice number for this sale is 10-221 and the customer's subsidiary account number is 801. As this transaction is entered, the subsidiary account 801 for Leland High School is debited for $1,500

Accounts Receivable Subsidiary Ledger

Leland High School			801
August 5 SJ1	1,500		

As cash is collected from this customer, the cash receipts journal records the transaction with a credit to the accounts receivable control account and a debit to cash. At the same time, the accounts receivable subsidiary ledger account number 801 also is credited. After the postings are made from the special journals, the balance in the accounts receivable control account should equal the sum of the balances in the accounts receivable subsidiary ledger accounts.

Cash Receipts Journal

All cash receipts are recorded in the *cash receipts journal.*

The purpose of the cash receipts journal is to record all cash receipts, regardless of the source. Every transaction recorded in this journal produces a debit entry to the cash account with the credit to various other accounts. Illustration 2C–2 shows a cash receipts journal using transactions of the Dress Right Clothing Corporation for the month of August 2018.

Illustration 2C–2

Cash Receipts Journal, Dress Right Clothing Corporation, August 2018

Page 1

Date	Explanation or Account Name	Dr. Cash (100)	Cr. Accounts Receivable (110)	Cr. Sales Revenue (400)	Cr. Other	Other Accounts
2018						
Aug. 7	Cash sale	500		500		
11	Borrowed cash	10,000			10,000	Note payable (220)
17	Leland High School	750	750			
20	Cash sale	300		300		
25	Mr. John Smith	200	200			
		11,750	950	800	10,000	

Because every transaction results in a debit to the cash account, No. 100, a column is provided for that account. At the end of August, an $11,750 debit is posted to the general ledger cash account with the source labeled CR1, cash receipts journal, page 1.

Because cash and credit sales are common, separate columns are provided for these accounts. At the end of August, a $950 credit is posted to the accounts receivable general ledger account, No. 110, and an $800 credit is posted to the sales revenue account, No. 400. Two additional credit columns are provided for uncommon cash receipt transactions, one for the credit amount and one for the account being credited. We can see that in August, Dress Right borrowed $10,000 requiring a credit to the note payable account, No. 220.

In addition to the postings to the general ledger control accounts, each time an entry is recorded in the accounts receivable column, a credit is posted to the accounts receivable subsidiary ledger account for the customer making the payment. For example, on August 17, Leland High School paid $750 on account. The subsidiary ledger account for Leland High School is credited for $750.

Accounts Receivable Subsidiary Ledger

Leland High School			801
August 5 SJ1	1,500		
		750	August 17 CR1

Questions For Review of Key Topics

Q 2–1 Explain the difference between external events and internal events. Give an example of each type of event.

Q 2–2 Each economic event or transaction will have a dual effect on financial position. Explain what is meant by this dual effect.

Q 2–3 What is the purpose of a journal? What is the purpose of a general ledger?

Q 2–4 Explain the difference between permanent accounts and temporary accounts. Why does an accounting system include both types of accounts?

Q 2–5 Describe how debits and credits affect assets, liabilities, and permanent owners' equity accounts.

Q 2–6 Describe how debits and credits affect temporary owners' equity accounts.

Q 2–7 What is the first step in the accounting processing cycle? What role do source documents fulfill in this step?

Q 2–8 Describe what is meant by transaction analysis.

Q 2–9 Describe what is meant by posting, the fourth step in the processing cycle.

Q 2–10 Describe the events that correspond to the following two journal entries:

1. Inventory	20,000	
Accounts payable		20,000
2. Accounts receivable	30,000	
Sales revenue		30,000
Cost of goods sold	18,000	
Inventory		18,000

Q 2–11 What is an unadjusted trial balance? An adjusted trial balance?

Q 2–12 Define adjusting entries and discuss their purpose.

Q 2–13 Define closing entries and their purpose.

Q 2–14 Define prepaid expenses and provide at least two examples.

Q 2–15 Deferred revenues represent liabilities recorded when cash is received from customers in advance of providing a good or service. What adjusting journal entry is required at the end of a period to recognize the amount of deferred revenues that were recognized during the period?

Q 2–16 Define accrued liabilities. What adjusting journal entry is required to record accrued liabilities?

Q 2–17 Describe the purpose of each of the five primary financial statements.

Q 2–18 [Based on Appendix A] What is the purpose of a worksheet? In a columnar worksheet similar to Illustration 2A–1, what would be the result of incorrectly transferring the balance in a liability account to column K, the credit column under income statement?

Q 2–19 [Based on Appendix B] Define reversing entries and discuss their purpose.

Q 2–20 [Based on Appendix C] What is the purpose of special journals? In what ways do they simplify the recording process?

Q 2–21 [Based on Appendix C] Explain the difference between the general ledger and a subsidiary ledger.

Brief Exercises

connect

BE 2–1
Transaction analysis
● LO2–1

The Marchetti Soup Company entered into the following transactions during the month of June: (1) purchased inventory on account for $165,000 (assume Marchetti uses a perpetual inventory system); (2) paid $40,000 in salaries to employees for work performed during the month; (3) sold merchandise that cost $120,000 to credit customers for $200,000; (4) collected $180,000 in cash from credit customers; and (5) paid suppliers of inventory $145,000. Analyze each transaction and show the effect of each on the accounting equation for a corporation.

BE 2–2
Journal entries
● LO2–2

Prepare journal entries for each of the transactions listed in BE 2–1.

BE 2–3
T-accounts
● LO2–3

Post the journal entries prepared in BE 2–2 to T-accounts. Assume that the opening balances in each of the accounts is zero except for cash, accounts receivable, and accounts payable that had opening balances of $65,000, $43,000, and $22,000, respectively.

BE 2–4
Journal entries
● LO2–2

Prepare journal entries for each of the following transactions for a company that has a fiscal year-end of December 31: (1) on October 1, $12,000 was paid for a one-year fire insurance policy; (2) on June 30 the company lent its chief financial officer $10,000; principal and interest at 6% are due in one year; and (3) equipment costing $60,000 was purchased at the beginning of the year for cash.

BE 2–5
Adjusting entries
● LO2–5

Prepare the necessary adjusting entries at December 31 for each of the items listed in BE 2–4. Depreciation on the equipment is $12,000 per year.

BE 2–6
Adjusting entries; income determination
● LO2–4, LO2–5

If the adjusting entries prepared in BE 2–5 were not recorded, would net income be higher or lower and by how much?

BE 2–7
Adjusting entries
● LO2–5

Prepare the necessary adjusting entries at its year-end of December 31, 2018, for the Jamesway Corporation for each of the following situations. No adjusting entries were recorded during the year.

1. On December 20, 2018, Jamesway received a $4,000 payment from a customer for services to be rendered early in 2019. Service revenue was credited.
2. On December 1, 2018, the company paid a local radio station $2,000 for 40 radio ads that were to be aired, 20 per month, throughout December and January. Prepaid advertising was debited.
3. Employee salaries for the month of December totaling $16,000 will be paid on January 7, 2019.
4. On August 31, 2018, Jamesway borrowed $60,000 from a local bank. A note was signed with principal and 8% interest to be paid on August 31, 2019.

BE 2–8
Income determination
● LO2–4

If none of the adjusting journal entries prepared in BE 2–7 were recorded, would assets, liabilities, and shareholders' equity on the 12/31/18 balance sheet be higher or lower and by how much?

BE 2–9
Adjusting entries
● LO2–5

Prepare the necessary adjusting entries for Johnstone Controls at the end of its December 31, 2018, fiscal year-end for each of the following situations. No adjusting entries were recorded during the year.

1. On March 31, 2018, the company lent $50,000 to another company. A note was signed with principal and interest at 6% payable on March 31, 2019.
2. On September 30, 2018, the company paid its landlord $12,000 representing rent for the period September 30, 2018, to September 30, 2019.
3. Supplies on hand at the end of 2017 totaled $3,000. Additional supplies costing $5,000 were purchased during 2018 and debited to the supplies account. At the end of 2018, supplies costing $4,200 remain on hand.
4. Vacation pay of $6,000 for the year that had been earned by employees was not paid or recorded. The company records vacation pay as salaries and wages expense.

BE 2–10
Financial statements
● LO2–6

The following account balances were taken from the 2018 adjusted trial balance of the Bowler Corporation: sales revenue, $325,000; cost of goods sold, $168,000; salaries expense, $45,000; rent expense, $20,000; depreciation expense, $30,000; and miscellaneous expense, $12,000. Prepare an income statement for 2018.

BE 2–11
Financial statements
● LO2–6

The following account balances were taken from the 2018 post-closing trial balance of the Bowler Corporation: cash, $5,000; accounts receivable, $10,000; inventory, $16,000; equipment, $100,000; accumulated depreciation—equipment, $40,000; accounts payable, $20,000; salaries payable, $12,000; retained earnings, $9,000; and common stock, $50,000. Prepare a 12/31/18 balance sheet.

BE 2–12
Closing entries
● LO2–7

The year-end adjusted trial balance of the Timmons Tool and Die Corporation included the following account balances: retained earnings, $220,000; sales revenue, $850,000; cost of goods sold, $580,000; salaries expense, $180,000; rent expense, $40,000; and interest expense, $15,000. Prepare the necessary closing entries.

BE 2–13
Cash versus accrual accounting
● LO2–8

Newman Consulting Company maintains its records on a cash basis. During 2018 the following cash flows were recorded: cash received from customers, $420,000; and cash paid for salaries, utilities, and advertising, $240,000, $35,000, and $12,000, respectively. You also determine that customers owed the company $52,000 and $60,000 at the beginning and end of the year, respectively, and that the company owed the utility company $6,000 and $4,000 at the beginning and end of the year, respectively. Determine accrual net income for the year.

Exercises

E 2–1
Transaction analysis
● LO2–1

The following transactions occurred during March 2018 for the Wainwright Corporation. The company owns and operates a wholesale warehouse.

1. Issued 30,000 shares of common stock in exchange for $300,000 in cash.
2. Purchased equipment at a cost of $40,000. $10,000 cash was paid and a note payable was signed for the balance owed.
3. Purchased inventory on account at a cost of $90,000. The company uses the perpetual inventory system.
4. Credit sales for the month totaled $120,000. The cost of the goods sold was $70,000.
5. Paid $5,000 in rent on the warehouse building for the month of March.
6. Paid $6,000 to an insurance company for fire and liability insurance for a one-year period beginning April 1, 2018.
7. Paid $70,000 on account for the merchandise purchased in 3.
8. Collected $55,000 from customers on account.
9. Recorded depreciation expense of $1,000 for the month on the equipment.

Required:

Analyze each transaction and show the effect of each on the accounting equation for a corporation.

Example:

	Assets	= Liabilities	+ Paid-In Capital + Retained Earnings
1.	+ 300,000 (cash)		+ 300,000 (common stock)

E 2–2
Journal entries
● LO2–2

Prepare journal entries to record each of the transactions listed in E 2–1.

E 2–3
T-accounts and trial balance
● LO2–3

Post the journal entries prepared in E 2–2 to T-accounts. Assume that the opening balances in each of the accounts is zero. Prepare a trial balance from the ending account balances.

E 2–4
Journal entries
● LO2–2

The following transactions occurred during the month of June 2018 for the Stridewell Corporation. The company owns and operates a retail shoe store.

1. Issued 100,000 shares of common stock in exchange for $500,000 cash.
2. Purchased office equipment at a cost of $100,000. $40,000 was paid in cash and a note payable was signed for the balance owed.
3. Purchased inventory on account at a cost of $200,000. The company uses the perpetual inventory system.
4. Credit sales for the month totaled $280,000. The cost of the goods sold was $140,000.
5. Paid $6,000 in rent on the store building for the month of June.
6. Paid $3,000 to an insurance company for fire and liability insurance for a one-year period beginning June 1, 2018.
7. Paid $120,000 on account for the merchandise purchased in 3.
8. Collected $55,000 from customers on account.
9. Paid shareholders a cash dividend of $5,000.
10. Recorded depreciation expense of $2,000 for the month on the office equipment.
11. Recorded the amount of prepaid insurance that expired for the month.

Required:

Prepare journal entries to record each of the transactions and events listed above.

E 2–5
The accounting processing cycle
● LO2–2 through LO2–7

Listed below are several terms and phrases associated with the accounting processing cycle. Pair each item from List A (by letter) with the item from List B that is most appropriately associated with it.

List A	List B
_____ 1. Source documents	a. Record of the dual effect of a transaction in debit/credit form.
_____ 2. Transaction analysis	b. Internal events recorded at the end of a reporting period.
_____ 3. Journal	c. Primary means of disseminating information to external decision makers.

(continued)

(concluded)

List A	List B
_____ 4. Posting	d. To zero out the owners' equity temporary accounts.
_____ 5. Unadjusted trial balance	e. Determine the dual effect on the accounting equation.
_____ 6. Adjusting entries	f. List of accounts and their balances before recording adjusting entries.
_____ 7. Adjusted trial balance	g. List of accounts and their balances after recording closing entries.
_____ 8. Financial statements	h. List of accounts and their balances after recording adjusting entries.
_____ 9. Closing entries	i. A means of organizing information: not part of the formal accounting system.
_____ 10. Post-closing trial balance	j. Transferring balances from the journal to the ledger.
_____ 11. Worksheet	k. Used to identify and process external transactions.

E 2–6
Debits and credits
● LO2–2

Indicate whether a *debit* will increase (I) or decrease (D) each of the following accounts listed in items 1 through 15.

Increase (I) or Decrease (D)	Account
1. _____	Inventory
2. _____	Depreciation expense
3. _____	Accounts payable
4. _____	Prepaid rent
5. _____	Sales revenue
6. _____	Common stock
7. _____	Salaries and wages payable
8. _____	Cost of goods sold
9. _____	Utility expense
10. _____	Equipment
11. _____	Accounts receivable
12. _____	Utilities payable
13. _____	Rent expense
14. _____	Interest expense
15. _____	Interest revenue

E 2–7
Transaction analysis; debits and credits
● LO2–2

Some of the ledger accounts for the Sanderson Hardware Company are numbered and listed below. For each of the October 2018 transactions numbered 1 through 12 below, indicate by account number which accounts should be debited and which should be credited. The company uses the perpetual inventory system. Assume that appropriate adjusting entries were recorded at the end of September.

(1) Accounts payable	(2) Equipment	(3) Inventory
(4) Accounts receivable	(5) Cash	(6) Supplies
(7) Supplies expense	(8) Prepaid rent	(9) Sales revenue
(10) Retained earnings	(11) Note payable	(12) Common stock
(13) Deferred revenue	(14) Rent expense	(15) Salaries and wages payable
(16) Cost of goods sold	(17) Salaries and wages expense	(18) Interest expense

	Account(s) Debited	Account(s) Credited
Example: Purchased inventory for cash	3	5

1. Paid a cash dividend.
2. Paid rent for the next three months.
3. Sold goods to customers on account.
4. Purchased inventory on account.
5. Purchased supplies for cash.
6. Paid employee salaries and wages for September.
7. Issued common stock in exchange for cash.
8. Collected cash from customers for goods sold in 3.
9. Borrowed cash from a bank and signed a note.
10. At the end of October, recorded the amount of supplies that had been used during the month.
11. Received cash for advance payment from customer.
12. Accrued employee salaries and wages for October.

E 2–8
Adjusting entries
● **LO2–5**

Prepare the necessary adjusting entries at December 31, 2018, for the Falwell Company for each of the following situations. Assume that no financial statements were prepared during the year and no adjusting entries were recorded.

1. A three-year fire insurance policy was purchased on July 1, 2018, for $12,000. The company debited insurance expense for the entire amount.
2. Depreciation on equipment totaled $15,000 for the year.
3. Employee salaries of $18,000 for the month of December will be paid in early January 2019.
4. On November 1, 2018, the company borrowed $200,000 from a bank. The note requires principal and interest at 12% to be paid on April 30, 2019.
5. On December 1, 2018, the company received $3,000 in cash from another company that is renting office space in Falwell's building. The payment, representing rent for December and January, was credited to deferred rent revenue.

E 2–9
Adjusting entries
● **LO2–5**

Prepare the necessary adjusting entries at December 31, 2018, for the Microchip Company for each of the following situations. Assume that no financial statements were prepared during the year and no adjusting entries were recorded.

1. On October 1, 2018, Microchip lent $90,000 to another company. A note was signed with principal and 8% interest to be paid on September 30, 2019.
2. On November 1, 2018, the company paid its landlord $6,000 representing rent for the months of November through January. Prepaid rent was debited.
3. On August 1, 2018, collected $12,000 in advance rent from another company that is renting a portion of Microchip's factory. The $12,000 represents one year's rent and the entire amount was credited to rent revenue.
4. Depreciation on office equipment is $4,500 for the year.
5. Vacation pay for the year that had been earned by employees but not paid to them or recorded is $8,000. The company records vacation pay as salaries expense.
6. Microchip began the year with $2,000 in its asset account, supplies. During the year, $6,500 in supplies were purchased and debited to supplies. At year-end, supplies costing $3,250 remain on hand.

E 2–10
Adjusting entries; solving for unknowns
● **LO2–4, LO2–5**

The Eldorado Corporation's controller prepares adjusting entries only at the end of the fiscal year. The following adjusting entries were prepared on December 31, 2018:

	Debit	Credit
Interest expense	7,200	
Interest payable		7,200
Rent expense	35,000	
Prepaid rent		35,000
Interest receivable	500	
Interest revenue		500

Additional information:

1. The company borrowed $120,000 on March 31, 2018. Principal and interest are due on March 31, 2019. This note is the company's only interest-bearing debt.
2. Rent for the year on the company's office space is $60,000. The rent is paid in advance.
3. On October 31, 2018, Eldorado lent money to a customer. The customer signed a note with principal and interest at 6% due in one year.

Required:

Determine the following:

1. What is the interest rate on the company's note payable?
2. The 2018 rent payment was made at the beginning of which month?
3. How much did Eldorado lend its customer on October 31?

E 2–11
Adjusting entries
● **LO2–5**

The Mazzanti Wholesale Food Company's fiscal year-end is June 30. The company issues quarterly financial statements requiring the company to prepare adjusting entries at the end of each quarter. Assuming all quarterly adjusting entries were properly recorded, prepare the necessary year-end adjusting entries at the end of June 30, 2018, for the following situations.

1. On December 1, 2017, the company paid its annual fire insurance premium of $6,000 for the year beginning December 1 and debited prepaid insurance.

2. On August 31, 2017, the company borrowed $80,000 from a local bank. The note requires principal and interest at 8% to be paid on August 31, 2018.
3. Mazzanti owns a warehouse that it rents to another company. On January 1, 2018, Mazzanti collected $24,000 representing rent for the 2018 calendar year and credited deferred rent revenue.
4. Depreciation on the office building is $20,000 for the fiscal year.
5. Employee salaries and wages for the month of June 2018 of $16,000 will be paid on July 20, 2018.

E 2–12
Financial statements and closing entries
● LO2–6, LO2–7

The December 31, 2018, adjusted trial balance for the Blueboy Cheese Corporation is presented below.

Account Title	Debits	Credits
Cash	21,000	
Accounts receivable	300,000	
Prepaid rent	10,000	
Inventory	50,000	
Office equipment	600,000	
Accumulated depreciation—office equipment		250,000
Accounts payable		60,000
Note payable (due in six months)		60,000
Salaries payable		8,000
Interest payable		2,000
Common stock		400,000
Retained earnings		100,000
Sales revenue		800,000
Cost of goods sold	480,000	
Salaries expense	120,000	
Rent expense	30,000	
Depreciation expense	60,000	
Interest expense	4,000	
Advertising expense	5,000	
Totals	1,680,000	1,680,000

Required:
1. Prepare an income statement for the year ended December 31, 2018, and a classified balance sheet as of December 31, 2018.
2. Prepare the necessary closing entries at December 31, 2018.

E 2–13
Closing entries
● LO2–7

American Chip Corporation's fiscal year-end is December 31. The following is a partial adjusted trial balance as of December 31, 2018.

Account Title	Debits	Credits
Retained earnings		80,000
Sales revenue		750,000
Interest revenue		3,000
Cost of goods sold	420,000	
Salaries expense	100,000	
Rent expense	15,000	
Depreciation expense	30,000	
Interest expense	5,000	
Insurance expense	6,000	

Required:
Prepare the necessary closing entries at December 31, 2018.

E 2–14
Closing entries
● LO2–7

Presented below is income statement information of the Schefter Corporation for the year ended December 31, 2018.

Sales revenue	$492,000	Cost of goods sold	284,000
Salaries expense	80,000	Insurance expense	12,000
Interest revenue	6,000	Interest expense	4,000
Advertising expense	10,000	Income tax expense	30,000
Gain on sale of investments	8,000	Depreciation expense	20,000

Required:
Prepare the necessary closing entries at December 31, 2018.

E 2–15
Cash versus accrual accounting; adjusting entries
● LO2–4, LO2–5, LO2–8

The Righter Shoe Store Company prepares monthly financial statements for its bank. The November 30 and December 31, 2018, trial balances contained the following account information:

	Nov. 30		Dec. 31	
	Dr.	**Cr.**	**Dr.**	**Cr.**
Supplies	1,500		3,000	
Prepaid insurance	6,000		4,500	
Salaries and wages payable		10,000		15,000
Deferred rent revenue		2,000		1,000

The following information also is known:

a. The December income statement reported $2,000 in supplies expense.
b. No insurance payments were made in December.
c. $10,000 was paid to employees during December for salaries and wages.
d. On November 1, 2018, a tenant paid Righter $3,000 in advance rent for the period November through January. Deferred rent revenue was credited.

Required:

1. What was the cost of supplies purchased during December?
2. What was the adjusting entry recorded at the end of December for prepaid insurance?
3. What was the adjusting entry recorded at the end of December for accrued salaries and wages?
4. What was the amount of rent revenue recognized in December? What adjusting entry was recorded at the end of December for deferred rent revenue?

E 2–16
External transactions and adjusting entries
● LO2–2, LO2–5

The following transactions occurred during 2018 for the Beehive Honey Corporation:

Feb. 1	Borrowed $12,000 from a bank and signed a note. Principal and interest at 10% will be paid on January 31, 2019.
Apr. 1	Paid $3,600 to an insurance company for a two-year fire insurance policy.
July 17	Purchased supplies costing $2,800 on account. The company records supplies purchased in an asset account. At the year-end on December 31, 2018, supplies costing $1,250 remained on hand.
Nov. 1	A customer borrowed $6,000 and signed a note requiring the customer to pay principal and 8% interest on April 30, 2019.

Required:

1. Record each transaction in general journal form. Omit explanations.
2. Prepare any necessary adjusting entries at the year-end on December 31, 2018. No adjusting entries were recorded during the year for any item.

E 2–17
Accrual accounting income determination
● LO2–4, LO2–8

During the course of your examination of the financial statements of the Hales Corporation for the year ended December 31, 2018, you discover the following:

a. An insurance policy covering three years was purchased on January 1, 2018, for $6,000. The entire amount was debited to insurance expense and no adjusting entry was recorded for this item.
b. During 2018, the company received a $1,000 cash advance from a customer for merchandise to be manufactured and shipped in 2019. The $1,000 was credited to sales revenue. No entry was recorded for the cost of merchandise.
c. There were no supplies listed in the balance sheet under assets. However, you discover that supplies costing $750 were on hand at December 31.
d. Hales borrowed $20,000 from a local bank on October 1, 2018. Principal and interest at 12% will be paid on September 30, 2019. No accrual was recorded for interest.
e. Net income reported in the 2018 income statement is $30,000 before reflecting any of the above items.

Required:

Determine the proper amount of net income for 2018.

E 2–18
Cash versus accrual accounting
● LO2–8

Stanley and Jones Lawn Service Company (S&J) maintains its books on a cash basis. However, the company recently borrowed $100,000 from a local bank and the bank requires S&J to provide annual financial statements prepared on an accrual basis. During 2018, the following cash flows were recorded:

Cash collected from customers		$320,000
Cash paid for:		
Salaries	$180,000	
Supplies	25,000	
Rent	12,000	
Insurance	6,000	
Miscellaneous	20,000	243,000
Net operating cash flow		$ 77,000

You are able to determine the following information about accounts receivable, prepaid expenses, and accrued liabilities:

	January 1, 2018	December 31, 2018
Accounts receivable	$32,000	$27,000
Prepaid insurance	–0–	2,000
Supplies	1,000	1,500
Accrued liabilities (for miscellaneous expenses)	2,400	3,400

In addition, you learn that the bank loan was dated September 30, 2018, with principal and interest at 6% due in one year. Depreciation on the company's equipment is $10,000 for the year.

Required:
Prepare an accrual basis income statement for 2018. (Ignore income taxes.)

E 2–19
Cash versus accrual accounting
● LO2–8

Haskins and Jones, Attorneys-at-Law, maintain its books on a cash basis. During 2018, the company collected $545,000 in fees from its clients and paid out $412,000 in expenses. You are able to determine the following information about accounts receivable, prepaid expenses, deferred fee revenue, and accrued liabilities:

	January 1, 2018	December 31, 2018
Accounts receivable	$62,000	$55,000
Prepaid insurance	4,500	6,000
Prepaid rent	9,200	8,200
Deferred fee revenue	9,200	11,000
Accrued liabilities (for various expenses)	12,200	15,600

In addition, 2018 depreciation expense on office equipment is $22,000.

Required:
Determine accrual basis net income for 2018.

E 2–20
Worksheet
● Appendix 2A

The December 31, 2018, unadjusted trial balance for the Wolkstein Drug Company is presented below. December 31 is the company's fiscal year-end.

Account Title	Debits	Credits
Cash	20,000	
Accounts receivable	35,000	
Prepaid rent	5,000	
Inventory	50,000	
Equipment	100,000	
Accumulated depreciation—equipment		30,000
Accounts payable		25,000
Salaries and wages payable		–0–
Common stock		100,000
Retained earnings		29,000
Sales revenue		323,000
Cost of goods sold	180,000	
Salaries and wages expense	71,000	
Rent expense	30,000	
Depreciation expense	–0–	
Utility expense	12,000	
Advertising expense	4,000	
Totals	507,000	507,000

The following year-end adjusting entries are required:

a. Depreciation expense for the year on the equipment is $10,000.
b. Accrued salaries and wages payable at year-end should be $4,000.

Required:

1. Prepare and complete a worksheet similar to Illustration 2A–1.
2. Prepare an income statement for 2018 and a balance sheet as of December 31, 2018.

E 2–21
Reversing entries
● Appendix 2B

The employees of Xitrex, Inc., are paid each Friday. The company's fiscal year-end is June 30, which falls on a Wednesday for the current year. Salaries and wages are earned evenly throughout the five-day work week, and $10,000 will be paid on Friday, July 2.

Required:

1. Prepare an adjusting entry to record the accrued salaries and wages as of June 30, a reversing entry on July 1, and an entry to record the payment of salaries and wages on July 2.
2. Prepare journal entries to record the accrued salaries and wages as of June 30 and the payment of salaries and wages on July 2 assuming a reversing entry is not recorded.

E 2–22
Reversing entries
● Appendix 2B

Refer to E 2–9 and respond to the following requirements.

Required:

1. If Microchip's accountant employed reversing entries for accruals, which adjusting entries would she likely reverse at the beginning of the following year?
2. Prepare the adjusting entries at the end of 2018 for the adjustments you identified in requirement 1.
3. Prepare the appropriate reversing entries at the beginning of 2019.

E 2–23
Reversing entries
● Appendix 2B

Refer to E 2–9 and respond to the following requirements.

Required:

1. If Microchip's accountant employed reversing entries for prepaid expenses, which transactions would be affected?
2. Prepare the original transactions creating the prepaid expenses and the adjusting entries at the end of 2018 for the transactions you identified in requirement 1.
3. Prepare the appropriate reversing entries at the beginning of 2019.

E 2–24
Special journals
● Appendix 2C

The White Company's accounting system consists of a general journal (GJ), a cash receipts journal (CR), a cash disbursements journal (CD), a sales journal (SJ), and a purchases journal (PJ). For each of the following, indicate which journal should be used to record the transaction.

Transaction	Journal
1. Purchased merchandise on account.	______
2. Collected an account receivable.	______
3. Borrowed $20,000 and signed a note.	______
4. Recorded depreciation expense.	______
5. Purchased equipment for cash.	______
6. Sold merchandise for cash (the sale only, not the cost of the merchandise).	______
7. Sold merchandise on credit (the sale only, not the cost of the merchandise).	______
8. Recorded accrued salaries and wages payable.	______
9. Paid employee salaries and wages.	______
10. Sold equipment for cash.	______
11. Sold equipment on credit.	______
12. Paid a cash dividend to shareholders.	______
13. Issued common stock in exchange for cash.	______
14. Paid accounts payable.	______

E 2–25
Special journals
● Appendix 2C

The accounting system of K and M Manufacturing consists of a general journal (GJ), a cash receipts journal (CR), a cash disbursements journal (CD), a sales journal (SJ), and a purchases journal (PJ). For each of the following, indicate which journal should be used to record the transaction.

Transaction	Journal
1. Paid interest on a loan.	______
2. Recorded depreciation expense.	______
3. Purchased furniture for cash.	______

(continued)

(concluded)

Transaction	Journal
4. Purchased merchandise on account.	_____
5. Sold merchandise on credit (the sale only, not the cost of the merchandise).	_____
6. Sold merchandise for cash (the sale only, not the cost of the merchandise).	_____
7. Paid rent.	_____
8. Recorded accrued interest payable.	_____
9. Paid advertising bill.	_____
10. Sold equipment on credit.	_____
11. Collected cash from customers on account.	_____
12. Paid employee salaries and wages.	_____
13. Collected interest on a note receivable.	_____

Problems

P 2–1
Accounting cycle through unadjusted trial balance
● LO2–2, LO2–3

Halogen Laminated Products Company began business on January 1, 2018. During January, the following transactions occurred:

Jan. 1	Issued common stock in exchange for $100,000 cash.
2	Purchased inventory on account for $35,000 (the perpetual inventory system is used).
4	Paid an insurance company $2,400 for a one-year insurance policy.
10	Sold merchandise on account for $12,000. The cost of the merchandise was $7,000.
15	Borrowed $30,000 from a local bank and signed a note. Principal and interest at 10% is to be repaid in six months.
20	Paid employees $6,000 salaries and wages for the first half of the month.
22	Sold merchandise for $10,000 cash. The cost of the merchandise was $6,000.
24	Paid $15,000 to suppliers for the merchandise purchased on January 2.
26	Collected $6,000 on account from customers.
28	Paid $1,000 to the local utility company for January gas and electricity.
30	Paid $4,000 rent for the building. $2,000 was for January rent, and $2,000 for February rent.

Required:

1. Prepare general journal entries to record each transaction. Omit explanations.
2. Post the entries to T-accounts.
3. Prepare an unadjusted trial balance as of January 30, 2018.

P 2–2
Accounting cycle through unadjusted trial balance
● LO2–2, LO2–3

The following is the post-closing trial balance for the Whitlow Manufacturing Corporation as of December 31, 2017.

Account Title	Debits	Credits
Cash	5,000	
Accounts receivable	2,000	
Inventory	5,000	
Equipment	11,000	
Accumulated depreciation—equipment		3,500
Accounts payable		3,000
Common stock		10,000
Retained earnings		6,500
Sales revenue		–0–
Cost of goods sold	–0–	
Salaries and wages expense	–0–	
Rent expense	–0–	
Advertising expense	–0–	
Totals	23,000	23,000

The following transactions occurred during January 2018:

Jan. 1	Sold merchandise for cash, $3,500. The cost of the merchandise was $2,000. The company uses the perpetual inventory system.
2	Purchased equipment on account for $5,500 from the Strong Company.
4	Received a $150 bill from the local newspaper for an advertisement that appeared in the paper on January 2.
8	Sold merchandise on account for $5,000. The cost of the merchandise was $2,800.
10	Purchased merchandise on account for $9,500.

(continued)

(concluded)

13	Purchased equipment for cash, $800.
16	Paid the entire amount due to the Strong Company.
18	Received $4,000 from customers on account.
20	Paid $800 to the owner of the building for January's rent.
30	Paid employees $3,000 for salaries and wages for the month of January.
31	Paid a cash dividend of $1,000 to shareholders.

Required:

1. Set up T-accounts and enter the beginning balances as of January 1, 2018.
2. Prepare general journal entries to record each transaction. Omit explanations.
3. Post the entries to T-accounts.
4. Prepare an unadjusted trial balance as of January 31, 2018.

P 2–3
Adjusting entries
● LO2–5

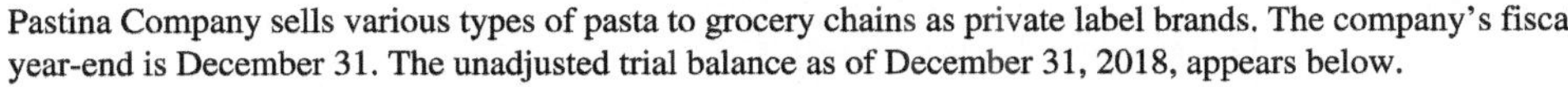

Pastina Company sells various types of pasta to grocery chains as private label brands. The company's fiscal year-end is December 31. The unadjusted trial balance as of December 31, 2018, appears below.

Account Title	Debits	Credits
Cash	30,000	
Accounts receivable	40,000	
Supplies	1,500	
Inventory	60,000	
Note receivable	20,000	
Interest receivable	–0–	
Prepaid rent	2,000	
Prepaid insurance	–0–	
Office equipment	80,000	
Accumulated depreciation—office equipment		30,000
Accounts payable		31,000
Salaries and wages payable		–0–
Note payable		50,000
Interest payable		–0–
Deferred revenue		–0–
Common stock		60,000
Retained earnings		24,500
Sales revenue		148,000
Interest revenue		–0–
Cost of goods sold	70,000	
Salaries and wages expense	18,900	
Rent expense	11,000	
Depreciation expense	–0–	
Interest expense	–0–	
Supplies expense	1,100	
Insurance expense	6,000	
Advertising expense	3,000	
Totals	343,500	343,500

Information necessary to prepare the year-end adjusting entries appears below.

1. Depreciation on the office equipment for the year is $10,000.
2. Employee salaries and wages are paid twice a month, on the 22nd for salaries and wages earned from the 1st through the 15th, and on the 7th of the following month for salaries and wages earned from the 16th through the end of the month. Salaries and wages earned from December 16 through December 31, 2018, were $1,500.
3. On October 1, 2018, Pastina borrowed $50,000 from a local bank and signed a note. The note requires interest to be paid annually on September 30 at 12%. The principal is due in 10 years.
4. On March 1, 2018, the company lent a supplier $20,000 and a note was signed requiring principal and interest at 8% to be paid on February 28, 2019.
5. On April 1, 2018, the company paid an insurance company $6,000 for a two-year fire insurance policy. The entire $6,000 was debited to insurance expense.
6. $800 of supplies remained on hand at December 31, 2018.
7. A customer paid Pastina $2,000 in December for 1,500 pounds of spaghetti to be delivered in January 2019. Pastina credited sales revenue.
8. On December 1, 2018, $2,000 rent was paid to the owner of the building. The payment represented rent for December 2018 and January 2019 at $1,000 per month.

Required:
Prepare the necessary December 31, 2018, adjusting journal entries.

P 2–4
Accounting cycle; adjusting entries through post-closing trial balance
● LO2–3, LO2–5 through LO2–7

Refer to P 2–3 and complete the following steps:

1. Enter the unadjusted balances from the trial balance into T-accounts.
2. Post the adjusting entries prepared in P 2–3 to the accounts.
3. Prepare an adjusted trial balance.
4. Prepare an income statement and a statement of shareholders' equity for the year ended December 31, 2018, and a classified balance sheet as of December 31, 2018. Assume that no common stock was issued during the year and that $4,000 in cash dividends were paid to shareholders during the year. The $4,000 reduction in cash and in retained earnings is reflected in the unadjusted trial balance amounts. That is, the retained earnings balance at the beginning of the year was $28,500.
5. Prepare closing entries and post to the accounts.
6. Prepare a post-closing trial balance.

P 2–5
Adjusting entries
● LO2–5

Howarth Company's fiscal year-end is December 31. Below are the unadjusted and adjusted trial balances for December 31, 2018.

	Unadjusted		Adjusted	
Account Title	**Debits**	**Credits**	**Debits**	**Credits**
Cash	50,000		50,000	
Accounts receivable	35,000		35,000	
Prepaid rent	2,000		1,200	
Supplies	1,500		800	
Inventory	60,000		60,000	
Note receivable	30,000		30,000	
Interest receivable	–0–		1,500	
Office equipment	45,000		45,000	
Accumulated depreciation		15,000		21,500
Accounts payable		34,000		34,000
Salaries and wages payable		–0–		6,200
Note payable		50,000		50,000
Interest payable		–0–		2,500
Deferred rent revenue		–0–		2,000
Common stock		46,000		46,000
Retained earnings		20,000		20,000
Sales revenue		244,000		244,000
Rent revenue		6,000		4,000
Interest revenue		–0–		1,500
Cost of goods sold	126,000		126,000	
Salaries and wages expense	45,000		51,200	
Rent expense	11,000		11,800	
Depreciation expense	–0–		6,500	
Supplies expense	1,100		1,800	
Interest expense	5,400		7,900	
Advertising expense	3,000		3,000	
Totals	415,000	415,000	431,700	431,700

Required:
Prepare the adjusting journal entries that were recorded at December 31, 2018.

P 2–6
Accounting cycle
● LO2–2 through LO2–7

The general ledger of the Karlin Company, a consulting company, at January 1, 2018, contained the following account balances:

Account Title	Debits	Credits
Cash	30,000	
Accounts receivable	15,000	
Equipment	20,000	
Accumulated depreciation		6,000
Salaries payable		9,000
Common stock		40,500
Retained earnings		9,500
Total	65,000	65,000

The following is a summary of the transactions for the year:

a. Sales of services, $100,000, of which $30,000 was on credit.
b. Collected on accounts receivable, $27,300.
c. Issued shares of common stock in exchange for $10,000 in cash.
d. Paid salaries, $50,000 (of which $9,000 was for salaries payable).
e. Paid miscellaneous expenses, $24,000.
f. Purchased equipment for $15,000 in cash.
g. Paid $2,500 in cash dividends to shareholders.

Required:

1. Set up the necessary T-accounts and enter the beginning balances from the trial balance.
2. Prepare a general journal entry for each of the summary transactions listed above.
3. Post the journal entries to the accounts.
4. Prepare an unadjusted trial balance.
5. Prepare and post adjusting journal entries. Accrued salaries at year-end amounted to $1,000. Depreciation for the year on the equipment is $2,000.
6. Prepare an adjusted trial balance.
7. Prepare an income statement for 2018 and a balance sheet as of December 31, 2018.
8. Prepare and post closing entries.
9. Prepare a post-closing trial balance.

P 2–7
Adjusting entries and income effects
● LO2–2, LO2–5

The information necessary for preparing the 2018 year-end adjusting entries for Vito's Pizza Parlor appears below. Vito's fiscal year-end is December 31.

a. On July 1, 2018, purchased $10,000 of IBM Corporation bonds at face value. The bonds pay interest twice a year on January 1 and July 1. The annual interest rate is 12%.
b. Vito's depreciable equipment has a cost of $30,000, a five-year life, and no salvage value. The equipment was purchased in 2016. The straight-line depreciation method is used.
c. On November 1, 2018, the bar area was leased to Jack Donaldson for one year. Vito's received $6,000 representing the first six months' rent and credited deferred rent revenue.
d. On April 1, 2018, the company paid $2,400 for a two-year fire and liability insurance policy and debited insurance expense.
e. On October 1, 2018, the company borrowed $20,000 from a local bank and signed a note. Principal and interest at 12% will be paid on September 30, 2019.
f. At year-end, there is a $1,800 debit balance in the supplies (asset) account. Only $700 of supplies remain on hand.

Required:

1. Prepare the necessary adjusting journal entries at December 31, 2018.
2. Determine the amount by which net income would be misstated if Vito's failed to record these adjusting entries. (Ignore income tax expense.)

P 2–8
Adjusting entries
● LO2–5

Excalibur Corporation sells video games for personal computers. The unadjusted trial balance as of December 31, 2018, appears below. December 31 is the company's fiscal year-end. The company uses the perpetual inventory system.

Account Title	Debits	Credits
Cash	23,300	
Accounts receivable	32,500	
Supplies	–0–	
Prepaid rent	–0–	
Inventory	65,000	
Office equipment	75,000	
Accumulated depreciation—office equipment		10,000
Accounts payable		26,100
Salaries and wages payable		3,000
Note payable		30,000
Common stock		80,000
Retained earnings		16,050
Sales revenue		180,000

(continued)

(concluded)

Account Title	Debits	Credits
Cost of goods sold	95,000	
Interest expense	–0–	
Salaries and wages expense	32,350	
Rent expense	14,000	
Supplies expense	2,000	
Utility expense	6,000	
Totals	345,150	345,150

Information necessary to prepare the year-end adjusting entries appears below.

1. The office equipment was purchased in 2016 and is being depreciated using the straight-line method over an eight-year useful life with no salvage value.
2. Accrued salaries and wages at year-end should be $4,500.
3. The company borrowed $30,000 on September 1, 2018. The principal is due to be repaid in 10 years. Interest is payable twice a year on each August 31 and February 28 at an annual rate of 10%.
4. The company debits supplies expense when supplies are purchased. Supplies on hand at year-end cost $500.
5. Prepaid rent at year-end should be $1,000.

Required:

Prepare the necessary December 31, 2018, adjusting entries.

P 2–9

Accounting cycle; unadjusted trial balance through closing

● LO2–3, LO2–5, LO2–7

The unadjusted trial balance as of December 31, 2018, for the Bagley Consulting Company appears below. December 31 is the company's fiscal year-end.

Account Title	Debits	Credits
Cash	8,000	
Accounts receivable	9,000	
Prepaid insurance	3,000	
Land	200,000	
Buildings	50,000	
Accumulated depreciation—buildings		20,000
Office equipment	100,000	
Accumulated depreciation—office equipment		40,000
Accounts payable		35,050
Salaries and wages payable		–0–
Deferred rent revenue		–0–
Common stock		200,000
Retained earnings		56,450
Sales revenue		90,000
Interest revenue		3,000
Rent revenue		7,500
Salaries and wages expense	37,000	
Depreciation expense	–0–	
Insurance expense	–0–	
Utility expense	30,000	
Maintenance expense	15,000	
Totals	452,000	452,000

Required:

1. Enter the account balances in T-accounts.
2. From the trial balance and information given, prepare adjusting entries and post to the accounts.
   a. The buildings have an estimated useful life of 50 years with no salvage value. The company uses the straight-line depreciation method.
   b. The office equipment is depreciated at 10 percent of original cost per year.
   c. Prepaid insurance expired during the year, $1,500.
   d. Accrued salaries and wages at year-end, $1,500.
   e. Deferred rent revenue at year-end should be $1,200.
3. Prepare an adjusted trial balance.
4. Prepare closing entries.
5. Prepare a post-closing trial balance.

P 2–10
Accrual accounting; financial statements
● LO2–4, LO2–6, LO2–8

McGuire Corporation began operations in 2018. The company purchases computer equipment from manufacturers and then sells to retail stores. During 2018, the bookkeeper used a check register to record all cash receipts and cash disbursements. No other journals were used. The following is a recap of the cash receipts and disbursements made during the year.

Cash receipts:	
Sale of common stock	$ 50,000
Collections from customers	320,000
Borrowed from local bank on April 1, note signed requiring principal and interest at 12% to be paid on March 31, 2019	40,000
Total cash receipts	$ 410,000
Cash disbursements:	
Purchase of merchandise	$ 220,000
Payment of salaries and wages	80,000
Purchase of office equipment	30,000
Payment of rent on building	14,000
Miscellaneous expenses	10,000
Total cash disbursements	$ 354,000

You are called in to prepare financial statements at December 31, 2018. The following additional information was provided to you:

1. Customers owed the company $22,000 at year-end.
2. At year-end, $30,000 was still due to suppliers of merchandise purchased on credit.
3. At year-end, merchandise inventory costing $50,000 still remained on hand.
4. Salaries and wages owed to employees at year-end amounted to $5,000.
5. On December 1, $3,000 in rent was paid to the owner of the building used by McGuire. This represented rent for the months of December through February.
6. The office equipment, which has a 10-year life and no salvage value, was purchased on January 1, 2018. Straight-line depreciation is used.

Required:

Prepare an income statement for 2018 and a balance sheet as of December 31, 2018.

P 2–11
Cash versus accrual accounting
● LO2–8

Selected balance sheet information for the Wolf Company at November 30, and December 31, 2018, is presented below. The company uses the perpetual inventory system and all sales to customers are made on credit.

	Nov. 30		Dec. 31	
	Debits	**Credits**	**Debits**	**Credits**
Accounts receivable	10,000		3,000	
Prepaid insurance	5,000		7,500	
Inventory	7,000		6,000	
Accounts payable		12,000		15,000
Salaries and wages payable		5,000		3,000

The following cash flow information also is available:

a. Cash collected from credit customers, $80,000
b. Cash paid for insurance, $5,000
c. Cash paid to suppliers of inventory, $60,000 (the entire accounts payable amounts relate to inventory purchases)
d. Cash paid to employees for salaries and wages, $10,000

Required:

1. Determine the following for the month of December:
   a. Sales revenue
   b. Cost of goods sold
   c. Insurance expense
   d. Salaries and wages expense
2. Prepare summary journal entries to record the month's sales and cost of those sales.

P 2–12
Cash versus accrual accounting
● LO2–8

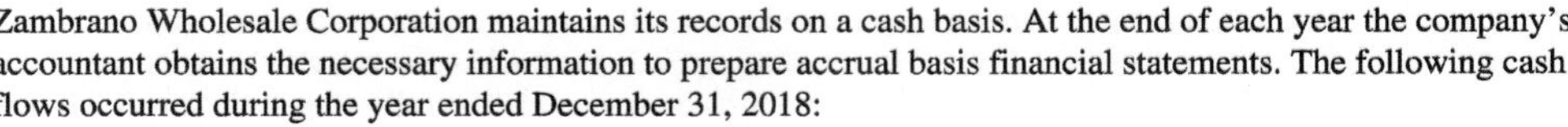

Zambrano Wholesale Corporation maintains its records on a cash basis. At the end of each year the company's accountant obtains the necessary information to prepare accrual basis financial statements. The following cash flows occurred during the year ended December 31, 2018:

Cash receipts:	
From customers	$675,000
Interest on note	4,000
Loan from a local bank	100,000
Total cash receipts	$779,000
Cash disbursements:	
Purchase of merchandise	$390,000
Annual insurance payment	6,000
Payment of salaries and wages	210,000
Dividends paid to shareholders	10,000
Annual rent payment	24,000
Total cash disbursements	$640,000

Selected balance sheet information:

	12/31/17	12/31/18
Cash	$ 25,000	$164,000
Accounts receivable	62,000	92,000
Inventory	80,000	62,000
Prepaid insurance	2,500	?
Prepaid rent	11,000	?
Interest receivable	3,000	?
Note receivable	50,000	50,000
Equipment	100,000	100,000
Accumulated depreciation—equipment	(40,000)	(50,000)
Accounts payable (for merchandise)	110,000	122,000
Salaries and wages payable	20,000	24,000
Note payable	–0–	100,000
Interest payable	–0–	?

Additional information:

1. On March 31, 2017, Zambrano lent a customer $50,000. Interest at 8% is payable annually on each March 31. Principal is due in 2021.
2. The annual insurance payment is paid in advance on April 30. The policy period begins on May 1.
3. On October 31, 2018, Zambrano borrowed $100,000 from a local bank. Principal and interest at 6% are due on October 31, 2019.
4. Annual rent on the company's facilities is paid in advance on June 30. The rental period begins on July 1.

Required:

1. Prepare an accrual basis income statement for 2018 (ignore income taxes).
2. Determine the following balance sheet amounts on December 31, 2018:
   a. Prepaid insurance
   b. Prepaid rent
   c. Interest receivable
   d. Interest payable

P 2–13
Worksheet
● Appendix 2A

Using the information from P 2–8, prepare and complete a worksheet similar to Illustration 2A–1. Use the information in the worksheet to prepare an income statement and a statement of shareholders' equity for 2018 and a balance sheet as of December 31, 2018. Cash dividends paid to shareholders during the year amounted to $6,000. Also prepare the necessary closing entries assuming that adjusting entries have been correctly posted to the accounts.

Broaden Your Perspective

Apply your critical-thinking ability to the knowledge you've gained. These cases will provide you an opportunity to develop your research, analysis, judgment, and communication skills. You also will work with other students, integrate what you've learned, apply it in real-world situations, and consider its global and ethical ramifications. This practice will broaden your knowledge and further develop your decision-making abilities.

Judgment Case 2–1
Cash versus accrual accounting; adjusting entries; Chapters 1 and 2
● LO2–4, LO2–8

You have recently been hired by Davis & Company, a small public accounting firm. One of the firm's partners, Alice Davis, has asked you to deal with a disgruntled client, Mr. Sean Pitt, owner of the city's largest hardware store. Mr. Pitt is applying to a local bank for a substantial loan to remodel his store. The bank requires accrual based financial statements but Mr. Pitt has always kept the company's records on a cash basis. He doesn't see the purpose of accrual based statements. His most recent outburst went something like this: "After all, I collect cash from customers, pay my bills in cash, and I am going to pay the bank loan with cash. And, I already show my building and equipment as assets and depreciate them. I just don't understand the problem."

Required:

1. Explain the difference between a cash basis and an accrual basis measure of performance.
2. Why, in most cases, does accrual basis net income provide a better measure of performance than net operating cash flow?
3. Explain the purpose of adjusting entries as they relate to the difference between cash and accrual accounting.

Judgment Case 2–2
Cash versus accrual accounting
● LO2–8

Refer to Case 2–1 above. Mr. Pitt has relented and agrees to provide you with the information necessary to convert his cash basis financial statements to accrual basis statements. He provides you with the following transaction information for the fiscal year ending December 31, 2018:

1. A new comprehensive insurance policy requires an annual payment of $12,000 for the upcoming year. Coverage began on September 1, 2018, at which time the first payment was made.
2. Mr. Pitt allows customers to pay using a credit card. At the end of the current year, various credit card companies owed Mr. Pitt $6,500. At the end of last year, customer credit card charges outstanding were $5,000.
3. Employees are paid once a month, on the 10th of the month following the work period. Cash disbursements to employees were $8,200 and $7,200 for January 10, 2019, and January 10, 2018, respectively.
4. Utility bills outstanding totaled $1,200 at the end of 2018 and $900 at the end of 2017.
5. A physical count of inventory is always taken at the end of the fiscal year. The merchandise on hand at the end of 2018 cost $35,000. At the end of 2017, inventory on hand cost $32,000.
6. At the end of 2017, Mr. Pitt did not have any bills outstanding to suppliers of merchandise. However, at the end of 2018, he owed suppliers $4,000.

Required:

1. Mr. Pitt's 2018 cash basis net income (including depreciation expense) is $26,000. Determine net income applying the accrual accounting model.
2. Explain the effect on Mr. Pitt's balance sheet of converting from cash to accrual. That is, would assets, liabilities, and owner's equity be higher or lower and by what amounts?

Communication Case 2–3
Adjusting entries
● LO2–4

"I don't understand," complained Chris, who responded to your bulletin board posting for tutoring in introductory accounting. The complaint was in response to your statements that recording adjusting entries is a critical step in the accounting processing cycle, and the two major classifications of adjusting entries are prepayments and accruals.

Required:

Respond to Chris.

1. When do prepayments occur? Accruals?
2. Describe the appropriate adjusting entry for prepaid expenses and for deferred revenues. What is the effect on net income, assets, liabilities, and shareholders' equity of not recording a required adjusting entry for prepayments?
3. Describe the required adjusting entry for accrued liabilities and for accrued receivables. What is the effect on net income, assets, liabilities, and shareholders' equity of not recording a required adjusting entry for accruals?

Continuing Cases

Target Case

● LO2–4, LO2–8

Target Corporation prepares its financial statements according to U.S. GAAP. Target's financial statements and disclosure notes for the year ended January 30, 2016, are available in Connect. This material is also available under the Investor Relations link at the company's website (www.target.com).

Required:

1. Refer to Target's balance sheet for the years ended January 30, 2016 and January 31, 2015. Based on the amounts reported for accumulated depreciation, and assuming no depreciable assets were sold during the year, prepare an adjusting entry to record Target's depreciation for the year.
2. Refer to Target's statement of cash flows for the year ended January 30, 2016. Assuming your answer to Requirement 1 includes all depreciation expense recognized during the year, how much amortization expense was recognized during the year?
3. Note 13 provides information on Target's current assets. Assume all prepaid expenses are for prepaid insurance and that insurance expense comprises $50 million of the $14,665 million of Selling, general and administrative expenses reported in the income statement for the year ended January 30, 2016. How much cash did Target pay for insurance coverage during the year? Prepare the adjusting entry Target would make to record all insurance expense for the year. What would be the effect on the income statement and balance sheet if Target didn't record an adjusting entry for prepaid expenses?

Air France–KLM Case

● LO2–4

IFRS

Air France-KLM (AF), a Franco-Dutch company, prepares its financial statements according to International Financial Reporting Standards. AF's financial statements and disclosure notes for the year ended December 31, 2015, are provided in Connect. This material is also available under the Finance link at the company's website (www.airfranceklm.com).

Required:

1. Refer to AF's balance sheet and compare it to the balance sheet presentation in Illustration 2–14. What differences do you see in the format of the two balance sheets?
2. What differences do you see in the terminology used in the two balance sheets?

CPA Exam Questions and Simulations

Sample CPA Exam questions from Roger CPA Review are available in Connect as support for the topics in this chapter. These Multiple Choice Questions and Task-Based Simulations include expert-written explanations and solutions, and provide a starting point for students to become familiar with the content and functionality of the actual CPA Exam.

CHAPTER

3

The Balance Sheet and Financial Disclosures

OVERVIEW

Chapter 1 stressed the importance of the financial statements to investors and creditors, and Chapter 2 reviewed the preparation of those financial statements. In this chapter, we'll take a closer look at the balance sheet, along with accompanying disclosures. The balance sheet provides relevant information useful in helping investors and creditors not only to predict future cash flows, but also to make the related assessments of liquidity and long-term solvency. In Chapter 4 we'll continue our conversation about the financial statements with discussion of the income statement, statement of comprehensive income, and statement of cash flows.

LEARNING OBJECTIVES

After studying this chapter, you should be able to:

- **LO3–1** Describe the purpose of the balance sheet and understand its usefulness and limitations. (*p. 110*)
- **LO3–2** Identify and describe the various asset classifications. (*p. 112*)
- **LO3–3** Identify and describe the various liability and shareholders' equity classifications. (*p. 116*)
- **LO3–4** Explain the purpose of financial statement disclosures. (*p. 120*)
- **LO3–5** Describe disclosures related to management's discussion and analysis, responsibilities, and compensation. (*p. 123*)
- **LO3–6** Explain the purpose of an audit and describe the content of the audit report. (*p. 126*)
- **LO3–7** Describe the techniques used by financial analysts to transform financial information into forms more useful for analysis. (*p. 128*)
- **LO3–8** Identify and calculate the common liquidity and solvency ratios used to assess risk. (*p. 129*)
- **LO3–9** Discuss the primary differences between U.S. GAAP and IFRS with respect to the balance sheet, financial disclosures, and segment reporting. (*pp. 118* and *136*)

© G Fiume/Maryland Terrapins/Getty Images

FINANCIAL REPORTING CASE

What's It Worth?

"I can't believe it. Why don't you accountants prepare financial statements that are relevant?" Your friend Jerry is a finance major and is constantly badgering you about what he perceives to be a lack of relevance of financial statements prepared according to generally accepted accounting principles. "For example, take a look at this balance sheet for Under Armour that I just downloaded off the Internet. The equity (or book value) of the company according to the 2015 balance sheet was nearly $1.7 billion. But if you multiply the number of outstanding shares by the stock price per share at the same point in time, the company's market value was about $9 billion. I thought equity was supposed to represent the value of the company, but those two numbers aren't close." You decide to look at the company's balance sheet and try to set Jerry straight.

QUESTIONS

By the time you finish this chapter, you should be able to respond appropriately to the questions posed in this case. Compare your response to the solution provided at the end of the chapter.

1. Respond to Jerry's criticism that shareholders' equity does not represent the market value of the company. What information does the balance sheet provide? (*p. 111*)
2. The usefulness of the balance sheet is enhanced by classifying assets and liabilities according to common characteristics. What are the classifications used in Under Armour's balance sheet and what elements do those categories include? (*p. 111*)

The SEC's EDGAR system improves the efficiency with which company information is collected and disseminated.

Most companies provide their financial statements and accompanying disclosures on their website in an "Investor Relations" link, but this information also can be found at the SEC's website (www.sec.gov) through its electronic filing system known as EDGAR (Electronic Data Gathering, Analysis, and Retrieval system). Companies are required to file their financial information in a timely manner using the EDGAR system. As stated by the SEC, "Its (EDGAR system's) primary purpose is to increase the efficiency and fairness of the securities market for the benefit of investors, corporations, and the economy by accelerating the receipt, acceptance, dissemination, and analysis of time-sensitive corporate information filed with the agency."

The first part of this chapter begins our discussion of the financial statements by providing an overview of the balance sheet. The balance sheet reports a company's assets, liabilities, and shareholders' equity. You can see an example of Under Armour on the next page. In the second part of this chapter, we discuss additional disclosures that companies are required to provide beyond the basic financial statements. These disclosures are critical to understanding the financial statements and to evaluating a firm's performance and financial health. In the third part of this chapter, we discuss how information in the financial statements can be used by decision makers to assess business risk (liquidity and long-term solvency).

Real World Financials

UNDER ARMOUR INC. AND SUBSIDIARIES
Consolidated Balance Sheet
December 31, 2015
($ in thousands)

Assets		
Current assets:		
Cash and cash equivalents	$ 129,852	
Accounts receivable, net	433,638	
Inventories	783,031	
Prepaid expenses and other current assets	152,242	
Total current assets		$1,498,763
Property and equipment, net	538,531	
Goodwill	585,181	
Intangible assets, net	75,686	
Deferred income taxes	92,157	
Other long-term assets	78,582	
Total long-term assets		1,370,137
Total assets		$2,868,900
Liabilities and Stockholders' Equity		
Current liabilities:		
Accounts payable	$ 200,460	
Accrued expenses	192,935	
Current maturities of long-term debt	42,000	
Other current liabilities	43,415	
Total current liabilities		478,810
Long-term debt, net of current maturities	352,000	
Revolving credit facility, long-term	275,000	
Other long-term liabilities	94,868	
Total long-term liabilities		721,868
Total liabilities		$1,200,678
Stockholders' equity:		
Common stock	72	
Additional paid-in capital	636,630	
Retained earnings	1,076,533	
Accumulated other comprehensive loss	(45,013)	
Total stockholders' equity		1,668,222
Total liabilities and stockholders' equity		$2,868,900

PART A

The Balance Sheet

● LO3–1

The purpose of the balance sheet, sometimes referred to as the **statement of financial position**, is to report a company's financial position on a particular date. The balance sheet presents an organized array of assets, liabilities, and shareholders' equity *at a point in time.* It is a freeze frame or snapshot of financial position at the end of a particular day marking the end of an accounting period.

Usefulness

The balance sheet provides information useful for assessing future cash flows, liquidity, and long-term solvency.

The balance sheet provides a list of assets and liabilities that are classified (grouped) according to common characteristics. These classifications, which we explore in the next section, along with related disclosure notes, help the balance sheet to provide useful information about liquidity and long-term solvency. Liquidity most often refers to the ability of a company to convert its assets to cash to pay its *current* obligations. Long-term solvency refers to an assessment of whether a company will be able to pay its long-term debts. Other things being equal, the risk that a company will not be able to pay its debt increases as its liabilities, relative to equity, increases.

Solvency also provides information about *financial flexibility*—the ability of a company to alter cash flows in order to take advantage of unexpected investment opportunities and needs. For example, the higher the percentage of a company's liabilities to its equity, the more difficult it typically will be to borrow additional funds either to take advantage of a promising investment opportunity or to meet obligations. In general, the less financial flexibility, the more risk there is that an enterprise will fail. In Part C of this chapter, we introduce some common ratios used to assess liquidity and long-term solvency.[1]

Limitations

Despite its usefulness, the balance sheet has limitations. One important limitation is that a company's book value, its reported assets minus liabilities as shown in the balance sheet, usually *will not directly measure the company's market value.* Market value is the amount someone would be willing to pay to own the company. For a company with publicly traded stock, market value can easily be computed as the current stock price times the number of shares outstanding.

FINANCIAL Reporting Case

Q1, p. 109

Assets minus liabilities, measured according to GAAP, is not likely to be representative of the market value of the entity.

The two primary reasons that the balance sheet does not portray the company's market value are:

1. Many assets, like land and buildings, are measured at their historical costs rather than their fair values. For example, if a company owns land and the value of that land increases, the increase in value is not reported in the balance sheet but it would be reflected in market value.
2. Many aspects of a company may represent valuable resources (such as trained employees, experienced management team, loyal customer relationships, and product knowledge), but these items are not recorded as assets in the balance sheet.

As an example of the second item, in 2015 Facebook spent almost $5 billion on research and development to design new products and improve existing services. While these costs likely improve the company's ability to generate future profits (and therefore increase the market value of the company to shareholders), these items are expensed when incurred and not reported in the balance sheet as an asset. As a result of this and other items, Facebook's ratio of market value to book value at the end of 2015 was 7.1. The average ratio of market value to book value for companies in the S&P 500 index was about 2.8.

Another limitation of the balance sheet is that many items in the balance sheet are heavily reliant on *estimates and judgments rather than determinable amounts.* For example, companies estimate: (a) the amount of receivables they will be able to actually collect, (b) the amount of warranty costs they will eventually incur for products already sold, (c) the residual values and useful lives of their long-term assets, and (d) amounts used to calculate employee pension obligations. Each of these estimates affects amounts reported in the balance sheet.

In summary, even though the balance sheet *does not directly measure* the market value of the entity, it provides valuable information that can be used to *help judge* market value.

Classification of Elements

The usefulness of the balance sheet is enhanced when assets and liabilities are grouped according to common characteristics. *The broad distinction made in the balance sheet is the current versus long-term (noncurrent) classification of both assets and liabilities.* The remainder of Part A provides an overview of the balance sheet. We discuss each of the three primary elements of the balance sheet (assets, liabilities, and shareholders' equity) in the

FINANCIAL Reporting Case

Q2, p. 109

The key classification of assets and liabilities in the balance sheet is the current versus long-term distinction.

[1]Another way the balance sheet is useful is in combination with income statement items. We explore some of these relationships in Chapter 4.

order they are reported in the statement as well as the classifications typically made within the elements. The balance sheet elements were defined in Chapter 1 as follows:

> **Assets** are probable future economic benefits obtained or controlled by a particular entity as a result of past transactions or events. Simply, these are the economic resources of a company.
>
> **Liabilities** are probable future sacrifices of economic benefits arising from present obligations of a particular entity to transfer assets or provide services to other entities in the future as a result of past transactions or events. Simply, these are the obligations of a company.
>
> **Equity** (or net assets), called **shareholders' equity** or **stockholders' equity** for a corporation, is the residual interest in the assets of an entity that remains after deducting liabilities. Stated another way, equity equals total assets minus total liabilities.

Illustration 3–1 shows the relationship among assets, liabilities, and shareholders' equity, often referred to as the accounting equation. Included in the illustration are the subclassifications of each element. We will discuss each of these subclassifications next.

Illustration 3–1
Classification of Elements within a Balance Sheet

Assets	=	Liabilities	+	Shareholders' Equity
1. Current assets		1. Current liabilities		1. Paid-in capital
2. Long-term assets		2. Long-term liabilities		2. Retained earnings

Assets

● LO3–2

Current assets include cash and all other assets expected to become cash or be consumed within one year or the *operating cycle*, whichever is longer.

CURRENT ASSETS. Current assets include cash and other assets that are reasonably expected to be converted to cash or consumed within the coming year, or within the normal operating cycle of the business if that's longer than one year. The operating cycle for a typical merchandising or manufacturing company refers to the period of time from the initial outlay of cash for the purchase of inventory until the time the company collects cash from a customer from the sale of inventory.

For a merchandising company, the initial purchase of inventory often is for a finished good, although some preparation may be necessary to get the inventory ready for sale (such as packaging or distribution). *For a manufacturing company,* the initial outlay of cash often involves the purchase of raw materials, which are then converted into a finished product through the manufacturing process. The concept of an operating cycle is shown in Illustration 3–2.

Illustration 3–2
Operating Cycle of a Typical Merchandising or Manufacturing Company

1
Use cash to acquire inventory
2
Prepare inventory for sale to customers
3
Deliver inventory to customer
4
Collect cash from customer

In some businesses, such as shipbuilding or distilleries, the operating cycle extends far beyond one year. For example, if it takes two years to build an oil-carrying supertanker, then the shipbuilder will classify as current those assets that will be converted to cash or consumed within two years. But for most businesses the operating cycle will be shorter than one year. In these situations the one-year convention is used to classify both assets and liabilities. Where a company has no clearly defined operating cycle, the one-year convention is used.

Illustration 3–3 presents the current asset sections of Nike's balance sheets for the years ended May 31, 2015, and May 31, 2014. In keeping with common practice, the individual current assets are listed in the order of their liquidity (the ability to convert the asset to cash).

Cash and Cash Equivalents. The most liquid asset, cash, is listed first. Cash includes cash on hand and in banks that is available for use in the operations of the business and such items as bank drafts, cashier's checks, and money orders. Cash equivalents frequently include certain negotiable items such as commercial paper, money market funds, and U.S. treasury bills. These are highly liquid investments that can be quickly

	May 31, 2015	May 31, 2014
	($ in millions)	
Current assets:		
Cash and cash equivalents	$ 3,852	$ 2,220
Short-term investments	2,072	2,922
Accounts receivable, net	3,358	3,434
Inventories	4,337	3,947
Deferred income taxes	389	355
Prepaid expenses and other current assets	1,968	818
Total current assets	$15,976	$13,696

Illustration 3–3

Current Assets—Nike, Inc.

Real World Financials

converted into cash. Most companies draw a distinction between investments classified as cash equivalents and the next category of current assets, short-term investments, according to the scheduled maturity of the investment. *It is common practice to classify investments that have a maturity date of three months or less from the date of purchase as cash equivalents.* Nike's policy follows this practice and is disclosed in the summary of significant accounting policies disclosure note. The portion of the note from the company's financial statements is shown in Illustration 3–4.

Cash and equivalents represent cash and short-term, highly liquid investments, including commercial paper, U.S. Treasury, U.S. Agency, money market funds, time deposits and corporate debt securities with maturities of 90 days or less at the date of purchase.

Illustration 3–4

Disclosure of Cash Equivalents—Nike, Inc.

Real World Financials

Cash that is restricted for a special purpose and not available for current operations should not be included in the primary balance of cash and cash equivalents. These restrictions could include future plans to repay debt, purchase equipment, or make investments. Restricted cash is classified as a current asset if it is expected to be used within one year. Otherwise, restricted cash is classified as a long-term asset.

Short-Term Investments. Liquid investments not classified as cash equivalents are reported as short-term investments, sometimes called *temporary investments* or *short-term marketable securities.* Investments in stock and debt securities of other corporations are included as short-term investments *if* the company has the ability and intent to sell those securities within the next 12 months or operating cycle, whichever is longer. We discuss accounting for debt and equity investments in Chapter 12.

Accounts Receivable. Accounts receivable result from the sale of goods or services on credit (discussed in Chapter 7). Accounts receivable often are referred to as *trade receivables* because they arise in the course of a company's normal trade. *Nontrade receivables* result from loans or advances by the company to individuals and other entities. When receivables are supported by a formal agreement or note that specifies payment terms they are called notes receivable.

Accounts receivable usually are due in 30 to 60 days, depending on the terms offered to customers and are, therefore, classified as current assets. Any receivable, regardless of the source, not expected to be collected within one year or the operating cycle, whichever is longer, is classified as a long-term asset, investments. In addition, receivables are typically reported at the net amount expected to be collected. The net amount is calculated as total receivables less an allowance for the estimate of uncollectible accounts.

Inventories consist of assets that a retail or wholesale company acquires for resale or goods that manufacturers produce for sale.

Inventories. Inventories for a wholesale or retail company consist of finished goods for sale to customers. For example, you buy finished goods such as shoes and athletic wear from Nike, potato chips at Costco, school supplies at Staples, and a new shirt at Gap.

However, the inventory of a manufacturer will include not only finished goods, but also goods in the course of production (work in process) and goods to be consumed directly or indirectly in production (raw materials). Manufacturers typically report all three types of inventory either directly in the balance sheet or in a disclosure note. Illustration 3–5 demonstrates how Intel Corp., a semiconductor chip manufacturer, discloses its components of inventory.

Illustration 3–5

Inventories Disclosure—Intel Corp.

Real World Financials

	December 26, 2015	December 27, 2014
	($ in millions)	
Raw materials	$ 532	$ 462
Work in process	2,893	2,375
Finished goods	1,742	1,436
Total inventories	$ 5,167	$4,273

Inventories are reported as current assets because they normally are sold within the operating cycle.

Prepaid Expenses. Recall from Chapter 2 that a prepaid expense represents an asset recorded when an expense is paid in advance, creating benefits beyond the current period. Examples are prepaid rent and prepaid insurance. Even though these assets are not converted to cash, they would involve an outlay of cash if not prepaid.

Whether a prepaid expense is current or noncurrent depends on when its benefits will be realized. For example, if rent on an office building were prepaid for one year, then the prepayment is classified as a current asset. However, if rent were prepaid for a period extending beyond the coming year, a portion of the prepayment is classified as an other asset, a long-term asset.[2] Nike includes prepaid expenses along with other current assets. Other current assets also could include assets such as nontrade receivables, that, because their amounts are not material, did not warrant separate disclosure.

LONG-TERM ASSETS. When assets are expected to provide economic benefits beyond the next year, or operating cycle, they are reported as *long-term* (or *noncurrent) assets.* Typical classifications of long-term assets are as follows:

1. Investments
2. Property, plant, and equipment
3. Intangible assets
4. Other long-term assets

Next, we'll discuss each of these categories of long-term assets.

Investments are assets not used directly in operations.

Investments. Most companies occasionally acquire assets that are not used directly in the operations of the business. These assets include investments in equity and debt securities of other corporations, land held for speculation, long-term receivables, and cash set aside for special purposes (such as for future plant expansion). These assets are classified as long-term because management does not intend to convert the assets into cash in the next year (or the operating cycle if that's longer).

Tangible, long-lived assets used in the operations of the business are classified as *property, plant, and equipment.*

Property, Plant, and Equipment. Virtually all companies own assets classified as property, plant, and equipment. The common characteristics these assets share are that they are *tangible, long-lived,* and *used in the operations of the business.* Property, plant, and equipment often are the primary revenue-generating assets of the business.

[2]Companies often include prepayments for benefits extending beyond one year as current assets when the amounts are not material.

Property, plant, and equipment includes land, buildings, equipment, machinery, furniture, and vehicles, as well as natural resources, such as mineral mines, timber tracts, and oil wells. These various assets usually are reported as a single amount in the balance sheet, with details provided in a note. They are reported at original cost less accumulated depreciation (or depletion for natural resources) to date. Quite often, a company will present only the net amount of property, plant, and equipment in the balance sheet and provide details in a disclosure note. Land often is listed as a separate item in this classification because it has an unlimited useful life and thus is not depreciated.

Intangible Assets. Some assets used in the operations of a business have no physical substance. These assets are appropriately called intangible assets. Many intangible assets grant an exclusive right to a company to provide a product or service. This right can be a valuable resource in generating future revenues. Patents, copyrights, franchises, and trademarks are examples. Intangible assets generally are reported in the balance sheet at their purchase price less accumulated *amortization* (similar to how we account for property, plant, and equipment at their purchase price less accumulated *depreciation*).

Intangible assets **generally represent exclusive rights that a company can use to generate future revenues.**

Not all intangible assets are purchased; some are developed internally. For example, instead of purchasing a patent granting the exclusive right to manufacture a certain drug, a pharmaceutical company may spend significant amounts in research and development to discover the drug and obtain a patent on its own. For internally developed intangibles, none of the research and development costs incurred in developing the intangible asset are included in reported cost. Instead, research and development costs are expensed as incurred. Pfizer, one of the world's largest pharmaceutical companies, spent $7.7 billion on researching and developing new medicines, vaccines, medical devices, and other health care products in 2015. These costs may help to generate future profits, but none of them were reported as an asset.

Another common type of intangible asset is *goodwill.* Goodwill isn't associated with any specific identifiable right, but instead arises when one company acquires another company. The amount reported for goodwill equals the acquisition price above the fair value of the identifiable net assets acquired. We'll discuss goodwill and other intangible assets in more detail in Chapter 10.

Illustration 3–6 shows the long-term asset section of Nike's balance sheets, including its disclosure of goodwill and identifiable intangible assets.

Illustration 3–6

Long-term Assets—Nike, Inc.

Real World Financials

	May 31, 2015	May 31, 2014
	($ in millions)	
Long-term assets:		
Property, plant, and equipment, net	$3,011	$2,834
Identifiable intangible assets	281	282
Goodwill	131	131
Deferred income taxes and other assets	2,201	1,651
Total long-term assets	$5,624	$4,898

Other Long-Term Assets. This category of long-term assets (reported by most companies) represents a catch-all classification of long-term assets that were not reported separately in one of the other long-term classifications. This amount most often includes long-term prepaid expenses, called *deferred charges.* For instance, Nike includes promotional expenditures related to long-term endorsement contracts and long-term advertising in this category. Nike also includes deferred charges related to income taxes.

This category might also include any long-term investments that are not material in amount and that were not reported separately in the long-term investments category discussed earlier. In the disclosure notes to its financial statements, Nike revealed that it did have a small amount of long-term investments as well as long-term receivables that were combined with deferred charges and reported in this category (instead of being reported separately in a long-term investments category).

Asset classification is affected by management intent.

A key to understanding which category an asset is reported is *management intent.* For example, in which category will land be reported? It depends on management intent. Management may intend to use land for long-term operating purposes (property, plant, and equipment), hold it for future resale (investment), or sell it in its ordinary course of business (inventory for a real estate company).

● LO3–3

Liabilities

Liabilities represent obligations to other entities. The information value of reporting these amounts is enhanced by classifying them as current liabilities and long-term liabilities. Illustration 3–7 shows the liability section of Nike's balance sheets.

Illustration 3–7

Liabilities—Nike, Inc.

Real World Financials

	May 31, 2015	May 31, 2014
	($ in millions)	
Current liabilities:		
Current portion of long-term debt	$ 107	$ 7
Notes payable	74	167
Accounts payable	2,131	1,930
Accrued liabilities	3,951	2,491
Income tax payable	71	432
Total current liabilities	6,334	5,027
Long-term debt	1,079	1,199
Deferred income taxes and other liabilities	1,480	1,544
Total liabilities	$8,893	$7,770

Current liabilities are expected to be satisfied within one year or the operating cycle, whichever is longer.

CURRENT LIABILITES. Current liabilities are those obligations that are expected to be satisfied through the use of current assets or the creation of other current liabilities. So, this classification includes all liabilities that are expected to be satisfied within one year or the operating cycle, whichever is longer. As of May 31, 2015, Nike had current liabilities of $6,334 million that it planned to pay in the next 12 months.

The most common current liabilities are accounts payable, notes payable (short-term borrowings), deferred revenues, accrued liabilities, and the currently maturing portion of long-term debt.

Accounts payable are obligations to suppliers of merchandise or of services purchased on open account, with payment usually due in 30 to 60 days.

Notes payable are written promises to pay cash at some future date (I.O.U.s). Unlike accounts payable, notes usually require the payment of explicit interest in addition to the original obligation amount. Notes maturing in the next year or operating cycle, whichever is longer, will be classified as current liabilities.

Deferred revenues, sometimes called *unearned revenues,* represent cash received from a customer for goods or services to be provided in a future period. For example, a company records deferred revenue when it sells gift cards and then waits to record the (actual) revenue until the cards are redeemed or expire.

Accrued liabilities represent obligations created when expenses have been incurred but amounts owed will not be paid until a subsequent reporting period. For example, a company might owe salaries at the end of the fiscal year to be paid some time in the following year. In this case, the company would report *salaries payable* as an accrued liability in the current year's balance sheet (as well as the related salaries expense in the income statement). Other common examples of accrued liabilities include interest payable, taxes payable, utilities payable, and legal fees payable. In most financial statements these items are reported in the balance sheet as accrued liabilities and the categories may be found listed in the disclosure notes.

Current maturities of long-term debt refer to the portion of long-term notes, loans, mortgages, and bonds payable that is payable within the next year (or operating cycle if that's longer).[3] For example, a $1,000,000 note payable requiring $100,000 in principal payments to be made in each of the next 10 years is classified as a $100,000 current liability and a $900,000 long-term liability. Nike classifies the current portion of its long-term debt as a current liability.

An exception for the current liability classification is a liability that management intends to refinance on a long-term basis. For example, if management intends to refinance a six-month note payable by substituting a two-year note payable and has the ability to do so, then the liability would not be classified as current even though it's due within the coming year. This exception and issues related to current liabilities are discussed in more detail in Chapter 13.

LONG-TERM LIABILITIES. Long-term liabilities are obligations that will *not* be satisfied in the next year or operating cycle, whichever is longer. They do not require the use of current assets or the creation of current liabilities for payment. Examples are long-term notes, bonds, pension obligations, and lease obligations.

Noncurrent, or long-term liabilities, usually are those payable beyond the current year.

But simply classifying a liability as long-term doesn't provide complete information to external users. For instance, long-term could mean anything from 2 to 20, 30, or 40 years. Payment terms, interest rates, and other details needed to assess the impact of these obligations on future cash flows and long-term solvency are reported in a disclosure note. Nike reports long-term liabilities related to corporate bonds and promissory notes.

Shareholders' Equity

Recall from our discussions in Chapters 1 and 2 that owners' equity is simply a residual amount derived by subtracting liabilities from assets. For that reason, it's sometimes referred to as *net assets* or *book value.* Also recall that owners of a corporation are its shareholders, so owners' equity for a corporation is referred to as *shareholders' equity* or *stockholders' equity.* Here's a simple way to think of equity. If someone buys a house for $200,000 by making an initial $50,000 payment and borrowing the remaining $150,000, then the house's owner has an asset of $200,000, a liability of $150,000, and equity of $50,000.

Shareholders' equity for a corporation arises primarily from:

1. Paid-in capital
2. Retained earnings

Paid-in capital is the amount that shareholders have invested in the company. It most often arises when the company issues stock. As shown in Illustration 3–8, the shareholders' equity section of Nike's balance sheets reports the full amount of paid-in capital in two accounts—common stock and additional paid-in capital. Information about the number of shares the company has authorized and how many shares have been issued and are outstanding also must be disclosed either directly in the balance sheet or in a note.

	May 31, 2015	May 31, 2014
	($ in millions)	
Stockholders' equity:		
Common stock, 679 and 692 shares outstanding	$ 3	$ 3
Additional paid-in capital	6,773	5,865
Retained earnings	4,685	4,871
Accumulated other comprehensive income	1,246	85
Total stockholders' equity	$12,707	$10,824

Illustration 3–8
Shareholders' Equity—Nike, Inc.

Real World Financials

[3]Payment can be with current assets or the creation of other current liabilities.

Retained earnings represents the accumulated net income reported by a company since its inception minus all dividends paid to shareholders. In other words, it's the accumulated lifetime profits a company has earned for its shareholders but has not yet distributed to those shareholders. The fact that a company does not pay all of its profits each year as dividends is not necessarily a bad thing from the shareholders' perspective. Instead of paying additional cash dividends, Nike's management can put those undistributed profits to productive use, such as buying additional inventory or equipment or paying liabilities as they come due.

Nike also reports a *third component of stockholders' equity*—**accumulated other comprehensive income (AOCI)**. Comprehensive income refers to the total change in stockholders' equity other than transactions with owners. While most of this change is reported in the income statement as net income, there are some items of other comprehensive income not reported in the income statement. We accumulate these items in the *accumulated other comprehensive income* account, just like we accumulate each year's net income (that hasn't been distributed as dividends) in the *retained earnings* account.

While accumulated other comprehensive income typically is much smaller than the amount of paid-in capital or retained earnings, it is reported by many companies. We will discuss specific examples of items included in other comprehensive income in Chapters 4, 12, and 18.

We also will discuss other transactions affecting equity, such as a company's purchase of its own stock that is not retired (*treasury stock*) in Chapter 18. Reacquired shares are essentially the same as shares that never were issued at all. A company may decide to re-issue those shares in the future, but until then, they are reported as negative (or contra) shareholders' equity. Nike does not report any treasury stock but many companies do.

International Financial Reporting Standards

● LO3–9

Balance Sheet Presentation. There are more similarities than differences in balance sheets prepared according to U.S. GAAP and those prepared applying IFRS. Some of the differences are:

- International standards specify a minimum list of items to be presented in the balance sheet. U.S. GAAP has no minimum requirements.
- *IAS No. 1, revised,*[4] changed the title of the balance sheet to *statement of financial position,* although companies are not required to use that title. Some U.S. companies use the statement of financial position title as well.
- Under U.S. GAAP, we present current assets and liabilities before noncurrent assets and liabilities. *IAS No. 1* doesn't prescribe the format of the balance sheet, but balance sheets prepared using IFRS often report noncurrent items first. A recent survey of large companies that prepare their financial statements according to IFRS reports that 73% of the surveyed companies list noncurrent items first.[5] For example, H&M, a Swedish-based clothing company, reported assets, liabilities, and shareholders' equity in its balance sheet in the following order:

	(SEK in millions)
Noncurrrent assets (including property, plant, and equipment)	26,488
Current assets	39,188
Total assets	65,676
Shareholders' equity	45,248
Long-term liabilities	3,031
Current liabilities	17,397
Total liabilities and equity	65,676

[4]"Financial Statement Presentation,"*International Accounting Standard No. 1* (IASCF), as amended effective January 1, 2016.
[5]*IFRS Accounting Trends and Techniques–2011* (New York, AICPA, 2011), p.133.

Where We're Headed 

In 2004, the FASB and IASB began working together on a project, Financial Statement Presentation, to establish a common standard for presenting information in the financial statements, including classifying and displaying line items and aggregating line items into subtotals and totals. This project could have a dramatic impact on the format of financial statements. An important part of the proposal involves the organization of elements of the balance sheet (statement of financial position), statement of comprehensive income (including the income statement), and statement of cash flows into a common set of classifications.

Progress was slow, and in 2011 both Boards suspended activity on the project to concentrate on other convergence projects. In 2014, the project was moved back on the FASB's agenda. It is not known if the project will retain its original scope of encompassing all of the financial statements or if it will focus on one or two statements. In August 2016, the FASB issued an Exposure Draft to propose adding "Chapter 7: Presentation" to *Concepts Statement 8—Conceptual Framework for Financial Reporting*. The Exposure Draft proposes a framework for the Board to consider in developing standards related to the presentation of information in the financial statements.

Concept Review Exercise

BALANCE SHEET CLASSIFICATION

The following is a post-closing trial balance for the Sepia Paint Corporation at December 31, 2018, the end of the company's fiscal year:

Account Title	Debits	Credits
Cash	$ 80,000	
Accounts receivable	200,000	
Allowance for uncollectible accounts		$ 20,000
Inventories	300,000	
Prepaid expenses	30,000	
Note receivable (due in one month)	60,000	
Investments	50,000	
Land	120,000	
Buildings	550,000	
Machinery	500,000	
Accumulated depreciation—buildings and machinery		450,000
Patent (net of amortization)	50,000	
Accounts payable		170,000
Salaries payable		40,000
Interest payable		10,000
Note payable		100,000
Bonds payable (due in 10 years)		500,000
Common stock, no par		400,000
Retained earnings		250,000
Totals	$1,940,000	$1,940,000

The $50,000 balance in the investment account consists of marketable equity securities of other corporations. The company's intention is to hold the securities for at least three years. The $100,000 note payable is an installment loan. $10,000 of the principal, plus interest, is due on each July 1 for the next 10 years. At the end of the year, 100,000 shares of common stock were issued and outstanding. The company has 500,000 shares of common stock authorized.

Required:

Prepare a classified balance sheet for the Sepia Paint Corporation at December 31, 2018.

Solution:

SEPIA PAINT CORPORATION
Balance Sheet
At December 31, 2018

Assets		
Current assets:		
Cash		$ 80,000
Accounts receivable	$ 200,000	
Less: Allowance for uncollectible accounts	(20,000)	180,000
Note receivable		60,000
Inventories		300,000
Prepaid expenses		30,000
Total current assets		650,000
Investments		50,000
Property, plant, and equipment:		
Land	120,000	
Buildings	550,000	
Machinery	500,000	
	1,170,000	
Less: Accumulated depreciation	(450,000)	
Net property, plant, and equipment		720,000
Intangible assets:		
Patent		50,000
Total assets		$1,470,000
Liabilities and Shareholders' Equity		
Current liabilities:		
Accounts payable		$ 170,000
Salaries payable		40,000
Interest payable		10,000
Current maturities of long-term debt		10,000
Total current liabilities		230,000
Long-term liabilities:		
Note payable	$ 90,000	
Bonds payable	500,000	
Total long-term liabilities		590,000
Shareholders' equity:		
Common stock, no par, 500,000 shares authorized, 100,000 shares issued and outstanding	400,000	
Retained earnings	250,000	
Total shareholders' equity		650,000
Total liabilities and shareholders' equity		$1,470,000

The usefulness of the balance sheet, as well as the other financial statements, is significantly enhanced by financial statement disclosures. We now turn our attention to these disclosures.

PART B

Financial Disclosures

● LO3–4

At the end of each fiscal year, companies with public securities are required to provide shareholders with an *annual report.* The annual report includes financial statements such as the balance sheet. Financial statements, though, are only part of the information provided in the annual report. Critical to understanding the financial statements and to evaluating a firm's performance and financial health are additional disclosures included as part of the financial statements.

Financial disclosures make up a significant portion of the information reported to shareholders.

The amount of information provided by financial disclosures can be significant. For example, Nike's 2015 annual report included five pages of financial statements followed by 32 pages of related disclosures. Nike's full Form 10-K (annual report filed with the SEC) included another 50 pages of disclosures related to business conditions, risk factors, legal proceedings, the company's stock performance, management's discussion and analysis, and internal control procedures. We will discuss some of these disclosures in the next section.

Disclosure Notes

Some financial statement disclosures are provided by including additional information, often parenthetically, on the face of the statement. Common examples of disclosures included on the face of the balance sheet are the allowance for uncollectible accounts and information about common stock. Other disclosures include supporting discussion, calculations, and schedules in notes following the financial statements. These notes are the most common means of providing additional disclosure. For instance, the fair values of financial instruments and "off-balance-sheet" risk associated with financial instruments are disclosed in notes. Information providing details of many financial statement items is provided using disclosure notes. Some examples include:

The full-disclosure principle requires that financial statements provide all material relevant information concerning the reporting entity.

- Pension plans
- Leases
- Long-term debt
- Investments
- Income taxes
- Property, plant, and equipment
- Employee benefit plans

Disclosure notes must include certain specific notes such as a summary of significant accounting policies, descriptions of subsequent events, and related third-party transactions, but many notes are fashioned to suit the disclosure needs of the particular reporting enterprise. Actually, any explanation that contributes to investors' and creditors' understanding of the results of operations, financial position, and cash flows of the company should be included. Let's take a look at just a few disclosure notes.

Summary of Significant Accounting Policies

There are many areas where management chooses from among equally acceptable alternative accounting methods. For example, management chooses whether to use accelerated or straight-line depreciation, whether to use FIFO, LIFO, or average cost to measure inventories, and whether to measure certain financial investments at fair value or cost. The company also defines which securities it considers to be cash equivalents and its policies regarding the timing of recognizing revenues. Typically, the first disclosure note consists of a summary of significant accounting policies that discloses the choices the company makes.[6] Illustration 3–9 shows a portion of a typical summary note from a recent annual report of the Starbucks Corporation.

The *summary of significant accounting policies* conveys valuable information about the company's choices from among various alternative accounting methods.

Studying this note is an essential step in analyzing financial statements. Obviously, knowing which methods were used to derive certain accounting numbers is critical to assessing the adequacy of those amounts.

Subsequent Events

When an event that has a material effect on the company's financial position occurs after the fiscal year-end but before the financial statements are issued or "available to be issued," the event is described in a subsequent event disclosure note.[7] Examples include the issuance of

A *subsequent event* is a significant development that occurs after a company's fiscal year-end but before the financial statements are issued or available to be issued.

[6]FASB ASC 235–10–50: Notes to Financial Statements–Overall–Disclosure (previously "Disclosure of Accounting Policies," *Accounting Principles Board Opinion No. 22* (New York: AICPA, 1972)).

[7]Financial statements are viewed as issued if they have been widely distributed to financial statement users in a format consistent with GAAP. Some entities (for example, private companies) don't widely distribute their financial statements to users. For those entities, the key date for subsequent events is not the date of issuance but rather the date upon which the financial statements are "available to be issued," which occurs when the financial statements are complete, in a format consistent with GAAP, and have obtained the necessary approvals for issuance. Companies must disclose the date through which subsequent events have been evaluated. FASB ASC 855: Subsequent Events (previously "Subsequent Events," *Statement of Financial Accounting Standards No. 165* (Stamford, Conn.: FASB, 2009)).

Illustration 3–9 Summary of Significant Accounting Policies—Starbucks Corporation

Real World Financials

Note 1: Summary of Accounting Policies (in part)

Principles of Consolidation
The consolidated financial statements reflect the financial position and operating results of Starbucks, including wholly owned subsidiaries and investees that we control.

Cash and Cash Equivalents
We consider all highly liquid instruments with a maturity of three months or less at the time of purchase to be cash equivalents.

Inventories
Inventories are stated at the lower of cost (primarily moving average cost) or market. We record inventory reserves for obsolete and slow-moving inventory and for estimated shrinkage between physical inventory counts.

Property, Plant, and Equipment
Property, plant, and equipment are carried at cost less accumulated depreciation. Cost includes all direct costs necessary to acquire and prepare assets for use, including internal labor and overhead in some cases. Depreciation of property, plant, and equipment, which includes assets under capital leases, is provided on the straight-line method over estimated useful lives, generally ranging from 2 to 15 years for equipment and 30 to 40 years for buildings. Leasehold improvements are amortized over the shorter of their estimated useful lives or the related lease life, generally 10 years.

Revenue Recognition
Company-operated stores' revenues are recognized when payment is tendered at the point of sale. Revenues from our stored value cards, primarily Starbucks Cards, are recognized when redeemed or when the likelihood of redemption, based on historical experience, is deemed to be remote. Outstanding customer balances are included in deferred revenue on the consolidated balance sheets.

debt or equity securities, a business combination or the sale of a business, the sale of assets, an event that sheds light on the outcome of a loss contingency, or any other event having a material effect on operations. Illustration 3–10 illustrates an event that Target Corporation disclosed in its annual report for the year ending January 31, 2015, but before the release of those financial statements. We cover subsequent events in more depth in Chapter 13.

Illustration 3–10
Subsequent Event—Target Corp.

Real World Financials

29. Subsequent Events
In March 2015, we announced a headquarters workforce reduction. As a result, we expect to record approximately $100 million of severance and other benefits-related charges within SG&A in the first quarter of 2015, the vast majority of which are expected to require cash expenditures.

Noteworthy Events and Transactions

Some transactions and events occur only occasionally but, when they do occur, they are potentially important to evaluating a company's financial statements. In this category are related-party transactions, errors and fraud, and illegal acts. The more frequent of these is related-party transactions.

The economic substance of *related-party* transactions should be disclosed, including dollar amounts involved.

Sometimes a company will engage in transactions with owners, management, families of owners or management, affiliated companies, and other parties that can significantly influence or be influenced by the company. The potential problem with related-party transactions is that their economic substance may differ from their legal form. For instance, borrowing or lending money at an interest rate that differs significantly from the market interest rate is an example of a transaction that could result from a related-party involvement. As a result of the potential for misrepresentation, financial statement users are particularly interested in more details about these transactions.

When related-party transactions occur, companies must disclose the nature of the relationship, provide a description of the transactions, and report the dollar amounts of transactions and any amounts due from or to related parties.[8] Illustration 3–11 shows a disclosure note from a recent annual report of Champions Oncology, Inc. The note describes payments for consulting services to a member of its Board of Directors.

[8]FASB ASC 850–10–50: Related Party Disclosures–Overall–Disclosure (previously "Related Party Disclosures," *Statement of Financial Accounting Standards No. 57* (Stamford, Conn.: FASB, 1982)).

Note 4. Related-Party Transactions
Related party transactions include transactions between the Company and its shareholders, management, or affiliates. The following transactions were in the normal course of operations and were measured and recorded at the exchange amount, which is the amount of consideration established and agreed to by the parties.

Consulting Services
During the three months ended July 31, 2015 and 2014, the Company paid a member of its Board of Directors $18,000 and $37,500, respectively, for consulting services unrelated to his duties as a board member. During the three months ended July 31, 2015 and 2014, the Company paid a board member's company $5,900 and nil, respectively, for consulting services. All of the amounts paid to these related parties have been recognized and expensed in the period the services were performed.

Illustration 3–11

Related-Party Transactions Disclosure—Champions Oncology, Inc.

Real World Financials

Less frequent events are errors and fraud. The distinction between these two terms is that errors are unintentional while fraud is intentional misappropriation of assets or fraudulent financial reporting.[9] Errors and fraud may require disclosure (e.g., of assets lost through either errors or fraud). Obviously, the existence of fraud involving management might cause a user to approach financial analysis from an entirely different and more cautious viewpoint.

Closely related to fraud are illegal acts such as bribes, kickbacks, illegal contributions to political candidates, and other violations of the law. Accounting for illegal practices has been influenced by the Foreign Corrupt Practices Act passed by Congress in 1977. The Act is intended to discourage illegal business practices through tighter controls and also encourage better disclosure of those practices when encountered. The nature of such disclosures should be influenced by the materiality of the impact of illegal acts on amounts disclosed in the financial statements.[10] However, the SEC issued guidance expressing its view that exclusive reliance on quantitative benchmarks to assess materiality in preparing financial statements is inappropriate.[11] A number of other factors, including whether the item in question involves an unlawful transaction, should also be considered when determining materiality.

As you might expect, any disclosures of related-party transactions, fraud, and illegal acts can be quite sensitive. Although auditors must be considerate of the privacy of the parties involved, that consideration cannot be subordinate to users' needs for full disclosure.

We've discussed only a few of the disclosure notes most frequently included in annual reports. Other common disclosures include details concerning earnings per share calculations, income taxes, property and equipment, contingencies, long-term debt, leases, pensions, stock options, changes in accounting methods, fair values of financial instruments, and exposure to market risk and credit risk. We discuss and illustrate these in later chapters in the context of related financial statement elements.

Disclosure notes for some financial statement elements are required. Others are provided when required by specific situations in the interest of full disclosure.

Management's Discussion and Analysis

● LO3–5

In addition to the financial statements and accompanying disclosure notes, each annual report of a public company requires a fairly lengthy discussion and analysis provided by the company's management. In this section, which precedes the financial statements and the auditor's report, management provides its views on significant events, trends, and uncertainties pertaining to the company's (a) operations, (b) liquidity, and (c) capital resources. Although the management's discussion and analysis (MD&A) section may embody management's biased perspective, it can offer an informed insight that might not be available elsewhere. As an example, Illustration 3–12 contains a portion of GameStop Corporation's MD&A regarding liquidity and capital resources that is in its annual report.

Management's discussion and analysis provides a biased but informed perspective of a company's (a) operations, (b) liquidity, and (c) capital resources.

[9]"Consideration of Fraud in a Financial Statement Audit," *AICPA Professional Standards AU 240* (New York: AICPA, 2012).
[10]"Consideration of Laws and Regulations in an Audit of Financial Statements," *AICPA Professional Standards AU 250* (New York: AICPA, 2012).
[11]FASB ASC 250–10–S99–1, SAB Topic 1.M: Assessing Materiality (originally "Materiality," *Staff Accounting Bulletin No. 99* (Washington, D.C.: SEC, August 1999)).

Illustration 3–12

Management's Discussion and Analysis—GameStop Corp.

Real World Financials

Management's Discussion and Analysis of Financial Condition and Results of Operations
(In part: Liquidity and Capital Resources)

Overview

Based on our current operating plans, we believe that available cash balances, cash generated from our operating activities, funds available under our $400.0 million asset-based revolving credit facility (the "Revolver") and the proceeds from our recently issued 2021 Senior Notes together will provide sufficient liquidity to fund our operations, store openings and remodeling activities and corporate capital allocation programs, including acquisitions, share repurchases and the payment of dividends declared by the Board of Directors, for at least the next 12 months.

Cash Flow

During fiscal 2015, cash provided by operations was $656.8 million, compared to cash provided by operations of $480.5 million in fiscal 2014. The increase in cash provided by operations of $176.3 million from fiscal 2014 to fiscal 2015 was primarily due to an increase in cash provided by working capital of $167.7 million, due primarily to the timing of payments for income taxes as well as accounts payable and accrued liabilities when compared to fiscal 2014.

Use of Capital

We opened 85 Video Game Brands stores and opened or acquired 568 Technology Brands stores in fiscal 2015, and we expect to open 140 stores in fiscal 2016, as well as make significant investments in our Technology Brands businesses through acquisitions. Capital expenditures for fiscal 2016 are projected to be approximately $160-170 million.

We used cash to expand our operations through acquisitions. During fiscal 2015, fiscal 2014 and fiscal 2013, we used $267.5 million, $89.7 million and $77.4 million, respectively, for acquisitions, primarily related to the growth of our Technology Brands business and ThinkGeek.

Since January 2010, our Board of Directors has authorized several share repurchase programs authorizing our management to repurchase our Class A Common Stock. For fiscal 2015, we repurchased 5.2 million shares for an average price per share of $38.68 and a total of $202.0 million.

In fiscal 2015, we paid dividends of $1.44 per share of Class A Common Stock, totaling $154.1 million for the year.

Management's Responsibilities

Management acknowledges responsibility and certifies accuracy of financial statements.

Management prepares and is responsible for the financial statements and other information in the annual report. To enhance the awareness of the users of financial statements concerning the relative roles of management and the auditor, annual reports of public companies include a management's responsibilities section that asserts the responsibility of management for the information contained in the annual report as well as an assessment of the company's internal control procedures.

Illustration 3–13 contains Management's Report on Internal Control Over Financial Reporting for Nike, included with the company's financial statements for the year ended May 31, 2015. Recall from our discussion of financial reporting reform in Chapter 1, that the *Sarbanes-Oxley Act of 2002* requires corporate executives to personally certify the financial statements. Submission of false statements carries a penalty of up to 20 years in jail. Mark G. Parker, Nike's president and chief executive officer, and Donald W. Blair, the chief financial officer, signed the required certifications.

Compensation of Directors and Top Executives

The compensation large U.S. corporations pay their top executives is an issue of considerable public debate and controversy. Shareholders, employees, politicians, and the public in general sometimes question the huge pay packages received by company officials at the

Management's Responsibility for Financial Statements (in part)

Management of NIKE, Inc. is responsible for the information and representations contained in this report. The financial statements have been prepared in conformity with the generally accepted accounting principles we considered appropriate in the circumstances and include some amounts based on our best estimates and judgments.

The Audit Committee is responsible for the appointment of the independent registered public accounting firm and reviews, with the independent registered public accounting firm, management and the internal audit staff, the scope and the results of the annual examination, the effectiveness of the accounting control system and other matters relating to the financial affairs of NIKE as the Audit Committee deems appropriate. The independent registered public accounting firm and the internal auditors have full access to the Committee, with and without the presence of management, to discuss any appropriate matters.

Management's Report on Internal Control over Financial Reporting (in part)

Management is responsible for establishing and maintaining adequate internal control over financial reporting, as such term is defined in Rule 13(a)-15(f) and Rule 15(d)-15(f) of the Securities Exchange Act of 1934, as amended. Internal control over financial reporting is a process designed to provide reasonable assurance regarding the reliability of financial reporting and the preparation of the financial statements for external purposes in accordance with generally accepted accounting principles in the United States of America.

While "reasonable assurance" is a high level of assurance, it does not mean absolute assurance. Because of its inherent limitations, internal control over financial reporting may not prevent or detect every misstatement and instance of fraud. Controls are susceptible to manipulation, especially in instances of fraud caused by the collusion of two or more people, including our senior management.

Under the supervision and with the participation of our Chief Executive Officer and Chief Financial Officer, our management conducted an evaluation of the effectiveness of our internal control over financial reporting based upon the framework in Internal Control — Integrated Framework (2013) issued by the Committee of Sponsoring Organizations of the Treadway Commission (COSO). Based on the results of our evaluation, our management concluded that our internal control over financial reporting was effective as of May 31, 2015.

Mark G. Parker
President & Chief Executive Officer

Donald W. Blair
Chief Financial Officer

Illustration 3–13

Management's Responsibilities and Certification—Nike, Inc.

Real World Financials

same time that more and more rank-and-file employees are being laid off as a result of company cutbacks. Contributing to the debate is the realization that the compensation gap between executives and lower-level employees is much wider in the United States than in most other industrialized countries.

Historically, disclosures related to executive compensation were not clear. In addition, a substantial portion of executive pay often is in the form of stock options, further confusing the total compensation paid to executives. Executive stock options give their holders the right to buy stock at a specified price, usually equal to the market price when the options are granted. When stock prices rise, executives can exercise their options and realize a profit. In some cases, options have made executive compensation extremely high. Stock options are discussed in depth in Chapter 19.

To help shareholders and others sort out the content of executive pay packages and better understand the commitments of the company in this regard, SEC requirements provide for disclosures on compensation to directors and executives, and in particular, concerning stock options. The proxy statement must be reported each year to all shareholders, usually along with the annual report. The statement invites shareholders to the annual meeting to elect board members and to vote on issues before the shareholders, or to vote by proxy. The **proxy statement** also includes compensation and stock option information for directors and top executives. Illustration 3–14 shows a portion of Best Buy's summary compensation table included in a recent proxy statement.

The proxy statement contains disclosures on compensation to directors and executives.

Illustration 3–14 Summary Compensation Table—Best Buy Co., Inc. Real World Financials

Summary Compensation Table (in part)

Name and Principal Position	Salary	Stock Awards	Option Awards	Short-Term Incentive Plan Payout	All Other Compensation	Total
Hubert July Chairman and Chief Executive Officer	$1,175,000	$8,011,688	$1,842,715	$3,814,050	$29,028	$14,872,481
Sharon L. McCollam Chief Administrative and Chief Financial Officer	925,000	3,039,724	1,397,391	2,251,913	9,669	7,623,697
Shari L. Ballard President, U S Retail	790,385	2,672,270	1,228,476	1,927,311	24,641	6,643,083
R. Michael Mohan Chief Merchandising Officer	790,385	1,336,135	614,238	1,927,311	10,323	4,678,392
Keith Nelsen General Counsel and Secretary	640,385	1,102,314	506,742	1,027,899	10,482	3,287,822

Auditors' Report

LO3–6

Auditors examine financial statements and the internal control procedures designed to support the content of those statements. Their role is to attest to the fairness of the financial statements based on that examination. The auditors' attest function for public business entities results in an opinion stated in the **auditors' report**.

There are four basic types of auditors' reports:

1. Unqualified
2. Unqualified with an explanatory paragraph
3. Qualified
4. Adverse or disclaimer

An auditor issues an *unqualified* (or "clean") opinion when the auditor has undertaken professional care to ensure that the financial statements are presented in conformity with generally accepted accounting principles (GAAP). Professional care would include sufficient planning of the audit, understanding the company's internal control procedures, and gather evidence to attest to the accuracy of the amounts reported in the financial statements.

The abbreviated unqualified auditors' report prepared by PricewaterhouseCoopers (PwC) for the financial statements of Nike is shown in Illustration 3–15.

In most cases, including the report for Nike, the auditors will be satisfied that the financial statements "present fairly" the financial position, results of operations, and cash flows and are "in conformity with U.S. generally accepted accounting principles." These situations prompt an unqualified opinion. Notice that the report also references the auditors' opinion on the effectiveness of the company's internal control over financial reporting.[12]

[12] The auditors' reports of public companies must be in compliance with the specifications of the PCAOB as specified in AS 2201: An Audit of Internal Control over Financial Reporting That Is Integrated with An Audit of Financial Statements.

Report of Independent Registered Public Accounting Firm (in part)

To the Board of Directors and Shareholders of Nike, Inc.:

In our opinion, the consolidated financial statements present fairly, in all material respects, the financial position of NIKE, Inc. and its subsidiaries at May 31, 2015 and 2014, and the results of their operations and their cash flows for each of the three years in the period ended May 31, 2015 in conformity with accounting principles generally accepted in the United States of America.

Also in our opinion, the Company maintained, in all material respects, effective internal control over financial reporting as of May 31, 2015, based on criteria established in Internal Control—Integrated Framework (2013) issued by the Committee of Sponsoring Organizations of the Treadway Commission (COSO).

The Company's management is responsible for these financial statements and financial statement schedule, for maintaining effective internal control over financial reporting and for its assessment of the effectiveness of internal control over financial reporting, included in Management's Annual Report on Internal Control Over Financial Reporting.

Our responsibility is to express opinions on these financial statements, on the financial statement schedule and on the Company's internal control over financial reporting based on our integrated audits.

PRICEWATERHOUSECOOPERS LLP
Portland, Oregon
July 23, 2015

Illustration 3–15

Auditors' Report—Nike, Inc.

Real World Financials

Sometimes circumstances cause the auditor to issue an opinion that is *unqualified with an explanatory paragraph.* In these circumstances, the auditor believes the financial statements are in conformity with GAAP (unqualified), but the auditor feels that other important information needs to be emphasized to financial statement users. Most notably, these situations include:

- *Lack of consistency* due to a change in accounting principle such that comparability is affected even though the auditor concurs with the desirability of the change.
- *Going concern* when the auditor determines there is significant doubt as to whether the company will be able to pay its debts as they come due. Indicators of a going concern include significant operating losses, loss of a major customer, or legal proceedings that might jeopardize the company's ability to continue operations.[13]
- *Emphasis of a matter* concerning the financial statements that does not affect the existence of an unqualified opinion but relates to a significant event such as a related-party transaction.

An example of a going concern paragraph in the 2015 auditors' report of Timberline Resources is shown in Illustration 3–16.

The accompanying financial statements have been prepared assuming that the Company will continue as a going concern. As discussed in Note 2 to the financial statements, the Company has incurred substantial losses, has no recurring source of revenue and has an accumulated deficit. These factors raise substantial doubt about its ability to continue as a going concern. Management's plans in regards to these matters are also described in Note 2. The consolidated financial statements do not include any adjustments that might result from the outcome of this uncertainty.

Illustration 3–16

Going Concern Paragraph—Timberline Resources Corp.

Real World Financials

Some audits result in the need to issue other than an unqualified opinion due to exceptions such as (a) nonconformity with generally accepted accounting principles, (b) inadequate

[13] "The Auditor's Consideration of an Entity's Ability to Continue as a Going Concern (Redrafted)," *Statement on Auditing Standards No. 126, AICPA Professional Standards AU 570* (New York: AICPA, 2012). Management is also required to assess the company's ability to continue as a going concern and provide certain disclosures when substantial doubt exists (ASC 205-40).

The auditors' report calls attention to problems that might exist in the financial statements.

disclosures, and (c) a limitation or restriction of the scope of the examination. In these situations the auditor will issue a (an):

- *Qualified opinion* when either the audit process has been limited (scope limitation) or there has been a departure from GAAP, but neither is of sufficient seriousness to invalidate the financial statements as a whole.
- *Adverse opinion* when the auditor has specific knowledge that financial statements or disclosures are seriously misstated or misleading. Adverse opinions are rare because auditors usually are able to persuade management to rectify problems to avoid this undesirable report.
- *Disclaimer* when the auditor is not able to gather sufficient information that financial statements are in conformity with GAAP.

Obviously, the auditors' report is most informative when any of these deviations from the standard unqualified opinion are present. These departures from the norm should raise a red flag to a financial analyst and prompt additional search for information.

PART C Risk Analysis

Using Financial Statement Information

LO3–7

Investors and others use information that companies provide in corporate financial reports to make decisions. Although the financial reports focus primarily on the past performance and the present financial condition of the reporting company, users are most interested in information about the future. Investors want to know a company's **default risk**. This is the risk that a company won't be able to pay its obligations when they come due. Another aspect of risk is **operational risk**, which relates more to how adept a company is at withstanding various events and circumstances that might impair its ability to earn profits.

Trying to gain a glimpse of the future from past and present data entails using various tools and techniques to formulate predictions. This is the goal of financial statement analysis. Common methods for analyzing financial statements include:

1. **Comparative financial statements**. Financial statements that are accompanied by the corresponding financial statement of the preceding year, and often the previous two years.
2. **Horizontal analysis**. Each item in a financial statement is expressed as a percentage of that same item in the financial statements of another year (base amount). For example, comparing inventory this year to inventory last year would provide the percentage change in inventory.
3. **Vertical analysis**. Each item in the financial statements is expressed as a percentage of an appropriate corresponding total, or base amount, but within the same year. For example, cash, receivables, and inventory in the current year can be restated as a percentage of total assets in the current year.
4. **Ratio analysis**. Financial statement items are converted to ratios for evaluating the performance and risk of a company.

As an example, we presented the current asset section of **Nike**'s comparative balance sheets in Illustration 3–3. From this, we could easily calculate the current year's percentage change in cash (horizontal analysis) or cash as a percentage of total current assets (vertical analysis). Understanding Nike's cash position, either relative to the previous year or relative to other current assets, provides some information for assessing the cash available to pay debt or to respond to other operating concerns.

However, the most common way to analyze financial statements is ratio analysis. Next, we'll analyze Nike's risk by using ratio analysis to investigate **liquidity** and **long-term solvency**. In Chapter 4, we introduce ratios related to profitability analysis. You will also employ ratios in Decision Makers' Perspective sections of many of the chapters in this text.

Analysis cases that benefit from ratio analysis are included in many of these chapters as well.

We use ratios every day. Batting averages indicate how well our favorite baseball players are performing. We evaluate basketball players by field goal percentage and rebounds per game. Speedometers measure the speed of our cars in terms of miles per hour. We compare grocery costs on the basis of price per pound or ounce. In each of these cases, the ratio is more meaningful than a single number by itself. Do 45 hits indicate satisfactory performance? It depends on the number of at-bats. Is $2 a good price for cheese? It depends on how many ounces the $2 buys. Ratios make these measurements meaningful.

Likewise, we can use ratios to help evaluate a firm's performance and financial position. Is net income of $4 million a cause for shareholders to celebrate? Probably not if shareholders' equity is $10 billion. But if shareholders equity is $10 million, that's a 40% return on equity! Although ratios provide more meaningful information than absolute numbers alone, the ratios are most useful when analyzed relative to some standard of comparison. That standard of comparison may be previous performance of the same company, the performance of a competitor company, or an industry average for the particular ratio.

Evaluating information in ratio form allows analysts to control for size differences over time and among firms.

Liquidity Ratios

● LO3–8

Liquidity most often refers to the ability of a company to convert its assets to cash to pay its *current* obligations. By examining a company's liquidity, we can obtain a general idea of the firm's ability to pay its short-term debts as they come due.

Current assets usually are thought of as the most liquid of a company's assets, because these assets are easier to convert to cash than are long-term assets. Obviously, though, some current assets are more liquid than others, so it's important also to evaluate the specific makeup of current assets.

Two common measures of liquidity are (1) the current ratio and (2) the acid-test ratio (or quick ratio) calculated as follows:

$$\text{Current ratio} = \frac{\text{Current assets}}{\text{Current liabilities}}$$

$$\text{Acid-test (or quick ratio)} = \frac{\text{Quick assets}}{\text{Current liabilities}}$$

CURRENT RATIO. Implicit in the definition of a current liability is the relationship between current assets and current liabilities. The difference between current assets and current liabilities is called working capital. By comparing a company's obligations that will shortly become due with the company's cash and other assets that, by definition, are expected to shortly be converted to cash, the analysis offers some indication of an ability to pay those debts. Although used in a variety of decisions, it is particularly useful to those considering whether to extend short-term credit. Nike's working capital (in millions) at the end of its May 31, 2015, fiscal year is $9,642. This amount is computed as Nike's current assets of $15,976 (Illustration 3–3) minus its current liabilities of $6,334 (Illustration 3–7).

***Working capital*, the difference between current assets and current liabilities, is a popular measure of a company's ability to satisfy its short-term obligations.**

The current ratio is computed by dividing current assets by current liabilities. Nike's current ratio of 2.52 indicates that the company has $2.52 of current assets for each $1 of current liabilities.

$$\text{Current ratio} = \frac{\$15{,}976}{\$6{,}334} = 2.52$$

Care should be taken, however, in assessing liquidity based solely on working capital. Liabilities usually are paid with cash, not other components of working capital. A company could have difficulty paying its liabilities even with a current ratio significantly greater than 1.0. For example, if a significant portion of current assets consisted of inventories, and inventories usually are not converted to cash for several months, there could be a problem in paying accounts payable due in 30 days. On the other hand, a current ratio of less than 1.0 doesn't necessarily mean the company will have difficulty meeting its current obligations. A line of credit, for instance, which the company can use to borrow funds, provides financial flexibility. That also must be considered in assessing liquidity.

The *acid-test ratio* provides a more stringent indication of a company's ability to pay its current obligations.

ACID-TEST RATIO (OR QUICK RATIO). Some analysts like to modify the current ratio to consider only current assets that are readily available to pay current liabilities. One such variation in common use is the acid-test ratio. This ratio excludes inventories, prepaid items, restricted cash, and deferred taxes from current assets before dividing by current liabilities. The numerator, then, consists of (unrestricted) cash, short-term investments, and accounts receivable, the "quick assets." By eliminating current assets that are less readily convertible into cash, the acid-test ratio provides a more rigorous indication of liquidity than does the current ratio.

Illustration 3–3 shows that Nike's quick assets (in millions) total $9,282 ($3,852 + 2,072 + 3,358). The acid-test ratio can be computed as follows:

$$\text{Acid-test ratio} = \frac{\$9{,}282}{\$6{,}334} = 1.47$$

Are these liquidity ratios adequate? It's generally difficult to say without some point of comparison. As indicated previously, common standards for such comparisons are industry averages for similar ratios or ratios of the same company in prior years. Industry averages for the above two ratios are as follows:

Industry Average
Current ratio = 1.41
Acid-test ratio = 1.12

Nike's ratios are higher than the industry average, so Nike's liquidity appears to be in good shape. What if the ratios were lower? Would that indicate a liquidity problem? Not necessarily, but it would raise a red flag that calls for caution in analyzing other areas. Remember that each ratio is but one piece of the entire puzzle. For instance, profitability is perhaps the best indication of liquidity in the long run. We discuss ratios that measure profitability in Chapter 4.

Liquidity ratios should be assessed in the context of both profitability and efficiency of managing assets.

Also, management may be very efficient in managing current assets so that, let's say, receivables are collected faster than normal or inventory is sold faster than normal, making those assets more liquid than they otherwise would be. Higher turnover ratios, relative to those of a competitor or the industry, generally indicate a more liquid position for a given level of the current ratio. We discuss these turnover ratios in Chapter 4.

Solvency Ratios

Investors and creditors, particularly long-term creditors, are vitally interested in long-term solvency, a company's ability to pay its long-term debts. Two common solvency ratios are (1) the debt to equity ratio and (2) the times interest earned ratio:

$$\text{Debt to equity ratio} = \frac{\text{Total liabilities}}{\text{Shareholders' equity}}$$

$$\text{Times interest earned ratio} = \frac{\text{Net income} + \text{Interest expense} + \text{Income taxes}}{\text{Interest expense}}$$

Ethical Dilemma

The Raintree Cosmetic Company has several loans outstanding with a local bank. The debt agreements all contain a covenant stipulating that Raintree must maintain a current ratio of at least 0.9. Jackson Phillips, company controller, estimates that the 2018 year-end current assets and current liabilities will be $2,100,000 and $2,400,000, respectively. These estimates provide a current ratio of only 0.875. Violation of the debt agreement will increase Raintree's borrowing costs as the loans are renegotiated at higher rates.

Jackson proposes to the company president that Raintree purchase inventory of $600,000 on credit before year-end. This will cause both current assets and current liabilities to increase by the same amount, but the current ratio will increase to 0.9. The extra $600,000 in inventory will be used over the later part of 2019. However, the purchase will cause warehousing costs and financing costs to increase.

Jackson is concerned about the ethics of his proposal. What do you think?

DEBT TO EQUITY RATIO. The debt to equity ratio compares resources provided by creditors with resources provided by owners. It is calculated by dividing total liabilities (current and long-term) by total shareholders' equity (including retained earnings).[14]

The *debt to equity ratio* indicates the extent of reliance on creditors, rather than owners, in providing resources.

Other things being equal, the higher the ratio, the higher the risk. The higher the ratio, the greater the creditor claims on assets, so the higher the likelihood an individual creditor would not be paid in full if the company is unable to meet its obligations.

Nike's liabilities (in millions) are \$8,893 (Illustration 3–7), and stockholders' equity is \$12,707 (Illustration 3–8). The debt to equity ratio can be computed as follows:

$$\text{Debt to equity ratio} = \frac{\$8,893}{\$12,707} = 0.70$$

As with all ratios, the debt to equity ratio is more meaningful if compared to some standard such as an industry average or a competitor. For example, an industry average debt to equity ratio of 0.95 would indicate that Nike has a lower portion of liabilities in its capital structure than does the average firm in its industry. Does this mean that Nike's default risk is lower? Other things equal—yes. Is that good? Not necessarily. As discussed in the next section, it may be that debt is being underutilized by Nike. More debt might increase the potential for return to shareholders, but with higher debt comes higher risk. This is a fundamental trade-off faced by virtually all firms when trying to settle on the optimal amount of debt versus equity in its capital structure.

The makeup of liabilities also is important. For example, liabilities could include deferred services revenue. Recall that deferred revenues are liabilities recorded when cash is received from customers in advance of providing a good or service. Companies satisfy these liabilities not by paying cash, but by providing a service to their customers.

TIMES INTEREST EARNED RATIO. A ratio that is commonly used in conjunction with the debt to equity ratio is the times interest earned ratio. This ratio is calculated as income before subtracting interest expense and income taxes, divided by interest expense. To remain solvent or to take on more debt if needed, a company needs to have funds available in the current year to pay interest charges. The ability of a company to "cover" its interest charges commonly is measured by the extent to which income exceeds interest charges in the current period.

The *times interest earned ratio* indicates the margin of safety provided to creditors.

If income is many times greater than interest expense, creditors' interests are more protected than if income just barely covers this expense. For this purpose, income should be the amount available to pay interest, which is income before subtracting interest and income taxes, calculated by adding back to net income the interest and income taxes that were deducted.

As an example, Nike reports the following:

	(\$ in millions)
Net income	\$3,273
Interest expense	+ 34
Income taxes	+ 932
Income before interest and taxes	\$4,239

The times interest earned ratio can be computed as follows:

$$\text{Times interest earned ratio} = \frac{\$4,239}{\$34} = 124.68$$

The ratio of 124.68 times indicates a considerable margin of safety for creditors. Income could decrease many times and the company would still be able to meet its interest payment obligations.[15] Nike is a highly profitable company with little interest-bearing debt. In comparison, the average times interest earned ratio for its industry is approximately 36.4 times.

[14]A commonly used variation of the debt to equity ratio is found by dividing total liabilities by *total assets*, rather than by shareholders' equity only. Of course, in this configuration the ratio measures precisely the same attribute of the firm's capital structure but can be interpreted as the percentage of a company's total assets provided by funds from creditors, rather than by owners.

[15]Of course, interest is paid with cash, not with "income." The times interest earned ratio often is calculated by using cash flow from operations before subtracting either interest payments or tax payments as the numerator and interest payments as the denominator.

Relationship Between Risk and Profitability. Now that we've assessed a company's liquidity and solvency, let's look at why a company might want to borrow money. While there are default risks associated with borrowing, a company can use those borrowed funds to provide greater returns to its shareholders. This is referred to as favorable **financial leverage** and is a very common (but risky) business activity.

To see how financial leverage works, consider a newly formed corporation attempting to determine the appropriate mix of debt and equity. The initial capitalization goal is $50 million. The capitalization mix alternatives have been narrowed to two: (1) $10 million in debt and $40 million in equity and (2) $30 million in debt and $20 million in equity.

Also assume that regardless of the capitalization mix chosen, the corporation will be able to generate a 16% annual return, *before payment of interest and income taxes,* on the $50 million in assets acquired. In other words, income before interest and taxes will be $8 million (16% × $50 million). If the interest rate on debt is 8% and the income tax rate is 40%, comparative net income for the first year of operations for the two capitalization alternatives can be calculated as follows:

	Alternative 1 **Debt = $10 million** **Equity = $40 million**	**Alternative 2** **Debt = $30 million** **Equity = $20 million**
Income before interest and income taxes	$ 8,000,000	$8,000,000
Less: Interest expense	(800,000)*	(2,400,000)†
Income before income taxes	$ 7,200,000	$5,600,000
Less: Income tax expense (40%)	(2,880,000)	(2,240,000)
Net income	$4,320,000	$3,360,000

*8% × $10,000,000

†8% × $30,000,000

Favorable financial leverage means earning a return on borrowed funds that exceeds the cost of borrowing the funds.

Would shareholders be in favor of alternative 1? Probably not. Although alternative 1 provides a higher net income, the return on the shareholders' equity (net income divided by shareholders' equity) is higher for alternative 2. Under alternative 1, shareholders had to invest $40 million to earn $4.32 million. Under alternative 2, shareholders had to invest only $20 million to earn $3.36 million.

	Alternative 1	Alternative 2
Return on shareholders' equity[16] =	$\frac{\$4,320,000}{\$40,000,000}$	$\frac{\$3,360,000}{\$20,000,000}$
=	10.8%	16.8%

Alternative 2 generated a higher return for each dollar invested by shareholders. This is because the company leveraged its $20 million equity investment with additional debt. *Any time the cost of the additional debt (8%) is less than the return on assets invested (16%), the return to shareholders is higher with borrowing.* This is the essence of favorable financial leverage.

Be aware, though, leverage is risky and not always favorable; the cost of borrowing the funds might exceed the returns they provide. If the return on assets invested turned out to be less than expected, the additional debt could result in a lower return on equity for alternative 2. If, for example, the return on assets invested (before interest and income taxes) had been 6% of $50,000,000 (or $3,000,000), rather than 16%, alternative 1 would have provided the better return on equity:

[16]If return is calculated on *average* shareholders' equity, we're technically assuming that all income is paid to shareholders in cash dividends, so that beginning, ending, and average shareholders' equity are the same If we assume *no* dividends are paid, rates of return would be

	Alternative 1	Alternative 2
Return on shareholders' equity =	$\frac{\$4,320,000}{(\$44,320,000 + 40,000,000)/2}$	$\frac{\$3,360,000}{(\$20,000,000 + 23,360,000)/2}$
=	10.25%	15.50%

In any case our conclusions are the same.

	Alternative 1 Debt = $10 million Equity = $40 million	Alternative 2 Debt = $30 million Equity = $20 million
Income before interest and income taxes	$ 3,000,000	$3,000,000
Less: Interest expense	(800,000)*	(2,400,000)†
Income before income taxes	$ 2,200,000	$ 600,000
Less: Income tax expense (40%)	(880,000)	(240,000)
Net income	$1,320,000	$ 360,000

*8% × $10,000,000

†8% × $30,000,000

		Alternative 1	Alternative 2
Return on shareholders' equity[17]	=	$\frac{\$1,320,000}{\$40,000,000}$	$\frac{\$360,000}{\$20,000,000}$
	=	3.3%	1.8%

If the return on assets are too low and the company has become too leveraged, it faces the risk of not being able to make its interest and debt payments. So, shareholders typically are faced with a trade-off between the risk that high debt denotes and the potential for a higher return from having the higher debt. Liquidity and solvency ratios can help with that decision.

Financial Reporting Case Solution

© G Flume/Maryland Terrapins/Getty Images

1. **Respond to Jerry's criticism that shareholders' equity does not represent the market value of the company. What information does the balance sheet provide?** *(p. 111)* Jerry is correct. The financial statements are supposed to help investors and creditors value a company. However, the balance sheet is not intended to portray the market value of the entity. The assets of a company minus its liabilities as shown in the balance sheet (shareholders' equity) usually will not equal the company's market value for several reasons. For example, many assets are measured at their historical costs rather than their fair values. Also, many company resources, including its trained employees, its experienced management team, and its reputation are not recorded as assets at all. The balance sheet must be used in conjunction with other financial statements, disclosure notes, and other publicly available information.

   The balance sheet does, however, provide valuable information that can be used by investors and creditors to help determine market value. After all, it is the balance sheet that describes many of the resources a company has available for generating future cash flows. The balance sheet also provides important information about liquidity and long-term solvency.

2. **The usefulness of the balance sheet is enhanced by classifying assets and liabilities according to common characteristics. What are the classifications used in Under Armour's balance sheet and what elements do those categories include?** *(p. 111)* Under Armour's balance sheet contains the following classifications:

Assets:

- *Current assets* include cash and several other assets that are reasonably expected to be converted to cash or consumed within the coming year, or within the normal operating cycle of the business if that's longer than one year.
- *Property and equipment* are the tangible long-lived assets used in the operations of the business. This category includes land, buildings, equipment, machinery, and furniture, as well as natural resources.

(continued)

[17]If we assume *no* dividends are paid, rates of return would be

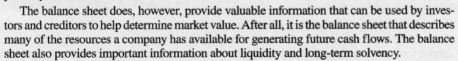

		Alternative 1	Alternative 2
Return on shareholders' equity	=	$\frac{\$1,320,000}{(\$41,320,000 + 40,000,000)/2}$	$\frac{\$360,000}{(\$20,000,000 + 20,360,000)/2}$
	=	3.25%	1.78%

In any case our conclusions are the same.

(concluded)

- *Goodwill* is a unique intangible asset in that its cost can't be directly associated with any specifically identifiable right and is not separable from the company as a whole. It represents the unique value of the company as a whole over and above all identifiable tangible and intangible assets.
- *Intangible assets* are assets that represent exclusive rights to something such as a product, a process, or a name. Patents, copyrights, and franchises are examples.
- *Deferred income taxes* result from temporary differences between taxable income and accounting income.
- *Other long-term assets* is a "catch-all" classification of long-term (noncurrent) assets and could include long-term prepaid expenses and any long-term asset not included in one of the other categories.

Liabilities:

- *Current liabilities* are those obligations that are expected to be satisfied through the use of current assets or the creation of other current liabilities. Usually, this means liabilities that are expected to be paid within one year, or the operating cycle if that's longer than one year.
- *Long-term liabilities* are payable further in the future and include bonds, deferred income taxes, and pension obligations. Under Armour lists *long-term debt, revolving credit facilities,* and *other long-term liabilities* as its long-term liabilities.

Shareholders' equity:

- *Common stock* and *additional paid-in capital* collectively equal the amounts invested by shareholders in the corporation.
- *Retained earnings* represents the accumulated net income or net loss reported since inception of the corporation less dividends paid out to shareholders. If this amount is negative, it is called *accumulated deficit.*
- *Accumulated other comprehensive loss* is the cumulative amount of other comprehensive income/loss items. This topic is addressed in subsequent chapters. ●

The Bottom Line

- **LO3–1** The balance sheet is a position statement that presents an organized array of assets, liabilities, and shareholders' equity at a particular point in time. The statement does not portray the market value of the entity. However, the information in the statement can be useful in assessing market value, as well as in providing important information about liquidity and long-term solvency. *(p. 110)*
- **LO3–2** Current assets include cash and other assets that are reasonably expected to be converted to cash or consumed during one year or within the normal operating cycle of the business if the operating cycle is longer than one year. All other assets are classified as various types of noncurrent assets. In addition to cash and cash equivalents, current assets include short-term investments, accounts receivable, inventories, and prepaid expenses. Other asset classifications include investments; property, plant, and equipment; intangible assets; and other assets. *(p. 112)*
- **LO3–3** Current liabilities are those obligations that are expected to be satisfied through the use of current assets or the creation of other current liabilities. All other liabilities are classified as long term. Current liabilities include notes and accounts payable, deferred revenues, accrued liabilities, and the current maturities of long-term debt. Long-term liabilities include long-term notes, loans, mortgages, bonds, pension and lease obligations, as well as deferred income taxes. Shareholders' equity for a corporation arises primarily from two sources: (1) paid-in capital—amounts invested by shareholders in the corporation, and (2) retained earnings—accumulated net income reported by a company since its inception minus all dividends paid to shareholders. *(p. 116)*
- **LO3–4** Financial statement disclosures are used to convey additional information about the account balances in the basic financial statements as well as to provide supplemental information. This information is disclosed, often parenthetically in the basic financial statements, or in disclosure notes that often include supporting schedules. *(p. 120)*

- **LO3–5** Annual reports of public companies will include management's discussion and analysis of key aspects of the company's business. The purpose of this disclosure is to provide external parties with management's insight into certain transactions, events, and circumstances that affect the enterprise, including their financial impact. *(p. 123)*
- **LO3–6** The purpose of an audit is to provide a professional, independent opinion as to whether or not the financial statements are prepared in conformity with generally accepted accounting principles. The standard audit report of a public company contains four paragraphs; the first two deal with the scope of the audit and the third paragraph states the auditors' opinion regarding the financial statements. The fourth paragraph provides the auditors' opinion on the effectiveness of the company's internal control. *(p. 126)*
- **LO3–7** Financial analysts use various techniques to transform financial information into forms more useful for analysis. Horizontal analysis and vertical analysis provide a usesful way of analyzing year-to-year changes. Ratio analysis allows analysts to control for size differences over time and among firms while investigating important relationships among financial variables. *(p. 128)*
- **LO3–8** The balance sheet provides information that can be useful in assessing risk. A key element of risk analysis is investigating a company's ability to pay its obligations when they come due. Liquidity ratios and solvency ratios provide information about a company's ability to pay its obligations. *(p. 129)*
- **LO3–9** There are more similarities than differences in balance sheets and financial disclosures prepared according to U.S. GAAP and those prepared applying IFRS. Balance sheet presentation is one important difference. Under U.S. GAAP, we present current assets and liabilities before long-term assets and liabilities. IFRS doesn't prescribe the format of the balance sheet, but balance sheets prepared using IFRS often report long-term items first. Reportable segment disclosures also are similar. However, IFRS requires an additional disclosure, the amount of segment liabilities (Appendix 3). *(pp. 118 and 136)*

APPENDIX 3

Reporting Segment Information

Financial analysis of diversified companies is especially difficult. Consider, for example, a company that operates in several distinct business segments including computer peripherals, home health care systems, textiles, and consumer food products. The results of these distinctly different activities will be aggregated into a single set of financial statements, making difficult an informed projection of future performance. It may well be that the five-year outlook differs greatly among the areas of the economy represented by the different segments. To make matters worse for an analyst, the integrated financial statements do not reveal the relative investments in each of the business segments nor the success the company has had within each area. Given the fact that so many companies these days have chosen to balance their operating risks through diversification, aggregated financial statements pose a widespread problem for analysts, lending and credit officers, and other financial forecasters.

Many companies operate in several business segments as a strategy to achieve growth and to reduce operating risk through diversification.

Reporting by Operating Segment

To address the problem, the accounting profession requires companies engaged in more than one significant business to provide supplemental information concerning individual operating segments. The supplemental disaggregated data do not include complete financial statements for each reportable segment, only certain specified items.

Segment reporting facilitates the financial statement analysis of diversified companies.

WHAT IS A REPORTABLE OPERATING SEGMENT? According to U.S. GAAP guidelines, a *management approach* is used in determining which segments of a company are reportable. This approach is based on the way that management organizes the segments within the enterprise for making operating decisions and assessing performance. The segments are, therefore, evident from the structure of the enterprise's internal organization.

More formally, the following characteristics define an operating segment[18] as a component of an enterprise:

- That engages in business activities from which it may recognize revenues and incur expenses (including revenues and expenses relating to transactions with other components of the same enterprise)

[18]FASB ASC 280–10–50–1: Segment Reporting–Overall–Disclosure (previously "Disclosures about Segments of an Enterprise and Related Information," *Statement of Financial Accounting Standards No. 131* (Norwalk, Conn.: FASB, 1997), par. 10).

- Whose operating results are regularly reviewed by the enterprise's chief operating decision maker to make decisions about resources to be allocated to the segment and assess its performance
- For which discrete financial information is available

The FASB hopes that this approach provides insights into the risk and opportunities management sees in the various areas of company operations. Also, reporting information based on the enterprise's internal organization should reduce the incremental cost to companies of providing the data. In addition, there are quantitative thresholds for the definition of an operating segment to limit the number of reportable segments. Only segments of material size (10% or more of total company revenues, assets, or net income) must be disclosed. However, a company must account for at least 75% of consolidated revenue through segment disclosures.

WHAT AMOUNTS ARE REPORTED BY AN OPERATING SEGMENT? For areas determined to be reportable operating segments, the following disclosures are required:

a. General information about the operating segment
b. Information about reported segment profit or loss, including certain revenues and expenses included in reported segment profit or loss, segment assets, and the basis of measurement
c. Reconciliations of the totals of segment revenues, reported profit or loss, assets, and other significant items to corresponding enterprise amounts
d. Interim period information[19]

Illustration 3A–1 shows the business segment information reported by Abbott Laboratories, in its 2015 annual report.

Illustration 3A–1
Business Segment Information Disclosure—Abbott Laboratories, Inc.

Real World Financials

Business Segment Information
($ in millions)

Segments	Net Sales	Operating Earnings	Total Assets	Depr. and Amort.	Capital Expenditures
Established Pharmaceuticals	$ 3,720	$ 658	$ 2,210	$ 83	$ 112
Nutritionals	6,975	1,741	3,187	157	142
Diagnostics	4,646	1,171	2,844	310	321
Vascular	2,792	1,061	1,536	74	32
Other	2,272	(1,448)	31,470*	247	747
Total	$20,405	$3,183	$41,247	$ 871	$1,354

*This amount includes items such as cash and investments, assets of non-reportable segments, goodwill and other intangible assets, and deferred income taxes.

International Financial Reporting Standards

● LO3–9

Segment Reporting. U.S. GAAP requires companies to report information about reported segment profit or loss, including certain revenues and expenses included in reported segment profit or loss, segment assets, and the basis of measurement. The international standard on segment reporting, *IFRS No. 8,*[20] requires that companies also disclose total *liabilities* of its reportable segments.

[19]FASB ASC 280–10–50–20 through 26 and 280–10–50–32: Segment Reporting–Overall–Disclosure (previously "Disclosures about Segments of an Enterprise and Related Information," *Statement of Financial Accounting Standards No. 131* (Norwalk, Conn.: FASB, 1997), par. 25).

[20]"Operating Segments," *International Financial Reporting Standard No. 8* (IASCF), as amended effective January 1, 2016.

REPORTING BY GEOGRAPHIC AREA. In today's global economy it is sometimes difficult to distinguish domestic and foreign companies. Most large U.S. firms conduct significant operations in other countries in addition to having substantial export sales from this country. Differing political and economic environments from country to country means risks and associated rewards sometimes vary greatly among the various operations of a single company. For instance, manufacturing facilities in a South American country embroiled in political unrest pose different risks from having a plant in Vermont, or even Canada. Without disaggregated financial information, these differences cause problems for analysts.

U.S. GAAP requires an enterprise to report certain geographic information unless it is impracticable to do so. This information includes:

a. Revenues from external customers (1) attributed to the enterprise's country of domicile and (2) attributed to all foreign countries in total from which the enterprise derives revenues, and
b. Long-lived assets other than financial instruments, long-term customer relationships of a financial institution, mortgage and other servicing rights, deferred policy acquisition costs, and deferred tax assets (1) located in the enterprise's country of domicile and (2) located in all foreign countries in total in which the enterprise holds material assets.[21]

Abbott Laboratories reports its geographic sales by separate countries in 2015, as shown in Illustration 3A–2. Notice that both the business segment (Illustration 3A–1) and geographic information disclosures include a reconciliation to company totals. In both illustrations, net sales of both the business segments and the geographic areas are reconciled to the company's total net sales of $20,405 million.

Illustration 3A–2

Geographic Area Sales Disclosure—Abbott Laboratories, Inc.

Real World Financials

Geographic Areas
($ in millions)

Net Sales			
U.S.	$6,270	U.K.	430
China	1,796	Canada	428
India	1,053	Colombia	388
Germany	1,004	Italy	383
Japan	895	Brazil	381
Netherlands	855	France	375
Switzerland	784	All Others	4,880
Russia	483	Total	$20,405

INFORMATION ABOUT MAJOR CUSTOMERS. Financial analysts are extremely interested in information concerning the extent to which a company's prosperity depends on one or more major customers. For this reason, if 10% or more of the revenue of an enterprise is derived from transactions with a single customer, the enterprise must disclose that fact, the total amount of revenue from each such customer, and the identity of the operating segment or segments reporting the revenue. The identity of the major customer or customers need not be disclosed, although companies routinely provide that information. In its 2015 annual report, Abbott Laboratories did not report any major customer information.

Revenues from major customers must be disclosed.

However, in its 2015 segment disclosures, Lockheed Martin Corporation reports that the U.S. government accounts for 78% of its revenues. Many companies in the defense industry derive substantial portions of their revenues from contracts with the Defense Department. When cutbacks occur in national defense or in specific defense systems, the impact on a company's operations can be considerable. ●

[21]FASB ASC 280–10–50–41: Segment Reporting–Overall–Disclosure (previously "Disclosures about Segments of an Enterprise and Related Information," *Statement of Financial Accounting Standards No. 131* (Norwalk, Conn.: FASB, 1997), par. 38).

Questions For Review of Key Topics

Q 3–1 Describe the purpose of the balance sheet.

Q 3–2 Explain why the balance sheet does not portray the market value of the entity.

Q 3–3 Define current assets and list the typical asset categories included in this classification.

Q 3–4 Define current liabilities and list the typical liability categories included in this classification.

Q 3–5 Describe what is meant by an operating cycle for a typical manufacturing company.

Q 3–6 Explain the difference(s) between investments in equity securities classified as current assets versus those classified as long-term (noncurrent) assets.

Q 3–7 Describe the common characteristics of assets classified as property, plant, and equipment and identify some assets included in this classification.

Q 3–8 Distinguish between property, plant, and equipment and intangible assets.

Q 3–9 Explain how each of the following liabilities would be classified in the balance sheet:

- A note payable of $100,000 due in five years
- A note payable of $100,000 payable in annual installments of $20,000 each, with the first installment due next year

Q 3–10 Define the terms *paid-in-capital* and *retained earnings.*

Q 3–11 Disclosure notes are an integral part of the information provided in financial statements. In what ways are the notes critical to understanding the financial statements and to evaluating the firm's performance and financial health?

Q 3–12 A summary of the company's significant accounting policies is a required disclosure. Why is this disclosure important to external financial statement users?

Q 3–13 Define a subsequent event.

Q 3–14 Every annual report of a public company includes an extensive discussion and analysis provided by the company's management. Specifically, which aspects of the company must this discussion address? Isn't management's perspective too biased to be of use to investors and creditors?

Q 3–15 What is a proxy statement? What information does it provide?

Q 3–16 The auditors' report provides the analyst with an independent and professional opinion about the fairness of the representations in the financial statements. What are the four main types of opinion an auditor of a public company might issue? Describe each.

Q 3–17 Define the terms *working capital, current ratio,* and *acid-test ratio* (or *quick ratio*).

Q 3–18 Show the calculation of the following solvency ratios: (1) the debt to equity ratio, and (2) the times interest earned ratio.

IFRS **Q 3–19** Where can we find authoritative guidance for balance sheet presentation under IFRS?

IFRS **Q 3–20** Describe at least two differences between U.S. GAAP and IFRS in balance sheet presentation.

Q 3–21 (Based on Appendix 3) Segment reporting facilitates the financial statement analysis of diversified companies. What determines whether an operating segment is a reportable segment for this purpose?

Q 3–22 (Based on Appendix 3) For segment reporting purposes, what amounts are reported by each operating segment?

IFRS **Q 3–23** (Based on Appendix 3) Describe any differences in segment disclosure requirements between U.S. GAAP and IFRS.

Brief Exercises

BE 3–1
Current versus long-term classification
● LO3–2, LO3–3

Indicate whether each of the following assets and liabilities should be classified as current or long-term: (a) accounts receivable; (b) prepaid rent for the next six months; (c) note receivable due in two years; (d) note payable due in 90 days; (e) note payable due in five years; and (f) patent.

BE 3–2
Balance sheet classification
● LO3–2, LO3–3

The trial balance for K and J Nursery, Inc., listed the following account balances at December 31, 2018, the end of its fiscal year: cash, $16,000; accounts receivable, $11,000; inventories, $25,000; equipment (net), $80,000; accounts payable, $14,000; wages payable, $9,000; interest payable, $1,000; note payable (due in 18 months), $30,000; common stock, $50,000. Calculate total current assets and total current liabilities that would appear in the company's year-end balance sheet.

BE 3–3
Balance sheet classification
● LO3–2, LO3–3

Refer to the situation described in BE 3–2. Determine the year-end balance in retained earnings for K and J Nursery, Inc.

BE 3–4
Balance sheet classification
● LO3–2, LO3–3

Refer to the situation described in BE 3–2. Prepare a classified balance sheet for K and J Nursery, Inc. The equipment originally cost $140,000.

BE 3–5
Balance sheet classification
● LO3–2, LO3–3

The following is a December 31, 2018, post-closing trial balance for Culver City Lighting, Inc. Prepare a classified balance sheet for the company.

Account Title	Debits	Credits
Cash	$ 55,000	
Accounts receivable	39,000	
Inventories	45,000	
Prepaid insurance	15,000	
Equipment	100,000	
Accumulated depreciation—equipment		$ 34,000
Patent, net	40,000	
Accounts payable		12,000
Interest payable		2,000
Note payable (due in 10, equal annual installments)		100,000
Common stock		70,000
Retained earnings		76,000
Totals	$294,000	$294,000

BE 3–6
Balance sheet classification
● LO3–2, LO3–3

You have been asked to review the December 31, 2018, balance sheet for Champion Cleaning. After completing your review, you list the following three items for discussion with your superior:

1. An investment of $30,000 is included in current assets. Management has indicated that it has no intention of liquidating the investment in 2019.
2. A $100,000 note payable is listed as a long-term liability, but you have determined that the note is due in 10, equal annual installments with the first installment due on March 31, 2019.
3. Deferred revenue of $60,000 is included as a current liability even though only two-thirds will be recognized as revenue in 2019, and the other one-third in 2020.

Determine the appropriate classification of each of these items.

BE 3–7
Balance sheet preparation; missing elements
● LO3–2, LO3–3

The following information is taken from the balance sheet of Raineer Plumbing: cash and cash equivalents, $40,000; accounts receivable, $120,000; inventories, ?; total current assets, $235,000; property, plant, and equipment (net), ?; total assets, $400,000; accounts payable, $32,000; note payable (due in two years), $50,000; common stock; $100,000; and retained earnings, ?. Determine the missing amounts.

BE 3–8
Financial statement disclosures
● LO3–4

For each of the following note disclosures, indicate whether the disclosure would likely appear in (A) the summary of significant accounts policies or (B) a separate note: (1) depreciation method; (2) contingency information; (3) significant issuance of common stock after the fiscal year-end; (4) cash equivalent designation; (5) long-term debt information; and (6) inventory costing method.

BE 3–9
Calculating ratios
● LO3–8

Refer to the trial balance information in BE 3–5. Calculate the (a) current ratio, (b) acid-test ratio, and (c) debt to equity ratio.

BE 3–10
Effect of decisions on ratios
● LO3–8

At the end of 2018, Barker Corporation's preliminary trial balance indicated a current ratio of 1.2. Management is contemplating paying some of its accounts payable balance before the end of the fiscal year. Explain the effect this transaction would have on the current ratio. Would your answer be the same if the preliminary trial balance indicated a current ratio of 0.8?

BE 3–11
Calculating ratios; solving for unknowns
● LO3–8

The current asset section of Stibbe Pharmaceutical Company's balance sheet included cash of $20,000 and accounts receivable of $40,000. The only other current asset is inventories. The company's current ratio is 2.0 and its acid-test ratio is 1.5. Determine the ending balance in inventories and total current liabilities.

Exercises

E 3–1
Balance sheet; missing elements
● LO3–2, LO3–3, LO3–8

The following December 31, 2018, fiscal year-end account balance information is available for the Stonebridge Corporation:

Cash and cash equivalents	$ 5,000
Accounts receivable (net)	20,000
Inventories	60,000
Property, plant, and equipment (net)	120,000
Accounts payable	44,000
Wages payable	15,000
Paid-in-capital	100,000

The only asset not listed is short-term investments. The only liabilities not listed are a $30,000 note payable due in two years and related accrued interest of $1,000 due in four months. The current ratio at year-end is 1.5:1.

Required:

Determine the following at December 31, 2018:
1. Total current assets
2. Short-term investments
3. Retained earnings

E 3–2
Balance sheet classification
● LO3–2, LO3–3

The following are the typical classifications used in a balance sheet:

a. Current assets
b. Investments and funds
c. Property, plant, and equipment
d. Intangible assets
e. Other assets
f. Current liabilities
g. Long-term liabilities
h. Paid-in-capital
i. Retained earnings

Required:

For each of the following balance sheet items, use the letters above to indicate the appropriate classification category. If the item is a contra account, place a minus sign before the chosen letter.

1. _____ Equipment
2. _____ Accounts payable
3. _____ Allowance for uncollectible accounts
4. _____ Land, held for investment
5. _____ Note payable, due in 5 years
6. _____ Deferred rent revenue for the next 12 months
7. _____ Note payable, due in 6 months
8. _____ Income less dividends, accumulated
9. _____ Investment in XYZ Corp., long-term
10. _____ Inventories
11. _____ Patent
12. _____ Land, in use
13. _____ Accrued liabilities
14. _____ Prepaid rent for the next 9 months
15. _____ Common stock
16. _____ Building, in use
17. _____ Cash
18. _____ Taxes payable

E 3–3
Balance sheet classification
● LO3–2, LO3–3

The following are the typical classifications used in a balance sheet:

a. Current assets
b. Investments and funds
c. Property, plant, and equipment
d. Intangible assets
e. Other assets
f. Current liabilities
g. Long-term liabilities
h. Paid-in-capital
i. Retained earnings

Required:

For each of the following 2018 balance sheet items, use the letters above to indicate the appropriate classification category. If the item is a contra account, place a minus sign before the chosen letter.

1. _____ Accrued interest payable
2. _____ Franchise
3. _____ Accumulated depreciation
4. _____ Prepaid insurance, for 2019
5. _____ Bonds payable, due in 10 years
6. _____ Current maturities of long-term debt
7. _____ Note payable, due in three months
8. _____ Long-term receivables
9. _____ Restricted cash, will be used to retire bonds in 10 years
10. _____ Supplies
11. _____ Machinery
12. _____ Land, in use
13. _____ Deferred revenue, for 2019
14. _____ Copyrights
15. _____ Preferred stock
16. _____ Land, held for speculation
17. _____ Cash equivalents
18. _____ Wages payable

E 3–4
Balance sheet preparation
● LO3–2, LO3–3

The following is a December 31, 2018, post-closing trial balance for the Jackson Corporation.

Account Title	Debits	Credits
Cash	$ 40,000	
Accounts receivable	34,000	
Inventories	75,000	
Prepaid rent for the next 8 months	16,000	
Marketable securities (short term)	10,000	
Machinery	145,000	
Accumulated depreciation—machinery		$ 11,000
Patent (net of amortization)	83,000	
Accounts payable		8,000
Wages payable		4,000
Taxes payable		32,000
Bonds payable (due in 10 years)		200,000
Common stock		100,000
Retained earnings		48,000
Totals	$403,000	$403,000

Required:
Prepare a classified balance sheet for Jackson Corporation at December 31, 2018.

E 3–5
Balance sheet preparation
● LO3–2, LO3–3

The following are the ending balances of accounts at December 31, 2018, for the Valley Pump Corporation.

Account Title	Debits	Credits
Cash	$ 25,000	
Accounts receivable	56,000	
Inventories	81,000	
Interest payable		$ 10,000
Marketable securities	44,000	
Land	120,000	
Buildings	300,000	
Accumulated depreciation—buildings		100,000
Equipment	75,000	
Accumulated depreciation—equipment		25,000
Copyright (net of amortization)	12,000	
Prepaid expenses (next 12 months)	32,000	
Accounts payable		65,000
Deferred revenues (next 12 months)		20,000
Notes payable		250,000
Allowance for uncollectible accounts		5,000
Common stock		200,000
Retained earnings		70,000
Totals	$745,000	$745,000

Additional Information:

1. The $120,000 balance in the land account consists of $100,000 for the cost of land where the plant and office buildings are located. The remaining $20,000 represents the cost of land being held for speculation.
2. The $44,000 in the marketable securities account represents an investment in the common stock of another corporation. Valley intends to sell one-half of the stock within the next year.
3. The notes payable account consists of a $100,000 note due in six months and a $150,000 note due in three annual installments of $50,000 each, with the first payment due in August of 2019.

Required:
Prepare a classified balance sheet for the Valley Pump Corporation at December 31, 2018.

E 3–6
Balance sheet; Current versus long-term classification
● LO3–2, LO3–3

Presented next are the ending balances of accounts for the Kansas Instruments Corporation at December 31, 2018.

Account Title	Debits	Credits
Cash	$ 20,000	
Accounts receivable	130,000	
Raw materials	24,000	
Note receivable	100,000	
Interest receivable	3,000	
Interest payable		$ 5,000
Marketable securities	32,000	
Land	50,000	
Buildings	1,300,000	
Accumulated depreciation—buildings		620,000
Work in process	42,000	
Finished goods	89,000	
Equipment	300,000	
Accumulated depreciation—equipment		130,000
Patent (net of amortization)	120,000	
Prepaid rent (for the next two years)	60,000	
Deferred revenue (next 12 months)		36,000
Accounts payable		180,000
Note payable		400,000
Cash restricted for payment of note payable	80,000	
Allowance for uncollectible accounts		13,000
Sales revenue		800,000
Cost of goods sold	450,000	
Rent expense	28,000	

Additional Information:

1. The note receivable, along with any accrued interest, is due on November 22, 2019.
2. The note payable is due in 2022. Interest is payable annually.
3. The marketable securities consist of treasury bills, all of which mature in the next year.
4. Deferred revenue will be recognized as revenue equally over the next two years.

Required:

Determine the company's working capital (current assets minus current liabilities) at December 31, 2018.

E 3–7
Balance sheet preparation; errors
● LO3–2, LO3–3

The following balance sheet for the Los Gatos Corporation was prepared by a recently hired accountant. In reviewing the statement you notice several errors.

LOS GATOS CORPORATION
Balance Sheet
At December 31, 2018

Assets	
Cash	$ 40,000
Accounts receivable	80,000
Inventories	55,000
Machinery (net)	120,000
Franchise (net)	30,000
Total assets	$325,000
Liabilities and Shareholders' Equity	
Accounts payable	$ 50,000
Allowance for uncollectible accounts	5,000
Note payable	55,000
Bonds payable	110,000
Shareholders' equity	105,000
Total liabilities and shareholders' equity	$325,000

Additional Information:

1. Cash includes a $20,000 restricted amount to be used for repayment of the bonds payable in 2022.
2. The cost of the machinery is $190,000.
3. Accounts receivable includes a $20,000 note receivable from a customer due in 2021.

4. The note payable includes accrued interest of $5,000. Principal and interest are both due on February 1, 2019.
5. The company began operations in 2013. Income less dividends since inception of the company totals $35,000.
6. 50,000 shares of no par common stock were issued in 2013. 100,000 shares are authorized.

Required:
Prepare a corrected, classified balance sheet.

E 3–8
Balance sheet; current versus long-term classification
● LO3–2, LO3–3

Cone Corporation is in the process of preparing its December 31, 2018, balance sheet. There are some questions as to the proper classification of the following items:

a. $50,000 in cash restricted in a savings account to pay bonds payable. The bonds mature in 2022.
b. Prepaid rent of $24,000, covering the period January 1, 2019, through December 31, 2020.
c. Note payable of $200,000. The note is payable in annual installments of $20,000 each, with the first installment payable on March 1, 2019.
d. Accrued interest payable of $12,000 related to the note payable.
e. Investment in marketable securities of other corporations, $80,000. Cone intends to sell one-half of the securities in 2019.

Required:
Prepare a partial classified balance sheet to show how each of the above items should be reported.

E 3–9
Balance sheet preparation
● LO3–2, LO3–3

The following is the balance sheet of Korver Supply Company at December 31, 2017.

KORVER SUPPLY COMPANY
Balance Sheet
At December 31, 2017

Assets	
Cash	$120,000
Accounts receivable	300,000
Inventories	200,000
Furniture and fixtures, net	150,000
Total assets	$770,000
Liabilities and Shareholders' Equity	
Accounts payable (for merchandise)	$190,000
Note payable	200,000
Interest payable	6,000
Common stock	100,000
Retained earnings	274,000
Total liabilities and shareholders' equity	$770,000

Transactions during 2018 were as follows:

1. Sales to customers on account	$800,000
2. Cash collected from customers	780,000
3. Purchase of merchandise on account	550,000
4. Cash payment to suppliers	560,000
5. Cost of merchandise sold	500,000
6. Cash paid for operating expenses	160,000
7. Cash paid for interest on note	12,000

The note payable is dated June 30, 2017 and is due on June 30, 2019. Interest at 6% is payable annually on June 30. Depreciation on the furniture and fixtures for the year is $20,000. The furniture and fixtures originally cost $300,000.

Required:
Prepare a classified balance sheet at December 31, 2018 (ignore income taxes).

E 3–10
Financial statement disclosures
● LO3–4

The following are typical disclosures that would appear in the notes accompanying financial statements. For each of the items listed, indicate where the disclosure would likely appear—either in (A) the significant accounting policies note or (B) a separate note.

1. Inventory costing method	A
2. Information on related party transactions	____
3. Composition of property, plant, and equipment	____
4. Depreciation method	____
5. Subsequent event information	____
6. Measurement basis for certain financial instruments	____
7. Important merger occurring after year-end	____
8. Composition of receivables	____

E 3–11
Disclosure notes
● LO3–4

Hallergan Company produces car and truck batteries that it sells primarily to auto manufacturers. Dorothy Hawkins, the company's controller, is preparing the financial statements for the year ended December 31, 2018. Hawkins asks for your advice concerning the following information that has not yet been included in the statements. The statements will be issued on February 28, 2019.

1. Hallergan leases its facilities from the brother of the chief executive officer.
2. On January 8, 2019, Hallergan entered into an agreement to sell a tract of land that it had been holding as an investment. The sale, which resulted in a material gain, was completed on February 2, 2019.
3. Hallergan uses the straight-line method to determine depreciation on all of the company's depreciable assets.
4. On February 8, 2019, Hallergan completed negotiations with its bank for a $10,000,000 line of credit.
5. Hallergan uses the first-in, first-out (FIFO) method to value inventory.

Required:

For each of the above items, discuss any additional disclosures that Hawkins should include in Hallergan's financial statements.

E 3–12
Financial statement disclosures
● LO3–4

Parkman Sporting Goods is preparing its annual report for its 2018 fiscal year. The company's controller has asked for your help in determining how best to disclose information about the following items:

1. A related-party transaction
2. Depreciation method
3. Allowance for uncollectible accounts
4. Composition of investments
5. Composition of long-term debt
6. Inventory costing method
7. Number of shares of common stock authorized, issued, and outstanding
8. Employee benefit plans

Required:

Indicate whether the above items should be disclosed (A) in the summary of significant accounting policies note, (B) in a separate disclosure note, or (C) on the face of the balance sheet.

E 3–13
FASB codification research
● LO3–4

The *FASB Accounting Standards Codification* represents the single source of authoritative U.S. generally accepted accounting principles.

Required:

1. Obtain the relevant authoritative literature on the disclosure of accounting policies using the *FASB Accounting Standards Codification* at the FASB website (www.fasb.org). Identify the topic number that provides guidance on information contained in the notes to the financial statements.
2. What is the specific citation that requires a company to identify and describe in the notes to the financial statements the accounting principles and methods used to prepare the financial statements?
3. Describe the disclosure requirements.

E 3–14
FASB codification research
● LO3–2, LO3–4

Access the *FASB Accounting Standards Codification* at the FASB website (www.fasb.org). Determine the specific citation for each of the following items:

1. What is the balance sheet classification for a note payable due in six months that was used to purchase a building?
2. Which assets may be excluded from current assets?
3. Should a note receivable from a related party be included in the balance sheet with notes receivable or accounts receivable from customers?
4. What items are nonrecognized subsequent events that require a disclosure in the notes to the financial statements?

E 3–15
Concepts; terminology
● LO3–2 through LO3–4, LO3–6

Listed below are several terms and phrases associated with the balance sheet and financial disclosures. Pair each item from List A (by letter) with the item from List B that is most appropriately associated with it.

List A	List B
_____ 1. Balance sheet	a. Will be satisfied through the use of current assets
_____ 2. Liquidity	b. Items expected to be converted to cash or consumed within one year or the operating cycle, whichever is longer
_____ 3. Current assets	c. The statements are presented fairly in conformity with GAAP
_____ 4. Operating cycle	d. An organized array of assets, liabilities, and equity
_____ 5. Current liabilities	e. Important to a user in comparing financial information across companies
_____ 6. Cash equivalent	f. Scope limitation or a departure from GAAP
_____ 7. Intangible asset	g. Recorded when an expense is incurred but not yet paid
_____ 8. Working capital	h. Refers to the ability of a company to convert its assets to cash to pay its current obligations
_____ 9. Accrued liabilities	i. Occurs after the fiscal year-end but before the statements are issued
_____ 10. Summary of significant accounting policies	j. Period of time from payment of cash to collection of cash
_____ 11. Subsequent events	k. One-month U.S. Treasury bill
_____ 12. Unqualified opinion	l. Current assets minus current liabilities
_____ 13. Qualified opinion	m. Lacks physical substance

E 3–16
Calculating ratios
● LO3–8

The 2018 balance sheet for Hallbrook Industries, Inc., is shown below.

HALLBROOK INDUSTRIES, INC.
Balance Sheet
December 31, 2018
($ in thousands)

Assets	
Cash	$ 200
Short-term investments	150
Accounts receivable	200
Inventories	350
Property, plant, and equipment (net)	1,000
Total assets	$1,900
Liabilities and Shareholders' Equity	
Current liabilities	$ 400
Long-term liabilities	350
Paid-in capital	750
Retained earnings	400
Total liabilities and shareholders' equity	$1,900

The company's 2018 income statement reported the following amounts ($ in thousands):

Net sales	$4,600
Interest expense	40
Income tax expense	100
Net income	160

Required:

Determine the following ratios for 2018:

1. Current ratio
2. Acid-test ratio
3. Debt to equity ratio
4. Times interest earned ratio

E 3–17
Calculating ratios; Best Buy
● LO3–8

Best Buy Co, Inc., is a leading retailer specializing in consumer electronics. A condensed income statement and balance sheet for the fiscal year ended January 30, 2016, are shown next.

Real World Financials

Best Buy Co., Inc.
Balance Sheet
At January 30, 2016
($ in millions)
Assets

Current assets:	
Cash and cash equivalents	$ 1,976
Short-term investments	1,305
Accounts receivable, net	1,162
Merchandise inventories	5,051
Other current assets	392
Total current assets	9,886
Long-term assets	3,633
Total assets	$13,519
Liabilities and Shareholders' Equity	
Current liabilities:	
Accounts payable	$ 4,450
Other current liabilities	2,475
Total current liabilities	6,925
Long-term liabilities	2,216
Shareholders' equity	4,378
Total liabilities and shareholders' equity	$13,519

Best Buy Co., Inc.
Income Statement
For the Year Ended January 30, 2016
($ in millions)

Revenues	$ 39,528
Costs and expenses	38,153
Operating income	1,375
Other income (expense)*	(65)
Income before income taxes	1,310
Income tax expense	503
Net income	$ 807

*Includes $80 of interest expense.

Liquidity and solvency ratios for the industry are as follows:

	Industry Average
Current ratio	1.23
Acid-test ratio	0.60
Debt to equity	0.70
Times interest earned	5.66 times

Required:

1. Determine the following ratios for Best Buy for its fiscal year ended January 30, 2016.
   a. Current ratio
   b. Acid-test ratio
   c. Debt to equity ratio
   d. Times interest earned ratio
2. Using the ratios from requirement 1, assess Best Buy's liquidity and solvency relative to its industry.

E 3–18 Calculating ratios; solve for unknowns ● LO3–8

The current asset section of the Excalibur Tire Company's balance sheet consists of cash, marketable securities, accounts receivable, and inventories. The December 31, 2018, balance sheet revealed the following:

Inventories	$ 840,000
Total assets	$ 2,800,000
Current ratio	2.25
Acid-test ratio	1.2
Debt to equity ratio	1.8

Required:

Determine the following 2018 balance sheet items:

1. Current assets
2. Shareholders' equity
3. Long-term assets
4. Long-term liabilities

E 3–19 Calculating ratios; solve for unknowns ● LO3–8

The current asset section of Guardian Consultant's balance sheet consists of cash, accounts receivable, and prepaid expenses. The 2018 balance sheet reported the following: cash, \$1,300,000; prepaid expenses, \$360,000; long-term assets, \$2,400,000; and shareholders' equity, \$2,500,000. The current ratio at the end of the year was 2.0 and the debt to equity ratio was 1.4.

Required:

Determine the following 2018 amounts and ratios:

1. Current liabilities
2. Long-term liabilities
3. Accounts receivable
4. The acid-test ratio

E 3–20 Effect of management decisions on ratios ● LO3–8

Most decisions made by management impact the ratios analysts use to evaluate performance. Indicate (by letter) whether each of the actions listed below will immediately increase (I), decrease (D), or have no effect (N) on the ratios shown. Assume each ratio is less than 1.0 before the action is taken.

Action	Current Ratio	Acid-Test Ratio	Debt to Equity Ratio
1. Issuance of long-term bonds	_____	_____	_____
2. Issuance of short-term notes	_____	_____	_____
3. Payment of accounts payable	_____	_____	_____
4. Purchase of inventory on account	_____	_____	_____
5. Purchase of inventory for cash	_____	_____	_____
6. Purchase of equipment with a 4-year note	_____	_____	_____
7. Retirement of bonds	_____	_____	_____
8. Sale of common stock	_____	_____	_____
9. Write-off of obsolete inventory	_____	_____	_____
10. Purchase of short-term investment for cash	_____	_____	_____
11. Decision to refinance on a long-term basis some currently maturing debt	_____	_____	_____

E 3–21 Segment reporting ● Appendix 3

The Canton Corporation operates in four distinct business segments. The segments, along with 2018 information on revenues, assets, and net income, are listed below (\$ in thousands):

Segment	Revenues	Assets	Net Income
Pharmaceuticals	\$2,000	\$1,000	\$200
Plastics	3,000	1,500	270
Farm equipment	2,500	1,250	320
Electronics	500	250	40
Total company	\$8,000	\$4,000	\$830

Required:

1. For which segments must Canton report supplementary information according to U.S. GAAP?
2. What amounts must be reported for the segments you identified in requirement 1?

E 3–22 Segment reporting ● Appendix 3 LO3–9

IFRS

Refer to E 3–21.

Required:

How might your answers differ if Canton Corporation prepares its segment disclosure according to International Financial Reporting Standards?

Problems

P 3–1
Balance sheet preparation
● LO3–2, LO3–3

Presented below is a list of balance sheet accounts.

Accounts payable	Cash
Accounts receivable	Common stock
Accumulated depreciation—buildings	Copyright
Accumulated depreciation—equipment	Equipment
Allowance for uncollectible accounts	Interest receivable (due in three months)
Restricted cash (to be used in 10 years)	Inventories
Bonds payable (due in 10 years)	Land (in use)
Buildings	Long-term investments
Notes payable (due in 6 months)	Rent payable (current)
Notes receivable (due in 2 years)	Retained earnings
Patent	Short-term investments
Preferred stock	Taxes payable
Prepaid expenses	Wages payable

Required:
Prepare a classified balance sheet ignoring monetary amounts.

P 3–2
Balance sheet preparation; missing elements
● LO3–2, LO3–3

The data listed below are taken from a balance sheet of Trident Corporation at December 31, 2018. Some amounts, indicated by question marks, have been intentionally omitted.

	($ in thousands)
Cash and cash equivalents	$ 239,186
Short-term investments	353,700
Accounts receivable (net of allowance)	504,944
Inventories	?
Prepaid expenses (current)	83,259
Total current assets	1,594,927
Long-term receivables	110,800
Property and equipment (net)	?
Total assets	?
Notes payable and short-term debt	31,116
Accounts payable	?
Accrued liabilities	421,772
Other current liabilities	181,604
Total current liabilities	693,564
Long-term debt and deferred taxes	?
Total liabilities	956,140
Shareholders' equity	1,370,627

Required:
1. Determine the missing amounts.
2. Prepare Trident's classified balance sheet.

P 3–3
Balance sheet preparation
● LO3–2, LO3–3

The following is a December 31, 2018, post-closing trial balance for Almway Corporation.

Account Title	Debits	Credits
Cash	$ 45,000	
Investments	110,000	
Accounts receivable	60,000	
Inventories	200,000	
Prepaid insurance (for the next 9 months)	9,000	
Land	90,000	
Buildings	420,000	
Accumulated depreciation—buildings		$100,000
Equipment	110,000	
Accumulated depreciation—equipment		60,000
Patents (net of amortization)	10,000	
Accounts payable		75,000

(continued)

(concluded)

Account Title	Debits	Credits
Notes payable		130,000
Interest payable		20,000
Bonds payable		240,000
Common stock		300,000
Retained earnings		129,000
Totals	$1,054,000	$1,054,000

Additional Information:

1. The investment account includes an investment in common stock of another corporation of $30,000 which management intends to hold for at least three years. The balance of these investments is intended to be sold in the coming year.
2. The land account includes land which cost $25,000 that the company has not used and is currently listed for sale.
3. The cash account includes $15,000 restricted in a fund to pay bonds payable that mature in 2021 and $23,000 restricted in a three-month Treasury bill.
4. The notes payable account consists of the following:
   a. a $30,000 note due in six months
   b. a $50,000 note due in six years
   c. a $50,000 note due in five annual installments of $10,000 each, with the next installment due February 15, 2019
5. The $60,000 balance in accounts receivable is net of an allowance for uncollectible accounts of $8,000.
6. The common stock account represents 100,000 shares of no par value common stock issued and outstanding. The corporation has 500,000 shares authorized.

Required:

Prepare a classified balance sheet for the Almway Corporation at December 31, 2018.

P 3–4
Balance sheet preparation
● LO3–2, LO3–3

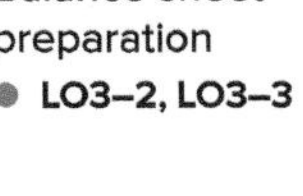

The following is the ending balances of accounts at December 31, 2018, for the Weismuller Publishing Company.

Account Title	Debits	Credits
Cash	$ 65,000	
Accounts receivable	160,000	
Inventories	285,000	
Prepaid expenses	148,000	
Machinery and equipment	320,000	
Accumulated depreciation—equipment		$ 110,000
Investments	140,000	
Accounts payable		60,000
Interest payable		20,000
Deferred revenue		80,000
Taxes payable		30,000
Notes payable		200,000
Allowance for uncollectible accounts		16,000
Common stock		400,000
Retained earnings		202,000
Totals	$1,118,000	$1,118,000

Additional Information:

1. Prepaid expenses include $120,000 paid on December 31, 2018, for a two-year lease on the building that houses both the administrative offices and the manufacturing facility.
2. Investments include $30,000 in Treasury bills purchased on November 30, 2018. The bills mature on January 30, 2019. The remaining $110,000 includes investments in marketable equity securities that the company intends to sell in the next year.
3. Deferred revenue represents customer prepayments for magazine subscriptions. Subscriptions are for periods of one year or less.
4. The notes payable account consists of the following:
   a. a $40,000 note due in six months
   b. a $100,000 note due in six years

c. a $60,000 note due in three annual installments of $20,000 each, with the next installment due August 31, 2019

5. The common stock account represents 400,000 shares of no par value common stock issued and outstanding. The corporation has 800,000 shares authorized.

Required:

Prepare a classified balanced sheet for the Weismuller Publishing Company at December 31, 2018.

P 3–5
Balance sheet preparation
● LO3–2, LO3–3

The following is the ending balances of accounts at June 30, 2018 for Excell Company.

Account Title	Debits	Credits
Cash	$ 83,000	
Short-term investments	65,000	
Accounts receivable	280,000	
Prepaid expenses (for the next 12 months)	32,000	
Land	75,000	
Buildings	320,000	
Accumulated depreciation—buildings		$ 160,000
Equipment	265,000	
Accumulated depreciation—equipment		120,000
Accounts payable		173,000
Accrued expenses		45,000
Notes payable		100,000
Mortgage payable		250,000
Common stock		100,000
Retained earnings		172,000
Totals	$1,120,000	$1,120,000

Additional Information:

1. The short-term investments account includes $18,000 in U.S. treasury bills purchased in May. The bills mature in July.
2. The accounts receivable account consists of the following:

a. Amounts owed by customers	$225,000
b. Allowance for uncollectible accounts—trade customers	(15,000)
c. Nontrade note receivable (due in three years)	65,000
d. Interest receivable on note (due in four months)	5,000
Total	$280,000

3. The notes payable account consists of two notes of $50,000 each. One note is due on September 30, 2018, and the other is due on November 30, 2019.
4. The mortgage payable is payable in *semiannual* installments of $5,000 each plus interest. The next payment is due on October 31, 2018. Interest has been properly accrued and is included in accrued expenses.
5. Five hundred thousand shares of no par common stock are authorized, of which 200,000 shares have been issued and are outstanding.
6. The land account includes $50,000 representing the cost of the land on which the company's office building resides. The remaining $25,000 is the cost of land that the company is holding for investment purposes.

Required:

Prepare a classified balance sheet for the Excell Company at June 30, 2018.

P 3–6
Balance sheet preparation; disclosures
● LO3–2 through LO3–4

The following is the ending balances of accounts at December 31, 2018 for the Vosburgh Electronics Corporation.

Account Title	Debits	Credits
Cash	$ 67,000	
Short-term investments	182,000	
Accounts receivable	123,000	
Long-term investments	35,000	
Inventories	215,000	
Loans to employees	40,000	
Prepaid expenses (for 2019)	16,000	
Land	280,000	
Building	1,550,000	

(continued)

(concluded)

Account Title	Debits	Credits
Machinery and equipment	637,000	
Patent	152,000	
Franchise	40,000	
Note receivable	250,000	
Interest receivable	12,000	
Accumulated depreciation—building		$ 620,000
Accumulated depreciation—equipment		210,000
Accounts payable		189,000
Dividends payable (payable on 1/16/2019)		10,000
Interest payable		16,000
Taxes payable		40,000
Deferred revenue		60,000
Notes payable		300,000
Allowance for uncollectible accounts		8,000
Common stock		2,000,000
Retained earnings		146,000
Totals	$3,599,000	$3,599,000

Additional Information:

1. The common stock represents 1 million shares of no par stock authorized, 500,000 shares issued and outstanding.
2. The loans to employees are due on June 30, 2019.
3. The note receivable is due in installments of $50,000, payable on each September 30. Interest is payable annually.
4. Short-term investments consist of marketable equity securities that the company plans to sell in 2019 and $50,000 in treasury bills purchased on December 15 of the current year that mature on February 15, 2019. Long-term investments consist of marketable equity securities that the company does not plan to sell in the next year.
5. Deferred revenue represents customer payments for extended service contracts. Eighty percent of these contracts expire in 2019, the remainder in 2020.
6. Notes payable consists of two notes, one for $100,000 due on January 15, 2020, and another for $200,000 due on June 30, 2021.

Required:

1. Prepare a classified balance sheet for Vosburgh at December 31, 2018.
2. Identify the items that would require additional disclosure, either on the face of the balance sheet or in a disclosure note.

P 3–7
Balance sheet preparation; errors
● LO3–2, LO3–3

The following balance sheet for the Hubbard Corporation was prepared by the company:

HUBBARD CORPORATION
Balance Sheet
At December 31, 2018

Assets	
Buildings	$ 750,000
Land	250,000
Cash	60,000
Accounts receivable (net)	120,000
Inventories	240,000
Machinery	280,000
Patent (net)	100,000
Investment in marketable equity securities	60,000
Total assets	$1,860,000
Liabilities and Shareholders' Equity	
Accounts payable	$ 215,000
Accumulated depreciation	255,000
Notes payable	500,000
Appreciation of inventories	80,000
Common stock, authorized and issued 100,000 shares of no par stock	430,000
Retained earnings	380,000
Total liabilities and shareholders' equity	$1,860,000

Additional Information:

1. The buildings, land, and machinery are all stated at cost except for a parcel of land that the company is holding for future sale. The land originally cost $50,000 but, due to a significant increase in market value, is listed at $120,000. The increase in the land account was credited to retained earnings.
2. Marketable equity securities consist of stocks of other corporations and are recorded at cost, $20,000 of which will be sold in the coming year. The remainder will be held indefinitely.
3. Notes payable are all long-term. However, a $100,000 note requires an installment payment of $25,000 due in the coming year.
4. Inventories are recorded at current resale value. The original cost of the inventories is $160,000.

Required:

Prepare a corrected classified balance sheet for the Hubbard Corporation at December 31, 2018.

P 3–8
Balance sheet; errors; missing amounts
● LO3–2, LO3–3

The following incomplete balance sheet for the Sanderson Manufacturing Company was prepared by the company's controller. As accounting manager for Sanderson, you are attempting to reconstruct and revise the balance sheet.

Sanderson Manufacturing Company
Balance Sheet
At December 31, 2018
($ in thousands)

Assets		
Current assets:		
Cash		$ 1,250
Accounts receivable		3,500
Allowance for uncollectible accounts		(400)
Finished goods inventory		6,000
Prepaid expenses		1,200
Total current assets		11,550
Long-term assets:		
Investments		3,000
Raw materials and work in process inventory		2,250
Equipment		15,000
Accumulated depreciation—equipment		(4,200)
Patent		?
Total assets		$?
Liabilities and Shareholders' Equity		
Current liabilities:		
Accounts payable		$ 5,200
Note payable		4,000
Interest payable—note		100
Deferred revenue		3,000
Total current liabilities		12,300
Long-term liabilities:		
Bonds payable		5,500
Interest payable—bonds		200
Shareholders' equity:		
Common stock	$?	
Retained earnings	?	?
Total liabilities and shareholders' equity		?

Additional Information ($ in thousands):

1. Certain records that included the account balances for the patent and shareholders' equity items were lost. However, the controller told you that a complete, preliminary balance sheet prepared before the records were lost showed a debt to equity ratio of 1.2. That is, total liabilities are 120% of total shareholders' equity. Retained earnings at the beginning of the year was $4,000. Net income for 2018 was $1,560 and $560 in cash dividends were declared and paid to shareholders.
2. Management intends to sell the investments in the next six months.
3. Interest on both the note and the bonds is payable annually.
4. The note payable is due in annual installments of $1,000 each.
5. Deferred revenue will be recognized as revenue equally over the next two fiscal years.
6. The common stock represents 400,000 shares of no par stock authorized, 250,000 shares issued and outstanding.

Required:
Prepare a complete, corrected, classified balance sheet.

P 3–9
Balance sheet preparation
● LO3–2 , LO3–3

Presented below is the balance sheet for HHD, Inc., at December 31, 2018.

Current assets	$ 600,000	Current liabilities	$ 400,000
Investments	500,000	Long-term liabilities	1,100,000
Property, plant, and equipment	2,000,000	Shareholders' equity	1,800,000
Intangible assets	200,000		
Total assets	$3,300,000	Total liabilities and shareholders' equity	$3,300,000

The captions shown in the summarized statement above include the following:

a. Current assets: cash, $150,000; accounts receivable, $200,000; inventories, $225,000; and prepaid insurance, $25,000.

b. Investments: investments in common stock, short term, $90,000, and long term, $160,000; and restricted cash, long term, $250,000.

c. Property, plant, and equipment: buildings, $1,500,000 less accumulated depreciation, $600,000; equipment, $500,000 less accumulated depreciation, $200,000; and land, $800,000.

d. Intangible assets: patent, $110,000; and copyright, $90,000.

e. Current liabilities: accounts payable, $100,000; notes payable, short term, $150,000, and long term, $90,000; and taxes payable, $60,000.

f. Long-term liabilities: bonds payable due 2023.

g. Shareholders' equity: common stock, $1,000,000; retained earnings, $800,000. Five hundred thousand shares of no par common stock are authorized, of which 200,000 shares were issued and are outstanding.

Required:
Prepare a corrected classified balance sheet for HHD, Inc., at December 31, 2018.

P 3–10
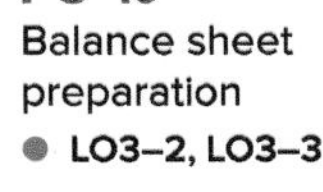
Balance sheet preparation
● LO3–2, LO3–3

Melody Lane Music Company was started by John Ross early in 2018. Initial capital was acquired by issuing shares of common stock to various investors and by obtaining a bank loan. The company operates a retail store that sells records, tapes, and compact discs. Business was so good during the first year of operations that John is considering opening a second store on the other side of town. The funds necessary for expansion will come from a new bank loan. In order to approve the loan, the bank requires financial statements.

John asks for your help in preparing the balance sheet and presents you with the following information for the year ending December 31, 2018:

a. Cash receipts consisted of the following:

From customers	$360,000
From issue of common stock	100,000
From bank loan	100,000

b. Cash disbursements were as follows:

Purchase of inventory	$300,000
Rent	15,000
Salaries	30,000
Utilities	5,000
Insurance	3,000
Purchase of equipment and furniture	40,000

c. The bank loan was made on March 31, 2018. A note was signed requiring payment of interest and principal on March 31, 2019. The interest rate is 12%.

d. The equipment and furniture were purchased on January 3, 2018, and have an estimated useful life of 10 years with no anticipated salvage value. Depreciation per year is $4,000.

e. Inventories on hand at the end of the year cost $100,000.

f. Amounts owed at December 31, 2018, were as follows:

To suppliers of inventory	$20,000
To the utility company	1,000

g. Rent on the store building is $1,000 per month. On December 1, 2018, four months' rent was paid in advance.

h. Net income for the year was $76,000. Assume that the company is not subject to federal, state, or local income tax.

i. One hundred thousand shares of no par common stock are authorized, of which 20,000 shares were issued and are outstanding.

Required:
Prepare a balance sheet at December 31, 2018.

Broaden Your Perspective

Apply your critical-thinking ability to the knowledge you've gained. These cases will provide you an opportunity to develop your research, analysis, judgment, and communication skills. You also will work with other students, integrate what you've learned, apply it in real-world situations, and consider its global and ethical ramifications. This practice will broaden your knowledge and further develop your decision-making abilities.

Communication Case 3–1
Current versus long-term classification
● LO3–2

A first-year accounting student is confused by a statement made in a recent class. Her instructor stated that the assets listed in the balance sheet of the IBM Corporation include computers that are classified as current assets as well as computers that are classified as long-term (noncurrent) assets. In addition, the instructor stated that investments in marketable securities of other corporations could be classified in the balance sheet as either current or long-term assets.

Required:

Explain to the student the distinction between current and long-term assets pertaining to the IBM computers and the investments in marketable securities.

Analysis Case 3–2
Current versus long-term classification
● LO3–2, LO3–3

The usefulness of the balance sheet is enhanced when assets and liabilities are grouped according to common characteristics. The broad distinction made in the balance sheet is the current versus long-term classification of both assets and liabilities.

Required:

1. Discuss the factors that determine whether an asset or liability should be classified as current or long-term in a balance sheet.
2. Identify six items that under different circumstances could be classified as either current or long-term. Indicate the factors that would determine the correct classification.

Communication Case 3–3
FASB codification research; inventory or property, plant, and equipment
● LO3–2

The Red Hen Company produces, processes, and sells fresh eggs. The company is in the process of preparing financial statements at the end of its first year of operations and has asked for your help in determining the appropriate treatment of the cost of its egg-laying flock. The estimated life of a laying hen is approximately two years, after which they are sold to soup companies.

The controller considers the company's operating cycle to be two years and wants to present the cost of the egg-producing flock as inventory in the current asset section of the balance sheet. He feels that the hens are "goods awaiting sale." The chief financial officer does not agree with this treatment. He thinks that the cost of the flock should be classified as property, plant, and equipment because the hens are used in the production of product—the eggs.

The focus of this case is the balance sheet presentation of the cost of the egg-producing flock. Your instructor will divide the class into two to six groups depending on the size of the class. The mission of your group is to reach consensus on the appropriate presentation.

Required:

1. Each group member should deliberate the situation independently and draft a tentative argument prior to the class session for which the case is assigned.
2. In class, each group will meet for 10 to 15 minutes in different areas of the classroom. During that meeting, group members will take turns sharing their suggestions for the purpose of arriving at a single group treatment.
3. After the allotted time, a spokesperson for each group (selected during the group meetings) will share the group's solution with the class. The goal of the class is to incorporate the views of each group into a consensus approach to the situation.

IFRS Case 3–4
Balance sheet presentation; Vodafone Group, Plc.
● LO3–2, LO3–3, LO3–9

Real World Financials

Vodafone Group, Plc., a U.K. company, is the largest mobile telecommunications network company in the world. The company prepares its financial statements in accordance with International Financial Reporting Standards. Below are partial company balance sheets (statements of financial position) included in a recent annual report:

Vodafone Group, Plc.
Consolidated Statements of Financial Position
At March 31

	2015	2014
	£m	£m
Long-term assets:		
Goodwill	22,537	23,315
Other intangible assets	20,953	23,373
Property, plant, and equipment	26,603	22,851

(continued)

(concluded)	2015	2014
	£m	£m
Investments in associates and joint ventures	(3)	114
Other investments	3,757	3,553
Deferred tax assets	23,845	20,607
Post employment benefits	169	35
Trade and other receivables	4,865	3,270
	102,726	97,118
Current assets:		
Inventory	482	441
Taxation recoverable	575	808
Trade and other receivables	8,053	8,886
Other investments	3,855	4,419
Cash and cash equivalents	6,882	10,134
Assets held for sale	—	34
	19,847	24,722
Total assets	122,573	121,840
Equity (details provided in complete statements)	67,733	71,781
Long-term liabilities:		
Long-term borrowings	22,435	21,454
Taxation liabilities	—	50
Deferred tax liabilities	595	747
Post employment benefits	567	584
Provisions	1,082	846
Trade and other payables	1,264	1,339
	25,943	25,020
Current liabilities:		
Short-term borrowings	12,623	7,747
Taxation liabilities	599	873
Provisions	767	963
Trade and other payables	14,908	15,456
	28,897	25,039
Total equity and liabilities	122,573	121,840

Required:

1. Describe the differences between Vodafone's balance sheets and a typical U.S. company balance sheet.
2. What type of liabilities do you think are included in the *provisions* category in Vodafone's balance sheets?

Judgment Case 3–5
Balance sheet; errors
● LO3–2 through LO3–4

You recently joined the internal auditing department of Marcus Clothing Corporation. As one of your first assignments, you are examining a balance sheet prepared by a staff accountant.

MARCUS CLOTHING CORPORATION
Balance Sheet
At December 31, 2018
Assets

Current assets:		
Cash		$ 137,000
Accounts receivable, net		80,000
Note receivable		53,000
Inventories		240,000
Investments		66,000
Total current assets		576,000
Other assets:		
Land	$ 200,000	
Equipment, net	320,000	
Prepaid expenses (for the next 12 months)	27,000	
Patent	22,000	
Total other assets		569,000
Total assets		$1,145,000

(continued)

(concluded)

Liabilities and Shareholders' Equity		
Current liabilities:		
Accounts payable		$ 125,000
Salaries payable		32,000
Total current liabilities		157,000
Long-term liabilities:		
Note payable	$ 100,000	
Bonds payable (due in 5 years)	300,000	
Interest payable	20,000	
Total long-term liabilities		420,000
Shareholders' equity:		
Common stock	500,000	
Retained earnings	68,000	
Total shareholders' equity		568,000
Total liabilities and shareholders' equity		$1,145,000

In the course of your examination you uncover the following information pertaining to the balance sheet:

1. The company rents its facilities. The land that appears in the statement is being held for future sale.
2. The note receivable is due in 2020. The balance of $53,000 includes $3,000 of accrued interest. The next interest payment is due in July 2019.
3. The note payable is due in installments of $20,000 per year. Interest on both the notes and bonds is payable annually.
4. The company's investments consist of marketable equity securities of other corporations. Management does not intend to liquidate any investments in the coming year.

Required:

Identify and explain the deficiencies in the statement prepared by the company's accountant. Include in your answer items that require additional disclosure, either on the face of the statement or in a note.

Judgment Case 3–6
Financial disclosures
● LO3–4

You recently joined the auditing staff of Best, Best, and Krug, CPAs. You have been assigned to the audit of Clearview, Inc., and have been asked by the audit senior to examine the balance sheet prepared by Clearview's accountant.

CLEARVIEW, INC.
Balance Sheet
At December 31, 2018
($ in millions)

Assets		
Current assets:		
Cash		$ 10.5
Accounts receivable		112.1
Inventories		220.6
Prepaid expenses		5.5
Total current assets		348.7
Investments		22.0
Property, plant, and equipment, net		486.9
Total assets		$857.6
Liabilities and Shareholders' Equity		
Current liabilities:		
Accounts payable		$ 83.5
Accrued taxes and interest		25.5
Current maturities of long-term debt		20.0
Total current liabilities		129.0
Long-term liabilities:		420.0
Total liabilities		549.0
Shareholders' equity:		
Common stock	$100.0	
Retained earnings	208.6	
Total shareholders' equity		308.6
Total liabilities and shareholders' equity		$857.6

Required:

Identify the items in the statement that most likely would require further disclosure either on the face of the statement or in a note. Further identify those items that would require disclosure in the significant accounting policies note.

Real World Case 3–7
Balance sheet and significant accounting policies disclosure; Walmart

● LO3–2 through LO3–4, LO3–8

Real World Financials

The balance sheet and disclosure of significant accounting policies taken from the 2016 annual report of Wal-Mart Stores, Inc., appear below. Use this information to answer the following questions:

1. What are the asset classifications contained in Walmart's balance sheet?
2. What amounts did Walmart report for the following items for 2016:
   a. Total assets
   b. Current assets
   c. Current liabilities
   d. Total equity
   e. Retained earnings
   f. Inventories
3. What is Walmart's largest current asset? What is its largest current liability?
4. Compute Walmart's current ratio for 2016.
5. Identify the following items:
   a. The company's inventory valuation method
   b. The definition of cash equivalents

WAL-MART STORES, INC.
Consolidated Balance Sheets
($ in millions except per share data)

	As of January 31,	
	2016	**2015**
Assets		
Current assets:		
Cash and cash equivalents	$ 8,705	$ 9,135
Receivables, net	5,624	6,778
Inventories	44,469	45,141
Prepaid expenses and other	1,441	2,224
Total current assets	60,239	63,278
Property and equipment:		
Property and equipment	176,958	177,395
Less accumulated depreciation	(66,787)	(63,115)
Property and equipment, net	110,171	114,280
Property under capital leases:		
Property under capital lease and financing obligations	11,096	5,239
Less accumulated amortization	(4,751)	(2,864)
Property under capital leases and financing obligations, net	6,345	2,375
Goodwill	16,695	18,102
Other assets and deferred charges	6,131	5,455
Total assets	$199,581	$203,490
Liabilities, Redeemable Noncontrolling Interest and Equity		
Current liabilities:		
Short-term borrowings	$ 2,708	$ 1,592
Accounts payable	38,487	38,410
Accrued liabilities	19,607	19,152
Accrued income taxes	521	1,021
Long-term debt due within one year	2,745	4,791
Capital lease and financing obligations due within one year	551	287
Total current liabilities	64,619	65,253
Long-term debt	38,214	40,889
Long-term capital lease and financing obligations	5,816	2,606
Deferred income taxes and other	7,321	8,805
Commitments and contingencies Equity:		
Common stock	317	323
Capital in excess of par value	1,805	2,462
Retained earnings	90,021	85,777
Accumulated other comprehensive income (loss)	(11,597)	(7,168)
Total Walmart shareholders' equity	80,546	81,394
Nonredeemable noncontrolling interest	3,065	4,543
Total equity	83,611	85,937
Total liabilities, redeemable noncontrolling interest and equity	$199,581	$203,490

NOTES TO CONSOLIDATED FINANCIAL STATEMENTS
WAL-MART STORES, INC.

1 Summary of Significant Accounting Policies (in part)

Cash and Cash Equivalents
The Company considers investments with a maturity of three months or less when purchased to be cash equivalents.

Inventories
The Company values inventories at the lower of cost or market as determined primarily by the retail method of accounting, using the last-in, first-out ("LIFO") method for substantially all of the Walmart U.S. segment's merchandise inventories. Inventories for the Walmart International operations are primarily valued by the retail method of accounting, using the first-in, first-out ("FIFO") method. At January 31, 2016 and 2015, our inventories valued at LIFO approximate those inventories as if they were valued at FIFO.

Revenue Recognition
The Company recognizes sales revenue net of sales taxes and estimated sales returns at the time it sells merchandise to the customer. Customer purchases of shopping cards are not recognized as revenue until the card is redeemed and the customer purchases merchandise by using the shopping card. The Company also recognizes revenue from service transactions at the time the service is performed. Generally, revenue from services is classified as a component of net sales on our consolidated statements of income.

Judgment Case 3–8
Post fiscal year-end events
● LO3–4

The fiscal year-end for the Northwest Distribution Corporation is December 31. The company's 2018 financial statements were issued on March 15, 2019. The following events occurred between December 31, 2018, and March 15, 2019.

1. On January 22, 2019, the company negotiated a major merger with Blandon Industries. The merger will be completed by the middle of 2019.
2. On February 3, 2019, Northwest negotiated a $10 million long-term note with the Credit Bank of Ohio. The amount of the note is material.
3. On February 25, 2019, a flood destroyed one of the company's manufacturing plants causing $600,000 of uninsured damage.

Required:

Determine the appropriate treatment of each of these events in the 2018 financial statements of Northwest Distribution Corporation.

Research Case 3–9
FASB codification; locate and extract relevant information and cite authoritative support for a financial reporting issue; related-party disclosures; Enron Corporation
● LO3–4

Real World Financials

CODE

Enron Corporation was a darling in the energy-provider arena, and in January 2001 its stock price rose above $100 per share. A collapse of investor confidence in 2001 and revelations of accounting fraud led to one of the largest bankruptcies in U.S. history. By the end of the year, Enron's stock price had plummeted to less than $1 per share. Investigations and lawsuits followed. One problem area concerned transactions with related parties that were not adequately disclosed in the company's financial statements. Critics stated that the lack of information about these transactions made it difficult for analysts following Enron to identify problems the company was experiencing.

Required:

1. Obtain the relevant authoritative literature on related-party transactions using the *FASB Accounting Standards Codification* at the FASB website (www.fasb.org). What is the specific citation that outlines the required information on related-party disclosures that must be included in the notes to the financial statements?
2. Describe the disclosures required for related-party transactions.
3. Use EDGAR (www.sec.gov) or another method to locate the December 31, 2000, financial statements of Enron. Search for the related-party disclosure. Briefly describe the relationship central to the various transactions described.
4. Why is it important that companies disclose related-party transactions? Use the Enron disclosure of the sale of dark fiber inventory in your answer.

Real World Case 3–10
Disclosures; proxy statement; Coca-Cola
● LO3–4, LO3–5

Real World Financials

EDGAR, the Electronic Data Gathering, Analysis, and Retrieval system, performs automated collection, validation, indexing, and forwarding of submissions by companies and others who are required by law to file forms with the SEC. All publicly traded domestic companies use EDGAR to make the majority of their filings. (Some foreign companies file voluntarily.) Form 10-K, which includes the annual report, is required to be filed on EDGAR. The SEC makes this information available on the Internet.

Required:

1. Access EDGAR on the Internet. The web address is www.sec.gov.
2. Search for The Coca-Cola Company. Access the 10-K for the year ended December 31, 2015. Search or scroll to find the disclosure notes and audit report.
3. Answer the following questions:
   a. Describe the subsequent events disclosed by the company.
   b. Which firm is the company's auditor? What type of audit opinion did the auditor render?
4. Access the proxy statement filed with the SEC on March 10, 2016 (the proxy statement designation is Def 14A), locate the executive officers summary compensation table and answer the following questions:
   a. What is the principal position of Muhtar Kent?
   b. What was the salary paid to Mr. Kent during the year ended December 31, 2015?

Judgment Case 3–11
Debt versus equity
● LO3–7

A common problem facing any business entity is the debt versus equity decision. When funds are required to obtain assets, should debt or equity financing be used? This decision also is faced when a company is initially formed. What will be the mix of debt versus equity in the initial capital structure? The characteristics of debt are very different from those of equity as are the financial implications of using one method of financing as opposed to the other.

Cherokee Plastics Corporation is formed by a group of investors to manufacture household plastic products. Their initial capitalization goal is $50,000,000. That is, the incorporators have decided to raise $50,000,000 to acquire the initial assets of the company. They have narrowed down the financing mix alternatives to two:

1. All equity financing
2. $20,000,000 in debt financing and $30,000,000 in equity financing

No matter which financing alternative is chosen, the corporation expects to be able to generate a 10% annual return, before payment of interest and income taxes, on the $50,000,000 in assets acquired. The interest rate on debt would be 8%. The effective income tax rate will be approximately 50%.

Alternative 2 will require specified interest and principal payments to be made to the creditors at specific dates. The interest portion of these payments (interest expense) will reduce the taxable income of the corporation and hence the amount of income tax the corporation will pay. The all-equity alternative requires no specified payments to be made to suppliers of capital. The corporation is not legally liable to make distributions to its owners. If the board of directors does decide to make a distribution, it is not an expense of the corporation and does not reduce taxable income and hence the taxes the corporation pays.

Required:

1. Prepare abbreviated income statements that compare first-year profitability for each of the two alternatives.
2. Which alternative would be expected to achieve the highest first-year profits? Why?
3. Which alternative would provide the highest rate of return on shareholders' equity? Why?
4. What other related implications of the decision should be considered?

Analysis Case 3–12
Obtain and critically evaluate an actual annual report
● LO3–4, LO3–6 through LO3–8

Real World Financials

Financial reports are the primary means by which corporations report their performance and financial condition. Financial statements are one component of the annual report mailed to their shareholders and to interested others.

Required:

Obtain an annual report from a corporation with which you are familiar. Using techniques you learned in this chapter and any analysis you consider useful, respond to the following questions:

1. Do the firm's auditors provide a clean opinion on the financial statements?
2. Has the company made changes in any accounting methods it uses?
3. Have there been any subsequent events, errors and fraud, illegal acts, or related-party transactions that have a material effect on the company's financial position?
4. What are two trends in the company's operations or capital resources that management considers significant to the company's future?
5. Is the company engaged in more than one significant line of business? If so, compare the relative profitability of the different segments.
6. How stable are the company's operations?
7. Has the company's situation deteriorated or improved with respect to liquidity, solvency, asset management, and profitability?

Note: You can obtain a copy of an annual report from a local company, from a friend who is a shareholder, from the investor relations department of the corporation, from a friendly stockbroker, or from EDGAR (Electronic Data Gathering, Analysis, and Retrieval) on the Internet (www.sec.gov).

Analysis Case 3–13
Obtain and compare annual reports from companies in the same industry
● LO3–4, LO3–7, LO3–8

Real World Financials

Insight concerning the performance and financial condition of a company often comes from evaluating its financial data in comparison with other firms in the same industry.

Required:

Obtain annual reports from three corporations in the same primary industry. Using techniques you learned in this chapter and any analysis you consider useful, respond to the following questions:

1. Are there differences in accounting methods that should be taken into account when making comparisons?
2. How do earnings trends compare in terms of both the direction and stability of income?
3. Which of the three firms had the greatest earnings relative to resources available?
4. Which corporation has made most effective use of financial leverage?
5. Of the three firms, which seems riskiest in terms of its ability to pay short-term obligations? Long-term obligations?

Note: You can obtain copies of annual reports from friends who are shareholders, from the investor relations department of the corporations, from a friendly stockbroker, or from EDGAR (Electronic Data Gathering, Analysis, and Retrieval) on the Internet (www.sec.gov).

Analysis Case 3–14
Balance sheet information
● LO3–2 through LO3–4

Real World Financials

Target Corporation prepares its financial statements according to U.S. GAAP. Target's financial statements and disclosure notes for the year ended January 30, 2016, are available in the Connect library. This material also is available under the Investor Relations link at the company's website (www.target.com).

Required:

1. What categories does the company use to classify its assets? Its liabilities?
2. Why are investments shown as a current asset?
3. Explain the current liability "Accrued and other current liabilities."
4. What purpose do the disclosure notes serve?
5. What method does the company use to depreciate its property and equipment?

Analysis Case 3–15
Segment reporting concepts
● Appendix 3, LO3–9

 IFRS

Levens Co. operates in several distinct business segments. The company does not have any reportable foreign operations or major customers.

Required:

1. What is the purpose of operating segment disclosures?
2. Define an operating segment.
3. List the amounts to be reported by operating segment.
4. How would your answer to requirement 3 differ if Levens Co. prepares its segment disclosure according to International Financial Reporting Standards?

Ethics Case 3–16
Segment reporting
● Appendix 3

You are in your third year as an accountant with McCarver-Lynn Industries, a multidivisional company involved in the manufacturing, marketing, and sales of surgical prosthetic devices. After the fiscal year-end, you are working with the controller of the firm to prepare geographic area disclosures. Yesterday you presented her with the following summary information:

	($ in millions)					
	Domestic	**Libya**	**Egypt**	**France**	**Cayman Islands**	**Total**
Revenues	$ 845	$222	$265	$343	$2,311	$3,986
Operating income	145	76	88	21	642	972
Assets	1,005	301	290	38	285	1,919

Upon returning to your office after lunch, you find the following memo:

Nice work. Let's combine the data this way:

	($ in millions)			
	Domestic	**Africa**	**Europe and Other Foreign**	**Total**
Revenues	$ 845	$487	$2,654	$3,986
Capital expenditures	145	164	663	972
Assets	1,005	591	323	1,919

Because of political instability in North Africa, let's not disclose specific countries. In addition, we restructured most of our French sales and some of our U.S. sales to occur through our offices in the Cayman Islands. This allows us to avoid paying higher taxes in those countries. The Cayman Islands has a 0% corporate income tax rate. We don't want to highlight our ability to shift profits to avoid taxes.

Required:

Do you perceive an ethical dilemma? What would be the likely impact of following the controller's suggestions? Who would benefit? Who would be injured?

Continuing Cases

Target Case

● LO3–2, LO3–3, LO3–8

Target Corporation prepares its financial statements according to U.S. GAAP. Target's financial statements and disclosure notes for the year ended January 30, 2016, are provided in available in Connect. This material is also available under the Investor Relations link at the company's website (www.target.com).

Required:

1. By what name does Target label its balance sheet?
2. What amounts did Target report for the following items on January 30, 2016?
   a. Current assets
   b. Long-term assets
   c. Total assets
   d. Current liabilities
   e. Long-term liabilities
   f. Total liabilities
   g. Total shareholders' equity
3. What was Target's largest current asset? What was its largest current liability?
4. Compute Target's current ratio and debt to equity ratio in 2016?
5. Assuming Target's industry had an average current ratio of 1.0 and an average debt to equity ratio of 2.5, comment on Target's liquidity and long-term solvency.

Air France–KLM Case

● LO3–9

IFRS

Air France-KLM (AF), a Franco-Dutch company, prepares its financial statements according to International Financial Reporting Standards. AF's financial statements and disclosure notes for the year ended December 31, 2015, are provided in Connect. This material is also available under the Finance link at the company's website (www.airfranceklm.com).

Required:

Describe the apparent differences in the order of presentation of the components of the balance sheet between IFRS as applied by Air France–KLM (AF) and a typical balance sheet prepared in accordance with U.S. GAAP.

CPA Exam Questions and Simulations

Sample CPA Exam questions from Roger CPA Review are available in Connect as support for the topics in this chapter. These Multiple Choice Questions and Task-Based Simulations include expert-written explanations and solutions, and provide a starting point for students to become familiar with the content and functionality of the actual CPA Exam.

CHAPTER

4 The Income Statement, Comprehensive Income, and the Statement of Cash Flows

OVERVIEW

This chapter has three purposes: (1) to consider important issues dealing with the content, presentation, and disclosure of net income and other components of comprehensive income, (2) to provide an *overview* of the statement of cash flows, which is covered in depth in Chapter 21, and (3) to examine common ratios used in profitability analysis.

The income statement summarizes the profit-generating activities that occurred during a particular reporting period. Comprehensive income includes net income as well as other gains and losses that are not part of net income.

The statement of cash flows provides information about the cash receipts and cash disbursements of an enterprise's operating, investing, and financing activities that occurred during the period.

Profitability ratios measure how well a company manages its operations and utilizes resources to generate a profit. Profitability is a key metric in understanding the company's ability to generate cash in the future.

LEARNING OBJECTIVES

After studying this chapter, you should be able to:

- **LO4–1** Discuss the importance of income from continuing operations and describe its components. (*p. 164*)
- **LO4–2** Describe earnings quality and how it is impacted by management practices to alter reported earnings. (*p. 168*)
- **LO4–3** Discuss the components of operating and nonoperating income and their relationship to earnings quality. (*p. 169*)
- **LO4–4** Define what constitutes discontinued operations and describe the appropriate income statement presentation for these transactions. (*p. 173*)
- **LO4–5** Discuss additional reporting issues related to accounting changes, error corrections, and earnings per share (EPS). (*p. 178*)
- **LO4–6** Explain the difference between net income and comprehensive income and how we report components of the difference. (*p. 181*)
- **LO4–7** Describe the purpose of the statement of cash flows. (*p. 185*)
- **LO4–8** Identify and describe the various classifications of cash flows presented in a statement of cash flows. (*p. 186*)
- **LO4–9** Discuss the primary differences between U.S. GAAP and IFRS with respect to the income statement, statement of comprehensive income, and statement of cash flows. (*pp. 168, 182, 191,* and *202*)
- **LO4–10** Identify and calculate the common ratios used to assess profitability. (*p. 193*)

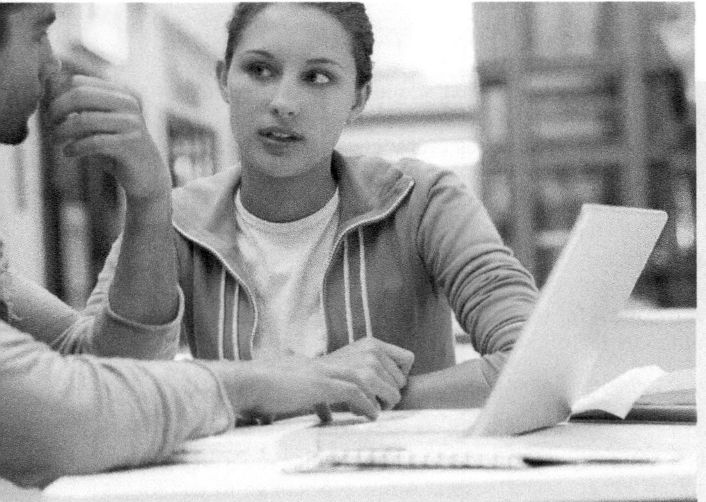

© Onoky/SuperStock

FINANCIAL REPORTING CASE

Abbott Laboratories

Your friend, Becky Morgan, just received a generous gift from her grandfather. Accompanying a warm letter were 200 shares of stock of Abbott Laboratories, a global health care company, along with the most recent annual financial statements of the company. Becky knows that you are an accounting major and pleads with you to explain some items in the company's income statement. "I remember studying the income statement in my introductory accounting course," says Becky, "but I am still confused. What is this item *discontinued operations?* I also read in the annual report the company has *restructuring costs?* These don't sound good. Are they something I should worry about? We studied earnings per share briefly, but what does *earnings per common share—diluted* mean?" You agree to try to help.

ABBOTT LABORATORIES AND SUBSIDIARY COMPANIES
Statements of Earnings For the Year Ended December 31
($ in millions, except per share data)

	2015	2014
Net sales	$20,405	$20,247
Costs and expenses:		
Cost of products sold	8,747	9,218
Amortization of intangible assets	601	555
Research and development expenses	1,405	1,345
Selling, general and administrative	6,785	6,530
Operating income	2,867	2,599
Other income (deductions)	316	(81)
Income from continuing operations before income taxes	3,183	2,518
Provision for taxes on income	577	797
Income from continuing operations	2,606	1,721
Income from discontinued operations, net of tax	1,817	563
Net income	$ 4,423	$ 2,284
Earnings per common share—basic:		
Continuing operations	$ 1.73	$ 1.13
Discontinued operations	1.21	0.37
Net income	$ 2.94	$ 1.50
Earnings per common share—diluted:		
Continuing operations	$ 1.72	$ 1.12
Discontinued operations	1.20	0.37
Net income	$ 2.92	$ 1.49

QUESTIONS

By the time you finish this chapter, you should be able to respond appropriately to the questions posed in this case. Compare your response to the solution provided at the end of the chapter.

1. How would you explain restructuring costs to Becky? Are restructuring costs something Becky should worry about? (*p. 170*)
2. Explain to Becky what is meant by discontinued operations and describe to her how that item is reported in an income statement. (*p. 173*)
3. Describe to Becky the difference between basic and diluted earnings per share. (*p. 180*)

In Chapter 1, we discussed the critical role of financial accounting information in allocating resources within our economy. Ideally, resources should be allocated to private enterprises that will (1) provide the goods and services our society desires and (2) at the same time provide a fair rate of return to those who supply the resources. A company will be able to achieve these goals only if it can generate enough cash to stay in business. A company's ability to generate cash relates to its ability to sell products and services for amounts greater than the costs of providing those products and services (that is, generate a profit).

Two financial statements that are critical for understanding the company's ability to earn profits and generate cash in the future are as follows:

1. **Income statement** (also called *statement of operations* or *statement of earnings*).
2. **Statement of cash flows.**

The income statement reports a company's profit during a particular reporting period. Profit equals revenues and gains minus expenses and losses. A few types of gains and losses are excluded from the income statement but are included in the broader concept of comprehensive income. We refer to these other gains and losses as other comprehensive income (OCI).

The statement of cash flows provides information about the cash receipts and cash payments of a company during a particular reporting period. The difference between cash receipts and cash payments represents the change in cash for the period. To help investors and creditors better understand the sources and uses of cash during the period, the statement of cash flows distinguishes among operating, investing, and financing activities.

PART A

The Income Statement and Comprehensive Income

Before we discuss the specific components of an income statement in much depth, let's take a quick look at the general makeup of the statement. Illustration 4–1 offers an income statement for McAllister's Manufacturing, a hypothetical company, that you can refer to as we proceed through the chapter. At this point, our objective is only to gain a general perspective on the items reported and classifications contained in corporate income statements. In addition, each income statement should include in the heading the name of the company, the title of the statement, and the date or time period. McAllister's income statement is for the year ended December 31. This means that amounts in the income statement are the result of transactions from January 1 to December 31 of that year. In reality, many companies have reporting periods (often referred to as *fiscal years*) that end in months other than December, as you'll see demonstrated later in this chapter. Illustration 4–1 shows comparative income statements for two consecutive years.

Let's first look closer at the components of net income. At the end of this part, we'll see how net income fits within the concept of comprehensive income and how comprehensive income is reported.

Income from Continuing Operations

Revenues, Expenses, Gains, and Losses

● LO4–1

Income from continuing operations includes the revenues, expenses, gains and losses from operations that are more likely to continue into the future.

Unlike the balance sheet, which is a position statement *at a point in time,* the income statement measures activity *over a period of time.* The income statement reports the revenues, expenses, gains, and losses that have occurred during the reporting period. For example, if a company reports revenues of $100 million in its income statement for the year ended December 31, 2018, this means that the company had revenue transactions from January 1, 2018, to December 31, 2018, equal to $100 million. Next, we will formally define each of the elements of the income statement.

Revenues are inflows of resources resulting from providing goods or services to customers. For merchandising companies like Walmart, the main source of revenue is sales

Illustration 4–1

Income Statement

McAllister's Manufacturing
Income Statement
($ in millions, except per share data)

		Year Ended December 31	
		2018	**2017**
Income from Continuing Operations	Sales revenue	$1,450.6	$1,380.0
	Cost of goods sold	832.6	800.4
	Gross profit	618.0	579.6
	Operating expenses:		
	Selling	123.5	110.5
	General and administrative	147.8	139.1
	Research and development	55.0	65.0
	Restructuring costs	125.0	—
	Total operating expenses	451.3	314.6
	Operating income	166.7	265.0
	Other income (expense):		
	Interest income	12.4	11.1
	Interest expense	(25.9)	(24.8)
	Gain on sale of investments	18.0	19.0
	Income from continuing operations before income taxes	171.2	270.3
	Income tax expense	59.9	94.6
	Income from continuing operations	111.3	175.7
Discontinued Operations	Discontinued operations:		
	Loss from operations of discontinued component (including gain on disposal in 2018 of $47)	(7.6)	(45.7)
	Income tax benefit	2.0	13.0
	Loss on discontinued operations	(5.6)	(32.7)
	Net income	$ 105.7	$ 143.0
Earnings per Share	Earnings per common share—basic:		
	Income from continuing operations	$ 2.14	$ 3.38
	Discontinued operations	(0.11)	(0.63)
	Net income	$ 2.03	$ 2.75
	Earnings per common share—diluted:		
	Income from continuing operations	$ 2.06	$ 3.25
	Discontinued operations	(0.10)	(0.61)
	Net income	$ 1.96	$ 2.64

revenue derived from selling merchandise. Service firms such as FedEx and State Farm Insurance generate revenue by providing services.

Expenses are outflows of resources incurred while generating revenue. They represent the costs of providing goods and services. When recognizing expenses, we attempt to establish a causal relationship between revenues and expenses. If causality can be determined, expenses are reported in the same period that the related revenue is recognized. If a causal relationship cannot be established, we relate the expense to a particular period, allocate it over several periods, or expense it as incurred.

Gains and losses are increases or decreases in equity from peripheral or incidental transactions of an entity. In general, these gains and losses result from changes in equity that do not result directly from operations but nonetheless are related to those activities. For example, the sale of equipment, buildings, or other operating assets for an amount that differs from their recorded amount results in a gain or loss.

To understand a company's ability to generate cash in the future, investors and creditors assess which components of net income are likely to continue into the future. Income from continuing operations includes revenues, expenses (including income taxes), gains, and losses arising from operations that are more likely to continue. In contrast, income from *discontinued operations* will not continue into the future.[1]

The three major components of income from continuing operations include:

1. Operating income
2. Nonoperating income
3. Income tax expense

Operating income versus Nonoperating Income

Operating income includes revenues and expenses directly related to the *primary revenue-generating activities* of the company. For example, operating income for a manufacturing company includes sales revenue from selling the products it manufactures as well as all expenses related to this activity.[2] As shown in Illustration 4–1, operating income is often presented as gross profit (sales revenue minus cost of goods sold) minus other operating expenses.

Nonoperating income relates to *peripheral or incidental activities* of the company. For example, a manufacturer would include interest and dividend revenue, gains and losses from selling investments, and interest expense in nonoperating income. These items are not directly related to the primary revenue-generating activities of a manufacturing company. On the other hand, a financial institution like a bank would consider those items to be a part of operating income because they relate to the primary revenue-generating activities for that type of business. As shown in Illustration 4–1, nonoperating items often are included in the income statement under the heading *Other income (expense).*

Income Tax Expense

Income tax expense is reported in a separate line in the income statement.

Income taxes are levied on taxpayers in proportion to the amount of taxable income that is reported to taxing authorities. Like individuals, corporations are income-tax-paying entities.[3] Because of the importance and size of income tax expense (sometimes called *provision for income taxes*), it always is reported in a separate line in corporate income statements. When tax rules and GAAP differ regarding the timing of revenue or expense recognition, the actual payment of taxes may occur in a period different from when income tax expense is reported in the income statement. We discuss this and other issues related to accounting for income taxes in Chapter 16. At this point, consider income tax expense to be simply a percentage of income before taxes.

Illustration 4–2 presents the 2015 income statement for Sherwin Williams Company, a company that manufactures paint. Notice that Sherwin Williams distinguishes between operating income, nonoperating income, and income tax expense. Operating income includes revenues and expenses from primary business activities related to producing and selling paint. After operating income is determined, nonoperating items are added or subtracted to arrive at income before income taxes. For a paint manufacturer like Sherwin Williams, activities related to interest and investments are not primary operations and therefore are listed as nonoperating items. Finally, income tax expense is subtracted to arrive at net income.

Now let's consider the formats used to report the components of net income.

Income Statement Formats

No specific standards dictate how income from continuing operations must be displayed, so companies have considerable latitude in how they present the components of income from continuing operations. This flexibility has resulted in a variety of income statement

[1]Discontinued operations are addressed in a subsequent section.

[2]In certain situations, operating income might also include gains and losses from selling equipment and other assets used in the manufacturing process. FASB ASC 360-10-45-5: Property, plant, and equipment-Overall-Other Presentation Matters (previously "Accounting for the Impairment of Long-Lived Assets and for Long-Lived Assets to Be Disposed Of," *Statement of Financial Accounting Standards No. 144* (Norwalk, Conn.: FASB, 2001)).

[3]Partnerships are not tax-paying entities. Their taxable income or loss is included in the taxable income of the individual partners.

Statement of Consolidated Income
($ in thousands, except per share data)

	Year ended December 31, 2015
Net sales	$ 11,339,304
Cost of goods sold	5,780,078
Gross profit	5,559,226
Selling, general, and administrative expenses	3,943,786
Operating income	1,615,440
Interest expense	(61,791)
Interest and investment income	1,399
Other expenses	(6,082)
Income before income taxes	1,548,966
Income tax expense	495,117
Net income	$ 1,053,849

Illustration 4–2

Income Statement–Sherwin Williams Company

Real World Financials

presentations. However, we can identify two general approaches, the single-step and the multiple-step formats, that might be considered the two extremes, with the income statements of most companies falling somewhere in between.

The **single-step** format first lists all the revenues and gains included in income from continuing operations. Then, expenses and losses are grouped, subtotaled, and subtracted—in a single step—from revenues and gains to derive income from continuing operations. In a departure from that, though, companies usually report income tax expense in a separate line in the statement. Operating and nonoperating items are not separately classified. Illustration 4–3 shows an example of a single-step income statement for a hypothetical manufacturing company, Maxwell Gear Corporation.

A *single-step* income statement format groups all revenues and gains together and all expenses and losses together.

MAXWELL GEAR CORPORATION
Income Statement
For the Year Ended December 31, 2018

Revenues and gains:		
Sales	$573,522	
Interest and dividends	26,400	
Gain on sale of investments	5,500	
Total revenues and gains		$605,422
Expenses and losses:		
Cost of goods sold	$302,371	
Selling	47,341	
General and administrative	24,888	
Research and development	16,300	
Interest	14,522	
Total expenses and losses		405,422
Income before income taxes		200,000
Income tax expense		80,000
Net income		$120,000

Illustration 4–3

Single-Step Income Statement

The **multiple-step** format reports a series of intermediate subtotals such as gross profit, operating income, and income before taxes. Most of the real-world income statements are in this format. Illustration 4–4 presents a multiple-step income statement for the Maxwell Gear Corporation.

A primary advantage of the multiple-step format is that, by separately classifying operating and nonoperating items, it provides information that might be useful in analyzing trends. Similarly, the classification of expenses by function also provides useful information. For example,

A *multiple-step* income statement format includes a number of intermediate subtotals before arriving at income from continuing operations.

Illustration 4–4
Multiple-Step Income Statement

MAXWELL GEAR CORPORATION
Income Statement
For the Year Ended December 31, 2018

Sales revenue		$573,522
Cost of goods sold		302,371
Gross profit		271,151
Operating expenses:		
Selling	$47,341	
General and administrative	24,888	
Research and development	16,300	
Total operating expenses		88,529
Operating income		182,622
Other income (expense):		
Interest and dividend revenue	26,400	
Gain on sale of investments	5,500	
Interest expense	(14,522)	
Total other income, net		17,378
Income before income taxes		200,000
Income tax expense		80,000
Net income		$120,000

reporting *gross profit* for merchandising companies highlights the important relationship between sales revenue and cost of goods sold. *Operating income* provides a measure of profitability for core (or normal) operations, a key performance measure for predicting the future profit-generating ability of the company. *Income before taxes* could be useful for comparing the performance of companies in different tax jurisdictions or comparing corporations (tax-paying entities) with sole proprietorships or partnerships (typically non-tax-paying entities).

It is important to note that the difference between the single-step and multiple-step income statement is one of presentation. The bottom line, *net income,* is the same regardless of the format used. Most companies use the multiple-step format. We use the multiple-step format for illustration purposes throughout the remainder of this chapter.

International Financial Reporting Standards

Income Statement Presentation. There are more similarities than differences between income statements prepared according to U.S. GAAP and those prepared applying international standards. Some of the differences are as follows:

LO4–9

- International standards require certain minimum information to be reported on the face of the income statement. U.S. GAAP has no minimum requirements.
- International standards allow expenses to be classified either by function (e.g., cost of goods sold, general and administrative, etc.), or by natural description (e.g., salaries, rent, etc.). SEC regulations require that expenses be classified by function.
- In the United States, the "bottom line" of the income statement usually is called either *net income* or *net loss.* The descriptive term for the bottom line of the income statement prepared according to international standards is either *profit* or *loss.*

Earnings Quality

LO4–2

Investors, creditors, and financial analysts are concerned with more than just the bottom line of the income statement—net income. The presentation of the components of net income and the related supplemental disclosures provide clues to the user of the statement in an assessment of *earnings quality.* Earnings quality is used as a framework for more in-depth discussions of operating and nonoperating income.

One meaning of **earnings quality** is the ability of reported earnings (income) to predict a company's future earnings. The relevance of any historical-based financial statement hinges on its predictive value. To enhance predictive value, analysts try to separate a company's *temporary earnings* from its *permanent earnings.* Temporary earnings effects result from transactions or events that are not likely to occur again in the foreseeable future or that are likely to have a different impact on earnings in the future. In contrast, permanent earnings relate to operations that are expected to generate similar profits in the future. Analysts begin their assessment of permanent earnings with income before discontinued operations, that is, income from continuing operations. Later in the chapter we address discontinued operations that, because of their nature, are required to be reported separately at the bottom of the income statement.

Earnings quality refers to the ability of reported earnings (income) to predict a company's future earnings.

It would be a mistake, though, to assume that all items included in income from continuing operations reflect permanent earnings. Some income items that fall under this category may be temporary. In a sense, the label *continuing* may be misleading.

Income Smoothing and Classification Shifting

An often-debated contention is that, within GAAP, managers have the power to change reported income by altering assumptions and estimates. And these alternatives are not always in the direction of higher income. Survey evidence suggests that managers often alter income upwards in one year but downward in other years.[4] For example, in a year when income is high, managers may create reserves by overestimating certain expenses (such as future bad debts or warranties). These reserves reduce reported income in the current year. Then, in later years, they can use those reserves by underestimating expenses, which will increase reported income. By shifting income in this manner, managers effectively smooth the pattern in reported income over time, portraying a steadier income stream to investors, creditors, and other financial statement users.[5]

Management's *income smoothing* behavior is controversial. While some believe that a smoother income pattern helps investors and creditors to better predict future performance, others believe that managers are doing this to hide the true risk (volatility) of operations. By hiding this underlying volatility through manipulation of the income pattern over time, managers may be "fooling" investors and creditors into believing that the company's operations are lower-risk than they really are.

Income smoothing may help investors to predict future performance but it could also hide underlying risk.

Another way that managers affect reported income is through *classification shifting* in the income statement.[6] The most common example of this involves misclassifying operating expenses as nonoperating expenses. By shifting operating expenses to a nonoperating expense classification (often referred to as "special charges" or "special items"), managers report fewer operating expenses and therefore higher operating income. This type of manipulation creates the appearance of stronger performance for core operations. While bottom-line net income remains unaffected, investors and creditors may believe the core business is stronger than it really is.

Classification shifting inflates core performance.

Operating Income and Earnings Quality

● LO4–3

Should all items of revenue and expense included in operating income be considered indicative of a company's permanent earnings? No, not necessarily. Sometimes a company will have an unusual or infrequent event. Even though these events may be unlikely to occur again in the near future, we report them as part of operating income because they are so closely related to the company's core business.[7]

[4]See, for example, Dichev, I., J. Graham, H. Campbell, and S. Rajgopal. 2013. "Earnings quality: Evidence from the field," *Journal of Accounting and Economics* 56, pp. 1–33.

[5]Graham, J., H. Campbell, and S. Rajgopal, 2005, "The economic implications of corporate financial reporting," *Journal of Accounting and Economics* 40, pp. 3–73.

[6]McVay, S., 2006, "Earnings Management Using Classification Shifting: An Examination of Core Earnings and Special Items," *The Accounting Review* 81, pp. 501–531.

[7]Until recently, GAAP required events that were both unusual and infrequent to be classified as "extraordinary items" and reported net of tax after income from continuing operations. As part of the FASB's Simplification Initiative, Accounting Standards Update No. 2015-01 eliminated the extraordinary classification. International accounting standards also do not recognize the extraordinary classification.

What kind of items might be included in this category? Look closely at the partial income statements of The Hershey Company, the largest producer of chocolate in North America, presented in Illustration 4–5. Which items appear unusual? Certainly not net sales, cost of sales, or selling, marketing and administrative expenses. But what about "Goodwill and other intangible asset impairment charges" and "Business realignment charges"? Let's consider both.

Illustration 4–5

Partial Income Statement—The Hershey Company

Real World Financials

Income Statements (in part) ($ in thousands)	Year Ended	
	December 31, 2015	December 31, 2014
Net sales	$7,386,626	$7,421,768
Cost of sales	4,003,951	4,085,602
Selling, marketing and administrative expenses	1,969,308	1,898,284
Goodwill and other intangible asset impairment charges	280,802	15,900
Business realignment charges	94,806	29,721
Operating profit	$1,037,759	$1,392,261

FINANCIAL Reporting Case

Q1, p. 163

Restructuring costs include costs associated with shutdown or relocation of facilities or downsizing of operations.

GAAP requires that restructuring costs be recognized only in the period incurred.

RESTRUCTURING COSTS. It's not unusual for a company to reorganize its operations to attain greater efficiency. When this happens, the company often incurs significant associated restructuring costs (sometimes referred to as *reorganization costs* or *realignment costs*). Restructuring costs are associated with management's plans to materially change the scope of business operations or the manner in which they are conducted.[8] For example, facility closings and related employee layoffs translate into costs incurred for severance pay and relocation costs. The Hershey Company had restructuring costs related to reorganization of operations in Brazil to enhance distribution of the company's products, as well as employee severance costs related to eliminating several positions as part of the company's Productivity Initiative.

Restructuring costs are recognized in the period the exit or disposal cost obligation actually is incurred. Suppose, as part of a restructuring plan, employees to be terminated are offered various benefits but only if they complete a certain period of work for the company. In that case, a liability for termination benefits, and corresponding expense, should be accrued in the required period(s) of work. On the other hand, if future work by the employee is not required to receive the termination benefits, the liability and corresponding expense for benefits are recognized at the time the company communicates the arrangement to employees. Similarly, costs associated with closing facilities and relocating employees are recognized when goods or services associated with those activities are received.

Because it usually takes considerable time to sell or terminate a line of business, or to close a location or facility, many restructuring costs represent long-term liabilities. GAAP requires initial measurement of these liabilities to be at fair value, which often is determined as the present value of future estimated cash outflows. Companies also are required to provide many disclosures in the notes, including the years over which the restructuring is expected to take place.

Should restructuring costs be considered part of a company's permanent earnings stream?

Now that we understand the nature of restructuring costs, we can address the important question: Should financial statement users attempting to forecast future earnings consider these costs to be part of a company's permanent earnings stream, or are they unlikely to occur again? There is no easy answer. For example, Hershey has reported some amount of restructuring costs in each year from 2005-2015. Will the company incur these costs again in the near future? Probably. A recent survey reports that of the 500 companies surveyed, 40% included restructuring costs in their income statements.[9] The inference: a financial statement user must interpret restructuring charges in light of a company's past history and financial statement note disclosures which outline the plan and the period over which it will

[8]FASB ASC 420-10-20: Exit or Disposal Cost Obligations-Overall-Glossary (previously "Accounting for Costs Associated with Exit or Disposal Activities," *Statement of Financial Accounting Standards No. 146* (Norwalk, Conn.: FASB, 2002)).

[9]*U.S. GAAP Financial Statements-Best Practices in Presentation and Disclosure*-2013 (New York: AICPA, 2013).

take place. In general, the more frequently these sorts of unusual charges occur, the more appropriate it is that financial statement users include them in their estimation of the company's permanent earnings stream.[10]

OTHER UNUSUAL ITEMS. Two other expenses in Hershey's income statements that warrant additional scrutiny are *goodwill impairments* and *asset impairments.* Any long-lived asset, whether tangible or intangible, should have its balance reduced if there has been a significant impairment of value. We explore property, plant, and equipment and intangible assets in Chapters 10 and 11. After discussing this topic in more depth in those chapters, we revisit the concept of earnings quality as it relates to asset impairment.

These aren't the only components of operating expenses that call into question this issue of earnings quality. For example, in Chapter 9 we discuss the write-down of inventory that can occur with obsolete or damaged inventory. Other possibilities include losses from natural disasters such as earthquakes and floods and gains and losses from litigation settlements. Earnings quality also is influenced by the way a company records income from investments (Chapter 12) and accounts for its pension plans (Chapter 17).

Unusual items included in operating income require investigation to determine their permanent or temporary nature.

Earnings quality is affected by revenue issues as well. As an example, suppose that toward the end of its fiscal year, a company loses a major customer that can't be replaced. That would mean the current year's revenue number includes a component that will not occur again next year. Of course, in addition to its effect on revenues, losing the customer would have implications for certain related expenses and net income.

Another issue affecting earnings quality is the intentional misstatement of revenue. In 2014, the Securities and Exchange Commission (SEC) charged AgFeed Industries with reporting nonexistent revenues. The allegations include executives faking the sale of hogs that didn't really exist. These executives tried to hide their actions by saying the fake hogs died. Also, because larger hogs can be sold for higher prices, the executives inflated the weights of actual hogs sold, inflating sales revenues.

Companies also misstate revenue by accelerating the timing of its recognition. This happens when companies record revenue before actually performing its obligation to the customer. In 2014, the SEC alleged that Saba Software accelerated the timing of revenue by recognizing consulting revenue prior to actually providing those services to its clients. This manipulation was done to help the company achieve quarterly revenue targets. We explore additional issues of revenue recognition in Chapter 5. Now, though, let's discuss earnings quality issues related to *nonoperating* items.

Nonoperating Income and Earnings Quality

Most of the components of earnings in an income statement relate directly to the ordinary, continuing operations of the company. Some, though, such as interest and gains or losses on the sale of investments or property and equipment relate only tangentially to normal operations. We refer to these as nonoperating items. How should these items be interpreted in terms of their relationship to future earnings? Are these expenses likely to occur again next year? Investors need to understand that some of these items may recur, such as interest expense, while others are less likely to recur, such as gains and losses.

Gains and losses from the sale of assets typically relate only tangentially to normal operations.

Home Depot's partial income statement is shown in Illustration 4–6. There are two nonoperating amounts reported after operating income. The first one is "Interest and investment income" that primarily includes gains on the sale of investments in another company's stock. Because Home Depot's primary business includes selling home improvement products, sales of investments are not considered normal operations. Therefore, Home Depot reports these amounts as nonoperating items. Home Depot disclosed in the notes of its 2016 and 2015 reports that gains on the sale of investments were $144 million and $323 million, respectively. Once these investments are sold, their gains are not expected to continue into future profitability, so investors would not consider these gains to be a permanent component of profit. The remaining relatively minor amount in this nonoperating category comes from interest income.

[10]Arthur Levitt, Jr. "The Numbers Game," *The CPA Journal*, December 1998, p. 16.

Illustration 4–6

Income Statements (in part)—The Home Depot, Inc.

Real World Financials

Income Statements (in part)
($ in millions)

	Year Ended	
	January 31, 2016	**February 1, 2015**
Operating income	$11,774	$10,469
Interest and investment income	166	337
Interest expense	(919)	(830)
Income before taxes	$11,021	$ 9,976

Another large nonoperating item reported by most companies is interest expense. In its 2016 report, Home Depot reported $919 million in interest expense. The company also reported long-term debt of nearly $21 billion in the balance sheet. Because this long-term debt will not be repaid for several years, the company will have to pay interest for several years. Therefore, interest expense represents a type of nonoperating item that is expected by investors to be a more permanent component of future profitability.

Non-GAAP Earnings

Many companies voluntarily provide *non-GAAP earnings*—management's assessment of permanent earnings.

Companies are required to report earnings based on Generally Accepted Accounting Principles (GAAP). This number includes *all revenues and expenses.* Most companies, however, also voluntarily provide **non-GAAP earnings** when they announce annual or quarterly earnings. Non-GAAP earnings *exclude certain expenses* and sometimes certain revenues. Common expenses excluded are restructuring costs, acquisition costs, write-downs of impaired assets, and stock-based compensation. Supposedly, non-GAAP earnings are management's view of "permanent earnings," in the sense of being a better long-run measure of its company's performance.

Nearly all major companies report non-GAAP earnings. For example, Hewlett-Packard Company reported GAAP earnings in 2015 of $4.6 billion or $2.48 per share. At the same time, the company announced that its non-GAAP earnings for the year were $6.6 billion or $3.59 per share (nearly 50% higher than GAAP earnings). The difference in earnings numbers relates primarily to management excluding certain restructuring charges, amortization of intangible assets, and employee separation costs in the calculation of non-GAAP earnings.

Non-GAAP earnings are controversial.

Non-GAAP earnings are controversial because determining which expenses to exclude is at the discretion of management. By removing certain expenses from reported GAAP earnings, management has the potential to report misleadingly higher profits. In 2015, companies in the S&P 500 reported non-GAAP earnings that were 33% *higher* than GAAP earnings.[11] Some companies that reported non-GAAP profits actually had GAAP losses. The issue is: Do non-GAAP earnings represent management's true belief of core, long-term performance (so excluding certain temporary expenses is helpful to investors), or do non-GAAP earnings represent management's attempt to mislead investors into believing the company is more profitable than it actually is (and therefore harming investors)? Many are concerned that the latter is more likely.

The Sarbanes-Oxley Act requires reconciliation between non-GAAP earnings and earnings determined according to GAAP.

The Sarbanes-Oxley Act addressed non-GAAP earnings in its Section 401. One of the act's important provisions requires that if non-GAAP earnings are included in any periodic or other report filed with the SEC or in any public disclosure or press release, the company also must provide a reconciliation with earnings determined according to GAAP.[12]

We now turn our attention to discontinued operations, an item that is not part of a company's permanent earnings and, appropriately, is excluded from continuing operations.

[11]"S&P 500 Earnings: Far Worse Than Advertised," *Wall Street Journal* (February 24, 2016).

[12]The Congress of the United States of America, *The Sarbanes-Oxley Act of 2002,* Section 401 (b) (2), Washington, D.C., 2004.

Discontinued Operations

● LO4–4

Sometimes a company decides to discontinue (or sell) part of its business. For example, in 2015 Abbott Laboratories decided to sell its businesses related to developed markets branded generic pharmaceuticals and animal health. Obviously, profits from these discontinued operations *will not continue.* Because profits from these operations are considered to have a material effect[13] on the income statement, Abbott Laboratories reported them separately to allow statement users to focus on continuing operations. We saw in the introduction of this chapter how Abbott Laboratories reported discontinued operations separately, below income from continuing operations.

Although a company has considerable flexibility in reporting income from *continuing operations,* the presentation of discontinued operations is mandated as follows (using simple numbers to demonstrate the reporting):[14]

Income from continuing operations before income taxes	$1,000
Income tax expense (assuming 40%)	400
Income from continuing operations	600
Income from discontinued operations, **$100** net of **$40** tax expense	60
Net income	$ 660

FINANCIAL Reporting Case

Q2, p. 163

The objective of this format is to inform financial statements users of which components of net income are continuing. We do this by separately reporting income from continuing operations ($600) and income from discontinued operations ($60). All else the same, investors should not expect next year's net income to be $660, because only $600 of profits from this year are part of continuing operations.

Income from discontinued operations (and its tax effect) are reported separately.

Separate reporting includes taxes as well. The income tax expense associated with continuing operations ($400) is reported separately from the income tax of discontinued operations ($40). Also, in the case that there is a loss from discontinued operations, there would be an *income tax benefit* (instead of income tax expense); losses from discontinued operations are tax deductible and would reduce overall taxes owed, thereby providing a benefit. The process of associating income tax effects with the income statement components that create those effects is referred to as *intraperiod tax allocation,* something we discuss in depth in Chapter 16.

What are some examples of discontinued operations? Pfizer Inc. is a global biopharmaceutical company. In addition to its drug and consumer healthcare divisions, the company also operated a nutrition business prior to 2013 focusing primarily on infants. Late in 2012 the nutrition business was sold to Nestlé for $11.85 billion. In 2013 Campbell Soup Company sold its European simple meals business to Soppa Investments. Google sold its Motorola Mobility smartphone subsidiary to Lenovo for $2.9 billion in 2013. Pfizer's sale of its nutrition business, Campbell Soup's sale of its European simple meals business, and Google's sale of its smartphone subsidiary are examples of discontinued operations.

What Constitutes a Discontinued Operation?

Discontinued operations are reported when:

1. A *component of an entity* or group of components has been sold or disposed of, or is considered held for sale,
2. If the disposal represents a *strategic shift* that has, or will have, a major effect on a company's operations and financial results.[15]

[13]We discussed the concept of materiality in Chapter 1.

[14]The presentation of discontinued operations is the same for single-step and multiple-step income statement formats. The single-step versus multiple-step distinction applies to items included in income from continuing operations.

[15]A discontinued operation is also defined as business or nonprofit activity that is considered held for sale *when acquired* (FASB ASC 205-20-15-2). A business is a set of activities and assets that is managed for purposes of providing economic benefits to the company. A nonprofit activity is similar to a business but is not intended to provide goods and services to customers at a profit.

For the first item, a *component of an entity* includes activities and cash flows that can be clearly distinguished, operationally and for financial reporting purposes, from the rest of the company. A component could include an operating segment, a reporting unit, a subsidiary, or an asset group.[16]

For the second item, whether the disposal represents a *strategic shift* requires the judgment of company management. Examples of possible strategic shifts include the disposal of operations in a major geographical area, a major line of business, a major equity method investment,[17] or other major parts of the company.

As part of the continuing process to converge U.S. GAAP and international standards, the FASB and IASB have developed a common definition and a common set of disclosures for discontinued operations.[18]

Reporting Discontinued Operations

By definition, the income or loss stream from a discontinued operation no longer will continue. A financial statement user is more interested in the results of their operations that will continue. It is informative, then, for companies to separate the effects of the discontinued operations from the results of operations that will continue. For this reason, the revenues, expenses, gains, losses, and income tax related to a *discontinued* operation must be removed from *continuing* operations and reported separately *for all years presented.*

For example, even though Abbott Laboratories did not sell its generic pharmaceuticals and animal health businesses until 2015, it's important for comparative purposes to separate the effects for any prior years presented. This allows an apples-to-apples comparison of income from *continuing* operations. So, in its 2015 three-year comparative income statements, the 2014 and 2013 income statements reclassified income from generic pharmaceuticals and animal health businesses to income from discontinued operations. In addition, there was a disclosure note to inform readers that prior years were reclassified.[19]

Sometimes a discontinued component actually has been sold by the end of a reporting period. Often, though, the disposal transaction has not yet been completed as of the end of the reporting period. We consider these two possibilities next.

WHEN THE COMPONENT HAS BEEN SOLD. When the discontinued component is sold before the end of the reporting period, the reported income effects of a discontinued operation will include two elements.

1. Income or loss from operations (revenues, expenses, gains, and losses) of the component from the beginning of the reporting period *to the disposal date*
2. Gain or loss on disposal of the component's assets

The first element would consist primarily of income from daily operations of this discontinued component of the company. This would include typical revenues from sales to customers and ordinary expenses such as cost of goods sold, salaries, rent, and insurance. The second element includes gains and losses on the sale of assets, such as selling a building or office equipment of this discontinued component.

These two elements can be combined or reported separately, net of their tax effects. If combined, the gain or loss component must be indicated. In our illustrations to follow, we combine the income effects. Illustration 4–7 describes a situation in which the discontinued component is sold before the end of the reporting period.

Notice that an *income tax benefit* occurs because a *loss* reduces taxable income, saving the company $800,000 in taxes.

On the other hand, suppose Duluth's discontinued division had a pretax loss from operations of only $1,000,000 (and still had a gain on disposal of $3,000,000). In this case, the

---

[16]FASB ASC 205-20-20: Presentation of Financial Statements-Discontinued Operations-Glossary.

[17]Equity method investments are discussed in Chapter 12.

[18]"Noncurrent Assets Held for Sale and Discontinued Operations," *International Financial Reporting Standard No. 5* (IASCF), as amended effective January 1, 2016.

[19]The presentation of discontinued operations in comparative income statements enhances the qualitative characteristics of comparability and consistency. We discussed the concepts of comparability and consistency in Chapter 1.

Illustration 4–7

Discontinued Operations—Loss

In October 2018, management of Duluth Holding Company decided to sell one of its divisions that qualifies as a separate component according to generally accepted accounting principles. The division was sold on December 18, 2018. Consider the following facts related to the division:

1. From January 1 through disposal, the division had a pretax loss from operations of $5,000,000.
2. The assets of the division had a net selling price of $15,000,000 and book value of $12,000,000.

Duluth's income statement for 2018, beginning with after-tax income from continuing operations of $20,000,000, would be reported as follows (assuming a 40% tax rate):

Income from continuing operations		$ 20,000,000
Discontinued operations:		
Loss from operations of discontinued component (including gain on disposal of $3,000,000*)	$(2,000,000)†	
Income tax benefit	800,000‡	
Loss on discontinued operations		(1,200,000)
Net income		$18,800,000

*Net selling price of $15 million less book value of $12 million
†Loss from operations of $5 million less gain on disposal of $3 million
‡$2,000,000 × 40%

combined amount of $2,000,000 represents *income* from operations of the discontinued component, and the company would have an additional *income tax expense* of $800,000, as demonstrated below.

Income from continuing operations		$20,000,000
Discontinued operations:		
Income from operations of discontinued component (including gain on disposal of $3,000,000*)	$2,000,000†	
Income tax expense	(800,000)‡	
Income on discontinued operations		1,200,000
Net income		$21,200,000

*Net selling price of $15 million less book value of $12 million
†Loss from operations of $1 million plus gain on disposal of $3 million
‡$2,000,000 × 40%

Additional Consideration

For reporting discontinued operations in the income statement, some companies separate the income/loss from operations and the gain/loss on disposal. For example, in Illustration 4–7, Duluth Holding Company could have reported the $5,000,000 loss from operations separately from the $3,000,000 gain on disposal, with each shown net of their tax effects.

Income from continuing operations		$20,000,000
Discontinued operations:		
Loss from operations (net of tax benefit)	$(3,000,000)†	
Gain on disposal (net of tax expense)	1,800,000‡	
Loss on discontinued operations		(1,200,000)
Net income		$18,800,000

†$5,000,000 − ($5,000,000 × 40%)
‡$15,000,000 − $12,000,000 = $3,000,000; $3,000,000 − ($3,000,000 × 40%) = $1,800,000

(continued)

(concluded)

The amount of the loss on discontinued operations of $1,200,000 is the same with either presentation. In practice, most companies report on the face of the income statement a single net amount for discontinued operations, with a note disclosure providing details of the calculation.

Income from continuing operations	$20,000,000
Loss on discontinued operations, net of tax	(1,200,000)
Net income	$18,800,000

If a component to be discontinued has not yet been sold, its income effects, including any impairment loss, usually still are reported separately as discontinued operations.

WHEN THE COMPONENT IS CONSIDERED HELD FOR SALE. What if a company has decided to discontinue a component but, when the reporting period ends, the component has not yet been sold? If the situation indicates that the component is likely to be sold within a year, the component is considered "held for sale."[20] In that case, the income effects of the discontinued operation still are reported, but the two components of the reported amount are modified as follows:

1. Income or loss from operations (revenues, expenses, gains and losses) of the component from the beginning of the reporting period *to the end of the reporting period*
2. An impairment loss if the book value (sometimes called carrying value or carrying amount) of the assets of the component is more than fair value minus cost to sell

The two income elements can be combined or reported separately, net of their tax effects. In addition, if the amounts are combined and there is an impairment loss, the loss must be disclosed, either parenthetically on the face of the statement or in a disclosure note. Consider the example in Illustration 4–8.

Illustration 4–8

Discontinued Operations—Impairment Loss

In October 2018, management of Duluth Holding Company decided to sell one of its divisions that qualifies as a separate component according to generally accepted accounting principles. On December 31, 2018, the end of the company's fiscal year, **the division had not yet been sold.** Consider the following facts related to the division:

1. For the year, the division reported a pretax loss from operations of $5,000,000.
2. On December 31, assets of the division had a book value of $12,000,000 and a fair value, minus anticipated cost to sell, of $9,000,000.

Duluth's income statement for 2018, beginning with after-tax income from continuing operations of $20,000,000, would be reported as follows (assuming a 40% tax rate):

Income from continuing operations		$20,000,000
Discontinued operations:		
Loss from operations of discontinued component (including impairment loss of $3,000,000*)	$(8,000,000)†	
Income tax benefit	3,200,000‡	
Loss on discontinued operations		(4,800,000)
Net income		$15,200,000

*Book value of $12 million less fair value net of cost to sell of $9 million
†Loss from operations of $5 million plus impairment loss of $3 million
‡$8,000,000 × 40%

Also, the net-of-tax income or loss from operations of the component being discontinued is reported separately from continuing operations for any prior year that is presented for comparison purposes along with the 2018 income statement. Then, in the year of actual

[20]Six criteria are used to determine whether the component is likely to be sold and therefore considered "held for sale." You can find these criteria in FASB ASC 360-10-45-9: Property, Plant, and Equipment-Overall-Other Presentation Matters-Long-Lived Assets Classified as Held for Sale (previously "Accounting for the Impairment or Disposal of Long-Lived Assets," *Statement of Financial Accounting Standards No. 144* (Norwalk, Conn.: FASB, 2001), par. 30).

disposal, the discontinued operations section of the income statement will include the final gain or loss on the sale of the discontinued segment's assets. The gain or loss is determined relative to the revised book values of the assets after the impairment write-down.

Important information about discontinued operations, whether sold or held for sale, is reported in a disclosure note. The note provides additional details about the discontinued component, including its identity, its major classes of assets and liabilities, the major revenues and expenses constituting pretax income or loss from operations, the reason for the discontinuance, and the expected manner of disposition if held for sale.[21]

In Illustration 4–8, if the fair value of the division's assets minus cost to sell exceeded the book value of $12,000,000, there is no impairment loss and the income effects of the discontinued operation would include only the loss from operations of $5,000,000, less the income tax benefit.

The balance sheet is affected, too. The assets and liabilities of the component considered held for sale are reported at the lower of their book value or fair value minus cost to sell. And, because it's not in use, an asset classified as held for sale is no longer reported as part of property, plant, and equipment or intangible assets and is not depreciated or amortized.[22]

The sales of discontinued operations by Abbott Laboratories were completed by the end of 2015, but some assets and liabilities of the sold businesses had not yet been transferred. The 2015 year-end balance sheet reported $107 million in "Current assets held for disposition," and $373 million in "Current liabilities held for disposition." Information about the discontinued operations was included in the disclosure note shown in Illustration 4–9.

Illustration 4–9

Discontinued Operations Disclosure—Abbott Laboratories.

Real World Financials

NOTE 3—DISCONTINUED OPERATIONS (in part)

The following is a summary of the assets and liabilities held for disposition:

($ in millions)	December 31, 2015
Cash and Trade receivables, net	$ 54
Total inventories	43
Prepaid expenses and other receivables	8
Other assets	2
Current assets held for disposition	$107
Trade accounts payable	$359
Salaries, wages, commissions and other accrued liabilities	14
Current liabilities held for disposition	$373

Notice that the assets and liabilities held for sale are classified as *current* because the company expects to complete the transfer of these assets and liabilities in the next fiscal year.

INTERIM REPORTING. Remember that companies whose ownership shares are publicly traded in the United States must file quarterly reports with the Securities and Exchange Commission. If a component of an entity is considered held for sale at the end of a quarter, the income effects of the discontinued component must be separately reported in the quarterly income statement. These effects would include the income or loss from operations for the quarter as well as an impairment loss if the component's assets have a book value more than fair value minus cost to sell. If the assets are impaired and written down, any gain or loss on disposal in a subsequent quarter is determined relative to the new, written-down book value.

[21]For a complete list of disclosure requirements, see FASB ASC 205-20-50: Presentation of Financial Statements-Discontinued Operations-Disclosure.

[22]The assets and liabilities held for sale are not offset and presented as a single net amount, but instead are listed separately (ASC 205-20-45-10).

Accounting Changes

LO4–5

Accounting changes fall into one of three categories: (1) a change in an accounting principle, (2) a change in estimate, or (3) a change in reporting entity. The correction of an error is another adjustment that is accounted for in the same way as certain accounting changes. A brief overview of a change in accounting principle, a change in estimate, and correction of errors is provided here. We cover accounting changes, including changes in reporting entities, and accounting errors in detail in subsequent chapters, principally in Chapter 20.

Change in Accounting Principle

A change in accounting principle refers to a change from one acceptable accounting method to another. There are many situations that allow alternative treatments for similar transactions. Common examples of these situations include the choice among FIFO, LIFO, and average cost for the measurement of inventory and among alternative revenue recognition methods. New accounting standard updates issued by the FASB also may require companies to change their accounting methods.

MANDATED CHANGES IN ACCOUNTING PRINCIPLES. Sometimes the FASB requires a change in accounting principle. These changes in accounting principles potentially hamper the ability of external users to compare financial information among reporting periods because information lacks consistency. The board considers factors such as this, as well as the cost and complexity of adopting new standards, and chooses among various approaches to require implementation by companies.

1. **Retrospective approach.** The new standard is applied to all periods presented in the financial statements. That is, we restate prior period financial statements as if the new accounting method had been used in those prior periods. We revise the balance of each account affected to make those statements appear as if the newly adopted accounting method had been applied all along.
2. **Modified retrospective approach.** The new standard is applied to the adoption period only. Prior period financial statements are not restated. The cumulative effect of the change on prior periods' net income is shown as an adjustment to the beginning balance of retained earnings in the adoption period.
3. **Prospective approach.** This approach requires neither a modification of prior period financial statements nor an adjustment to account balances. Instead, the change is simply implemented in the current period and all future periods.

VOLUNTARY CHANGES IN ACCOUNTING PRINCIPLES. Occasionally, without being required by the FASB, a company will change from one generally accepted accounting principle to another. For example, a company may decide to change its inventory method from LIFO to FIFO. When this occurs, inventory and cost of goods sold are measured in one reporting period using LIFO, but then are measured using FIFO in a subsequent period. Inventory and cost of goods sold, and hence net income, for the two periods are not comparable. To improve comparability and consistency, GAAP typically requires that voluntary accounting changes be accounted for retrospectively.[23,24]

We will see these aspects of accounting for the change in accounting principle demonstrated in Chapter 9 in the context of our discussion of inventory methods. We'll also discuss changes in accounting principles in depth in Chapter 20.

[23]FASB ASC 250-10-45-5: Accounting Changes and Error Corrections-Overall-Other Presentation Matters (previously "Accounting Changes and Error Corrections-a replacement of APB Opinion No. 20 and FASB Statement No. 3," *Statement of Financial Accounting Standard No. 154* (Norwalk, Conn.: FASB, 2005)).

[24]Sometimes a lack of information makes it impracticable to report a change retrospectively so the new method is simply applied prospectively, that is, we simply use the new method from now on. Also, if a new standard specifically requires prospective accounting, that requirement is followed.

Change in Depreciation, Amortization, or Depletion Method

A change in depreciation, amortization, or depletion method is considered to be a change in accounting estimate that is achieved by a change in accounting principle. We account for this change prospectively, almost exactly as we would any other change in estimate. One difference is that most changes in estimate don't require a company to justify the change. However, this change in estimate is a result of changing an accounting principle and therefore requires a clear justification as to why the new method is preferable. Chapter 11 provides an illustration of a change in depreciation method.

Changes in depreciation, amortization, or depletion methods are accounted for the same way as a change in an accounting estimate.

Change in Accounting Estimate

Estimates are a necessary aspect of accounting. A few of the more common accounting estimates are the amount of future bad debts on existing accounts receivable, the useful life and residual value of a depreciable asset, and future warranty expenses.

A *change in accounting estimate* is reflected in the financial statements of the current period and future periods.

Because estimates require the prediction of future events, it's not unusual for them to turn out to be wrong. When an estimate is modified as new information comes to light, accounting for the change in estimate is quite straightforward. We do not revise prior years' financial statements to reflect the new estimate. Instead, we merely incorporate the new estimate in any related accounting determinations from that point on, that is, we account for a change in accounting estimate prospectively.[25] If the effect of the change is material, a disclosure note is needed to describe the change and its effect on both net income and earnings per share. Chapters 11 and 20 provide illustrations of changes in accounting estimates.

Correction of Accounting Errors

Errors occur when transactions are either recorded incorrectly or not recorded at all. We briefly discuss the correction of errors here as an overview and in later chapters in the context of the effect of errors on specific chapter topics. In addition, Chapter 20 provides comprehensive coverage of the correction of errors.

Accountants employ various control mechanisms to ensure that transactions are accounted for correctly. In spite of this, errors occur. When errors do occur, they can affect any one or several of the financial statement elements on any of the financial statements a company prepares. In fact, many kinds of errors simultaneously affect more than one financial statement. When errors are discovered, they should be corrected.

Most errors are discovered in the same year that they are made. These errors are simple to correct. The original erroneous journal entry is reversed and the appropriate entry is recorded. If an error is discovered in a year subsequent to the year the error is made, the accounting treatment depends on whether or not the error is material with respect to its effect on the financial statements. In practice, the vast majority of errors are not material and are, therefore, simply corrected in the year discovered. However, material errors that are discovered in subsequent periods require a prior period adjustment.

Prior Period Adjustments

Assume that after its financial statements are published and distributed to shareholders, Roush Distribution Company discovers a material error in the statements. What does it do? Roush must make a **prior period adjustment**.[26] Roush would record a journal entry that adjusts any balance sheet accounts to their appropriate levels and would account for the income effects of the error by increasing or decreasing the beginning retained earnings balance in a statement of shareholders' equity. Remember, net income in prior periods was closed to retained earnings so, by adjusting retained earnings, the prior period adjustment accounts for the error's effect on prior periods' net income.

[25] If the original estimate had been based on erroneous information or calculations or had not been made in good faith, the revision of that estimate would constitute the correction of an error (discussed in the next section).

[26] FASB ASC 250-10-45-23: Accounting Changes and Error Corrections-Overall-Other Presentation Matters (previously "Prior Period Adjustments," *Statement of Financial Accounting Standards No. 16* (Norwalk, Conn.: FASB, 1977)).

Simply reporting a corrected retained earnings amount might cause misunderstanding for someone familiar with the previously reported amount. Explicitly reporting a prior period adjustment in the statement of shareholders' equity (or statement of retained earnings if that's presented instead) highlights the adjustment and avoids this confusion.

In addition to reporting the prior period adjustment to retained earnings, previous years' financial statements that are incorrect as a result of the error are retrospectively restated to reflect the correction. Also, a disclosure note communicates the impact of the error on prior periods' net income.

Earnings per Share

We've discussed that the income statement reports a company's net income for the period. Net income is reported in total dollars (total dollars of revenues minus total dollars of expenses) and represents the total profits that the company has generated for *all shareholders* during the period. However, for individual decision making, investors want to know how much profit has been generated for *each shareholder*. To know this, we calculate **earnings per share (EPS)** to relate the amount of net income a company generates to the number of common shares outstanding.

EPS provides a convenient way for investors to link the company's profitability to the value of an individual share of ownership. The ratio of stock price per share to earnings per share (the PE ratio) is one of the most widely used financial metrics in the investment world. EPS also makes it easier to compare the performance of the company over time or with other companies. Larger companies may naturally have larger dollar amounts of net income, but they do not always generate more profit for each shareholder.

All corporations whose common stock is publicly traded must disclose EPS.

FINANCIAL Reporting Case

Q3, p. 163

U.S. GAAP requires that public companies report two specific calculations of EPS: (1) basic EPS and (2) diluted EPS. **Basic EPS** equals total net income (less any dividends to preferred shareholders) divided by the weighted-average number of common shares outstanding. Dividends to preferred shareholders are subtracted from net income in the numerator because those dividends are distributions of the company not available to common shareholders. The denominator is the weighted-average number of common shares outstanding, rather than the number of shares outstanding at the beginning or end of the period, because the goal is to relate performance for the period to the shares that were in place throughout that period. The number of common shares may change over the year from additional issuances or company buybacks, so a weighted average better reflects the number of shares outstanding for the period. The resulting EPS provides a measure of net income generated for each share of common stock during the period.

For example, suppose the Fetzer Corporation reported net income of $600,000 for its fiscal year ended December 31, 2018. Preferred stock dividends of $75,000 were declared during the year. Fetzer had one million shares of common stock outstanding at the beginning of the year and issued an additional one million shares on March 31, 2018. Basic EPS of $0.30 per share for 2018 is computed as follows:

$$\frac{\$600{,}000 - 75{,}000}{\underbrace{1{,}000{,}000}_{\text{Shares at Jan. 1}} + \underbrace{1{,}000{,}000\ (9/12)}_{\text{New shares}}} = \frac{\$525{,}000}{1{,}750{,}000} = \$0.30$$

Diluted EPS incorporates the dilutive effect of all *potential* common shares in the calculation of EPS. Dilution refers to the reduction in EPS that occurs as the number of common shares outstanding increases. Companies may have certain securities outstanding that could be converted into common shares, or they could have stock options outstanding that create additional common shares if the options were exercised. Because these items could cause the number of shares in the denominator to increase, they potentially decrease EPS. We devote a substantial portion of Chapter 19 to understanding these two measures of EPS. Here, we provide only an overview.

When the income statement includes discontinued operations, we report per-share amounts for both income (loss) from continuing operations and for net income (loss), as well as for the discontinued operations. We see this demonstrated for Abbott Laboratories in Illustration 4–10.

Abbott Laboratories
Statements of Earnings For the Year Ended December 31 (in part)

($ in millions, except per share amounts)	2015	2014
Income from continuing operations	$2,606	$1,721
Income from discontinued operations, net of tax	1,817	563
Net income	$4,423	$2,284
Earnings per common share—basic:		
Continuing operations	$ 1.73	$ 1.13
Discontinued operations	1.21	0.37
Net income	$ 2.94	$ 1.50
Earnings per common share—diluted:		
Continuing operations	$ 1.72	$ 1.12
Discontinued operations	1.20	0.37
Net income	$ 2.92	$ 1.49

Illustration 4–10

EPS Disclosures—Abbott Laboratories.

Real World Financials

Comprehensive Income

LO4–6

Comprehensive income is the total change in equity for a reporting period other than from transactions with owners.

Net income, as we have already discussed, includes all revenues, expenses, gains, and losses reported in the income statement. Comprehensive income provides a broader perspective of income and includes *all* revenues, expenses, gains, and losses for the period. In other words, comprehensive income includes net income plus other changes in shareholders' equity that do not represent transactions with owners. The relation between comprehensive income and net income is shown below:

Comprehensive income = Net income + Other comprehensive income

Accounting professionals have engaged in an ongoing debate concerning whether certain gains and losses should be included as components of net income or as part of other comprehensive income. As we discuss below and in later chapters, current standards allow some items initially to be recorded as other comprehensive income and then later reclassified into net income. However, there is *no conceptual basis* for determining which items qualify for net income versus other comprehensive income. The FASB addresses this distinction by requiring presentation of net income in the income statement and also the expanded concept of comprehensive income.

Other Comprehensive Income

Comprehensive income includes net income as well as other gains and losses that change shareholders' equity but are not included in traditional net income.

The calculation of net income omits certain types of gains, losses, and other adjustments that are instead included in other comprehensive income (OCI). As one example, in Chapter 12 you will learn that certain investments are reported in the balance sheet at their fair values, but that the gains and losses resulting from adjusting those investments to fair value might not be included in net income. Instead, they are reported as other comprehensive income (loss).

Companies must report both net income and comprehensive income and reconcile the difference between the two.[27] *Be sure to remember that net income actually is a part of comprehensive income.* The reconciliation simply extends net income to include other comprehensive income items, reported net of tax, as shown in Illustration 4–11.

Reporting comprehensive income can be accomplished with a single, continuous statement or in two separate, but consecutive statements.

Flexibility in Reporting

The information in the income statement and other comprehensive income items shown in Illustration 4–11 can be presented either (1) in a single, continuous statement of

[27]FASB ASC 220-10-45-1A and 1B: Comprehensive Income-Overall-Other Presentation Matters (previously "Reporting Comprehensive Income," *Statement of Financial Accounting Standards No. 130* (Norwalk, Conn.: FASB, 1997)).

Illustration 4–11
Comprehensive Income

		($ in millions)
Net income		$xxx
Other comprehensive income:		
Net unrealized holding gains (losses) on investments (net of tax)*	$x	
Gains (losses) from and amendments to postretirement benefit plans (net of tax)†	(x)	
Deferred gains (losses) from derivatives (net of tax)‡	(x)	
Foreign currency translation adjustment (net of tax)§	x	xx
Comprehensive income		$xxx

*Changes in the market value of certain investments (described in Chapter 12)
†Gains and losses due to revising assumptions or market returns differing from expectations and prior service cost from amending the plan (described in Chapter 17).
‡When a derivative designated as a cash flow hedge is adjusted to fair value, the gain or loss is deferred as a component of comprehensive income and included in earnings later, at the same time as earnings are affected by the hedged transaction (described in the Derivatives Appendix to the text).
§The amount could be an addition to or reduction in shareholders' equity. (This item is discussed elsewhere in your accounting curriculum.)

comprehensive income or (2) in two separate, but consecutive statements, an income statement and a statement of comprehensive income. Each component of other comprehensive income can be displayed net of tax, as in Illustration 4–11, or alternatively, before tax with one amount shown for the aggregate income tax expense (or benefit).[28]

Some companies choose to present comprehensive income in a single statement. On the other hand, in its financial statements, AstroNova, Inc., a manufacturer of a broad range of specialty technology products, chose to use the separate statement approach, as shown in Illustration 4–12.

Illustration 4–12
Comprehensive Income Presented as a Separate Statement—AstroNova, Inc.

Real World Financials

ASTRONOVA, INC.
Consolidated Statements of Comprehensive Income
For the Years Ended January 31

($ in thousands)	**2015**	**2014**
Net income	$4,662	$3,212
Other comprehensive income (loss), net of taxes		
Foreign currency translation adjustments	(866)	(14)
Unrealized gain (loss) on securities available for sale	(9)	17
Other comprehensive income	(875)	3
Comprehensive income	$3,787	$3,215

International Financial Reporting Standards

Comprehensive Income. Both U.S. GAAP and IFRS allow companies to report comprehensive income in either a single statement of comprehensive income or in two separate statements.

LO4–9

Other comprehensive income items are similar under the two sets of standards. However, an additional OCI item, *changes in revaluation surplus,* is possible under IFRS. In Chapter 11 you will learn that *IAS No. 16*[29] permits companies to value property, plant, and equipment at (1) cost less accumulated depreciation or (2) fair value (revaluation). *IAS No. 38*[30] provides a similar option for the valuation of intangible assets. U.S. GAAP prohibits revaluation.

If the revaluation option is chosen and fair value is higher than book value, the difference, changes in revaluation surplus, is reported as *other comprehensive income* and then accumulates in a revaluation surplus account in equity.

[28]GAAP does not require the reporting of comprehensive earnings per share.
[29]"Property, Plant and Equipment," *International Accounting Standard No. 16* (IASCF), as amended effective January 1, 2016.
[30]"Intangible Assets," *International Accounting Standard No. 38* (IASCF), as amended effective January 1, 2016.

Accumulated Other Comprehensive Income

In addition to reporting OCI that occurs in the current reporting period, we must also report these amounts on a cumulative basis in the balance sheet. This is consistent with the way we report net income for the period in the income statement and also report accumulated net income (that hasn't been distributed as dividends) in the balance sheet as retained earnings. Similarly, we report OCI for the period in the statement of comprehensive income and also report **accumulated other comprehensive income (AOCI)** in the balance sheet. This is demonstrated in Illustration 4–13 for AstroNova, Inc.

The cumulative total of OCI (or comprehensive loss) is reported as accumulated other comprehensive income (AOCI), an additional component of shareholders' equity that is displayed separately.

Illustration 4–13

Shareholders' Equity—AstroNova, Inc.

Real World Financials

ASTRONOVA, INC.
Consolidated Balance Sheets (in part)
For the Years ended January 31

($ in thousands)	2015	2014
Shareholders' equity:		
Common stock	477	465
Additional paid-in capital	43,589	41,235
Retained earnings	39,735	37,201
Treasury stock, at cost	(19,591)	(12,463)
Accumulated other comprehensive income	(699)	176
Total shareholders' equity	$ 63,511	$ 66,614

Supplementing information in Illustration 4–13 with numbers reported in Illustration 4–12 along with dividends declared by AstroNova, we can reconcile the changes in both retained earnings and AOCI:

($ in thousands)	Retained Earnings	Accumulated Other Comprehensive Income
Balance, 1/31/2014	$37,201	$ 176
Add: Net income	4,662	
Deduct: Dividends	(2,128)	
Other comprehensive income		(875)
Balance, 1/31/2015	$39,735	$(699)

To further understand the relationship between net income and other comprehensive income, consider the following example. Philips Corporation began the year with retained earnings of $700 million and accumulated other comprehensive income of $30 million. Let's also assume that net income for the year, before considering the gain discussed below, is $100 million, of which $40 million was distributed to shareholders as dividends. Now assume that Philips had a $10 million net-of-tax gain that was also reported in one of two ways:

1. As a gain in net income, or
2. As a gain in other comprehensive income.

Under the first alternative, the gain will be included in shareholders' equity through retained earnings.

($ in millions)	Retained Earnings	Accumulated Other Comprehensive Income
Beginning Balance	$700	$30
Net income ($100 + 10)	110	
Dividends	(40)	
Other comprehensive income		–0–
Ending Balance	$770	$30

$800

Under the second alternative, the net-of-tax gain of $10 million is reported as a component of *other comprehensive income (loss)*. The gain will be included in shareholders' equity through *accumulated other comprehensive income (loss)*, rather than retained earnings, as demonstrated below. The total of retained earnings and accumulated other comprehensive income is $800 million either way.

($ in millions)	Retained Earnings	Accumulated Other Comprehensive Income
Beginning Balance	$700	$30
Net income	100	
Dividends	(40)	
Other comprehensive income		10
Ending Balance	$760	$40

$800

Net income and comprehensive income are identical for an enterprise that has no other comprehensive income items. When this occurs for all years presented, a statement of comprehensive income is not required. Components of other comprehensive income are described in subsequent chapters.

Concept Review Exercise

INCOME STATEMENT PRESENTATION; COMPREHENSIVE INCOME

The Barrington Construction Company builds office buildings. It also owns and operates a chain of motels throughout the Northwest. On September 30, 2018, the company decided to sell the entire motel business for $40 million. The sale was completed on December 15, 2018. Income statement information for 2018 is provided below for the two components of the company.

	($ in millions)	
	Construction Component	Motel Component
Sales revenue	$450.0	$200.0
Operating expenses	226.0	210.0
Operating income	224.0	(10.0)
Other income (loss)*	16.0	(30.0)
Income (loss) before income taxes	240.0	(40.0)
Income tax expense (benefit)†	96.0	(16.0)
Net income (loss)	$144.0	$ (24.0)

*For the motel component, the entire Other income (loss) amount represents the loss on sale of assets of the component for $40 million when their book value was $70 million.
†A 40% tax rate applies to all items of income or loss.

In addition, in 2018 the company had pretax net unrealized holding gains on investment securities of $3 million and a positive foreign currency translation adjustment of $1 million.

Required:

1. Prepare a single, continuous 2018 statement of comprehensive income for the Barrington Construction Company including EPS disclosures. There were 100 million shares of common stock outstanding throughout 2018. The company had no potentially dilutive securities outstanding or stock options that could cause additional common shares. Use the multiple-step approach for the income statement portion of the statement.

2. Prepare a separate 2018 statement of comprehensive income.

Solution:

1. Prepare a single, continuous 2018 statement of comprehensive income.

BARRINGTON CONSTRUCTION COMPANY
Statement of Comprehensive Income
For the Year Ended December 31, 2018
($ in millions, except per share amounts)

Sales revenue		$450.0
Operating expenses		226.0
Operating income		224.0
Other income		16.0
Income from continuing operations before income taxes		240.0
Income tax expense		96.0
Income from continuing operations		144.0
Discontinued operations:		
Loss from operations of discontinued motel component (including loss on disposal of $30)	$(40)	
Income tax benefit	16	
Loss on discontinued operations		(24.0)
Net income		120.0
Other comprehensive income:		
Unrealized gains on investment securities, net of tax	1.8	
Foreign currency translation adjustment, net of tax	0.6	
Total other comprehensive income		2.4
Comprehensive income		$122.4
Earnings per share:		
Income from continuing operations		$ 1.44
Discontinued operations		(0.24)
Net income		$ 1.20

2. Prepare a separate 2018 statement of comprehensive income.

BARRINGTON CONSTRUCTION COMPANY
Statement of Comprehensive Income
For the Year Ended December 31, 2018
($ in millions)

Net income		$120.0
Other comprehensive income:		
Unrealized gains on investment securities, net of tax	$1.8	
Foreign currency translation adjustment, net of tax	0.6	
Total other comprehensive income		2.4
Comprehensive income		$122.4

Now that we have discussed the presentation and content of the income statement, we turn our attention to the statement of cash flows.

The Statement of Cash Flows

PART B

When a balance sheet and an income statement are presented, a statement of cash flows (SCF) is required for each income statement period.[31] The purpose of the SCF is to provide information about the cash receipts and cash disbursements of an enterprise. Similar to the income statement, it is a *change* statement, summarizing the transactions that affected cash during the period. The term *cash* in the statement of cash flows refers to the total of cash, cash

● LO4–7

A statement of cash flows is presented for each period for which an income statement is provided.

[31]FASB ASC 230-10-45: Statement of Cash Flows-Overall-Other Presentation Matters (previously "Statement of Cash Flows," *Statement of Financial Accounting Standards No. 95* (Norwalk, Conn.: FASB, 1987)).

equivalents, and restricted cash. Cash equivalents, discussed in Chapter 3, include highly liquid (easily converted to cash) investments such as Treasury bills. Chapter 21 is devoted exclusively to the SCF. A brief overview is provided here.

Usefulness of the Statement of Cash Flows

We discussed the difference between cash and accrual accounting in Chapter 1. It was pointed out and illustrated that over short periods of time, operating cash flows may not be indicative of the company's long-run cash-generating ability, and that accrual-based net income provides a more accurate prediction of future operating cash flows. Nevertheless, information about cash flows from operating activities, when combined with information about cash flows from other activities, can provide information helpful in assessing future profitability, liquidity, and long-term solvency. After all, a company must pay its debts with cash, not with income.

Of particular importance is the amount of cash generated from operating activities. In the long run, a company must be able to generate positive cash flow from activities related to selling its product or service. These activities must provide the necessary cash to pay debts, provide dividends to shareholders, and provide for future growth.

Classifying Cash Flows

LO4–8

A list of cash flows is more meaningful to investors and creditors if they can determine the type of transaction that gave rise to each cash flow. Toward this end, the statement of cash flows classifies all transactions affecting cash into one of three categories: (1) operating activities, (2) investing activities, and (3) financing activities.

Operating Activities

Operating activities **are inflows and outflows of cash related to the transactions entering into the determination of net operating income.**

The inflows and outflows of cash that result from activities reported in the income statement are classified as cash flows from operating activities. In other words, this classification of cash flows includes the elements of net income reported on a cash basis rather than an accrual basis.[32]

Cash inflows include cash received from the following:

1. Customers from the sale of goods or services
2. Interest and dividends from investments

These amounts may differ from sales and investment income reported in the income statement. For example, sales revenue measured on the accrual basis reflects revenue recognized during the period, not necessarily the cash actually collected. Revenue will not equal cash collected from customers if receivables from customers or deferred revenue changed during the period.

Cash outflows include cash paid for the following:

1. The purchase of inventory
2. Salaries, wages, and other operating expenses
3. Interest on debt
4. Income taxes

Likewise, these amounts may differ from the corresponding accrual expenses reported in the income statement. Expenses are reported when incurred, not necessarily when cash is actually paid for those expenses. Also, some revenues and expenses, like depreciation expense, don't affect cash at all and aren't included as cash outflows from operating activities.

The difference between the inflows and outflows is called *net cash flows from operating activities.* This is equivalent to net income if the income statement had been prepared on a cash basis rather than an accrual basis.

[32]Cash flows related to gains and losses from the sale of assets shown in the income statement are reported as investing activities in the SCF.

DIRECT AND INDIRECT METHODS OF REPORTING. Two generally accepted formats can be used to report operating activities, the direct method and the indirect method. Under the **direct method**, the cash effect of each operating activity is reported directly in the statement. For example, *cash received from customers* is reported as the cash effect of sales activities. Income statement transactions that have no cash flow effect, such as depreciation, are simply not reported.

By the *direct method*, the cash effect of each operating activity is reported directly in the SCF.

By the **indirect method**, on the other hand, we arrive at net cash flow from operating activities indirectly by starting with reported net income and working backwards to convert that amount to a cash basis. Two types of adjustments to net income are needed. First, components of net income that do not affect cash are reversed. That means that noncash revenues and gains are subtracted, while noncash expenses and losses are added. For example, depreciation expense does not reduce cash, but it is subtracted in the income statement. To reverse this, then, we add back depreciation expense to net income to arrive at the amount that we would have had if depreciation had not been subtracted in the first place.

By the *indirect method*, cash flow from operating activities is derived indirectly by starting with reported net income and adding or subtracting items to convert that amount to a cash basis.

Second, we make adjustments for changes in operating assets and liabilities during the period that indicate that amounts included as components of net income are not the same as cash flows for those components. For instance, suppose accounts receivable increases during the period because cash collected from customers is less than sales revenue. This increase in accounts receivable would then be subtracted from net income to arrive at *cash flow from operating activities.* In the indirect method, positive adjustments to net income are made for decreases in related assets and increases in related liabilities, while negative adjustments are made for increases in those assets and decreases in those liabilities.

To contrast the direct and indirect methods further, consider the income statement and balance sheet for Arlington Lawn Care (ALC) in Illustration 4–14. We'll use these to construct the operating activities section of the statement of cash flows.

DIRECT METHOD. Let's begin with the direct method of presentation. We illustrated this method previously in Chapter 2. In that chapter, specific cash transactions were provided and we simply included them in the appropriate cash flow category in the SCF. Here, we start with account balances, so the direct method requires a bit more reasoning.

From the income statement, we see that ALC's net income has four components. Three of those—service revenue, general and administrative expenses, and income tax expense—affect cash flows, but not by the accrual amounts reported in the income statement. One component—depreciation—reduces net income but not cash; it's simply an allocation over time of a prior year's expenditure for a depreciable asset. So, to report these operating activities on a cash basis, rather than an accrual basis, we take the three items that affect cash and adjust the amounts to reflect cash inflow rather than revenue earned and cash outflows rather than expenses incurred. Let's start with service revenue.

Service revenue is $90,000, but ALC did not collect that much cash from its customers. We know that because accounts receivable increased from $0 to $12,000, ALC must have collected to date only $78,000 of the amount earned.

Accounts receivable			
Beg. bal.	0		
Revenue	90		
		78	Cash
End bal.	12		

Similarly, general and administrative expenses of $32,000 were incurred, but $7,000 of that hasn't yet been paid. We know that because accounts payable increased by $7,000. Also, prepaid insurance increased by $4,000 so ALC must have paid $4,000 more cash for insurance coverage than the amount that expired and was reported as insurance expense. That means cash paid thus far for general and administrative expenses was only $29,000 ($32,000 less the $7,000 increase in accounts payable plus the $4,000 increase in prepaid insurance). The other expense, income tax, was $15,000, but that's the amount by which income taxes payable increased so no cash has yet been paid for income taxes.

We can report ALC's cash flows from operating activities using the direct method as shown in Illustration 4–14A.

INDIRECT METHOD. To report operating cash flows using the indirect method, we take a different approach. We start with ALC's net income but realize that the $35,000 includes both cash and noncash components. We need to adjust net income, then, to eliminate the noncash effects so that we're left with only the cash flows. We start by eliminating the only noncash component of net income in our illustration—depreciation expense. Depreciation

Depreciation expense does not reduce cash, but is subtracted in the income statement. So, we add back depreciation expense to net income to eliminate it.

Illustration 4–14
Contrasting the Direct and Indirect Methods of Presenting Cash Flows from Operating Activities

Arlington Lawn Care (ALC) began operations at the beginning of 2018. ALC's 2018 income statement and its year-end balance sheet are shown below ($ in thousands).

Net income is $35,000, but cash flow from these same activities is not necessarily the same amount.

ARLINGTON LAWN CARE
Income Statement
For the Year Ended December 31, 2018

Service revenue		$90
Operating expenses:		
General and administrative	$32*	
Depreciation	8	
Total operating expenses		40
Income before income taxes		50
Income tax expense		15
Net income		$35

*Includes $6 in insurance expense

Changes in assets and liabilities can indicate that cash inflows are different from revenues and cash outflows are different from expenses.

ARLINGTON LAWN CARE
Balance Sheet
At December 31, 2018

Assets		Liabilities and Shareholders' Equity	
Current assets:		Current liabilities:	
Cash	$ 54	Accounts payable**	$ 7
Accounts receivable	12	Income taxes payable	15
Prepaid insurance	4	Total current liabilities	22
Total current assets	70	Shareholders' equity:	
Equipment	40	Common stock	50
Less: Accumulated depreciation	(8)	Retained earnings	30†
Total assets	$102	Total liabilities and shareholders' equity	$102

**For general and administrative expenses
†Net income of $35 less $5 in cash dividends paid

Illustration 4–14A
Direct Method of Presenting Cash Flows from Operating Activities

By the direct method, we report the components of net income on a cash basis.

ARLINGTON LAWN CARE
Statement of Cash Flows
For the Year Ended December 31, 2018

	($ in thousands)
Cash Flows from Operating Activities	
Cash received from customers*	$78
Cash paid for general and administrative expenses**	(29)
Net cash flows from operating activities	$49

*Service revenue of $90 thousand, less increase of $12 thousand in accounts receivable.
**General and administrative expenses of $32 thousand, less increase of $7 thousand in accounts payable, plus increase of $4 thousand in prepaid insurance.

of $8,000 was subtracted in the income statement, so to eliminate its negative effect on net income, we simply add it back.

We make adjustments for changes in assets and liabilities that indicate that components of net income are not the same as cash flows.

That leaves us with three components of net income that do affect cash but not necessarily by the amounts reported—service revenue, general and administrative expenses, and income tax expense. For those, we need to make adjustments to net income to cause it to reflect cash flows rather than accrual amounts. For instance, we saw earlier that even though $90,000 in service revenue is reflected in net income, only $78,000 cash was received from customers. That means we need to include an adjustment to reduce net income by $12,000, the increase in accounts receivable.

In a similar manner, we include adjustments for the changes in prepaid insurance, accounts payable, and income tax payable to adjust net income to reflect cash payments rather than expenses incurred. For prepaid insurance, because insurance expense in the income statement was less than cash paid for insurance, we need to subtract the difference, which equals the increase in prepaid insurance. If this asset had decreased, we would have added, rather than subtracted, the change. For accounts payable and taxes payable, because the related expense in the income statement was more than cash paid for those expenses, we need to add back the differences. If these liabilities had decreased, we would have subtracted, rather than added, the changes.

Cash flows from operating activities using the indirect method are shown in Illustration 4–14B.

ARLINGTON LAWN CARE
Statement of Cash Flows
For the Year Ended December 31, 2018

		($ in thousands)
Cash Flows from Operating Activities		
Net income		$35
Adjustments for noncash effects:		
Depreciation expense	$ 8	
Changes in operating assets and liabilities:		
Increase in accounts receivable	(12)	
Increase in prepaid insurance	(4)	
Increase in accounts payable	7	
Increase in income taxes payable	15	14
Net cash flows from operating activities		$49

Illustration 4–14B
Indirect Method of Presenting Cash Flows from Operating Activities

By the indirect method, we start with net income and work backwards to convert that amount to a cash basis.

Both the direct and the indirect methods produce the same net cash flows from operating activities ($49,000 in our illustration); they are merely alternative approaches to reporting the cash flows. The FASB, in promulgating GAAP for the statement of cash flows, stated its preference for the direct method. However, nearly all U.S. companies use the indirect method.

The choice of presentation method for cash flow from operating activities has no effect on how investing activities and financing activities are reported. We now look at how cash flows are classified into those two categories.

Investing Activities

Cash flows from **investing activities** include inflows and outflows of cash related to the acquisition and disposition of long-lived assets used in the operations of the business (such as property, plant, and equipment) and investment assets (except those classified as cash equivalents and trading securities). The purchase and sale of inventories are not considered investing activities. Inventories are purchased for the purpose of being sold as part of the company's operations, so their purchase and sale are included with operating activities rather than investing activities.

Investing activities involve the acquisition and sale of (1) long-term assets used in the business and (2) nonoperating investment assets.

Cash outflows from investing activities include cash paid for the following:

1. The purchase of long-lived assets used in the business
2. The purchase of investment securities like stocks and bonds of other entities (other than those classified as cash equivalents and trading securities)
3. Loans to other entities

Later, when the assets are disposed of, cash inflow from the sale of the assets (or collection of loans and notes) also is reported as cash flows from investing activities. As a result, cash inflows from these transactions are considered investing activities as follows:

1. The sale of long-lived assets used in the business

2. The sale of investment securities (other than cash equivalents and trading securities)
3. The collection of a nontrade receivable (excluding the collection of interest, which is an operating activity)

Net cash flows from investing activities represents the difference between the inflows and outflows. The only investing activity indicated in Illustration 4–14 is ALC's investment of $40,000 cash for equipment.

Financing Activities

Financing activities involve cash inflows and outflows from transactions with creditors (excluding trade creditors) and owners.

Financing activities relate to the external financing of the company. Cash inflows occur when cash is borrowed from creditors or invested by owners. Cash outflows occur when cash is paid back to creditors or distributed to owners. The payment of interest to a creditor, however, is classified as an operating activity.

Cash inflows include cash received from the following:

1. Owners when shares are sold to them
2. Creditors when cash is borrowed through notes, loans, mortgages, and bonds

Cash outflows include cash paid to the following:

1. Owners in the form of dividends or other distributions
2. Owners for the reacquisition of shares previously sold
3. Creditors as repayment of the principal amounts of debt (excluding trade payables that relate to operating activities)

Net cash flows from financing activities is the difference between the inflows and outflows. The only financing activities indicated in Illustration 4–14 are ALC's receipt of $50,000 cash from issuing common stock and the payment of $5,000 in cash dividends.

The 2018 statement of cash flows for ALC, beginning with net cash flows from operating activities, is shown in Illustration 4–15.

Illustration 4–15

Statement of Cash Flows (beginning with net cash flows from operating activities)

ARLINGTON LAWN CARE
Statement of Cash Flows (in part)
For the Year Ended December 31, 2018

		($ in thousands)
Net cash flows from operating activities (from Illustration 4–14A or 4–14B)		$49
Cash flows from investing activities:		
Purchase of equipment		(40)
Cash flows from financing activities:		
Sale of common stock	$50	
Payment of cash dividends	(5)	
Net cash flows from financing activities		45
Net increase in cash		54
Cash balance, January 1		0
Cash balance, December 31		$54

We know $40,000 was paid to buy equipment because that balance sheet account increased from no balance to $40,000. Likewise, because common stock increased from zero to $50,000, we include that amount as a cash inflow from financing activities. Finally, Illustration 4–14 told us that $5,000 was paid as a cash dividend, also a financing activity.

Noncash Investing and Financing Activities

As we just discussed, the statement of cash flows provides useful information about the investing and financing activities in which a company is engaged. Even though these

International Financial Reporting Standards

LO4–9

Classification of Cash Flows. Like U.S. GAAP, international standards also require a statement of cash flows. Consistent with U.S. GAAP, cash flows are classified as operating, investing, or financing. However, the U.S. standard designates cash outflows for interest payments and cash inflows from interest and dividends received as operating cash flows. Dividends paid to shareholders are classified as financing cash flows.

IAS No. 7,[33] on the other hand, allows more flexibility. Companies can report interest and dividends paid as either operating or financing cash flows and interest and dividends received as either operating or investing cash flows. Interest and dividend payments usually are reported as financing activities. Interest and dividends received normally are classified as investing activities.

Typical Classification of Cash Flows from Interest and Dividends

U.S. GAAP	IFRS
Operating Activities	*Operating Activities*
Dividends received	
Interest received	
Interest paid	
Investing Activities	*Investing Activities*
	Dividends received
	Interest received
Financing Activities	*Financing Activities*
Dividends paid	Dividends paid
	Interest paid

Siemens AG, a German company, prepares its financial statements according to IFRS. In its statement of cash flows for the first three months of the 2014 fiscal year, the company reported interest and dividends received as operating cash flows, as would a U.S. company. However, Siemens classified interest paid as a financing cash flow.

SIEMENS AG
Statement of Cash Flows (partial)
For the First Three Months of Fiscal 2014

	(€ in millions)
Cash flows from financing activities:	
Transactions with owners	(6)
Repayment of long-term debt	(5)
Change in short-term debt and other financing activities	1,138
Interest paid	(78)
Dividends paid	(4)
Financing discontinued operations	(107)
Cash flows from financing activities—continuing operations	938

primarily result in cash inflows and cash outflows, there may be significant investing and financing activities occurring during the period that do not involve cash flows at all. In order to provide complete information about these activities, any significant noncash investing and financing activities (that is, noncash exchanges) are reported either on the face of the SCF or in a disclosure note. An example of a significant noncash investing and financing activity is the acquisition of equipment (an investing activity) by issuing either a long-term note payable or equity securities (a financing activity).

[33]"Statement of Cash Flows," *International Accounting Standard No. 7* (IASCF), as amended effective January 1, 2016.

Concept Review Exercise

STATEMENT OF CASH FLOWS

Dublin Enterprises, Inc. (DEI), owns a chain of retail electronics stores located in shopping malls. The following are the company's 2018 income statement and comparative balance sheets ($ in millions):

Income Statement
For the Year Ended December 31, 2018

Revenue		$2,100
Cost of goods sold		1,400
Gross profit		700
Operating expenses:		
Selling and administrative	$ 355	
Depreciation	85	
Total operating expenses		440
Income before income taxes		260
Income tax expense		78
Net income		$ 182

Comparative Balance Sheets	**12/31/2018**	**12/31/2017**
Assets:		
Cash	$ 300	$ 220
Accounts receivable (net)	227	240
Inventory	160	120
Property, plant, and equipment	960	800
Less: Accumulated depreciation	(405)	(320)
Total assets	$1,242	$1,060
Liabilities and shareholders' equity:		
Accounts payable	$ 145	$ 130
Payables for selling and admin. expenses	147	170
Income taxes payable	95	50
Long-term debt	–0–	100
Common stock	463	400
Retained earnings	392	210
Total liabilities and shareholders' equity	$1,242	$1,060

Required:

1. Prepare DEI's 2018 statement of cash flows using the direct method.
2. Prepare the cash flows from operating activities section of DEI's 2018 statement of cash flows using the indirect method.

Solution:

1. Prepare DEI's 2018 statement of cash flows using the direct method.

DUBLIN ENTERPRISES, INC.
Statement of Cash Flows
For the Year Ended December 31, 2018
($ in millions)

Cash Flows from Operating Activities		
Collections from customers*	$ 2,113	
Purchase of inventory**	(1,425)	
Payment of selling and administrative expenses†	(378)	
Payment of income taxes‡	(33)	
Net cash flows from operating activities		$277
Cash Flows from Investing Activities		
Purchase of property, plant, and equipment		(160)

*Sales revenue of $2,100 million, plus $13 million decrease in accounts receivable (net).
**Cost of goods sold of $1,400 million, plus $40 million increase in inventory, less $15 million increase in accounts payable.
†Selling and administrative expenses of $355 million, plus $23 million decrease in payables for selling and administrative expenses.
‡Income tax expense of $78 million, less $45 million increase in income taxes payable.

(continued)

(concluded)

Cash Flows from Financing Activities		
Issuance of common stock	63	
Payment on long-term debt	(100)	
Net cash flows from financing activities		(37)
Net increase in cash		80
Cash, January 1		220
Cash, December 31		$300

2. Prepare the cash flows from operating activities section of DEI's 2018 statement of cash flows using the indirect method.

DUBLIN ENTERPRISES, INC.
Statement of Cash Flows
For the Year Ended December 31, 2018
($ in millions)

Cash Flows from Operating Activities		
Net income	$182	
Adjustments for noncash effects:		
Depreciation expense	85	
Changes in operating assets and liabilities:		
Decrease in accounts receivable (net)	13	
Increase in inventory	(40)	
Increase in accounts payable	15	
Increase in income taxes payable	45	
Decrease in payables for selling and administrative expenses	(23)	
Net cash flows from operating activities		$277

Profitability Analysis

PART C

● LO4–10

Chapter 3 provided an overview of financial statement analysis and introduced some of the common ratios used in risk analysis to investigate a company's liquidity and long-term solvency. We now look at ratios related to profitability analysis.

Activity Ratios

Activity ratios measure a company's efficiency in managing its assets.

One key to profitability is how well a company manages and utilizes its assets. Some ratios are designed to evaluate a company's effectiveness in managing assets. Of particular interest are the activity, or turnover ratios, of certain assets. The greater the number of times an asset turns over—the higher the ratio—the fewer assets are required to maintain a given level of activity (revenue). Therefore, high turnovers usually are preferred.

Although, in concept, the activity or turnover can be measured for any asset, activity ratios are most frequently calculated for total assets, accounts receivable, and inventory. These ratios are calculated as follows:

$$\text{Asset turnover ratio} = \frac{\text{Net sales}}{\text{Average total assets}}$$

$$\text{Receivables turnover ratio} = \frac{\text{Net sales}}{\text{Average accounts receivable (net)}}$$

$$\text{Inventory turnover ratio} = \frac{\text{Cost of goods sold}}{\text{Average inventory}}$$

The *asset turnover ratio* measures a company's efficiency in using assets to generate revenue.

ASSET TURNOVER A broad measure of asset efficiency is the asset turnover ratio. The ratio is computed by dividing a company's net sales by the average total assets available for use during a period. The denominator, average assets, is determined by adding beginning and ending total assets and dividing by two. The asset turnover ratio provides an indication of how efficiently a company utilizes all of its assets to generate revenue.

The *receivables turnover ratio* offers an indication of how quickly a company is able to collect its accounts receivable.

RECEIVABLES TURNOVER. The receivables turnover ratio is calculated by dividing a period's net credit sales by the average net accounts receivable. Because income statements seldom distinguish between cash sales and credit sales, this ratio usually is computed using total net sales as the numerator. The denominator, average accounts receivable, is determined by adding beginning and ending net accounts receivable (gross accounts receivable less allowance for uncollectible accounts) and dividing by two.[34]

The receivables turnover ratio provides an indication of a company's efficiency in collecting cash from customers. The ratio shows the number of times during a period that the average accounts receivable balance is collected. The higher the ratio, the shorter the average time between sales and cash collection.

The *average collection period* indicates the average age of accounts receivable.

A convenient extension is the average collection period. This measure is computed by dividing 365 days by the receivables turnover ratio. The result is an approximation of the number of days the average accounts receivable balance is outstanding.

$$\text{Average collection period} = \frac{365}{\text{Receivables turnover ratio}}$$

Monitoring the receivables turnover ratio (and average collection period) over time can provide useful information about a company's future prospects. For example, a decline in the receivables turnover ratio (an increase in the average collection period) could be an indication that sales are declining because of customer dissatisfaction with the company's products. Another possible explanation is that the company has changed its credit policy and is granting extended credit terms in order to maintain customers. Either explanation could signal a future increase in bad debts. Ratio analysis does not explain what is wrong. It does provide information that highlights areas for further investigation. We cover additional details of the receivables turnover ratio and average collection period in Chapter 7.

The *inventory turnover ratio* measures a company's efficiency in managing its investment in inventory.

INVENTORY TURNOVER. An important activity measure for a merchandising company (a retail, wholesale, or manufacturing company) is the inventory turnover ratio. The ratio shows the number of times the average inventory balance is sold during a reporting period. It indicates how quickly inventory is sold. The more frequently a business is able to sell, or turn over, its inventory, the lower its investment in inventory must be for a given level of sales. The ratio is computed by dividing the period's cost of goods sold by the average inventory balance. The denominator, average inventory, is determined by adding beginning and ending inventory and dividing by two.[35]

A relatively high ratio, say compared to a competitor, usually is desirable. A high ratio indicates comparative strength, perhaps caused by a company's superior sales force or maybe a successful advertising campaign. However, it might also be caused by a relatively low inventory level, which could mean either very efficient inventory management or stockouts and lost sales in the future.

On the other hand, a relatively low ratio, or a decrease in the ratio over time, usually is perceived to be unfavorable. Too much capital may be tied up in inventory. A relatively low ratio may result from overstocking, the presence of obsolete items, or poor marketing and sales efforts.

Similar to the receivables turnover, we can divide the inventory turnover ratio into 365 days to compute the average days in inventory. This measure indicates the number of days it normally takes to sell inventory.

$$\text{Average days in inventory} = \frac{365}{\text{Inventory turnover ratio}}$$

[34]Although net accounts receivable typically is used in practice for the denominator of receivables turnover, some prefer to use gross accounts receivable. Why? As the allowance for bad debts increases, net accounts receivable decreases, so if net accounts receivable is in the denominator, more bad debts have the effect of decreasing the denominator and therefore increasing receivables turnover. All else equal, an analyst would rather see receivables turnover improve because of more sales or less gross receivables, and not because of an increase in the allowance for bad debts.

[35]Notice the consistency in the measure used for the numerator and denominator of the two turnover ratios. For the receivables turnover ratio, both numerator and denominator are based on sales dollars, whereas they are both based on cost for the inventory turnover ratio.

Profitability Ratios

A fundamental element of an analyst's task is to develop an understanding of a firm's profitability. Profitability ratios attempt to measure a company's ability to earn an adequate return relative to sales or resources devoted to operations. Resources devoted to operations can be defined as total assets or only those assets provided by owners, depending on the evaluation objective.

Profitability ratios assist in evaluating various aspects of a company's profit-making activities.

Three common profitability measures are (1) the profit margin on sales, (2) the return on assets, and (3) the return on shareholders' equity. These ratios are calculated as follows:

$$\text{Profit margin on sales} = \frac{\text{Net income}}{\text{Net sales}}$$

$$\text{Return on assets} = \frac{\text{Net income}}{\text{Average total assets}}$$

$$\text{Return on shareholders' equity} = \frac{\text{Net income}}{\text{Average shareholders' equity}}$$

Notice that for all of the profitability ratios, our numerator is net income. Recall our discussion earlier in this chapter on earnings quality. The relevance of any historical-based financial statement hinges on its predictive value. To enhance predictive value, analysts often adjust net income in these ratios to separate a company's *temporary earnings* from its *permanent earnings.* Analysts begin their assessment of permanent earnings with income from continuing operations. Then, adjustments are made for any unusual, one-time gains or losses included in income from continuing operations. It is this adjusted number that they use as the numerator in these ratios.

When calculating profitability ratios, analysts often adjust net income for any temporary income effects.

PROFIT MARGIN ON SALES. The profit margin on sales is simply net income divided by net sales. The ratio measures an important dimension of a company's profitability. It indicates the portion of each dollar of revenue that is available after all expenses have been covered. It offers a measure of the company's ability to withstand either higher expenses or lower revenues.

The *profit margin on sales* measures the amount of net income achieved per sales dollar.

What is considered to be a desirable profit margin is highly sensitive to the nature of the business activity. For instance, you would expect a specialty shop to have a higher profit margin than, say, Walmart. A low profit margin can be compensated for by a high asset turnover rate, and vice versa, which brings us to considering the trade-offs inherent in generating return on assets.

RETURN ON ASSETS. The return on assets (ROA) ratio expresses income as a percentage of the average total assets available to generate that income. Because total assets are partially financed with debt and partially by equity funds, this is an inclusive way of measuring earning power that ignores specific sources of financing.

A company's return on assets is related to both profit margin and asset turnover. Specifically, profitability can be achieved by either a high profit margin, high asset turnover, or a combination of the two. In fact, the return on assets can be calculated by multiplying the profit margin and the asset turnover.

Profit margin and asset turnover combine to yield *return on assets*, which measures the return generated by a company's assets.

$$\textbf{Return on assets} = \textbf{Profit margin} \times \textbf{Asset turnover}$$

$$\frac{\text{Net income}}{\text{Average total assets}} = \frac{\text{Net income}}{\text{Net sales}} \times \frac{\text{Net sales}}{\text{Average total assets}}$$

Industry standards are particularly important when evaluating asset turnover and profit margin. Some industries are characterized by low turnover but typically make up for it with higher profit margins. Others have low profit margins but compensate with high turnover. Grocery stores typically have relatively low profit margins but relatively high asset turnover. In comparison, a manufacturer of specialized equipment will have a higher profit margin but a lower asset turnover ratio.

Additional Consideration

The return on assets ratio often is computed as follows:

$$\text{Return on assets} = \frac{\text{Net income} + \text{Interest expense } (1 - \text{Tax rate})}{\text{Average total assets}}$$

The reason for adding back interest expense (net of tax) is that interest represents a return to suppliers of debt capital and should not be deducted in the computation of net income when computing the return on total assets. In other words, the numerator is the total amount of income available to both debt and equity capital.

The *return on shareholders' equity* measures the return to suppliers of equity capital.

The DuPont framework shows that return on equity depends on profitability, activity, and financial leverage.

RETURN ON SHAREHOLDERS' EQUITY. Equity investors typically are concerned about the amount of profit that management can generate from the resources that owners provide. A closely watched measure that captures this concern is **return on equity (ROE)**, calculated by dividing net income by average shareholders' equity.

In addition to monitoring return on equity, investors want to understand how that return can be improved. The **DuPont framework** provides a convenient basis for analysis that breaks return on equity into three key components:[36]

- **Profitability,** measured by the profit margin (Net income ÷ Sales). As discussed already, a higher profit margin indicates that a company generates more profit from each dollar of sales.
- **Activity,** measured by asset turnover (Sales ÷ Average total assets). As discussed already, higher asset turnover indicates that a company uses its assets efficiently to generate more sales from each dollar of assets.
- **Financial Leverage,** measured by the equity multiplier (Average total assets ÷ Average total equity). A high equity multiplier indicates that relatively more of the company's assets have been financed with debt; that is, the company is more leveraged. As discussed in Chapter 3, leverage can provide additional return to the company's equity holders.

In equation form, the DuPont framework looks like this:

$$\textbf{Return on equity} = \textbf{Profit margin} \times \textbf{Asset turnover} \times \textbf{Equity multiplier}$$

$$\frac{\text{Net income}}{\text{Avg. total equity}} = \frac{\text{Net income}}{\text{Net sales}} \times \frac{\text{Net sales}}{\text{Avg. total assets}} \times \frac{\text{Avg. total assets}}{\text{Avg. total equity}}$$

Notice that net sales and average total assets appear in the numerator of one ratio and the denominator of another, so they cancel to yield net income ÷ average total equity, or ROE.

We have already seen that ROA is determined by profit margin and asset turnover, so another way to compute ROE is by multiplying ROA by the equity multiplier:

$$\textbf{Return on equity} = \textbf{Return on assets} \times \textbf{Equity multiplier}$$

$$\frac{\text{Net income}}{\text{Avg. total equity}} = \frac{\text{Net income}}{\text{Avg. total assets}} \times \frac{\text{Avg. total assets}}{\text{Avg. total equity}}$$

We can see from this equation that an equity multiplier of greater than 1 will produce a return on equity that is higher than the return on assets. However, as with all ratio analysis, there are trade-offs. If leverage is too high, creditors become concerned about the potential for default on the company's debt and require higher interest rates. Because interest is recognized as an expense, net income is reduced, so at some point the benefits of a higher equity multiplier are offset by a lower profit margin. Part of the challenge of managing a

[36]DuPont analysis is so named because the basic model was developed by F. Donaldson Brown, an electrical engineer who worked for DuPont in the early part of the twentieth century.

Additional Consideration

Sometimes when return on equity is calculated, shareholders' equity is viewed more narrowly to include only common shareholders. In that case, preferred stock is excluded from the denominator, and preferred dividends are deducted from net income in the numerator. The resulting rate of return on common shareholders' equity focuses on profits generated on resources provided by common shareholders.

company is to identify the combination of profitability, activity, and leverage that produces the highest return for equity holders.

Illustration 4–16 provides a recap of the ratios we have discussed.

Illustration 4–16
Summary of Profitability Analysis Ratios

Activity ratios

$$\text{Asset turnover} = \frac{\text{Net sales}}{\text{Average total assets}}$$

$$\text{Receivables turnover} = \frac{\text{Net sales}}{\text{Average accounts receivable (net)}}$$

$$\text{Average collection period} = \frac{365}{\text{Receivables turnover ratio}}$$

$$\text{Inventory turnover} = \frac{\text{Cost of goods sold}}{\text{Average inventory}}$$

$$\text{Average days in inventory} = \frac{365}{\text{Inventory turnover ratio}}$$

Profitability ratios

$$\text{Profit margin on sales} = \frac{\text{Net income}}{\text{Net sales}}$$

$$\text{Return on assets} = \frac{\text{Net income}}{\text{Average total assets}}$$

$$\text{Return on shareholders' equity} = \frac{\text{Net income}}{\text{Average shareholders' equity}}$$

Leverage ratio

$$\text{Equity multiplier} = \frac{\text{Average total assets}}{\text{Average total equity}}$$

Profitability Analysis—An Illustration

To illustrate the application of the DuPont framework and the computation of the activity and profitability ratios, we analyze the 2015 financial statements of two well-known retailers, Costco Wholesale Corporation and Wal-Mart Stores, Inc.[37] The operations of these two companies are similar in their focus on operating large general merchandising and food discount stores. Illustration 4–17 presents selected financial statement information for the two companies (all numbers are in millions of dollars).

On the surface, it appears that Walmart is far more profitable than Costco. As shown at the bottom of Illustration 4–17, Walmart's 2015 net income was $17,099 million, compared to Costco's $2,377 million. But that's not the whole story. Even though both are very large companies, Walmart is more than six times the size of Costco in terms of total assets, so how can they be compared? Focusing on financial ratios helps adjust for size differences, and the DuPont framework helps identify the determinants of profitability from the perspective of shareholders.

Illustration 4–18 includes the DuPont analysis for Walmart and Costco, as well as some additional activity ratios we've discussed. Walmart's return on assets (ROA) is higher than

[37]Walmart's financial statements are for the fiscal year ended January 31, 2015. Walmart refers to this as its 2015 fiscal year. Costco's financial statements are for the fiscal year ended August 30, 2015.

Illustration 4–17 Selected Financial Information for Costco Wholesale Corporation and Wal-Mart Stores, Inc. **Real World Financials**

	Costco			Walmart		
($ in millions)	**2015**		**2014**	**2015**		**2014**
Accounts receivable (net)	$ 1,224		$ 1,148	$ 6,778		$ 6,677
Inventories	8,908		8,456	45,141		44,858
Total assets	33,440		33,024	203,706		204,751
Total liabilities	22,597		20,509	117,769		121,921
Total shareholders' equity	10,843		12,515	85,937		82,830
Average for 2015:						
Accounts receivable (net)		$ 1,186			$ 6,727.5	
Inventories		8,682			44,999.5	
Total assets		33,232			204,228.5	
Total shareholders' equity		11,679			84,383.5	
Income Statement—2015						
Net sales		113,666			482,229	
Cost of goods sold		101,065			365,086	
Net Income		2,377			17,099	

Illustration 4–18 DuPont Framework and Activity Ratios—Costco Wholesale Corporation and Walmart Stores, Inc. **Real World Financials**

DuPont analysis	**Costco**	**Walmart**	**Industry Average***
Profit margin on sales	$= \frac{\$2,377}{\$113,666} = 2.09\%$	$\frac{\$17,099}{\$482,229} = 3.55\%$	4.42%
×	×	×	
Asset turnover	$= \frac{\$113,666}{\$33,232} = 3.42$	$\frac{\$482,229}{\$204,228.5} = 2.36$	1.85
=	=	=	
Return on assets	$= \frac{\$2,377}{\$33,232} = 7.15\%$	$\frac{\$17,099}{\$204,228.5} = 8.37\%$	8.09%
×	×	×	
Equity Multiplier	$= \frac{\$33,232}{\$11,679} = 2.85$	$\frac{\$204,228.5}{\$84,383.5} = 2.42$	2.24
=	=	=	
Return on equity	$= \frac{\$2,377}{\$11,679} = 20.35\%$	$\frac{\$17,099}{\$84,383.5} = 20.26\%$	16.61%
Other activity ratios			
Receivables turnover	$= \frac{\$113,666}{\$1,186} = 95.84$	$\frac{\$482,229}{\$6,727.5} = 71.68$	79.35
Average collection period	$= \frac{365}{95.84} = 3.81$ days	$\frac{365}{71.68} = 5.09$ days	4.60 days
Inventory turnover	$= \frac{\$101,065}{\$8,682} = 11.64$	$\frac{\$365,086}{\$44,999.5} = 8.11$	7.17
Average days in inventory	$= \frac{365}{11.64} = 31.36$ days	$\frac{365}{8.11} = 45.01$ days	50.91 days

*www.reuters.com.

Costco's (8.37% for Walmart compared to 7.15% for Costco). Why? Remember that both profitability and activity combine to determine return on assets. Costco's asset turnover is much higher than Walmart's (3.42 compared to 2.36), but its profit margin is much lower than Walmart's (2.09% compared to 3.55%). So, even though Costco makes significantly more sales with each dollar of its assets, Walmart makes more profit on each dollar of sales, and Walmart ends up coming out ahead on return on assets.

The average days in inventory provides insight into Costco's higher asset turnover. Inventory takes only 31 days on average before being sold by Costco, compared with 45 days for Walmart. Costco also turns over its accounts receivable faster than Walmart does, but accounts receivable are relatively small so attention would be focused on other ratios for both companies.

What matters most to the shareholders of these companies is not return on assets, but the return on equity (ROE). Even though Walmart's return on assets is higher, its equity multiplier is lower (2.42 for Walmart compared to 2.85 for Costco). As a result, the two companies' ROEs are close, with Costco's ROE of 20.35% and Walmart's ROE of 20.26%. The ROE of both companies is above the industry average.

A Costco shareholder looking at these numbers might wonder how best to increase Costco's ROE. Should Costco attempt to increase operational efficiency on the asset turnover dimension? That might be tough, given its already high asset turnover. Or, should Costco attempt to increase profit margin? Given competitive pressures on retail pricing, can Costco generate a much higher profit margin with its current product mix and low-price strategy, or should it consider including more upscale, high-margin items in its inventory? Or, should Costco attempt to increase leverage and improve its equity multiplier, so that debt holders are financing a greater percentage of its assets?

The essential point of our discussion here, and in Part C of Chapter 3, is that raw accounting numbers alone mean little to decision makers. The numbers gain value when viewed in relation to other numbers. Similarly, the financial ratios formed by those relationships provide even greater perspective when compared with similar ratios of other companies, or with averages for several companies in the same industry. Accounting information is useful in making decisions. Financial analysis that includes comparisons of financial ratios enhances the value of that information.

Financial Reporting Case Solution

© Onoky/SuperStock

1. **How would you explain restructuring costs to Becky? Are restructuring costs something Becky should worry about?** *(p. 170)* Restructuring costs include employee severance and termination benefits plus other costs associated with the shutdown or relocation of facilities or downsizing of operations. Restructuring costs are not necessarily bad. In fact, the objective is to make operations more efficient. The costs are incurred now in hopes of better earnings later.
2. **Explain to Becky what is meant by discontinued operations and describe to her how that item is reported in an income statement.** *(p. 173)* Separate reporting as a discontinued operation is required when the disposal of a component represents a strategic shift that has, or will have, a major effect on a company's operations and financial results. The net-of-tax effect of discontinued operations is separately reported below income from continuing operations. If the component has been disposed of by the end of the reporting period, the income effects include: (1) income or loss from operations of the discontinued component from the beginning of the reporting period through the disposal date and (2) gain or loss on disposal of the component's assets. If the component has not been disposed of by the end of the reporting period, the income effects include: (1) income or loss from operations of the discontinued component from the beginning of the reporting period through the end of the reporting period, and (2) an impairment loss if the fair value minus cost to sell of the component's assets is less than their book value.

3. **Describe to Becky the difference between basic and diluted earnings per share.** *(p. 180)* Basic earnings per share is computed by dividing net income available to common shareholders (net income less any preferred stock dividends) by the weighted- average number of common shares outstanding for the period. Diluted earnings per share reflects the potential dilution that could occur for companies that have certain securities outstanding that are convertible into common shares or stock options that could create additional common shares if the options were exercised. These items could cause earnings per share to decrease (become diluted). Because of the complexity of the calculation and the importance of earnings per share to investors, the text devotes a substantial portion of Chapter 19 to this topic. ●

The Bottom Line

- **LO4–1** The components of income from continuing operations are revenues, expenses (including income taxes), gains, and losses, excluding those related to discontinued operations. Companies often distinguish between operating and nonoperating income within continuing operations. (*p. 164*)
- **LO4–2** The term *earnings quality* refers to the ability of reported earnings (income) to predict a company's future earnings. The relevance of any historical-based financial statement hinges on its predictive value. To enhance predictive value, analysts try to separate a company's *temporary earnings* from its *permanent earnings.* Many believe that manipulating income reduces earnings quality because it can mask permanent earnings. Two major methods used by managers to manipulate earnings are (1) income shifting and (2) income statement classification. (*p. 168*)
- **LO4–3** Analysts begin their assessment of permanent earnings with income from continuing operations. It would be a mistake to assume income from continuing operations reflects permanent earnings entirely. In other words, there may be temporary earnings effects included in both operating and nonoperating income. (*p. 169*)
- **LO4–4** A discontinued operation refers to the disposal or planned disposal of a component of the entity. The net-of-tax effect of discontinued operations is separately reported below income from continuing operations. (*p. 173*)
- **LO4–5** Accounting changes include changes in principle, changes in estimate, or changes in reporting entity. Their effects on the current period and prior period financial statements are reported using various approaches—retrospective, modified retrospective, and prospective. Error corrections are made by restating prior period financial statements. Any correction to retained earnings is made with an adjustment to the beginning balance in the current period. Earnings per share (EPS) is the amount of income achieved during a period expressed per share of common stock outstanding. EPS must be disclosed for income from continuing operations and for discontinued operations. (*p. 178*)
- **LO4–6** The FASB's Concept Statement 6 defines the term *comprehensive income* as the change in equity from nonowner transactions. The calculation of net income, however, excludes certain transactions that are included in comprehensive income. To convey the relationship between the two measures, companies must report both net income and comprehensive income and reconcile the difference between the two. The presentation can be (1) in a single, continuous statement of comprehensive income, or (2) in two separate, but consecutive statements—an income statement and a statement of comprehensive income. (*p. 181*)
- **LO4–7** When a company provides a balance sheet and income statement, a statement of cash flows also is provided. The purpose of the statement of cash flows is to provide information about the cash receipts and cash disbursements that occurred during the period. (*p. 185*)
- **LO4–8** To enhance the usefulness of the information, the statement of cash flows classifies all transactions affecting cash into one of three categories: (1) operating activities, (2) investing activities, or (3) financing activities. (*p. 186*)
- **LO4–9** There are more similarities than differences between income statements and statements of cash flows prepared according to U.S. GAAP and those prepared applying international standards. In a statement of

cash flows, some differences are possible in the classifications of interest and divided revenue, interest expense, and dividends paid. (*p. 168, 182, 191 and 202*)

● **LO4–10** Activity and profitability ratios provide information about a company's profitability. Activity ratios include the receivables turnover ratio, the inventory turnover ratio, and the asset turnover ratio. Profitability ratios include the profit margin on sales, the return on assets, and the return on shareholders' equity. DuPont analysis explains return on stockholders' equity as determined by profit margin, asset turnover, and the extent to which assets are financed with equity versus debt. (*p. 193*) ●

APPENDIX 4

Interim Reporting

Financial statements covering periods of less than a year are called *interim reports*. Companies registered with the SEC, which includes most public companies, must submit quarterly reports, and you will see excerpts from these reports throughout this book.[38] Though there is no requirement to do so, most also provide quarterly reports to their shareholders and typically include abbreviated, unaudited interim reports as supplemental information within their annual reports. For instance, Illustration 4A–1 shows the quarterly information disclosed in the annual report of Sherwin Williams Company, a company that manufactures paint, for the fiscal year ended December 31, 2015. Amounts for each of the four quarters sum to the reported amount for the full year. Compare these numbers to the annual income statement in Illustration 4–2.

Interim reports are issued for periods of less than a year, typically as quarterly financial statements.

Illustration 4A–1

Interim Data in Annual Report—Sherwin Williams Company

Real World Financials

Note 16 – Summary of Quarterly Results of Operations (Unaudited)

Year Ended December 31, 2015	1st Quarter	2nd Quarter	3rd Quarter	4th Quarter	Full Year
	($ in thousands, except per share data)				
Net sales	$2,450,284	$3,132,139	$3,152,285	$2,604,596	$11,339,304
Gross profit	1,132,449	1,529,986	1,574,552	1,322,239	5,559,226
Net income	131,404	349,937	374,491	198,017	1,053,849
Basic	$ 1.41	$ 3.78	$ 4.04	$ 2.15	$ 11.38
Diluted	$ 1.38	$ 3.70	$ 3.96	$ 2.12	$ 11.16

For accounting information to be useful to decision makers, it must be available on a timely basis. One of the objectives of interim reporting is to enhance the timeliness of financial information. In addition, quarterly reports provide investors and creditors with additional insight on the seasonality of business operations that might otherwise get lost in annual reports. Why are sales and net income higher in the 2nd and 3rd quarters (compared to the 1st and 4th quarters) for Sherwin Williams? Most outside painting occurs in the warmer months. These months occur in the 2nd and 3rd quarters, so it is expected that sales would be higher in these quarters. Because the company sells paint for a profit, profitability is also higher in quarters with greater sales.

However, the downside to these benefits is the relative unreliability of interim reporting. With a shorter reporting period, questions associated with estimation and allocation are magnified. For example, certain expenses often benefit an entire year's operations and yet are incurred primarily within a single interim period. Similarly, should smaller companies use lower tax rates in the earlier quarters and higher rates in later quarters as higher tax brackets are reached? Another result of shorter reporting periods is the intensified effect of unusual events such as material gains and losses. A second quarter casualty loss, for instance, that would reduce annual profits by 10% might reduce second quarter profits by 40% or more. Is it more realistic to allocate such a loss over the entire year? These and similar questions tend to hinge on the way we view an interim period in relation to the fiscal year. More specifically, should each interim period be viewed as a *discrete* reporting period or as an *integral part* of the annual period?

The fundamental debate regarding interim reporting centers on the choice between the *discrete* and *integral part* approaches.

[38]Quarterly reports are filed with the SEC on Form 10-Q. Annual reports to the SEC are on Form 10-K.

Reporting Revenues and Expenses

With only a few exceptions, the same accounting principles applicable to annual reporting are used for interim reporting.

Existing practice and current reporting requirements for interim reporting generally follow the viewpoint that interim reports are an integral part of annual statements, although the discrete approach is applied to some items. Most revenues and expenses are recognized using the same accounting principles applicable to annual reporting. Some modifications are necessary to help cause interim statements to relate better to annual statements. This is most evident in the way costs and expenses are recognized. Most are recognized in interim periods as incurred. But when an expenditure clearly benefits more than just the period in which it is incurred, the expense should be allocated among the periods benefited on an allocation basis consistent with the company's annual allocation procedures. For example, annual repair expenses, property tax expense, and advertising expenses incurred in the first quarter that clearly benefit later quarters are assigned to each quarter through the use of accruals and deferrals. Costs and expenses subject to year-end adjustments, such as depreciation expense, are estimated and allocated to interim periods in a systematic way. Similarly, income tax expense at each interim date should be based on estimates of the effective tax rate for the whole year. This would mean, for example, that if the estimated effective rate has changed since the previous interim period(s), the tax expense in the current period would be determined as the new rate times the cumulative pretax income to date, less the total tax expense reported in previous interim periods.

Reporting Unusual Items

Discontinued operations and unusual items are reported entirely within the interim period in which they occur.

On the other hand, major events such as discontinued operations should be reported separately in the interim period in which they occur. That is, these amounts should not be allocated among individual quarters within the fiscal year. The same is true for items that are unusual. Treatment of these items is more consistent with the discrete view than the integral part view.

Earnings Per Share

Quarterly EPS calculations follow the same procedures as annual calculations.

A second item that is treated in a manner consistent with the discrete view is earnings per share. EPS calculations for interim reports follow the same procedures as annual calculations that you will study in Chapter 19. The calculations are based on conditions actually existing during the particular interim period rather than on conditions estimated to exist at the end of the fiscal year.

Reporting Accounting Changes

Recall that we account for a change in accounting principle retrospectively, meaning we recast prior years' financial statements when we report those statements again in comparative

International Financial Reporting Standards

● LO4–9

Interim Reporting. *IAS No. 34* requires that a company apply the same accounting policies in its interim financial statements as it applies in its annual financial statements. Therefore, IFRS takes much more of a discrete-period approach than does U.S. GAAP. For example, costs for repairs, property taxes, and advertising that do not meet the definition of an asset at the end of an interim period are expensed entirely in the period in which they occur under IFRS, but are accrued or deferred and then charged to each of the periods they benefit under U.S. GAAP. This difference would tend to make interim period income more volatile under IFRS than under U.S. GAAP. However, as in U.S. GAAP, income taxes are accounted for based on an estimate of the tax rate expected to apply for the entire year.[39]

[39]"Interim Financial Reporting," *International Accounting Standard No. 34* (IASCF), as amended effective January 1, 2016, par. 28–30.

form. In other words, we make those statements appear as if the newly adopted accounting method had been used in those prior years. It's the same with interim reporting. We retrospectively report a change made during an interim period in similar fashion. Then in financial reports of subsequent interim periods of the same fiscal year, we disclose how that change affected (a) income from continuing operations, (b) net income, and (c) related per share amounts for the postchange interim period.

Accounting changes made in an interim period are reported by retrospectively applying the changes to prior financial statements.

Minimum Disclosures

Complete financial statements are not required for interim period reporting, but certain minimum disclosures are required as follows:[40]

- Sales, income taxes, and net income
- Earnings per share
- Seasonal revenues, costs, and expenses
- Significant changes in estimates for income taxes
- Discontinued operations and unusual items
- Contingencies
- Changes in accounting principles or estimates
- Information about fair value of financial instruments and the methods and assumptions used to estimate fair values
- Significant changes in financial position

When fourth quarter results are not separately reported, material fourth quarter events, including year-end adjustments, should be reported in disclosure notes to annual statements.

Questions For Review of Key Topics

Q 4–1 The income statement is a change statement. Explain what is meant by this.

Q 4–2 What transactions are included in income from continuing operations? Briefly explain why it is important to segregate income from continuing operations from other transactions affecting net income.

Q 4–3 Distinguish between operating and nonoperating income in relation to the income statement.

Q 4–4 Briefly explain the difference between the single-step and multiple-step income statement formats.

Q 4–5 Explain what is meant by the term *earnings quality*.

Q 4–6 What are restructuring costs and where are they reported in the income statement?

Q 4–7 Define intraperiod tax allocation. Why is the process necessary?

Q 4–8 How are discontinued operations reported in the income statement?

Q 4–9 What is meant by a change in accounting principle? Describe the possible accounting treatments for a mandated change in accounting principle.

Q 4–10 Accountants very often are required to make estimates, and very often those estimates prove incorrect. In what period(s) is the effect of a change in an accounting estimate reported?

Q 4–11 The correction of a material error discovered in a year subsequent to the year the error was made is considered a prior period adjustment. Briefly describe the accounting treatment for prior period adjustments.

Q 4–12 Define earnings per share (EPS). For which income statement items must EPS be disclosed?

Q 4–13 Define comprehensive income. What are the two ways companies can present comprehensive income?

Q 4–14 Describe the purpose of the statement of cash flows.

Q 4–15 Identify and briefly describe the three categories of cash flows reported in the statement of cash flows.

Q 4–16 Explain what is meant by noncash investing and financing activities pertaining to the statement of cash flows. Give an example of one of these activities.

Q 4–17 Distinguish between the direct method and the indirect method for reporting the results of operating activities in the statement of cash flows.

[40]FASB ASC 270-10-50: Interim Reporting-Overall-Disclosure (previously "Interim Financial Reporting," *Accounting Principles Board Opinion No 28* (New York: AICPA, 1973)).

IFRS **Q 4–18** Describe the potential statement of cash flows classification differences between U.S. GAAP and IFRS.

Q 4–19 Show the calculation of the following activity ratios: (1) the receivables turnover ratio, (2) the inventory turnover ratio, and (3) the asset turnover ratio. What information about a company do these ratios offer?

Q 4–20 Show the calculation of the following profitability ratios: (1) the profit margin on sales, (2) the return on assets, and (3) the return on shareholders' equity. What information about a company do these ratios offer?

Q 4–21 Show the DuPont framework's calculation of the three components of return on shareholders' equity. What information about a company do these ratios offer?

Q 4–22 Interim reports are issued for periods of less than a year, typically as quarterly financial statements. Should these interim periods be viewed as separate periods or integral parts of the annual period?

IFRS **Q 4–23** [Based on Appendix 4] What is the primary difference between interim reports under IFRS and U.S. GAAP?

Brief Exercises

BE 4–1 Single-step income statement ● LO4–1

The adjusted trial balance of Pacific Scientific Corporation on December 31, 2018, the end of the company's fiscal year, contained the following income statement items ($ in millions): sales revenue, $2,106; cost of goods sold, $1,240; selling expenses, $126; general and administrative expenses, $105; interest expense, $35; and gain on sale of investments, $45. Income tax expense has not yet been recorded. The income tax rate is 40%. Prepare a single-step income statement for 2018. Ignore EPS disclosures.

BE 4–2 Multiple-step income statement ● LO4–1, LO4–3

Refer to the situation described in BE 4–1. If the company's accountant prepared a multiple-step income statement, what amount would appear in that statement for (a) operating income and (b) nonoperating income?

BE 4–3 Multiple-step income statement ● LO4–1, LO4–3

Refer to the situation described in BE 4–1. Prepare a multiple-step income statement for 2018. Ignore EPS disclosures.

BE 4–4 Multiple-step income statement ● LO4–1, LO4–3

The following is a partial year-end adjusted trial balance.

Account Title	Debits	Credits
Sales revenue		300,000
Loss on sale of investments	22,000	
Interest revenue		4,000
Cost of goods sold	160,000	
General and administrative expenses	40,000	
Restructuring costs	50,000	
Selling expenses	25,000	
Income tax expense	0	

Income tax expense has not yet been recorded. The income tax rate is 40%. Determine the following: (a) operating income (loss), (b) income (loss) before income taxes, and (c) net income (loss).

BE 4–5 Income from continuing operations ● LO4–3, LO4–5

The following are partial income statement account balances taken from the December 31, 2018, year-end trial balance of White and Sons, Inc.: restructuring costs, $300,000; interest revenue, $40,000; before-tax loss on discontinued operations, $400,000; and loss on sale of investments, $50,000. Income tax expense has not yet been recorded. The income tax rate is 40%. Prepare the lower portion of the 2018 income statement beginning with $850,000 income from continuing operations before income taxes. Include appropriate EPS disclosures. The company had 100,000 shares of common stock outstanding throughout the year.

BE 4–6 Discontinued operations ● LO4–4

On December 31, 2018, the end of the fiscal year, Revolutionary Industries completed the sale of its robotics business for $9 million. The business segment qualifies as a component of the entity according to GAAP. The book value of the assets of the segment was $7 million. The income from operations of the segment during 2018 was $4 million. Pretax income from continuing operations for the year totaled $12 million. The income tax rate is 40%. Prepare the lower portion of the 2018 income statement beginning with pretax income from continuing operations. Ignore EPS disclosures.

BE 4–7 Discontinued operations ● LO4–4

On December 31, 2018, the end of the fiscal year, California Microtech Corporation completed the sale of its semiconductor business for $10 million. The business segment qualifies as a component of the entity according to GAAP. The book value of the assets of the segment was $8 million. The loss from operations of the segment during 2018 was $3.6 million. Pretax income from continuing operations for the year totaled $5.8 million. The income tax rate is 30%. Prepare the lower portion of the 2018 income statement beginning with pretax income from continuing operations. Ignore EPS disclosures.

BE 4–8
Discontinued operations
● LO4–4

Refer to the situation described in BE 4–7. Assume that the semiconductor segment was not sold during 2018 but was held for sale at year-end. The estimated fair value of the segment's assets, less costs to sell, on December 31 was $10 million. Prepare the lower portion of the 2018 income statement beginning with pretax income from continuing operations. Ignore EPS disclosures.

BE 4–9
Discontinued operations
● LO4–4

Refer to the situation described in BE 4–8. Assume instead that the estimated fair value of the segment's assets, less costs to sell, on December 31 was $7 million rather than $10 million. Prepare the lower portion of the 2018 income statement beginning with pretax income from continuing operations. Ignore EPS disclosures.

BE 4–10
Comprehensive income
● LO4–6

O'Reilly Beverage Company reported net income of $650,000 for 2018. In addition, the company deferred a $60,000 pretax loss on derivatives and had pretax net unrealized holding gains on investment securities of $40,000. Prepare a separate statement of comprehensive income for 2018. The company's income tax rate is 40%.

BE 4–11
Statement of cash flows; direct method
● LO4–8

The following are summary cash transactions that occurred during the year for Hilliard Healthcare Co. (HHC):

Cash received from:	
Customers	$660,000
Interest on note receivable	12,000
Collection of note receivable	100,000
Sale of land	40,000
Issuance of common stock	200,000
Cash paid for:	
Interest on note payable	18,000
Purchase of equipment	120,000
Operating expenses	440,000
Dividends to shareholders	30,000

Prepare the cash flows from operating activities section of HHC's statement of cash flows using the direct method.

BE 4–12
Statement of cash flows; investing and financing activities
● LO4–8

Refer to the situation described in BE 4–11. Prepare the cash flows from investing and financing activities sections of HHC's statement of cash flows.

BE 4–13
Statement of cash flows; indirect method
● LO4–8

Net income of Mansfield Company was $45,000. The accounting records reveal depreciation expense of $80,000 as well as increases in prepaid rent, salaries payable, and income taxes payable of $60,000, $15,000, and $12,000, respectively. Prepare the cash flows from operating activities section of Mansfield's statement of cash flows using the indirect method.

BE 4–14
IFRS; Statement of cash flows
● LO4–8, LO4–9

 IFRS

Refer to the situation described in BE 4–11 and BE 4–12. How might your solution to those brief exercises differ if Hilliard Healthcare Co. prepares its statement of cash flows according to International Financial Reporting Standards?

BE 4–15
Receivables and inventory turnover ratios
● LO4–10

Universal Calendar Company began the year with accounts receivable (net) and inventory balances of $100,000 and $80,000, respectively. Year-end balances for these accounts were $120,000 and $60,000, respectively. Sales for the year of $600,000 generated a gross profit of $200,000. Calculate the receivables and inventory turnover ratios for the year.

BE 4–16
Profitability ratios
● LO4–10

The 2018 income statement for Anderson TV and Appliance reported sales revenue of $420,000 and net income of $65,000. Average total assets for 2018 was $800,000. Shareholders' equity at the beginning of the year was $500,000 and $20,000 was paid to shareholders as dividends. There were no other shareholders' equity transactions that occurred during the year. Calculate the profit margin on sales, return on assets, and return on shareholders' equity for 2018.

BE 4–17
Profitability ratios
● LO4–10

Refer to the facts described in BE 4–16. Show the DuPont framework's calculation of the three components of the 2018 return on shareholders' equity for Anderson TV and Appliance.

BE 4–18
Inventory turnover ratio
● LO4–10

During 2018, Rogue Corporation reported sales revenue of $600,000. Inventory at both the beginning and end of the year totaled $75,000. The inventory turnover ratio for the year was 6.0. What amount of gross profit did the company report in its 2018 income statement?

Exercises

E 4–1
Operating versus Nonoperating Income
● LO4–1

Pandora Corporation operates several factories in the Midwest that manufacture consumer electronics. The December 31, 2018, year-end trial balance contained the following income statement items:

Account Title	Debits	Credits
Sales revenue		12,500,000
Interest revenue		50,000
Loss on sale of investments	100,000	
Cost of goods sold	6,200,000	
Selling expenses	620,000	
General and administrative expenses	1,520,000	
Interest expense	40,000	
Research and development expense	1,200,000	
Income tax expense	900,000	

Required:
Calculate the company's operating income for the year.

E 4–2
Income statement format; single step and multiple step
● LO4–1, LO4–5

The following is a partial trial balance for the Green Star Corporation as of December 31, 2018:

Account Title	Debits	Credits
Sales revenue		1,300,000
Interest revenue		30,000
Gain on sale of investments		50,000
Cost of goods sold	720,000	
Selling expenses	160,000	
General and administrative expenses	75,000	
Interest expense	40,000	
Income tax expense	130,000	

100,000 shares of common stock were outstanding throughout 2018.

Required:
1. Prepare a single-step income statement for 2018, including EPS disclosures.
2. Prepare a multiple-step income statement for 2018, including EPS disclosures.

E 4–3
Income statement format; single step and multiple step
● LO4–1, LO4–3, LO4–5

The following is a partial trial balance for General Lighting Corporation as of December 31, 2018:

Account Title	Debits	Credits
Sales revenue		2,350,000
Interest revenue		80,000
Loss on sale of investments	22,500	
Cost of goods sold	1,200,300	
Loss from write-down of inventory due to obsolescence	200,000	
Selling expenses	300,000	
General and administrative expenses	150,000	
Interest expense	90,000	

300,000 shares of common stock were outstanding throughout 2018. Income tax expense has not yet been recorded. The income tax rate is 40%.

Required:

1. Prepare a single-step income statement for 2018, including EPS disclosures.
2. Prepare a multiple-step income statement for 2018, including EPS disclosures.

E 4–4
Multiple-step continuous statement of comprehensive income
● LO4–1, LO4–5, LO4–6

The trial balance for Lindor Corporation, a manufacturing company, for the year ended December 31, 2018, included the following income accounts:

Account Title	Debits	Credits
Sales revenue		2,300,000
Cost of goods sold	1,400,000	
Selling and administrative expenses	420,000	
Interest expense	40,000	
Unrealized holding gains on investment securities		80,000

The trial balance does not include the accrual for income taxes. Lindor's income tax rate is 30%. One million shares of common stock were outstanding throughout 2018.

Required:

Prepare a single, continuous multiple-step statement of comprehensive income for 2018, including appropriate EPS disclosures.

E 4–5
Income statement presentation
● LO4–1, LO4–5

The following *incorrect* income statement was prepared by the accountant of the Axel Corporation:

AXEL CORPORATION
Income Statement
For the Year Ended December 31, 2018

Revenues and gains:		
Sales		$592,000
Interest and dividends		32,000
Gain on sale of investments		86,000
Total revenues and gains		710,000
Expenses and losses:		
Cost of goods sold	$325,000	
Selling expenses	67,000	
Administrative expenses	87,000	
Interest	26,000	
Restructuring costs	55,000	
Income taxes	60,000	
Total expenses and losses		620,000
Net Income		$ 90,000
Earnings per share		$ 0.90

Required:

Prepare a multiple-step income statement for 2018 applying generally accepted accounting principles. The income tax rate is 40%.

E 4–6
Discontinued operations
● LO4–4, LO4–5

Chance Company had two operating divisions, one manufacturing farm equipment and the other office supplies. Both divisions are considered separate components as defined by generally accepted accounting principles. The farm equipment component had been unprofitable, and on September 1, 2018, the company adopted a plan to sell the assets of the division. The actual sale was completed on December 15, 2018, at a price of $600,000. The book value of the division's assets was $1,000,000, resulting in a before-tax loss of $400,000 on the sale.

The division incurred a before-tax operating loss from operations of $130,000 from the beginning of the year through December 15. The income tax rate is 40%. Chance's after-tax income from its continuing operations is $350,000.

Required:

Prepare an income statement for 2018 beginning with income from continuing operations. Include appropriate EPS disclosures assuming that 100,000 shares of common stock were outstanding throughout the year.

E 4–7
Income statement presentation; discontinued operations; restructuring costs
● LO4–1, LO4–3, LO4–4

Esquire Comic Book Company had income before tax of $1,000,000 in 2018 *before* considering the following material items:

1. Esquire sold one of its operating divisions, which qualified as a separate component according to generally accepted accounting principles. The before-tax loss on disposal was $350,000. The division generated before-tax income from operations from the beginning of the year through disposal of $500,000. Neither the loss on disposal nor the operating income is included in the $1,000,000 before-tax income the company generated from its other divisions.
2. The company incurred restructuring costs of $80,000 during the year.

Required:
Prepare a 2018 income statement for Esquire beginning with income from continuing operations. Assume an income tax rate of 40%. Ignore EPS disclosures.

E 4–8
Discontinued operations; disposal in subsequent year
● LO4–4

Kandon Enterprises, Inc., has two operating divisions; one manufactures machinery and the other breeds and sells horses. Both divisions are considered separate components as defined by generally accepted accounting principles. The horse division has been unprofitable, and on November 15, 2018, Kandon adopted a formal plan to sell the division. The sale was completed on April 30, 2019. At December 31, 2018, the component was considered held for sale.

On December 31, 2018, the company's fiscal year-end, the book value of the assets of the horse division was $250,000. On that date, the fair value of the assets, less costs to sell, was $200,000. The before-tax loss from operations of the division for the year was $140,000. The company's effective tax rate is 40%. The after-tax income from continuing operations for 2018 was $400,000.

Required:

1. Prepare a partial income statement for 2018 beginning with income from continuing operations. Ignore EPS disclosures.
2. Repeat requirement 1 assuming that the estimated net fair value of the horse division's assets was $400,000, instead of $200,000.

E 4–9
Discontinued operations; disposal in subsequent year; solving for unknown
● LO4–4

On September 17, 2018, Ziltech, Inc., entered into an agreement to sell one of its divisions that qualifies as a component of the entity according to generally accepted accounting principles. By December 31, 2018, the company's fiscal year-end, the division had not yet been sold, but was considered held for sale. The net fair value (fair value minus costs to sell) of the division's assets at the end of the year was $11 million. The pretax income from operations of the division during 2018 was $4 million. Pretax income from continuing operations for the year totaled $14 million. The income tax rate is 40%. Ziltech reported net income for the year of $7.2 million.

Required:
Determine the book value of the division's assets on December 31, 2018.

E 4–10
Earnings per share
● LO4–5

The Esposito Import Company had 1 million shares of common stock outstanding during 2018. Its income statement reported the following items: income from continuing operations, $5 million; loss from discontinued operations, $1.6 million. All of these amounts are net of tax.

Required:
Prepare the 2018 EPS presentation for the Esposito Import Company.

E 4–11
Comprehensive income
● LO4–6

The Massoud Consulting Group reported net income of $1,354,000 for its fiscal year ended December 31, 2018. In addition, during the year the company experienced a positive foreign currency translation adjustment of $240,000 and had unrealized losses on investment securities of $80,000. The company's effective tax rate on all items affecting comprehensive income is 30%. Each component of other comprehensive income is displayed net of tax.

Required:
Prepare a separate statement of comprehensive income for 2018.

E 4–12
Statement of cash flows; classifications
● LO4–8

The statement of cash flows classifies all cash inflows and outflows into one of the three categories shown below and lettered from a through c. In addition, certain transactions that do not involve cash are reported in the statement as noncash investing and financing activities, labeled d.

a. Operating activities
b. Investing activities
c. Financing activities
d. Noncash investing and financing activities

Required:

For each of the following transactions, use the letters above to indicate the appropriate classification category.

1. _____ Purchase of equipment for cash
2. _____ Payment of employee salaries
3. _____ Collection of cash from customers
4. _____ Cash proceeds from a note payable
5. _____ Purchase of common stock of another corporation for cash
6. _____ Issuance of common stock for cash
7. _____ Sale of equipment for cash
8. _____ Payment of interest on note payable
9. _____ Issuance of bonds payable in exchange for land and building
10. _____ Payment of cash dividends to shareholders
11. _____ Payment of principal on note payable

E 4–13
Statement of cash flows preparation
● LO4–8

The following summary transactions occurred during 2018 for Bluebonnet Bakers:

Cash Received from:	
Customers	$380,000
Interest on note receivable	6,000
Principal on note receivable	50,000
Sale of investments	30,000
Proceeds from note receivable	100,000
Cash Paid for:	
Purchase of inventory	160,000
Interest on note payable	5,000
Purchase of equipment	85,000
Salaries to employees	90,000
Principal on note payable	25,000
Payment of dividends to shareholders	20,000

The balance of cash and cash equivalents at the beginning of 2018 was $17,000.

Required:

Prepare a statement of cash flows for 2018 for Bluebonnet Bakers. Use the direct method for reporting operating activities.

E 4–14
IFRS; statement of cash flows
● LO4–8, LO4–9

 IFRS

Refer to the situation described in E 4–13.

Required:

Prepare the statement of cash flows assuming that Bluebonnet prepares its financial statements according to International Financial Reporting Standards. Where IFRS allows flexibility, use the classification used most often in IFRS financial statements.

E 4–15
Indirect method; reconciliation of net income to net cash flows from operating activities
● LO4–8

The accounting records of Hampton Company provided the data below ($ in thousands).

Net income	$17,300
Depreciation expense	7,800
Increase in accounts receivable	4,000
Decrease in inventory	5,500
Decrease in prepaid insurance	1,200
Decrease in salaries payable	2,700
Increase in interest payable	800

Required:

Prepare a reconciliation of net income to net cash flows from operating activities.

E 4–16
Statement of cash flows; directly from transactions
● LO4–8

The following transactions occurred during March 2018 for the Wainwright Corporation. The company owns and operates a wholesale warehouse. [These are the same transactions analyzed in Exercise 2–1, when we determined their effect on elements of the accounting equation.]

1. Issued 30,000 shares of capital stock in exchange for $300,000 in cash.

2. Purchased equipment at a cost of $40,000. $10,000 cash was paid and a note payable to the seller was signed for the balance owed.
3. Purchased inventory on account at a cost of $90,000. The company uses the perpetual inventory system.
4. Credit sales for the month totaled $120,000. The cost of the goods sold was $70,000.
5. Paid $5,000 in rent on the warehouse building for the month of March.
6. Paid $6,000 to an insurance company for fire and liability insurance for a one-year period beginning April 1, 2018.
7. Paid $70,000 on account for the merchandise purchased in 3.
8. Collected $55,000 from customers on account.
9. Recorded depreciation expense of $1,000 for the month on the equipment.

Required:

1. Analyze each transaction and classify each as a financing, investing, and/or operating activity (a transaction can represent more than one type of activity). In doing so, also indicate the cash effect of each, if any. If there is no cash effect, simply place a check mark (√) in the appropriate column(s).

   Example:

Operating	Investing	Financing
1.		$300,000

2. Prepare a statement of cash flows, using the direct method to present cash flows from operating activities. Assume the cash balance at the beginning of the month was $40,000.

E 4–17
Statement of cash flows; indirect method
● LO4–8

Cemptex Corporation prepares its statement of cash flows using the indirect method to report operating activities. Net income for the 2018 fiscal year was $624,000. Depreciation and amortization expense of $87,000 was included with operating expenses in the income statement. The following information describes the changes in current assets and liabilities other than cash:

Decrease in accounts receivable	$22,000
Increase in inventories	9,200
Increase prepaid expenses	8,500
Increase in salaries payable	10,000
Decrease in income taxes payable	14,000

Required:
Prepare the operating activities section of the 2018 statement of cash flows.

E 4–18
Statement of cash flows; indirect method
● LO4–8

Chew Corporation prepares its statement of cash flows using the indirect method of reporting operating activities. Net income for the 2018 fiscal year was $1,250,000. Depreciation expense of $140,000 was included with operating expenses in the income statement. The following information describes the changes in current assets and liabilities other than cash:

Increase in accounts receivable	$152,000
Decrease in inventories	108,000
Decrease prepaid expenses	62,000
Decrease in salaries payable	30,000
Increase in income taxes payable	44,000

Required:
Calculate cash flows from operating activities for 2018.

E 4–19
IFRS; statement of cash flows
● LO4–8, LO4–9

IFRS

The statement of cash flows for the year ended December 31, 2018, for Bronco Metals is presented below.

BRONCO METALS
Statement of Cash Flows
For the Year Ended December 31, 2018

Cash flows from operating activities:	
Collections from customers	$353,000
Interest on note receivable	4,000
Dividends received from investments	2,400
Purchase of inventory	(186,000)
Payment of operating expenses	(67,000)

(continued)

(concluded)

Payment of interest on note payable	(8,000)	
Net cash flows from operating activities		$ 98,400
Cash flows from investing activities:		
Collection of note receivable	100,000	
Purchase of equipment	(154,000)	
Net cash flows from investing activities		(54,000)
Cash flows from financing activities:		
Proceeds from issuance of common stock	200,000	
Dividends paid	(40,000)	
Net cash flows from financing activities		160,000
Net increase in cash		204,400
Cash and cash equivalents, January 1		28,600
Cash and cash equivalents, December 31		$233,000

Required:

Prepare the statement of cash flows assuming that Bronco prepares its financial statements according to International Financial Reporting Standards. Where IFRS allows flexibility, use the classification used most often in IFRS financial statements.

E 4–20
Statement of cash flows; indirect method
● LO4–8

Presented below is the 2018 income statement and comparative balance sheet information for Tiger Enterprises.

TIGER ENTERPRISES
Income Statement
For the Year Ended December 31, 2018

($ in thousands)		
Sales revenue		$7,000
Operating expenses:		
Cost of goods sold	$3,360	
Depreciation	240	
Insurance	100	
Administrative and other	1,800	
Total operating expenses		5,500
Income before income taxes		1,500
Income tax expense		600
Net income		$ 900

Balance Sheet Information ($ in thousands)	**Dec. 31, 2018**	**Dec. 31, 2017**
Assets:		
Cash	$ 300	$ 200
Accounts receivable	750	830
Inventory	640	600
Prepaid insurance	50	20
Plant and equipment	2,100	1,800
Less: Accumulated depreciation	(840)	(600)
Total assets	$3,000	$2,850
Liabilities and Shareholders' Equity:		
Accounts payable	$ 300	$360
Payables for administrative and other expenses	300	400
Income taxes payable	200	150
Note payable (due 12/31/2019)	800	600
Common stock	900	800
Retained earnings	500	540
Total liabilities and shareholders' equity	$3,000	$2,850

Required:

Prepare Tiger's statement of cash flows, using the indirect method to present cash flows from operating activities. (*Hint:* You will have to calculate dividend payments).

E 4–21
Statement of cash flows; direct method
● LO4–8

Refer to the situation described in E 4–20.

Required:

Prepare the cash flows from operating activities section of Tiger's 2018 statement of cash flows using the direct method. Assume that all purchases and sales of inventory are on account, and that there are no anticipated bad debts for accounts receivable. (Hint: Use T-accounts for the pertinent items to isolate the information needed for the statement).

E 4–22
FASB codification research
● LO4–5

The *FASB Accounting Standards Codification* represents the single source of authoritative U.S. generally accepted accounting principles.

Required:

1. Obtain the relevant authoritative literature on earnings per share using the *FASB Accounting Standards Codification* at the FASB website (www.fasb.org). Identify the Codification topic number that provides the accounting for earnings per share.
2. What is the specific citation that describes the additional information for earnings per share that must be included in the notes to the financial statements?
3. Describe the required disclosures.

E 4–23
FASB codification research
● LO4–5, LO4–6, LO4–8

Access the *FASB Accounting Standards Codification* at the FASB website (www.fasb.org). Determine the specific citation for each of the following items:

1. The calculation of the weighted average number of shares for basic earnings per share purposes
2. The alternative formats permissible for reporting comprehensive income
3. The classifications of cash flows required in the statement of cash flows

E 4–24
Concepts; terminology
● LO4–1, LO4–2, LO4–3, LO4–4, LO4–5, LO4–6, LO4–7, LO4–8

Listed below are several terms and phrases associated with income statement presentation and the statement of cash flows. Pair each item from List A (by letter) with the item from List B that is most appropriately associated with it.

List A	List B
______ 1. Intraperiod tax allocation	a. An other comprehensive income item
______ 2. Comprehensive income	b. Starts with net income and works backwards to convert to cash
______ 3. Unrealized holding gain on investments	c. Reports the cash effects of each operating activity directly on the statement
______ 4. Operating income	d. Correction of a material error of a prior period
______ 5. A discontinued operation	e. Related to the external financing of the company
______ 6. Earnings per share	f. Associates tax with income statement item
______ 7. Prior period adjustment	g. Total nonowner change in equity
______ 8. Financing activities	h. Related to the transactions entering into the determination of net income
______ 9. Operating activities (SCF)	i. Related to the acquisition and disposition of long-term assets
______ 10. Investing activities	j. Required disclosure for publicly traded corporation
______ 11. Direct method	k. A component of an entity
______ 12. Indirect method	l. Directly related to principal revenue-generating activities

E 4–25
Inventory turnover; calculation and evaluation
● LO4–10

The following is a portion of the condensed income statement for Rowan, Inc., a manufacturer of plastic containers:

Net sales		$2,460,000
Less: Cost of goods sold:		
Inventory, January 1	$ 630,000	
Net purchases	1,900,000	
Inventory, December 31	(690,000)	1,840,000
Gross profit		$ 620,000

Required:

1. Determine Rowan's inventory turnover.
2. What information does this ratio provide?

E 4–26
Evaluating efficiency of asset management
● LO4–10

The 2018 income statement of Anderson Medical Supply Company reported net sales of $8 million, cost of goods sold of $4.8 million, and net income of $800,000. The following table shows the company's comparative balance sheets for 2018 and 2017:

	($ in thousands)	
	2018	2017
Assets		
Cash	$ 300	$ 380
Accounts receivable	700	500
Inventory	900	700
Property, plant, and equipment (net)	2,400	2,120
Total assets	$4,300	$3,700
Liabilities and Shareholders' Equity		
Current liabilities	$ 960	$ 830
Bonds payable	1,200	1,200
Paid-in capital	1,000	1,000
Retained earnings	1,140	670
Total liabilities and shareholders' equity	$4,300	$3,700

Some industry averages for Anderson's line of business are

Inventory turnover	5 times
Average collection period	25 days
Asset turnover	1.8 times

Required:

1. Determine the following ratios for 2018:
   a. Inventory turnover
   b. Receivables turnover
   c. Average collection period
   d. Asset turnover
2. Assess Anderson's asset management relative to its industry.

E 4–27
Profitability ratios
● LO4–10

The following condensed information was reported by Peabody Toys, Inc., for 2018 and 2017:

	($ in thousands)	
	2018	2017
Income statement information		
Net sales	$5,200	$4,200
Net income	180	124
Balance sheet information		
Current assets	$ 800	$ 750
Property, plant, and equipment (net)	1,100	950
Total assets	$1,900	$1,700
Current liabilities	$ 600	$ 450
Long-term liabilities	750	750
Paid-in capital	400	400
Retained earnings	150	100
Liabilities and shareholders' equity	$1,900	$1,700

Required:

1. Determine the following ratios for 2018:
   a. Profit margin on sales
   b. Return on assets
   c. Return on shareholders' equity
2. Determine the amount of dividends paid to shareholders during 2018.

E 4–28
DuPont analysis
● LO4–10

This exercise is based on the Peabody Toys, Inc., data from E 4–27.

Required:

1. Determine the following components of the DuPont framework for 2018:
   a. Profit margin on sales

b. Asset turnover
c. Equity multiplier
d. Return on shareholders' equity

2. Write an equation that relates these components in calculating ROE. Use the Peabody Toys data to show that the equation is correct.

E 4–29
Interim financial statements; income tax expense
● Appendix 4

Joplin Laminating Corporation reported income before income taxes during the first three quarters, and management's estimates of the annual effective tax rate at the end of each quarter as shown below:

	Quarter		
	First	**Second**	**Third**
Income before income taxes	$50,000	$40,000	$100,000
Estimated annual effective tax rate	34%	30%	36%

Required:
Determine the income tax expense to be reported in the income statement in each of the three quarterly reports.

E 4–30
Interim reporting; recognizing expenses
● Appendix 4

Security-Rand Corporation determines executive incentive compensation at the end of its fiscal year. At the end of the first quarter, management estimated that the amount will be $300 million. Depreciation expense for the year is expected to be $60 million. Also during the quarter, the company realized a gain of $23 million from selling two of its manufacturing plants.

Required:
What amounts for these items should be reported in the first quarter's income statement?

E 4–31
Interim financial statements; reporting expenses
● Appendix 4

Shields Company is preparing its interim report for the second quarter ending June 30. The following payments were made during the first two quarters:

Required:

Expenditure	Date	Amount
Annual advertising	January	$800,000
Property tax for the fiscal year	February	350,000
Annual equipment repairs	March	260,000
One-time research and development fee to consultant	May	96,000

For each expenditure, indicate the amount that would be reported in the quarterly income statements for the periods ending March 31, June 30, September 30, and December 31.

E 4–32
Interim financial statements
● Appendix 4

IFRS

Assume the same facts as in E 4–31, but that Shields Company reports under IFRS. For each expenditure, indicate the amount that would be reported in the quarterly income statements for the periods ending March 31, June 30, September 30, and December 31.

Problems

P 4–1
Comparative income statements; multiple-step format
● LO4–1, LO4–3, LO4–4, LO4–5

Selected information about income statement accounts for the Reed Company is presented below (the company's fiscal year ends on December 31).

	2018	2017
Sales	$4,400,000	$3,500,000
Cost of goods sold	2,860,000	2,000,000
Administrative expenses	800,000	675,000
Selling expenses	360,000	312,000
Interest revenue	150,000	140,000
Interest expense	200,000	200,000
Loss on sale of assets of discontinued component	50,000	—

On July 1, 2018, the company adopted a plan to discontinue a division that qualifies as a component of an entity as defined by GAAP. The assets of the component were sold on September 30, 2018, for $50,000 less than their book value. Results of operations for the component (*included* in the above account balances) were as follows:

	1/1/2018–9/30/2018	2017
Sales	$400,000	$500,000
Cost of goods sold	(290,000)	(320,000)
Administrative expenses	(50,000)	(40,000)
Selling expenses	(20,000)	(30,000)
Operating income before taxes	$ 40,000	$110,000

In addition to the account balances above, several events occurred during 2018 that have *not* yet been reflected in the above accounts:

1. A fire caused $50,000 in uninsured damages to the main office building. The fire was considered to be an infrequent but not unusual event.
2. Inventory that had cost $40,000 had become obsolete because a competitor introduced a better product. The inventory was sold as scrap for $5,000.
3. Income taxes have not yet been recorded.

Required:

Prepare a multiple-step income statement for the Reed Company for 2018, showing 2017 information in comparative format, including income taxes computed at 40 percent and EPS disclosures assuming 300,000 shares of common stock.

P 4–2
Discontinued operations
● LO4–4

The following condensed income statements of the Jackson Holding Company are presented for the two years ended December 31, 2018 and 2017:

	2018	2017
Sales	$15,000,000	$9,600,000
Cost of goods sold	9,200,000	6,000,000
Gross profit	5,800,000	3,600,000
Operating expenses	3,200,000	2,600,000
Operating income	2,600,000	1,000,000
Gain on sale of division	600,000	—
	3,200,000	1,000,000
Income tax expense	1,280,000	400,000
Net income	$ 1,920,000	$ 600,000

On October 15, 2018, Jackson entered into a tentative agreement to sell the assets of one of its divisions. The division qualifies as a component of an entity as defined by GAAP. The division was sold on December 31, 2018, for $5,000,000. Book value of the division's assets was $4,400,000. The division's contribution to Jackson's operating income before-tax for each year was as follows:

2018	$400,000
2017	$300,000

Assume an income tax rate of 40 percent.

Required:

1. Prepare revised income statements according to generally accepted accounting principles, beginning with income from continuing operations before income taxes. Ignore EPS disclosures.
2. Assume that by December 31, 2018, the division had not yet been sold but was considered held for sale. The fair value of the division's assets on December 31 was $5,000,000. What would be the amount presented for discontinued operations?
3. Assume that by December 31, 2018, the division had not yet been sold but was considered held for sale. The fair value of the division's assets on December 31 was $3,900,000. What would be the amount presented for discontinued operations?

P 4–3
Income statement presentation; Discontinued operations; Accounting error
● LO4–4, LO4–5

For the year ending December 31, 2018, Micron Corporation had income from continuing operations before taxes of $1,200,000 before considering the following transactions and events. All of the items described below are before taxes and the amounts should be considered material.

1. In November 2018, Micron sold its Waffle House restaurant chain that qualified as a component of an entity. The company had adopted a plan to sell the chain in May 2018. The income from operations of the chain from January 1, 2018, through November was $160,000 and the loss on sale of the chain's assets was $300,000.
2. In 2018, Micron sold one of its six factories for $1,200,000. At the time of the sale, the factory had a book value of $1,100,000. The factory was not considered a component of the entity.
3. In 2016, Micron's accountant omitted the annual adjustment for patent amortization expense of $120,000. The error was not discovered until December 2018.

Required:

Prepare Micron's income statement, beginning with income from continuing operations before taxes, for the year ended December 31, 2018. Assume an income tax rate of 30%. Ignore EPS disclosures.

P 4–4
Restructuring costs; Discontinued operations; Accounting error
● LO4–3, LO4–4, LO4–5

The preliminary 2018 income statement of Alexian Systems, Inc., is presented below:

ALEXIAN SYSTEMS, INC.
Income Statement
For the Year Ended December 31, 2018
($ in millions, except earnings per share)

Revenues and gains:	
Net sales	$ 425
Interest	3
Other income	126
Total revenues and gains	554
Expenses:	
Cost of goods sold	270
Selling and administrative	154
Income taxes	52
Total expenses	476
Net income	$ 78
Earnings per share	$3.90

Additional Information:

1. Selling and administrative expenses include $26 million in restructuring costs.
2. Included in other income is $120 million in income from a discontinued operation. This consists of $90 million in operating income and a $30 million gain on disposal. The remaining $6 million is from the gain on sale of investments.
3. Cost of goods sold was increased by $5 million to correct an error in the calculation of 2017's ending inventory. The amount is material.

Required:

For each of the three additional facts listed in the additional information, discuss the appropriate presentation of the item described. Do not prepare a revised statement.

P 4–5
Income statement presentation; Restructuring costs; Discontinued operations; Accounting error
● LO4–1, LO4–3, LO4–4, LO4–5

[This is a variation of the previous problem focusing on income statement presentation.]

Required:

Refer to the information presented in P 4–4. Prepare a revised income statement for 2018 reflecting the additional facts. Use a multiple-step format. Assume that an income tax rate of 40% applies to all income statement items, and that 20 million shares of common stock were outstanding throughout the year.

P 4–6
Income statement presentation; Discontinued operations; EPS
● LO4–1, LO4–3, LO4–4, LO4–5

Rembrandt Paint Company had the following income statement items for the year ended December 31, 2018 ($ in thousands):

Net sales	$18,000
Interest income	200
Interest expense	350
Cost of goods sold	10,500
Selling and administrative expenses	2,500
Restructuring costs	800

In addition, during the year the company completed the disposal of its plastics business and incurred a loss from operations of $1.6 million and a gain on disposal of the component's assets of $2 million. 500,000 shares of common stock were outstanding throughout 2018. Income tax expense has not yet been recorded. The income tax rate is 30% on all items of income (loss).

Required:

Prepare a multiple-step income statement for 2018, including EPS disclosures.

P 4–7
Income statement presentation; statement of comprehensive income; unusual items
● LO4–1, LO4–3 through LO4–6

The following income statement items appeared on the adjusted trial balance of Schembri Manufacturing Corporation for the year ended December 31, 2018 ($ in thousands): sales revenue, $15,300; cost of goods sold, $6,200; selling expenses, $1,300; general and administrative expenses, $800; interest revenue, $85; interest expense, $180. Income taxes have not yet been recorded. The company's income tax rate is 40% on all items of income or loss. These revenue and expense items appear in the company's income statement every year. The company's controller, however, has asked for your help in determining the appropriate treatment of the following nonrecurring transactions that also occurred during 2018 ($ in thousands). All transactions are material in amount.

1. Investments were sold during the year at a loss of $220. Schembri also had unrealized gains of $320 for the year on investments.
2. One of the company's factories was closed during the year. Restructuring costs incurred were $1,200.
3. During the year, Schembri completed the sale of one of its operating divisions that qualifies as a component of the entity according to GAAP. The division had incurred a loss from operations of $560 in 2018 prior to the sale, and its assets were sold at a gain of $1,400.
4. In 2018, the company's accountant discovered that depreciation expense in 2017 for the office building was understated by $200.
5. Negative foreign currency translation adjustment for the year totaled $240.

Required:

1. Prepare Schembri's single, continuous multiple-step statement of comprehensive income for 2018, including earnings per share disclosures. One million shares of common stock were outstanding at the beginning of the year and an additional 400,000 shares were issued on July 1, 2018.
2. Prepare a separate statement of comprehensive income for 2018.

P 4–8
Multiple-step statement of income and comprehensive income
● LO4–1, LO4–3, LO4–5, LO4–6

Duke Company's records show the following account balances at December 31, 2018:

Sales	$15,000,000
Cost of goods sold	9,000,000
General and administrative expenses	1,000,000
Selling expenses	500,000
Interest expense	700,000

Income tax expense has not yet been determined. The following events also occurred during 2018. All transactions are material in amount.

1. $300,000 in restructuring costs were incurred in connection with plant closings.
2. Inventory costing $400,000 was written off as obsolete. Material losses of this type are considered to be unusual.
3. It was discovered that depreciation expense for 2017 was understated by $50,000 due to a mathematical error.
4. The company experienced a negative foreign currency translation adjustment of $200,000 and had unrealized gains on investments of $180,000.

Required:

Prepare a single, continuous multiple-step statement of comprehensive income for 2018. The company's effective tax rate on all items affecting comprehensive income is 40%. Each component of other comprehensive income should be displayed net of tax. Ignore EPS disclosures.

P 4–9
Statement of cash flows
● LO4–8

The Diversified Portfolio Corporation provides investment advice to customers. A condensed income statement for the year ended December 31, 2018, appears below:

Service revenue	$900,000
Operating expenses	700,000
Income before income taxes	200,000
Income tax expense	80,000
Net income	$120,000

The following balance sheet information also is available:

	12/31/2018	12/31/2017
Cash	$275,000	$ 70,000
Accounts receivable	120,000	100,000
Accounts payable (operating expenses)	70,000	60,000
Income taxes payable	10,000	15,000

In addition, the following transactions took place during the year:

1. Common stock was issued for $100,000 in cash.
2. Long-term investments were sold for $50,000 in cash. The original cost of the investments also was $50,000.
3. $80,000 in cash dividends was paid to shareholders.
4. The company has no outstanding debt, other than those payables listed above.
5. Operating expenses include $30,000 in depreciation expense.

Required:

1. Prepare a statement of cash flows for 2018 for the Diversified Portfolio Corporation. Use the direct method for reporting operating activities.
2. Prepare the cash flows from operating activities section of Diversified's 2018 statement of cash flows using the indirect method.

P 4–10
Integration of financial statements; Chapters 3 and 4
● LO4–8

The chief accountant for Grandview Corporation provides you with the company's 2018 statement of cash flows and income statement. The accountant has asked for your help with some missing figures in the company's comparative balance sheets. These financial statements are shown next ($ in millions).

GRANDVIEW CORPORATION
Statement of Cash Flows
For the Year Ended December 31, 2018

Cash Flows from Operating Activities:		
Collections from customers	$71	
Payment to suppliers	(30)	
Payment of general & administrative expenses	(18)	
Payment of income taxes	(9)	
Net cash flows from operating activities		$14
Cash Flows from Investing Activities:		
Sale of investments		65
Cash Flows from Financing Activities:		
Issuance of common stock	10	
Payment of dividends	(3)	
Net cash flows from financing activities		7
Net increase in cash		$86

GRANDVIEW CORPORATION
Income Statement
For the Year Ended December 31, 2018

Sales revenue		$80
Cost of goods sold		32
Gross profit		48
Operating expenses:		
General and administrative	$18	
Depreciation	10	
Total operating expenses		28
Operating income		20
Other income:		
Gain on sale of investments		15
Income before income taxes		35
Income tax expense		7
Net income		$28

(continued)

(concluded)

GRANDVIEW CORPORATION
Balance Sheets
At December 31

	2018	2017
Assets:		
Cash	$145	$?
Accounts receivable	?	84
Investments	—	50
Inventory	60	?
Property, plant & equipment	150	150
Less: Accumulated depreciation	(65)	?
Total assets	?	?
Liabilities and Shareholders' Equity:		
Accounts payable to suppliers	$ 40	$ 30
Payables for selling & admin. expenses	9	9
Income taxes payable	22	?
Common stock	240	230
Retained earnings	?	47
Total liabilities and shareholders' equity	?	?

Required:

1. Calculate the missing amounts.
2. Prepare the operating activities section of Grandview's 2018 statement of cash flows using the indirect method.

P 4–11
Statement of cash flows; indirect method
● LO4–8

Presented below are the 2018 income statement and comparative balance sheets for Santana Industries.

SANTANA INDUSTRIES
Income Statement
For the Year Ended December 31, 2018
($ in thousands)

Sales revenue	$14,250	
Service revenue	3,400	
Total revenue		$17,650
Operating expenses:		
Cost of goods sold	7,200	
Selling	2,400	
General and administrative	1,500	
Total operating expenses		11,100
Operating income		6,550
Interest expense		200
Income before income taxes		6,350
Income tax expense		2,500
Net income		$ 3,850

Balance Sheet Information ($ in thousands)	Dec. 31, 2018	Dec. 31, 2017
Assets:		
Cash	$ 7,350	$ 2,200
Accounts receivable	2,500	2,200
Inventory	4,000	3,000
Prepaid rent	150	300
Plant and equipment	14,500	12,000
Less: Accumulated depreciation	(5,100)	(4,500)
Total assets	$23,400	$15,200
Liabilities and shareholders' equity:		
Accounts payable	$ 1,400	$ 1,100
Interest payable	100	0
Deferred service revenue	800	600
Income taxes payable	550	800
Loan payable (due 12/31/2020)	5,000	0
Common stock	10,000	10,000
Retained earnings	5,550	2,700
Total liabilities and shareholders' equity	$23,400	$15,200

Additional information for the 2018 fiscal year ($ in thousands):

1. Cash dividends of $1,000 were declared and paid.
2. Equipment costing $4,000 was purchased with cash.
3. Equipment with a book value of $500 (cost of $1,500 less accumulated depreciation of $1,000) was sold for $500.
4. Depreciation of $1,600 is included in operating expenses.

Required:
Prepare Santana Industries' 2018 statement of cash flows, using the indirect method to present cash flows from operating activities.

P 4–12
Calculating activity and profitability ratios
● LO4–10

Financial statements for Askew Industries for 2018 are shown below (in thousands):

2018 Income Statement

Sales	$9,000
Cost of goods sold	(6,300)
Gross profit	2,700
Operating expenses	(2,000)
Interest expense	(200)
Tax expense	(200)
Net income	$ 300

Comparative Balance Sheets

	Dec. 31	
	2018	2017
Assets		
Cash	$ 600	$ 500
Accounts receivable	600	400
Inventory	800	600
Property, plant, and equipment (net)	2,000	2,100
	$4,000	$3,600
Liabilities and Shareholders' Equity		
Current liabilities	$1,100	$ 850
Bonds payable	1,400	1,400
Paid-in capital	600	600
Retained earnings	900	750
	$4,000	$3,600

Required:
Calculate the following ratios for 2018.

1. Inventory turnover ratio
2. Average days in inventory
3. Receivables turnover ratio
4. Average collection period
5. Asset turnover ratio
6. Profit margin on sales
7. Return on assets
8. Return on shareholders' equity
9. Equity multiplier
10. Return on shareholders' equity (using the DuPont framework)

P 4–13
Use of ratios to compare two companies in the same industry
● LO4–10

Presented below are condensed financial statements adapted from those of two actual companies competing in the pharmaceutical industry—Johnson and Johnson (J&J) and Pfizer, Inc. ($ in millions, except per share amounts).

Required:
Evaluate and compare the two companies by responding to the following questions. ***Note:*** Because two-year comparative statements are not provided, you should use year-end balances in place of average balances as appropriate.

1. Which of the two companies appears more efficient in collecting its accounts receivable and managing its inventory?
2. Which of the two firms had greater earnings relative to resources available?
3. Have the two companies achieved their respective rates of return on assets with similar combinations of profit margin and turnover?
4. From the perspective of a common shareholder, which of the two firms provided a greater rate of return?
5. From the perspective of a common shareholder, which of the two firms appears to be using leverage more effectively to provide a return to shareholders above the rate of return on assets?

Balance Sheets
($ in millions, except per share data)

	J&J	Pfizer
Assets:		
Cash	$ 5,377	$ 1,520
Short-term investments	4,146	10,432
Accounts receivable (net)	6,574	8,775
Inventories	3,588	5,837
Other current assets	3,310	3,177
Current assets	22,995	29,741
Property, plant, and equipment (net)	9,846	18,287
Intangibles and other assets	15,422	68,747
Total assets	$48,263	$116,775
Liabilities and Shareholders' Equity:		
Accounts payable	$ 4,966	$ 2,601
Short-term notes	1,139	8,818
Other current liabilities	7,343	12,238
Current liabilities	13,448	23,657
Long-term debt	2,955	5,755
Other long-term liabilities	4,991	21,986
Total liabilities	21,394	51,398
Capital stock (par and additional paid-in capital)	3,120	67,050
Retained earnings	30,503	29,382
Accumulated other comprehensive income (loss)	(590)	195
Less: Treasury stock and other equity adjustments	(6,164)	(31,250)
Total shareholders' equity	26,869	65,377
Total liabilities and shareholders' equity	$48,263	$116,775
Income Statements		
Net sales	$41,862	$ 45,188
Cost of goods sold	12,176	9,832
Gross profit	29,686	35,356
Operating expenses	19,763	28,486
Other (income) expense—net	(385)	3,610
Income before taxes	10,308	3,260
Tax expense	3,111	1,621
Net income	$ 7,197	$ 1,639*
Basic net income per share	$ 2.42	$ 0.22

*This is before income from discontinued operations.

P 4–14
Creating a balance sheet from ratios; Chapters 3 and 4
● LO4–10

Cadux Candy Company's income statement for the year ended December 31, 2018, reported interest expense of $2 million and income tax expense of $12 million. Current assets listed in its balance sheet include cash, accounts receivable, and inventories. Property, plant, and equipment is the company's only noncurrent asset. Financial ratios for 2018 are listed below. Profitability and turnover ratios with balance sheet items in the denominator were calculated using year-end balances rather than averages.

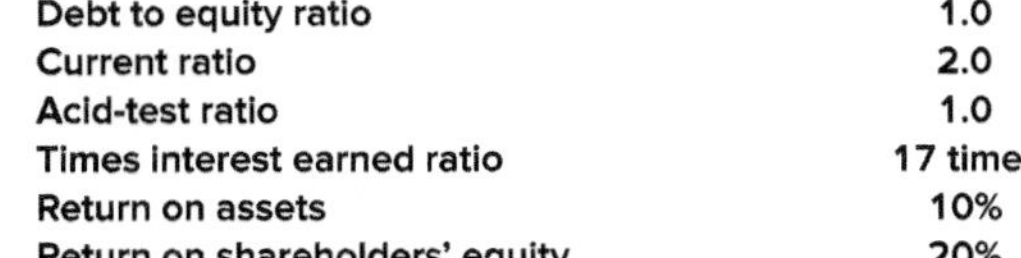

Debt to equity ratio	1.0
Current ratio	2.0
Acid-test ratio	1.0
Times interest earned ratio	17 times
Return on assets	10%
Return on shareholders' equity	20%

(continued)

(concluded)

Profit margin on sales	5%
Gross profit margin (gross profit divided by net sales)	40%
Inventory turnover	8 times
Receivables turnover	20 times

Required:

Prepare a December 31, 2018, balance sheet for the Cadux Candy Company.

P 4–15
Compare two companies in the same industry; Chapters 3 and 4
● LO4–10

Presented below are condensed financial statements adapted from those of two actual companies competing as the primary players in a specialty area of the food manufacturing and distribution industry ($ in millions, except per share amounts).

	Balance Sheets	
	Metropolitan	**Republic**
Assets:		
Cash	$ 179.3	$ 37.1
Accounts receivable (net)	422.7	325.0
Short-term investments	—	4.7
Inventories	466.4	635.2
Prepaid expenses and other current assets	134.6	476.7
Current assets	1,203.0	1,478.7
Property, plant, and equipment (net)	2,608.2	2,064.6
Intangibles and other assets	210.3	464.7
Total assets	$4,021.5	$4,008.0
Liabilities and Shareholders' Equity		
Accounts payable	$ 467.9	$ 691.2
Short-term notes	227.1	557.4
Accruals and other current liabilities	585.2	538.5
Current liabilities	1,280.2	1,787.1
Long-term debt	535.6	542.3
Deferred tax liability	384.6	610.7
Other long-term liabilities	104.0	95.1
Total liabilities	2,304.4	3,035.2
Common stock (par and additional paid-in capital)	144.9	335.0
Retained earnings	2,476.9	1,601.9
Less: Treasury stock	(904.7)	(964.1)
Total liabilities and shareholders' equity	$4,021.5	$4,008.0
Income Statements		
Net sales	$5,698.0	$7,768.2
Cost of goods sold	(2,909.0)	(4,481.7)
Gross profit	2,789.0	3,286.5
Operating expenses	(1,743.7)	(2,539.2)
Interest expense	(56.8)	(46.6)
Income before taxes	988.5	700.7
Tax expense	(394.7)	(276.1)
Net income	$ 593.8	$ 424.6
Net income per share	$ 2.40	$ 6.50

Required:

Evaluate and compare the two companies by responding to the following questions.

Note: Because comparative statements are not provided you should use year-end balances in place of average balances as appropriate.

1. Which of the two firms had greater earnings relative to resources available?
2. Have the two companies achieved their respective rates of return on assets with similar combinations of profit margin and turnover?
3. From the perspective of a common shareholder, which of the two firms provided a greater rate of return?
4. Which company is most highly leveraged and which has made most effective use of financial leverage?
5. Of the two companies, which appears riskier in terms of its ability to pay short-term obligations?
6. How efficiently are current assets managed?

7. From the perspective of a creditor, which company offers the most comfortable margin of safety in terms of its ability to pay fixed interest charges?

P 4–16
Interim financial reporting
● Appendix 4

Branson Electronics Company is a small, publicly traded company preparing its first quarter interim report to be mailed to shareholders. The following information for the quarter has been compiled:

Revenues		$180,000
Cost of goods sold		35,000
Operating expenses:		
Fixed	$59,000	
Variable	48,000	107,000

Fixed operating expenses include payments of $50,000 to an advertising firm to promote Branson through various media throughout the year. The income tax rate for Branson's level of operations in the first quarter is 30%, but management estimates the effective rate for the entire year will be 36%.

Required:
Prepare the income statement to be included in Branson's first quarter interim report.

Broaden Your Perspective

Apply your critical-thinking ability to the knowledge you've gained. These cases will provide you an opportunity to develop your research, analysis, judgment, and communication skills. You also will work with other students, integrate what you've learned, apply it in real-world situations, and consider its global and ethical ramifications. This practice will broaden your knowledge and further develop your decision-making abilities.

Judgment Case 4–1
Earnings quality
● LO4–2, LO4–3

The financial community in the United States has become increasingly concerned with the quality of reported company earnings.

Required:
1. Define the term *earnings quality.*
2. Explain the distinction between permanent and temporary earnings as it relates to the concept of earnings quality.
3. How do earnings management practices affect the quality of earnings?
4. Assume that a manufacturing company's annual income statement included a large gain from the sale of investment securities. What factors would you consider in determining whether or not this gain should be included in an assessment of the company's permanent earnings?

Judgment Case 4–2
Restructuring costs
● LO4–3

The appearance of restructuring costs in corporate income statements increased significantly in the 1980s and 1990s and continues to be relevant today.

Required:
1. What types of costs are included in restructuring costs?
2. When are restructuring costs recognized?
3. How would you classify restructuring costs in a multi-step income statement?
4. What factors would you consider in determining whether or not restructuring costs should be included in an assessment of a company's permanent earnings?

Judgment Case 4–3
Earnings management
● LO4–2, LO4–3

Companies often are under pressure to meet or beat Wall Street earnings projections in order to increase stock prices and also to increase the value of stock options. Some resort to earnings management practices to artificially create desired results.

Required:
Is *earnings management* always intended to produce higher income? Explain.

Real World Case 4–4
Earnings quality and non-GAAP earnings
● LO4–3

Companies often voluntarily provide non-GAAP earnings when they announce annual or quarterly earnings.

Required:
1. What is meant by the term *non-GAAP earnings* in this context?
2. How do non-GAAP earnings relate to the concept of earnings quality?

Research Case 4–5
FASB codification; locate and extract relevant information and cite authoritative support for a financial reporting issue; restructuring costs; exit or disposal cost obligations
● LO4–2, LO4–3

The accrual of restructuring costs creates obligations (liabilities) referred to as *exit or disposal cost obligations.*

Required:

1. Obtain the relevant authoritative literature on exit or disposal cost obligations using the *FASB Accounting Standards Codification.* You might gain access at the FASB website (www.fasb.org). What is the Codification topic number that addresses this issue?
2. What is the specific citation that addresses the initial measurement of these obligations?
3. How are these obligations and related costs to be measured?
4. What is the specific citation that describes the disclosure requirements in the notes to the financial statements for exit or disposal obligations?
5. List the required disclosures.

Judgment Case 4–6
Income statement presentation
● LO4–3, LO4–4, LO4–5

Each of the following situations occurred during 2018 for one of your audit clients:

1. The write-off of inventory due to obsolescence.
2. Discovery that depreciation expenses were omitted by accident from 2017's income statement.
3. The useful lives of all machinery were changed from eight to five years.
4. The depreciation method used for all equipment was changed from the declining-balance to the straight-line method.
5. Restructuring costs were incurred.
6. The Stridewell Company, a manufacturer of shoes, sold all of its retail outlets. It will continue to manufacture and sell its shoes to other retailers. A loss was incurred in the disposition of the retail stores. The retail stores are considered a component of the entity.
7. The inventory costing method was changed from FIFO to average cost.

Required:

1. For each situation, identify the appropriate reporting treatment from the list below (consider each event to be material):
   a. As an unusual gain or loss
   b. As a prior period adjustment
   c. As a change in accounting principle
   d. As a discontinued operation
   e. As a change in accounting estimate
   f. As a change in accounting estimate achieved by a change in accounting principle
2. Indicate whether each situation would be included in the income statement in continuing operations (CO) or below continuing operations (BC), or if it would appear as an adjustment to retained earnings (RE). Use the format shown below to answer requirements 1 and 2.

Situation	Treatment (a–f)	Financial Statement Presentation (CO, BC, or RE)
1.		
2.		
3.		
4.		
5.		
6.		
7.		

Judgment Case 4–7
Income statement presentation
● LO4–3, LO4–4, LO4–5

The following events occurred during 2018 for various audit clients of your firm. Consider each event to be independent and the effect of each event to be material.

1. A manufacturing company recognized a loss on the sale of investments.

2. An automobile manufacturer sold all of the assets related to its financing component. The operations of the financing business is considered a component of the entity.
3. A company changed its depreciation method from the double-declining-balance method to the straight-line method.
4. Due to obsolescence, a company engaged in the manufacture of high-technology products incurred a loss on the write-down of inventory.
5. One of your clients discovered that 2017's depreciation expense was overstated. The error occurred because of a miscalculation of depreciation for the office building.
6. A cosmetics company decided to discontinue the manufacture of a line of women's lipstick. Other cosmetic lines will be continued. A loss was incurred on the sale of assets related to the lipstick product line. The operations of the discontinued line is not considered a component of the entity.

Required:
Discuss the 2018 financial statement presentation of each of the above events. Do not consider earnings per share disclosures.

IFRS Case 4–8
Statement of cash flows; GlaxoSmithKline Plc.
● LO4–8, LO4–9

Real World Financials

GlaxoSmithKline Plc. (GSK) is a global pharmaceutical and consumer health-related products company located in the United Kingdom. The company prepares its financial statements in accordance with International Financial Reporting Standards. Below is a portion of the company's statements of cash flows included in recent financial statements:

GLAXOSMITHKLINE PLC.
Consolidated Cash Flow Statement
For the Year Ended 31 December 2013

	Notes	2013 £m	2012 (restated) £m	2011 (restated) £m
Cash flow from operating activities				
Profit after taxation for the year		5,628	4,678	5,405
Adjustments reconciling profit after tax to operating cash flows	36	2,871	1,370	2,308
Cash generated from operations		8,499	6,048	7,713
Taxation paid		(1,277)	(1,673)	(1,463)
Net cash inflow from operating activities		7,222	4,375	6,250
Cash flow from investing activities				
Purchase of property, plant and equipment		(1,188)	(1,051)	(923)
Proceeds from sale of property, plant and equipment		46	68	100
Purchase of intangible assets		(513)	(469)	(405)
Proceeds from sale of intangible assets		136	1,056	237
Purchase of equity investments		(133)	(229)	(76)
Proceeds from sale of equity investments		59	28	68
Purchase of businesses, net of cash acquired	38	(247)	(2,235)	(264)
Disposal of businesses	38	1,851	—	—
Investments in associates and joint ventures	20	(8)	(99)	(35)
Proceeds from disposal of subsidiary and interest in associate		429	—	1,034
Decrease in liquid investments		15	224	30
Interest received		59	30	97
Dividends from associates and joint ventures		18	46	25
Net cash inflow/(outflow) from investing activities		524	(2,631)	(112)
Cash flow from financing activities				
Proceeds from own shares for employee share options		—	58	45
Shares acquired by ESOP Trusts		(45)	(37)	(36)
Issue of share capital	33	585	356	250
Purchase of own shares for cancellation or to be held as Treasury shares		(1,504)	(2,493)	(2,191)
Purchase of non-controlling interests		(588)	(14)	—
Increase in long-term loans		1,913	4,430	—
Increase in short-term loans		—	1,743	45
Repayment of short-term loans		(1,872)	(2,559)	(8)
Net repayment of obligations under finance leases		(31)	(35)	(38)
Interest paid		(749)	(779)	(769)
Dividends paid to shareholders		(3,680)	(3,814)	(3,406)
Distributions to non-controlling interests		(238)	(171)	(234)

(continued)

(concluded)

Other financing cash flows		(64)	(36)	110
Net cash outflow from financing activities		(6,273)	(3,351)	(6,232)
Increase/(decrease) in cash and bank overdrafts	37	1,473	(1,607)	(94)
Cash and bank overdrafts at beginning of year		3,906	5,605	5,807
Exchange adjustments		(148)	(92)	(108)
Increase/(decrease) in cash and bank overdrafts		1,473	(1,607)	(94)
Cash and bank overdrafts at end of year		5,231	3,906	5,605
Cash and bank overdrafts at end of year comprise:				
Cash and cash equivalents		5,534	4,184	5,714
Overdrafts		(303)	(278)	(109)
		5,231	3,906	5,605

Required:

Identify the items in the above statements that would be reported differently if GlaxoSmithKline prepared its financial statements according to U.S. GAAP rather than IFRS.

Judgment Case 4–9
Income statement presentation; unusual items; comprehensive income
● LO4–3, LO4–4, LO4–5, LO4–6

Norse Manufacturing Inc. prepares an annual single, continuous statement of income and comprehensive income. The following situations occurred during the company's 2018 fiscal year:

1. Restructuring costs were incurred due to the closing of a factory.
2. Investments were sold, and a loss was recognized.
3. A positive foreign currency translation adjustment was recognized.
4. Interest expense was incurred.
5. A division was sold that qualifies as a separate component of the entity according to GAAP.
6. Obsolete inventory was written off.
7. The controller discovered an error in the calculation of 2017's patent amortization expense.

Required:

1. For each situation, identify the appropriate reporting treatment from the list below (consider each event to be material):
   a. As a component of operating income
   b. As a nonoperating income item (other income or expense)
   c. As a discontinued operation
   d. As an other comprehensive income item
   e. As an adjustment to retained earnings
2. Identify the situations that would be reported net-of-tax.

Judgment Case 4–10
Management incentives for change
● LO4–2

It has been suggested that not all accounting choices are made by management in the best interest of fair and consistent financial reporting.

Required:

What motivations can you think of for management's choice of accounting methods?

Research Case 4–11
Non-GAAP earnings
● LO4–3

Companies often voluntarily provide non-GAAP earnings when they announce annual or quarterly earnings. These numbers are controversial as they represent management's view of permanent earnings. The Sarbanes-Oxley Act (SOX), issued in 2002, requires that if non-GAAP earnings are included in any periodic or other report filed with the SEC or in any public disclosure or press release, the company also must provide a reconciliation with earnings determined according to GAAP.

Professors Entwistle, Feltham, and Mbagwu, in "Financial Reporting Regulation and the Reporting of Pro Forma Earnings," examine whether firms changed their reporting practice in response to the regulations included in SOX.

Required:

1. In your library or from some other source, locate the indicated article in *Accounting Horizons,* March 2006.
2. What sample of firms did the authors use in their examination?
3. What percent of firms reported non-GAAP earnings (referred to as *pro forma earnings* by the authors) in 2001? In 2003?
4. What percent of firms had non-GAAP earnings greater than GAAP earnings in 2001? In 2003?

5. What was the most frequently reported adjusting item in 2001? In 2003?
6. What are the authors' main conclusions of the impact of SOX on non-GAAP reporting?

Integrating Case 4–12
Balance sheet and income statement; Chapters 3 and 4
● LO4–3

Rice Corporation is negotiating a loan for expansion purposes and the bank requires financial statements. Before closing the accounting records for the year ended December 31, 2018, Rice's controller prepared the following financial statements:

RICE CORPORATION
Balance Sheet At December 31, 2018
($ in thousands)

Assets	
Cash	$ 275
Marketable securities	78
Accounts receivable	487
Inventories	425
Allowance for uncollectible accounts	(50)
Property and equipment, net	160
Total assets	$1,375
Liabilities and Shareholders' Equity	
Accounts payable and accrued liabilities	$ 420
Notes payable	200
Common stock	260
Retained earnings	495
Total liabilities and shareholders' equity	$1,375

RICE CORPORATION
Income Statement
For the Year Ended December 31, 2018
($ in thousands)

Net sales		$1,580
Expenses:		
Cost of goods sold	$755	
Selling and administrative	385	
Miscellaneous	129	
Income taxes	100	
Total expenses		1,369
Net income		$ 211

Additional Information:

1. The company's common stock is traded on an organized stock exchange.
2. The investment portfolio consists of short-term investments valued at $57,000. The remaining investments will not be sold until the year 2020.
3. Notes payable consist of two notes:

   Note 1: $80,000 face value dated September 30, 2018. Principal and interest at 10% are due on September 30, 2019.

   Note 2: $120,000 face value dated April 30, 2018. Principal is due in two equal installments of $60,000 plus interest on the unpaid balance. The two payments are scheduled for April 30, 2019, and April 30, 2020.

   Interest on both loans has been correctly accrued and is included in accrued liabilities on the balance sheet and selling and administrative expenses on the income statement.
4. Selling and administrative expenses include $90,000 representing costs incurred by the company in restructuring some of its operations. The amount is material.

Required:

Identify and explain the deficiencies in the presentation of the statements prepared by the company's controller. Do not prepare corrected statements. Include in your answer a list of items which require additional disclosure, either on the face of the statement or in a note.

Analysis Case 4–13
Income statement information
● LO4–1

Refer to the income statement of Sherwin Williams Company in Illustration 4–2 of this chapter.

Required:

1. Is this income statement presented in the single-step or multiple-step format?

2. What is the company's approximate income tax rate?
3. What is the percentage of net income relative to net sales?

Real World Case 4–14
Income statement information
● LO4–1, LO4–3, LO4–4

Real World Financials

EDGAR, the Electronic Data Gathering, Analysis, and Retrieval system, performs automated collection, validation, indexing, and forwarding of submissions by companies and others who are required by law to file forms with the U.S. Securities and Exchange Commission (SEC). All publicly traded domestic companies use EDGAR to make the majority of their filings. (Some foreign companies file voluntarily.) Form 10-K, which includes the annual report, is required to be filed on EDGAR. The SEC makes this information available on the Internet.

Required:

1. Access EDGAR on the Internet. The web address is www.sec.gov.
2. Search for a public company with which you are familiar. Access the most recent 10-K filing. Search or scroll to find the financial statements and related notes.
3. Answer the following questions related to the company's income statement:
   a. Does the company use the single-step or multiple-step format, or a variation?
   b. Does the income statement contain any income or loss on discontinued operations? If it does, describe the component of the company that was discontinued. (*Hint:* there should be a related disclosure note.)
   c. Describe the trend in net income over the years presented.
4. Repeat requirements 2 and 3 for two additional companies.

Real World Case 4–15
Income statement format; restructuring costs; earnings per share; comprehensive income; statement of cash flows; Ralph Lauren
● LO4–1, LO4–3, LO4–5, LO4–6, LO4–8

Real World Financials

Ralph Lauren Corporation is a global leader in the design, marketing, and distribution of premium lifestyle products, including men's, women's and children's apparel. Below are selected financial statements taken from a recent 10-K filing.

Required:

Use the information in the financial statements to answer the following questions.

1. Does the company use the single-step or multiple-step format to present its income statements?
2. What are restructuring costs? Why are they reported as a line item?
3. Describe the fiscal 2014 restructuring and other costs. (Note: this will require access to the company's 10-K which you can find using EDGAR on the Internet at www.sec.gov, or on the investor relations page at the company website: www.ralphlauren.com).
4. Using the information you find in the company's 10-K, describe the 2013 asset impairments.
5. Explain the difference between basic and diluted earnings per share.
6. The company chose to report comprehensive income in two consecutive statements, a statement of income and a statement of comprehensive income. What other alternative did the company have to report the information in these two statements?
7. What "other comprehensive items (OCI)" did the company report in fiscal 2014? What other possible transactions would be reported as OCI if the company had experienced those transactions?
8. What method does the company use to report net cash provided by operating activities? What other method(s) could the company have used?
9. What is the largest cash outflow from investing activities?

RALPH LAUREN CORPORATION
CONSOLIDATED STATEMENTS OF INCOME

	Fiscal Years Ended		
	March 29, 2014	**March 30, 2013**	**March 31, 2012**
	($ in millions, except per share data)		
Net sales	$ 7,284	$ 6,763	$ 6,679
Licensing revenue	166	182	181
Net revenues	7,450	6,945	6,860
Cost of goods sold	(3,140)	(2,789)	(2,862)
Gross profit	4,310	4,156	3,998
Other costs and expenses:			
Selling, general, and administrative expenses	(3,142)	(2,971)	(2,916)
Amortization of intangible assets	(35)	(27)	(29)
Gain on acquisition of Chaps	16	—	—
Impairments of assets	(1)	(19)	(2)

(continued)

(concluded)

RALPH LAUREN CORPORATION
CONSOLIDATED STATEMENTS OF INCOME

	Fiscal Years Ended		
	March 29, 2014	**March 30, 2013**	**March 31, 2012**
	($ in millions, except per share data)		
Restructuring and other costs	(18)	(12)	(12)
Total other costs and expenses, net	(3,180)	(3,029)	(2,959)
Operating income	1,130	1,127	1,039
Foreign currency losses	(8)	(12)	(2)
Interest expense	(20)	(22)	(24)
Interest and other income, net	3	6	11
Equity in losses of equity-method investees	(9)	(10)	(9)
Income before provision for income taxes	1,096	1,089	1,015
Provision for income taxes	(320)	(339)	(334)
Net income	$ 776	$ 750	$ 681
Net income per common share:			
Basic	$ 8.55	$ 8.21	$ 7.35
Diluted	$ 8.43	$ 8.00	$ 7.13

RALPH LAUREN CORPORATION
CONSOLIDATED STATEMENTS OF COMPREHENSIVE INCOME

	Fiscal Years Ended		
	March 29, 2014	**March 30, 2013**	**March 31, 2012**
	($ in millions)		
Net income	$776	$750	$681
Other comprehensive income (loss), net of tax:			
Foreign currency translation adjustments	52	(93)	(50)
Gains (losses) on derivatives	(27)	(13)	32
Net unrealized gains (losses) on available-for-sale investments	(5)	4	1
Losses on defined benefit plans	—	(1)	(2)
Other comprehensive income (loss), net of tax	20	(103)	(19)
Total comprehensive income	$796	$647	$662

RALPH LAUREN CORPORATION
CONSOLIDATED STATEMENTS OF CASH FLOWS

	Fiscal Years Ended		
	March 29, 2014	March 30, 2013	March 31, 2012
	($ in millions)		
Cash flows from operating activities:			
Net income	$776	$750	$ 681
Adjustments to reconcile net income to net cash provided by operating activities:			
Depreciation and amortization expense	258	233	225
Deferred income tax expense (benefit)	1	14	(15)
Equity in losses of equity-method investees	9	10	9
Non-cash stock-based compensation expense	93	88	78
Gain on acquisition of Chaps	(16)	—	—
Non-cash impairment of assets	1	19	2
Other non-cash charges, net	6	3	3
Excess tax benefits from stock-based compensation arrangements	(34)	(41)	(40)
Changes in operating assets and liabilities:			
Accounts receivable	(104)	82	(114)
Inventories	(77)	(68)	(148)

(continued)

(concluded)

RALPH LAUREN CORPORATION
CONSOLIDATED STATEMENTS OF CASH FLOWS

	Fiscal Years Ended		
	March 29, 2014	March 30, 2013	March 31, 2012
		($ in millions)	
Prepaid expenses and other current assets	(56)	4	(39)
Accounts payable and accrued liabilities	43	(57)	33
Income tax receivables and payables	59	(13)	122
Deferred income	(18)	(30)	(19)
Other balance sheet changes, net	(34)	25	107
Net cash provided by operating activities	907	1,019	885
Cash flows from investing activities:			
Capital expenditures	(390)	(276)	(272)
Purchases of investments	(1,067)	(876)	(1,360)
Proceeds from sales and maturities of investments	1,011	1,058	1,394
Acquisitions and ventures, net of cash acquired	(40)	(22)	(12)
Change in restricted cash deposits	(2)	3	1
Net cash used in investing activities	(488)	(113)	(249)
Cash flows from financing activities:			
Proceeds from issuance of debt	300	—	108
Repayment of debt	(269)	—	(108)
Payments of capital lease obligations	(9)	(9)	(8)
Payments of dividends	(149)	(128)	(74)
Repurchases of common stock, including shares surrendered for tax withholdings	(558)	(497)	(419)
Prepayments of common stock repurchases	—	(50)	—
Proceeds from exercise of stock options	52	49	61
Excess tax benefits from stock-based compensation arrangements	34	41	40
Payment on interest rate swap termination	—	—	(8)
Other financing activities	—	(1)	—
Net cash used in financing activities	(599)	(595)	(408)
Effect of exchange rate changes on cash and cash equivalents	3	(9)	(9)
Net increase (decrease) in cash and cash equivalents	(177)	302	219
Cash and cash equivalents at beginning of period	974	672	453
Cash and cash equivalents at end of period	$ 797	$ 974	$ 672

Analysis Case 4–16
Evaluating profitability and asset management; obtain and compare annual reports from companies in the same industry
● LO4–10

Performance and profitability of a company often are evaluated using the financial information provided by a firm's annual report in comparison with other firms in the same industry. Ratios are useful in this assessment.

Required:

Obtain annual reports from two corporations in the same primary industry. Using techniques you learned in this chapter and any analysis you consider useful, respond to the following questions:

1. How do earnings trends compare in terms of both the direction and stability of income?
2. Which of the two firms had greater earnings relative to resources available?
3. How efficiently are current assets managed?
4. Has each of the companies achieved its respective rate of return on assets with similar combinations of profit margin and turnover?
5. Are there differences in accounting methods that should be taken into account when making comparisons?

Note: You can obtain copies of annual reports from friends who are shareholders, the investor relations department of the corporations, from a friendly stockbroker, or from EDGAR (Electronic Data Gathering, Analysis, and Retrieval) on the Internet (www.sec.gov).

Judgment Case 4–17
Relationships among ratios; Chapters 3 and 4
● LO4–10

You are a part-time financial advisor. A client is considering an investment in common stock of a waste recycling firm. One motivation is a rumor the client heard that the company made huge investments in a new fuel creation process. Unable to confirm the rumor, your client asks you to determine whether the firm's assets had recently increased significantly.

Because the firm is small, information is sparse. Last quarter's interim report showed total assets of $324 million, approximately the same as last year's annual report. The only information more current than that is a press release last week in which the company's management reported "record net income for the year of $21 million, representing a 14.0% return on shareholders' equity. Performance was enhanced by the Company's judicious use of financial leverage on a debt/equity ratio of 2 to 1."

Required:

Use the information available to provide your client with an opinion as to whether the waste recycling firm invested in the new fuel creation process during the last quarter of the year.

Integrating Case 4–18
Using ratios to test reasonableness of data; Chapters 3 and 4
● LO4–10

You are a new staff accountant with a large regional CPA firm, participating in your first audit. You recall from your auditing class that CPAs often use ratios to test the reasonableness of accounting numbers provided by the client. Since ratios reflect the relationships among various account balances, if it is assumed that prior relationships still hold, prior years' ratios can be used to estimate what current balances should approximate. However, you never actually performed this kind of analysis until now. The CPA in charge of the audit of Covington Pike Corporation brings you the list of ratios shown below and tells you these reflect the relationships maintained by Covington Pike in recent years.

Profit margin on sales = 5%
Return on assets = 7.5%
Gross profit margin = 40%
Inventory turnover ratio = 6 times
Receivables turnover ratio = 25 times
Acid-test ratio = 0.9 to one
Current ratio = 2 to 1
Return on shareholders' equity = 10%
Debt to equity ratio = 1/3
Times interest earned ratio = 12 times

Jotted in the margins are the following notes:

- Net income $15,000.
- Only one short-term note ($5,000); all other current liabilities are trade accounts.
- Property, plant, and equipment are the only noncurrent assets.
- Bonds payable are the only noncurrent liabilities.
- The effective interest rate on short-term notes and bonds is 8%.
- No investment securities.
- Cash balance totals $15,000.

Required:

You are requested to approximate the current year's balances in the form of a balance sheet and income statement, to the extent the information allows. Accompany those financial statements with the calculations you use to estimate each amount reported.

Continuing Cases

Target Case
● LO4–3, LO4–4, LO4–6, LO4–8

Target Corporation prepares its financial statements according to U.S. GAAP. Target's financial statements and disclosure notes for the year ended January 30, 2016, are available in Connect. This material is also available under the Investor Relations link at the company's website (www.target.com).

Required:

1. By what name does Target label its income statement?
2. What amounts did Target report for the following items for the year ended January 30, 2016?
    a. Sales
    b. Gross margin
    c. Earnings from continuing operations before income taxes
    d. Net earnings from continuing operations
    e. Net earnings
3. What additional items, if any, does Target report as part of its comprehensive income?
4. Does target prepare the statement of cash flows using the direct method or the indirect method?
5. Which is higher, net earnings or operating cash flows? Which line item is the biggest reason for this difference? Explain why.
6. What is the largest investing cash flow and the largest financing cash flow reported by the company for the year ended January 30, 2016?

Air France–KLM Case

● LO4–9

 IFRS

Air France–KLM (AF), a Franco-Dutch company, prepares its financial statements according to International Financial Reporting Standards. AF's financial statements and disclosure notes for the year ended December 31, 2015, are provided Connect. This material is also available under the Finance link at the company's website (www.airfranceklm.com).

Required:

1. How does AF classify operating expenses in its income statement? How are these expenses typically classified in a U.S. company income statement?
2. How does AF classify interest paid, interest received, and dividends received in its statement of cash flows? What other alternatives, if any, does the company have for the classification of these items? How are these items classified under U.S. GAAP?

CPA Exam Questions and Simulations

Sample CPA Exam questions from Roger CPA Review are available in Connect as support for the topics in this chapter. These Multiple Choice Questions and Task-Based Simulations include expert-written explanations and solutions, and provide a starting point for students to become familiar with the content and functionality of the actual CPA Exam.

CHAPTER

5 Revenue Recognition

OVERVIEW

In Chapter 4, we discussed net income and its presentation in the income statement. In Chapter 5 we focus on revenue recognition, which determines when and how much revenue appears in the income statement. In Part A of this chapter, we discuss the general approach for recognizing revenue in three situations—at a point in time, over a period of time, and for contracts that include multiple parts that might require recognizing revenue at different times. In Part B, we see how to deal with special issues that affect the revenue recognition process. In Part C, we discuss how to account for revenue in long-term contracts. In an appendix, we consider some aspects of GAAP that were eliminated by recent changes in accounting standards but that still will be used in practice until the end of 2017.

LEARNING OBJECTIVES

After studying this chapter, you should be able to:

- **LO5–1** State the core revenue recognition principle and the five key steps in applying it. *(p. 236)*
- **LO5–2** Explain when it is appropriate to recognize revenue at a single point in time. *(p. 238)*
- **LO5–3** Explain when it is appropriate to recognize revenue over a period of time. *(p. 239)*
- **LO5–4** Allocate a contract's transaction price to multiple performance obligations. *(p. 241)*
- **LO5–5** Determine whether a contract exists, and whether some frequently encountered features of contracts qualify as performance obligations. *(p. 245)*
- **LO5–6** Understand how variable consideration and other aspects of contracts affect the calculation and allocation of the transaction price. *(p. 248)*
- **LO5–7** Determine the timing of revenue recognition with respect to licenses, franchises, and other common arrangements. *(p. 254)*
- **LO5–8** Understand the disclosures required for revenue recognition, accounts receivable, contract assets, and contract liabilities. *(p. 259)*
- **LO5–9** Demonstrate revenue recognition for long-term contracts, both at a point in time when the contract is completed and over a period of time according to the percentage completed. *(p. 261)*
- **LO5–10** Discuss the primary differences between U.S. GAAP and IFRS with respect to revenue recognition. *(pp. 246, 249 and 256)*

© Hero Images/Getty Images

FINANCIAL REPORTING CASE

Ask the Oracle

"Good news! I got the job," she said, closing the door behind her.

Your roommate, a software engineer, goes on to explain that she accepted a position at Oracle Corporation, a world leader in enterprise software, computer hardware, and cloud-computing services.

"The salary's good, too," she continued. "Plus, Mr. Watson, my supervisor, said I'll be getting a bonus tied to the amount of revenue my projects produce. So I started looking at Oracle's financial statements, but I can't even understand when they get to recognize revenue. Sometimes they recognize it all at once, sometimes over time, and sometimes they seem to break apart a sale and recognize revenue for different parts at different times. And sometimes they recognize revenue before they are even done with a project, according to the percentage they have completed so far. You're the accountant. What determines when Oracle gets to recognize revenue?"

QUESTIONS

By the time you finish this chapter, you should be able to respond appropriately to the questions posed in this case. Compare your response to the solution provided at the end of the chapter.

1. Under what circumstances do companies recognize revenue at a point in time? Over a period of time? (*p. 238*)
2. When do companies break apart a sale and treat its parts differently for purposes of recognizing revenue? (*p. 241*)
3. How do companies account for long-term contracts that qualify for revenue recognition over time? (*p. 262*)

What is revenue? According to the FASB's conceptual framework, "Revenues are inflows or other enhancements of assets of an entity or settlements of its liabilities (or a combination of both) from delivering or producing goods, rendering services, or other activities that constitute the entity's ongoing major or central operations."[1] In simpler terms, revenue is the inflow of cash or accounts receivable that a business receives when it provides goods or services to its customers.

For many companies, revenue is the single largest number reported in the financial statements. Its pivotal role in the picture painted by the financial statements makes measuring and reporting revenue one of the most critical aspects of financial reporting. It is important not only to determine *how much* revenue to recognize (record), but also *when* to recognize it. A one-year income statement should report a company's revenues for only that one-year period. Sometimes, though, it's difficult to determine how much revenue to recognize in a particular period. Also, you can imagine that a manager who is evaluated according to how much revenue she generates each period might be tempted to recognize more revenue than is appropriate. In fact, the SEC has cracked down on revenue-recognition abuses in the past, and its enforcement division continues to do so.[2]

[1]"Elements of Financial Statements," *Statement of Financial Concepts No. 6* (Stamford, Conn.: FASB, 1985, par. 78).

[2]For SEC guidance that provides examples of appropriate and inappropriate revenue recognition, see FASB ASC 605–10–S99: Revenue Recognition–Overall–SEC Materials (originally "Revenue Recognition in Financial Statements," *Staff Accounting Bulletin No. 101* (Washington, D.C.: SEC, December 1999) and *Staff Accounting Bulletin No. 104* (Washington, D.C.: SEC, December 2003)).

Revenue recognition criteria help ensure that an income statement reflects the actual accomplishments of a company for the period.

Revenue recognition accounting standards help ensure that the appropriate amount of revenue appears in each period's income statement. That guidance has changed recently.

Revenue recognition previously was based on the "realization principle," which required that we recognize revenue when both the earnings process is virtually complete and there is reasonable certainty as to the collectibility of the assets to be received in exchange for goods and services. That approach to revenue recognition created some problems. Revenue recognition was poorly tied to the FASB's conceptual framework, which places more emphasis on recognizing assets and liabilities rather than on the earnings process. The focus on the earnings process led to similar transactions being treated differently in different industries. And, the realization principle was difficult to apply to complex arrangements that involved multiple goods or services.

To address these concerns, the FASB and IASB worked together to develop a new revenue recognition standard, which the FASB issued as *Accounting Standards Update (ASU) No. 2014–09*, "Revenue from Contracts with Customers," on May 28, 2014.[3] The ASU provides a unified approach that replaces more than 200 different pieces of specialized guidance that had developed over time in U.S. GAAP for revenue recognition under various industries and circumstances. Public companies reporting under U.S. GAAP must adopt the ASU for periods beginning after December 15, 2017.[4] Companies have two options for adopting *ASU No 2014–09*: they can restate prior years presented in comparative financial statements to appear as if the company had always accounted for revenue under the ASU, or they can leave prior year financial statements unchanged and in the beginning of 2018 record the adjustments necessary to convert to the ASU.

Because you need to understand the revenue recognition requirements that will be in effect during your career, we focus on the revenue recognition approach described in *ASU No. 2014–09* (and clarified in subsequent guidance). In the chapter appendix, we consider aspects of GAAP that were eliminated by the ASU but that still will appear in practice for public companies until the end of 2017.

PART A Introduction to Revenue Recognition

● LO5–1

Let's start with the core revenue recognition principle and the key steps we use to apply that principle. These are shown in Illustration 5–1.

Illustration 5–1 Core Revenue Recognition Principle and the Five Steps Used to Apply the Principle

Core Revenue Recognition Principle

Companies recognize revenue when goods or services are transferred to customers for the amount the company expects to be entitled to receive in exchange for those goods or services.*

Five Steps Used to Apply the Principle

Step 1	• Identify the contract with a customer.
Step 2	• Identify the performance obligation(s) in the contract.
Step 3	• Determine the transaction price.
Step 4	• Allocate the transaction price to each performance obligation.
Step 5	• Recognize revenue when (or as) each performance obligation is satisfied.

*FASB ASC 606-10-05-4: Revenue from Contracts with Customers–Overall–Overview and Background–General (previously "Revenue from Contracts with Customers (Topic 606)" Accounting Standards Update 2014–09 (Norwalk, Conn: FASB, 2014)).

[3]"Revenue from Contracts with Customers (Topic 606)" *Accounting Standards Update 2014–09* (Norwalk, Conn: FASB, 2014).

[4]The new revenue recognition standard is required for nonpublic companies for annual reporting periods beginning after December 15, 2018. All U.S. companies can adopt the ASU for periods starting after December 15, 2016 if they so choose. For companies issuing reports under IFRS, the IFRS version of this standard, IFRS 15, is effective for periods beginning January 1, 2018. Early adoption of IFRS 15 is permitted.

All revenue recognition starts with a contract between a seller and a customer. You may not have realized it, but you have been a party to several such contracts very recently. Maybe you bought a cup of Starbucks coffee or a breakfast biscuit at McDonald's this morning. Or maybe you bought this textbook through Amazon or had a checkup at your doctor's office. Even though these transactions weren't accompanied by written and signed agreements, they are considered contracts for purposes of revenue recognition. The key is that, implicitly or explicitly, you entered into an arrangement that specifies the legal rights and obligations of a seller and a customer.

Performance obligations **are promises to transfer goods or services to a customer.**

Contracts between a seller and a customer contain one or more performance obligations, which are promises by the seller to transfer goods or services to a customer. The seller recognizes revenue when it satisfies a performance obligation by transferring the promised good or service. We consider transfer to have occurred when the customer has *control* of the good or service. *Control* means that the customer has direct influence over the use of the good or service and obtains its benefits.

Performance obligations are satisfied when the seller transfers *control* of goods or services to the customer.

For many contracts, following this approach is very straightforward. In particular, if a contract includes only one performance obligation, we typically just have to decide when the seller delivers the good or provides the service to a customer, and then make sure that the seller recognizes revenue at that time.

As a simple example, assume Macy's sells a skirt to Susan for $75 that Macy's previously purchased from a wholesaler for $40. How would Macy's account for the sale to Susan?

1. **Identify the contract with a customer:** In this case, the contract may not be written, but it is clear—Macy's delivers the skirt to Susan, and Susan agrees to pay $75 to Macy's.
2. **Identify the performance obligation(s) in the contract:** Macy's has only a single performance obligation—to deliver the skirt.
3. **Determine the transaction price:** Macy's is entitled to receive $75 from Susan.
4. **Allocate the transaction price to each performance obligation:** With only one performance obligation, Macy's allocates the full transaction price of $75 to delivery of the skirt.
5. **Recognize revenue when (or as) each performance obligation is satisfied:** Macy's satisfies its performance obligation when it delivers the skirt to Susan, so Macy's records the following journal entries at that time:

Cash	75	
Sales revenue		75
Cost of goods sold*	40	
Inventory		40

*This second journal entry assumes that Macy's uses a "perpetual" inventory system, by which we record increases and decreases in inventory as they occur ("perpetually"). We reviewed this method briefly in Chapter 2 and explore it in more depth in Chapter 8.

Revenue recognition gets more complicated when a contract contains more than one performance obligation. For example, when Verizon signs up a new cell phone customer, the sales contract might require Verizon to provide (1) a smartphone, (2) related software, (3) a warranty on the phone, (4) ongoing network access, and (5) optional future upgrades. Verizon must determine which of these goods and services constitute performance obligations, allocate the transaction price to those performance obligations, and recognize revenue when (or as) each performance obligation is satisfied.

In Part A of this chapter, we apply the five steps for recognizing revenue to various types of contracts. First we'll focus on contracts that have only one performance obligation to deliver a good or service at a single point in time, like when Macy's sells a skirt to Susan. Then we'll consider situations in which one performance obligation to deliver goods and services is satisfied over time, like a landlord renting an apartment or a bank lending money. After that, we'll consider contracts that contain multiple performance obligations, like the Verizon example we just discussed. Illustration 5–2 summarizes some key considerations we will return to throughout this chapter.

Illustration 5–2 Key Considerations When Applying the Five Steps to Revenue Recognition

Five Steps to Recognizing Revenue	For Transactions Involving Single and Multiple Performance Obligations		
Step 1 Identify the contract	Legal rights of seller and customer established		
Step 2 Identify the performance obligation(s)	***Single*** performance obligation		***Multiple*** performance obligations
Step 3 Determine the transaction price	Amount seller is entitled to receive from customer		Amount seller is entitled to receive from customer
Step 4 Allocate the transaction price	No allocation required		Allocate a portion to each performance obligation
Step 5 Recognize revenue when (or as) each performance obligation is satisfied	At a point in time	Over a period of time	At whatever time is appropriate for each performance obligation

Recognizing Revenue at a Single Point in Time

● LO5–2

FINANCIAL Reporting Case

Q1, p. 235

First we consider a simple contract that includes only one performance obligation and is satisfied at a single point in time. The performance obligation is satisfied when control of the goods or services is transferred from the seller to the customer. Usually it's obvious that transfer occurs at the time of delivery. In our Macy's example above, for instance, the performance obligation is satisfied at the time of the sale when the skirt is transferred to Susan.

In other cases transfer of control can be harder to determine. Illustration 5–3 lists five key indicators we use to decide whether control has passed from the seller to the customer. Sellers should evaluate these indicators individually and in combination to decide whether control has been transferred and revenue can be recognized.

Illustration 5–3
Indicators that Control Has Been Transferred from the Seller to the Customer

The customer is more likely to control a good or service if the customer has:

- An obligation to pay the seller.
- Legal title to the asset.
- Physical possession of the asset.
- Assumed the risks and rewards of ownership.
- Accepted the asset.*

*These indicators apply to both goods and services. It may seem strange to talk about the customer accepting an asset with respect to a service, but think of a service as an asset that is consumed as the customer receives it.

In Illustration 5–4 we apply these indicators to TrueTech Industries, a company we will revisit throughout this chapter to illustrate revenue recognition.

Illustration 5–4
Recognizing Revenue at a Point in Time

TrueTech Industries sells the Tri-Box, a gaming console that allows users to play video games individually or in multiplayer environments over the Internet. A Tri-Box is only a gaming module and includes no other goods or services. When should TrueTech recognize revenue for the following sale of 1,000 Tri-Boxes to CompStores?

- **December 20, 2017: CompStores orders 1,000 Tri-Boxes at a price of $240 each, promising payment within 30 days after delivery.** TrueTech has received the order but hasn't fulfilled its performance obligation to deliver Tri-Boxes. In light of this and other indicators, TrueTech's judgment is that control has not been transferred and revenue should not be recognized.

(continued)

Illustration 5–4
(concluded)

- **January 1, 2018: TrueTech delivers 1,000 Tri-Boxes to CompStores, and title to the Tri-Boxes transfers to CompStores.** TrueTech has delivered the Tri-Boxes, and CompStores has accepted delivery, so CompStores has physical possession, legal title, the risks and rewards of ownership, and an obligation to pay TrueTech. TrueTech's performance obligation has been satisfied, so TrueTech can recognize revenue and a related account receivable of $240,000.*

Accounts receivable ($240 × 1,000)	240,000	
Sales revenue		240,000

- **January 25, 2018: TrueTech receives $240,000 from CompStores.** This transaction does not affect revenue. We recognize revenue when performance obligations are satisfied, not when cash is received. TrueTech simply records collection of the account receivable.

Cash	240,000	
Accounts receivable		240,000

*TrueTech also would debit cost of goods sold and credit inventory to recognize the cost of inventory sold.

Recognizing Revenue over a Period of Time

● LO5–3

Services such as lending money, performing audits, and providing consulting advice are performed over a period of time. Some construction contracts require construction over months or even years. In these situations, should a company recognize revenue continuously over time as a product or service is being provided, or wait to recognize revenue at the single point in time when the company has finished providing the product or service? As we'll see next, in most situations like these, companies should recognize revenue over time as the service or product is being provided.

Criteria for Recognizing Revenue over Time

Let's assume once again that we have a contract with a customer that includes a single performance obligation and a known transaction price. As indicated in Illustration 5–5, we recognize revenue over time if any one of three criteria is met.

Illustration 5–5
Criteria for Recognizing Revenue over Time

Revenue is recognized over time if either:

1. **The customer consumes the benefit of the seller's work as it is performed,** as when a company provides cleaning services to a customer for a period of time, or
2. **The customer controls the asset as it is created,** as when a contractor builds an extension onto a customer's existing building, or
3. **The seller is creating an asset that has no alternative use to the seller, and the seller has the legal right to receive payment for progress to date,** as when a company manufactures customized fighter jets for the U.S. Air Force.

We recognize revenue over time if one of three criteria is met.

When a performance obligation is satisfied over time, revenue is recognized in proportion to the amount of the performance obligation that has been satisfied.

If a performance obligation meets at least one of these criteria, we recognize revenue over time, in proportion to the amount of the performance obligation that has been satisfied. If, say, one-third of a service has been performed, then one-third of the performance obligation has been satisfied, so one-third of the revenue should be recognized. For example, Gold's Gym recognizes revenue from a two-year membership over the 24-month membership period, and Six Flags Entertainment recognizes revenue for season passes over the operating season. Often these arrangements involve receiving cash in advance of satisfying a performance obligation, which requires recognition of a liability, deferred revenue. For example, consider Illustration 5–6.

Most long-term construction contracts qualify for revenue recognition over time.

Most long-term construction contracts qualify for revenue recognition over time. For example, many long-term construction contracts are structured such that the customer owns the work-in-process (WIP) as it is constructed, which satisfies the second criterion in Illustration 5–5. Also, the third criterion is satisfied if the asset the seller is constructing has no alternate use to the

Illustration 5–6

Recognizing Revenue over a Period of Time

TrueTech Industries sells one-year subscriptions to the Tri-Net multiuser platform of Internet-based games. TrueTech sells 1,000 subscriptions for $60 each on January 1, 2018.

TrueTech has a single performance obligation—to provide a service to subscribers by allowing them access to the gaming platform for one year. Because Tri-Net users consume the benefits of access to that service over time, under the first criterion in Illustration 5–5 TrueTech recognizes revenue from the subscriptions over the one-year time period.

On January 1, 2018, TrueTech records the following journal entry:

	Debit	Credit
Cash ($60 × 1,000)	60,000	
Deferred revenue		60,000

TrueTech recognizes no revenue on January 1. Rather, TrueTech recognizes a deferred revenue liability for $60,000 associated with receiving cash prior to satisfying its performance obligation to provide customers with access to the Tri-Net games for a year.

Tri-Net subscribers receive benefits each day they have access to the Tri-Net network, so TrueTech uses "proportion of time" as its measure of progress toward completion. At the end of each of the 12 months following the sale, TrueTech would record the following entry to recognize Tri-Net subscription revenue:

	Debit	Credit
Deferred revenue ($60,000 ÷ 12)	5,000	
Service revenue		5,000

After 12 months TrueTech will have recognized the entire $60,000 of Tri-Net subscription revenue, and the deferred revenue liability will be reduced to zero.

Deferred Revenue

	Debit	Credit
1/1		60,000
1/31	5,000	
2/28	5,000	
. . .	. . .	
12/31	5,000	
12/31		-0-

Service Revenue

	Debit	Credit
1/1		-0-
1/31		5,000
2/28		5,000
. . .		. . .
12/31		5,000
12/31		60,000

seller and the contract stipulates that the seller is paid for performance. We discuss accounting for long-term construction contracts in more detail in Part C of this chapter.

If a performance obligation doesn't meet any of the three criteria for recognizing revenue over time, we recognize revenue at the point in time when the performance obligation has been completely satisfied, which usually occurs at the end of the contract.

Many services are so short term in nature that companies don't bother with recognizing revenue over time even if they qualify for doing so. For example, UPS picks up a package and delivers it to its destination within a few days. The company's summary of significant accounting policies disclosure note indicates that "Revenue is recognized upon delivery of a letter or package." In other words, UPS recognizes revenue upon completion of service rather than over time during the service period. This departure from GAAP is immaterial given the short duration of UPS's services and the lack of additional useful information that would be provided by more precise timing of revenue recognition.

Determining Progress toward Completion

Because progress toward completion is the basis for recognizing revenue over time, the seller needs to estimate that progress in a way that reflects when the control of goods or services is transferred to the customer.

Input or *output* methods can be used to estimate progress toward completion when performance obligations are satisfied over time.

Sellers sometimes use an *output-based* estimate of progress toward completion, measured as the proportion of the goods or services transferred to date. For our Tri-Net example in Illustration 5–6, output is measured by the passage of time, because the performance obligation being satisfied is to provide access to the Tri-Net gaming platform. Other times sellers use an *input-based* estimate of progress toward completion, measured as the proportion of effort expended thus far relative to the total effort expected to satisfy the performance obligation. For example, sellers often use the ratio of costs incurred to date compared to total costs estimated to complete the job.[5] In Part C of this chapter, we continue our discussion of output- and input-based measures of progress toward completion, and also consider how to deal with changes in estimates of progress toward completion.

[5]If for some reason the seller can't make a reasonable estimate of progress to completion using either input or output methods, the seller must wait to recognize revenue until the performance obligation has been completely satisfied. However, if the seller expects to be able to at least recover its costs from the customer, the seller can recognize an amount of revenue equal to the costs incurred until it can make a reasonable estimate of progress toward completion.

Recognizing Revenue for Contracts that Contain Multiple Performance Obligations

● LO5–4

Revenue recognition becomes more complicated when a contract contains multiple performance obligations. As an example, in Illustration 5–7 we combine the two TrueTech examples we already have discussed. In the first example (Illustration 5–4), TrueTech sold Tri-Box modules and recognized revenue at a single point in time (upon delivery). In the second example (Illustration 5–6), TrueTech sold one-year subscriptions to the Tri-Net platform and recognized revenue over time (one-twelfth each month over the year). Now, let's consider how TrueTech would recognize revenue if these two items were sold as a package deal for a single price.

FINANCIAL Reporting Case

Q2, p. 235

Illustration 5–7
Contract Containing Multiple Performance Obligations

TrueTech Industries manufactures the Tri-Box System, a multiplayer gaming system allowing players to compete with each other over the Internet.

- The Tri-Box System includes the physical Tri-Box module as well as a one-year subscription to the Tri-Net multiuser platform of Internet-based games and other applications.
- TrueTech sells individual one-year subscriptions to the Tri-Net platform for $60. Customers can access the Tri-Net using a Tri-Box as well as other gaming modules.
- TrueTech sells individual Tri-Box modules for $240. Customers can use a Tri-Box to access the Tri-Net as well as other multiuser gaming platforms.
- As a package deal, TrueTech sells the Tri-Box System (module plus subscription) for $250.

On January 1, 2018, TrueTech delivers 1,000 Tri-Box Systems to CompStores at a price of $250 per system. TrueTech receives $250,000 from CompStores on January 25, 2018.

We'll assume TrueTech has concluded that it has a contract with CompStores, so step 1 of revenue recognition is satisfied. We'll start with step 2.

Step 2: Identify the Performance Obligation(s)

Sellers account for a promise to provide a good or service as a performance obligation if the good or service is distinct from other goods or services in the contract. The idea is to separate contracts into parts that can be viewed on a stand-alone basis. That way the financial statements can better reflect the timing of the transfer of separate goods and services and the profit generated on each one. Goods or services that are not distinct are combined and treated as a single performance obligation.

Promises to provide goods and services are performance obligations when the goods and services are *distinct*.

A good or service is distinct if it is both:

1. *Capable of being distinct.* The customer could use the good or service on its own or in combination with other goods or services it could obtain elsewhere, and
2. *Separately identifiable from other goods or services in the contract.* The promises to transfer goods and services are distinct in the *context of the contract,* because the seller is promising to provide goods and services *individually* as opposed to promising to provide a *combined* good or service for which the individual goods or services are inputs.

As an example of applying these criteria, think of going to a store like Home Depot to purchase lumber, paint, and other building supplies for a home project. Each of those products is capable of being distinct, because you can buy it individually and use it however you desire. Each also is separately identifiable from other goods and services, because Home Depot's only performance obligation is to deliver the individual items. So, Home Depot can view its promise to deliver each of these items as a separate performance obligation.

Now think about signing an agreement with a construction contractor like Toll Brothers to build a house for you. Like Home Depot, the contractor is selling you lumber, paint, and other building supplies. However, while those items are capable of being distinct, they aren't separately identifiable in the context of the contract, because the contractor's performance obligation is to combine those inputs and deliver a completed building. Therefore, Toll Brothers views itself as having a single performance obligation. As we discuss further in Part C of this chapter, most long-term construction contracts are viewed as including a single performance obligation because the seller provides the service of combining goods and services into a combined output.

Construction contracts aren't the only ones that fail the "separately identifiable" criterion. Goods and services also aren't considered separately identifiable if they are highly interdependent, or if one significantly modifies or customizes another. For example, consider a company that offers online access to a clip-art library. The only way customers can access the clip art is by using the online access service. Even though a clip art library and an online access service might be capable of being distinct outside the context of the contract, within the contract they are so intertwined that they are more appropriately thought of as a single performance obligation.[6]

In Illustration 5–8 we apply these criteria to identify the performance obligations for our TrueTech example.

Illustration 5–8

Determining Whether Goods or Services Are Distinct

Assume the same facts as in Illustration 5–7. Do the Tri-Box module and the Tri-Net subscription qualify as performance obligations in TrueTech's contract with CompStores?

Which of the goods and services promised in the contract are distinct? Both the Tri-Box module and the Tri-Net subscription can be used on their own by a customer, so they are capable of being distinct. The module and subscription are not highly interrelated and do not modify or customize each other, and the nature of TrueTech's promise is not to integrate the module and service into a combined unit, so they are separately identifiable in the context of the contract.

Conclusion: The module and subscription are distinct so the contract has two performance obligations: (1) delivery of a Tri-Box module and (2) fulfillment of a one-year Tri-Net subscription.

Step 3: Determine the Transaction Price

The *transaction price* is the amount the seller expects to be entitled to receive from the customer in exchange for providing goods or services.

The **transaction price** is the amount the seller expects to be entitled to receive from the customer in exchange for providing goods or services.[7] Determining the transaction price is simple if the customer pays a fixed amount immediately or soon after the sale. That's the case with our TrueTech example. The transaction price is $250,000, equal to $250 per system × 1,000 systems.

Step 4: Allocate the Transaction Price to Each Performance Obligation

We allocate the transaction price to performance obligations in proportion to their relative *stand-alone selling prices.*

If a contract includes more than one performance obligation, the seller allocates the transaction price to each one in proportion to the stand-alone selling prices of the goods or services underlying all the performance obligations in the contract. The **stand-alone selling price** is the amount at which the good or service is sold separately under similar circumstances.[8] If a stand-alone selling price can't be directly observed, the seller should estimate it.

Look at Illustration 5–9 to see how we allocate the transaction price to each of the performance obligations in our TrueTech example.

Step 5: Recognize Revenue When (Or As) Each Performance Obligation Is Satisfied

Revenue with respect to each performance obligation is recognized when (or as) that performance obligation is satisfied.

As we discussed earlier, performance obligations can be satisfied either at a point in time or over a period of time, and revenue with respect to a performance obligation is recognized when (or as) the performance obligation is satisfied. That timing doesn't depend on whether

[6]Sellers also treat as a single performance obligation a series of distinct goods or services that are substantially the same and have the same pattern of transfer.

[7]Normally, sellers are immediately or eventually paid in cash, but sometimes sellers are paid with other assets like property. In that case, the seller measures the assets received at fair value at the start of the contract.

[8]A contractually stated "list price" doesn't necessarily represent a stand-alone selling price, because the seller might actually sell the good or service for a different amount. The seller has to reference actual stand-alone selling prices, or estimate those prices.

Assume the same facts as in Illustration 5–7. The transaction price of one Tri-Box System is $250. Because the stand-alone price of a Tri-Box module ($240) represents 80% of the sum of the stand-alone selling prices [$240 ÷ ($240 + 60)], and the stand-alone price of a Tri-Net subscription comprises 20% of the total [$60 ÷ ($240 + 60)], we allocate 80% of the transaction price to the Tri-Box module and 20% of the transaction price to the Tri-Net subscription, as follows:

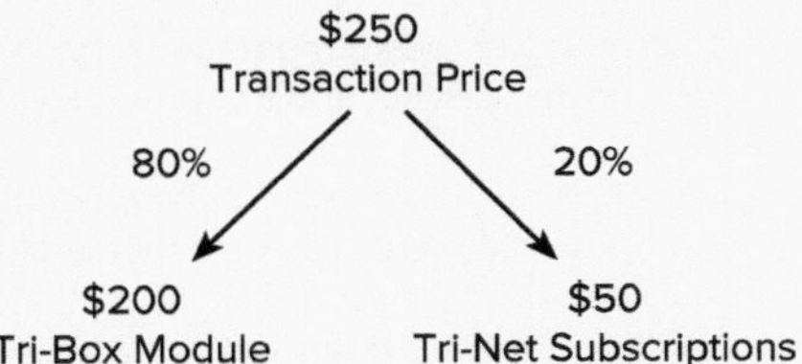

Illustration 5–9
Allocating the Transaction Price to Performance Obligations Based on Relative Selling Prices

Additional Consideration

Discounts in Contracts with Multiple Performance Obligations. Note that Illustration 5–7 shows that Tri-Box systems are sold at a discount—TrueTech sells the system for a transaction price ($250) that's less than the $300 sum of the stand-alone selling prices of the Tri-Box module ($240) and the subscription to Tri-Net ($60). Because there is no evidence that the discount relates to only one of the performance obligations, it is spread between them in the allocation process. If TrueTech had clear evidence from sales of those goods and services that the discount related to only one of them, the entire discount would be allocated to that good or service.

a performance obligation is the only one in a contract or is one of several performance obligations in a contract. We determine the timing of revenue recognition for each performance obligation individually.

Returning to our TrueTech example, the $200,000 of revenue associated with the Tri-Box modules is recognized when those modules are delivered to CompStores on January 1, but the $50,000 of revenue associated with the Tri-Net subscriptions is recognized over the one-year subscription term. The timing of revenue recognition for each performance obligation is shown in Illustration 5–10.

Assume the same facts as in Illustration 5–7. TrueTech records the following journal entry at the time of the sale to CompStores (ignoring any entry to record the reduction in inventory and the corresponding cost of goods sold):

January 1, 2018:		
Accounts receivable	250,000	
Sales revenue ($250,000 × 80%)		200,000
Deferred revenue ($250,000 × 20%)		50,000

In each of the 12 months following the sale, TrueTech records the following entry to recognize Tri-Net subscription revenue:

Deferred revenue ($50,000 ÷ 12)	4,167	
Service revenue		4,167

After 12 months TrueTech will have recognized the entire $50,000 of Tri-Net subscription revenue, and the deferred revenue liability will have been reduced to zero.

Illustration 5–10
Recognizing Revenue for Multiple Performance Obligations

Deferred Revenue

	Debit	Credit
1/1		50,000
1/31	4,167	
2/28	4,167	
. . .	. . .	
12/31	4,167	
12/31		-0-

Service Revenue

	Debit	Credit
1/1		-0-
1/31		4,167
2/28		4,167
. . .		. . .
12/31		4,167
12/31		50,000

Illustration 5–11 summarizes Part A's discussion of the fundamental issues related to recognizing revenue.

Illustration 5–11 Summary of Fundamental Issues Related to Recognizing Revenue

Revenue Recognition	Fundamental Issues	
Step 1 Identify the contract	A contract establishes the legal rights and obligations of the seller and customer with respect to one or more performance obligations.	
Step 2 Identify the performance obligation(s)	A performance obligation is a promise to transfer a good or service that is distinct, which is the case if the good or service is both (a) capable of being distinct and (b) separately identifiable.	
Step 3 Determine the transaction price	The transaction price is the amount the seller is entitled to receive from the customer.	
Step 4 Allocate the transaction price	The seller allocates the transaction price to performance obligations based on the relative stand-alone selling prices of the goods or services in each performance obligation.	
Step 5 Recognize revenue when (or as) each performance obligation is satisfied	The seller recognizes revenue **at a single point in time** when control passes to the customer, which is more likely if the customer has: • Obligation to pay the seller. • Legal title to the asset. • Possession of the asset. • Assumed the risks and rewards of ownership. • Accepted the asset.	The seller recognizes revenue **over a period of time** if: • Customer consumes benefit as work performed, • Customer controls asset as it's created, or • Seller is creating an asset that has no alternative use to the seller and the seller has right to receive payment for work completed.

Concept Review Exercise

REVENUE RECOGNITION FOR CONTRACTS WITH MULTIPLE PERFORMANCE OBLIGATIONS

Macrovision sells a variety of satellite TV packages. The popular $600 Basic Package includes a hardware component (consisting of a satellite dish and receiver) along with a twelve-month subscription to 130 TV channels. Macrovision sells the hardware component without a subscription for $180, and sells a twelve-month subscription to the same 130 channels without hardware for $540/year. Let's account for the sale of one Basic Package for $600 on January 1, 2018.

Required:

1. Identify the performance obligations in the Basic Package contract, and determine when revenue for each should be recognized.
2. For the single Basic Package sold on January 1, 2018, allocate the $600 transaction price to the performance obligations in the contract, and prepare a journal entry to record the sale (ignoring any entry to record the reduction in inventory and the corresponding cost of goods sold).
3. Prepare any journal entry necessary to record revenue related to the same contract on January 31, 2018.

Solution:

1. Identify the performance obligations in the Basic Package contract, and determine when revenue for each should be recognized.

   The hardware component and the twelve-month subscription are *capable of being distinct* (they are sold separately) and are *separately identifiable* (the hardware and services are not highly intertwined so it makes sense to consider them separately). Therefore, the hardware component and the twelve-month subscription are distinct from each other and should be treated as separate performance obligations. Revenue for the hardware component should be recognized on January 1, 2018, because transfer of control of the hardware occurs when the hardware is delivered to the customer. Revenue for the subscription should be recognized over the next twelve months as the customer receives the benefit of having access to TV channels.

2. For the single Basic Package sold on January 1, 2018, allocate the $600 transaction price to the performance obligations in the contract, and prepare a journal entry to record the sale (ignoring any entry to record the reduction in inventory and the corresponding cost of goods sold).

   Because the stand-alone price of the hardware component ($180) represents 25% of the total of all the stand-alone selling prices ($180 ÷ [$180 + 540]), and the stand-alone price of the twelve-month subscription comprises 75% of the total ($540 ÷ [$180 + 540]), we allocate 25% of the transaction price to the hardware component and 75% of the transaction price to the twelve-month subscription. The transaction price of $600 would be allocated as follows:

   Hardware Component: $600 × 25% = $150.
   Twelve-Month Subscription: $600 × 75% = $450.

   The journal entry recorded on January 1, 2018, would be:

Cash	600	
Sales revenue (for delivery of hardware)		150
Deferred revenue (for subscription)		450

3. Prepare any journal entry necessary to record revenue for the same contract on January 31, 2018.

Deferred revenue ($450 ÷ 12)	37.50	
Service revenue		37.50

Special Topics in Revenue Recognition

PART B

Now that we've covered the basics, let's consider some important issues that occur in practice with respect to each of the five steps. We'll cover each step in turn.

● LO5–5

Special Issues for Step 1: Identify the Contract

A **contract** is an agreement that creates legally enforceable rights and obligations. We normally think of a contract as being specified in a written document, but contracts can be oral rather than written. Contracts also can be *implicit* based on the typical business practices that a company follows. Remember from our example in Part A, just buying a skirt from Macy's implies a contract for purposes of recognizing revenue. The key is that all parties to the contract are committed to performing their obligations and enforcing their rights.[9]

A *contract* is an agreement that creates legally enforceable rights and obligations.

A contract only exists for purposes of revenue recognition if the seller believes it's probable that it will collect substantially all of the amount it's entitled to receive in exchange for the goods or services that it will provide to the customer. This collectibility threshold makes sure that revenue really reflects an inflow of net assets from the customer. However, even if a contract doesn't exist, the seller still can recognize an amount of revenue equal to any nonrefundable payments it has received, so long as it has already transferred control of the

A seller must believe collectibility is probable for a contract to exist for purposes of revenue recognition.

[9]Specifically, *ASU No. 2014–09* indicates that a contract exists for purposes of revenue recognition only if it (a) has commercial substance, affecting the risk, timing or amount of the seller's future cash flows, (b) has been approved by both the seller and the customer, indicating commitment to fulfilling their obligations, (c) specifies the seller's and customer's rights regarding the goods or services to be transferred, (d) specifies payment terms, and (e) is probable that the seller will collect substantially all of the amount it is entitled to receive. These criteria are very similar to requirements previously indicated by the SEC in the Staff Accounting Bulletins No. 101 and No. 104 mentioned earlier in this chapter.

goods or services and it does not have any further obligations to transfer goods or services to the customer.

A contract does not exist if (a) neither the seller nor the customer has performed any obligations under the contract and (b) both the seller and the customer can terminate the contract without penalty. In other words, either the seller or the customer must have done something that has commercial substance for the seller to start accounting for revenue. Illustration 5–12 provides an example.

Illustration 5–12
Determining Whether a Contract Exists for Revenue Recognition Purposes

Recall from Illustration 5–7 that CompStores ordered 1,000 Tri-Box systems on December 20, 2017, at a price of $250 per unit. Assume that CompStores and TrueTech can cancel the order without penalty prior to delivery. TrueTech made delivery on January 1, 2018, and received $250,000 on January 25, 2018. When does TrueTech's arrangement with CompStores qualify as a contract for purposes of revenue recognition?

The arrangement qualifies as a contract on January 1, 2018. That's the date TrueTech makes delivery to CompStores. Prior to delivery, neither TrueTech nor CompStores had performed an obligation under the contract, and both parties could cancel the order without penalty, so the arrangement didn't qualify as a contract for purposes of revenue recognition.

International Financial Reporting Standards

● LO5–10

ASU No. 2014–09 defines "probable" as "likely to occur." Similarly, *SFAC No. 6* defines "probable" to mean an amount can "reasonably be expected or believed on the basis of available evidence or logic but is neither certain nor proved," which implies a relatively high likelihood of occurrence. IFRS defines "probable" as a likelihood that is greater than 50%, which is lower than the definition in U.S. GAAP. Therefore, some contracts might not meet this threshold under U.S. GAAP that do meet it under IFRS.

Additional Consideration

Contract Modifications. A customer and seller might agree to modify a contract in some way. For instance, they might change the transaction price, change the performance obligations, or add another performance obligation. The way we account for a contract modification depends on the nature of the modification:

1. Sometimes a modification is really just a separate new contract. That happens when the modification adds another distinct good or service and requires the customer to pay an additional amount equal to the stand-alone selling price of the added good or service. In that case, we view the modification as a separate contract.
2. Other times a modification is to a contract for which the remaining goods and services are distinct from those already transferred, but the modification doesn't qualify as a separate contract. In that case, the seller acts as if the old contract has been terminated and a new contract has been created. The new contract includes whatever performance obligations remain after the modification, and its transaction price is equal to the amount that hasn't yet been recognized as revenue under the old contract plus or minus any change in price required by the modification. We allocate the revised transaction price to all performance obligations remaining in the contract based on their stand-alone selling prices at that time.
3. Finally, sometimes we modify a contract for which the remaining performance obligations are not distinct and therefore form a single performance obligation that is being satisfied over time. In that case, we need to update our assessment of progress toward completion and adjust revenue as appropriate to reflect progress to date, just like we treat other changes in estimates.

Special Issues for Step 2: Identify the Performance Obligation(s)

Previously we saw that promises to provide goods and services are treated as performance obligations when the goods and services are distinct. Now let's consider several aspects of contracts we often encounter and determine if they qualify as performance obligations. We discuss prepayments, warranties, and options.

PREPAYMENTS. Some contracts require nonrefundable up-front fees for particular activities (for example, LA Fitness charges up-front registration fees for gym memberships). We don't consider such *prepayments* to be performance obligations because they aren't a promise to transfer a product or service to a customer. Instead, the up-front fee is an advance payment by the customer for future products or services and should be included in the transaction price, allocated to the various performance obligations in the contract, initially recorded as deferred revenue, and recognized as revenue when (or as) each performance obligation is satisfied.

A *prepayment* is not a performance obligation.

WARRANTIES. Most products are sold with a warranty that obligates the seller to make repairs or replace products that later are found to be defective or unsatisfactory. These warranties are not sold separately, and either can be stated explicitly or be implicit based on normal business practice. We call these quality-assurance warranties. A quality-assurance warranty (sometimes called an "assurance-type warranty") is not a performance obligation. Rather, it is a cost of satisfying the performance obligation to deliver products of acceptable quality. The seller recognizes this cost in the period of sale as a warranty expense and related contingent liability. Because the exact amount of the cost usually is not known at the time of the sale, it must be estimated. For example, Deere & Company, which manufactures equipment used for construction, landscaping and other purposes, reported a quality-assurance warranty liability of $807 million at the end of its 2015 fiscal year.

A *quality-assurance warranty* obligates the seller to repair or replace defective products.

A quality-assurance warranty is not a performance obligation.

Extended warranties, on the other hand, are offered as an additional service that covers new problems arising after the customer takes control of the product. It's unusual these days to buy a phone, digital tablet, car, or almost any durable consumer product without being asked to buy an extended warranty. An extended warranty (sometimes called a "service-type warranty") provides protection beyond the manufacturer's quality-assurance warranty. Because an extended warranty usually is priced and sold separately from the product, it constitutes a performance obligation and can be viewed as a separate sales transaction. The price is recorded as a deferred revenue liability and then recognized as revenue over the extended warranty period. If an extended warranty is included along with the related product as part of a single contract, the extended warranty still is treated as a separate performance obligation, allocated a portion of the transaction price, and that portion of the transaction price is recorded as deferred revenue. Deere & Company reported a liability for deferred extended warranty revenue of $454 million at the end of its 2015 fiscal year.

An *extended warranty* is an additional service that covers new problems arising after a customer takes control of a product.

An extended warranty is a separate performance obligation.

How can you tell if a warranty should be treated as a quality-assurance warranty or an extended warranty? A warranty should be treated as an extended warranty if either (a) the customer has the option to purchase the warranty separately from the seller or (b) the warranty provides a service to the customer beyond only assuring that the seller delivered a product or service that was free from defects. The specifics of the warranty have to be considered when making this determination. For example, if the warranty period is very long, it's likely the warranty is covering more than just the quality of the product at the date of delivery, so it likely would represent an extended warranty.

We discuss accounting for warranties more in Chapter 13.

CUSTOMER OPTIONS FOR ADDITIONAL GOODS OR SERVICES. In some contracts the seller grants to the customer an *option* to receive additional goods or services at no cost or at a discount. Examples include software upgrades, customer loyalty programs (frequent flier miles, credit card points), discounts on future goods or services, and contract renewal options. Options for additional goods or services are considered performance obligations if they provide a *material right* to the customer that the customer would not receive otherwise.[10] For example, if a shoe seller normally discounts its products by 5%, but customers who purchase a pair of shoes receive a 20% discount off the next pair of shoes purchased at

[10]Be careful not to confuse these types of options with stock options, which are financial instruments that allow purchase of shares of stock at a specific price at a future date.

the same store, the extra discount of 15% (20% – 5%) is a material right, as it is a discount customers would not receive otherwise.

An *option* for additional goods or services is a performance obligation if it confers a material right to the customer.

When a contract includes an option that provides a material right, the seller must allocate part of the contract's transaction price to the option. Just like for other performance obligations, that allocation process requires the seller to estimate the stand-alone selling price of the option, taking into account the likelihood that the customer will actually exercise the option. The seller recognizes revenue associated with the option when the option is exercised or expires. Illustration 5–13 provides an example.

Illustration 5–13

Customer options for additional goods or services.

TrueTech offers a promotional coupon with every Tri-Box it sells for the normal price of $240. The coupon gives the Tri-Box customer an opportunity to buy a headset that normally sells for $150 for only $90 (a 40% discount). The coupon must be redeemed within one year of the Tri-Box purchase. TrueTech estimates that 80% of customers will take advantage of the coupon. How would TrueTech account for the cash sale of 100 Tri-Boxes sold under this promotion on January 1, 2018?

The coupon provides a material right to the customer, because it provides a discount of $150 × 40% = $60, so it is a performance obligation. Therefore, TrueTech must allocate the $240 transaction price to two performance obligations: the Tri-Box and the coupon.

Because TrueTech expects only 80% of the coupons to be used, it estimates the stand-alone selling price of a coupon to be $60 × 80% = $48.* The sum of the stand-alone selling prices of the performance obligations is $288, equal to the Tri-Box module ($240) plus the coupon ($48). The Tri-Box module ($240) represents five-sixths (or 83.33%) of the total ($240 ÷ $288), and the coupon comprises one-sixth (or 16.67%) of the total ($48 ÷ $288), so TrueTech allocates five-sixths of the $240 transaction price to the Tri-Box module and one-sixth to the coupon, as follows:

January 1, 2018:		
Cash	24,000	
Sales revenue ($240 × 5/6 × 100 units)		20,000
Deferred revenue—coupons ($240 × 1/6 × 100 units)		4,000

When the coupons are later redeemed or expire, TrueTech will debit deferred revenue—coupons and credit revenue.

*It may seem strange that we consider the likelihood that the customer will use the coupon when estimating the coupon's stand-alone selling price, but think about it from TrueTech's perspective. Each coupon saves a customer $60, but on average TrueTech will only have to provide discounts of $48, so $48 is its estimate of the average stand-alone value of its performance obligation.

Special Issues for Step 3: Determine the Transaction Price

● LO5–6

The *transaction price* is the amount the seller expects to be entitled to receive from the customer.

Until now we've assumed that contracts indicate a fixed **transaction price** that will be paid at or soon after delivery. However, in some contracts the transaction price is less clear. Specific situations affecting the transaction price are (a) variable consideration and the constraint on its recognition, (b) sales with a right of return (a particular type of variable consideration), (c) identifying whether the seller is acting as a principal or an agent, (d) the time value of money, and (e) payments by the seller to the customer. Let's consider these one at a time to see how recording revenue will be affected when there is variable consideration.

Variable consideration is the portion of a transaction price that depends on the outcome of future events.

VARIABLE CONSIDERATION. Sometimes a transaction price is uncertain because some of the price depends on the outcome of future events. Contracts that include this **variable consideration** are commonplace in many industries, including construction (incentive payments), entertainment and media (royalties), health care (Medicare and Medicaid reimbursements), manufacturing (volume discounts and product returns), and telecommunications (rebates).

Variable consideration is estimated as either the expected value or the most likely amount.

Estimating Variable Consideration. When an amount to be received depends on some uncertain future event, the seller still should include the uncertain amount in the transaction price by estimating it. A seller estimates variable consideration as either (a) the *expected*

Additional Consideration

Shipping Costs. Amazon Prime includes "free" two-day shipping. You pay one price but Amazon has two obligations: to provide a good and to ship that good. Are these considered separate performance obligations that require Amazon to allocate the transaction price for purposes of revenue recognition? It depends.

If shipping is provided *prior* to the seller transferring control of goods to the buyer (for example, if title passes to the customer upon delivery), then shipping is viewed as just another cost of doing business.[11] In that case, shipping is not treated as a separate performance obligation, and none of the transaction price would be allocated to it.

If shipping is provided *after* the customer has taken control of goods, then shipping could be viewed as a separate service and treated as a separate performance obligation. Note 1 of Amazon's 2015 10-K provides an example of this situation: "Retail sales to customers are made pursuant to a sales contract that provides for transfer of both title and risk of loss upon our delivery to the carrier." Amazon could view these arrangements as including two separate performance obligations: providing goods and then shipping those goods. However, allocating a small portion of the transaction price to "shipping revenue" might be more trouble than it's worth. Therefore, the FASB allows companies to choose whether to treat shipping provided after the customer takes control as either (a) just a cost of doing business or (b) a separate performance obligation (which requires sellers to allocate a portion of the transaction price to shipping and then to recognize shipping revenue when shipping is completed). The seller's policy must be disclosed clearly.[12] The IASB does not allow this choice, so some companies that apply IFRS might be forced to recognize "shipping revenue" when they would prefer not to go to the trouble of doing so.

value (calculated as the sum of each possible amount multiplied by its probability), or (b) the *most likely amount,* depending on which estimation approach better predicts the amount that the seller will receive. If there are several possible outcomes, the expected value will be more appropriate. On the other hand, if only two outcomes are possible, the most likely amount might be the best indication of the amount the seller will likely receive. Illustration 5–14 provides an example.

The seller must reassess its estimate of the transaction price in each period to determine whether circumstances have changed. If the seller revises its estimate of the amount of variable consideration it will receive, it must revise any receivable it has recorded and reflect the adjustment in that period's revenue, as we see in Illustration 5–15.

Constraint on Recognizing Variable Consideration. Sometimes sellers lack sufficient information to make a good estimate of variable consideration. The concern is that a seller might overestimate variable consideration, recognize revenue based on a transaction price that is too high, and later have to reverse that revenue (and reduce net income) to correct the estimate. To guard against this, sellers only include an estimate of variable consideration in the transaction price to the extent it is "probable" that a significant reversal of revenue

International Financial Reporting Standards

IFRS uses the term "highly probable" instead of "probable" in this case. Because IFRS defines "probable" to mean a likelihood greater than 50%, its use of "highly probable" is intended to convey the same likelihood as is conveyed by "probable" in U.S. GAAP.

● LO5–10

[11] In Chapter 8 we'll distinguish between situations in which title transfers before shipment and after shipment.

[12] FASB ASC 606-10-25-18B: Revenue from Contracts with Customers–Overall–Identifying Performance Obligations (previously "Revenue from Contracts with Customers" (Topic 606) – Identifying Performance Obligations and Licensing" *Accounting Standards Update 2016-10* (Norwalk, Conn: FASB, 2016)).

Illustration 5–14

Accounting for Variable Consideration

TrueTech enters into a contract with ProSport Gaming to add ProSport's online games to the Tri-Net network. ProSport offers popular games like Brawl of Bands, and wants those games offered on the Tri-Net so ProSport can sell gems, weapons, health potions, and other game features that allow players to advance more quickly in a game.

On January 1, 2018, ProSport pays TrueTech an up-front fixed fee of $300,000 for six months of featured access. ProSport also will pay TrueTech a bonus of $180,000 if Tri-Net users access ProSport games for at least 15,000 hours during the six-month period. TrueTech estimates a 75% chance that it will achieve the usage target and receive the $180,000 bonus.

TrueTech would record the following entry for the receipt of the cash on January 1, 2018:

Cash	300,000	
Deferred revenue		300,000

Subsequent entries to recognize revenue depend on whether TrueTech estimates the transaction price as the expected value or the most likely amount.

Alternative 1: Expected Value

The expected value would be calculated as a probability-weighted transaction price.

Possible Amounts	Probabilities		Expected Amounts
$480,000 ($300,000 fixed fee + 180,000 bonus)	× 75%	=	$ 360,000
$300,000 ($300,000 fixed fee + 0 bonus)	× 25%	=	75,000
Expected value of the contract price at inception			**$435,000**

Alternative 2: Most Likely Amount

Because there is a greater chance of qualifying for the bonus than of not qualifying for the bonus, a transaction price based on the most likely amount would be $300,000 + $180,000, or $480,000.

Let's assume that TrueTech bases the estimate on the most likely amount, $480,000. In each successive month TrueTech would recognize one month's revenue based on a total transaction price of $480,000. Because it previously recorded $300,000 as deferred revenue, at the end of each month TrueTech would reduce deferred revenue by one-sixth of the $300,000 as well as recognizing a bonus receivable for one-sixth of the $180,000 bonus it expects to receive.

Deferred revenue ($300,000 ÷ 6 months)	50,000	
Bonus receivable ($180,000 ÷ 6 months)	30,000	
Service revenue ($480,000 ÷ 6 months)*		80,000

After six months, TrueTech's deferred revenue account would have been reduced to a zero balance, and the bonus receivable account would have a balance of $180,000 ($30,000 × 6). At that point, TrueTech would know if the usage of ProSport products had reached the bonus threshold and would record one of the following two journal entries:

If TrueTech receives the bonus			If TrueTech does not receive the bonus		
Cash	180,000		Service revenue	180,000	
Bonus receivable		180,000	Bonus receivable		180,000

*If TrueTech instead used the expected value as its estimate of the transaction price, the journal entries would be the same except that the amount of revenue recognized each month would be $72,500 (**$435,000** ÷ 6 months). The reduction in the deferred revenue liability each month would still be $50,000, and the amount of bonus receivable accrued each month would be $22,500 ($135,000 ÷ 6 months).

Bonus Receivable

	Debit	Credit
1/1	-0-	
1/31	30,000	
2/28	30,000	
3/31	30,000	
4/30	30,000	
5/31	30,000	
6/30	30,000	180,000
6/30	-0-	

Service Revenue

	Debit	Credit
1/1		-0-
1/31		80,000
2/28		80,000
3/31		80,000
4/30		80,000
5/31		80,000
6/30		80,000
6/30		480,000

Illustration 5–15 Accounting for Variable Consideration

Assume the same facts as in Illustration 5–14, but that after three months TrueTech concludes that, due to low usage of ProSport's games, the most likely outcome is that True-Tech will *not* receive the $180,000 bonus. TrueTech would record the following entry in April to reduce its bonus receivable to zero and reflect the adjustment in revenue:

Service revenue	90,000	
Bonus receivable (reducing the account to zero)		90,000

For the remainder of the contract, TrueTech only recognizes revenue in each month associated with the up-front fixed payment of $300,000.

Deferred revenue ($300,000 ÷ 6 months)	50,000	
Service revenue		50,000

Bonus Receivable

	Debit	Credit
1/1	-0-	
1/31	30,000	
2/28	30,000	
3/31	30,000	
4/30		90,000
4/30	-0-	

Service Revenue

	Debit	Credit
1/1		-0-
1/31		80,000
2/28		80,000
3/31		80,000
4/30	90,000	50,000
5/31		50,000
6/30		50,000
6/30		300,000

recognized to date will not occur when the uncertainty associated with the variable consideration is resolved in the future.

Applying this constraint requires judgment on the part of the seller, taking into account all information available. Indicators that a significant revenue reversal could occur include (a) poor evidence on which to base an estimate, (b) dependence of the estimate on factors outside the seller's control, (c) a history of the seller changing payment terms on similar contracts, (d) a broad range of outcomes that could occur, and (e) a long delay before uncertainty resolves.

Sellers are limited to recognizing variable consideration to the extent that it is probable that a significant revenue reversal will not occur in the future.

If a seller changes its opinion regarding whether a constraint on variable consideration is necessary, the seller should update the transaction price in the current reporting period, just as the seller would do for other changes in estimated variable consideration. Illustration 5–16 provides an example.

Illustration 5–16

Constraint on Recognizing Variable Consideration

Assume the same facts as in Illustration 5–14, but that initially TrueTech can't conclude that it is probable that a significant revenue reversal will not occur in the future. In that case, TrueTech is constrained from recognizing revenue associated with variable consideration. It includes only the up-front fixed payment of $300,000 in the transaction price, and recognizes revenue of $50,000 each month.

Deferred revenue ($300,000 ÷ 6 months)	50,000	
Service revenue		50,000

On March 31, after three months of the contract have passed, TrueTech concludes it can make an accurate enough bonus estimate for it to be probable that a significant revenue reversal will not occur. As in Illustration 5–14, TrueTech estimates a 75% likelihood it will receive the bonus and bases its estimate on the "most likely amount" of $180,000. Since on March 31 the contract is one-half finished (3 of the 6 months have passed), TrueTech records a bonus receivable and service revenue for $90,000 ($180,000 × 3/6), the cumulative amount that would have been recognized over the first three months of the contract if an estimate of variable consideration had been included in the transaction price to begin with:

Bonus receivable ($180,000 × 3/6)	90,000	
Service revenue		90,000

In the final three months of the contract, TrueTech recognizes the remaining revenue assuming a transaction price of $480,000, exactly as if it had included an estimate of variable consideration in the transaction price all along:

Deferred revenue ($300,000 ÷ 6 months)	50,000	
Bonus receivable ($180,000 ÷ 6 months)	30,000	
Service revenue ($480,000 ÷ 6 months)		80,000

Bonus Receivable

Date	Debit	Credit
1/1	-0-	
3/31	90,000	
4/30	30,000	
5/31	30,000	
6/30	30,000	
6/30	180,000	

Service Revenue

Date	Debit	Credit
1/1		-0-
1/31		50,000
2/28		50,000
3/31		50,000
3/31		90,000
4/30		80,000
5/31		80,000
6/30		80,000
6/30		480,000

RIGHT OF RETURN. Retailers usually give customers the right to return merchandise if customers decide they don't want it, are not satisfied with it, or are unable to resell it. For example, video-game manufacturers like Take-Two Interactive Software often give customers a right of return for unsold products.

The right to return merchandise does not create a performance obligation for the seller. Instead, it represents a potential failure to satisfy the original performance obligation to provide goods that the customer wants to keep.

A *right of return* is not a performance obligation.

Because the total amount of cash a seller is entitled to receive depends on the amount of returns, a right of return creates a situation involving variable consideration. Based on past experience, a seller usually can estimate the returns that will result for a given volume of sales, so the seller reduces revenue by the estimated returns and records a liability for cash the seller anticipates refunding to customers. For example, assume that TrueTech sold 1,000 Tri-Boxes to CompStores for $240 each. TrueTech would record the following entry:

A *right of return* is a form of variable consideration.

Cash ($240 × 1,000)	240,000	
Sales revenue		240,000

If TrueTech estimates that CompStores will return five percent of the Tri-Boxes purchased, TrueTech would record a liability for that amount:

Sales returns ($240,000 × 5% estimated returns)	12,000	
Refund liability		12,000

Sales revenue
Less: Sales returns
Net sales

The sales returns account is a "contra revenue" account that has the effect of reducing revenue. As a result, we report sales revenues net of the amount expected to be returned.[13] We also have to consider the effect of expected returns on cost of goods sold and inventory. When TrueTech recorded the sale, it would have reduced inventory and recognized cost of goods sold. To account for expected returns, it would need to reduce cost of goods sold and record an asset, "Inventory—estimated returns," to reflect the cost of inventory expected to be returned.

In practice, most companies find it impractical to record an estimated refund liability each time they make a sale. Instead, they debit sales returns and credit cash as returns occur and then, at the end of each reporting period, make appropriate adjustments to sales returns and a refund liability to account for their estimate of remaining returns. We discuss these and other aspects of accounting for returns in more detail in Chapter 7.

What if TrueTech had sold the Tri-Boxes on account rather than for cash? When TrueTech accounts for estimated returns, it might not want to record a refund liability to return cash it hadn't yet received. Instead, TrueTech might credit a contra asset, *allowance for sales returns,* that reduces the book value, sometimes called the carrying value or carrying amount, of accounts receivable to $228,000 ($240,000 − 12,000).

If the seller lacks sufficient information to be able to accurately estimate returns, the constraint on recognizing variable consideration we discussed earlier applies, and the seller should recognize revenue only to the extent it is probable that a significant revenue reversal will not occur later if the estimate of returns changes. In fact, the seller might postpone recognizing any revenue until the uncertainty about returns is resolved. Illustration 5–17 provides an example.

Illustration 5–17

Disclosure of Revenue Recognition Policy—Intel Corporation.

Real World Financials

Revenue Recognition

Because of frequent sales price reductions and rapid technology obsolescence in the industry, we defer product revenue and related costs of sales from component sales made to distributors under agreements allowing price protection or right of return until the distributors sell the merchandise.

Source: Excerpts taken from the Intel Corporation 10-K filed February 23, 2009.

IS THE SELLER A PRINCIPAL OR AGENT? Sometimes more than one company is involved in providing goods or services to a customer. In those situations, we need to determine whether a company is acting as a **principal** and providing the good or service to the customer, or an **agent** and only arranging for another company to provide the good or service.

A *principal* controls goods or services and is responsible for providing them to the customer.

An *agent* doesn't control goods or services, but rather facilitates transfers between sellers and customers.

We view the seller as a principal if it obtains control of the goods or services before they are transferred to the customer. Various indicators help determine whether a seller obtains control. Control is indicated if the seller has primary responsibility for providing a product or service that the customer finds acceptable, if the seller has discretion in setting prices, and/or if the seller is vulnerable to risks associated with holding inventory or having inventory returned to it.

A principal's performance obligation is to provide goods and services. In contrast, an agent doesn't primarily provide goods or services, but acts as a facilitator that receives a commission for helping sellers provide goods and services to buyers. An

[13]Alternatively, the seller could combine the journal entries and record net revenue as:

Cash	240,000	
Sales revenue (net)		228,000
Refund liability		12,000

agent's performance obligation is to facilitate a transaction between a principal and a customer.

Many examples of agents occur in business. One you're familiar with is a real estate agent. Real estate agents don't own the houses they sell, but rather charge a commission to help home owners transact with home buyers. Similarly, online auction houses like eBay, travel facilitators like Expedia, Inc. and priceline.com, and broad web-based retailers like Amazon.com act as agents for a variety of sellers. Complicating matters, these same companies also act as principals on some other arrangements, selling their own products and services directly to customers.

The distinction between a principal and an agent is important because it affects the amount of revenue that a company can record. If the company is a principal, it records revenue equal to the total sales price paid by customers as well as cost of goods sold equal to the cost of the item to the company. On the other hand, if the company is an agent, it records as revenue only the commission it receives on the transaction.

An agent only records its commission as revenue.

We see from Illustration 5–18 that whether the seller is a principal or an agent can have a significant effect on its revenue. This is particularly important for start-ups or growth-oriented companies that may be valued more for growth in revenue than for growth in net income.

Illustration 5–18
Comparison of Revenue Recognition by Principals and Agents

Mike buys a Tri-Box module from an online retailer for $290. Let's consider accounting for that sale by two retailers, PrinCo and AgenCo.

- PrinCo purchases Tri-Box modules directly from TrueTech for $240, has the modules shipped to its distribution center in Kansas, and then ships individual modules to buyers when a sale is made. PrinCo offers occasional price discounts according to its marketing strategy. Because PrinCo is responsible for fulfilling the contract, bears the risk of holding inventory, and has latitude in setting sales prices, the evidence suggests that PrinCo is a principal in this transaction.
- AgenCo serves as a web portal by which multiple game module manufacturers like TrueTech can offer their products for sale. The manufacturers ship directly to buyers when a sale is made. AgenCo receives a $50 commission on each sale that occurs via its web portal. Given that AgenCo is not primarily responsible for fulfilling the contract, bears no inventory risk, has no latitude in setting sales prices, and is paid on commission, the evidence suggests AgenCo is an agent in this transaction.

The first part of the income statement for each retailer is shown below. Notice that the same amount of gross profit, $50, is recognized by the principal and the agent. What differ are the amounts of revenue and expense that are recognized and reported.

A Principal Records Gross Revenue (PrinCo)		An Agent Records Net Revenue (AgenCo)	
Revenue	$290	Revenue	$50
Less: Cost of goods sold	240	Less: Cost of goods sold	0
Gross profit	$ 50	Gross profit	$50

THE TIME VALUE OF MONEY. It's common for contracts to specify that payment occurs either before or after delivery. We recognize an account receivable when payment occurs after delivery, and we recognize deferred revenue when payment occurs before delivery. We can think of these arrangements in part as financing transactions. In the case of an account receivable, the seller is making a loan to the customer between delivery and payment. In the case of a payment prior to delivery, the customer is making a loan to the seller by paying in advance. As with any other loan, there is an interest charge (a "time value of money") implicit in these arrangements.

If delivery and payment occur relatively near each other, the time value of money is not significant and can be ignored. As a practical matter, a seller can assume the time value of money is not significant if the period between delivery and payment is less than a year. However, if the time value of money is significant, the seller views the transaction price as

Sellers must account for the financing component of transactions when it is significant.

consisting of (a) the cash price of the good or service and (b) a "financing component" representing the interest for the time between the sale and the cash payment. The seller then adjusts the transaction price to remove the financing component. That way, the seller recognizes the same amount of revenue for goods or services that it would recognize if the customer paid cash at the time the seller delivers those goods or services. The seller separately accounts for the financing component of the contract by recognizing interest revenue (in the case of an account receivable) or interest expense (in the case of a customer prepayment) over time. We discuss the time value of money in detail in Chapter 6. We discuss how sellers make adjustments for the time value of money for accounts receivable in Chapter 7 and for prepayments in Chapter 13.

PAYMENTS BY THE SELLER TO THE CUSTOMER. Usually it's the customer who pays the seller for goods or services. Occasionally, though, a *seller* also makes payments to a *customer*. For example, Samsung sells TVs, smartphones, tablets, and other products to BestBuy. However, Samsung also might pay BestBuy for dedicated space in BestBuy stores or to conduct special Samsung-focused advertising programs. The question is whether a payment by Samsung is a purchase of goods or services from BestBuy, or really just a refund of some of the price paid by BestBuy to purchase Samsung products.

The way we account for payments by a seller to a customer depends on the specifics of the arrangement. If the seller is purchasing distinct goods or services from the customer at the fair value of those goods or services, we account for that purchase as a separate transaction. If a seller pays more for distinct goods or services purchased from its customer than the fair value of those goods or services, those excess payments are viewed as a refund. They are subtracted from the amount the seller is entitled to receive when calculating the transaction price of the sale to the customer. In our Samsung example, if Samsung pays more for dedicated floor space at BestBuy than the fair value of that floor space, Samsung should treat that excess payment as a refund to BestBuy of part of the price paid by BestBuy for Samsung products.

Special Issues for Step 4: Allocate the Transaction Price to the Performance Obligations

We already discussed the need for the seller to allocate the transaction price to each performance obligation in a contract in proportion to the stand-alone selling prices of the goods or services. We also noted that when goods and services aren't normally sold separately, sellers must estimate those stand-alone selling prices. Various approaches are available to estimate stand-alone selling prices. Examples include the following:

The *residual approach* is used to estimate a stand-alone selling price that is very uncertain.

1. **Adjusted market assessment approach:** The seller considers what it could sell the product or services for in the market in which it normally conducts business, perhaps referencing prices charged by competitors.
2. **Expected cost plus margin approach:** The seller estimates its costs of satisfying a performance obligation and then adds an appropriate profit margin.
3. **Residual approach:** The seller estimates an unknown (or highly uncertain) stand-alone selling price by subtracting the sum of the known or estimated stand-alone selling prices of other goods or services in the contract from the total transaction price of the contract. The residual approach is allowed only if the stand-alone selling price is highly uncertain, either because the seller hasn't previously sold the good or service and hasn't yet determined a price for it, or because the seller provides the same good or service to different customers at substantially different prices. Illustration 5–19 provides an example of the residual approach.

Special Issues for Step 5: Recognize Revenue When (Or As) Each Performance Obligation Is Satisfied

● LO5–7

Previously, we discussed recognizing revenue at a point in time and over a period of time. Now let's look at a few commonplace arrangements that occur in practice that make it more

Illustration 5–19
Allocating Transaction Price to Performance Obligations Using the Residual Approach

Assume the same facts as Illustration 5–7, except that the stand-alone selling price of the one-year Tri-Net subscription is highly uncertain because TrueTech hasn't sold that service previously and hasn't established a price for it. Under the residual approach, the value of the subscription would be estimated as follows:

Total price of Tri-Box with Tri-Net subscription ($250 × 1,000)	$250,000
Stand-alone price of Tri-Box sold without subscription ($240 × 1,000)	240,000
Estimated stand-alone price of Tri-Net subscription	$ 10,000

Based on these relative stand-alone selling prices, if CompStores orders 1,000 Tri-Box Systems at the normal wholesale price of $250 each, TrueTech records the following journal entry (ignoring any entry to record the reduction in inventory and corresponding cost of goods sold):

Accounts receivable	250,000	
Sales revenue		240,000
Deferred revenue		10,000

TrueTech would convert the $10,000 of deferred revenue to revenue (debit deferred revenue; credit service revenue) over the one-year term of the Tri-Net subscription.

Additional Consideration

Allocating Variable Consideration. What if a contract that has variable consideration includes multiple performance obligations? Typically the seller would include the variable consideration in the transaction price that is allocated to each of those performance obligations according to their relative stand-alone selling prices. Also, changes in estimated variable consideration are allocated to performance obligations on the same basis. However, if the variable consideration relates only to one performance obligation, it is allocated to only that performance obligation.

difficult to determine when revenue should be recognized. In particular, we discuss licenses, franchises, bill-and-hold sales, consignment arrangements, and gift cards.

Licenses allow the customer to use the seller's intellectual property.

LICENSES. Customers sometimes pay a licensing fee to use a company's intellectual property ("IP"). Licenses are common in the software, technology, media, and entertainment (including motion pictures and music) industries. The accounting question is when to recognize revenue for these arrangements, which the FASB recently addressed in ASU 2016-10.[14]

Licenses of functional IP transfer a *right of use*, so sellers typically recognize revenue at a point in time.

Functional intellectual property: Some licenses transfer a *right of use* to IP that has *significant standalone functionality,* meaning that it can perform a function or a task, or be played or aired. The benefit the customer receives from the license isn't affected by the seller's ongoing activity. Examples of this *functional IP* include software like Microsoft Office, drug formulas, and media content like books, music, and movies. For licenses of functional IP, sellers typically recognize revenue at the *point in time* that the customer can start using the IP.

For example, once you download a Beyoncé hit from Apple's iTunes, you can enjoy listening to that song as often as you like, regardless of future actions by Beyoncé or iTunes. You probably didn't realize it, but you had just purchased a license to use IP (and that license came with some restrictions, like not being able to copy and sell the music or broadcast

[14]FASB ASC 606-10-55-59-62: Revenue from Contracts with Customers–Overall–Implementation Guidance and Illustrations—Determining the Nature of the Entity's Promise (previously "Revenue from Contracts with Customers" (Topic 606)–Identifying Performance Obligations and Licensing" *Accounting Standards Update 2016-10* (Norwalk, Conn: FASB, 2016)).

it publicly). Apple recognized revenue at the point in time that the download occurred, because that is when you could start listening to the downloaded music.

Licenses of symbolic IP transfer a *right of access*, so sellers recognize revenue over time.

Symbolic intellectual property: Other licenses provide the customer with the *right of access* to the seller's IP with the understanding that the IP does not have significant stand-alone functionality. Rather, the seller will undertake ongoing activities during the license period that benefit the customer. The seller might make changes to the IP over the course of the license, or could perform marketing or other activities that affect the value of the license to the customer. Examples of this *symbolic IP* include trademarks, logos, brand names and franchise rights. For licenses of symbolic IP, sellers recognize revenue *over time,* because that is when they satisfy their performance obligation.

For example, suppose the NBA sells a five-year license that allows Adidas to manufacture shirts and hats with NBA team logos. Adidas agrees to the license arrangement with the understanding that the NBA will continue to play games and promote the league during the license period. These activities affect the value of the shirts and hats and thus the license to Adidas. Therefore, the NBA satisfies its performance obligation under the license agreement through its ongoing activities and will recognize revenue over the *period of time* for which access is provided.

Licenses of functional IP transfer a *right of use*, so sellers typically recognize revenue at a point in time.

Sometimes functional IP also requires revenue recognition over time. This happens when the seller is expected to change the functionality over the license period and the customer is required to use the updated version. For example, that's the case with some software products, like virus protection. In that case, even though the license involves functional IP, we view the license as transferring a right of access, so revenue must be recognized over the license period.

Finally, sometimes a license isn't considered to be a separate performance obligation because it's not *distinct* from other goods or services provided in the same transaction. For example, an online service might grant a license to customers to access content at a website. In that case, the license isn't distinct from the website content, because the purpose of the license is to access the content. As result, the website access and license would be treated as

International Financial Reporting Standards

● LO5–10

The IASB's licensing guidance doesn't rely on the functional/symbolic classifications, so it differs from U.S. GAAP by not requiring revenue recognition over time for all symbolic intellectual property. Instead, the IASB requires the seller to recognize revenue over time only if the seller's ongoing activities affect the benefits the customer obtains from the IP. This distinction usually doesn't matter, but there are exceptions. For example, given that the Brooklyn Dodgers played their last baseball game in 1957, it is unlikely that their ongoing activities affect the benefit of licensing the Brooklyn Dodgers logo. Therefore, under IFRS, the seller would recognize license revenue for licensing that logo at the point in time the customer can use the logo. However, because U.S. GAAP would focus on the logo being symbolic IP, U.S. GAAP would require the seller to recognize revenue over the license period.

Additional Consideration

Variable Consideration and Licenses. Previously you learned about sellers being able to recognize revenue associated with variable consideration. There's an exception if variable consideration is based on sales or usage of a license. Those amounts (often called "royalties") are only included in the transaction price when the sales or usage has actually occurred, such that they are known rather than needing to be estimated.

a single performance obligation, and revenue would be recognized over time as customers are provided access to the website.

FRANCHISES. Many retail outlets for fast food, restaurants, hotels, and auto rental agencies are operated as franchises. In franchise arrangements, the **franchisor**, such as **Subway**, grants to the **franchisee**, quite often an individual, a right to sell the franchisor's products and use its name for a specified period of time. The franchisor also typically provides initial start-up services (such as identifying locations, remodeling or constructing facilities, selling equipment, and providing training to the franchisee) as well as providing ongoing products and services (such as franchise-branded products and advertising and administrative services). So, a franchise involves a *license* to use the franchisor's intellectual property, but also involves *initial sales* of products and services as well as *ongoing sales* of products and services. The franchisor must evaluate each part of the franchise arrangement to identify the performance obligations. Illustration 5–20 gives an example.

In a *franchise* arrangement, a franchisor grants to the franchisee the right to sell the franchisor's products and use its name.

Illustration 5–20

Franchise Arrangements

Assume that TrueTech starts selling TechStop franchises. TrueTech charges franchisees an initial fee in exchange for (a) the exclusive right to operate the only TechStop in a particular area for a five-year period, (b) the equipment necessary to distribute and repair TrueTech products, and (c) training services to be provided over a two-year period. Similar equipment and training can be purchased elsewhere. What are the performance obligations in this arrangement, and when would TrueTech recognize revenue for each of them?

1. The exclusive five-year right to operate the only TechStop in a particular area is distinct because it can be used with other goods or services (furnishings, equipment, products) that the customer could obtain elsewhere.
2. The equipment is distinct because similar equipment is sold separately.
3. The training is distinct because similar training could be acquired elsewhere.

TrueTech would allocate the initial franchise fee to three separate performance obligations based on their relative stand-alone prices: (1) the right to operate a TechStop, (2) equipment, and (3) training. TrueTech would recognize revenue for the right to operate a TechStop over the five-year license period, because TrueTech's ongoing activities over the license period affect the value of the right to run a TechStop. TrueTech would recognize revenue for the equipment at the time the equipment is delivered to the franchisee, and would recognize revenue for the training over the two-year period that the training is provided.

What if TrueTech also charges franchisees an additional fee for ongoing services provided by TrueTech? In that case, TrueTech would recognize revenue associated with that fee over time as it provides the ongoing services.

BILL-AND-HOLD ARRANGEMENTS. A **bill-and-hold** arrangement exists when a customer purchases goods but requests that the seller retain physical possession of the goods until a later date. For example, a customer might buy equipment and ask the seller to store the equipment until an installation site has been prepared.

A *bill-and-hold* arrangement occurs when a customer purchases goods but requests that shipment occur at a later date.

For bill-and-hold arrangements, the key issue is that the customer doesn't have physical possession of the asset until the seller has delivered it. Remember, physical possession is one of the indicators that control may have been transferred as listed in Illustration 5–3. Bill-and-hold arrangements might arise normally in the course of business, but they also have been abused by some companies in the past. Managers at companies like **Sunbeam**, **NutraCea**, and **Nortel Networks** are alleged to have overstated revenue by falsely claiming that unsold inventory has been sold under a bill-and-hold arrangement.

The physical possession indicator normally overshadows other control indicators in a bill-and-hold arrangement, so sellers usually conclude that control has not been transferred and revenue should not be recognized until actual delivery to the customer occurs.

Revenue recognition usually occurs at delivery for a *bill-and-hold* arrangement.

Ethical Dilemma

The Precision Parts Corporation manufactures automobile parts. The company has reported a profit every year since the company's inception in 1980. Management prides itself on this accomplishment and believes one important contributing factor is the company's incentive plan that rewards top management a bonus equal to a percentage of operating income if the operating income goal for the year is achieved. However, 2018 has been a tough year, and prospects for attaining the income goal for the year are bleak.

Tony Smith, the company's chief financial officer, has determined a way to increase December sales by an amount sufficient to boost operating income over the goal for the year and secure bonuses for all top management. A reputable customer ordered $120,000 of normally stocked parts to be shipped on January 15, 2019. Tony told the rest of top management "I know we can get that order ready by December 31. We can then just leave the order on the loading dock until shipment. I see nothing wrong with recognizing the sale in 2018, since the parts will have been manufactured and we do have a firm order from a reputable customer." The company's normal procedure is to ship goods f.o.b. destination and to recognize sales revenue when the customer receives the parts.

Consistent with SEC guidance, sellers can recognize revenue prior to delivery only if (a) they conclude that the customer controls the product, (b) there is a good reason for the bill-and-hold arrangement, and (c) the product is specifically identified as belonging to the customer and is ready for shipment.[15]

CONSIGNMENT ARRANGEMENTS. Sometimes a company arranges for another company to sell its product under consignment. In these arrangements, the "consignor" physically transfers the goods to the other company (the consignee), but the consignor retains legal title. If a buyer is found, the consignee remits the selling price (less commission and approved expenses) to the consignor. If the consignee can't find a buyer within an agreed-upon time, the consignee returns the goods to the consignor.

Revenue recognition occurs upon sale to an end customer in a *consignment* arrangement.

When does control transfer from the consignor, allowing the consignor to recognize revenue? Referring to the indicators listed in Illustration 5–3, the consignor still has title and retains many of the risks and rewards of ownership for goods it has placed on consignment. Therefore, it's likely that the consignor would be judged to retain control after transfer to the consignee and would postpone recognizing revenue until sale to an end customer occurs. Illustration 5–21 provides an example of a consignment arrangement by Boston Scientific Corporation from a recent annual report. We discuss accounting for consignment arrangements further in Chapter 8.

Illustration 5–21

Disclosure of Revenue Recognition Policy for Consignment Arrangements—Boston Scientific Corporation

Real World Financials

Note 1: Business and Summary of Significant Accounting Policies: Revenue Recognition (in part)

We generally meet these criteria at the time of shipment, unless a consignment arrangement exists or we are required to provide additional services. We recognize revenue from consignment arrangements based on product usage, or implant, which indicates that the sale is complete.

Source: Excerpts taken from the Boston Scientific Corporation 10-K filed February 28, 2008.

Sales of gift cards are recognized as deferred revenue.

GIFT CARDS. Let's assume you received an iTunes gift card that allows you to download songs or audiobooks later. When your friend bought that gift card, Apple recorded a deferred revenue liability in anticipation of recording revenue when you used your gift card to get songs. But, what if you lose the card or fail to redeem it for some other reason?

[15]FASB ASC 605–10–S99: Revenue Recognition–Overall–SEC Materials (originally "Revenue Recognition in Financial Statements," *Staff Accounting Bulletin No. 101* (Washington, D.C.: SEC, 1999) and *Staff Accounting Bulletin No. 104* (Washington, D.C.: SEC, 2003)).

Sellers like Apple, Target, Amazon, and others will recognize revenue at the point when they have concluded based on past experience that there is only a "remote likelihood" that customers will use the cards.[16] We discuss accounting for gift card liabilities further in Chapter 13.

Disclosures

INCOME STATEMENT DISCLOSURE. Of course, a seller reports revenue in its income statement. In addition, that seller is required to either include in its income statement or disclosure notes any bad debt expense and any interest revenue or interest expense associated with significant financing components of long-term contracts.

● LO5–8

BALANCE SHEET DISCLOSURE. A seller reports accounts receivable, "contract liabilities," and "contract assets" on separate lines of its balance sheet. We discuss each in turn.

The seller recognizes *contract liabilities, contract assets,* and *accounts receivable* on separate lines of its balance sheet.

If a customer pays the seller before the seller has satisfied a performance obligation, we saw earlier that the seller records deferred revenue. For example, we recorded deferred revenue in Illustration 5–6 when TrueTech received payment for Tri-Net subscriptions prior to providing that service. A contract liability is a label we give to deferred revenue (or unearned revenue) accounts.

The seller has a contract *liability* if it received payment prior to satisfying a performance obligation.

On the other hand, if the seller satisfies a performance obligation *before* the customer has paid for it, the seller records either a contract asset or accounts receivable. The seller recognizes an account receivable if the seller has an unconditional right to receive payment, which is the case if only the passage of time is required before the payment is due. In other words, the seller has satisfied all of its performance obligations and is just waiting to be paid.

If, instead, the seller satisfies a performance obligation but payment depends on something other than the passage of time, the seller recognizes a contract asset. For example, construction companies sometimes complete a significant amount of work prior to when the construction contract indicates they can bill their clients for progress payments. As we will see in Part C of this chapter, a construction company in that situation reports a contract asset called "construction-in-progress in excess of billings" to reflect that the company will be able to bill its client in the future for the work that has been completed.

A seller has an *account receivable* if it has an unconditional right to receive payment after satisfying a performance obligation.

A seller has a *contract asset* if it has a conditional right to receive payment after satisfying a performance obligation.

DISCLOSURE NOTES. Several important aspects of revenue recognition must be disclosed in the notes to the financial statements. For example, sellers must separate their revenue into categories that help investors understand the nature, amount, timing, and uncertainty of revenue and cash flows. Categories might include product lines, geographic regions, types of customers, or types of contracts. Sellers also must disclose amounts included in revenue that were previously recognized as deferred revenue or that resulted from changes in transaction prices.

Sellers also must describe their outstanding performance obligations, discuss how performance obligations typically are satisfied, and describe important contractual provisions like payment terms and policies for refunds, returns, and warranties. They also must disclose any significant judgments used to estimate transaction prices, to allocate transaction prices to performance obligations, and to determine when performance obligations have been satisfied.

Companies provide detailed disclosures about revenues.

Sellers also must explain significant changes in contract assets and contract liabilities that occurred during the period.

The objective of these disclosures is to help users of financial statements understand the revenue and cash flows arising from contracts with customers. Of course, the downside of these disclosures is that sellers also are providing information to competitors, suppliers, and customers.

Illustration 5–22 provides a summary of both Parts A and Parts B of this chapter to provide a comprehensive review of revenue recognition.

[16]This is sometimes referred to as "breakage" of the gift card.

Illustration 5–22 Summary of Fundamental and Special Issues Related to Recognizing Revenue

Revenue Recognition	Fundamental Issues (Part A)	Special Issues (Part B)
Step 1 Identify the contract	A contract establishes the legal rights and obligations of the seller and customer with respect to one or more performance obligations.	A contract exists if it (a) has commercial substance, (b) has been approved by both the seller and the customer, (c) specifies the seller's and customer's rights and obligations, (d) specifies payment terms, and (e) is probable that the seller will collect the amounts it is entitled to receive. A contract does ***not*** exist if (a) neither the seller nor the customer has performed any obligations under the contract, and (b) both the seller and the customer can terminate the contract without penalty.
Step 2 Identify the performance obligation(s)	A performance obligation is a promise to transfer a good or service that is distinct, which is the case if the good or service is both (a) capable of being distinct and (b) separately identifiable.	The following ***do not*** qualify as performance obligations: • Quality assurance warranties • Customer prepayments The following ***do*** qualify as performance obligations: • Extended warranties • Customer options for additional goods and services that provide a material right
Step 3 Determine the transaction price	The transaction price is the amount the seller is entitled to receive from the customer.	The seller adjusts the transaction price for: • Variable consideration (estimated as either the expected value or the most likely amount). Constraint: Variable consideration is recognized only to the extent it is probable that a significant revenue reversal will not occur in the future. • Whether the seller is acting as a principal or agent • A significant financing component • Any payments by the seller to the customer
Step 4 Allocate the transaction price	The seller allocates the transaction price to performance obligations based on relative stand-alone selling prices of the goods or services in each performance obligation.	Various approaches are available to estimate stand-alone selling prices: • Adjusted market assessment approach • Expected cost plus margin approach • Residual approach
Step 5 Recognize revenue when (or as) each performance obligation is satisfied	The seller recognizes revenue **at a single point in time** when control passes to the customer, which is more likely if the customer has: • Obligation to pay seller. • Legal title to the asset. • Possession of the asset. • Assumed the risks and rewards of ownership. • Accepted the asset. The seller recognizes revenue **over a period of time** if: • Customer consumes benefit as work performed, • Customer controls asset as it's created, or • Seller is creating an asset that has no alternative use to the seller and the seller has right to receive payment for work completed.	The seller must determine the timing of revenue recognition for: • Licenses (if functional intellectual property, usually recognize revenue at beginning of license; if symbolic intellectual property, recognize revenue over license period). • Franchises (initial fees recognized when goods and services are transferred; continuing fees recognized over time). • Bill-and-hold arrangements (typically do not transfer control, so recognize upon delivery of goods to customer). • Consignment arrangements (do not transfer control, so recognize after sale to end customer occurs). • Gift cards (initially deferred and then recognized as redeemed or expire).

PART C

Accounting for Long-Term Contracts

● LO5–9

A recent survey of reporting practices of 500 large public companies indicates that approximately one in every eight companies participates in long-term contracts.[17] These are not only construction companies. Illustration 5–23 lists just a sampling of companies that use long-term contracts, many of which you might recognize.

Illustration 5–23

Companies Engaged in Long-Term Contracts

Company	Type of Industry or Product
Oracle Corp.	Computer software, license and consulting fees
Lockheed Martin Corporation	Aircraft, missiles, and spacecraft
HP	Information technology
Northrop Grumman Corporation	Shipbuilding
Nortel Networks Corp.	Networking solutions and services to support the Internet
SBA Communications Corp.	Telecommunications
Layne Christensen Company	Water supply services and geotechnical construction
Kaufman & Broad Home Corp.	Commercial and residential construction
Raytheon Company	Defense electronics
Amec Foster Wheeler Corp.	Construction, petroleum and chemical facilities
Halliburton	Construction, energy services
Allied Construction Products Corp.	Large metal stamping presses

The five-step process for recognizing revenue described in Parts A and B of this chapter also applies to long-term contracts. However, steps 2 and 5 merit special attention.

Step 2, "Identify the performance obligation(s) in the contract," is important because long-term contracts typically include many products and services that could be viewed as separate performance obligations. For example, constructing a building requires the builder to deliver many different materials and other products (concrete, lumber, furnace, bathroom fixtures, carpeting) and to provide many different services (surveying, excavating, construction, fixture installation, painting, landscaping). These products and services are capable of being distinct, but they are not separately identifiable, because the seller's role is to combine those products and services for purposes of delivering a completed building to the customer. Therefore, it's the bundle of products and services that comprise a single performance obligation. Most long-term contracts should be viewed as including a single performance obligation.

Step 5, "Recognize revenue when (or as) each performance obligation is satisfied," is important because there can be a considerable difference for long-term contracts between recognizing revenue over time and recognizing revenue only when the contract has been completed. Imagine a builder who spends years constructing a skyscraper but only gets to recognize revenue at the end of the contract. Such delayed revenue recognition would do a poor job of informing financial statement users about the builder's economic activity. Fortunately, most long-term contracts qualify for revenue recognition over time. Often the customer owns the seller's work in process, such that the seller is creating an asset that the customer controls as it is completed. Also, often the seller is creating an asset that is customized for the customer, so the seller has no other use for the asset and has the right to be paid for progress even if the customer cancels the contract. In either of those cases, the seller recognizes revenue over time.

Long-term contracts are complex, and specialized accounting approaches have been developed to handle that complexity. For many years, long-term contracts that qualified for revenue recognition over time were accounted for using an approach called the *percentage-of-completion method,* which recognized revenue in each year of the contract according to the progress toward completion that occurred during that year. Long-term contracts that didn't qualify for revenue recognition over time were accounted for using an approach

[17] *U.S. GAAP Financial Statements–Best Practices in Presentation and Disclosure–2013* (New York: AICPA, 2013).

called the *completed contract method,* because all revenue was recognized at a single point in time—upon completion of the contract.

ASU No. 2014–09 removes the terms "percentage-of-completion method" and "completed contract method" from the Accounting Standards Codification, and changes the criteria that determine whether revenue should be recognized over a period of time or at a point in time. However, the journal entries necessary to account for revenue over time are the same as those that were used under the percentage-of-completion method, and those used to account for revenue at a point in time are the same as those used under the completed contract method. We demonstrate those journal entries next.

Accounting for a Profitable Long-Term Contract

FINANCIAL Reporting Case

Q3, p. 235

Much of the accounting for long-term contracts is the same regardless of whether we recognize revenue over the contract period or upon completion of the contract. So, we start by discussing the similarities between the two approaches, and then the differences. You'll see that we recognize the same total amounts of revenue and profit over the life of the contract either way. Only the timing of recognition differs.

Illustration 5–24 provides information for a typical long-term construction contract that we'll use to consider accounting for long-term contracts.

Illustration 5–24

Example of Long-Term Construction Contract

At the beginning of 2018, the Harding Construction Company received a contract to build an office building for $5 million. Harding will construct the building according to specifications provided by the buyer, and the project is estimated to take three years to complete. According to the contract, Harding will bill the buyer in installments over the construction period according to a prearranged schedule. Information related to the contract is as follows:

	2018	2019	2020
Construction costs incurred during the year	$ 1,500,000	$ 1,000,000	$1,600,000
Construction costs incurred in prior years	-0-	1,500,000	2,500,000
Cumulative actual construction costs	1,500,000	2,500,000	4,100,000
Estimated costs to complete at end of year	2,250,000	1,500,000	-0-
Total estimated and actual construction costs	$3,750,000	$4,000,000	$4,100,000
Billings made during the year	$ 1,200,000	$ 2,000,000	$1,800,000
Cash collections during year	1,000,000	1,400,000	2,600,000

Construction costs include the labor, materials, and overhead costs directly related to the construction of the building. Notice how the total of estimated and actual construction costs changes from period to period. Cost revisions are typical in long-term contracts because costs are estimated over long periods of time.

ACCOUNTING FOR THE COST OF CONSTRUCTION AND ACCOUNTS RECEIVABLE. Summary journal entries are shown in Illustration 5–24A for actual construction costs, billings, and cash receipts. These journal entries are not affected by the timing of revenue recognition.

Construction in progress (CIP) is the contractor's work-in-process inventory.

The first journal entry shows Harding incurring various costs during the construction process and recording them in an asset account called **construction in progress** (or "CIP" for short). This asset account is equivalent to work-in-process inventory in a manufacturing company. This is logical because the construction project is essentially an inventory item in process for the contractor.

Accounting for costs, billings, and cash receipts does not depend on the timing of revenue recognition.

The second journal entry occurs when Harding bills its customer according to whatever schedule the contract permits. Notice that periodic billings are credited to **billings on construction contract**. This account is a contra account to the CIP asset. At the end of each period, the balances in these two accounts are compared. If the net amount is a debit, it is reported in the balance sheet as a contract asset. Conversely, if the net amount is a credit, it is reported as a contract liability.[18]

[18]If the company is engaged in more than one long-term contract, all contracts for which construction in progress exceeds billings are reported in the balance sheet as contract assets, and all contracts for which billings exceed construction in progress are reported as contract liabilities.

Illustration 5–24A Journal Entries—Costs, Billings, and Cash Collections

	2018		2019		2020	
Construction in progress (CIP)	1,500,000		1,000,000		1,600,000	
Cash, materials, etc.		1,500,000		1,000,000		1,600,000
To record construction costs.						
Accounts receivable	1,200,000		2,000,000		1,800,000	
Billings on construction contract		1,200,000		2,000,000		1,800,000
To record progress billings.						
Cash	1,000,000		1,400,000		2,600,000	
Accounts receivable		1,000,000		1,400,000		2,600,000
To record cash collections.						

To understand why we use the billings on construction contract account (or "billings" for short), consider a key difference between accounting for a long-term contract and accounting for a more normal sale of inventory to a customer. In the normal case, the seller debits an account receivable and credits revenue, and also debits cost of goods sold and credits inventory. Thus, the seller gives up its physical asset (inventory) and recognizes cost of goods sold at the same time it gets a financial asset (an account receivable) and recognizes revenue. First the physical asset is in the balance sheet, and then the financial asset, but the two are not in the balance sheet at the same time.

Now consider our Harding Construction example. Harding is creating a physical asset (CIP) in the same periods it recognizes a financial asset (first recognizing accounts receivable when the customer is billed and then recognizing cash when the receivable is collected). Having both the physical asset and the financial asset in the balance sheet at the same time constitutes double counting the same arrangement. The billings account solves this problem. Whenever an account receivable is recognized, the other side of the journal entry increases the billings account, which is contra to (and thus reduces) CIP. As a result, the financial asset (accounts receivable) increases and the physical asset (the net amount of CIP and billings) decreases, and no double counting occurs.

The *billings on construction contract* account prevents "double counting" assets by reducing CIP whenever an account receivable is recognized.

Remember, we recognize accounts receivable when the seller has an unconditional right to receive payment, which is the case if only the passage of time is required before the payment is due, and we recognize a contract asset when the seller's right to receive payment depends on something other than the passage of time. Consistent with those definitions, Harding will report an account receivable for amounts it has billed the client and not yet been paid, and will report a contract asset (CIP – Billings) for the remaining amount of work completed, for which it eventually will be paid once it is able to bill the client.

REVENUE RECOGNITION—GENERAL APPROACH. Now let's consider revenue recognition. The top portion of Illustration 5–24B shows the single journal entry to recognize

Illustration 5–24B Journal Entries—Revenue Recognition

	2018		2019		2020	
Recognizing Revenue upon Completion						
Construction in progress (CIP)					900,000	
Cost of construction					4,100,000	
Revenue from long-term contracts						5,000,000
To record gross profit.						
Recognizing Revenue Over Time According to Percentage of Completion						
Construction in progress (CIP)	500,000		125,000		275,000	
Cost of construction	1,500,000		1,000,000		1,600,000	
Revenue from long-term contracts		2,000,000		1,125,000		1,875,000
To record gross profit.						

revenue, cost of construction (think of this as cost of goods sold), and gross profit when recognizing revenue upon completion of the contract, while the bottom portion shows the journal entries that achieve this when recognizing revenue over the term of the contract. At this point focus on the structure of the journal entries (what is debited and credited). We'll discuss how to calculate the specific amounts later in the chapter.

The same total amount of revenue is recognized whether it's over the term of the contract or only upon completion, but the timing of recognition differs.

It's important to understand two key aspects of Illustration 5–24B. First, the same amounts of revenue (the $5 million contract price), cost, and gross profit are recognized whether it's over the term of the contract or only upon completion. The only difference is timing. To check this, we can add together all of the revenue recognized for both methods over the three years, as follows:

	Revenue Recognition	
	Over Time	**Upon Completion**
Revenue recognized:		
2018	$2,000,000	$ –0–
2019	1,125,000	–0–
2020	1,875,000	5,000,000
Total revenue	$5,000,000	$5,000,000

Second, notice that, regardless of the timing of revenue recognition, we add gross profit (the difference between revenue and cost) to the CIP asset. That seems odd—why add profit to what is essentially an inventory account? The key here is that, when Harding recognizes gross profit, Harding is acting like it has sold some portion of the asset to the customer, but Harding keeps the asset in Harding's own balance sheet (in the CIP account) until delivery to the customer. Putting recognized gross profit into the CIP account just updates that account to reflect the total value (cost + gross profit = sales price) of the customer's asset. But don't forget that the billings account is contra to the CIP account. Over the life of the construction project, Harding will bill the customer for the entire sales price of the asset. Therefore, at the end of the contract, the CIP account (containing total cost and gross profit) and the billings account (containing all amounts billed to the customer) will have equal balances that exactly offset to create a net value of zero.

CIP includes profits and losses on the contract that have been recognized to date.

Now let's discuss the timing of revenue recognition in more detail.

REVENUE RECOGNITION UPON THE COMPLETION OF THE CONTRACT. If a contract doesn't qualify for revenue recognition over time, revenue is recognized at the point in time that control transfers from the seller to the customer, which typically occurs when the contract has been completed. At that time, the seller views itself as selling the asset and recognizes revenues and expenses associated with the sale. As shown in Illustration 5–24B and in the T-accounts below, completion occurs in 2020 for our Harding example. Prior to then, CIP includes only costs, showing a cumulative balance of $1,500,000 and $2,500,000 at the end of 2018 and 2019, respectively, and totaling $4,100,000 ($1,500,000 + 1,000,000 + 1,600,000) when the project is completed in 2020. Upon completion, Harding recognizes revenue of $5,000,000 and cost of construction (similar to cost of goods sold) of $4,100,000, because the asset is viewed as "sold" on that date. Harding includes the resulting $900,000 gross profit in CIP, increasing its balance to the $5,000,000 total cost + gross profit for the project.

If a contract doesn't qualify for revenue recognition over time, revenue is recognized when the project is completed.

Recognizing Revenue upon Completion

	Construction in Progress (CIP)		Billings on Construction Contract		
2018 construction costs	1,500,000			1,200,000	2018 billings
End balance, 2018	1,500,000			1,200,000	End balance, 2018
2019 construction costs	1,000,000			2,000,000	2019 billings
End balance, 2019	2,500,000			3,200,000	End balance, 2019
2020 construction costs	1,600,000			1,800,000	2020 billings
Total gross profit	900,000				
Balance, before closing	5,000,000			5,000,000	Balance, before closing

If revenue is recognized upon completion of the contract, CIP is updated to include gross profit at that point in time.

RECOGNIZING REVENUE OVER TIME ACCORDING TO PERCENTAGE OF COMPLETION. If a contract qualifies for revenue recognition over time, revenue is recognized based on progress towards completion. How should progress to date be estimated?

If a contract qualifies for revenue recognition over time, revenue is recognized over time as the project is completed.

As discussed in Part A of this chapter, one approach to estimating progress towards completion is to use output-based measures, like number of units produced or delivered, achievement of milestones, and surveys or appraisals of performance completed to date. A shortcoming of output measures is that they may provide a distorted view of actual progress to date.[19] For example, an output measure for highway construction might be finished miles of road, but that measure could be deceptive if not all miles of road require the same effort. A highway contract for the state of Arizona would likely pay the contractor more for miles of road blasted through the mountains than for miles paved across flat desert. Another shortcoming of some output measures is that the information they require, such as surveys or appraisals, might be costly to obtain.

Another way to estimate progress is to base it on the seller's *input,* measured as the proportion of effort expended thus far relative to the total effort expected to satisfy the performance obligation. Measures of effort include costs incurred, labor hours expended, machine hours used, or time lapsed. The most common approach to estimating progress toward completion is to use a "cost-to-cost ratio" that compares total cost incurred to date to the total estimated cost to complete the project.[20] When using that approach, sellers have to make sure to exclude from the ratio costs that don't reflect progress toward completion. For example, inefficiencies in production could lead to wasted materials, labor, or other resources. Those costs must be expensed as incurred, but not included in the cost-to-cost ratio.

Regardless of the specific approach used to estimate progress towards completion, we determine the amount of revenue recognized in each period using the following logic:

$$\text{Revenue recognized this period} = \underbrace{\left(\text{Total estimated revenue} \times \text{Percentage completed to date}\right)}_{\text{Cumulative revenue to be recognized to date}} - \text{Revenue recognized in prior periods}$$

Illustration 5–24C shows the calculation of revenue for each of the years for our Harding Construction Company example, with progress to date estimated using the cost-to-cost ratio. Notice that this approach automatically includes changes in estimated cost to complete the job, and therefore in estimated percentage completion, by first calculating the cumulative amount of revenue to be recognized to date and then subtracting revenue recognized in prior periods to determine revenue recognized in the current period. Refer to the following T-accounts to see that the gross profit recognized in each period is added to the CIP account.

When recognizing revenue over the term of the contract, CIP is updated each period to include gross profit.

Recognizing Revenue Over the Term of the Contract

	Construction in Progress (CIP)		Billings on Construction Contract	
2018 construction costs	1,500,000		1,200,000	2018 billings
2018 gross profit	500,000			
End balance, 2018	2,000,000		1,200,000	End balance, 2018
2019 construction costs	1,000,000		2,000,000	2019 billings
2019 gross profit	125,000			
End balance, 2019	3,125,000		3,200,000	End balance, 2019
2020 construction costs	1,600,000		1,800,000	2020 billings
2020 gross profit	275,000			
Balance, before closing	5,000,000		5,000,000	Balance, before closing

[19]Number of units produced or delivered is not an appropriate basis for measuring progress toward completion if these measures are distorted by the seller having material amounts of work-in-progress or finished-goods inventory at the end of the period.

[20]R. K. Larson and K. L. Brown, "Where Are We with Long-Term Contract Accounting?" *Accounting Horizons,* September 2004, pp. 207–219.

Illustration 5–24C
Allocation of Revenue to Each Period

	2018	2019	2020
Construction costs:			
Construction costs incurred during the year	$1,500,000	$1,000,000	$1,600,000
Construction costs incurred in prior years	–0–	1,500,000	2,500,000
Actual costs to date	1,500,000	2,500,000	4,100,000
Estimated remaining costs to complete	2,250,000	1,500,000	–0–
Total cost (estimated + actual)	$3,750,000	$4,000,000	$4,100,000
Contract price	$5,000,000	$5,000,000	$5,000,000
Multiplied by:	×	×	×
Percentage of completion Actual costs to date / Total cost (est. + actual)	($1,500,000 / $3,750,000 = 40%)	($2,500,000 / $4,000,000 = 62.5%)	($4,100,000 / $4,100,000 = 100%)
Equals:			
Cumulative revenue to be recognized to date	$2,000,000	$3,125,000	$5,000,000
Less:			
Revenue recognized in prior periods	–0–	(2,000,000)	(3,125,000)
Equals:			
Revenue recognized in the current period	$2,000,000	$1,125,000	$1,875,000
Journal entries to recognize revenue:			
Construction in progress (CIP)	500,000	125,000	275,000
Cost of construction	1,500,000	1,000,000	1,600,000
Revenue from long-term contracts	$2,000,000	$1,125,000	$1,875,000

The income statement includes revenue, cost of construction and gross profit.

If a contract qualifies for revenue recognition over time, the income statement for each year will report the appropriate revenue and cost of construction amounts. For example, in 2018, the income statement will report revenue of $2,000,000 (40% of the $5,000,000 contract price) less $1,500,000 cost of construction, yielding gross profit of $500,000.[21] The table in Illustration 5–24D shows the revenue, cost of construction, and gross profit recognized in each of the three years of our example.

Illustration 5–24D
Recognition of Revenue and Cost of Construction in Each Period

2018		
Revenue recognized ($5,000,000 × 40%)		$2,000,000
Cost of construction		(1,500,000)
Gross profit		$ 500,000
2019		
Revenue recognized to date ($5,000,000 × 62.5%)	$3,125,000	
Less: Revenue recognized in 2018	2,000,000	
Revenue recognized		$ 1,125,000
Cost of construction		(1,000,000)
Gross profit		$ 125,000
2020		
Revenue recognized to date ($5,000,000 × 100%)	$5,000,000	
Less: Revenue recognized in 2018 and 2019	3,125,000	
Revenue recognized		$ 1,875,000
Cost of construction		(1,600,000)
Gross profit		$ 275,000

We record the same journal entry to close out the billings and CIP accounts regardless of whether revenue is recognized over time or upon completion.

COMPLETION OF THE CONTRACT. After the job is finished, the only task remaining is for Harding to officially transfer title to the finished asset to the customer. At that time, Harding will prepare a journal entry that removes the contract from its balance sheet by

[21]In most cases, cost of construction also equals the construction costs incurred during the period. Cost of construction does not equal the construction costs incurred during the year when a loss is projected on the entire project. This situation is illustrated later in the chapter.

debiting billings and crediting CIP for the entire value of the contract. As shown in Illustration 5–24E, the same journal entry is recorded to close out the billings on construction contract and CIP accounts whether revenue is recognized over the term of the contract or at the completion of the contract.

	2018	2019	2020	
Billings on construction contract......			5,000,000	
Construction in progress (CIP)......				5,000,000
To close accounts.				

Illustration 5–24E

Journal Entry to Close Billings and CIP Accounts Upon Contract Completion

A Comparison of Revenue Recognized Over the Term of the Contract and at the Completion of Contract

INCOME RECOGNITION. Illustration 5–24B shows the journal entries that would determine the amount of revenue, cost, and therefore gross profit that would appear in the income statement when we recognize revenue over the term of the contract and at the completion of contract. Comparing the gross profit patterns produced by each method of revenue recognition demonstrates the essential difference between them:

	Revenue Recognition	
	Over Time	**Upon Completion**
Gross profit recognized:		
2018	$500,000	$ –0–
2019	125,000	–0–
2020	275,000	900,000
Total gross profit	$ 900,000	$900,000

Timing of revenue recognition does not affect the total amount of profit or loss recognized.

Whether revenue is recognized over time or upon completion does not affect the total gross profit of $900,000 recognized over the three-year contract, but the timing of gross profit recognition is affected. When the contract does not qualify for recognizing revenue over time, we defer all gross profit to 2020, when the project is completed. Obviously, recognizing revenue over the term of the contract provides a better measure of the company's economic activity and progress over the three-year term. As indicated previously, most long-term contracts qualify for revenue recognition over time.[22] Revenue is deferred until the completion of the contract only if the seller doesn't qualify for revenue recognition over time according to the criteria listed in Illustration 5–5.

BALANCE SHEET RECOGNITION. The balance sheet presentation for the construction-related accounts for both methods is shown in Illustration 5–24F.

Balance Sheet (End of Year)	**2018**	**2019**
Projects for which Revenue Recognized Upon Completion:		
Current assets:		
Accounts receivable	$200,000	$800,000
Costs ($1,500,000) in excess of billings ($1,200,000)	300,000	
Current liabilities:		
Billings ($3,200,000) in excess of costs ($2,500,000)		$700,000
Projects for which Revenue Recognized Over Time:		
Current assets:		
Accounts receivable	$200,000	$800,000
Costs and profit ($2,000,000) in excess of billings ($1,200,000)	800,000	
Current liabilities:		
Billings ($3,200,000) in excess of costs and profit ($3,125,000)		$ 75,000

Illustration 5–24F

Balance Sheet Presentation

[22] For income tax purposes, revenue can be recognized at completion for home construction contracts and certain other real estate construction contracts. All other contracts must recognize revenue over time according to percentage of completion.

Billings on construction contracts are subtracted from CIP to determine balance sheet presentation.

In the balance sheet, the construction in progress (CIP) account is offset against the billings on construction contract account, with CIP > Billings shown as a contract asset and Billings > CIP shown as a contract liability. Rather than referring to CIP, companies sometimes refer to what the CIP account contains, as is done in Illustration 5–24F. When revenue is recognized over the term of the contract, CIP contains cost and gross profit; if revenue is recognized upon the completion of the contract, CIP typically contains only costs. Because a company may have some contracts that have a net asset position and others that have a net liability position, it is not unusual to see both contract assets and contract liabilities shown in a balance sheet at the same time.

CIP in excess of billings is treated as a contract asset rather than an accounts receivable because something other than the passage of time must occur for the company to be paid for that amount. Although Harding has incurred construction costs (and is recognizing gross profit over the term of the contract) for which it will be paid by the buyer, those amounts are not yet billable according to the construction contract. Once Harding has made progress sufficient to bill the customer, it will debit accounts receivable and credit billings, which will increase the accounts receivable asset and reduce CIP in excess of billings (by increasing billings).

On the other hand, *Billings in excess of CIP* is treated as a contract liability. It reflects that Harding has billed its customer for more work than it actually has done. This is similar to the deferred revenue liability that is recorded when a customer pays for a product or service in advance. The advance is properly shown as a liability that represents the obligation to provide the good or service in the future.

Long-Term Contract Losses

The Harding Construction Company example above involves a situation in which an overall profit was anticipated at each stage of the contract. Unfortunately, losses sometimes occur on long-term contracts. As facts change, sellers must update their estimates and recognize losses if necessary to properly account for the amount of revenue that should have been recognized to date. How we treat losses in any one period depends on whether the contract is profitable overall.

PERIODIC LOSS OCCURS FOR PROFITABLE PROJECT. When a project qualifies for revenue recognition over time, a loss sometimes must be recognized in at least one period along the way, even though the project as a whole is expected to be profitable. We determine the loss in precisely the same way we determine the profit in profitable years. For example, assume the same $5 million contract for Harding Construction Company described earlier in Illustration 5–24 but with the following cost information:

	2018	2019	2020
Construction costs incurred during the year	$1,500,000	$ 1,260,000	$1,840,000
Construction costs incurred in prior years	–0–	1,500,000	2,760,000
Cumulative construction costs	1,500,000	2,760,000	4,600,000
Estimated costs to complete at end of year	2,250,000	1,840,000	–0–
Total estimated and actual construction costs	$3,750,000	$4,600,000	$4,600,000

At the end of 2018, 40% of the project is complete ($1,500,000 ÷ 3,750,000). Revenue of $2,000,000 – cost of construction of $1,500,000 = gross profit of $500,000 is recognized in 2018, as previously determined.

At the end of 2019, though, the company now forecasts a total profit of $400,000 ($5,000,000 – 4,600,000) on the project and, at that time, the project is estimated to be 60% complete ($2,760,000 ÷ 4,600,000). Applying this percentage to the anticipated revenue of $5,000,000 results in revenue *to date* of $3,000,000. This implies that gross profit recognized to date should be $240,000 ($3,000,000 – 2,760,000). But remember, gross profit of $500,000 was recognized the previous year.

We treat a situation like this as a *change in accounting estimate* because it results from a change in the estimation of costs to complete at the end of 2018. Total estimated costs to complete the project at the end of 2019—$4,600,000—were much higher than the 2018 year-end estimate of $3,750,000. Recall from our discussion of changes in accounting estimates in Chapter 4 that we don't go back and restate the prior year's income statement. Instead, the 2019 income statement reports *a loss of $260,000* ($500,000 – 240,000) so that the cumulative amount of gross profit recognized to date is $240,000. The loss consists of 2019 revenue of $1,000,000 (computed as $5,000,000 × 60% = $3,000,000 revenue to be recognized by end of 2019 less 2018 revenue of $2,000,000) less cost of construction of $1,260,000 (cost incurred in 2019). Just as gross profit gets debited to the CIP account, this gross loss gets credited to the CIP account, so that CIP includes the cumulative amount of gross profit or loss recognized to date. The following journal entry records the loss in 2019:

Cost of construction	1,260,000	
Revenue from long-term contracts (below)		1,000,000
Construction in progress (CIP)		260,000

Recognized losses on long-term contracts reduce the CIP account.

In 2020 the company recognizes $2,000,000 in revenue ($5,000,000 less revenue of $3,000,000 recognized in 2018 and 2019) and $1,840,000 in cost of construction (cost incurred in 2020), yielding a gross profit of $160,000.

Revenue	$2,000,000
Less: Cost of construction	(1,840,000)
Gross profit	$ 160,000

Of course, if revenue is instead recognized upon the completion of the contract, rather than over time, no profit or loss is recorded in 2018 or 2019. Instead, revenue of $5,000,000, cost of construction of $4,600,000, and gross profit of $400,000 are recognized in 2020.

LOSS IS PROJECTED ON THE ENTIRE PROJECT. If an overall loss is projected on the entire contract, the total loss must be recognized in the period in which that loss becomes evident, regardless of whether revenue is recognized over the term of the contract or only upon the completion of the contract. Again, consider the Harding Construction Company example but with the following cost information:

	2018	2019	2020
Construction costs incurred during the year	$1,500,000	$ 1,260,000	$2,440,000
Construction costs incurred in prior years	–0–	1,500,000	2,760,000
Cumulative construction costs	1,500,000	2,760,000	5,200,000
Estimated costs to complete at end of year	2,250,000	2,340,000	–0–
Total estimated and actual construction costs	$3,750,000	$5,100,000	$5,200,000

At the end of 2019, revised costs indicate an estimated loss of $100,000 for the entire project (contract revenue of $5,000,000 less estimated construction costs of $5,100,000). In this situation, the *total* anticipated loss must be recognized in 2019 regardless of whether revenue is recognized over the term of the contract or only upon the completion of the contract. If revenue is being recognized over the term of the contract, a gross profit of $500,000 was recognized in 2018, so a *$600,000 loss is recognized in 2019* to make the cumulative amount recognized to date total a $100,000 loss. Once again, this situation is treated as a change in accounting estimate, with no restatement of 2018 income. On the other hand, if revenue is being recognized only upon the completion of the contract, no gross profit is recognized in 2018, and the $100,000 loss for the project is recognized in 2019. This is accomplished by debiting a loss from long-term contracts and crediting CIP for $100,000.

An estimated loss on a long-term contract is fully recognized in the first period the loss is anticipated, regardless of the whether revenue is recognized over time or upon completion.

Why recognize the estimated overall loss of $100,000 in 2019, rather than at the end of the contract? If the loss is not recognized in 2019, CIP would be valued at an amount greater than the company expects to realize from the contract. To avoid that problem, the loss reduces the CIP account to $2,660,000 ($2,760,000 in costs to date less $100,000 estimated total loss). This amount combined with the estimated costs to complete of $2,340,000 equals the contract price of $5,000,000. Recognizing losses on long-term contracts in the period the losses become known is similar to measuring inventory at the lower of cost or net realizable value, a concept we will study in Chapter 9.

The pattern of gross profit (loss) over the contract term is summarized in the following table. Notice that in 2020 an additional unanticipated increase in costs of $100,000 causes a further loss of $100,000 to be recognized.

	Revenue Recognition	
	Over Time	Upon Completion
Gross profit (loss) recognized:		
2018	$ 500,000	$ –0–
2019	(600,000)	(100,000)
2020	(100,000)	(100,000)
Total project loss	$ (200,000)	$(200,000)

The table in Illustration 5–24G shows the revenue and cost of construction recognized in each of the three years, assuming the contract qualifies for recognizing revenue over time. Revenue is recognized in the usual way by multiplying a percentage of completion by the total contract price. In situations where a loss is expected on the entire project, cost of construction for the period will no longer be equal to cost incurred during the period. The easiest way to compute the cost of construction is to add the amount of the loss recognized to the amount of revenue recognized. For example, in 2019 revenue recognized of $706,000 is added to the loss of $600,000 to arrive at the cost of construction of $1,306,000.[23]

Illustration 5–24G

Allocation of Revenue and Cost of Construction to Each Period—Loss on Entire Project

2018		
Revenue recognized ($5,000,000 × 40%)		$ 2,000,000
Cost of construction		(1,500,000)
Gross profit		$ 500,000
2019		
Revenue recognized to date ($5,000,000 × 54.12%)*	$2,706,000	
Less: Revenue recognized in 2018	(2,000,000)	
Revenue recognized		$ 706,000
Cost of construction†		(1,306,000)
Loss		$ (600,000)
2020		
Revenue recognized to date ($5,000,000 × 100%)	$5,000,000	
Less: Revenue recognized in 2018 and 2019	(2,706,000)	
Revenue recognized		$ 2,294,000
Cost of construction†		(2,394,000)
Loss		$ (100,000)

*$2,760,000 ÷ $5,100,000 = 54.12%
†The difference between revenue and loss

The journal entries to record the losses in 2019 and 2020 are as follows:

2019		
Cost of construction	1,306,000	
Revenue from long-term contracts		706,000
Construction in progress (CIP)		600,000
2020		
Cost of construction	2,394,000	
Revenue from long-term contracts		2,294,000
Construction in progress (CIP)		100,000

[23]The cost of construction also can be determined as follows:

Loss to date (100% recognized)		$ 100,000
Add:		
Remaining total project cost, not including the loss ($5,100,000 − 100,000)	$5,000,000	
Multiplied by the percentage of completion	× .5412*	2,706,000
Total		2,806,000
Less: Cost of construction recognized in 2016		(1,500,000)
Cost of construction recognized in 2017		$1,306,000

*$2,760,000 ÷ 5,100,000

Recognizing revenue over time in this case produces a large overstatement of income in 2018 and a large understatement in 2019 because of a change in the estimation of future costs. These estimate revisions happen occasionally when revenue is recognized over time.

When the contract does not qualify for recognizing revenue over time, no revenue or cost of construction is recognized until the contract is complete. In 2019, a loss on long-term contracts (an income statement account) of $100,000 is recognized. In 2020, the income statement will report revenue of $5,000,000 and cost of construction of $5,100,000, combining for an additional loss of $100,000. The journal entries to record the losses in 2019 and 2020 are as follows:

2019		
Loss on long-term contracts	100,000	
Construction in progress (CIP)		100,000
2020		
Cost of construction	5,100,000	
Revenue from long-term contracts		5,000,000
Construction in progress (CIP)		100,000

Concept Review Exercise

LONG-TERM CONSTRUCTION CONTRACTS

During 2018, the Samuelson Construction Company began construction on an office building for the City of Gernon. The contract price is $8,000,000 and the building will take approximately 18 months to complete. Completion is scheduled for early in 2020. The company's fiscal year ends on December 31.

The following is a year-by-year recap of construction costs incurred and the estimated costs to complete the project as of the end of each year. Progress billings and cash collections also are indicated.

	2018	2019	2020
Actual costs incurred during the year	$ 1,500,000	$4,500,000	$ 1,550,000
Actual costs incurred in prior years	–0–	1,500,000	6,000,000
Cumulative actual costs incurred to date	1,500,000	6,000,000	7,550,000
Estimated costs to complete at end of year	4,500,000	1,500,000	–0–
Total costs (actual + estimated)	$ 6,000,000	$7,500,000	$ 7,550,000
Billings made during the year	$ 1,400,000	$5,200,000	$ 1,400,000
Cash collections during year	1,000,000	4,000,000	3,000,000

Required:

1. Determine the amount of construction revenue, construction cost, and gross profit or loss to be recognized in each of the three years assuming (a) the contract qualifies for recognizing revenue over time and (b) the contract does *not* qualify for recognizing revenue over time.
2. Assuming the contract qualifies for recognizing revenue over time, prepare the necessary summary journal entries for each of the three years to account for construction costs, construction revenue, contract billings, and cash collections, and to close the construction accounts in 2020.
3. Assuming the contract qualifies for recognizing revenue over time, prepare a partial balance sheet for 2018 and 2019 that includes all construction-related accounts.

Solution:

1. Determine the amount of construction revenue, construction cost, and gross profit or loss to be recognized in each of the three years assuming (a) the contract qualifies for recognizing revenue over time and (b) the contract does *not* qualify for recognizing revenue over time.

	The Contract Qualifies for Recognizing Revenue Over Time		
	2018	**2019**	**2020**
Contract price	$8,000,000	$8,000,000	$8,000,000
Multiplied by % of completion*	25%	80%	100%
Cumulative revenue to be recognized to date	2,000,000	6,400,000	8,000,000
Less revenue recognized in prior years	–0–	(2,000,000)	(6,400,000)
Revenue recognized this year	2,000,000	4,400,000	1,600,000
Less actual costs incurred this year	(1,500,000)	(4,500,000)	1,550,000
Gross profit (loss) recognized this year	$ 500,000	$ (100,000)	$ 50,000

*Estimated percentage of completion:

2018	2019	2020
$\frac{1,500,000}{6,000,000} = 25\%$	$\frac{6,000,000}{7,500,000} = 80\%$	Project complete = 100%

	The Contract Does *Not* Qualify for Recognizing Revenue Over Time		
	2018	**2019**	**2020**
Revenue recognized	$-0-	$-0-	$ 8,000,000
Less cost of construction recognized	-0-	-0-	(7,550,000)
Gross profit recognized	$-0-	$-0-	$ 450,000

2. Assuming the contract qualifies for recognizing revenue over time, prepare the necessary summary journal entries for each of the three years to account for construction costs, construction revenue, contract billings, and cash collections, and to close the construction accounts in 2020.

	2018		2019		2020	
Construction in progress (CIP)	1,500,000		4,500,000		1,550,000	
Cash, materials, etc.		1,500,000		4,500,000		1,550,000
To record construction costs.						
Construction in progress (CIP)	500,000				50,000	
Cost of construction	1,500,000				1,550,000	
Revenue		2,000,000				1,600,000
To record revenue and gross profit.						
Cost of construction			4,500,000			
Revenue				4,400,000		
Construction in progress (CIP)				100,000		
To record revenue and gross loss.						
Accounts receivable	1,400,000		5,200,000		1,400,000	
Billings on construction contract		1,400,000		5,200,000		1,400,000
To record progress billings.						
Cash	1,000,000		4,000,000		3,000,000	
Accounts receivable		1,000,000		4,000,000		3,000,000
To record cash collections.						
Billings on construction contract					8,000,000	
Construction in progress (CIP)						8,000,000
To close accounts.						

3. Assuming the contract qualifies for recognizing revenue over time, prepare a partial balance sheet for 2018 and 2019 that includes all construction-related accounts.

Balance Sheet
(End of Year)

	2018	**2019**
Current assets:		
Accounts receivable	$400,000	$1,600,000
Costs and profit ($2,000,000) in excess of billings ($1,400,000)	600,000	
Current liabilities:		
Billings ($6,600,000) in excess of costs and profit ($6,400,000)		$ 200,000

Financial Reporting Case Solution

© Hero Images/Getty Images

1. **Under what circumstances do companies recognize revenue at a point in time? Over a period of time?** *(p. 238)* A seller recognizes revenue when it satisfies a performance obligation, which happens when the seller transfers control of a good or service to the customer. Indicators that transfer of control has occurred include customer acceptance and physical possession of the good or service as well as the seller having a right to receive payment. Some performance obligations are satisfied at a point in time, when the seller has finished transferring the good or service to the customer. Other performance obligations are satisfied over time. For example, the customer might consume the benefit of the seller's work as it is performed, or the customer might control an asset as the seller creates it.
2. **When do companies break apart a sale and treat its parts differently for purposes of recognizing revenue?** *(p. 241)* Sellers must break apart a contract if the contract contains more than one performance obligation. Goods and services are viewed as separate performance obligations if they are both capable of being distinct (for example, if the goods and services could be sold separately) and if they are separately identifiable (which isn't the case if the point of the contract is to combine various goods and services into a completed product, as occurs with construction contracts). To account for contracts with multiple performance obligations, the seller allocates the contract's transaction price to the performance obligations according to their stand-alone selling prices and then recognizes revenue for each performance obligation when it is satisfied.
3. **How do companies account for long-term contracts that qualify for revenue recognition over time?** *(p. 262)* When contracts qualify for revenue recognition over time, the seller recognizes revenue each period as the contract is being fulfilled. The amount recognized is based on progress to date, which usually is estimated as the fraction of the project's cost incurred to date divided by total estimated costs. To calculate the total amount of revenue that should be recognized up to a given date, the estimated percentage of completion is multiplied by the contract price. To calculate the amount of revenue to be recognized in the current period, the amount of revenue recognized in prior periods is subtracted from the total amount of revenue that should be recognized as of the end of the current period. ●

The Bottom Line

- **LO5–1** Companies recognize revenue when goods or services are transferred to customers for the amount the company expects to be entitled to receive in exchange for those goods or services. That core principle is implemented by (1) identifying a contract with a customer, (2) identifying the performance obligations in the contract, (3) determining the transaction price of the contract, (4) allocating that price to the performance obligations, and (5) recognizing revenue when (or as) each performance obligation is satisfied. *(p. 236)*
- **LO5–2** Revenue should be recognized *at a single point in time* when control of a good or service is transferred to the customer on a specific date. Indicators that transfer has occurred and that revenue should be recognized include the seller having the right to receive payment, the customer having legal title and physical possession of the asset, the customer formally accepting the asset, and the customer assuming the risks and rewards of ownership. *(p. 238)*
- **LO5–3** Revenue should be recognized *over time* when a performance obligation is satisfied over time. That occurs if (1) the customer consumes the benefit of the seller's work as it is performed, (2) the customer controls the asset as the seller creates it, or (3) the asset has no alternative use to the seller and the seller can be paid for its progress even if the customer cancels the contract. *(p. 239)*

- **LO5–4** A contract's transaction price is allocated to its performance obligations. The allocation is based on the *stand-alone selling prices* of the goods and services underlying those performance obligations. The stand-alone selling price must be estimated if a good or service is not sold separately. (*p. 241*)
- **LO5–5** A contract exists when it has commercial substance and all parties to the contract are committed to performing the obligations and enforcing the rights that it specifies. Performance obligations are promises by the seller to transfer goods or services to a customer. A promise to transfer a good or service is a separate performance obligation if it is *distinct,* which is the case if it is both *capable of being distinct* (meaning that the customer could use the good or service on its own or in combination with other goods and services it could obtain elsewhere), and *it is separately identifiable* (meaning that the good or service is not highly interrelated with other goods and services in the contract, so it is distinct in the context of the contract). Prepayments, rights to return merchandise, and normal quality-assurance warranties do not qualify as performance obligations, because they don't transfer a good or service to the customer. On the other hand, extended warranties and customer options to receive goods or services in some preferred manner (for example, at a discount) qualify as performance obligations. (*p. 245*)
- **LO5–6** When a contract includes consideration that depends on the outcome of future events, sellers estimate that variable consideration and include it in the contract's transaction price. The seller's estimate is based either on the most likely outcome or the expected value of the outcome. However, a constraint applies—variable consideration only should be included in the transaction price to the extent it is probable that a significant revenue reversal will not occur. The estimate of variable consideration is updated each period to reflect changes in circumstances. A seller also needs to determine if it is a principal (and recognizes as revenue the amount received from the customer) or an agent (and recognizes its commission as revenue), consider time value of money, and consider the effect of any payments by the seller to the customer. Once the transaction price is estimated, we allocate it to performance obligations according to their stand-alone selling prices, which can be estimated using the adjusted market assessment approach, the expected cost plus margin approach, or the residual approach. (*p. 248*)
- **LO5–7** If the seller's activity over the license period is expected to affect the benefits the customer receives from the intellectual property being licensed, as with symbolic IP, the seller recognizes revenue over the license period. Otherwise, the seller recognizes revenue at the point in time that the customer obtains access to the seller's intellectual property. Franchises are an example of contracts that typically include licenses as well as other performance obligations. Revenue for bill-and-hold sales should be recognized when the seller transfers control of goods to the customer, even if the seller retains physical possession of the goods, and for consignment sales when goods are delivered to the end customer. Revenue for gift cards should be recognized when the gift card is redeemed, expires, or viewed as broken. (*p. 254*)
- **LO5–8** Much disclosure is required for revenue recognition. For example, a seller recognizes contract liabilities, contract assets, and accounts receivable on separate lines of its balance sheet. If the customer makes payment to the seller before the seller has satisfied performance obligations, the seller records a contract liability, such as deferred revenue. If the seller satisfies a performance obligation before the customer has paid for it, the seller records either a contract asset or an account receivable. The seller recognizes an account receivable if only the passage of time is required before the payment is due. If instead the seller's right to payment depends on something other than the passage of time, the seller recognizes a contract asset. (*p. 259*)
- **LO5–9** Long-term contracts usually qualify for revenue recognition over time. We recognize revenue over time by assigning a share of the project's revenues and costs to each reporting period over the life of the project according to the percentage of the project completed to date. If long-term contracts don't qualify for revenue recognition over time, we recognize revenues and expenses at the point in time when the project is complete. (*p. 261*)
- **LO5–10** IFRS interprets the word "probable" as indicating a lower probability threshold than does U.S. GAAP. As a consequence, a seller could conclude a contract meets the "probable that it will collect the amounts its entitled to receive" threshold and recognize revenue under IFRS but not under U.S. GAAP. Also, IFRS doesn't tie the timing of revenue recognition for licenses to whether a license involves "functional" versus "symbolic" intellectual property, so IFRS might allow revenue recognition at a point in time for "symbolic IP" licenses that would require revenue recognition over time under U.S. GAAP. (*pp. 246, 249* and *256*)

Questions For Review of Key Topics

Q 5–1 What are the five key steps a company follows to apply the core revenue recognition principle?

Q 5–2 What indicators suggest that a performance obligation has been satisfied at a single point in time?

Q 5–3 What criteria determine whether a company can recognize revenue over time?

Q 5–4 We recognize service revenue either at one point in time or over a period of time. Explain the rationale for recognizing service revenue using these two approaches.

Q 5–5 What characteristics make a good or service a performance obligation?

Q 5–6 How does a seller allocate a transaction price to a contract's performance obligations?

Q 5–7 What must a contract include for the contract to exist for purposes of revenue recognition?

IFRS **Q 5–8** How might the definition of "probable" affect determining whether a contract exists under IFRS as compared to U.S. GAAP?

Q 5–9 When a contract includes an option to buy additional goods or services, when does that option give rise to a performance obligation?

Q 5–10 Is variable consideration included in the calculation of a contract's transaction price? If so, how is the amount of variable consideration estimated?

Q 5–11 How are sellers constrained from recognizing variable consideration, and under what circumstances does the constraint apply?

Q 5–12 Is a customer's right to return merchandise a performance obligation of the seller? How should sellers account for a right of return?

Q 5–13 What is the difference between a principal and an agent for determining the amount of revenue to recognize?

Q 5–14 Under what circumstances should sellers consider the time value of money when recognizing revenue?

Q 5–15 When should a seller view a payment to its customer as a refund of part of the price paid by the customer for the seller's products or services?

Q 5–16 What are three methods for estimating stand-alone selling prices of goods and services that normally are not sold separately?

Q 5–17 When is revenue recognized with respect to licenses?

Q 5–18 In a franchise arrangement, what are a franchisor's typical performance obligations?

Q 5–19 When does a company typically recognize revenue for a bill-and-hold sale?

Q 5–20 How might a license for symbolic intellectual property be treated differently under IFRS as compared to U.S. GAAP?

Q 5–21 When does a consignor typically recognize revenue for a consignment sale?

Q 5–22 When does a company recognize revenue for a sale of a gift card?

Q 5–23 Must bad debt expense be reported on its own line on the income statement? If not, how should it be disclosed?

Q 5–24 Explain the difference between contract assets, contract liabilities, and accounts receivable.

Q 5–25 Explain how to account for revenue on a long-term contract over time as opposed to at a point in time. Under what circumstances should revenue be recognized at the point in time a contract is completed?

Q 5–26 Periodic billings to the customer for a long-term construction contract are recorded as billings on construction contract. How is this account reported in the balance sheet?

Q 5–27 When is an estimated loss on a long-term contract recognized, both for contracts that recognize revenue over time and those that recognize revenue at the point in time the contract is completed?

Brief Exercises

BE 5–1
Revenue recognition at a point in time
● LO5–2

On July 1, 2018, Apache Company, a real estate developer, sold a parcel of land to a construction company for $3,000,000. The book value of the land on Apache's books was $1,200,000. Terms of the sale required a down payment of $150,000 and 19 annual payments of $150,000 plus interest at an appropriate interest rate due on each July 1 beginning in 2019. How much revenue will Apache recognize for the sale (ignoring interest), assuming that it recognizes revenue at the point in time at which it transfers the land to the construction company?

BE 5–2
Timing of revenue recognition
● LO5–3

Estate Construction is constructing a building for CyberB, an online retailing company. Under the construction agreement, if for any reason Estate can't complete construction, CyberB would own the partially completed building and could hire another construction company to complete the job. When should Estate recognize revenue: as the building is constructed, or after construction is completed?

BE 5–3
Timing of revenue recognition
● LO5–3

On May 1, 2018, Varga Tech Services signed a $6,000 consulting contract with Shaffer Holdings. The contract requires Varga to provide computer technology support services whenever requested over the period from May 1, 2018, to April 30, 2019, with Shaffer paying the entire $6,000 on May 1, 2018. How much revenue should Varga recognize in 2018?

BE 5–4
Allocating the transaction price
● LO5–4

Sarjit Systems sold software to a customer for $80,000. As part of the contract, Sarjit promises to provide "free" technical support over the next six months. Sarjit sells the same software without technical support for $70,000 and a stand-alone six-month technical support contract for $30,000, so these products would sell for $100,000 if sold separately. Prepare Sarjit's journal entry to record the sale of the software.

BE 5–5
Existence of a contract
● LO5-5

Tulane Tires wrote a contract for a $100,000 sale to the new Garden District Tour Company. Tulane only anticipates a slightly greater than fifty percent chance that Garden will be able to pay the amounts that Tulane is entitled to receive under the contract. Upon delivery of the tires, assuming no payment has yet been made by Garden, how much revenue should Tulane recognize under U.S. GAAP?

BE 5–6
Existence of a contract; IFRS
● LO5-5, LO5-10
IFRS

Assume the same facts as in BE 5-5 but that Tulane Tires reports under IFRS. How much revenue should Tulane recognize under IFRS?

BE 5–7
Performance obligations; prepayments
● LO5–5

eLean is an online fitness community, offering access to workout routines, nutrition advice, and eLean coaches. Customers pay a $50 fee to become registered on the website, and then pay $5 per month for access to all eLean services. How many performance obligations exist in the implied contract when a customer registers for the services?

BE 5–8
Performance obligations; warranties
● LO5–5

Vroom Vacuums sells the Tornado vacuum cleaner. Each Tornado has a one-year warranty that covers any product defects. When customers purchase a Tornado, they also have the option to purchase an extended three-year warranty that covers any breakage or maintenance. The extended warranty sells for the same amount regardless of whether it is purchased at the same time as the Tornado or at some other time. How many performance obligations exist in the implied contract for the purchase of a vacuum cleaner?

BE 5–9
Performance obligations; warranties
● LO5–5

Assume the same facts as in BE 5–8 but that customers pay 20% less for the extended warranty if they buy it at the same time they buy a Tornado. How many performance obligations exist in the implied contract for the purchase of a vacuum cleaner?

BE 5–10
Performance obligations; options
● LO5–5

McAfee sells a subscription to its antivirus software along with a subscription renewal option that allows renewal at half the prevailing price for a new subscription. How many performance obligations exist in this contract?

BE 5–11
Performance obligations; construction
● LO5–5

Precision Equipment, Inc., specializes in designing and installing customized manufacturing equipment. On February 1, 2018, it signs a contract to design a fully automated wristwatch assembly line for $2 million, which will be settled in cash upon completion of construction. Precision Equipment will install the equipment on the client's property, furnish it with a customized software package that is integral to operations, and provide consulting services that integrate the equipment with Precision's other assembly lines. How many performance obligations exist in this contract?

BE 5–12
Performance obligations; construction
● LO5–5

On January 1, 2018, Lego Construction Company signed a contract to build a custom garage for a customer and received $10,000 in advance for the job. The new garage will be built on the customer's land. To complete this project, Lego must first build a concrete floor, construct wooden pillars and walls, and finally install a roof. Lego normally charges stand-alone prices of $3,000, $4,000, and $5,000, respectively, for each of these three smaller tasks if done separately. How many performance obligations exist in this contract?

BE 5–13
Performance obligations; right of return
● LO5–5, LO5–6

Aria Perfume, Inc., sold 3,210 boxes of white musk soap during January of 2018 at the price of $90 per box. The company offers a full refund to unsatisfied customers for any product returned within 30 days from the date of purchase. Based on historical experience, Aria expects that 3% of sales will be returned. How many performance obligations are there in each sale of a box of soap? How much revenue should Aria recognize in January?

BE 5–14
Variable consideration
● LO5–6

Leo Consulting enters into a contract with Highgate University to restructure Highgate's processes for purchasing goods from suppliers. The contract states that Leo will earn a fixed fee of $25,000 and earn an additional $10,000 if Highgate achieves $100,000 of cost savings. Leo estimates a 50% chance that Highgate will achieve $100,000 of cost savings. Assuming that Leo determines the transaction price as the expected value of expected consideration, what transaction price will Leo estimate for this contract?

BE 5–15
Variable consideration
● LO5–6

In January 2018, Continental Fund Services, Inc., enters into a one-year contract with a client to provide investment advisory services. The company will receive a management fee, prepaid at the beginning of the contract, that is calculated as 1% of the client's $150 million total assets being managed. In addition, the contract specifies that Continental will receive a performance bonus of 20% of any returns in excess of the return on the Dow Jones Industrial Average market index. Continental estimates that it will earn a $2 million performance bonus, but is very uncertain of that estimate, given that the bonus depends on a highly volatile stock market. On what transaction price should Continental base revenue recognition?

BE 5–16
Right of return
● LO5–6

Finerly Corporation sells cosmetics through a network of independent distributors. Finerly shipped cosmetics to its distributors and is considering whether it should record $300,000 of revenue upon shipment of a new line of cosmetics. Finerly expects the distributors to be able to sell the cosmetics, but is uncertain because it has little experience with selling cosmetics of this type. Finerly is committed to accepting the cosmetics back from the distributors if the cosmetics are not sold. How much revenue should Finerly recognize upon delivery to its distributors?

BE 5–17
Principal or agent
● LO5–6

Assume that Amazon.com sells the MacBook Pro, a computer produced by Apple, for a retail price of $1,500. Amazon arranges its operations such that customers receive products directly from Apple Stores rather than Amazon. Customers purchase from Amazon using credit cards, and Amazon forwards cash to Apple equal to the retail price minus a $150 commission that Amazon keeps. In this arrangement, how much revenue will Amazon recognize for the sale of one MacBook Pro?

BE 5–18
Payments by the seller to the customer
● LO5–6

Lewis Co. sold merchandise to AdCo for $60,000 and received $60,000 for that sale one month later. One week prior to receiving payment from AdCo, Lewis made a $10,000 payment to AdCo for advertising services that have a fair value of $7,500. After accounting for any necessary adjustments, how much revenue should Lewis Co. record for the merchandise sold to AdCo?

BE 5–19
Estimating stand-alone selling prices: adjusted market assessment approach
● LO5–6

O'Hara Associates sells golf clubs, and with each sale of a full set of clubs provides complementary club-fitting services. A full set of clubs with the fitting services sells for $1,500. Similar club-fitting services are offered by other vendors for $110, and O'Hara generally charges approximately 10% more than do other vendors for similar services. Estimate the stand-alone selling price of the club-fitting services using the adjusted market assessment approach.

BE 5–20
Estimating stand-alone selling prices: expected cost plus margin approach
● LO5–6

O'Hara Associates sells golf clubs, and with each sale of a full set of clubs provides complementary club-fitting services. A full set of clubs with the fitting services sells for $1,500. O'Hara estimates that it incurs $60 of staff compensation and other costs to provide the fitting services, and normally earns 30% over cost on similar services. Assuming that the golf clubs and the club-fitting services are separate performance obligations, estimate the stand-alone selling price of the club-fitting services using the expected cost plus margin approach.

BE 5–21
Estimating stand-alone selling prices; residual approach
● LO5–6

O'Hara Associates sells golf clubs, and with each sale of a full set of clubs provides complementary club-fitting services. A full set of clubs with the fitting services sells for $1,500. O'Hara sells the same clubs without the fitting service for $1,400. Assuming that the golf clubs and the club-fitting services are separate performance obligations, estimate the stand-alone selling price of the club fitting services using the residual approach.

BE 5–22
Timing of revenue recognition; licenses
● LO5–7

Saar Associates sells two licenses to Kim & Company on September 1, 2018. First, in exchange for $100,000, Saar provides Kim with a copy of its proprietary investment management software, which Saar does not anticipate updating and which Kim can use permanently. Second, in exchange for $90,000, Saar provides Kim with a three-year right to market Kim's financial advisory services under the name of

Saar Associates, which Saar advertises on an ongoing basis. How much revenue will Saar recognize in 2018 under this arrangement?

BE 5-23 Timing of revenue recognition; licenses ● LO5-7 IFRS

Assume the same facts as in BE 5-22 except that the trade name "Saar Associates" is not well known in the marketplace and the owner provides no advertising or other benefits to a licensee of the Saar Associates trade name during the license period. How much revenue will Saar recognize in 2018 under this arrangement if Saar reports under U.S. GAAP?

BE 5-24 Timing of revenue recognition; licenses ● LO5-7, LO5-10

IFRS

Assume the same facts as in BE 5-23 . How much revenue will Saar recognize in 2018 under this arrangement if Saar reports under IFRS?

BE 5–25 Timing of revenue recognition; franchises ● LO5–7

TopChop sells hairstyling franchises. TopChop receives $50,000 from a new franchisee for providing initial training, equipment and furnishings that have a stand-alone selling price of $50,000. TopChop also receives $30,000 per year for use of the TopChop name and for ongoing consulting services (starting on the date the franchise is purchased). Carlos became a TopChop franchisee on July 1, 2018, and on August 1, 2018, had completed training and was open for business. How much revenue in 2018 will TopChop recognize for its arrangement with Carlos?

BE 5–26 Timing of revenue recognition; bill-and-hold ● LO5–7

Dowell Fishing Supply, Inc., sold $50,000 of Dowell Rods on December 15, 2018, to Bassadrome. Because of a shipping backlog, Dowell held the inventory in Dowell's warehouse until January 12, 2019 (having assured Bassadrome that it would deliver sooner if necessary). How much revenue should Dowell recognize in 2018 for the sale to Bassadrome?

BE 5–27 Timing of revenue recognition; consignment ● LO5–7

Kerianne paints landscapes, and in late 2018 placed four paintings with a retail price of $250 each in the Holmstrom Gallery. Kerianne's arrangement with Holmstrom is that Holmstrom will earn a 20% commission on paintings sold to gallery patrons. As of December 31, 2018, one painting had been sold by Holmstrom to gallery patrons. How much revenue with respect to these four paintings should Kerianne recognize in 2018?

BE 5–28 Timing of revenue recognition; gift card ● LO5–7

GoodBuy sells gift cards redeemable for GoodBuy products either in store or online. During 2018, GoodBuy sold $1,000,000 of gift cards, and $840,000 of the gift cards were redeemed for products. As of December 31, 2018, $30,000 of the remaining gift cards had passed the date at which GoodBuy concludes that the cards will never be redeemed. How much gift card revenue should GoodBuy recognize in 2018?

BE 5–29 Contract assets and contract liabilities ● LO5–8

Holt Industries received a $2,000 prepayment from the Ramirez Company for the sale of new office furniture. Holt will bill Ramirez an additional $3,000 upon delivery of the furniture to Ramirez. Upon receipt of the $2,000 prepayment, how much should Holt recognize for a contract asset, a contract liability, and accounts receivable?

BE 5–30 Contract assets and contract liabilities ● LO5–8, LO5–9

As of December 31, 2018, Cady Construction has one construction job for which the construction in progress (CIP) account has a balance of $20,000 and the billings on construction contract account has a balance of $14,000. Cady has another construction job for which the construction in progress account has a balance of $3,000 and the billings on construction contract account has a balance of $5,000. Indicate the amount of contract asset and/or contract liability that Cady would show in its December 31, 2018, balance sheet.

BE 5–31 Long-term contract; revenue recognition over time; profit recognition ● LO5–9

A construction company entered into a fixed-price contract to build an office building for $20 million. Construction costs incurred during the first year were $6 million and estimated costs to complete at the end of the year were $9 million. The company recognizes revenue over time according to percentage of completion. How much revenue and gross profit or loss will appear in the company's income statement in the first year of the contract?

BE 5–32
Long-term contract; revenue recognition over time; balance sheet
● LO5–9

Refer to the situation described in BE 5–31. Assume that, during the first year the company billed its customer $7 million, of which $5 million was collected before year-end. What would appear in the year-end balance sheet related to this contract?

BE 5–33
Long-term contract; revenue recognition upon completion
● LO5–9

Refer to the situation described in BE 5–31. Assume that the building was completed during the second year, and construction costs incurred during the second year were $10 million. How much revenue and gross profit or loss will the company recognize in the first and second year if it recognizes revenue upon contract completion?

BE 5–34
Long-term contract; revenue recognition; loss on entire project
● LO5–9

Franklin Construction entered into a fixed-price contract to build a freeway-connecting ramp for $30 million. Construction costs incurred in the first year were $16 million and estimated remaining costs to complete at the end of the year were $17 million. How much gross profit or loss will Franklin recognize in the first year if it recognizes revenue over time according to percentage of completion? What if instead Franklin recognizes revenue upon contract completion?

Exercises

E 5–1
FASB codification research
● LO5–1, LO5–2, LO5–3

Access the *FASB's Accounting Standards Codification* at the FASB website (www.fasb.org).

Required:

Determine the specific citation for accounting for each of the following items:

1. What are the five key steps to applying the revenue recognition principle?
2. What are indicators that control has passed from the seller to the buyer, such that it is appropriate to recognize revenue at a point in time?
3. Under what circumstances can sellers recognize revenue over time?

E 5–2
Service revenue
● LO5–3

Ski West, Inc., operates a downhill ski area near Lake Tahoe, California. An all-day adult lift ticket can be purchased for $85. Adult customers also can purchase a season pass that entitles the pass holder to ski any day during the season, which typically runs from December 1 through April 30. Ski West expects its season pass holders to use their passes equally throughout the season. The company's fiscal year ends on December 31.

On November 6, 2018, Jake Lawson purchased a season pass for $450.

Required:

1. When should Ski West recognize revenue from the sale of its season passes?
2. Prepare the appropriate journal entries that Ski West would record on November 6 and December 31.
3. What will be included in the Ski West 2018 income statement and balance sheet related to the sale of the season pass to Jake Lawson?

E 5–3
Allocating transaction price
● LO5–4

Video Planet (VP) sells a big screen TV package consisting of a 60-inch plasma TV, a universal remote, and on-site installation by VP staff. The installation includes programming the remote to have the TV interface with other parts of the customer's home entertainment system. VP concludes that the TV, remote, and installation service are separate performance obligations. VP sells the 60-inch TV separately for $1,700, sells the remote separately for $100, and offers the installation service separately for $200. The entire package sells for $1,900.

Required:

How much revenue would be allocated to the TV, the remote, and the installation service?

E 5–4
FASB codification research
● LO5–4, LO5–5

Access the *FASB Standards Codification* at the FASB website (www.fasb.org).

Required:

Determine the specific citation for accounting for each of the following items:

1. On what basis is a contract's transaction price allocated to its performance obligations?
2. What are indicators that a promised good or service is separately identifiable from other goods and services promised in the contract?
3. Under what circumstances is an option viewed as a performance obligation?

E 5–5
Performance obligations
● LO5–2, LO5–4, LO5–5

On March 1, 2018, Gold Examiner receives $147,000 from a local bank and promises to deliver 100 units of certified 1-oz. gold bars on a future date. The contract states that ownership passes to the bank when Gold Examiner delivers the products to Brink's, a third-party carrier. In addition, Gold Examiner has agreed to provide a replacement shipment at no additional cost if the product is lost in transit. The stand-alone price of a gold bar is $1,440 per unit, and Gold Examiner estimates the stand-alone price of the replacement insurance service to be $60 per unit. Brink's picked up the gold bars from Gold Examiner on March 30, and delivery to the bank occurred on April 1.

Required:

1. How many performance obligations are in this contract?
2. Prepare the journal entry Gold Examiner would record on March 1.
3. Prepare the journal entry Gold Examiner would record on March 30.
4. Prepare the journal entry Gold Examiner would record on April 1.

E 5–6
Performance obligations; customer option for additional goods or services
● LO5–2, LO5–4, LO5–5

Clarks Inc., a shoe retailer, sells boots in different styles. In early November the company starts selling "SunBoots" to customers for $70 per pair. When a customer purchases a pair of SunBoots, Clarks also gives the customer a 30% discount coupon for any additional future purchases made in the next 30 days. Customers can't obtain the discount coupon otherwise. Clarks anticipates that approximately 20% of customers will utilize the coupon, and that on average those customers will purchase additional goods that normally sell for $100.

Required:

1. How many performance obligations are in a contract to buy a pair of SunBoots?
2. Prepare a journal entry to record revenue for the sale of 1,000 pairs of SunBoots, assuming that Clarks uses the residual method to estimate the stand-alone selling price of SunBoots sold without the discount coupon.

E 5–7
Performance obligations; customer option for additional goods or services; prepayment
● LO5–3, LO5–4, LO5–5

A New York City daily newspaper called "Manhattan Today" charges an annual subscription fee of $135. Customers prepay their subscriptions and receive 260 issues over the year. To attract more subscribers, the company offered new subscribers the ability to pay $130 for an annual subscription that also would include a coupon to receive a 40% discount on a one-hour ride through Central Park in a horse-drawn carriage. The list price of a carriage ride is $125 per hour. The company estimates that approximately 30% of the coupons will be redeemed.

Required:

1. How much revenue should Manhattan Today recognize upon receipt of the $130 subscription price?
2. How many performance obligations exist in this contract?
3. Prepare the journal entry to recognize sale of 10 new subscriptions, clearly identifying the revenue or deferred revenue associated with each performance obligation.

E 5–8
Performance obligations; customer option for additional goods or services
● LO5–4, LO5–5

On May 1, 2018, Meta Computer, Inc., enters into a contract to sell 5,000 units of Comfort Office Keyboard to one of its clients, Bionics, Inc., at a fixed price of $95,000, to be settled by a cash payment on May 1. Delivery is scheduled for June 1, 2018. As part of the contract, the seller offers a 25% discount coupon to Bionics for any purchases in the next six months. The seller will continue to offer a 5% discount on all sales during the same time period, which will be available to all customers. Based on experience, Meta Computer estimates a 50% probability that Bionics will redeem the 25% discount voucher, and that the coupon will be applied to $20,000 of purchases. The stand-alone selling price for the Comfort Office Keyboard is $19.60 per unit.

Required:

1. How many performance obligations are in this contract?
2. Prepare the journal entry that Meta would record on May 1, 2018.
3. Assume the same facts and circumstances as above, except that Meta gives a 5% discount option to Bionics instead of 25%. In this case, what journal entry would Meta record on May 1, 2018?

E 5–9
Variable consideration; estimation and constraint
● LO5–6

Thomas Consultants provided Bran Construction with assistance in implementing various cost-savings initiatives. Thomas's contract specifies that it will receive a flat fee of $50,000 and an additional $20,000 if Bran reaches a prespecified target amount of cost savings. Thomas estimates that there is a 20% chance that Bran will achieve the cost-savings target.

Required:

1. Assuming Thomas uses the expected value as its estimate of variable consideration, calculate the transaction price.
2. Assuming Thomas uses the most likely value as its estimate of variable consideration, calculate the transaction price.
3. Assume Thomas uses the expected value as its estimate of variable consideration, but is very uncertain of that estimate due to a lack of experience with similar consulting arrangements. Calculate the transaction price.

E 5–10
Variable consideration—most likely amount; change in estimate
● LO5–3, LO5–6

Rocky Guide Service provides guided 1–5 day hiking tours throughout the Rocky Mountains. Wilderness Tours hires Rocky to lead various tours that Wilderness sells. Rocky receives $1,000 per tour day, and shortly after the end of each month Rocky learns whether it will receive a $100 bonus per tour day it guided during the previous month if its service during that month received an average evaluation of "excellent" by Wilderness customers. The $1,000 per day and any bonus due are paid in one lump payment shortly after the end of each month.

- On July 1, based on prior experience, Rocky estimated there is a 30% chance it will earn the bonus for July tours. It guided a total of 10 days from July 1–July 15.
- On July 16, based on Rocky's view that it had provided excellent service during the first part of the month, Rocky revised its estimate to an 80% chance it would earn the bonus for July tours. Rocky also guided customers for 15 days from July 16–July 31.
- On August 5 Rocky learned it did not receive an average evaluation of "excellent" for its July tours, so it would not receive any bonus for July, and received all payment due for the July tours.

Rocky bases estimates of variable consideration on the most likely amount it expects to receive.

Required:

1. Prepare Rocky's July 15 journal entry to record revenue for tours given from July 1–July 15.
2. Prepare Rocky's July 31 journal entry to record revenue for tours given from July 16–July 31.
3. Prepare Rocky's August 5 journal entry to record any necessary adjustments to revenue and receipt of payment from Wilderness.

E 5–11
Variable consideration–expected value; change in estimate
● LO5–3, LO5–6

Assume the same facts as in E 5–10.

Required:

Complete the requirements of E 5–10 assuming that Rocky bases estimates of variable consideration on the expected value it expects to receive.

E 5–12
Consideration payable to customer; collectibility of transaction price
● LO5–2, LO5–5, LO5–6

Furtastic manufactures imitation fur garments. On June 1, 2018, Furtastic made a sale to Willett's Department Store under terms that require Willett to pay $150,000 to Furtastic on June 30, 2018. In a separate transaction on June 15, 2018, Furtastic purchased brand advertising services from Willett for $12,000. The fair value of those advertising services is $5,000. Furtastic expects that 3% of all sales will prove uncollectible.

Required:

1. Prepare the journal entry to record Furtastic's sale on June 1, 2018.
2. Prepare the journal entry to record Furtastic's purchase of advertising services from Willett on June 15, 2018. Assume all of the advertising services are delivered on June 15, 2018.
3. Prepare the journal entry to record Furtastic's receipt of $150,000 from Willett on June 30, 2018.
4. How would Furtastic's expectation regarding uncollectible accounts affect its recognition of revenue from the sale to Willett's Department Store on June 1, 2018? Explain briefly.

E 5–13
Approaches for estimating stand-alone selling prices
● LO5–6

(This exercise is a variation of E 5–3.)

Video Planet (VP) sells a big screen TV package consisting of a 60-inch plasma TV, a universal remote, and on-site installation by VP staff. The installation includes programming the remote to have the TV interface with other parts of the customer's home entertainment system. VP concludes that the TV, remote, and installation service are separate performance obligations. VP sells the 60-inch TV separately for $1,750 and sells the remote separately for $100, and offers the entire package for $1,900. VP does not sell the installation service separately. VP is aware that other similar vendors charge $150 for the installation service. VP also estimates that it incurs approximately $100 of compensation and other costs for VP staff to provide the installation service. VP typically charges 40% above cost on similar sales.

Required:

1. Estimate the stand-alone selling price of the installation service using the adjusted market assessment approach.
2. Estimate the stand-alone selling price of the installation service using the expected cost plus margin approach.
3. Estimate the stand-alone selling price of the installation service using the residual approach.

E 5–14
FASB codification research
● LO5–6, LO5–7

Access the *FASB Accounting Standards Codification* at the FASB website (www.fasb.org).

Required:

Determine the specific citation for accounting for each of the following items:

1. What alternative approaches can be used to estimate variable consideration?
2. What alternative approaches can be used to estimate the stand-alone selling price of performance obligations that are not sold separately?

3. What determines the timing of revenue recognition with respect to licenses of symbolic intellectual property?
4. What indicators suggest that a seller is a principal rather than an agent?

E 5–15
Franchises; residual method
● LO5–6, LO5–7

Monitor Muffler sells franchise arrangements throughout the United States and Canada. Under a franchise agreement, Monitor receives $600,000 in exchange for satisfying the following separate performance obligations: (1) franchisees have a five-year right to operate as a Monitor Muffler retail establishment in an exclusive sales territory, (2) franchisees receive initial training and certification as a Monitor Mechanic, and (3) franchisees receive a Monitor Muffler building and necessary equipment. The stand-alone selling price of the initial training and certification is $15,000, and $450,000 for the building and equipment. Monitor estimates the stand-alone selling price of the five-year right to operate as a Monitor Muffler establishment using the residual approach.

Monitor received $75,000 on July 1, 2018, from Perkins and accepted a note receivable for the rest of the franchise price. Monitor will construct and equip Perkins's building and train and certify Perkins by September 1, and Perkins's five-year right to operate as a Monitor Muffler establishment will commence on September 1 as well.

Required:

1. What amount would Monitor calculate as the stand-alone selling price of the five-year right to operate as a Monitor Muffler retail establishment?
2. What journal entry would Monitor record on July 1, 2018, to reflect the sale of a franchise to Dan Perkins?
3. How much revenue would Monitor recognize in the year ended December 31, 2018, with respect to its franchise arrangement with Perkins? (Ignore any interest on the note receivable.)

E 5–16
FASB codification research
● LO5–8

Access the *FASB Accounting Standards Codification* at the FASB website (www.fasb.org).

Required:

Determine the specific citation for accounting for each of the following items:

1. What disclosures are required with respect to performance obligations that the seller is committed to satisfying but that are not yet satisfied?
2. What disclosures are required with respect to uncollectible accounts receivable, also called impairments of receivables?
3. What disclosures are required with respect to significant changes in contract assets and contract liabilities?

E 5–17
Long-term contract; revenue recognition over time and at a point in time
● LO5–9

Assume Nortel Networks contracted to provide a customer with Internet infrastructure for $2,000,000. The project began in 2018 and was completed in 2019. Data relating to the contract are summarized below:

	2018	2019
Costs incurred during the year	$ 300,000	$ 1,575,000
Estimated costs to complete as of 12/31	1,200,000	–0–
Billings during the year	380,000	1,620,000
Cash collections during the year	250,000	1,750,000

Required:

1. Compute the amount of revenue and gross profit or loss to be recognized in 2018 and 2019 assuming Nortel recognizes revenue over time according to percentage of completion.
2. Compute the amount of revenue and gross profit or loss to be recognized in 2018 and 2019 assuming this project does not qualify for revenue recognition over time.
3. Prepare a partial balance sheet to show how the information related to this contract would be presented at the end of 2018 assuming Nortel recognizes revenue over time according to percentage of completion.
4. Prepare a partial balance sheet to show how the information related to this contract would be presented at the end of 2018 assuming this project does not qualify for revenue recognition over time.

E 5–18
Long-term contract; revenue recognition over time vs. upon project completion
● LO5–9

On June 15, 2018, Sanderson Construction entered into a long-term construction contract to build a baseball stadium in Washington, D.C., for $220 million. The expected completion date is April 1, 2020, just in time for the 2020 baseball season. Costs incurred and estimated costs to complete at year-end for the life of the contract are as follows ($ in millions):

	2018	2019	2020
Costs incurred during the year	$ 40	$80	$50
Estimated costs to complete as of December 31	120	60	—

Required:

1. How much revenue and gross profit will Sanderson report in its 2018, 2019, and 2020 income statements related to this contract assuming Sanderson recognizes revenue over time according to percentage of completion?

2. How much revenue and gross profit will Sanderson report in its 2018, 2019, and 2020 income statements related to this contract assuming this project does not qualify for revenue recognition over time?
3. Suppose the estimated costs to complete at the end of 2019 are $80 million instead of $60 million. Determine the amount of revenue and gross profit or loss to be recognized in 2019 assuming Sanderson recognizes revenue over time according to percentage of completion.

E 5–19
Long-term contract; revenue recognition over time; loss projected on entire project
● LO5–9

On February 1, 2018, Arrow Construction Company entered into a three-year construction contract to build a bridge for a price of $8,000,000. During 2018, costs of $2,000,000 were incurred with estimated costs of $4,000,000 yet to be incurred. Billings of $2,500,000 were sent, and cash collected was $2,250,000.

In 2019, costs incurred were $2,500,000 with remaining costs estimated to be $3,600,000. 2019 billings were $2,750,000, and $2,475,000 cash was collected. The project was completed in 2020 after additional costs of $3,800,000 were incurred. The company's fiscal year-end is December 31. Arrow recognizes revenue over time according to percentage of completion.

Required:
1. Calculate the amount of revenue and gross profit or loss to be recognized in each of the three years.
2. Prepare journal entries for 2018 and 2019 to record the transactions described (credit "various accounts" for construction costs incurred).
3. Prepare a partial balance sheet to show the presentation of the project as of December 31, 2018 and 2019.

E 5–20
Long-term contract; revenue recognition upon project completion; loss projected on entire project
● LO5–8, LO5–9

[This is a variation of E 5–19 focusing on the revenue recognition upon project completion.]

On February 1, 2018, Arrow Construction Company entered into a three-year construction contract to build a bridge for a price of $8,000,000. During 2018, costs of $2,000,000 were incurred, with estimated costs of $4,000,000 yet to be incurred. Billings of $2,500,000 were sent, and cash collected was $2,250,000.

In 2019, costs incurred were $2,500,000 with remaining costs estimated to be $3,600,000. 2019 billings were $2,750,000, and $2,475,000 cash was collected. The project was completed in 2020 after additional costs of $3,800,000 were incurred. The company's fiscal year-end is December 31. This project does not qualify for revenue recognition over time.

Required:
1. Calculate the amount of gross profit or loss to be recognized in each of the three years.
2. Prepare journal entries for 2018 and 2019 to record the transactions described (credit "various accounts" for construction costs incurred).
3. Prepare a partial balance sheet to show the presentation of the project as of December 31, 2018 and 2019. Indicate whether any of the amounts shown are contract assets or contract liabilities.

E 5–21
Income (loss) recognition; Long-term contract; revenue recognition over time vs. upon project completion
● LO5–9

Brady Construction Company contracted to build an apartment complex for a price of $5,000,000. Construction began in 2018 and was completed in 2020. The following is a series of independent situations, numbered 1 through 6, involving differing costs for the project. All costs are stated in thousands of dollars.

	Costs Incurred During Year			Estimated Costs to Complete (As of the End of the Year)		
Situation	**2018**	**2019**	**2020**	**2018**	**2019**	**2020**
1	1,500	2,100	900	3,000	900	—
2	1,500	900	2,400	3,000	2,400	—
3	1,500	2,100	1,600	3,000	1,500	—
4	500	3,000	1,000	3,500	875	—
5	500	3,000	1,300	3,500	1,500	—
6	500	3,000	1,800	4,600	1,700	—

Required:

Copy and complete the following table:

	Gross Profit (Loss) Recognized					
	Over Time			Upon Completion		
Situation	**2018**	**2019**	**2020**	**2018**	**2019**	**2020**
1						
2						
3						
4						
5						
6						

E 5–22
Long-term contract; revenue recognition over time; solve for unknowns
● LO5–9

In 2018, Long Construction Corporation began construction work under a three-year contract. The contract price is $1,600,000. Long recognizes revenue over time according to percentage of completion for financial reporting purposes. The financial statement presentation relating to this contract at December 31, 2018, is as follows:

Balance Sheet		
Accounts receivable (from construction progress billings)		$30,000
Construction in progress	$100,000	
Less: Billings on construction contract	(94,000)	
Cost and profit of uncompleted contracts in excess of billings		6,000
Income Statement		
Income (before tax) on the contract recognized in 2018		$20,000

Required:

1. What was the cost of construction actually incurred in 2018?
2. How much cash was collected in 2018 on this contract?
3. What was the estimated cost to complete as of the end of 2018?
4. What was the estimated percentage of completion used to calculate revenue in 2018? *(AICPA adapted)*

Problems

connect

P 5–1
Upfront fees; performance obligations
● LO5–4, LO5–5

Fit & Slim (F&S) is a health club that offers members various gym services.

Required:

1. Assume F&S offers a deal whereby enrolling in a new membership for $700 provides a year of unlimited access to facilities and also entitles the member to receive a voucher redeemable for 25% off yoga classes for one year. The yoga classes are offered to gym members as well as to the general public. A new membership normally sells for $720, and a one-year enrollment in yoga classes sells for an additional $500. F&S estimates that approximately 40% of the vouchers will be redeemed. F&S offers a 10% discount on all one-year enrollments in classes as part of its normal promotion strategy.
   a. How many performance obligations are included in the new member deal?
   b. How much of the contract price would be allocated to each performance obligation? Explain your answer.
   c. Prepare the journal entry to recognize revenue for the sale of a new membership. Clearly identify revenue or deferred revenue associated with each performance obligation.
2. Assume F&S offers a "Fit 50" coupon book with 50 prepaid visits over the next year. F&S has learned that Fit 50 purchasers make an average of 40 visits before the coupon book expires. A customer purchases a Fit 50 book by paying $500 in advance, and for any additional visits over 50 during the year after the book is purchased, the customer can pay a $15 visitation fee per visit. F&S typically charges $15 to nonmembers who use the facilities for a single day.
   a. How many separate performance obligations are included in the Fit 50 member deal? Explain your answer.
   b. How much of the contract price would be allocated to each separate performance obligation? Explain your answer.
   c. Prepare the journal entry to recognize revenue for the sale of a new Fit 50 book.

P 5–2
Performance obligations; warranties; option
● LO5–2, LO5–4, LO5–5

Creative Computing sells a tablet computer called the Protab. The $780 sales price of a Protab Package includes the following:

- One Protab computer.
- A 6-month limited warranty. This warranty guarantees that Creative will cover any costs that arise due to repairs or replacements associated with defective products for up to six months.
- A coupon to purchase a Creative Probook e-book reader for $200, a price that represents a 50% discount from the regular Probook price of $400. It is expected that 20% of the discount coupons will be utilized.
- A coupon to purchase a one-year extended warranty for $50. Customers can buy the extended warranty for $50 at other times as well. Creative estimates that 40% of customers will purchase an extended warranty.
- Creative does not sell the Protab without the limited warranty, option to purchase a Probook, and the option to purchase an extended warranty, but estimates that if it did so, a Protab alone would sell for $760.

Required:

1. How many performance obligations are included in a Protab Package? Explain your answer.

2. List the performance obligations in the Protab Package in the following table, and complete it to allocate the transaction price of 100,000 Protab Packages to the performance obligations in the contract.

Performance obligation:	Stand-alone selling price of the performance obligation:	Percentage of the sum of the stand-alone selling prices of the performance obligations (to two decimal places):	Allocation of total transaction price to the performance obligation:

3. Prepare a journal entry to record sales of 100,000 Protab Packages (ignore any sales of extended warranties).

P 5–3
Performance obligations; warranties; option
● LO5–2, LO5–4, LO5–5

Assume the same facts as in P5–2, except that customers must pay $75 to purchase the extended warranty if they don't purchase it with the $50 coupon that was included in the Protab Package. Creative estimates that 40% of customers will use the $50 coupon to purchase an extended warranty. Complete the same requirements as in P 5–2.

P 5–4
Performance obligations; customer options for additional goods and services
● LO5–2, LO5–4, LO5–5

Supply Club, Inc., sells a variety of paper products, office supplies, and other products used by businesses and individual consumers. During July 2018 it started a loyalty program through which qualifying customers can accumulate points and redeem those points for discounts on future purchases. Redemption of a loyalty point reduces the price of one dollar of future purchases by 20% (equal to 20 cents). Customers do not earn additional loyalty points for purchases on which loyalty points are redeemed. Based on past experience, Supply Club estimates a 60% probability that any point issued will be redeemed for the discount. During July 2018, the company records $135,000 of revenue and awards 125,000 loyalty points. The aggregate stand-alone selling price of the purchased products is $135,000. Eighty percent of sales were cash sales, and the remainder were credit sales.

Required:

1. Prepare Supply Club's journal entry to record July sales.
2. During August, customers redeem loyalty points on $60,000 of merchandise. Seventy-five percent of those sales were for cash, and the remainder were credit sales. Prepare Supply Club's journal entry to record those sales.

P 5–5
Variable consideration
● LO5–3, LO5–6

On January 1, Revis Consulting entered into a contract to complete a cost reduction program for Green Financial over a six-month period. Revis will receive $20,000 from Green at the end of each month. If total cost savings reach a specific target, Revis will receive an additional $10,000 from Green at the end of the contract, but if total cost savings fall short, Revis will refund $10,000 to Green. Revis estimates an 80% chance that cost savings will reach the target and calculates the contract price based on the expected value of future payments to be received.

Required:

Prepare the following journal entries for Revis:

1. Prepare the journal entry on January 31 to record the collection of cash and recognition of the first month's revenue.
2. Assuming total cost savings exceed target, prepare the journal entry on June 30 to record receipt of the bonus.
3. Assuming total cost savings fall short of target, prepare the journal entry on June 30 to record payment of the penalty.

P 5–6
Variable consideration; change of estimate
● LO5–3, LO5–6

Since 1970, Super Rise, Inc., has provided maintenance services for elevators. On January 1, 2018, Super Rise obtains a contract to maintain an elevator in a 90-story building in New York City for 10 months and receives a fixed payment of $80,000. The contract specifies that Super Rise will receive an additional $40,000 at the end of the 10 months if there is no unexpected delay, stoppage, or accident during the year. Super Rise estimates variable consideration to be the most likely amount it will receive.

Required:

1. Assume that, because the building sees a constant flux of people throughout the day, Super Rise is allowed to access the elevators and related mechanical equipment only between 3am and 5am on any given day, which

is insufficient to perform some of the more time-consuming repair work. As a result, Super Rise believes that unexpected delays are likely and that it will not earn the bonus. Prepare the journal entry Super Rise would record on January 1.

2. Assume instead that Super Rise knows at the inception of the contract that it will be given unlimited access to the elevators and related equipment each day, with the right to schedule repair sessions any time. When given these terms and conditions, Super Rise has never had any delays or accidents in the past. Prepare the journal entry Super Rise would record on January 31 to record one month of revenue.
3. Assume the same facts as requirement 1. In addition assume that, on May 31, Super Rise determines that it does not need to spend more than two hours on any given day to operate the elevator safely because the client's elevator is relatively new. Therefore, Super Rise believes that unexpected delays are very unlikely. Prepare the journal entry Super Rise would record on May 31 to recognize May revenue and any necessary revision in its estimated bonus receivable.

P 5–7
Variable consideration; constraint and change of estimate
● LO5–3, LO5–6

Assume the same facts as P 5–6.

Required:

1. Assume that Super Rise anticipates it will earn the performance bonus, but is highly uncertain about its estimate given unfamiliarity with the building and uncertainty about its access to the elevators and related equipment. Prepare the journal entry Super Rise would record on January 1.
2. Assume the same facts as requirement 1. In addition assume that, on May 31, Super Rise determines that it has sufficient experience with the company to make an accurate estimate of the likelihood that it will earn the performance bonus, and concludes that it is likely to earn the performance bonus. Prepare the journal entry Super Rise would record on May 31 to recognize May revenue and any necessary revision in its estimated bonus receivable.

P 5–8
Variable transaction price
● LO5–3, LO5–6

Velocity, a consulting firm, enters into a contract to help Burger Boy, a fast-food restaurant, design a marketing strategy to compete with Burger King. The contract spans eight months. Burger Boy promises to pay $60,000 at the beginning of each month. At the end of the contract, Velocity either will give Burger Boy a refund of $20,000 or will be entitled to an additional $20,000 bonus, depending on whether sales at Burger Boy at year-end have increased to a target level. At the inception of the contract, Velocity estimates an 80% chance that it will earn the $20,000 bonus and calculates the contract price based on the expected value of future payments to be received. After four months, circumstances change, and Velocity revises to 60% its estimate of the probability that it will earn the bonus. At the end of the contract, Velocity receives the additional consideration of $20,000.

Required:

1. Prepare the journal entry to record revenue each month for the first four months of the contract.
2. Prepare the journal entry that the Velocity Company would record after four months to recognize the change in estimate associated with the reduced likelihood that the $20,000 bonus will be received.
3. Prepare the journal entry to record the revenue each month for the second four months of the contract.
4. Prepare the journal entry after eight months to record receipt of the $20,000 cash bonus.

P 5–9
Variable transaction price
● LO5–3, LO5–6, LO5–7

Tran Technologies licenses its functional intellectual property to Lyon Industries. Terms of the arrangement require Lyon to pay Tran $500,000 on April 1, 2018, when Lyon first obtains access to Tran's intellectual property, and then to pay Tran a royalty of 4% of future sales of products that utilize that intellectual property. Tran anticipates receiving sales-based royalties of $1,000,000 during 2018 and $1,500,000/year for the years 2019–2021. Assume Tran accounts for the Lyon license as a right of use, because Tran's actions subsequent to April 1, 2018, will affect the benefits that Lyon receives from access to Tran's intellectual property.

Required:

1. Access the *FASB Accounting Standards Codification* at the FASB website (www.fasb.org). Identify the specific citation for accounting for variable consideration arising from sales-based royalties on licenses of intellectual property, and consider the relevant GAAP. When can Tran recognize revenue from sales-based royalties associated with the Lyon license?
2. What journal entry would Tran record on April 1, 2018, when it receives the $500,000 payment from Lyon?
3. Assume on December 31, 2018, Tran receives $1,000,000 for all sales-based royalties earned from Lyon in 2018. What journal entry would Tran record on December 31, 2018, to recognize any revenue that should be recognized in 2018 with respect to the Lyon license that it has not already recognized?
4. Assume Tran accounts for the Lyon license as a five-year right to access Tran's symbolic intellectual property from April 1, 2018, through March 31, 2023. Tran expects that its ongoing marketing efforts will affect the value of the license to Lyon during the five-year license period. Repeat requirements 2 and 3.

P 5–10
Long-term contract; revenue recognition over time
● LO5–8, LO5–9

In 2018, the Westgate Construction Company entered into a contract to construct a road for Santa Clara County for $10,000,000. The road was completed in 2020. Information related to the contract is as follows:

	2018	2019	2020
Cost incurred during the year	$2,400,000	$3,600,000	$2,200,000
Estimated costs to complete as of year-end	5,600,000	2,000,000	–0–
Billings during the year	2,000,000	4,000,000	4,000,000
Cash collections during the year	1,800,000	3,600,000	4,600,000

Westgate recognizes revenue over time according to percentage of completion.

Required:

1. Calculate the amount of revenue and gross profit to be recognized in each of the three years.
2. Prepare all necessary journal entries for each of the years (credit "various accounts" for construction costs incurred).
3. Prepare a partial balance sheet for 2018 and 2019 showing any items related to the contract. Indicate whether any of the amounts shown are contract assets or contract liabilities.
4. Calculate the amount of revenue and gross profit to be recognized in each of the three years assuming the following costs incurred and costs to complete information:

	2018	2019	2020
Costs incurred during the year	$2,400,000	$3,800,000	$3,200,000
Estimated costs to complete as of year-end	5,600,000	3,100,000	–0–

5. Calculate the amount of revenue and gross profit to be recognized in each of the three years assuming the following costs incurred and costs to complete information:

	2018	2019	2020
Costs incurred during the year	$2,400,000	$3,800,000	$3,900,000
Estimated costs to complete as of year-end	5,600,000	4,100,000	–0–

P 5–11
Long-term contract; revenue recognition upon completion
● LO5–9

[This is a variation of P 5–10 modified to focus on revenue recognition upon project completion.]

Required:

Complete the requirements of P 5–10 assuming that Westgate Construction's contract with Santa Clara County does *not* qualify for revenue recognition over time.

P 5–12
Long-term contract; revenue recognized over time; loss projected on entire project
● LO5–9

Curtiss Construction Company, Inc., entered into a fixed-price contract with Axelrod Associates on July 1, 2018, to construct a four-story office building. At that time, Curtiss estimated that it would take between two and three years to complete the project. The total contract price for construction of the building is $4,000,000. Curtiss concludes that the contract does not qualify for revenue recognition over time. The building was completed on December 31, 2020. Estimated percentage of completion, accumulated contract costs incurred, estimated costs to complete the contract, and *accumulated* billings to Axelrod under the contract were as follows:

	At 12-31-2018	At 12-31-2019	At 12-31-2020
Percentage of completion	10%	60%	100%
Costs incurred to date	$ 350,000	$2,500,000	$4,250,000
Estimated costs to complete	3,150,000	1,700,000	–0–
Billings to Axelrod, to date	720,000	2,170,000	3,600,000

Required:

1. For each of the three years, prepare a schedule to compute total gross profit or loss to be recognized as a result of this contract.
2. Assuming Curtiss recognizes revenue over time according to percentage of completion, compute gross profit or loss to be recognized in each of the three years.
3. Assuming Curtiss recognizes revenue over time according to percentage of completion, compute the amount to be shown in the balance sheet at the end of 2018 and 2019 as either cost in excess of billings or billings in excess of costs.

(AICPA adapted)

P 5–13
Long-term contract; revenue recognition over time vs. upon project completion
● LO5–9

Citation Builders, Inc., builds office buildings and single-family homes. The office buildings are constructed under contract with reputable buyers. The homes are constructed in developments ranging from 10–20 homes and are typically sold during construction or soon after. To secure the home upon completion, buyers must pay a deposit of 10% of the price of the home with the remaining balance due upon completion of the house and transfer of title. Failure to pay the full amount results in forfeiture of the down payment. Occasionally, homes remain unsold for as long as three months after construction. In these situations, sales price reductions are used to promote the sale.

During 2018, Citation began construction of an office building for Altamont Corporation. The total contract price is $20 million. Costs incurred, estimated costs to complete at year-end, billings, and cash collections for the life of the contract are as follows:

	2018	2019	2020
Costs incurred during the year	$ 4,000,000	$ 9,500,000	$4,500,000
Estimated costs to complete as of year-end	12,000,000	4,500,000	—
Billings during the year	2,000,000	10,000,000	8,000,000
Cash collections during the year	1,800,000	8,600,000	9,600,000

Also during 2018, Citation began a development consisting of 12 identical homes. Citation estimated that each home will sell for $600,000, but individual sales prices are negotiated with buyers. Deposits were received for eight of the homes, three of which were completed during 2018 and paid for in full for $600,000 each by the buyers. The completed homes cost $450,000 each to construct. The construction costs incurred during 2018 for the nine uncompleted homes totaled $2,700,000.

Required:

1. Briefly explain the difference between recognizing revenue over time and upon project completion when accounting for long-term construction contracts.
2. Answer the following questions assuming that Citation concludes it does not qualify for revenue recognition over time for its office building contracts:
   a. How much revenue related to this contract will Citation report in its 2018 and 2019 income statements?
   b. What is the amount of gross profit or loss to be recognized for the Altamont contract during 2018 and 2019?
   c. What will Citation report in its December 31, 2018, balance sheet related to this contract? (Ignore cash.)
3. Answer requirements 2a through 2c assuming that Citation recognizes revenue over time according to percentage of completion for its office building contracts.
4. Assume the same information for 2018 and 2019, but that as of year-end 2019 the estimated cost to complete the office building is $9,000,000. Citation recognizes revenue over time according to percentage of completion for its office building contracts.
   a. How much revenue related to this contract will Citation report in the 2019 income statement?
   b. What is the amount of gross profit or loss to be recognized for the Altamont contract during 2019?
   c. What will Citation report in its 2019 balance sheet related to this contract? (Ignore cash.)
5. When should Citation recognize revenue for the sale of its single-family homes?
6. What will Citation report in its 2018 income statement and 2018 balance sheet related to the single-family home business (ignore cash in the balance sheet)?

Broaden Your Perspective

Apply your critical-thinking ability to the knowledge you've gained. These cases will provide you an opportunity to develop your research, analysis, judgment, and communication skills. You also will work with other students, integrate what you've learned, apply it in real-world situations, and consider its global and ethical ramifications. This practice will broaden your knowledge and further develop your decision-making abilities.

Research Case 5–1
Earnings management with respect to revenues
● LO5–1

An article published in *Accounting Horizons* describes various techniques that companies use to manage their earnings.

Required:

In your library, on the Internet, or from some other source, locate the article "How Are Earnings Managed? Evidence from Auditors" in *Accounting Horizons,* 2003 (Supplement), and answer the following questions:

1. What are the four most common revenue-recognition abuses identified by auditors in that article? From the examples provided in the article, briefly explain each abuse.

2. What is the revenue-recognition abuse identified in the article related to the percentage-of-completion method?
3. Did revenue-recognition abuses tend to increase or decrease net income in the year they occurred?
4. Did auditors tend to require their clients to make adjustments that reduced the revenue-recognition abuses they detected?

Judgment Case 5–2
Satisfaction of performance obligations
● LO5–2

Assume McDonald's enters into a contract to sell Billy Bear dolls for Toys4U Stores. Based on the contract, McDonald's displays the dolls in selected stores. Toys4U is not paid until the dolls have been sold by McDonald's, and unsold dolls are returned to Toys4U.

Required:
Determine whether Toys4U has satisfied its performance obligation when it delivers the dolls to McDonald's. Explain your answer.

Judgment Case 5–3
Satisfaction of performance obligations
● LO5–2

Cutler Education Corporation developed a software product to help children under age 12 learn mathematics. The software contains two separate parts: Basic Level (Level I) and Intermediate Level (Level II). Parents purchase each level separately and are eligible to purchase the access code for Level II only if their children pass the Level I exam.

Kerry purchases the Level I software at a price of $50 for his son, Tom, on December 1. Suppose Tom passed the Level I test on December 10, and Kerry immediately purchased the access code for Level II for an additional $30. Cutler provided Kerry with the access code to Level II on December 20.

Required:
When would Cutler recognize revenue for the sale of Level I and Level II software?

Ethics Case 5–4
Revenue recognition
● LO5–2

Horizon Corporation manufactures personal computers. The company began operations in 2013 and reported profits for the years 2013 through 2016. Due primarily to increased competition and price slashing in the industry, 2017's income statement reported a loss of $20 million. Just before the end of the 2018 fiscal year, a memo from the company's chief financial officer to Jim Fielding, the company controller, included the following comments:

If we don't do something about the large amount of unsold computers already manufactured, our auditors will require us to write them off. The resulting loss for 2018 will cause a violation of our debt covenants and force the company into bankruptcy. I suggest that you ship half of our inventory to J.B. Sales, Inc., in Oklahoma City. I know the company's president and he will accept the merchandise and acknowledge the shipment as a purchase. We can record the sale in 2018 which will boost profits to an acceptable level. Then J.B. Sales will simply return the merchandise in 2019 after the financial statements have been issued.

Required:
Discuss the ethical dilemma faced by Jim Fielding.

Judgment Case 5–5
Satisfying performance obligations
● LO5–2, LO5–3

Consider each of the following scenarios separately:

Scenario 1: Crown Construction Company entered into a contract with Star Hotel for building a highly sophisticated, customized conference room to be completed for a fixed price of $400,000. Nonrefundable progress payments are made on a monthly basis for work completed during the month. Legal title to the conference room equipment is held by Crown until the end of the construction project, but if the contract is terminated before the conference room is finished, Star retains the partially completed job and must pay for any work completed to date.

Scenario 2: Regent Company entered into a contract with Star Hotel for constructing and installing a standard designed gym for a fixed price of $400,000. Nonrefundable progress payments are made on a monthly basis for work completed during the month. Legal title to the gym passes to Star upon completion of the building process. If Star cancels the contract before the gym construction is completed, Regent removes all the installed equipment and Star must compensate Regent for any loss of profit on sale of the gym to another customer.

Scenario 3: On January 1, the CostDriver Company, a consulting firm, entered into a three-month contract with Coco Seafood Restaurant to analyze its cost structure in order to find a way to reduce operating costs and increase profits. CostDriver promises to share findings with the restaurant every two weeks and to provide the restaurant with a final analytical report at the end of the contract. This service is customized to Coco, and CostDriver would need to start from scratch if it provided a similar service to another client. Coco promises to pay $5,000 per month. If Coco chooses to terminate the contract, it is entitled to receive a report detailing analyses to that stage.

Scenario 4: Assume Trump International Tower (Phase II) is developing luxury residential real estate and begins to market individual apartments during their construction. The Tower entered into a contract with Edwards for the sale of a specific apartment. Edwards pays a deposit that is refundable only if the Tower fails to deliver the completed apartment in accordance with the contract. The remainder of the purchase price is paid on completion of the contract when Edwards obtains possession of the apartment.

Required:

For each of the scenarios, determine whether the seller should recognize revenue (a) over time or (b) when the product or service is completed. Explain your answer.

Judgment Case 5–6
Performance obligation; licensing
● LO5–5, LO5–7

Assume that Pfizer, a large research-based pharmaceutical company, enters into a contract with a start-up biotechnology company called HealthPro and promises to:

1. Grant HealthPro the exclusive rights to use Pfizer's Technology A for the life of its patent. The license gives HealthPro the exclusive right to market, distribute, and manufacture Drug B as developed using Technology A. Pfizer views the patent as functional intellectual property.
2. Assign four full-time equivalent employees to perform research and development services for HealthPro in a specially designated Pfizer lab facility. The primary objective of these services is to receive regulatory approval to market and distribute Drug B using Technology A.

HealthPro is required to use Pfizer's lab to perform the research and development services necessary to develop Drug B using Technology A, because the expertise related to Technology A is proprietary to Pfizer and not available elsewhere.

Required:

What parts of this contract are separate performance obligations? Explain your reasoning for each obligation.

Communication Case 5–7
Performance obligations; loyalty program
● LO5–5

Jerry's Ice Cream Parlor is considering a marketing plan to increase sales of ice cream cones. The plan will give customers a free ice cream cone if they buy 10 ice cream cones at regular prices. Customers will be issued a card that will be punched each time an ice cream cone is purchased. After 10 punches, the card can be turned in for a free cone.

Jerry Donovan, the company's owner, is not sure how the new plan will affect accounting procedures. He realizes that the company will be incurring costs each time a free ice cream cone is awarded, but there will be no corresponding revenue or cash inflow.

The focus of this case is on how to account for revenue if the new plan is adopted. Your instructor will divide the class into two to six groups depending on the size of the class. The mission of your group is to reach consensus on the appropriate accounting treatment for the new plan. That treatment should describe when revenue is recognized and how it will be calculated.

Required:

1. Each group member should deliberate the situation independently and draft a tentative argument prior to the class session for which the case is assigned.
2. In class, each group will meet for 10–15 minutes in different areas of the classroom. During that meeting, group members will take turns sharing their suggestions for the purpose of arriving at a single group treatment.
3. After the allotted time, a spokesperson for each group (selected during the group meetings) will share the group's solution with the class. The goal of the class is to incorporate the views of each group into a consensus approach to the situation.

Judgment Case 5–8
Principal or agent
● LO5–6

AuctionCo.com sells used products collected from different suppliers. Assume a customer purchases a used bicycle through AuctionCo.com for $300. AuctionCo.com agrees to pay the supplier $200 for the bicycle. The bicycle will be shipped to the customer by the original bicycle owner.

Required:

1. Assume AuctionCo.com takes control of this used bicycle before the sale and pays $200 to the supplier. Under this assumption, how much revenue would AuctionCo.com recognize at the time of the sale to the customer?
2. Assume AuctionCo.com never takes control of this used bicycle before the sale. Instead, the bicycle is shipped directly to the customer by the original bicycle owner, and then AuctionCo.com pays $200 to the supplier. Under this assumption, how much revenue would AuctionCo.com recognize at the time of the sale to the customer?
3. Assume AuctionCo.com promises to pay $200 to the supplier regardless of whether the bicycle is sold, but the bicycle will continue to be shipped directly from the supplier to the customer. Under this assumption, how much revenue would AuctionCo.com recognize at the time of the sale to the customer?

Real World Case 5–9
Principal agent considerations
● LO5–6

EDGAR, the Electronic Data Gathering, Analysis, and Retrieval system, performs automated collection, validation, indexing, and forwarding of submissions by companies and others who are required by law to file forms with the U.S. Securities and Exchange Commission (SEC). All publicly traded domestic companies use EDGAR to make the majority of their filings. (Some foreign companies file voluntarily.) Form 10-K, which includes the annual report, is required to be filed on EDGAR. The SEC makes this information available on the Internet.

Required:

1. Access EDGAR on the Internet. The web address is www.sec.gov.

2. Search for the most recent 10-K's of Expedia, Inc., and Priceline Group Inc. Search or scroll to find the revenue recognition note in the financial statements.
3. For each of the following types of revenue, indicate whether the amount shown in the income statement is "net" or "gross" (the terms used with respect to revenue recognition in the chapter), and briefly explain your answer.
   a. Expedia's "merchant hotel model" revenues
   b. Priceline's "'Name Your Own Price'® services"
   c. Priceline's "merchant retail services"
   d. Priceline's agency revenues
4. Consider your responses to 3a through 3d. Does it look like there is the potential for noncomparability when readers consider Expedia and Priceline? Indicate "yes" or "no," and briefly explain your answer.

Research Case 5–10
FASB codification; locate and extract relevant information and authoritative support for a financial reporting issue; reporting revenue as a principal or as an agent
● LO5–6

The birth of the Internet in the 1990s led to the creation of a new industry of online retailers such as Amazon, Overstock.com, and PCM, Inc., Many of these companies often act as intermediaries between the manufacturer and the customer without ever taking possession of the merchandise sold. Revenue recognition for this type of transaction has been controversial.

Assume that Overstock.com sold you a product for $200 that cost $150. The company's profit on the transaction clearly is $50. Should Overstock recognize $200 in revenue and $150 in cost of goods sold (the gross method), or should it recognize only the $50 in gross profit (the net method) as commission revenue?

Required:
1. Access the *FASB Accounting Standards Codification* at the FASB website (www.fasb.org). Determine the specific Codification citation that indicates what an entity assesses to determine whether the nature of its promise is to act as a principal or agent.
2. What indicators does the Codification list that suggest an entity is a principal? Determine the specific Codification citation.
3. Using EDGAR (www.sec.gov), access Google, Inc.'s 2013 10-K. Locate the disclosure note that discusses the company's revenue recognition policy.
4. Does Google discuss determining whether they should report revenue on a gross versus net basis with respect to any of their products or services? What is the reason Google provides for its choices? Do you agree with Google's reasoning?

Real World Case 5–11
Chainsaw Al; revenue recognition and earnings management
● LO5–7

In May 2001, the Securities and Exchange Commission sued the former top executives at Sunbeam, charging the group with financial reporting fraud that allegedly cost investors billions in losses. Sunbeam Corporation is a recognized designer, manufacturer, and marketer of household and leisure products, including Coleman, Eastpak, First Alert, Grillmaster, Mixmaster, Mr. Coffee, Oster, Powermate, and Campingaz. In the mid-1990s, Sunbeam needed help: its profits had declined by over 80% percent, and in 1996, its stock price was down over 50% from its high. To the rescue: Albert Dunlap, also known as "Chainsaw Al" based on his reputation as a ruthless executive known for his ability to restructure and turn around troubled companies, largely by eliminating jobs.

The strategy appeared to work. In 1997, Sunbeam's revenues had risen by 18 percent. However, in April 1998, the brokerage firm of Paine Webber downgraded Sunbeam's stock recommendation. Why the downgrade? Paine Webber had noticed unusually high accounts receivable, massive increases in sales of electric blankets in the third quarter 1997, which usually sell best in the fourth quarter, as well as unusually high sales of barbeque grills for the fourth quarter. Soon after, Sunbeam announced a first quarter loss of $44.6 million, and Sunbeam's stock price fell 25 percent.

It eventually came to light that Dunlap and Sunbeam had been using a "bill-and-hold" strategy with retail buyers. This involved selling products at large discounts to retailers before they normally would buy and then holding the products in third-party warehouses, with delivery at a later date.

Many felt Sunbeam had deceived shareholders by artificially inflating earnings and the company's stock price. A class-action lawsuit followed, alleging that Sunbeam and Dunlap violated federal securities laws, suggesting the motivation to inflate the earnings and stock price was to allow Sunbeam to complete hundreds of millions of dollars of debt financing in order to complete some ongoing mergers. Shareholders alleged damages when Sunbeam's subsequent earnings decline caused a huge drop in the stock price.

Required:
1. How might Sunbeam's 1997 "bill-and-hold" strategy have contributed to artificially high earnings in 1997?
2. How would the strategy have led to the unusually high accounts receivable Paine Webber noticed?
3. How might Sunbeam's 1997 "bill-and-hold" strategy have contributed to a 1998 earnings decline?
4. How does earnings management of this type affect earnings quality?

Judgment Case 5–12
Revenue recognition; long-term construction contracts
● LO5–9

Two accounting students were discussing the timing of revenue recognition for long-term construction contracts. The discussion focused on which method was most like the typical revenue recognition method of recognizing revenue at the point of product delivery. Bill argued that recognizing revenue upon project completion was preferable because it was analogous to recognizing revenue at the point of delivery. John disagreed and supported recognizing revenue over time, stating that it was analogous to accruing revenue as a performance obligation was satisfied. John also pointed out that an advantage of recognizing revenue over time is that it provides information sooner to users.

Required:

Discuss the arguments made by both students. Which argument do you support? Why?

Communication Case 5–13
Long-term contract; revenue recognition over time vs. upon project completion
● LO5–9

Willingham Construction is in the business of building high-priced, custom, single-family homes. The company, headquartered in Anaheim, California, operates throughout the Southern California area. The construction period for the average home built by Willingham is six months, although some homes have taken as long as nine months.

You have just been hired by Willingham as the assistant controller and one of your first tasks is to evaluate the company's revenue recognition policy. The company presently recognizes revenue upon completion for all of its projects and management is now considering whether revenue recognition over time is appropriate.

Required:

Write a 1- to 2-page memo to Virginia Reynolds, company controller, describing the differences between the effects of recognizing revenue over time and upon project completion on the income statement and balance sheet. Indicate any criteria specifying when revenue should be recognized. Be sure to include references to GAAP as they pertain to the choice of method. Do not address the differential effects on income taxes nor the effect on the financial statements of switching between methods.

Continuing Cases

Target Case
● LO5-2, LO5-6, LO5-7

Target Corporation prepares its financial statements according to U.S. GAAP. Target's financial statements and disclosure notes for the year ended January 30, 2016, are available in Connect. This material also is available under the Investor Relations link at the company's website (www.target.com).

Required:

1. On what line of Target's income statement is revenue reported? What was the amount of revenue Target reported for the fiscal year ended January 30, 2016?
2. Disclosure Note 2 indicates that Target generally records revenue in retail stores at the point of sale. Does that suggest that Target generally records revenue at a point in time or over a period of time? Explain.
3. Disclosure Note 2 indicates that customers ("guests") can return some merchandise within 90 days of purchase and can return other merchandise within a year of purchase. How is Target's revenue and net income affected by returns, given that it does not know at the time a sale is made which items will be returned?
4. Disclosure Note 2 indicates that "Commissions earned on sales generated by leased departments are included within sales and were $37 million . . . in 2015." Do you think it likely that Target is accounting for those sales as a principal or an agent? Explain.
5. Disclosure Note 2 discusses Target's accounting for gift card sales. Does Target recognize revenue when it sells a gift card to a customer? If not, when does it recognize revenue? Explain.
6. Disclosure Note 4 discussed how Target accounts for consideration received from vendors, which they call "vendor income". Does that consideration produce revenue for Target? Does that consideration produce revenue for Target's vendors? Explain.

Air France–KLM Case
● LO5-2, LO5-4, LO5-5
IFRS

Air France–KLM (AF), a Franco-Dutch company, prepares its financial statements according to International Financial Reporting Standards. AF's financial statements and disclosure notes for the year ended December 31, 2015, are available in Connect. This material is also available under the Finance link at the company's website (www.airfranceklm.com).

Required:

1. In note 4.6, AF indicates that "Sales related to air transportation are recognized when the transportation service is provided," so passenger and freight tickets "are consequently recorded as "Deferred revenue upon issuance date"."
   a. Examine AF's balance sheet. What is the total amount of deferred revenue on ticket sales as of December 31, 2015?
   b. When transportation services are provided with respect to the deferred revenue on ticket sales, what journal entry would AF make to reduce deferred revenue?

c. Does AF's treatment of deferred revenue under IFRS appear consistent with how these transactions would be handled under U.S. GAAP? Explain.

2. AF has a frequent flyer program, "Flying Blue," which allows members to acquire "miles" as they fly on AF or partner airlines that are redeemable for free flights or other benefits.
   a. How does AF account for these miles?
   b. Does AF report any liability associated with these miles as of December 31, 2015?
   c. Although AF's 2015 annual report was issued prior to the effective date of *ASU No. 2014-09*, consider whether the manner in which AF accounts for its frequent flier program appears consistent with the revenue recognition guidelines included in the ASU.

CPA Exam Questions and Simulations

Sample CPA Exam questions from Roger CPA Review are available in Connect as support for the topics in this chapter. These Multiple Choice Questions and Task-Based Simulations include expert-written explanations and solutions, and provide a starting point for students to become familiar with the content and functionality of the actual CPA Exam.

REVENUE RECOGNITION

GAAP in Effect Prior to *ASU No. 2014-09*

A Chapter Supplement

PREFACE

Chapter 5 is based on the revenue recognition approach established in *ASU No. 2014-09*, which must be adopted by companies issuing reports under U.S. GAAP for periods beginning after December 15, 2017, and for companies issuing reports under IFRS for periods beginning January 1, 2018. Companies may adopt the ASU one year earlier than required. This appendix discusses GAAP that is eliminated by the ASU but that is traditionally covered in intermediate accounting courses. GAAP covered in this appendix will be relevant until the ASU becomes effective, and students taking the CPA or CMA exams will be responsible for this GAAP until six months after the effective date of the ASU.

Summary of GAAP Changes

Over 200 specific items of revenue recognition guidance were replaced by *ASU No. 2014-09* (hereafter "the ASU"). Illustration 5–S1 summarizes some important changes in GAAP that occurred.

The rest of this supplement discusses some of these changes in more detail, focusing on aspects of GAAP that usually are featured in intermediate accounting courses but that are eliminated by the ASU. We start by discussing the realization principle, which guided revenue recognition prior to the ASU. Then we discuss the installment sales and cost recovery

Additional Consideration

Transitioning to *ASU No. 2014-09*. Given the importance of revenue recognition and the changes in information systems and reporting practices necessary to implement the new ASU, the FASB gave companies over two years before requiring that it be adopted. The FASB also allowed companies to choose between two alternatives to transition to the ASU.

- Full Retroactive Restatement: This approach restates prior years to appear as if the ASU had been used all along, similar to the approach used for other accounting changes. For example, prior-year revenue, net income, and retained earnings are adjusted to reflect the ASU.
- Partial Retroactive Restatement: This approach applies the ASU only to new contracts and to contracts that have not been completed as of the date the ASU is initially adopted by the company. Under this approach, the company only adjusts the opening balance of retained earnings in the year the ASU is adopted to account for the cumulative effect of the ASU on net income recognized in prior years with respect to uncompleted contracts.

Allowing two approaches for adopting the ASU reduces comparability between companies.

Illustration 5–S1 Some Important Changes in Revenue Recognition GAAP Resulting from *ASU No. 2014-09*

	Previous GAAP	**New GAAP Under *ASU No. 2014-09***
Key concept underlying revenue recognition	The realization principle: Recognize revenue when both the earnings process is complete and there is reasonable certainty as to collectibility of the asset(s) to be received.	The core revenue recognition principle: Recognize revenue when goods or services are transferred to customers for the amount the company expects to be entitled to receive in exchange for those goods and services.
Role of collectibility in determining whether revenue is recognized.	Defer revenue recognition if cash collection is not reasonably certain. Use installment method or cost-recovery method to tie revenue recognition to subsequent cash collection.	Defer revenue recognition until cash collection is probable. Installment and cost-recovery methods eliminated.
Criteria for recognizing revenue over time	Depends on the earnings process. For long-term contracts, recognizing revenue over time is generally required unless reliable estimates can't be made.	Depends on characteristics of the contract and of the performance obligations being satisfied.
Accounting for multiple performance obligations	Depends on the industry. Sometimes performance obligations are ignored (e.g., "free" smartphones in cell phone contracts); sometimes revenue recognition is constrained (e.g., software for which there is not sufficient evidence of stand-alone prices).	Regardless of industry, apply criteria for determining whether goods and services are distinct to identify performance obligations, allocate transaction price to performance obligations, and recognize revenue when each performance obligation is satisfied.
Treatment of customer options for additional goods or services	Depends on the industry. Sometimes treated as a separate deliverable (e.g., software upgrades), other times ignored (e.g., frequent flyer miles).	Regardless of industry, treat an option as a separate performance obligation if it provides a material right to the customer that the customer would not otherwise have.
Treatment of variable consideration	Typically only recognize revenue associated with variable consideration when uncertainty has been resolved.	Include estimated variable consideration in the transaction price, but only to the extent it is probable that a significant revenue reversal will not occur in the future.
Treatment of time value of money	Interest revenue recognized for long-term receivables but interest expense typically not recognized for long-term customer prepayments.	Interest revenue or expense recognized for both long-term receivables and long-term customer prepayments if amount is significant.

methods, which were used when collectibility of receivables was very uncertain. We conclude with coverage of revenue recognition practices particular to software contracts, other multiple-deliverable arrangements, and franchises.

The Realization Principle

Revenue recognition used to be based on the **realization principle**. As shown in Illustration 5–S2, the realization principle required that two criteria be satisfied before revenue can be recognized (recorded).

Illustration 5–S2
The Realization Principle

The Realization Principle*

Revenue should only be recognized when *both:*

1. The earnings process is judged to be complete or virtually complete (the earnings process refers to the activity or activities performed by the company to generate revenue).
2. There is reasonable certainty as to the collectibility of the asset to be received (usually cash).

*These criteria are addressed in *SFAC 5*, "Recognition and Measurement in Financial Statements," *Statement of Financial Accounting Concepts No. 5* (Stamford, Conn.: FASB, 1984).

The *realization principle* bases revenue recognition on completion of the earnings process and reasonable certainty about collectibility.

The realization principle may sound similar to the approach discussed in Chapter 5, which bases revenue recognition on satisfaction of performance obligations and which requires that it be probable that receivables will be collected. However, it differs in important ways.

First, the idea of completion of the earnings process was interpreted and applied differently in various industries and for various types of products and services. As a consequence, revenue recognition standards and other guidance became very complicated, and sometimes transactions that were relatively similar were treated very differently. The ASU eliminates much of that industry-specific guidance, including special treatment of software sales and franchise arrangements. We cover that guidance in a later section of this appendix.

Second, the realization principle's requirement that there be reasonable certainty as to collectibility meant that revenue recognition sometimes was delayed until cash had been collected. As discussed in the next section of this appendix, the installment sales method and the cost recovery method were used to tie revenue recognition to cash collection. Those methods aren't allowed by the ASU.[24] Instead, the ASU only requires that collectibility be probable, and ties subsequent revenue recognition to satisfying performance obligations rather than cash collection.

International Financial Reporting Standards

Revenue Recognition Concepts. The IFRS version of *ASU No. 2014-09*, called *IFRS No. 15*, replaces preexisting IFRS. Prior to *IFRS No. 15*, *IAS No. 18* governed most revenue recognition under IFRS. It allowed revenue to be recognized when the following conditions had been satisfied:

- the amount of revenue and costs associated with the transaction can be measured reliably,
- it is probable that the economic benefits associated with the transaction will flow to the seller,
- (for sales of goods) the seller has transferred to the buyer the risks and rewards of ownership, and doesn't effectively manage or control the goods, and
- (for sales of services) the stage of completion can be measured reliably.

These general conditions typically led to revenue recognition at the same time and in the same amount as would occur under U.S. GAAP, but there were exceptions. Also, IFRS had much less industry-specific guidance than did U.S. GAAP, leading to fewer exceptions to applying these revenue recognition conditions.

Installment Sales

The *installment sales* and *cost recovery* methods are only used when extreme uncertainty exists regarding future cash collections.

Customers sometimes are allowed to pay for purchases in installments over a long period of time. Many large retail stores, such as Sears and J.C. Penney, sell products on such installment plans. In most situations, the increased uncertainty concerning the collection of cash from installment sales can be accommodated satisfactorily by estimating uncollectible amounts. However, if it is not possible to make a reasonable assessment of future bad debts, the seller lacks reasonable certainty as to collectibility, and the realization principle requires that revenue recognition be delayed.

These circumstances occur relatively rarely in practice, because sellers typically don't want to enter into transactions when they can't estimate how much cash they will be paid. However, exceptions do occur. For example, real estate sales often are made on an installment basis with relatively small down payments and long payment periods, perhaps 25 years or more. These payment characteristics, combined with the general speculative nature of many of these transactions, may translate into extreme uncertainty concerning the collectibility of the installment receivable.[25]

[24]The tax law still requires the use of the installment sales method for certain types of properties unless a taxpayer elects not to use the method.

[25]In fact, the installment sales method was required for retail land sales that met certain conditions. FASB ASC 360—20: Property, Plant, and Equipment–Real Estate Sales (previously "Accounting for Sales of Real Estate," *Statement of Financial Accounting Standards No. 66* (Stamford, Conn.: FASB, 1982)).

When extreme uncertainty exists regarding the ultimate collectibility of cash, GAAP previously required the use of one of two accounting techniques, the installment sales method or the cost recovery method. We discuss each in turn.

Installment Sales Method. The installment sales method recognizes revenue and costs only when cash payments are received. Each payment is assumed to be composed of two components: (1) a partial recovery of the cost of the item sold and (2) a gross profit component. These components are determined by the gross profit percentage applicable to the sale. For example, if the gross profit percentage (gross profit ÷ sales price) is 40%, then 40% of each dollar collected represents gross profit and the remaining 60% represents cost recovery. Consider the example in Illustration 5–S3.

Illustration 5–S3

Installment Sales Method

On November 1, 2018, the Belmont Corporation, a real estate developer, sold a tract of land for $800,000. The sales agreement requires the customer to make four equal annual payments of $200,000 plus interest on each November 1, beginning November 1, 2018. The land cost $560,000 to develop. The company's fiscal year ends on December 31.

The gross profit of $240,000 ($800,000 − 560,000) represents 30% of the sales price ($240,000 ÷ $800,000). The collection of cash and the recognition of gross profit under the installment method are summarized below. In this example, we ignore the collection of interest charges and the recognition of interest revenue to concentrate on the collection of the $800,000 sales price and the recognition of gross profit on the sale.

		Amount Allocated to	
Date	**Cash Collected**	**Cost (70%)**	**Gross Profit (30%)**
Nov. 1, 2018	$200,000	$140,000	$ 60,000
Nov. 1, 2019	200,000	140,000	60,000
Nov. 1, 2020	200,000	140,000	60,000
Nov. 1, 2021	200,000	140,000	60,000
Totals	$800,000	$560,000	$240,000

The *installment sales method* recognizes the gross profit by applying the gross profit percentage on the sale to the amount of cash actually received.

The gross profit recognized in a period will be equal to the gross profit percentage multiplied by the period's cash collection. The following journal entries are recorded (interest charges ignored):

Make Installment Sale: November 1, 2018

Installment receivables	800,000	
Inventory		560,000
Deferred gross profit		240,000
To record installment sale.		

The first entry records the installment receivable and the reduction of inventory. The difference between the $800,000 selling price and the $560,000 cost of sales represents the gross profit on the sale of $240,000. As gross profit will be recognized in net income only as collections are received, it is recorded initially in an account called deferred gross profit.

This is a contra account to the installment receivable. The deferred gross profit account will be reduced as collections are received until all profit has been recognized.[26]

[26]Accountants sometimes initially record installment sales in separate entries:

Installment receivables	800,000	
Installment sales		800,000
To record installment sales.		
Cost of installment sales	560,000	
Inventory		560,000
To record the cost of installment sales.		

Then at the end of the period, the following adjusting/closing entry is needed:

Installment sales	800,000	
Cost of installment sales		560,000
Deferred gross profit on installment sales		240,000

The text entries concentrate on the effect of the transactions and avoid this unnecessary procedural complexity.

Collect Cash: November 1, 2018		
Cash	200,000	
Installment receivables		200,000
To record cash collection from installment sale.		
Deferred gross profit	60,000	
Realized gross profit		60,000
To recognize gross profit from installment sale.		

The second set of entries records the collection of the first installment and recognizes the gross profit component of the payment, $60,000. Realized gross profit gets closed to income summary as part of the normal year-end closing process and is included in net income in the income statement. Journal entries to record the remaining three payments on November 1, 2019, 2020, and 2021, are identical.

At the end of 2018, the balance sheet would report the following:

Installment receivables ($800,000 − 200,000)	$600,000
Less: Deferred gross profit ($240,000 − 60,000)	(180,000)
Installment receivables (net)	$420,000

The net amount of the receivable reflects the portion of the remaining payments to be received that represents cost recovery (70% × $600,000). The installment receivables are classified as current assets if they will be collected within one year (or within the company's operating cycle, if longer); otherwise, they are classified as noncurrent assets.

The income statement for 2018 would report gross profit from installment sales of $60,000. Sales and cost of goods sold associated with installment sales usually are not reported in the income statement under the installment method, just the resulting gross profit. However, if those amounts aren't included in the income statement in the period in which the installment sale is made, they need to be included in the notes to the financial statements, along with the amount of gross profit that has not yet been recognized.

Additional Consideration

A company uses the installment method because it can't reliably estimate bad debts. Therefore, the company doesn't explicitly recognize bad debts or create an allowance for uncollectible accounts in the installment method. Rather, bad debts are dealt with implicitly by deferring gross profit until cash is collected. If the cash never is collected, the related deferred gross profit never gets included in net income. To illustrate, assume that in the example described in Illustration 5–A3, the Belmont Corporation collected the first payment but the customer was unable to make the remaining payments. Typically, the seller would repossess the item sold and make the following journal entry:

Repossessed inventory	420,000	
Deferred gross profit	180,000	
Installment receivable		600,000

This entry removes the receivable and the remaining deferred gross profit and records the repossessed land in an inventory account. This example assumes that the repossessed land's current fair value is equal to the net receivable of $420,000. If the land's fair value at the date of repossession is less than $420,000, a loss on repossession is recorded (debited).

The *cost recovery method* defers all gross profit recognition until cash equal to the cost of the item sold has been received.

Cost Recovery Method. In situations where there is an extremely high degree of uncertainty regarding the ultimate cash collection on an installment sale, an even more conservative approach, the **cost recovery method**, can be used. This method defers all gross profit recognition until the cost of the item sold has been recovered. The gross profit recognition pattern applying the cost recovery method to the Belmont Corporation situation used in Illustration 5–A3 is shown below.

Date	Cash Collected	Cost Recovery	Gross Profit Recognized
Nov. 1, 2018	$200,000	$200,000	$ –0–
Nov. 1, 2019	200,000	200,000	–0–
Nov. 1, 2020	200,000	160,000	40,000
Nov. 1, 2021	200,000	–0–	200,000
Totals	$800,000	$560,000	$240,000

The journal entries using this method are similar to those for the installment sales method except that $40,000 in gross profit is recognized in 2020 and $200,000 in 2021.

Make Installment Sale: November 1, 2018		
Installment receivables	800,000	
Inventory		560,000
Deferred gross profit		240,000
To record installment sale.		
Collect Cash: November 1, 2018, 2019, 2020, and 2021		
Cash	200,000	
Installment receivables		200,000
To record cash collection from installment sale.		
November 1, 2018 and 2019		
No entry for gross profit.		
November 1, 2020		
Deferred gross profit	40,000	
Realized gross profit		40,000
To recognize gross profit from installment sale.		
November 1, 2021		
Deferred gross profit	200,000	
Realized gross profit		200,000
To recognize gross profit from installment sale.		

A couple of points are apparent from these journal entries. First, the cost recovery method's initial journal entry is identical to what appears under the installment sales method. Second, when payments are received, gross profit only is recognized under the cost recovery method after all costs have been recovered.

Concept Review Exercise

INSTALLMENT SALES

Boatwright Implements, Inc., manufactures and sells farm machinery. For most of its sales, revenue and cost of sales are recognized at the delivery date. In 2018 Boatwright sold a cotton baler to a new customer for $100,000. The cost of the baler was $60,000. Payment will be made in five annual installments of $20,000 each, with the first payment due in 2018. Boatwright usually does not allow its customers to pay in installments. Due to the unusual nature of the payment terms and the uncertainty of collection of the installment payments, Boatwright is considering alternative methods of recognizing profit on this sale.

Required:

Ignoring interest charges, prepare a table showing the gross profit to be recognized from 2018 through 2022 on the cotton baler sale using the following three methods:

1. Revenue recognition upon delivery

2. The installment sales method
3. The cost recovery method

Solution:

	At Delivery	Installment Sales Method (40% × cash collection)	Cost Recovery Method
2018	$40,000	$ 8,000	$ 0
2019	0	8,000	0
2020	0	8,000	0
2021	0	8,000	20,000
2022	0	8,000	20,000
Totals	$40,000	$40,000	$40,000

Industry-Specific Revenue Issues

SOFTWARE AND OTHER MULTIPLE-ELEMENT ARRANGEMENTS

The software industry is a key economic component of our economy. Microsoft alone reported revenues of over $93 billion for its 2015 fiscal year. Yet, the recognition of software revenues has been a controversial accounting issue because of the way software vendors typically package their products. It is not unusual for these companies to sell multiple software elements in a bundle for a lump-sum contract price. The bundle often includes product, upgrades, post-contract customer support, and other services. The critical accounting question concerns the timing of revenue recognition.

Revenue for bundled software contracts was allocated based on vendor-specific objective evidence (VSOE).

Prior to *ASU No. 2014-09*, GAAP required that the revenue associated with a software contract that included multiple elements be allocated to the elements based on "vendor-specific objective evidence" ("VSOE") of fair values of the individual elements. The VSOE of fair values are the sales prices of the elements when sold separately by that vendor. If VSOE didn't exist, revenue recognition was deferred until VSOE became available or until all elements of the contract had been delivered.[27]

For example, suppose that a vendor sold software to a customer for $90,000. As part of the contract, the vendor promises to provide "free" technical support over the next six months. However, the vendor sells the same software without technical support for $80,000, and the vendor sells a stand-alone six-month technical support contract for $20,000, so those products would sell for $100,000 if sold separately. Based on that VSOE, the software comprises 80% of the total fair values, and the technical support 20%. Therefore, the seller would recognize $72,000 ($90,000 × 80%) in revenue up front when the software is delivered, and defer the remaining $18,000 ($90,000 × 20%) and recognize it ratably over the next six months as the technical support service is provided. If VSOE was not available, the vendor couldn't recognize any revenue initially, and instead would recognize the entire $90,000 ratably over the six-month period.

These revenue deferrals can be material. For example, in its 2013 balance sheet, Microsoft reported a liability for unearned (deferred) software revenue of over $22 billion.

Revenue for multiple-deliverable contracts is allocated based on actual or estimated stand-alone selling prices.

In 2009, the FASB's Emerging Issues Task Force (EITF) issued guidance to broaden the application of this basic perspective to other arrangements that involve "multiple deliverables."[28] Examples of such arrangements are sales of appliances with maintenance contracts and even painting services that include sales of paint as well as labor. Other examples are products that contain both hardware and software essential to the functioning of the product, such as computers and smartphones that are always sold with an operating system. The new guidance required that sellers allocate total revenue to the various parts of a multiple-deliverable arrangement on the basis of the relative stand-alone selling prices of the parts, similar to how

[27]FASB ASC 985–605–25: Software–Revenue Recognition–Recognition (previously "Software Revenue Recognition," *Statement of Position 97–2* (New York: AICPA, 1997), p. 14).

[28]FASB ASC 605–25-25: Revenue Recognition–Multiple-Element Arrangements-Recognition (Originally *EITF 08–1: Revenue Arrangements with Multiple Deliverables* (Stamford, Conn.: FASB, 2009)), and *EITF 09–3: Applicability of AICPA Statement of Position 97–2 to Certain Arrangements that Include Software Elements* (Stamford, Conn.: FASB, 2009)).

software contracts were handled. Sellers had to defer revenue recognition for parts that don't have stand-alone value, or whose value was contingent upon other undelivered parts. However, unlike software-only arrangements, sellers offering other multiple-deliverable contracts were allowed to estimate selling prices when they lacked VSOE from stand-alone sales prices. Using estimated selling prices allowed earlier revenue recognition than would be allowed if sellers had to have VSOE in order to recognize revenue.

For some sellers this change had a huge effect. As an example, consider Apple Inc. and the highly successful iPhone. Prior to the change, Apple deferred revenue on iPhones and other products because it didn't have VSOE of the sales price of future software upgrades included with the phones. This practice resulted in over $12 billion of unearned (deferred) revenue in its balance sheet at the end of the company's 2009 fiscal year. After this accounting change, Apple recognized almost all of the revenue associated with an iPhone at the time of sale. The only amount deferred was the small amount of revenue estimated for future software upgrade rights.

The ASU requires a similar process as was used to account for revenue on contracts that include multiple deliverables. Sellers allocate a contract's transaction price to the contract's performance obligations based on the stand-alone selling prices of those performance obligations. Important differences are that the ASU provides much more guidance concerning how to identify performance obligation and eliminates the need for VSOE for software contracts.

FRANCHISE SALES

The use of franchise arrangements is popular throughout the world. Many retail outlets for fast food, restaurants, motels, and auto rental agencies are operated as franchises. In franchise arrangements, the franchisor, such as McDonald's Corporation, grants to the franchisee, quite often an individual, the right to sell the franchisor's products and use its name for a specified period of time. The fees to be paid by the franchisee to the franchisor usually comprise (1) an *initial franchise fee* and (2) *continuing franchise fees.*

Initial franchise fees compensate the franchisor for the right to use its name and sell its products, as well as for such services as assistance in finding a location, constructing the facilities, and training employees. The initial franchise fee usually is a fixed amount, but it may be payable in installments.

In the early 1960s and 1970s, many franchisors recognized the entire initial franchise fee as revenue in the period in which the contract was signed. However, in many cases the fee included payment for significant services to be performed after that period and the fee was collectible in installments over an extended period of time, creating uncertainty as to cash collection. GAAP was modified to require that substantially all of the initial services of the franchisor required by the franchise agreement be performed before the initial franchise fee could be recognized as revenue. If the initial franchise fee was collectible in installments, and if a reasonable estimate of bad debts could not be made, the installment sales or cost recovery methods were required.

Unlike initial franchise fees, continuing franchise fees compensate the franchisor for ongoing rights and services provided over the life of the franchise agreement. These fees sometimes are a fixed annual or monthly amount, a percentage of the volume of business done by the franchise, or a combination of both. They usually do not present any accounting difficulty and previous GAAP required that they be recognized by the franchisor as revenue over time in the periods the services are performed by the franchisor, which generally corresponded to the periods they are received. Consider the example in Illustration 5–S4.

Illustration 5–S4
Franchise Sales

On March 31, 2018, the Red Hot Chicken Wing Corporation entered into a franchise agreement with Thomas Keller. In exchange for an initial franchise fee of $50,000, Red Hot will provide initial services to include the selection of a location, construction of the building, training of employees, and consulting services over several years. $10,000 is payable on March 31, 2018, with the remaining $40,000 payable in annual installments that include interest at an appropriate rate. In addition, the franchisee will pay continuing franchise fees of $1,000 per month for advertising and promotion provided by Red Hot, beginning immediately after the franchise begins operations. Thomas Keller opened his Red Hot franchise for business on September 30, 2018.

Initial Franchise Fee. Assuming that the initial services to be performed by Red Hot subsequent to the contract signing are substantial but that collectibility of the installment note receivable is reasonably certain, the following journal entry is recorded:

March 31, 2018		
Cash	10,000	
Note receivable	40,000	
Unearned franchise fee revenue		50,000
To record franchise agreement and down payment.		

Unearned franchise fee revenue (called "deferred franchise fee revenue" in the body of Chapter 5) is a liability. It would be reduced to zero and revenue would be recognized when the initial services have been performed. This could occur in increments or at one point in time, depending on the circumstances.[29] For example, in our illustration, if substantial performance was deemed to have occurred when the franchise began operations, the following entry would be recorded:

Sept. 30, 2018		
Unearned franchise fee revenue	50,000	
Franchise fee revenue		50,000
To recognize franchise fee revenue.		

If collectibility of the installment note receivable is uncertain and there is no basis for estimating uncollectible amounts, the September 30 entry would record a credit to deferred franchise fee revenue, which is then recognized as being earned using either the installment sales or cost recovery methods.

Continuing Franchise Fees. Continuing franchise fee revenue is recognized on a monthly basis as follows:

Cash (or accounts receivable)	1,000	
Service revenue		1,000
To recognize continuing franchise fee revenue.		

Expenses incurred by the franchisor in providing these continuing franchise services should be recognized in the same periods as the service revenue.

Accounting for franchise revenue under *ASU No. 2014-09* is similar to revenue recognition under previous GAAP. To the extent that the services underlying initial franchise fees constitute separate performance obligations, revenue associated with those fees is recognized when those services have been performed. Similarly, to the extent that continuing franchise fees constitute payments for services that are provided over time, revenue recognition over time is likely to be appropriate. However, the justification for the amount and timing of revenue recognition is based on the ASU, rather than on special guidance provided for franchise arrangements. Also, *ASU 2014-09* includes new guidance for recognizing licensing revenue.

Other unique industry-specific revenue recognition situations exist besides those we have discussed. The FASB and AICPA previously issued detailed revenue recognition guidance for such industries as insurance, record and music, cable television, and motion pictures. All of that guidance was replaced by *ASU No. 2014-09*.[30]

---

[29]Franchise agreements sometimes require that any payments made to the franchisor will be refunded if the franchise fails to open. If this condition is present, it would be an important factor in deciding whether to recognize revenue before the franchise opens.

[30]FASB ASC 944: Financial Services–Insurance (previously "Accounting and Reporting by Insurance Enterprises," *Statement of Financial Accounting Standards No. 60* (Stamford, Conn.: FASB, 1982)); FASB ASC 928–Entertainment–Music (previously "Financial Reporting in the Record and Music Industry," *Statement of Financial Accounting Standards No. 50* (Stamford, Conn.: FASB, 1981)); FASB ASC 922: Entertainment–Cable Television (previously "Financial Reporting by Cable Television Companies," *Statement of Financial Accounting Standards No. 51* (Stamford, Conn.: FASB, 1981)); FASB ASC 928: Entertainment–Films (previously "Accounting by Producers or Distributors of Films," *Statement of Position 00–2* (New York: AICPA, 2000)).

Additional Differences Between U.S. GAAP and IFRS

ASU No. 2014-09 is a converged standard, providing virtually identical guidance for U.S. GAAP and IFRS. However, prior to issuance of the ASU, there was incomplete convergence between U.S. GAAP and IFRS. In addition to differences in revenue recognition concepts discussed earlier in this appendix, key differences involved accounting for revenue on long-term contracts and multiple-deliverable arrangements. We provide an IFRS Box for each of these issues below.

International Financial Reporting Standards

Long-Term Construction Contracts. Prior to issuance of the ASU, *IAS No. 11* governed revenue recognition for long-term construction contracts.[31] Like U.S. GAAP, that standard required the use of the percentage-of-completion method when reliable estimates can be made. However, unlike U.S. GAAP, *IAS No. 11* required the use of the cost recovery method rather than the completed contract method when reliable estimates couldn't be made.[32] Under the cost recovery method, contract costs are expensed as incurred, and an offsetting amount of contract revenue is recognized to the extent that it is probable that costs will be recoverable from the customer. No gross profit is recognized until all costs have been recovered, which is why this method is also sometimes called the "zero-profit method." Note that under both the completed contract and cost recovery methods no gross profit is recognized until the contract is near completion, but revenue and construction costs will be recognized earlier under the cost recovery method than under the completed contract method. Also, under both methods an expected loss is recognized immediately.

To see this difference between the completed contract and cost recovery methods, here is a version of Illustration 5–24B that compares revenue, cost, and gross profit recognition under the two methods, as follows:

	2018		2019		2020	
Completed Contract						
Construction in progress (CIP)					900,000	
Cost of construction					4,100,000	
Revenue from long-term contracts						5,000,000
To record gross profit.						
Cost Recovery						
Construction in progress (CIP)					900,000	
Cost of construction	1,500,000		1,000,000		1,600,000	
Revenue from long-term contracts		1,500,000		1,000,000		2,500,000
To record gross profit.						

Revenue recognition occurs earlier under the cost recovery method than under the completed contract method, but gross profit recognition occurs near the end of the contract for both methods. As a result, gross profit as a percentage of revenue differs between the two methods at various points in the life of the contract.

[31] "Construction Contracts," *International Accounting Standard No. 11* (IASCF), as amended, effective January 1, 2011.

[32] Earlier in this appendix we referred to the "cost recovery method" in a different circumstance–when a company had already delivered a product to a customer but had to delay gross profit recognition until a point after delivery because of an inability to make reliable estimates of uncollectible accounts. In that case, gross profit only could be recognized after costs had been recovered (and cash collections exceeded cost of goods sold). IFRS use of "cost recovery method" is similar, in that gross profit recognition is delayed until after cost has been recovered, but note that in this case the product is being constructed for the customer and therefore has not yet been delivered.

International Financial Reporting Standards

Multiple-Deliverable Arrangements. IFRS contained very little guidance about multiple-deliverable arrangements. *IAS No. 18* simply states that: ". . . in certain circumstances, it is necessary to apply the recognition criteria to the separately identifiable components of a single transaction in order to reflect the substance of the transaction" and gives a couple of examples.[33] Allocations of total revenue to individual components were based on fair value, with no requirements to focus on VSOE. Also, IFRS tended to encourage focus on the underlying economics of revenue transactions, so particular contractual characteristics like contingencies mattered less under IFRS than they do under U.S. GAAP.

Questions For Review of Key Topics

Q 5–28 What are the two general criteria that must be satisfied before a company can recognize revenue?

Q 5–29 Explain why, in most cases, a seller recognizes revenue when it delivers its product rather than when it produces the product.

Q 5–30 Revenue recognition for most installment sales occurs at the point of delivery of the product or service. Under what circumstances would a seller delay revenue recognition for installment sales beyond the delivery date?

Q 5–31 Distinguish between the installment sales method and the cost recovery method of accounting for installment sales.

Q 5–32 How does a company report deferred gross profit resulting from the use of the installment sales method in its balance sheet?

IFRS **Q 5–33** When percentage-of-completion accounting is not appropriate, U.S. GAAP requires the use of the completed contract method, while IFRS requires the use of the cost recovery method. Explain how the two methods affect recognition of revenue, cost of construction, and gross profit over the life of a profitable contract.

Q 5–34 Briefly describe the guidelines for recognizing revenue from the sale of software and other multiple-deliverable arrangements.

IFRS **Q 5–35** Briefly describe how IFRS guidelines for recognizing revenue from multiple-deliverable arrangements differ from U.S. GAAP guidelines.

Q 5–36 Briefly describe the guidelines provided by GAAP for the recognition of revenue by a franchisor for an initial franchise fee.

Brief Exercises

BE 5–35
Installment sales method

On July 1, 2018, Apache Company sold a parcel of undeveloped land to a construction company for $3,000,000. The book value of the land on Apache's books was $1,200,000. Terms of the sale required a down payment of $150,000 and 19 annual payments of $150,000 plus interest at an appropriate interest rate due on each July 1 beginning in 2019. Apache has no significant obligations to perform services after the sale. How much gross profit will Apache recognize in both 2018 and 2019 applying the installment sales method?

BE 5–36
Installment sales method

Refer to the situation described in BE 5–35. What should be the balance in the deferred gross profit account at the end of 2019 applying the installment sales method?

BE 5–37
Cost recovery method

Refer to the situation described in BE 5–35. How much gross profit will Apache recognize in both 2018 and 2019 applying the cost recovery method?

BE 5–38
IFRS; long-term contracts; cost recovery method

A construction company entered into a fixed-price contract to build an office building for $20 million. Construction costs incurred during the first year were $6 million and estimated costs to complete at the end of the year were $9 million. The building was completed during the second year. Construction costs incurred during the

[33]"Revenue," *International Accounting Standards No. 18* (IASCF), as amended effective January 1, 2014, par. 13.

second year were $10 million. How much revenue, cost, and gross profit will the company recognize in the first and second year of the contract applying the cost recovery method that is required by IFRS?

BE 5–39
Revenue recognition; software contracts

Orange, Inc., sells a LearnIt-Plus software package that consists of their normal LearnIt math tutorial program along with a one-year subscription to the online LearnIt Office Hours virtual classroom. LearnIt-Plus retails for $200. When sold separately, the LearnIt math tutorial sells for $150, and access to the LearnIt Office Hours sells for $100 per year. When should Orange recognize revenue for the parts of this arrangement? Would your answer change if Orange did not sell the LearnIt Office Hours separately, but believed it would price it at $100 per year if they ever decided to do so?

BE 5–40
Revenue recognition; software contracts under IFRS
IFRS

Refer to the situation described in BE 5–39. How would your answer change if Orange reported under IFRS?

BE 5–41
Revenue recognition; franchise sales

Collins, Inc., entered into a 10-year franchise agreement with an individual. For an initial franchise fee of $40,000, Collins agrees to assist in design and construction of the franchise location and in all other necessary start-up activities. Also, in exchange for advertising and promotional services, the franchisee agrees to pay continuing franchise fees equal to 5% of revenue generated by the franchise. When should Collins recognize revenue for the initial and continuing franchise fees?

Exercises

E 5–23
Installment sales method

Charter Corporation, which began business in 2018, appropriately uses the installment sales method of accounting for its installment sales. The following data were obtained for sales made during 2018 and 2019:

	2018	2019
Installment sales	$360,000	$350,000
Cost of installment sales	234,000	245,000
Cash collections on installment sales during:		
2018	150,000	100,000
2019	—	120,000

Required:
1. How much gross profit should Charter recognize in 2018 and 2019 from installment sales?
2. What should be the balance in the deferred gross profit account at the end of 2018 and 2019?

E 5–24
Installment sales method; journal entries

[This is a variation of E 5–23 focusing on journal entries.]
Charter Corporation, which began business in 2018, appropriately uses the installment sales method of accounting for its installment sales. The following data were obtained for sales during 2018 and 2019:

	2018	2019
Installment sales	$360,000	$350,000
Cost of installment sales	234,000	245,000
Cash collections on installment sales during:		
2018	150,000	100,000
2019	—	120,000

Required:
Prepare summary journal entries for 2018 and 2019 to account for the installment sales and cash collections. The company uses the perpetual inventory system.

E 5–25
Installment sales; alternative recognition methods

On July 1, 2018, the Foster Company sold inventory to the Slate Corporation for $300,000. Terms of the sale called for a down payment of $75,000 and three annual installments of $75,000 due on each July 1, beginning July 1, 2019. Each installment also will include interest on the unpaid balance applying an appropriate interest rate. The inventory cost Foster $120,000. The company uses the perpetual inventory system.

Required:

1. Compute the amount of gross profit to be recognized from the installment sale in 2018, 2019, 2020, and 2021 if revenue was recognized upon delivery. Ignore interest charges.
2. Repeat requirement 1 applying the installment sales method.
3. Repeat requirement 1 applying the cost recovery method.

E 5–26
Journal entries; point of delivery, installment sales, and cost recovery methods

[This is a variation of E 5–25 focusing on journal entries.]
On July 1, 2018, the Foster Company sold inventory to the Slate Corporation for $300,000. Terms of the sale called for a down payment of $75,000 and three annual installments of $75,000 due on each July 1, beginning July 1, 2019. Each installment also will include interest on the unpaid balance applying an appropriate interest rate. The inventory cost Foster $120,000. The company uses the perpetual inventory system.

Required:

1. Prepare the necessary journal entries for 2018 and 2019 assuming revenue recognition upon delivery. Ignore interest charges.
2. Repeat requirement 1 applying the installment sales method.
3. Repeat requirement 1 applying the cost recovery method.

E 5–27
Installment sales and cost recovery methods; solve for unknowns

Wolf Computer Company began operations in 2018. The company allows customers to pay in installments for many of its products. Installment sales for 2018 were $1,000,000. If revenue is recognized at the point of delivery, $600,000 in gross profit would be recognized in 2018. If the company instead uses the cost recovery method, $100,000 in gross profit would be recognized in 2018.

Required:

1. What was the amount of cash collected on installment sales in 2018?
2. What amount of gross profit would be recognized if the company uses the installment sales method?

E 5–28
Installment sales; default and repossession

Sanchez Development Company uses the installment sales method to account for some of its installment sales. On October 1, 2018, Sanchez sold a parcel of land to the Kreuze Corporation for $4 million. This amount was not considered significant relative to Sanchez's other sales during 2018. The land had cost Sanchez $1.8 million to acquire and develop. Terms of the sale required a down payment of $800,000 and four annual payments of $800,000 plus interest at an appropriate interest rate, with payments due on each October 1 beginning in 2019. Kreuze paid the down payment, but on October 1, 2019, defaulted on the remainder of the contract. Sanchez repossessed the land. On the date of repossession the land had a fair value of $1.3 million.

Required:

Prepare the necessary entries for Sanchez to record the sale, receipt of the down payment, and the default and repossession applying the installment sales method. Ignore interest charges.

E 5–29
Real estate sales; gain recognition

On April 1, 2018, the Apex Corporation sold a parcel of underdeveloped land to the Applegate Construction Company for $2,400,000. The book value of the land on Apex's books was $480,000. Terms of the sale required a down payment of $120,000 and 19 annual payments of $120,000 plus interest at an appropriate interest rate due on each April 1 beginning in 2019. Apex has no significant obligations to perform services after the sale.

Required:

1. Prepare the necessary entries for Apex to record the sale, receipt of the down payment, and receipt of the first installment assuming that Apex is able to make a reliable estimate of possible uncollectible amounts (that is, profit is recognized upon delivery). Ignore interest charges.
2. Repeat requirement 1 assuming that Apex cannot make a reliable estimate of possible uncollectible amounts and decides to use the installment sales method for profit recognition.

E 5–30
FASB codification research

CODE

Access the *FASB Accounting Standards Codification* at the FASB website (www.fasb.org).

Required:

Determine the specific citation for accounting for each of the following items: Circumstances indicating when the installment method or cost recovery method is appropriate for revenue recognition.

E 5–31
Long-term contracts, Cost recovery method
IFRS

Assume the same information as in E 5–18.

Required:

Determine the amount of revenue, cost, and gross profit or loss to be recognized in each of the three years under IFRS, assuming that using the percentage-of-completion method is not appropriate.

E 5–32
Revenue recognition; software

Easywrite Software Company shipped software to a customer on July 1, 2018. The arrangement with the customer also requires the company to provide technical support over the next 12 months and to ship an expected software upgrade on January 1, 2019. The total contract price is $243,000, and Easywrite estimates that the individual fair values of the components of the arrangement if sold separately would be as follows:

Software	$210,000
Technical support	30,000
Upgrade	30,000

Required:

1. Determine the timing of revenue recognition for the $243,000.
2. Assume that the $243,000 contract price was paid on July 1, 2018. Prepare a journal entry to record the cash receipt. Disregard the cost of the items sold.

E 5–33 Multiple-deliverable arrangements

Richardson Systems sells integrated bottling manufacturing systems that involve a conveyer, a labeler, a filler, and a capper. All of this equipment is sold separately by other vendors, and the fair values of the separate equipment are as follows:

Conveyer	$20,000
Labeler	10,000
Filler	15,000
Capper	5,000
Total	$50,000

Richardson sells the integrated system for $45,000. Each of the components is shipped separately to the customer for the customer to install.

Required:

1. Assume that each of the components can be used independently, even though Richardson sells them as an integrated system. How much revenue should be allocated to each component?
2. Now assume that the labeler, filler, and capper can't be used in production without the conveyer, and that the conveyer is the last component installed. How much revenue should be recognized at the time the conveyer is installed?

E 5–34 Multiple-deliverable arrangements under IFRS

Assume the same facts as in E 5–33, but that Richardson Systems reports under IFRS. How would your answers change? (Assume for requirement 2 that separate shipment is part of the normal course of Richardson's operations, and successful customer installation is highly probable.)

E 5–35 Revenue recognition; franchise sales

On October 1, 2018, the Submarine Sandwich Company entered into a franchise agreement with an individual. In exchange for an initial franchise fee of $300,000, Submarine will provide initial services to the franchisee to include assistance in design and construction of the building, help in training employees, and help in obtaining financing. Ten percent of the initial franchise fee is payable on October 1, 2018, with the remaining $270,000 payable in nine equal annual installments beginning on October 1, 2019. These installments will include interest at an appropriate rate. The franchise opened for business on January 15, 2019.

Required:

Assume that the initial services to be performed by Submarine Sandwich subsequent to October 1, 2018, are substantial and that collectibility of the installment receivable is reasonably certain. Substantial performance of the initial services is deemed to have occurred when the franchise opened. Prepare the necessary journal entries for the following dates (ignoring interest charges):

1. October 1, 2018
2. January 15, 2019

Problems

P 5–14 Income statement presentation; installment sales method (Chapters 4 and 5)

Reagan Corporation computed income from continuing operations before income taxes of $4,200,000 for 2018. The following material items have not yet been considered in the computation of income:

1. The company sold equipment and recognized a gain of $50,000. The equipment had been used in the manufacturing process and was replaced by new equipment.
2. In December, the company received a settlement of $1,000,000 for a lawsuit it had filed based on antitrust violations of a competitor. The settlement was considered to be an unusual and infrequent event.

3. Inventory costing $400,000 was written off as obsolete. Material losses of this type were incurred twice in the last eight years.
4. It was discovered that depreciation expense on the office building of $50,000 per year was not recorded in either 2017 or 2018.

In addition, you learn that included in revenues is $400,000 from installment sales made during the year. The cost of these sales is $240,000. At year-end, $100,000 in cash had been collected on the related installment receivables. Because of considerable uncertainty regarding the collectibility of receivables from these sales, the company's accountant should have used the installment sales method to recognize revenue and gross profit on these sales.

Also, the company's income tax rate is 40% and there were 1 million shares of common stock outstanding throughout the year.

Required:

Prepare an income statement for 2018 beginning with income from continuing operations before income taxes. Include appropriate EPS disclosures.

P 5–15
Installment sales and cost recovery methods

Ajax Company appropriately accounts for certain sales using the installment sales method. The perpetual inventory system is used. Information related to installment sales for 2018 and 2019 is as follows:

	2018	2019
Sales	$300,000	$400,000
Cost of sales	180,000	280,000
Customer collections on:		
2018 sales	120,000	100,000
2019 sales	—	150,000

Required:

1. Calculate the amount of gross profit that would be recognized each year from installment sales.
2. Prepare all necessary journal entries for each year.
3. Repeat requirements 1 and 2 assuming that Ajax uses the cost recovery method to account for its installment sales.

P 5–16
Installment sales; alternative recognition methods

On August 31, 2018, the Silva Company sold merchandise to the Bendix Corporation for $500,000. Terms of the sale called for a down payment of $100,000 and four annual installments of $100,000 due on each August 31, beginning August 31, 2019. Each installment also will include interest on the unpaid balance applying an appropriate interest rate. The book value of the merchandise on Silva's books on the date of sale was $300,000. The perpetual inventory system is used. The company's fiscal year-end is December 31.

Required:

1. Prepare a table showing the amount of gross profit to be recognized in each of the five years of the installment sale applying each of the following methods:
   a. Point of delivery revenue recognition
   b. Installment sales method
   c. Cost recovery method
2. Prepare journal entries for each of the five years applying the three revenue recognition methods listed in requirement 1. Ignore interest charges.
3. Prepare a partial balance sheet as of the end of 2018 and 2019 listing the items related to the installment sale applying each of the three methods listed in requirement 1.

P 5–17
Installment sales and cost recovery methods

Mulcahey Builders (MB) remodels office buildings in low-income urban areas that are undergoing economic revitalization. MB typically accepts a 25% down payment when they complete a job and a note that requires that the remainder be paid in three equal installments over the next three years, plus interest. Because of the inherent uncertainty associated with receiving these payments, MB has historically used the cost recovery method to recognize revenue.

As of January 1, 2018, MB's outstanding gross installment accounts receivable (not net of deferred gross profit) consist of the following:

1. $400,000 due from the Bluebird Motel. MB completed the Bluebird job in 2016, and estimated gross profit on that job is 25%.
2. $150,000 due from the PitStop Gas and MiniMart. MB completed the PitStop job in 2015, and estimated gross profit on that job is 35%.

Dan Mulcahey has been considering switching from the cost recovery method to the installment sales method, because he wants to show the highest possible gross profit in 2018 and he understands that the installment sales method recognizes gross profit sooner than does the cost recovery method.

Required:

1. Calculate how much gross profit is expected to be earned on these jobs in 2018 under the cost recovery method, and how much would be earned if MB instead used the installment sales method. Ignore interest.
2. If Dan is primarily concerned about 2018, do you think he would be happy with a switch to the installment sales method? Explain.

P 5–18
Construction accounting under IFRS

[This is a variation of P 5–10 modified to focus on IFRS.]

Required:

Complete the requirements of P 5–10 assuming that Westgate Construction reports under IFRS and concludes that the percentage-of-completion method is not appropriate.

P 5–19
Franchise sales; installment sales method

Olive Branch Restaurant Corporation sells franchises throughout the western states. On January 30, 2018, the company entered into the following franchise agreement with Jim and Tammy Masters:

1. The initial franchise fee is $1.2 million. $200,000 is payable immediately and the remainder is due in ten, $100,000 installments plus 10% interest on the unpaid balance each January 30, beginning January 30, 2019. The 10% interest rate is an appropriate market rate.
2. In addition to allowing the franchisee to use the franchise name for the 10-year term of the agreement, in exchange for the initial fee Olive Branch agrees to assist the franchisee in selecting a location, obtaining financing, designing and constructing the restaurant building, and training employees.
3. All of the initial down payment of $200,000 is to be refunded by Olive Branch and the remaining obligation canceled if, for any reason, the franchisee fails to open the franchise.
4. In addition to the initial franchise fee, the franchisee is required to pay a monthly fee of 3% of franchise sales for advertising, promotion, menu planning, and other continuing services to be provided by Olive Branch over the life of the agreement. This fee is payable on the 10th of the following month.

Substantial performance of the initial services provided by Olive Branch, which are significant, is deemed to have occurred when the franchise opened on September 1, 2018. Franchise sales for the month of September 2018 were $40,000.

Required:

1. Assuming that collectibility of the installment receivable is reasonably certain, prepare the necessary journal entries for Olive Branch on the following dates (ignore interest charges on the installment receivable and the costs of providing franchise services):
   a. January 30, 2018
   b. September 1, 2018
   c. September 30, 2018
   d. January 30, 2019
2. Assume that significant uncertainty exists as to the collection of the installment receivable and that Olive Branch elects to recognize initial franchise fee revenue using the installment sales method. Prepare the necessary journal entries for the dates listed in requirement 1 (ignore interest charges on the installment receivable and the costs of providing franchise services).
3. Examine your answer to requirement 1a of this problem (the January 30, 2018, journal entry under the installment sales method). What is the effect of that journal entry on Olive Branch's balance sheet? (Ignore cash.) Briefly explain your answer.

Broaden Your Perspective

Apply your critical-thinking ability to the knowledge you've gained. These cases will provide you an opportunity to develop your research, analysis, judgment, and communication skills. You also will work with other students, integrate what you've learned, apply it in real-world situations, and consider its global and ethical ramifications. This practice will broaden your knowledge and further develop your decision-making abilities.

Judgment Case 5–14
Revenue recognition; installment sale

On October 1, 2018, the Marshall Company sold a large piece of machinery to the Hammond Construction Company for $80,000. The cost of the machine was $40,000. Hammond made a down payment of $10,000 and agreed to pay the remaining balance in seven equal monthly installments of $10,000, plus interest at 12% on the unpaid balance, beginning November 1.

Required:

1. Identify three alternative methods for recognizing revenue and costs for the situation described and compute the amount of gross profit that would be recognized in 2018 using each method.
2. Discuss the circumstances under which each of the three methods would be used.

IFRS Case 5–15
Comparison of revenue recognition in Sweden and the United States

Vodafone Group, Plc, headquartered in the United Kingdom, is one of the world's largest telecommunications companies. Excerpts from the revenue recognition disclosure included in its 2015 annual report are reproduced below.

Note A1: Significant accounting policies

Revenue

Revenue is recognised to the extent the Group has delivered goods or rendered services under an agreement, the amount of revenue can be measured reliably and it is probable that the economic benefits associated with the transaction will flow to the Group. Revenue is measured at the fair value of the consideration received, exclusive of sales taxes and discounts.

The Group principally obtains revenue from providing the following telecommunication services: access charges, airtime usage, messaging, interconnect fees, data services and information provision, connection fees and equipment sales. Products and services may be sold separately or in bundled packages.

Revenue for access charges, airtime usage and messaging by contract customers is recognised as services are performed, with unbilled revenue resulting from services already provided accrued at the end of each period and unearned revenue from services to be provided in future periods deferred. Revenue from the sale of prepaid credit is deferred until such time as the customer uses the airtime, or the credit expires.

Revenue from interconnect fees is recognised at the time the services are performed.

Revenue from data services and information provision is recognised when the Group has performed the related service and, depending on the nature of the service, is recognised either at the gross amount billed to the customer or the amount receivable by the Group as commission for facilitating the service.

Customer connection revenue is recognised together with the related equipment revenue to the extent that the aggregate equipment and connection revenue does not exceed the fair value of the equipment delivered to the customer. Any customer connection revenue not recognised together with related equipment revenue is deferred and recognised over the period in which services are expected to be provided to the customer.

Revenue for device sales is recognised when the device is delivered to the end customer and the significant risk and rewards of ownership have transferred. For device sales made to intermediaries, revenue is recognised if the significant risks associated with the device are transferred to the intermediary and the intermediary has no general right to return the device to receive a refund. If the significant risks are not transferred, revenue recognition is deferred until sale of the device to an end customer by the intermediary or the expiry of the right of return.

In revenue arrangements including more than one deliverable, the arrangements are divided into separate units of accounting. Deliverables are considered separate units of accounting if the following two conditions are met: (1) the deliverable has value to the customer on a stand-alone basis and (2) there is evidence of the fair value of the item. The arrangement consideration is allocated to each separate unit of accounting based on its relative fair value.

Required:

On the basis of the information the disclosures provide, compare revenue recognition under IFRS (as applied by Vodafone) with that in the United States.

IFRS Case 5–16
Comparison of revenue recognition for construction contracts

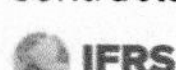

ThyssenKrupp AG, headquartered in Germany, is one of the world's largest technology companies, with almost 160,000 employees worldwide and primary segments in steel, technology, and capital goods and services.

Required:

1. Access ThyssenKrupp's most recent annual report using the Internet. Find the footnote describing significant accounting policies. Indicate the methods that ThyssenKrupp uses to account for long-term construction contracts when they can and cannot make an accurate estimate of the income on a construction contract.
2. If ThyssenKrupp was a U.S. company, how would you expect its accounting for these contracts to differ?

Trueblood Accounting Case 5–17
Revenue recognition for long-term contracts

The following Trueblood case is recommended for use with this chapter. The case provides an excellent opportunity for class discussion, group projects, and writing assignments. The case, along with Professor's Discussion Material, can be obtained from the Deloitte Foundation at its website www.deloitte.com/us/truebloodcases.

Case 12.5: *Aren't We Done Yet?*

This case concerns the appropriate timing of revenue recognition for a long-term construction contract, including percentage-of-completion, completed contract, and zero-profit methods used pre-*ASU No. 2014-09* under U.S. GAAP and IFRS.

Trueblood Accounting Case 5–18
Revenue recognition for multiple-deliverable contracts.

The following Trueblood case is recommended for use with this chapter. The case provides an excellent opportunity for class discussion, group projects, and writing assignments. The case, along with Professor's Discussion Material, can be obtained from the Deloitte Foundation at its website www.deloitte.com/us/truebloodcases.

Case 14-3: *Coconut Telegraph*

This case concerns accounting for revenue when multiple deliverables exist within an arrangement that includes software, as well as identifying the relevant standard used pre-*ASU No. 2014-09* under U.S. GAAP and IFRS.

Real World Case 5–19
Revenue recognition; franchise sales

EDGAR, the Electronic Data Gathering, Analysis, and Retrieval system, performs automated collection, validation, indexing, and forwarding of submissions by companies and others who are required by law to file forms with the U.S. Securities and Exchange Commission (SEC). All publicly traded domestic companies use EDGAR to make the majority of their filings. (Some foreign companies file voluntarily.) Form 10-K which includes the annual report, is required to be filed on EDGAR. The SEC makes this information available on the Internet.

Required:

1. Access EDGAR on the Internet. The web address is www.sec.gov.
2. Search for Jack in the Box, Inc. Access the most recent 10-K filing. Search or scroll to find the financial statements and related notes.
3. Answer the following questions related to the company's revenue recognition policies:
   a. When does the company recognize initial franchise license fee revenue?
   b. How are continuing fees determined?
4. Repeat requirements 2 and 3 for two additional companies that you suspect also earn revenues through the sale of franchise rights. Compare their revenue recognition policies with the policies of Jack in the Box.

CHAPTER

6 Time Value of Money Concepts

OVERVIEW

Time value of money concepts, specifically future value and present value, are essential in a variety of accounting situations. These concepts and the related computational procedures are the subjects of this chapter. Present values and future values of *single amounts* and present values and future values of *annuities* (series of equal periodic payments) are described separately but shown to be interrelated.

LEARNING OBJECTIVES

After studying this chapter, you should be able to:

- **LO6–1** Explain the difference between simple and compound interest. (*p. 314*)
- **LO6–2** Compute the future value of a single amount. (*p. 315*)
- **LO6–3** Compute the present value of a single amount. (*p. 316*)
- **LO6–4** Solve for either the interest rate or the number of compounding periods when present value and future value of a single amount are known. (*p. 317*)
- **LO6–5** Explain the difference between an ordinary annuity and an annuity due situation. (*p. 323*)
- **LO6–6** Compute the future value of both an ordinary annuity and an annuity due. (*p. 324*)
- **LO6–7** Compute the present value of an ordinary annuity, an annuity due, and a deferred annuity. (*p. 325*)
- **LO6–8** Solve for unknown values in annuity situations involving present value. (*p. 330*)
- **LO6–9** Briefly describe how the concept of the time value of money is incorporated into the valuation of bonds, long-term leases, and pension obligations. (*p. 333*)

© Shutterstock/Gabriel Petrescu

FINANCIAL REPORTING CASE

The Winning Ticket

Pedro Quezada, a former shop owner from a working-class suburb, had been in the United States for 26 years. On Monday, March 25, 2013, he walked out of a local liquor store with a lottery ticket. The next day the New Jersey resident learned he had won the $338 million Powerball lottery, the fourth-largest jackpot in Powerball history. "I felt pure joy, just happiness," he said. Imagine his surprise, though, when he was told that, having chosen a lump-sum payout rather than 30-year installment payments, he would get a check for "only" $152 million. Sure, federal tax was withheld at a 25% rate and New Jersey added another 3%, but this difference was far more than the amount of the tax.

QUESTIONS

By the time you finish this chapter, you should be able to respond appropriately to the questions posed in this case. Compare your response to the solution provided at the end of the chapter.

1. Why was Quezada to receive $152 million rather than the $338 million lottery prize? (*p. 326*)
2. What interest rate did the state of New Jersey use to calculate the $152 million lump-sum payment? (*p. 331*)
3. What are some of the accounting applications that incorporate the time value of money into valuation? (*p. 334*)

PART A

Basic Concepts

Time Value of Money

The *time value of money* means that money can be invested today to earn interest and grow to a larger dollar amount in the future.

The key to solving the problem described in the financial reporting case is an understanding of the concept commonly referred to as the time value of money. This concept means that money invested today will grow to a larger dollar amount in the future. For example, $100 invested in a savings account at your local bank yielding 6% annually will grow to $106 in one year. The difference between the $100 invested now—the present value of the investment—and its $106 future value represents the time value of money.

This concept has nothing to do with the worth or buying power of those dollars. Prices in our economy can change. If the inflation rate were higher than 6%, then the $106 you would have in the savings account actually would be worth less than the $100 you had a year earlier. The time value of money concept concerns only the growth in the dollar amounts of money, ignoring inflation.

Time value of money concepts are useful in valuing several assets and liabilities.

The concepts you learn in this chapter are useful in solving business decisions such as determining the lottery award presented in the financial reporting case. More important, the concepts are necessary when valuing assets and liabilities for financial reporting purposes. Most accounting applications that incorporate the time value of money involve the concept of present value. The valuation of leases, bonds, pension obligations, and certain notes receivable and payable are a few prominent examples. It is important that you master the concepts and tools we review here as it is essential for the remainder of your accounting education.

Simple versus Compound Interest

● LO6–1

Interest is the amount of money paid or received in excess of the amount borrowed or lent.

Interest is the "rent" paid for the use of money for some period of time. In dollar terms, it is the amount of money paid or received in excess of the amount of money borrowed or lent. If you lend someone $100 today and "receive" $106 a year from now, your interest would be $6. Interest also can be expressed as a rate at which money will grow. In this case, that rate is 6%. It is this interest that gives money its time value.

Simple interest is computed by multiplying an initial investment times both the applicable interest rate and the period of time for which the money is used. For example, simple interest earned each year on a $1,000 investment paying 10% is $100 ($1,000 × 10%).

Compound interest includes interest not only on the initial investment but also on the accumulated interest in previous periods.

Compound interest occurs when money remains invested for multiple periods. It results in increasingly larger interest amounts for each period of the investment. The reason is that interest is then being generated not only on the initial investment amount but also on the accumulated interest earned in previous periods.

For example, Cindy Johnson invested $1,000 in a savings account paying 10% interest *compounded* annually. How much interest will she earn each year, and what will be her investment balance after three years?

Date	Interest (Interest rate × Outstanding balance = Interest)	Balance
Initial deposit		$ 1,000
End of year 1	10% × $1,000 = $100	$ 1,100
End of year 2	10% × $1,100 = $110	$ 1,210
End of year 3	10% × $1,210 = $121	$1,331

With compound interest at 10% annually, the $1,000 investment would grow to $1,331 at the end of the three-year period. If Cindy withdrew the interest earned each year, she would earn only $100 in interest each year (the amount of simple interest). If the investment period had been 20 years, 20 calculations would be needed. However, calculators, Excel, and compound interest tables, like those in an appendix to this textbook, make these calculations easier.

Interest rates are typically stated as annual rates.

Most banks compound interest more frequently than once a year. Daily compounding is common for savings accounts. More rapid compounding has the effect of increasing the actual rate, which is called the effective rate, at which money grows per year. It is important to note that interest is typically stated as an annual rate regardless of the length of the compounding period involved. In situations when the compounding period is less than a year, the interest rate per compounding period is determined by dividing the annual rate by the number of periods. Assuming an annual rate of 12%:

Compounded	Interest Rate Per Compounding Period
Semiannually	12% ÷ 2 = 6%
Quarterly	12% ÷ 4 = 3%
Monthly	12% ÷ 12 = 1%

As an example, now let's assume Cindy Johnson invested $1,000 in a savings account paying 10% interest *compounded* twice a year. There are two six-month periods paying interest at 5% (the annual rate divided by two periods). How much interest will she earn the first year, and what will be her investment balance at the end of the year?

Date	Interest (Interest rate × Outstanding balance = Interest)	Balance
Initial deposit		$ 1,000.00
After six months	5% × $1,000 = $50.00	$ 1,050.00
End of year 1	5% × $1,050 = $52.50	$1,102.50

The *effective interest* rate is the rate at which money actually will grow during a full year.

The $1,000 would grow by $102.50, the interest earned, to $1,102.50, $2.50 more than if interest were compounded only once a year. The effective annual interest rate, often referred to as the annual *yield,* is 10.25% ($102.50 ÷ $1,000).

Valuing a Single Cash Flow Amount

Future Value of a Single Amount

● LO6–2

In the first Cindy example, in which $1,000 was invested for three years at 10% compounded annually, the $1,331 is referred to as the **future value (FV)**. A time diagram is a useful way to visualize this relationship, with 0 indicating the date of the initial investment.

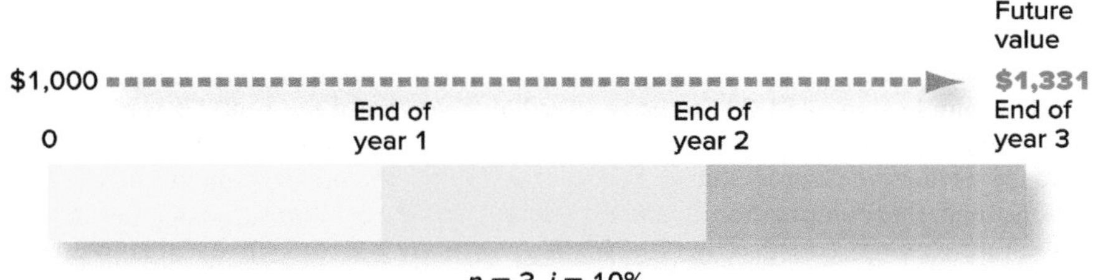

$n = 3, i = 10\%$

The future value after one year can be calculated as $1,000 × 1.10 (1.00 + .10) = $1,100. After three years, the future value is $1,000 × 1.10 × 1.10 × 1.10 = $1,331. In fact, the future value of any invested amount can be determined as follows:

$$FV = I(1 + i)^n$$

The *future value* of a single amount is the amount of money that a dollar will grow to at some point in the future.

where: FV = Future value of the invested amount
I = Amount invested at the beginning of the period
i = Interest rate
n = Number of compounding periods

The future value can be determined by using Table 1, Future Value of $1, located at the end of this textbook. The table contains the future value of $1 invested for various periods of time, n, and at various rates, i.

Use this table to determine the future value of any invested amount simply by multiplying it by the table value at the *intersection* of the column for the desired rate and the row for the number of compounding periods. Illustration 6–1 contains an excerpt from Table 1.

Illustration 6–1

Future Value of $1 (excerpt from Table 1 located at the end of this book)

	Interest Rates (i)					
Periods (n)	**7%**	**8%**	**9%**	**10%**	**11%**	**12%**
1	1.07000	1.08000	1.09000	1.10000	1.11000	1.12000
2	1.14490	1.16640	1.18810	1.21000	1.23210	1.25440
3	1.22504	1.25971	1.29503	1.33100	1.36763	1.40493
4	1.31080	1.36049	1.41158	1.46410	1.51807	1.57352
5	1.40255	1.46933	1.53862	1.61051	1.68506	1.76234

The table shows various values of $(1 + i)^n$ for different combinations of i and n. From the table you can find the future value factor for three periods at 10% to be 1.331. This means that $1 invested at 10% compounded annually will grow to approximately $1.33 in three years. So, the future value of $1,000 invested for three years at 10% is $1,331:

FV = I × FV factor
FV = $1,000 × 1.331* = $1,331

*Future value of $1; $n = 3, i = 10\%$

The future value function in financial calculators or in an Excel spreadsheet calculates future values in the same way. Determining future values (and present values) electronically avoids the need for tables such as those in the appendix. But, we use the tables extensively in the book to make it easier for you to visualize how the amounts are actually determined. It's important to remember that the n in the future value formula refers to the number of compounding periods, not necessarily the number of years. For example, suppose you wanted to know the future value *two* years from today of $1,000 invested at 12% with *quarterly* compounding. The number of periods is therefore eight, and the compounding rate is 3% (12% annual rate divided by four, the number of quarters in a year). The future value factor from Table 1 is 1.26677, so the future value is $1,266.77 ($1,000 × 1.26677).[1]

Present Value of a Single Amount

● LO6–3

The present value of a single amount is today's equivalent to a particular amount in the future.

The example used to illustrate future value reveals that $1,000 invested today is equivalent to $1,100 received after one year, $1,210 after two years, or $1,331 after three years, assuming 10% interest compounded annually. Thus, the $1,000 investment (I) is the **present value (PV)** of the single sum of $1,331 to be received at the end of three years. It is also the present value of $1,210 to be received in two years or $1,100 in one year.

Remember that the future value of a present amount is the present amount *times* $(1 + i)^n$. Logically, then, that computation can be reversed to find the *present value* of a future amount to be the future amount *divided* by $(1 + i)^n$. We substitute PV for I (invested amount) in the future value formula above.

$$FV = PV(1 + i)^n$$

$$PV = \frac{FV}{(1 + i)^n}$$

In our example,

$$PV = \frac{\$1{,}331}{(1 + .10)^3} = \frac{\$1{,}331}{1.331} = \$1{,}000$$

Of course, dividing by $(1 + i)^n$ is the same as multiplying by its reciprocal, $1/(1 + i)^n$.

$$PV = \$1{,}331 \times \frac{1}{(1 + .10)^3} = \$1{,}331 \times .75131 = \$1{,}000$$

As with future value, these computations are simplified by using calculators, Excel, or present value tables. Table 2, Present Value of $1, provides the solutions of $1/(1 + i)^n$ for various interest rates (i) and compounding periods (n). These amounts represent the present value of $1 to be received at the *end* of the different periods. The table can be used to find the present value of any single amount to be received in the future by *multiplying* that amount by the value in the table that lies at the *intersection* of the column for the appropriate rate and the row for the number of compounding periods.[2] Illustration 6–2 contains an excerpt from Table 2.

Illustration 6–2
Present Value of $1 (excerpt from Table 2)

	Interest Rates (*i*)					
Periods (*n*)	**7%**	**8%**	**9%**	**10%**	**11%**	**12%**
1	0.93458	0.92593	0.91743	0.90909	0.90090	0.89286
2	0.87344	0.85734	0.84168	0.82645	0.81162	0.79719
3	0.81630	0.79383	0.77218	0.75131	0.73119	0.71178
4	0.76290	0.73503	0.70843	0.68301	0.65873	0.63552
5	0.71299	0.68058	0.64993	0.62092	0.59345	0.56743

Notice that the further into the future the $1 is to be received, the less valuable it is now. This is the essence of the concept of the time value of money. Given a choice between $1,000 now and $1,000 three years from now, you would choose to have the money now. If you have

[1]When interest is compounded more frequently than once a year, the effective annual interest rate, or yield, can be determined using the following equation:

$$\text{Yield} = (1 + \frac{i}{p})^p - 1$$

with i being the annual interest rate and p the number of compounding periods per year. In this example, the annual yield would be 12.55%, calculated as follows:

$$\text{Yield} = (1 + \frac{.12}{4})^4 - 1 = 1.1255 - 1 = .1255$$

Determining the yield is useful when comparing returns on investment instruments with different compounding period length.

[2]The factors in Table 2 are the reciprocals of those in Table 1. For example, the future value factor for 10%, three periods is 1.331, while the present value factor is .75131. $1 ÷ 1.331 = $.75131, and $1 ÷ 0.75131 = $1.331.

it now, you could put it to use. But the choice between, say, $740 now and $1,000 three years from now would depend on your time value of money. If your time value of money is 10%, you would choose the $1,000 in three years, because the $740 invested at 10% for three years would grow to only $984.94 [$740 × 1.331 (FV of $1, i = 10%, n = 3)]. On the other hand, if your time value of money is 11% or higher, you would prefer the $740 now.[3] Presumably, you would invest the $740 now and have it grow to $1,012.05 ($740 × 1.36763) in three years.

Using the present value table in Illustration 6-2, the present value of $1,000 to be received in three years assuming a time value of money of 10% is $751.31 [$1,000 × 0.75131 (PV of $1, i = 10% and n = 3)]. Because the present value of the future amount, $1,000, is higher than $740 we could have today, we again determine that with a time value of money of 10%, the $1,000 in three years is preferred to the $740 now.

In our earlier example, $1,000 now is equivalent to $1,331 in three years, assuming the time value of money is 10%. Graphically, the relation between the present value and the future value can be viewed this way:

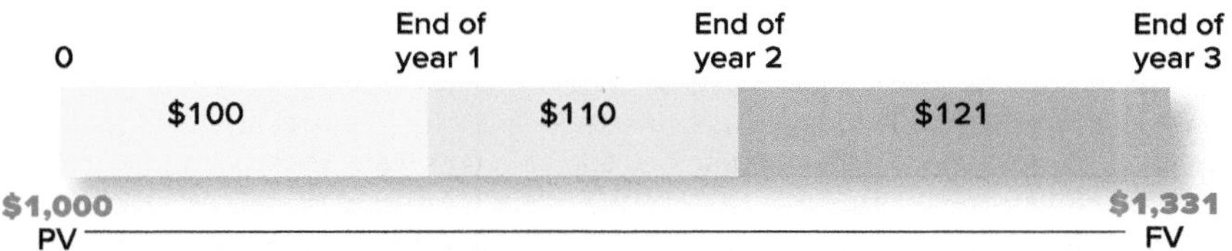

While the calculation of *future value* of a single sum invested today requires the *inclusion* of compound interest, *present value* problems require the *removal* of compound interest. The process of computing present value *removes* the $331 of interest earned over the three-year period from the future value of $1,331, just as the process of computing future value *adds* $331 of interest to the present value of *$1,000* to arrive at the future value of *$1,331*.

The calculation of future value requires the addition of interest, while the calculation of present value requires the removal of interest.

As we demonstrate later in this chapter and in subsequent chapters, present value calculations are incorporated into accounting valuation much more frequently than future value.

Accountants use PV calculations much more frequently than FV.

Solving for Other Values When FV and PV are Known

● LO6–4

There are four variables in the process of adjusting single cash flow amounts for the time value of money: the present value (PV), the future value (FV), the number of compounding periods (n), and the interest rate (i). If you know any three of these, the fourth can be determined. Illustration 6–3 solves for an unknown interest rate and Illustration 6–4 determines an unknown number of periods.

DETERMINING THE UNKNOWN INTEREST RATE

Illustration 6–3
Determining i When PV, FV, and n are Known

Suppose a friend asks to borrow $500 today and promises to repay you $605 two years from now. What is the annual interest rate you would be agreeing to?

The following time diagram illustrates the situation:

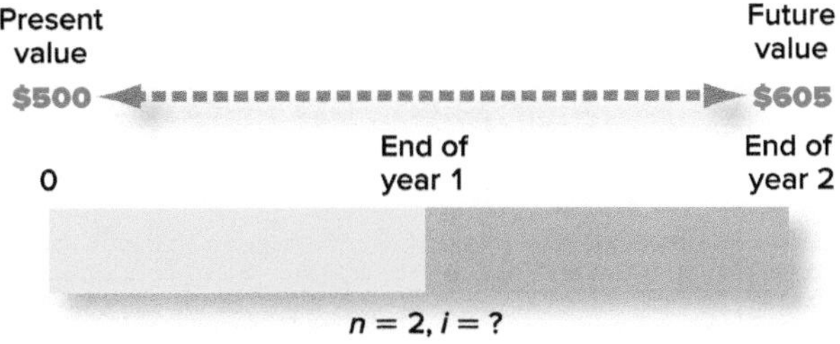

[3]The interest rate used to find the present value sometimes is called the *discount rate,* and finding the present value is sometimes called "discounting" a future amount to its present value.

The interest rate is the rate that will provide a present value of \$500 when determining the present value of the \$605 to be received in two years:

\$500 (present value) = \$605 (future value) × ?*

*Present value of \$1: $n = 2, i = ?$

Rearranging algebraically, we find that the present value table factor is 0.82645.

\$500 (present value) ÷ \$605 (future value) = 0.82645*

*Present value of \$1: $n = 2, i = ?$

The unknown variable is the annuity amount.

When you consult the present value table, Table 2, you search row two ($n = 2$) for this value and find it in the 10% column. So the effective interest rate is 10%. Notice that the computed factor value exactly equals the table factor value.[4]

DETERMINING THE UNKNOWN NUMBER OF PERIODS

Illustration 6–4

Determining n When PV, FV, and i are Known

> You want to invest \$10,000 today to accumulate \$16,000 for graduate school. If you can invest at an interest rate of 10% compounded annually, how many years will it take to accumulate the required amount?

The following time diagram illustrates the situation:

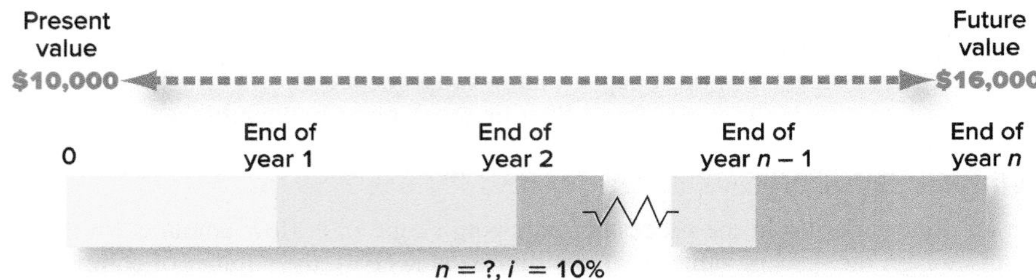

The years it will take is the value of n that will provide a present value of \$10,000 when finding the present value of \$16,000 at a rate of 10%:

The unknown variable is the interest rate.

\$10,000 (present value) = \$16,000 (future value) × ?*

*Present value of \$1; $n = ?, i = 10\%$

Rearranging algebraically, we find that the present value table factor is 0.625.

\$10,000 (present value) ÷ \$16,000 (future value) = 0.625*

*Present value of \$1: $n = ?, i = 10\%$

When you consult the present value table, Table 2, you search the 10% column ($i = 10\%$) for this value and find 0.62092 in row five. So it would take approximately five years to accumulate \$16,000 in the situation described.

[4]If the calculated factor lies between two table factors, interpolation is useful in finding the unknown value. For example, if the future value in our example is \$600, instead of \$605, the calculated PV factor is 0.83333 (\$500 ÷ \$600). This factor lies between the 9% factor of 0.84168 and the 10% factor of 0.82645. The total difference between these factors is .01523 (0.84168 − 0.82645). The difference between the calculated factor of 0.83333 and the 10% factor of 0.82645 is 0.00688. This is 45% of the difference between the 9% and 10% factors:

$$\frac{0.00688}{0.01523} = 0.45$$

Therefore, the interpolated interest rate is 9.55% (10 − 0.45).

Additional Consideration

Solving for the unknown factor in either of these examples could just as easily be done using the future value tables. The number of years is the value of n that will provide a present value of $10,000 when $16,000 is the future amount and the interest rate is 10%.

$16,000 (future value) = $10,000 (present value) × ?*

*Future value of $1: n = ?, i = 10%

Rearranging algebraically, the future value table factor is 1.6.

$16,000 (future value) ÷ $10,000 (present value) = 1.6*

*Future value of $1: n = ?, i = 10%

When you consult the future value table, Table 1, you search the 10% column (i = 10%) for this value and find 1.61051 in row five. So it would take approximately five years to accumulate $16,000 in the situation described.

Concept Review Exercise

VALUING A SINGLE CASH FLOW AMOUNT

Using the appropriate table, answer each of the following independent questions.

1. What is the future value of $5,000 at the end of six periods at 8% compound interest?
2. What is the present value of $8,000 to be received eight periods from today assuming a compound interest rate of 12%?
3. What is the present value of $10,000 to be received two *years* from today assuming an annual interest rate of 24% and *monthly* compounding?
4. If an investment of $2,000 grew to $2,520 in three periods, what is the interest rate at which the investment grew? Solve using both present and future value tables.
5. Approximately how many years would it take for an investment of $5,250 to accumulate to $15,000, assuming interest is compounded at 10% annually? Solve using both present and future value tables.

Solution:

1. FV = $5,000 × 1.58687* = $7,934

   *Future value of $1: n = 6, i = 8% (from Table 1)

2. PV = $8,000 × 0.40388* = $3,231

   *Present value of $1: n = 8, i = 12% (from Table 2)

3. PV = $10,000 × 0.62172* = $6,217

   *Present value of $1: n = 24, i = 2% (from Table 2)

4. Using present value table,

   $2,000/$2,520 = 0.7937*

   *Present value of $1: n = 3, i = ? (from Table 2, i approximately **8%**)

   Using future value table,

   $$\frac{\$2,520}{\$2,000} = 1.260^*$$

   *Future value of $1: n = 3, i = ? (from Table 1, i approximately **8%**)

5. Using present value table,

   $$\frac{\$5,250}{\$15,000} = 0.35^*$$

   *Present value of $1: n = ?, i = 10% (from Table 2, n approximately **11 years**)

   Using future value table,

   $$\frac{\$15,000}{\$5,250} = 2.857^*$$

   *Future value of $1: n = ?. i = 10% (from Table 1, n approximately **11 years**)

Preview of Accounting Applications of Present Value Techniques—Single Cash Amount

Doug Smith switched off his television set immediately after watching the Super Bowl game and swore to himself that this would be the last year he would watch the game on his 10-year-old 24-inch TV. "Next year, a big screen 4K LED," he promised himself. Soon after, he saw an advertisement in the local newspaper from Slim Jim's TV and Appliance offering a Samsung 78-inch television on sale for $1,800. And the best part of the deal was that Doug could take delivery immediately but would not have to pay the $1,800 for one whole year! "In a year, I can easily save the $1,800," he thought.

In the above scenario, the seller, Slim Jim's TV and Appliance, records a sale when the TV is delivered to Doug. How should the company value its receivable and corresponding sales revenue? We provide a solution to this question at the end of this section. The following discussion will help you to understand that solution.

Most *monetary assets* and *monetary liabilities* are valued at the present value of future cash flows.

Many assets and most liabilities are monetary in nature. **Monetary assets** include money and claims to receive money, the amount of which is fixed or determinable. Examples include cash and most receivables. **Monetary liabilities** are obligations to pay amounts of cash, the amount of which is fixed or determinable. Most liabilities are monetary. For example, if you borrow money from a bank and sign a note payable, the amount of cash to be repaid to the bank is fixed. Monetary receivables and payables are valued based on the fixed amount of cash to be received or paid in the future taking into account the time value of money. In other words, we value most receivables and payables at the present value of future cash flows, reflecting an appropriate time value of money.[5]

The example in Illustration 6–5 demonstrates this concept.

Illustration 6–5

Valuing a Note: One Payment, Explicit Interest

Explicit Interest

The Stridewell Wholesale Shoe Company manufactures athletic shoes for sale to retailers. The company recently sold a large order of shoes to Harmon Sporting Goods for $50,000. Stridewell agreed to accept a note in payment for the shoes requiring payment of $50,000 in one year plus interest at 10%.

How should Stridewell value the note receivable and corresponding sales revenue earned? How should Harmon value the note payable and corresponding inventory purchased? As long as the interest rate explicitly stated in the agreement properly reflects the time value of money, the answer is $50,000, the face value of the note. It's important to realize that this amount also equals the present value of future cash flows at 10%. Future cash flows equal $55,000, the $50,000 note itself plus $5,000 interest ($50,000 × 10%). Using a time diagram, it's illustrated as follows:

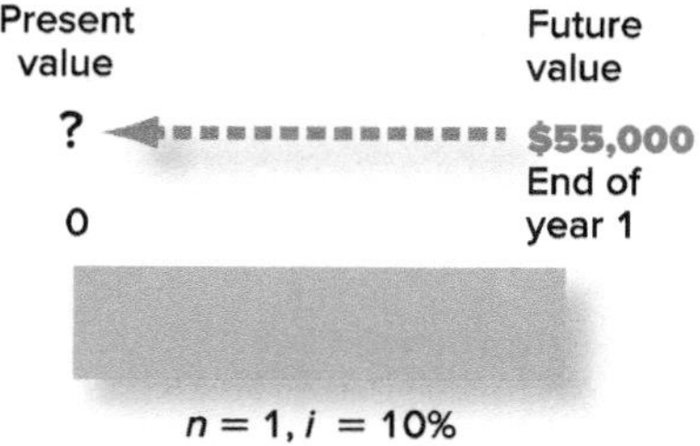

In equation form, we can solve for present value as follows:

$55,000 (future value) × 0.90909* = $50,000 (present value)

*Present value of $1: $n = 1, i = 10\%$

[5]FASB ASC 835–30: Interest–Imputation of Interest (previously "Interest on Receivables and Payables," *Accounting Principles Board Opinion No. 21* (New York: AICPA, 1971)). As you will learn in Chapter 7, we value normal trade accounts receivable and accounts payable at the amounts expected to be received or paid, not the present value of those amounts. The difference between the amounts expected to be received or paid and present values often is immaterial.

By calculating the present value of $55,000 to be received in one year, the interest of $5,000 is removed from the future value, resulting in the appropriate note receivable/sales revenue value of $50,000 for Stridewell and a $50,000 note payable/inventory value for Harmon.

While most notes, loans, and mortgages explicitly state an interest rate that will properly reflect the time value of money, there can be exceptions. Consider the example in Illustration 6–6.

Illustration 6–6

Valuing a Note: One Payment, Explicit Interest

No Explicit Interest
The Stridewell Wholesale Shoe Company recently sold a large order of shoes to Harmon Sporting Goods. Terms of the sale require Harmon to sign a noninterest-bearing note of $60,500 with payment due in two years.

How should Stridewell and Harmon value the note receivable/payable and corresponding sales revenue/inventory? Even though the agreement states a noninterest-bearing note, the $60,500 does, in fact, include interest for the two-year period of the loan. We need to remove the interest portion of the $60,500 to determine the portion that represents the sales price of the shoes. We do this by computing the present value. The following time diagram illustrates the situation assuming that a rate of 10% reflects the appropriate interest rate for a loan of this type:

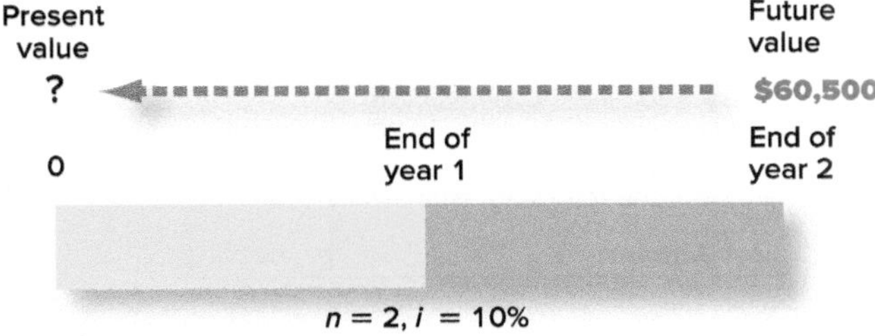

Again, using the present value of $1 table,

$60,500 (future value) × 0.82645* = $50,000 (present value)

*Present value of $1: $n = 2, i = 10\%$

Both the note receivable for Stridewell and the note payable for Harmon initially will be valued at $50,000. The difference of $10,500 ($60,500 − 50,000) represents interest revenue/expense to be recognized over the life of the note. The appropriate journal entries are illustrated in later chapters.

Now can you answer the question posed in the scenario at the beginning of this section? Assuming that a rate of 10% reflects the appropriate interest rate in this situation, Slim Jim's TV and Appliance records a receivable and sales revenue of $1,636 which is the present value of the $1,800 to be received from Doug Smith one year from the date of sale.

$1,800 (future value) × 0.90909* = $1,636 (present value)

*Present value of $1: $n = 1, i = 10\%$ (from Table 2)

Additional Consideration

In Illustration 6–6, if Harmon Sporting Goods had prepaid Stridewell for delivery of the shoes in two years, rather than buying now and paying later, Harmon would be viewed as providing a two-year loan to Stridewell. Assuming that Harmon pays Stridewell $41,323, the present value of $50,000 for two-periods at 10%, Stridewell would record interest expense and Harmon would record interest revenue of $8,677 ($50,000 – 41,323) over the two-year period. When delivery occurs in two years, Stridewell records sales revenue of $50,000 and Harmon values the inventory acquired at $50,000.

Expected Cash Flow Approach

SFAC No. 7 provides a framework for using future cash flows in accounting measurements.

Present value measurement has long been integrated with accounting valuation and is specifically addressed in several accounting standards. Because of its increased importance, the FASB issued *Statement of Financial Accounting Concepts No. 7,* "Using Cash Flow Information and Present Value in Accounting Measurements."[6] This statement provides a framework for using future cash flows as the basis for accounting measurement and asserts that the objective in valuing an asset or liability using present value is to approximate the fair value of that asset or liability. Key to that objective is determining the present value of future cash flows associated with the asset or liability, *taking into account any uncertainty concerning the amounts and timing of the cash flows.* Although future cash flows in many instances are contractual and certain, the amounts and timing of cash flows are less certain in other situations.

For example, lease payments are provided in the contract between lessor and lessee. On the other hand, the future cash flows to be paid to settle a pending lawsuit may be highly uncertain. Traditionally, the way uncertainty has been considered in present value calculations has been by finding the present value of the "best estimate" of future cash flows applying an interest rate that has been adjusted to reflect the uncertainty or risk of those cash flows. With the approach described by *SFAC No. 7,* though, the adjustment for uncertainty or risk of cash flows is applied to the cash flows, not the interest rate. This new *expected cash flow approach* incorporates specific probabilities of cash flows into the analysis. Consider Illustration 6–7.

Illustration 6–7
Expected Cash Flow Approach

Dalton Corporation faces the likelihood of having to pay an uncertain amount in five years in connection with an environmental cleanup. The future cash flow estimate is in the range of $100 million to $300 million with the following estimated probabilities:

Loss Amount	Probability
$100 million	10%
$200 million	60%
$300 million	30%

The expected cash flow, then, is $220 million as shown below:

$100 × 10% =	$ 10 million
200 × 60% =	120 million
300 × 30% =	90 million
	$220 million

If the company's risk-free rate of interest is 5%, Dalton Corporation will report a liability of $172,376,600, the present value of the expected cash outflow as follows:

$220,000,000
× 0.78353*
$ 172,376,600

*Present value of $1, $n = 5$, $i = 5\%$ (from Table 2)

The company's risk-free rate of interest is used when applying the expected cash flow approach to the calculation of present value.

Compare the approach described in Illustration 6–7 to the traditional approach that uses the present value of the most likely estimate of $200 million and ignores information about cash flow probabilities.

The interest rate used to determine present value when applying the expected cash flow approach should be the company's *risk-free rate of interest.* Uncertainty is incorporated

[6] "Using Cash Flow Information and Present Value in Accounting Measurements," *Statement of Financial Accounting Concepts No. 7* (Norwalk, Conn.: FASB, 2000). Recall that Concept Statements do not directly prescribe GAAP, but instead provide structure and direction to financial accounting.

into the determination of the probability-weighted expected cash flows. In the traditional approach, uncertainty is incorporated into a risk-adjusted interest rate.

The FASB expects that the traditional approach to calculating present value will continue to be used in many situations, particularly those where future cash flows are contractual. The board also believes that the expected cash flow approach is more appropriate in more complex situations. In fact, the board has incorporated the concepts developed in *SFAC No. 7* into standards on asset retirement obligations, impairment losses, and business combinations. In Chapter 10, we illustrate the use of the expected cash flow approach as it would be applied to the measurement of an asset retirement obligation. In Chapter 13, we use the approach to measure the liability associated with a loss contingency.

Basic Annuities

PART B

● LO6–5

The previous examples involved the receipt or payment of a single future amount. Financial instruments frequently involve multiple receipts or payments of cash. If the same amount is to be received or paid each period, the series of cash flows is referred to as an **annuity**. A common annuity encountered in practice is a loan on which periodic interest is paid in equal amounts. For example, bonds typically pay interest semiannually in an amount determined by multiplying a stated rate by a fixed principal amount. Some loans and most leases are paid in equal installments during a specified period of time.

In an *ordinary annuity*, cash flows occur at the end of each period.

An agreement that creates an annuity can produce either an **ordinary annuity** or an **annuity due** (sometimes referred to as an annuity in advance) situation. The first cash flow (receipt or payment) of an ordinary annuity is made one compounding period *after* the date on which the agreement begins. The final cash flow takes place on the *last* day covered by the agreement. For example, an installment note payable dated December 31, 2018, might require the debtor to make three equal annual payments, with the first payment due on December 31, 2019, and the last one on December 31, 2021. The following time diagram illustrates an ordinary annuity:

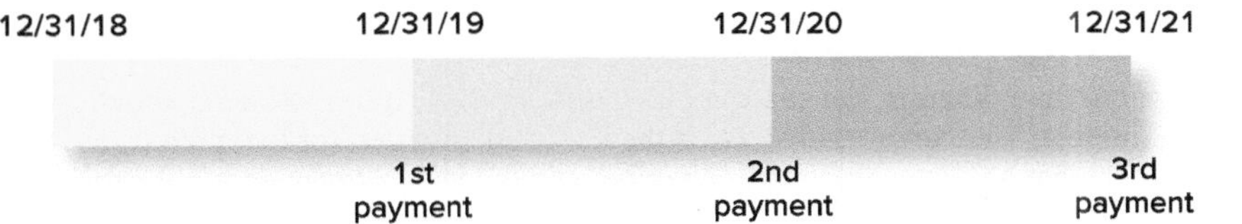

Ordinary annuity.

The first payment of an annuity due is made on the *first* day of the agreement, and the last payment is made one period *before* the end of the agreement. For example, a three-year lease of a building that begins on December 31, 2018, and ends on December 31, 2021, may require the first year's lease payment in advance on December 31, 2018. The third and last payment would take place on December 31, 2020, the beginning of the third year of the lease. The following time diagram illustrates this situation:

In an *annuity due*, cash flows occur at the *beginning* of each period.

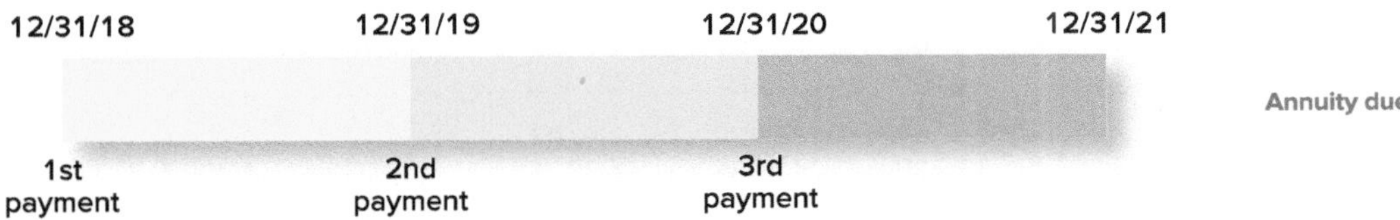

Annuity due.

Future Value of an Annuity

Future Value of an Ordinary Annuity

● LO6–6 Let's first consider the future value of an ordinary annuity in Illustration 6–8.

Illustration 6–8
Future Value of an Ordinary Annuity

Rita Grant wants to accumulate a sum of money to pay for graduate school. Rather than investing a single amount today that will grow to a future value, she decides to invest $10,000 a year over the next three years in a savings account paying 10% interest compounded annually. She decides to make the first payment to the bank one year from today.

The following time diagram illustrates this ordinary annuity situation. Time 0 is the start of the first period.

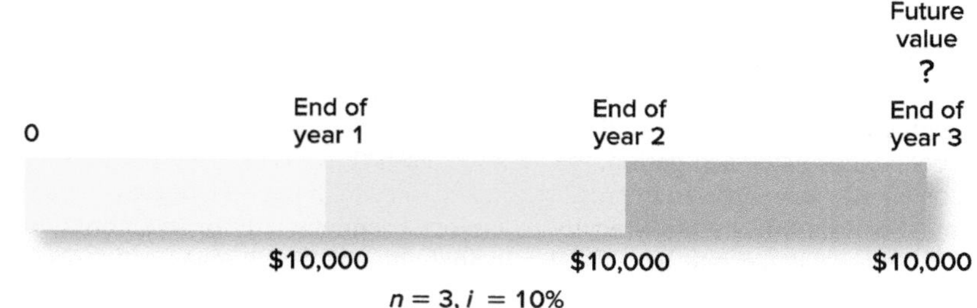

Using the FV of $1 factors from Table 1, we can calculate the future value of this annuity by calculating the future value of each of the individual payments as follows:

	Payment		FV of $1 $i = 10\%$		Future Value (at the end of year 3)	n
First payment	$10,000	×	1.21	=	$ 12,100	2
Second payment	10,000	×	1.10	=	11,000	1
Third payment	10,000	×	1.00	=	10,000	0
Total			3.31		$33,100	

In the future value of an ordinary annuity, the last cash payment will not earn any interest.

From the time diagram, we can see that the first payment has two compounding periods to earn interest. The factor used, 1.21, is the FV of $1 invested for two periods at 10%. The second payment has one compounding period, and the last payment does not earn any interest because it is invested on the last day of the three-year annuity period. Therefore, the factor used is 1.00.

This illustration shows that it's possible to calculate the future value of the annuity by separately calculating the FV of each payment and then adding these amounts together. Fortunately, that's not necessary. Table 3, Future Value of an Ordinary Annuity of $1, simplifies the computation by summing the individual FV of $1 factors for various factors of n and i. Illustration 6–9 contains an excerpt from Table 3.

Illustration 6–9
Future Value of an Ordinary Annuity of $1 (excerpt from Table 3)

	Interest Rates (i)					
Periods (n)	7%	8%	9%	10%	11%	12%
1	1.0000	1.0000	1.0000	1.0000	1.0000	1.0000
2	2.0700	2.0800	2.0900	2.1000	2.1100	2.1200
3	3.2149	3.2464	3.2781	3.3100	3.3421	3.3744
4	4.4399	4.5061	4.5731	4.6410	4.7097	4.7793
5	5.7507	5.8666	5.9847	6.1051	6.2278	6.3528

The future value of $1 at the end of each of three periods invested at 10% is shown in Table 3 to be $3.31. We can simply multiply this factor by $10,000 to derive the FV of our ordinary annuity (FVA):

FVA = $10,000 (annuity amount) × 3.31* = $33,100

*Future value of an ordinary annuity of $1: $n = 3, i = 10\%$

Future Value of an Annuity Due

Let's modify the previous illustration to create an annuity due in Illustration 6–10.

Rita Grant wants to accumulate a sum of money to pay for graduate school. Rather than investing a single amount today that will grow to a future value, she decides to invest $10,000 a year over the next three years in a savings account paying 10% interest compounded annually. She decides to make the first payment to the bank immediately. How much will Sally have available in her account at the end of three years?

Illustration 6–10

Future Value of an Annuity Due

The following time diagram depicts the situation. Again, note that 0 is the start of the first period.

0	End of year 1	End of year 2	End of year 3 (Future value ?)
$10,000	$10,000	$10,000	

$n = 3, i = 10\%$

The future value can be found by separately calculating the FV of each of the three payments and then summing those individual future values:

	Payment		FV of $1 i = 10%		Future Value (at the end of year 3)	n
First payment	$10,000	×	1.331	=	$ 13,310	3
Second payment	10,000	×	1.210	=	12,100	2
Third payment	10,000	×	1.100	=	11,000	1
Total			3.641		$36,410	

In the future value of an annuity due, the last cash payment will earn interest.

And, again, this same future value can be found by using the future value of an annuity due (FVAD) factor from Table 5, Future Value of an Annuity Due of $1 as follows:

FVAD = $10,000 (annuity amount) × 3.641* = $36,410

*Future value of an annuity due of $1: $n = 3, i = 10\%$

Of course, if *unequal* amounts are invested each year, we can't solve the problem by using the annuity tables. The future value of each payment would have to be calculated separately.

Present Value of an Annuity

Present Value of an Ordinary Annuity

● LO6–7

You will learn in later chapters that liabilities and receivables, with the exception of certain trade receivables and payables, are reported in financial statements at their present values. Most of these financial instruments specify equal periodic interest payments or installment payments. As a result, the most common accounting applications of the time value of money involve determining present value of annuities. As in the future value applications we discussed above, an annuity can be either an ordinary annuity or an annuity due. Let's look at an ordinary annuity first.

FINANCIAL Reporting Case

Q1, p. 313

In Illustration 6–8, we determined that Rita Grant could accumulate $33,100 for graduate school by investing $10,000 at the end of each of three years at 10%. The $33,100 is the future value of the ordinary annuity described. Another alternative is to invest one single amount at the beginning of the three-year period. (See Illustration 6–11.) This single amount will equal the present value at the beginning of the three-year period of the $33,100 future value. It will also equal the present value of the $10,000 three-year annuity.

Illustration 6–11

Present Value of an Ordinary Annuity

Rita Grant wants to accumulate a sum of money to pay for graduate school. She wants to invest a single amount today in a savings account earning 10% interest compounded annually that is equivalent to investing $10,000 at the end of each of the next three years.

The present value can be found by separately calculating the PV of each of the three payments and then summing those individual present values as follows:

	Payment		PV of $1 i = 10%		Present Value (at the beginning of year 1)	n
First payment	$10,000	×	0.90909	=	$ 9,091	1
Second payment	10,000	×	0.82645	=	8,264	2
Third payment	10,000	×	0.75131	=	7,513	3
Total			2.48685		$24,868	

A more efficient method of calculating present value is to use Table 4, Present Value of an Ordinary Annuity of $1. Illustration 6–12 contains an excerpt from Table 4.

Illustration 6–12

Present Value of an Ordinary Annuity of $1 (excerpt from Table 4)

	Interest Rates (i)					
Periods (n)	**7%**	**8%**	**9%**	**10%**	**11%**	**12%**
1	0.93458	0.92593	0.91743	0.90909	0.90090	0.89286
2	1.80802	1.78326	1.75911	1.73554	1.71252	1.69005
3	2.62432	2.57710	2.53129	2.48685	2.44371	2.40183
4	3.38721	3.31213	3.23972	3.16987	3.10245	3.03735
5	4.10020	3.99271	3.88965	3.79079	3.69590	3.60478

Using Table 4, we calculate the PV of the ordinary annuity (PVA) as follows:

PVA = $10,000 (annuity amount) × 2.48685* = $24,868

*Present value of an ordinary annuity of $1: $n = 3$, $i = 10\%$

The relationship between the present value and the future value of the annuity can be depicted graphically as follows:

Present value $24,868 | Future value $33,100

0	End of year 1	End of year 2	End of year 3
	$10,000	$10,000	$10,000

$n = 3, i = 10\%$

This can be interpreted in several ways.

1. $10,000 invested at 10% at the end of each of the next three years will accumulate to $33,100 at the end of the third year.
2. $24,868 invested at 10% now will grow to $33,100 after three years.
3. Someone whose time value of money is 10% would be willing to pay $24,868 now to receive $10,000 at the end of each of the next three years.
4. If your time value of money is 10%, you should be indifferent with respect to paying/receiving (a) $24,868 now, (b) $33,100 three years from now, or (c) $10,000 at the end of each of the next three years.

Additional Consideration

We also can verify that these are the present value and future value of the same annuity by calculating the present value of a single cash amount of $33,100 three years hence:

PV = $33,100 (future value) × 0.75131* = $24,868

*Present value of $1: $n = 3, i = 10\%$

Present Value of an Annuity Due

In the previous illustration, suppose that the three equal payments of $10,000 are to be made at the *beginning* of each of the three years. Recall from Illustration 6–10 that the future value of this annuity is $36,410. What is the present value?

Illustration 6–13
Present Value of an Annuity Due

The following time diagram depicts this situation:

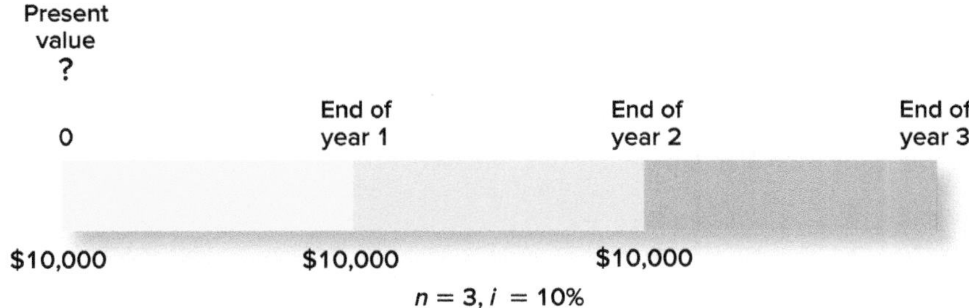

Once again, using individual PV factors of $1 from Table 2, the PV of the annuity due can be calculated as follows:

	Payment		PV of $1 $i = 10\%$		Present Value (at the beginning of year 1)	n
First payment	$10,000	×	1.00000	=	$ 10,000	0
Second payment	10,000	×	0.90909	=	9,091	1
Third payment	10,000	×	0.82645	=	8,264	2
Total			2.73554		$27,355	

The first payment does not contain any interest since it is made on the first day of the three-year annuity period. Therefore, the factor used is 1.00. The second payment has one compounding period and the factor used of 0.90909 is the PV factor of $1 for one period and 10%, and we need to remove two compounding periods of interest from the third payment. The factor used of 0.82645 is the PV factor of $1 for two periods and 10%.

In the present value of an annuity due, no interest needs to be removed from the first cash payment.

The relationship between the present value and the future value of the annuity can be depicted graphically as follows:

Present value $27,355 | Future value $36,410

0 | End of year 1 | End of year 2 | End of year 3

$10,000 | $10,000 | $10,000

$n = 3, i = 10\%$

Using Table 6, Present Value of an Annuity Due, we can more efficiently calculate the PV of the annuity due (PVAD):

$$\text{PVAD} = \$10{,}000 \text{ (annuity amount)} \times 2.73554^{*} = \$27{,}355$$

*Present value of an annuity due of $1: $n = 3, i = 10\%$

To better understand the relationship between Tables 4 and 6, notice that the PVAD factor for three periods, 10%, from Table 6 is 2.73554. This is simply the PVA factor for two periods, 10%, of 1.73554, plus 1.0. The addition of 1.0 reflects the fact that the first payment does not require the removal of any interest.

Present Value of a Deferred Annuity

A ***deferred annuity*** **exists when the first cash flow occurs more than one period after the date the agreement begins.**

Accounting valuations often involve the present value of annuities in which the first cash flow is expected to occur more than one time period after the date of the agreement. As the inception of the annuity is deferred beyond a single period, this type of annuity is referred to as a **deferred annuity**.[7]

Illustration 6–14
Deferred Annuity

> At January 1, 2018, you are considering acquiring an investment that will provide three equal payments of $10,000 each to be received at the end of three consecutive years. However, the first payment is not expected until *December 31, 2020.* The time value of money is 10%. How much would you be willing to pay for this investment?

The following time diagram depicts this situation:

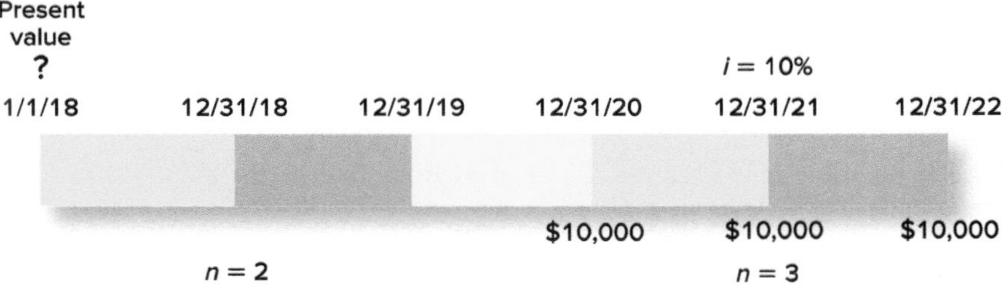

The present value of the deferred annuity can be calculated by summing the present values of the three individual cash flows, as of today.

	Payment		PV of \$1 $i = 10\%$		Present Value	n
First payment	$10,000	×	0.75131	=	$ 7,513	3
Second payment	10,000	×	0.68301	=	6,830	4
Third payment	10,000	×	0.62092	=	6,209	5
					$20,552	

[7]The future value of a deferred annuity is the same as the future amount of an annuity not deferred. That is because there are no interest compounding periods prior to the beginning of the annuity period.

A more efficient way of calculating the present value of a deferred annuity involves a two-step process.

1. Calculate the PV of the annuity *as of the beginning of the annuity period.*
2. Reduce the single amount calculated in (1) to its present value *as of today.*

In this case, we compute the present value of the annuity as of December 31, 2019, by multiplying the annuity amount by the three-period ordinary annuity factor:

$$PVA = \$10{,}000 \text{ (annuity amount)} \times 2.48685^* = \$24{,}868$$

*Present value of an ordinary annuity of \$1: $n = 3$, $i = 10\%$

This is the present value as of December 31, 2019. This single amount is then reduced to present value as of January 1, 2018, by making the following calculation:

$$PV = \$24{,}868 \text{ (future amount)} \times 0.82645^* = \$20{,}552$$

*Present value of \$1: $n = 2$, $i = 10\%$

The following time diagram illustrates this two-step process:

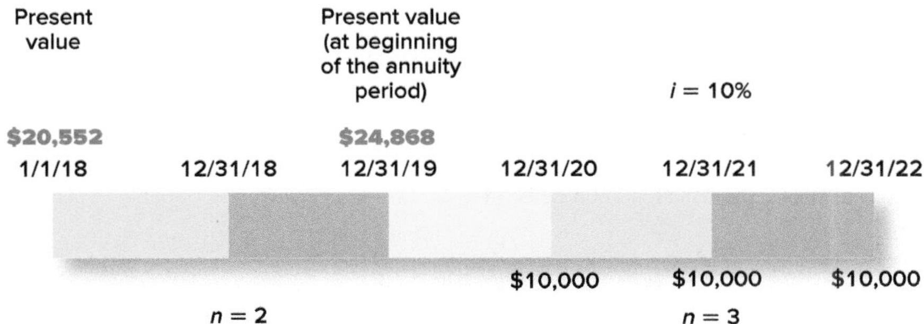

If you recall the concepts you learned in this chapter, you might think of other ways the present value of a deferred annuity can be determined. Among them:

1. Calculate the PV of an annuity due, rather than an ordinary annuity, and then reduce that amount three periods rather than two:

   $$PVAD = \$10{,}000 \text{ (annuity amount)} \times 2.73554^* = \$27{,}355$$

   *Present value of an annuity due of \$1: $n = 3$, $i = 10\%$

   This is the present value as of December 31, 2020. This single amount is then reduced to present value as of January 1, 2018 by making the following calculation:

   $$PV = \$27{,}355 \times 0.75131^* = \$20{,}552$$

   *Present value of \$1: $n = 3$, $i = 10\%$

2. From Table 4, subtract the two-period PVA factor (1.73554) from the five-period PVA factor (3.79079) and multiply the difference (2.05525) by \$10,000 to get \$20,552.

Financial Calculators and Excel

As previously mentioned, financial calculators can be used to solve future and present value problems. For example, a Texas Instruments model BA-35 has the following pertinent keys:

[N] [%I] [PV] [FV] [PMT] [CPT]

These keys are defined as follows:

N = number of periods
%I = interest rate
PV = present value

FV = future value
PMT = annuity payments
CPT = compute button

Using a calculator:
enter: N 10 I 10
PMT −200
Output: PV 1,229

Using Excel, enter:
PV(.10,10,-200)
Output: 1,229

To illustrate its use, assume that you need to determine the present value of a 10-period ordinary annuity of $200 using a 10% interest rate. You would enter N 10, %I 10, PMT −200, then press CPT and PV to obtain the answer of $1,229.

Many professionals choose to use spreadsheet software, such as Excel, to solve time value of money problems. These spreadsheets can be used in a variety of ways. A template can be created using the formulas shown in Illustration 6–22. An alternative is to use the software's built-in financial functions. For example, Excel has a function called PV that calculates the present value of an ordinary annuity. To use the function, you would select the pull-down menu for "Insert," click on "Function" and choose the category called "Financial." Scroll down to PV and double-click. You will then be asked to input the necessary variables—interest rate, the number of periods, and the payment amount.

In subsequent chapters we illustrate the use of both a calculator and Excel in addition to present value tables to solve present value calculations for selected examples and illustrations.

Solving for Unknown Values in Present Value Situations

LO6–8

In present value problems involving annuities, there are four variables: (1) present value of an ordinary annuity (PVA) or present value of an annuity due (PVAD), (2) the amount of each annuity payment, (3) the number of periods, *n*, and (4) the interest rate, *i*. If you know any three of these, the fourth can be determined.

Illustration 6–15
Determining the Annuity Amount When Other Variables Are Known

Assume that you borrow $700 from a friend and intend to repay the amount in four equal annual installments beginning one year from today. Your friend wishes to be reimbursed for the time value of money at an 8% annual rate. What is the required annual payment that must be made (the annuity amount), to repay the loan in four years?

The following time diagram illustrates the situation:

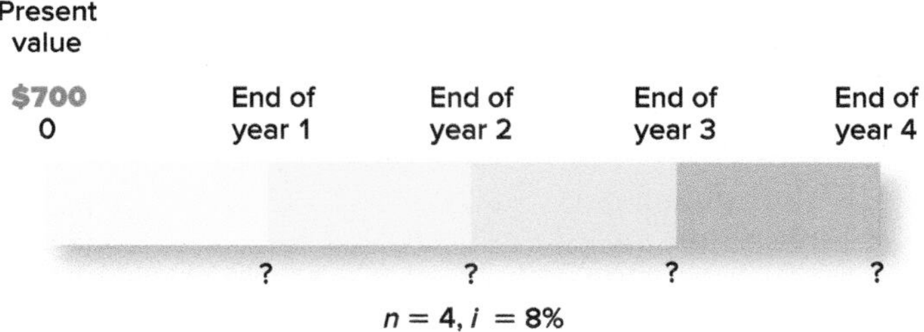

The required payment is the annuity amount that will provide a present value of $700 when using an interest rate of 8%.

$700 (present value) = 3.31213* × annuity amount

*Present value of an ordinary annuity of $1: $n = 4, i = 8\%$

Rearranging algebraically, we find that the annuity amount is $211.34.

The unknown variable is the annuity amount.

$700 (present value) ÷ 3.31213* = $211.34 (annuity amount)

*Present value of an ordinary annuity of $1: $n = 4, i = 8\%$

You would have to make four annual payments of $211.34 to repay the loan. Total payments of $845.36 (4 × $211.34) would include $145.36 in interest ($845.36 – 700.00).

Assume that you borrow $700 from a friend and intend to repay the amount in equal installments of $100 per year over a period of years. The payments will be made at the end of each year beginning one year from now. Your friend wishes to be reimbursed for the time value of money at a 7% annual rate. How many years would it take before you repaid the loan?

Illustration 6–16

Determining n When Other Variables Are Known

Once again, this is an ordinary annuity situation because the first payment takes place one year from now. The following time diagram illustrates the situation:

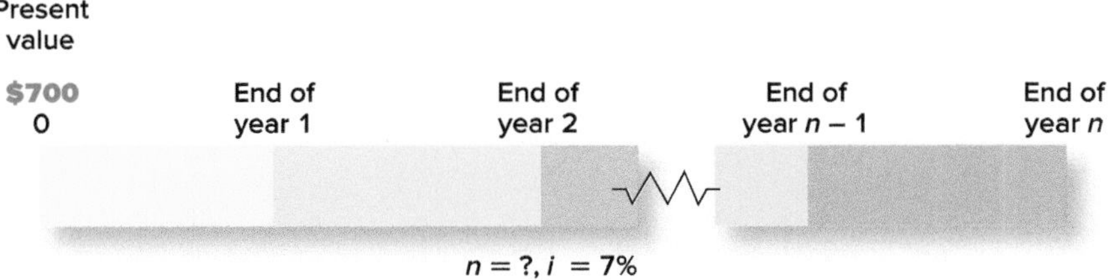

The number of years is the value of n that will provide a present value of $700 when finding the present value of $100 payments using an interest rate of 7%:

$700 (present value) = $100 (annuity amount) × ?*

*Present value of an ordinary annuity of $1: $n = ?, i = 7\%$

The unknown variable is the number of periods.

Rearranging algebraically, we find that the PVA table factor is 7.0.

$700 (present value) ÷ $100 (annuity amount) = 7.0*

*Present value of an ordinary annuity of $1: $n = ?, i = 7\%$

When you consult the PVA table, Table 4, you search the 7% column ($i = 7\%$) for this value and find 7.02358 in row 10. So it would take approximately 10 years to repay the loan in the situation described.

Suppose that a friend asked to borrow $331 today (present value) and promised to repay you $100 (the annuity amount) at the end of each of the next four years. What is the annual interest rate implicit in this agreement?

Illustration 6–17

Determining i When Other Variables Are Known

First of all, we are dealing with an ordinary annuity situation as the payments are at the end of each period. The following time diagram illustrates the situation:

FINANCIAL Reporting Case

Q2, p. 313

Present value
$331
0
End of year 1 — $100
End of year 2 — $100
End of year 3 — $100
End of year 4 — $100

$n = 4, i = ?$

The interest rate is the rate that will provide a present value of $331 when finding the present value of the $100 four-year ordinary annuity.

$331 (present value) = $100 (annuity amount) × ?*

*Present value of an ordinary annuity of $1: $n = 4, i = ?$

The unknown variable is the interest rate.

Rearranging algebraically, we find that the PVA table factor is 3.31.

$331 (present value) ÷ $100 (annuity amount) = 3.31*

*Present value of an ordinary annuity of $1: $n = 4, i = ?$

When you consult the PVA table, Table 4, you search row four ($n = 4$) for this value and find it in the 8% column. So the effective interest rate is 8%.

Illustration 6–18

Determining i When Other Variables Are Known—Unequal Cash Flows

Suppose that you borrowed $400 from a friend and promised to repay the loan by making three annual payments of $100 at the end of each of the next three years plus a final payment of $200 at the end of year four. What is the interest rate implicit in this agreement?

The following time diagram illustrates the situation:

Present value				
$400	End of year 1	End of year 2	End of year 3	End of year 4
0				
	$100	$100	$100	$200

$100 annuity has $n = 3$, $i = ?$
$200 single payment has $n = 4$, $i = ?$

The interest rate is the rate that will provide a present value of $400 when finding the present value of the $100 three-year ordinary annuity plus the $200 to be received in four years:

The unknown variable is the interest rate.

$400 (present value) = $100 (annuity amount) × ?* + $200 (single payment) × ?†

*Present value of an ordinary annuity of $1: $n = 3$, $i = ?$

†Present value of $1: $n = 4$, $i = ?$

This equation involves two unknowns and is not as easily solved as the two previous examples. One way to solve the problem is to trial-and-error the answer. For example, if we assumed i to be 9%, the total PV of the payments would be calculated as follows:

PV = $100 (2.53129*) + $200 (0.70843†) = $395

*Present value of an ordinary annuity of $1: $n = 3$, $i = 9\%$

†Present value of $1: $n = 4$, $i = 9\%$

Because the present value computed is less than the $400 borrowed, using 9% removes too much interest. Recalculating PV with $i = 8\%$ results in a PV of $405. This indicates that the interest rate implicit in the agreement is between 8% and 9%.

Concept Review Exercise

ANNUITIES

Using the appropriate table, answer each of the following independent questions.

1. What is the future value of an annuity of $2,000 invested at the *end* of each of the next six periods at 8% interest?
2. What is the future value of an annuity of $2,000 invested at the *beginning* of each of the next six periods at 8% interest?
3. What is the present value of an annuity of $6,000 to be received at the *end* of each of the next eight periods assuming an interest rate of 10%?
4. What is the present value of an annuity of $6,000 to be received at the *beginning* of each of the next eight periods assuming an interest rate of 10%?
5. Jane bought a $3,000 audio system and agreed to pay for the purchase in 10 equal annual installments of $408 beginning one year from today. What is the interest rate implicit in this agreement?
6. Jane bought a $3,000 audio system and agreed to pay for the purchase in 10 equal annual installments beginning one year from today. The interest rate is 12%. What is the amount of the annual installment?

7. Jane bought a $3,000 audio system and agreed to pay for the purchase by making nine equal annual installments beginning one year from today plus a lump-sum payment of $1,000 at the end of 10 periods. The interest rate is 10%. What is the required annual installment?
8. Jane bought an audio system and agreed to pay for the purchase by making four equal annual installments of $800 beginning one year from today plus a lump-sum payment of $1,000 at the end of five years. The interest rate is 12%. What was the cost of the audio system? (Hint: What is the present value of the cash payments?)
9. Jane bought an audio system and agreed to pay for the purchase by making five equal annual installments of $1,100 beginning four years from today. The interest rate is 12%. What was the cost of the audio system? (Hint: What is the present value of the cash payments?)

Solution:

1. FVA = $2,000 × 7.3359* = $14,672

   *Future value of an ordinary annuity of $1: $n = 6, i = 8\%$ (from Table 3)

2. FVAD = $2,000 × 7.9228* = $15,846

   *Future value of an annuity due of $1: $n = 6, i = 8\%$ (from Table 5)

3. PVA = $6,000 × 5.33493* = $32,010

   *Present value of ordinary annuity of $1: $n = 8, i = 10\%$ (from Table 4)

4. PVAD = $6,000 × 5.86842* = $35,211

   *Present value of an annuity due of $1: $n = 8, i = 10\%$ (from Table 6)

5. $\frac{\$3{,}000}{\$408} = 7.35^*$

   *Present value of an ordinary annuity of $1: $n = 10, i = ?$ (from Table 4, i approximately 6%)

6. Each annuity payment $= \frac{\$3{,}000}{5.65022^*} = \$531$

   *Present value of an ordinary annuity of $1: $n = 10, i = 12\%$ (from Table 4)

7. Each annuity payment $= \frac{\$3{,}000 - [\text{PV of } \$1{,}000(n = 10, i = 10\%)]}{5.75902^*}$

   Each annuity payment $= \frac{\$3{,}000 - (\$1{,}000 \times .38554^\dagger)}{5.75902^*}$

   Each annuity payment $= \frac{\$2{,}614}{5.75902^*} = \$454$

   *Present value of an ordinary annuity of $1: $n = 9, i = 10\%$ (from Table 4)
   †Present value of $1: $n = 10, i = 10\%$ (from Table 2)

8. PV = $800 × 3.03735* + $1,000 × 0.56743† = $2,997

   *Present value of an ordinary annuity of $1: $n = 4, i = 12\%$ (from Table 4)
   †Present value of $1: $n = 5, i = 12\%$ (from Table 2)

9. PVA = $1,100 × 3.60478* = $3,965

   *Present value of an ordinary annuity of $1: $n = 5, i = 12\%$ (from Table 4)

   This is the present value three years from today (the beginning of the five-year ordinary annuity). This single amount is then reduced to present value as of today by making the following calculation:

   PV = $3,965 × 0.71178† = $2,822
   †Present value of $1: $n = 3, i = 12\%$, (from Table 2)

Preview of Accounting Applications of Present Value Techniques—Annuities

The time value of money has many applications in accounting. Most of these applications involve the concept of present value. Because financial instruments typically specify equal periodic payments, these applications quite often involve annuity situations. For example, let's consider one accounting situation using both an ordinary annuity and the present value of a single amount (long-term bonds), one using an annuity due (long-term leases), and a third using a deferred annuity (pension obligations). ● LO6–9

Valuation of Long-Term Bonds

FINANCIAL Reporting Case

Q3, p. 313

You will learn in Chapter 14 that a long-term bond usually requires the issuing (borrowing) company to repay a specified amount at maturity and make periodic stated interest payments over the life of the bond. The *stated* interest payments are equal to the contractual stated rate multiplied by the face value of the bonds. At the date the bonds are issued (sold), the marketplace will determine the price of the bonds based on the *market* rate of interest for investments with similar characteristics. The market rate at date of issuance may not equal the bonds' stated rate in which case the price of the bonds (the amount the issuing company actually is borrowing) will not equal the bonds' face value. Bonds issued at more than face value are said to be issued at a premium, while bonds issued at less than face value are said to be issued at a discount. Consider the example in Illustration 6–19.

Illustration 6–19

Valuing a Long-Term Bond Liability

On June 30, 2018, Fumatsu Electric issued 10% stated rate bonds with a face amount of $200 million. The bonds mature on June 30, 2038 (20 years). The market rate of interest for similar issues was 12%. Interest is paid semiannually (5%) on June 30 and December 31, beginning December 31, 2018. The interest payment is $10 million (5% × $200 million). What was the price of the bond issue? What amount of interest expense will Fumatsu record for the bonds in 2018?

To determine the price of the bonds, we calculate the present value of the 40-period annuity (40 semiannual interest payments of $10 million) and the lump-sum payment of $200 million paid at maturity using the semiannual market rate of interest of 6%. In equation form,

$$\text{PVA} = \$10 \text{ million (annuity amount)} \times 15.04630^{*} = \$150{,}463{,}000$$
$$\text{PV} = \$200 \text{ million (lump-sum)} \times 0.09722^{\dagger} = \underline{19{,}444{,}000}$$
$$\text{Price of the bond issue} = \underline{\underline{\$169{,}907{,}000}}$$

*Present value of an ordinary annuity of $1: $n = 40$, $i = 6\%$
†Present value of $1: $n = 40$, $i = 6\%$

The bonds will sell for $169,907,000, which represents a discount of $30,093,000 ($200,000,000 − 169,907,000). The discount results from the difference between the semiannual stated rate of 5% and the market rate of 6%. Fumatsu records a $169,907,000 increase in cash and a corresponding liability for bonds payable.

Interest expense for the first six months is determined by multiplying the carrying value (book value) of the bonds ($169,907,000) by the semiannual effective rate (6%) as follows:

$$\$169{,}907{,}000 \times 6\% = \$10{,}194{,}420$$

The difference between interest expense ($10,194,420) and interest paid ($10,000,000) increases the carrying value of the bond liability. Interest for the second six months of the bonds' life is determined by multiplying the new carrying value by the 6% semiannual effective rate.[8]

We discuss the specific accounts used to record these transactions in Chapters 12 and 14.

Valuation of Long-Term Leases

Companies frequently acquire the use of assets by leasing rather than purchasing them. Leases usually require the payment of fixed amounts at regular intervals over the life of the lease. You will learn in Chapter 15 that certain leases are treated in a manner similar to an installment purchase by the lessee. In other words, the lessee records an asset and corresponding lease liability at the present value of the lease payments. Consider the example in Illustration 6–20.

Leases require the recording of an asset and corresponding liability at the present value of future lease payments.

Once again, by computing the present value of the lease payments, we remove the portion of the payments that represents interest, leaving the portion that represents payment for the asset itself. Because the first payment is due immediately, as is common for leases, this is an annuity due situation. In equation form:

$$\text{PVAD} = \$10{,}000 \text{ (annuity amount)} \times 9.98474^{*} = \$99{,}847$$

*Present value of an annuity due of $1: $n = 25$, $i = 10\%$

[8]In Chapters 12 and 14, we refer to the process of determining interest as the effective interest rate times the loan balance as the *effective interest method.*

On January 1, 2018, the Stridewell Wholesale Shoe Company signed a 25-year lease agreement for an office building. Terms of the lease call for Stridewell to make annual lease payments of $10,000 at the beginning of each year, with the first payment due on January 1, 2018. Assuming an interest rate of 10% properly reflects the time value of money in this situation, how should Stridewell value the asset acquired and the corresponding lease liability?

Illustration 6–20

Valuing a Long-Term Lease Liability

Stridewell initially will value the leased asset and corresponding lease liability at $99,847.

Right-of-use asset	99,847	
Lease payable		99,847

Journal entry at the beginning of the lease.

The difference between this amount and total future cash payments of $250,000 ($10,000 × 25) represents the interest that is implicit in this agreement. That difference is recorded as interest over the life of the lease.

Valuation of Pension Obligations

Pension plans are important compensation vehicles used by many U.S. companies. These plans are essentially forms of deferred compensation as the pension benefits are paid to employees after they retire. You will learn in Chapter 17 that some pension plans create obligations during employees' service periods that must be paid during their retirement periods. These obligations are funded during the employment period. This means companies contribute cash to pension funds annually with the intention of accumulating sufficient funds to pay employees the retirement benefits they have earned. The amounts contributed are determined using estimates of retirement benefits. The actual amounts paid to employees during retirement depend on many factors including future compensation levels and length of life. Consider Illustration 6–21.

On January 1, 2018, the Stridewell Wholesale Shoe Company hired Terry Elliott. Terry is expected to work for 25 years before retirement on December 31, 2042. Annual retirement payments will be paid at the end of each year during his retirement period, expected to be 20 years. The first payment will be on December 31, 2043. During 2018 Terry earned an annual retirement benefit estimated to be $2,000 per year. The company plans to contribute cash to a pension fund that will accumulate to an amount sufficient to pay Terry this benefit. Assuming that Stridewell anticipates earning 6% on all funds invested in the pension plan, how much would the company have to contribute at the end of 2018 to pay for pension benefits earned in 2018?

Illustration 6–21

Valuing a Pension Obligation

To determine the required contribution, we calculate the present value on December 31, 2018, of the deferred annuity of $2,000 that begins on December 31, 2043, and is expected to end on December 31, 2062.

The following time diagram depicts this situation:

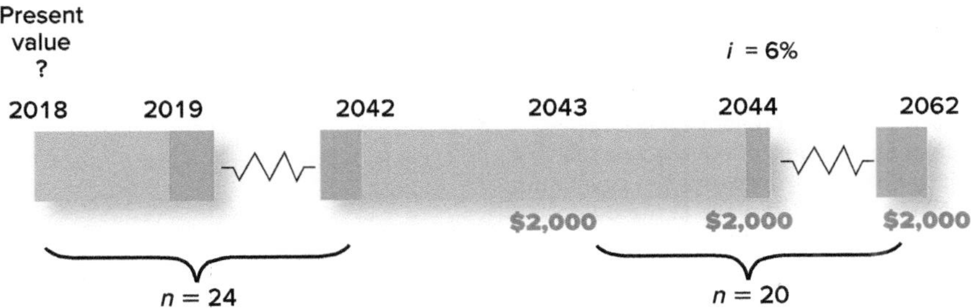

We can calculate the present value of the annuity using a two-step process. The first step computes the present value of the annuity as of December 31, 2042, by multiplying the annuity amount by the 20-period ordinary annuity factor.

$$PVA = \$2{,}000 \text{ (annuity amount)} \times 11.46992^{*} = \$22{,}940$$

*Present value of an ordinary annuity of \$1: $n = 20$, $i = 6\%$

This is the present value as of December 31, 2042. This single amount is then reduced to present value as of December 31, 2018, by a second calculation.

$$PV = \$22{,}940 \text{ (future amount)} \times 0.24698^{*} = \$5{,}666$$

*Present value of \$1: $n = 24$, $i = 6\%$

Stridewell would have to contribute \$5,666 at the end of 2018 to fund the estimated pension benefits earned by its employee in 2018. Viewed in reverse, \$5,666 invested now at 6% will accumulate a fund balance of \$22,940 at December 31, 2042. If the fund balance remains invested at 6%, \$2,000 can be withdrawn each year for 20 years before the fund is depleted.

Among the other situations you'll encounter using present value techniques are valuing notes (Chapters 10 and 14) and other postretirement benefits (Chapter 17).

Summary of Time Value of Money Concepts

Illustration 6–22 summarizes the time value of money concepts discussed in this chapter.

Illustration 6–22
Summary of Time Value of Money Concepts

Concept	Summary	Formula	Table
Future value (FV) of \$1	The amount of money that a dollar will grow to at some point in the future.	$FV = \$1\,(1+i)^n$	1
Present value (PV) of \$1	The amount of money today that is equivalent to a given amount to be received or paid in the future.	$PV = \frac{\$1}{(1+i)^n}$	2
Future value of an ordinary annuity (FVA) of \$1	The future value of a series of equal-sized cash flows with the first payment taking place at the end of the first compounding period.	$FVA = \frac{(1+i)^n - 1}{i}$	3
Present value of an ordinary annuity (PVA) of \$1	The present value of a series of equal-sized cash flows with the first payment taking place at the end of the first compounding period.	$PVA = \frac{1 - \frac{1}{(1+i)^n}}{i}$	4
Future value of an annuity due (FVAD) of \$1	The future value of a series of equal-sized cash flows with the first payment taking place at the beginning of the annuity period.	$FVAD = \left[\frac{(1+i)^n - 1}{i}\right] \times (1+i)$	5
Present value of an annuity due (PVAD) of \$1	The present value of a series of equal-sized cash flows with the first payment taking place at the beginning of the annuity period.	$PVAD = PVA\left[\frac{1 - \frac{1}{(1+i)^n}}{i}\right] \times (1+i)$	6

Financial Reporting Case Solution

© Shutterstock/Gabriel Petrescu

1. **Why was Quezada to receive $152 million rather than the $338 million lottery prize?** *(p. 326)* Quezada chose to receive his lottery winnings in one lump payment immediately rather than in 30 installment payments. The state calculates the present value of the payments, withholds the necessary federal and state income tax, and pays Quezada the remainder.
2. **What interest rate did the state of New Jersey use to calculate the $152 million lump-sum payment** *(p. 331)* Assuming equal annual installment payments beginning immediately, the amount of the payments is determined by dividing $338 million by 30 periods:

$338 million ÷ 30 =	$11,266,667
Less: 28% income tax	(3,154,667)
Net-of-tax payment	$ 8,112,000

Because the first payment is made immediately, this is an annuity due situation. We must find the interest rate that provides a present value of $152 million. $152,000,000 ÷ $8,112,000 is 18.738, the present value factor that equates the payments and their present value. Searching for that factor in row 30 of Table 6 at the end of the text, we find the factor closest to 18.738 in the 3.5% column. So, the interest rate used by the state was approximately 3.5%.

3. **What are some of the accounting applications that incorporate the time value of money into valuation?** *(p. 334)* Accounting applications that incorporate the time value of money techniques into valuation include the valuation of long-term notes receivable and various long-term liabilities that include bonds, notes, leases, pension obligations, and other postretirement benefits. We study these in detail in later chapters. ●

The Bottom Line

- **LO6–1** A dollar today is worth more than a dollar to be received in the future. The difference between the present value of cash flows and their future value represents the time value of money. Interest is the rent paid for the use of money over time. (*p. 314*)
- **LO6–2** The future value of a single amount is the amount of money that a dollar will grow to at some point in the future. It is computed by *multiplying* the single amount by $(1 + i)^n$, where i is the interest rate and n the number of compounding periods. The Future Value of $1 table allows for the calculation of future value for any single amount by providing the factors for various combinations of i and n. (*p. 315*)
- **LO6–3** The present value of a single amount is the amount of money today that is equivalent to a given amount to be received or paid in the future. It is computed by *dividing* the future amount by $(1 + i)^n$. The Present Value of $1 table simplifies the calculation of the present value of any future amount. (*p. 316*)
- **LO6–4** There are four variables in the process of adjusting single cash flow amounts for the time value of money: present value (PV), future value (FV), i and n. If you know any three of these, the fourth can be computed easily. (*p. 317*)
- **LO6–5** An annuity is a series of equal-sized cash flows occurring over equal intervals of time. An ordinary annuity exists when the cash flows occur at the end of each period. An annuity due exists when the cash flows occur at the beginning of each period. (*p. 323*)
- **LO6–6** The future value of an ordinary annuity (FVA) is the future value of a series of equal-sized cash flows with the first payment taking place at the end of the first compounding period. The last payment will not earn any interest since it is made at the end of the annuity period. The future value of an annuity due (FVAD) is the future value of a series of equal-sized cash flows with the first payment taking place at the beginning of the annuity period (the beginning of the first compounding period). (*p. 324*)
- **LO6–7** The present value of an ordinary annuity (PVA) is the present value of a series of equal-sized cash flows with the first payment taking place at the end of the first compounding period. The present value of an

annuity due (PVAD) is the present value of a series of equal-sized cash flows with the first payment taking place at the beginning of the annuity period. The present value of a deferred annuity is the present value of a series of equal-sized cash flows with the first payment taking place more than one time period after the date of the agreement. (*p. 325*)

- LO6–8 In present value problems involving annuities, there are four variables: PVA or PVAD, the annuity amount, the number of compounding periods (n) and the interest rate (i). If you know any three of these, you can determine the fourth. (*p. 330*)
- LO6–9 Most accounting applications of the time value of money involve the present values of annuities. The initial valuation of long-term bonds is determined by calculating the present value of the periodic stated interest payments and the present value of the lump-sum payment made at maturity. Certain leases require the lessee to compute the present value of future lease payments to value the leased asset and corresponding lease obligation. Also, pension plans require the payment of deferred annuities to retirees. (*p. 333*)

Questions For Review of Key Topics

Q 6–1 Define interest.

Q 6–2 Explain compound interest.

Q 6–3 What would cause the annual interest rate to be different from the annual effective rate or yield?

Q 6–4 Identify the three items of information necessary to calculate the future value of a single amount.

Q 6–5 Define the present value of a single amount.

Q 6–6 Explain the difference between monetary and nonmonetary assets and liabilities.

Q 6–7 What is an annuity?

Q 6–8 Explain the difference between an ordinary annuity and an annuity due.

Q 6–9 Explain the relationship between Table 2, Present Value of $1, and Table 4, Present Value of an Ordinary Annuity of $1.

Q 6–10 Prepare a time diagram for the present value of a four-year ordinary annuity of $200. Assume an interest rate of 10% per year.

Q 6–11 Prepare a time diagram for the present value of a four-year annuity due of $200. Assume an interest rate of 10% per year.

Q 6–12 What is a deferred annuity?

Q 6–13 Assume that you borrowed $500 from a friend and promised to repay the loan in five equal annual installments beginning one year from today. Your friend wants to be reimbursed for the time value of money at an 8% annual rate. Explain how you would compute the required annual payment.

Q 6–14 Compute the required annual payment in Question 6–13.

Q 6–15 Explain how the time value of money concept is incorporated into the valuation of certain leases.

Brief Exercises

BE 6–1
Simple versus compound interest
● LO6–1

Fran Smith has two investment opportunities. The interest rate for both investments is 8%. Interest on the first investment will compound annually while interest on the second will compound quarterly. Which investment opportunity should Fran choose? Why?

BE 6–2
Future value; single amount
● LO6–2

Bill O'Brien would like to take his wife, Mary, on a trip three years from now to Europe to celebrate their 40th anniversary. He has just received a $20,000 inheritance from an uncle and intends to invest it for the trip. Bill estimates the trip will cost $23,500 and he believes he can earn 5% interest, compounded annually, on his investment. Will he be able to pay for the trip with the accumulated investment amount?

BE 6–3
Future value; solving for unknown; single amount
● LO6–4

Refer to the situation described in BE 6–2. Assume that the trip will cost $26,600. What interest rate, compounded annually, must Bill earn to accumulate enough to pay for the trip?

BE 6–4
Present value; single amount
● LO6–3

John has an investment opportunity that promises to pay him $16,000 in four years. He could earn a 6% annual return investing his money elsewhere. What is the maximum amount he would be willing to invest in this opportunity?

BE 6–5
Present value; solving for unknown; single amount
● LO6–4

Refer to the situation described in BE 6–4. Suppose the opportunity requires John to invest $13,200 today. What is the interest rate John would earn on this investment?

BE 6–6
Future value; ordinary annuity
● LO6–6

Leslie McCormack is in the spring quarter of her freshman year of college. She and her friends already are planning a trip to Europe after graduation in a little over three years. Leslie would like to contribute to a savings account over the next three years in order to accumulate enough money to take the trip. Assuming an interest rate of 4%, compounded quarterly, how much will she accumulate in three years by depositing $500 at the *end* of each of the next 12 quarters, beginning three months from now?

BE 6–7
Future value; annuity due
● LO6–6

Refer to the situation described in BE 6–6. How much will Leslie accumulate in three years by depositing $500 at the *beginning* of each of the next 12 quarters?

BE 6–8
Present value; ordinary annuity
● LO6–7

Canliss Mining Company borrowed money from a local bank. The note the company signed requires five annual installment payments of $10,000 beginning one year from today. The interest rate on the note is 7%. What amount did Canliss borrow?

BE 6–9
Present value; annuity due
● LO6–7

Refer to the situation described in BE 6–8. What amount did Canliss borrow assuming that the first $10,000 payment was due immediately?

BE 6–10
Deferred annuity
● LO6–7

Refer to the situation described in BE 6–8. What amount did Canliss borrow assuming that the first of the five annual $10,000 payments was not due for three years?

BE 6–11
Solve for unknown; annuity
● LO6–8

Kingsley Toyota borrowed $100,000 from a local bank. The loan requires Kingsley to pay 10 equal annual installments beginning one year from today. Assuming an interest rate of 8%, what is the amount of each annual installment payment?

BE 6–12
Price of a bond
● LO6–9

On December 31, 2018, Interlink Communications issued 6% stated rate bonds with a face amount of $100 million. The bonds mature on December 31, 2048. Interest is payable annually on each December 31, beginning in 2019. Determine the price of the bonds on December 31, 2018, assuming that the market rate of interest for similar bonds was 7%.

BE 6–13
Lease payment
● LO6–9

On September 30, 2018, Ferguson Imports leased a warehouse. Terms of the lease require Ferguson to make 10 annual lease payments of $55,000 with the first payment due immediately. Accounting standards require the company to record a lease liability when recording this type of lease. Assuming an 8% interest rate, at what amount should Ferguson record the lease liability on September 30, 2018, before the first payment is made?

Exercises

E 6–1
Future value; single amount
● LO6–2

Determine the future value of the following single amounts:

	Invested Amount	Interest Rate	No. of Periods
1.	$15,000	6%	12
2.	20,000	8	10
3.	30,000	12	20
4.	50,000	4	12

E 6–2
Future value; single amounts
● LO6–2

Determine the future value of $10,000 under each of the following sets of assumptions:

	Annual Rate	Period Invested	Interest Compounded
1.	10%	10 years	Semiannually
2.	12	5 years	Quarterly
3.	24	30 months	Monthly

E 6–3
Present value; single amounts
● LO6–3

Determine the present value of the following single amounts:

	Future Amount	Interest Rate	No. of Periods
1.	$20,000	7%	10
2.	14,000	8	12
3.	25,000	12	20
4.	40,000	10	8

E 6–4
Present value; multiple, unequal amounts
● LO6–3

Determine the combined present value as of December 31, 2018, of the following four payments to be received at the end of each of the designated years, assuming an annual interest rate of 8%.

Payment	Year Received
$5,000	2019
6,000	2020
8,000	2022
9,000	2024

E 6–5
Noninterest-bearing note; single payment
● LO6–3

The Field Detergent Company sold merchandise to the Abel Company on June 30, 2018. Payment was made in the form of a noninterest-bearing note requiring Abel to pay $85,000 on June 30, 2020. Assume that a 10% interest rate properly reflects the time value of money in this situation.

Required:
Calculate the amount at which Field should record the note receivable and corresponding sales revenue on June 30, 2018.

E 6–6
Solving for unknowns; single amounts
● LO6–4

For each of the following situations involving single amounts, solve for the unknown (?). Assume that interest is compounded annually. (i = interest rate, and n = number of years)

	Present Value	Future Value	i	n
1.	?	$ 40,000	10%	5
2.	$36,289	65,000	?	10
3.	15,884	40,000	8	?
4.	46,651	100,000	?	8
5.	15,376	?	7	20

E 6–7
Future value; annuities
● LO6–6

Wiseman Video plans to make four annual deposits of $2,000 each to a special building fund. The fund's assets will be invested in mortgage instruments expected to pay interest at 12% on the fund's balance. Using the appropriate annuity table, determine how much will be accumulated in the fund on December 31, 2021, under each of the following situations:

1. The first deposit is made on December 31, 2018, and interest is compounded annually.
2. The first deposit is made on December 31, 2017, and interest is compounded annually.
3. The first deposit is made on December 31, 2017, and interest is compounded quarterly.
4. The first deposit is made on December 31, 2017, interest is compounded annually, *and* interest earned is withdrawn at the end of each year.

E 6–8
Present value; annuities
● LO6–7

Using the appropriate present value table and assuming a 12% annual interest rate, determine the present value on December 31, 2018, of a five-period annual annuity of $5,000 under each of the following situations:

1. The first payment is received on December 31, 2019, and interest is compounded annually.
2. The first payment is received on December 31, 2018, and interest is compounded annually.
3. The first payment is received on December 31, 2019, and interest is compounded quarterly.

E 6–9
Solving for unknowns; annuities
● LO6–8

For each of the following situations involving annuities, solve for the unknown (?). Assume that interest is compounded annually and that all annuity amounts are received at the *end* of each period. (i = interest rate, and n = number of years)

	Present Value	Annuity Amount	*i*	*n*
1.	?	$ 3,000	8%	5
2.	$242,980	75,000	?	4
3.	161,214	20,000	9	?
4.	500,000	80,518	?	8
5.	250,000	?	10	4

E 6–10
Future value; solving for annuities and single amount
● LO6–4, LO6–8

John Rider wants to accumulate $100,000 to be used for his daughter's college education. He would like to have the amount available on December 31, 2023. Assume that the funds will accumulate in a certificate of deposit paying 8% interest compounded annually.

Required:

Answer each of the following independent questions.

1. If John were to deposit a single amount, how much would he have to invest on December 31, 2018?
2. If John were to make five equal deposits on each December 31, beginning on December 31, 2019, what is the required amount of each deposit?
3. If John were to make five equal deposits on each December 31, beginning on December 31, 2018, what is the required amount of each deposit?

E 6–11
Future and present value
● LO6–3, LO6–6, LO6–7

Answer each of the following independent questions.

1. Alex Meir recently won a lottery and has the option of receiving one of the following three prizes: (1) $64,000 cash immediately, (2) $20,000 cash immediately and a six-period annuity of $8,000 beginning one year from today, or (3) a six-period annuity of $13,000 beginning one year from today. Assuming an interest rate of 6%, which option should Alex choose?
2. The Weimer Corporation wants to accumulate a sum of money to repay certain debts due on December 31, 2027. Weimer will make annual deposits of $100,000 into a special bank account at the end of each of 10 years beginning December 31, 2018. Assuming that the bank account pays 7% interest compounded annually, what will be the fund balance after the last payment is made on December 31, 2027?

E 6–12
Deferred annuities
● LO6–7

Lincoln Company purchased merchandise from Grandville Corp. on September 30, 2018. Payment was made in the form of a noninterest-bearing note requiring Lincoln to make six annual payments of $5,000 on each September 30, beginning on September 30, 2021.

Required:

Calculate the amount at which Lincoln should record the note payable and corresponding purchases on September 30, 2018, assuming that an interest rate of 10% properly reflects the time value of money in this situation.

E 6–13
Solving for unknown annuity payment
● LO6–8

Don James purchased a new automobile for $20,000. Don made a cash down payment of $5,000 and agreed to pay the remaining balance in 30 monthly installments, beginning one month from the date of purchase. Financing is available at a 24% *annual* interest rate.

Required:

Calculate the amount of the required monthly payment.

E 6–14
Solving for unknown interest rate
● LO6–8

Lang Warehouses borrowed $100,000 from a bank and signed a note requiring 20 annual payments of $13,388 beginning one year from the date of the agreement.

Required:

Determine the interest rate implicit in this agreement.

E 6–15
Solving for unknown annuity amount
● LO6–8

Sandy Kupchack just graduated from State University with a bachelor's degree in history. During her four years at the university, Sandy accumulated $12,000 in student loans. She asks for your help in determining the amount of the *quarterly* loan payment. She tells you that the loan must be paid back in five years and that the annual interest rate is 8%. Payments begin in three months.

Required:

Determine Sandy's quarterly loan payment.

E 6–16
Deferred annuities; solving for annuity amount
● LO6–7, LO6–8

On April 1, 2018, John Vaughn purchased appliances from the Acme Appliance Company for $1,200. In order to increase sales, Acme allows customers to pay in installments and will defer any payments for six months. John will make 18 equal monthly payments, beginning October 1, 2018. The annual interest rate implicit in this agreement is 24%.

Required:

Calculate the monthly payment necessary for John to pay for his purchases.

E 6–17
Price of a bond
● LO6–9

On September 30, 2018, the San Fillipo Corporation issued 8% stated rate bonds with a face amount of $300 million. The bonds mature on September 30, 2038 (20 years). The market rate of interest for similar bonds was 10%. Interest is paid semiannually on March 31 and September 30.

Required:
Determine the price of the bonds on September 30, 2018.

E 6–18
Price of a bond; interest expense
● LO6–9

On June 30, 2018, Singleton Computers issued 6% stated rate bonds with a face amount of $200 million. The bonds mature on June 30, 2033 (15 years). The market rate of interest for similar bond issues was 5% (2.5% semiannual rate). Interest is paid semiannually (3%) on June 30 and December 31, beginning on December 31, 2018.

Required:
1. Determine the price of the bonds on June 30, 2018.
2. Calculate the interest expense Singleton reports in 2018 for these bonds.

E 6–19
Lease payments
● LO6–9

On June 30, 2018, Fly-By-Night Airlines leased a jumbo jet from Boeing Corporation. The terms of the lease require Fly-By-Night to make 20 annual payments of $400,000 on each June 30. Generally accepted accounting principles require this lease to be recorded as a liability for the present value of scheduled payments. Assume that a 7% interest rate properly reflects the time value of money in this situation.

Required:
1. At what amount should Fly-By-Night record the lease liability on June 30, 2018, assuming that the first payment will be made on June 30, 2019?
2. At what amount should Fly-By-Night record the lease liability on June 30, 2018, *before* any payments are made, assuming that the first payment will be made on June 30, 2018?

E 6–20
Lease payments; solve for unknown interest rate
● LO6–8, LO6–9

On March 31, 2018, Southwest Gas leased equipment from a supplier and agreed to pay $200,000 annually for 20 years beginning March 31, 2019. Generally accepted accounting principles require that a liability be recorded for this lease agreement for the present value of scheduled payments. Accordingly, at inception of the lease, Southwest recorded a $2,293,984 lease liability.

Required:
Determine the interest rate implicit in the lease agreement.

E 6–21
Concepts; terminology
● LO6–1 through LO6–3, LO6–5

Listed below are several terms and phrases associated with concepts discussed in the chapter. Pair each item from List A with the item from List B (by letter) that is most appropriately associated with it.

List A	List B
____ 1. Interest	a. First cash flow occurs one period after agreement begins
____ 2. Monetary asset	b. The rate at which money will actually grow during a year
____ 3. Compound interest	c. First cash flow occurs on the first day of the agreement
____ 4. Simple interest	d. The amount of money that a dollar will grow to
____ 5. Annuity	e. Amount of money paid/received in excess of amount borrowed/lent
____ 6. Present value of a single amount	f. Obligation to pay a sum of cash, the amount of which is fixed
____ 7. Annuity due	g. Money can be invested today and grow to a larger amount
____ 8. Future value of a single amount	h. No fixed dollar amount attached
____ 9. Ordinary annuity	i. Computed by multiplying an invested amount by the interest rate
____ 10. Effective rate or yield	j. Interest calculated on invested amount plus accumulated interest
____ 11. Nonmonetary asset	k. A series of equal-sized cash flows
____ 12. Time value of money	l. Amount of money required today that is equivalent to a given future amount
____ 13. Monetary liability	m. Claim to receive a fixed amount of money

Problems

P 6–1
Analysis of alternatives
● LO6–3, LO6–7

Esquire Company needs to acquire a molding machine to be used in its manufacturing process. Two types of machines that would be appropriate are presently on the market. The company has determined the following:

Machine A could be purchased for $48,000. It will last 10 years with annual maintenance costs of $1,000 per year. After 10 years the machine can be sold for $5,000.

Machine B could be purchased for $40,000. It also will last 10 years and will require maintenance costs of $4,000 in year three, $5,000 in year six, and $6,000 in year eight. After 10 years, the machine will have no salvage value.

Required:
Determine which machine Esquire should purchase. Assume an interest rate of 8% properly reflects the time value of money in this situation and that maintenance costs are paid at the end of each year. Ignore income tax considerations.

P 6–2
Present and future value
● LO6–6, LO6–7, LO6–9

Johnstone Company is facing several decisions regarding investing and financing activities. Address each decision independently.

1. On June 30, 2018, the Johnstone Company purchased equipment from Genovese Corp. Johnstone agreed to pay Genovese $10,000 on the purchase date and the balance in five annual installments of $8,000 on each June 30 beginning June 30, 2019. Assuming that an interest rate of 10% properly reflects the time value of money in this situation, at what amount should Johnstone value the equipment?
2. Johnstone needs to accumulate sufficient funds to pay a $400,000 debt that comes due on December 31, 2023. The company will accumulate the funds by making five equal annual deposits to an account paying 6% interest compounded annually. Determine the required annual deposit if the first deposit is made on December 31, 2018.
3. On January 1, 2018, Johnstone leased an office building. Terms of the lease require Johnstone to make 20 annual lease payments of $120,000 beginning on January 1, 2018. A 10% interest rate is implicit in the lease agreement. At what amount should Johnstone record the lease liability on January 1, 2018, *before* any lease payments are made?

P 6–3
Analysis of alternatives
● LO6–3, LO6–7

Harding Company is in the process of purchasing several large pieces of equipment from Danning Machine Corporation. Several financing alternatives have been offered by Danning:

1. Pay $1,000,000 in cash immediately.
2. Pay $420,000 immediately and the remainder in 10 annual installments of $80,000, with the first installment due in one year.
3. Make 10 annual installments of $135,000 with the first payment due immediately.
4. Make one lump-sum payment of $1,500,000 five years from date of purchase.

Required:
Determine the best alternative for Harding, assuming that Harding can borrow funds at an 8% interest rate.

P 6–4
Investment analysis
● LO6–3, LO6–7

John Wiggins is considering the purchase of a small restaurant. The purchase price listed by the seller is $800,000. John has used past financial information to estimate that the net cash flows (cash inflows less cash outflows) generated by the restaurant would be as follows:

Years	Amount
1–6	$80,000
7	70,000
8	60,000
9	50,000
10	40,000

If purchased, the restaurant would be held for 10 years and then sold for an estimated $700,000.

Required:
Assuming that John desires a 10% rate of return on this investment, should the restaurant be purchased? (Assume that all cash flows occur at the end of the year.)

P 6–5
Investment decision; varying rates
● LO6–3, LO6–7

John and Sally Claussen are considering the purchase of a hardware store from John Duggan. The Claussens anticipate that the store will generate cash flows of $70,000 per year for 20 years. At the end of 20 years, they intend to sell the store for an estimated $400,000. The Claussens will finance the investment with a variable rate mortgage. Interest rates will increase twice during the 20-year life of the mortgage. Accordingly, the Claussens' desired rate of return on this investment varies as follows:

Years 1–5	8%
Years 6–10	10%
Years 11–20	12%

Required:
What is the maximum amount the Claussens should pay John Duggan for the hardware store? (Assume that all cash flows occur at the end of the year.)

P 6–6
Solving for unknowns
● LO6–3, LO6–8

The following situations should be considered independently.

1. John Jamison wants to accumulate $60,000 for a down payment on a small business. He will invest $30,000 today in a bank account paying 8% interest compounded annually. Approximately how long will it take John to reach his goal?
2. The Jasmine Tea Company purchased merchandise from a supplier for $28,700. Payment was a noninterest-bearing note requiring Jasmine to make five annual payments of $7,000 beginning one year from the date of purchase. What is the interest rate implicit in this agreement?
3. Sam Robinson borrowed $10,000 from a friend and promised to pay the loan in 10 equal annual installments beginning one year from the date of the loan. Sam's friend would like to be reimbursed for the time value of money at a 9% annual rate. What is the annual payment Sam must make to pay back his friend?

P 6–7
Solving for unknown
● LO6–8

Lowlife Company defaulted on a $250,000 loan that was due on December 31, 2018. The bank has agreed to allow Lowlife to repay the $250,000 by making a series of equal annual payments beginning on December 31, 2019.

Required:

1. Calculate the required annual payment if the bank's interest rate is 10% and four payments are to be made.
2. Calculate the required annual payment if the bank's interest rate is 8% and five payments are to be made.
3. If the bank's interest rate is 10%, how many annual payments of $51,351 would be required to repay the debt?
4. If three payments of $104,087 are to be made, what interest rate is the bank charging Lowlife?

P 6–8
Deferred annuities
● LO6–7

On January 1, 2018, the Montgomery Company agreed to purchase a building by making six payments. The first three are to be $25,000 each, and will be paid on December 31, 2018, 2019, and 2020. The last three are to be $40,000 each and will be paid on December 31, 2021, 2022, and 2023. Montgomery borrowed other money at a 10% annual rate.

Required:

1. At what amount should Montgomery record the note payable and corresponding cost of the building on January 1, 2018?
2. How much interest expense on this note will Montgomery recognize in 2018?

P 6–9
Deferred annuities
● LO6–7

John Roberts is 55 years old and has been asked to accept early retirement from his company. The company has offered John three alternative compensation packages to induce John to retire.

1. $180,000 cash payment to be paid immediately
2. A 20-year annuity of $16,000 beginning immediately
3. A 10-year annuity of $50,000 beginning at age 65

Required:

Which alternative should John choose assuming that he is able to invest funds at a 7% rate?

P 6–10
Noninterest-bearing note; annuity and lump-sum payment
● LO6–3, LO6–7

On January 1, 2018, The Barrett Company purchased merchandise from a supplier. Payment was a noninterest-bearing note requiring five annual payments of $20,000 on each December 31 beginning on December 31, 2018, and a lump-sum payment of $100,000 on December 31, 2022. A 10% interest rate properly reflects the time value of money in this situation.

Required:

Calculate the amount at which Barrett should record the note payable and corresponding merchandise purchased on January 1, 2018.

P 6–11
Solving for unknown lease payment
● LO6–8, LO6–9

Benning Manufacturing Company is negotiating with a customer for the lease of a large machine manufactured by Benning. The machine has a cash price of $800,000. Benning wants to be reimbursed for financing the machine at an 8% annual interest rate.

Required:

1. Determine the required lease payment if the lease agreement calls for 10 equal annual payments beginning immediately.
2. Determine the required lease payment if the first of 10 annual payments will be made one year from the date of the agreement.
3. Determine the required lease payment if the first of 10 annual payments will be made immediately and Benning will be able to sell the machine to another customer for $50,000 at the end of the 10-year lease.

P 6–12
Solving for unknown lease payment; compounding periods of varying length
● LO6–8, LO6–9

[This is a variation of P 6-11 focusing on compounding periods of varying length.]

Benning Manufacturing Company is negotiating with a customer for the lease of a large machine manufactured by Benning. The machine has a cash price of $800,000. Benning wants to be reimbursed for financing the machine at a 12% annual interest rate over the five-year lease term.

Required:

1. Determine the required lease payment if the lease agreement calls for 10 equal semiannual payments beginning six months from the date of the agreement.
2. Determine the required lease payment if the lease agreement calls for 20 equal quarterly payments beginning immediately.
3. Determine the required lease payment if the lease agreement calls for 60 equal monthly payments beginning one month from the date of the agreement. The present value of an ordinary annuity factor for $n = 60$ and $i = 1\%$ is 44.9550.

P 6–13
Lease vs. buy alternatives
● LO6–3, LO6–7, LO6–9

Kiddy Toy Corporation needs to acquire the use of a machine to be used in its manufacturing process. The machine needed is manufactured by Lollie Corp. The machine can be used for 10 years and then sold for $10,000 at the end of its useful life. Lollie has presented Kiddy with the following options:

1. *Buy machine.* The machine could be purchased for $160,000 in cash. All insurance costs, which approximate $5,000 per year, would be paid by Kiddy.
2. *Lease machine.* The machine could be leased for a 10-year period for an annual lease payment of $25,000 with the first payment due immediately. All insurance costs will be paid for by the Lollie Corp. and the machine will revert back to Lollie at the end of the 10-year period.

Required:

Assuming that a 12% interest rate properly reflects the time value of money in this situation and that all maintenance and insurance costs are paid at the end of each year, determine which option Kiddy should choose. Ignore income tax considerations.

P 6–14
Deferred annuities; pension obligation
● LO6–7, LO6–9

Three employees of the Horizon Distributing Company will receive annual pension payments from the company when they retire. The employees will receive their annual payments for as long as they live. Life expectancy for each employee is 15 years beyond retirement. Their names, the amount of their annual pension payments, and the date they will receive their first payment are shown below:

Employee	Annual Payment	Date of First Payment
Tinkers	$20,000	12/31/21
Evers	25,000	12/31/22
Chance	30,000	12/31/23

Required:

1. Compute the present value of the pension obligation to these three employees as of December 31, 2018. Assume an 11% interest rate.
2. The company wants to have enough cash invested at December 31, 2021, to provide for all three employees. To accumulate enough cash, they will make three equal annual contributions to a fund that will earn 11% interest compounded annually. The first contribution will be made on December 31, 2018. Compute the amount of this required annual contribution.

P 6–15
Bonds and leases; deferred annuities
● LO6–3, LO6–7, LO6–9

On the last day of its fiscal year ending December 31, 2018, the Sedgwick & Reams (S&R) Glass Company completed two financing arrangements. The funds provided by these initiatives will allow the company to expand its operations.

1. S&R issued 8% stated rate bonds with a face amount of $100 million. The bonds mature on December 31, 2036 (20 years). The market rate of interest for similar bond issues was 9% (4.5% semiannual rate). Interest is paid semiannually (4%) on June 30 and December 31, beginning on June 30, 2019.
2. The company leased two manufacturing facilities. Lease A requires 20 annual lease payments of $200,000 beginning on January 1, 2019. Lease B also is for 20 years, beginning January 1, 2019. Terms of the lease require 17 annual lease payments of $220,000 beginning on January 1, 2022. Generally accepted accounting principles require both leases to be recorded as liabilities for the present value of the scheduled payments. Assume that a 10% interest rate properly reflects the time value of money for the lease obligations.

Required:

What amounts will appear in S&R's December 31, 2018, balance sheet for the bonds and for the leases?

Broaden Your Perspective

Apply your critical-thinking ability to the knowledge you've gained. These cases will provide you an opportunity to develop your research, analysis, judgment, and communication skills. You also will work with other students, integrate what you've learned, apply it in real-world situations, and consider its global and ethical ramifications. This practice will broaden your knowledge and further develop your decision-making abilities.

Ethics Case 6–1
Rate of return
● LO6–1

The Damon Investment Company manages a mutual fund composed mostly of speculative stocks. You recently saw an ad claiming that investments in the funds have been earning a rate of return of 21%. This rate seemed quite high so you called a friend who works for one of Damon's competitors. The friend told you that the 21% return figure was determined by dividing the two-year appreciation on investments in the fund by the average investment. In other words, $100 invested in the fund two years ago would have grown to $121 ($21 ÷ $100 = 21%).

Required:
Discuss the ethics of the 21% return claim made by the Damon Investment Company.

Analysis Case 6–2
Bonus alternatives; present value analysis
● LO6–3, LO6–7

Sally Hamilton has performed well as the chief financial officer of the Maxtech Computer Company and has earned a bonus. She has a choice among the following three bonus plans:

1. A $50,000 cash bonus paid now.
2. A $10,000 annual cash bonus to be paid each year over the next six years, with the first $10,000 paid now.
3. A three-year $22,000 annual cash bonus with the first payment due three years from now.

Required:
Evaluate the three alternative bonus plans. Sally can earn a 6% annual return on her investments.

Communication Case 6–3
Present value of annuities
● LO6–7

Harvey Alexander, an all-league professional football player, has just declared free agency. Two teams, the San Francisco 49ers and the Dallas Cowboys, have made Harvey the following offers to obtain his services:

49ers:	$1 million signing bonus payable immediately and an annual salary of $1.5 million for the five-year term of the contract.
Cowboys:	$2.5 million signing bonus payable immediately and an annual salary of $1 million for the five-year term of the contract.

With both contracts, the annual salary will be paid in one lump sum at the end of the football season.

Required:
You have been hired as a consultant to Harvey's agent, Phil Marks, to evaluate the two contracts. Write a short letter to Phil with your recommendation including the method you used to reach your conclusion. Assume that Harvey has no preference between the two teams and that the decision will be based entirely on monetary considerations. Also assume that Harvey can invest his money and earn an 8% annual return.

Analysis Case 6–4
Present value of an annuity
● LO6–7

On a rainy afternoon two years ago, John Smiley left work early to attend a family birthday party. Eleven minutes later, a careening truck slammed into his SUV on the freeway causing John to spend two months in a coma. Now he can't hold a job or make everyday decisions and is in need of constant care. Last week, the 40-year-old Smiley won an out-of-court settlement from the truck driver's company. He was awarded payment for all medical costs and attorney fees, plus a lump-sum settlement of $2,330,716. At the time of the accident, John was president of his family's business and earned approximately $200,000 per year. He had anticipated working 25 more years before retirement.[9]

John's sister, an acquaintance of yours from college, has asked you to explain to her how the attorneys came up with the settlement amount. "They said it was based on his lost future income and a 7% rate of some kind," she explained. "But it was all 'legal-speak' to me."

Required:
How was the amount of the lump-sum settlement determined? Create a calculation that might help John's sister understand.

Judgment Case 6–5
Replacement decision
● LO6–3, LO6–7

Hughes Corporation is considering replacing a machine used in the manufacturing process with a new, more efficient model. The purchase price of the new machine is $150,000 and the old machine can be sold for $100,000. Output for the two machines is identical; they will both be used to produce the same amount of product for five years. However, the annual operating costs of the old machine are $18,000 compared to $10,000 for the new

[9]This case is based on actual events.

machine. Also, the new machine has a salvage value of $25,000, but the old machine will be worthless at the end of the five years.

Required:

Should the company sell the old machine and purchase the new model? Assume that an 8% rate properly reflects the time value of money in this situation and that all operating costs are paid at the end of the year. Ignore the effect of the decision on income taxes.

Real World Case 6–6
Zero-coupon bonds; Johnson & Johnson
● LO6–3, LO6–9
Real World Financials

Johnson & Johnson is one of the world's largest manufacturers of health care products. The company's December 31, 2015, financial statements included the following information in the long-term debt disclosure note:

	($ in millions) 2015
Zero-coupon convertible subordinated debentures, due 2020	$137

The bonds were issued at the beginning of 2000. The disclosure note stated that the effective interest rate for these bonds is 3% annually. Some of the original convertible bonds have been converted into Johnson & Johnson shares of stock. The $137 million is the present value of the bonds not converted and thus reported in the financial statements. Each individual bond has a maturity value (face amount) of $1,000. The maturity value indicates the amount that Johnson & Johnson will pay bondholders at the beginning of 2020. Zero-coupon bonds pay no cash interest during the term to maturity. The company is "accreting" (gradually increasing) the issue price to maturity value using the bonds' effective interest rate computed on a semiannual basis.

Required:

1. Determine the maturity value of the zero-coupon bonds that Johnson & Johnson will pay bondholders at the beginning of 2020.
2. Determine the issue price at the beginning of 2000 of a single, $1,000 maturity-value bond.

Real World Case 6–7
Leases; Southwest Airlines
● LO6–3, LO6–9
Real World Financials

Southwest Airlines provides scheduled air transportation services in the United States. Like many airlines, Southwest leases many of its planes from Boeing Company. In its long-term debt disclosure note included in the financial statements for the year ended December 31, 2015, the company listed $324 million in lease obligations. The existing leases had an approximate ten-year remaining life and future lease payments average approximately $45 million per year.

Required:

1. Determine the effective interest rate the company used to determine the lease liability assuming that lease payments are made at the end of each fiscal year.
2. Repeat requirement 1 assuming that lease payments are made at the beginning of each fiscal year.

Continuing Cases

Target Case
● LO6-3, LO6-7
LO6-9

Target Corporation prepares its financial statements according to U.S. GAAP. Target's financial statements and disclosure notes for the year ended January 30, 2016, are available in Connect. This material is also available under the Investor Relations link at the company's website (www.target.com). Target leases most of its facilities.

Required:

1. Refer to disclosure note 22 following Target's financial statements. What is the amount reported for "capital" leases (shown as the present value of minimum lease payments)? What is the total of those lease payments? What accounts for the difference between the two amounts?
2. What is the total of the operating lease payments? New lease accounting guidance (discussed in Chapter 15) will require companies to report operating leases at present value as well as capital leases (now called finance leases). If Target had used the new lease accounting guidance in its 2016 financial statements, what would be the amount reported for operating leases? Hint: Assume the payments "after 2020" are to be paid evenly over a 16 years period and all payments are at the end of years indicated. Target indicates elsewhere in its financial statements that 6% is an appropriate discount rate for its leases.

Air France–KLM Case

● LO6–9

IFRS

Air France–KLM (AF), a Franco-Dutch company, prepares its financial statements according to International Financial Reporting Standards. AF's financial statements and disclosure notes for the year ended December 31, 2015, are available in Connect. This material is also available under the Finance link at the company's website (www.airfranceklm.com.) The presentation of financial statements often differs between U.S. GAAP and IFRS, particularly with respect to the balance sheet.

Using IFRS, companies discount their pension obligations using an interest rate approximating the average interest rate on high quality corporate bonds. U.S. GAAP allows much more flexibility in the choice of a discount rate. By both sets of standards, the rate used is reported in the disclosure note related to pensions.

Required:

Refer to AF's Note 31.2 "Description of the actuarial assumptions and related sensitivities."

1. What are the average discount rates used to measure AF's (a) 10-15 year and (b) 15 year and more pension obligations in the "euro" geographic zone in 2015?
2. If the rate used had been 1% (100 basis points) higher, what change would have occurred in the pension obligation in 2015? What if the rate had been 1% lower?

CPA Exam Questions and Simulations

Sample CPA Exam questions from Roger CPA Review are available in Connect as support for the topics in this chapter. These Multiple Choice Questions and Task-Based Simulations include expert-written explanations and solutions, and provide a starting point for students to become familiar with the content and functionality of the actual CPA Exam.

Assets

CHAPTER

7 Cash and Receivables

OVERVIEW

We begin our study of assets by looking at cash and receivables—the two assets typically listed first in a balance sheet. For cash, the key issues are internal control and classification in the balance sheet. For receivables, the key issues are valuation and the related income statement effects of transactions involving accounts receivable and notes receivable.

LEARNING OBJECTIVES

After studying this chapter, you should be able to:

- **LO7–1** Define what is meant by internal control and describe some key elements of an internal control system for cash receipts and disbursements. (*p. 352*)
- **LO7–2** Explain the possible restrictions on cash and their implications for classification in the balance sheet. (*p. 353*)
- **LO7–3** Distinguish between the gross and net methods of accounting for cash discounts. (*p. 357*)
- **LO7–4** Describe the accounting treatment for merchandise returns. (*p. 358*)
- **LO7–5** Describe the accounting treatment of anticipated uncollectible accounts receivable. (*p. 362*)
- **LO7–6** Describe how to estimate the allowance for uncollectible accounts. (*p. 364*)
- **LO7–7** Describe the accounting treatment of notes receivable. (*p. 368*)
- **LO7–8** Differentiate between the use of receivables in financing arrangements accounted for as a secured borrowing and those accounted for as a sale. (*p. 374*)
- **LO7–9** Describe the variables that influence a company's investment in receivables and calculate the key ratios used by analysts to monitor that investment. (*p. 382*)
- **LO7–10** Discuss the primary differences between U.S. GAAP and IFRS with respect to cash and receivables. (*pp. 355, 373, 381,* and *392*)

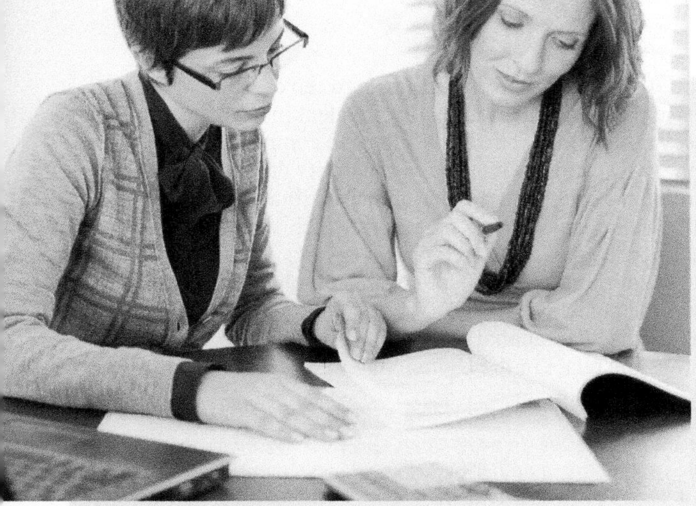
© Rob Daly / age fotostock

FINANCIAL REPORTING CASE

Bad Debt Trouble

Your roommate, Karen Buckley, was searching for some information about her future employer, Community Health Systems. Karen, a nursing major, noticed an article online titled "CHS Missed Big in Q4." "This doesn't look good," Karen said. "This article says my new employer's provision for bad debts jumped by over $200 million. Does that mean those patients haven't paid? What is CHS doing for cash—I want my paycheck to clear!" You look over the article and start to explain. "First of all, the term *provision* just means expense. The company uses what is called the allowance method to account for bad debts. It looks like CHS recorded more in expense and increased the allowance for uncollectible accounts. That doesn't necessarily mean they have a cash flow problem." Karen was not happy with your answer. "So, it isn't that the patients haven't paid, it's that they aren't going to pay? How does CHS know what they are going to do? And here is another article saying that CHS is securitizing its receivables to get more cash. Does that mean they are making the receivables more secure?" "Okay," you offer, "let's start at the beginning."

QUESTIONS

By the time you finish this chapter, you should be able to respond appropriately to the questions posed in this case. Compare your response to the solution provided at the end of the chapter.

1. Explain the allowance method of accounting for bad debts. (*p. 362*)
2. What approaches might CHS have used to arrive at the $200 million increase in its bad debt provision? (*p. 364*)
3. Are there any alternatives to the allowance method? (*p. 365*)
4. What does it mean for CHS to securitize its receivables? (*p. 376*)

In the earlier chapters of this text, we studied the underlying measurement and reporting concepts for the basic financial statements presented to external decision makers. Now we turn our attention to the elements of those financial statements. Specifically, we further explore the elements of the balance sheet, and also consider the income statement effects of transactions involving these elements. We first address assets, then liabilities, and finally shareholders' equity. This chapter focuses on the current assets cash and cash equivalents and receivables.

PART A

Cash and Cash Equivalents

Cash includes currency and coins, balances in checking accounts, and items acceptable for deposit in these accounts, such as checks and money orders received from customers. These forms of cash represent amounts readily available to pay off debt or to use in operations, without any legal or contractual restriction.

Managers typically invest temporarily idle cash to earn interest on those funds rather than keep an unnecessarily large checking account. These amounts are essentially equivalent to cash because they can quickly become available for use as cash. So, short-term, highly liquid investments that can be readily converted to cash with little risk of loss are viewed as cash equivalents. For financial reporting we make no distinction between cash in the form of currency or bank account balances and amounts held in cash-equivalent investments.

A company's policy concerning which short-term, highly liquid investments it classifies as *cash equivalents* should be described in a disclosure note.

Cash equivalents include money market funds, treasury bills, and commercial paper. To be classified as cash equivalents, these investments must have a maturity date no longer than three months *from the date of purchase.* Companies are permitted flexibility in designating cash equivalents and must establish individual policies regarding which short-term, highly liquid investments are classified as cash equivalents. A company's policy should be consistent with the usual motivation for acquiring these investments. The policy should be disclosed in the notes to the financial statements.

Illustration 7–1 shows a note from the 2015 annual report of Walgreen Boots Alliance, Inc., which operates the largest drugstore chain in the United States.

Illustration 7–1

Disclosure of Cash Equivalents—Walgreen Boots Alliance, Inc.

Real World Financials

Note 2: Summary of Major Accounting Policies (in part) Cash and Cash Equivalents
Cash and cash equivalents include cash on hand and all highly liquid investments with an original maturity of three months or less. Credit and debit card receivables from banks, which generally settle within two to seven business days, of $165 million and $229 million were included in cash and cash equivalents at August 31, 2015 and 2014, respectively.

Credit and debit card receivables often are included in cash equivalents.

The measurement and reporting of cash and cash equivalents are largely straightforward because cash generally presents no measurement problems. It is the standard medium of exchange and the basis for measuring assets and liabilities. Cash and cash equivalents usually are combined and reported as a single amount in the balance sheet. However, cash that is not available for use in current operations because it is restricted for a special purpose usually is classified in one of the noncurrent asset categories. Restricted cash is discussed later in this chapter.

All assets must be safeguarded against possible misuse. However, cash is the most liquid asset and the asset most easily stolen. As a result, a system of internal control of cash is a key accounting issue.

Internal Control

LO7–1

The success of any business enterprise depends on an effective system of internal control. Internal control refers to a company's plan to (a) encourage adherence to company policies and procedures, (b) promote operational efficiency, (c) minimize errors and theft, and (d) enhance the reliability and accuracy of accounting data. From a financial accounting perspective, the focus is on controls intended to improve the accuracy and reliability of accounting information and to safeguard the company's assets.

The Sarbanes-Oxley Act requires a company to document and assess its internal controls. Auditors express an opinion on management's assessment.

Recall from our discussion in Chapter 1 that Section 404 of the *Sarbanes-Oxley Act of 2002* requires that companies document their internal controls and assess their adequacy. The Public Company Accounting Oversight Board AS 2201 further requires the auditor to express its own opinion on whether the company has maintained effective internal control over financial reporting.

Many companies have incurred significant costs in an effort to comply with the requirements of Section 404.[1] A framework for designing an internal control system is provided by the *Committee of Sponsoring Organizations (COSO)* of the Treadway Commission.[2] Formed in 1985, the organization is dedicated to improving the quality of financial reporting through, among other things, effective internal controls.

COSO defines internal control as a process, undertaken by an entity's board of directors, management and other personnel, designed to provide reasonable assurance regarding the achievement of objectives in the following categories:

- Effectiveness and efficiency of operations

[1]PCAOB AS 2201 emphasizes audit efficiency with a focused, risk-based testing approach that is intended to reduce the total costs of 404 compliance.

[2]The sponsoring organizations include the AICPA, the Financial Executives International, the Institute of Internal Auditors, the American Accounting Association, and the Institute of Management Accountants.

- Reliability of financial reporting
- Compliance with applicable laws and regulations[3]

Internal Control Procedures—Cash Receipts

As cash is the most liquid of all assets, a well-designed and functioning system of internal control must surround all cash transactions. Separation of duties is critical. Individuals that have physical responsibility for assets should not also have access to accounting records. So, employees who handle cash should not be involved in or have access to accounting records nor be involved in the reconciliation of cash book balances to bank balances.

Employees involved in recordkeeping should not also have physical access to the assets.

Consider the cash receipt process. Most nonretail businesses receive payment for goods by checks received through the mail. An approach to internal control over cash receipts that utilizes separation of duties might include the following steps:

1. Employee A opens the mail each day and prepares a multicopy listing of all checks including the amount and payor's name.
2. Employee B takes the checks, along with one copy of the listing, to the person responsible for depositing the checks in the company's bank account.
3. A second copy of the check listing is sent to the accounting department, where Employee C enters receipts into the accounting records.

Good internal control helps ensure accuracy as well as safeguard against theft. The bank-generated deposit slip can be compared with the check listing to verify that the amounts received were also deposited. And, because the person opening the mail is not the person who maintains the accounting records, it's impossible for one person to steal checks and alter accounting records to cover up their theft.

Internal Control Procedures—Cash Disbursements

Proper controls for cash disbursements should be designed to prevent any unauthorized payments and ensure that disbursements are recorded in the proper accounts. Important elements of a cash disbursement control system include:

1. All disbursements, other than very small disbursements from petty cash, should be made by check. This provides a permanent record of all disbursements.
2. All expenditures should be *authorized* before a check is prepared. For example, a vendor invoice for the purchase of inventory should be compared with the purchase order and receiving report to ensure the accuracy of quantity, price, part numbers, and so on. This process should include verification of the proper ledger accounts to be debited.
3. Checks should be signed only by authorized individuals.

Once again, separation of duties is important. Responsibilities for check signing, check writing, check mailing, cash disbursement documentation, and recordkeeping should be separated whenever possible. That way, a single person can't write checks to himself and disguise that theft as a payment to an approved vendor.

An important part of any system of internal control of cash is the periodic reconciliation of book balances and bank balances to the correct balance. In addition, a petty cash system is employed by many business enterprises. We cover these two topics in Appendix 7A.

Restricted Cash and Compensating Balances

We discussed the classification of assets and liabilities in Chapter 3. You should recall that only cash available for current operations or to satisfy current liabilities is classified as a current asset. Cash that is restricted in some way and not available for current use usually is reported as a noncurrent asset such as *investments and funds* or *other assets.* ● LO7–2

[3]www.coso.org.

Restrictions on cash can be informal, arising from management's intent to use a certain amount of cash for a specific purpose. For example, a company may set aside funds for future plant expansion. This cash, if material, should be classified as investments and funds or other assets. Sometimes restrictions are contractually imposed. Debt instruments, for instance, frequently require the borrower to set aside funds (often referred to as a sinking fund) for the future payment of a debt. In these instances, the restricted cash is classified as noncurrent investments and funds or other assets if the debt is classified as noncurrent. On the other hand, if the liability is current, the restricted cash also is classified as current. Disclosure notes should describe any material restrictions of cash.

Banks frequently require cash restrictions in connection with loans or loan commitments (lines of credit). Typically, the borrower is asked to maintain a specified balance in a low interest or noninterest-bearing account at the bank (creditor). The required balance usually is some percentage of the committed amount (say 2% to 5%). These are known as **compensating balances** because they compensate the bank for granting the loan or extending the line of credit.

The effect of a *compensating balance* is a higher effective interest rate on the debt.

A compensating balance results in the borrower's paying an effective interest rate higher than the stated rate on the debt. For example, suppose that a company borrows $10,000,000 from a bank at an interest rate of 12%. If the bank requires a compensating balance of $2,000,000 to be held in a noninterest-bearing checking account, the company really is borrowing only $8,000,000 (the loan less the compensating balance). This means an effective interest rate of 15% ($1,200,000 interest divided by $8,000,000 cash available for use).

A material compensating balance must be disclosed regardless of the classification of the cash.

The classification and disclosure of a compensating balance depends on the nature of the restriction and the classification of the related debt.[4] If the restriction is legally binding, the cash is classified as either current or noncurrent (investments and funds or other assets) depending on the classification of the related debt. In either case, note disclosure is appropriate.

If the compensating balance arrangement is informal with no contractual agreement that restricts the use of cash, the compensating balance can be reported as part of cash and cash equivalents, with note disclosure of the arrangement.

Illustration 7–2 provides an example of a note disclosure from Walgreen's annual report.

Illustration 7–2

Disclosure of Restricted Cash—Walgreen Boots Alliance, Inc.

Real World Financials

Note 2: Summary of Major Accounting Policies (in part) Restricted Cash

The Company is required to maintain cash deposits with certain banks which consist of deposits restricted under contractual agency agreements and cash restricted by law and other obligations. As of August 31, 2015, the amount of such restricted cash was $184 million. There was no restricted cash as of August 31, 2014.

Where We're Headed

Restricted Cash and the Statement of Cash Flows. In mid-2016, the FASB issued an exposure draft of an ASU that would require more complete disclosure of restricted cash and its changes during each reporting period. In the statement of cash flows, companies would reconcile the beginning and ending balance in the total of cash, cash equivalents, restricted cash and restricted cash equivalents (rather than reconciling only unrestricted amounts). Also, companies would be required to disclose in the statement of cash flows or in the notes to the financial statements the amounts and line items in which restricted cash appears in the balance sheet. It is likely this ASU will be adopted, improving disclosure of restricted cash.

[4]FASB ASC 210–10–S99–2: SAB Topic 6.H–Balance Sheet–Overall–SEC Materials, *Accounting Series Release 148* (originally "Amendments to Regulations S-X and Related Interpretations and Guidelines Regarding the Disclosure of Compensating Balances and Short-Term Borrowing Arrangements," *Accounting Series Release No. 148,* Securities and Exchange Commission (November 13, 1973)).

International Financial Reporting Standards

Cash and Cash Equivalents. In general, cash and cash equivalents are treated similarly under IFRS and U.S. GAAP. One difference relates to bank overdrafts, which occur when withdrawals from a bank account exceed the available balance. U.S. GAAP requires that overdrafts typically be treated as liabilities. In contrast, *IAS No. 7* allows bank overdrafts to be offset against other cash accounts when overdrafts are payable on demand and fluctuate between positive and negative amounts as part of the normal cash management program that a company uses to minimize its cash balance.[5] For example, LaDonia Company has two cash accounts with the following balances as of December 31, 2018:

● LO7–10

National Bank	$300,000
Central Bank	(15,000)

Under U.S. GAAP, LaDonia's 12/31/18 balance sheet would report a cash asset of $300,000 and an overdraft current liability of $15,000. Under IFRS, LaDonia would report a cash asset of $285,000.

Decision Makers' Perspective

Cash often is referred to as a *nonearning* asset because it earns no interest. For this reason, managers invest idle cash in either cash equivalents or short-term investments, both of which provide a return. Management's goal is to hold the minimum amount of cash necessary to conduct normal business operations, meet its obligations, and take advantage of opportunities. Too much cash reduces profits through lost returns, while too little cash increases risk. This trade-off between risk and return is an ongoing choice made by management (internal decision makers). Whether the choice made is appropriate is an ongoing assessment made by investors and creditors (external decision makers).

A company must have cash available for the compensating balances we discussed in the previous section as well as for planned disbursements related to normal operating, investing, and financing cash flows. However, because cash inflows and outflows can vary from planned amounts, a company needs an additional cash cushion as a precaution against unexpected events. The size of the cushion depends on the company's ability to convert cash equivalents and short-term investments into cash quickly, along with its short-term borrowing capacity.

Companies hold cash to pay for planned and unplanned transactions and to satisfy compensating balance requirements.

Liquidity is a measure of a company's cash position and overall ability to obtain cash in the normal course of business to pay liabilities as they come due. A company is assumed to be liquid if it has sufficient cash or is capable of converting its other assets to cash in a relatively short period of time so that current needs can be met. Frequently, liquidity is measured with respect to the ability to pay currently maturing debt. The current ratio is one of the most common ways of measuring liquidity and is calculated by dividing current assets by current liabilities. By comparing liabilities that must be satisfied in the near term with assets that either are cash or will be converted to cash in the near term we have a base measure of a company's liquidity. We can refine the measure by adjusting for the implicit assumption of the current ratio that all current assets are equally liquid. In the acid-test or quick ratio, the numerator consists of "quick assets," which include only cash and cash equivalents, short-term investments, and accounts receivable. By eliminating inventories and prepaid expenses, the current assets that are less readily convertible into cash, we get a more precise indication of a company's short-term liquidity than with the current ratio. We discussed and illustrated these liquidity ratios in Chapter 3.

We should evaluate the adequacy of any ratio in the context of the industry in which the company operates and other specific circumstances. Bear in mind, though, that industry averages are only one indication of acceptability and any ratio is but one indication of liquidity. Profitability, for instance, is perhaps the best long-run indication of liquidity. And

[5]"Statement of Cash Flows," *International Accounting Standard No. 7* (IASCF), as amended effective January 1, 2016, par. 8.

a company may be very efficient in managing its current assets so that, say, receivables are more liquid than they otherwise would be. The receivables turnover ratio we discuss in Part B of this chapter offers a measure of management's efficiency in this regard.

A manager should actively monitor the company's cash position.

There are many techniques that a company can use to manage cash balances. A discussion of these techniques is beyond the scope of this text. However, it is sufficient here to understand that management must make important decisions related to cash that have a direct impact on a company's profitability and risk. Because the lack of prudent cash management can lead to the failure of an otherwise sound company, it is essential that managers as well as outside investors and creditors maintain close vigil over this facet of a company's health. ●

PART B

Current Receivables

Receivables represent a company's claims to the future collection of cash, other assets, or services. Receivables resulting from the sale of goods or services on account are called **accounts receivable** and often are referred to as *trade receivables.* Nontrade receivables are those other than trade receivables and include tax refund claims, interest receivable, and loans by the company to other entities including stockholders and employees. When a receivable, trade or nontrade, is accompanied by a formal promissory note, it is referred to as a note receivable. We consider notes receivable after first discussing accounts receivable.

An account receivable and an account payable reflect opposite sides of the same transaction.

As you study receivables, realize that one company's claim to the future collection of cash corresponds to another company's (or individual's) obligation to pay cash. One company's account receivable will be the mirror image of another company's account payable. Chapter 13 addresses accounts payable and other current liabilities.

Accounts Receivable

Typically, revenue and related accounts receivable are recognized at the point of delivery of the product or service.

Accounts receivable are created when sellers recognize revenue associated with a credit sale. Recall from Chapter 5 that revenue is recognized when a seller satisfies a performance obligation. For most products or services, the performance obligation is satisfied at the point of delivery of the product or service, so revenue and the related receivable are recognized at that time.

Accounts receivable are current assets because they will be converted to cash within the normal operating cycle.

Most businesses provide credit to their customers, either because it's not practical to require immediate cash payment or to encourage customers to purchase the company's product or service. Accounts receivable are *informal* credit arrangements supported by an invoice and normally are due in 30 to 60 days after the sale. They almost always are classified as current assets because their normal collection period, even if longer than a year, is part of, and therefore less than, the operating cycle of the business.

Initial Valuation of Accounts Receivable

You learned in Chapter 5 that sellers recognize an amount of revenue equal to the amount they are entitled to receive in exchange for satisfying a performance obligation. Sellers allocate the transaction price to the various performance obligations in a contract and then recognize revenue (and the corresponding receivable for credit sales) when performance obligations are satisfied. Clearly, revenue recognition and accounts receivable recognition are closely related. That means that some of the complexities that affect revenue recognition also affect accounts receivable.

Accounts receivable typically are not shown at present value.

One potential complexity relates to time value of money. Because credit sales allow a customer to get goods or services now but pay for them in the future, you can view a credit sale as providing a loan in addition to whatever goods or services are included in a contract. However, as you learned in Chapter 5, sellers can ignore this "financing component" when it is not significant, which typically is the case when receivables are due in less than one year. Therefore, sellers usually record relatively short-term accounts receivable at the entire amount the seller expects to receive, rather than at the present value of that amount.[6] For

[6]FASB ASC 606-10-32-15: Revenue from Contracts with Customers—Overall—Measurement—The Existence of a Significant Financing Component" (previously "Revenue from Contracts with Customers (Topic 606)" *Accounting Standards Update 2014-09* (Norwalk, Conn: FASB, 2014)).

long-term receivables the financing component is more significant and sellers have to account for it, as you will see when we cover notes receivable later in this section.

Another type of complexity relates to variable consideration. As you learned in Chapter 5, contracts can include some aspect of variable consideration that must be estimated when determining the transaction price, and therefore the amount of the receivable. In particular, contracts can allow cash discounts as well as sales returns and allowances. Let's discuss each of those complexities in turn.

DISCOUNTS. There are two types of discounts that companies commonly offer, trade discounts and cash discounts. Companies frequently offer **trade discounts** to customers, usually a percentage reduction from the list price. For example, a manufacturer might list a machine part at $2,500 but sell it to an important customer at a 10% discount. That discount of $250 is reflected by recording the sale at the agreed-upon price of $2,250.

Trade discounts allow a customer to pay an amount that is below the list price.

Trade discounts are not variable consideration. Rather, they are simply a way to specify a transaction price. Trade discounts allow a seller to offer different prices without publishing a new catalog, to disguise real prices from competitors, and to give quantity discounts to large customers.

Trade discounts are not variable consideration.

● LO7–3

Cash discounts, often called *sales discounts,* represent reductions in the amount to be paid by a credit customer if the customer makes payment within a specified period of time. A cash discount provides an incentive for quick payment. The amount of a cash discount and the time period within which it's available usually are conveyed by terms like 2/10, n/30 (meaning a 2% discount if paid within 10 days, otherwise full payment within 30 days).

Cash discounts reduce the amount to be paid if payment occurs within a specified short period of time.

Cash discounts are variable consideration, because there is uncertainty about whether the customer will pay quickly enough to qualify for the discount. However, it is usually difficult for a seller to estimate the amount of discount that will be taken with every sale. Therefore, sellers use two methods in practice that simplify the process of recording cash discounts: the gross method and the net method. With both methods, sales revenue ends up being reduced by only those discounts that are actually taken. To see how these methods work, consider the example in Illustration 7–3.

Cash discounts are variable consideration.

Illustration 7–3
Cash Discounts

The Hawthorne Manufacturing Company offers credit customers a 2% cash discount if the sales price is paid within 10 days. Any amounts not paid within 10 days are due in 30 days. These repayment terms are stated as 2/10, n/30. On October 5, 2018, Hawthorne sold merchandise at a price of $20,000. The customer paid $13,720 ($14,000 less the 2% cash discount) on October 14 and the remaining balance of $6,000 on November 4.

The appropriate journal entries to record the sale and cash collection, comparing the gross and net methods are as follows:

Gross Method			**Net Method**		
October 5, 2018			**October 5, 2018**		
Accounts receivable	20,000		Accounts receivable	19,600	
Sales revenue		20,000	Sales revenue		19,600
October 14, 2018			**October 14, 2018**		
Cash	13,720		Cash	13,720	
Sales discounts	280		Accounts receivable		13,720
Accounts receivable		14,000			
November 4, 2018			**November 4, 2018**		
Cash	6,000		Cash	6,000	
Accounts receivable		6,000	Accounts receivable		5,880
			Sales discounts forfeited		120

Both methods get us to the same place from the perspective of total revenue and therefore total net income recognized, as shown in the table below. They just get us to that place in slightly different ways.

Revenue comparison of the gross method and the net method.

	Gross Method	Net Method
Sales revenue	$20,000	$19,600
Less: Sales discounts	(280)	–0–
Add: Discounts forfeited	0	120
Net sales revenue	$ 19,720	$ 19,720

The *gross method* assumes customers won't take cash discounts and then reduces revenue for discounts taken.

Using the gross method, we initially record the revenue and related receivable at the full $20,000 price. If payment occurs within the discount period, the $280 discount is recorded as a debit to an account called *sales discounts.* This is a contra account to sales revenue and is deducted from sales revenue to derive the net sales revenue reported in the income statement. If payment occurs after the discount period, cash is simply increased and accounts receivable decreased by the gross amount originally recorded.

The *net method* assumes customers will take cash discounts and then increases revenue for discounts forfeited.

Using the net method, we record revenue and the related accounts receivable at the agreed-upon price *less* the 2% discount, yielding $19,600. If payment occurs within the discount period, we simply debit cash and credit accounts receivable for the amount received. If payment occurs after the discount period, the discount not taken is recorded to an account called *sales discounts forfeited.* This account is added to sales revenue to calculate net sales revenue. Conceptually, sales discounts forfeited is similar to interest revenue, since it is extra revenue received because a receivable is outstanding for a longer period of time.[7] In this case, customers forfeited $120 ($6,000 × 2%) of cash discounts.

The net method is more correct conceptually.

Which method is correct? Remember from Chapter 5 that sales revenue and the corresponding accounts receivable should be stated at the amount of consideration the seller expects to be entitled to receive. The net method typically better reflects that amount, because the discount is a savings that prudent customers are unwilling to forgo. To appreciate the size of that savings, reconsider Illustration 7–3. In order to save $2, the customer must pay $98 twenty days earlier than otherwise due, effectively "investing" $98 to "earn" $2, a rate of return of 2.04% ($2/$98) for a 20-day period. To convert this 20-day rate to an annual rate, we multiply by 365/20:

$$2.04\% \times 365/20 = 37.23\% \text{ effective rate}$$

Would you like to earn a sure return of over 37%? You can see why customers try to take the discount if at all possible. That's why recording the receivable net of the discount is more accurate. Still, even though the net method is more correct conceptually, both methods are used in practice, because many sellers prefer to record receivables at gross and then make downward adjustments at the time payment is made. The dollar value of the difference between methods usually is viewed as immaterial.

● LO7–4

SALES RETURNS. Customers frequently are given the right to return merchandise they purchase. When practical, a customer might be given a special price reduction as an incentive to keep the merchandise purchased.[8] We use the term sales returns to refer to these returns and other adjustments. Sales returns are common in industries such as food products, publishing, and retailing.

Sales returns are variable consideration.

As we discussed in Chapter 5, sales returns are a form of variable consideration. Because products might be returned or prices adjusted, there is uncertainty as to the final amount the seller will be entitled to receive (the seller's consideration). Recognizing returns only at the time they happen might cause receivables, revenue, and profit to be overstated in the period the sale is made and understated in the return period. For example, assume merchandise is sold to a customer for $10,000 in December 2018, the last month in the selling company's fiscal year, and that the merchandise cost $6,000. The company would recognize gross profit of $4,000 in 2018 ($10,000 – 6,000). If all of the

[7]In fact, prior to the effective date of *ASU 2014-09* (which specified how variable consideration should be treated in revenue recognition), sales discounts forfeited were often disclosed as interest revenue or other revenue in the income statement.

[8]Price reductions sometimes are referred to as *sales allowances* and are distinguished from situations when the products actually are returned for a refund or credit (sales returns).

merchandise is returned in 2019, after financial statements for 2018 are issued, gross profit will be overstated in 2018 and understated in 2019 by $4,000. Assets at the end of 2018 also will be overstated by $4,000, because a $10,000 receivable would be recorded instead of $6,000 in inventory.

Sellers should reduce revenue and accounts receivable for estimated future returns.

To avoid this problem, the seller should estimate sales returns and reduce both revenue and accounts receivable accordingly. Technically, the seller should estimate returns at the time of sale and adjust the transaction price at that time. However, as noted in Chapter 5, it is impractical for most sellers to estimate returns every time they make a sale. For that reason, sellers typically account for returns as they actually occur and then make an adjusting entry at the end of the accounting period to reflect any remaining returns they expect to occur in the future. That is the approach we demonstrate.

Sales revenue
Less: Sales returns
Net sales revenue

To account for returns, rather than reducing sales revenue directly, we debit a contra-revenue account, *sales returns,* which reduces sales revenue indirectly. Sales revenue minus sales returns equals the sales that aren't returned (referred to as *net sales* or *net sales revenue* in the income statement). As shown in Illustration 7–4, the corresponding credit in the journal entry that debits sales returns depends on whether cash has already been collected or we have an outstanding receivable.

Accounts receivable
Less: Allow. for sales returns
Net accounts receivable

As shown in Illustration 7–4, for cash sales (or if cash already has been collected for credit sales), Hawthorne refunds the cash when a customer returns a product. At the end of the period, Hawthorne also records a **refund liability** for its estimate of additional cash that it will have to refund in the future.

When returns occur for credit sales with the receivable still outstanding, Hawthorne reduces the receivable, because Hawthorne no longer is entitled to receive payment from the customer. At the end of the period, Hawthorne also must estimate returns for accounts receivable still outstanding. In this text, we'll record this estimate as a credit to **allowance for sales return**. This allowance is a contra account that is offset against accounts receivable to reduce the net balance of accounts receivable for Hawthorne's estimate of future returns. We use this allowance account, instead of a separate refund liability account, to avoid showing a liability to return cash that hasn't yet been received. (In practice, some companies instead might show a refund liability, just as if cash had already been collected.)

Regardless of whether cash has been collected or a receivable is outstanding, the 2018 income statement reports net sales revenue of $1,800,000, which is gross sales revenue of $2,000,000 reduced by actual and estimated returns of $200,000 ($130,000 + 70,000).

Hawthorne also must adjust inventory to account for the returned merchandise. In a perpetual inventory system we record increases (debits) and decreases (credits) in the inventory account as events occur. So, when actual returns occur, Hawthorne increases inventory to include the $78,000 of returned items. Later, when Hawthorne estimates returns at the end of the period, the $42,000 of inventory *expected* to be returned in 2019 is included as an asset, "inventory—estimated returns," in Hawthorne's 2018 balance sheet, even though the actual merchandise still belongs to customers, because ownership of the merchandise is expected to revert back to the Hawthorne. As a result, 2018 cost of goods sold equals $1,080,000, which is $1,200,000 reduced by the cost of actual and estimated returns of $120,000 ($78,000 + $42,000).[9]

Sometimes a customer will return damaged or defective merchandise. This possibility is included in a company's estimate of returns. As we will see in Chapter 9, the amount recorded in inventory for damaged or defective merchandise reflects a value less than its original cost.

[9]As indicated in Chapter 5, companies technically should estimate all variable consideration, including sales returns, at the time a sale is made. The financial statement outcomes of that approach are the same as those shown in Illustration 7–4, but the journal entries that get us there are somewhat different. To adapt our example to account for estimated returns at the time of sale, look at the journal entries that Hawthorne makes at the end of 2018 to account for estimated future returns. Hawthorne would record the same journal entries at the time of sale, but for the full amount of estimated sales returns ($200,000) and estimated inventory to be returned ($200,000 × 60% = $120,000). After recording the estimated returns at the time of the sale, all *actual* returns would be accounted for as shown in our example for actual returns occurring in 2019, reducing the refund liability for cash sales or reducing the allowance for sales returns for credit sales.

Illustration 7–4 Accounting for Sales Returns

During 2018, its first year of operations, the Hawthorne Manufacturing Company sold merchandise for $2,000,000. This merchandise cost Hawthorne $1,200,000 (60% of the selling price). Industry experience indicates that 10% of all sales will be returned, which equals $200,000 ($2,000,000 × 10%) in this case. Customers returned $130,000 of sales during 2018. Hawthorne uses a perpetual inventory system.

	Cash Sales			Credit Sales (A/R Outstanding)*		
Sales of $2,000,000 occurred in 2018, with cost of goods sold of $1,200,000.	Cash	2,000,000		Accounts receivable	2,000,000	
	Sales revenue		2,000,000	Sales revenue		2,000,000
	Cost of goods sold	1,200,000		Cost of goods sold	1,200,000	
	Inventory		1,200,000	Inventory		1,200,000
Sales returns of $130,000 occurred during 2018. The cost of returned inventory is $78,000 ($130,000 × 60%).	Sales returns	130,000		Sales returns	130,000	
	Cash		130,000	Accounts receivable		130,000
	Inventory	78,000		Inventory	78,000	
	Cost of goods sold		78,000	Cost of goods sold		78,000
At the end of 2018, an additional $70,000 of sales returns are expected. The cost of the inventory expected to be returned is $42,000 ($70,000 × 60%).	Sales returns	70,000		Sales returns	70,000	
	Refund liability		70,000	Allow. for sales returns		70,000
	Inventory—est. returns	42,000		Inventory—est. returns	42,000	
	Cost of goods sold		42,000	Cost of goods sold		42,000
Sales returns of $70,000 occurred during 2019. The cost of returned inventory is $42,000.	Refund liability	70,000		Allow. for sales returns	70,000	
	Cash		70,000	Accounts receivable		70,000
	Inventory	42,000		Inventory	42,000	
	Inventory—est. returns		42,000	Inventory—est. returns		42,000

*If a sale was made on credit and cash already has been collected, returns are handled the same way they are for cash sales.

Changes in estimated returns are recorded in whatever period the estimate changes.

What happens if Hawthorne's estimate of future returns is wrong, such that returns end up being more or less than $70,000? We don't revise prior years' financial statements to reflect the new estimate. Instead, as you learned in Chapter 5, we adjust the accounts to reflect the change in estimated returns, with any effect on income recognized in the period in which the adjustment is made. For example, suppose in our illustration that only $60,000 of 2018 sales were returned in 2019, instead of the $70,000 that Hawthorne anticipated. Also suppose that the estimated returns relate to outstanding accounts receivable, and that Hawthorne estimates that no more returns will occur. In that case, the allowance for sales returns still has a pre-adjustment balance of **$10,000** remaining from 2018 sales. Likewise, inventory—estimated returns still has a pre-adjustment balance of **$6,000** (60% × $10,000) remaining from 2018 sales.

Allowance for sales returns

	Debit	Credit
1/1/2019		70,000
2019 returns	60,000	
Pre-adjustment balance		**10,000**
Change in estimate	10,000	
12/31/2019		-0-

Inventory—estimated returns

	Debit	Credit
1/1/2019	42,000	
2019 returns		36,000
Pre-adjustment balance	**6,000**	
Change in estimate		6,000
12/31/2019	-0-	

In 2019, Hawthorne would record its change in estimated returns of 2018 sales as follows:

Allowance for sales returns	10,000	
Sales returns ($70,000 – 60,000)		10,000
Cost of goods sold (60% × $10,000)	6,000	
Inventory—estimated returns		6,000

These adjustments remove the remaining 2018 balance from the allowance for sales returns and inventory—estimated returns. They also increase net sales revenue (by reducing sales returns) and cost of goods sold in 2019, the period in which the change in estimate occurs.

Experience guides firms when estimating returns.

How do companies estimate returns? They rely on past history, but they also consider any changes that might affect future experience. For example, changes in customer base, payment terms offered to customers, and overall economic conditions might suggest that future returns will differ from past returns. The task of estimating returns is made easier for many large retail companies whose fiscal year-end is the end of January. Since retail companies generate a large portion of their annual sales during the Christmas season, most returns from these sales already have been accounted for by the end of January. In fact, that's an important motivation for those companies to choose to end their fiscal years at the end of January.

AVX Corporation is a leading manufacturer of electronic components. Illustration 7–5, drawn from AVX's 2015 annual report, describes the company's approach to estimating returns.

Revenue Recognition and Accounts Receivable (in part): Returns
Sales revenue and cost of sales reported in the income statement are reduced to reflect estimated returns. We record an estimated sales allowance for returns at the time of sale based on historical trends, current pricing and volume information, other market specific information, and input from sales, marketing, and other key management personnel. The amount accrued reflects the return of value of the customer's inventory. These procedures require the exercise of significant judgments. We believe that these procedures enable us to make reliable estimates of future returns. Our actual results have historically approximated our estimates. When the product is returned and verified, the customer is given credit against their accounts receivable.

Illustration 7–5

Disclosure of Sales Returns Policy—AVX Corporation

Real World Financials

If sales returns are immaterial, they can be recorded as they occur.

In some industries, returns typically are small and infrequent. Companies in these industries usually don't bother to estimate returns and simply record returns in the period they occur, because the effect on income measurement and asset valuation is immaterial. Also, companies sometimes lack sufficient information to make a good estimate of returns. As you learned in Chapter 5, companies must recognize only the amount of revenue that is probable to not require reversal in the future. That way, sales are less likely to be overstated in the period of the transfer of goods or services. Difficulty estimating returns requires a larger estimate of returns (and therefore a smaller amount of net sales revenue recognized) than would be the case if a more precise estimate was possible.

Subsequent Valuation of Accounts Receivable

● LO7–5

You learned in Chapter 5 that revenue and a corresponding receivable are recognized for the amount the seller is *entitled* to receive for satisfying a performance obligation. However, being entitled to receive payment doesn't necessarily mean that the seller *will* be paid. In fact, credit losses (bad debts) are an inherent cost of granting credit. How should we account for the fact that not every account receivable is likely to be collected?

DIRECT WRITE-OFF METHOD (NOT GAAP). A simple approach to recognizing bad debts that is ***not*** allowed by GAAP is to wait until a particular account is deemed uncollectible and write it off at that time. For example, if a customer goes bankrupt and it becomes clear that a $15,000 account receivable will not be collected, the following journal entry could be recorded under the direct write-off method:

Bad debt expense	15,000	
Accounts receivable		15,000

A shortcoming of the direct write-off method is that it overstates the balance in accounts receivable in the periods prior to the write off, because it fails to anticipate that some accounts receivable will prove uncollectible. Also, it distorts net income by postponing recognition of any bad debt expense until the period in which the customer actually fails to pay, even though some bad debts expense was predictable before that time. These conceptual problems are why the direct write-off method isn't allowed for financial-reporting purposes unless the amount of bad debts is not material. However, the direct write-off method is required for income tax purposes for most companies.

The carrying value of accounts receivable is reduced by the allowance for uncollectible accounts.

FINANCIAL Reporting Case

Q1, p. 351

ALLOWANCE METHOD (GAAP). GAAP requires use of the allowance method whenever the amount of bad debts is material. Under the allowance method, companies use a contra-asset account, the allowance for uncollectible accounts, to reduce the carrying value of accounts receivable to the amount of cash they expect to collect.[10] Both the carrying value and the amount of the allowance typically are shown on the face of the balance sheet. For example, Illustration 7–6 shows how Johnson & Johnson, the large pharmaceutical company, reported accounts receivable in its comparative balance sheets for 2015 and 2014.

Illustration 7–6

Disclosure of Accounts Receivable—Johnson & Johnson

Real World Financials

	($ in millions)	
	2015	**2014**
Accounts receivable trade, less allowances for doubtful accounts $268 (2014, $275)	10,734	10,985

Johnson & Johnson's balance sheet communicates that, as of year-end 2015, it had net accounts receivable of $10,734 and an allowance for doubtful accounts of $268, which implies a gross accounts receivable of $10,734 + 268 = $11,002.

The allowance method recognizes bad debt expense when the allowance is adjusted for estimated bad debts, not when specific accounts are written off.

Under the allowance method, bad debt expense is ***not*** recognized when specific accounts are written off. Rather, bad debt expense is recognized earlier, when the allowance is created and subsequently adjusted to reflect new sales and changes in customer's credit quality. Later, when a specific account receivable is deemed uncollectible, both the allowance and the specific account receivable are reduced to write off the receivable.

An example will clarify how the allowance method works. Assume the Hawthorne Manufacturing Company started operations in 2018. It had sales of $1,200,000 and collections of $895,000, leaving a balance of $305,000 in accounts receivable as of December 31, 2018.

[10]You may see this carrying value referred to as "net realizable value". However, as you will learn in Chapter 9, that term has a very specific definition in GAAP that should not be misused.

Accounts Receivable

	Debit	Credit
1/1/2018	-0-	
Sales	1,200,000	
Collections		895,000
12/31/2018	305,000	

Recognizing allowance for uncollectible accounts (end of first year). Hawthorne's analysis indicates it expects to collect **$280,000** of its accounts receivable, so it must establish an allowance for uncollectible accounts of $25,000 ($305,000 – **280,000**). (Later we'll talk about how Hawthorne would estimate the allowance. For now let's assume that number.)

Hawthorne establishes the necessary allowance with the following journal entry:

Allowance for Uncollectible Accounts

	Debit	Credit
1/1/2018		-0-
Bad debt expense		25,000
12/31/2018		25,000

	Debit	Credit
Bad debt expense	25,000	
Allowance for uncollectible accounts		25,000

The balances in accounts receivable ($305,000) and the contra asset allowance for uncollectible accounts ($25,000) offset to carry receivables at a net amount of **$280,000** on the balance sheet.

Of course, at this point Hawthorne doesn't know which particular accounts receivable will prove uncollectible. (If it could predict that perfectly, it wouldn't have made those sales to begin with!) Hawthorne only can record an estimate of the amount of uncollectible accounts for its outstanding receivables. That estimate both reduces net income (through bad debt expense) and reduces the carrying value of Hawthorne's accounts receivable.

When accounts are deemed uncollectible. On April 24, 2019, Hawthorne concludes that it will not collect a $15,000 account receivable from a customer that recently has gone bankrupt. Hawthorne would make the following journal entry:

	Debit	Credit
Allowance for uncollectible accounts	15,000	
Accounts receivable		15,000

Accounts Receivable

	Debit	Credit
1/1/2019	305,000	
Specific write-off		15,000
	290,000	

Allowance for Uncollectible Accounts

	Debit	Credit
1/1/2019		25,000
Specific write-off	15,000	
		10,000

Note that the journal entry didn't affect net income, and that accounts receivable still are carried at a net amount of **$280,000** ($290,000 – 10,000) on the balance sheet.

The write-off of an account receivable *reduces* both gross receivables and the allowance, thus having no effect on net income or financial position.

When previously written-off accounts are reinstated. Occasionally, a receivable that has been written off is later reinstated because the company gets new information and now believes the receivable will be collected in part or in full. When this happens, the entry to write off the account is reversed. For example, assume Hawthorne learns on May 30 that the financial situation of its customer has improved and it will collect $1,200 of the receivable that previously was written off. Hawthorne reinstates that amount of the receivable with the following journal entry:

FINANCIAL Reporting Case

Q2, p. 351

	Debit	Credit
Accounts receivable	1,200	
Allowance for uncollectible accounts		1,200

Accounts Receivable

	Debit	Credit
	290,000	
Reinstatement	1,200	
	291,200	

Allowance for Uncollectible Accounts

	Debit	Credit
		10,000
Reinstatement		1,200
		11,200

Reinstating a previously written off accounts receivable *increases* both gross receivables and the allowance, thus having no effect on net income or financial position.

Note that, once again, the journal entry didn't affect net income, and that accounts receivable still are carried at a net amount of **$280,000** ($291,200 – 11,200) on the balance sheet. Just as the carrying value of accounts receivable was not affected by writing off a specific receivable, it also is not affected by reversing the write-off of a specific receivable.

Once the receivable is reinstated, collection is recorded the same way it would be if the receivable had never been written off, debiting cash and crediting accounts receivable.

● LO7–6

ESTIMATING THE ALLOWANCE FOR UNCOLLECTIBLE ACCOUNTS. Basing bad debt expense on the appropriate carrying value of accounts receivable is very much a balance sheet approach. The company determines what the ending balance of the allowance for uncollectible accounts should be, and then records the amount of bad debt expense that's necessary to adjust the allowance to that desired balance.

Past history as well as current conditions guide estimation of the necessary balance in the allowance for uncollectible accounts. Estimation could be done by analyzing each customer account, by applying an estimate of the percentage of bad debts to the entire outstanding receivable balance, or by applying different percentages to accounts receivable balances depending on the length of time outstanding. This latter approach employs an accounts receivable aging schedule, and is very common in practice. For example, Illustration 7–7 shows the aging schedule for Hawthorne's December 31, 2018 accounts receivable balance of $305,000.

Illustration 7–7

Accounts Receivable Aging Schedule

Customer	Accounts Receivable 12/31/2018	0–60 Days	61–90 Days	91–120 Days	Over 120 Days
Axel Manufacturing Co.	$ 20,000	$ 14,000	$ 6,000		
Banner Corporation	33,000		20,000	$10,000	$ 3,000
Dando Company	60,000	50,000	10,000		
"	"	"	"	"	"
"	"	"	"	"	"
Xicon Company	18,000	10,000	4,000	3,000	1,000
Totals	$305,000	$220,000	$50,000	$25,000	$10,000

Summary

Age Group	Amount	Estimated Percent Uncollectible	Estimated Allowance
0–60 days	$220,000	5%	$ 11,000
61–90 days	50,000	10%	5,000
91–120 days	25,000	20%	5,000
Over 120 days	10,000	40%	4,000
Allowance for uncollectible accounts			$25,000

The schedule classifies the year-end receivable balances according to their length of time outstanding. Therefore, the schedule applies higher estimated default percentages to groups of older receivables. Typically, the longer an account has been outstanding, the more likely it will prove uncollectible. Because the schedule calculates a necessary balance in the allowance of $25,000, Hawthorn would adjust the balance of the allowance to that amount, as shown previously in this section.

A/R	$400,000
Less allowance	40,000
Net A/R	$360,000

Recognizing allowance for uncollectible accounts (end of second year). At the end of the second year of operations (and each year thereafter), Hawthorne must once again estimate what the carrying value of its accounts receivable should be, and adjust the allowance as necessary to produce that carrying value. Let's suppose that at the end of 2019 Hawthorne has a gross accounts receivable balance of $400,000 but believes it only will collect **$360,000.** That implies that Hawthorne needs an allowance of $40,000 ($400,000 – **360,000**). Unlike the first year, the balance of the allowance for uncollectible accounts in later years may not be zero at the time Hawthorne makes the adjustment. In our example, the pre-adjustment balance is $11,200 (see T-account above). What adjustment is needed to update the allowance account from $11,200 to the new estimate of $40,000? The adjusting entry is a "plug" of $28,800.

Allowance for Uncollectible Accounts	
(*Pre*-adjustment balance)	11,200
Bad debt expense	28,800
(*Post*-adjustment balance)	40,000

Bad debt expense	28,800	
Allowance for uncollectible accounts		28,800

Be sure to understand that the amount of bad debt expense recognized in this journal entry is purely a plug that is determined by the difference between the pre-adjustment balance and the necessary post-adjustment balance in the allowance. For example, if Hawthorne had written off so many accounts receivable during 2019 that the adjustment account had a pre-adjustment balance that was a debit of $2,000, Hawthorne would have to credit the allowance for $42,000 (and debit bad debt expense for the same amount) to reach the necessary $40,000 post-adjustment balance.

Allowance for Uncollectible Accounts		
Beg. Bal.	2,000	
Bad Debt Exp.		42,000
End Bal.		40,000

On the other hand, if the pre-adjustment balance in the allowance was a credit of $11,200 and the quality of Hawthorne's receivables improved so much that Hawthorne believed the post-adjustment balance in the allowance should be only $5,000, Hawthorne would need to *debit* the allowance for $6,200.

Allowance for Uncollectible Accounts		
Beg. Bal		11,200
Bad Debt Exp.	6,200	
End Bal.		5,000

A debit to the allowance requires a credit to bad debt expense. While crediting an expense looks weird, think of it as driven by a change in an estimate. The allowance was increased by too much in a prior period, so Hawthorne has to reduce it this period. As with changes in other estimates, we don't restate prior year financial statements, but instead show the effect of the change in estimate in current-period net income.

Income statement approach. An alternative to the balance sheet approach is to estimate bad debt expense directly as a percentage of each period's net credit sales. This percentage usually is determined by reviewing the company's recent history of the relationship between credit sales and actual bad debts. For a relatively new company, this percentage may be estimated by referring to other sources such as industry averages. For example, if Hawthorne had sales of $1,200,000 in 2018, and estimated that 2% of those sales would prove uncollectible, it would debit bad debts expense and credit the allowance for uncollectible accounts for $24,000 ($1,200,000 × 2%).

FINANCIAL Reporting Case

Q3, p. 351

It's important to notice that this income statement approach focuses on the current year's credit sales, so the effect on the balance sheet—the allowance for uncollectible accounts and hence net accounts receivable—is an incidental result of estimating the expense. An income statement approach should be used only if it doesn't provide a distorted estimate of the net amount of cash that is expected to be collected from accounts receivable.

Combined approaches. Some companies use a combination of approaches when estimating bad debts. For example, Hawthorne might decide it's more convenient to estimate bad debts on a quarterly basis using the income statement approach and then refine the

Allowance for Uncollectible Accounts	
	24,000
	1,000
	25,000

estimate by employing the balance sheet approach at the end of the year based on an aging of receivables. In our example, Hawthorne recognized $24,000 in the allowance and the bad debt expense accounts during the year under the income statement approach. If at the end of the year Hawthorne's aging schedule indicated that a total of $25,000 was needed in the allowance, Hawthorne would recognize an additional $1,000 of allowance and bad debt expense to adjust the total to the necessary balance.

Bad debt expense	1,000	
Allowance for uncollectible accounts		1,000

Ethical Dilemma 

The management of the Auto Parts Division of the Santana Corporation receives a bonus if the division's income achieves a specific target. For 2018 the target will be achieved by a wide margin. Mary Beth Williams, the controller of the division, has been asked by Philip Stanton, the head of the division's management team, to try to reduce this year's income and "bank" some of the profits for future years. Mary Beth suggests that the division's bad debt expense as a percentage of the gross accounts receivable balance for 2018 be increased from 3% to 5%. She believes that 3% is the more accurate estimate but knows that both the corporation's internal auditors as well as the external auditors allow some flexibility when estimates are involved. Does Mary Beth's proposal present an ethical dilemma?

Illustration 7–8 summarizes the key issues involving measuring and reporting accounts receivable.

Illustration 7–8
Measuring and Reporting Accounts Receivable

Recognition	Depends on revenue recognition; for most credit sales, revenue and the related receivables are recognized at the point of delivery.
Initial valuation	Initially recorded at the amount of consideration the seller is entitled to receive. Affected by cash discounts and variable consideration such as sales discounts and sales returns.
Subsequent valuation	Initial valuation reduced by allowance for uncollectible accounts, so accounts receivable are shown at the amount of cash the seller expects to receive.
Classification	Almost always classified as a current asset.

CURRENT EXPECTED CREDIT LOSS (CECL) MODEL FOR ACCOUNTS RECEIVABLE. Under current GAAP, the potential for bad debts is viewed as a loss contingency (meaning that the amount of loss depends on some future event, like a customer's failure to pay). We'll discuss loss contingencies more in Chapter 13, but for now you only need to understand that an allowance and corresponding expense is recognized for any amount of loss that is both probable to occur and can be reasonably estimated. When a company has many accounts receivable, it is probable that some bad debts will occur, so companies recognize an allowance and accrue bad debt expense to adjust the carrying value of accounts receivable to the amount expected to be collected.

Guidance in this area is changing. Starting in 2020, companies will be required to use the **CECL ("Current Expected Credit Loss") model** to account for bad debts, and companies can choose to use that approach starting in 2019.[11] The CECL model is designed to give a more accurate and forward-looking estimate of bad debt expense. It still uses the allowance method, and it still uses the same journal entries, but it differs from current GAAP in two important ways. First, the "probable" threshold for identifying bad debts is removed. Therefore, even if the seller is considering a single receivable for which the likelihood of default

[11]"Financial Instruments—Credit Losses (Topic 326)" *Accounting Standards Update 2016-13* (Norwalk, Conn: FASB, 2016).

is low (and thus not "probable"), the seller typically will make some estimate of bad debts. Second, while current practice tends to focus on events that already have occurred when considering the potential for bad debts, the CECL model explicitly requires creditors to also consider additional information such as reasonable and supportable forecasts about the future.

Concept Review Exercise

UNCOLLECTIBLE ACCOUNTS RECEIVABLE

The Crowe Company offers 30 days of credit to its customers. At the end of the year, bad debts expense is estimated and the allowance for uncollectible accounts is adjusted based on an aging of accounts receivable. The company began 2019 with the following balances in its accounts:

Accounts receivable	$350,000
Allowance for uncollectible accounts	(32,000)
Net accounts receivable	$318,000

During 2019, sales on credit were $1,300,000, cash collections from customers were $1,253,000, and actual write-offs of accounts were $25,000.

Crowe Company Accounts Receivable Aging
December 31, 2019

	Summary	
Age Group	**Amount**	**Estimated Percent Uncollectible**
0–60 days	$250,000	6%
61–90 days	80,000	15%
91–120 days	32,000	25%
Over 121 days	10,000	50%
Total	$372,000	

Required:

1. Determine the balances in accounts receivable and allowance for uncollectible accounts at the end of 2019.
2. Determine bad debt expense for 2019.
3. Prepare journal entries to write off receivables and to recognize bad debt expense for 2019.

Solution:

1. Determine the balances in accounts receivable and allowance for uncollectible accounts at the end of 2019.

Accounts Receivable

	Debit	Credit
12/31/2018	350,000	
Sales	1,300,000	
Collections		1,253,000
Write-offs		25,000
12/31/2019	372,000	

Crowe Company Accounts Receivable Aging
December 31, 2019

	Summary		
Age Group	**Amount**	**Estimated Percent Uncollectible**	**Estimated Allowance**
0–60 days	$250,000	6%	$15,000
61–90 days	80,000	15%	12,000
91–120 days	32,000	25%	8,000
Over 121 days	10,000	50%	5,000
Total	$372,000		$40,000

Allowance for Uncollectible Accounts		
		32,000
Write-offs	25,000	
Bad debt expense (12/31/2019) adjustment		33,000
		40,000

As shown in the T-account, the ending balance in Accounts Receivable is $372,000. As shown in the calculation within the aging of accounts receivable, the ending balance in the Allowance for Uncollectible Accounts is $40,000.

2. Determine bad debt expense for 2019.

   As shown in the T-account above, the plug necessary to reach the required ending balance in the Allowance for Uncollectible Accounts is $33,000, so that is bad debt expense for 2019.

3. Prepare journal entries to write off receivables and to recognize bad debt expense for 2019.

Allowance for uncollectible accounts	25,000	
Accounts receivable		25,000
Write-off of accounts receivable as they are determined uncollectible.		
Bad debt expense	33,000	
Allowance for uncollectible accounts		33,000
Year-end adjusting entry for bad debts.		

Notes Receivable

LO7–7 **Notes receivable** are formal credit arrangements between a creditor (lender) and a debtor (borrower) that specify payment terms. Notes arise from loans made to people and companies who need cash, including stockholders and employees, as well as from the sale of merchandise, other assets, or services under relatively long-term payment arrangements. Notes receivable are classified as either current or noncurrent depending on the expected collection date(s).

When the term of a note is less than a year, it is reported as a short-term note. We start by discussing short-term notes, and then discuss long-term notes.

Short-Term Interest-Bearing Notes

The typical **interest-bearing note receivable** requires payment of a specified face amount, also called *principal,* at a specified maturity date or dates. In addition, interest is paid at a stated percentage of the face amount. Interest on notes is calculated as:

Face amount × Annual rate × Fraction of the annual period

For an example, consider Illustration 7–9.

If the sale in the illustration instead occurred on August 1, 2018, and the company's fiscal year-end is December 31, a year-end adjusting entry accrues interest earned.

December 31, 2018		
Interest receivable	35,000	
Interest revenue ($700,000 × 12% × $\frac{5}{12}$)		35,000

The February 1 collection is then recorded as follows:

February 1, 2019		
Cash ($700,000 + [$700,000 × 12% × $\frac{6}{12}$])	742,000	
Interest revenue ($700,000 × 12% × $\frac{1}{12}$)		7,000
Interest receivable (accrued at December 31)		35,000
Note receivable		700,000

Illustration 7–9
Note Receivable

The Stridewell Wholesale Shoe Company manufactures athletic shoes that it sells to retailers. On May 1, 2018, the company sold shoes to Harmon Sporting Goods. Stridewell agreed to accept a $700,000, 6-month, 12% note in payment for the shoes. Interest is payable at maturity. Assume that an interest rate of 12% is appropriate for a note of this type.

Stridewell would account for the note as follows:*

May 1, 2018		
Note receivable	700,000	
Sales revenue		700,000
To record the sale of goods in exchange for a note receivable.		
November 1, 2018		
Cash ($700,000 + $42,000)	742,000	
Interest revenue ($700,000 × 12% × 6/12)		42,000
Note receivable		700,000
To record the collection of the note at maturity.		

*To focus on recording the note we intentionally omit the entry required for the cost of the goods sold if the perpetual inventory system is used.

Short-Term Noninterest-Bearing Notes

Sometimes a receivable assumes the form of a so-called **noninterest-bearing note**. The name is a misnomer, though. Noninterest-bearing notes actually do bear interest, but the interest is deducted (or *discounted*) from the face amount to determine the cash proceeds made available to the borrower at the outset. For example, what if Stridewell accepted a six-month, $700,000 noninterest-bearing note with a 12% discount rate? If Stridewell views the financing component of the note to be insignificant, it would ignore the interest rate and simply record an account receivable for $700,000. However, Stridewell could view the financing component of the contract to be significant. In that case, $42,000 ($700,000 × 12% × 6/12 year) interest would be discounted at the outset rather than explicitly stated, and the selling price of the shoes would be only $658,000.[12] Stridewell still receives $700,000, but that total revenue is recognized as sales revenue of $658,000 and interest revenue of $42,000. Assuming a May 1, 2018 sale, the transaction is recorded as follows:[13]

May 1, 2018		
Note receivable (face amount)	700,000	
Discount on note receivable ($700,000 × 12% × 6/12)		42,000
Sales revenue (difference)		658,000
November 1, 2018		
Discount on note receivable	42,000	
Interest revenue		42,000
Cash	700,000	
Note receivable (face amount)		700,000

[12]Sometimes the terms *discount rate* and *effective interest rate* are used interchangeably, so don't be confused by the different use of the term *discount rate* with respect to noninterest-bearing notes. Here, *discount rate* refers only to a rate that is multiplied by the face amount of the note (in Stridewell's case, $700,000) to calculate how much interest is included in the note (in Stridewell's case, $42,000). That discount rate is different from the *effective interest rate* that Stridewell earns on the outstanding receivable balance, and that Stridewell would use to calculate the present value of future cash flows.

[13]The entries shown assume the note is recorded by the gross method. By the net method, the interest component is netted against the face amount of the note as follows:

May 1, 2016		
Note receivable	658,000	
Sales revenue		658,000
November 1, 2016		
Cash	700,000	
Note receivable		658,000
Interest revenue ($700,000 × 12% × 6/12)		42,000

When interest is discounted from the face amount of a note, the effective interest rate is higher than the stated discount rate.

The discount on note receivable is a contra account to the note receivable account. That is, the note receivable would be reported in the balance sheet net (less) any remaining discount. The discount represents future interest revenue that will be recognized as it is earned over time. The sales revenue under this arrangement is only $658,000, but the total amount of interest is calculated as the discount rate times the $700,000 face amount. This causes the *effective* interest rate to be higher than the 12% discount rate.

Using a calculator, enter: N 1 I .06383 PMT − 700000
Output: PV 658,000

	$ 42,000	Interest for 6 months
÷	$658,000	Sales price
=	6.383%	Rate for 6 months
×	2*	To annualize the rate
=	12.766%	Effective interest rate

*Two 6-month periods

Using Excel, enter: = PV(.06383,1,700000)
Output: 658,000

This note should be valued at the present value of future cash receipts. The present value of $700,000 to be received in six months using an effective interest rate of 6.383% is $658,000 ($700,000 ÷ 1.06383 = $658,000). The use of present value techniques for valuation purposes was introduced in Chapter 6, and we'll use these techniques extensively in subsequent chapters to value various long-term notes receivable, investments, and liabilities.

In the illustration, if the sale occurs on August 1, the December 31, 2018, adjusting entry and the entry to record the cash collection on February 1, 2019, are recorded as follows:

December 31, 2018		
Discount on note receivable	35,000	
Interest revenue ($700,000 × 12% × 5/12)*		35,000
February 1, 2019		
Discount on note receivable	7,000	
Interest revenue ($700,000 × 12% × 1/12)		7,000
Cash	700,000	
Note receivable (face amount)		700,000

*We also can calculate interest revenue by multiplying the net note receivable balance by the effective interest rate ($658,000 × 12.766% × 5/12 = $35,000).

In the December 31, 2018 balance sheet, the note receivable is shown at $693,000: the face amount ($700,000) less remaining discount ($7,000).

Long-Term Notes Receivable

We account for long-term notes receivable the same way we account for short-term notes receivable, but the time value of money has a larger effect. Therefore, if long-term notes are received in exchange for goods and services, the financing component of the transaction typically is viewed as significant for revenue recognition purposes. To provide an example, Illustration 7–10 modifies the facts in Illustration 7–9 to have Stridewell agree on January 1, 2018, to accept a two-year noninterest-bearing note.

Using a calculator, enter: N 2 I .12 PMT − 700000
Output: PV 558,036

It's useful to consider a couple of aspects of Illustration 7–10. First, notice that the sales revenue in 2018 is not recorded for the full $700,000. Instead, sales revenue is calculated as ($558,036), the *present value* of the amount ($700,000) to be received in two years. The net amount of the note receivable equals its present value ($558,036), which is the note receivable of $700,000 less the discount on note receivable of $141,964. Recall from Chapter 5 that sellers need to recognize the financing component of a contract when the time value of money is significant. That is what Stridewell is doing. It earns sales revenue of $558,036 from selling shoes, and interest revenue totaling $141,964 ($66,964 + 75,000) for financing the transaction.

Using Excel, enter: = PV(.12,2,700000)
Output: 558,036

Second, interest revenue each period is calculated based on the *net* note receivable as of the beginning of that period. As a consequence, interest revenue differs between periods because the net note receivable increases over time. In our example, Stridewell's 2018 interest revenue of $66,964 is calculated based on the initial net note receivable balance

Illustration 7–10

Long-Term Noninterest-Bearing Note Receivable

The Stridewell Wholesale Shoe Company manufactures athletic shoes that it sells to retailers. On January 1, 2018, the company sold shoes to Harmon Sporting Goods. Stridewell agreed to accept a $700,000, two-year note in payment for the shoes. Assuming a 12% effective interest rate, Stridewell would account for the note as follows:*

January 1, 2018		
Notes receivable	700,000	
Discount on note receivable		141,964
Sales revenue[†]		558,036
To record the sale of goods in exchange for a two-year note receivable.		
December 31, 2018		
Discount on note receivable	66,964	
Interest revenue ($558,036 × 12%)		66,964
To record interest revenue in 2018.		
December 31, 2019		
Cash	700,000	
Discount on note receivable	75,000	
Interest revenue [($558,036 + $66,964) × 12%]		75,000
Notes receivable		700,000
To record interest revenue in 2019 and collection of the note		

*To focus on recording the note we intentionally omit the entry required for the cost of the goods sold if the perpetual inventory system is used.
[†]$700,000 × Present value of $1; $n = 2$, $i = 12\%$

In the ***effective interest method***, interest is determined by multiplying the outstanding balance by the effective interest rate.

($558,036 × 12%). We reduce the discount on note receivable for 2018 interest revenue, which increases the net note receivable balance to $625,000 ($558,036 + $66,964). So, Stridewell's 2019 interest revenue of $75,000 is calculated based on that higher net note receivable balance ($625,000 × 12%), reducing the discount on note receivable to zero by the end of 2019. At that point, the book value of the note, sometimes called the carrying value, carrying amount, or amortized cost basis, is $700,000, and that is the amount of cash that is collected. The effective interest rate stays the same over time, but interest revenue increases as that rate is multiplied by a receivable balance that increases over time. This is an application of the effective interest method, by which we calculate interest revenue or interest expense by multiplying the outstanding balance of a long-term receivable or liability by the effective interest rate. As you will see in later chapters, that method is used for all long-term receivables and liabilities.

We discuss long-term notes receivable in much greater detail in Chapter 14 at the same time we discuss accounting for long-term notes payable. That discussion provides more examples of accounting for long-term noninterest-bearing notes, as well as long-term interest-bearing notes, and also considers accounting for notes receivable that are collected in equal installment payments.

Marriott International accepts both interest-bearing and noninterest-bearing notes from developers and franchisees of new hotels. The 2015 disclosure note shown in Illustration 7–11 describes the company's accounting policy for these notes.

When a noninterest-bearing note is received solely in exchange for cash, the amount of cash exchanged is the basis for valuing the note.

NOTES RECEIVED SOLELY FOR CASH. If a note with an unrealistic interest rate—even a noninterest-bearing note—is received *solely* in exchange for cash, the cash paid to the issuer is considered to be the note's present value.[14] Even if this means recording interest at a ridiculously low or zero rate, the amount of cash exchanged is the basis for valuing the

[14]This assumes that no other present or future considerations are included in the agreement. For example, a noninterest-bearing note might be given to a vendor in exchange for cash *and* a promise to provide future inventories at prices lower than anticipated market prices. The issuer values the note at the present value of cash payments using a realistic interest rate, and the difference between present value and cash payments is recognized as interest revenue over the life of the note. This difference also increases future inventory purchases to realistic market prices.

Illustration 7–11
Disclosure of Notes Receivable—Marriott International

Real World Financials

Summary of Significant Accounting Policies (in part)

We may make senior, mezzanine, and other loans to owners of hotels that we operate or franchise, generally to facilitate the development of a hotel and sometimes to facilitate brand programs or initiatives. We expect the owners to repay the loans in accordance with the loan agreements, or earlier as the hotels mature and capital markets permit.

Note 9: Notes Receivable (in part)

Notes Receivable Principal Payments (net of reserves and unamortized discounts) and Interest Rates ($ in millions)	**Amount**
Balance at year-end 2015	$221
Range of stated interest rates at year-end 2015	0 to 15%

note. If the noninterest-bearing note in the previous example had been received solely in exchange for $700,000 cash, the transaction would be recorded as follows:

Note receivable (face amount)	700,000	
Cash (given)		700,000

Subsequent Valuation of Notes Receivable

Similar to accounts receivable, if a company anticipates bad debts (also called credit losses) on short-term notes receivable, it uses an allowance account to reduce the receivable to the appropriate carrying value. The process of recording bad debt expense is the same as with accounts receivable.

One of the more difficult measurement problems facing banks and other lending institutions is the estimation of bad debts on their long-term notes (loans). It's difficult to predict uncollectible accounts for these arrangements. As an example, Wells Fargo & Company, a large bank holding company, reported the following in the asset section of its December 31, 2015, balance sheet:

($ in millions)	December 31, 2015	December 31, 2014
Loans	$916,559	$862,551
Allowance for loan losses	(11,545)	(12,319)
Net loans	$905,014	$850,232

A disclosure note, reproduced in Illustration 7–12, describes Wells Fargo's loan loss policy.

Illustration 7–12
Disclosure of Allowance for Loan Losses—Wells Fargo & Company

Real World Financials

Allowance for Credit Losses (ACL) (in part)

The allowance for credit losses is management's estimate for credit losses inherent in the loan portfolio, including unfunded credit commitments, at the balance sheet date. We have an established process to determine the appropriateness of the allowance for credit losses that assesses the losses inherent in our portfolio and related unfunded credit commitments. While we attribute portions of the allowance to our respective commercial and consumer portfolio segments, the entire allowance is available to absorb credit losses inherent in the total loan portfolio and unfunded credit commitments.

GAAP requires that companies disclose the fair value of their notes receivable in the disclosure notes (they don't have to disclose the fair value of accounts receivable when the book value of the receivables approximates fair value).[15] Also, companies can choose

[15]FASB ASC 825–10–50–10: Financial Instruments–Overall–Disclosure–Fair Value of Financial Instruments (previously "Disclosures about Fair Value of Financial Instruments" *Statement of Financial Accounting Standards No. 107* (Norwalk, Conn.: FASB, 1991)).

to carry receivables at fair value in their balance sheets, with changes in fair value recognized as gains or losses in the income statements.[16] This "fair value option" is discussed in Chapter 12.

Usually creditors account for bad debts for a portfolio of notes, just as they do for a portfolio of accounts receivable. However, when it becomes *probable* that a creditor will be unable to collect all amounts due according to the contractual terms of a *particular* note receivable, that receivable is considered impaired and accounted for separately. The receivable is remeasured as the present value of currently expected cash flows, discounted at the loan's original effective rate. Impairments of receivables are discussed in Appendix 7B.

CURRENT EXPECTED CREDIT LOSS (CDCL) MODEL FOR NOTES RECEIVABLE. As with accounts receivable, the CECL model will be used to estimate credit losses with respect to notes receivable starting in 2020, and companies can choose to use that approach starting in 2019. Under the CECL model, creditors consider all relevant information when assessing credit losses, including reasonable and supportable forecasts about the future. Creditors can use a variety of approaches to estimate uncollectible notes receivable, including the aging method illustrated for accounts receivable. Often creditors use discounted cash flow techniques, estimating the amount of necessary allowance by comparing the balance in the note receivable to the present value of the cash flows expected to be received, discounted at the interest rate that was effective when the receivable was initially recognized. An example of that approach is included in Appendix 7B.

International Financial Reporting Standards

LO7–10

Accounts and Notes Receivable. Until recently, *IAS No. 39* was the standard that specified appropriate accounting for accounts and notes receivable, under the category of Loans and Receivables.[17] However, *IFRS No. 9* currently is scheduled to be required after January 1, 2018, and earlier adoption is allowed.[18] Therefore, until 2018 either standard could be in effect for a particular company that reports under IFRS (although countries in the European Union may not report under *IFRS No. 9,* as the European Commission has not yet ratified it). Still, both of the IFRS standards are very similar to U.S. GAAP with respect to accounting for accounts and notes receivable, with similar treatment of trade and cash discounts, sales returns, recognizing interest on notes receivable, and using an allowance for uncollectible accounts (which typically is called a "provision for bad debts" under IFRS).

A few key differences remain. IFRS and U.S. GAAP both allow a "fair value option" for accounting for receivables, but the IFRS standards restrict the circumstances in which that option is allowed (we discuss this more in Chapter 12). Also, *IAS No. 39* permits accounting for receivables as "available for sale" investments if that approach is elected upon initial recognition of the receivable. *IFRS No. 9* does not allow that option for receivables, and U.S. GAAP only allows "available for sale" accounting for investments in debt securities (we also discuss that approach further in Chapter 12). Also, U.S. GAAP requires more disaggregation of accounts and notes receivable in the balance sheet or notes to the financial statements. For example, companies need to separately disclose accounts receivable from customers, from related parties, and from others. IFRS recommends but does not require separate disclosure.

A final important difference relates to estimating bad debts. IFRS uses the ECL ("Expected Credit Loss") model. For most receivables, the ECL model reports a "12-month ECL," which bases expected credit losses only on defaults that could occur within the next twelve months. Only if a receivable's credit quality has deteriorated significantly does the creditor instead report the "lifetime ECL," which also includes credit losses expected to occur from defaults after twelve months, as is done for all receivables under the CECL model that will be used in U.S. GAAP. As a result of this lack of convergence, it is likely that accruals for credit losses under IFRS will be lower, and occur later, than under U.S. GAAP.

[16]FASB ASC 825–10–25: Financial Instruments–Overall–Recognition Fair Value Option (previously "The Fair Value Option for Financial Assets and Financial Liabilities" *Statement of Financial Accounting Standards No. 159* (Norwalk, Conn.: FASB, 2007)).

[17]"Financial Instruments: Recognition and Measurement," *International Accounting Standard No. 39* (IASCF), as amended effective January 1, 2016.

[18]"Financial Instruments," *International Financial Reporting Standard No. 9* (IASCF), as amended effective January 1, 2016.

Financing with Receivables

LO7–8

Financial institutions have developed a wide variety of ways for companies to use their receivables to obtain immediate cash. Companies can find this attractive because it shortens their operating cycles by providing cash immediately rather than having to wait until credit customers pay the amounts due. Also, many companies avoid the difficulties of servicing (billing and collecting) receivables by having financial institutions take on that role. Of course, financial institutions require compensation for providing these services, usually interest and/or a finance charge.

The various approaches used to finance with receivables differ with respect to which rights and risks are retained by the *transferor* (the company who was the original holder of the receivables) and which are passed on to the *transferee* (the new holder, the financial institution). Despite this diversity, any of these approaches can be described as either:

1. A *secured borrowing*. Under this approach, the transferor (borrower) simply acts like it borrowed money from the transferee (lender), with the receivables remaining in the transferor's balance sheet and serving as collateral for the loan. On the other side of the transaction, the transferee recognizes a note receivable.
2. *A sale of receivables*. Under this approach, the transferor (seller) "derecognizes" (removes) the receivables from its balance sheet, acting like it sold them to the transferee (buyer). On the other side of the transaction, the transferee recognizes the receivables as assets in its balance sheet and measures them at their fair value.

As you will see in the examples that follow, the transferor (borrower) debits cash regardless of whether the transaction is treated as a secured borrowing or a sale of receivables. What differs is whether the borrower credits a liability (for a secured borrowing) or credits the receivable asset (for a sale of receivables). Let's discuss each of these approaches in more detail as they apply to accounts receivable and notes receivable. Then we'll discuss the circumstances under which GAAP requires each approach.

Secured Borrowing

When companies *pledge* accounts receivable as collateral for debt, a disclosure note describes the arrangement.

Sometimes companies pledge accounts receivable as collateral for a loan. No particular receivables are associated with the loan. Rather, the entire receivables balance serves as collateral. The responsibility for collection of the receivables remains solely with the company. No special accounting treatment is needed for pledged receivables, but the arrangement should be described in a disclosure note. For example, Illustration 7–13 shows a portion of the long-term debt disclosure note included in the 2015 annual report of Virco Mfg. Corporation, a manufacturer of office furniture.

Illustration 7–13

Disclosure of Receivables Used as Collateral—Virco Mfg. Corporation

Real World Financials

Liquidity and Capital Resources (in part) Working Capital Requirements (in part)

The Revolving Credit Facility is an asset-based line of credit that is subject to a borrowing base limitation and generally provides for advances of up to 85% of eligible accounts receivable . . .

Alternatively, financing arrangements can require that companies assign particular receivables to serve as collateral for loans. You already may be familiar with the concept of assigning an asset as collateral if you or someone you know has a mortgage on a home. The bank or other financial institution holding the mortgage will require that, if the homeowner defaults on the mortgage payments, the home be sold and the proceeds used to pay off the mortgage debt. Similarly, in the case of an assignment of receivables, nonpayment of a debt will require the proceeds from collecting the assigned receivables to go directly toward repayment of the debt.

In these arrangements, the lender typically lends an amount of money that is less than the amount of receivables assigned by the borrower. The difference provides some protection for the lender to allow for possible uncollectible accounts. Also, the lender (sometimes called an *assignee*) usually charges the borrower (sometimes called an *assignor*) an upfront finance charge in addition to stated interest on the loan. The receivables might be collected either by the lender or the borrower, depending on the details of the arrangement. Illustration 7–14 provides an example.

Illustration 7–14

Assignment of Accounts Receivable

On December 1, 2018, the Santa Teresa Glass Company borrowed $500,000 from Finance Bank and signed a promissory note. Interest at 12% is payable monthly. The company assigned $620,000 of its receivables as collateral for the loan. Finance Bank charges a finance fee equal to 1.5% of the accounts receivable assigned.

Santa Teresa Glass records the borrowing as follows:

Cash (difference)	490,700	
Finance charge expense* (1.5% × $620,000)	9,300	
Liability—financing arrangement		500,000

*In theory, this fee should be allocated over the entire period of the loan rather than recorded as an expense in the initial period. However, amounts usually are small and the loan period usually is short. For expediency, then, we expense the entire fee immediately.

Santa Teresa will continue to collect the receivables, and will record any discounts, sales returns, and bad debt write-offs, but will remit the cash to Finance Bank, usually on a monthly basis. If $400,000 of the receivables assigned are collected in December, Santa Teresa Glass records the following entries:

Cash	400,000	
Accounts receivable		400,000
Interest expense ($500,000 × 12% × ¹⁄₁₂)	5,000	
Liability—financing arrangement	400,000	
Cash		405,000

Accounts Receivable

Debit	Credit
620,000	
	400,000
220,000	

Note Payable

Debit	Credit
	500,000
400,000	
	100,000

In Santa Teresa's financial statements, the arrangement is described in a disclosure note.

Sale of Receivables

Accounts and notes receivable, like any other assets, can be sold at a gain or a loss. The basic accounting treatment for the sale of receivables is similar to accounting for the sale of other assets. The seller (transferor) (a) removes from the accounts the receivables (and any allowance for bad debts associated with them), (b) recognizes at fair value any assets acquired or liabilities assumed by the seller in the transaction, and (c) records the difference as a gain or loss.

The sale of accounts receivable is a popular method of financing. A technique once used by companies in a few industries or with poor credit ratings, the sale of receivables is now a common occurrence for many different types of companies. For example, General Motors, Deere & Co., and Bank of America all sell receivables. The two most common types of selling arrangements are **factoring** and **securitization**. We'll now discuss each type.

Two popular arrangements used for the sale of receivables are *factoring* and *securitization*.

In a factoring arrangement, the company sells its accounts receivable to a financial institution. The financial institution typically buys receivables for cash, handles the billing and collection of the receivables, and charges a fee for this service. Actually, credit cards like VISA and Mastercard are forms of factoring arrangements. The seller relinquishes all rights to the future cash receipts in exchange for cash from the buyer (the *factor*).

As an example, Illustration 7–15 shows an excerpt from the website of BusinessCash.Com, a financial institution that offers factoring as one of its services.

Notice that the factor, BusinessCash.com, advances only between 70%–92% of the factored receivables. The remaining balance is retained as security until all of the receivables are collected and then remitted to the transferor, net of the factor's fee. The interest rate charged by this factor might seem low, but realize it is a 30-day rate. Multiply it by 12, and you will see a range of annual interest rates from 7% to almost 18%. The specific rate charged depends on, among other things, the quality of the receivables and the length of time before payment is required.

Illustration 7–15
Advertisement of Factoring BusinessCash. Com

Real World Financials

Accounts Receivable Factoring

0.59-1.49% 30-Day Rates! Funding in 24-48 hours!

Accounts Receivable Financing is the sale of a company's receivables at a discount in exchange for immediate cash. The percentage of working capital a company can receive upfront ranges from 70-92%. AR financing can be a perfect solution for many industries, including to textiles, to wine distributors, and to start-ups.

FINANCIAL Reporting Case

Q4, p. 351

Another popular arrangement used to sell receivables is securitization. In a typical accounts receivable securitization, the company creates a "special purpose entity" (SPE), usually a trust or a subsidiary. The SPE buys a pool of trade receivables, credit card receivables, or loans from the company, and then sells related securities, typically debt such as bonds or commercial paper, that are backed (collateralized) by the receivables. Securitizing receivables using an SPE can provide significant economic advantages, allowing companies to reach a large pool of investors and to obtain more favorable financing terms.[19]

As an example of a securitization, Illustration 7–16 shows a portion of the disclosure note included in the 2015 annual report of Flextronics International Limited, a worldwide leader in design, manufacturing and logistics services, describing the securitization of its trade accounts receivables.

Illustration 7–16
Description of Securitization Program—Flextronics International Limited

Real World Financials

Note 10: Trade Receivables Securitization

The Company continuously sells designated pools of trade receivables . . . to affiliated special purpose entities, each of which in turns sells 100% of the receivables to unaffiliated financial institutions . . . The company services, administers and collects the receivables on behalf of the special purpose entities and receives a servicing fee of 0.1% to 0.5% of serviced receivables per annum.

The specifics of sale accounting vary depending on the particular arrangement between the seller and buyer (transferee).[20] One key feature is whether the receivables are transferred without recourse or with recourse.

The buyer assumes the risk of uncollectibility when accounts receivable are sold *without recourse.*

SALE WITHOUT RECOURSE. If a factoring arrangement is made without recourse, the buyer can't ask the seller for more money if the receivables prove to be uncollectible. Therefore, the buyer assumes the risk of bad debts. Illustration 7–17 provides an example of receivables factored without recourse.

Note that in Illustration 7–17 the fair value ($50,000) of the last 10% of the receivables to be collected is less than 10% of the total book value of the receivables (10% × $600,000 = $60,000). That's common, because the last receivables to be collected are likely to be reduced by sales returns and allowances, and therefore have a lower fair value.

The seller retains the risk of uncollectibility when accounts receivable are sold *with recourse.*

SALE WITH RECOURSE. When a company sells accounts receivable with recourse, the seller retains all of the risk of bad debts. In effect, the seller guarantees that the buyer will be paid even if some receivables prove to be uncollectible. To compensate the seller for retaining the risk of bad debts, the buyer usually charges a lower factoring fee when receivables are sold with recourse.

In Illustration 7–17, even if the receivables were sold with recourse, Santa Teresa Glass still could account for the transfer as a sale so long as the conditions for sale treatment are met. The only difference is the additional requirement that Santa Teresa record the estimated

[19]Although SPEs usually aren't viewed as separate entities for accounting purposes, they typically are separate entities for legal purposes. As a consequence, an SPE typically is viewed as "bankruptcy remote," meaning that the transferor's creditors can't access the receivables if the transferor goes bankrupt. This increases the safety of the SPE's assets and typically allows it to obtain more favorable financing terms than could the transferor.

[20]FASB ASC 860: Transfers and Servicing (previously "Accounting for Transfers of Financial Assets, an amendment of FASB Statement No. 140," *Statement of Financial Accounting Standards No. 166* (Norwalk, Conn.: FASB, 2009)).

Illustration 7–17
Accounts Receivable Factored without Recourse

In December 2018, the Santa Teresa Glass Company factored accounts receivable that had a book value of $600,000 to Factor Bank. The transfer was made without recourse. Under this arrangement, Santa Teresa transfers the $600,000 of receivables to Factor, and Factor immediately remits to Santa Teresa cash equal to 90% of the factored amount (90% × $600,000 = $540,000). Factor retains the remaining 10% to cover its factoring fee (equal to 4% of the total factored amount; 4% × $600,000 = $24,000) and to provide a cushion against potential sales returns and allowances. After Factor has collected cash equal to the amount advanced to Santa Teresa plus their factoring fee, Factor remits the excess to Santa Teresa. Therefore, under this arrangement Factor provides Santa Teresa with cash upfront and a "beneficial interest" in the transferred receivables equal to the fair value of the last 10% of the receivables to be collected (which management estimates to equal $50,000), less the 4% factoring fee.*

Santa Teresa Glass records the transfer as follows:

Cash (90% × $600,000)	540,000	
Loss on sale of receivables (to balance)	34,000	
Receivable from factor ($50,000 − 24,000 fee)	26,000	
Accounts receivable (book value sold)		600,000

*Illustration 7–17 depicts an arrangement in which the factor's fee is paid out of the 10% of receivables retained by the factor. Alternatively, a factoring arrangement could be structured to have the factor's fee withheld from the cash advanced to the company at the start of the arrangement. In that case, in Illustration 7–17 the journal entry recorded by Santa Teresa would be:

Cash ([90% × $600,000] − $24,000 fee)	516,000	
Loss on sale of receivables (to balance)	34,000	
Receivable from factor	50,000	
Accounts receivable (book value sold)		600,000

fair value of its recourse obligation as a liability. The recourse obligation is the estimated amount that Santa Teresa will have to pay Factor Bank as a reimbursement for uncollectible receivables. Illustration 7–18 provides an example of receivables factored with recourse.

Illustration 7–18
Accounts Receivable Factored with Recourse

Assume the same facts as in Illustration 7–17, except that Santa Teresa sold the receivables to Factor *with recourse* and estimates the fair value of the recourse obligation to be $5,000. Santa Teresa records the transfer as follows:

Cash (90% × $600,000)	540,000	
Loss on sale of receivables (to balance)	39,000	
Receivable from factor ($50,000 − 24,000 fee)	26,000	
Recourse liability		5,000
Accounts receivable (book value sold)		600,000

When comparing Illustration 7–17 and 7–18, notice that the estimated recourse liability of $5,000 increases the loss on sale by $5,000. If the factor eventually collects all of the receivables, Santa Teresa eliminates the recourse liability and recognizes a gain.

Transfers of Notes Receivable

We handle transfers of notes receivable in the same manner as transfers of accounts receivable. A note receivable can be used to obtain immediate cash from a financial institution either by pledging the note as collateral for a loan or by selling the note. Notes also can be securitized.

The transfer of a note receivable to a financial institution is called *discounting*.

The transfer of a note to a financial institution is referred to as **discounting**. The financial institution accepts the note and gives the seller cash equal to the maturity value of the note reduced by a discount. The discount is computed by applying a discount rate to the maturity value and represents the financing fee the financial institution charges for the transaction. Illustration 7–19 provides an example of the calculation of the proceeds received by the transferor.

Illustration 7–19
Discounting a Note Receivable

On December 31, 2018, the Stridewell Wholesale Shoe Company sold land in exchange for a nine-month, 10% note. The note requires the payment of $200,000 plus interest on September 30, 2019. The company's fiscal year-end is December 31. The 10% rate properly reflects the time value of money for this type of note. On March 31, 2019, Stridewell discounted the note at the Bank of the East. The bank's discount rate is 12%.

Because the note had been outstanding for three months before it's discounted at the bank, Stridewell first records the interest that has accrued prior to being discounted:

STEP 1: Accrue interest earned on the note receivable prior to its being discounted.

March 31, 2019

Interest receivable	5,000	
Interest revenue ($200,000 × 10% × 3/12)		5,000

Next, the value of the note if held to maturity is calculated. Then the discount for the time remaining to maturity is deducted to determine the cash proceeds from discounting the note:

STEP 2: Add interest to maturity to calculate maturity value.

STEP 3: Deduct discount to calculate cash proceeds.

$200,000	Face amount
15,000	Interest to maturity ($200,000 × 10% × 9/12)
215,000	Maturity value
(12,900)	Discount ($215,000 × 12% × 6/12)
$202,100	Cash proceeds

Similar to accounts receivable, Stridewell potentially could account for the transfer as a sale or a secured borrowing. For example, Illustration 7–20 shows the appropriate journal entries to account for the transfer as a sale without recourse.

Illustration 7–20
Discounted Note Treated as a Sale

Cash (proceeds determined above)	202,100	
Loss on sale of note receivable (to balance)	2,900	
Note receivable (face amount)		200,000
Interest receivable (accrued interest determined above)		5,000

Deciding Whether to Account for a Transfer as a Sale or a Secured Borrowing

Transferors usually prefer to use the sale approach rather than the secured borrowing approach to account for the transfer of a receivable, because the sale approach makes the transferor seem less leveraged, more liquid, and perhaps more profitable than does the secured borrowing approach. Illustration 7–21 explains why by describing particular effects on key accounting metrics.

Illustration 7–21
Why Do Transferors of Receivables Generally Want to Account for the Transfer as a Sale?

	Transfer of Receivables Accounted for as		
Does the Accounting Approach	**Sale**	**Secured Borrowing**	**Why Sales Approach is Preferred by the Transferor**
Derecognize A/R, reducing assets?	Yes	No	Sale approach produces lower total assets and higher return on assets (ROA).
Recognize liability for cash received?	No	Yes	Sale approach produces lower liabilities and less leverage (debt/equity).
Where is cash received shown in the statement of cash flows?	May be in operating or financing sections	Always in financing section	Sale approach can produce higher cash flow from operations at time of transfer.
Recognize gain on transfer?	More likely	Less likely	Sale approach can produce higher income at time of transfer.

So when is a company allowed to account for the transfer of receivables as a sale? The most critical element is the extent to which the company (the transferor) *surrenders control over the assets transferred.* For some arrangements, surrender of control is clear (e.g., when a receivable is sold without recourse and without any other involvement by the transferor). However, for other arrangements this distinction is not obvious. Indeed, some companies appear to structure transactions in ways that qualify for sale treatment but retain enough involvement to have control. This led the FASB to provide guidelines designed to constrain inappropriate use of the sale approach. Specifically, the transferor (defined to include the company, its consolidated affiliates, and people acting on behalf of the company) is determined to have surrendered control over the receivables if and only if all of the following conditions are met:[21]

a. The transferred assets have been isolated from the transferor—beyond the reach of the transferor and its creditors.
b. Each transferee has the right to pledge or exchange the assets it received.
c. The transferor does not maintain *effective control* over the transferred assets, for example, by structuring the transfer such that the assets are likely to end up returned to the transferor.

If the transferor is deemed to have surrendered control over the transferred receivables, the arrangement is accounted for as a sale; otherwise as a secured borrowing.

If *all* of these conditions are met, the transferor accounts for the transfer as a sale. If *any* of the conditions are not met, the transferor treats the transaction as a secured borrowing.

It is not surprising that some companies have aggressively tried to circumvent these conditions by creating elaborate transactions to qualify for sale treatment. The most famous recent case was Lehman Brothers' use of "Repo 105" transactions, discussed in Illustration 7–22.

Illustration 7–22

Repo 105 Transactions—Lehman Brothers

Real World Financials

Lehman Brothers' bankruptcy in 2008 was the largest ever to occur in the United States. One factor that likely contributed to investor losses was Lehman's use of "Repo 105" transactions that concealed how overburdened with liabilities the company had become. Here is how a Repo 105 transaction worked. Near the end of each quarter, Lehman would transfer financial assets like receivables to a bank or other financial institution in exchange for cash, and would account for that transfer as a sale of the financial assets. Lehman would use the cash obtained from the transfer to pay down liabilities, so the net effect of the transaction was to reduce assets, reduce liabilities, and therefore make Lehman appear less leveraged and less risky. Lehman also agreed to repurchase ("repo") the assets in the next quarter for an amount of cash that exceeded the amount it initially received.

In substance, this transaction is a loan, since Lehman ended up retaining the financial assets and paying amounts equivalent to principal and interest. However, Lehman argued that the assets were beyond its *effective control,* because the cash it received for transferring the assets was insufficient to enable Lehman to repurchase those assets (the "105" in "Repo 105" refers to the assets being worth at least 105% of the cash Lehman was getting for them). Although Lehman's interpretation was supported by the GAAP in effect at the time, these transactions were very poorly disclosed, and when they eventually came to light, the financial markets and investing public reacted very negatively. In response to the Lehman debacle, the FASB has taken steps to close the loophole that allowed Repo 105 transactions to be accounted for as sales.*

*FASB ASC 860–10–55: Transfers and Servicing–Overall–Implementation Guidance and Illustrations (previously *ASU 2011-03*: Transfers and Servicing (Topic 860): *Reconsideration of Effective Control for Repurchase Agreements* (Norwalk, Conn.: FASB 2011)).

Illustration 7–23 summarizes the decision process that is used to determine whether a transfer of a receivable is accounted for as a secured borrowing or a sale.

Disclosures

Much disclosure is required when the transferor has continuing involvement in the transferred assets but accounts for the transfer as a sale. Why? Those are the circumstances under

[21]FASB ASC 860–10–40: Transfers and Servicing–Overall–Derecognition (previously "Accounting for Transfers and Servicing of Financial Assets and Extinguishments of Liabilities," *Statement of Financial Accounting Standards No. 140* (Norwalk, Conn.: FASB, 2000), as amended by *SFAS No. 166*).

Additional Consideration

Participating Interests. What if, rather than transferring all of a particular receivable, a company transfers only part of it? For example, what if a company transfers the right to receive future interest payments on a note, but retains the right to receive the loan principal? U.S. GAAP requires that a partial transfer be treated as a secured borrowing unless the amount transferred qualifies as a "participating interest" as well as meeting the "surrender of control" requirements described above. Participating interests are defined as having a proportionate ownership interest in the receivable and sharing proportionally in the cash flows of the receivable. Many common securitization arrangements do not qualify as participating interests, so this change in GAAP makes it harder for partial transfers to qualify for the sale approach.

Illustration 7–23
Accounting for the Financing of Receivables

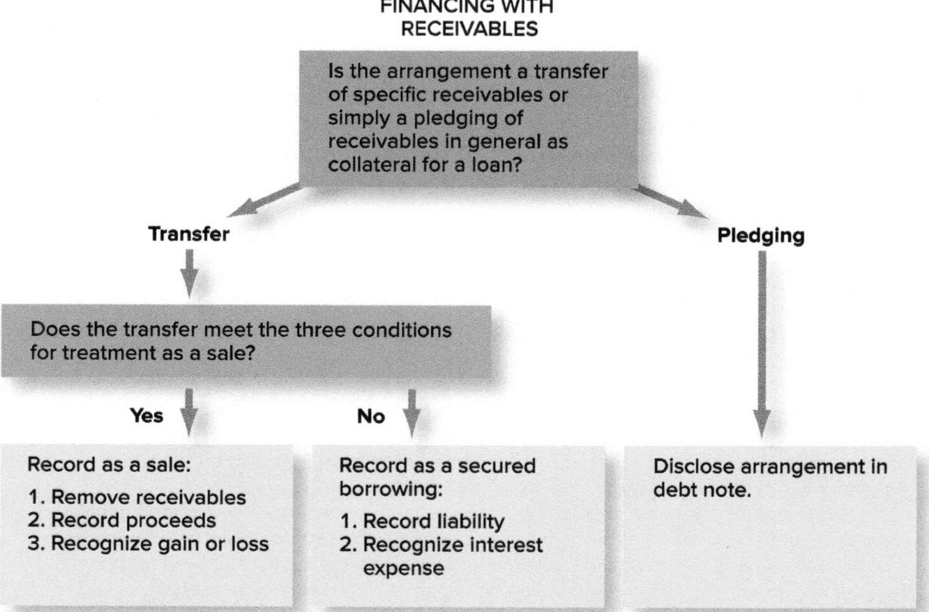

which it's most likely that the transferor may still bear significant risk associated with the arrangement, so those are the arrangements that analysts often view instead as a secured borrowing. As a result, transferors must provide enough information about the transfer to allow financial statement users to fully understand (a) the transfer, (b) any continuing involvement with the transferred assets, and (c) any ongoing risks to the transferor.

The company also has to provide information about the quality of the transferred assets. For example, for transferred receivables, the company needs to disclose the amount of receivables that are past due and any credit losses occurring during the period. Among the other information the company must disclose are these:

- How fair values were estimated when recording the transaction
- Any cash flows occurring between the transferor and the transferee
- How any continuing involvement in the transferred assets will be accounted for on an ongoing basis[22]

[22]FASB ASC 860–10–40: Transfers and Servicing–Overall–Derecognition (previously "Accounting for Transfers of Financial Assets, an amendment of FASB Statement No. 140," *Statement of Financial Accounting Standards No. 166* (Norwalk, Conn.: FASB, 2009), par. 17).

International Financial Reporting Standards

● LO7–10

Transfers of Receivables. *IAS No. 39* and *FASB ASC 860* cover financing with receivables under IFRS and U.S. GAAP, respectively.[23,24] The international and U.S. guidance often lead to similar accounting treatments. Both seek to determine whether an arrangement should be treated as a secured borrowing or a sale, and, having concluded which approach is appropriate, both account for the approaches in a similar fashion.

Where IFRS and U.S. GAAP most differ is in the conceptual basis for their choice of accounting approaches and in the decision process they require to determine which approach to use. As you have seen in this chapter, U.S. GAAP focuses on whether control of assets has shifted from the transferor to the transferee. In contrast, IFRS requires a more complex decision process. The company has to have transferred the rights to receive the cash flows from the receivable, and then considers whether the company has transferred "substantially all of the risks and rewards of ownership," as well as whether the company has transferred control. Under IFRS:

1. If the company *transfers* substantially all of the risks and rewards of ownership, the transfer is treated as a sale.
2. If the company *retains* substantially all of the risks and rewards of ownership, the transfer is treated as a secured borrowing.
3. If neither conditions 1 or 2 hold, the company accounts for the transaction as a sale if it has transferred control, and as a secured borrowing if it has retained control.

Whether risks and rewards have been transferred is evaluated by comparing how variability in the amounts and timing of the cash flows of the transferred asset affect the company before and after the transfer.

This is a broad overview of the IFRS guidance. Application of the detailed rules is complex, and depending on the specifics of an arrangement, a company could have different accounting under IFRS and U.S. GAAP.

Concept Review Exercise

FINANCING WITH RECEIVABLES

The Hollywood Lumber Company obtains financing from the Midwest Finance Company by factoring (or discounting) its receivables. During June 2018, the company factored $1,000,000 of accounts receivable to Midwest. The transfer was made *without* recourse. The factor, Midwest Finance, remits 80% of the factored receivables and retains 20%. When the receivables are collected by Midwest, the retained amount, less a 3% fee (3% of the total factored amount), will be remitted to Hollywood Lumber. Hollywood estimates that the fair value of the amount retained by Midwest is $180,000.

In addition, on June 30, 2018, Hollywood discounted a note receivable without recourse. The note, which originated on March 31, 2018, requires the payment of $150,000 *plus* interest at 8% on March 31, 2019. Midwest's discount rate is 10%. The company's fiscal year-end is December 31.

Required:

Prepare journal entries for Hollywood Lumber for the factoring of accounts receivable and the note receivable discounted on June 30. Assume that the required criteria are met and the transfers are accounted for as sales.

[23] "Financial Instruments: Recognition and Measurement," *International Accounting Standard No. 39* (IASCF), as amended effective January 1, 2014.

[24] FASB ASC 860: Transfers and Servicing (previously "Accounting for Transfers of Financial Assets, an amendment of FASB Statement No. 140," *Statement of Financial Accounting Standards No. 166* (Norwalk, Conn.: FASB, 2009)).

Solution:

The Factoring of Receivables		
Cash (80% × $1,000,000)	800,000	
Loss on sale of receivables (to balance)	50,000	
Receivable from factor ($180,000 − 30,000 fee)	150,000	
Accounts receivable (balance sold)		1,000,000
The Note Receivable Discounted		
Interest receivable	3,000	
Interest revenue ($150,000 × 8% × 3/12)		3,000
Cash (proceeds determined below)	149,850	
Loss on sale of note receivable (difference)	3,150	
Note receivable (face amount)		150,000
Interest receivable (accrued interest determined above)		3,000

$150,000	Face amount
12,000	Interest to maturity ($150,000 × 8%)
162,000	Maturity value
(12,150)	Discount ($162,000 × 10% × 9/12)
$149,850	Cash proceeds

Decision Makers' Perspective

LO7–9

RECEIVABLES MANAGEMENT. A company's investment in receivables is influenced by several variables, including the level of sales, the nature of the product or service sold, and credit and collection policies. These variables are, of course, related. For example, a change in credit policies could affect sales. In fact, more liberal credit policies—allowing customers a longer time to pay or offering cash discounts for early payment—often are initiated with the specific objective of increasing sales volume.

Management must evaluate the costs and benefits of any change in credit and collection policies.

Management's choice of credit and collection policies often involves trade-offs. For example, offering cash discounts may increase sales volume, accelerate customer payment, and reduce bad debts. These benefits are not without cost. The cash discounts reduce the amount of cash collected from customers who take advantage of the discounts. Extending payment terms also may increase sales volume. However, this creates an increase in the required investment in receivables and may increase bad debts.

The ability to use receivables as a method of financing also offers management alternatives. Assigning, factoring, and discounting receivables are alternative methods of financing operations that must be evaluated relative to other financing methods such as lines of credit or other types of short-term borrowing.

Investors, creditors, and financial analysts can gain important insights by monitoring a company's investment in receivables. Chapter 4 introduced the receivables turnover ratio and the related average collection period, ratios designed to monitor receivables. Recall that these ratios are calculated as follows:

$$\text{Receivables turnover ratio} = \frac{\text{Net sales}}{\text{Average accounts receivable (net)}}$$

$$\text{Average collection period} = \frac{\text{365 days}}{\text{Receivables turnover ratio}}$$

The turnover ratio shows the number of times during a period that the average accounts receivable balance is collected, and the average collection period is an approximation of the number of days the average accounts receivable balance is outstanding.

As a company's sales grow, receivables also will increase. If the percentage increase in receivables is greater than the percentage increase in sales, the receivables turnover ratio will decline (the average collection period will increase). This could indicate customer dissatisfaction with the product or that the company has extended too generous payment terms in order to attract new customers, which, in turn, could increase sales returns and bad debts.

These ratios also can be used to compare the relative effectiveness of companies in managing the investment in receivables. Of course, it would be meaningless to compare the receivables turnover ratio of a computer products company such as IBM with that of, say, a food products company like Hershey. A company selling high-priced, low-volume products like mainframe computers generally will grant customers longer payment terms than a company selling lower priced, higher volume food products. Illustration 7–24 lists the 2015 receivables turnover ratio for some well-known companies. The differences are as expected, given the nature of the companies' products and operations. In particular, companies designing expensive products for medical and business applications turn over their receivables less frequently than do consumer-goods manufacturers and wholesalers.

Company	**2015 Receivables Turnover Ratio**
Medtronic (medical technology)	4.54
Autodesk (design software)	4.84
General Mills (wholesale consumer foods)	8.28

Illustration 7–24
Receivables Turnover Ratios

To illustrate receivables analysis in more detail, let's compute the 2015 receivables turnover ratio and the average collection period for two companies in the software industry, Symantec Corp. and CA, Inc.

	($ in millions)					
	Symantec Corp.			**CA, Inc.**		
	2015		**2014**	**2015**		**2014**
Accounts receivable (net)	$993		$1,007	$652		$800
Two-year averages		$1,000			$ 726	
Net sales—2015		**$6,508**			**$4,262**	

	Symantec Corp.	**CA, Inc.**	**Industry Average**
Receivables Turnover	$= \frac{\$6,508}{\$1,000} = 6.51$ times	$\frac{\$4,262}{\$726} = 5.87$ times	6.85 times
Average Collection Period	$= \frac{365}{6.51} = 56.07$ days	$\frac{365}{5.87} = 62.18$ days	53.28 days

On average, Symantec collects its receivables 6 days sooner than does CA, but 3 days slower than the industry average. A major portion of Symantec's sales of products like Norton antivirus software are made directly to consumers online who pay immediately with credit cards, significantly accelerating payment. CA, on the other hand, sells primarily to businesses, which take longer to pay.

EARNINGS QUALITY. Recall our discussion in Chapter 4 concerning earnings quality. We learned that managers have the ability, to a limited degree, to manipulate reported income and that many observers believe this practice diminishes earnings quality because it can mask "permanent" earnings. Former SEC Chairman Arthur Levitt listed discretionary accruals, which he called "Miscellaneous Cookie Jar Reserves," as one of the most popular methods companies use to manipulate income.

Bad debt expense is one of a variety of discretionary accruals that provide management with the opportunity to manipulate income.

Sometimes financial statement users can examine accounts receivable, the allowance for bad debts, and other accounts to detect low earnings quality. For example, in an analysis that eventually led to an important SEC fraud case, PaineWebber Inc. downgraded its stock recommendation for Sunbeam, Inc., after noticing unusually high accounts receivable and unexpected increases in sales of certain products. Also, Sunbeam's allowance for uncollectible accounts had shown large increases in prior periods. It eventually came to light that Sunbeam had been manipulating its income by using a "bill and hold" strategy with retail buyers. This involved selling products at large discounts to retailers before they normally would buy and then holding the products in third-party warehouses, with delivery at a later date. More generally, research indicates that companies sometimes manage earnings by building up large allowances for bad debts in good periods and then reducing those allowances to increase earnings in bad periods.[25]

Another area for accounting-quality concern is the sale method used to account for transfers of receivables. Research suggests that some companies manage earnings by distorting the fair value estimates that are made as part of recording securitizations.[26] Also, some firms classify cash flows associated with selling their accounts receivable in the operating section of the statement of cash flows, such that changes in the extent to which accounts receivable are sold can be used to manipulate cash flow from operations. In fact, evidence suggests that sophisticated investors and bond-rating agencies undo sales accounting to treat transfers of receivables as secured borrowings before assessing the riskiness of a company's debt.[27] Still, Wall Street is very good at identifying clever ways to structure transactions around accounting standards, so it is important to be vigilant regarding the accounting for these transactions. ●

Financial Reporting Case Solution

© Rob Daly / age fotostock

1. **Explain the allowance method of accounting for bad debts.** *(p. 362)* The allowance method is used to carry accounts receivable at the amount expected to be collected. In an adjusting entry, we record bad debt expense and reduce accounts receivable indirectly by crediting a contra account to accounts receivable for an estimate of the amount that eventually will prove uncollectible.
2. **What approaches might CHS have used to arrive at the $275 million bad debt provision?** *(p. 364)* CHS would determine the balance in the allowance for uncollectible accounts that is necessary to show net accounts receivable at the appropriate carrying value, and then would record whatever adjustment and corresponding bad debt expense resulted in that balance. It likely would use an aging of accounts receivable to calculate the appropriate balance. It might also use a percentage of net sales to estimate bad debt expense, particularly on an interim basis, but that approach would only be allowed if it produced a similar carrying value as the balance sheet approach.
3. **Are there any alternatives to the allowance method?** *(p. 365)* An alternative to the allowance method is the direct write-off method. Using this method, adjusting entries are not recorded and any bad debt that does arise simply is written off as bad debt expense. The direct write-off method is not permitted by GAAP except in limited circumstances.
4. **What does it mean for CHS to securitize its receivables?** *(p. 376)* Securitization is a method used to sell accounts receivables. In a typical securitization, a company creates a "special purpose entity" that buys receivables from the company and issues securities that are collateralized by the securities. Securitization allows CHS to obtain cash for its receivables sooner than it could otherwise, and to reach a large pool of investors at favorable financing rates.

[25] S.B. Jackson and X. Liu, "The Allowance for Uncollectible Accounts, Conservatism, and Earnings Management," Journal of Accounting Research 48, No. 3 (2010): 565-601.

[26] P. M. Dechow, L. A. Myers, and C. Shakespeare, "Fair Value Accounting and Gains from Asset Securitizations: A Convenient Earnings Management Tool with Compensation Side-Benefits," *Journal of Accounting and Economics* 49, No. 2 (2010): 2–25.

[27] Other recent research provides evidence that investors treat securitizations as loans rather than asset sales, suggesting that they are unconvinced that a sale has truly taken place. For example, see W. R. Landsman, K. Peasnell, and C. Shakespeare, "Are Asset Securitizations Sales or Loans?" *The Accounting Review 83,* No. 5 (2008), pp. 1251–72.

The Bottom Line

- **LO7–1** Internal control refers to the plan designed to encourage adherence to company policies and procedures; promote operational efficiency; minimize errors, thefts or fraud; and maximize the reliability and accuracy of accounting data. Key elements of an internal control system for cash receipts and disbursements include separation of record keeping from control of cash duties and the periodic preparation of a bank reconciliation. *(p. 352)*
- **LO7–2** Cash can be informally restricted by management for a particular purpose. Restrictions also can be contractually imposed. If restricted cash is available for current operations or to pay current liabilities, it's classified as a current asset; otherwise, it's classified as investments and funds or other assets. *(p. 353)*
- **LO7–3** The gross method of accounting for cash discounts considers a discount not taken as part of sales revenue. The net method considers a discount not taken as sales discount forfeited. *(p. 357)*
- **LO7–4** When merchandise returns are anticipated, an allowance for sales returns should be recorded as a contra account to accounts receivable and sales revenue also should be reduced by the anticipated sales returns. *(p. 358)*
- **LO7–5** At the end of each period, the company estimates the necessary balance in the allowance for uncollectible accounts and then records whatever adjustment to the allowance and corresponding bad debt expense is necessary to reach that balance. *(p. 362)*
- **LO7–6** The balance sheet approach determines bad debt expense by estimating the appropriate carrying value of accounts receivable to be reported in the balance sheet and then adjusting the allowance for uncollectible accounts as necessary to reach that carrying value. The income statement approach estimates bad debt expense based on the notion that a certain percentage of each period's credit sales will prove to be uncollectible. *(p. 364)*
- **LO7–7** Notes receivable are formal credit arrangements between a creditor (lender) and a debtor (borrower). The typical note receivable requires the payment of a specified face amount, also called principal, at a specified maturity date or dates. In addition, interest is paid at a stated percentage of the face amount. Interest on notes is calculated by multiplying the face amount by the annual rate by the fraction of the annual period. *(p. 368)*
- **LO7–8** A wide variety of methods exists for companies to use their receivables to obtain immediate cash. These methods can be described as either a secured borrowing or a sale of receivables. If three conditions indicating surrender of control are met, the transferor accounts for the transfer of receivables as a sale; otherwise as a secured borrowing. *(p. 374)*
- **LO7–9** A company's investment in receivables is influenced by several related variables, to include the level of sales, the nature of the product or service, and credit and collection policies. Investors, creditors, and financial analysts can gain important insights by monitoring a company's investment in receivables. The receivables turnover and average collection period ratios are designed to monitor receivables. *(p. 382)*
- **LO7–10** Accounting for cash and accounts receivable are similar under U.S. GAAP and IFRS. Other than some differences in terminology and balance sheet classifications, the most important differences involve accounting for transfers of receivables. Both IFRS and U.S. GAAP seek to distinguish between determining whether a sales treatment or secured borrowing treatment is appropriate, but they use different conceptual frameworks to guide that choice. U.S. GAAP focuses on whether control of the receivables is transferred, while IFRS use a more complex decision process that also considers whether substantially all of the risks and rewards of ownership have been transferred. *(pp. 355, 373, 381,* and *392)*

Cash Controls

APPENDIX 7A

Bank Reconciliation

One of the most important tools used in the control of cash is the **bank reconciliation**. Since all cash receipts are deposited into the bank account and cash disbursements are made by check, the bank account provides a separate record of cash. It's desirable to periodically compare the bank balance with the balance in the company's own records and reconcile any differences.

You probably know from your own personal experience that the ending balance in your checking account reported on your monthly bank statement rarely equals the balance you have recorded in your checkbook. Differences arise from two types of items: timing differences and errors.

Differences between the cash book and bank balance occur due to differences in the timing of recognition of certain transactions and errors.

Timing differences occur when the company and the bank record transactions at different times. At any point in time the company may have adjusted the cash balance for items of which the bank is not yet aware. Likewise, the bank may have adjusted its record of that balance by items of which the company is not yet aware. For example, checks written and cash deposits are not all processed by the bank in the same month that they are recorded by the company. Also, the bank may adjust the company's account for items such as service charges that the company is not aware of until the bank statement is received.

Errors can be made either by the company or the bank. For example, a check might be written for $210 but recorded on the company's books as a $120 disbursement; a deposit of $500 might be processed incorrectly by the bank as a $50 deposit. In addition to serving as a safeguard of cash, the bank reconciliation also uncovers errors such as these and helps ensure that the proper cash balance is reported in the balance sheet.

STEP 1: Adjust the bank balance to the corrected cash balance.

Bank reconciliations include adjustments to the balance per bank for timing differences involving transactions already reflected in the company's accounting records that have not yet been processed by the bank. These adjustments usually include *checks outstanding* and *deposits outstanding* (also called *deposits in transit*). In addition, the balance per bank would be adjusted for any bank errors discovered. These adjustments produce an adjusted bank balance that represents the corrected cash balance.

STEP 2: Adjust the book balance to the corrected cash balance.

The balance per books is similarly adjusted for timing differences involving transactions already reflected by the bank of which the company is unaware until the bank statement is received. These would include service charges, charges for NSF (nonsufficient funds) checks, and collections made by the bank on the company's behalf. In addition, the balance per books is adjusted for any company errors discovered, resulting in an adjusted book balance that will also represent the corrected cash balance. *Each of these adjustments requires a journal entry to correct the book balance.* Only adjustments to the book balance require journal entries. Illustration 7A–1 recaps these reconciling items.

Illustration 7A–1

Bank Reconciliation—Reconciling Items

Balance per Bank
+ Deposits outstanding
− Checks outstanding
± Errors
Corrected balance

Balance per Book
+ Collections by bank
− Service charges
− NSF checks
± Errors
Corrected balance

The two corrected balances must equal.

Step 1: Adjustments to Bank Balance

1. *Add deposits outstanding.* These represent cash amounts received by the company and debited to cash that have not been deposited in the bank by the bank statement cutoff date and cash receipts deposited in the bank near the end of the period that are not recorded by the bank until after the cutoff date.
2. *Deduct checks outstanding.* These represent checks written and recorded by the company as credits to cash that have not yet been processed by the bank before the cutoff date.
3. *Bank errors.* These will either be increases or decreases depending on the nature of the error.

Step 2: Adjustments to Book Balance

1. *Add collections made by the bank* on the company's behalf and other increases in cash that the company is unaware of until the bank statement is received.
2. *Deduct service and other charges* made by the bank that the company is unaware of until the bank statement is received.
3. *Deduct NSF (nonsufficient funds) checks.* These are checks previously deposited for which the payors do not have sufficient funds in their accounts to cover the amount of the checks. The checks are returned to the company whose responsibility it is to seek payment from payors.
4. *Company errors.* These will either be increases or decreases depending on the nature of the error.

To demonstrate the bank reconciliation process, consider Illustration 7A–2.

Illustration 7A–2
Bank Reconciliation

The Hawthorne Manufacturing Company maintains a general checking account at the First Pacific Bank. First Pacific provides a bank statement and canceled checks once a month. The cutoff date is the last day of the month. The bank statement for the month of May is summarized as follows:

Balance, May 1, 2018	$ 32,120
Deposits	82,140
Checks processed	(78,433)
Service charges	(80)
NSF checks	(2,187)
Note payment collected by bank (includes $120 interest)	1,120
Balance, May 31, 2018	$ 34,680

The company's general ledger cash account has a balance of $35,276 at the end of May. A review of the company records and the bank statement reveals the following:

1. Cash receipts not yet deposited totaled $2,965.
2. A deposit of $1,020 was made on May 31 that was not credited to the company's account until June.
3. All checks written in April have been processed by the bank. Checks written in May that had not been processed by the bank total $5,536.
4. A check written for $1,790 was incorrectly recorded by the company as a $790 disbursement. The check was for payment to a supplier of raw materials.

The bank reconciliation prepared by the company appears as follows:

Step 1: Bank Balance to Corrected Balance	
Balance per bank statement	$34,680
Add: Deposits outstanding	3,985*
Deduct: Checks outstanding	(5,536)
Corrected cash balance	$ 33,129

Step 2: Book Balance to Corrected Balance	
Balance per books	$35,276
Add: Note collected by bank	1,120
Deduct:	
Service charges	(80)
NSF checks	(2,187)
Error—understatement of check	(1,000)
Corrected cash balance	$ 33,129

*$2,965 + 1,020 = $3,985

The next step is to prepare adjusting journal entries to reflect each of the adjustments to the balance per books. These represent amounts the company was not previously aware of until receipt of the bank statement. No adjusting entries are needed for the adjustments to the balance per bank because the company has already recorded these items. However, the bank needs to be notified of any errors discovered.

To record the receipt of principal and interest on note collected directly by the bank		
Cash	1,120	
Notes receivable		1,000
Interest revenue		120

(continued)

(concluded)

To record credits to cash revealed by the bank reconciliation		
Miscellaneous expense (bank service charges)	80	
Accounts receivable (NSF checks)	2,187	
Accounts payable (error in check to supplier)	1,000	
Cash		3,267

After these entries are posted, the general ledger cash account will equal the corrected balance of $33,129.

Petty Cash

Most companies keep a small amount of cash on hand to pay for low-cost items such as postage, office supplies, delivery charges, and entertainment expenses. It would be inconvenient, time consuming, and costly to process a check each time these small payments are made. A petty cash fund provides a more efficient way to handle these payments.

The petty cash fund always should have cash and receipts that together equal the amount of the fund.

A petty cash fund is established by transferring a specified amount of cash from the company's general checking account to an employee designated as the petty cash custodian. The amount of the fund should approximate the expenditures made from the fund during a relatively short period of time (say a week or a month). The custodian disburses cash from the fund when the appropriate documentation is presented, such as a receipt for the purchase of office supplies. At any point in time, the custodian should be in possession of cash and appropriate receipts that sum to the amount of the fund. The receipts serve as the basis for recording appropriate expenses each time the fund is replenished. Consider the example in Illustration 7A–3.

Illustration 7A–3
Petty Cash Fund

On May 1, 2018, the Hawthorne Manufacturing Company established a $200 petty cash fund. John Ringo is designated as the petty cash custodian. The fund will be replenished at the end of each month. On May 1, 2018, a check is written for $200 made out to John Ringo, petty cash custodian. During the month of May, John paid bills totaling $160 summarized as follows:

Postage	$ 40
Office supplies	35
Delivery charges	55
Entertainment	30
Total	$160

In journal entry form, the transaction to establish the fund would be recorded as follows:

May 1, 2018		
Petty Cash	200	
Cash (checking account)		200

A petty cash fund is established by writing a check to the custodian.

No entries are recorded at the time the actual expenditures are made from the fund. The expenditures are recorded when reimbursement is requested at the end of the month. At that time, a check is written to John Ringo, petty cash custodian, for the total of the fund receipts, $160 in this case. John cashes the check and replenishes the fund to $200. In journal entry form, replenishing the fund would be recorded as follows:

May 31, 2018		
Postage expense	40	
Office supplies expense	35	
Delivery expense	55	
Entertainment expense	30	
Cash (checking account)		160

The petty cash account is not debited when replenishing the fund. If, however, the size of the fund is increased at time of replenishment, the account is debited for the increase. Similarly, petty cash would be credited if the size of the fund is decreased.

The appropriate expense accounts are debited when the petty cash fund is reimbursed.

To maintain the control objective of separation of duties, the petty cash custodian should not be involved in the process of writing or approving checks, nor in record-keeping. In addition, management should arrange for surprise counts of the fund.

APPENDIX 7B

Accounting for Impairment of a Receivable and a Troubled Debt Restructuring[28]

Impairment of a Receivable

Earlier in this chapter you learned about the allowance method of accounting for bad debts. Because it is difficult to determine which individual receivables will ultimately prove uncollectible, the allowance method recognizes bad debt expense for a large group of receivables and reduces the book value of that group of receivables by establishing an allowance for uncollectible accounts. Later, when an individual receivable proves uncollectible, the receivable and the allowance are both reduced. The allowance method is used for many types of receivables, including normal trade receivables, notes receivable, and loans receivable.

However, for long-term receivables like notes receivable and loans receivable, companies also can consider information specific to an *individual* receivable when estimating bad debt (credit loss) expense. For example, a bank might learn that one of its borrowers is having financial difficulties. In that case, a more precise estimate of a credit loss for that receivable can be made.

Under current GAAP, an impairment loss (credit loss) on a receivable is recognized if the creditor (lender) believes it is *probable* that it will not receive all of the cash flows (principal and any interest payments) that have been promised by the debtor (borrower). In that case, the creditor remeasures the receivable based on the present value of currently expected cash flows, discounted at the receivable's original effective interest rate.[29] The necessary adjustment should seem familiar—a loss is included in current income by debiting bad debt expense (or a separate impairment loss account) and crediting the allowance for uncollectible accounts. Illustration 7B–1 provides an example.

In the future, if additional information indicates that conditions have changed, bad debt expense and the allowance for uncollectible accounts are increased or decreased as necessary to reflect the change.

You may be wondering whether recognizing an impairment loss leads to a double counting of bad debt expense. After all, the receivable first was included in a group of receivables for which bad debt expense was estimated, and then was singled out for recognition of an impairment loss. Creditors have to be careful to avoid this problem by excluding an impaired receivable and estimating bad debt expense as appropriate for the rest of the receivables. That way, bad debt expense for the impaired receivable and for the rest of the receivables is calculated separately, and there is no double counting.

CURRENT EXPECTED CREDIT LOSS (CECL) MODEL: EXAMPLE As mentioned earlier in the chapter, the CECL model, required starting in 2020 and adopted as early as 2019, removes the "probable" criterion for recognizing bad debts.[30] The FASB provides firms with broad latitude concerning how they will estimate credit losses under CECL. As an example of how the CECL model could be applied, Illustration 7B–2 considers a long-term receivable for which there is a relatively lower likelihood of credit loss than you saw in Illustration 7B-1.

[28]This appendix discusses accounting for the impairment of individual accounts and notes receivable, as specified in ASC 310–10–35: Receivables–Overall–Subsequent Measurement (previously "Accounting by Creditors for Impairment of a Loan–An amendment of FASB Statements No. 5 and 15," *Statement of Financial Accounting Standards No. 114* (Norwalk, Conn.: FASB, 1993)). When a receivable has been securitized, or when a company has elected to account for a receivable under the fair value option, the receivable is viewed as an investment and different GAAP applies, as described in Appendix 12B.

[29]Rather than calculating the present value of the loan, as a practical expediency the creditor can base the new value of the loan on the loan's market price or the fair value of collateral that supports the loan.

[30]"Financial Instruments–Credit Losses (Topic 326)" *Accounting Standards Update 2016-13* (Norwalk, Conn: FASB, 2016).

Illustration 7B–1
Receivable Impairment

The discounted present value of the cash flows prior to the impairment is the same as the receivable's book value.

The discounted present value of the cash flows after the impairment is less than book value.

The difference is a loss, debited to bad debt expense.

Brillard Properties owes First Prudent Bank $30 million under a 10% note with two years remaining to maturity. Due to Brillard's financial difficulties, the previous year's interest ($3 million) was not paid. First Prudent estimates that it will not receive the $3 million of accrued interest, that it will receive only $2 million of interest in each of the next two years, and that it will receive only $25 million of principal at the end of two years.

Analysis

Previous Value			
Accrued interest (10% × $30,000,000)		$ 3,000,000	
Principal		30,000,000	
Book value of the receivable			$ 33,000,000
New Value (based on estimated cash flows to be received)			
Present value of accrued interest to be received	=	$ 0	
Present value of future interest	$ 2 million × 1.73554* =	3,471,080	
Present value of estimated principal	$25 million × 0.82645† =	20,661,250	
Present value of the receivable			(24,132,330)
Loss			$ 8,867,670

*Present value of an ordinary annuity of $1: $n = 2$, $i = 10\%$
†Present value of $1: $n = 2$, $i = 10\%$

Journal Entry

Bad debt expense (to balance)	8,867,670	
Accrued interest receivable		3,000,000
Allowance for uncollectible accounts ($30,000,000 – 24,132,330)		5,867,670

Illustration 7B–2
Receivable Impairment Under CECL Model

Hart Industries owes Second National Bank $20 million under a 10% note with two years remaining to maturity. Due to Hart's financial difficulties, the previous year's interest ($2 million) was not paid. Based on its experience with similar loans and its projections regarding Hart's ability to generate cash in the future, Second National estimates that there is a 75% chance it will be paid in full and a 25% chance that Hart will default and Second National will (a) not receive the $2 million of accrued interest, (b) receive only $1 million of interest in each of the next two years, and (c) receive only $15 million of principal at the end of two years.

Analysis

Previous Value			
Accrued interest (10% × $20,000,000)		$ 2,000,000	
Principal		20,000,000	
Amortized cost basis of the receivable			$22,000,000
Value Assuming Default (based on estimated cash flows to be received)			
Present value of accrued interest to be received	=	$ 0	
Present value of future interest	$ 1 million × 1.73554* =	1,735,540	
Present value of estimated principal	$15 million × 0.82645† =	12,396,750	
Present value of the receivable			(14,132,290)
Loss if Default Occurs			$ 7,867,710

*Present value of an ordinary annuity of $1: $n = 2$, $i = 10\%$
†Present value of $1: $n = 2$, $i = 10\%$

Calculation of CECL Impairment		
Amortized cost basis of the receivable (see Illustration 7B–2)		$22,000,000
Expected credit loss		
(25%) × $7,867,710 (see Illustration 7B–2)	$1,966,928	
(75%) × $0 loss	0	
Expected credit loss		(1,966,928)
Revised amortized cost basis of the receivable		$ 20,033,072

Note that, under current GAAP, Second National would recognize *zero* impairment, because a loss is *not probable*. The receivable still would be grouped with other similar receivables to consider the potential for bad debts for the group. When you compare the write down of $0 under current GAAP with the write down of almost $2 million under the CECL model, you can see why banks are concerned that the CECL model will increase the amount of bad debt expense they have to recognize.

Second National would account for the expected credit loss as a credit loss (bad debt) expense, adjusting upward or downward its allowance for credit losses (bad debts) with respect to the Second National loan as necessary to state the net receivable at $20,033,072.

Troubled Debt Restructurings

A troubled debt restructuring occurs when the creditor makes concessions to the debtor in response to the debtor's financial difficulties.

Sometimes a creditor changes the original terms of a debt agreement in response to the debtor's financial difficulties. The creditor makes concessions to the debtor that make it easier for the debtor to pay, with the goal of maximizing the amount of cash that the creditor can collect. In that case, the new arrangement is referred to as a **troubled debt restructuring**. Because identifying an arrangement as a troubled debt restructuring requires recognizing any impairment loss associated with the arrangement, creditors might be reluctant to conclude that a troubled debt restructuring has occurred, so the FASB provides guidance to help ensure that all troubled debt restructurings are properly identified.[31]

WHEN THE RECEIVABLE IS CONTINUED, BUT WITH MODIFIED TERMS. In a troubled debt restructuring, it's likely that the bank allows the receivable to continue but with the terms of the debt agreement modified to make it easier for the debtor to comply. The lender might agree to reduce or delay the scheduled interest payments. Or, it may agree to reduce or delay the maturity amount. Often a troubled debt restructuring will call for some combination of these concessions.

Consider again Illustration 7B–1. What if First Prudent Bank and Brillard Properties actually *renegotiated* Brillard's debt to (1) forgive the interest accrued from last year, (2) reduce the two remaining interest payments from $3 million each to $2 million each, and (3) reduce the face amount from $30 million to $25 million? In that case, First Prudent would account for its loss in exactly the same way as shown in Illustration 7B–1. The only difference would be that, whereas we originally based calculations on First Prudent's estimates of future cash flows, we now base calculations on the cash flows that were specified in the restructured debt agreement.

WHEN THE RECEIVABLE IS SETTLED OUTRIGHT. Sometimes a receivable in a troubled debt restructuring is actually settled at the time of the restructuring by the debtor making a payment of cash, some other noncash assets, or even shares of the debtor's stock. In that case, the creditor simply records a loss for the difference between the carrying amount of the receivable and the fair value of the asset(s) or equity securities received. Illustration 7B–3 provides an example.

[31]A troubled debt restructuring occurs when a creditor makes concessions in response to a debtor's financial difficulties. These terms have been clarified recently (ASC 310–40–15: Receivables–Troubled Debt Restructurings by Creditors–Scope and Scope Exceptions; previously "A Creditor's Determination of Whether a Restructuring is a Troubled Debt Restructuring," *Accounting Standards Update No. 2011–02* (Norwalk, Conn.: FASB, 2011)). A debtor is viewed as experiencing *financial difficulties* if it is probable that the debtor will default on any of its liabilities unless the creditor restructures the debt. A *concession* has occurred if, as a result of the restructuring, the creditor does not expect to collect all amounts due, including accrued interest. A concession also can occur if the creditor restructures the terms of the debt in a way that provides the debtor with funds at a better rate of interest than the debtor could receive if the debtor tried to obtain new debt with similar terms (for example, a similar payment schedule, collateral, and guarantees) as the restructured debt. But, not all changes are concessions. For example, a restructuring that results in an insignificant delay of payment is not a concession.

Illustration 7B–3

Debt Settled at the Time of a Restructuring

First Prudent Bank is owed $30 million by Brillard Properties under a 10% note with two years remaining to maturity. Due to Brillard's financial difficulties, the previous year's interest ($3 million) was not received. The bank agrees to settle the receivable (and accrued interest receivable) in exchange for property having a fair value of $20 million.

	($ in millions)	
Land (fair value)	20	
Bad debt expense (to balance)*	13	
Accrued interest receivable (10% × $30 million)		3
Note receivable (account balance)		30

*Rather than debiting bad debt expense, First Prudent might debit Loss on troubled debt restructuring.

International Financial Reporting Standards

LO7–10

Impairments. IFRS (IAS 39) and current U.S. GAAP (ASC 310) generally provide similar treatments of impairments of receivables, but the specific impairment evaluation process and criteria are somewhat different regarding:[32,33]

- Level of analysis:
  - Under U.S. GAAP we examine impairment of individual receivables (whether or not they are significant). If impairment isn't indicated, we group the receivables with other receivables of similar risk characteristics when estimating bad debts for the group.
  - Under IFRS we first consider whether individually significant receivables are impaired. If impairment isn't indicated, the individually significant receivables are grouped with other receivables of similar risk characteristics to test impairment.
- Impairment indicators:
  - U.S. GAAP provides an illustrative list of information we might consider when evaluating receivables for impairment, and requires measurement of potential impairment if impairment (a) is viewed as probable and (b) can be estimated reliably.
  - IFRS provides an illustrative list of "loss events" and requires measurement of an impairment if there is objective evidence that a loss event has occurred that has an impact on the future cash flows to be collected and that can be estimated reliably. Requiring the occurrence of a loss event may result in recognizing a loss later under IFRS than U.S. GAAP.
- Reversal of impairments: Under both U.S. GAAP and IFRS, if an impaired receivable's estimated future cash flows improve, the creditor recalculates the impairment and adjusts the valuation allowance up or down as appropriate. The net book value of the receivable can't exceed the original amount of the receivable (as adjusted for any normal amortization of any discount or premium). Reversals increase income (for example, by crediting bad debt expense in the period of reversal).

Also, as indicated earlier in this chapter, IFRS requirements are moving to an ECL ("Expected Credit Loss") model for recognizing credit losses on long-term receivables, while U.S. GAAP is moving to the CECL model. The primary difference between the two approaches is that the ECL model used in IFRS does not accrue post-twelve-month credit losses for receivables that have not as yet deteriorated in credit quality. Therefore, U.S. GAAP will tend to recognize credit losses earlier, and in higher amounts, than are recognized under IFRS. Further convergence in this area is unlikely in the near future.

In this appendix we have focused on creditors' accounting for loan losses and troubled debt restructurings. We discuss those topics from the standpoint of the debtor in Chapter 14, Appendix B.

[32]"Financial Instruments: Recognition and Measurement," *International Accounting Standard No. 39* (IASCF), as amended effective January 1, 2014.

[33]34FASB ASC 310–10–35: Receivables–Overall–Subsequent Measurement.

Questions For Review of Key Topics

Q 7–1 Define cash equivalents.

Q 7–2 Explain the primary functions of internal controls procedures in the accounting area. What is meant by separation of duties?

Q 7–3 What are the responsibilities of management described in Section 404 of the Sarbanes-Oxley Act? What are the responsibilities of the company's auditor?

Q 7–4 Define a compensating balance. How are compensating balances reported in financial statements?

IFRS **Q 7–5** Do U.S. GAAP and IFRS differ in how bank overdrafts are treated? Explain.

Q 7–6 Explain the difference between a trade discount and a cash discount.

Q 7–7 Distinguish between the gross and net methods of accounting for cash discounts.

Q 7–8 Briefly explain the accounting treatment for sales returns.

Q 7–9 Explain the typical way companies account for uncollectible accounts receivable (bad debts). When is it permissible to record bad debt expense only at the time when receivables actually prove uncollectible?

Q 7–10 Briefly explain the difference between the income statement approach and the balance sheet approach to estimating bad debts.

IFRS **Q 7–11** If a company has accounts receivable from ordinary customers and from related parties, can they combine those receivables in their financial statements under U.S. GAAP? Under IFRS?

Q 7–12 Is any special accounting treatment required for the assigning of accounts receivable in general as collateral for debt?

Q 7–13 Explain any possible differences between accounting for an account receivable factored with recourse compared with one factored without recourse.

IFRS **Q 7–14** Do U.S. GAAP and IFRS differ in the criteria they use to determine whether a transfer of receivables is treated as a sale? Explain.

Q 7–15 What is meant by the discounting of a note receivable? Describe the four-step process used to account for discounted notes.

Q 7–16 What are the key variables that influence a company's investment in receivables? Describe the two ratios used by financial analysts to monitor a company's investment in receivables.

Q 7–17 Explain how the CECL model (introduced in *ASU No. 2016-13* and required in 2020) differs from current GAAP in its calculation of bad debt expense.

Q 7–18 (Based on Appendix 7A) In a two-step bank reconciliation, identify the items that might be necessary to adjust the bank balance to the corrected cash balance. Identify the items that might be necessary to adjust the book balance to the corrected cash balance.

Q 7–19 (Based on Appendix 7A) How is a petty cash fund established? How is the fund replenished?

Q 7–20 (Based on Appendix 7B) Marshall Companies, Inc., holds a note receivable from a former subsidiary. Due to financial difficulties, the former subsidiary has been unable to pay the previous year's interest on the note. Marshall agreed to restructure the debt by both delaying and reducing remaining cash payments. The concessions impair the creditor's investment in the receivable. How is this impairment recorded?

IFRS **Q 7–21** (Based on Appendix 7B) Do U.S. GAAP and IFRS differ in the ability of a company to recognize in net income the recovery of impairment losses of accounts and notes receivable?

Brief Exercises

BE 7–1
Internal control
● LO7–1

Janice Dodds opens the mail for the Ajax Plumbing Company. She lists all customer checks on a spreadsheet that includes the name of the customer and the check amount. The checks, along with the spreadsheet, are then sent to Jim Seymour in the accounting department who records the checks and deposits them daily in the company's checking account. How could the company improve its internal control procedure for the handling of its cash receipts?

BE 7–2
Bank overdrafts
● LO7–2, LO7–10

Cutler Company has a cash account with a balance of $250,000 with Wright Bank and a cash account with an overdraft of $5,000 at Lowe Bank. What would the current assets section of Cutler's balance sheet include for "cash" under IFRS? Under U.S. GAAP?

BE 7–3
Cash and cash equivalents
● LO7–2

The following items appeared on the year-end trial balance of Consolidated Freight Corporation: cash in a checking account, U.S. Treasury bills that mature in six months, undeposited customer checks, cash in a savings account, and currency and coins. Which of these items would be included in the company's balance sheet as cash and cash equivalents?

BE 7–4
Cash discounts; gross method
● LO7–3

On December 28, 2018, Tristar Communications sold 10 units of its new satellite uplink system to various customers for $25,000 each. The terms of each sale were 1/10, n/30. Tristar uses the gross method to account for sales discounts. In what year will income before tax be affected by discounts, assuming that all customers paid the net-of-discount amount on January 6, 2019? By how much?

BE 7–5
Cash discounts; net method
● LO7–3

Refer to the situation described in BE 7–4. Answer the questions assuming that Tristar uses the net method to account for sales discounts.

BE 7–6
Sales returns
● LO7–4

During 2018, its first year of operations, Hollis Industries recorded sales of $10,600,000 and experienced returns of $720,000. Cost of goods sold totaled $6,360,000 (60% of sales). The company estimates that 8% of all sales will be returned. Prepare the year-end adjusting journal entries to account for anticipated sales returns, assuming that all sales are made on credit and all accounts receivable are outstanding.

BE 7–7
Sales returns
● LO7–4

Refer to the situation described in BE 7–6. Prepare the year-end adjusting journal entries to account for anticipated sales returns under the assumption that all sales are made for cash (no accounts receivable are outstanding).

BE 7–8
Accounts receivable classification
● LO7–5, LO7–10

 IFRS

Singletary Associates has accounts receivable due from normal credit customers, and also has an account receivable due from a director of the company. Singletary would like to combine both of those receivables on one line in the current assets section of their balance sheet and in the disclosure notes. Is that permissible under U.S. GAAP? Under IFRS? Explain.

BE 7–9
Uncollectible accounts; income statement approach
● LO7–5, LO7–6

The following information relates to a company's accounts receivable: accounts receivable balance at the beginning of the year, $300,000; allowance for uncollectible accounts at the beginning of the year, $25,000 (credit balance); credit sales during the year, $1,500,000; accounts receivable written off during the year, $16,000; cash collections from customers, $1,450,000. Assuming the company estimates bad debts at an amount equal to 2% of credit sales, calculate (1) bad debt expense for the year and (2) the year-end balance in the allowance for uncollectible accounts.

BE 7–10
Uncollectible accounts; balance sheet approach
● LO7–5, LO7–6

Refer to the situation described in BE 7–9. Answer the two questions assuming the company estimates that future bad debts will equal 10% of the year-end balance in accounts receivable.

BE 7–11
Uncollectible accounts; solving for unknown
● LO7–5, LO7–6

A company's year-end balance in accounts receivable is $2,000,000. The allowance for uncollectible accounts had a beginning-of-year credit balance of $30,000. An aging of accounts receivable at the end of the year indicates a required allowance of $38,000. If bad debt expense for the year was $40,000, what was the amount of bad debts written off during the year?

BE 7–12
Uncollectible accounts; solving for unknown
● LO7–5, LO7–6

Refer to the situation described in BE 7–11. If credit sales for the year were $8,200,000 and $7,950,000 was collected from credit customers, what was the beginning-of-year balance in accounts receivable?

BE 7–13
Note receivable
● LO7–7

On December 1, 2018, Davenport Company sold merchandise to a customer for $20,000. In payment for the merchandise, the customer signed a 6% note requiring the payment of interest and principal on March 1, 2019. How much interest revenue will the company recognize during 2018? In 2019?

BE 7–14
Long-term notes receivable
● LO7–4

On April 19, 2018, Millipede Machinery sold a tractor to Thomas Hartwood, accepting a note promising payment of $120,000 in five years. The applicable effective interest rate is 7%. What amount of sales revenue would Millipede recognize on April 19, 2018, for the Hartwood transaction?

BE 7–15
Factoring of accounts receivable
● LO7–8

Logitech Corporation transferred $100,000 of accounts receivable to a local bank. The transfer was made without recourse. The local bank remits 85% of the factored amount to Logitech and retains the remaining 15%. When the bank collects the receivables, it will remit to Logitech the retained amount less a fee equal to 3% of the total amount factored. Logitech estimates a fair value of its 15% interest in the receivables of $11,000 (not including the 3% fee). What is the effect of this transaction on the company's assets, liabilities, and income before income taxes?

BE 7–16
Factoring of accounts receivable
● LO7–8

Refer to the situation described in BE 7–15. Assuming that the sale criteria are not met, describe how Logitech would account for the transfer.

BE 7–17
Transfers of accounts receivable
● LO7–8, LO7–10

 IFRS

Huling Associates plans to transfer $300,000 of accounts receivable to Mitchell Inc. in exchange for cash. Huling has structured the arrangement so that it retains substantially all the risks and rewards of ownership but shifts control over the receivables to Mitchell. Assuming all other criteria are met for recognizing the transfer as a sale, how would Huling account for this transaction under IFRS? Under U.S. GAAP?

BE 7–18
Discounting a note
● LO7–8

On March 31, Dower Publishing discounted a $30,000 note at a local bank. The note was dated February 28 and required the payment of the principal amount and interest at 6% on May 31. The bank's discount rate is 8%. How much cash will Dower receive from the bank on March 31?

BE 7–19
Receivables turnover
● LO7–8

Camden Hardware's credit sales for the year were $320,000. Accounts receivable at the beginning and end of the year were $50,000 and $70,000, respectively. Calculate the accounts receivable turnover ratio and the average collection period for the year.

BE 7–20
Bank Reconciliation
● Appendix 7A

Marin Company's general ledger indicates a cash balance of $22,340 as of September 30, 2018. Early in October Marin received a bank statement indicating that during September Marin had an NSF check of $1,500 returned to a customer and incurred service charges of $45. Marin also learned it had incorrectly recorded a check received from a customer on September 15 as $500 when in fact the check was for $550. Calculate Marin's correct September 30, 2018, cash balance.

BE 7–21
Bank Reconciliation
● Appendix 7A

Shan Enterprises received a bank statement listing its May 31, 2018, bank balance as $47,582. Shan determined that as of May 31 it had cash receipts of $2,500 that were not yet deposited and checks outstanding of $7,224. Calculate Shan's correct May 31, 2018, cash balance.

BE 7–22
Impairments of Accounts Receivable
● Appendix 7B

Einhorn Industries believes it is not probable that Thaler Inc. will default on an account receivable, but given the possibility of default, Einhorn believes it will collect $30,000 less than the receivable's current carrying value on Einhorn's balance sheet. Under current GAAP, how much impairment charge should Einhorn recognize?

BE 7–23
Credit Losses on Accounts Receivable (CECL Model)
● Appendix 7B

Assume the same facts as in BE 7–22, but that Einhorn determines credit losses using the CECL model introduced in *ASU 2016-13* and required in 2020. How much credit loss should Einhorn recognize?

Exercises

E 7–1
Cash and cash equivalents; restricted cash
● LO7–2

The controller of the Red Wing Corporation is in the process of preparing the company's 2018 financial statements. She is trying to determine the correct balance of cash and cash equivalents to be reported as a current asset in the balance sheet. The following items are being considered:

a. Balances in the company's accounts at the First National Bank; checking $13,500, savings $22,100.
b. Undeposited customer checks of $5,200.

c. Currency and coins on hand of $580.

d. Savings account at the East Bay Bank with a balance of $400,000. This account is being used to accumulate cash for future plant expansion (in 2020).

e. $20,000 in a checking account at the East Bay Bank. The balance in the account represents a 20% compensating balance for a $100,000 loan with the bank. Red Wing may not withdraw the funds until the loan is due in 2021.

f. U.S. Treasury bills; 2-month maturity bills totaling $15,000, and 7-month bills totaling $20,000.

Required:

1. Determine the correct balance of cash and cash equivalents to be reported in the current asset section of the 2018 balance sheet.
2. For each of the items not included in your answer to requirement 1, explain the correct classification of the item.

E 7–2
Cash and cash equivalents
● LO7–2

Delta Automotive Corporation has the following assets listed in its 12/31/2018 trial balance:

Cash in bank—checking account	$22,500
U.S. Treasury bills (mature in 60 days)*	5,000
Cash on hand (currency and coins)	1,350
U.S. Treasury bills (mature in six months)*	10,000
Undeposited customer checks	1,840

*Purchased on 11/30/2018

Required:

1. Determine the correct balance of cash and cash equivalents to be reported in the current asset section of the 2018 balance sheet.
2. For each of the items not included in your answer to requirement 1, explain the correct classification of the item.

E 7–3
FASB codification research
● LO7–2, LO7–6, LO7–7

Access the *FASB Accounting Standards Codification* at the FASB website (www.fasb.org).

Required:

Determine the specific citation for accounting for each of the following items:

1. Accounts receivables from related parties should be shown separately from trade receivables
2. The definition of cash equivalents
3. The requirement to value notes exchanged for cash at the cash proceeds
4. The two conditions that must be met to accrue a loss on an accounts receivable

E 7–4
Bank overdrafts
● LO7–2, LO7–10
IFRS

Parker Inc. has the following cash balances:

First Bank	$150,000
Second Bank	(10,000)
Third Bank	25,000
Fourth Bank	(5,000)

Required:

1. Prepare the current assets and current liabilities section of Parker's 2018 balance sheet, assuming Parker reports under U.S. GAAP.
2. Prepare the current assets and current liabilities section of Parker's 2018 balance sheet, assuming Parker reports under IFRS.

E 7–5
Trade and cash discounts; the gross method and the net method compared
● LO7–3

Tracy Company, a manufacturer of air conditioners, sold 100 units to Thomas Company on November 17, 2018. The units have a list price of $600 each, but Thomas was given a 30% trade discount. The terms of the sale were 2/10, n/30.

Required:

1. Prepare the journal entries to record the sale on November 17 (ignore cost of goods) and collection on November 26, 2018, assuming that the gross method of accounting for cash discounts is used.
2. Prepare the journal entries to record the sale on November 17 (ignore cost of goods) and collection on December 15, 2018, assuming that the gross method of accounting for cash discounts is used.
3. Repeat requirements 1 and 2 assuming that the net method of accounting for cash discounts is used.

E 7–6
Cash discounts; the gross method
● LO7–3

Harwell Company manufactures automobile tires. On July 15, 2018, the company sold 1,000 tires to the Nixon Car Company for $50 each. The terms of the sale were 2/10, n/30. Harwell uses the gross method of accounting for cash discounts.

Required:

1. Prepare the journal entries to record the sale on July 15 (ignore cost of goods) and collection on July 23, 2018.
2. Prepare the journal entries to record the sale on July 15 (ignore cost of goods) and collection on August 15, 2018.

E 7–7
Cash discounts; the net method
● LO7–3

[This is a variation of E 7–6 modified to focus on the net method of accounting for cash discounts.]
Harwell Company manufactures automobile tires. On July 15, 2018, the company sold 1,000 tires to the Nixon Car Company for $50 each. The terms of the sale were 2/10, n/30. Harwell uses the net method of accounting for cash discounts.

Required:

1. Prepare the journal entries to record the sale on July 15 (ignore cost of goods) and payment on July 23, 2018.
2. Prepare the journal entries to record the sale on July 15 (ignore cost of goods) and payment on August 15, 2018.

E 7–8
Sales returns
● LO7–4

Halifax Manufacturing allows its customers to return merchandise for any reason up to 90 days after delivery and receive a credit to their accounts. All of Halifax's sales are for credit (no cash is collected at the time of sale). The company began 2018 with an allowance for sales returns of $300,000. During 2018, Halifax sold merchandise on account for $11,500,000. This merchandise cost Halifax $7,475,000 (65% of selling prices). Also during the year, customers returned $450,000 in sales for credit. Sales returns, estimated to be 4% of sales, are recorded as an adjusting entry at the end of the year.

Required:

1. Prepare an entry to record actual merchandise returns as they occur (not adjusting the allowance for sales returns), and then record a year-end entry to adjust the allowance for sales returns to its appropriate balance.
2. What is the amount of the year-end allowance for sales returns after the adjusting entry is recorded?

E 7–9
FASB codification research
● LO7–5

The *FASB Accounting Standards Codification* represents the single source of authoritative U.S. generally accepted accounting principles.

Required:

1. Obtain the relevant authoritative literature on accounting for accounts receivable using the FASB's Codification Research System at the FASB website (www.fasb.org). What is the specific citation that describes the information about loans and trade receivables that is to be disclosed in the summary of significant accounting policies?
2. List the disclosure requirements.

E 7–10
Uncollectible accounts; allowance method vs. direct write-off method
● LO7–5, LO7–6

Johnson Company uses the allowance method to account for uncollectible accounts receivable. Bad debt expense is established as a percentage of credit sales. For 2018, net credit sales totaled $4,500,000, and the estimated bad debt percentage is 1.5%. The allowance for uncollectible accounts had a credit balance of $42,000 at the beginning of 2018 and $40,000, after adjusting entries, at the end of 2018.

Required:

1. What is bad debt expense for 2018 as a percent of net credit sales?
2. Assume Johnson makes no other adjustment of bad debt expense during 2018. Determine the amount of accounts receivable written off during 2018.
3. If the company uses the direct write-off method, what would bad debt expense be for 2018?

E 7–11
Uncollectible accounts; allowance method; balance sheet approach
● LO7–5, LO7–6

Colorado Rocky Cookie Company offers credit terms to its customers. At the end of 2018, accounts receivable totaled $625,000. The allowance method is used to account for uncollectible accounts. The allowance for uncollectible accounts had a credit balance of $32,000 at the beginning of 2018 and $21,000 in receivables were written off during the year as uncollectible. Also, $1,200 in cash was received in December from a customer whose account previously had been written off. The company estimates bad debts by applying a percentage of 10% to accounts receivable at the end of the year.

Required:

1. Prepare journal entries to record the write-off of receivables, the collection of $1,200 for previously written off receivables, and the year-end adjusting entry for bad debt expense.
2. How would accounts receivable be shown in the 2018 year-end balance sheet?

E 7–12
Uncollectible accounts; allowance method and direct write-off method compared; solving for unknown
● LO7–6

Castle Company provides estimates for its uncollectible accounts. The allowance for uncollectible accounts had a credit balance of $17,280 at the beginning of 2018 and a $22,410 credit balance at the end of 2018 (after adjusting entries). If the direct write-off method had been used to account for uncollectible accounts (bad debt expense equals actual write-offs), the income statement for 2018 would have included bad debt expense of $17,100 and revenue of $2,200 from the collection of previously written off bad debts.

Required:
Determine bad debt expense for 2018 according to the allowance method.

E 7–13
Uncollectible accounts; allowance method; solving for unknowns; General Mills
● LO7–5, LO7–6
Real World Financials

General Mills reported the following information in its 2015 financial statements ($ in millions):

	2015	2014
Balance Sheet:		
Accounts receivable, net	$ 1,386.7	$1,483.6
Income statement:		
Sales revenue	$17,630.3	

A note disclosed that the allowance for uncollectible accounts had a balance of $25.3 million and $21.0 million at the end of 2015 and 2014, respectively. Bad debt expense for 2015 was $19.8 million.

Required:
Determine the amount of cash collected from customers during 2015.

E 7–14
Note receivable
● LO7–7

On June 30, 2018, the Esquire Company sold some merchandise to a customer for $30,000. In payment, Esquire agreed to accept a 6% note requiring the payment of interest and principal on March 31, 2019. The 6% rate is appropriate in this situation.

Required:
1. Prepare journal entries to record the sale of merchandise (omit any entry that might be required for the cost of the goods sold), the December 31, 2018 interest accrual, and the March 31, 2019 collection.
2. If the December 31 adjusting entry for the interest accrual is not prepared, by how much will income before income taxes be over- or understated in 2018 and 2019?

E 7–15
Noninterest-bearing note receivable
● LO7–7

[This is a variation of E 7–14 modified to focus on a noninterest-bearing note.]

On June 30, 2018, the Esquire Company sold some merchandise to a customer for $30,000 and agreed to accept as payment a noninterest-bearing note with an 8% discount rate requiring the payment of $30,000 on March 31, 2019. The 8% rate is appropriate in this situation. Esquire views the financing component of this contract as significant.

Required:
1. Prepare journal entries to record the sale of merchandise (omit any entry that might be required for the cost of the goods sold), the December 31, 2018 interest accrual, and the March 31, 2019 collection.
2. What is the *effective* interest rate on the note?

E 7–16
Long-term notes receivable
● LO7–7

On January 1, 2018, Wright Transport sold four school buses to the Elmira School District. In exchange for the buses, Wright received a note requiring payment of $515,000 by Elmira on December 31, 2020. The effective interest rate is 8%.

Required:
1. How much sales revenue would Wright recognize on January 1, 2018, for this transaction?
2. Prepare journal entries to record the sale of merchandise on January 1, 2018 (omit any entry that might be required for the cost of the goods sold), the December 31, 2018, interest accrual, the December 31, 2019, interest accrual, and receipt of payment of the note on December 31, 2020.

E 7–17
Interest-bearing note receivable; solving for unknown rate
● LO7–7

On January 1, 2018, the Apex Company exchanged some shares of common stock it had been holding as an investment for a note receivable. The note principal plus interest is due on January 1, 2019. The 2018 income statement reported $2,200 in interest revenue from this note and a $6,000 gain on sale of investment in stock. The stock's book value was $16,000. The company's fiscal year ends on December 31.

Required:
1. What is the note's effective interest rate?
2. Reconstruct the journal entries to record the sale of the stock on January 1, 2018, and the adjusting entry to record interest revenue at the end of 2018. The company records adjusting entries only at year-end.

E 7–18
Assigning of specific accounts receivable
● LO7–8

On June 30, 2018, the High Five Surfboard Company had outstanding accounts receivable of $600,000. On July 1, 2018, the company borrowed $450,000 from the Equitable Finance Corporation and signed a promissory note. Interest at 10% is payable monthly. The company assigned specific receivables totaling $600,000 as collateral for the loan. Equitable Finance charges a finance fee equal to 1.8% of the accounts receivable assigned.

Required:

Prepare the journal entry to record the borrowing on the books of High Five Surfboard.

E 7–19
Factoring of accounts receivable without recourse
● LO7–8

Mountain High Ice Cream Company transferred $60,000 of accounts receivable to the Prudential Bank. The transfer was made *without recourse.* Prudential remits 90% of the factored amount to Mountain High and retains 10%. When the bank collects the receivables, it will remit to Mountain High the retained amount (which Mountain estimates has a fair value of $5,000) less a 2% fee (2% of the total factored amount).

Required:

Prepare the journal entry to record the transfer on the books of Mountain High assuming that the sale criteria are met.

E 7–20
Factoring of accounts receivable with recourse
● LO7–8

[This is a variation of E 7–19 modified to focus on factoring with recourse.]
Mountain High Ice Cream Company transferred $60,000 of accounts receivable to the Prudential Bank. The transfer was made *with recourse.* Prudential remits 90% of the factored amount to Mountain High and retains 10% to cover sales returns and allowances. When the bank collects the receivables, it will remit to Mountain High the retained amount (which Mountain estimates has a fair value of $5,000). Mountain High anticipates a $3,000 recourse obligation. The bank charges a 2% fee (2% of $60,000), and requires that amount to be paid at the start of the factoring arrangement.

Required:

Prepare the journal entry to record the transfer on the books of Mountain High assuming that the sale criteria are met.

E 7–21
Factoring of accounts receivable with recourse under IFRS
● LO7–8, LO7–10
IFRS

This is a variation of E 7–20 modified to focus on factoring with recourse under IFRS.]
Mountain High Ice Cream Company reports under IFRS. Mountain High transferred $60,000 of accounts receivable to the Prudential Bank. The transfer was made *with recourse.* Prudential remits 90% of the factored amount to Mountain High and retains 10% to cover sales returns and allowances. When the bank collects the receivables, it will remit to Mountain High the retained amount (which Mountain estimates has a fair value of $5,000). Mountain High anticipates a $3,000 recourse obligation. The bank charges a 2% fee (2% of $60,000), and requires that amount to be paid at the start of the factoring arrangement. Mountain High has transferred control over the receivables, but determines that it still retains substantially all risks and rewards associated with them.

Required:

Prepare the journal entry to record the transfer on the books of Mountain High, considering whether the sale criteria under IFRS have been met.

E 7–22
Discounting a note receivable
● LO7–8

Selkirk Company obtained a $15,000 note receivable from a customer on January 1, 2018. The note, along with interest at 10%, is due on July 1, 2018. On February 28, 2018, Selkirk discounted the note at Unionville Bank. The bank's discount rate is 12%.

Required:

Prepare the journal entries required on February 28, 2018, to accrue interest and to record the discounting (round all calculations to the nearest dollar) for Selkirk. Assume that the discounting is accounted for as a sale.

E 7–23
Concepts; terminology
● LO7–1 through LO7–8

Listed below are several terms and phrases associated with cash and receivables. Pair each item from List A (by letter) with the item from List B that is most appropriately associated with it.

List A	List B
_____ 1. Internal control	a. Restriction on cash
_____ 2. Trade discount	b. Cash discount not taken is sales revenue
_____ 3. Cash equivalents	c. Includes separation of duties
_____ 4. Allowance for uncollectibles	d. Bad debt expense a % of credit sales
_____ 5. Cash discount	e. Recognizes bad debts as they occur
_____ 6. Balance sheet approach	f. Sale of receivables to a financial institution
_____ 7. Income statement approach	g. Include highly liquid investments
_____ 8. Net method	h. Estimate of bad debts
_____ 9. Compensating balance	i. Reduction in amount paid by credit customer
_____ 10. Discounting	j. Reduction below list price
_____ 11. Gross method	k. Cash discount not taken is sales discount forfeited
_____ 12. Direct write-off method	l. Bad debt expense determined by estimating amount of accounts receivable expected to be received
_____ 13. Factoring	m. Sale of note receivable to a financial institution

E 7–24
Receivables; transaction analysis
● LO7–3, LO7–5 through LO7–8

Weldon Corporation's fiscal year ends December 31. The following is a list of transactions involving receivables that occurred during 2018:

Mar. 17	Accounts receivable of $1,700 were written off as uncollectible. The company uses the allowance method.
30	Loaned an officer of the company $20,000 and received a note requiring principal and interest at 7% to be paid on March 30, 2019.
May 30	Discounted the $20,000 note at a local bank. The bank's discount rate is 8%. The note was discounted without recourse and the sale criteria are met.
June 30	Sold merchandise to the Blankenship Company for $12,000. Terms of the sale are 2/10, n/30. Weldon uses the gross method to account for cash discounts.
July 8	The Blankenship Company paid its account in full.
Aug. 31	Sold stock in a nonpublic company with a book value of $5,000 and accepted a $6,000 noninterest-bearing note with a discount rate of 8%. The $6,000 payment is due on February 28, 2019. The stock has no ready market value.
Dec. 31	Bad debt expense is estimated to be 2% of credit sales for the year. Credit sales for 2018 were $700,000.

Required:

1. Prepare journal entries for each of the above transactions (round all calculations to the nearest dollar).
2. Prepare any additional year-end adjusting entries indicated.

E 7–25
Ratio analysis; Microsoft
● LO7–9
Real World Financials

Microsoft Corporation reported the following information in its financial statements for three successive quarters ($ in millions):

	Three Months Ended		
	12/31/2015 (Q2)	9/30/2015 (Q1)	6/30/2015 (Q4)
Balance sheets:			
Accounts receivable, net	$14,507	$11,444	$17,908
Income statements:			
Sales revenue	$23,796	$20,379	$22,180

Required:

Compute the receivables turnover ratio and the average collection period for Q1 and Q2. Assume that each quarter consists of 91 days.

E 7–26
Ratio analysis
● LO7–9

The current asset section of the Moorcroft Outboard Motor Company's balance sheet reported the following amounts:

	12/31/2018	12/31/2017
Accounts receivable, net	$400,000	$300,000

The average collection period for 2018 is 50 days.

Required:

Determine net sales for 2018.

E 7–27
Petty cash
● Appendix 7A

Loucks Company established a $200 petty cash fund on October 2, 2018. The fund is replenished at the end of each month. At the end of October 2018, the fund contained $37 in cash and the following receipts:

Office supplies	$76
Lunch with client	48
Postage	20
Miscellaneous	19

Required:

Prepare the necessary general journal entries to establish the petty cash fund on October 2 and to replenish the fund on October 31.

E 7–28
Petty cash
● Appendix 7A

The petty cash fund of Ricco's Automotive contained the following items at the end of September 2018:

Currency and coins		$ 58
Receipts for the following expenditures:		
Delivery charges	$16	
Printer paper	11	
Paper clips and rubber bands	8	35
An I.O.U. from an employee		25
Postage		32
Total		$150

The petty cash fund was established at the beginning of September with a transfer of $150 from cash to the petty cash account.

Required:

Prepare the journal entry to replenish the fund at the end of September.

E 7–29
Bank reconciliation
● **Appendix 7A**

Jansen Company's general ledger showed a checking account balance of $23,820 at the end of May 2018. The May 31 cash receipts of $2,340, included in the general ledger balance, were placed in the night depository at the bank on May 31 and were processed by the bank on June 1. The bank statement dated May 31, 2018, showed bank service charges of $38. All checks written by the company had been processed by the bank by May 31 and were listed on the bank statement except for checks totaling $1,890.

Required:

Prepare a bank reconciliation as of May 31, 2018. [*Hint:* You will need to compute the balance that would appear on the bank statement.]

E 7–30
Bank reconciliation and adjusting entries
● **Appendix 7A**

Harrison Company maintains a checking account at the First National City Bank. The bank provides a bank statement along with canceled checks on the last day of each month. The July 2018 bank statement included the following information:

Balance, July 1, 2018	$ 55,678
Deposits	179,500
Checks processed	(192,610)
Service charges	(30)
NSF checks	(1,200)
Monthly loan payment deducted directly by bank from account (includes $320 in interest)	(3,320)
Balance, July 31, 2018	$ 38,018

The company's general ledger account had a balance of $38,918 at the end of July. Deposits outstanding totaled $6,300 and all checks written by the company were processed by the bank except for those totaling $8,420. In addition, a $2,000 July deposit from a credit customer was recorded as a $200 debit to cash and credit to accounts receivable, and a check correctly recorded by the company as a $30 disbursement was incorrectly processed by the bank as a $300 disbursement.

Required:

1. Prepare a bank reconciliation for the month of July.
2. Prepare the necessary journal entries at the end of July to adjust the general ledger cash account.

E 7–31
Impairments of Notes Receivable
● **Appendix 7B**

At January 1, 2018, Lewis Enterprises has the following individual notes receivable that it is considering for impairment:

- A $2 million note (including accrued interest) from Bebko Inc. Lewis believes it is probable that Bebko will default on the note, and calculates the net realizable value of the receivable to be $1.4 million.
- A $3 million note (including accrued interest) from Dutta Associates. Lewis believes it is possible but not probable that Dutta will default on the note, and calculates the net realizable value of the receivable to be $2.5 million.

Required:

Determine the amount of impairment that Lewis would recognize for these two loans.

E 7–32
Credit Losses from Notes Receivable (CECL Model)
● **Appendix 7B**

Assume the same facts as in E 7–31, but that Lewis determines credit losses using the CECL model introduced in *ASU 2016-13* and required in 2020. Determine the amount of credit losses that Lewis would recognize for these two loans.

E 7–33
Impairment of notes receivable; troubled debt restructuring
● **Appendix 7B**

At January 1, 2018, Clayton Hoists Inc. owed Third BancCorp $12 million, under a 10% note due December 31, 2019. Interest was paid last on December 31, 2016. Clayton was experiencing severe financial difficulties and asked Third BancCorp to modify the terms of the debt agreement. After negotiation Third BancCorp agreed to do the following:

- Forgive the interest accrued for the year just ended.
- Reduce the remaining two years' interest payments to $1 million each.
- Reduce the principal amount to $11 million.

Required:

Prepare the journal entries by Third BancCorp necessitated by the restructuring of the debt at

1. January 1, 2018
2. December 31, 2018
3. December 31, 2019

E 7–34
Impairment of notes receivable; troubled debt restructuring
● Appendix 7B

At January 1, 2018, NCI Industries, Inc., was indebted to First Federal Bank under a $240,000, 10% unsecured note. The note was signed January 1, 2016, and was due December 31, 2019. Annual interest was last paid on December 31, 2016. NCI was experiencing severe financial difficulties and negotiated a restructuring of the terms of the debt agreement. First Federal agreed to reduce last year's interest and the remaining two years' interest payments to $11,555 each and delay all payments until December 31, 2019, the maturity date.

Required:

Prepare the journal entries by First Federal Bank necessitated by the restructuring of the debt at

1. January 1, 2018
2. December 31, 2018
3. December 31, 2019

Problems

P 7–1
Uncollectible accounts; allowance method; income statement and balance sheet approach
● LO7–5, LO7–6

Swathmore Clothing Corporation grants its customers 30 days' credit. The company uses the allowance method for its uncollectible accounts receivable. During the year, a monthly bad debt accrual is made by multiplying 3% times the amount of credit sales for the month. At the fiscal year-end of December 31, an aging of accounts receivable schedule is prepared and the allowance for uncollectible accounts is adjusted accordingly.

At the end of 2017, accounts receivable were $574,000 and the allowance account had a credit balance of $54,000. Accounts receivable activity for 2018 was as follows:

Beginning balance	$ 574,000
Credit sales	2,620,000
Collections	(2,483,000)
Write-offs	(68,000)
Ending balance	$ 643,000

The company's controller prepared the following aging summary of year-end accounts receivable:

	Summary	
Age Group	**Amount**	**Percent Uncollectible**
0–60 days	$430,000	4%
61–90 days	98,000	15
91–120 days	60,000	25
Over 120 days	55,000	40
Total	$643,000	

Required:

1. Prepare a summary journal entry to record the monthly bad debt accrual and the write-offs during the year.
2. Prepare the necessary year-end adjusting entry for bad debt expense.
3. What is total bad debt expense for 2018? How would accounts receivable appear in the 2018 balance sheet?

P 7–2
Uncollectible accounts; Amdahl
● LO7–5
Real World Financials

Amdahl Corporation manufactures large-scale, high performance computer systems. In a recent annual report, the balance sheet included the following information ($ in thousands):

	Current Year	Previous Year
Current assets:		
Receivables, net of allowances of $5,042 and $6,590 in the previous year	$504,944	$580,640

In addition, the income statement reported sales revenue of $2,158,755 ($ in thousands) for the current year. All sales are made on a credit basis. The statement of cash flows indicates that cash collected from customers during the current year was $2,230,065 ($ in thousands). There were no recoveries of accounts receivable previously written off.

Required:

1. Compute the following ($ in thousands):
   a. The amount of uncollectibles written off by Amdahl during the current year
   b. The amount of bad debt expense that Amdahl would include in its income statement for the current year
   c. The approximate percentage that Amdahl used to estimate uncollectibles for the current year, assuming that it uses the income statement approach
2. Suppose that Amdahl had used the direct write-off method to account for uncollectibles. Compute the following ($ in thousands):
   a. The accounts receivable information that would be included in the year-end balance sheet
   b. The amount of bad debt expense that Amdahl would include in its income statement for the current year

P 7–3
Bad debts; Nike, Inc.
● LO7–5
Real World Financials

Nike, Inc., is a leading manufacturer of sports apparel, shoes, and equipment. The company's 2015 financial statements contain the following information ($ in millions):

	2015	2014
Balance sheets:		
Accounts receivable, net	$ 3,358	$ 3,434
Income statements:		
Sales revenue	$30,601	$27,799

A note disclosed that the allowance for uncollectible accounts had a balance of $78 million and $78 million at the end of 2015 and 2014, respectively. Bad debt expense for 2015 was $20 million. Assume that all sales are made on a credit basis.

Required:

1. What is the amount of gross (total) accounts receivable due from customers at the end of 2015 and 2014?
2. What is the amount of bad debt write-offs during 2015?
3. Analyze changes in the gross accounts receivable account to calculate the amount of cash received from customers during 2015.
4. Analyze changes in net accounts receivable to calculate the amount of cash received from customers during 2015.

P 7–4
Uncollectible accounts
● LO7–5, LO7–6

Raintree Cosmetic Company sells its products to customers on a credit basis. An adjusting entry for bad debt expense is recorded only at December 31, the company's fiscal year-end. The 2017 balance sheet disclosed the following:

Current assets:	
Receivables, net of allowance for uncollectible accounts of $30,000	$432,000

During 2018, credit sales were $1,750,000, cash collections from customers $1,830,000, and $35,000 in accounts receivable were written off. In addition, $3,000 was collected from a customer whose account was written off in 2017. An aging of accounts receivable at December 31, 2018, reveals the following:

Age Group	Percentage of Year-End Receivables in Group	Percent Uncollectible
0–60 days	65%	4%
61–90 days	20	15
91–120 days	10	25
Over 120 days	5	40

Required:

1. Prepare summary journal entries to account for the 2018 write-offs and the collection of the receivable previously written off.
2. Prepare the year-end adjusting entry for bad debts according to each of the following situations:
   a. Bad debt expense is estimated to be 3% of credit sales for the year.
   b. Bad debt expense is estimated by computing net realizable value of the receivables. The allowance for uncollectible accounts is estimated to be 10% of the year-end balance in accounts receivable.
   c. Bad debt expense is estimated by computing net realizable value of the receivables. The allowance for uncollectible accounts is determined by an aging of accounts receivable.
3. For situations (a)–(c) in requirement 2 above, what would be the net amount of accounts receivable reported in the 2018 balance sheet?

P 7–5
Receivables; bad debts and returns; Avon Products, Inc.
● LO7–4, LO7–5
Real World Financials

Avon Products, Inc., located in New York City, is one of the world's largest producers of beauty and related products. The company's consolidated balance sheets for the 2015 and 2014 fiscal years included the following ($ in thousands):

	2015	2014
Current assets:		
Receivables, less allowances of $86,700 in 2015 and $106,900 in 2014	$443,000	$515,600

A disclosure note accompanying the financial statements reported the following ($ in thousands):

	Year Ended	
	2015	**2014**
Calculation of account receivables, net:		
Receivables	$529,700	$622,500
Less: allowance for doubtful accounts	(77,600)	(93,700)
Less: reserve for product returns	(9,100)	(13,200)
Trade accounts receivable, net:	$443,000	$515,600

Assume that the company reported bad debt expense in 2015 of $144,100 and had products returned for credit totaling $6,800 (sales price). Net sales for 2015 were $6,076,500 ($ in thousands).

Required:
1. What is the amount of accounts receivable due from customers at the end of 2015 and 2014?
2. What amount of accounts receivable did Avon write off during 2015?
3. What is the amount of Avon's gross sales for the 2015 fiscal year?
4. Assuming that all sales are made on a credit basis, what is the amount of cash Avon collected from customers during the 2015 fiscal year?

P 7–6
Notes receivable; solving for unknowns
● LO7–7

Cypress Oil Company's December 31, 2018, balance sheet listed $645,000 of notes receivable and $16,000 of interest receivable included in current assets. The following notes make up the notes receivable balance:

Note 1	Dated 8/31/2018, principal of $300,000 and interest at 10% due on 2/28/2019.
Note 2	Dated 6/30/2018, principal of $150,000 and interest due 3/31/2019.
Note 3	$200,000 face value noninterest-bearing note dated 9/30/2018, due 3/31/2019. Note was issued in exchange for merchandise.

The company records adjusting entries only at year-end. There were no other notes receivable outstanding during 2018.

Required:
1. Determine the rate used to discount the noninterest-bearing note.
2. Determine the explicit interest rate on Note 2.
3. What is the amount of interest revenue that appears in the company's 2018 income statement related to these notes?

P 7–7
Factoring versus assigning of accounts receivable
● LO7–8

Lonergan Company occasionally uses its accounts receivable to obtain immediate cash. At the end of June 2018, the company had accounts receivable of $780,000. Lonergan needs approximately $500,000 to capitalize on a unique investment opportunity. On July 1, 2018, a local bank offers Lonergan the following two alternatives:

a. Borrow $500,000, sign a note payable, and assign the entire receivable balance as collateral. At the end of each month, a remittance will be made to the bank that equals the amount of receivables collected plus 12% interest on the unpaid balance of the note at the beginning of the period.
b. Transfer $550,000 of specific receivables to the bank without recourse. The bank will charge a 2% factoring fee on the amount of receivables transferred. The bank will collect the receivables directly from customers. The sale criteria are met.

Required:
1. Prepare the journal entries that would be recorded on July 1 for each of the alternatives.
2. Assuming that 80% of all June 30 receivables are collected during July, prepare the necessary journal entries to record the collection and the remittance to the bank.

3. For each alternative, explain any required note disclosures that would be included in the July 31, 2018, financial statements.

P 7–8
Factoring of accounts receivable; without recourse
● LO7–8

Samson Wholesale Beverage Company regularly factors its accounts receivable with the Milpitas Finance Company. On April 30, 2018, the company transferred $800,000 of accounts receivable to Milpitas. The transfer was made without recourse. Milpitas remits 90% of the factored amount and retains 10%. When Milpitas collects the receivables, it remits to Samson the retained amount less a 4% fee (4% of the total factored amount). Samson estimates the fair value of the last 10% of its receivables to be $60,000.

Required:

Prepare the journal entry for Samson Wholesale Beverage for the transfer of accounts receivable on April 30, assuming the sale criteria are met.

P 7–9
Cash and accounts receivable under IFRS
● LO7–2, LO7–5, LO7–8, LO7–10

IFRS

The following facts apply to Walken Company during December 2018:

a. Walken began December with an accounts receivable balance (net of bad debts) of €25,000.
b. Walken had credit sales of €85,000.
c. Walken had cash collections of €30,000.
d. Walken factored €20,000 of net accounts receivable with Reliable Factor Company, transferring all risks and rewards associated with the receivable, and otherwise meeting all criteria necessary to qualify for treating the transfer of receivables as a sale.
e. Walken factored €15,000 of net accounts receivable with Dependable Factor Company, retaining all risks and rewards associated with the receivable, and otherwise meeting all criteria necessary to qualify for treating the transfer of receivables as a sale.
f. Walken did not recognize any additional bad debts expense, and had no write-offs of bad debts during the month.
g. At December 31, 2018, Walken had a balance of €40,000 of cash at M&V Bank and an overdraft of (€5,000) at First National Bank. (That cash balance includes any effects on cash of the other transactions described in this problem.)

Required:

Prepare the cash and accounts receivable lines of the current assets section of Walken's balance sheet, as of December 31, 2018.

P 7–10
Miscellaneous receivable transactions
● LO7–3, LO7–4, LO7–7, LO7–8

Evergreen Company sells lawn and garden products to wholesalers. The company's fiscal year-end is December 31. During 2018, the following transactions related to receivables occurred:

Feb. 28	Sold merchandise to Lennox, Inc., for $10,000 and accepted a 10%, 7-month note. 10% is an appropriate rate for this type of note.
Mar. 31	Sold merchandise to Maddox Co. and accepted a noninterest-bearing note with a discount rate of 10%. The $8,000 payment is due on March 31, 2019.
Apr. 3	Sold merchandise to Carr Co. for $7,000 with terms 2/10, n/30. Evergreen uses the gross method to account for cash discounts.
11	Collected the entire amount due from Carr Co.
17	A customer returned merchandise costing $3,200. Evergreen reduced the customer's receivable balance by $5,000, the sales price of the merchandise. Sales returns are recorded by the company as they occur.
30	Transferred receivables of $50,000 to a factor without recourse. The factor charged Evergreen a 1% finance charge on the receivables transferred. The sale criteria are met.
June 30	Discounted the Lennox, Inc., note at the bank. The bank's discount rate is 12%. The note was discounted without recourse.
Sep. 30	Lennox, Inc., paid the note amount plus interest to the bank.

Required:

1. Prepare the necessary journal entries for Evergreen for each of the above dates. For transactions involving the sale of merchandise, ignore the entry for the cost of goods sold (round all calculations to the nearest dollar).
2. Prepare any necessary adjusting entries at December 31, 2018. Adjusting entries are only recorded at year-end (round all calculations to the nearest dollar).
3. Prepare a schedule showing the effect of the journal entries in requirements 1 and 2 on 2018 income before taxes.

P 7–11
Discounting a note receivable
● LO7–7

Descriptors are provided below for six situations involving notes receivable being discounted at a bank. In each case, the maturity date of the note is December 31, 2018, and the principal and interest are due at maturity. For each, determine the proceeds received from the bank on discounting the note.

Note	Note Face Value	Date of Note	Interest Rate	Date Discounted	Discount Rate
1	$50,000	3/31/2018	8%	6/30/2018	10%
2	50,000	3/31/2018	8	9/30/2018	10
3	50,000	3/31/2018	8	9/30/2018	12
4	80,000	6/30/2018	6	10/31/2018	10
5	80,000	6/30/2018	6	10/31/2018	12
6	80,000	6/30/2018	6	11/30/2018	10

P 7–12
Accounts and notes receivable; discounting a note receivable; receivables turnover ratio
● LO7–5, LO7–6, LO7–7, LO7–8, LO7–9

Chamberlain Enterprises Inc. reported the following receivables in its December 31, 2018, year-end balance sheet:

Current assets:	
Accounts receivable, net of $24,000 in allowance for uncollectible accounts	$218,000
Interest receivable	6,800
Notes receivable	260,000

Additional Information:

1. The notes receivable account consists of two notes, a $60,000 note and a $200,000 note. The $60,000 note is dated October 31, 2018, with principal and interest payable on October 31, 2019. The $200,000 note is dated June 30, 2018, with principal and 6% interest payable on June 30, 2019.
2. During 2019, sales revenue totaled $1,340,000, $1,280,000 cash was collected from customers, and $22,000 in accounts receivable were written off. All sales are made on a credit basis. Bad debt expense is recorded at year-end by adjusting the allowance account to an amount equal to 10% of year-end accounts receivable.
3. On March 31, 2019, the $200,000 note receivable was discounted at the Bank of Commerce. The bank's discount rate is 8%. Chamberlain accounts for the discounting as a sale.

Required:

1. In addition to sales revenue, what revenue and expense amounts related to receivables will appear in Chamberlain's 2019 income statement?
2. What amounts will appear in the 2019 year-end balance sheet for accounts receivable?
3. Calculate the receivables turnover ratio for 2019.

P 7–13
Bank reconciliation and adjusting entries; cash and cash equivalents
● Appendix 7A

The bank statement for the checking account of Management Systems Inc. (MSI) showed a December 31, 2018, balance of $14,632.12. Information that might be useful in preparing a bank reconciliation is as follows:

a. Outstanding checks were $1,320.25.
b. The December 31, 2018, cash receipts of $575 were not deposited in the bank until January 2, 2019.
c. One check written in payment of rent for $246 was correctly recorded by the bank but was recorded by MSI as a $264 disbursement.
d. In accordance with prior authorization, the bank withdrew $450 directly from the checking account as payment on a mortgage note payable. The interest portion of that payment was $350. MSI has made no entry to record the automatic payment.
e. Bank service charges of $14 were listed on the bank statement.
f. A deposit of $875 was recorded by the bank on December 13, but it did not belong to MSI. The deposit should have been made to the checking account of MIS, Inc.
g. The bank statement included a charge of $85 for an NSF check. The check was returned with the bank statement and the company will seek payment from the customer.
h. MSI maintains a $200 petty cash fund that was appropriately reimbursed at the end of December.
i. According to instructions from MSI on December 30, the bank withdrew $10,000 from the account and purchased U.S. Treasury bills for MSI. MSI recorded the transaction in its books on December 31 when it received notice from the bank. Half of the Treasury bills mature in two months and the other half in six months.

Required:

1. Prepare a bank reconciliation for the MSI checking account at December 31, 2018. You will have to compute the balance per books.
2. Prepare any necessary adjusting journal entries indicated.
3. What amount would MSI report as cash and cash equivalents in the current asset section of the December 31, 2018, balance sheet?

P 7–14
Bank reconciliation and adjusting entries
● Appendix 7A

El Gato Painting Company maintains a checking account at American Bank. Bank statements are prepared at the end of each month. The November 30, 2018, reconciliation of the bank balance is as follows:

Balance per bank, November 30		$3,231
Add: Deposits outstanding		1,200
Less: Checks outstanding		
#363	$123	
#365	201	
#380	56	
#381	86	
#382	340	(806)
Adjusted balance per bank, November 30		$3,625

The company's general ledger checking account showed the following for December:

Balance, December 1	$ 3,625
Receipts	42,650
Disbursements	(41,853)
Balance, December 31	$ 4,422

The December bank statement contained the following information:

Balance, December 1	$ 3,231
Deposits	43,000
Checks processed	(41,918)
Service charges	(22)
NSF checks	(440)
Balance, December 31	$ 3,851

The checks that were processed by the bank in December include all of the outstanding checks at the end of November except for check #365. In addition, there are some December checks that had not been processed by the bank by the end of the month. Also, you discover that check #411 for $320 was correctly recorded by the bank but was incorrectly recorded on the books as a $230 disbursement for advertising expense. Included in the bank's deposits is a $1,300 deposit incorrectly credited to the company's account. The deposit should have been posted to the credit of the Los Gatos Company. The NSF checks have not been redeposited and the company will seek payment from the customers involved.

Required:
1. Prepare a bank reconciliation for the El Gato checking account at December 31, 2018.
2. Prepare any necessary adjusting journal entries indicated.

P 7–15
Impairment of receivables
● Appendix 7B

National Bank loaned the Lyon Company $10 million, at an interest rate of 8%. The note was signed January 1, 2008, and was due December 31, 2022. Annual interest was last paid on December 31, 2016. At January 1, 2018, National Bank concluded it was probable that the note was impaired. National believes it will not collect accrued interest, that it will only receive $500,000 of interest each year, and that it will only receive $8 million of principal at the end of the life of the note.

Required:
Calculate the amount of impairment that National Bank would recognize for the Lyon note.

P 7–16
Impairment of receivables
● Appendix 7B

Assume the same facts as in P 7–15, but that National Bank believes there is only a 40% chance that the loan is impaired (suffers a credit loss).

Required:
1. Calculate the amount of impairment that National Bank would recognize for the Lyon note under current U.S. GAAP.
2. Calculate the amount of credit loss that National Bank would recognize for the Lyon note, but assuming that since 2017 National has determined credit losses using the CECL model introduced in *ASU 2016-13*.

P 7–17
Impairment of receivables; troubled debt restructuring
● Appendix 7B

Rothschild Chair Company, Inc., was indebted to First Lincoln Bank under a $20 million, 10% unsecured note. The note was signed January 1, 2008, and was due December 31, 2021. Annual interest was last paid on December 31, 2016. At January 1, 2018, Rothschild Chair Company was experiencing severe financial difficulties and negotiated a restructuring of the terms of the debt agreement.

Required:

Prepare all journal entries by First Lincoln Bank to record the restructuring and any remaining transactions, for current and future years, relating to the debt under each of the independent circumstances below:

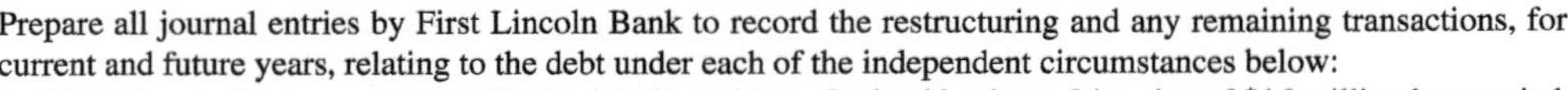

1. First Lincoln Bank agreed to settle the debt in exchange for land having a fair value of $16 million but carried on Rothschild Chair Company's books at $13 million.
2. First Lincoln Bank agreed to (a) forgive the interest accrued from last year, (b) reduce the remaining four interest payments to $1 million each, and (c) reduce the principal to $15 million.
3. First Lincoln Bank agreed to defer all payments (including accrued interest) until the maturity date and accept $27,775,000 at that time in settlement of the debt.

Broaden Your Perspective

Apply your critical-thinking ability to the knowledge you've gained. These cases will provide you an opportunity to develop your research, analysis, judgment, and communication skills. You also will work with other students, integrate what you've learned, apply it in real-world situations, and consider its global and ethical ramifications. This practice will broaden your knowledge and further develop your decision-making abilities.

Judgment Case 7–1
Accounts and notes receivable
● LO7–5, LO7–6, LO7–8

Magrath Company has an operating cycle of less than one year and provides credit terms for all of its customers. On April 1, 2018, the company factored, without recourse, some of its accounts receivable. Magrath transferred the receivables to a financial institution, and will have no further association with the receivables.

Magrath uses the allowance method to account for uncollectible accounts. During 2018, some accounts were written off as uncollectible and other accounts previously written off as uncollectible were collected.

Required:

1. How should Magrath account for and report the accounts receivable factored on April 1, 2018? Why is this accounting treatment appropriate?
2. How should Magrath account for the collection of the accounts previously written off as uncollectible?
3. What are the two basic approaches to estimating uncollectible accounts under the allowance method? What is the rationale for each approach?

(AICPA adapted)

Communication Case 7–2
Uncollectible accounts
● LO7–5

You have been hired as a consultant by a parts manufacturing firm to provide advice as to the proper accounting methods the company should use in some key areas. In the area of receivables, the company president does not understand your recommendation to use the allowance method for uncollectible accounts. She stated, "Financial statements should be based on objective data rather than the guesswork required for the allowance method. Besides, since my uncollectibles are fairly constant from period to period, with significant variations occurring infrequently, the direct write-off method is just as good as the allowance method."

Required:

Draft a one-page response in the form of a memo to the president in support of your recommendation for the company to use the allowance method.

Judgment Case 7–3
Accounts receivable
● LO7–3, LO7–7, LO7–8

Hogan Company uses the net method of accounting for sales discounts. Hogan offers trade discounts to various groups of buyers.

On August 1, 2018, Hogan factored some accounts receivable on a without recourse basis. Hogan incurred a finance charge.

Hogan also has some notes receivable bearing an appropriate rate of interest. The principal and total interest are due at maturity. The notes were received on October 1, 2018, and mature on September 30, 2019. Hogan's operating cycle is less than one year.

Required:

1. a. Using the net method, how should Hogan account for the sales discounts at the date of sale? What is the rationale for the amount recorded as sales under the net method?
   b. Using the net method, what is the effect on Hogan's sales revenues and net income when customers do not take the sales discounts?
2. What is the effect of trade discounts on sales revenues and accounts receivable? Why?
3. How should Hogan account for the accounts receivable factored on August 1, 2018? Why?
4. How should Hogan report the effects of the interest-bearing notes receivable in its December 31, 2018, balance sheet and its income statement for the year ended December 31, 2018? Why?

(AICPA adapted)

Real World Case 7–4
Sales returns; Green Mountain Coffee Roasters
● LO7–4

Real World Financials

The following is an excerpt from Sam Antar, "Is Green Mountain Coffee Roasters Shuffling the Beans to Beat Earnings Expectations?" (*Phil's Stock World delivered by Newstex,* May 9, 2011.)

> On May 3, 2011, Green Mountain Coffee Roasters (NASDAQ: GMCR) beat analysts' earnings estimates by $0.10 per share for the thirteen-week period ended March 26, 2011. The next day, the stock price had risen to $11.91 per share to close at $75.98 per share, a staggering 18.5% increase over the previous day's closing stock price. CNBC Senior Stocks Commentator Herb Greenberg raised questions about the quality of Green Mountain Coffees earnings because its provision for sales returns dropped $22 million in the thirteen-week period. He wanted to know if there was a certain adjustment to reserves ("a reversal") that helped Green Mountain Coffee beat analysts' earnings estimates. . . .
>
> During the thirteen-week period ended March 26, 2011, it was calculated that Green Mountain Coffee had a negative $22.259 million provision for sales returns. In its latest 10-Q report, Green Mountain Coffee disclosed that its provision for sales returns was $5.262 million for the twenty-six week period ending March 26, 2011, but the company did not disclose amounts for the thirteen-week period ended March 26, 2011. In its previous 10-Q report for the thirteen-week period ended December 25, 2010, Green Mountain Coffee disclosed that its provision for sales returns was $27.521 million. Therefore, the provision for sales returns for the thirteen-week period ended March 26, 2011 was a negative $22.259 million ($5.262 million minus $27.521 million).

Required:

1. Access EDGAR on the Internet. The web address is www.sec.gov.
2. Search for Green Mountain Coffee Roasters, Inc.'s 10-K for the fiscal year ended September 25, 2010 (filed December 9, 2010). (*Note*: the company now is named Keurig Green Mountain, Inc.) Answer the following questions related to the company's 2010 accounting for sales returns:
   a. What type of an account (for example, asset, contraliability) is Sales Returns Reserve? Explain.
   b. Prepare a T-account for fiscal 2010's sales returns reserve. Include entries for the beginning and ending balance, acquisitions, amounts charged to cost and expense, and deductions.
   c. Prepare journal entries for amounts charged to cost and expense and for deductions. Provide a brief explanation of what each of those journal entries represents.
   d. For any of the amounts included in your journal entries that appear in Green Mountain's statement of cash flows on page F-8, explain why the amount appears as an increase or decrease to cash flows.
3. Now consider the information provided by Antar in the excerpt at the beginning of this case.
   a. Prepare a T-account for the first quarter of fiscal 2011's sales returns reserve. Assume amounts associated with acquisitions and deductions are zero, such that the only entry affecting the account during the first quarter of fiscal 2011 is to record amounts charged or recovered from cost and expense. Compute the ending balance of the account.
   b. Prepare a T-account for the second quarter of fiscal 2011's sales returns reserve. Assume amounts associated with acquisitions and deductions are zero, such that the only entry affecting the account during the first quarter of fiscal 2011 is to record amounts charged or recovered from cost and expense. Compute the ending balance of the account.
   c. Assume that actual returns were zero during the second quarter of fiscal 2011. Prepare a journal entry to record amounts charged or recovered from cost and expense during the second quarter of fiscal 2011. How would that journal entry affect 2011 net income?
   d. Speculate as to what might have caused the activity in Green Mountain's sales returns account during the second quarter of fiscal 2011. Consider how this result could occur unintentionally, or why it might occur intentionally as a way to manage earnings.

Ethics Case 7–5
Uncollectible accounts
● LO7–5

You have recently been hired as the assistant controller for Stanton Industries, a large, publicly held manufacturing company. Your immediate superior is the controller who, in turn, is responsible to the vice president of finance.

The controller has assigned you the task of preparing the year-end adjusting entries. In the receivables area, you have prepared an aging of accounts receivable and have applied historical percentages to the balances of each of the age categories. The analysis indicates that an appropriate balance for the allowance for uncollectible accounts is $180,000. The existing balance in the allowance account prior to any adjusting entry is a $20,000 credit balance.

After showing your analysis to the controller, he tells you to change the aging category of a large account from over 120 days to current status and to prepare a new invoice to the customer with a revised date that agrees with the new aging category. This will change the required allowance for uncollectible accounts from $180,000 to $135,000. Tactfully, you ask the controller for an explanation for the change and he tells you "We need the extra income; the bottom line is too low."

Required:

1. What is the effect on income before taxes of the change requested by the controller?
2. Discuss the ethical dilemma you face. Consider your options and responsibilities along with the possible consequences of any action you might take.

Judgment Case 7–6
Internal control
● LO7–1

For each of the following independent situations, indicate the apparent internal control weaknesses and suggest alternative procedures to eliminate the weaknesses.

1. John Smith is the petty cash custodian. John approves all requests for payment out of the $200 fund, which is replenished at the end of each month. At the end of each month, John submits a list of all accounts and amounts to be charged and a check is written to him for the total amount. John is the only person ever to tally the fund.
2. All of the company's cash disbursements are made by check. Each check must be supported by an approved voucher, which is in turn supported by the appropriate invoice and, for purchases, a receiving document. The vouchers are approved by Dean Leiser, the chief accountant, after reviewing the supporting documentation. Betty Hanson prepares the checks for Leiser's signature. Leiser also maintains the company's check register (the cash disbursements journal) and reconciles the bank account at the end of each month.
3. Fran Jones opens the company's mail and makes a listing of all checks and cash received from customers. A copy of the list is sent to Jerry McDonald who maintains the general ledger accounts. Fran prepares and makes the daily deposit at the bank. Fran also maintains the subsidiary ledger for accounts receivable, which is used to generate monthly statements to customers.

Real World Case 7–7
Receivables; bad debts; Cisco Systems, Inc.
● LO7–5

EDGAR, the Electronic Data Gathering, Analysis, and Retrieval system, performs automated collection, validation, indexing, and forwarding of submissions by companies and others who are required by law to file forms with the U.S. Securities and Exchange Commission (SEC). All publicly traded domestic companies use EDGAR to make the majority of their filings. (Some foreign companies file voluntarily). Form 10-K or 10-KSB, which include the annual report, is required to be filed on EDGAR. The SEC makes this information available on the Internet.

Real World Financials

Required:

1. Access EDGAR on the Internet. The web address is www.sec.gov.
2. Search for Cisco Systems, Inc. Access the 10-K filing for the most recent fiscal year. Search or scroll to find the financial statements.
3. Answer the following questions related to the company's accounts receivable and bad debts:
   a. What is the amount of gross trade accounts receivable at the end of the year?
   b. What is the amount of bad debt expense for the year? (*Hint:* check the statement of cash flows).
   c. Determine the amount of actual bad debt write-offs made during the year. Assume that all bad debts relate only to trade accounts receivable.
   d. Using only information from the balance sheets, income statements, and your answer to requirement 3(c), determine the amount of cash collected from customers during the year. Assume that all sales are made on a credit basis, that the company provides no allowances for sales returns, that no previously written-off receivables were collected, and that all sales relate to trade accounts receivable.

Integrating Case 7–8
Change in estimate of bad debts
● LO7–5

McLaughlin Corporation uses the allowance method to account for bad debts. At the end of the company's fiscal year, accounts receivable are analyzed and the allowance for uncollectible accounts is adjusted. At the end of 2018, the company reported the following amounts:

Accounts receivable	$10,850,000
Less: Allowance for uncollectible accounts	(450,000)
Accounts receivable, net	$10,400,000

In 2019, it was determined that $1,825,000 of year-end 2018 receivables had to be written off as uncollectible. This was due in part to the fact that Hughes Corporation, a long-standing customer that had always paid its bills, unexpectedly declared bankruptcy in 2019. Hughes owed McLaughlin $1,400,000. At the end of 2018, none of the Hughes receivable was considered uncollectible.

Required:

Describe the appropriate accounting treatment and required disclosures for McLaughlin's underestimation of bad debts at the end of 2018.

Analysis Case 7–9
Financing with receivables
● LO7–8

Financial institutions have developed a wide variety of methods for companies to use their receivables to obtain immediate cash. The methods differ with respect to which rights and risks are retained by the transferor (the original holder of the receivable) and those passed on to the transferee (the new holder, usually a financial institution).

Required:

1. Describe the alternative methods available for companies to use their receivables to obtain immediate cash.
2. Discuss the alternative accounting treatments for these methods.

Real World Case 7–10
Financing with receivables; Sanofi-Aventis
● LO7–5, LO7–8, LO7–10

IFRS

Search on the Internet for the 2015 annual report for Sanofi-Aventis. Find the accounts receivable disclosure note.

Required:

1. Sanofi-Aventis subtracts "impairment" from the gross value of accounts receivable to obtain the net value. Interpret the impairment of (€167) in 2015 in terms of how that amount would typically be described in U.S. GAAP.
2. To what extent does Sanofi-Aventis factor or securitize accounts receivable? How do you know?
3. Assume that Sanofi-Aventis decided to increase the extent to which it securitizes its accounts receivable, changing to a policy of securitizing accounts receivable immediately upon making a sale and treating the securitization as a sale of accounts receivable. Indicate the likely effect of that change in policy on:
   a. Accounts receivable in the period of the change
   b. Cash flow from operations in the period of the change
   c. Accounts receivable in subsequent periods
   d. Cash flow from operations in subsequent periods
4. Given your answers to requirement 3, could a company change the extent to which it factors or securitizes receivables to create one-time changes in its cash flow? Explain.

Research Case 7–11
Locate and extract relevant information and authoritative support for a financial reporting issue; financing with receivables
● LO7–8

You are spending the summer working for a local wholesale furniture company, Samson Furniture, Inc. The company is considering a proposal from a local financial institution, Old Reliant Financial, to factor Samson's receivables. The company controller is unfamiliar with the prevailing GAAP that deals with accounting for the transfer of financial assets and has asked you to do some research. The controller wants to make sure the arrangement with the financial institution is structured in such a way as to allow the factoring to be accounted for as a sale.

Old Reliant has offered to factor all of the company's receivables on a "without recourse" basis. Old Reliant will remit to Samson 90% of the factored amount, collect the receivables from Samson's customers, and retain the remaining 10% until all of the receivables have been collected. When Old Reliant collects all of the receivables, it will remit to Samson the retained amount, less a 4% fee (4% of the total factored amount).

Required:

1. Explain the meaning of the term *without recourse.*
2. Access the relevant authoritative literature on accounting for the transfer of financial assets using the *FASB Accounting Standards Codification.* You might gain access at the FASB website (www.fasb.org), from your school library, or some other source. What conditions must be met for a transfer of receivables to be accounted for as a sale (or in accounting terms, "derecognized")? What is the specific citation that Samson would rely on in applying that accounting treatment?
3. Assuming that the conditions for treatment as a sale are met, prepare Samson's journal entry to record the factoring of $400,000 of receivables. Assume that the fair value of the last 10% of Samson's receivables is equal to $25,000.
4. An agreement that both entitles and obligates the transferor, Samson, to repurchase or redeem transferred assets from the transferee, Old Reliant, maintains the transferor's effective control over those assets and the transfer is accounted for as a secured borrowing, not a sale, if and only if what conditions are met?

Analysis Case 7–12
Compare receivables management using ratios; Tyson Foods Inc. and Pilgrim's Pride Corp.
● LO7–9

Real World Financials

The table below contains selected financial information included in the 2015 financial statements of Tyson Foods Inc. and Pilgrim's Pride Corp.

	($ in millions)			
	Tyson		Pilgrim's Pride	
	2015	2014	2015	2014
Balance sheets:				
Accounts receivable, net	$ 1,620	$ 1,684	$ 349	$ 379
Income statements:				
Net sales	$41,373	$37,580	$8,180	$8,583

Required:

1. Calculate the 2015 receivables turnover ratio and average collection period for both companies. Evaluate the management of each company's investment in receivables.
2. Obtain annual reports from three corporations in the same primary industry and compare the management of each company's investment in receivables.

Note: You can obtain copies of annual reports from your library, from the investor relations department of the corporations, or from EDGAR (Electronic Data Gathering, Analysis, and Retrieval) on the Internet (www.sec.gov).

Continuing Cases

Target Case

● LO7–2, LO7–5

Target Corporation prepares its financial statements according to U.S. GAAP. Target's financial statements and disclosure notes for the year ended January 30, 2016, are available in Connect. This material also is available under the Investor Relations link at the company's website (www.target.com).

Required:

1. What is Target's policy for designating investments as cash equivalents?
2. What is Target's balance of cash equivalents for the fiscal year ended January 30, 2016?
3. What is Target's policy with respect to accounting for merchandise returns?
4. Does Target have accounts receivable? Speculate as to why it has the balance that it has. (Hint, see Disclosure Notes 9, 11 and 13).

Air France–KLM Case

● LO7–8

Air France–KLM (AF), a Franco-Dutch company, prepares its financial statements according to International Financial Reporting Standards. AF's financial statements and disclosure notes for the year ended December 31, 2015, are available in Connect. This material is also available under the Finance link at the company's website (www.airfranceklm.com).

Required:

1. In note 4.11, AF describes how it values trade receivables. How does the approach used by AF compare to U.S. GAAP?
2. In note 26, AF reconciles the beginning and ending balances of its valuation allowances for trade accounts receivable. Prepare a T-account for the valuation allowance and include entries for the beginning and ending balances as well as any reconciling items that affected the account during 2015.
3. Examine note 28. Does AF have any bank overdrafts? If so, are the overdrafts shown in the balance sheet the same way they would be shown under U.S. GAAP?

CPA Exam Questions and Simulations

Sample CPA Exam questions from Roger CPA Review are available in Connect as support for the topics in this chapter. These Multiple Choice Questions and Task-Based Simulations include expert-written explanations and solutions, and provide a starting point for students to become familiar with the content and functionality of the actual CPA Exam.

CHAPTER

8 Inventories: Measurement

OVERVIEW

The next two chapters continue our study of assets by investigating the measurement and reporting issues involving inventories and the related expense—cost of goods sold. Inventory refers to the assets a company (1) intends to sell in the normal course of business, (2) has in production for future sale, or (3) uses currently in the production of goods to be sold.

LEARNING OBJECTIVES

After studying this chapter, you should be able to:

- **LO8–1** Explain the types of inventory and the differences between a perpetual inventory system and a periodic inventory system. (*p. 416*)
- **LO8–2** Explain which physical units of goods should be included in inventory. (*p. 420*)
- **LO8–3** Account for transactions that affect net purchases and prepare a cost of goods sold schedule. (*p. 421*)
- **LO8–4** Differentiate between the specific identification, FIFO, LIFO, and average cost methods used to determine the cost of ending inventory and cost of goods sold. (*p. 424*)
- **LO8–5** Discuss the factors affecting a company's choice of inventory method. (*p. 431*)
- **LO8–6** Understand supplemental LIFO disclosures and the effect of LIFO liquidations on net income. (*p. 432*)
- **LO8–7** Calculate the key ratios used by analysts to monitor a company's investment in inventories. (*p. 438*)
- **LO8–8** Determine ending inventory using the dollar-value LIFO inventory method. (*p. 441*)
- **LO8–9** Discuss the primary difference between U.S. GAAP and IFRS with respect to determining the cost of inventory. (*p. 431*)

© Dave and Les Jacobs LLC

FINANCIAL REPORTING CASE

Inventory Measurement at Kroger Company

As you were reading the annual report of Kroger Company, one of the world's largest grocery retailers, you notice the company accounts for nearly all of its grocery inventory based on a LIFO method (last-in, first-out). This means the company reports its most recent inventory purchases as sold *first.* However, you understand that most grocery inventory consists of perishable food items, meaning that the company in reality almost certainly sells its most recent purchases *last.* Otherwise, there would be considerable inventory spoilage. You decide to look a little deeper and notice the following discussion in the company's annual report:

Inventories (in part)

Inventories are stated at the lower of cost (principally on a last-in, first-out "LIFO" basis) or market. In total, approximately 95% of inventories were valued using the LIFO method. Replacement cost was higher than the carrying amount by $1,272 at January 30, 2016 and $1,245 at January 31, 2015.

($ in millions)	2016	2015
FIFO Inventory	$7,440	$6,933
LIFO reserve	(1,272)	(1,245)
Reported inventories	$6,168	$5,688

After seeing this information, you are further confused because you don't understand why Kroger would choose to report inventory for more than $1 billion below its replacement cost. Doesn't that make the company's inventory look less valuable and therefore the company less profitable?

You do some more research and find that other retail companies, as well as companies in industries such as automobiles, consumer products, energy, manufacturing, and mining, also use the LIFO method. Each of these companies most likely sells its actual inventory on a first-in, first-out (FIFO) basis, so why are they assuming the opposite?

QUESTIONS

By the time you finish this chapter, you should be able to respond appropriately to the questions posed in this case. Compare your response to the solution provided at the end of the chapter.

1. How is the LIFO method used to calculate inventories? Is this permissible according to GAAP? (*p. 430*)
2. What is the purpose of disclosing the difference between the reported LIFO inventory amounts and replacement cost, assuming that replacement cost is equivalent to a FIFO basis? (*p. 432*)
3. Are you correct that, by using LIFO, Kroger reports lower inventory and lower profits? Why would Kroger do that? (*p. 438*)

Recording and Measuring Inventory

PART A

Inventory refers to the assets a company (1) intends to sell in the normal course of business, (2) has in production for future sale (work in process), or (3) uses currently in the production of goods to be sold (raw materials). The computers produced by

Inventories consist of assets that a retail or wholesale company acquires for resale or goods that manufacturers produce for sale.

Hewlett-Packard (HP), that are intended for sale to customers are inventory, as are partially completed components, the computer chips, and memory modules that will go into computers produced later. The computers *used* by HP's employees to maintain its accounting system and other company operations, however, are not available for sale to customers and therefore are classified and accounted for as equipment. Similarly, the stocks and bonds a securities dealer holds for sale are inventory, whereas HP would classify the securities it holds as investments.

Cost of goods sold is the expense related to inventory. The inventory amount in the balance sheet represents the cost of the inventory still on hand (not yet sold) at the end of the period, while cost of goods sold in the income statement represents the cost of the inventory sold during the period.

Inventory usually is one of the most valuable assets listed in the balance sheet for manufacturing, wholesale, and retail companies (enterprises that produce revenue by selling goods). Similarly, cost of goods sold typically is the largest expense in the income statement of these companies. For example, a recent balance sheet for Best Buy reported inventories of $5.1 billion, which represented 51% of current assets. The company's income statement for the year ended January 30, 2016, reported cost of goods sold of $30.3 billion representing 80% of operating expenses.

As we'll see in this and the next chapter, it's usually difficult to measure inventory and cost of goods sold at the exact cost of the actual physical quantities on hand and sold. Fortunately, accountants can use one of several techniques to approximate the desired result and satisfy our measurement objectives.

Types of Inventory

Merchandising Inventory

● LO8–1

Wholesale and retail companies purchase goods that are primarily in finished form. These companies are intermediaries in the process of moving goods from the manufacturer to the end-user. They often are referred to as merchandising companies and their inventory as merchandise inventory. *The cost of merchandise inventory includes the purchase price plus any other costs necessary to get the goods in condition and location for sale.* We discuss the concept of condition and location and the types of costs that typically constitute inventory later in this chapter.

Manufacturing Inventories

Inventory for a manufacturing company consists of raw materials, work in process, and finished goods.

Unlike merchandising companies, manufacturing companies actually produce the goods they sell to wholesalers, retailers, other manufacturers, or consumers. Inventory for a manufacturer consists of (1) raw materials, (2) work in process, and (3) finished goods.

Raw materials represent the cost of components purchased from suppliers that will become part of the finished product. For example, Hewlett-Packard's raw materials inventory includes semiconductors, circuit boards, plastic, and glass that go into the production of personal computers.

Work-in-process inventory refers to the products that are not yet complete in the manufacturing process. The cost of work in process includes the cost of raw materials used in production, the cost of labor that can be directly traced to the goods in process, and an allocated portion of other manufacturing costs, called *manufacturing overhead.* Overhead costs include electricity and other utility costs to operate the manufacturing facility, depreciation of manufacturing equipment, and many other manufacturing costs that cannot be directly linked to the production of specific goods.

Finished goods are goods that have been completed in the manufacturing process but have not yet been sold. They have reached their final stage and now await sale to a customer. Their cost includes the cost of all raw materials and work-in-process used in production.

Manufacturing companies generally disclose, either in a note or directly in the balance sheet, the dollar amount of each inventory category. For example, Intel, one of the world's largest semiconductor chip manufacturers, reports inventory as shown in Illustration 8–1.

	($ in millions)	
	December 26, 2015	**December 27, 2014**
Raw materials	$ 532	$ 462
Work in process	2,893	2,375
Finished goods	1,742	1,436
Total Inventories	$5,167	$4,273

Illustration 8–1

Inventories Disclosure—Intel Corporation

Real World Financials

The inventory accounts and the cost flows for a typical manufacturing company are shown using T-accounts in Illustration 8–2. The costs of raw materials used, direct labor applied, and manufacturing overhead applied flow into work in process and then to finished goods. When the goods are sold, the cost of those goods flows to cost of goods sold.

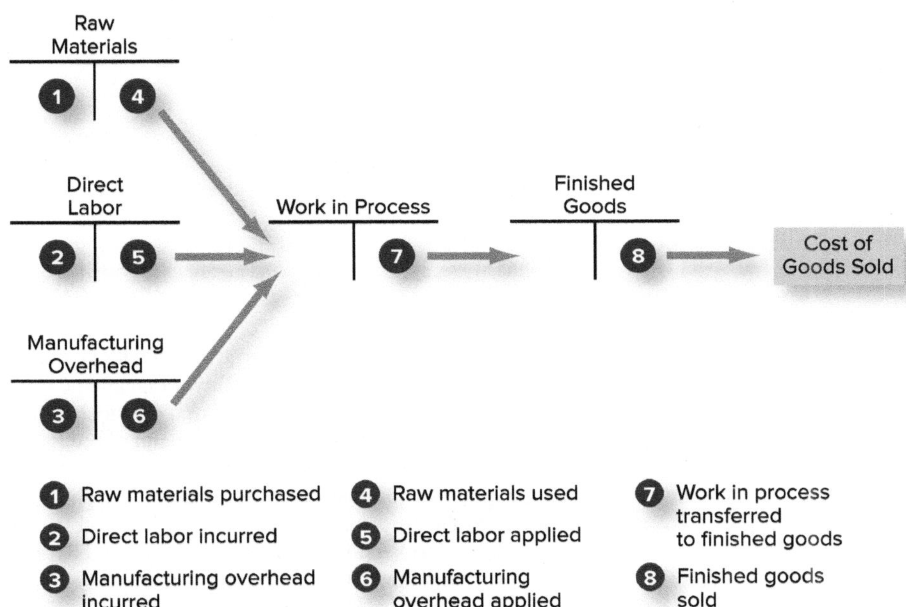

1 Raw materials purchased
2 Direct labor incurred
3 Manufacturing overhead incurred
4 Raw materials used
5 Direct labor applied
6 Manufacturing overhead applied
7 Work in process transferred to finished goods
8 Finished goods sold

Illustration 8–2

Inventory Components and Cost Flow for a Manufacturing Company

The costs of inventory units follow their physical movement from one stage of activity to another.

We focus in this text primarily on merchandising companies (wholesalers and retailers). Still, most of the accounting principles and procedures discussed here also apply to manufacturing companies. The unique problems involved with accumulating the direct costs of raw materials and labor and with allocating manufacturing overhead are addressed in managerial and cost accounting textbooks.

Types of Inventory Systems

Perpetual Inventory System

Two accounting systems are used to record transactions involving inventory: the **perpetual inventory system** and the **periodic inventory system**. The perpetual system was introduced in Chapter 2. The system is aptly termed perpetual because the account *inventory* is continually adjusted for each change in inventory, whether it's caused by a purchase, a sale, or a return of merchandise by the company to its supplier (a *purchase return* for the buyer, a *sales return* for the seller).[1] The cost of goods sold account, along with the inventory account, is adjusted each time goods are sold or are returned by a customer. This concept is applied to the Lothridge Wholesale Beverage Company for which inventory information is provided in Illustration 8–3. This hypothetical company also will be used in the next several illustrations.

[1]We discussed accounting for sales returns in Chapter 7.

Illustration 8–3
Perpetual Inventory System

The Lothridge Wholesale Beverage Company purchases soft drinks from producers and then sells them to retailers. The company begins 2018 with inventory of $120,000 on hand. The following information relates to inventory transactions during 2018:

1. Additional soft drink inventory is purchased on account at a cost of $600,000.
2. Sales for the year, all on account, totaled $820,000.
3. The cost of the soft drink inventory sold is $540,000.

Lothridge uses the *perpetual inventory system* to keep track of both inventory quantities and inventory costs. The system indicates that the cost of inventory on hand at the end of the year is $180,000.

The following summary journal entries record the inventory transactions for the Lothridge Company:

2018		
Inventory	600,000	
Accounts payable		600,000
To record the purchase of inventory.		
2018		
Accounts receivable	820,000	
Sales revenue		820,000
To record sales on account.		
Cost of goods sold	540,000	
Inventory		540,000
To record the cost of sales.		

An important feature of a perpetual system is that it is designed to track inventory quantities from their acquisition to their sale. If the system is accurate, it allows management to determine how many goods are on hand on any date without having to take a physical count. However, physical counts of inventory usually are made anyway, either at the end of the fiscal year or on a sample basis throughout the year, to verify that the perpetual system is correctly tracking quantities. Differences between the quantity of inventory determined by the physical count and the quantity of inventory according to the perpetual system could be caused by system errors, theft, breakage, or spoilage. In addition to keeping up with inventory purchases, a perpetual system also directly determines how many items are sold during a period.

A perpetual inventory system **continuously tracks both inventory quantities and inventory costs.**

When a company uses a perpetual inventory system to record inventory and cost of goods sold transactions, merchandise cost data also is included in the system. That way, when merchandise is purchased/sold, the system records not only the addition/reduction in inventory quantity but also the addition/reduction in the *cost* of the inventory.

The perpetual inventory system is becoming increasingly popular among companies. You probably are familiar with the scanning mechanisms used at grocery stores and other checkout counters. The scanners not only record each item sold but also can be used to track the purchase of merchandise for inventory management purposes. Inventory software and barcode tracking systems reduce the burden of physical inventory counts and make the use of the perpetual inventory system easier and more efficient.

Periodic Inventory System

A periodic inventory system **adjusts inventory and records cost of goods sold only at the end of each reporting period.**

A **periodic inventory system** is not designed to track either the quantity or cost of merchandise. The merchandise inventory account balance is not adjusted as purchases and sales are made but only periodically at the end of a reporting period. A physical count of the period's ending inventory is made and costs are assigned to the quantities determined. Merchandise purchases, purchase returns, purchase discounts, and freight-in (purchases plus freight-in less returns and discounts equals net purchases) are recorded in temporary accounts and the period's cost of goods sold is determined at the end of the period by combining the temporary accounts with the inventory account:

Cost of goods sold equation

Beginning inventory + Net purchases − Ending inventory = Cost of goods sold

The cost of goods sold equation assumes that all inventory quantities not on hand at the end of the period were sold. This may not be the case if inventory items were either damaged or stolen. If damaged and stolen inventory are identified, they must be removed from beginning inventory or purchases before calculating cost of goods sold and then classified as a separate expense item.

Illustration 8–4 looks at the periodic system using the Lothridge Wholesale Beverage Company example.

Illustration 8–4
Periodic Inventory System

The Lothridge Wholesale Beverage Company purchases soft drinks from producers and then sells them to retailers. The company begins 2018 with inventory of $120,000 on hand. The following information relates to inventory transactions during 2018:

1. Additional soft drink inventory is purchased on account at a cost of $600,000.
2. Sales for the year, all on account, totaled $820,000.

Lothridge uses the **periodic inventory system**. A physical count determined the cost of inventory at the end of the year to be $180,000.

The following summary journal entries record the inventory transactions for the Lothridge Company:

2018		
Purchases	600,000	
Accounts payable		600,000
To record the purchase of inventory.		
2018		
Accounts receivable	820,000	
Sales revenue		820,000
To record sales on account.		

No entry is recorded for the cost of inventory sold.

Because cost of goods sold isn't determined automatically and continually by the periodic system, it must be determined indirectly after a physical inventory count. Cost of goods sold for 2018 is determined as follows:

Beginning inventory	$ 120,000
Plus: Purchases	600,000
Cost of goods available for sale	720,000
Less: Ending inventory (per physical count)	(180,000)
Cost of goods sold	$540,000

The following journal entry combines the components of cost of goods sold into a single expense account and updates the balance in the inventory account:

December 31, 2018		
Cost of goods sold	540,000	
Inventory (ending)	180,000	
Inventory (beginning)		120,000
Purchases		600,000
To adjust inventory, close the purchases account, and record cost of goods sold.		

This entry adjusts the inventory account to the correct period-end amount, closes the temporary purchases account, and records the residual as cost of goods sold. Now let's compare the two inventory accounting systems.

A Comparison of the Perpetual and Periodic Inventory Systems

Beginning inventory plus net purchases during the period is the *cost of goods available for sale.* The main difference between a perpetual and a periodic system is that the periodic system allocates cost of goods available for sale between ending inventory and cost of goods sold (periodically) *at the end of the period.* In contrast, the perpetual system performs this allocation by decreasing inventory and increasing cost of goods sold (perpetually) *each time goods are sold.*

The impact on the financial statements of choosing one system over the other generally is not significant. The choice between the two approaches usually is motivated by management control considerations as well as the comparative costs of implementation. Perpetual systems can provide more information about the dollar amounts of inventory levels on a continuous basis. They also facilitate the preparation of interim financial statements by providing fairly accurate information without the necessity of a physical count of inventory.

A perpetual system provides more timely information but generally is more costly.

On the other hand, a perpetual system may be more expensive to implement than a periodic system. This is particularly true for inventories consisting of large numbers of low-cost items. Perpetual systems are more workable with inventories of high-cost items such as construction equipment or automobiles. However, with the help of computers and electronic sales devices such as cash register systems with barcode scanners, the perpetual inventory system now is available to many small businesses that previously could not afford them and is economically feasible for a broader range of inventory items than before.

The periodic system is less costly to implement during the period but requires a physical count before ending inventory and cost of goods sold can be determined. This makes the preparation of interim financial statements more costly unless an inventory estimation technique is used.[2] And, perhaps most importantly, the inventory monitoring features provided by a perpetual system are not available. However, it is important to remember that a perpetual system involves the tracking of both inventory quantities *and* costs. Many companies that determine costs only periodically employ systems to constantly monitor inventory quantities.

What is Included in Inventory?

Physical Units Included in Inventory

● LO8–2

Regardless of the system used, the measurement of inventory and cost of goods sold starts with determining the physical units of goods. Typically, determining the physical units that should be included in inventory is a simple matter because it consists of items in the possession of the company. However, in some situations the identification of items that should be included in inventory is more difficult. Consider, for example, goods in transit, goods on consignment, and sales returns.

GOODS IN TRANSIT. At the end of a reporting period, it's important to ensure a proper inventory cutoff. This means ownership must be determined for goods that are in transit between the company and its customers as well as between the company and its suppliers.

For example, in December 2018, the Lothridge Wholesale Beverage Company sold goods to the Jabbar Company.

1. The goods were shipped from Lothridge on December 29, 2018, but
2. The goods didn't arrive at Jabbar until January 3, 2019.

If both companies have December 31 fiscal year ends, whose inventory is it on December 31, 2018? In other words, which company will report these goods in ending inventory in the balance sheet as of December 31, 2018? The answer depends on who owns the goods on December 31. Ownership depends on the terms of the agreement between the two companies.

Inventory shipped *f.o.b. shipping point* is included in the purchaser's inventory as soon as the merchandise is shipped.

If the goods are shipped **f.o.b. (free on board) shipping point**, then legal title to the goods changes hands at the *point of shipment* when the seller delivers the goods to the common carrier (for example, a trucking company). In this case, the purchaser is responsible for shipping costs and transit insurance. Lothridge records the sale of inventory on December

[2]In Chapter 9 we discuss inventory estimation techniques that avoid the necessity of a physical count to determine ending inventory and cost of goods sold.

29, 2018, and Jabbar records the purchase of inventory on that same day. Jabbar will include these goods in its 2018 ending inventory even though the company is not in physical possession of the goods on the last day of the fiscal year.

On the other hand, if the goods are shipped f.o.b. destination, the seller is responsible for shipping, and legal title does not pass until the goods arrive at their *destination* (the customer's location). In our example, if the goods are shipped f.o.b. destination, Lothridge includes the goods in its 2018 ending inventory and the sale is not recorded until January 3, 2019, when those goods reach Jabbar. Jabbar also will wait until 2019 to record the purchase.

Inventory shipped *f.o.b. destination* is included in the purchaser's inventory only after it reaches the purchaser's destination.

GOODS ON CONSIGNMENT. Sometimes a company arranges for another company to sell its product under consignment. The goods are physically transferred to the other company (the consignee), but the transferor (consignor) retains legal title. If the consignee can't find a buyer, the goods are returned to the consignor. If a buyer is found, the consignee remits the selling price (less commission and approved expenses) to the consignor.

Goods held on *consignment* are included in the inventory of the consignor until sold by the consignee.

As we discussed in Chapter 5, because risk is retained by the consignor, the sale is not complete (revenue is not recognized) until an eventual sale to a third party occurs. As a result, goods held on consignment generally are not included in the consignee's inventory. While in stock, they belong to the consignor and should be included in inventory of the consignor even though not in the company's physical possession. A sale is recorded by the consignor only when the goods are sold by the consignee and title passes to the customer.

SALES RETURNS. Recall from our discussions in Chapters 5 and 7 that when the right of return exists, a seller must be able to estimate those returns before revenue can be recognized. The adjusting entry for estimated sales returns includes a debit to sales returns and a credit to refund liability (or some companies might credit an allowance for sales returns in the case of credit sales). At the same time, cost of goods sold is reduced and an estimate of inventory to be returned is made (see Illustration 7–4). As a result, a company includes in ending inventory the cost of merchandise sold it anticipates will be returned.

Now that we've considered which goods are part of inventory, let's examine the types of costs that should be associated with those inventory units.

Transactions Affecting Net Purchases

● LO8–3

As mentioned earlier, the cost of inventory includes all necessary expenditures to acquire the inventory and bring it to its desired *condition* and *location* for sale or for use in the manufacturing process. Obviously, the cost includes the purchase price of the goods. But usually the cost of acquiring inventory also includes freight charges on incoming goods borne by the buyer; insurance costs incurred by the buyer while the goods are in transit (if shipped f.o.b. shipping point); and the costs of unloading, unpacking, and preparing merchandise inventory for sale or raw materials inventory for use.[3] The costs included in inventory are called product costs. They are associated with products and *expensed as cost of goods sold only when the related products are sold.*[4]

Expenditures necessary to bring inventory to its *condition* and *location* for sale or use are included in its cost.

FREIGHT-IN ON PURCHASES. Freight-in on purchases is commonly included in the cost of inventory. These costs clearly are necessary to get the inventory in location for sale or use and can generally be associated with particular goods. Freight costs are added to the *inventory* account in a perpetual system.

The cost of *freight-in* paid by the purchaser generally is part of the cost of inventory.

In a periodic system, freight costs generally are recorded in a temporary account called freight-in or transportation-in, which is added to total purchases in determining net purchases for inclusion in cost of goods sold. (See also the cost of goods sold schedule in

[3]Generally accepted accounting principles require that abnormal amounts of certain costs be recognized as current period expenses rather than being included in the cost of inventory, specifically idle facility costs, freight, handling costs, and waste materials (spoilage). FASB ASC 330–10–30: Inventory–Overall–Initial Measurement (previously "Inventory Costs–An Amendment of *ARB No. 43,* Chapters 4," *Statement of Financial Accounting Standards No. 151* (Norwalk, Conn.: FASB, 2004)).

[4]For practical reasons, though, some of these expenditures often are not included in inventory cost and are treated as **period costs.** They often are immaterial or it is impractical to associate the expenditures with particular units of inventory (for example, unloading and unpacking costs). Period costs are not associated with products and are expensed in the *period* incurred.

Illustration 8–6 later in this section.) From a control perspective, by recording freight-in as a separate item, management can more easily track its freight costs. The same perspectives pertain to purchase returns and purchase discounts, which are discussed in the next sections.

Shipping charges on outgoing goods are reported either as part of cost of goods sold or as an operating expense, usually among selling expenses.

Shipping charges on outgoing goods (freight-out) are not included in the cost of inventory. They are reported in the income statement either as part of cost of goods sold or as an operating expense, usually among selling expenses. If a company adopts a policy of not including shipping charges in cost of goods sold, both the amounts incurred during the period as well as the income statement classification of the expense must be disclosed.[5]

PURCHASE RETURNS. In Chapter 7 we discussed merchandise returns from the perspective of the selling company. At the time a customer returns merchandise, the seller records a sales return (a contra revenue account). We now address returns from the buyer's point of view. When merchandise is returned, the buyer records a **purchase return**. In a perpetual inventory system, the purchase return is recorded directly as a reduction to the *inventory* account. In a periodic system, we use a *purchase returns* account to temporarily accumulate these amounts. Recall our earlier discussion of the cost of goods sold calculation (Beginning inventory + *Net purchases* − Ending inventory = Cost of goods sold). Purchase returns are subtracted from total purchases to calculate net purchases. (See also the cost of goods sold schedule in Illustration 8–6 later in this section.)

Purchase discounts represent reductions in the amount to be paid if remittance is made within a designated period of time.

PURCHASE DISCOUNTS. Cash discounts also were discussed from the seller's perspective in Chapter 7. These discounts really are quick-payment discounts because they represent reductions in the amount to be paid by the buyer in the event payment is made within a specified period of time. The amount of the discount and the time period within which it's available are conveyed by terms like 2/10, n/30 (meaning a 2% discount if paid within 10 days, otherwise full payment within 30 days). As with the seller, the purchaser can record these **purchase discounts** using either the **gross method** or the **net method**. Consider Illustration 8–5, which is similar to the cash discount illustration in Chapter 7.

Illustration 8–5
Purchase Discounts

On October 5, 2018, the Lothridge Wholesale Beverage Company purchased merchandise at a price of $20,000. The repayment terms are stated as 2/10, n/30. Lothridge paid $13,720 ($14,000 less the 2% cash discount) on October 14 and the remaining balance of $6,000 on November 4. Lothridge employs a periodic inventory system.

The gross and net methods of recording the purchase and cash payment are compared as follows:

By either method, net purchases are reduced by discounts taken.

Gross Method			Net Method		
October 5, 2018			**October 5, 2018**		
Purchases*	20,000		Purchases*	19,600	
Accounts payable		20,000	Accounts payable		19,600
October 14, 2018			**October 14, 2018**		
Accounts payable	14,000		Accounts payable	13,720	
Purchase discounts*		280	Cash		13,720
Cash		13,720			
November 4, 2018			**November 4, 2018**		
Accounts payable	6,000		Accounts payable	5,880	
Cash		6,000	Interest expense	120	
			Cash		6,000

*The inventory account is used in a perpetual system.

Conceptually, the gross method views a discount not taken as part of the cost of inventory. The net method considers the cost of inventory to include the net, after-discount amount, and any discounts not taken are reported as *interest expense*.[6] The discount is viewed as compensation to the seller for providing financing to the buyer.

[5]FASB ASC 605–45–50–2: Revenue Recognition–Principal Agent Considerations–Disclosure–Shipping and Handling Fees and Costs (previously "Accounting for Shipping and Handling Fees and Costs," *EITF Issue No. 00–10* (Norwalk, Conn.: FASB, 2000), par. 6).

[6]An alternative treatment is to debit an expense account called *purchase discounts lost* rather than interest expense. This enables a company to more easily identify the forgone discounts. Some companies might prefer to include discounts lost as part of cost of goods sold.

Purchase discounts recorded under the gross method are subtracted from total purchases when determining net purchases. Under the perpetual inventory system, purchase discounts are treated as a reduction in the inventory account.

The effect on the financial statements of the difference between the two methods usually is immaterial. Net income over time will be the same using either method. *There will, however, be a difference in gross profit between the two methods equal to the amount of discounts not taken.* In Illustration 8–5, the $120 in discounts not taken is included as interest expense using the net method and in cost of goods sold using the gross method.

Illustration 8–6 compares the perpetual and periodic inventory systems, using the gross method. A schedule to demonstrate the calculation of cost of goods sold is provided at the end.

Illustration 8–6

Inventory Transactions—Perpetual and Periodic Systems

The Lothridge Wholesale Beverage Company purchases soft drinks from producers and then sells them to retailers. The company began 2018 with merchandise inventory of $120,000 on hand. During 2018 additional inventory transactions include:

- Purchases of merchandise on account totaled $620,000, with terms 2/10, n/30.
- Freight charges paid by Lothridge were $16,000.
- Merchandise with a cost of $20,000 was returned to suppliers for credit.
- All purchases on account were paid within the discount period.
- Sales on account totaled $830,000. The cost of soft drinks sold was $550,000.
- Inventory remaining on hand at the end of 2018 totaled $174,000.

The above transactions are recorded in summary form according to both the perpetual and periodic inventory systems using the gross method:

($ in thousands)

Perpetual System			Periodic System		
			Purchases		
Inventory	620		Purchases	620	
Accounts payable		620	Accounts payable		620
			Freight		
Inventory	16		Freight-in	16	
Cash		16	Cash		16
			Returns		
Accounts payable	20		Accounts payable	20	
Inventory		20	Purchase returns		20
			Discounts		
Accounts Payable	600		Accounts Payable	600	
Inventory ($600 × 2%)		12	Purchase discounts ($600 × 2%)		12
Cash		588	Cash		588
			Sales		
Accounts receivable	830		Accounts receivable	830	
Sales revenue		830	Sales revenue		830
Cost of goods sold	550		No entry		
Inventory		550			
			End of period		
No entry			Cost of goods sold (below)	550	
			Inventory (ending)	174	
			Purchase returns	20	
			Purchase discounts	12	
			Inventory (beginning)		120
			Purchases		620
			Freight-in		16

(continued)

(concluded)

Supporting Schedule

Cost of goods sold:		
Beginning inventory		$120
Purchases	$620	
Plus: Freight-in	16	
Less: Returns	(20)	
Less: Discounts	(12)	
Net purchases		604
Cost of goods available		724
Less: Ending inventory		(174)
Cost of goods sold		$550

Inventory Cost Flow Assumptions

● LO8–4

Regardless of whether the perpetual or periodic system is used, it's necessary to assign dollar amounts to the physical quantities of goods sold and goods remaining in ending inventory. Unless each item of inventory is specifically identified and traced through the system, assigning dollars is accomplished by making an assumption regarding how units of goods (and their associated costs) flow through the system. We examine the common cost flow assumptions next. In previous illustrations, dollar amounts of the cost of goods sold and the cost of ending inventory were assumed known. However, if various portions of inventory are acquired at different costs, we need a way to decide which units were sold and which remain in inventory. Illustration 8–7 will help explain.

Illustration 8–7

Inventory Information

Goods available for sale include beginning inventory plus purchases.

The Browning Company has the following inventory information for 2018:

Beginning Inventory and Purchases During 2018

Date	**Units**	**Unit Cost***	**Total Cost**
Jan. 1 (Beginning Inventory)	4,000	$5.50	$22,000
Purchases:			
Jan. 17	1,000	6.00	6,000
Mar. 22	3,000	7.00	21,000
Oct. 15	3,000	7.50	22,500
Goods available for sale	11,000		$71,500

Sales

Date of Sale	**Units**
Jan. 10	2,000
Apr. 15	1,500
Nov. 20	3,000
Total	6,500

*Includes purchase price and cost of freight.

Browning began the year with 4,000 units and purchased another 7,000 units, so there were 11,000 units available for sale. Of this amount, 6,500 units were sold. This means 4,500 units remain in ending inventory. This allocation of units is depicted in Illustration 8–7A.

What is the cost of the 6,500 units sold? In other words, which of the 11,000 units available for sale were sold? If all units, including beginning inventory, were purchased at the

Beginning inventory (4,000 units)
+
Purchases (7,000 units)
Units available (11,000)
Units on hand at end of period
4,500
Units sold during the period
6,500
Total units = 11,000

Illustration 8–7A
Allocation of Units Available

same price, then the answer would be simple. However, that rarely is the case. Using the numbers given, let's consider the question as follows:

Beginning inventory (4,000 units @ \$5.50)	\$ 22,000
Plus: Purchases (7,000 units @ various prices)	49,500
Cost of goods available for sale (11,000 units)	\$71,500
Less: Ending inventory (4,500 units @ ?)	?
Cost of goods sold (6,500 units @ ?)	?

The \$71,500 in cost of goods available for sale must be allocated to ending inventory and cost of goods sold. The allocation decision is depicted in Illustration 8–7B.

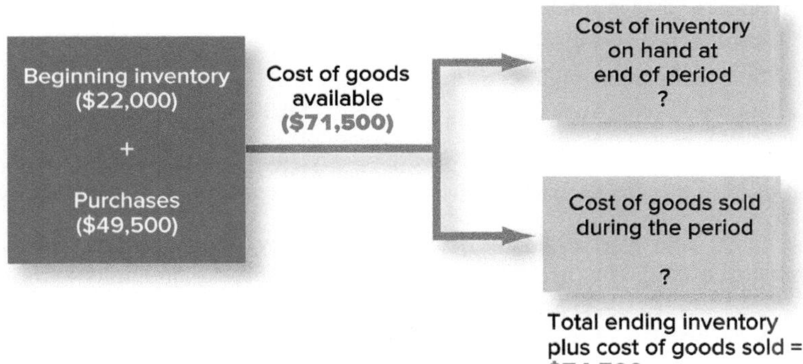

Illustration 8–7B
Allocation of Cost of Goods Available

Let's turn our attention now to the various inventory methods that can be used to achieve the allocation between ending inventory and cost of goods sold.

Specific Identification

It's sometimes possible for each unit sold during the period or each unit on hand at the end of the period to be matched with its actual cost. Actual costs can be determined by reference to the invoice representing the purchase of the item. The **specific identification** is used frequently by companies selling unique, expensive products with low sales volume which makes it relatively easy and economically feasible to associate each item with its actual cost. For example, automobiles have unique serial numbers that can be used to match a specific auto with the invoice identifying the actual purchase price.

The specific identification method, however, is not feasible for many types of products either because items are not uniquely identifiable or because it's too costly to match a specific purchase price with each item sold or each item remaining in ending inventory. For this reason, most companies use other cost flow methods that *assume* which units of inventory have been sold and which units remain in ending inventory. It's important to note that the *actual flow of a company's inventory does not have to match management's assumed flow*.

The three most common cost flow assumption methods are average cost; first-in, first-out (FIFO); and last-in, first-out (LIFO). We discuss each of these next. Later in this chapter we will discuss the various motivating factors that influence management's choice among various methods.

Average Cost

The *average cost method* assumes that items sold and items in ending inventory come from a mixture of all the goods available for sale.

The average cost method assumes that cost of goods sold and ending inventory consist of a mixture of all the goods available for sale. The average unit cost applied to goods sold or to ending inventory is not simply an average of the various unit costs of purchases during the period but an average unit cost *weighted* by the number of units acquired at the various unit costs.

In a periodic inventory system, the average cost is computed only at the end of the period.

PERIODIC AVERAGE COST. In a periodic inventory system, this weighted average is calculated only at the end of the period as follows:

$$\text{Weighted-average unit cost} = \frac{\text{Cost of goods available for sale}}{\text{Quantity available for sale}}$$

The calculation of average cost is demonstrated in Illustration 8–7C using data from Illustration 8–7.

Illustration 8–7C

Average Cost—Periodic Inventory System

Beginning inventory (4,000 units @ $5.50)	$ 22,000
Plus: Purchases (7,000 units @ various prices)	49,500
Cost of goods available for sale (11,000 units)	71,500
Less: Ending inventory* (determined below)	(29,250)
Cost of goods sold (6,500 units)	$42,250

***Cost of Ending Inventory:**

$$\text{Weighted-average unit cost} = \frac{\$71,500}{11,000 \text{ units}} = \$6.50$$

4,500 units × $6.50 = $29,250

Cost of goods sold also could be determined directly by multiplying the weighted-average unit cost of $6.50 by the number of units sold ($6.50 × 6,500 units = $42,250).

In a perpetual inventory system, the average cost method is applied by computing a moving-average unit cost each time additional inventory is purchased.

PERPETUAL AVERAGE COST. The weighted-average unit cost in a perpetual inventory system becomes a moving-average unit cost. *A new weighted-average unit cost is calculated each time additional units are purchased.* The new average is determined after each purchase by (1) summing the cost of the previous inventory balance and the cost of the new purchase, and (2) dividing this new total cost (cost of goods available for sale) by the number of units on hand (the inventory units that are available for sale). This average is then used to cost any units sold before the next purchase is made. The moving-average concept is applied in Illustration 8–7D.

On January 17 the new average of $5.667 (rounded) is calculated by dividing the $17,000 cost of goods available ($11,000 from beginning inventory + $6,000 purchased on January 17) by the 3,000 units available (2,000 units from beginning inventory + 1,000 units acquired on January 17). The average is updated to $6.333 (rounded) with the March 22 purchase. The 1,500 units sold on April 15 are then costed at the average cost of $6.333.

Periodic average cost and perpetual average cost generally produce different allocations to cost of goods sold and ending inventory.

First-In, First-Out (FIFO)

The *first-in, first-out (FIFO) method* assumes that items sold are those that were acquired first.

Ending inventory applying FIFO consists of the most recently acquired items.

The first-in, first-out (FIFO) method assumes that units sold are the first units acquired. Beginning inventory is sold first, followed by purchases during the period in the chronological order of their acquisition. In our illustration, 6,500 units were sold during 2018. Applying FIFO, these would be the 4,000 units in beginning inventory, the 1,000 units purchased on January 17, and 1,500 of the 3,000 units from the March 22 purchase.

Illustration 8–7D Average Cost—Perpetual Inventory System

	Date	Purchased	Sold	Balance
	Beginning inventory	4,000 @ $5.50 = $22,000		4,000 @ $5.50 = $22,000
	Jan. 10		2,000 @ $5.50 = $ 11,000	2,000 @ $5.50 = $11,000
	Jan. 17	1,000 @ $6.00 = $6,000		$11,000 + $6,000 = $17,000
Average cost per unit	→	[$17,000 / 3,000 units] = $5.667/unit		2,000 + 1,000 = 3,000 units
	Mar. 22	3,000 @ $7.00 = $21,000		$17,000 + $21,000 = $38,000
Average cost per unit	→	[$38,000 / 6,000 units] = $6.333/unit		3,000 + 3,000 = 6,000 units
	Apr. 15		1,500 @ $6.333 = $9,500	4,500 @ $6.333 = $28,500
	Oct. 15	3,000 @ $7.50 = $22,500		$28,500 + $22,500 = $51,000
Average cost per unit	→	[$51,000 / 7,500 units] = $6.80/unit		4,500 + 3,000 = 7,500 units
	Nov. 20		3,000 @ $6.80 = $ 20,400	4,500 @ $6.80 = **$30,600**
		Total cost of goods sold	= **$40,900**	

Ending inventory consists of the remaining units assumed not to be sold. In this case, the 4,500 units in ending inventory consist of 1,500 of the 3,000 units purchased on March 22 and all of the 3,000 units purchased on October 15. Graphically, the flow is as follows:

Units Available		
Beg. inv.	4,000	6,500 units sold
Jan. 17	1,000	
Mar. 22	1,500	
Mar. 22	1,500	4,500 units in ending inventory
Oct. 15	3,000	
Total	11,000	

PERIODIC FIFO Recall that we determine physical quantities on hand in a periodic inventory system by taking a physical count. Costing the 4,500 units in ending inventory this way automatically gives us the cost of goods sold as well. Using the numbers from our illustration, we determine cost of goods sold to be $38,500 by subtracting the $33,000 ending inventory from $71,500 cost of goods available for sale as shown in Illustration 8–7E.

Illustration 8–7E

FIFO—Periodic Inventory System

Beginning inventory (4,000 units @ $5.50)	$22,000
Plus: Purchases (7,000 units @ various prices)	49,500
Cost of goods available for sale (11,000 units)	71,500
Less: Ending inventory* (determined below)	(33,000)
Cost of goods sold (6,500 units)	$38,500

***Cost of Ending Inventory:**

Date of Purchase	Units	Unit Cost	Total Cost
Mar. 22	1,500	$7.00	$ 10,500
Oct. 15	3,000	7.50	22,500
Total	4,500		$33,000

Of course, the 6,500 units sold could be costed directly as follows:

Date of Purchase	Units	Unit Cost	Total Cost
Jan. 1 (Beginning inventory)	4,000	$5.50	$22,000
Jan. 17	1,000	6.00	6,000
Mar. 22	1,500	7.00	10,500
Total	6,500		$38,500

Perpetual FIFO results in cost of goods sold and ending inventory amounts that are the same as those obtained using periodic FIFO.

PERPETUAL FIFO *The ending inventory and cost of goods sold will have the same amounts in a perpetual inventory system as in a periodic inventory system when FIFO is used.* This is because the same units and costs are first in and first out whether cost of goods sold is determined as each sale is made or at the end of the period as a residual amount. The application of FIFO in a perpetual system is shown in Illustration 8–7F.

Illustration 8–7F

FIFO—Perpetual Inventory System

Date	Purchased	Sold	Balance	
Beginning inventory	4,000 @ $5.50 = $22,000		4,000 @ $5.50 = $22,000	
Jan. 10		2,000 @ $5.50 = $ 11,000	2,000 @ $5.50 = $11,000	
Jan. 17	1,000 @ $6.00 = $ 6,000		2,000 @ $5.50 1,000 @ $6.00	$17,000
Mar. 22	3,000 @ $7.00 = $21,000		2,000 @ $5.50 1,000 @ $6.00 3,000 @ $7.00	$38,000
Apr. 15		1,500 @ $5.50 = $ 8,250	500 @ $5.50 1,000 @ $6.00 3,000 @ $7.00	$29,750
Oct. 15	3,000 @ $7.50 = $22,500		500 @ $5.50 1,000 @ $6.00 3,000 @ $7.00 3,000 @ $7.50	$52,250
Nov. 20		500 @ $5.50 + 1,000 @ $6.00 + 1,500 @ $7.00 = $ 19,250	1,500 @ $7.00 3,000 @ $7.50	$33,000
	Total cost of goods sold	= $38,500		

Last-In, First-Out (LIFO)

The *last-in, first-out (LIFO) method* assumes that items sold are those that were most recently acquired.

Ending inventory applying LIFO consists of the items acquired first.

The last-in, first-out (LIFO) method assumes that the units sold are the most recent units purchased. In our illustration, the 6,500 units assumed sold would be the 6,500 units acquired most recently: the 3,000 units acquired on October 15, the 3,000 units acquired on March 22, and 500 of the 1,000 units purchased on January 17. Ending inventory, then, consists of the remaining units assumed not sold; in this case, 500 of the 1,000 units purchased on January 17 and all of the 4,000 units from beginning inventory. Graphically, the flow is as follows:

Units Available		
Beg. inv.	4,000	4,500 units in ending inventory
Jan. 17	500	
Jan. 17	500	6,500 units sold
Mar. 22	3,000	
Oct. 15	3,000	
Total	11,000	

PERIODIC LIFO The cost of ending inventory determined to be $25,000 (calculated below) by the LIFO assumption and using a periodic system is subtracted from cost of goods available for sale to arrive at the cost of goods sold of $46,500 as shown in Illustration 8–7G.

Illustration 8–7G

LIFO—Periodic Inventory System

Beginning inventory (4,000 units @ $5.50)	$22,000
Plus: Purchases (7,000 units @ various prices)	49,500
Cost of goods available for sale (11,000 units)	71,500
Less: Ending inventory* (determined below)	(25,000)
Cost of goods sold (6,500 units)	$46,500

***Cost of Ending Inventory:**

Date of Purchase	Units	Unit Cost	Total Cost
Jan. 1 (Beginning inventory)	4,000	$5.50	$22,000
Jan. 17	500	6.00	3,000
Total	4,500		$25,000

The 6,500 sold could be costed directly as follows:

Date of Purchase	Units	Unit Cost	Total Cost
Jan. 17	500	$6.00	$ 3,000
Mar. 22	3,000	7.00	21,000
Oct. 15	3,000	7.50	22,500
Total	6,500		$46,500

PERPETUAL LIFO The application of LIFO in a perpetual system is shown in Illustration 8–7H. Each time inventory is purchased or sold, the LIFO layers are adjusted. For example, after the March 22 purchase, we have three layers of inventory at different unit costs listed in the chronological order of their purchase. When 1,500 units are sold on April 15, we assume they come from the most recent layer of 3,000 units purchased at $7.00.

Perpetual LIFO generally results in cost of goods sold and inventory amounts that are different from those obtained by applying periodic LIFO.

Notice that the total cost of goods available for sale is allocated $44,000 to cost of goods sold by perpetual LIFO and $27,500 to ending inventory (the balance after the last

Illustration 8–7H

LIFO—Perpetual Inventory System

Date	Purchased	Sold	Balance	
Beginning inventory	4,000 @ $5.50 = $22,000		4,000 @ $5.50 =	$22,000
Jan. 10		2,000 @ $5.50 = $ 11,000	2,000 @ $5.50 =	$11,000
Jan. 17	1,000 @ $6.00 = $6,000		2,000 @ $5.50 1,000 @ $6.00	$17,000
Mar. 22	3,000 @ $7.00 = $21,000		2,000 @ $5.50 1,000 @ $6.00 3,000 @ $7.00	$38,000
Apr. 15		1,500 @ $7.00 = $ 10,500	2,000 @ $5.50 1,000 @ $6.00 1,500 @ $7.00	$27,500
Oct. 15	3,000 @ $7.50 = $22,500		2,000 @ $5.50 1,000 @ $6.00 1,500 @ $7.00 3,000 @ $7.50	$50,000
Nov. 20		3,000 @ $7.50 = $ 22,500	2,000 @ $5.50 1,000 @ $6.00 1,500 @ $7.00	$27,500
	Total cost of goods sold	= $44,000		

transaction), which is different from the periodic LIFO result of $46,500 and $25,000. *Unlike FIFO, applying LIFO in a perpetual inventory system will generally result in an ending inventory and cost of goods sold different from the allocation arrived at when applying LIFO in a periodic system.* Periodic LIFO applies the last-in, first-out concept to total sales and total purchases only at the conclusion of the reporting period. Perpetual LIFO applies the same concept, but several times during the period—every time a sale is made.

For example, when 2,000 units are sold on January 10, perpetual LIFO costs those units at $5.50, the beginning inventory unit cost, because those were the last units acquired *before the sale.* Periodic LIFO, by contrast, would be applied at year-end. By the end of the year, enough purchases have been made that the beginning inventory would be assumed to remain intact, and the January 10 units sold would be costed at a price from the most recent acquisition *before the end of the year.*

Comparison of cost flow methods

Comparison of Cost Flow Methods

The three cost flow methods are compared below assuming a periodic inventory system.

	Average	FIFO	LIFO
Cost of goods sold	$42,250	$38,500	$46,500
Ending inventory	29,250	33,000	25,000
Total	$71,500	$71,500	$71,500

Notice that the average cost method in this example produces amounts that fall in between the FIFO and LIFO amounts for both cost of goods sold and ending inventory. This will usually be the case. Whether it will be FIFO or LIFO that produces the highest or lowest value of cost of goods sold depends on the pattern of the actual unit cost changes during the period.

If unit costs are increasing, LIFO will result in a higher cost of goods sold and lower ending inventory than FIFO.

During periods of rising costs, as in our example, FIFO results in a lower cost of goods sold than LIFO because the lower costs of the earliest purchases are assumed sold. LIFO cost of goods sold will include the more recent higher cost purchases. On the other hand, FIFO ending inventory includes the most recent higher cost purchases which results in a higher ending inventory than LIFO. LIFO ending inventory includes the lower costs of the earliest purchases. Conversely, if costs are declining, then FIFO will result in a higher cost of goods sold and lower ending inventory than LIFO.[7]

FINANCIAL Reporting Case

Q1, p. 415

A company must disclose the inventory method(s) it uses.

Each of the three methods is permissible according to generally accepted accounting principles and frequently is used. Also, a company need not use the same method for its entire inventory. For example, International Paper Company uses LIFO for its raw materials and finished pulp and paper products, and both the FIFO and average cost methods for other inventories. Because of the importance of inventories and the possible differential effects of different methods on the financial statements, a company must identify in a disclosure note the method(s) it uses. The chapter's opening case included an example of this disclosure for Kroger, and you will encounter additional examples later in the chapter.

Illustration 8–8 shows the results of a recent survey of inventory methods used by 500 large public companies.[8] FIFO is the most popular method, but both LIFO and average cost are used

Illustration 8–8
Inventory Cost Flow Methods Used in Practice
Real World Financials

	# of Companies	% of Companies
FIFO	312	47%
LIFO	163	24
Average	133	20
Other* and not disclosed	61	9
Total	669	100%

*"Other" includes the specific identification method and miscellaneous less popular methods.

[7]The differences between the various methods also hold when a perpetual inventory system is used.

[8]*U.S. GAAP Financial Statements-Best Practices in Presentation and Disclosure-2013* (New York, New York: AICPA, 2013).

by many companies. Notice that the column total for the number of companies is greater than 500, indicating that many companies included in this sample do use multiple methods.

International Financial Reporting Standards

LO8–9

Inventory Cost Flow Assumptions. *IAS No. 2* does not permit the use of LIFO.[9] Because of this restriction, many U.S. multinational companies use LIFO only for their domestic inventories and FIFO or average cost for their foreign subsidiaries. A disclosure note included in a recent annual report of General Mills provides an example:

Real World Financials

Inventories (in part)

All inventories in the United States other than grain are valued at the lower of cost, using the last-in, first-out (LIFO) method, or market. Inventories outside of the United States generally are valued at the lower of cost, using the first-in, first-out (FIFO) method, or market.

This difference could prove to be a significant impediment to U.S. convergence to international standards. Unless the U.S. Congress repeals the LIFO conformity rule, convergence would cause many corporations to lose a valuable tax shelter, the use of LIFO for tax purposes. If these companies were immediately taxed on the difference between LIFO inventories and inventories valued using another method, it would cost companies billions of dollars. Some industries would be particularly hard hit. Most oil companies and auto manufacturers, for instance, use LIFO. The government estimates that the repeal of the LIFO method would increase federal tax revenues by $76 billion over a ten-year period.[10] The companies affected most certainly will lobby heavily to retain the use of LIFO for tax purposes.

Decision Makers' Perspective—Factors Influencing Method Choice

LO8–5

What factors motivate companies to choose one method over another? What factors have caused the increased popularity of LIFO? Choosing among alternative accounting methods is a complex issue. Often such choices are not made in isolation but in such a way that the combination of inventory cost flow assumptions, depreciation methods, pension assumptions, and other choices meet a particular objective. Also, many believe managers sometimes make these choices to maximize their own personal benefits rather than those of the company or its external constituents. But regardless of the motive, the impact on reported numbers is an important consideration in each choice of method. The inventory choice determines (a) how closely reported costs reflect the actual physical flow of inventory, (b) the timing of reported income and income tax expense, and (c) how well costs are matched with associated revenues.

PHYSICAL FLOW. If a company wanted to choose a method that most closely approximates specific identification, then the actual physical flow of inventory in and out of the company would motivate the choice of method.

A company is not required to choose an inventory method that approximates actual physical flow.

For example, companies often attempt to sell the oldest goods in inventory first for some of their products. This certainly is the case with perishable goods such as many grocery items. The FIFO method best mirrors the physical flow in these situations. The average cost method might be used for liquids such as chemicals where items sold are taken from a mixture of inventory acquired at different times and different prices. There are very few inventories that actually flow in a LIFO manner. It is important for you to understand that there is no requirement that companies choose an inventory method that approximates actual

[9] "Inventories," *International Accounting Standard No. 2* (IASCF), as amended effective January 1, 2016.

[10] Andrew Lundeen, "Proposed Tax Changes in President Obama's Fiscal Year 2016 Budget," (taxfoundation.org).

physical flow and few companies make the choice on this basis. In fact, as we discuss next, the effect of inventory method on income and income taxes is the primary motivation that influences method choice.

INCOME TAXES AND NET INCOME. If the unit cost of inventory changes during a period, the inventory method chosen can have a significant effect on the amount of income reported by the company to external parties and also on the amount of income taxes paid to the Internal Revenue Service (IRS) and state and local taxing authorities. Over the entire life of a company, cost of goods sold for all years will equal actual costs of items sold regardless of the inventory method used. However, as we have discussed, different inventory methods can produce significantly different results in each particular year.

Many companies choose LIFO in order to reduce income taxes in periods when prices are rising.

When prices rise and inventory quantities are not decreasing, LIFO produces a higher cost of goods sold and therefore lower net income than the other methods. The company's income tax returns will report a lower taxable income using LIFO and lower taxes will be paid currently. Taxes are not reduced permanently, only deferred. The reduced amount will be paid to the taxing authorities when either the unit cost of inventory or the quantity of inventory subsequently declines. However, we know from our discussion of the time value of money that it is advantageous to save a dollar today even if it must be paid back in the future. In the past, high inflation (increasing prices) periods motivated many companies to switch to LIFO in order to gain this tax benefit.

If a company uses LIFO to measure its taxable income, IRS regulations require that LIFO also be used to measure income reported to investors and creditors (the *LIFO conformity rule*).

A corporation's taxable income comprises revenues, expenses (including cost of goods sold), gains, and losses measured according to the regulations of the appropriate taxing authority. Income before tax as reported in the income statement does not always equal taxable income. In some cases, differences are caused by the use of different measurement methods.[11] However, IRS regulations, which determine federal taxable income, require that if a company uses LIFO to measure taxable income, the company also must use LIFO for external financial reporting. This is known as the **LIFO conformity rule** with respect to inventory methods.

Because of the LIFO conformity rule, to obtain the tax advantages of using LIFO in periods of rising prices, lower net income is reported to shareholders, creditors, and other external parties. The income tax motivation for using LIFO may be offset by a desire to report higher net income. Reported net income could have an effect on a corporation's share price,[12] on bonuses paid to management, or on debt agreements with lenders. For example, research has indicated that the managers of companies with bonus plans tied to income measures are more likely to choose accounting methods that maximize their bonuses (often those that increase net income).[13]

FINANCIAL Reporting Case

Q2, p. 415

The LIFO conformity rule permits LIFO users to report non-LIFO inventory valuations in a disclosure note, but not on the face of the income statement. For example, Illustration 8–9 shows the notes provided in a recent annual report of **Dollar General Corporation**, a large variety store chain, disclosing its use of LIFO to value its inventories.

LIFO RESERVES. Many companies use LIFO for external reporting and income tax purposes but maintain their internal records using FIFO or average cost. There is a variety of reasons, including: (1) the high recordkeeping costs for LIFO, (2) contractual agreements such as bonus or profit sharing plans that calculate net income with a method other than LIFO, and (3) using FIFO or average cost information for pricing decisions.

● LO8–6

[11]For example, a corporation can take advantage of incentives offered by Congress by deducting more depreciation in the early years of an asset's life in its federal income tax return than it reports in its income statement.

[12]The concept of capital market efficiency has been debated for many years. In an efficient capital market, the market is not fooled by differences in accounting method choice that do not translate into real cash flow differences. The only apparent cash flow difference caused by different inventory methods is the amount of income taxes paid currently. In an efficient market, we would expect the share price of a company that switched its method to LIFO and saved tax dollars to increase even though it reported lower net income than if LIFO had not been adopted. Research on this issue is mixed. For example, see William E. Ricks, "Market's Response to the 1974 LIFO Adoptions," *Journal of Accounting Research* (Autumn 1982); and Robert Moren Brown, "Short-Range Market Reaction to Changes to LIFO Using Preliminary Earnings Announcement Dates," *Journal of Accounting Research* (Spring 1980).

[13]For example, see P. M. Healy, "The Effect of Bonus Schemes on Accounting Decisions," *Journal of Accounting and Economics* (April 1985); and D. Dhaliwal, G. Salamon, and E. Smith, "The Effect of Owner Versus Management Control on the Choice of Accounting Methods," *Journal of Accounting and Economics* (July 1982).

Inventories

Inventories are stated at the lower of cost or market with cost determined using the retail last-in, first-out (LIFO) method as this method results in a better matching of costs and revenues.

The excess of current cost over LIFO cost was approximately $92.9 million and $95.1 million at January 29, 2016 and January 30, 2015, respectively. Current cost is determined using the retail inventory method on a first-in, first-out basis.

Illustration 8–9

Inventories Disclosures—Dollar General Corporation

Real World Financials

Generally, the conversion to LIFO from the internal records occurs at the end of the reporting period without actually entering the adjustment into the company's records. Some companies, though, enter the conversion adjustment—the difference between the internal method and LIFO—directly into the records as a "contra account" to inventory. This contra account is called the **LIFO reserve** or the *LIFO allowance*.

For illustration, let's say that the Doubletree Corporation began 2018 with a balance of $475,000 in its LIFO reserve account. This balance means that at the beginning of the year, the inventory balance under LIFO is $475,000 lower than it would be under FIFO. By the end of 2018, assume the difference between LIFO and FIFO inventory balances is then $535,000. The LIFO reserve needs to be adjusted to reflect the increase in the reserve during the year. The LIFO reserve has a normal credit balance, so the entry to increase its balance is recorded as:

Cost of goods sold ($535,000 − 475,000)	60,000	
LIFO reserve		60,000

The entry to increase the LIFO reserve also involves an increase to cost of goods sold. The debit to cost of goods sold increases total expenses and therefore lowers reported profitability.

An increase in the LIFO reserve reduces reported profits.

If the difference between inventory valued internally using FIFO and inventory valued using LIFO had *decreased* over the year, the LIFO reserve would need to be decreased with a debit. The corresponding credit would be to cost of goods sold. In this situation, when cost of goods sold is decreased, profits will increase. This situation demonstrates that even though reported inventory is lower under LIFO than FIFO, LIFO profits might be larger than FIFO profits when the LIFO reserve decreases during the year.

A decrease in the LIFO reserve increases reported profits.

As an example of the disclosure of the LIFO reserve, Illustration 8–10 provides a disclosure note of **Books-A-Million, Inc.**, a leading book retailer primarily located in the eastern United States that operates both superstores and traditional bookstores. The note shows the company's inventories valued at FIFO (the internal method), less the LIFO reserve, to arrive at the LIFO amount reported in the company's balance sheet.

Inventories (in part)

($ in thousands)	2015	2014
Inventories (at FIFO)	$192,605	$204,220
Less: LIFO reserve	(4,645)	(4,636)
Net inventories (at LIFO)	$187,960	$199,584

Illustration 8–10

Inventories Disclosure—Books-A-Million

Real World Financials

Under LIFO, inventory is reported in the 2015 balance sheet at a lower amount, which indicates the need for a LIFO reserve of $4,645. The LIFO reserve at the beginning of 2015 was already $4,636, so its balance needs to be increased by only $9 thousand ($4,645 − $4,636). The increase is recorded with a credit to the LIFO reserve. At the same time, we increase (or debit) cost of goods sold, thereby reducing reported profit.

LIFO LIQUIDATIONS Earlier in the text, we demonstrated the importance of matching revenues and expenses in creating an income statement that is useful in predicting future

Proponents of LIFO argue that it results in a better match of revenues and expenses.

cash flows. Under LIFO, sales reflect the most recent selling prices, and cost of goods sold includes the costs of the most recent purchases.

For the same reason, though, inventory costs in the balance sheet with LIFO generally are out of date because they reflect old purchase transactions. It is not uncommon for a company's LIFO inventory balance to be based on unit costs actually incurred several years earlier.

This distortion sometimes carries over to the income statement as well. When inventory quantities decline during a period, then these out-of-date inventory layers are liquidated and cost of goods sold will partially match noncurrent costs with current selling prices. If costs have been increasing (decreasing), LIFO liquidations produce higher (lower) net income than would have resulted if the liquidated inventory were included in cost of goods sold at current costs. The paper profits (losses) caused by including out-of-date, low (high) costs in cost of goods sold is referred to as the effect on income of liquidations of LIFO inventory.

To illustrate this problem, consider the example in Illustration 8–11.

Illustration 8–11
LIFO Liquidation

National Distributors, Inc., uses the LIFO inventory method. The company began 2018 with inventory of 10,000 units that cost $20 per unit. During 2018, 30,000 units were purchased for $25 each and 35,000 units were sold.

National's LIFO cost of goods sold for 2018 consists of:

30,000	units @ $25 per unit =	$750,000
5,000	units @ $20 per unit =	100,000
35,000		$850,000

Included in cost of goods sold are 5,000 units from beginning inventory that now have been liquidated. If the company had purchased at least 35,000 units, no liquidation would have occurred. Then cost of goods sold would have been $875,000 (35,000 units × $25 per unit) instead of $850,000. The difference between these two cost of goods sold figures is $25,000 ($875,000 – 850,000). This is the before-tax income effect of the LIFO liquidation.

We also can determine the $25,000 before-tax LIFO liquidation profit by multiplying the 5,000 units liquidated by the difference between the $25 *current cost* per unit and the $20 *acquisition cost* per unit we included in cost of goods sold (5,000 units × [$25 − 20] = $25,000). Assuming a 40% income tax rate, the net effect of the liquidation is to increase net income by $15,000 [$25,000 × (1 − 0.40)]. The lower the costs of the units liquidated, the more severe the effect on income.

A company must disclose in a note any material effect of **LIFO liquidation** on net income. For example, Illustration 8–12 shows the disclosure note included with recent financial statements of **Genuine Parts Company**, a distributor of automotive replacement parts, industrial replacement parts, office products, and electrical parts.

Illustration 8–12
LIFO Liquidation Disclosure—Genuine Parts Company

Real World Financials

Summary of Significant Accounting Policies (in part)

Merchandise Inventories

During 2014 and 2013, reductions in inventory levels in automotive parts inventories (2013) and industrial parts inventories (2014 and 2013) resulted in liquidations of LIFO inventory layers. The effect of the LIFO liquidations in 2014 and 2013 was to reduce cost of goods sold by approximately $8,000,000 and $5,000,000, respectively.

In Illustration 8–11, National Distributors would disclose that LIFO liquidations increased income by $15,000 in 2018, assuming that this effect on income is considered material.

We've discussed several factors that influence companies in their choice of inventory method. A company could be influenced by the actual physical flow of its inventory, by the effect of inventory method on reported net income and the amount of income taxes payable currently, or by a desire to provide a better match of expenses with revenues. You've seen that the direction of the change in unit costs determines the effect of using different methods on net income and income taxes. While the United States has experienced persistent inflation for many years (increases in the general price-level), the prices of many goods and services have experienced periods of declining prices (for example, personal computers). ●

Concept Review Exercise

INVENTORY COST FLOW METHODS

The Rogers Company had beginning inventory in 2018 of 10 million units at a cost of $5 each.

The following inventory transactions occurred during the first six months of 2018.

Date	Transaction
Feb. 15	Purchased, on account, 5 million units at a cost of $6.50 each.
Mar. 20	Sold, on account, 8 million units at a selling price of $12 each.
Apr. 30	Purchased, on account, 5 million units at a cost of $7 each.

On June 30, 2018, 12 million units were on hand.

Required:

1. Prepare journal entries to record the above transactions. The company uses a periodic inventory system.
2. Prepare the required adjusting entry on June 30, 2018, applying each of the following inventory methods:
   a. Average
   b. FIFO
   c. LIFO
3. Repeat requirement 1 assuming that the company uses a perpetual inventory system.

Solution:

1. Prepare journal entries to record the above transactions. The company uses a periodic inventory system.

	($ in millions)	
February 15		
Purchases (5 million × $6.50)	32.5	
Accounts payable		32.5
To record the purchase of inventory.		
March 20		
Accounts receivable (8 million × $12)	96	
Sales revenue		96
To record sales on account.		
No entry is recorded for the cost of inventory sold.		
April 30		
Purchases (5 million × $7)	35	
Accounts payable		35
To record the purchase of inventory.		

2. Prepare the required adjusting entry on June 30, 2018, applying each method.

		($ in millions)					
Date	**Journal entry**	**Average**		**FIFO**		**LIFO**	
June 30	Cost of goods sold (determined below)	47.0		40.0		54.5	
	Inventory (ending—determined below)	70.5		77.5		63.0	
	Inventory [beginning—(10 million @ $5)]		50.0		50.0		50.0
	Purchases ($32.5 million + 35 million)		67.5		67.5		67.5

Calculation of ending inventory and cost of goods sold:

a. Average:

	($ in millions)
Beginning inventory (10 million units @ $5.00)	$50.0
Plus: Purchases (10 million units @ various prices)	67.5
Cost of goods available for sale (20 million units)	117.5
Less: Ending inventory* (determined below)	(70.5)
Cost of goods sold	$47.0

*Cost of ending inventory:

$$\text{Weighted-average unit cost} = \frac{\$117.5}{20 \text{ million units}} = \$5.875$$

$$12 \text{ million units} \times \$5.875 = \$70.5 \text{ million}$$

b. FIFO:

Cost of goods available for sale (20 million units)	$117.5
Less: Ending inventory* (determined below)	(77.5)
Cost of goods sold	$ 40.0

*Cost of ending inventory:

Date of Purchase	Units	Unit Cost	Total Cost
Beg. inv.	2 million	$5.00	$10.0
Feb. 15	5 million	6.50	32.5
April 30	5 million	7.00	35.0
Total	12 million		$77.5

c. LIFO:

Cost of goods available for sale (20 million units)	$117.5
Less: Ending inventory* (determined below)	(63.0)
Cost of goods sold	$ 54.5

*Cost of ending inventory:

Date of Purchase	Units	Unit Cost	Total Cost
Beg. inv.	10 million	$5.00	$50.0
Feb. 15	2 million	6.50	13.0
Total	12 million		$63.0

3. Repeat requirement 1 assuming that the company uses a perpetual inventory system.

	($ in millions)	
February 15		
Inventory (5 million × $6.50)	32.5	
Accounts payable		32.5
To record the purchase of inventory.		
April 30		
Inventory (5 million × $7.00)	35.0	
Accounts payable		35.0
To record the purchase of inventory.		

	($ in millions)					
Journal Entries—March 20	**Average**		**FIFO**		**LIFO**	
Accounts receivable (8 million × $12)	96.0		96.0		96.0	
Sales revenue		96.0		96.0		96.0
To record sales on account.						
Cost of goods sold (determined below)	44.0		40.0		47.5	
Inventory		44.0		40.0		47.5
To record cost of goods sold.						

Calculation of cost of goods sold:

a. Average:

Cost of goods sold:

	($ in millions, except unit costs)		
Date	**Purchased**	**Sold**	**Balance**
Beg. inv.	10 million @ $5.00 = $50.0		10 million @ $5.00 = $50.0
Feb. 15	5 million @ $6.50 = $32.5		$50.0 + $32.5 = $82.5
	$\frac{\$82.5}{15 \text{ million units}} = \$5.50/\text{unit}$		
Mar. 20		8 million @ $5.50 = $44.0	

b. FIFO:

Cost of goods sold:

Units Sold	**Cost of Units Sold**	**Total Cost**
8 million (from Beg. inv.)	$5.00	$40.0

c. LIFO:

Cost of goods sold:

Units Sold	**Cost of Units Sold**	**Total Cost**
5 million (from Feb. 15 purchase)	$6.50	$32.5
3 million (from Beg. inv.)	5.00	15.0
8 million		$47.5

Decision Makers' Perspective—Inventory Management

Managers closely monitor inventory levels to (1) ensure that the inventories needed to sustain operations are available, and (2) hold the cost of ordering and carrying inventories to the lowest possible level.[14] Unfortunately, these objectives often conflict with one another. Companies must maintain sufficient quantities of inventory to meet customer demand. However, maintaining inventory is costly. Fortunately, a variety of tools are available, including computerized inventory control systems and the outsourcing of inventory component production, to help balance these conflicting objectives.[15]

Real World Financials

A company should maintain sufficient inventory quantities to meet customer demand while at the same time minimizing inventory ordering and carrying costs.

A just-in-time (JIT) system is another valuable technique that many companies have adopted to assist them with inventory management. JIT is a system used by a manufacturer to coordinate production with suppliers so that raw materials or components arrive just as they are needed in the production process. Harley Davidson is a company known for its custom-ordered motorcycles, and the company's JIT inventory system in an important part of the

[14]The cost of carrying inventory includes the possible loss from the write-down of obsolete inventory. We discuss inventory write-downs in Chapter 9. There are analytical models available to determine the appropriate amount of inventory a company should maintain. A discussion of these models is beyond the scope of this text.

[15]Eugene Brigham and Joel Houston, *Fundamentals of Financial Management,* 12th ed. (Florence, Kentucky: South-Western, 2010).

company's success. This system enables Harley Davidson to maintain relatively low inventory balances. At the same time, the company's efficient production techniques, along with its excellent relationships with suppliers ensuring prompt delivery of components, enables it to quickly meet customer demand. For the year ended December 31, 2015, Harley Davidson reported motorcycle sales of $5,308.7 million on cost of goods sold of only $3,356.3 million. That's a gross profit of $1,952.4 (or 36.8% of sales), far outpacing the industry average.

As we discussed in Chapter 4, one factor financial analysts use to evaluate management's success is how well the company utilizes its assets. This evaluation, which often is based on the calculation of certain ratios, is influenced by the company's inventory method choice. The different inventory methods affect reported amounts, requiring analysts must make adjustments when comparing companies that use different methods. For companies that use LIFO, supplemental disclosures help to convert inventory amounts to those that would have been reported using FIFO, allowing a better comparison to a company that reports using FIFO.

FINANCIAL Reporting Case

Q3, p. 415

For example, Harley Davidson uses the LIFO method. Additional inventory information from the company's recent financial statements is provided below.

Real World Financials

($ in millions)	For the Year Ended December 31, 2015	December 31, 2014
Balance sheets:		
Inventories	$ 585.9	$ 448.9
Income statements:		
Net sales	$5,308.7	$5,567.7
Cost of goods sold	3,356.3	3,542.6

Supplemental LIFO disclosures can be used to convert LIFO inventories and cost of goods sold amounts.

Suppose an analyst wanted to compare Harley Davidson with a competitor that used all FIFO, or that used both LIFO and FIFO but with different percentages of LIFO and FIFO. To compare apples with apples, we can convert Harley Davidson's inventories and cost of goods sold (and the competitor's if necessary) to a 100% FIFO basis before comparing the two companies. The information necessary for this conversion is provided as a supplemental disclosure by Harley Davidson:

	2015	2014
Inventories (LIFO)	$585.9	$448.9
Add: conversion to FIFO	49.3	49.9
Inventories (100% FIFO)	$635.2	$498.8

If Harley Davidson had used FIFO instead of LIFO, ending inventory in 2015 would have been $49.3 million higher. The large difference in reported inventory can have a material affect on financial ratios (as demonstrated below).

The use of FIFO versus LIFO has less of an effect on cost of goods sold. For Harley Davidson, the *difference* between FIFO and LIFO inventory decreased by $0.6 million during 2015 (from $49.9 to $49.3 million). This means the company would have recorded a decrease of $0.6 million in the LIFO reserve in 2015, along with a decrease in cost of goods sold (see earlier discussion of the LIFO reserve adjustment). The decrease in cost of goods sold indicates that reported profits under LIFO were slightly higher than if FIFO had been used. If the LIFO reserve had increased during the year, profits would have been lower under LIFO than FIFO.

● LO8–7

One useful profitability indicator that involves cost of goods sold is gross profit. The gross profit ratio is computed as follows:

$$\text{Gross profit ratio} = \frac{\text{Gross profit}}{\text{Net sales}}$$

The *gross profit ratio* indicates the percentage of each sales dollar available to cover expenses other than cost of goods sold and to provide a profit.

The higher the ratio, the higher the markup a company is able to achieve on its products. For example, a product that costs $100 and sells for $150 provides a gross profit of $50 ($150 − 100) and the gross profit ratio is 33% ($50 ÷ $150). If that same product can be sold for $200, the gross profit increases to $100 and the gross profit ratio increases to 50% ($100 ÷ $200), so more dollars are available to cover expenses other than cost of goods sold.

As we discussed previously, the 2015 gross profit for Harley Davidson's motorcycle sales is \$1,952.4 million (equal to sales of \$5,308.7 million minus cost of goods sold of \$3,356.3 million). That's a gross profit ratio of 36.8%. The industry average is 20.5%. Harley Davidson is able to sell its products at significantly higher markups. Even if we adjust cost of goods sold slightly upward (by \$0.6 million) to its FIFO amount, Harley Davidson remains relatively profitable.

Monitoring this ratio over time can provide valuable insights. For example, a declining ratio might indicate that the company is unable to offset rising costs with corresponding increases in selling price, or perhaps that sales prices are declining without a commensurate reduction in costs. In either case, the decline in the ratio has important implications for future profitability.

In Chapter 4 we were introduced to an important ratio, the **inventory turnover ratio**, which is designed to evaluate a company's effectiveness in managing its investment in inventory. The ratio shows the number of times the average inventory balance is sold during a reporting period. The more frequently a business is able to sell or turn over its inventory, the lower its investment in inventory must be for a given level of sales. Monitoring the inventory turnover ratio over time can highlight potential problems. A declining ratio generally is unfavorable and could be caused by the presence of obsolete or slow-moving products, or poor marketing and sales efforts.

Recall that the ratio is computed as follows:

$$\text{Inventory turnover ratio} = \frac{\text{Cost of goods sold}}{\text{Average inventory}}$$

If the analysis is prepared for the fiscal year reporting period, we can divide the inventory turnover ratio into 365 days to calculate the **average days in inventory**, which indicates the average number of days it normally takes the company to sell its inventory. In 2015, Harley Davidson's inventory turnover ratio using reported LIFO amounts is 6.49 {\$3,356.3 ÷ [(\$585.9 + 448.9) ÷ 2]} and the average days in inventory is 56.2 days (365 ÷ 6.49).

Alternatively, if we convert amounts to those under FIFO, we see that Harley Davidson's inventory turnover ratio would have been only 5.92 {\$3,356.9 ÷ [(\$635.2 + 498.8) ÷ 2]} and the average days in inventory would have been 61.7 days (365 ÷ 5.92). The difference in inventory turnover ratios between LIFO and FIFO is caused primarily by lower average inventory under LIFO and demonstrates the noticeable effect that the choice of inventory method can have on financial ratios.

EARNINGS QUALITY. Changes in the ratios we discussed above often provide information about the quality of a company's current period earnings. For example, a slowing turnover ratio combined with higher than normal inventory levels may indicate the potential for decreased production, obsolete inventory, or a need to decrease prices to sell inventory (which will then decrease gross profit ratios and net income). This proposition was tested in an important academic research study. Professors Lev and Thiagarajan empirically demonstrated the importance of a set of 12 fundamental variables in valuing companies' common stock. The set of variables included inventory (change in inventory minus change in sales). The inventory variable was found to be a significant indicator of returns on investments in common stock, particularly during high and medium inflation years.[16]

The choice of which inventory method to use also affects earnings quality, particularly in times of rapidly changing prices. Earlier in this chapter we discussed the effect of a LIFO liquidation on company profits. A LIFO liquidation profit (or loss) reduces the quality of current period earnings. Fortunately for analysts, companies must disclose these profits or losses, if material. In addition, LIFO cost of goods sold determined using a periodic inventory system is more susceptible to manipulation than is FIFO. Year-end purchases can have a dramatic effect on LIFO cost of goods sold in rapid cost-change environments. Recall again our discussion in Chapter 4 concerning earnings quality. Many believe that manipulating income reduces earnings quality because it can mask permanent earnings. Inventory write-downs and changes in inventory method are two additional inventory-related techniques a company could use to manipulate earnings. We discuss these issues in the next chapter. ●

[16]B. Lev and S. R. Thiagarajan, "Fundamental Information Analysis," *Journal of Accounting Research* (Autumn 1993). The main conclusion of the study was that fundamental variables, not just earnings, are useful in firm valuation, particularly when examined in the context of macroeconomic conditions such as inflation.

PART B

Methods of Simplifying LIFO

The recordkeeping costs of unit LIFO can be significant.

The LIFO method described and illustrated to this point is called *unit LIFO*[17] because the last-in, first-out concept is applied to individual units of inventory. One problem with unit LIFO is that it can be very costly to implement. It requires records of each unit of inventory. The costs of maintaining these records can be significant, particularly when a company has numerous individual units of inventory and when unit costs change often during a period.

Another disadvantage of unit LIFO is the possibility of LIFO liquidation.

In the previous section, a second disadvantage of unit LIFO was identified—the possibility that LIFO layers will be liquidated if the quantity of a particular inventory unit declines below its beginning balance. Even if a company's total inventory quantity is stable or increasing, if the quantity of any particular inventory unit declines, unit LIFO will liquidate all or a portion of a LIFO layer of inventory. When inventory quantity declines in a period of rising costs, noncurrent lower costs will be included in cost of goods sold and matched with current selling prices, resulting in LIFO liquidation profit.

This part of the chapter discusses techniques that can be used to significantly reduce the recordkeeping costs of LIFO and to minimize the probability of LIFO inventory layers being liquidated. Specifically, we discuss the use of inventory pools and the dollar-value LIFO method.

LIFO Inventory Pools

A pool consists of inventory units grouped according to natural physical similarities.

The objectives of using **LIFO inventory pools** are to simplify recordkeeping by grouping inventory units into pools based on physical similarities of the individual units and to reduce the risk of LIFO layer liquidation. For example, a glass company might group its various grades of window glass into a single window pool. Other pools might be auto glass and sliding-door glass. A lumber company might pool its inventory into hardwood, framing lumber, paneling, and so on.

The average cost for all of the pool purchases during the period is applied to the current year's LIFO layer.

This allows a company to account for a few inventory pools rather than every specific type of inventory separately. Within pools, all purchases during a period are considered to have been made at the same time and at the same cost. Individual unit costs are converted to an average cost for the pool. If the quantity of ending inventory for the pool increases, then ending inventory will consist of the beginning inventory plus a single layer added during the period at the average acquisition cost for that pool.

Here's an example. Let's say Diamond Lumber Company has a rough-cut lumber inventory pool that includes three types: pine, oak, and maple. The beginning inventory consisted of the following:

	Quantity (Board Feet)	Cost (Per Foot)	Total Cost
Pine	16,000	$2.20	$35,200
Oak	10,000	3.00	30,000
Maple	14,000	2.40	33,600
	40,000		$98,800

The average cost for this pool is $2.47 per board foot ($98,800 ÷ 40,000 board feet). Now assume that during the next reporting period Diamond purchased 50,000 board feet of lumber as follows:

	Quantity (Board Feet)	Cost (Per Foot)	Total Cost
Pine	20,000	$2.25	$ 45,000
Oak	14,000	3.00	42,000
Maple	16,000	2.50	40,000
	50,000		$127,000

[17]Unit LIFO sometimes is called *specific goods LIFO*.

The average cost for this pool is $2.54 per board foot ($127,000 ÷ 50,000 board feet). Assuming that Diamond sold 46,000 board feet during this period, the quantity of inventory for the pool increased by 4,000 board feet (50,000 purchased less 46,000 sold). Ending inventory includes the beginning 40,000 feet of inventory and a new LIFO layer consisting of the 4,000 board feet purchased this period. We would add this LIFO layer at the average cost of purchases made during the period, $2.54. The ending inventory of $108,960 now consists of two layers:

	Quantity (Board Feet)	Cost (Per Foot)	Total Cost
Beginning inventory	40,000	$2.47	$ 98,800
LIFO layer added	4,000	2.54	10,160
Ending inventory	44,000		$108,960

Despite the advantages of LIFO inventory pools, it's easy to imagine situations in which its benefits are not achieved. Suppose, for instance, that a company discontinues a certain product included in one of its pools. The old costs that existed in prior layers of inventory would be recognized as cost of goods sold and produce LIFO liquidation profit. Even if the product is replaced with another product, the replacement may not be similar enough to be included in the same inventory pool. In fact, the process itself of having to periodically redefine pools as changes in product mix occur can be expensive and time consuming. Next we discuss the dollar-value LIFO approach which helps overcome these problems.

Dollar-Value LIFO

Many companies that report inventory using LIFO actually use a method called dollar-value LIFO (DVL). DVL extends the concept of inventory pools by allowing a company to combine a large variety of goods into one pool. Pools are not based on physical units. Instead, an inventory pool is viewed as comprising layers of dollar value from different periods. Specifically, a pool should consist of those goods that are likely to be subject to the same cost change pressures.

A DVL pool is made up of items that are likely to face the same cost change pressures.

● LO8–8

Cost Indexes

In either the unit LIFO approach or the pooled LIFO approach, we determine whether a new LIFO layer was added by comparing the ending quantity with the beginning quantity. The focus is on *units* of inventory. Under DVL, we determine whether a new LIFO layer was added by comparing the ending dollar amount with the beginning dollar amount. The focus is on inventory *value,* not units. However, if the price level has changed, we need a way to determine whether an observed increase is a real increase (an increase in the quantity of inventory) or one caused by an increase in prices. *So before we compare the beginning and ending inventory amounts, we need to deflate inventory dollar amounts by any increase in prices so that both the beginning and ending amounts are measured in terms of the same price level.* We accomplish this by using cost indexes. A cost index for a particular layer year is determined as follows:

$$\text{Cost index in layer year} = \frac{\text{Cost in layer year}}{\text{Cost in base year}}$$

The base year is the year in which the DVL method is adopted and the layer year is any subsequent year in which an inventory layer is created. The cost index for the base year is set at 1.00. Subsequent years' indexes reflect cost changes relative to the base year. For example, if a "basket" of inventory items cost $120 at the end of the current year, and $100 at the end of the base year, the cost index for the current year would be: $120 ÷ $100 = 120%, or 1.20. This index simply tells us that costs in the layer year are 120% of what they were in the base year (i.e., costs increased by 20%).

The cost index for the base year (the year DVL is initially adopted) is set at 1.00.

There are several techniques that can be used to determine an index for a DVL pool. An external index like the Consumer Price Index (CPI) or the Producer Price Index (PPI) can be used. For example, assume that a company adopted the DVL method on January 1, 2018, when the CPI was 200. This amount is set equivalent to 1.00, the base year index. Then, the index in the layer year, say the end of 2018, would be determined relative to 200. So, if the CPI is 210 at the end of 2018, the 2018 index for DVL purposes would be 1.05 (210 ÷ 200).

However, in most cases these indexes would not properly reflect cost changes for any individual DVL pool. Instead, most companies use an internally generated index. These indexes can be calculated using one of several techniques such as the *double-extension method* or the *link-chain method.* A discussion of these methods is beyond the scope of this text. In our examples and illustrations, we assume cost indexes are given.

The DVL Inventory Estimation Technique

To see the calculation of ending inventory using DVL, consider the following example. Assume that Hanes Company adopted DVL on January 1, 2018, when the inventory cost was $400,000. On December 31, 2018, Hanes determines the year-end cost of inventory is $462,000. This amount is obtained by taking the physical units of inventory on hand at the end of the year and multiplying by year-end costs. It's not necessary for Hanes to track the item-by-item cost of purchases during the year.

Assuming a cost index for 2018 of 1.05 (105%), we'll use three steps to calculate the amount to report for ending inventory using dollar-value LIFO.

STEP 1: Convert ending inventory to base year cost. Notice inventory increased from $400,000 at the beginning of the year to $462,000 at the end of the year. Does this $62,000 increase in inventory represent an increase in the *quantity* and/or an increase in the *cost* of inventory? To determine this, the first step is to convert the ending inventory from year-end costs to base year costs. We do this by dividing ending inventory by the year's cost index.

$$\text{Ending inventory at } \textit{base year} \text{ cost} = \frac{\$462{,}000}{1.05} = \$440{,}000$$

STEP 2: Identify the layers of ending inventory created each year. The 2018 ending inventory deflated to base year cost is $440,000. From this, we can determine that the $62,000 increase in the cost of total inventory for the year consists of a $40,000 increase due to quantity (new inventory layer added in 2018) plus $22,000 due to an increase in the cost index of inventory (= $440,000 × 5%).

$400,000	(beginning inventory cost in 2018; beginning layer)
+ 40,000	(increase in *quantity* in 2018; new layer)
+ 22,000	(increase in *cost* = $440,000 × 5%)
$462,000	(ending inventory cost in 2018)

The calculation above is important for identifying the two layers of inventory *quantity* for applying the LIFO concept: (1) beginning inventory layer of $400,000 and (2) $40,000 layer added in 2018. These are the costs as if each layer was acquired at base year prices. The increase in inventory due to rising costs ($22,000) does not represent more units purchased.

STEP 3: Restate each layer using the cost index in the year acquired. Once the layers are identified, each is restated to prices existing when the layers were acquired. This is done by multiplying each layer by the cost index for the year it was acquired. The $400,000 layer was acquired when prices were 1.00, and the $40,000 layer was acquired when prices were 1.05. All layers are added, and ending inventory under DVL would be reported at $442,000.[18]

Date	Ending Inventory at Base Year Cost	×	Cost Index	=	Ending Inventory at DVL Cost
1/1/2018	$400,000		1.00		$ 400,000
2018 layer	40,000		1.05		42,000
Totals	$440,000				$442,000

[18]It is important to note that the costs of the year's layer are only an approximation of actual acquisition cost. DVL assumes that all inventory quantities added during a particular year were acquired at a single cost.

In cases where the quantity of inventory *decreases,* no layer would be added in the current year. In our example, if inventory at the end of 2018 had a base year cost of only $380,000, then no layer would have been added in 2018. Instead, the decrease of $20,000 would reduce old inventory layers in LIFO order (backwards in time). In addition, any future increases in inventory quantity (in 2019 or after) would add new layers beyond the $380,000 layer.

The identification of inventory layers is demonstrated further in the Concept Review Exercise below. In years when there is an increase in inventory at base year cost (2019 and 2021), a new inventory layer is added. In years when there is a decrease in inventory at base year cost (2020), we use LIFO and assume the inventory sold was from the last layer added.

Concept Review Exercise

DOLLAR-VALUE LIFO

On January 1, 2018, the Johnson Company adopted the dollar-value LIFO method. The inventory value on this date was $500,000. Inventory data for 2018 through 2021 are as follows:

Date	Ending Inventory at Year-End Costs	Cost Index
12/31/2018	$556,500	1.05
12/31/2019	596,200	1.10
12/31/2020	615,250	1.15
12/31/2021	720,000	1.25

Required:

Calculate Johnson's ending inventory for the years 2018 through 2021.

Solution:

JOHNSON COMPANY

Date	Ending Inventory at Year-End Cost	Step 1 Ending Inventory at Base Year Cost	Step 2 Inventory Layers at Base Year Cost	Step 3 Inventory Layers Converted to Acquisition Year Cost	Ending Inventory at DVL Cost
1/1/2018	$500,000 (base year)	$\frac{\$500,000}{1.00} = \$500,000$	$500,000 (base)	$500,000 × 1.00 = $500,000	**$500,000**
12/31/2018	556,500	$\frac{\$556,500}{1.05} = \$530,000$	$500,000 (base)	$500,000 × 1.00 = $500,000	
			30,000 (2018)	30,000 × 1.05 = 31,500	**531,500**
12/31/2019	596,200	$\frac{\$596,200}{1.10} = \$542,000$	$500,000 (base)	$500,000 × 1.00 = $500,000	
			30,000 (2018)	30,000 × 1.05 = 31,500	
			12,000 (2019)	12,000 × 1.10 = 13,200	**544,700**
12/31/2020	615,250	$\frac{\$615,250}{1.15} = \$535,000$*	$500,000 (base)	$500,000 × 1.00 = $500,000	
			30,000 (2018)	30,000 × 1.05 = 31,500	
			5,000 (2019)	5,000 × 1.10 = 5,500	**537,000**
12/31/2021	720,000	$\frac{\$720,000}{1.25} = \$576,000$	$500,000 (base)	$500,000 × 1.00 = $500,000	
			30,000 (2018)	30,000 × 1.05 = 31,500	
			5,000 (2019)	5,000 × 1.10 = 5,500	
			41,000 (2021)	41,000 × 1.25 = 51,250	**588,250**

*Since inventory declined during 2020 (from $542,000 to $535,000 at base year costs), no new layer is added. Instead the most recently acquired layer, 2019, is reduced by $7,000 (from $12,000 to $5,000).

Advantages of DVL

The DVL method has important advantages. First, it simplifies the recordkeeping procedures compared to unit LIFO because no information is needed about unit flows. Second, it minimizes the probability of the liquidation of LIFO inventory layers, even more so than the use of pools alone, through the aggregation of many types of inventory into larger pools. In addition, the method can be used by firms that do not replace units sold with new units of the same kind. For firms whose products are subject to annual model changes, for example, the items in one year's inventory are not the same as those of the prior year. Under pooled LIFO, however, the new replacement items must be substantially identical to previous models to be included in the same pool. Under DVL, no distinction is drawn between the old and new merchandise on the basis of their physical characteristics, so a much broader range of goods can be included in the pool. That is, the acquisition of the new items is viewed as replacement of the dollar value of the old items. Because the old layers are maintained, this approach retains the benefits of LIFO by matching the most recent acquisition cost of goods with sales measured at current selling prices.

Financial Reporting Case Solution

© Dave and Les Jacobs LLC

1. **How is the LIFO method used to calculate inventories? Is this permissible according to GAAP?** *(p. 430)* The LIFO method uses the assumption that the most recent inventory purchased is sold first. Yes, this method is permissible according to generally accepted accounting principles. A company need not use the same method that represents its actual inventory flow.
2. **What is the purpose of disclosing the difference between the reported LIFO inventory amounts and replacement cost, assuming that replacement cost is equivalent to a FIFO basis?** *(p. 432)* The LIFO conformity rule requires that if a company uses LIFO to measure taxable income, it also must use LIFO for external financial reporting. Kroger does this. However, the LIFO conformity rule allows LIFO users to report non-LIFO inventory valuations in a disclosure note, but not on the face of the income statement. The company's disclosure note offers this additional information.
3. **Are you correct that, by using LIFO, Kroger reports lower inventory and lower profits? Why would Kroger do that?** *(p. 438)* Yes. Because Kroger uses LIFO instead of FIFO, reported inventory in the balance sheet is lower. For the year ended January 30, 2016, Kroger reported LIFO inventory of only $6,168 million, compared to $7,440 million that it would have reported under FIFO. This is a difference of $1,272 million. In the previous year, the difference between LIFO and FIFO was $1,245 million. This means the LIFO effect (or LIFO reserve) has increased by $27 million ($1,272 million minus $1,245 million). An increase in the LIFO reserve is recorded to cost of goods sold, lowering profits. However, if the LIFO reserve had decreased in the current year, cost of goods sold would be reduced and profits would have been higher. ●

The Bottom Line

- **LO8–1** In a perpetual inventory system, inventory is continually adjusted for each change in inventory. Cost of goods sold is adjusted each time goods are sold or returned by a customer. A periodic inventory system adjusts inventory and records cost of goods sold only at the end of a reporting period. *(p. 416)*
- **LO8–2** Generally, determining the physical quantity that should be included in inventory is a simple matter, because it consists of items in the possession of the company. However, at the end of a reporting period it's important to determine the ownership of goods that are in transit between the company and its customers as well as between the company and its suppliers. Also, goods on consignment should be included in inventory of the consignor even though the company doesn't have physical possession of the goods. In addition, a company anticipating sales returns includes in inventory the cost of merchandise it estimates will be returned. *(p. 420)*

- **LO8–3** The cost of inventory includes all expenditures necessary to acquire the inventory and bring it to its desired condition and location for sale or use. Generally, these expenditures include the purchase price of the goods reduced by any returns and purchase discounts, plus freight-in charges. *(p. 421)*
- **LO8–4** Once costs are determined, the cost of goods available for sale must be allocated between cost of goods sold and ending inventory. Unless each item is specifically identified and traced through the system, the allocation requires an assumption regarding the flow of costs. First-in, first-out (FIFO) assumes that units sold are the first units acquired. Last-in, first-out (LIFO) assumes that the units sold are the most recent units purchased. The average cost method assumes that cost of goods sold and ending inventory consist of a mixture of all the goods available for sale. *(p. 424)*
- **LO8–5** A company's choice of inventory method will be influenced by (a) how closely cost flow reflects the actual physical flow of its inventory, (b) the timing of income tax expenses, and (c) how costs are matched with revenues. *(p. 431)*
- **LO8–6** The LIFO conformity rule requires that if a company uses LIFO to measure taxable income, it also must use LIFO for external financial reporting. LIFO users often provide a disclosure note describing the effect on inventories of using another method for inventory valuation rather than LIFO. If a company uses LIFO and inventory quantities decline during a period, then out-of-date inventory layers are liquidated and the cost of goods sold will partially match noncurrent costs with current selling prices. If costs have been increasing (decreasing), LIFO liquidations produce higher (lower) net income than would have resulted if the liquidated inventory were included in cost of goods sold at current costs. The paper profits (losses) caused by including out-of-date, low (high) costs in cost of goods sold is referred to as the effect on income of liquidations of LIFO inventory. *(p. 432)*
- **LO8–7** Investors, creditors, and financial analysts can gain important insights by monitoring a company's investment in inventories. The gross profit ratio, inventory turnover ratio, and average days in inventory are designed to monitor inventories. *(p. 438)*
- **LO8–8** The dollar-value LIFO method converts ending inventory at year-end cost to base year cost using a cost index. After identifying the layers in ending inventory with the years they were created, each year's base year cost measurement is converted to layer year cost measurement using the layer year's cost index. The layers are then summed to obtain total ending inventory at cost. *(p. 441)*
- **LO8–9** The primary difference between U.S. GAAP and IFRS with respect to determining the cost of inventory is that IFRS does not allow the use of the LIFO method to value inventory. *(p. 431)*

Questions For Review of Key Topics

Q 8–1 Describe the three types of inventory of a manufacturing company.

Q 8–2 What is the main difference between a perpetual inventory system and a periodic inventory system?

Q 8–3 The Cloud Company employs a perpetual inventory system and the McKenzie Corporation uses a periodic system. Describe the differences between the two systems in accounting for the following events: (1) purchase of merchandise, (2) sale of merchandise, (3) return of merchandise to supplier, and (4) payment of freight charge on merchandise purchased. Indicate which inventory-related accounts would be debited or credited for each event.

Q 8–4 The Bockner Company shipped merchandise to Laetner Corporation on December 28, 2018. Laetner received the shipment on January 3, 2019. December 31 is the fiscal year-end for both companies. The merchandise was shipped f.o.b. shipping point. Explain the difference in the accounting treatment of the merchandise if the shipment had instead been designated f.o.b. destination.

Q 8–5 What is a consignment arrangement? Explain the accounting treatment of goods held on consignment.

Q 8–6 Distinguish between the gross and net methods of accounting for purchase discounts.

Q 8–7 The Esquire Company employs a periodic inventory system. Indicate the effect (increase or decrease) of the following items on cost of goods sold:

1. Beginning inventory
2. Purchases
3. Ending inventory
4. Purchase returns
5. Freight-in

Q 8–8 Identify four methods of assigning cost to ending inventory and cost of goods sold and briefly explain the difference in the methods.

Q 8–9 It's common in the electronics industry for unit costs of raw materials inventories to decline over time. In this environment, explain the difference between LIFO and FIFO, in terms of the effect on income and financial position. Assume that inventory quantities remain the same for the period.

Q 8–10 Explain why proponents of LIFO argue that it provides a better match of revenue and expenses. In what situation would it not provide a better match?

Q 8–11 Explain what is meant by the Internal Revenue Service conformity rule with respect to the inventory method choice.

Q 8–12 Describe the ratios used by financial analysts to monitor a company's investment in inventories.

Q 8–13 What is a LIFO inventory pool? How is the cost of ending inventory determined when pools are used?

Q 8–14 Identify two advantages of dollar-value LIFO compared with unit LIFO.

Q 8–15 The Austin Company uses the dollar-value LIFO inventory method with internally developed price indexes. Assume that ending inventory at year-end cost has been determined. Outline the remaining steps used in the dollar-value LIFO computations.

IFRS **Q 8–16** Identify any differences between U.S. GAAP and International Financial Reporting Standards in the methods allowed to value inventory.

Brief Exercises

BE 8–1
Determining ending inventory; periodic system
● LO8–1

A company began its fiscal year with inventory of $186,000. Purchases and cost of goods sold for the year were $945,000 and $982,000, respectively. What was the amount of ending inventory?

BE 8–2
Perpetual system; journal entries
● LO8–1

Litton Industries uses a perpetual inventory system. The company began its fiscal year with inventory of $267,000. Purchases of merchandise on account during the year totaled $845,000. Merchandise costing $902,000 was sold on account for $1,420,000. Prepare the journal entries to record these transactions.

BE 8–3
Goods in transit
● LO8–2

Kelly Corporation shipped goods to a customer f.o.b. destination on December 29, 2018. The goods arrived at the customer's location in January. In addition, one of Kelly's major suppliers shipped goods to Kelly f.o.b. shipping point on December 30. The merchandise arrived at Kelly's location in January. Which shipments should be included in Kelly's December 31 inventory?

BE 8–4
Purchase discounts; gross method
● LO8–3

On December 28, 2018, Videotech Corporation (VTC) purchased 10 units of a new satellite uplink system from Tristar Communications for $25,000 each. The terms of each sale were 1/10, n/30. VTC uses the gross method to account for purchase discounts and a perpetual inventory system. VTC paid the net-of-discount amount on January 6, 2019. Prepare the journal entries on December 28 and January 6 to record the purchase and payment.

BE 8–5
Purchase discounts; net method
● LO8–3

Refer to the situation described in BE 8–4. Prepare the necessary journal entries assuming that VTC uses the net method to account for purchase discounts.

BE 8–6
Inventory cost flow methods; periodic system
● LO8–4

Samuelson and Messenger (SAM) began 2018 with 200 units of its one product. These units were purchased near the end of 2017 for $25 each. During the month of January, 100 units were purchased on January 8 for $28 each and another 200 units were purchased on January 19 for $30 each. Sales of 125 units and 100 units were made on January 10 and January 25, respectively. There were 275 units on hand at the end of the month. SAM uses a *periodic* inventory system. Calculate ending inventory and cost of goods sold for January using (1) FIFO, and (2) average cost.

BE 8–7
Inventory cost flow methods; perpetual system
● LO8–4

Refer to the situation described in BE 8–6. SAM uses a *perpetual* inventory system. Calculate ending inventory and cost of goods sold for January using (1) FIFO, and (2) average cost.

BE 8–8
LIFO method
● LO8–4

Esquire Inc. uses the LIFO method to value its inventory. Inventory at January 1, 2018, was $500,000 (20,000 units at $25 each). During 2018, 80,000 units were purchased, all at the same price of $30 per unit. 85,000 units were sold during 2018. Esquire uses a periodic inventory system. Calculate the December 31, 2018, ending inventory and cost of goods sold for 2018.

BE 8–9
LIFO method
● LO8–4

AAA Hardware uses the LIFO method to value its inventory. Inventory at the beginning of the year consisted of 10,000 units of the company's one product. These units cost $15 each. During the year, 60,000 units were purchased at a cost of $18 each and 64,000 units were sold. Near the end of the fiscal year, management is considering the purchase of an additional 5,000 units at $18. What would be the effect of this purchase on income before income taxes? Would your answer be the same if the company used FIFO instead of LIFO?

BE 8–10
LIFO liquidation
● LO8–6

Refer to the situation described in BE 8–8. Assuming an income tax rate of 40%, what is LIFO liquidation profit or loss that the company would report in a disclosure note accompanying its financial statements?

BE 8–11
Supplemental LIFO disclosures; Walgreen
● LO8–6
Real World Financials

Walgreens Boots Alliance, Inc. reported inventories of $8,678 million and $6,076 million in its August 31, 2015, and August 31, 2014, balance sheets, respectively. Cost of goods sold for the year ended August 31, 2015, was $76,520 million. The company uses primarily the LIFO inventory method. A disclosure note reported that if FIFO had been used instead of LIFO, inventory would have been higher by $2,500 million and $2,300 million at the end of the August 31, 2015, and August 31, 2014, periods, respectively. Calculate cost of goods sold for the year ended August 31, 2015, assuming Walgreens used FIFO instead of LIFO.

BE 8–12
Ratio analysis
● LO8–7

Selected financial statement data for Schmitzer Inc. is shown below:

	2018	2017
Balance sheet:		
Inventories	60,000	48,000
Ratios:		
Gross profit ratio for 2018	40%	
Inventory turnover ratio for 2018	5	

What was the amount of net sales for 2018?

BE 8–13
Dollar-value LIFO
● LO8–8

At the beginning of 2018, a company adopts the dollar-value LIFO inventory method for its one inventory pool. The pool's value on that date was $1,400,000. The 2018 ending inventory valued at year-end costs was $1,664,000 and the year-end cost index was 1.04. Calculate the inventory value at the end of 2018 using the dollar-value LIFO method.

Exercises

E 8–1
Perpetual inventory system; journal entries
● LO8–1

John's Specialty Store uses a perpetual inventory system. The following are some inventory transactions for the month of May 2018:

1. John's purchased merchandise on account for $5,000. Freight charges of $300 were paid in cash.
2. John's returned some of the merchandise purchased in (1). The cost of the merchandise was $600 and John's account was credited by the supplier.
3. Merchandise costing $2,800 was sold for $5,200 in cash.

Required:
Prepare the necessary journal entries to record these transactions.

E 8–2
Periodic inventory system; journal entries
● LO8–1

[This is a variation of E 8–1 modified to focus on the periodic inventory system.]

John's Specialty Store uses a periodic inventory system. The following are some inventory transactions for the month of May 2018:

1. John's purchased merchandise on account for $5,000. Freight charges of $300 were paid in cash.
2. John's returned some of the merchandise purchased in (1). The cost of the merchandise was $600 and John's account was credited by the supplier.
3. Merchandise costing $2,800 was sold for $5,200 in cash.

Required:
Prepare the necessary journal entries to record these transactions.

E 8–3
Determining cost of goods sold; periodic inventory system
● LO8–1

Askew Company uses a periodic inventory system. The June 30, 2018, year-end trial balance for the company contained the following information:

Account	Debit	Credit
Merchandise inventory, 7/1/17	32,000	
Sales		380,000
Sales returns	12,000	
Purchases	240,000	
Purchase discounts		6,000
Purchase returns		10,000
Freight-in	17,000	

In addition, you determine that the June 30, 2018, inventory balance is $40,000.

Required:
1. Calculate the cost of goods sold for the Askew Company for the year ending June 30, 2018.
2. Prepare the year-end adjusting entry to record cost of goods sold.

E 8–4
Perpetual and periodic inventory systems compared
● LO8–1

The following information is available for the Johnson Corporation for 2018:

Beginning inventory	$ 25,000
Merchandise purchases (on account)	155,000
Freight charges on purchases (paid in cash)	10,000
Merchandise returned to supplier (for credit)	12,000
Ending inventory	30,000
Sales (on account)	250,000
Cost of merchandise sold	148,000

Required:
Applying both a perpetual and a periodic inventory system, prepare the journal entries that summarize the transactions that created these balances. Include all end-of-period adjusting entries indicated.

E 8–5
Periodic inventory system; missing data
● LO8–1

The Playa Company uses a periodic inventory system. The following information is taken from Playa's records. Certain data have been intentionally omitted ($ in thousands).

	2018	2019	2020
Beginning inventory	?	?	225
Cost of goods sold	627	621	?
Ending inventory	?	225	216
Cost of goods available for sale	876	?	800
Purchases (gross)	630	?	585
Purchase discounts	18	15	?
Purchase returns	24	30	14
Freight-in	13	32	16

Required:
Determine the missing numbers. Show computations where appropriate.

E 8–6
Goods in transit
● LO8–2

The Kwok Company's inventory balance on December 31, 2018, was $165,000 (based on a 12/31/2018 physical count) *before* considering the following transactions:

1. Goods shipped to Kwok f.o.b. destination on December 20, 2018, were received on January 4, 2019. The invoice cost was $30,000.
2. Goods shipped to Kwok f.o.b. shipping point on December 28, 2018, were received on January 5, 2019. The invoice cost was $17,000.
3. Goods shipped from Kwok to a customer f.o.b. destination on December 27, 2018, were received by the customer on January 3, 2019. The sales price was $40,000 and the merchandise cost $22,000.
4. Goods shipped from Kwok to a customer f.o.b. destination on December 26, 2018, were received by the customer on December 30, 2018. The sales price was $20,000 and the merchandise cost $13,000.
5. Goods shipped from Kwok to a customer f.o.b. shipping point on December 28, 2018, were received by the customer on January 4, 2019. The sales price was $25,000 and the merchandise cost $12,000.

Required:
Determine the correct inventory amount to be reported in Kwok's 2018 balance sheet.

E 8–7 Goods in transit; consignment ● LO8–2

The December 31, 2018, year-end inventory balance of the Raymond Corporation is $210,000. You have been asked to review the following transactions to determine if they have been correctly recorded.

1. Goods shipped to Raymond f.o.b. destination on December 26, 2018, were received on January 2, 2019. The invoice cost of $30,000 *is* included in the preliminary inventory balance.
2. At year-end, Raymond held $14,000 of merchandise on consignment from the Harrison Company. This merchandise *is* included in the preliminary inventory balance.
3. On December 29, merchandise costing $6,000 was shipped to a customer f.o.b. shipping point and arrived at the customer's location on January 3, 2019. The merchandise is *not* included in the preliminary inventory balance.
4. At year-end, Raymond had merchandise costing $15,000 on consignment with the Joclyn Corporation. The merchandise is *not* included in the preliminary inventory balance.

Required:

Determine the correct inventory amount to be reported in Raymond's 2018 balance sheet.

E 8–8 Physical quantities and costs included in inventory ● LO8–2

The Phoenix Corporation's fiscal year ends on December 31. Phoenix determines inventory quantity by a physical count of inventory on hand at the close of business on December 31. The company's controller has asked for your help in deciding if the following items should be included in the year-end inventory count.

1. Merchandise held on consignment for Trout Creek Clothing.
2. Goods shipped f.o.b. destination on December 28 that arrived at the customer's location on January 4.
3. Goods purchased from a vendor shipped f.o.b. shipping point on December 26 that arrived on January 3.
4. Goods shipped f.o.b. shipping point on December 28 that arrived at the customer's location on January 5.
5. Phoenix had merchandise on consignment at Lisa's Markets, Inc.
6. Goods purchased from a vendor shipped f.o.b. destination on December 27 that arrived on January 3.
7. Freight charges on goods purchased in 3.

Required:

Determine if each of the items above should be included or excluded from the company's year-end inventory.

E 8–9 Purchase discounts; the gross method ● LO8–3

On July 15, 2018, the Nixon Car Company purchased 1,000 tires from the Harwell Company for $50 each. The terms of the sale were 2/10, n/30. Nixon uses a periodic inventory system and the *gross* method of accounting for purchase discounts.

Required:

1. Prepare the journal entries to record the purchase on July 15 and payment on July 23, 2018.
2. Prepare the journal entry to record the payment on August 15, 2018.
3. If Nixon instead uses a perpetual inventory system, explain any changes to the journal entries created in requirements 1 and 2.

E 8–10 Purchase discounts; the net method ● LO8–3

[This is a variation of E 8–9 modified to focus on the net method of accounting for purchase discounts.]

On July 15, 2018, the Nixon Car Company purchased 1,000 tires from the Harwell Company for $50 each. The terms of the sale were 2/10, n/30. Nixon uses a periodic inventory system and the *net* method of accounting for purchase discounts.

Required:

1. Prepare the journal entries to record the purchase on July 15 and payment on July 23, 2018.
2. Prepare the journal entry to record the payment on August 15, 2018.
3. If Nixon instead uses a perpetual inventory system, explain any changes to the journal entries created in requirements 1 and 2.

E 8–11 Trade and purchase discounts; the gross method and the net method compared ● LO8–3

Tracy Company, a manufacturer of air conditioners, sold 100 units to Thomas Company on November 17, 2018. The units have a list price of $500 each, but Thomas was given a 30% trade discount. The terms of the sale were 2/10, n/30. Thomas uses a periodic inventory system.

Required:

1. Prepare the journal entries to record the purchase by Thomas on November 17 and payment on November 26, 2018, using the gross method of accounting for purchase discounts.
2. Prepare the journal entry to record the payment on December 15, 2018, using the gross method of accounting for purchase discounts.
3. Repeat requirements 1 and 2 using the net method of accounting for purchase discounts.

E 8–12
FASB codification research
● LO8–2, LO8–3

Access the *FASB Accounting Standards Codification* at the FASB website (www.fasb.org). Determine the specific citation for each of the following items:

1. Define the meaning of cost as it applies to the initial measurement of inventory.
2. Indicate the circumstances when it is appropriate to initially measure agricultural inventory at fair value.
3. What is a major objective of accounting for inventory?
4. Are abnormal freight charges included in the cost of inventory?

E 8–13
Inventory cost flow methods; periodic system
● LO8–1, LO8–4

Altira Corporation uses a periodic inventory system. The following information related to its merchandise inventory during the month of August 2018 is available:

Aug. 1	Inventory on hand—2,000 units; cost $6.10 each.
8	Purchased 10,000 units for $5.50 each.
14	Sold 8,000 units for $12.00 each.
18	Purchased 6,000 units for $5.00 each.
25	Sold 7,000 units for $11.00 each.
31	Inventory on hand—3,000 units.

Required:
Determine the inventory balance Altira would report in its August 31, 2018, balance sheet and the cost of goods sold it would report in its August 2018 income statement using each of the following cost flow methods:

1. First-in, first-out (FIFO)
2. Last-in, first-out (LIFO)
3. Average cost

E 8–14
Inventory cost flow methods; perpetual system
● LO8–1, LO8–4

[This is a variation of E 8–13 modified to focus on the perpetual inventory system and alternative cost flow methods.]
Altira Corporation uses a perpetual inventory system. The following transactions affected its merchandise inventory during the month of August 2018:

Aug. 1	Inventory on hand—2,000 units; cost $6.10 each.
8	Purchased 10,000 units for $5.50 each.
14	Sold 8,000 units for $12.00 each.
18	Purchased 6,000 units for $5.00 each.
25	Sold 7,000 units for $11.00 each.
31	Inventory on hand—3,000 units.

Required:
Determine the inventory balance Altira would report in its August 31, 2018, balance sheet and the cost of goods sold it would report in its August 2018 income statement using each of the following cost flow methods:

1. First-in, first-out (FIFO)
2. Last-in, first-out (LIFO)
3. Average cost

E 8–15
Comparison of FIFO and LIFO; periodic system
● LO8–1, LO8–4

Alta Ski Company's inventory records contained the following information regarding its latest ski model. The company uses a periodic inventory system.

Beginning inventory, January 1, 2018	600 units @ $80 each
Purchases:	
January 15	1,000 units @ $95 each
January 21	800 units @ $100 each
Sales:	
January 5	400 units @ $120 each
January 22	800 units @ $130 each
January 29	400 units @ $135 each
Ending inventory, January 31, 2018	800 units

Required:

1. Which method, FIFO or LIFO, will result in the highest cost of goods sold figure for January 2018? Why? Which method will result in the highest ending inventory balance? Why?
2. Compute cost of goods sold for January and the ending inventory using both the FIFO and LIFO methods.

E 8–16
Average cost method; periodic and perpetual systems
● LO8–1, LO8–4

The following information is taken from the inventory records of the CNB Company for the month of September:

Beginning inventory, 9/1/2018	5,000 units @ $10.00
Purchases:	
9/7	3,000 units @ $10.40
9/25	8,000 units @ $10.75
Sales:	
9/10	4,000 units
9/29	5,000 units
7,000 units were on hand at the end of September.	

Required:

1. Assuming that CNB uses a periodic inventory system and employs the average cost method, determine cost of goods sold for September and September's ending inventory.
2. Repeat requirement 1 assuming that the company uses a perpetual inventory system.

E 8–17
FIFO, LIFO, and average cost methods
● LO8–1, LO8–4

Causwell Company began 2018 with 10,000 units of inventory on hand. The cost of each unit was $5.00. During 2018 an additional 30,000 units were purchased at a single unit cost, and 20,000 units remained on hand at the end of 2018 (20,000 units therefore were sold during 2018). Causwell uses a periodic inventory system. Cost of goods sold for 2018, applying the average cost method, is $115,000. The company is interested in determining what cost of goods sold would have been if the FIFO or LIFO methods were used.

Required:

1. Determine the cost of goods sold for 2018 using the FIFO method. [*Hint:* Determine the cost per unit of 2018 purchases.]
2. Determine the cost of goods sold for 2018 using the LIFO method.

E 8–18
Supplemental LIFO disclosures; LIFO reserve; AEP Industries
● LO8–6
Real World Financials

AEP Industries Inc. is a leading manufacturer of plastic packing films. The company uses the LIFO inventory method for external reporting but maintains its internal records using FIFO. The following disclosure note was included in a recent quarterly report:

4. Inventories (in part)
Inventories are comprised of the following ($ in thousands):

	January 31, 2016	October 31, 2015
Raw materials	$ 42,881	$ 47,593
Finished goods	71,547	66,484
Supplies	5,240	5,280
	119,668	119,357
Less: LIFO reserve	(13,655)	(18,093)
Inventories (under LIFO)	$106,013	$101,264

The company's income statements reported cost of goods sold of $209,826 thousand for the quarter ended January 31, 2016.

Required:

1. Assume that AEP adjusts the LIFO reserve at the end of its quarter. Prepare the January 31, 2016, adjusting entry to record the cost of goods sold adjustment.
2. If AEP had used FIFO to value its inventories, what would cost of goods sold have been for the quarter ended January 31, 2016?

E 8–19
LIFO liquidation
● LO8–1, LO8–4, LO8–6

The Reuschel Company began 2018 with inventory of 10,000 units at a cost of $7 per unit. During 2018, 50,000 units were purchased for $8.50 each. Sales for the year totaled 54,000 units leaving 6,000 units on hand at the end of 2018. Reuschel uses a periodic inventory system and the LIFO inventory cost method.

Required:

1. Calculate cost of goods sold for 2018.
2. From a financial reporting perspective, what problem is created by the use of LIFO in this situation? Describe the disclosure required to report the effects of this problem.

E 8–20
LIFO liquidation
● LO8–4, LO8–6

The Churchill Corporation uses a periodic inventory system and the LIFO inventory cost method for its one product. Beginning inventory of 20,000 units consisted of the following, listed in chronological order of acquisition:

12,000 units at a cost of $8.00 per unit = $96,000
8,000 units at a cost of $9.00 per unit = 72,000

During 2018, inventory quantity declined by 10,000 units. All units purchased during 2018 cost $12.00 per unit.

Required:
Calculate the before-tax LIFO liquidation profit or loss that the company would report in a disclosure note, assuming the amount determined is material.

E 8–21
FASB codification research
● LO8–6

CODE

The *FASB Accounting Standards Codification* represents the single source of authoritative U.S. generally accepted accounting principles.

Required:

1. Obtain the relevant authoritative literature on the disclosure of accounting policies using the *FASB Accounting Standards Codification* at the FASB website (www.fasb.org).
2. What is the specific citation that describes the disclosure requirements that must be made by publicly traded companies for a LIFO liquidation?
3. Describe the disclosure requirements.

E 8–22
Ratio analysis; Home Depot and Lowe's
● LO8–7

Real World Financials

The table below contains selected information from recent financial statements of The Home Depot, Inc., and Lowe's Companies, Inc., two companies in the home improvement retail industry ($ in millions):

	Home Depot		Lowe's	
	1/31/16	2/1/15	1/29/16	1/30/15
Net sales	$88,519	$83,176	$59,074	$56,223
Cost of goods sold	58,254	54,787	38,504	36,665
Year-end inventory	11,809	11,079	9,458	8,911
Industry averages:				
Gross profit ratio	33%			
Inventory turnover ratio	3.9 times			
Average days in inventory	94 days			

Required:
Calculate the gross profit ratio, the inventory turnover ratio, and the average days in inventory for the two companies for their fiscal years ending in 2016. Compare your calculations for the two companies, taking into account the industry averages.

E 8–23
Dollar-value LIFO
● LO8–8

On January 1, 2018, the Haskins Company adopted the dollar-value LIFO method for its one inventory pool. The pool's value on this date was $660,000. The 2018 and 2019 ending inventory valued at year-end costs were $690,000 and $760,000, respectively. The appropriate cost indexes are 1.04 for 2018 and 1.08 for 2019.

Required:
Calculate the inventory value at the end of 2018 and 2019 using the dollar-value LIFO method.

E 8–24
Dollar-value LIFO
● LO8–8

Mercury Company has only one inventory pool. On December 31, 2018, Mercury adopted the dollar-value LIFO inventory method. The inventory on that date using the dollar-value LIFO method was $200,000. Inventory data are as follows:

Year	Ending Inventory at Year-End Costs	Ending Inventory at Base Year Costs
2019	$231,000	$220,000
2020	299,000	260,000
2021	300,000	250,000

Required:
Compute the inventory at December 31, 2019, 2020, and 2021, using the dollar-value LIFO method.

(AICPA adapted)

E 8–25
Dollar-value LIFO
● LO8–8

Carswell Electronics adopted the dollar-value LIFO method on January 1, 2018, when the inventory value of its one inventory pool was $720,000. The company decided to use an external index, the Consumer Price Index (CPI), to adjust for changes in the cost level. On January 1, 2018, the CPI was 240. On December 31, 2018, inventory valued at year-end cost was $880,000 and the CPI was 264.

Required:

Calculate the inventory value at the end of 2018 using the dollar-value LIFO method.

E 8–26
Concepts; terminology
● LO8–1 through LO8–5

Listed below are several terms and phrases associated with inventory measurement. Pair each item from List A with the item from List B (by letter) that is most appropriately associated with it.

List A	List B
_____ 1. Perpetual inventory system	a. Legal title passes when goods are delivered to common carrier.
_____ 2. Periodic inventory system	b. Goods are transferred to another company but title remains with transferor.
_____ 3. F.o.b. shipping point	c. Purchase discounts not taken are included in inventory cost.
_____ 4. Gross method	d. If LIFO is used for taxes, it must be used for financial reporting.
_____ 5. Net method	e. Assumes items sold are those acquired first.
_____ 6. Cost index	f. Assumes items sold are those acquired last.
_____ 7. F.o.b. destination	g. Purchase discounts not taken are considered interest expense.
_____ 8. FIFO	h. Used to convert ending inventory at year-end cost to base year cost.
_____ 9. LIFO	i. Continuously records changes in inventory.
_____ 10. Consignment	j. Assumes items sold come from a mixture of goods acquired during the period.
_____ 11. Average cost	k. Legal title passes when goods arrive at location.
_____ 12. IRS conformity rule	l. Adjusts inventory at the end of the period.

Problems

P 8–1
Various inventory transactions; journal entries
● LO8–1 through LO8–3

James Company began the month of October with inventory of $15,000. The following inventory transactions occurred during the month:

a. The company purchased merchandise on account for $22,000 on October 12, 2018. Terms of the purchase were 2/10, n/30. James uses the net method to record purchases. The merchandise was shipped f.o.b. shipping point and freight charges of $500 were paid in cash.
b. On October 31, James paid for the merchandise purchased on October 12.
c. During October merchandise costing $18,000 was sold on account for $28,000.
d. It was determined that inventory on hand at the end of October cost $19,060.

Required:

1. Assuming that the James Company uses a periodic inventory system, prepare journal entries for the above transactions including the adjusting entry at the end of October to record cost of goods sold.
2. Assuming that the James Company uses a perpetual inventory system, prepare journal entries for the above transactions.

P 8–2
Items to be included in inventory
● LO8–2

The following inventory transactions took place near December 31, 2018, the end of the Rasul Company's fiscal year-end:

1. On December 27, 2018, merchandise costing $2,000 was shipped to the Myers Company on consignment. The shipment arrived at Myers's location on December 29, but none of the merchandise was sold by the end of the year. The merchandise was *not* included in the 2018 ending inventory.
2. On January 5, 2019, merchandise costing $8,000 was received from a supplier and recorded as a purchase on that date and *not* included in the 2018 ending inventory. The invoice revealed that the shipment was made f.o.b. shipping point on December 28, 2018.
3. On December 29, 2018, the company shipped merchandise costing $12,000 to a customer f.o.b. destination. The goods, which arrived at the customer's location on January 4, 2019, were *not* included in Rasul's 2018 ending inventory. The sale was recorded in 2018.
4. Merchandise costing $4,000 was received on December 28, 2018, on consignment from the Aborn Company. A purchase was *not* recorded and the merchandise was *not* included in 2018 ending inventory.
5. Merchandise costing $6,000 was received and recorded as a purchase on January 8, 2019. The invoice revealed that the merchandise was shipped from the supplier on December 28, 2018, f.o.b. destination. The merchandise was *not* included in 2018 ending inventory.

Required:
State whether Rasul correctly accounted for each of the above transactions. Give the reason for your answer.

P 8–3
Costs included in inventory
● LO8–2, LO8–3

Reagan Corporation is a wholesale distributor of truck replacement parts. Initial amounts taken from Reagan's records are as follows:

Inventory at December 31 (based on a physical count of goods in Reagan's warehouse on December 31)	$1,250,000
Accounts payable at December 31:	

Vendor	Terms	Amount
Baker Company	2%, 10 days, net 30	$ 265,000
Charlie Company	Net 30	210,000
Dolly Company	Net 30	300,000
Eagler Company	Net 30	225,000
Full Company	Net 30	—
Greg Company	Net 30	—
Accounts payable, December 31		$1,000,000
Sales for the year		$9,000,000

Additional Information:

1. Parts held by Reagan on consignment from Charlie, amounting to $155,000, were included in the physical count of goods in Reagan's warehouse and in accounts payable at December 31.
2. Parts totaling $22,000, which were purchased from Full and paid for in December, were sold in the last week of the year and *appropriately* recorded as sales of $28,000. The parts were included in the physical count of goods in Reagan's warehouse on December 31 because the parts were on the loading dock waiting to be picked up by customers.
3. Parts in transit on December 31 to customers, shipped f.o.b. shipping point on December 28, amounted to $34,000. The customers received the parts on January 6 of the following year. Sales of $40,000 to the customers for the parts were recorded by Reagan on January 2.
4. Retailers were holding goods on consignment from Reagan, which had a cost of $210,000 and a retail value of $250,000.
5. Goods were in transit from Greg to Reagan on December 31. The cost of the goods was $25,000, and they were shipped f.o.b. shipping point on December 29.
6. A freight bill in the amount of $2,000 specifically relating to merchandise purchased in December, all of which was still in the inventory at December 31, was received on January 3. The freight bill was not included in either the inventory or in accounts payable at December 31.
7. All the purchases from Baker occurred during the last seven days of the year. These items have been recorded in accounts payable and accounted for in the physical inventory at cost before discount. Reagan's policy is to pay invoices in time to take advantage of all discounts, adjust inventory accordingly, and record accounts payable net of discounts.

Required:
Prepare a schedule of adjustments to the initial amounts using the format shown below. Show the effect, if any, of each of the transactions separately and if the transactions would have no effect on the amount shown, state *none*.

	Inventory	Accounts Payable	Sales
Initial amounts	$1,250,000	$1,000,000	$9,000,000
Adjustments—increase (decrease):			
1.			
2.			
3.			
4.			
5.			
6.			
7.			
Total adjustments			
Adjusted amounts	$	$	$

(AICPA adapted)

P 8–4
Various inventory transactions; determining inventory and cost of goods
● LO8–1 through LO8–4

Johnson Corporation began 2018 with inventory of 10,000 units of its only product. The units cost $8 each. The company uses a periodic inventory system and the LIFO cost method. The following transactions occurred during 2018:

a. Purchased 50,000 additional units at a cost of $10 per unit. Terms of the purchases were 2/10, n/30, and 100% of the purchases were paid for within the 10-day discount period. The company uses the gross method to record purchase discounts. The merchandise was purchased f.o.b. shipping point and freight charges of $0.50 per unit were paid by Johnson.
b. 1,000 units purchased during the year were returned to suppliers for credit. Johnson was also given credit for the freight charges of $0.50 per unit it had paid on the original purchase. The units were defective and were returned two days after they were received.
c. Sales for the year totaled 45,000 units at $18 per unit.
d. On December 28, 2018, Johnson purchased 5,000 additional units at $10 each. The goods were shipped f.o.b. destination and arrived at Johnson's warehouse on January 4, 2019.
e. 14,000 units were on hand at the end of 2018.

Required:
1. Determine ending inventory and cost of goods sold for 2018.
2. Assuming that operating expenses other than those indicated in the above transactions amounted to $150,000, determine income before income taxes for 2018.

P 8–5
Various inventory costing methods
● LO8–1, LO8–4

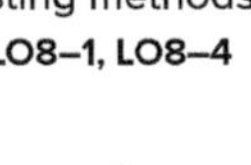

Ferris Company began 2018 with 6,000 units of its principal product. The cost of each unit is $8. Merchandise transactions for the month of January 2018 are as follows:

	Purchases		
Date of Purchase	**Units**	**Unit Cost***	**Total Cost**
Jan. 10	5,000	$ 9	$ 45,000
Jan. 18	6,000	10	60,000
Totals	11,000		$105,000

*Includes purchase price and cost of freight.

Sales	
Date of Sale	**Units**
Jan. 5	3,000
Jan. 12	2,000
Jan. 20	4,000
Total	9,000

8,000 units were on hand at the end of the month.

Required:
Calculate January's ending inventory and cost of goods sold for the month using each of the following alternatives:
1. FIFO, periodic system
2. LIFO, periodic system
3. LIFO, perpetual system
4. Average cost, periodic system
5. Average cost, perpetual system

P 8–6
Various inventory costing methods; gross profit ratio
● LO8–1, LO8–4, LO8–7

Topanga Group began operations early in 2018. Inventory purchase information for the quarter ended March 31, 2018, for Topanga's only product is provided below. The unit costs include the cost of freight. The company uses a periodic inventory system.

Date of Purchase	Units	Unit Cost	Total Cost
Jan. 7	5,000	$4.00	$ 20,000
Feb. 16	12,000	4.50	54,000
March 22	17,000	5.00	85,000
Totals	34,000		$159,000

Sales for the quarter, all at $7.00 per unit, totaled 20,000 units leaving 14,000 units on hand at the end of the quarter.

Required:

1. Calculate the Topanga's gross profit ratio for the first quarter using:
   a. FIFO
   b. LIFO
   c. Average cost
2. Comment on the relative effect of each of the three inventory methods on the gross profit ratio.

P 8–7
Various inventory costing methods
● LO8–1, LO8–4

Carlson Auto Dealers Inc. sells a handmade automobile as its only product. Each automobile is identical; however, they can be distinguished by their unique ID number. At the beginning of 2018, Carlson had three cars in inventory, as follows:

Car ID	Cost
203	$60,000
207	60,000
210	63,000

During 2018, each of the three autos sold for $90,000. Additional purchases (listed in chronological order) and sales for the year were as follows:

Car ID	Cost	Selling Price
211	$63,000	$ 90,000
212	63,000	93,000
213	64,500	not sold
214	66,000	96,000
215	69,000	100,500
216	70,500	not sold
217	72,000	105,000
218	72,300	106,500
219	75,000	not sold

Required:

1. Calculate 2018 ending inventory and cost of goods sold assuming the company uses the specific identification inventory method.
2. Calculate ending inventory and cost of goods sold assuming FIFO and a periodic inventory system.
3. Calculate ending inventory and cost of goods sold assuming LIFO and a periodic inventory system.
4. Calculate ending inventory and cost of goods sold assuming the average cost method and a periodic inventory system.

P 8–8
Supplemental LIFO disclosures; Caterpillar
● LO8–4, LO8–6
Real World Financials

Caterpillar, Inc., is one of the world's largest manufacturers of construction, mining, and forestry machinery. The following disclosure note is included in the company's 2015 financial statements:

> **D. Inventories** ($ in millions)
> Inventories are stated at the lower of cost or market. Cost is principally determined using the last-in, first-out (LIFO) method. If the FIFO (first-in, first-out) method had been in use, inventories would have been $2,498 million and $2,430 million higher than reported at December 31, 2015 and 2014, respectively.

Required:

1. The company reported LIFO cost of goods sold of $33,742 million. Calculate the amount that would be reported for cost of goods sold had Caterpillar used the FIFO inventory method for all of its inventory.
2. How does the amount in requirement 1 affect income before taxes?
3. Why might the information contained in the disclosure note be useful to a financial analyst?

P 8–9
LIFO liquidation
● LO8–4, LO8–6

Taylor Corporation has used a periodic inventory system and the LIFO cost method since its inception in 2011. The company began 2018 with the following inventory layers (listed in chronological order of acquisition):

10,000 units @ $15	$150,000
15,000 units @ $20	300,000
Beginning inventory	$450,000

During 2018, 30,000 units were purchased for $25 per unit. Due to unexpected demand for the company's product, 2018 sales totaled 40,000 units at various prices, leaving 15,000 units in ending inventory.

Required:

1. Calculate cost of goods sold for 2018.
2. Determine the amount of LIFO liquidation profit that the company must report in a disclosure note to its 2018 financial statements. Assume an income tax rate of 40%.
3. If the company decided to purchase an additional 10,000 units at $25 per unit at the end of the year, how much income tax currently payable would be saved?

P 8–10
LIFO liquidation
● LO8–4, LO8–6

Cansela Corporation uses a periodic inventory system and the LIFO method to value its inventory. The company began 2018 with inventory of 4,500 units of its only product. The beginning inventory balance of $64,000 consisted of the following layers:

2,000 units at $12 per unit	=	$24,000
2,500 units at $16 per unit	=	40,000
Beginning inventory		$64,000

During the three years 2018–2020 the cost of inventory remained constant at $18 per unit. Unit purchases and sales during these years were as follows:

	Purchases	Sales
2018	10,000	11,000
2019	13,000	14,500
2020	12,000	13,000

Required:

1. Calculate cost of goods sold for 2018, 2019, and 2020.
2. Disregarding income tax, determine the LIFO liquidation profit or loss, if any, for each of the three years.
3. Prepare the company's LIFO liquidation disclosure note that would be included in the 2020 financial statements to report the effects of any liquidation on cost of goods sold and net income. Assume any liquidation effects are material and that Cansela's effective income tax rate is 40%. Cansela's 2020 financial statements include income statements for two prior years for comparative purposes.

P 8–11
Inventory cost flow methods: LIFO liquidation; ratios
● LO8–4, LO8–6, LO8–7

Cast Iron Grills, Inc., manufactures premium gas barbecue grills. The company uses a periodic inventory system and the LIFO cost method for its grill inventory. Cast Iron's December 31, 2018, fiscal year-end inventory consisted of the following (listed in chronological order of acquisition):

Units	Unit Cost
5,000	$700
4,000	800
6,000	900

The replacement cost of the grills throughout 2019 was $1,000. Cast Iron sold 27,000 grills during 2019. The company's selling price is set at 200% of the current replacement cost.

Required:

1. Compute the gross profit (sales minus cost of goods sold) and the gross profit ratio for 2019 assuming that Cast Iron purchased 28,000 units during the year.
2. Repeat requirement 1 assuming that Cast Iron purchased only 15,000 units.
3. Why does the number of units purchased affect your answers to the above requirements?
4. Repeat requirements 1 and 2 assuming that Cast Iron uses the FIFO inventory cost method rather than the LIFO method.
5. Why does the number of units purchased have no effect on your answers to requirements 1 and 2 when the FIFO method is used?

P 8–12
Integrating problem; inventories and accounts receivable; Chapters 7 and 8
● LO8–4, LO8–6, LO8–7

Inverness Steel Corporation is a producer of flat-rolled carbon, stainless and electrical steels, and tubular products. The company's income statement for the 2018 fiscal year reported the following information ($ in millions):

Sales	$6,255
Cost of goods sold	5,190

The company's balance sheets for 2018 and 2017 included the following information ($ in millions):

	2018	2017
Current assets:		
Accounts receivable, net	$703	$583
Inventories	880	808

The statement of cash flows reported bad debt expense for 2018 of $8 million. The summary of significant accounting policies included the following notes ($ in millions):

Accounts Receivable (in part)

The allowance for uncollectible accounts was $10 and $7 at December 31, 2018 and 2017, respectively. All sales are on credit.

Inventories

Inventories are valued at the lower of cost or market. The cost of the majority of inventories is measured using the last in, first out (LIFO) method. Other inventories are measured principally at average cost and consist mostly of foreign inventories and certain raw materials. If the entire inventory had been valued on an average cost basis, inventory would have been higher by $480 and $350 at the end of 2018 and 2017, respectively.

During 2018, 2017, and 2016, liquidation of LIFO layers generated income of $6, $7, and $25, respectively.

Required:

Using the information provided:

1. Determine the amount of accounts receivable Inverness wrote off during 2018.
2. Calculate the amount of cash collected from customers during 2018.
3. Calculate what cost of goods sold would have been for 2018 if the company had used average cost to value its entire inventory.
4. Calculate the following ratios for 2018:
   a. Receivables turnover ratio
   b. Inventory turnover ratio
   c. Gross profit ratio
5. Explain briefly what caused the income generated by the liquidation of LIFO layers. Assuming an income tax rate of 35%, what was the effect of the liquidation of LIFO layers on cost of goods sold in 2018?

P 8–13
Dollar-value LIFO
● LO8–8

On January 1, 2018, the Taylor Company adopted the dollar-value LIFO method. The inventory value for its one inventory pool on this date was $400,000. Inventory data for 2018 through 2020 are as follows:

Date	Ending Inventory at Year-End Costs	Cost Index
12/31/2018	$441,000	1.05
12/31/2019	487,200	1.12
12/31/2020	510,000	1.20

Required:

Calculate Taylor's ending inventory for 2018, 2019, and 2020.

P 8–14
Dollar-value LIFO
● LO8–8

Kingston Company uses the dollar-value LIFO method of computing inventory. An external price index is used to convert ending inventory to base year. The company began operations on January 1, 2018, with an inventory of $150,000. Year-end inventories at year-end costs and cost indexes for its one inventory pool were as follows:

Year Ended December 31	Ending Inventory at Year-End Costs	Cost Index (Relative to Base Year)
2018	$200,000	1.08
2019	245,700	1.17
2020	235,980	1.14
2021	228,800	1.10

Required:

Calculate inventory amounts at the end of each year.

P 8–15
Dollar-value LIFO
● LO8–8

On January 1, 2018, Avondale Lumber adopted the dollar-value LIFO inventory method. The inventory value for its one inventory pool on this date was $260,000. An internally generated cost index is used to convert ending inventory to base year. Year-end inventories at year-end costs and cost indexes for its one inventory pool were as follows:

Year Ended December 31	Inventory Year-End Costs	Cost Index (Relative to Base Year)
2018	$340,000	1.02
2019	350,000	1.06
2020	400,000	1.07
2021	430,000	1.10

Required:
Calculate inventory amounts at the end of each year.

P 8–16
Dollar-value LIFO; solving for unknowns
● LO8–8

At the beginning of 2018, Quentin and Kopps (Q&K) adopted the dollar-value LIFO (DVL) inventory method. On that date the value of its one inventory pool was $84,000. The company uses an internally generated cost index to convert ending inventory to base year. Inventory data for 2018 through 2021 are as follows:

Year Ended December 31	Ending Inventory at Year-End Costs	Ending Inventory at Base-Year Costs	Cost Index	Ending Inventory at DVL cost
2018	$100,800	$ 96,000	1.05	?
2019	136,800	?	1.14	?
2020	150,000	125,000	?	?
2021	?	?	1.25	$133,710

Required:
Determine the missing amounts.

Broaden Your Perspective

Apply your critical-thinking ability to the knowledge you've gained. These cases will provide you an opportunity to develop your research, analysis, judgment, and communication skills. You also will work with other students, integrate what you've learned, apply it in real-world situations, and consider its global and ethical ramifications. This practice will broaden your knowledge and further develop your decision-making abilities.

Judgment Case 8–1
Riding the Merry-Go-Round
● LO8–7

Real World Financials

Merry-Go-Round Enterprises, the clothing retailer for dedicated followers of young men's and women's fashion, was looking natty as a company. It was March 1993, and the Joppa, Maryland-based outfit had just announced the acquisition of Chess King, a rival clothing chain, a move that would give it the biggest share of the young men's clothing market. Merry-Go-Round told brokerage firm analysts that the purchase would add $13 million, or 15 cents a share, to profits for the year. So some Wall Street analysts raised their earnings estimates for Merry-Go-Round. The company's stock rose $2.25, or 15 percent, to $17 on the day of the Chess King news. Merry-Go-Round was hot—$100 of its stock in January 1988 was worth $804 five years later. In 1993 the chain owned 1,460 stores in 44 states, mostly under the Cignal, Chess King, and Merry-Go-Round names.

Merry-Go-Round's annual report for the fiscal year ended January 30, 1993, reported a 15% sales growth, to $877.5 million from $761.2 million. A portion of the company's balance sheet is reproduced below:

	Jan. 30, 1993	Feb. 1, 1992
Assets		
Cash and cash equivalents	$40,115,000	$29,781,000
Marketable securities	—	9,703
Receivables	6,466,000	6,195
Merchandise inventories	82,197,000	59,971,000

But Merry-Go-Round spun out. The company lost $544,000 in the first six months of 1993, compared with earnings of $13.5 million in the first half of 1992. In the fall of 1992, Leonard "Boogie" Weinglass, Merry-Go-Round's flamboyant founder and chairman who had started the company in 1968, boarded up his Merry-Go-Ranch in Aspen, Colorado, and returned to management after a 12-year hiatus. But the pony-tailed, shirtsleeved entrepreneur—the inspiration for the character Boogie in the movie *Diner*—couldn't save his company from bankruptcy. In January 1994, the company filed for Chapter 11 protection in Baltimore. Shares crumbled below $3.

Required:

In retrospect, can you identify any advance warning at the date of the financial statements of the company's impending bankruptcy?

[Adapted from Jonathan Burton, "Due Diligence," *Worth*, June 1994, pp. 89–96.]

Real World Case 8–2
Physical quantities and costs included in inventory; Sport Chalet
● LO8–2
Real World Financials

Determining the physical quantity that should be included in inventory normally is a simple matter because that amount consists of items in the possession of the company. The cost of inventory includes all necessary expenditures to acquire the inventory and bring it to its desired *condition* and *location* for sale or for use in the manufacturing process.

Required:

1. Identify and describe the situations in which physical quantity included in inventory is more difficult than simply determining items in the possession of the company.
2. In addition to the direct acquisition costs such as the price paid and transportation costs to obtain inventory, what other expenditures might be necessary to bring the inventory to its desired condition and location?
3. Access EDGAR on the Internet. The web address is www.sec.gov. Search for Sport Chalet Inc., a leading operator of full-service, specialty sporting goods stores in California and Nevada. Access the 10-K filing for the most recent fiscal year. Search or scroll to find the disclosure notes (footnotes). What costs does Sport Chalet include in its inventory?

Judgment Case 8–3
The specific identification inventory method; inventoriable costs
● LO8–3, LO8–4

Happlia Co. imports household appliances. Each model has many variations and each unit has an identification number. Happlia pays all costs for getting the goods from the port to its central warehouse in Des Moines. After repackaging, the goods are consigned to retailers. A retailer makes a sale, simultaneously buys the appliance from Happlia, and pays the balance due within one week.

To alleviate the overstocking of refrigerators at a Minneapolis retailer, some were reshipped to a Kansas City retailer where they were still held in inventory at December 31, 2018. Happlia paid the costs of this reshipment. Happlia uses the specific identification inventory costing method.

Required:

1. In regard to the specific identification inventory costing method:
   a. Describe its key elements.
   b. Discuss why it is appropriate for Happlia to use this method.
2. a. What general criteria should Happlia use to determine inventory carrying amounts at December 31, 2018?
   b. Give four examples of costs included in these inventory carrying amounts.
3. What costs should be reported in Happlia's 2018 income statement? Ignore lower of cost or market considerations.

(AICPA adapted)

Communication Case 8–4
LIFO versus FIFO
● LO8–4, LO8–5

You have just been hired as a consultant to Tangier Industries, a newly formed company. The company president, John Meeks, is seeking your advice as to the appropriate inventory method Tangier should use to value its inventory and cost of goods sold. Mr. Meeks has narrowed the choice to LIFO and FIFO. He has heard that LIFO might be better for tax purposes, but FIFO has certain advantages for financial reporting to investors and creditors. You have been told that the company will be profitable in its first year and for the foreseeable future.

Required:

Prepare a report for the president describing the factors that should be considered by Tangier in choosing between LIFO and FIFO.

Communication Case 8–5
LIFO versus FIFO
● LO8–4, LO8–5

An accounting intern for a local CPA firm was reviewing the financial statements of a client in the electronics industry. The intern noticed that the client used the FIFO method of determining ending inventory and cost of goods sold. When she asked a colleague why the firm used FIFO instead of LIFO, she was told that the client used FIFO to minimize its income tax liability. This response puzzled the intern because she thought that LIFO would minimize income tax liability.

Required:

What would you tell the intern to resolve the confusion?

Judgment Case 8–6
Goods in transit
● LO8–2

At the end of 2018, the Biggie Company performed its annual physical inventory count. John Lawrence, the manager in charge of the physical count, was told that an additional $22,000 in inventory that had been sold and was in transit to the customer should be included in the ending inventory balance. John was of the opinion that the merchandise shipped should be excluded from the ending inventory since Biggie was not in physical possession of the merchandise.

Required:

Discuss the situation and indicate why John's opinion might be incorrect.

Ethics Case 8–7
Profit manipulation
● LO8–4

In 2017 the Moncrief Company purchased from Jim Lester the right to be the sole distributor in the western states of a product called Zelenex. In payment, Moncrief agreed to pay Lester 20% of the gross profit recognized from the sale of Zelenex in 2018.

Moncrief uses a periodic inventory system and the LIFO inventory method. Late in 2018, the following information is available concerning the inventory of Zelenex:

Beginning inventory, 1/1/2018 (10,000 units @ $30)	$ 300,000
Purchases (40,000 units @ $30)	1,200,000
Sales (35,000 units @ $60)	2,100,000

By the end of the year, the purchase price of Zelenex had risen to $40 per unit. On December 28, 2018, three days before year-end, Moncrief is in a position to purchase 20,000 additional units of Zelenex at the $40 per unit price. Due to the increase in purchase price, Moncrief will increase the selling price in 2019 to $80 per unit. Inventory on hand before the purchase, 15,000 units, is sufficient to meet the next six months' sales and the company does not anticipate any significant changes in purchase price during 2019.

Required:
1. Determine the effect of the purchase of the additional 20,000 units on the 2018 gross profit from the sale of Zelenex and the payment due to Jim Lester.
2. Discuss the ethical dilemma Moncrief faces in determining whether or not the additional units should be purchased.

Real World Case 8–8
Effects of inventory valuation methods; supplemental LIFO disclosures; Wolverine World Wide, Inc.
● LO8–4, LO8–6

Real World Financials

Income statement and balance sheet information abstracted from a recent annual report of Wolverine World Wide, Inc. appears below:

Balance Sheets
($ in millions)

	January 2, 2016	January 3, 2015
Current assets:		
Inventories	$466.6	$414.0

Income Statements
($ in millions)

	For the Year Ended	
	January 2, 2016	January 3, 2015
Net sales	$2,691.6	$2,761.1
Cost of goods sold	1,636.9	1,673.8
Gross profit	$1,054.7	$1,087.3

The significant accounting policies note disclosure contained the following:

Inventories

The Company used the LIFO method to value inventories. If the FIFO method had been used, inventories would have been $27.0 million and $25.1 million higher than reported at January 2, 2016 and January 3, 2015, respectively.

Required:
1. Why is Wolverine disclosing the FIFO cost of its LIFO inventory?
2. Calculate what beginning inventory and ending inventory would have been for the year ended January 2, 2016, if Wolverine had used FIFO for all of its inventories.
3. Calculate what cost of goods sold would have been for the year ended January 2, 2016, if Wolverine had used FIFO for all of its inventories.

Real World Case 8–9
Effects of inventory valuation methods; Whole Foods Market
● LO8–4, LO8–5, LO8–7

Real World Financials

EDGAR, the Electronic Data Gathering, Analysis, and Retrieval system, performs automated collection, validation, indexing, and forwarding of submission by companies and others who are required by law to file forms with the U.S. Securities and Exchange Commission (SEC). All publicly traded domestic companies use EDGAR to make the majority of their filings. (Some foreign companies file voluntarily.) Form 10-K, which includes the annual report, is required to be filed on EDGAR. The SEC makes this information available on the Internet.

Required:
1. Access EDGAR on the Internet. The web address is www.sec.gov.
2. Search for Whole Foods Market, Inc. Access the 10-K filing for the most recent fiscal year. Search or scroll to find the financial statements and related notes.

3. Answer the following questions related to the company's inventories:
   a. What method(s) does the company use to value its inventories?
   b. Calculate what cost of sales would have been for the year if the company had used FIFO to value its inventories.
   c. Calculate inventory turnover for the year using the reported numbers.

Communication Case 8–10
Dollar-value LIFO method
● LO8–8

Maxi Corporation uses the unit LIFO inventory method. The costs of the company's products have been steadily rising since the company began operations in 2008 and cost increases are expected to continue. The chief financial officer of the company would like to continue using LIFO because of its tax advantages. However, the controller, Sally Hamel, would like to reduce the recordkeeping costs of LIFO that have steadily increased over the years as new products have been added to the company's product line. Sally suggested the use of the dollar-value LIFO method. The chief financial officer has asked Sally to describe the dollar-value LIFO procedure.

Required:

Describe the dollar-value LIFO procedure.

Research Case 8–11
FASB codification; locate and extract relevant information and authoritative support for a financial reporting issue; product financing arrangement
● LO8–2, LO8–3

You were recently hired to work in the controller's office of the Balboa Lumber Company. Your boss, Alfred Eagleton, took you to lunch during your first week and asked a favor. "Things have been a little slow lately, and we need to borrow a little cash to tide us over. Our inventory has been building up and the CFO wants to pledge the inventory as collateral for a short-term loan. But I have a better idea." Mr. Eagleton went on to describe his plan. "On July 1, 2018, the first day of the company's third quarter, we will sell $100,000 of inventory to the Harbaugh Corporation for $160,000. Harbaugh will pay us immediately and then we will agree to repurchase the merchandise in two months for $164,000. The $4,000 is Harbaugh's fee for holding the inventory and for providing financing. I already checked with Harbaugh's controller and he has agreed to the arrangement. Not only will we obtain the financing we need, but the third quarter's before-tax profits will be increased by $56,000, the gross profit on the sale less the $4,000 fee. Go research the issue and make sure we would not be violating any specific accounting standards related to product financing arrangements."

Required:

1. Obtain the relevant authoritative literature on product financing arrangements using the *FASB Accounting Standards Codification*. You might gain access at the FASB website (www.fasb.org). What is the specific citation that provides guidance for determining whether an arrangement involving the sale of inventory is "in substance" a financing arrangement?
2. What is the specific citation that addresses the recognition of a product financing arrangement?
3. Determine the appropriate treatment of product financing arrangements like the one proposed by Mr. Eagleton.
4. Prepare the journal entry for Balboa Lumber to record the "sale" of the inventory and subsequent repurchase.

Analysis Case 8–12
Compare inventory management using ratios; Kohl's and Dillards
● LO8–7

Real World Financials

The table below contains selected financial information included in the 2016 financial statements of Kohl's Corporation and Dillards, Inc., two companies in the department store industry.

	($ in millions)			
	Kohl's Corp.		Dillards, Inc.	
	2016	2015	2016	2015
Balance sheet:				
Inventories	$ 4,038	$3,814	$1,375	$1,374
Income statement—2016:				
Net sales	$19,204		$6,755	
Cost of goods sold	12,265		4,351	

Required:

1. Calculate the 2016 gross profit ratio, inventory turnover ratio, and average days in inventory for both companies. Evaluate the management of each company's investment in inventory.
2. Obtain annual reports from three corporations in an industry other than department stores and compare the management of each company's investment in inventory.

Note: You can obtain copies of annual reports from your library, from friends who are shareholders, from the investor relations department of the corporations, from a friendly stockbroker, or from EDGAR (Electronic Data Gathering, Analysis, and Retrieval) on the Internet (www.sec.gov).

Continuing Cases

Target Case

● LO8–1, LO8–4, LO8–7

Target Corporation prepares its financial statements according to U.S. GAAP. Target's financial statements and disclosure notes for the year ended January 30, 2016, are available in Connect. This material is also available under the Investor Relations link at the company's website (www.target.com).

Required:

1. What inventory method(s) does Target use to value its inventories?
2. In addition to the purchase price, what additional expenditures does the company include in the initial cost of merchandise?
3. Calculate the gross profit ratio and the inventory turnover ratio for the fiscal year ended January 30, 2016. Compare Target's ratios with the industry averages of 24.5% and 7.1 times.

Air France–KLM Case

● LO8–9

Air France–KLM (AF), a Franco-Dutch company, prepares its financial statements according to International Financial Reporting Standards. AF's financial statements and disclosure notes for the year ended December 31, 2015, are available in Connect. This material is also available under the Finance link at the company's website (www.airfranceklm.com).

Required:

What method does the company use to value its inventory? What other alternatives are available under IFRS? Under U.S. GAAP?

CPA Exam Questions and Simulations

ROGER CPA Review

Sample CPA Exam questions from Roger CPA Review are available in Connect as support for the topics in this chapter. These Multiple Choice Questions and Task-Based Simulations include expert-written explanations and solutions, and provide a starting point for students to become familiar with the content and functionality of the actual CPA Exam.

CHAPTER

9 Inventories: Additional Issues

OVERVIEW

We covered most of the principal measurement and reporting issues involving the asset inventory and the corresponding expense cost of goods sold in the previous chapter. In this chapter, we complete our discussion of inventory measurement by explaining how inventories are measured at the end of the period. In addition, we investigate inventory estimation techniques, methods of simplifying LIFO, changes in inventory method, and inventory errors.

LEARNING OBJECTIVES

After studying this chapter, you should be able to:

- **LO9–1** Understand and apply rules for measurement of inventory at the end of the reporting period. (*p. 465*)
- **LO9–2** Estimate ending inventory and cost of goods sold using the gross profit method. (*p. 473*)
- **LO9–3** Estimate ending inventory and cost of goods sold using the retail inventory method, applying the various cost flow methods. (*p. 475*)
- **LO9–4** Explain how the retail inventory method can be made to approximate the lower of cost or market rule. (*p. 478*)
- **LO9–5** Determine ending inventory using the dollar-value LIFO retail inventory method. (*p. 483*)
- **LO9–6** Explain the appropriate accounting treatment required when a change in inventory method is made. (*p. 486*)
- **LO9–7** Explain the appropriate accounting treatment required when an inventory error is discovered. (*p. 488*)
- **LO9–8** Discuss the primary differences between U.S. GAAP and IFRS with respect to the lower of cost or net realizable value rule for valuing inventory. (*p. 468*)

© Justin Sullivan/Getty Images

FINANCIAL REPORTING CASE

Does It Count?

Today you drove over to Dollar General to pick up a few items. You recall from class yesterday that your accounting professor had discussed inventory measurement issues and the different methods (FIFO, LIFO, and average) used by companies to determine ending inventory and cost of goods sold. As of February 26, 2016, Dollar General had 12,575 store locations. You can't imagine actually counting the inventory in all of the stores around the country. You consider that there must be some way Dollar General can avoid counting all of that inventory every time they want to produce financial statements. When you get home, you check their financial statements on the Internet to see what kind of inventory method they use. You find the following in the summary of significant accounting policies included in Dollar General's most recent financial statements:

Merchandise Inventories (in part):

Merchandise inventories are stated at the lower of cost or market ("LCM") with cost determined using the retail last in, first out ("LIFO") method. We use the retail inventory method ("RIM") to calculate gross profit and the resulting valuation of inventories at cost, which are computed utilizing a calculated cost-to-retail inventory ratio at an inventory department level. The RIM will result in valuing inventories at LCM if permanent markdowns are currently taken as a reduction of the retail value of inventories.

We perform an annual LIFO analysis whereby all merchandise units are considered for inclusion in the index formulation. An actual valuation of inventory under the LIFO method is made at the end of each year based on the inventory levels and costs at that time.

QUESTIONS

By the time you finish this chapter, you should be able to respond appropriately to the questions posed in this case. Compare your response to the solution provided at the end of the chapter.

1. How does Dollar General avoid counting all its inventory every time it produces financial statements? (*p. 483*)
2. What is the index formulation used for? (*p. 483*)

Subsequent Measurement of Inventory

PART A

● LO9–1

As you would expect, companies hope to sell their inventory for more than its cost. Yet, this doesn't always happen. Sometimes circumstances arise after (or *subsequent* to) the purchase or production of inventory that indicate the company will have to sell its inventory for less than its cost. This might happen because of inventory damage, physical deterioration, obsolescence, changes in price levels, or any situation that lessens demand for the inventory. Consider, for example, the value of unsold electronics inventory when the next generation comes out, or the leftover clothing inventory at the end of the selling season. Usually, the only way these items can be sold is at deeply discounted prices (well-below their purchase cost).

An inventory write-down has the effect of reducing inventory and reducing net income.

GAAP requires that companies evaluate their unsold inventory at the end of each reporting period (for reasons mentioned above). When the expected benefit of unsold inventory is estimated to have fallen below its cost, companies must depart from the cost basis of reporting ending inventory; an adjusting entry is needed to reduce the reported amount of inventory and to reduce net income for the period. This end-of-period adjusting entry is known as an *inventory write-down.*

The two measurement approaches for recording an inventory write-down are listed in Illustration 9–1. The approach chosen by a company depends on which inventory costing method the company uses.[1] For companies that use a cost method other than LIFO or the retail inventory method, we report inventory at the *lower of cost or net realizable value.* For companies that use LIFO or the retail inventory method (discussed later in this chapter), we report inventory at the *lower of cost or market.*

Illustration 9–1
Subsequent Inventory Measurement

Measurement Approach	For Companies that Use	Financial Statement Effects of Inventory Write-Downs
1. Lower of cost or net realizable value (LCNRV)	FIFO, average cost, or any other method besides LIFO or the retail inventory method	a. Reduce reported inventory b. Reduce net income
2. Lower of cost or market (LCM)	LIFO or retail inventory method	a. Reduce reported inventory b. Reduce net income

For both measurement approaches, the financial statement effects of an inventory write-down are the same: (a) reduce reported inventory and (b) reduce net income. Both approaches have the same conceptual purpose of reporting inventory conservatively at the lower of two amounts. The difference between the two approaches is the measurement of the *amount* of the inventory write-down. We discuss those measurements next.[2]

Lower of Cost or Net Realizable Value (LCNRV)

Net realizable value (NRV) is the estimated selling price reduced by any costs of completion, disposal, and transportation.

Companies that use FIFO, average cost, or any other method besides LIFO or the retail inventory method report inventory using the **lower of cost or net realizable value** (LCNRV) approach. To do this, a company compares the inventory's cost to the inventory's net realizable value (NRV). NRV is the estimated selling price of the inventory in the ordinary course of business reduced by reasonably predictable costs of completion, disposal, and transportation (such as sales commissions and shipping costs).

Another way to think about NRV is that it's the *net* amount a company expects to *realize* (or collect in cash) from the sale of the inventory. Companies often estimate the "costs to sell" by applying a predetermined percentage to the selling price. For example, if the selling price of Product A is $10 per unit, and the company estimates that sales commissions and shipping costs average approximately 10% of selling price, NRV would be $9 [$10 − ($10 × 10%)].

After comparing cost and NRV, a company reports inventory at the lower of the two amounts.

When NRV is lower than cost, an inventory write down is recorded.

1. If NRV is lower than cost, we need an adjusting entry to reduce inventory from its already recorded purchase cost to the lower NRV. NRV then becomes the new carrying value of inventory reported in the balance sheet.
2. If cost is lower than NRV, no adjusting entry is needed. Inventory already is recorded at cost at the time it was purchased, and this cost is lower than total NRV at the end of the period.

The LCNRV approach avoids reporting inventory at an amount greater than the cash it can provide to the company. Reporting inventories this way causes income to be reduced in the period the value of inventory declines below its cost rather than in the period in which the goods ultimately are sold.[3]

[1]FASB ASC 330-10-35-1A through 35-1C: Inventory-Overall-Subsequent Measurement.
[2]Interestingly, the two approaches to subsequent measurement of inventory arose out of *Accounting Standards Update (ASU) No. 2015–11*, which was part of the FASB's Simplification Initiative aimed at *reducing* reporting complexity. However, *ASU 2015–11 increases* the number of subsequent measurement approaches. Prior to *ASU 2015–11*, all companies reported inventory using a single approach - the lower of cost or market. Some may argue that the introduction of a second approach increases reporting complexity.
[3]In other words, if the inventory was not written down to NRV (and instead remained at cost) at the end of the current period, the full cost amount would become cost of goods sold and thus reduce net income when the inventory is sold in a subsequent period.

Applying Lower of Cost or Net Realizable Value

The LCNRV rule can be applied to individual inventory items, major inventory categories, or the entire inventory.

For financial reporting purposes, LCNRV can be applied (a) to individual inventory items, (b) to major categories of inventory, or (c) to the entire inventory.[4] Illustration 9–2 demonstrates the LCNRV approach with each of the three possible applications.

Illustration 9–2

Lower of Cost or Net Realizable Value—Application at Different Levels of Aggregation

The Collins Company has five inventory items on hand at the end of the year. The year-end cost (determined by applying the FIFO cost method) and net realizable value (current selling prices less costs of completion, disposal, and transportation) for each of the items are presented below.

Items A and B are a collection of similar items, and items C, D, and E are another collection of similar items. Each collection can be considered a category of inventory.

			Lower of Cost or NRV		
Item	**Cost**	**NRV**	**By Individual Items**	**By Category**	**By Total Inventory**
A	$ 50,000	$ 85,000	$ 50,000		
B	100,000	90,000	90,000		
Total A and B	$150,000	$175,000		$150,000	
C	$ 80,000	$ 75,000	75,000		
D	90,000	85,000	85,000		
E	95,000	96,000	95,000		
Total C, D, and E	$265,000	$256,000		256,000	
Total	$415,000	$431,000	$395,000	$406,000	$415,000

If we first consider LCNRV *by individual items,* we see that cost is lower than NRV for items A and E (see "By Individual Items" column). These inventory items were initially recorded at cost at the time of purchase. So, under the LCNRV approach, they are currently recorded at their proper amounts. No adjustment is needed. However, for items B, C, and D, we see that NRV is below cost. Therefore, we need to adjust the carrying value of these items downward and report them at NRV in the balance sheet. After determining the lower of cost or NRV for each individual item, the total amount to report for inventory is $395,000.

Now let's see what happens if we apply the LCNRV approach *by inventory category* (see "By Category" column). The first category of inventory (items A and B) has a combined cost of $150,000 and a combined NRV of $175,000, so we report this second inventory group at its cost of $150,000. For the second category (items C, D, and E), the combined NRV ($256,000) is lower than the combined cost ($265,000), so we report this second inventory group at its NRV of $256,000. We report inventory at $406,000 ($150,000 + $256,000).

Finally, if we apply the LCNRV approach *by total inventory,* we see that inventory's total cost ($415,000) is lower than its total NRV ($431,000). Inventory would be reported at its cost of $415,000.

As shown in this illustration, applying the LCNRV rule to groups of inventory items will cause a higher inventory valuation than if applied on an item-by-item basis. The reason is that group application permits increases in the net realizable value of some items to offset decreases in others. Each approach is acceptable but should be applied consistently from one period to another.

[4]FASB ASC 330–10–35–8: Inventory–Overall–Subsequent Measurement. In addition, for income tax purposes, the rule must be applied on an individual item basis.

Ethical Dilemma

The Hartley Company, owned and operated by Bill Hartley, manufactures and sells high-end ergonomic office chairs and custom bookshelves. The company has reported profits in the majority of years since the company's inception in 1975 and is projecting a profit in 2018 of $65,000, down from $96,000 in 2017.

Near the end of 2018, the company is in the process of applying for a bank loan. The loan proceeds will be used to replace manufacturing equipment to modernize the manufacturing operation. In preparing the financial statements for the year, the chief accountant, Don Davis, mentioned to Bill Hartley that net realizable value (NRV) of the bookshelf inventory is below its cost by $40,000 and should be written off in 2018. However, no write-off is necessary for office chairs because their NRV is $50,000 above cost.

Bill is worried that the write-down would lower 2018 income to a level that might cause the bank to refuse the loan. Without the loan, it would be difficult for the company to compete. This could decrease future business, and employees might have to be laid off. Bill suggests to Don that the company combine the office chairs and bookshelves into a single inventory category (office furniture) for reporting purposes, so that the combined NRV is above the combined cost. In this case, no inventory write-down would be needed. The company has not previously combined these inventory items and has no stated policy on the matter. Don is contemplating his responsibilities in this situation.

Adjusting Cost to Net Realizable Value

When NRV is below cost, companies are required to write down inventory to the lower NRV. This is accomplished in one of two ways depending on the nature of the decline in inventory value. These write-downs usually are included in cost of goods sold because they are a natural consequence of holding inventory and therefore part of the inventory's cost. However, when a write-down is substantial and unusual, the write-down should be recorded in a loss account instead. That loss must be expressly disclosed in the financial statements. This could be accomplished with a disclosure note alone or by also reporting the loss in a separate line of the income statement, usually among operating expenses.

Referring back to Illustration 9–2, assume that we report inventory using the LCNRV approach by individual items. The recorded cost of inventory ($415,000) needs to be written down to its NRV ($395,000) at the end of the period. The amount of the reduction is $20,000. The period-end adjusting entry would be one of the following, depending on whether the inventory write-down is usual (cost of goods sold) or unusual (loss):

Inventory

415,000	
	20,000
395,000	

Cost of goods sold......	20,000			Loss on write-down of inventory...	20,000	
Inventory*..................		20,000	or	Inventory*.......................................		20,000

*Or, inventory can be reduced indirectly with a credit to an allowance account.

Regardless of which entry we use to report the write-down, the reduced inventory amount becomes the new cost basis for subsequent reporting. If the inventory value later increases prior to its sale, we do not write it back up.[5]

[5]The SEC, in *Staff Accounting Bulletin* No. 100, "Restructuring and Impairment Charges" (Washington, D.C.: SEC, November, 1999), paragraph B.B., (FASB ASC 330–10–S35–1: SAB Topic 5.BB), reaffirmed the provisions of GAAP literature on this issue. For interim reporting purposes, however, recoveries of losses on the same inventory in subsequent interim periods of the same fiscal year through market price recoveries should be recognized as gains in the later interim period, not to exceed the previously recognized losses.

International Financial Reporting Standards

Lower of cost or net realizable value. You just learned that in the United States some companies report inventory at the *lower of cost or net realizable value.* This is the same approach used under IFRS. However, there are some differences between U.S. GAAP and IFRS in the application of lower of cost or net realizable value.

● LO9–8

First, *IAS No. 2* specifies that if circumstances indicate that an inventory write-down is no longer appropriate, it must be reversed.[6] Reversals are not permitted under U.S. GAAP.

Second, under U.S. GAAP, the lower of cost or net realizable value rule can be applied to individual items, inventory categories, or the entire inventory. Under the international standard, the assessment usually is applied to individual items, although using inventory categories is allowed under certain circumstances.

Siemens AG, a German electronics and electrical engineering company, prepares its financial statements according to IFRS. The following disclosure note illustrates the valuation of inventory at the lower of cost or net realizable value.

Inventories (in part)
Inventory is valued at the lower of acquisition or production cost and net realizable value, cost being generally determined on the basis of an average or first-in, first-out method.

Concept Review Exercise

LOWER OF COST OR NET REALIZABLE VALUE

The Strand Company sells four products that can be grouped into two major categories and employs the FIFO cost method. Information needed to apply the lower of cost or NRV (LCNRV) rule on December 31, 2018 (end of the period), for each of the four products is presented below. Sales commissions and transportation costs average 10% of selling price. Inventory write-downs are a normal occurrence for Strand.

Product	Cost	Selling Price
101	$120,000	$160,000
102	175,000	180,000
201	160,000	160,000
202	45,000	60,000

Products 101 and 102 are in category A, and products 201 and 202 are in category B.

Required:

Determine the reported amount of ending inventory and record any necessary year-end adjusting entry to write down inventory, applying the LCNRV approach to the following:

1. Individual items
2. Major categories
3. Total inventory

Solution:

Determine the reported amount of ending inventory and record any necessary year-end adjusting entry to write down inventory, applying the LCNRV approach.

[6]"Inventories," *International Accounting Standard No. 2* (IASCF), as amended effective January 1, 2016.

			Lower of Cost or NRV		
Product	**Cost**	**NRV***	**By Individual Products**	**By Category**	**By Total Inventory**
101	$120,000	$144,000	$120,000		
102	175,000	162,000	162,000		
Total 101 + 102	$295,000	$306,000		$295,000	
201	$160,000	$144,000	144,000		
202	45,000	54,000	45,000		
Total 201 + 202	$205,000	$198,000		198,000	
Total	$500,000	$504,000	$471,000	$493,000	$500,000

*NRV = Selling price less costs to sell. For product 101, $160,000 – ($160,000 × 10%) = $144,000.

The NRV for both the individual product and category applications are lower than cost so inventory write-downs are needed. On the other hand, cost is lower than NRV at the total inventory level, so no adjustment would be needed.

1. Individual items

Reported ending inventory = $471,000 (NRV)

December 31, 2018		
Cost of goods sold†	29,000*	
Inventory		29,000
*$500,000 (recorded cost) – $471,000 (NRV)		

2. Major categories

Reported ending inventory = $493,000 (NRV)

December 31, 2018		
Cost of goods sold†	7,000*	
Inventory		7,000
*$500,000 (recorded cost) – $493,000 (NRV)		

†For the two entries above, we record the adjustment to the cost of goods sold account because the inventory write-down is considered usual. If the write-down had been unusual, we record the adjustment to a Loss account.

3. Total inventory

Reported ending inventory = $500,000 (Cost)

Because inventory already is recorded at cost as of December 31, 2018, and because total cost is lower than total NRV ($504,000), no year-end adjustment is needed.

Additional Consideration

Critics of reporting inventory lower than its cost contend that this causes losses to be recognized that haven't actually occurred. Others maintain that it introduces needless inconsistency in order to be conservative, because decreases in value are recognized as they occur, but not increases. As you learned in Chapter 1, conservatism is not part of the conceptual framework. So, why not record increases as well? Recall the revenue recognition guidance we discussed in Chapter 5. Recognizing increases in the value of inventory prior to sale would, in most cases, result in premature revenue recognition, because the seller would be acting as if it had satisfied a performance obligation (selling inventory) before that actually occurred. For example, let's say that merchandise costing $100 now has a net realizable value of $150. Recognizing a gain for the increase in value would increase pretax income by $50. This is equivalent to recognizing revenue of $150, cost of goods sold of $100, and gross profit of $50. The effect is to increase pretax income in a period prior to sale of the product. That's not allowed.

Lower of Cost or Market (LCM)

Companies that use LIFO or the retail inventory method report inventory using the lower of cost or market (LCM) approach. You might interpret the term *market* to mean the amount that could be realized if the inventory were sold. This would be similar to the concept of *net realizable value* discussed above. However, market is defined differently.

Market is current replacement cost, but not above the ceiling or below the floor.

Market is the inventory's current replacement cost (by purchase or reproduction) except that:

1. Market should not be greater than the net realizable value (this forms a "ceiling" on market), and
2. Market should not be less than net realizable value reduced by an allowance for an approximately normal profit margin (this forms a "floor" on market).

In effect, we have a ceiling and a floor between which market (that is, replacement cost) must fall. If replacement cost is between the ceiling and the floor, it represents market; if replacement cost is above the ceiling or below the floor, the ceiling or the floor becomes market. The designated market amount is compared with cost, and the lower of the two is used to value inventory.

To see an example, let's look at Illustration 9–3. In the top part of the illustration, we calculate the ceiling and the floor. In the bottom part, we calculate LCM.

Illustration 9–3
Lower of Cost or Market (LCM)

The Collins Company has five inventory items on hand at the end of the year. The year-end selling prices, and estimated costs of completion, disposal, and transportation (selling costs) for each of the items are given below. The normal gross profit ratio for each of the products is 20% of selling price. These amounts are used to calculate the ceiling and floor as follows:

Item	Selling Price	Estimated Selling Costs	NRV [Ceiling]*	Normal Profit Margin (20% of Selling Price)	NRV – NPM [Floor]†
A	$100,000	$15,000	$85,000	$20,000	$65,000
B	120,000	30,000	90,000	24,000	66,000
C	90,000	15,000	75,000	18,000	57,000
D	100,000	15,000	85,000	20,000	65,000
E	110,000	14,000	96,000	22,000	74,000

Additional information related to year-end inventory cost (determined by applying the LIFO cost method) and replacement cost are given in the first two columns. Determination of LCM is a two-step process: (1) calculate the market amount using replacement cost, subject to a ceiling and floor, and (2) select the lower of cost or market.

		Market				
	(1)	(2)	(3)	(4)	(5)	
Item	Cost	Replacement Cost	NRV [Ceiling]	NRV – NPM [Floor]	Market [Middle of (2), (3), (4)]	LCM [Lower of (1) or (5)]
A	**$ 50,000**	$55,000	$85,000	$65,000	**$65,000**	$ 50,000
B	**100,000**	97,000	90,000	66,000	**90,000**	90,000
C	**80,000**	70,000	75,000	57,000	**70,000**	70,000
D	**90,000**	95,000	85,000	65,000	**85,000**	85,000
E	**95,000**	92,000	96,000	74,000	**92,000**	92,000
Total	**$415,000**					$387,000

*NRV = Estimated selling price less estimated selling costs. For item A, $100,000 – $15,000 = $85,000.
†NRV – NPM = NRV less a normal profit margin. For item A, $85,000 – ($100,000 selling price × 20%) = $65,000.

Notice the market amount for each inventory item is simply the middle value among replacement cost, NRV (ceiling), and NRV – NPM (floor). When replacement cost is:

a. *Below the floor* (item A), we select the floor as the market.
b. *Above the ceiling* (items B and D), we select the ceiling as the market.
c. *Between the ceiling and the floor* (items C and E), we select replacement cost as the market.

We then compare each item's designated market amount to its cost and choose the lower of the two. After doing this, ending inventory under LCM is $387,000. This means that the recorded cost of $415,000 needs to be reduced by $28,000 ($415,000 – $387,000). We record that adjustment to cost of goods sold if the decrease to market is considered normal for this company. Otherwise, the reduction is recorded as a loss.

Inventory	
415,000	
	28,000
387,000	

Cost of goods sold......	28,000		Loss on write-down of inventory...	28,000	
Inventory*..................		28,000 or	Inventory*....................................		28,000

*Or, inventory can be reduced indirectly with a credit to an allowance account.

The example in Illustration 9–3 calculates LCM on an individual items basis. The LCM method also can be applied to major categories of inventory or to the entire inventory, just like we saw in Illustration 9–2 under the LCNRV approach. As shown in Illustration 9–3A, inventory using the LCM approach applied *by category* would be reported as $397,000. If we calculate LCM *by total inventory,* the amount to report for ending inventory would be $402,000.

Illustration 9–3A

Lower of Cost or Market-Application at Different Levels of Aggregation

From the information in Illustration 9–3, also assume items A and B are a collection of similar items, and items C, D, and E are another collection of similar items. Each collection can be considered a category of inventory.

			Lower of Cost or Market		
Item	**Cost**	**Market**	**By Individual Items**	**By Category**	**By Total Inventory**
A	$ 50,000	$ 65,000	$ 50,000		
B	100,000	90,000	90,000		
Total A and B	$150,000	$155,000		$ 150,000	
C	$ 80,000	$ 70,000	70,000		
D	90,000	85,000	85,000		
E	95,000	92,000	92,000		
Total C, D, and E	$265,000	$247,000		247,000	
Total	$415,000	$402,000	$387,000	$397,000	$402,000

PART B

Inventory Estimation Techniques

For some companies or in certain situations, it becomes difficult or impossible to physically count each unit of inventory. For example, consider a large retail company that has locations over the entire nation and sells many different items. Trying to track the cost of each item would be nearly impossible. In these situations, companies have developed methods for estimating inventory. We'll study those methods next.

The Gross Profit Method

The gross profit method, also known as the gross margin method, is useful in situations where estimates of inventory are desirable. The technique is valuable in a variety of situations, including the following:

● LO9–2

1. In determining the cost of inventory that has been lost, destroyed, or stolen
2. In estimating inventory and cost of goods sold for interim reports, avoiding the expense of a physical inventory count
3. In auditors' testing of the overall reasonableness of inventory amounts reported by clients
4. In budgeting and forecasting

The technique relies on a relationship you learned in the previous chapter—ending inventory and cost of goods sold always equal the cost of goods available for sale. Even when inventory is unknown, we can estimate it because accounting records usually indicate the cost of goods available for sale (beginning inventory plus net purchases), and the cost of goods sold can be estimated from available information. So by subtracting the cost of goods sold estimate from the cost of goods available for sale, we obtain an estimate of ending inventory. Let's compare that with the way inventory and cost of goods sold normally are determined.

Usually, in a periodic inventory system, ending inventory is known from a physical count and cost of goods sold is *derived* as follows:

Beginning inventory	(from the accounting records)
Plus: Net purchases	(from the accounting records)
Goods available for sale	
Less: Ending inventory	(from a physical count)
Cost of goods sold	

However, when using the gross profit method, the ending inventory is *not* known. Instead, the amount of sales is known—from which we can estimate the cost of goods sold—and ending inventory is the amount calculated.

Beginning inventory	(from the accounting records)
Plus: Net purchases	(from the accounting records)
Goods available for sale	
Less: Cost of goods sold	(estimated)
Ending inventory	(estimated)

So, a first step in estimating inventory is to estimate cost of goods sold. This estimate relies on the historical relationship among (a) net sales, (b) cost of goods sold, and (c) gross profit. Gross profit, you will recall, is simply net sales minus cost of goods sold. So, if we know what net sales are, and if we know what percentage of net sales the gross profit is, we can fairly accurately estimate cost of goods sold. Companies often sell products that have similar gross profit ratios. As a result, accounting records usually provide the information necessary to estimate the cost of ending inventory, even when a physical count is impractical.

Suppose a company began 2018 with inventory of $600,000, and on March 17 a warehouse fire destroyed the entire inventory. Company records indicate net purchases of $1,500,000 and net sales of $2,000,000 prior to the fire. The gross profit ratio in each of the previous three years has been very close to 40%. Illustration 9–4 shows how the company can estimate the cost of the inventory destroyed for its insurance claim.

A Word of Caution

The gross profit method provides only an estimate. The key to obtaining good estimates is the reliability of the gross profit ratio. The ratio usually is estimated from relationships between sales and cost of goods sold. However, the current relationship may differ from the past. In that case, all available information should be used to make necessary adjustments. For example, the company may have made changes in the markup percentage of some of its

The key to obtaining good estimates is the reliability of the gross profit ratio.

Illustration 9–4
Gross Profit Method

Beginning inventory (from records)		$ 600,000
Plus: Net purchases (from records)		1,500,000
Goods available for sale		2,100,000
Less: Cost of goods sold:		
Net sales	$2,000,000	
Less: Estimated gross profit of 40%	(800,000)	
Estimated cost of goods sold*		(1,200,000)
Estimated ending inventory		$ 900,000

*Alternatively, cost of goods sold can be calculated as $2,000,000 × (1 – 0.40) = $1,200,000.

products. Very often different products have different markups. In these situations, a blanket ratio should not be applied across the board. The accuracy of the estimate can be improved by grouping inventory into pools of products that have similar gross profit relationships rather than using one gross profit ratio for the entire inventory.

The company's cost flow assumption should be implicitly considered when estimating the gross profit ratio. For example, if LIFO is used and the relationship between cost and selling price has changed for recent acquisitions, this would suggest a ratio different from one where the average cost method was used.

Another difficulty with the gross profit method is that it does not explicitly consider possible theft or spoilage of inventory. The method assumes that if the inventory was not sold, then it must be on hand at the end of the period. Suspected theft or spoilage would require an adjustment to estimates obtained using the gross profit method.

The *gross profit method* is not acceptable for the preparation of annual financial statements.

Because of these deficiencies, the gross profit method is not allowed under generally accepted accounting principles for annual financial statements. The method can be used for interim reports.

Additional Consideration

The gross profit ratio is, by definition, a percentage of sales. Sometimes, though, the gross profit is stated as a percentage of cost instead. In that case, it is referred to as the **markup on cost**. For instance, a 66% markup on cost is equivalent to a gross profit ratio of 40%. Here's why:

A gross profit ratio of 40% can be formulated as follows:

$$\text{Sales} = \text{Cost} + \text{Gross profit}$$
$$100\% = 60\% + 40\%$$

Now, expressing gross profit as a percentage of cost we get the following:

$$\text{Gross profit \%} \div \text{Cost\%} = \text{Gross profit as a \% of cost}$$
$$40\% \div 60\% = 66\tfrac{2}{3}\%$$

Conversely, gross profit as a percentage of cost can be converted to gross profit as a percentage of sales (the gross profit ratio) as follows:

$$\text{Gross profit as a \% of sales} = \frac{\text{Gross profit as a \% of cost}}{1 + \text{Gross profit as a \% of cost}}$$

$$\frac{66\tfrac{2}{3}\%}{1 + 66\tfrac{2}{3}\%} = 40\%$$

Be careful to note which way the percentage is being stated. If stated as a markup on cost, it can be converted to the gross profit ratio, and the gross profit method can be applied the usual way.

The Retail Inventory Method

● LO9–3

The retail inventory method is used to estimate ending inventory and cost of goods sold.

As the name implies, the retail inventory method is used by many retail companies such as Target, Walmart, Sears Holding Corporation, J.C. Penney, and Macy's. Certain retailers like auto dealers and jewelry stores, whose inventory consists of few, high-priced items, can economically use the specific identification inventory method. However, high-volume retailers selling many different items at low unit prices find the retail inventory method ideal. Its principal benefit is that a physical count of inventory is not required to estimate ending inventory and cost of goods sold.[7]

In its simplest form, the retail inventory method first estimates the amount of ending inventory (at retail) by subtracting sales (at retail) from goods available for sale (at retail). *Retail* amounts refer to current selling prices. Ending inventory (at retail) is then multiplied by the current cost-to-retail percentage to estimate ending inventory (at cost). The cost-to-retail percentage is found by dividing goods available for sale at *cost* by goods available for sale at *current selling price.*

Illustration 9–5 provides an example of the retail inventory method. It shows how Home Improvement Stores, Inc., can use the relation between its inventory's cost and retail to estimate ending inventory and cost of goods sold for the month of June.

Illustration 9–5

Retail Inventory Method—Estimating ending inventory and cost of goods sold

Home Improvement Stores, Inc., uses a periodic inventory system and the retail inventory method to estimate ending inventory and cost of goods sold. The following data are available from the company's records for the month of June:

	Cost	Retail
Beginning inventory	$ 60,000	$ 100,000
Plus: Net purchases	287,200	460,000
Goods available for sale	347,200	560,000
Cost-to-retail percentage: $\frac{\$347,200}{\$560,000} = 62\%$		
Less: Net sales		(400,000)
Estimated ending inventory at retail		$160,000
Estimated ending inventory at cost ($160,000 × 62%)	**(99,200)**	
Estimated cost of goods sold	**$248,000***	

*Goods available for sale (at cost) minus ending inventory (at cost)

Home Improvement Stores first estimates ending inventory at retail ($160,000) by subtracting net sales from goods available for sale (at retail). Ending inventory at retail is multiplied by the cost-to-retail percentage (62%), which is found by dividing goods available for sale at *cost* by goods available for sale at *current selling price.* This multiplication leads to an estimate of ending inventory of **$99,200**. This amount is subtracted from the cost of goods available for sale to estimate cost of goods sold of **$248,000.**

The retail inventory method tends to provide a more accurate estimate than the gross profit method because it's based on the current relation between cost and selling prices rather than the historical gross profit ratio. This is one reason the retail inventory method is allowed for financial reporting purposes.

Another advantage of the retail inventory method is that different cost flow methods can be explicitly incorporated into the estimation technique. In other words, we can modify the application of the method to estimate ending inventory and cost of goods sold using FIFO, LIFO, or average cost.

As shown in Illustration 9–6, American Eagle Outfitters uses the retail inventory method with average cost to value its inventory.

[7]The retail inventory method is acceptable for external financial reporting if the results of applying the method are sufficiently close to what would have been achieved using a more rigorous determination of the cost of ending inventory. Also, it's allowed by the Internal Revenue Service as a method that can be used to determine cost of goods sold for income tax purposes.

Illustration 9–6
Inventory Method Disclosure—American Eagle Outfitters
Real World Financials

Summary of Significant Accounting Policies (in part)
Merchandise Inventory
Merchandise inventory is valued at the lower of average cost and net realizable value, utilizing the retail method.

Later in the chapter we illustrate average cost and LIFO with the retail inventory method. We do not illustrate the FIFO method with the retail inventory method because it is used infrequently in practice.

Like the gross profit method, the retail inventory method also can be used to estimate the cost of inventory lost, stolen, or destroyed; for testing the overall reasonableness of physical counts; in budgeting and forecasting as well as in generating information for interim financial statements. Even though the retail method provides fairly accurate estimates, a physical count of inventory usually is performed at least once a year to verify accuracy and detect spoilage, theft, and other irregularities.[8]

Retail Terminology

Changes in the selling prices must be included in the determination of ending inventory at retail.

Our example above is simplified in that we implicitly assumed that the selling prices of beginning inventory and of merchandise purchased did not change from date of acquisition to the end of the period. This frequently is an unrealistic assumption. After the initial markup of inventory but before it has been sold, companies sometimes increase the selling price further (additional markup) or reduce the selling price (markdown). For applying the retail inventory method, we need to track the movement in the selling price until it is sold. The terms in Illustration 9–7 are associated with changing retail prices of merchandise inventory.

Illustration 9–7
Terminology Used in Applying the Retail Method

Initial markup	Original amount of markup from cost to selling price
Additional markup	Increase in selling price subsequent to initial markup
Markup cancellation	Elimination of an additional markup
Markdown	Reduction in selling price below the original selling price
Markdown cancellation	Elimination of a markdown

To illustrate, assume that a product purchased for $6 is initially listed with a selling price of $10 (that is, there is a $4 initial markup). If the selling price is subsequently increased to $12, the additional markup is $2. If the selling price is then subsequently decreased to $10.50, the markup cancellation is $1.50. A markup cancellation reduces an additional markup but not below the original selling price. We refer to the net effect of additional markups and markup cancellations ($2.00 – 1.50 = $0.50) as the **net markup**. Illustration 9–8A depicts these events.

Now, let's say the selling price of the product, purchased for $6 and initially marked up to $10, is reduced to $7. The markdown is $3. If the selling price is later increased to $8, the markdown cancellation is $1. A markdown cancellation reduces a markdown but not above the original selling price. We refer to the net effect of markdowns and markdown cancellations ($3 – 1 = $2) as the **net markdown**. Illustration 9–8B depicts this possibility.

Net markups and *net markdowns* are included in the retail column to determine ending inventory at retail.

When applying the retail inventory method, *net markups and net markdowns must be included in the determination of ending inventory at retail.* We now continue our illustration of the retail inventory method, but expand it to incorporate markups and markdowns as well as to approximate cost by each of the alternative inventory cost flow methods.

[8]The retail inventory method also is allowable under IFRS. "Inventories," *International Accounting Standard No. 2 (IASCF)*, as amended effective January 1, 2016, par. 22.

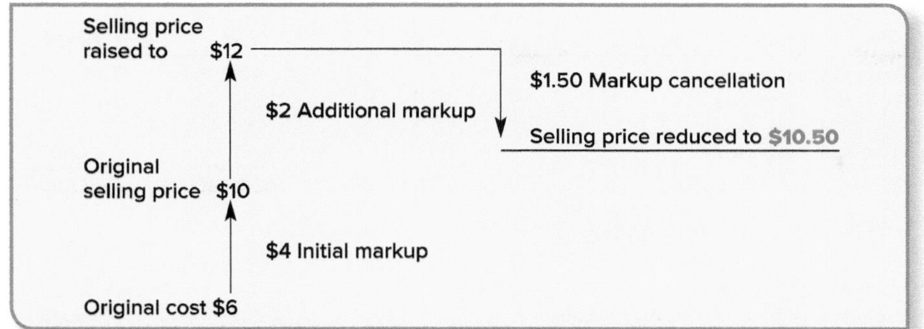

Illustration 9–8A
Retail Inventory Method Terminology

Illustration 9–8B
Retail Inventory Method Terminology

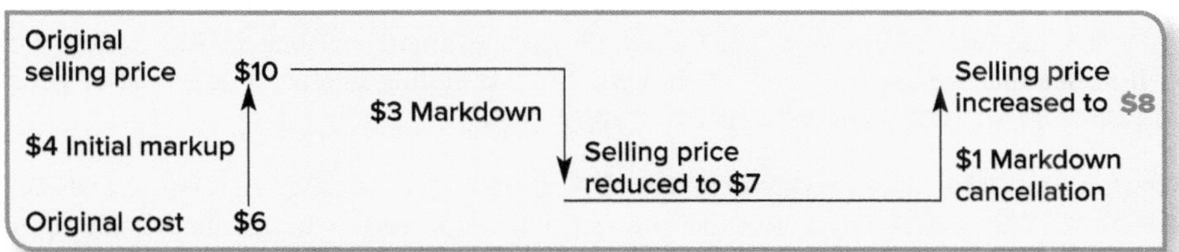

Cost Flow Methods

Let's continue our example of Home Improvement Stores, Inc., from Illustration 9–5. We'll use the data in Illustration 9–9 to see how the retail inventory method can be used to approximate different cost flow assumptions.

Illustration 9–9
The Retail Inventory Method—Various Cost Flow Methods

Home Improvement Stores, Inc., uses a periodic inventory system and the retail inventory method to estimate ending inventory and cost of goods sold. The following data are available from the company's records for the month of July:

	Cost	Retail
Beginning inventory	$ 99,200	$160,000
Net purchases	305,280*	470,000**
Net markups		10,000
Net markdowns		8,000
Net sales		434,000†

*Purchases at cost less returns, plus freight-in.
**Original selling price of purchased goods less returns at retail.
†Gross sales less returns.

APPROXIMATING AVERAGE COST. Recall that the average cost method assumes that cost of goods sold and ending inventory each consist of a *mixture* of all the goods available for sale. So when we use the retail method to approximate average cost, the cost-to-retail percentage should be based on the weighted averages of the costs and retail amounts for *all* goods available for sale. This is achieved by calculating the cost-to-retail percentage by dividing the total cost of goods available for sale by total goods available for sale at retail. When this average percentage is applied to ending inventory at retail, we get an estimate of ending inventory at average cost.

To approximate average cost, the cost-to-retail percentage is determined for *all* goods available for sale.

We demonstrate the retail inventory method approximating average costs for July in Illustration 9–10. Notice that both markups and markdowns are included in the determination of goods available for sale at retail.

Illustration 9–10

Retail Inventory Method—Average Cost

	Cost	Retail
Beginning inventory	$ 99,200	$ 160,000
Plus: Net purchases	305,280	470,000
Net markups		10,000
Less: Net markdowns		(8,000)
Goods available for sale	404,480	632,000
Cost-to-retail percentage: $\frac{\$404,480}{\$632,000} = 64\%$		
Less: Net sales		(434,000)
Estimated ending inventory at retail		$198,000
Estimated ending inventory at cost ($198,000 × 64%)	**(126,720)**	
Estimated cost of goods sold	**$ 277,760**	

If you look back to our simplified example for the month of June in Illustration 9–5, you'll notice that we used this approach there. So, our ending inventory and cost of goods sold estimates for June were estimates of average cost.[9]

● LO9–4

APPROXIMATING AVERAGE LOWER OF COST OR MARKET—THE CONVENTIONAL RETAIL METHOD. Recall from our discussion earlier in the chapter that companies using the retail inventory method report inventory in the balance sheet at the lower of cost or market. Fortunately, we can apply the retail inventory method in such a way that the lower of average cost or market is approximated. This method often is referred to as the **conventional retail method**. We apply the method by *excluding markdowns from the calculation of the cost-to-retail percentage.* Markdowns still are subtracted in the retail column but only after the percentage is calculated. To approximate lower of average cost or market, the retail method is modified as shown in Illustration 9–11.

To approximate the lower of average cost or market, markdowns are not included in the calculation of the cost-to-retail percentage.

Illustration 9–11

Retail Inventory Method—Conventional

	Cost	Retail
Beginning inventory	$ 99,200	$ 160,000
Plus: Net purchases	305,280	470,000
Net markups		10,000
Goods available for sale (excluding net markdowns)	404,480	640,000
Cost-to-retail percentage: $\frac{\$404,480}{\$640,000} = 63.2\%$		
Less: Net markdowns		(8,000)
Goods available for sale (including net markdowns)		632,000
Less: Net sales		(434,000)
Estimated ending inventory at retail		$198,000
Estimated ending inventory at cost ($198,000 × 63.2%)	**(125,136)**	
Estimated cost of goods sold	**$ 279,344**	

Notice that by not subtracting net markdowns from the denominator, the cost-to-retail percentage is lower than it was previously (63.2% versus 64%). This always will be the case when markdowns exist. As a result, the cost approximation of ending inventory always will be less when markdowns exist.

The logic for using this approximation is that a markdown is evidence of a reduction in the utility of inventory.

To understand why this lower amount approximates the lower of average cost or market, we need to realize that markdowns usually occur when obsolescence, spoilage, overstocking, price declines, or competition has lessened the utility of the merchandise. To recognize

[9]We also implicitly assumed no net markups or markdowns in Illustration 9–5.

this decline in utility in the period it occurs, we exclude net markdowns from the calculation of the cost-to-retail percentage. It should be emphasized that this approach provides only an *approximation* of what ending inventory might be as opposed to applying the lower of cost or market rule in the more exact way described earlier in the chapter.

Also notice that the ending inventory at retail is the same using both approaches ($198,000). This will be the case regardless of the cost flow method used because in all approaches this amount reflects the ending inventory at current retail prices.

The conventional retail variation generally is not used in combination with LIFO. This does not mean that a company using LIFO ignores the lower of cost or market rule. Any obsolete or slow-moving inventory that has not been marked down by year-end can be written down to market after the estimation of inventory using the retail method. This usually is not a significant problem. If prices are rising, LIFO ending inventory includes old lower-priced items whose costs are likely to be lower than current market. The conventional retail variation could be applied to the FIFO method.

Assume retail prices remain stable.

THE LIFO RETAIL METHOD. The last-in, first-out (LIFO) method assumes that units sold are those most recently acquired. When there's a net increase in inventory quantity during a period, the use of LIFO results in ending inventory that includes the beginning inventory as well as one or more additional layers added during the period. When there's a net decrease in inventory quantity, LIFO layer(s) are liquidated. In applying LIFO to the retail method in the simplest way, we assume that the retail prices of goods remained stable during the period. This assumption, which is relaxed later in the chapter, allows us to look at the beginning and ending inventory in dollars to determine if inventory quantity has increased or decreased.

If inventory at retail increases during the year, a new layer is added.

We'll use the numbers from our previous example to illustrate using the retail method to approximate LIFO so we can compare the results with those of the conventional retail method. Recall that beginning inventory at retail is $160,000 and ending inventory at retail is $198,000. If we assume stable retail prices, inventory quantity must have increased during the year. This means ending inventory includes the beginning inventory layer of $160,000 ($99,200 at cost) as well as some additional merchandise purchased during the period. To estimate total ending inventory at LIFO cost, we also need to determine the inventory layer added during the period. When using the LIFO retail method, we assume no more than one inventory layer is added per period if inventory increases.[10] Each layer will carry its own cost-to-retail percentage.

Illustration 9–12 shows how Home Improvement Stores would estimate total ending inventory and cost of goods sold for the period using the LIFO retail method. The beginning inventory layer carries a cost-to-retail percentage of 62% ($99,200 ÷ $160,000). The layer of inventory added during the period is $38,000 at retail, which is determined by subtracting beginning inventory at retail from ending inventory at retail ($198,000 – $160,000). This layer will be converted to cost by multiplying it by its own cost-to-retail percentage reflecting the *current* period's ratio of cost to retail amounts, in this case 64.68%.

The next period's (August's) beginning inventory will include the two distinct layers (June and July), each of which carries its own unique cost-to-retail percentage. Notice in the illustration that both net markups and net markdowns are included in the calculation of the current period's cost-to-retail percentage.

Other Issues Pertaining to the Retail Method

To focus on the key elements of the retail method, we've so far ignored some of the details of the retail process. Fundamental elements such as returns and allowances, discounts, freight, spoilage, and shortages can complicate the retail method.

Recall that net purchases is found by adding freight-in to purchases and subtracting both purchase returns and purchase discounts. When these components are considered separately in the retail method, purchase returns are deducted from purchases on both the cost and

[10]Of course, any number of layers at different costs can actually be added through the years. When using the regular LIFO method, rather than LIFO retail, we would keep track of each of those layers.

Illustration 9–12
LIFO Retail Method

	Cost	Retail
Beginning inventory	$ 99,200	$160,000
Plus: Net purchases	305,280	470,000
Net markups		10,000
Less: Net markdowns		(8,000)
Goods available for sale (excluding beginning inventory)	305,280	472,000
Goods available for sale (including beginning inventory)	404,480	632,000
Beginning inventory cost-to-retail percentage: $\frac{\$99,200}{\$160,000} = 62.00\%$		
July cost-to-retail percentage: $\frac{\$305,280}{\$472,000} = 64.68\%$		
Less: Net sales		(434,000)
Estimated ending inventory at retail		$198,000
Estimated ending inventory at cost (calculated below)	**(123,778)**	
Estimated cost of goods sold	**$280,702**	

Calculation of ending inventory at cost:

	Retail	Cost
Beginning inventory	$160,000 × 62.00% =	$ 99,200
Current period's layer	38,000 × 64.68% =	24,578
Estimated ending inventory	$198,000	**$123,778**

Each layer has its own cost-to-retail percentage.

retail side (at different amounts) and freight-in is added only to the cost side in determining net purchases. If the gross method is used to record purchases, purchase discounts taken also are deducted in determining the cost of net purchases.

If sales are recorded net of employee discounts, the discounts are added to sales.

Likewise, net sales is determined by subtracting sales returns from sales. However, sales discounts are *not* subtracted because to do so would cause the inventory to be overstated. Sales discounts do not represent an adjustment in selling price but a financial incentive for customers to pay early. On the other hand, when sales are recorded net of employee discounts, the discounts are *added* to net sales before sales are deducted in the retail column.

For example, suppose an item of merchandise purchased for $6 is initially marked up to $10. Original selling price is therefore $10. When the item is sold, we deduct sales of $10 from the retail column. But if the item is sold to an employee for $7 (a $3 employee discount) and recorded as a $7 sale, the $3 employee discount must be added back to sales so the full $10 is deducted from goods available at retail to arrive at ending inventory at retail.

We also need to consider spoilage, breakage, and theft. So far we've assumed that by subtracting goods sold from goods available for sale, we find ending inventory. It's possible, though, that some of the goods available for sale were lost to such shortages and therefore do not remain in ending inventory.

Normal shortages are deducted in the retail column *after* the calculation of the cost-to-retail percentage.

Abnormal shortages are deducted in both the cost and retail columns *before* the calculation of the cost-to-retail percentage.

To take these shortages into account when using the retail method, we deduct the retail value of inventory lost due to spoilage, breakage, or theft in the retail column. These losses are expected for most retail ventures so they are referred to as *normal shortages* (spoilage, breakage, etc.), and are deducted in the retail column *after* the calculation of the cost-to-retail percentage. Because these losses are anticipated, they are included implicitly in the determination of selling prices. Including normal spoilage in the calculation of the percentage would distort the normal relationship between cost and retail. *Abnormal shortages* should be deducted in both the cost and retail columns *before* the calculation of the cost-to-retail percentage. These losses are not anticipated and are not included in the determination of selling prices.

We recap the treatment of special elements in the application of the retail method in Illustration 9–13 and illustrate the use of some of them in the concept review exercise that follows.

Illustration 9–13 Recap of Other Retail Method Elements

Element	Treatment
Before calculating the cost-to-retail percentage:	
Freight-in	*Added* in the cost column.
Purchase returns	*Deducted* in both the cost and retail columns.
Purchase discounts taken (if gross method used to record purchases)	*Deducted* in the cost column.
Abnormal shortages (spoilage, breakage, theft)	*Deducted* in both the cost and retail columns.
After calculating the cost-to-retail percentage:	
Normal shortages (spoilage, breakage, theft)	*Deducted* in the retail column.
Employee discounts (if sales recorded net of discounts)	*Added* to net sales.

Concept Review Exercise

RETAIL INVENTORY METHOD

The Henderson Company uses the retail inventory method to estimate ending inventory and cost of goods sold. The following data are available in Henderson's accounting records:

	Cost	Retail
Beginning inventory	$ 8,000	$12,000
Purchases	68,000	98,000
Freight-in	3,200	
Purchase returns	3,000	4,200
Net markups		6,000
Net markdowns		2,400
Normal spoilage		1,800
Net sales		92,000

The company records sales net of employee discounts. These discounts totaled $2,300.

Required:

1. Estimate Henderson's ending inventory and cost of goods sold for the year using the average cost retail method.
2. Estimate Henderson's ending inventory and cost of goods sold for the year using the conventional retail method.
3. Estimate Henderson's ending inventory and cost of goods sold for the year using the LIFO retail method.

Solution:

1. Estimate Henderson's ending inventory and cost of goods sold for the year using the average cost retail method.

	Cost	Retail
Beginning inventory	$ 8,000	$ 12,000
Plus: Purchases	68,000	98,000
Freight-in	3,200	
Less: Purchase returns	(3,000)	(4,200)
Plus: Net markups		6,000
Less: Net markdowns		(2,400)
Goods available for sale	76,200	109,400

Cost-to-retail percentage: $\frac{\$76,200}{\$109,400} = 69.65\%$

(continued)

		Cost	Retail
Less: Normal spoilage			(1,800)
Sales:			
Net sales	$92,000		
Add back employee discounts	2,300		(94,300)
Estimated ending inventory at retail			$ 13,300
Estimated ending inventory at cost (69.65% × $13,300)		(9,263)	
Estimated cost of goods sold		$66,937	

2. Estimate Henderson's ending inventory and cost of goods sold for the year using the conventional retail method.

		Cost	Retail
Beginning inventory		$ 8,000	$ 12,000
Plus: Purchases		68,000	98,000
Freight-in		3,200	
Less: Purchase returns		(3,000)	(4,200)
Plus: Net markups			6,000
			111,800
Cost-to-retail percentage: $\frac{\$76,200}{\$111,800} = 68.16\%$			
Less: Net markdowns			(2,400)
Goods available for sale		76,200	109,400
Less: Normal spoilage			(1,800)
Sales:			
Net sales	$92,000		
Add back employee discounts	2,300		(94,300)
Estimated ending inventory at retail			$ 13,300
Estimated ending inventory at cost (68.16% × $13,300)		(9,065)	
Estimated cost of goods sold		$67,135	

3. Estimate Henderson's ending inventory and cost of goods sold for the year using the LIFO retail method.

		Cost	Retail
Beginning inventory		$ 8,000	$ 12,000
Plus: Purchases		68,000	98,000
Freight-in		3,200	
Less: Purchase returns		(3,000)	(4,200)
Plus: Net markups			6,000
Less: Net markdowns			(2,400)
Goods available for sale (excluding beginning inventory)		68,200	97,400
Goods available for sale (including beginning inventory)		76,200	109,400
Cost-to-retail percentage: $\frac{\$68,200}{\$97,400} = 70.02\%$			
Less: Normal spoilage			(1,800)
Sales:			
Net sales	$92,000		
Add back employee discounts	2,300		(94,300)
Estimated ending inventory at retail			$ 13,300
Estimated ending inventory at cost (see below)		(8,910)	
Estimated cost of goods sold		$67,290	

	Retail	Cost
Beginning inventory	$12,000 × 66.67%* =	$8,000
Current period's layer	1,300 × 70.02% =	910
Estimated Ending Inventory	$13,300	$8,910

*$8,000 ÷ $12,000 = 66.67%

PART C

Dollar-Value LIFO Retail

● LO9–5

In our earlier discussion of the LIFO retail method, we assumed that the retail prices of the inventory remained stable during the period. If you recall from Illustration 9–12, we compared the ending inventory (at retail) with the beginning inventory (at retail) to see if inventory had increased. If the dollar amount of ending inventory exceeded the beginning amount, we assumed a new LIFO layer had been added. But this isn't necessarily true. It may be that the dollar amount of ending inventory exceeded the beginning amount simply because retail prices increased, without an actual change in the quantity of goods. So, to see if there's been a "real" increase in quantity, we need a way to eliminate the effect of any price changes before we compare the ending inventory with the beginning inventory. Fortunately, we can accomplish this by combining two methods we've already discussed—the LIFO retail method (Part B of this chapter) and dollar-value LIFO (previous chapter). The combination is called the **dollar-value LIFO retail method**.

FINANCIAL Reporting Case

Q1, p. 465

Allow for retail prices to change during the period.

Using the retail method

To illustrate, we return to the Home Improvement Stores situation (Illustration 9–12) in which we applied LIFO retail. We keep the same inventory data, but change the illustration from the month of July to the fiscal year 2018. This allows us to build into Illustration 9–12A a significant change in retail prices over the year of 10% (an increase in the retail price index from 1.00 to 1.10). We follow the LIFO retail procedure up to the point of comparing the ending inventory with the beginning inventory. However, because prices have risen, the apparent increase in inventory is only partly due to an additional layer of inventory and partly due to the increase in retail prices. The real increase is found by deflating the ending inventory amount to beginning of the year prices before comparing beginning and ending amounts. We did this with the dollar-value LIFO technique discussed in the previous chapter.[11]

FINANCIAL Reporting Case

Q2, p. 465

Illustration 9–12A

The Dollar-Value LIFO Retail Method

	Cost	Retail
Beginning inventory	$ 99,200	$160,000
Plus: Net purchases	305,280	470,000
Net markups		10,000
Less: Net markdowns		(8,000)
Goods available for sale (excluding beginning inventory)	305,280	472,000
Goods available for sale (including beginning inventory)	404,480	632,000
Base layer cost-to-retail percentage: $\frac{\$99,200}{\$160,000} = 62\%$		
2018 layer cost-to-retail percentage: $\frac{\$305,280}{\$472,000} = 64.68\%$		
Less: Net sales		(434,000)
Ending inventory at current year retail prices		$198,000
Estimated ending inventory at cost (calculated below)	**(113,430)**	
Estimated cost of goods sold	**$ 291,050**	

Calculation of ending inventory at cost:

Ending Inventory at Year-End Retail Prices	Step 1 Ending Inventory at Base Year Retail Prices	Step 2 Inventory Layers at Base Year Retail Prices	Step 3 Inventory Layers Converted to LIFO Cost
$198,000 (assumed) →	$\frac{\$198,000}{1.10} = \$180,000$ →	$180,000	
		160,000 (base) × 1.00 × 0.62	= $ 99,200
		20,000 (2018) × 1.10 × 0.6468 =	14,230
Total ending inventory at dollar-value LIFO retail cost			$113,430

[11]The index used here is analogous to the cost index used in regular DVL except that it reflects the change in retail prices rather than in acquisition costs.

Each layer year carries its unique retail price index and its unique cost-to-retail percentage.

In this illustration, the ending inventory (at retail) of $198,000 is restated to base year prices ($180,000). Comparing this restated amount to beginning inventory layer of $160,000 reveals that a layer of $20,000 has been added in 2018. Multiplying each layer by its retail price index and by its cost-to-retail percentage converts it from retail to cost. The two layers are added to derive ending inventory at dollar-value LIFO retail cost.

When additional layers are added in subsequent years, their LIFO amounts are determined the same way. For illustration, let's assume ending inventory in 2019 is $226,200 at current retail prices and the price level has risen to 1.16. Also assume that the cost-to-retail percentage for 2019 net purchases is 63%. In Illustration 9–12B, the ending inventory is converted to base year retail prices (step 1). This amount is apportioned into layers, each at base year retail prices (step 2). Layers then are converted to LIFO costs (step 3).

Illustration 9–12B

The Dollar-Value LIFO Retail Inventory Method

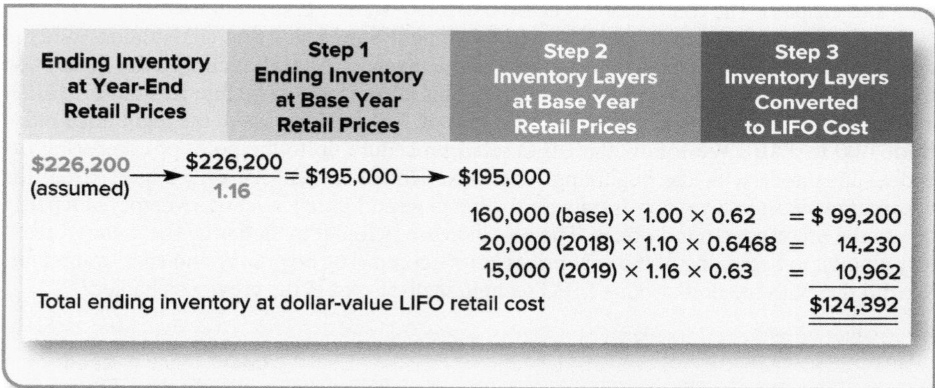

Ending Inventory at Year-End Retail Prices	Step 1 Ending Inventory at Base Year Retail Prices	Step 2 Inventory Layers at Base Year Retail Prices	Step 3 Inventory Layers Converted to LIFO Cost
$226,200 (assumed) →	$226,200 / 1.16 = $195,000 →	$195,000	
		160,000 (base) × 1.00 × 0.62	= $ 99,200
		20,000 (2018) × 1.10 × 0.6468	= 14,230
		15,000 (2019) × 1.16 × 0.63	= 10,962
Total ending inventory at dollar-value LIFO retail cost			$124,392

Now, let's assume that ending inventory in 2019 is $204,160 at current retail prices (instead of $226,200 as in the previous example) and the price level has risen to 1.16. Also assume that the cost-to-retail percentage for 2019 net purchases is 63%. Step 1 converts the ending inventory to a base year price of $176,000 ($204,160 ÷ 1.16).

Recall from the prior example that ending inventory in 2018 at base year prices was $180,000 (see Illustration 9–12B). The decrease in ending inventory to $176,000 at base year prices indicates that inventory *decreased* during 2019. In this case, no 2019 layer is added, and 2019 ending inventory at dollar-value LIFO retail of $110,584 is determined in Illustration 9–12C.

Illustration 9–12C

The Dollar-Value LIFO Retail Inventory Method

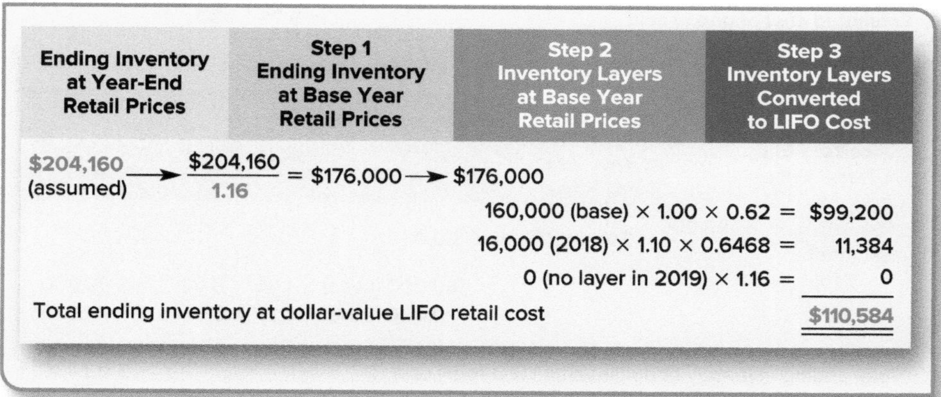

Ending Inventory at Year-End Retail Prices	Step 1 Ending Inventory at Base Year Retail Prices	Step 2 Inventory Layers at Base Year Retail Prices	Step 3 Inventory Layers Converted to LIFO Cost
$204,160 (assumed) →	$204,160 / 1.16 = $176,000 →	$176,000	
		160,000 (base) × 1.00 × 0.62 =	$99,200
		16,000 (2018) × 1.10 × 0.6468 =	11,384
		0 (no layer in 2019) × 1.16 =	0
Total ending inventory at dollar-value LIFO retail cost			$110,584

When inventory decreases, a layer is liquidated.

A portion of the 2018 inventory layer has been liquidated—reduced from $20,000 to $16,000 at base year prices—to reduce total inventory at base year prices to $176,000.

As we mentioned earlier in this section, many high-volume retailers selling many different items use the retail method. Costco Wholesale Corporation, for example, uses the dollar-value LIFO variation of the retail method. Illustration 9–13 shows the inventory disclosure note included in the company's recent financial statements.

Merchandise Inventories (in part)

Merchandise inventories are valued at the lower of cost or market, as determined primarily by the retail inventory method, and are stated using the last-in, first-out (LIFO) method for substantially all U.S. merchandise inventories. The Company records an adjustment each quarter, if necessary, for the projected annual effect of inflation or deflation, and these estimates are adjusted to actual results determined at year-end, after actual inflation rates and inventory levels for the year have been determined.

Illustration 9–13

Disclosure of Inventory Method—Costco Wholesale Corporation

Real World Financials

Concept Review Exercise

DOLLAR-VALUE LIFO RETAIL METHOD

On January 1, 2018, the Nicholson Department Store adopted the dollar-value LIFO retail inventory method. Inventory transactions at both cost and retail and cost indexes for 2018 and 2019 are as follows:

	2018		2019	
	Cost	Retail	Cost	Retail
Beginning inventory	$16,000	$24,000		
Net purchases	42,000	58,500	$45,000	$58,700
Net markups		3,000		2,400
Net markdowns		1,500		1,100
Net sales		56,000		57,000
Price index:				
January 1, 2018	1.00			
December 31, 2018	1.08			
December 31, 2019	1.15			

Required:

Estimate the 2018 and 2019 ending inventory and cost of goods sold using the dollar-value LIFO retail inventory method.

Solution:

	2018		2019	
	Cost	Retail	Cost	Retail
Beginning inventory	$ 16,000	$ 24,000	$ 17,456	$ 28,000
Plus: Net purchases	42,000	58,500	45,000	58,700
Net markups		3,000		2,400
Less: Net markdowns		(1,500)		(1,100)
Goods available for sale (excluding beg. inv.)	42,000	60,000	45,000	60,000
Goods available for sale (including beg. inv.)	58,000	84,000	62,456	88,000
Base layer				
Cost-to-retail percentage: $\frac{\$16,000}{\$24,000} = 66.67\%$				
2018				
Cost-to-retail percentage: $\frac{\$42,000}{\$60,000} = 70.00\%$				
2019				
Cost-to-retail percentage: $\frac{\$45,000}{\$60,000} = 75.00\%$				
Less: Net sales		(56,000)		(57,000)
Estimated ending inv. at current year retail prices		$ 28,000		$ 31,000
Less: Estimated ending inventory at cost (below)	(17,456)		(18,345)	
Estimated cost of goods sold	$ 40,544		$ 44,111	

2018

Ending Inventory at Year-End Retail Prices	Step 1 Ending Inventory at Base Year Retail Prices	Step 2 Inventory Layers at Base Year Retail Prices	Step 3 Inventory Layers Converted to Cost
$28,000 (above)	$\frac{\$28,000}{1.08}$ = $25,926	$24,000 (base) × 1.00 × 66.67% =	$16,000
		1,926 (2018) × 1.08 × 70.00% =	1,456
Total ending inventory at dollar-value LIFO retail cost			$17,456

2019

Ending Inventory at Year-End Retail Prices	Step 1 Ending Inventory at Base Year Retail Prices	Step 2 Inventory Layers at Base Year Retail Prices	Step 3 Inventory Layers Converted to Cost
$31,000 (above)	$\frac{\$31,000}{1.15}$ = $26,957	$24,000 (base) × 1.00 × 66.67% =	$16,000
		1,926 (2018) × 1.08 × 70.00% =	1,456
		1,031 (2019) × 1.15 × 75.00% =	889
Total ending inventory at dollar-value LIFO retail cost			$18,345

PART D

Change in Inventory Method and Inventory Errors

Change in Inventory Method

LO9–6

Accounting principles should be applied consistently from period to period to allow for comparability of operating results. However, changes within a company as well as changes in the external economic environment may require a company to change an accounting method. As we mentioned in Chapter 8, in the past, high inflation periods motivated many companies to switch to LIFO for the tax benefit.

Specific accounting treatment and disclosures are prescribed for companies that change accounting principles. Chapter 4 introduced the subject of accounting changes and Chapter 20 provides in-depth coverage of the topic. Here we provide an overview of how changes in inventory methods are reported.

Most Inventory Changes

Changes in inventory methods, other than a change to LIFO, are accounted for retrospectively.

Recall from our brief discussion in Chapter 4 that most voluntary changes in accounting principles are reported retrospectively. This means reporting all previous periods' financial statements as if the new method had been used in all prior periods. Changes in inventory methods, other than a change to LIFO, are treated this way. We discuss the *change to LIFO* exception in the next section. In Chapter 4, we briefly discussed the steps a company undertakes to account for a change in accounting principle. We demonstrate those steps in Illustration 9–14.

Illustration 9–14
Change in Inventory Method

Autogeek, Inc., a wholesale distributor of auto parts, began business in 2015. Inventory reported in the 2017 year-end balance sheet, determined using the average cost method, was $123,000. In 2018, the company decided to change its inventory method to FIFO. If the company had used the FIFO method in 2017, ending inventory would have been $146,000. What steps should Autogeek take to report this change?

Step 1: Revise comparative financial statements.

The first step is to revise prior years' financial statements. That is, for each year reported in the comparative statements, Autogeek makes those statements appear as if the newly adopted inventory method, FIFO, had been applied all along. In its balance sheets, assuming that the company presents balance sheets for two years for comparative purposes, the company would report 2018 inventory by its newly adopted method, FIFO, and also would revise the amounts it reported last year for its 2017 inventory. In its 2018 and prior year income statements, cost of goods sold would also reflect the new method.

In its statements of shareholders' equity, Autogeek would report retained earnings each year as if it had used FIFO all along. And, for the earliest year reported, the company would revise beginning retained earnings that year to reflect the cumulative income effect of the difference in inventory methods for all prior years. You will see this step illustrated in Chapter 20 after you have studied the statement of shareholders' equity in more depth.

Step 2: The affected accounts are adjusted.

Autogeek also would record a journal entry to adjust the book balances from their current amounts to what those balances would have been using FIFO. Because differences in cost of goods sold and income are reflected in retained earnings, as are the income tax effects, the journal entry updates inventory, retained earnings, and the appropriate income tax account. We ignore the income tax effects here but include those effects in an illustration in Chapter 20. The journal entry below, *ignoring income taxes,* increases the 2018 beginning inventory to the FIFO basis amount of $146,000 and increases retained earnings by the same amount, because that's what the increase in prior years' income would have been had FIFO been used.

Inventory ($146,000 − 123,000)	23,000	
Retained earnings		23,000

Step 3: A disclosure note provides additional information.

Autogeek must provide in a disclosure note clear explanation of why the change to FIFO is preferable. The note also would indicate the effects of the change on (a) income from continuing operations, (b) net income, (c) each line-item affected, (d) earnings per share, and (e) the cumulative effect of the change on retained earnings or other components of equity as of the beginning of the earliest period presented.

We see in Illustration 9–15 an example of such a note in a recent annual report of CVS Health Corporation when it changed its inventory method for retail/LTC inventories to the average cost method.

Inventory (in part)

Effective January 1, 2015, the Company changed its methods of accounting for "front store" inventories in the Retail/LTC Segment. Prior to 2015, the Company valued front store inventories at the lower of cost or market on a first-in, first-out ("FIFO") basis in retail stores using the retail inventory method and in distribution centers using the FIFO cost method. Effective January 1, 2015, all front store inventories in the Retail/LTC Segment have been valued at the lower of cost or market using the weighted average cost method.

These changes were made primarily to provide the Company with better information to manage its retail front store operations and to bring all of the Company's inventories to a common inventory valuation methodology. The Company believes the weighted average cost method is preferable to the retail inventory method and the FIFO cost method because it results in greater precision in the determination of cost of revenues and inventories at the stock keeping unit ("SKU") level and results in a consistent inventory valuation method for all of the Company's inventories as all of the Company's remaining inventories, which consist of prescription drugs, were already being valued using the weighted average cost method.

The Company recorded the cumulative effect of these changes in accounting principle as of January 1, 2015. The effect of these changes in accounting principle as of January 1, 2015, was a decrease in inventories of $7 million, an increase in current deferred income tax assets of $3 million and a decrease in retained earnings of $4 million.

Illustration 9–15

Disclosure of Change in Inventory Method—CVS Health Corporation

Real World Financials

Change to the LIFO Method

Accounting records usually are inadequate for a company changing to *LIFO* to report the change retrospectively.

When a company changes *to the LIFO inventory method* from any other method, it usually is impossible to calculate the income effect on prior years. To do so would require assumptions as to when specific LIFO inventory layers were created in years prior to the change.

As a result, a company changing to LIFO usually does not report the change retrospectively. Instead, the LIFO method simply is used from that point on. The base year inventory for all future LIFO determinations is the beginning inventory in the year the LIFO method is adopted.[12]

A disclosure note is needed to explain (a) the nature of and justification for the change, (b) the effect of the change on current year's income and earnings per share, and (c) why retrospective application was impracticable. When Seneca Foods Corporation adopted the LIFO inventory method, it reported the change in the note shown in Illustration 9–16.

Illustration 9–16

Change in Inventory Method Disclosure—Seneca Foods Corporation

Real World Financials

10. Inventories (in part)

The Company decided to change its inventory valuation method from the FIFO method to the LIFO method. In the high inflation environment that the Company is experiencing, the Company believes that the LIFO inventory method is preferable over the FIFO method because it better compares the cost of current production to current revenue. Selling prices are established to reflect current market activity, which recognizes the increasing costs. Under FIFO, revenue and costs are not aligned. Under LIFO, the current cost of sales is matched to the current revenue.

The Company determined that retrospective application of LIFO for periods prior to the current fiscal year was impracticable because the period-specific information necessary to analyze inventories, including inventories acquired as part of the prior fiscal year's Signature acquisition, were not readily available and could not be precisely determined at the appropriate level of detail, including the commodity, size and item code information necessary to perform the detailed calculations required to retrospectively compute the internal LIFO indices applicable to prior fiscal years. The effect of this change was to reduce net earnings by $37,917,000 and $18,307,000 in the current and prior fiscal year, respectively, below that which would have been reported using the Company's previous inventory method. The reduction in earnings per share was $3.12 ($3.09 diluted) and $1.50 per share ($1.49 diluted) in the current and prior fiscal year, respectively.

As we discussed in Chapter 8, an important motivation for using LIFO in periods of rising costs is that it produces higher cost of goods sold and lowers net income and income taxes. Notice in the Seneca Foods disclosure note that the switch to LIFO did cause a decrease in net income and therefore income taxes in the year of the switch indicating an environment of increasing costs.

Additional Consideration

When changing from one generally accepted accounting principle to another, a company must justify that the change results in financial information that more properly portrays operating results and financial position. For income tax purposes, a company generally must obtain consent from the Internal Revenue Service before changing an accounting method. A special form also must be filed with the IRS when a company intends to adopt the LIFO inventory method. When a company changes from LIFO for tax purposes, it can't change back to LIFO until five tax returns have been filed using the non-LIFO method.

Inventory Errors

● LO9–7

Accounting errors must be corrected when they are discovered. In Chapter 4, we briefly discussed the correction of accounting errors, and Chapter 20 provides in-depth coverage. Here we provide an overview of the accounting treatment and disclosures in the context of inventory errors. Inventory errors include the over- or understatement of ending inventory

[12]A change to LIFO is handled the same way for income tax purposes.

due to a mistake in physical count or a mistake in pricing inventory quantities. Also, errors include the over- or understatement of purchases which could be caused by the cutoff errors described in Chapter 8.

If an inventory error is discovered in the same accounting period it occurred, the original erroneous entry should simply be reversed and the appropriate entry recorded. This situation presents no particular reporting problem.

If a *material* inventory error is discovered in an accounting period subsequent to the period in which the error was made, any previous years' financial statements that were incorrect as a result of the error are retrospectively restated to reflect the correction.[13] And, of course, any account balances that are incorrect as a result of the error are corrected by journal entry. If, due to an error affecting net income, retained earnings is one of the incorrect accounts, the correction is reported as a prior period adjustment to the beginning balance on the statement of shareholders' equity.[14] In addition, a disclosure note is needed to describe the nature of the error and the impact of its correction on net income, each line-item affected, and earnings per share.

For material errors, previous years' financial statements are retrospectively restated.

Incorrect balances are corrected.

When analyzing inventory errors, it's helpful to visualize the way cost of goods sold, net income, and retained earnings are determined (see Illustration 9–17). Beginning inventory and net purchases are *added* in the calculation of cost of goods sold. If either of these is overstated (understated) then cost of goods sold would be overstated (understated). On the other hand, ending inventory is *deducted* in the calculation of cost of goods sold, so if ending inventory is overstated (understated) then cost of goods sold is understated (overstated). Of course, errors that affect income also will affect income taxes. In the illustration that follows, we ignore the tax effects of the errors and focus on the errors themselves rather than their tax aspects.

A correction of retained earnings is reported as a prior period adjustment.

A disclosure note describes the nature and the impact of the error.

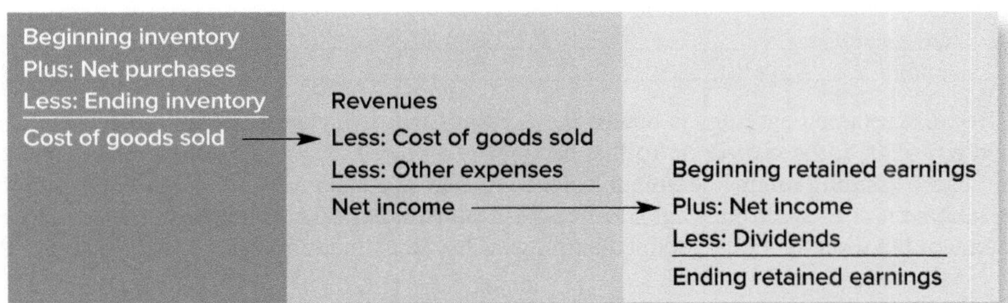

Illustration 9–17
Visualizing the Effect of Inventory Errors

Let's look at an example in Illustration 9–18.

Illustration 9–18
Inventory Error Correction

The Barton Company uses a periodic inventory system. At the end of 2017, a mathematical error caused an $800,000 overstatement of ending inventory. Ending inventories for 2018 and 2019 are correctly determined.

The way we correct this error depends on when the error is discovered. Assuming that the error is not discovered until after 2018, the 2017 and 2018 effects of the error, ignoring income tax effects, are shown below. The overstated and understated amounts are $800,000 in each instance.

(continued)

[13]If the effect of the error is not material, it is simply corrected in the year of discovery.

[14]The prior period adjustment is applied to beginning retained earnings for the year following the error, or for the earliest year being reported in the comparative financial statements when the error occurs prior to the earliest year presented. The retained earnings balances in years after the first year also are adjusted to what those balances would be if the error had not occurred, but a company may choose not to explicitly report those adjustments as separate line items.

(concluded)

Analysis: U = Understated O = Overstated

2017		2018	
Beginning inventory		Beginning inventory	O – 800,000
Plus: Net purchases		Plus: Net purchases	
Less: Ending inventory	O – 800,000	Less: Ending inventory	
Cost of goods sold	U – 800,000	Cost of goods sold	O – 800,000
Revenues		Revenues	
Less: Cost of goods sold	U – 800,000	Less: Cost of goods sold	O – 800,000
Less: Other expenses		Less: Other expenses	
Net income	O – 800,000	Net income	U – 800,000
↓		↓	
Retained earnings	O – 800,000	Retained earnings	*corrected*

When the Inventory Error Is Discovered the Following Year

Previous years' financial statements are retrospectively restated.

First, let's assume the error is discovered in 2018. The 2017 financial statements that were incorrect as a result of the error are retrospectively restated to reflect the correct inventory amount, cost of goods sold, net income, and retained earnings when those statements are reported again for comparative purposes in the 2018 annual report. The following journal entry, *ignoring income taxes,* corrects the error.

A journal entry corrects any incorrect account balance.

Retained earnings	800,000	
Inventory		800,000

When retained earnings requires correction, a *prior period adjustment* is made on the statement of shareholders' equity.

Because retained earnings is one of the accounts that is incorrect, when the error is discovered in 2018, the correction to that account is reported as a *prior period adjustment* to the 2018 beginning retained earnings balance in Barton's statement of shareholders' equity (or statement of retained earnings). Prior period adjustments do not flow through the income statement but directly adjust retained earnings. This adjustment is illustrated in Chapter 20.

When the Inventory Error Is Discovered Two Years Later

If the error in 2017 isn't discovered until 2019, the 2018 financial statements also are retrospectively restated to reflect the correct cost of goods sold and net income even though no correcting entry would be needed at that point. Inventory and retained earnings would not require adjustment. The error has self-corrected and no prior period adjustment is needed.

A disclosure note describes the nature of the error and the impact of the correction on income.

Also, a disclosure note in Barton's annual report should describe the nature of the error and the impact of its correction on each year's net income (overstated by $800,000 in 2017; understated by $800,000 in 2018), the line items affected, and earnings per share.

Concept Review Exercise

INVENTORY ERRORS

In 2018, the controller of the Fleischman Wholesale Beverage Company discovered the following material errors related to the 2016 and 2017 financial statements:

a. Inventory at the end of 2016 was understated by $50,000.

b. Late in 2017, a $3,000 purchase was incorrectly recorded as a $33,000 purchase. The invoice has not yet been paid.

c. Inventory at the end of 2017 was overstated by $20,000.

The company uses a periodic inventory system.

Required:

1. Assuming that the errors were discovered after the 2017 financial statements were issued, analyze the effect of the errors on 2016 and 2017 cost of goods sold, net income, and retained earnings. Ignore income taxes.
2. Prepare a journal entry to correct the errors.

Solution:

1. **Analysis: U = Understated O = Overstated**

2016		2017	
Beginning inventory		Beginning inventory	U – 50,000
Plus: Net purchases		Plus: Net purchases	O – 30,000
Less: Ending inventory	U – 50,000	Less: Ending inventory	O – 20,000
Cost of goods sold	O – 50,000	Cost of goods sold	U – 40,000
Revenues		Revenues	
Less: Cost of goods sold	O – 50,000	Less: Cost of goods sold	U – 40,000
Less: Other expenses		Less: Other expenses	
Net income	U – 50,000	Net income	O – 40,000
↓		↓	
Retained earnings	U – 50,000	Retained earnings	U – 10,000

2. Prepare a journal entry to correct the errors.

	Debit	Credit
Accounts payable	30,000	
Inventory		20,000
Retained earnings		10,000

Earnings Quality

A change in the accounting method a company uses to value inventory is one way managers can artificially manipulate income. However, this method of income manipulation is transparent. As we learned in a previous section, the effect on income of switching from one inventory method to another must be disclosed. That disclosure restores comparability between periods and enhances earnings quality.

Inventory write-downs often are cited as a method used to shift income between periods.

On the other hand, inventory write-downs are included in the broader category of "big bath" accounting techniques some companies use to manipulate earnings. By overstating the write-down, profits are increased in future periods as the inventory is used or sold. When the demand for many high technology products decreased significantly in late 2000 and early 2001, several companies, including Sycamore Networks, Cisco Systems, Lucent Technologies, and JDS Uniphase, recorded large inventory write-offs, some in the billions of dollars. Certainly, these write-offs reflected the existing economic environment. However, some analysts questioned the size of some of the write-offs. For example, William Schaff, an investment officer at Bay Isle Financial, noted that Cisco's $2 billion write-off was approximately equal to the balance of inventory on hand at the end of the previous quarter and about equal to the cost of goods actually sold during the quarter.

A financial analyst must carefully consider the effect of any significant asset write-down on the assessment of a company's permanent earnings.

Financial Reporting Case Solution

© Justin Sullivan/Getty Images

1. **How does Dollar General avoid counting all its inventory every time it produces financial statements? *(p. 483)*** Dollar General uses the dollar-value LIFO retail inventory method. The retail inventory estimation technique avoids the counting of ending inventory by keeping track of goods available for sale not only at cost but also at retail prices. Each period's sales, at sales prices, are deducted from the retail amount of goods available for sale to arrive at ending inventory at retail. This amount is then converted to cost using a cost-to-retail percentage.
2. **What is the index formulation used for? *(p. 483)*** The dollar-value LIFO retail method uses a price index to first convert ending inventory at retail to base year prices. Yearly LIFO layers are then determined and each layer is converted to that year's current year retail prices using the year's price index and then to cost using the layer's cost-to-retail percentage. ●

The Bottom Line

- **LO9–1** Companies that use FIFO, average cost, or any other method besides LIFO or the retail inventory method report inventory at the lower of cost or net realizable value (NRV). Net realizable value is selling price less costs to sell. Companies that use LIFO or the retail inventory method report inventory at the lower of cost or market. Market equals replacement cost, except that market should not (a) be greater than NRV (ceiling) or (b) be less than NRV minus an approximately normal profit margin (floor). (*p. 465*)
- **LO9–2** The gross profit method estimates cost of goods sold which is then subtracted from cost of goods available for sale to estimate ending inventory. The estimate of cost of goods sold is determined by subtracting an estimate of gross profit from net sales. The estimate of gross profit is determined by multiplying the historical gross profit ratio times net sales. (*p. 473*)
- **LO9–3** The retail inventory method determines the amount of ending inventory at retail by subtracting sales for the period from goods available for sale at retail. Ending inventory at retail is then converted to *cost* by multiplying it by the cost-to-retail percentage, which is based on a current relationship between cost and selling price. (*p. 475*)
- **LO9–4** By the conventional retail method, we estimate average cost at lower of cost or market. Average cost is estimated by including beginning inventory in the calculation of the cost-to-retail percentage. The lower of average cost or market is estimated by excluding markdowns from the calculation. Markdowns are subtracted in the retail column after the percentage is calculated. (*p. 478*)
- **LO9–5** By the LIFO retail method, ending inventory includes the beginning inventory plus the current year's layer. To determine layers, we compare ending inventory at retail to beginning inventory at retail and assume that no more than one inventory layer is added if inventory increases. Each layer carries its own cost-to-retail percentage which is used to convert each layer from retail to cost. The dollar-value LIFO retail inventory method combines the LIFO retail method and the dollar-value LIFO method (Chapter 8) to estimate LIFO from retail prices when the price level has changed. (*p. 483*)
- **LO9–6** Most changes in inventory methods are reported retrospectively. This means revising all previous periods' financial statements to appear as if the newly adopted inventory method had been applied all along. An exception is a change to the LIFO method. In this case, it usually is impossible to calculate the income effect on prior years. To do so would require assumptions as to when specific LIFO inventory layers were created in years prior to the change. As a result, a company changing to LIFO usually does not report the change retrospectively. Instead, the LIFO method simply is used from that point on. (*p. 486*)
- **LO9–7** If a material inventory error is discovered in an accounting period subsequent to the period in which the error is made, previous years' financial statements that were incorrect as a result of the error are retrospectively restated to reflect the correction. Account balances are corrected by journal entry. A correction of retained earnings is reported as a prior period adjustment to the beginning balance in the statement of shareholders' equity. In addition, a disclosure note is needed to describe the nature of the error and the impact of its correction on continuing operations, net income, and earnings per share. (*p. 488*)

● LO9–8 *IAS No. 2* specifies that if circumstances reveal that an inventory write-down is no longer appropriate, it must be reversed. Reversals are not permitted under U.S. GAAP. Under U.S. GAAP, the lower of cost or net realizable value rule can be applied to individual items, inventory categories, or the entire inventory. Using the international standard, the assessment usually is applied to individual items, although using inventory categories is allowed under certain circumstances. (*p. 468*) ●

Purchase Commitments

APPENDIX 9

Purchase commitments are contracts that obligate a company to purchase a specified amount of merchandise or raw materials at specified prices on or before specified dates. Companies enter into these agreements to make sure they will be able to obtain important inventory as well as to protect against increases in purchase price. However, if the purchase price decreases before the agreement is exercised, the commitment has the disadvantage of requiring the company to purchase inventory at a higher than market price. If this happens, a loss on the purchase commitment is recorded.

Purchase commitments protect the buyer against price increases and provide a supply of product.

Because purchase commitments create the possibility of this kind of loss, the loss occurs when the market price falls below the commitment price rather than when the inventory eventually is sold. This means recording the loss when the product is purchased or, if the commitment is still outstanding, at the end of the reporting period. In other words, purchases are recorded at market price when that price is lower than the contract price, and a loss is recognized for the difference. Also, losses are recognized for any purchase commitments outstanding at the end of a reporting period when market price is less than contract price. This is best understood by the example in Illustration 9A–1.

Purchases made pursuant to a purchase commitment are recorded at the lower of contract price or market price on the date the contract is executed.

Illustration 9A–1
Purchase Commitments

In July 2018, the Lassiter Company signed two purchase commitments. The first requires Lassiter to purchase inventory for $500,000 by November 15, 2018. The second requires Lassiter to purchase inventory for $600,000 by February 15, 2019. Lassiter's fiscal year-end is December 31. The company uses a perpetual inventory system.

Contract Period within Fiscal Year

The contract period for the first commitment is contained within a single fiscal year. Lassiter would record the purchase at the contract price if the market price of inventory at date of acquisition is *equal to or greater than* the contract price of $500,000.[15]

Inventory (contract price)	500,000	
Cash (or accounts payable)		500,000

Purchase inventory at the contract price.

If the market price of inventory at acquisition is *less* than the contract price, inventory is recorded at the market price and a loss is recognized.[16] For example, if the market price is $425,000 at the time of acquisition, Lassiter must still pay $500,000 (contract price) and would record the following entry:

Inventory (market price)	425,000	
Loss on purchase commitment	75,000	
Cash (or accounts payable)		500,000

If market price is less than the contract price at acquisition, a loss is recorded.

[15]In each of the following situations, if a periodic inventory system is used, purchases is debited instead of inventory.

[16]Recall from the chapter that one method of recording losses from inventory write-downs is to report the loss as a line item in the income statement.

The objective of this treatment is to associate the loss with the period in which the price declines rather than with the period in which the company eventually sells the inventory. This is consistent with recording inventory at the lower of cost or market, as you studied in the chapter.

Contract Period Extends beyond Fiscal Year

Now let's consider Lassiter's second purchase commitment that is outstanding at the end of the fiscal year 2018 (that is, the purchases have not yet been made). If the market price of inventory at the end of the year is *equal to or greater than* the contract price of $600,000, no entry is recorded. However, if the market price at year-end is *less* than the contract price, a loss must be recognized. The objective is to associate the loss with the period in which the price declines rather than with the period in which the company eventually sells the inventory. Let's say the year-end market price of the inventory for Lassiter's second purchase commitment is $540,000. The following adjusting entry is recorded:

If the market price at year-end is less than the contract price, a loss is recorded for the difference.

December 31, 2018		
Estimated loss on purchase commitment ($600,000 − 540,000)	60,000	
Estimated liability on purchase commitment		60,000

A liability is credited for estimated losses on purchase commitments.

At this point, the loss is an *estimated* loss. The actual loss, if any, will not be known until the inventory actually is purchased. The best estimate of the market price on date of purchase is the current market price, in this case $540,000. Because no inventory has been acquired, we can't credit inventory for the loss. Instead, a liability is credited because, in a sense, the loss represents an obligation to purchase inventory above market price.

The entry to record the actual purchase on or before February 15, 2019, will vary depending on the market price of the inventory at date of purchase. If the market price is unchanged or has increased from the year-end price, the following entry is made:

If market price on purchase date has not declined from year-end price, the purchase is recorded at the year-end market price.

Inventory (accounting cost)	540,000	
Estimated liability on purchase commitment	60,000	
Cash (or accounts payable)		600,000

Even if the market price of the inventory increases, there is no recovery of the $60,000 loss recognized in 2018. Similar to the method of recording inventory at the lower of cost or market, the reduced inventory value, in this case the reduced value of purchases, is considered to be the new cost and any recovery of value is ignored.

If the market price declines even further from year-end levels, an additional loss is recognized. For example, if the market price of the inventory covered by the commitment declines to $510,000, the following entry is recorded:

If market price declines further from year-end, an additional loss is recorded at acquisition.

Inventory (market price)	510,000	
Loss on purchase commitment ($540,000 − 510,000)	30,000	
Estimated liability on purchase commitment	60,000	
Cash (or accounts payable)		600,000

The total loss on this purchase commitment of $90,000 is thus allocated between 2018 and 2019 according to when the decline in value of the inventory covered by the commitment occurred.

If there are material amounts of purchase commitments outstanding at the end of a reporting period, the contract details are disclosed in a note. This disclosure is required even if no loss estimate has been recorded.

Questions For Review of Key Topics

Q 9–1 Explain the (a) lower of cost or net realizable value (LCNRV) approach and the (b) lower of cost or market (LCM) approach to valuing inventory.

Q 9–2 What are the various levels of aggregation to which the LCNRV and LCM approaches can be applied?

Q 9–3 Describe the alternative approaches for recording inventory write-downs.

Q 9–4 Explain the gross profit method of estimating ending inventory.

Q 9–5 The Rider Company uses the gross profit method to estimate ending inventory and cost of goods sold. The cost percentage is determined based on historical data. What factors could cause the estimate of ending inventory to be overstated?

Q 9–6 Explain the retail inventory method of estimating ending inventory.

Q 9–7 Both the gross profit method and the retail inventory method provide a way to estimate ending inventory. What is the main difference between the two estimation techniques?

Q 9–8 Define each of the following retail terms: initial markup, additional markup, markup cancellation, markdown, markdown cancellation.

Q 9–9 Explain how to estimate the average cost of inventory when using the retail inventory method.

Q 9–10 What is the conventional retail method?

Q 9–11 Explain the LIFO retail inventory method.

Q 9–12 Discuss the treatment of freight-in, net markups, normal spoilage, and employee discounts in the application of the retail inventory method.

Q 9–13 Explain the difference between the retail inventory method using LIFO and the dollar-value LIFO retail method.

Q 9–14 Describe the accounting treatment for a change in inventory method other than to LIFO.

Q 9–15 When a company changes its inventory method to LIFO, an exception is made for the way accounting changes usually are reported. Explain the difference in the accounting treatment of a change *to* the LIFO inventory method from other inventory method changes.

Q 9–16 Explain the accounting treatment of material inventory errors discovered in an accounting period subsequent to the period in which the error is made.

Q 9–17 It is discovered in 2018 that ending inventory in 2016 was understated. What is the effect of the understatement on the following:

2016:	Cost of goods sold
	Net income
	Ending retained earnings
2017:	Net purchases
	Cost of goods sold
	Net income
	Ending retained earnings

IFRS Q 9–18 Identify any differences between U.S. GAAP and IFRS when applying the lower of cost or net realizable value rule to inventory valuation.

Q 9–19 (Based on Appendix 9) Define purchase commitments. What is the advantage(s) of these agreements to buyers?

Q 9–20 (Based on Appendix 9) Explain how purchase commitments are recorded for the lower of contract price or market price.

Brief Exercises

BE 9–1
Lower of cost or net realizable value
● LO9–1

Ross Electronics has one product in its ending inventory. Per unit data consist of the following: cost, $20; selling price, $30; selling costs, $4. What unit value should Ross use when applying the lower of cost or net realizable value rule to ending inventory?

BE 9–2
Lower of cost or net realizable value
● LO9–1

SLR Corporation has 1,000 units of each of its two products in its year-end inventory. Per unit data for each of the products are as follows:

	Product 1	Product 2
Cost	$50	$34
Selling price	70	36
Costs to sell	6	4

Determine the carrying value of SLR's inventory assuming that the lower of cost or net realizable value (LCNRV) rule is applied to individual products. What is the before-tax income effect of the LCNRV adjustment?

BE 9–3
Lower of cost or market
● LO9–1

[This is a variation of BE 9–1, modified to focus on the lower of cost or market.] Ross Electronics has one product in its ending inventory. Per unit data consist of the following: cost, $20; replacement cost, $18; selling price, $30; selling costs, $4. The normal profit margin is 30% of selling price. What unit value should Ross use when applying the lower of cost or market (LCM) rule to ending inventory?

BE 9–4
Lower of cost or market
● LO9–1

[This is a variation of BE 9–2, modified to focus on the lower of cost or market.] SLR Corporation has 1,000 units of each of its two products in its year-end inventory. Per unit data for each of the products are as follows:

	Product 1	Product 2
Cost	$50	$34
Replacement cost	48	26
Selling price	70	36
Selling costs	6	4
Normal profit margin	10	8

Determine the carrying value of SLR's inventory assuming that the lower of cost or market (LCM) rule is applied to individual products. What is the before-tax income effect of the LCM adjustment?

BE 9–5
Gross profit method
● LO9–2

On February 26 a hurricane destroyed the entire inventory stored in a warehouse owned by the Rockford Corporation. The following information is available from the records of the company's periodic inventory system: beginning inventory, $220,000; purchases and net sales from the beginning of the year through February 26, $400,000 and $600,000, respectively; gross profit ratio, 30%. Estimate the cost of the inventory destroyed by the hurricane using the gross profit method.

BE 9–6
Gross profit method; solving for unknown
● LO9–2

Adams Corporation estimates that it lost $75,000 in inventory from a recent flood. The following information is available from the records of the company's periodic inventory system: beginning inventory, $150,000; purchases and net sales from the beginning of the year through the date of the flood, $450,000 and $700,000, respectively. What is the company's gross profit ratio?

BE 9–7
Retail inventory method; average cost
● LO9–3

Kiddie World uses a periodic inventory system and the retail inventory method to estimate ending inventory and cost of goods sold. The following data are available for the quarter ending September 30, 2018:

	Cost	Retail
Beginning inventory	$300,000	$ 450,000
Net purchases	861,000	1,210,000
Freight-in	22,000	
Net markups		48,000
Net markdowns		18,000
Net sales		1,200,000

Estimate ending inventory and cost of goods sold (average cost).

BE 9–8
Retail inventory method; LIFO
● LO9–3

Refer to the situation described in BE 9–7. Estimate ending inventory and cost of goods sold (LIFO).

BE 9–9
Conventional retail method
● LO9–4

Refer to the situation described in BE 9–7. Estimate ending inventory and cost of goods sold using the conventional method.

BE 9–10
Conventional retail method
● LO9–4

Roberson Corporation uses a periodic inventory system and the retail inventory method. Accounting records provided the following information for the 2018 fiscal year:

	Cost	Retail
Beginning inventory	$220,000	$ 400,000
Net purchases	640,000	1,180,000
Freight-in	17,800	
Net markups		16,000
Net markdowns		6,000
Normal spoilage		3,000
Net sales		1,300,000

The company records sales to employees net of discounts. These discounts totaled $15,000 for the year. Estimate ending inventory and cost of goods sold using the conventional method.

BE 9–11
Dollar-value LIFO retail
● LO9–5

On January 1, 2018, Sanderson Variety Store adopted the dollar-value LIFO retail inventory method. Accounting records provided the following information:

	Cost	Retail
Beginning inventory	$ 40,800	$ 68,000
Net purchases	155,440	270,000
Net markups		6,000
Net markdowns		8,000
Net sales		250,000
Retail price index, end of year		1.02

Estimate ending inventory using the dollar-value LIFO retail method.

BE 9–12
Dollar-value LIFO retail
● LO9–5

This exercise is a continuation of BE 9–11. During 2019, purchases at cost and retail were $168,000 and $301,000, respectively. Net markups, net markdowns, and net sales for the year were $3,000, $4,000, and $280,000, respectively. The retail price index at the end of 2019 was 1.06. Estimating ending inventory in 2019 using the dollar-value LIFO retail method.

BE 9–13
Change in inventory costing methods
● LO9–6

In 2018, Hopyard Lumber changed its inventory method from LIFO to FIFO. Inventory at the end of 2017 of $127,000 would have been $145,000 if FIFO had been used. Inventory at the end of 2018 is $162,000 using the new FIFO method but would have been $151,000 if the company had continued to use LIFO. Describe the steps Hopyard should take to report this change. What is the effect of the change on 2018 cost of goods sold?

BE 9–14
Change in inventory costing methods
● LO9–6

In 2018, Wade Window and Glass changed its inventory method from FIFO to LIFO. Inventory at the end of 2017 is $150,000. Describe the steps Wade Window and Glass should take to report this change.

BE 9–15
Inventory error
● LO9–7

In 2018, Winslow International, Inc.'s controller discovered that ending inventories for 2016 and 2017 were overstated by $200,000 and $500,000, respectively. Determine the effect of the errors on retained earnings at January 1, 2018. (Ignore income taxes.)

BE 9–16
Inventory error
● LO9–7

Refer to the situation described in BE 9–15. What steps would be taken to report the error in the 2018 financial statements?

Exercises

connect

E 9–1
Lower of cost or net realizable value
● LO9–1

Herman Company has three products in its ending inventory. Specific per unit data at the end of the year for each of the products are as follows:

	Product 1	Product 2	Product 3
Cost	$20	$ 90	$50
Selling price	40	120	70
Costs to sell	6	40	10

Required:
What unit values should Herman use for each of its products when applying the lower of cost or net realizable value (LCNRV) rule to ending inventory?

E 9–2
Lower of cost or net realizable value
● LO9–1

The inventory of Royal Decking consisted of five products. Information about the December 31, 2018, inventory is as follows:

	Per Unit	
Product	**Cost**	**Selling Price**
A	$ 40	$ 60
B	80	100
C	40	80
D	100	130
E	20	30

Costs to sell consist of a sales commission equal to 10% of selling price and shipping costs equal to 5% of cost.

Required:

What unit value should Royal Decking use for each of its products when applying the lower of cost or net realizable value (LCNRV) rule to units of ending inventory?

E 9–3
Lower of cost or net realizable value
● LO9–1

Tatum Company has four products in its inventory. Information about the December 31, 2018, inventory is as follows:

Product	Total Cost	Total Net Realizable Value
101	$120,000	$100,000
102	90,000	110,000
103	60,000	50,000
104	30,000	50,000

Required:

1. Determine the carrying value of inventory at December 31, 2018, assuming the lower of cost or net realizable value (LCNRV) rule is applied to individual products.
2. Assuming that inventory write-downs are common for Tatum Company, record any necessary year-end adjusting entry.

E 9–4
Lower of cost or market
● LO9–1

[This is a variation of E 9–1, modified to focus on the lower of cost or market.] Herman Company has three products in its ending inventory. Specific per unit data at the end of the year for each of the products are as follows:

	Product 1	Product 2	Product 3
Cost	$20	$ 90	$50
Replacement cost	18	85	40
Selling price	40	120	70
Selling costs	6	40	10
Normal profit margin	5	30	12

Required:

What unit values should Herman use for each of its products when applying the lower of cost or market (LCM) rule to ending inventory?

E 9–5
Lower of cost or market
● LO9–1

[This is a variation of E 9–2, modified to focus on the lower of cost or market.] The inventory of Royal Decking consisted of five products. Information about the December 31, 2018, inventory is as follows:

	Per Unit		
Product	**Cost**	**Replacement Cost**	**Selling Price**
A	$ 40	$35	$ 60
B	80	70	100
C	40	55	80
D	100	70	130
E	20	28	30

Selling costs consist of a sales commission equal to 10% of selling price and shipping costs equal to 5% of cost. The normal gross profit percentage is 30% of selling price.

Required:

What unit value should Royal Decking use for each of its products when applying the lower of cost or market (LCM) rule to units of ending inventory?

E 9–6
Lower of cost or market
● LO9–1

[This is a variation of E 9–3, modified to focus on the lower of cost or market.] Tatum Company has four products in its inventory. Information about the December 31, 2018, inventory is as follows:

Product	Total Cost	Total Replacement Cost	Total Net Realizable Value
101	$120,000	$100,000	$100,000
102	90,000	85,000	110,000
103	60,000	40,000	50,000
104	30,000	28,000	50,000

The normal gross profit percentage is 25% of *total cost.*

Required:

1. Determine the carrying value of inventory at December 31, 2018, assuming the lower of cost or market (LCM) rule is applied to individual products.
2. Assuming that inventory write-downs are common for Tatum Company, record any necessary year-end adjusting entry.

E 9–7
FASB codification research
● LO9–3, LO9–6, LO9–7

Access the *FASB Accounting Standards Codification* at the FASB website (www.fasb.org). Determine the specific citation for each of the following items:

1. Measurement of ending inventory using the lower of cost or net realizable value (LCNRV) rule
2. Measurement of ending inventory using the lower of cost or market (LCM) rule
3. The level of aggregation that should be used in applying the LCNRV or LCM rule

E 9–8
Gross profit method
● LO9–2

On September 22, 2018, a flood destroyed the entire merchandise inventory on hand in a warehouse owned by the Rocklin Sporting Goods Company. The following information is available from the records of the company's periodic inventory system:

Inventory, January 1, 2018	$140,000
Net purchases, January 1 through September 22	370,000
Net sales, January 1 through September 22	550,000
Gross profit ratio	25%

Required:

Estimate the cost of inventory destroyed in the flood using the gross profit method.

E 9–9
Gross profit method
● LO9–2

On November 21, 2018, a fire at Hodge Company's warehouse caused severe damage to its entire inventory of Product Tex. Hodge estimates that all usable damaged goods can be sold for $12,000. The following information was available from the records of Hodge's periodic inventory system:

Inventory, November 1	$100,000
Net purchases from November 1, to the date of the fire	140,000
Net sales from November 1, to the date of the fire	220,000

Based on recent history, Hodge's gross profit ratio on Product Tex is 35% of net sales.

Required:

Calculate the estimated loss on the inventory from the fire, using the gross profit method.

E 9–10
Gross profit method
● LO9–2

A fire destroyed a warehouse of the Goren Group, Inc., on May 4, 2018. Accounting records on that date indicated the following:

(AICPA adapted)

Merchandise inventory, January 1, 2018	$1,900,000
Purchases to date	5,800,000
Freight-in	400,000
Sales to date	8,200,000

The gross profit ratio has averaged 20% of sales for the past four years.

Required:

Use the gross profit method to estimate the cost of the inventory destroyed in the fire.

E 9–11
Gross profit method
● LO9–2

Royal Gorge Company uses the gross profit method to estimate ending inventory and cost of goods sold when preparing monthly financial statements required by its bank. Inventory on hand at the end of October was $58,500. The following information for the month of November was available from company records:

Purchases	$110,000
Freight-in	3,000
Sales	180,000
Sales returns	5,000
Purchases returns	4,000

In addition, the controller is aware of $8,000 of inventory that was stolen during November from one of the company's warehouses.

Required:
1. Calculate the estimated inventory at the end of November, assuming a gross profit ratio of 40%.
2. Calculate the estimated inventory at the end of November, assuming a markup on cost of 100%.

E 9–12
Gross profit method; solving for unknown cost percentage
● LO9–2

National Distributing Company uses a periodic inventory system to track its merchandise inventory and the gross profit method to estimate ending inventory and cost of goods sold for interim periods. Net purchases for the month of August were $31,000. The July 31 and August 31, 2018, financial statements contained the following information:

Income Statements
For the Months Ending

	August 31, 2018	July 31, 2018
Net sales	$50,000	$40,000

Balance Sheets at

	August 31, 2018	July 31, 2018
Assets:		
Merchandise inventory	$28,000	$27,000

Required:
Determine the company's cost percentage.

E 9–13
Retail inventory method; average cost
● LO9–3

San Lorenzo General Store uses a periodic inventory system and the retail inventory method to estimate ending inventory and cost of goods sold. The following data are available for the month of October 2018:

	Cost	Retail
Beginning inventory	$35,000	$50,000
Net purchases	19,120	31,600
Net markups		1,200
Net markdowns		800
Net sales		32,000

Required:
Estimate the average cost of ending inventory and cost of goods sold for October.

E 9–14
Conventional retail method
● LO9–4

Campbell Corporation uses the retail method to value its inventory. The following information is available for the year 2018:

	Cost	Retail
Merchandise inventory, January 1, 2018	$190,000	$280,000
Purchases	600,000	840,000
Freight-in	8,000	
Net markups		20,000
Net markdowns		4,000
Net sales		800,000

Required:
Determine the December 31, 2018, inventory that approximates average cost.

E 9–15
Retail inventory method; LIFO
● LO9–3

Crosby Company owns a chain of hardware stores throughout the state. The company uses a periodic inventory system and the retail inventory method to estimate ending inventory and cost of goods sold. The following data are available for the three months ending March 31, 2018:

	Cost	Retail
Beginning inventory	$160,000	$280,000
Net purchases	607,760	840,000
Net markups		20,000
Net markdowns		4,000
Net sales		800,000

Required:
Estimate the LIFO cost of ending inventory and cost of goods sold for the three months ending March 31, 2018. Assume stable retail prices during the period.

E 9–16
Conventional retail method; normal spoilage
● LO9–4

Almaden Valley Variety Store uses the retail inventory method to estimate ending inventory and cost of goods sold. Data for 2018 are as follows:

	Cost	Retail
Beginning inventory	$ 12,000	$ 20,000
Purchases	102,600	165,000
Freight-in	3,480	
Purchase returns	4,000	7,000
Net markups		6,000
Net markdowns		3,000
Normal spoilage		4,200
Net sales		152,000

Required:
Estimate the ending inventory and cost of goods sold for 2018, applying the conventional retail method.

E 9–17
Conventional retail method; employee discounts
● LO9–3, LO9–4

LeMay Department Store uses the retail inventory method to estimate ending inventory for its monthly financial statements. The following data pertain to one of its largest departments for the month of March 2018:

	Cost	Retail
Beginning inventory	$ 40,000	$ 60,000
Purchases	207,000	400,000
Freight-in	14,488	
Purchase returns	4,000	6,000
Net markups		5,800
Net markdowns		3,500
Normal breakage		6,000
Net sales		280,000
Employee discounts		1,800

Sales are recorded net of employee discounts.

Required:
1. Compute estimated ending inventory and cost of goods sold for March applying the conventional retail method.
2. Recompute the cost-to-retail percentage using the average cost method.

E 9–18
Retail inventory method; solving for unknowns
● LO9–3

Adams Corporation uses a periodic inventory system and the retail inventory method to estimate ending inventory and cost of goods sold. The following data are available for the month of September 2018:

	Cost	Retail
Beginning inventory	$21,000	$35,000
Net purchases	10,500	?
Net markups		4,000
Net markdowns		1,000
Net sales		?

The company used the average cost flow method and estimated inventory at the end of September to be $17,437.50. If the company had used the LIFO cost flow method, the cost-to-retail percentage would have been 50%.

Required:
Compute net purchases at retail and net sales for the month of September.

E 9–19
Dollar-value LIFO retail
● LO9–5

On January 1, 2018, the Brunswick Hat Company adopted the dollar-value LIFO retail method. The following data are available for 2018:

	Cost	Retail
Beginning inventory	$ 71,280	$ 132,000
Net purchases	112,500	255,000
Net markups		6,000
Net markdowns		11,000
Net sales		232,000
Retail price index, 12/31/2018		1.04

Required:
Calculate the estimated ending inventory and cost of goods sold for 2018.

E 9–20
Dollar-value LIFO retail
● LO9–5

Canova Corporation adopted the dollar-value LIFO retail method on January 1, 2018. On that date, the cost of the inventory on hand was $15,000 and its retail value was $18,750. Information for 2018 and 2019 is as follows:

Date	Ending Inventory at Retail	Retail Price Index	Cost-to-Retail Percentage
12/31/2018	$25,000	1.25	82%
12/31/2019	28,600	1.30	85

Required:
1. What is the cost-to-retail percentage for the inventory on hand at 1/1/2018?
2. Calculate the inventory value at the end of 2018 and 2019 using the dollar-value LIFO retail method.

E 9–21
Dollar-value LIFO retail
● LO9–5

Lance-Hefner Specialty Shoppes decided to use the dollar-value LIFO retail method to value its inventory. Accounting records provide the following information:

	Cost	Retail
Merchandise inventory, January 1, 2018	$160,000	$250,000
Net purchases	350,200	510,000
Net markups		7,000
Net markdowns		2,000
Net sales		380,000

Related retail price indexes are as follows:

January 1, 2018	1.00
December 31, 2018	1.10

Required:
Determine ending inventory and cost of goods sold.

E 9–22
Dollar-value LIFO retail; solving for unknowns
● LO9–5

Bosco Company adopted the dollar-value LIFO retail method at the beginning of 2018. Information for 2018 and 2019 is as follows, with certain data intentionally omitted:

	Inventory			
Date	Cost	Retail	Retail Price Index	Cost-to-Retail Percentage
Inventory, 1/1/2018	$21,000	$28,000	1.00	?
Inventory, 12/31/2018	22,792	33,600	1.12	?
2019 net purchases	60,000	88,400		
2019 net sales		80,000		
Inventory, 12/31/2019	?	?	1.20	

Required:
Determine the missing data.

E 9–23
Change in inventory costing methods
● LO9–6

In 2018, CPS Company changed its method of valuing inventory from the FIFO method to the average cost method. At December 31, 2017, CPS's inventories were $32 million (FIFO). CPS's records indicated that the inventories would have totaled $23.8 million at December 31, 2017, if determined on an average cost basis.

Required:

1. Prepare the journal entry to record the adjustment. (Ignore income taxes.)
2. Briefly describe other steps CPS should take to report the change.

E 9–24
Change in inventory costing methods
● LO9–6

Goddard Company has used the FIFO method of inventory valuation since it began operations in 2015. Goddard decided to change to the average cost method for determining inventory costs at the beginning of 2018. The following schedule shows year-end inventory balances under the FIFO and average cost methods:

Year	FIFO	Average Cost
2015	$45,000	$54,000
2016	78,000	71,000
2017	83,000	78,000

Required:

1. Ignoring income taxes, prepare the 2018 journal entry to adjust the accounts to reflect the average cost method.
2. How much higher or lower would cost of goods sold be in the 2017 revised income statement?

E 9–25
Error correction; inventory error
● LO9–7

During 2018, WMC Corporation discovered that its ending inventories reported in its financial statements were misstated by the following material amounts:

2016	understated by	$120,000
2017	overstated by	150,000

WMC uses a periodic inventory system and the FIFO cost method.

Required:

1. Determine the effect of these errors on retained earnings at January 1, 2018, before any adjustments. Explain your answer. (Ignore income taxes.)
2. Prepare a journal entry to correct the errors.
3. What other step(s) would be taken in connection with the correction of the errors?

E 9–26
Inventory errors
● LO9–7

For each of the following inventory errors occurring in 2018, determine the effect of the error on 2018's cost of goods sold, net income, and retained earnings. Assume that the error is not discovered until 2019 and that a periodic inventory system is used. Ignore income taxes.

U = understated O = overstated NE = no effect

	Cost of Goods Sold	Net Income	Retained Earnings
1. Overstatement of ending inventory	U	O	O
2. Overstatement of purchases			
3. Understatement of beginning inventory			
4. Freight-in charges are understated			
5. Understatement of ending inventory			
6. Understatement of purchases			
7. Overstatement of beginning inventory			
8. Understatement of purchases plus understatement of ending inventory by the same amount			

E 9–27
Inventory error
● LO9–7

In 2018, the internal auditors of Development Technologies, Inc., discovered that a $4 million purchase of merchandise in 2018 was recorded in 2017 instead. The physical inventory count at the end of 2017 was correct.

Required:

Prepare the journal entry needed in 2018 to correct the error. Also, briefly describe any other measures Development Technologies would take in connection with correcting the error. (Ignore income taxes.)

E 9–28
Inventory errors
● LO9–7

In 2018, the controller of Sytec Corporation discovered that $42,000 of inventory purchases were incorrectly charged to advertising expense in 2017. In addition, the 2017 year-end inventory count failed to include $30,000 of company merchandise held on consignment by Erin Brothers. Sytec uses a periodic inventory system. Other than the omission of the merchandise on consignment, the year-end inventory count was correct. The amounts of the errors are deemed to be material.

Required:

1. Determine the effect of the errors on retained earnings at January 1, 2018. Explain your answer. (Ignore income taxes.)
2. Prepare a journal entry to correct the errors.
3. What other step(s) would be taken in connection with the correction of the errors?

E 9–29
Concepts; terminology
● LO9–1 through LO9–7

Listed below are several terms and phrases associated with inventory measurement. Pair each item from List A with the item from List B (by letter) that is most appropriately associated with it.

List A	List B
____ 1. Gross profit ratio	a. Reduction in selling price below the original selling price
____ 2. Cost-to-retail percentage	b. Beginning inventory is not included in the calculation of the cost-to-retail percentage
____ 3. Additional markup	c. Deducted in the retail column after the calculation of the cost-to-retail percentage
____ 4. Markdown	d. Requires base year retail to be converted to layer year retail and then to cost
____ 5. Net markup	e. Gross profit divided by net sales
____ 6. Retail method, FIFO and LIFO	f. Material inventory error discovered in a subsequent year
____ 7. Conventional retail method	g. Must be added to sales if sales are recorded net of discounts
____ 8. Change from LIFO	h. Deducted in the retail column to arrive at goods available for sale at retail
____ 9. Dollar-value LIFO retail	i. Divide cost of goods available for sale by goods available at retail
____ 10. Normal spoilage	j. Average cost, lower of cost or market
____ 11. Requires retrospective restatement	k. Added to the retail column to arrive at goods available for sale
____ 12. Employee discounts	l. Increase in selling price subsequent to initial markup
____ 13. Net markdowns	m. Selling price less estimated selling costs
____ 14. Net realizable value	n. Accounting change requiring retrospective treatment

E 9–30
Purchase commitments
● Appendix

On October 6, 2018, the Elgin Corporation signed a purchase commitment to purchase inventory for $60,000 on or before March 31, 2019. The company's fiscal year-end is December 31. The contract was exercised on March 21, 2019, and the inventory was purchased for cash at the contract price. On the purchase date of March 21, the market price of the inventory was $54,000. The market price of the inventory on December 31, 2018, was $56,000. The company uses a perpetual inventory system.

Required:

1. Prepare the necessary adjusting journal entry (if any is required) on December 31, 2018.
2. Prepare the journal entry to record the purchase on March 21, 2019.

E 9–31
Purchase commitments
● Appendix

In March 2018, the Phillips Tool Company signed two purchase commitments. The first commitment requires Phillips to purchase inventory for $100,000 by June 15, 2018. The second commitment requires the company to purchase inventory for $150,000 by August 20, 2018. The company's fiscal year-end is June 30. Phillips uses a periodic inventory system.

The first commitment is exercised on June 15, 2018, when the market price of the inventory purchased was $85,000. The second commitment was exercised on August 20, 2018, when the market price of the inventory purchased was $120,000.

Required:

Prepare the journal entries required on June 15, June 30, and August 20, 2018, to account for the two purchase commitments. Assume that the market price of the inventory related to the outstanding purchase commitment was $140,000 at June 30.

Problems

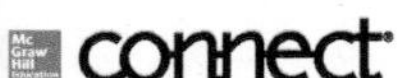

P 9–1
Lower of cost or net realizable value
● LO9–1

Decker Company has five products in its inventory. Information about the December 31, 2018, inventory follows.

Product	Quantity	Unit Cost	Unit Selling Price
A	1,000	$10	$16
B	800	15	18
C	600	3	8
D	200	7	6
E	600	14	13

The cost to sell for each product consists of a 15 percent sales commission.

Required:

1. Determine the carrying value of inventory at December 31, 2018, assuming the lower of cost or net realizable value (LCNRV) rule is applied to individual products.
2. Determine the carrying value of inventory at December 31, 2018, assuming the LCNRV rule is applied to the entire inventory. Also, assuming inventory write-downs are usual business practice for Decker, record any necessary year-end adjusting entry.

P 9–2
Lower of cost or net realizable value
● LO9–1

Almaden Hardware Store sells two product categories, tools and paint products. Information pertaining to its 2018 year-end inventory is as follows:

Inventory, by Product Category	Quantity	Per Unit Cost	Net Realizable Value
Tools:			
Hammers	100	$ 5.00	$5.50
Saws	200	10.00	9.00
Screwdrivers	300	2.00	2.60
Paint products:			
1-gallon cans	500	6.00	5.00
Paint brushes	100	4.00	4.50

Required:

1. Determine the carrying value of inventory at year-end, assuming the lower of cost or net realizable value (LCNRV) rule is applied to (a) individual products, (b) product categories, and (c) total inventory.
2. Assuming that the company reports an inventory write-down as a line item in the income statement, for each of the LCNRV applications determine the amount of the loss.

P 9–3
Lower of cost or market
● LO9–1

Forester Company has five products in its inventory. Information about the December 31, 2018, inventory follows.

Product	Quantity	Unit Cost	Unit Replacement Cost	Unit Selling Price
A	1,000	$10	$12	$16
B	800	15	11	18
C	600	3	2	8
D	200	7	4	6
E	600	14	12	13

The cost to sell for each product consists of a 15 percent sales commission. The normal profit percentage for each product is 40 percent of the selling price.

Required:

1. Determine the carrying value of inventory at December 31, 2018, assuming the lower of cost or market (LCM) rule is applied to individual products.
2. Determine the carrying value of inventory at December 31, 2018, assuming the LCM rule is applied to the entire inventory. Also, assuming inventory write-downs are usual business practice for Forester, record any necessary year-end adjusting entry.

P 9–4
Lower of cost or market
● LO9–1

Home Stop sells two product categories, furniture and accessories. Information pertaining to its 2018 year-end inventory is as follows:

Inventory, by Product Category	Quantity	Per Unit Cost	Market
Furniture:			
Chairs	50	$25	$31
Desks	10	73	58
Tables	20	84	92
Accessories:			
Rugs	40	60	48
Lamps	30	22	18

Required:

1. Determine the carrying value of inventory at year-end, assuming the lower of cost or market (LCM) rule is applied to (a) individual products, (b) product categories, and (c) total inventory.
2. Assuming that the company reports an inventory write-down as a line item in the income statement, for each of the LCM applications determine the amount of the loss.

P 9–5
Gross profit method
● LO9–2

Smith Distributors, Inc., supplies ice cream shops with various toppings for making sundaes. On November 17, 2018, a fire resulted in the loss of all of the toppings stored in one section of the warehouse. The company must provide its insurance company with an estimate of the amount of inventory lost. The following information is available from the company's accounting records:

	Fruit Toppings	Marshmallow Toppings	Chocolate Toppings
Inventory, January 1, 2018	$ 20,000	$ 7,000	$ 3,000
Net purchases through Nov. 17	150,000	36,000	12,000
Net sales through Nov. 17	200,000	55,000	20,000
Historical gross profit ratio	20%	30%	35%

Required:

1. Calculate the estimated cost of each of the toppings lost in the fire.
2. What factors could cause the estimates to be over- or understated?

P 9–6
Retail inventory method; various cost methods
● LO9–3, LO9–4

Sparrow Company uses the retail inventory method to estimate ending inventory and cost of goods sold. Data for 2018 are as follows:

	Cost	Retail
Beginning inventory	$ 90,000	$180,000
Purchases	355,000	580,000
Freight-in	9,000	
Purchase returns	7,000	11,000
Net markups		16,000
Net markdowns		12,000
Normal spoilage		3,000
Abnormal spoilage	4,800	8,000
Sales		540,000
Sales returns		10,000

The company records sales net of employee discounts. Discounts for 2018 totaled $4,000.

Required:

Estimate Sparrow's ending inventory and cost of goods sold for the year using the retail inventory method and the following applications:

1. Average cost
2. Conventional

P 9–7
Retail inventory method; conventional and LIFO
● LO9–3, LO9–4

Alquist Company uses the retail method to estimate its ending inventory. Selected information about its year 2018 operations is as follows:

a. January 1, 2018, beginning inventory had a cost of $100,000 and a retail value of $150,000.
b. Purchases during 2018 cost $1,387,500 with an original retail value of $2,000,000.
c. Freight costs were $10,000 for incoming merchandise.
d. Net additional markups were $300,000 and net markdowns were $150,000.
e. Based on prior experience, shrinkage due to shoplifting was estimated to be $15,000 of retail value.
f. Merchandise is sold to employees at a 20% of selling price discount. Employee sales are recorded in a separate account at the net selling price. The balance in this account at the end of 2018 is $250,000.
g. Sales to customers totaled $1,750,000 for the year.

Required:
1. Estimate ending inventory and cost of goods sold using the conventional retail method.
2. Estimate ending inventory and cost of goods sold using the LIFO retail method. (Assume stable prices.)

P 9–8
Retail inventory method; conventional
● LO9–4

Grand Department Store, Inc., uses the retail inventory method to estimate ending inventory for its monthly financial statements. The following data pertain to a single department for the month of October 2018:

Inventory, October 1, 2018:	
At cost	$ 20,000
At retail	30,000
Purchases (exclusive of freight and returns):	
At cost	100,151
At retail	146,495
Freight-in	5,100
Purchase returns:	
At cost	2,100
At retail	2,800
Additional markups	2,500
Markup cancellations	265
Markdowns (net)	800
Normal spoilage and breakage	4,500
Sales	135,730

Required:
1. Using the conventional retail method, prepare a schedule computing estimated lower of cost or market (LCM) inventory for October 31, 2018.
2. A department store using the conventional retail inventory method estimates the cost of its ending inventory as $29,000. An accurate physical count reveals only $22,000 of inventory at lower of cost or market. List the factors that may have caused the difference between computed inventory and the physical count.

(AICPA adapted)

P 9–9
Retail method—average cost and conventional
● LO9–3, LO9–4

Smith-Kline Company maintains inventory records at selling prices as well as at cost. For 2018, the records indicate the following data:

	($ in thousands)	
	Cost	**Retail**
Beginning inventory	$ 80	$ 125
Purchases	671	1,006
Freight-in on purchases	30	
Purchase returns	1	2
Net markups		4
Net markdowns		8
Net sales		916

Required:
Use the retail method to approximate cost of ending inventory in each of the following ways:
1. Average cost
2. Conventional

P 9–10
Dollar-value LIFO retail method
● LO9–5

[This is a variation of P 9–9, modified to focus on the dollar-value LIFO retail method.] Smith-Kline Company maintains inventory records at selling prices as well as at cost. For 2018, the records indicate the following data:

	($ in thousands)	
	Cost	**Retail**
Beginning inventory	$ 80	$ 125
Purchases	671	1,006
Freight-in on purchases	30	
Purchase returns	1	2
Net markups		4
Net markdowns		8
Net sales		916

Required:
Assuming the price level increased from 1.00 at January 1 to 1.10 at December 31, 2018, use the dollar-value LIFO retail method to approximate cost of ending inventory and cost of goods sold.

P 9–11
Dollar-value LIFO retail
● LO9–5

On January 1, 2018, HGC Camera Store adopted the dollar-value LIFO retail inventory method. Inventory transactions at both cost and retail, and cost indexes for 2018 and 2019 are as follows:

	2018		2019	
	Cost	**Retail**	**Cost**	**Retail**
Beginning inventory	$28,000	$ 40,000		
Net purchases	85,000	108,000	$90,000	$114,000
Freight-in	2,000		2,500	
Net markups		10,000		8,000
Net markdowns		2,000		2,200
Net sales to customers		100,000		104,000
Sales to employees (net of 20% discount)		2,400		4,000
Price Index:				
January 1, 2018				1.00
December 31, 2018				1.06
December 31, 2019				1.10

Required:
Estimate the 2018 and 2019 ending inventory and cost of goods sold using the dollar-value LIFO retail inventory method.

P 9–12
Retail inventory method; various applications
● LO9–3 through LO9–5

Raleigh Department Store uses the conventional retail method for the year ended December 31, 2016. Available information follows:

a. The inventory at January 1, 2016, had a retail value of $45,000 and a cost of $27,500 based on the conventional retail method.
b. Transactions during 2016 were as follows:

	Cost	**Retail**
Gross purchases	$282,000	$490,000
Purchase returns	6,500	10,000
Purchase discounts	5,000	
Gross sales		492,000
Sales returns		5,000
Employee discounts		3,000
Freight-in	26,500	
Net markups		25,000
Net markdowns		10,000

Sales to employees are recorded net of discounts.

c. The retail value of the December 31, 2017, inventory was $56,100, the cost-to-retail percentage for 2017 under the LIFO retail method was 62%, and the appropriate price index was 102% of the January 1, 2017, price level.

d. The retail value of the December 31, 2018, inventory was $48,300, the cost-to-retail percentage for 2018 under the LIFO retail method was 61%, and the appropriate price index was 105% of the January 1, 2017, price level.

Required:

1. Estimate ending inventory for 2016 using the conventional retail method.
2. Estimate ending inventory for 2016 assuming Raleigh Department Store used the LIFO retail method.
3. Assume Raleigh Department Store adopts the dollar-value LIFO retail method on January 1, 2017. Estimating ending inventory for 2017 and 2018.

(AICPA adapted)

P 9–13
Retail inventory method; various applications
● LO9–3 through LO9–5

On January 1, 2018, Pet Friendly Stores adopted the retail inventory method. Inventory transactions at both cost and retail, and cost indexes for 2018 and 2019 are as follows:

	2018		2019	
	Cost	**Retail**	**Cost**	**Retail**
Beginning inventory	$ 90,000	$150,000		
Purchases	478,000	730,000	$511,000	$760,000
Purchase returns	2,500	3,500	2,200	4,000
Freight-in	6,960		8,000	
Net markups		8,500		10,000
Net markdowns		4,000		6,000
Net sales to customers		650,000		680,000
Sales to employees (net of 30% discount)		14,000		17,500
Normal spoilage		5,000		6,600
Price Index:				
January 1, 2018	1.00			
December 31, 2018	1.03			
December 31, 2019	1.06			

Required:

1. Estimate the 2018 and 2019 ending inventory and cost of goods sold using the dollar-value LIFO retail method.
2. Estimate the 2018 ending inventory and cost of goods sold using the average cost retail method.
3. Estimate the 2018 ending inventory and cost of goods sold using the conventional retail method.

P 9–14
Change in methods
● LO9–6

Rockwell Corporation uses a periodic inventory system and has used the FIFO cost method since inception of the company in 1979. In 2018, the company decided to switch to the average cost method. Data for 2018 are as follows:

Beginning inventory, FIFO (5,000 units @ $30)		$150,000
Purchases:		
5,000 units @ $36	$180,000	
5,000 units @ $40	200,000	380,000
Cost of goods available for sale		$530,000
Sales for 2018 (8,000 units @ $70)		$560,000

Additional Information:

a. The company's effective income tax rate is 40% for all years.
b. If the company had used the average cost method prior to 2018, ending inventory for 2017 would have been $130,000.
c. 7,000 units remained in inventory at the end of 2018.

Required:

1. Ignoring income taxes, prepare the 2018 journal entry to adjust the accounts to reflect the average cost method.
2. What is the effect of the change in methods on 2018 net income?

P 9–15
Inventory errors
● LO9–7

You have been hired as the new controller for the Ralston Company. Shortly after joining the company in 2018, you discover the following errors related to the 2016 and 2017 financial statements:

a. Inventory at December 31, 2016, was understated by $6,000.
b. Inventory at December 31, 2017, was overstated by $9,000.

c. On December 31, 2017, inventory was purchased for $3,000. The company did not record the purchase until the inventory was paid for early in 2018. At that time, the purchase was recorded by a debit to purchases and a credit to cash.

The company uses a periodic inventory system.

Required:

1. Assuming that the errors were discovered after the 2017 financial statements were issued, analyze the effect of the errors on 2017 and 2016 cost of goods sold, net income, and retained earnings. (Ignore income taxes.)
2. Prepare a journal entry to correct the errors.
3. What other step(s) would be taken in connection with the errors?

P 9–16
Inventory errors
● LO9–7

The December 31, 2018, inventory of Tog Company, based on a physical count, was determined to be $450,000. Included in that count was a shipment of goods received from a supplier at the end of the month that cost $50,000. The purchase was recorded and paid for in 2019. Another supplier shipment costing $20,000 was correctly recorded as a purchase in 2018. However, the merchandise, shipped FOB shipping point, was not received until 2019 and was incorrectly omitted from the physical count. A third purchase, shipped from a supplier FOB shipping point on December 28, 2018, did not arrive until January 3, 2019. The merchandise, which cost $80,000, was not included in the physical count and the purchase has not yet been recorded.

The company uses a periodic inventory system.

Required:

1. Determine the correct December 31, 2018, inventory balance and, assuming that the errors were discovered after the 2018 financial statements were issued, analyze the effect of the errors on 2018 cost of goods sold, net income, and retained earnings. (Ignore income taxes.)
2. Prepare a journal entry to correct the errors.

P 9–17
Integrating problem; Chapters 8 and 9; inventory errors
● LO9–7

Capwell Corporation uses a periodic inventory system. The company's ending inventory on December 31, 2018, its fiscal-year end, based on a physical count, was determined to be $326,000. Capwell's unadjusted trial balance also showed the following account balances: Purchases, $620,000; Accounts payable; $210,000; Accounts receivable, $225,000; Sales revenue, $840,000.

The internal audit department discovered the following items:

1. Goods valued at $32,000 held on consignment from Dix Company were included in the physical count but not recorded as a purchase.
2. Purchases from Xavier Corporation were incorrectly recorded at $41,000 instead of the correct amount of $14,000. The correct amount was included in the ending inventory.
3. Goods that cost $25,000 were shipped from a vendor on December 28, 2018, terms f.o.b. destination. The merchandise arrived on January 3, 2019. The purchase and related accounts payable were recorded in 2018.
4. One inventory item was incorrectly included in ending inventory as 100 units, instead of the correct amount of 1,000 units. This item cost $40 per unit.
5. The 2017 balance sheet reported inventory of $352,000. The internal auditors discovered that a mathematical error caused this inventory to be understated by $62,000. This amount is considered to be material. Comparative financial statements will be issued.
6. Goods shipped to a customer f.o.b. destination on December 25, 2018, were received by the customer on January 4, 2019. The sales price was $40,000 and the merchandise cost $22,000. The sale and corresponding accounts receivable were recorded in 2018.
7. Goods shipped from a vendor f.o.b. shipping point on December 27, 2018, were received on January 3, 2019. The merchandise cost $18,000. The purchase was not recorded until 2019.

Required:

1. Determine the correct amounts for 2018 purchases, accounts payable, sales revenue, and accounts receivable.
2. Calculate ending inventory and cost of goods sold for 2018.
3. Describe the steps Capwell would undertake to correct the error in the 2017 ending inventory. What was the effect of the error on 2017 before-tax income?

P 9–18
Purchase commitments
● Appendix

In November 2018, the Brunswick Company signed two purchase commitments. The first commitment requires Brunswick to purchase 10,000 units of inventory at $10 per unit by December 15, 2018. The second commitment requires the company to purchase 20,000 units of inventory at $11 per unit by March 15, 2019. Brunswick's fiscal year-end is December 31. The company uses a periodic inventory system. Both contracts were exercised on their expiration date.

Required:

1. Prepare the journal entry to record the December 15 purchase for cash assuming the following alternative unit market prices on that date:
   a. $10.50
   b. $ 9.50
2. Prepare any necessary adjusting entry at December 31, 2018, for the second purchase commitment assuming the following alternative unit market prices on that date:
   a. $12.50
   b. $10.30
3. Assuming that the unit market price on December 31, 2018, was $10.30, prepare the journal entry to record the purchase on March 15, 2019, assuming the following alternative unit market prices on that date:
   a. $11.50
   b. $10.00

Broaden Your Perspective

Apply your critical-thinking ability to the knowledge you've gained. These cases will provide you an opportunity to develop your research, analysis, judgment, and communication skills. You also will work with other students, integrate what you've learned, apply it in real-world situations, and consider its global and ethical ramifications. This practice will broaden your knowledge and further develop your decision-making abilities.

Judgment Case 9–1
Inventoriable costs; lower of cost or market; retail inventory method
● LO9–1, LO9–3, LO9–4

Hudson Company, which is both a wholesaler and a retailer, purchases its inventories from various suppliers. Additional facts for Hudson's wholesale operations are as follows:

a. Hudson incurs substantial warehousing costs.
b. Hudson values inventory at the lower of cost or market. Market is below cost of the inventories.

Additional facts for Hudson's retail operations are as follows:

a. Hudson determines the estimated cost of its ending inventories held for sale at retail using the conventional retail inventory method, which approximates lower of average cost or market.
b. Hudson incurs substantial freight-in costs.
c. Hudson has net markups and net markdowns.

Required:

1. Theoretically, how should Hudson account for the warehousing costs related to its wholesale inventories? Why?
2. a. In general, why is inventory valued at the lower of cost or market?
   b. At which amount should Hudson's wholesale inventories be reported in the balance sheet?
3. In the calculation of the cost-to-retail percentage used to determine the estimated cost of its ending retail inventories, how should Hudson treat
   a. Freight-in costs?
   b. Net markups?
   c. Net markdowns?
4. Why does Hudson's retail inventory method approximate lower of average cost or market?

(AICPA adapted)

Communication Case 9–2
Lower of cost or net realizable value
● LO9–1

The lower of cost or net realizable value (LCNRV) approach to valuing inventory is a departure from the accounting principle of reporting assets at their historical costs. There are those who believe that inventory, as well as other assets, should be valued at NRV, regardless of whether NRV is above or below cost.

The focus of this case is the justification for the LCNRV rule for valuing inventories. Your instructor will divide the class into two to six groups depending on the size of the class. The mission of your group is to defend the LCNRV approach against the alternatives of valuing inventory at either historical cost or NRV.

Required:

1. Each group member should consider the situation independently and draft a tentative argument prior to the class session for which the case is assigned.
2. In class, each group will meet for 10 to 15 minutes in different areas of the classroom. During that meeting, group members will take turns sharing their suggestions for the purpose of arriving at a single group argument.

3. After the allotted time, a spokesperson for each group (selected during the group meetings) will share the group's solution with the class. The goal of the class is to incorporate the views of each group into a consensus approach to the situation.

Integrating Case 9–3
FIFO and lower of cost or net realizable value
● LO9–1

York Co. sells one product, which it purchases from various suppliers. York's trial balance at December 31, 2018, included the following accounts:

Sales (33,000 units @ $16)	$528,000
Sales discounts	7,500
Purchases	368,900
Purchase discounts	18,000
Freight-in	5,000
Freight-out	11,000

York Co.'s inventory purchases during 2018 were as follows:

	Units	Cost per Unit	Total Cost
Beginning inventory	7,000	$7.70	$ 53,900
Purchases, quarter ended March 31	13,000	7.50	97,500
Purchases, quarter ended June 30	15,000	7.90	118,500
Purchases, quarter ended September 30	12,000	8.25	99,000
Purchases, quarter ended December 31	8,000	8.20	65,600
	55,000		$434,500

Additional Information:

a. York's accounting policy is to report inventory in its financial statements at the lower of cost or net realizable value, applied to total inventory. Cost is determined under the first-in, first-out (FIFO) method.
b. York has determined that, at December 31, 2018, the net realizable value was $8.00 per unit.

Required:

1. Prepare York's schedule of cost of goods sold, with a supporting schedule of ending inventory. York includes inventory write-down losses in cost of goods sold.
2. Explain the rule of lower of cost or net realizable value and its application in this situation.

(AICPA adapted)

Judgment Case 9–4
The dollar-value LIFO method; the retail inventory method
● LO9–3, LO9–4

Huddell Company, which is both a wholesaler and retailer, purchases merchandise from various suppliers. The dollar-value LIFO method is used for the wholesale inventories.

Huddell determines the estimated cost of its retail ending inventories using the conventional retail inventory method, which approximates lower of average cost or market.

Required:

1. a. What are the advantages of using the dollar-value LIFO method as opposed to the traditional LIFO method?
   b. How does the application of the dollar-value LIFO method differ from the application of the traditional LIFO method?
2. a. In the calculation of the cost-to-retail percentage used to determine the estimated cost of its ending inventories, how should Huddell use
      - Net markups?
      - Net markdowns?
   b. Why does Huddell's retail inventory method approximate lower of average cost or market?

(AICPA adapted)

Communication Case 9–5
Retail inventory method
● LO9–3, LO9–4

The Brenly Paint Company, your client, manufactures paint. The company's president, Mr. Brenly, decided to open a retail store to sell paint as well as wallpaper and other items that would be purchased from other suppliers. He has asked you for information about the retail method of estimating inventories at the retail store.

Required:

Prepare a report to the president explaining the retail method of estimating inventories.

Analysis Case 9–6
Change in inventory method
● LO9–6

Generally accepted accounting principles should be applied consistently from period to period. However, changes within a company, as well as changes in the external economic environment, may force a company to change an accounting method. The specific reporting requirements when a company changes from one generally accepted inventory method to another depend on the methods involved.

Required:

Explain the accounting treatment for a change in inventory method (a) not involving LIFO, (b) from the LIFO method, and (c) to the LIFO method. Explain the logic underlying those treatments. Also, describe how disclosure requirements are designed to address the departure from consistency and comparability of changes in accounting principle.

Real World Case 9–7
Change in inventory method; Abercrombie & Fitch Co.
● LO9–6
Real World Financials

Abercrombie & Fitch Co. is a specialty retail company operating over 1,000 stores globally. The following disclosure note was included in recent financial statements:

4. Change in Accounting Principle

The Company elected to change its method of accounting for inventory from the retail method to the weighted average cost method effective February 2, 2013. In accordance with generally accepted accounting principles, all periods have been retroactively adjusted to reflect the period-specific effects of the change to the weighted average cost method. The Company believes that accounting under the weighted average cost method is preferable as it better aligns with the Company's focus on realized selling margin and improves the comparability of the Company's financial results with those of its competitors. Additionally, it will improve the matching of cost of goods sold with the related net sales and reflect the acquisition cost of inventory outstanding at each balance sheet date. The cumulative adjustment as of January 30, 2010, was an increase in its inventory of $73.6 million and an increase in retained earnings of $47.3 million.

Required:

Why does GAAP require Abercrombie to retroactively adjust all prior periods for this type of accounting change?

Real World Case 9–8
Various inventory issues; Chapters 8 and 9; Fred's Inc.
● LO9–1, LO9–5, LO9–6
Real World Financials

Fred's Inc. operates general merchandise retail discount stores and full-service pharmacies in the Southeastern United States. Access the company's 10-K for the fiscal year ended January 30, 2016. You can find the 10-K by using EDGAR at www.sec.gov. Answer the following questions.

Required:

1. What inventory methods does Fred's use to value its inventory?
2. Which price index does the company use in applying the retail inventory method?
3. A company that uses LIFO is allowed to provide supplemental disclosures reporting the effect of using another inventory method rather than LIFO. Using the supplemental LIFO disclosures provided by Fred's, determine the income effect of using LIFO versus another method for the current fiscal year.
4. Calculate the company's inventory turnover ratio for the fiscal year ended January 30, 2016.
5. Assume that in the next fiscal year the company decides to switch to the average cost method. Describe the accounting treatment required for the switch.

Communication Case 9–9
Change in inventory method; disclosure note
● LO9–6

Mayfair Department Stores, Inc., operates over 30 retail stores in the Pacific Northwest. Prior to 2018, the company used the FIFO method to value its inventory. In 2018, Mayfair decided to switch to the dollar value LIFO retail inventory method. One of your responsibilities as assistant controller is to prepare the disclosure note describing the change in method that will be included in the company's 2018 financial statements. Kenneth Meier, the controller, provided the following information:

a. Internally developed retail price indexes are used to adjust for the effects of changing prices.
b. If the change had not been made, cost of goods sold for the year would have been $22 million lower. The company's income tax rate is 40% and there were 100 million shares of common stock outstanding during 2018.
c. The cumulative effect of the change on prior years' income is not determinable.
d. The reasons for the change were (a) to provide a more consistent matching of merchandise costs with sales revenue, and (b) the new method provides a more comparable basis of accounting with competitors that also use the LIFO method.

Required:

1. Prepare for Kenneth Meier the disclosure note that will be included in the 2018 financial statements.
2. Explain why the "cumulative effect of the change on prior years' income is not determinable."

Judgment Case 9–10
Inventory errors
● LO9–7

Some inventory errors are said to be self-correcting in that the error has the opposite financial statement effect in the period following the error, thereby correcting the original account balance errors.

Required:

Despite this self-correcting feature, discuss why these errors should not be ignored and describe the steps required to account for the error correction.

Ethics Case 9–11
Overstatement of ending inventory
● LO9–7

Danville Bottlers is a wholesale beverage company. Danville uses the FIFO inventory method to determine the cost of its ending inventory. Ending inventory quantities are determined by a physical count. For the fiscal year-end June 30, 2018, ending inventory was originally determined to be $3,265,000. However, on July 17, 2018, John Howard, the company's controller, discovered an error in the ending inventory count. He determined that the correct ending inventory amount should be $2,600,000.

Danville is a privately owned corporation with significant financing provided by a local bank. The bank requires annual audited financial statements as a condition of the loan. By July 17, the auditors had completed their review of the financial statements which are scheduled to be issued on July 25. They did not discover the inventory error.

John's first reaction was to communicate his finding to the auditors and to revise the financial statements before they are issued. However, he knows that his and his fellow workers' profit-sharing plans are based on annual pretax earnings and that if he revises the statements, everyone's profit-sharing bonus will be significantly reduced.

Required:

1. Why will bonuses be negatively affected? What is the effect on pretax earnings?
2. If the error is not corrected in the current year and is discovered by the auditors during the following year's audit, how will it be reported in the company's financial statements?
3. Discuss the ethical dilemma John Howard faces.

Analysis Case 9–12
Purchase commitments
● Appendix

The management of the Esquire Oil Company believes that the wholesale price of heating oil that they sell to homeowners will increase again as the result of increased political problems in the Middle East. The company is currently paying $0.80 a gallon. If they are willing to enter an agreement in November 2018 to purchase a million gallons of heating oil during the winter of 2019, their supplier will guarantee the price at $0.80 per gallon. However, if the winter is a mild one, Esquire would not be able to sell a million gallons unless they reduced their retail price and thereby increase the risk of a loss for the year. On the other hand, if the wholesale price did increase substantially, they would be in a favorable position with respect to their competitors. The company's fiscal year-end is December 31.

Required:

Discuss the accounting issues related to the purchase commitment that Esquire is considering.

Continuing Cases

Target Case
● LO9–3, LO9–4, LO9–5

Target Corporation prepares its financial statements according to U.S. GAAP. Target's financial statements and disclosure notes for the year ended January 30, 2016, are available in Connect. This material is also available under the Investor Relations link at the company's website (www.target.com).

Required:

1. What indices does Target use to measure the LIFO provision?
2. Why does Target feel that the retail inventory method will result in inventory being valued at the lower of cost or market?
3. How does Target account for inventory when arrangements are made with vendors whereby Target does not purchase or pay for merchandise until the merchandise is ultimately sold to a customer?

Air France–KLM Case

● LO9–8

Air France–KLM (AF), a Franco-Dutch company, prepares its financial statements according to International Financial Reporting Standards. AF's financial statements and disclosure notes for the year ended December 31, 2015, are available in Connect. This material is also available under the Finance link at the company's website (www.airfranceklm.com).

Required:

AF's inventories are valued at the lower of cost or net realizable value. Does this approach differ from U.S. GAAP?

CPA Exam Questions and Simulations

Sample CPA Exam questions from Roger CPA Review are available in Connect as support for the topics in this chapter. These Multiple Choice Questions and Task-Based Simulations include expert-written explanations and solutions, and provide a starting point for students to become familiar with the content and functionality of the actual CPA Exam.

CHAPTER

10 Property, Plant, and Equipment and Intangible Assets: Acquisition

OVERVIEW

This chapter and the one that follows address the measurement and reporting issues involving property, plant, and equipment and intangible assets, the tangible and intangible long-lived assets that are used in the production of goods and services. This chapter covers the valuation at date of acquisition. In Chapter 11, we discuss the allocation of the cost of property, plant, and equipment and intangible assets to the periods benefited by their use, the treatment of expenditures made over the life of these assets to maintain and improve them, impairment, and disposition.

LEARNING OBJECTIVES

After studying this chapter, you should be able to:

- **LO10–1** Identify the various costs included in the initial cost of property, plant, and equipment, natural resources, and intangible assets. *(p. 520)*
- **LO10–2** Determine the initial cost of individual property, plant, and equipment and intangible assets acquired as a group for a lump-sum purchase price. *(p. 529)*
- **LO10–3** Determine the initial cost of property, plant, and equipment and intangible assets acquired in exchange for a deferred payment contract. *(p. 530)*
- **LO10–4** Determine the initial cost of property, plant, and equipment and intangible assets acquired in exchange for equity securities or through donation. *(p. 532)*
- **LO10–5** Calculate the fixed-asset turnover ratio used by analysts to measure how effectively managers use property, plant, and equipment. *(p. 534)*
- **LO10–6** Determine the initial cost of property, plant, and equipment and intangible assets acquired in exchange for other nonmonetary assets. *(p. 534)*
- **LO10–7** Identify the items included in the cost of a self-constructed asset and determine the amount of capitalized interest. *(p. 538)*
- **LO10–8** Explain the difference in the accounting treatment of costs incurred to purchase intangible assets versus the costs incurred to internally develop intangible assets. *(p. 544)*
- **LO10–9** Discuss the primary differences between U.S. GAAP and IFRS with respect to the acquisition of property, plant, and equipment and intangible assets. *(pp. 533, 547, and 549)*

© Preston Mack/Disney Parks via Getty Images

FINANCIAL REPORTING CASE

A Disney Adventure

"Now I'm really confused," confessed Stan, your study partner, staring blankly at the Walt Disney Company balance sheet that your professor handed out last week. "I thought that interest is always expensed in the income statement. Now I see that Disney is capitalizing interest. I'm not even sure what *capitalize* means! And what about this other account called *goodwill?* What's that all about?" We talked about these topics in our accounting class today. Let's take a look at the Disney financial statements and the disclosure note on capitalized interest and I'll try to explain it all to you."

Borrowings (in part):

The Company capitalizes interest on assets constructed for its parks and resorts and on theatrical productions. In fiscal years 2015, 2014, and 2013, total interest capitalized was $110 million, $73 million, and $77 million, respectively.

QUESTIONS

By the time you finish this chapter, you should be able to respond appropriately to the questions posed in this case. Compare your response to the solution provided at the end of the chapter.

1. Describe to Stan what it means to capitalize an expenditure. What is the general rule for determining which costs are capitalized when property, plant, and equipment or an intangible asset is acquired? (*p. 520*)
2. Which costs might be included in the initial cost of equipment? (*p. 520*)
3. What is goodwill and how is it measured? (*p. 527*)
4. In what situations is interest capitalized rather than expensed? (*p. 539*)
5. What is the three-step process used to determine the amount of interest capitalized? (*p. 541*)

General Motors Corporation has significant investments in the production facilities it uses to manufacture the automobiles it sells. On the other hand, the principal revenue-producing assets of Microsoft Corporation are the copyrights on its computer software that permit it the exclusive rights to earn profits from those products. Timber reserves provide major revenues to International Paper. From a reporting perspective, we classify GM's production facilities as property, plant, and equipment; Microsoft's copyrights as intangible assets; and International Paper's timber reserves as natural resources.[1] Together, these three noncurrent assets constitute the *long-lived, revenue-producing assets* of a company. Unlike manufacturers, many service firms and merchandising companies rely primarily on people or investments in inventories rather than on property, plant, and equipment and intangible assets to generate revenues. Even nonmanufacturing firms, though, typically have at least modest investments in buildings and equipment.

The measurement and reporting issues pertaining to this group of assets include valuation at date of acquisition, disposition, the treatment of expenditures made over the life of these assets to maintain and improve them, the allocation of cost to reporting periods that benefit from their use, and impairment. We focus on initial valuation in this chapter. In the next chapter, we examine subsequent expenditures, cost allocation, impairment, and disposition.

[1]These are sometimes called *plant assets* or *fixed assets.*

PART A

Valuation at Acquisition

Types of Assets

For financial reporting purposes, long-lived, revenue-producing assets typically are classified in two categories.

1. **Property, plant, and equipment.** Assets in this category include land, land improvements, buildings, machinery used in manufacturing, computers and other office equipment, vehicles, furniture, and fixtures. Natural resources such as oil and gas deposits, timber tracts, and mineral deposits also are included.
2. **Intangible assets.** Unlike property, plant, and equipment and natural resources, these lack physical substance and the extent and timing of their future benefits typically are uncertain. They include patents, copyrights, trademarks, franchises, and goodwill.

Of course, every company maintains its own unique mix of these assets. The way these assets are classified and combined for reporting purposes also varies from company to company. As an example, a recent balance sheet of Semtech Corporation, a leading supplier of semiconductor products, reported net property, plant, and equipment of $101,006 thousand and $115,471 thousand at the end of fiscal years 2016 and 2015, respectively. A disclosure note, shown in Illustration 10–1, provided the details.

Illustration 10–1

Property, Plant, and Equipment—Semtech Corporation

Real World Financials

Note 7. Property, Plant, and Equipment (in part):

The following is a summary of property and equipment, at cost less accumulated depreciation:

($ in thousands)	January 31, 2016	January 25, 2015
Property	$ 8,888	$ 9,022
Buildings	18,749	18,657
Leasehold improvements	10,182	10,429
Machinery and equipment	141,357	135,956
Enterprise resource planning systems	35,907	26,890
Furniture and office equipment	28,166	33,780
Construction in progress	1,539	1,325
Property, plant, and equipment, gross	244,788	236,059
Less: accumulated depreciation and amortization	(143,782)	(120,588)
Property, plant, and equipment, net	$101,006	$115,471

In practice, some companies report intangibles as part of property, plant, and equipment, and others show intangibles as a separate balance sheet category. For example, Layne Christensen Company, a leading construction and exploration company, reported goodwill of $8,915 thousand and other intangible assets of $6,991 thousand in a recent disclosure note, as shown in Illustration 10–2.

In this chapter, we'll first discuss how to record the acquisition cost of several types of property, plant, and equipment, and then we'll discuss the acquisition cost of intangible assets. You should find it helpful to study the overview of typical acquisition costs for each type of asset in Illustration 10–3. In Part B of this chapter, we examine how to record the acquisition of these assets when no cash is involved. Self-constructed assets and special issues related to research and development costs are addressed in Part C of the chapter. In the next chapter, we'll see how asset acquisition costs are expensed over time in a process called *depreciation* for plant and equipment, *depletion* for natural resources, and *amortization* for intangibles.

(5) Other Intangible Assets (in part)

	2016		2015	
($ in thousands)	Gross Amount	Accumulated Amortization	Gross Amount	Accumulated Amortization
Tradenames	$5,120	$(3,527)	$5,120	$(3,186)
Patents	905	(592)	905	(548)
Other	966	(653)	966	(590)
Total	$6,991	$(4,772)	$6,991	$(4,324)

Illustration 10–2
Intangible Assets—Layne Christensen Company

Real World Financials

Illustration 10–3 Property, Plant, and Equipment and Intangible Assets and Their Acquisition Costs

Asset	Description	Typical Acquisition Costs
Property, plant, and equipment	Productive assets that derive their value from long-term use in operations rather than from resale.	All expenditures necessary to get the asset in condition and location for its intended use.
Equipment	Broad term that includes machinery, computers and other office equipment, vehicles, furniture, and fixtures.	Purchase price (less discounts), taxes, transportation, installation, testing, trial runs, and reconditioning.
Land	Real property used in operations (land held for speculative investment or future use is reported as investments or other assets).	Purchase price, attorney's fees, title, recording fees, commissions, back taxes, mortgages, liens, clearing, filling, draining, and removing old buildings.
Land improvements	Enhancements to property such as parking lots, driveways, private roads, fences, landscaping, and sprinkler systems.	Separately identifiable costs.
Buildings	Structures that include warehouses, plant facilities, and office buildings.	Purchase price, attorney's fees, commissions, and reconditioning.
Natural resources	Productive assets that are physically consumed in operations such as timber, mineral deposits, and oil and gas reserves.	Acquisition, exploration, development, and restoration costs.
Intangible Assets	Productive assets that lack physical substance and have long-term but typically uncertain benefits.	All expenditures necessary to get the asset in condition and location for its intended use.
Patents	Exclusive 20-year right to manufacture a product or use a process.	Purchase price, legal fees, filing fees, not including internal R&D.
Copyrights	Exclusive right to benefit from a creative work such as a song, film, painting, photograph, or book.	Purchase price, legal fees, filing fees, not including internal R&D.
Trademarks (tradenames)	Exclusive right to display a word, a slogan, a symbol, or an emblem that distinctively identifies a company, product, or a service.	Purchase price, legal fees, filing fees, not including internal R&D.
Franchises	A contractual arrangement under which a franchisor grants the franchisee the exclusive right to use the franchisor's trademark or tradename and certain product rights.	Franchise fee plus any legal fees.
Goodwill	The unique value of the company as a whole over and above all identifiable assets.	Excess of the fair value of the consideration exchanged for the company over the fair value of the net assets acquired.

Costs to be Capitalized

LO10–1

Property, plant, and equipment and intangible assets can be acquired through purchase, exchange, lease, donation, self-construction, or a business combination. We address acquisitions through leasing in Chapter 15 and acquisitions through business combinations later in this chapter and in Chapter 12.

The initial cost of property, plant, and equipment and intangible assets includes the purchase price and all expenditures necessary to bring the asset to its desired condition and location for use.

The initial valuation of property, plant, and equipment and intangible assets usually is quite simple. We know from prior study that assets are valued on the basis of their original costs. In Chapter 8 we introduced the concept of condition and location in determining the cost of inventory. For example, if Thompson Company purchased inventory for $42,000 and incurred $1,000 in freight costs to have the inventory shipped to its location, the initial cost of the inventory is $43,000. This concept applies to the valuation of property, plant, and equipment and intangible assets as well. The initial cost of these assets includes the purchase price and all expenditures necessary to bring the asset to its desired condition and location for use. We discuss these additional expenditures in the next section.

FINANCIAL Reporting Case

Q1, p. 517

Our objective in identifying the costs of an asset is to distinguish the expenditures that produce future benefits from those that produce benefits only in the current period. The costs in the second group are recorded as expenses, but those in the first group are *capitalized;* that is, they are recorded as an asset and expensed in future periods.[2] For example, the cost of a major improvement to a delivery truck that extends its useful life generally would be capitalized. On the other hand, the cost of an engine tune-up for the delivery truck simply allows the truck to continue its productive activity but does not increase future benefits. These maintenance costs would be expensed. Subsequent expenditures for these assets are discussed in Chapter 11.

The distinction is not trivial. This point was unmistakably emphasized in the summer of 2002 when WorldCom, Inc., disclosed that it had improperly capitalized nearly $4 billion in expenditures related to the company's telecom network. This massive fraud resulted in one of the largest financial statement restatements in history and triggered the collapse of the once powerful corporation. Capitalizing rather than expensing these expenditures caused a substantial understatement of expenses and overstatement of reported income for 2001 and the first quarter of 2002. If the deception had not been discovered, not only would income for 2001 and 2002 have been overstated, but also income for many years into the future would have been understated as the fraudulent capitalized assets were depreciated. Of course, the balance sheet also would have overstated the assets and equity of the company.

Property, Plant, and Equipment

FINANCIAL Reporting Case

Q2 p. 517

COST OF EQUIPMENT. Equipment is a broad term that encompasses machinery used in manufacturing, computers and other office equipment, vehicles, furniture, and fixtures. The cost of equipment includes the purchase price plus any sales tax (less any discounts received from the seller), transportation costs paid by the buyer to transport the asset to the location in which it will be used, expenditures for installation, testing, legal fees to establish title, and any other costs of bringing the asset to its condition and location for use. To the extent that these costs can be identified and measured, they should be included in the asset's initial valuation rather than expensed currently.

Although most costs can be identified easily, others are more difficult. For example, the costs of training personnel to operate machinery could be considered a cost necessary to make the asset ready for use. However, because it is difficult to measure the amount of training costs associated with specific assets, these costs usually are expensed. Consider Illustration 10–4.

[2]Exceptions are land and certain intangible assets that have indefinite useful lives. Costs to acquire these assets also produce future benefits and therefore are capitalized, but unlike other property, plant, and equipment and intangible assets, their costs are not systematically expensed in future periods as depreciation or amortization.

Illustration 10–4

Initial Cost of Equipment

Central Machine Tools purchased an industrial machine to be used in its manufacturing process. The purchase price was $62,000. Central paid a freight company $1,000 to transport the machine to its plant location plus $300 shipping insurance. In addition, the machine had to be installed and mounted on a special platform built specifically for the machine at a cost of $1,200. After installation, several trial runs were made to ensure proper operation. The cost of these trials including wasted materials was $600. At what amount should Central capitalize the machine?

Purchase price	$62,000
Freight and handling	1,000
Insurance during shipping	300
Special platform	1,200
Trial runs	600
	$65,100

Each of the expenditures described was necessary to bring the machine to its condition and location for use and should be capitalized. These costs will be expensed in the future periods in which the asset is used.

COST OF LAND. The cost of land also should include expenditures needed to get the land ready for its intended use. These include the purchase price plus closing costs such as fees for the attorney, real estate agent commissions, title and title search, and recording. If the property is subject to back taxes, liens, mortgages, or other obligations, these amounts are included also. In addition, any expenditures such as clearing, filling, draining, and even removing (razing) old buildings that are needed to prepare the land for its intended use are part of the land's cost. Proceeds from the sale of salvaged materials from old buildings torn down after purchase reduce the cost of land. Illustration 10–5 provides an example.

Illustration 10–5

Initial Cost of Land

The Byers Structural Metal Company purchased a six-acre tract of land and an existing building for $500,000. The company plans to remove the old building and construct a new office building on the site. In addition to the purchase price, the company made the following expenditures at closing of the purchase:

Title insurance	$ 3,000
Commissions	16,000
Property taxes	6,000*

*The $6,000 in property taxes included $4,000 of delinquent taxes paid by Byers on behalf of the seller and $2,000 attributable to the portion of the current fiscal year after the purchase date.

In addition, shortly after closing, the Byers paid a contractor $10,000 to tear down the old building and remove it from the site. An additional $5,000 was paid to grade the land. What should be the capitalized cost of the land?

Capitalized cost of land:	
Purchase price of land (and building to be removed)	$500,000
Title insurance	3,000
Commissions	16,000
Delinquent property taxes	4,000
Cost of removing old building	10,000
Cost of grading	5,000
Total cost of land	$538,000

Property taxes of $2,000 were not included. These relate only to the current period and should be expensed separately. Other costs were necessary to acquire the land and are capitalized.

LAND IMPROVEMENTS. It's important to distinguish between the cost of land and the cost of land improvements because land has an indefinite life and land improvements usually have useful lives that are estimable. Examples of land improvements include the costs of establishing parking lots, driveways, and private roads and the costs of fences and lawn and garden sprinkler systems. Costs of these assets are separately identified and capitalized. We depreciate their cost over periods benefited by their use.

COST OF BUILDINGS. The cost of acquiring a building usually includes realtor commissions and legal fees in addition to the purchase price. Quite often a building must be refurbished, remodeled, or otherwise modified to suit the needs of the new owner. These reconditioning costs are part of the building's acquisition cost. When a building is constructed rather than purchased, unique accounting issues are raised. We discuss these in Part C in the "Self-Constructed Assets" section.

COST OF NATURAL RESOURCES. Natural resources that provide long-term benefits are reported as property, plant, and equipment. These include timber tracts, mineral deposits, and oil and gas deposits. They can be distinguished from other assets by the fact that their benefits are derived from their physical consumption. For example, mineral deposits are physically diminishing as the minerals are extracted from the ground and either sold or used in the production process.[3] On the contrary, equipment, land, and buildings produce benefits for a company through their *use* in the production of goods and services. Unlike those of natural resources, their physical characteristics usually remain unchanged during their useful lives.

Sometimes a company buys natural resources from another company. In that case, initial valuation is simply the purchase price plus any other costs necessary to bring the asset to condition and location for use. More frequently, though, the company will develop these assets. In this situation, the initial valuation can include (a) acquisition costs, (b) exploration costs, (c) development costs, and (d) restoration costs. Acquisition costs are the amounts paid to acquire the rights to explore for undiscovered natural resources or to extract proven natural resources. Exploration costs are expenditures such as drilling a well, or excavating a mine, or any other costs of searching for natural resources. Development costs are incurred after the resource has been discovered but before production begins. They include a variety of costs such as expenditures for tunnels, wells, and shafts. It is not unusual for the cost of a natural resource, either purchased or developed, to include estimated restoration costs. These are costs to restore land or other property to its original condition after extraction of the natural resource ends. Because restoration expenditures occur later—after production begins—they initially represent an obligation incurred in conjunction with an asset retirement. Restoration costs are one example of *asset retirement obligations,* the topic of the next subsection.

The cost of a natural resource includes the *acquisition costs* for the use of land, the *exploration* and *development costs* incurred before production begins, and *restoration costs* incurred during or at the end of extraction.

On the other hand, the costs of heavy equipment and other assets a company uses during drilling or excavation usually are not considered part of the cost of the natural resource itself. Instead, they are considered depreciable plant and equipment. However, if an asset used in the development of a natural resource cannot be moved and has no alternative use, its depreciable life is limited by the useful life of the natural resource.

ASSET RETIREMENT OBLIGATIONS. Sometimes a company incurs obligations associated with the disposition of property, plant, and equipment and natural resources, often as a result of acquiring those assets. For example, an oil and gas exploration company might be required to restore land to its original condition after extraction is completed. Before 2001, there was considerable diversity in the ways companies accounted for these obligations. Some companies recognized these asset retirement obligations (AROs) gradually over the life of the asset while others did not recognize the obligations until the asset was retired or sold.

An asset retirement obligation (ARO) is measured at fair value and is recognized as a liability and corresponding increase in asset valuation.

Generally accepted accounting principles require that an existing legal obligation associated with the retirement of a tangible, long-lived asset be recognized as a liability and

[3]Because of this characteristic, natural resources sometimes are called *wasting assets.*

measured at fair value, if value can be reasonably estimated. When the liability is credited, the offsetting debit is to the related asset.[4] These retirement obligations could arise in connection with several types of assets. We introduce the topic here because it often arises with natural resources. Let's consider some of the provisions of the standard that addresses these obligations.

Scope. AROs arise only from *legal* obligations associated with the retirement of a tangible long-lived asset that result from the acquisition, construction, or development and (or) normal operation of a long-lived asset.

Recognition. A retirement obligation might arise at the inception of an asset's life or during its operating life. For instance, an offshore oil-and-gas production facility typically incurs its removal obligation when it begins operating. On the other hand, a landfill or a mining operation might incur a reclamation obligation gradually over the life of the asset as space is consumed with waste or as the mine is excavated.

Measurement. A company recognizes the fair value of an ARO in the period it's incurred. The amount of the liability increases the valuation of the related asset. Usually, the fair value is estimated by calculating the present value of estimated future cash outflows.

Present value calculations. Traditionally, the way uncertainty has been considered in present value calculations has been by discounting the "best estimate" of future cash flows applying a discount rate that has been adjusted to reflect the uncertainty or risk of those cash flows. That's not the approach we take here. Instead, we follow the approach described in the FASB's *Concept Statement No. 7* which is to adjust the cash flows, not the discount rate, for the uncertainty or risk of those cash flows.[5] This **expected cash flow approach** incorporates specific probabilities of cash flows into the analysis. We use a discount rate equal to the *credit-adjusted risk free rate.* The higher a company's credit risk, the higher will be the discount rate. All other uncertainties or risks are incorporated into the cash flow probabilities. We first considered an illustration of this approach in Chapter 6. Illustration 10–6 demonstrates the approach in connection with the acquisition of a natural resource.

Illustration 10–6

Cost of Natural Resources

The Jackson Mining Company paid $1,000,000 for the right to explore for a coal deposit on 500 acres of land in Pennsylvania. Costs of exploring for the coal deposit totaled $800,000 and intangible development costs incurred in digging and erecting the mine shaft were $500,000. In addition, Jackson purchased new excavation equipment for the project at a cost of $600,000. After the coal is removed from the site, the equipment will be sold.

Jackson is required by its contract to restore the land to a condition suitable for recreational use after it extracts the coal. The company has provided the following three cash flow possibilities (A, B, and C) for the restoration costs to be paid in three years, after extraction is completed:

	Cash Outflow	Probability
A	$500,000	30%
B	600,000	50%
C	700,000	20%

The company's credit-adjusted risk free interest rate is 8%.

[4]FASB ASC 410–20–25: Asset Retirement and Environmental Obligations–Asset Retirement Obligations–Recognition (previously "Accounting for Asset Retirement Obligations," *Statement of Financial Accounting Standards No. 143* (Norwalk, Conn.: FASB, 2001)).

[5]"Using Cash Flow Information and Present Value in Accounting Measurements," *Statement of Financial Accounting Concepts No. 7* (Norwalk, Conn.: FASB, 2000).

Illustration 10–6

Continued

Total capitalized cost for the coal deposit is:

Purchase of rights to explore	$1,000,000
Exploration costs	800,000
Development costs	500,000
Restoration costs	468,360*
Total cost of coal deposit	$2,768,360

*Present value of expected cash outflow for restoration costs (asset retirement obligation):

$500,000 × 30% = $150,000
600,000 × 50% = 300,000
700,000 × 20% = 140,000
$590,000 × 0.79383 = $468,360
(0.79383 is the present value of $1, $n = 3$, $i = 8\%$)

Journal Entries

Coal mine (determined above)	2,768,360	
Cash ($1,000,000 + 800,000 + 500,000)		2,300,000
Asset retirement liability (determined above)		468,360
Excavation equipment	600,000	
Cash (cost)		600,000

As we discuss in Chapter 11, the cost of the coal mine is allocated to future periods as *depletion* using a depletion rate based on the estimated amount of coal discovered. The $600,000 cost of the excavation equipment, less any anticipated residual value, is allocated to future periods as *depreciation.*

Additionally, the difference between the asset retirement liability of $468,360 and the probability-weighted expected cash outflow of $590,000 is recognized as accretion expense, an additional expense that accrues as an operating expense, over the three-year excavation period. This process increases the liability to $590,000 by the end of the excavation period.

Year	Accretion Expense	Increase in Balance	Asset Retirement Obligation
			468,360
1	8% (468,360) = 37,469	37,469	505,829
2	8% (505,829) = 40,466	40,466	546,295
3	8% (546,295) = 43,705*	43,705	590,000

*Rounded

The journal entry to record accretion expense for the first year is as follows:

Accretion expense	37,469	
Asset retirement liability		37,469

If the actual restoration costs are more (less) than the $590,000, we recognize a loss (gain) on retirement of the obligation for the difference. For example, if the actual restoration costs were $625,000, we would record the transaction as follows:

Asset retirement liability	590,000	
Loss ($625,000 − 590,000)	35,000	
Cash		625,000

Asset retirement obligations could result from the acquisition of many different types of tangible assets, not just natural resources.

SM Energy Company is engaged in the exploration, development, acquisition, and production of natural gas and crude oil. For the year ended December 31, 2015, SM reported $137.5 million in asset retirement obligations in its balance sheet. A disclosure note included in a recent annual report shown in Illustration 10–7 describes the company's policy and provides a summary of disclosure requirements.

It is important to understand that asset retirement obligations could result from the acquisition of many different types of tangible assets, not just natural resources. For example,

Note 9—Asset Retirement Obligations (in part)

The Company recognizes an estimated liability for future costs associated with the plugging and abandonment of its oil and gas properties. A liability for the fair value of an asset retirement obligation ("ARO") and a corresponding increase to the carrying value of the related long-lived asset are recorded at the time a well is drilled or acquired. The increase in carrying value is included in proved oil and gas properties in the accompanying balance sheets. The Company depletes the amount added to proved oil and gas property costs and recognizes expense in connection with the accretion of the discounted liability over the remaining estimated economic lives of the respective oil and gas properties. Cash paid to settle asset retirement obligations is included in the operating section of the Company's accompanying statements of cash flows.

The Company's estimated asset retirement obligation liability is based on historical experience in plugging and abandoning wells, estimated economic lives, estimated plugging and abandonment cost, and federal and state regulatory requirements. The liability is discounted using the credit-adjusted risk-free rate estimated at the time the liability is incurred or revised. The credit-adjusted risk-free rates used to discount the Company's plugging and abandonment liabilities range from 5.5 percent to 12 percent. In periods subsequent to initial measurement of the liability, the Company must recognize period-to-period changes in the liability resulting from the passage of time, revisions to either the amount of the original estimate of undiscounted cash flows or changes in inflation factors or the Company's credit-adjusted risk-free rate as market conditions warrant.

Illustration 10–7

Disclosure of Asset Retirement Obligations—SM Energy Company

Real World Financials

Dow Chemical Company reported a $96 million asset retirement liability in its 2016 balance sheet related to anticipated demolition and remediation activities at its manufacturing sites in the United States, Canada, Brazil, China, Argentina, Australia, and Europe; and capping activities at landfill sites in the United States, Canada, Brazil, and Italy.

Sometimes, after exploration or development, it becomes apparent that continuing the project is economically infeasible. If that happens, any costs incurred are expensed rather than capitalized. An exception is in the oil and gas industry, where we have two generally accepted accounting alternatives for accounting for projects that prove unsuccessful. We discuss these alternatives in Appendix 10.

Intangible Assets

Intangible assets are assets, other than financial assets, that lack physical substance. They include such items as patents, copyrights, trademarks, franchises, and goodwill. Despite their lack of physical substance, these assets can be extremely valuable resources for a company. For example, Interbrand Sampson, the world's leading branding consulting company, recently estimated the value of the Coca-Cola trademark to be $78 billion.[6] In general, intangible assets refer to the ownership of exclusive rights that provide benefits to the owner in the production of goods and services.

Intangible assets generally represent exclusive rights that provide benefits to the owner.

The issues involved in accounting for intangible assets are similar to those of property, plant, and equipment. One key difference, though, is that the future benefits that we attribute to intangible assets usually are much less certain than those attributed to tangible assets. For example, will the new toy for which a company acquires a patent be accepted by the market? If so, will it be a blockbuster like Silly Bandz or Rubik's Cube, or will it be only a moderate success? Will it have lasting appeal like Barbie dolls, or will it be a short-term fad? In short, it's often very difficult to anticipate the timing, and even the existence, of future benefits attributable to many intangible assets. In fact, this uncertainty is a discriminating characteristic of intangible assets that perhaps better distinguishes them from tangible assets than their lack of physical substance. After all, other assets, too, do not exist physically but are not considered intangible assets. Accounts receivable and prepaid expenses, for example, have no physical substance and yet are reported among tangible assets.

Companies can either (1) *purchase* intangible assets from other entities (existing patent, copyright, trademark, or franchise rights) or (2) *develop* intangible assets internally (say, develop a new product or process that is then patented). For purchased intangible assets, the

Purchased intangible assets are valued at their original cost.

[6]This $78 billion represents an estimate of the fair value to the company at the time the estimate was made, not the historical cost valuation that appears in the balance sheet of Coca-Cola.

initial valuation usually is quite simple. We value a purchased intangible at its original cost, which includes its purchase price and all other costs necessary to bring it to condition and location for intended use. For example, if a company purchases a patent from another entity, it might pay legal fees and filing fees in addition to the purchase price. We value intangible assets acquired in exchange for stock, or for other nonmonetary assets, or with deferred payment contracts exactly as we do property, plant, and equipment.

The cost of an intangible asset is amortized over its useful life unless it has an indefinite useful life.[7] Also, just like property, plant, and equipment, intangibles are subject to asset impairment rules. We discuss amortization and impairment in Chapter 11. In this chapter, we consider the acquisition cost of intangible assets. Let's look briefly at the costs of purchasing some of the more common intangible assets.

PATENTS. A patent is an exclusive right to manufacture a product or to use a process. This right is granted by the U.S. Patent Office for a period of 20 years. In essence, the holder of a patent has a monopoly on the use, manufacture, or sale of the product or process. If a patent is purchased from an inventor or another individual or company, the amount paid is its initial valuation. The cost might also include such other costs as legal and filing fees to secure the patent. Holders of patents often need to defend a patent in court against infringement. Any attorney fees and other costs of successfully defending a patent are added to the patent account.

When a patent is *developed internally,* the research and development costs of doing so are expensed as incurred. We discuss research and development in more detail in a later section. We capitalize legal and filing fees to secure the patent, even if internally developed.

COPYRIGHTS. A copyright is an exclusive right of protection given to a creator of a published work, such as a song, film, painting, photograph, or book. Copyrights are protected by law and give the creator the exclusive right to reproduce and sell the artistic or published work for the life of the creator plus 70 years. Accounting for the costs of copyrights is virtually identical to that of patents.

Trademarks or tradenames often are considered to have indefinite useful lives.

TRADEMARKS. A trademark, also called tradename, is an exclusive right to display a word, a slogan, a symbol, or an emblem that distinctively identifies a company, a product, or a service. The trademark can be registered with the U.S. Patent Office which protects the trademark from use by others for a period of 10 years. The registration can be renewed for an indefinite number of 10-year periods, so a trademark is an example of an intangible asset whose useful life could be indefinite.

Trademarks or tradenames often are acquired through a business combination. As an example, in 2002, Hewlett-Packard Company (HP) acquired all of the outstanding stock of Compaq Computer Corporation for $24 billion. Of that amount, $1.4 billion was assigned to the Compaq tradename. HP stated in a disclosure note that this ". . . intangible asset will not be amortized because it has an indefinite remaining useful life based on many factors and considerations, including the length of time that the Compaq name has been in use, the Compaq brand awareness and market position and the plans for continued use of the Compaq brand within a portion of HP's overall product portfolio."

Trademarks or tradenames can be very valuable. The estimated value of $78 billion for the Coca-Cola trademark mentioned previously is a good example. Note that the cost of the trademark reported in the balance sheet is far less than the estimate of its worth to the company. The Coca-Cola Company's balance sheet at December 31, 2015, disclosed all trademarks at a cost of only $6 billion.

Franchise operations are among the most common ways of doing business.

FRANCHISES. A franchise is a contractual arrangement under which the franchisor grants the franchisee the exclusive right to use the franchisor's trademark or tradename and may include product and formula rights, within a geographical area, usually for a specified period of time. Many popular retail businesses such as fast food outlets, automobile dealerships, and motels are franchises. For example, the last time you ordered a hamburger at McDonald's, you were probably dealing with a franchise.

The owner of that McDonald's outlet paid McDonald's Corporation a fee in exchange for the exclusive right to use the McDonald's name and to sell its products within a specified geographical

[7]FASB ASC 350–30–35–1: Intangibles–Goodwill and Other–General Intangibles Other Than Goodwill–Subsequent Measurement, and FASB ASC 350–20–35–1: Intangibles–Goodwill and Other–Goodwill–Subsequent Measurement (previously "Goodwill and Other Intangible Assets," *Statement of Financial Accounting Standards No. 142* (Norwalk, Conn.: FASB, 2001)).

area. In addition, many franchisors provide other benefits to the franchisee, such as participating in the construction of the retail outlet, training of employees, and national advertising.

Payments to the franchisor usually include an initial payment plus periodic payments over the life of the franchise agreement. The franchisee capitalizes as an intangible asset the initial franchise fee plus any legal costs associated with the contract agreement. The franchise asset is then amortized over the life of the franchise agreement. The periodic payments usually relate to services provided by the franchisor on a continuing basis and are expensed as incurred.

Most purchased intangibles are *specifically identifiable.* That is, cost can be directly associated with a specific intangible right. An exception is goodwill, which we discuss next.

GOODWILL. Goodwill is a unique intangible asset in that its cost can't be directly associated with any specifically identifiable right and it is not separable from the company itself. It represents the unique value of a company as a whole over and above its identifiable tangible and intangible assets. Goodwill can emerge from a company's clientele and reputation, its trained employees and management team, its favorable business location, and any other unique features of the company that can't be associated with a specific asset.

Goodwill can only be purchased through the acquisition of another company.

Because goodwill can't be separated from a company, it's not possible for a buyer to acquire it without also acquiring the whole company or a portion of it. Goodwill will appear as an asset in a balance sheet only when it was purchased in connection with the acquisition of control over another company. In that case, the capitalized cost of goodwill equals the fair value of the consideration exchanged (acquisition price) for the company less the fair value of the net assets acquired. The fair value of the net assets equals the fair value of all identifiable tangible and intangible assets less the fair value of any liabilities of the selling company assumed by the buyer. Goodwill is a residual asset; it's the amount left after other assets are identified and valued. Consider Illustration 10–8.

FINANCIAL Reporting Case

Q3, p. 517

Goodwill is the excess of the fair value of the consideration exchanged over the fair value of the net assets acquired.

Illustration 10–8

Goodwill

The Smithson Corporation acquired all of the outstanding common stock of the Rider Corporation in exchange for $180 million cash.* Smithson assumed all of Rider's long-term liabilities, which have a fair value of $120 million at the date of acquisition. The fair values of all identifiable assets of Rider are as follows ($ in millions):

Receivables	$ 50
Inventory	70
Property, plant, and equipment	90
Patent	40
Total	$250

The cost of the goodwill resulting from the acquisition is $50 million:

Fair value of consideration exchanged		$180
Less: Fair value of net assets acquired:		
Fair value of identifiable assets acquired	$250	
Less: Fair value of liabilities assumed	(120)	(130)
Goodwill		$ 50

The following journal entry captures the effect of the acquisition on Smithson's assets and liabilities:

Receivables (fair value)	50	
Inventory (fair value)	70	
Property, plant, and equipment (fair value)	90	
Patent (fair value)	40	
Goodwill (difference)	50	
Liabilities (fair value)		120
Cash (acquisition price)		180

*Determining the amount an acquirer is willing to pay for a company in excess of the identifiable net assets is a question of determining the value of a company as a whole. This question is addressed in most introductory and advanced finance textbooks.

Of course, a company can develop its own goodwill through advertising, training, and other efforts. In fact, most do. However, a company must expense all such costs incurred in the internal generation of goodwill. By not capitalizing these items, accountants realize that this results in an improper match of expenses with revenues because many of these expenditures do result in significant future benefits. Also, it's difficult to compare two companies when one has acquired goodwill and the other has not. But imagine how difficult it would be to associate these expenditures with any objective measure of goodwill. In essence, we have a situation where the characteristic of faithful representation overshadows relevance.

Goodwill, along with other intangible assets with indefinite useful lives, is not amortized.

Just like for other intangible assets that have indefinite useful lives, *we do not amortize goodwill.* This makes it imperative that companies make every effort to identify specific intangibles other than goodwill that they acquire in a business combination since goodwill is the amount left after other assets are identified.

Additional Consideration

It's possible for the fair value of net assets to exceed the fair value of the consideration exchanged for those net assets. A "bargain purchase" situation could result from an acquisition involving a "forced sale" in which the seller is acting under duress. The FASB previously required this excess, deemed *negative goodwill,* to be allocated as a pro rata reduction of the amounts that otherwise would have been assigned to particular assets acquired. This resulted in assets acquired being recorded at amounts less than their fair values. However, current GAAP makes it mandatory that assets and liabilities acquired in a business combination be valued at their fair values.[8] Any negative goodwill is reported as a gain in the year of the combination.

In a business combination, an intangible asset must be recognized as an asset apart from goodwill if it arises from contractual or other legal rights or is separable.

In keeping with that goal, GAAP provides guidelines for determining which intangibles should be separately recognized and valued. Specifically, an intangible should be recognized as an asset apart from goodwill if it arises from contractual or other legal rights or is capable of being separated from the acquired entity. Possibilities are patents, trademarks, copyrights, and franchise agreements, and such items as customer lists, license agreements, order backlogs, employment contracts, and noncompetition agreements.[9] In past years, some of these intangibles, if present in a business combination, often were included in the cost of goodwill.[10]

Additional Consideration

Contract Acquisition Costs. Chapter 5 introduced you to the new guidance on revenue recognition issued by the FASB in 2014. Under the new standard, sellers of goods and services are required to capitalize, as an intangible asset, the incremental costs of obtaining and fulfilling a long-term (longer than one year) contract. A sales commission is an example of a contract acquisition cost that could be capitalized, rather than expensed, under this new guidance.

If capitalized, the cost of the resulting intangible asset is amortized on a systematic basis that is consistent with the pattern of transfer of the goods or services to which the asset relates. The intangible asset also is evaluated for impairment using the same approach used for other intangible assets. We discuss amortization and impairment testing of intangible assets in Chapter 11.

[8]FASB ASC 805: Business Combinations (previously "Business Combinations," *Statement of Financial Accounting Standards No. 141 (revised)* (Norwalk, Conn.: FASB, 2007)).

[9]Ibid.

[10]An assembled workforce is an example of an intangible asset that is not recognized as a separate asset. A workforce does not represent a contractual or legal right, nor is it separable from the company as a whole.

Lump-Sum Purchases

● LO10–2

It's not unusual for a group of assets to be acquired for a single sum. If these assets are indistinguishable, for example 10 identical delivery trucks purchased for a lump-sum price of $150,000, valuation is obvious. Each of the trucks would be valued at $15,000 ($150,000 ÷ 10). However, if the lump-sum purchase involves different assets, it's necessary to allocate the lump-sum acquisition price among the separate items. The assets acquired may have different characteristics and different useful lives. For example, the acquisition of a factory may include assets that are significantly different such as land, building, and equipment.

The allocation is made in proportion to the individual assets' relative fair values. This process is best explained by an example in Illustration 10–9.

Illustration 10–9

Lump-Sum Purchase

The Smyrna Hand & Edge Tools Company purchased an existing factory for a single sum of $2,000,000. The price included title to the land, the factory building, the manufacturing equipment in the building, a patent on a process the equipment uses, and inventories of raw materials. An independent appraisal estimated the fair values of the assets (if purchased separately) at:

	Fair Values	
Land	$ 330,000	15%
Building	550,000	25
Equipment	660,000	30
Patent	440,000	20
Inventories	220,000	10
Total	$2,200,000	100%

The lump-sum purchase price of $2,000,000 is allocated to the separate assets as follows:

Land	(15% × $2,000,000)	300,000	
Building	(25% × $2,000,000)	500,000	
Equipment	(30% × $2,000,000)	600,000	
Patent	(20% × $2,000,000)	400,000	
Inventories	(10% × $2,000,000)	200,000	
Cash			2,000,000

The total purchase price is allocated in proportion to the relative fair values of the assets acquired.

The relative fair value percentages are multiplied by the lump-sum purchase price to determine the initial valuation of each of the separate assets. Notice that the lump-sum purchase includes inventories. The procedure used here to allocate the purchase price in a lump-sum acquisition pertains to any type of asset mix, not just to property, plant, and equipment and intangible assets.

Ethical Dilemma

Grandma's Cookie Company purchased a factory building. The company controller, Don Nelson, is in the process of allocating the lump-sum purchase price between land and building. Don suggests to the company's chief financial officer, Judith Prince, that they fudge a little by allocating a disproportionately higher share of the price to land. Don reasons that this will reduce depreciation expense, boost income, increase their profit-sharing bonus, and hopefully, increase the price of the company's stock. Judith has some reservations about this because the higher reported income will also cause income taxes to be higher than they would be if a correct allocation of the purchase price is made.

What are the ethical issues? What stakeholders' interests are in conflict?

PART B

Noncash Acquisitions

Companies sometimes acquire assets without paying cash at the time of the purchase. In Part B, we examine four situations where this occurs.

1. Deferred payments (notes payable)
2. Issuance of equity securities
3. Donated assets
4. Exchanges of nonmonetary assets for other assets

Assets acquired in noncash transactions are valued at the fair value of the assets given or the fair value of the assets received, whichever is more clearly evident.

The controlling principle in each of these situations is that in any noncash transaction, the asset acquired is recorded at its fair value. The first indicator of fair value is the fair value of the assets, debt, or equity securities given. Sometimes the fair value of the assets received is used when their fair value is more clearly evident than the fair value of the assets given.

Deferred Payments

● LO10–3

A company can acquire an asset by giving the seller a promise to pay cash in the future and thus creating a liability, usually a note payable. The initial valuation of the asset is, again, quite simple as long as the note payable explicitly requires the payment of interest at a realistic interest rate. For example, suppose a machine is acquired for $15,000 and the buyer signs a note requiring the payment of $15,000 sometime in the future *plus* interest in the meantime at a realistic interest rate. The machine would be valued at $15,000 and the transaction recorded as follows:

Machine	15,000	
Note payable		15,000

We know from our discussion of the time value of money in Chapter 6 that most liabilities are valued at the present value of future cash payments, reflecting an appropriate time value of money. As long as the note payable explicitly contains a realistic interest rate, the present value will equal the face value of the note, $15,000 in our previous example. This also should be equal to the fair value of the machine purchased. On the other hand, when an interest rate is not specified or is unrealistic, determining the cost of the asset is less straight-forward. In that case, the accountant should look beyond the form of the transaction and record its substance. Consider Illustration 10–10.

Illustration 10–10

Asset Acquired with Debt—Present Value of Note Indicative of Fair Value

On January 2, 2018, the Midwestern Steam Gas Corporation purchased an industrial furnace. In payment, Midwestern signed a noninterest-bearing note requiring $50,000 to be paid on December 31, 2019. If Midwestern had borrowed cash to buy the furnace, the bank would have required an interest rate of 10%.

Some portion of the payment(s) required by a noninterest-bearing note in reality is interest.

On the surface, it might appear that Midwestern is paying $50,000 for the furnace, the eventual cash payment. However, when you recognize that the agreement specifies no interest even though the payment won't be made for two years, it becomes obvious that a portion of the $50,000 payment is not actually payment for the furnace, but instead is interest on the note. At what amount should Midwestern value the furnace and the related note payable?

Noncash transactions are recorded at the fair value of the items exchanged.

The answer is fair value, as it is for any noncash transaction. This might be the fair value of the furnace or the fair value of the note. Let's say, in this situation, that the furnace is custom-built, so its cash price is unavailable. But Midwestern can determine the fair value of the note payable by computing the present value of the cash payments at the appropriate interest rate of 10%. The amount actually paid for the furnace, then, is the present value of the cash flows called for by the loan agreement, discounted at the market rate—10% in this case.

$$PV = \$50,000\ (0.82645^{*}) = \$41,323$$

*Present value of $1: $n = 2$, $i = 10\%$ (from Table 2).

So the furnace should be recorded at its *real* cost, $41,323, as follows:[11]

Furnace (determined above)	41,323	
Discount on note payable (difference)	8,677	
Note payable (face amount)		50,000

The economic essence of a transaction should prevail over its outward appearance.

Notice that the note also is recorded at $41,323, its present value, but this is accomplished by using a contra account, called *discount on note payable,* for the difference between the face amount of the note ($50,000) and its present value ($41,323). The difference of $8,677 is the portion of the eventual $50,000 payment that represents interest and is recognized as interest expense over the life of the note.

Assuming that Midwestern's fiscal year-end is December 31 and that adjusting entries are recorded only at the end of each year, the company would record the following entries at the end of 2018 and 2019 to accrue interest and the payment of the note:

December 31, 2018		
Interest expense ($41,323 × 10%)	4,132	
Discount on note payable		4,132
December 31, 2019		
Interest expense [($41,323 + 4,132)* × 10%]	4,545	
Discount on note payable		4,545
Note payable (face amount)	50,000	
Cash		50,000

*The 2018 unpaid interest increases the amount owed by $4,132.

Note payable

Jan. 1, 2018	50,000
50,000	Dec. 31, 2019
Bal. 12/31/19	0

Discount on note payable

8,677	Jan. 1, 2018
Dec. 31, 2018	4,132
Dec. 31, 2019	4,545
0	Bal. 12/31/19

Sometimes, the fair value of an asset acquired in a noncash transaction is readily available from price lists, previous purchases, or otherwise. In that case, this fair value may be more clearly evident than the fair value of the note and it would serve as the best evidence of the exchange value of the transaction. As an example, let's consider Illustration 10–11.

Illustration 10–11

Noninterest-Bearing Note—Fair Value of Asset Is Known

On January 2, 2018, Dennison, Inc., purchased a machine and signed a noninterest-bearing note in payment. The note requires the company to pay $100,000 on December 31, 2020. Dennison is not sure what interest rate appropriately reflects the time value of money. However, price lists indicate the machine could have been purchased for cash at a price of $79,383.

Dennison records both the asset and liability at $79,383 on January 2 as shown:

Machine (cash price)	79,383	
Discount on note payable (difference)	20,617	
Note payable (face amount)		100,000

In this situation, we infer the present value of the note from the fair value of the asset. Again, the difference between the note's $79,383 present value and the cash payment of $100,000 represents interest. We can determine the interest rate that is implicit in the agreement as follows:

$$\$79{,}383 \text{ (present value)} = \$100{,}000 \text{ (face amount)} \times \text{PV factor}$$
$$\$79{,}383 \div \$100{,}000 = 0.79383^*$$

*Present value of $1: $n = 3$, $i = ?$ (from Table 2, $i = 8\%$).

We refer to the 8% rate as the *implicit rate of interest.* Dennison records interest each year at 8% in the same manner as demonstrated in Illustration 10–10 and discussed in greater depth in Chapter 14.

[11]The entry shown assumes the note is recorded using the gross method. By the net method, a discount account is not used and the note is simply recorded at present value.

Furnace	41,323	
Note payable		41,323

We now turn our attention to the acquisition of assets acquired in exchange for equity securities and through donation.

Issuance of Equity Securities

LO10–4

The most common situation in which equity securities are issued for property, plant, and equipment and intangible assets occurs when small companies incorporate and the owner or owners contribute assets to the new corporation in exchange for ownership securities, usually common stock. Because the common shares are not publicly traded, it's difficult to determine their fair value. In that case, the fair value of the assets received by the corporation is probably the better indicator of the transaction's exchange value. In other situations, particularly those involving corporations whose stock is actively traded, the market value of the shares is the best indication of fair value. Consider Illustration 10–12.

Illustration 10–12
Asset Acquired by Issuing Equity Securities

Assets acquired by issuing common stock are valued at the fair value of the securities or the fair value of the assets, whichever is more clearly evident.

On March 31, 2018, the Elcorn Company issued 10,000 shares of its nopar common stock in exchange for land. On the date of the transaction, the fair value of the common stock, evidenced by its market price, was $20 per share. The journal entry to record this transaction is shown below:

Land	200,000	
Common stock (10,000 shares × $20)		200,000

If the fair value of the common stock had not been reliably determinable, the value of the land as determined through an independent appraisal would be used as the cost of the land and the value of the common stock.

Donated Assets

Donated assets are recorded at their fair values.

On occasion, companies acquire assets through donation. The donation usually is an enticement to do something that benefits the donor. For example, the developer of an industrial park might pay some of the costs of building a manufacturing facility to entice a company to locate in its park. Companies record assets donated by unrelated parties at their fair values based on either an available market price or an appraisal value. This should not be considered a departure from historical cost valuation. Instead, it is equivalent to the donor contributing cash to the company and the company using the cash to acquire the asset.

Revenue is credited for the amount paid by an unrelated party.

As the recipient records the asset at its fair value, what account receives the offsetting credit? Over the years, there has been disagreement over this question. Should the recipient increase its paid-in capital—the part of shareholders' equity representing investments in the firm? Or, should the donated asset be considered revenue? GAAP requires that donated assets be recorded as *revenue*.[12] Recall that revenues generally are inflows of assets from delivering or producing goods, rendering services, or from other activities that constitute the entity's ongoing major or central operations. The rationale is that the company receiving the donation is performing a service for the donor in exchange for the asset donated.

Corporations occasionally receive donations from governmental units. A local governmental unit might provide land or pay all or some of the cost of a new office building or manufacturing plant to entice a company to locate within its geographical boundaries. For example, the city of San Jose, California, paid a significant portion of the cost of a new office building for IBM Corporation. The new office building, located in downtown San Jose, brought jobs to a revitalized downtown area and increased revenues to the city. The City of San Jose did not receive an equity interest in IBM through its donation, but significantly benefited nevertheless. Illustration 10–13 provides an example.

[12]FASB ASC 958–605–15–2 and FASB ASC 958–605–25–2: Not-for-Profit Entities–Revenue Recognition–Scope and Scope Exceptions–Contributions Received (previously "Accounting for Contributions Received and Contributions Made," *Statement of Financial Accounting Standards No. 116* (Norwalk, Conn.: FASB, 1993)).

Illustration 10–13
Asset Donation

Elcorn Enterprises decided to relocate its office headquarters to the city of Westmont. The city agreed to pay 20% of the $20 million cost of building the headquarters in order to entice Elcorn to relocate. The building was completed on May 3, 2018. Elcorn paid its portion of the cost of the building in cash. Elcorn records the transaction as follows:

Building	20,000,000	
Cash		16,000,000
Revenue—donation of asset (20% × $20 million)		4,000,000

International Financial Reporting Standards

● LO10–9

IFRS requires government grants to be recognized in income over the periods necessary to match them on a systematic basis with the related costs that they are intended to compensate.

Government Grants. Both U.S. GAAP and IFRS require that companies value donated assets at their fair values. For government grants, though, the way that value is recorded is different under the two sets of standards. Unlike U.S. GAAP, donated assets are not recorded as revenue under IFRS. *IAS No. 20* requires that government grants be recognized in income over the periods necessary to match them on a systematic basis with the related costs that they are intended to compensate. So, for example, *IAS No. 20* allows two alternatives for grants related to assets.[13]

1. Deduct the amount of the grant in determining the initial cost of the asset.
2. Record the grant as a liability, deferred income, in the balance sheet and recognize it in the income statement systematically over the asset's useful life.

In Illustration 10–13, if a company chose the first option, the building would be recorded at $16 million. If instead the company chose the second option, the building would be recorded at $20 million, but rather than recognizing $4 million in revenue as with U.S. GAAP, a $4 million credit to deferred income would be recorded and recognized as income over the life of the building.

Siemens, a global electronics and electrical engineering company based in Germany, prepares its financial statements according to IFRS, and sometimes receives government grants for the purchase or production of fixed assets. The following disclosure note included with recent financial statements indicates that Siemens uses the first option, deducting the amount of the grant from the initial cost of the asset.

Government Grants (in part)
Grants awarded for the purchase or the production of fixed assets (grants related to assets) are generally offset against the acquisition or production costs of the respective assets and reduce future depreciations accordingly.

Property, plant, and equipment and intangible assets also can be acquired in an exchange. Because an exchange transaction inherently involves a disposition of one asset as it is given up in exchange for another, we cover these transactions next under Exchanges.

Decision Makers' Perspective

The property, plant, and equipment and intangible asset acquisition decision is among the most significant decisions that management must make. A decision to acquire a new fleet of airplanes or to build or purchase a new office building or manufacturing plant could influence a company's performance for many years.

These decisions, often referred to as capital budgeting decisions, require management to forecast all future net cash flows (cash inflows minus cash outflows) generated by the asset(s). These cash flows are then used in a model to determine if the future cash flows are sufficient to warrant the capital expenditure. One such model, the net present value model, compares the present value of future net cash flows with the required initial acquisition cost

[13]"Government Grants," *International Accounting Standard No. 20* (IASCF), as amended effective January 1, 2016.

of the asset(s). If the present value is higher than the acquisition cost, the asset is acquired. You have studied or will study capital budgeting in considerable depth in a financial management course. The introduction to the time value of money concept in Chapter 6 provided you with important tools necessary to evaluate capital budgeting decisions.

● LO10–5

A key to profitability is how well a company manages and utilizes its assets. Financial analysts often use activity, or turnover, ratios to evaluate a company's effectiveness in managing assets. This concept was illustrated with receivables and inventory in previous chapters. Property, plant, and equipment (PP&E) usually are a company's primary revenue-generating assets. Their efficient use is critical to generating a satisfactory return to owners. One ratio analysts often use to measure how effectively managers use PP&E is the fixed-asset turnover ratio. This ratio is calculated as follows:

The *fixed-asset turnover ratio* measures a company's effectiveness in managing property, plant, and equipment.

$$\text{Fixed-asset turnover ratio} = \frac{\text{Net sales}}{\text{Average fixed assets}}$$

The ratio indicates the level of sales generated by the company's investment in fixed assets. The denominator usually is the book value, sometimes called carrying value or carrying amount (cost less accumulated depreciation and depletion) of property, plant, and equipment.[14]

As with other turnover ratios, we can compare a company's fixed-asset turnover with that of its competitors, with an industry average, or with the same company's ratio over time. Let's compare the fixed-asset turnover ratios for The Gap, Inc., and Ross Stores, Inc., two companies in the retail apparel industry.

	($ in millions)			
	Gap		**Ross Stores**	
	2016	**2015**	**2016**	**2015**
Property, plant, and equipment (net)	$2,850	$2,773	$2,343	$2,274
Net sales—2016	$15,797		$11,940	

The 2016 fixed-asset turnover for Gap is 5.62 ($15,797 ÷ [($2,850 + 2,773) ÷ 2]) compared to the turnover for Ross Stores of 5.17 ($11,940 ÷ [($2,343 + 2,274) ÷ 2]). Gap is able to generate $0.45 more in sales dollars than Ross Stores for each dollar invested in fixed assets. ●

Exchanges

An asset received in an exchange of nonmonetary assets generally is valued at fair value.

Sometimes a company will acquire an asset in exchange for an asset other than cash. This frequently involves a trade-in by which a new asset is acquired in exchange for an old asset, and cash is given to equalize the fair values of the assets exchanged. The basic principle followed in these nonmonetary asset[15] exchanges is to value the asset received at fair value.

● LO10–6

This amount can be based on the fair value of the asset(s) given up or the fair value of the asset(s) received plus (or minus) any cash exchanged. In practice, we expect the fair value of total assets received to equal fair value of total assets given up in a fair trade. *We recognize a gain or loss for the difference between the fair value and the book value of the asset given up.* See the example in Illustration 10–14A.

In Illustration 10–14A, the fair value of the old asset ($150,000) was known. However, in a trade-in, quite often the fair value of the new asset is more clearly evident than the second-hand value of the asset traded in. For example, if it was known that the fair value of the new asset was $580,000, then the fair value of the old asset could have been determined by subtracting the cash paid ($580,000 − $430,000).

Let's modify the illustration slightly by assuming that the fair value of the old equipment is $75,000 instead of $150,000. Illustration 10–14B shows the journal entry to record the transaction.

[14]If intangible assets are significant, their book value could be added to the denominator to produce a turnover that reflects all long-revenue-producing assets. The use of book value provides an approximation of the company's current investment in these assets.

[15]Monetary items are assets and liabilities whose *amounts are fixed*, by contract or otherwise, in terms of a specific number of dollars. Others are considered nonmonetary.

Illustration 10–14A

Nonmonetary Asset Exchange—Gain

The Elcorn Company traded its laser equipment for the newer air-cooled ion lasers manufactured by American Laser Corporation. The old equipment had a book value of $100,000 (cost of $500,000 less accumulated depreciation of $400,000) and a **fair value of $150,000**. Elcorn also paid American Laser **$430,000 in cash** as part of the exchange. The following journal entry records the transaction:

Equipment—new ($150,000 + 430,000)	580,000	
Accumulated depreciation—old (account balance)	400,000	
Equipment—old (account balance)		500,000
Cash (amount paid)		430,000
Gain (to balance; also: $150,000 fair value − 100,000 book value)		50,000

The new laser equipment is recorded at $580,000, the fair value of the old equipment, $150,000, plus the cash given, $430,000. The old asset's account and accumulated depreciation are written off for their balances at the date of the exchange, and cash paid is recorded. Elcorn recognizes a gain of $50,000 for the difference between the old equipment's fair value, $150,000, and its book value, $100,000. The gain of $50,000 also is the amount needed to allow the debits to equal credits in the journal entry.

A gain is recognized when the fair value of an asset given is more than its book value.

Illustration 10–14B

Nonmonetary Asset Exchange—Loss

The Elcorn Company traded its laser equipment for the newer air-cooled ion lasers manufactured by American Laser Corporation. The old equipment had a book value of $100,000 (cost of $500,000 less accumulated depreciation of $400,000) and a **fair value of $75,000.** Elcorn also paid American Laser **$430,000 in cash** as part of the exchange. The following journal entry records the transaction:

Equipment—new ($75,000 + 430,000)	505,000	
Accumulated depreciation—old (account balance)	400,000	
Loss (to balance; also: $100,000 book value − 75,000 fair value)	25,000	
Equipment—old (account balance)		500,000
Cash (amount paid)		430,000

The new laser equipment is recorded at $505,000, the fair value of the old equipment, $75,000, plus the cash given, $430,000. Elcorn recognizes a loss of $25,000 for the difference between the old equipment's fair value, $75,000, and its book value, $100,000. The loss of $25,000 also is the amount needed to allow the debits to equal credits in the journal entry.

A loss is recognized when the fair value of an asset given is less than its book value

It's important to understand that the gain or loss recognized in these transactions is the difference between the fair value and book value of the asset given. *The amount of cash given or received has no effect on the amount of gain or loss recognized.* The cash given or received simply serves to equalize the fair value of the assets exchanged.

Until 2005, the accounting treatment of nonmonetary asset exchanges depended on a number of factors including (1) whether the assets exchanged were similar or dissimilar, (2) whether a gain or loss was indicated in the exchange, and (3) whether cash was given or received. Then a new accounting standard[16] simplified accounting for exchanges by requiring the use of fair value except in rare situations in which the fair value can't be determined or the exchange lacks commercial substance.[17]

Let's discuss these two rare situations.

Fair Value Not Determinable

It would be unusual for a company to be unable to reasonably determine fair value of either asset in an exchange. Nevertheless, if the situation does occur, the company would simply use the book value of the asset given up, plus (minus) any cash given (received) to value the

[16]FASB ASC 845: Nonmonetary Transactions (previously "Exchanges of Nonmonetary Assets an amendment of APB Opinion No. 29," *Statement of Financial Accounting Standards No. 153* (Norwalk, Conn.: FASB, 2004)).

[17]There is a third situation which precludes the use of fair value in a nonmonetary exchange. The transaction is an exchange of inventories to facilitate sales to customers other than the parties to the exchange.

asset acquired. For example, if fair value had not been determinable in Illustration 10–14A, Elcorn would have recorded the exchange as follows:

If we can't determine the fair value of either asset in the exchange, the asset received is valued at the book value of the asset given.

Equipment—new (book value + cash: $100,000 + 430,000)	530,000	
Accumulated depreciation—old (account balance)	400,000	
Equipment—old (account balance)		500,000
Cash (amount paid)		430,000

The new equipment is valued at the book value of the old equipment ($100,000) plus the cash given ($430,000). No gain or loss is recognized.

Lack of Commercial Substance

If we record an exchange at fair value, we recognize a gain or loss for the difference between the fair value and book value of the asset(s) given up. To prevent a company from exchanging an asset whose fair value is greater than book value for the sole purpose of recognizing a gain, fair value can be used only in gain situations that have "commercial substance."

Commercial substance occurs when future cash flows change as a result of the exchange.

A nonmonetary exchange is considered to have commercial substance if future cash flows will change as a result of the exchange. Most exchanges are for business reasons and would not be transacted if there were no anticipated change in future cash flows. For example, newer models of equipment can increase production or improve manufacturing efficiency, causing an increase in revenue or a decrease in operating costs with a corresponding increase in future cash flows. The exchange of old laser equipment for the *newer* model in Illustration 10–14A is an example of an exchange transacted for business reasons.

GAIN SITUATION. Suppose a company owned a tract of land that had a book value of $1 million and a fair value of $5 million. The only ways to recognize the $4 million difference as a gain are to either sell the land or to exchange the land for another nonmonetary asset for a legitimate business purpose. For example, if the land were exchanged for a different type of asset, say an office building, then future cash flows most likely will change. In this case, the exchange has commercial substance, and the $4 million gain can be recognized. On the other hand, if the land were exchanged for a tract of land that has the identical characteristics as the land given, then it is unlikely that future cash flows would change. In this case, the exchange lacks commercial substance and the new land is valued at the book value of the old land. Illustration 10–15 provides an example.

Illustration 10–15
Nonmonetary Asset Exchange—Exchange Lacks Commercial Substance

The Elcorn Company traded a tract of land to Sanchez Development for a similar tract of land. The old land had a book value of $2,500,000 and a fair value of $4,500,000. Elcorn also paid Sanchez $500,000 in cash. The following journal entry records the transaction, *assuming that the exchange lacks commercial substance:*

Land—new (book value + cash: $2,500,000 + 500,000)	3,000,000	
Land—old (account balance)		2,500,000
Cash (amount paid)		500,000

The new land is recorded at $3,000,000, the book value of the old land, $2,500,000, plus the cash given, $500,000. No gain is recognized because the exchange does not have commercial substance.

The FASB's intent in including the commercial substance requirement for the use of fair value was to avoid companies' trading property for no business reason other than to recognize the gain.

When the fair value of the asset given is less than its book value, we always use fair value to record the exchange.

LOSS SITUATION. In Illustration 10–15, what if the fair value of the land given was less than its book value? It's unlikely that a company would enter into this type of transaction unless there was a good reason. When a loss is indicated in a nonmonetary exchange, it's okay to record the loss and we use fair value to value the asset acquired.

Additional Consideration

In Illustration 10–15, cash was *given*. What if cash was *received*? Suppose that $450,000 cash was received instead of the $500,000 given. The fair value of the old land was $4,500,000, which means that the fair value of the land received is $4,050,000 ($4,500,000 – $450,000). In that case, a portion of the transaction is considered monetary and we would recognize that portion of the $2,000,000 gain ($4,500,000 fair value – $2,500,000 book value). The amount of gain recognized is equal to the portion of cash received relative to the total received.[18]

$$\frac{\$450{,}000}{\$450{,}000 + 4{,}050{,}000} = 10\%$$

Elcorn would recognize a $200,000 gain ($2,000,000 × 10%) and would value the land received at $2,250,000, the book value of the land given ($2,500,000), plus the gain recognized ($200,000), less the cash received ($450,000). The following journal entry records the transaction:

Land—new ($2,500,000 + 200,000 – 450,000)	2,250,000	
Cash	450,000	
Land—old		2,500,000
Gain		200,000

Illustration 10–16 summarizes the treatment of gains and losses, as well as the amount to record for the asset received, for each type of exchange discussed above.

Illustration 10–16
Exchanges

Type of Exchange	Amount of Gain/Loss to Recognized on Exchange	Amount to Record for Asset Received*
Fair value determinable	Gain = FV given – BV given.†	FV given + cash paid (or – cash received).
	Loss = BV given – FV given.	Same as above.
Fair value not determinable	No gain or loss recognized.	BV given + cash paid (or – cash received).
Lack of commercial substance	Gain = (FV given – BV given) × (cash received ÷ total FV received).	BV given – cash received + gain recognized.
	Gain = 0, if no cash received.	BV given + cash paid.
	Loss = BV given – FV given.	FV given + cash paid (or – cash received).

*For each type of exchange, the asset given is written off at its book value (cost less accumulated depreciation) at the date of the exchange.
†FV = fair value; BV = book value. All references to FV and BV relate to the asset being given in the exchange.

When fair value is determinable, we record the asset received at total fair value. Gains and losses are recorded for the difference between the fair value and book value of the asset given, depending on which is higher.

When fair value is not determinable, fair value cannot be used to record the asset being received, and therefore we don't record a gain or loss on the asset being given. The asset received is simply recorded for the book value of the asset given, adjusted for the effects of any cash exchanged.

The rules for exchanges that lack commercial substance reflect a bias toward preventing gains from being recognized unless some cash is received so that a portion of the transaction represents a monetary exchange. Losses in exchanges that lack commercial substance are fully recognized regardless of cash received or paid, just like losses when fair value is determinable.

[18]If the amount of monetary consideration received is deemed significant, the transaction is considered to be monetary and the entire gain is recognized. In other words, the transaction is accounted for as if it had commercial substance. GAAP defines "significance" in this situation as 25% or more of the fair value of the exchange. FASB ASC 845–10–25–6: Nonmonetary transactions–Overall–Recognition (previously "Interpretations of *APB Opinion No. 29,*" *EITF Abstracts No. 01–02* (Norwalk, Conn.: FASB, 2002)).

Concept Review Exercise

EXCHANGES

The MD Corporation recently acquired new equipment to be used in its production process. In exchange, the company traded in an existing asset that had an original cost of $60,000 and accumulated depreciation on the date of the exchange of $45,000. In addition, MD paid $40,000 cash to the equipment manufacturer. The fair value of the old equipment is $17,000.

Required:

1. Prepare the journal entry MD would use to record the exchange transaction assuming that the transaction has commercial substance.
2. Prepare the journal entry MD would use to record the exchange transaction assuming that the transaction does *not* have commercial substance.
3. Prepare the journal entry MD would use to record the exchange transaction assuming that the fair value of the old equipment is only $10,000.

Solution:

1. Prepare the journal entry MD would use to record the exchange transaction assuming that the transaction has commercial substance.

Equipment—new ($17,000 + 40,000)	57,000	
Accumulated depreciation—old (account balance)	45,000	
Equipment—old (account balance)		60,000
Cash (amount paid)		40,000
Gain ($17,000 fair value − $15,000 book value)		2,000

2. Prepare the journal entry MD would use to record the exchange transaction assuming that the transaction does not have commercial substance.

Equipment—new ($15,000 + 40,000)	55,000	
Accumulated depreciation—old (account balance)	45,000	
Equipment—old (account balance)		60,000
Cash (amount paid)		40,000

3. Prepare the journal entry MD would use to record the exchange transaction assuming that the fair value of the old equipment is only $10,000.

Equipment—new ($10,000 + 40,000)	50,000	
Accumulated depreciation—old (account balance)	45,000	
Loss ($15,000 book value − $10,000 fair value)	5,000	
Equipment—old (account balance)		60,000
Cash (amount paid)		40,000

PART C

Self-Constructed Assets and Research and Development

Two types of expenditures relating to property, plant, and equipment and intangible assets whose accounting treatment has generated considerable controversy are interest costs pertaining to self-constructed assets and amounts spent for research and development. We now consider those expenditures and why those controversies have developed.

Self-Constructed Assets

LO10–7

A company might decide to construct an asset for its own use rather than buy an existing one. For example, a retailer like Nordstrom might decide to build its own store rather than purchase an existing building. A manufacturing company like Intel could construct its own manufacturing facility. In fact, Nordstrom and Intel are just two of the many companies that self-construct assets. Other recognizable examples include Walt Disney, Sears, and Caterpillar. Quite often these companies act as the main contractor and then subcontract most of the actual construction work.

The critical accounting issue in these instances is identifying the cost of the self-constructed asset. The task is more difficult than for purchased assets because there is no external transaction to establish an exchange price. Actually, two difficulties arise in connection with assigning costs to self-constructed assets: (1) determining the amount of the company's indirect manufacturing costs (overhead) to be allocated to the construction and (2) deciding on the proper treatment of interest (actual or implicit) incurred during construction.

Overhead Allocation

One difficulty of associating costs with self-constructed assets is the same difficulty encountered when determining cost of goods manufactured for sale. The costs of material and direct labor usually are easily identified with a particular construction project and are included in cost. However, the treatment of manufacturing overhead cost and its allocation between construction projects and normal production is a controversial issue.

The cost of a self-constructed asset includes identifiable materials and labor and a portion of the company's manufacturing overhead costs.

Some accountants advocate the inclusion of only the *incremental* overhead costs in the total cost of construction. That is, the asset's cost would include only those additional costs that are incurred because of the decision to construct the asset. This would exclude such indirect costs as depreciation and the salaries of supervisors that would be incurred whether or not the construction project is undertaken. If, however, a new construction supervisor was hired specifically to work on the project, then that salary would be included in asset cost.

Others advocate assigning overhead on the same basis that is used for a regular manufacturing process. That is, all overhead costs are allocated both to production and to self-constructed assets based on the relative amount of a chosen cost driver (for example, labor hours) incurred. This is known as the *full-cost approach* and is the generally accepted method used to determine the cost of a self-constructed asset.

Interest Capitalization

To reiterate, the cost of an asset includes all costs necessary to get the asset ready for its intended use. Unlike one purchased from another company, a self-constructed asset requires time to create it. During this construction period, the project must be financed in some way. This suggests the question as to whether interest costs during the construction period are one of the costs of acquiring the asset itself or simply costs of financing the asset.

FINANCIAL Reporting Case

Q4, p. 517

On the one hand, we might point to interest charges to finance inventories during their period of manufacture or to finance the purchase of plant assets from others and argue that construction period interest charges are merely costs of financing the asset that should be expensed as incurred like all other interest costs.

On the other hand, we might argue that self-constructed assets are different in that during the construction period, they are not yet ready for their intended use for producing revenues. And, so, in keeping with the historical cost principle, all costs during this period, including interest, should be capitalized. Those costs are then allocated as depreciation during later periods when the assets are providing benefits.

QUALIFYING ASSETS Generally accepted accounting principles are consistent with the second argument. Specifically, interest is capitalized during the construction period for (a) assets built for a company's own use as well as for (b) assets constructed *as discrete projects* for sale or lease (a ship or a real estate development, for example). This excludes from interest capitalization consideration inventories that are routinely manufactured in large quantities on a repetitive basis and assets that already are in use or are ready for their intended use.[19] Interest costs incurred during the productive life of the asset are expensed as incurred.

Only assets that are constructed as discrete projects qualify for interest capitalization.

[19]FASB ASC 835–20–25: Interest–Capitalization of Interest–Recognition (previously "Capitalization of Interest Costs," *Statement of Financial Accounting Standards No. 34* (Stamford, Conn.: FASB, 1979)).

The interest capitalization period begins when construction begins and the first expenditure is made as long as interest costs are actually being incurred.

PERIOD OF CAPITALIZATION. The capitalization period for a self-constructed asset starts with the first expenditure (materials, labor, or overhead) and ends either when the asset is substantially complete and ready for use or when interest costs no longer are being incurred. Interest costs incurred can pertain to borrowings other than those obtained specifically for the construction project. However, interest costs can't be imputed; actual interest costs must be incurred.

Average accumulated expenditures approximates the average debt necessary for construction.

AVERAGE ACCUMULATED EXPENDITURES. Because we consider interest to be a necessary cost of getting a self-constructed asset ready for use, the amount capitalized is only that portion of interest cost incurred during the construction period that *could have been avoided* if expenditures for the asset had not been made. In other words, if construction had not been undertaken, debt incurred for the project would not have been necessary and/or other interest-bearing debt could have been liquidated or employed elsewhere.

As a result, interest should be determined for only the construction expenditures *actually incurred* during the capitalization period. And unless all expenditures are made at the outset of the period, it's necessary to determine the *average* amount outstanding during the period. This is the amount of debt that would be required to finance the expenditures and thus the amount on which interest would accrue. For instance, if a company accumulated $1,500,000 of construction expenditures fairly evenly throughout the construction period, the average expenditures would be:

Total accumulated expenditures incurred evenly throughout the period	$1,500,000
	÷2
Average accumulated expenditures	$ 750,000

At the beginning of the period, no expenditures have accumulated, so no interest has accrued (on the equivalent amount of debt). But, by the end of the period interest is accruing on the total amount, $1,500,000. On average, then, interest accrues on half the total or $750,000.

Average accumulated expenditures is determined by time-weighting individual expenditures made during the construction period.

If expenditures are not incurred evenly throughout the period, a simple average is insufficient. In that case, a *weighted average* is determined by time-weighting individual expenditures or groups of expenditures by the number of months from their incurrence to the end of the construction period.

Let's use the expenditures and loan information in Illustration 10–17 to demonstrate the calculation of interest capitalization. This calculation will involve three steps: (1) determine the weighted-average accumulated expenditures, (2) calculate the amount of interest to be capitalized, and (3) compare calculated interest with actual interest incurred.

Illustration 10–17

Expenditures and Loan Information for Interest Capitalization

On January 1, 2018, the Mills Conveying Equipment Company began construction of a building to be used as its office headquarters. The building was completed on June 30, 2019. Expenditures on the project, mainly payments to subcontractors, were as follows:

January 1, 2018	$ 500,000
March 31, 2018	400,000
September 30, 2018	600,000
Accumulated expenditures at December 31, 2018 (before interest capitalization)	$1,500,000
January 31, 2019	600,000
April 30, 2019	300,000

On January 1, 2018, the company obtained a $1 million construction loan with an 8% interest rate. The loan was outstanding during the entire construction period. The company's other interest-bearing debt included two long-term notes of $2,000,000 and $4,000,000 with interest rates of 6% and 12%, respectively. Both notes were outstanding during the entire construction period.

The weighted-average accumulated expenditures by the end of 2018 are shown below:

FINANCIAL Reporting Case

Q5, p. 517

	Actual Expenditures		Portion of Year Outstanding		Time-Weighted Expenditures
January 1, 2018	$ 500,000	×	12/12	=	$ 500,000
March 31, 2018	400,000	×	9/12	=	300,000
September 30, 2018	600,000	×	3/12	=	150,000
	$1,500,000				$950,000

Notice that the weighted-average accumulated expenditures are less than the actual accumulated expenditures of $1,500,000. If Mills had borrowed exactly the amount necessary to finance the project, it would not have incurred interest on a loan of $1,500,000 for the whole year but only on an average loan of $950,000. The next step is to determine the interest to be capitalized for the weighted-average accumulated expenditures.

STEP 1: Determine the weighted-average accumulated expenditures.

INTEREST RATES. In this situation, debt financing was obtained specifically for the construction project, and the amount borrowed is sufficient to cover the average accumulated expenditures. To determine the interest capitalized, then, we simply multiply the construction loan rate of 8% by the weighted-average accumulated expenditures.

STEP 2: Calculate the amount of interest to be capitalized.

The amount of interest capitalized is determined by multiplying an interest rate by the average accumulated expenditures.

$$\text{Interest capitalized for 2018} = \$950{,}000 \times 8\% = \$76{,}000$$

Notice that this is the same answer we would get by assuming separate 8% construction loans were made for each expenditure at the time each expenditure was made.

Actual Expenditures		Annual Rate		Portion of Year Outstanding		Calculated Interest
$500,000	×	8%	×	12/12	=	$ 40,000
400,000	×	8%	×	9/12	=	24,000
600,000	×	8%	×	3/12	=	12,000
Interest capitalized for 2018						$76,000

The interest of $76,000 is added to the cost of the building, bringing accumulated expenditures at December 31, 2018, to $1,576,000 ($1,500,000 + 76,000). The remaining interest cost incurred but not capitalized is expensed.

It should be emphasized that interest capitalization does not require that funds actually be borrowed for this specific purpose, only that the company does have outstanding debt. The presumption is that even if the company doesn't borrow specifically for the project, funds from other borrowings must be diverted to finance the construction. Either way—directly or indirectly—interest costs are incurred. In our illustration, for instance, even without the construction loan, interest would be capitalized because other debt was outstanding. The capitalized interest would be the average accumulated expenditures multiplied by the weighted-average rate on these other loans. The weighted-average interest rate on all debt other than the construction loan would be 10%, calculated as follows:[20]

Loans		Annual Rate		Interest
$2,000,000	×	6%	=	$120,000
4,000,000	×	12%	=	480,000
$6,000,000				$600,000

$$\text{Weighted-average rate: } \frac{\$600{,}000}{\$6{,}000{,}000} = 10\%$$

[20]The same result can be obtained simply by multiplying the individual debt interest rates by the relative amount of debt at each rate. In this case, one-third of total debt is at 6% and two-thirds of the total debt is at 12% [(1/3 × 6%) + (2/3 × 12%) = 10%].

This is a weighted average because total interest is $600,000 on total debt of $6,000,000. Therefore, in our illustration, without any specific construction loan, interest capitalized for 2018 would have been $95,000 ($950,000 × 10%).

Additional Consideration

The weighted-average rate isn't used for 2018 in our illustration because the specific construction loan is sufficient to cover the average accumulated expenditures. If the specific construction loan had been insufficient to cover the average accumulated expenditures, its 8% interest rate would be applied to the average accumulated expenditures up to the amount of the specific borrowing, and any remaining average accumulated expenditures in excess of specific borrowings would be multiplied by the weighted-average rate on all other outstanding interest-bearing debt. Suppose, for illustration, that the 8% construction loan had been only $500,000 rather than $1,000,000. We would calculate capitalized interest using both the specific rate and the weighted-average rate:

	Time-Weighted Expenditures		Annual Rate		Calculated Interest
Total	$950,000				
Specific borrowing	500,000	×	8%	=	$40,000
Excess	$450,000	×	10%	=	45,000
Capitalized interest					$85,000

In our illustration, it's necessary to use this approach in 2019.

Interest capitalized is limited to interest incurred.

It's possible that the amount of interest calculated to be capitalized exceeds the amount of interest actually incurred. If that's the case, we limit the interest capitalized to the actual interest incurred. In our illustration, total interest cost incurred during 2018 far exceeds the $76,000 of capitalized interest calculated, so it's not necessary to limit the capitalized amount.

STEP 3: Compare calculated interest with actual interest incurred.

Loans		Annual Rate		Actual Interest	Calculated Interest
$1,000,000	×	8%	=	$ 80,000	
2,000,000	×	6%	=	120,000	
4,000,000	×	12%	=	480,000	
				$680,000	$76,000
					↑ Use lower amount

Continuing the example based on the information in Illustration 10–17, let's determine the amount of interest capitalized during 2019 for the building. The total accumulated expenditures by the end of the project are:

Accumulated expenditures at the beginning of 2019 (including interest capitalization)	$1,576,000
January 31, 2019 expenditures	600,000
April 30, 2019 expenditures	300,000
Accumulated expenditures at June 30, 2019 (before 2019 interest capitalization)	$2,476,000

The weighted-average accumulated expenditures by the end of the project are:

STEP 1: Determine the weighted-average accumulated expenditures.

	Actual Expenditures		Portion of Year by End of Project		Time-Weighted Expenditures
January 1, 2019	$1,576,000	×	6/6	=	$ 1,576,000
January 31, 2019	600,000	×	5/6	=	500,000
April 30, 2019	300,000	×	2/6	=	100,000
Weighted-average accumulated expenditures for 2019					$2,176,000

Notice that the 2019 expenditures are weighted relative to the construction period of six months because the project was finished on June 30, 2019. Interest capitalized for 2019 would be $98,800, calculated as follows:

STEP 2: Calculate the amount of interest to be capitalized.

	Time-Weighted Expenditures		Annual Rate		Portion of Year Outstanding		Calculated Interest
Total	$2,176,000						
Specific borrowing	1,000,000	×	8%	×	6/12	=	$40,000
Excess	$1,176,000	×	10%	×	6/12	=	58,800
Interest capitalized for 2019							$98,800

Multiplying by six-twelfths reflects the fact that the interest rates are annual rates (12-month rates) and the construction period is only 6 months. Next, we compare the calculated interest with the actual interest incurred.

STEP 3: Compare calculated interest with actual interest incurred.

Loans		Annual Rate		Portion of Year Oustanding		Actual Interest	Calculated Interest
$1,000,000	×	8%	×	6/12	=	$ 40,000	
2,000,000	×	6%	×	6/12	=	60,000	
4,000,000	×	12%	×	6/12	=	240,000	
						$340,000	$98,800
							↑ Use lower amount

For the first six months of 2019, $98,800 of interest would be capitalized, bringing the total capitalized cost of the building to $2,574,800 ($2,476,000 + 98,800), and $241,200 in interest would be expensed ($340,000 − 98,800).

Additional Consideration

To illustrate how the actual interest limitation might come into play, let's assume the nonspecific borrowings in our illustration were $200,000 and $400,000 (instead of $2,000,000 and $4,000,000). Our comparison would change as follows:

Loans		Annual Rate		Portion of Year Oustanding		Actual Interest	Calculated Interest
$1,000,000	×	8%	×	6/12	=	$40,000	
200,000	×	6%	×	6/12	=	6,000	
400,000	×	12%	×	6/12	=	24,000	
						$70,000	$98,800
						↑ Use lower amount	

The method of determining interest to capitalize that we've discussed is called the specific interest method because we use rates from specific construction loans to the extent of specific borrowings before using the average rate of other debt. Sometimes, though, it's difficult to associate specific borrowings with projects. In these situations, it's acceptable to just use the weighted-average rate on all interest-bearing debt, including all construction loans. This is known as the weighted-average method. In our illustration, for example, if the $1,000,000, 8% loan had not been specifically related to construction, we would calculate a single weighted-average rate as shown below.

Weighted-average method

Loans		Annual Rate		Interest
$1,000,000	×	8%	=	$ 80,000
2,000,000	×	6%	=	120,000
4,000,000	×	12%	=	480,000
$7,000,000				$680,000

$$\text{Weighted-average rate: } \frac{\$680{,}000}{\$7{,}000{,}000} = 9.7\%$$

If we were using the weighted-average method rather than the specific interest method, we would simply multiply this single rate times the average accumulated expenditures to determine capitalizable interest.

If material, the amount of interest capitalized during the period must be disclosed.

DISCLOSURE. For an accounting period in which interest costs are capitalized, the total amount of interest costs capitalized, if the amount is material, should be disclosed. Illustration 10–18 shows an interest capitalization disclosure note that was included in a recent annual report of Wal-Mart Stores, Inc., the world's largest retailer.

Illustration 10–18

Capitalized Interest Disclosure—Wal-Mart Stores, Inc.

Real World Financials

Property and equipment (in part)

Interest costs capitalized on construction projects were $39 million, $59 million, and $78 million in fiscal 2016, 2015, and 2014, respectively.

Research and Development (R&D)

LO10–8

"Innovation" is a word commonly used in the marketing and production departments of most companies. Companies compete fiercely to dream up the next top-selling product or service. In 2015, Volkswagen spent more than $15 billion to research new technology for its hybrid vehicles and improve CO_2 emissions. Microsoft spent $11.4 billion on discovering new technology products. Of the 118,000 people employed by Miscrosoft, 39,000 are in product research and development. Google spent $9.8 billion on futuristic ideas such as self-driving cars and computer eyewear. Merck invested $7.2 billion to test new drugs related to oncology, infectious diseases, vaccines, and diabetes.

R&D costs entail a high degree of uncertainty of future benefits and are difficult to match with future revenues.

R&D costs are expensed in the periods incurred.

Companies are willing to spend huge amounts on R&D because they believe the project will eventually provide benefits that exceed the current expenditures. Unfortunately, though, it's difficult to predict which individual research and development projects will ultimately provide benefits. Will Google's expenditures on self-driving cars ever generate enough revenue to cover its costs? Moreover, even for those projects that pan out, a direct relationship between research and development costs and specific future revenue is difficult to establish. In other words, even if R&D costs do lead to future benefits, it's difficult to objectively determine the size of the benefits and in which periods the costs should be expensed if they are capitalized. For these reasons, *the FASB takes a conservative approach and requires R&D costs to be expensed immediately.*[21]

The FASB's decision is controversial. Many companies would prefer to delay the recognition of these expenses until later years when presumably the expenditures bear fruit. In other words, many companies would prefer to record R&D expenditures initially as an asset, because

[21]FASB ASC 730–10–25–1: Research and Development–Overall–Recognition (previously "Accounting for Research and Development Costs," *Statement of Financial Accounting Standards No. 2* (Stamford, Conn.: FASB, 1974), par. 12).

at least some of the R&D expenditures will likely produce future benefits. The requirement to expense R&D immediately leads to assets being understated and expenses being overstated.

Determining R&D Costs

GAAP distinguishes research and development as follows:

- **Research** is planned search or critical investigation aimed at discovery of new knowledge with the hope that such knowledge will be useful in developing a new product or service or a new process or technique or in bringing about a significant improvement to an existing product or process.
- **Development** is the translation of research findings or other knowledge into a plan or design for a new product or process or for a significant improvement to an existing product or process whether intended for sale or use.[22]

R&D costs include salaries, wages, and other labor costs of personnel engaged in R&D activities, the costs of materials consumed, equipment, facilities, and intangibles used in R&D projects, the costs of services performed by others in connection with R&D activities, and a reasonable allocation of indirect costs related to those activities. General and administrative costs should not be included unless they are clearly related to the R&D activity.

If an asset is purchased specifically for a single R&D project, its cost is considered R&D and expensed immediately even though the asset's useful life extends beyond the current year. However, the cost of an asset that has an alternative future use beyond the current R&D project is *not* a current R&D expense. Instead, the depreciation or amortization of these alternative-use assets is included as R&D expenses in the current and future periods the assets are used for R&D activities.

R&D expense includes the depreciation and amortization of assets used in R&D activities.

In general, R&D costs pertain to activities that occur prior to the start of commercial production. Commercial production most often refers to the point in time where the company has no other plans to materially change the product prior to beginning production for intended sales to customers.

Costs incurred *before* the start of commercial production are expensed as R&D.

Any costs incurred after the start of commercial production are not classified as R&D costs. These costs would be either expensed or treated as manufacturing overhead and included in the cost of inventory.

Costs incurred *after* commercial production begins would be either expensed or included in the cost of inventory.

Illustration 10–19 captures this concept with a time line beginning with the start of an R&D project and ending with the ultimate sale of a developed product or the use of a

Illustration 10–19
Research and Development Expenditures

Start of R&D Activity — *Start of Commercial Production* — *Sale of Product or Process*

Examples of R&D Costs:	*Examples of Non-R&D Costs:*
• Laboratory research aimed at discovery of new knowledge	• Engineering follow-through in an early phase of commercial production
• Searching for applications of new research findings or other knowledge	• Quality control during commercial production including routine testing of products
• Design, construction, and testing of preproduction prototypes and models	• Routine ongoing efforts to refine, enrich, or otherwise improve on the qualities of an existing product
• Modification of the formulation or design of a product or process	• Adaptation of an existing capability to a particular requirement or customer's need as a part of a continuing commercial activity

[22]Ibid., section 730–10–20 (previously par. 8 of *SFAS No. 2*).

developed process. The illustration also provides examples of activities typically included as R&D and examples of activities typically excluded from R&D.[23] Let's look at an example in Illustration 10–20.

Illustration 10–20
Research and Development Costs

The Askew Company made the following cash expenditures during 2018 related to the development of a new industrial plastic:

R&D salaries and wages	$ 10,000,000
R&D supplies consumed during 2018	3,000,000
Purchase of R&D equipment	5,000,000
Patent filing and legal costs	100,000
Payments to others for services performed in connection with R&D activities	1,200,000
Total	$19,300,000

The project resulted in a new product to be manufactured in 2019. A patent was filed with the U.S. Patent Office. Amortization of the patent's filing and legal costs will begin in 2019. The equipment purchased will be employed in other projects. Depreciation on the equipment for 2018 was $500,000.

Filing and legal costs for patents, copyrights, and other developed intangibles are capitalized and amortized in future periods.

The salaries and wages, supplies consumed, and payments to others for R&D services are expensed in 2018 as R&D. The equipment is capitalized and the 2018 depreciation is expensed as R&D. Even though the costs to develop the patented product are expensed, the filing and legal costs for the patent are capitalized and amortized in future periods just as similar costs are capitalized for purchased intangibles. Amortization of the patent is discussed in Chapter 11.

The various expenditures would be recorded as follows:

R&D expense ($10,000,000 + 3,000,000 + 1,200,000)	14,200,000	
Cash		14,200,000
To record R&D expenses.		
Equipment	5,000,000	
Cash		5,000,000
To record the purchase of equipment.		
R&D expense	500,000	
Accumulated depreciation—equipment		500,000
To record R&D depreciation.		
Patent	100,000	
Cash		100,000
To capitalize the patent filing and legal costs.		

Expenditures reconciliation:	
Recorded as R&D	$ 14,200,000
Capitalized as equipment	5,000,000
Capitalized as patent	100,000
Total expenditures	$19,300,000

GAAP requires disclosure of total R&D expense incurred during the period.

GAAP requires that total R&D expense incurred must be disclosed either as a line item in the income statement or in a disclosure note. In our illustration, total R&D expense disclosed in 2018 would be $14,700,000 ($14,200,000 in expenditures and $500,000 in depreciation). Note that if Askew later sells this patent to another company for, say, $15 million, the buyer would capitalize the entire purchase price rather than only the filing and legal costs. Once again, the reason for the apparent inconsistency in accounting treatment of internally generated intangibles and externally purchased intangibles is the difficulty of associating costs and benefits.

[23]Ibid., section 730–10–55 (previously par. 9 of *SFAS No. 2*).

International Financial Reporting Standards

IAS No. 38 draws a distinction between research activities and development activities.[24] Research expenditures are *expensed* in the period incurred. However, development expenditures that meet specified criteria are *capitalized* as an intangible asset. Under both U.S. GAAP and IFRS, any direct costs to secure a patent, such as legal and filing fees, are capitalized.

IFRS requires companies to capitalize development expenditures that meet specified criteria.

Heineken, a company based in Amsterdam, prepares its financial statements according to IFRS. The following disclosure note describes the company's adherence to *IAS No. 38*. The note also describes the criteria for capitalizing development expenditures as well as the types of expenditures capitalized.

● LO10–9

Software, Research and Development and Other Intangible Assets (in part)

Expenditures on research activities, undertaken with the prospect of gaining new technical knowledge and understanding, are recognized in the income statement when incurred. Development activities involve a plan or design for the production of new or substantially improved products and processes. Development expenditures are capitalized only if development costs can be measured reliably, the product or process is technically and commercially feasible, future economic benefits are probable, and Heineken intends to and has sufficient resources to complete development and to use or sell the asset. The expenditures capitalized include the cost of materials, direct labor and overhead costs that are directly attributable to preparing the asset for its intended use, and capitalized borrowing costs.

Amortization of capitalized development costs begins when development is complete and the asset is available for use. Heineken disclosed that it amortizes its capitalized development costs using the straight-line method over an estimated three-year useful life.

We've just discussed that U.S. GAAP requires R&D costs to be expensed immediately. There are three types of costs related to R&D, however, that are capitalized (recorded as an asset). These exceptions are shown below:

1. Development costs for software that has reached the point of technological feasibility
2. R&D performed by the company for sale to others
3. R&D purchased in a business acquisition

Software Development Costs

The computer software industry has become a large and important U.S. business over the last two decades. Companies in this multibillion dollar industry include Microsoft, Oracle, IBM, Adobe Systems, and Intuit. A significant expenditure for these companies is the cost of developing software. In the early years of the software industry, some software companies were capitalizing software development costs and expensing them in future periods and others were expensing these costs in the period incurred.

GAAP requires the capitalization of software development costs incurred after technological feasibility is established.

Now GAAP establishes a timeline for purposes of accounting for software development costs. Any software costs incurred from initial development activity until technological feasibility of the software are treated like all other R&D costs (expensed as incurred). Technological feasibility refers to the point in time "when the enterprise has completed all planning, designing, coding, and testing activities that are necessary to establish that the product can be produced to meet its design specifications including functions, features, and technical performance requirements."[25]

Costs incurred after technological feasibility but before the software is available for general release to customers are capitalized as an intangible asset. These costs include items such

[24]"Intangible Assets," *International Accounting Standard No. 38* (IASCF), as amended effective January 1, 2016.

[25]FASB ASC 985–20–25–2: Software–Costs of Software to be Sold, Leased, or Marketed–Recognition (previously "Accounting for the Costs of Computer Software to be Sold, Leased, or Otherwise Marketed," *Statement of Financial Accounting Standards No. 86* (Stamford, Conn.: FASB, 1985) par. 4).

as further coding and testing and the production of product masters. Capitalized costs are then amortized over the economic life of the software (discussed and illustrated below). Any costs incurred after the software release date generally are expensed but not as part of R&D.

The discussion above relates to costs incurred to develop or purchase computer software to be sold, leased, or otherwise marketed (that is, *for external purposes*).[26] We account for the costs incurred to develop computer software *to be used internally* in a similar manner. Costs incurred during the preliminary project stage are expensed as R&D. After the application development stage is reached (for example, at the coding stage or installation stage), we capitalize any further costs.[27] If, instead, we *purchase* computer software for internal use, those costs generally are capitalized.

Illustration 10–21 shows the R&D time line introduced earlier in the chapter modified to include the point at which technological feasibility is established. Only the costs incurred between technological feasibility and the software release date are capitalized.

Illustration 10–21
Research and Development Expenditures—Computer Software

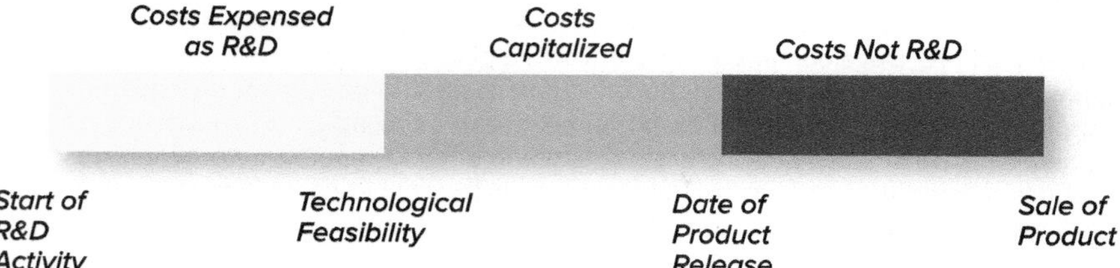

The amortization of capitalized computer software development costs begins when the product is available for general release to customers. The periodic amortization percentage is the greater of (1) the ratio of current revenues to current and anticipated revenues (percentage-of-revenue method) or (2) the straight-line percentage over the useful life of the asset, as shown in Illustration 10–22.

Illustration 10–22
Software Development Costs

The Astro Corporation develops computer software graphics programs for sale. A new development project begun in 2017 reached technological feasibility at the end of June 2018, and the product was available for release to customers early in 2019. Development costs incurred in 2018 prior to June 30 were \$1,200,000 and costs incurred from June 30 to the product availability date were \$800,000. 2019 revenues from the sale of the new product were \$3,000,000 and the company anticipates an additional \$7,000,000 in revenues in future years. The economic life of the software is estimated at four years.

Astro Corporation would expense the \$1,200,000 in costs incurred prior to the establishment of technological feasibility and capitalize the \$800,000 in costs incurred between technological feasibility and the product availability date. 2019 amortization of the intangible asset, software development costs, is calculated as follows:

1. **Percentage-of-revenue method:**

$$\frac{\$3{,}000{,}000}{\$3{,}000{,}000 + 7{,}000{,}000} = 30\% \times \$800{,}000 = \$240{,}000$$

2. **Straight-line method:**

$$\tfrac{1}{4} \text{ or } 25\% \times \$800{,}000 = \$200{,}000.$$

The percentage-of-revenue method is used because it produces the greater amortization, \$240,000.

Illustration 10–23 shows the software disclosure included in a recent annual report of CA, Inc. The note provides a good summary of the accounting treatment of software development costs.

[26]FASB ASC 985–20–25–1: Software–Costs of Software to be Sold, Leased, or Marketed–Recognition (previously "Accounting for the Costs of Computer Software to be Sold, Leased, or Otherwise Marketed," *Statement of Financial Accounting Standards No. 86* (Stamford, Conn.: FASB, 1985)).

[27]FASB ASC 350–40–25: Intangibles–Goodwill and Other–Internal-Use Software–Recognition (previously "Accounting for the Costs of Computer Software Developed or Obtained for Internal Use," *Statement of Position 98-1* (New York: AICPA, 1998)).

Internally Developed Software Products
Internally developed software products, which are included in "Capitalized software and other intangible assets, net" in the Consolidated Balance Sheets, consist of capitalized costs associated with the development of computer software to be sold, leased or otherwise marketed. Software development costs associated with new products and significant enhancements to existing software products are expensed as incurred until technological feasibility, as defined in FASB ASC Topic 985-20, has been established. Costs incurred thereafter are capitalized until the product is made generally available. The stage during the Company's development process for a new product or new release at which technological feasibility requirements are established affects the amount of costs capitalized.

Annual amortization of internally developed software products is the greater of the amount computed using the ratio that current gross revenues for a product bear to the total of current and anticipated future gross revenues for that product or the straight-line method over the remaining estimated economic life of the software product, generally estimated to be 5 years from the date the product became available for general release to customers. The Company generally recognizes amortization expense for capitalized software costs using the straight-line method, and such amortization is included in "Amortization of capitalized software costs" in the Consolidated Statements of Operations. Internally developed software products are reviewed for impairment quarterly and whenever events or changes in circumstances indicate that the carrying amount of an asset may not be recoverable.

Illustration 10–23

Software Disclosure—CA, Inc.

Real World Financials

Why do generally accepted accounting principles allow this exception to the general rule of expensing all R&D? We could attribute it to the political process. Software is a very important industry to our economy and perhaps its lobbying efforts resulted in the standard allowing software companies to capitalize certain R&D costs.

We could also attribute the exception to the nature of the software business. Recall that R&D costs in general are expensed in the period incurred for two reasons: (1) they entail a high degree of uncertainty of future benefits, and (2) they are difficult to match with future benefits. With software, there is an important identifiable engineering milestone, technological feasibility. When this milestone is attained, the probability of the software product's success increases significantly. And because the useful life of software is fairly short (one to five years in most cases), it is much easier to determine the periods of increased revenues than for R&D projects in other industries. Compare this situation with, say, the development of a new drug. Even after the drug has been developed, it must go through extensive testing to meet FDA (Food and Drug Administration) approval, which may never be attained. If attained, the useful life of the drug could be anywhere from a few months to many years.

International Financial Reporting Standards

Software Development Costs. The percentage we use to amortize computer software development costs under U.S. GAAP is the greater of (1) the ratio of current revenues to current and anticipated revenues or (2) the straight-line percentage over the useful life of the software. This approach is allowed under IFRS, but not required. Amortization under IFRS typically occurs over the useful life of the software, based on pattern of benefits, with straight-line as the default.

● LO10–9

R&D Performed for Others

The principle requiring the immediate expensing of R&D does not apply to companies that perform R&D for other companies under contract. In these situations, the R&D costs are capitalized as inventory and carried forward into future years until the project is completed. Of course, justification is that the benefits of these expenditures are the contract revenues that will eventually be recognized. Revenue from these contracts can be recognized over time or at a point in time, depending on the specifics of the contract. We discussed these alternatives in Chapter 5.

R&D Purchased in Business Acquisitions

It's not unusual for one company to buy another company in order to obtain technology that the acquired company has developed or is in the process of developing. Any time a company buys another, it values the tangible and intangible assets acquired at fair value. When part of the acquisition price involves technology, we distinguish between:

1. Developed technology
2. In-process research and development

In business acquisitions, the fair value of developed technology is capitalized as an finite-life intangible asset.

In business acquisitions, the fair value of in-process research and development is capitalized as an indefinite-life intangible asset.

To distinguish these two types of technology acquired, we borrow a criterion used in accounting for software development costs, and determine whether *technological feasibility* has been achieved. If it has, the technology is considered "developed," and we capitalize its fair value (record it as an asset) and amortize that amount over its useful life just like any other *finite-life* intangible asset.

For in-process R&D (technology that has not reached the feasibility stage), GAAP also requires capitalization of its fair value. However, unlike developed technology, we view in-process R&D as an *indefinite-life* intangible asset.[28] As you will learn in Chapter 11, we don't amortize indefinite-life intangibles. Instead, we monitor these assets and test them for impairment when required by GAAP.

If the acquired R&D project is completed successfully, we switch to the way we account for developed technology and amortize the capitalized amount over the estimated period the product or process developed will provide benefits. If the project instead is abandoned, we expense the entire balance immediately.

R&D costs incurred after the acquisition to complete the project are expensed as incurred, consistent with the treatment of usual R&D expenditures. Similarly, the purchase of R&D from third parties not associated with a business combination is expensed as incurred, just as if the company had performed the R&D activity itself. An exception is when the purchased R&D has an alternative use beyond a specific project.

As an example of R&D associated with a business acquisition, in 2015 AbbVie Inc., a global research-based biopharmaceutical company, acquired Pharmacyclics Inc. for approximately $20.8 billion. The fair values assigned included finite-life intangible assets of $11.4 billion, in-process R&D of $7.2 billion, and goodwill of $7.6 billion (as well as other identifiable assets of $1.7 billion and liabilities of $7.1 billion). AbbVie classified projects acquired that have not yet received regulatory approval as in-process R&D.

Illustration 10–24
Acquired In-Process Research and Development—Abbvie, Inc.

Real World Financials

Acquired In-Process Research and Development

The initial costs of rights to IPR&D projects acquired in an asset acquisition are expensed as IPR&D in the consolidated statements of earnings unless the project has an alternative future use. These costs include initial payments incurred prior to regulatory approval in connection with research and development collaboration agreements that provide rights to develop, manufacture, market and/or sell pharmaceutical products. The fair value of IPR&D projects acquired in a business combination are capitalized and accounted for as indefinite-lived intangible assets until the underlying project receives regulatory approval, at which point the intangible asset will be accounted for as a definite-lived intangible asset, or discontinuation, at which point the intangible asset will be written off. Development costs incurred after the acquisition are expensed as incurred. Indefinite- and definite-lived assets are subject to impairment reviews as discussed previously.

Start-Up Costs

Start-up costs are expensed in the period incurred.

Whenever a company introduces a new product or service, or commences business in a new territory or with a new customer, it incurs start-up costs. Start-up costs also include organization costs related to organizing a new entity, such as legal fees and state filing fees to incorporate. Prior to 1999, companies frequently capitalized start-up costs until the new business started and amortized organization costs over five years. Now, as with R&D expenditures, companies are required

[28]FASB ASC 805: Business Combinations (previously "Business Combinations," *Statement of Financial Accounting Standards No. 141 (revised)* (Norwalk, Conn.: FASB, 2007)).

to expense all the costs related to a company's start-up and organization activities in the period incurred, rather than capitalize those costs as an asset.[29]

For the year ended December 31, 2015, Chipotle Mexican Grill, Inc., opened 227 new restaurants. The company incurred a variety of one-time preopening costs for wages, benefits and travel for the training and opening teams, food and other restaurant operating costs totaling $17 million. These costs were expensed immediately.

Financial Reporting Case Solution

© Preston Mack/Disney Parks via Getty Images.

1. **Describe to Stan what it means to capitalize an expenditure. What is the general rule for determining which costs are capitalized when property, plant, and equipment or an intangible asset is acquired?** *(p. 520)* To capitalize an expenditure simply means to record it as an asset. All expenditures other than payments to shareholders and debt repayments are either expensed as incurred or capitalized. In general, the choice is determined by whether the expenditure benefits more than just the current period. Exceptions to this general principle are discussed in the chapter. The initial cost of an asset includes all expenditures necessary to bring the asset to its desired condition and location for use.
2. **Which costs might be included in the initial cost of equipment?** *(p. 520)* In addition to the purchase price, the cost of equipment might include the cost of transportation, installation, testing, and legal fees to establish title.
3. **What is goodwill and how is it measured?** *(p. 527)* Goodwill represents the unique value of a company as a whole over and above its identifiable tangible and intangible assets. Because goodwill can't be separated from a company, it's not possible for a buyer to acquire it without also acquiring the whole company or a controlling portion of it. Goodwill will appear as an asset in a balance sheet only when it was purchased in connection with the acquisition of another company. In that case, the capitalized cost of goodwill equals the fair value of the consideration exchanged for the company less the fair value of the net assets acquired. Goodwill is a residual asset; it's the amount left after other assets are identified and valued. Just like for other intangible assets that have indefinite useful lives, we do not amortize goodwill.
4. **In what situations is interest capitalized rather than expensed?** *(p. 539)* Interest is capitalized only for assets constructed for a company's own use or for assets constructed as discrete products for sale or lease. For example, Walt Disney capitalizes interest on assets constructed for its theme parks, resorts and other property, and on theatrical and television productions. During the construction period, interest is considered a cost necessary to get the asset ready for its intended use.
5. **What is the three-step process used to determine the amount of interest capitalized?** *(p. 541)* The first step is to determine the average accumulated expenditures for the period. The second step is to multiply the average accumulated expenditures by an appropriate interest rate or rates to determine the amount of interest capitalized. A final step compares the interest determined in step two with actual interest incurred. Interest capitalized is limited to the amount of interest incurred. ●

The Bottom Line

- **LO10–1** The initial cost of property, plant, and equipment and intangible assets acquired in an exchange transaction includes the purchase price and all expenditures necessary to bring the asset to its desired condition and location for use. The cost of a natural resource includes the acquisition costs for the use of land, the exploration and development costs incurred before production begins, and restoration costs incurred during or at the end of extraction. Purchased intangible assets are valued at their original cost to include the purchase price and legal and filing fees. *(p. 520)*

[29]FASB ASC 720–15–25–1: Other Expenses–Start-Up Costs–Recognition (previously "Reporting on the Costs of Start-Up Activities," *Statement of Position 98-5* (New York: AICPA, 1998)).

- LO10–2 If a lump-sum purchase involves different assets, it is necessary to allocate the lump-sum acquisition price among the separate items according to some logical allocation method. A widely used allocation method is to divide the lump-sum purchase price according to the individual assets' relative fair values. *(p. 529)*
- LO10–3 Assets acquired in exchange for deferred payment contracts are valued at their fair value or the present value of payments using a realistic interest rate. *(p. 530)*
- LO10–4 Assets acquired through the issuance of equity securities are valued at the fair value of the securities if known; if not known, the fair value of the assets received is used. Donated assets are valued at their fair value. *(p. 532)*
- LO10–5 A key to profitability is how well a company manages and utilizes its assets. Financial analysts often use activity, or turnover, ratios to evaluate a company's effectiveness in managing its assets. Property, plant, and equipment (PP&E) usually are a company's primary revenue-generating assets. Their efficient use is critical to generating a satisfactory return to owners. One ratio that analysts often use to measure how effectively managers use PP&E is the fixed-asset turnover ratio. This ratio is calculated by dividing net sales by average fixed assets. *(p. 534)*
- LO10–6 The basic principle used for nonmonetary exchanges is to value the asset(s) received based on the fair value of the asset(s) given up. In certain situations, the valuation of the asset(s) received is based on the book value of the asset(s) given up. *(p. 534)*
- LO10–7 The cost of a self-constructed asset includes identifiable materials and labor and a portion of the company's manufacturing overhead costs. In addition, GAAP provides for the capitalization of interest incurred during construction. The amount of interest capitalized is equal to the average accumulated expenditures for the period multiplied by the appropriate interest rates, not to exceed actual interest incurred. *(p. 538)*
- LO10–8 Research and development costs incurred to internally develop an intangible asset are expensed in the period incurred. Filing and legal costs for developed intangibles are capitalized. *(p. 544)*
- LO10–9 *IAS No. 20* requires that government grants be recognized in income over the periods necessary to match them on a systematic basis with the related costs that they are intended to compensate. Other than software development costs incurred after technological feasibility has been established, U.S. GAAP requires all research and development expenditures to be expensed in the period incurred. *IAS No. 38* draws a distinction between research activities and development activities. Research expenditures are expensed in the period incurred. However, development expenditures that meet specified criteria are capitalized as an intangible asset. *(pp. 533, 547,* and *549)*

APPENDIX 10 Oil and Gas Accounting

There are two generally accepted methods that companies can use to account for oil and gas exploration costs. The **successful efforts method** requires that exploration costs that are known *not* to have resulted in the discovery of oil or gas (sometimes referred to as *dry holes*) be included as expenses in the period the expenditures are made. The alternative, the **full-cost method**, allows costs incurred in searching for oil and gas within a large geographical area to be capitalized as assets and expensed in the future as oil and gas from the successful wells are removed from that area. Both of these methods are widely used. Illustration 10A–1 compares the two alternatives.

Illustration 10A–1
Oil and Gas Accounting

The Shannon Oil Company incurred $2,000,000 in exploration costs for each of 10 oil wells drilled in 2018 in west Texas. Eight of the 10 wells were dry holes.

The accounting treatment of the $20 million in total exploration costs will vary significantly depending on the accounting method used. The summary journal entries using each of the alternative methods are as follows:

Successful Efforts			**Full Cost**		
Oil Deposit	4,000,000		Oil Deposit	20,000,000	
Exploration Expense	16,000,000		Cash		20,000,000
Cash		20,000,000			

Using the full-cost method, Shannon would capitalize the entire $20 million which is expensed as oil from the two successful wells is depleted. On the other hand, using the successful efforts method, the cost of the unsuccessful wells is expensed in 2018, and only the $4 million cost related to the successful wells is capitalized and expensed in future periods as the oil is depleted.

Chapter 1 characterized the establishment of accounting and reporting standards as a political process. Standards, particularly changes in standards, can have significant differential effects on companies, investors and creditors, and other interest groups. The FASB must consider potential economic consequences of a change in an accounting standard or the introduction of a new standard. The history of oil and gas accounting provides a good example of this political process and the effect of possible adverse economic consequences on the standard-setting process.

In 1977 the FASB attempted to establish uniformity in the accounting treatment of oil and gas exploration costs. An accounting standard was issued requiring all companies to use the successful efforts method.[30]

This standard met with criticism from the oil and gas companies that were required to switch from full cost to successful efforts accounting. These companies felt that the switch would seriously depress their reported income over time. As a result, they argued, their ability to raise capital in the securities markets would be inhibited, which would result in a cutback of new exploration. The fear that the Standard would cause domestic companies to significantly reduce oil and gas exploration and thus increase our dependence on foreign oil was compelling to Congress, the SEC, and the U.S. Department of Energy.

Many feared that the requirement to switch to successful efforts accounting would cause a significant cutback in the exploration for new oil and gas in the United States.

Extensive pressure from Congress, the SEC, and affected companies forced the FASB to rescind the Standard. Presently, oil and gas companies can use either the successful efforts or full-cost method to account for oil and gas exploration costs. Of course, the method used must be disclosed. For example, Illustration 10A–2 shows how Chevron Corp. disclosed its use of the successful efforts method in a note to recent financial statements. ●

Properties, Plant, and Equipment (in part)

The successful efforts method is used for crude oil and natural gas exploration and production activities.

Illustration 10A–2

Oil and Gas Accounting Disclosure—Chevron Corp.

Real World Financials

Questions For Review of Key Topics

Q 10–1 Explain the difference between tangible and intangible long-lived, revenue-producing assets.

Q 10–2 What is included in the original cost of property, plant, and equipment and intangible assets acquired in an exchange transaction?

Q 10–3 Identify the costs associated with the initial valuation of a developed natural resource.

Q 10–4 Briefly summarize the accounting treatment for intangible assets, explaining the difference between purchased and internally developed intangible assets.

Q 10–5 What is goodwill and how is it measured?

Q 10–6 Explain the method generally used to allocate the cost of a lump-sum purchase to the individual assets acquired.

Q 10–7 When an asset is acquired and a note payable is assumed, explain how acquisition cost of the asset is determined when the interest rate for the note is less than the current market rate for similar notes.

Q 10–8 Explain how assets acquired in exchange for equity securities are valued.

Q 10–9 Explain how property, plant, and equipment and intangible assets acquired through donation are valued.

Q 10–10 What account is credited when a company receives donated assets? What is the rationale for this choice?

[30]The rescinded standard was "Financial Accounting and Reporting by Oil and Gas Producing Companies," *Statement of Financial Accounting Standards No. 19* (Stamford, Conn.: FASB, 1977). Authoritative guidance on this topic can now be found at FASB ASC 932: Extractive Activities–Oil and Gas.

Q 10–11 What is the basic principle for valuing property, plant, and equipment and intangible assets acquired in exchange for other nonmonetary assets?

Q 10–12 Identify the two exceptions to valuing property, plant, and equipment and intangible assets acquired in nonmonetary exchanges at the fair value of the asset(s) given up.

Q 10–13 In what situations is interest capitalized?

Q 10–14 Define average accumulated expenditures and explain how the amount is computed.

Q 10–15 Explain the difference between the specific interest method and the weighted-average method in determining the amount of interest to be capitalized.

Q 10–16 Define R&D according to U.S. GAAP.

Q 10–17 Explain the accounting treatment of equipment acquired for use in R&D projects.

Q 10–18 Explain the accounting treatment of costs incurred to develop computer software.

Q 10–19 Explain the difference in the accounting treatment of the cost of developed technology and the cost of in-process R&D in an acquisition.

IFRS **Q 10–20** Identify any differences between U.S. GAAP and International Financial Reporting Standards in accounting for government grants received.

IFRS **Q 10–21** Identify any differences between U.S. GAAP and International Financial Reporting Standards in the treatment of research and development expenditures.

IFRS **Q 10–22** Identify any differences between U.S. GAAP and International Financial Reporting Standards in the treatment of software development costs.

Q 10–23 (Based on Appendix 10) Explain the difference between the successful efforts and the full-cost methods of accounting for oil and gas exploration costs.

Brief Exercises

BE 10–1
Acquisition cost; machine
● LO10–1

Beaverton Lumber purchased a milling machine for $35,000. In addition to the purchase price, Beaverton made the following expenditures: freight, $1,500; installation, $3,000; testing, $2,000; personal property tax on the machine for the first year, $500. What is the initial cost of the machine?

BE 10–2
Acquisition cost; land and building
● LO10–1

Fullerton Waste Management purchased land and a warehouse for $600,000. In addition to the purchase price, Fullerton made the following expenditures related to the acquisition: broker's commission, $30,000; title insurance, $3,000; miscellaneous closing costs, $6,000. The warehouse was immediately demolished at a cost of $18,000 in anticipation of the building of a new warehouse. Determine the amounts Fullerton should capitalize as the cost of the land and the building.

BE 10–3
Lump-sum acquisition
● LO10–2

Refer to the situation described in BE 10–2. Assume that Fullerton decides to use the warehouse rather than demolish it. An independent appraisal estimates the fair values of the land and warehouse at $420,000 and $280,000, respectively. Determine the amounts Fullerton should capitalize as the cost of the land and the building.

BE 10–4
Cost of a natural resource; asset retirement obligation
● LO10–1

Smithson Mining operates a silver mine in Nevada. Acquisition, exploration, and development costs totaled $5.6 million. After the silver is extracted in approximately five years, Smithson is obligated to restore the land to its original condition, including constructing a wildlife preserve. The company's controller has provided the following three cash flow possibilities for the restoration costs: (1) $500,000, 20% probability; (2) $550,000, 45% probability; and (3) $650,000, 35% probability. The company's credit-adjusted, risk-free rate of interest is 6%. What is the initial cost of the silver mine?

BE 10–5
Asset retirement obligation
● LO10–1

Refer to the situation described in BE 10–4. What is the book value of the asset retirement liability at the end of one year? Assuming that the actual restoration costs incurred after extraction is completed are $596,000, what amount of gain or loss will Smithson recognize on retirement of the liability?

BE 10–6
Goodwill
● LO10–1

Pro-tech Software acquired all of the outstanding stock of Reliable Software for $14 million. The book value of Reliable's net assets (assets minus liabilities) was $8.3 million. The fair values of Reliable's assets and liabilities equaled their book values with the exception of certain intangible assets whose fair values exceeded book values by $2.5 million. Calculate the amount paid for goodwill.

BE 10–7
Acquisition cost; noninterest-bearing note
● LO10–3

On June 30, 2018, Kimberly Farms purchased custom-made harvesting equipment from a local producer. In payment, Kimberly signed a noninterest-bearing note requiring the payment of $60,000 in two years. The fair value of the equipment is not known, but an 8% interest rate properly reflects the time value of money for this type of loan agreement. At what amount will Kimberly initially value the equipment? How much interest expense will Kimberly recognize in its income statement for this note for the year ended December 31, 2018?

BE 10–8
Acquisition cost; issuance of equity securities
● LO10–4

Shackelford Corporation acquired a patent from its founder, Jim Shackelford, in exchange for 50,000 shares of the company's nopar common stock. On the date of the exchange, the common stock had a fair value of $22 per share. Determine the cost of the patent.

BE 10–9
Fixed-asset turnover ratio
● LO10–5

Huebert Corporation and Winslow Corporation reported the following information:

	($ in millions)			
	Huebert		Winslow	
	2018	2017	2018	2017
Property, plant, and equipment (net)	$210	$220	$680	$650
Net sales—2018	$1,850		$5,120	

Calculate each companies fixes-asset turnover ratio and determine which company utilizes its fixed assets most efficiently to generate sales.

BE 10–10
Fixed-asset turnover ratio; solve for unknown
● LO10–5

The balance sheets of Pinewood Resorts reported net fixed assets of $740,000 and $940,000 at the end of 2017 and 2018, respectively. The fixed-asset turnover ratio for 2018 was 3.25. Calculate Pinewood's net sales for 2018.

BE 10–11
Nonmonetary exchange
● LO10–6

Calaveras Tire exchanged equipment for two pickup trucks. The book value and fair value of the equipment were $20,000 (original cost of $65,000 less accumulated depreciation of $45,000) and $17,000, respectively. Calaveras also paid $8,000 in cash. At what amount will Calaveras value the pickup trucks? How much gain or loss will the company recognize on the exchange? Assume the exchange has commercial substance.

BE 10–12
Nonmonetary exchange
● LO10–6

Refer to the situation described in BE 10–11. Answer the questions assuming that the fair value of the equipment was $24,000, instead of $17,000.

BE 10–13
Nonmonetary exchange
● LO10–6

Refer to the situation described in BE 10–11. Answer the questions assuming that the exchange lacks commercial substance.

BE 10–14
Interest capitalization
● LO10–7

A company constructs a building for its own use. Construction began on January 1 and ended on December 30. The expenditures for construction were as follows: January 1, $500,000; March 31, $600,000; June 30, $400,000; October 30, $600,000. To help finance construction, the company arranged a 7% construction loan on January 1 for $700,000. The company's other borrowings, outstanding for the whole year, consisted of a $3 million loan and a $5 million note with interest rates of 8% and 6%, respectively. Assuming the company uses the *specific interest method,* calculate the amount of interest capitalized for the year.

BE 10–15
Interest capitalization
● LO10–7

Refer to the situation described in BE 10–14. Assuming the company uses the *weighted-average method,* calculate the amount of interest capitalized for the year.

BE 10–16
Research and development
● LO10–8

Maxtor Technology incurred the following costs during the year related to the creation of a new type of personal computer monitor:

Salaries	$220,000
Depreciation on R&D facilities and equipment	125,000
Utilities and other direct costs incurred for the R&D facilities	66,000
Patent filing and related legal costs	22,000
Payment to another company for performing a portion of the development work	120,000
Costs of adapting the new monitor for the specific needs of a customer	80,000

What amount should Maxtor report as research and development expense in its income statement?

BE 10–17
Software development costs
● LO10–8

In February 2018, Culverson Company began developing a new software to be sold to customers. The software allows people to enter health information and track daily eating and exercise habits to track their health status. The project was completed in November 2018 at a cost of $800,000. Of this amount, $300,000 was spent before technological feasibility was established. Culverson expects a useful life of two years for the new product and total revenues of $1,500,000. Determine the amount that Culverson should capitalize as software development costs in 2018.

BE 10–18
Research and development; various types
● LO10–8

Maltese Laboratories incurred the following research and developments costs related to its pharmaceutical business:

Internal projects (salaries, supplies, overhead for R&D facilities)	$620,000
Payment to acquire R&D from a third party related to a specific project	75,000
Costs of an R&D project to be sold under contract to Libo Pharmacy, a third party	82,000
In-process R&D associated with the acquisition of Curatics, an independent research company.	148,000

What amount should Maltese report as research and development expense in its income statement?

BE 10–19
Start-up costs
● LO10–8

In the current year, Big Burgers, Inc., expanded its fast food operations by opening several new stores in Texas. The company incurred the following costs in the current year: market appraisal ($50,000), consulting fees ($72,000), advertising ($47,000), and traveling to train employees ($31,000). The company is willing to incur these costs because it foresees strong customer demand in Texas for the next several years. What amount should Big Burgers report as an expense in its income statement associated with these costs?

Exercises

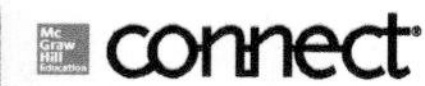

E 10–1
Acquisition costs; land and building
● LO10–1

On March 1, 2018, Beldon Corporation purchased land as a factory site for $60,000. An old building on the property was demolished, and construction began on a new building that was completed on December 15, 2018. Costs incurred during this period are listed below:

Demolition of old building	$ 4,000
Architect's fees (for new building)	12,000
Legal fees for title investigation of land	2,000
Property taxes on land (for period beginning March 1, 2018)	3,000
Construction costs	500,000
Interest on construction loan	5,000

Salvaged materials resulting from the demolition of the old building were sold for $2,000.

Required:
Determine the amounts that Beldon should capitalize as the cost of the land and the new building.

E 10–2
Acquisition cost; equipment
● LO10–1

Oaktree Company purchased new equipment and made the following expenditures:

Purchase price	$45,000
Sales tax	2,200
Freight charges for shipment of equipment	700
Insurance on the equipment for the first year	900
Installation of equipment	1,000

The equipment, including sales tax, was purchased on open account, with payment due in 30 days. The other expenditures listed above were paid in cash.

Required:
Prepare the necessary journal entries to record the above expenditures.

E 10–3
Acquisition costs; lump-sum acquisition
● LO10–1, LO10–2

Samtech Manufacturing purchased land and building for $4 million. In addition to the purchase price, Samtech made the following expenditures in connection with the purchase of the land and building:

Title insurance	$16,000
Legal fees for drawing the contract	5,000
Pro-rated property taxes for the period after acquisition	36,000
State transfer fees	4,000

An independent appraisal estimated the fair values of the land and building, if purchased separately, at $3.3 and $1.1 million, respectively. Shortly after acquisition, Samtech spent $82,000 to construct a parking lot and $40,000 for landscaping.

Required:
1. Determine the initial valuation of each asset Samtech acquired in these transactions.
2. Repeat requirement 1, assuming that immediately after acquisition, Samtech demolished the building. Demolition costs were $250,000 and the salvaged materials were sold for $6,000. In addition, Samtech spent $86,000 clearing and grading the land in preparation for the construction of a new building.

E 10–4
Cost of a natural resource; asset retirement obligation
● LO10–1

Jackpot Mining Company operates a copper mine in central Montana. The company paid $1,000,000 in 2018 for the mining site and spent an additional $600,000 to prepare the mine for extraction of the copper. After the copper is extracted in approximately four years, the company is required to restore the land to its original condition, including repaving of roads and replacing a greenbelt. The company has provided the following three cash flow possibilities for the restoration costs:

	Cash Outflow	Probability
1	$300,000	25%
2	400,000	40%
3	600,000	35%

To aid extraction, Jackpot purchased some new equipment on July 1, 2018, for $120,000. After the copper is removed from this mine, the equipment will be sold. The credit-adjusted, risk-free rate of interest is 10%.

Required:
1. Determine the cost of the copper mine.
2. Prepare the journal entries to record the acquisition costs of the mine and the purchase of equipment.

E 10–5
Intangibles
● LO10–1

In 2018, Bratten Fitness Company made the following cash purchases:
1. The exclusive right to manufacture and sell the X-Core workout machine from Symmetry Corporation for $200,000. Symmetry created the unique design for the machine. Bratten also paid an additional $10,000 in legal and filing fees to attorneys to complete the transaction.
2. An initial fee of $300,000 for a three-year agreement with Silver's Gym to use its name for a new facility in the local area. Silver's Gym has locations throughout the country. Bratten is required to pay an additional fee of $5,000 for each month it operates under the Silver's Gym name, with payments beginning in March 2018. Bratten also purchased $400,000 of exercise equipment to be placed in the new facility.
3. The exclusive right to sell Healthy Choice, a book authored by Kent Patterson, for $25,000. The book includes healthy recipes, recommendations for dietary supplements, and natural remedies. Bratten plans to display the book at the check-in counter at its new facility, as well as make it available online.

Required:
Prepare a summary journal entry to record expenditures related to initial acquisitions.

E 10–6
Goodwill
● LO10–1

On March 31, 2018, Wolfson Corporation acquired all of the outstanding common stock of Barney Corporation for $17,000,000 in cash. The book values and fair values of Barney's assets and liabilities were as follows:

	Book Value	Fair Value
Current assets	$ 6,000,000	$ 7,500,000
Property, plant, and equipment	11,000,000	14,000,000
Other assets	1,000,000	1,500,000
Current liabilities	4,000,000	4,000,000
Long-term liabilities	6,000,000	5,500,000

Required:
Calculate the amount paid for goodwill.

E 10–7
Goodwill
● LO10–1

Johnson Corporation acquired all of the outstanding common stock of Smith Corporation for $11,000,000 in cash. The book value of Smith's net assets (assets minus liabilities) was $7,800,000. The fair values of all of Smith's assets and liabilities were equal to their book values with the following exceptions:

	Book Value	Fair Value
Receivables	$1,300,000	$1,100,000
Property, plant, and equipment	8,000,000	9,400,000
Intangible assets	200,000	1,200,000

Required:
Calculate the amount paid for goodwill.

E 10–8
Lump-sum acquisition
● LO10–2

Pinewood Company purchased two buildings on four acres of land. The lump-sum purchase price was $900,000. According to independent appraisals, the fair values were $450,000 (building A) and $250,000 (building B) for the buildings and $300,000 for the land.

Required:
Determine the initial valuation of the buildings and the land.

E 10–9
Acquisition cost; noninterest-bearing note
● LO10–3

On January 1, 2018, Byner Company purchased a used tractor. Byner paid $5,000 down and signed a noninterest-bearing note requiring $25,000 to be paid on December 31, 2020. The fair value of the tractor is not determinable. An interest rate of 10% properly reflects the time value of money for this type of loan agreement. The company's fiscal year-end is December 31.

Required:
1. Prepare the journal entry to record the acquisition of the tractor. Round computations to the nearest dollar.
2. How much interest expense will the company include in its 2018 and 2019 income statements for this note?
3. What is the amount of the liability the company will report in its 2018 and 2019 balance sheets for this note?

E 10–10
Acquisition costs; noninterest-bearing note
● LO10–1, LO10–3

Teradene Corporation purchased land as a factory site and contracted with Maxtor Construction to construct a factory. Teradene made the following expenditures related to the acquisition of the land, building, and equipment for the factory:

Purchase price of the land	$1,200,000
Demolition and removal of old building	80,000
Clearing and grading the land before construction	150,000
Various closing costs in connection with acquiring the land	42,000
Architect's fee for the plans for the new building	50,000
Payments to Maxtor for building construction	3,250,000
Equipment purchased	860,000
Freight charges on equipment	32,000
Trees, plants, and other landscaping	45,000
Installation of a sprinkler system for the landscaping	5,000
Cost to build special platforms and install wiring for the equipment	12,000
Cost of trial runs to ensure proper installation of the equipment	7,000
Fire and theft insurance on the factory for the first year of use	24,000

In addition to the above expenditures, Teradene purchased four forklifts from Caterpillar. In payment, Teradene paid $16,000 cash and signed a noninterest-bearing note requiring the payment of $70,000 in one year. An interest rate of 7% properly reflects the time value of money for this type of loan.

Required:
Determine the initial valuation of each of the assets Teradene acquired in the above transactions.

E 10–11
IFRS; acquisition cost; issuance of equity securities and donation
● LO10–4, LO10–9

On February 1, 2018, the Xilon Corporation issued 50,000 shares of its nopar common stock in exchange for five acres of land located in the city of Monrovia. On the date of the acquisition, Xilon's common stock had a fair value of $18 per share. An office building was constructed on the site by an independent contractor. The building was completed on November 2, 2018, at a cost of $6,000,000. Xilon paid $4,000,000 in cash and the remainder was paid by the city of Monrovia.

Required:
1. Prepare the journal entries to record the acquisition of the land and the building.
2. Assuming that Xilon prepares its financial statements according to International Financial Reporting Standards, explain the alternatives the company has for recording the acquisition of the office building.

E 10–12
IFRS; acquisition cost; acquisition by donation; government grant
● LO10–9

 IFRS

Cranston LTD. prepares its financial statements according to International Financial Reporting Standards. In October 2018, the company received a $2 million government grant. The grant represents 20% of the total cost of equipment that will be used to improve the roads in the local area. Cranston recorded the grant and the purchase of the equipment as follows:

Cash	2,000,000	
Revenue		2,000,000
Equipment	10,000,000	
Cash		10,000,000

Required:
1. Explain the alternative accounting treatments available to Cranston for accounting for this government grant.
2. Prepare any necessary correcting entries under each of the alternatives described in requirement 1.

E 10–13
Fixed-asset turnover ratio; Nvidia
● LO10–5
Real World Financials

Nvidia Corporation, a global technology company located in Santa Clara, California, reported the following information in its 2016 financial statements ($ in millions):

	2016	2015
Balance sheets		
Property, plant, and equipment (net)	$ 466	$557
Income statement		
Net sales for 2016	$5,010	

Required:
1. Calculate the company's 2016 fixed-asset turnover ratio.
2. How would you interpret this ratio?

E 10–14
Nonmonetary exchange
● LO10–6

Cedric Company recently traded in an older model computer for a new model. The old model's book value was $180,000 (original cost of $400,000 less $220,000 in accumulated depreciation) and its fair value was $200,000. Cedric paid $60,000 to complete the exchange which has commercial substance.

Required:
Prepare the journal entry to record the exchange.

E 10–15
Nonmonetary exchange
● LO10–6

[This is a variation of the previous exercise.]

Required:
Assume the same facts as in Exercise 10–14, except that the fair value of the old equipment is $170,000. Prepare the journal entry to record the exchange.

E 10–16
Nonmonetary exchange
● LO10–6

The Bronco Corporation exchanged land for equipment. The land had a book value of $120,000 and a fair value of $150,000. Bronco paid the owner of the equipment $10,000 to complete the exchange which has commercial substance.

Required:
1. What is the fair value of the equipment?
2. Prepare the journal entry to record the exchange.

E 10–17
Nonmonetary exchange
● LO10–6

[This is a variation of the previous exercise.]

Required:
Assume the same facts as in Exercise 10–16 except that Bronco *received* $10,000 from the owner of the equipment to complete the exchange.
1. What is the fair value of the equipment?
2. Prepare the journal entry to record the exchange.

E 10–18
Nonmonetary exchange
● LO10–6

The Tinsley Company exchanged land that it had been holding for future plant expansion for a more suitable parcel located farther from residential areas. Tinsley carried the land at its original cost of $30,000. According to an independent appraisal, the land currently is worth $72,000. Tinsley paid $14,000 in cash to complete the transaction.

Required:
1. What is the fair value of the new parcel of land received by Tinsley?
2. Prepare the journal entry to record the exchange assuming the exchange has commercial substance.

3. Prepare the journal entry to record the exchange assuming the exchange lacks commercial substance.
4. Prepare the journal entry to record the exchange except that Tinsley *received* $18,000 in the exchange, and the exchange lacks commercial substance.

E 10–19
Acquisition cost; multiple methods
● LO10–1, LO10–3, LO10–4, LO10–6

Connors Corporation acquired manufacturing equipment for use in its assembly line. Below are four *independent* situations relating to the acquisition of the equipment.

1. The equipment was purchased on account for $25,000. Credit terms were 2/10, n/30. Payment was made within the discount period and the company records the purchases of equipment net of discounts.
2. Connors gave the seller a noninterest-bearing note. The note required payment of $27,000 one year from date of purchase. The fair value of the equipment is not determinable. An interest rate of 10% properly reflects the time value of money in this situation.
3. Connors traded in old equipment that had a book value of $6,000 (original cost of $14,000 and accumulated depreciation of $8,000) and paid cash of $22,000. The old equipment had a fair value of $2,500 on the date of the exchange. The exchange has commercial substance.
4. Connors issued 1,000 shares of its nopar common stock in exchange for the equipment. The market value of the common stock was not determinable. The equipment could have been purchased for $24,000 in cash.

Required:
For each of the above situations, prepare the journal entry required to record the acquisition of the equipment. Round computations to the nearest dollar.

E 10–20
FASB codification research
● LO10–6

The *FASB Accounting Standards Codification* represents the single source of authoritative U.S. generally accepted accounting principles.

Required:
1. Obtain the relevant authoritative literature on nonmonetary exchanges using the *FASB Accounting Standards Codification* at the FASB website (www.fasb.org). Identify the Codification topic number for nonmonetary transactions.
2. What are the specific citations that list the disclosure requirements for nonmonetary transactions?
3. Describe the disclosure requirements.

E 10–21
FASB codification research
● LO10–1, LO10–6, LO10–7, LO10–8

Access the *FASB Accounting Standards Codification* at the FASB website (www.fasb.org). Determine the specific citation for each of the following items:

1. The disclosure requirements in the notes to the financial statements for depreciation on property, plant, and equipment.
2. The criteria for determining commercial substance in a nonmonetary exchange.
3. The disclosure requirements for interest capitalization.
4. The elements of costs to be included as R&D activities.

E 10–22
Interest capitalization
● LO10–7

On January 1, 2018, the Marjlee Company began construction of an office building to be used as its corporate headquarters. The building was completed early in 2019. Construction expenditures for 2018, which were incurred evenly throughout the year, totaled $6,000,000. Marjlee had the following debt obligations which were outstanding during all of 2018:

Construction loan, 10%	$1,500,000
Long-term note, 9%	2,000,000
Long-term note, 6%	4,000,000

Required:
Calculate the amount of interest capitalized in 2018 for the building using the specific interest method.

E 10–23
Interest capitalization
● LO10–7

On January 1, 2018, the Shagri Company began construction on a new manufacturing facility for its own use. The building was completed in 2019. The only interest-bearing debt the company had outstanding during 2018 was long-term bonds with a book value of $10,000,000 and an effective interest rate of 8%. Construction expenditures incurred during 2018 were as follows:

January 1	$500,000
March 1	600,000
July 31	480,000
September 30	600,000
December 31	300,000

Required:
Calculate the amount of interest capitalized for 2018.

E 10–24
Interest capitalization
● LO10–7

On January 1, 2018, the Highlands Company began construction on a new manufacturing facility for its own use. The building was completed in 2019. The company borrowed $1,500,000 at 8% on January 1 to help finance the construction. In addition to the construction loan, Highlands had the following debt outstanding throughout 2018:

$5,000,000, 12% bonds
$3,000,000, 8% long-term note

Construction expenditures incurred during 2018 were as follows:

January 1	$ 600,000
March 31	1,200,000
June 30	800,000
September 30	600,000
December 31	400,000

Required:
Calculate the amount of interest capitalized for 2018 using the specific interest method.

E 10–25
Interest capitalization; multiple periods
● LO10–7

Thornton Industries began construction of a warehouse on July 1, 2018. The project was completed on March 31, 2019. No new loans were required to fund construction. Thornton does have the following two interest-bearing liabilities that were outstanding throughout the construction period:

$2,000,000, 8% note
$8,000,000, 4% bonds

Construction expenditures incurred were as follows:

July 1, 2018	$400,000
September 30, 2018	600,000
November 30, 2018	600,000
January 30, 2019	540,000

The company's fiscal year-end is December 31.

Required:
Calculate the amount of interest capitalized for 2018 and 2019.

E 10–26
Research and development
● LO10–8

In 2018, Space Technology Company modified its model Z2 satellite to incorporate a new communication device. The company made the following expenditures:

Basic research to develop the technology	$2,000,000
Engineering design work	680,000
Development of a prototype device	300,000
Acquisition of equipment	60,000
Testing and modification of the prototype	200,000
Legal and other fees for patent application on the new communication system	40,000
Legal fees for successful defense of the new patent	20,000
Total	$3,300,000

The equipment will be used on this and other research projects. Depreciation on the equipment for 2018 is $10,000.

During your year-end review of the accounts related to intangibles, you discover that the company has capitalized all of the above as costs of the patent. Management contends that the device simply represents an improvement of the existing communication system of the satellite and, therefore, should be capitalized.

Required:
Prepare correcting entries that reflect the appropriate treatment of the expenditures.

E 10–27
Research and development
● LO10–8

Delaware Company incurred the following research and development costs during 2018:

Salaries and wages for lab research	$ 400,000
Materials used in R&D projects	200,000
Purchase of equipment	900,000
Fees paid to third parties for R&D projects	320,000
Patent filing and legal costs for a developed product	65,000
Salaries, wages, and supplies for R&D work performed for another company under a contract	350,000
Total	$2,235,000

The equipment has a seven-year life and will be used for a number of research projects. Depreciation for 2018 is $120,000.

Required:

Calculate the amount of research and development expense that Delaware should report in its 2018 income statement.

E 10–28
IFRS; research and development
● LO10–8, LO10–9

Janson Pharmaceuticals incurred the following costs in 2018 related to a new cancer drug:

Research for new formulas	$2,425,000
Development of a new formula	1,600,000
Legal and filing fees for a patent for the new formula	60,000
Total	$4,085,000

The development costs were incurred after technological and commercial feasibility was established and after the future economic benefits were deemed probable. The project was successfully completed and the new drug was patented before the end of the 2018 fiscal year.

Required:

1. Calculate the amount of research and development expense Janson should report in its 2018 income statement related to this project.
2. Repeat requirement 1 assuming that Janson prepares its financial statements according to International Financial Reporting Standards.

E 10–29
IFRS; research and development
● LO10–9

IFRS

NXS Semiconductor prepares its financial statements according to International Financial Reporting Standards. The company incurred the following expenditures during 2018 related to the development of a chip to be used in mobile devices:

Salaries and wages for basic research	$3,450,000
Materials used in basic research	330,000
Other costs incurred for basic research	1,220,000
Development costs	1,800,000
Legal and filing fees for a patent for the new technology	50,000

The development costs were incurred after NXS established technological and commercial feasibility and after NXS deemed the future economic benefits to be probable. The project was successfully completed, and the new chip was patented near the end of the 2018 fiscal year.

Required:

1. Which of the expenditures should NXS expense in its 2018 income statement?
2. Explain the accounting treatment of the remaining expenditures.

E 10–30
Concepts; terminology
● LO10–1, LO10–4, LO10–6, LO10–7

Listed below are several terms and phrases associated with property, plant, and equipment and intangible assets. Pair each item from List A with the item from List B (by letter) that is most appropriately associated with it.

List A	List B
____ 1. Property, plant, and equipment	a. Exclusive right to display a word, a symbol, or an emblem
____ 2. Land improvements	b. Exclusive right to benefit from a creative work
____ 3. Capitalize	c. Assets that represent rights
____ 4. Average accumulated expenditures	d. Costs of establishing parking lots, driveways, and private roads
____ 5. Revenue	e. Purchase price less fair value of net identifiable assets
____ 6. Nonmonetary exchange	f. Assets such as land, buildings, and machines
____ 7. Natural resources	g. Approximation of average amount of debt if all construction funds were borrowed
____ 8. Intangible assets	h. Account credited when assets are donated to a corporation
____ 9. Copyright	i. Term meaning to record the cost as an asset
____ 10. Trademark	j. Basic principle is to value assets acquired using fair value of assets given other than cash
____ 11. Goodwill	k. Assets such as timber tracks and mineral deposits

E 10–31
Software development costs
● LO10–8

Early in 2018, the Excalibur Company began developing a new software package to be marketed. The project was completed in December 2018 at a cost of $6 million. Of this amount, $4 million was spent before technological feasibility was established. Excalibur expects a useful life of five years for the new product with total revenues of $10 million. During 2019, revenue of $3 million was recognized.

Required:

1. Prepare a journal entry to record the 2018 development costs.
2. Calculate the required amortization for 2019.
3. At what amount should the computer software costs be reported in the December 31, 2019, balance sheet?

E 10–32
Software development costs
● LO10–8

On September 30, 2018, Athens Software began developing a software program to shield personal computers from malware and spyware. Technological feasibility was established on February 28, 2019, and the program was available for release on April 30, 2019. Development costs were incurred as follows:

September 30 through December 31, 2018	$2,200,000
January 1 through February 28, 2019	800,000
March 1 through April 30, 2019	400,000

Athens expects a useful life of four years for the software and total revenues of $5,000,000 during that time. During 2019, revenue of $1,000,000 was recognized.

Required:

1. Prepare the journal entries to record the development costs in 2018 and 2019.
2. Calculate the required amortization for 2019.

E 10–33
Intangibles; start-up costs
● LO10–1, LO10–8

Freitas Corporation was organized early in 2018. The following expenditures were made during the first few months of the year:

Attorneys' fees in connection with the organization of the corporation	$ 12,000
State filing fees and other incorporation costs	3,000
Purchase of a patent	20,000
Legal and other fees for transfer of the patent	2,000
Purchase of equipment	30,000
Pre-opening salaries and employee training	40,000
Total	$107,000

Required:

Prepare a summary journal entry to record the $107,000 in cash expenditures.

E 10–34
Full-cost and successful efforts methods compared
● Appendix

The Manguino Oil Company incurred exploration costs in 2018 searching and drilling for oil as follows:

Well 101	$ 50,000
Well 102	60,000
Well 103	80,000
Wells 104–108	260,000
Total	$450,000

It was determined that Wells 104–108 were dry holes and were abandoned. Wells 101, 102, and 103 were determined to have sufficient oil reserves to be commercially successful.

Required:

1. Prepare a summary journal entry to record the indicated costs assuming that the company uses the full-cost method of accounting for exploration costs. All of the exploration costs were paid in cash.
2. Prepare a summary journal entry to record the indicated costs assuming that the company uses the successful efforts method of accounting for exploration costs. All of the exploration costs were paid in cash.

Problems

P 10–1
Acquisition costs
● LO10–1 through LO10–4

Tristar Production Company began operations on September 1, 2018. Listed below are a number of transactions that occurred during its first four months of operations.

1. On September 1, the company acquired five acres of land with a building that will be used as a warehouse. Tristar paid $100,000 in cash for the property. According to appraisals, the land had a fair value of $75,000 and the building had a fair value of $45,000.
2. On September 1, Tristar signed a $40,000 noninterest-bearing note to purchase equipment. The $40,000 payment is due on September 1, 2019. Assume that 8% is a reasonable interest rate.
3. On September 15, a truck was donated to the corporation. Similar trucks were selling for $2,500.

4. On September 18, the company paid its lawyer $3,000 for organizing the corporation.
5. On October 10, Tristar purchased maintenance equipment for cash. The purchase price was $15,000 and $500 in freight charges also were paid.
6. On December 2, Tristar acquired various items of office equipment. The company was short of cash and could not pay the $5,500 normal cash price. The supplier agreed to accept 200 shares of the company's nopar common stock in exchange for the equipment. The fair value of the stock is not readily determinable.
7. On December 10, the company acquired a tract of land at a cost of $20,000. It paid $2,000 down and signed a 10% note with both principal and interest due in one year. Ten percent is an appropriate rate of interest for this note.

Required:

Prepare journal entries to record each of the above transactions.

P 10–2
Acquisition costs; land and building
● LO10–1, LO10–2, LO10–7

On January 1, 2018, the Blackstone Corporation purchased a tract of land (site number 11) with a building for $600,000. Additionally, Blackstone paid a real estate broker's commission of $36,000, legal fees of $6,000, and title insurance of $18,000. The closing statement indicated that the land value was $500,000 and the building value was $100,000. Shortly after acquisition, the building was razed at a cost of $75,000.

Blackstone entered into a $3,000,000 fixed-price contract with Barnett Builders, Inc., on March 1, 2018, for the construction of an office building on land site 11. The building was completed and occupied on September 30, 2019. Additional construction costs were incurred as follows:

Plans, specifications, and blueprints	$12,000
Architects' fees for design and supervision	95,000

To finance the construction cost, Blackstone borrowed $3,000,000 on March 1, 2018. The loan is payable in 10 annual installments of $300,000 plus interest at the rate of 14%. Blackstone's average amounts of accumulated building construction expenditures were as follows:

For the period March 1 to December 31, 2018	$ 900,000
For the period January 1 to September 30, 2019	2,300,000

Required:

1. Prepare a schedule that discloses the individual costs making up the balance in the land account in respect of land site 11 as of September 30, 2019.
2. Prepare a schedule that discloses the individual costs that should be capitalized in the office building account as of September 30, 2019.

(AICPA adapted)

P 10–3
Acquisition costs
● LO10–1, LO10–4, LO10–6

The plant asset and accumulated depreciation accounts of Pell Corporation had the following balances at December 31, 2017:

	Plant Asset	Accumulated Depreciation
Land	$ 350,000	$ —
Land improvements	180,000	45,000
Building	1,500,000	350,000
Machinery and equipment	1,158,000	405,000
Automobiles	150,000	112,000

Transactions during 2018 were as follows:

a. On January 2, 2018, machinery and equipment were purchased at a total invoice cost of $260,000, which included a $5,500 charge for freight. Installation costs of $27,000 were incurred.
b. On March 31, 2018, a small storage building was donated to the company. The person donating the building originally purchased it three years ago for $25,000. The fair value of the building on the day of the donation was $17,000.
c. On May 1, 2018, expenditures of $50,000 were made to repave parking lots at Pell's plant location. The work was necessitated by damage caused by severe winter weather.
d. On November 1, 2018, Pell acquired a tract of land with an existing building in exchange for 10,000 shares of Pell's common stock that had a market price of $38 per share. Pell paid legal fees and title insurance totaling $23,000. Shortly after acquisition, the building was razed at a cost of $35,000 in anticipation of new building construction in 2019.
e. On December 31, 2018, Pell purchased a small storage building by giving $15,250 cash and an old automobile purchased for $18,000 in 2014. Depreciation on the old automobile recorded through December 31, 2018, totaled $13,500. The fair value of the old automobile was $3,750.

Required:

Prepare a schedule analyzing the changes in each of the plant assets during 2018, with detailed supporting computations.

(AICPA adapted)

P 10–4
Intangibles
● LO10–1, LO10–8

The Horstmeyer Corporation commenced operations early in 2018. A number of expenditures were made during 2018 that were debited to one account called *intangible asset.* A recap of the $144,000 balance in this account at the end of 2018 is as follows:

Date	Transaction	Amount
2/3/18	State incorporation fees and legal costs related to organizing the corporation	$ 7,000
3/1/18	Fire insurance premium for three-year period	6,000
3/15/18	Purchased a copyright	20,000
4/30/18	Research and development costs	40,000
6/15/18	Legal fees for filing a patent on a new product resulting from an R&D project	3,000
9/30/18	Legal fee for successful defense of patent developed above	12,000
10/13/18	Entered into a 10-year franchise agreement with franchisor	40,000
Various	Advertising costs	16,000
	Total	$144,000

Required:

Prepare the necessary journal entry to clear the intangible asset account and to set up accounts for separate intangible assets, other types of assets, and expenses indicated by the transactions.

P 10–5
Acquisition costs; journal entries
● LO10–1, LO10–3, LO10–6, LO10–8

Consider each of the transactions below. All of the expenditures were made in cash.

1. The Edison Company spent $12,000 during the year for experimental purposes in connection with the development of a new product.
2. In April, the Marshall Company lost a patent infringement suit and paid the plaintiff $7,500.
3. In March, the Cleanway Laundromat bought equipment. Cleanway paid $6,000 down and signed a noninterest-bearing note requiring the payment of $18,000 in nine months. The cash price for this equipment was $23,000.
4. On June 1, the Jamsen Corporation installed a sprinkler system throughout the building at a cost of $28,000.
5. The Mayer Company, plaintiff, paid $12,000 in legal fees in November, in connection with a successful infringement suit on its patent.
6. The Johnson Company traded its old machine with an original cost of $7,400 and a book value of $3,000 plus cash of $8,000 for a new one that had a fair value of $10,000. The exchange has commercial substance.

Required:

Prepare journal entries to record each of the above transactions.

P 10–6
Nonmonetary exchange
● LO10–6

Southern Company owns a building that it leases to others. The building's fair value is $1,400,000 and its book value is $800,000 (original cost of $2,000,000 less accumulated depreciation of $1,200,000). Southern exchanges this for a building owned by the Eastern Company. The building's book value on Eastern's books is $950,000 (original cost of $1,600,000 less accumulated depreciation of $650,000). Eastern also gives Southern $140,000 to complete the exchange. The exchange has commercial substance for both companies.

Required:

Prepare the journal entries to record the exchange on the books of both Southern and Eastern.

P 10–7
Nonmonetary exchange
● LO10–6

On September 3, 2018, the Robers Company exchanged equipment with Phifer Corporation. The facts of the exchange are as follows:

	Robers' Asset	Phifer's Asset
Original cost	$120,000	$140,000
Accumulated depreciation	55,000	63,000
Fair value	75,000	70,000

To equalize the exchange, Phifer paid Robers $5,000 in cash.

Required:

Record the exchange for both Robers and Phifer. The exchange has commercial substance for both companies.

P 10–8
Nonmonetary exchange
● LO10–6

Case A. Kapono Farms exchanged an old tractor for a newer model. The old tractor had a book value of $12,000 (original cost of $28,000 less accumulated depreciation of $16,000) and a fair value of $9,000. Kapono paid $20,000 cash to complete the exchange. The exchange has commercial substance.

Required:

1. What is the amount of gain or loss that Kapono would recognize on the exchange? What is the initial value of the new tractor?
2. Repeat requirement 1 assuming that the fair value of the old tractor is $14,000 instead of $9,000.

Case B. Kapono Farms exchanged 100 acres of farmland for similar land. The farmland given had a book value of $500,000 and a fair value of $700,000. Kapono paid $50,000 cash to complete the exchange. The exchange has commercial substance.

Required:

1. What is the amount of gain or loss that Kapono would recognize on the exchange? What is the initial value of the new land?
2. Repeat requirement 1 assuming that the fair value of the farmland given is $400,000 instead of $700,000.
3. Repeat requirement 1 assuming that the exchange lacked commercial substance.

P 10–9
Interest capitalization; specific interest method
● LO10–7

On January 1, 2018, the Mason Manufacturing Company began construction of a building to be used as its office headquarters. The building was completed on September 30, 2019. Expenditures on the project were as follows:

January 1, 2018	$1,000,000
March 1, 2018	600,000
June 30, 2018	800,000
October 1, 2018	600,000
January 31, 2019	270,000
April 30, 2019	585,000
August 31, 2019	900,000

On January 1, 2018, the company obtained a $3 million construction loan with a 10% interest rate. The loan was outstanding all of 2018 and 2019. The company's other interest-bearing debt included two long-term notes of $4,000,000 and $6,000,000 with interest rates of 6% and 8%, respectively. Both notes were outstanding during all of 2018 and 2019. Interest is paid annually on all debt. The company's fiscal year-end is December 31.

Required:

1. Calculate the amount of interest that Mason should capitalize in 2018 and 2019 using the specific interest method.
2. What is the total cost of the building?
3. Calculate the amount of interest expense that will appear in the 2018 and 2019 income statements.

P 10–10
Interest capitalization; weighted-average method
● LO10–7

[This is a variation of the previous problem, modified to focus on the weighted-average interest method.]

Required:

Refer to the facts in Problem 10–9 and answer the following questions:

1. Calculate the amount of interest that Mason should capitalize in 2018 and 2019 using the weighted-average method.
2. What is the total cost of the building?
3. Calculate the amount of interest expense that will appear in the 2018 and 2019 income statements.

P 10–11
Research and development
● LO10–8

In 2018, Starsearch Corporation began work on three research and development projects. One of the projects was completed and commercial production of the developed product began in December. The company's fiscal year-end is December 31. All of the following 2016 expenditures were included in the R&D expense account:

Salaries and wages for:	
Lab research	$ 300,000
Design and construction of preproduction prototype	160,000
Quality control during commercial production	20,000
Materials and supplies consumed for:	
Lab research	60,000
Construction of preproduction prototype	30,000
Purchase of equipment	600,000
Patent filing and legal fees for completed project	40,000
Payments to others for research	120,000
Total	$1,330,000

$200,000 of equipment was purchased solely for use in one of the projects. After the project is completed, the equipment will be abandoned. The remaining $400,000 in equipment will be used on future R&D projects. The useful life of equipment is five years. Assume that all of the equipment was acquired at the beginning of the year.

Required:

Prepare journal entries, reclassifying amounts in R&D expense, to reflect the appropriate treatment of the expenditures.

P 10–12
Acquisition costs; lump-sum acquisition; noninterest-bearing note; interest capitalization
● LO10–1, LO10–2, LO10–3, LO10–7

Early in its fiscal year ending December 31, 2018, San Antonio Outfitters finalized plans to expand operations. The first stage was completed on March 28 with the purchase of a tract of land on the outskirts of the city. The land and existing building were purchased for $800,000. San Antonio paid $200,000 and signed a noninterest-bearing note requiring the company to pay the remaining $600,000 on March 28, 2020. An interest rate of 8% properly reflects the time value of money for this type of loan agreement. Title search, insurance, and other closing costs totaling $20,000 were paid at closing.

During April, the old building was demolished at a cost of $70,000, and an additional $50,000 was paid to clear and grade the land. Construction of a new building began on May 1 and was completed on October 29. Construction expenditures were as follows:

May 1	$1,200,000
July 30	1,500,000
September 1	900,000
October 1	1,800,000

San Antonio borrowed $3,000,000 at 8% on May 1 to help finance construction. This loan, plus interest, will be paid in 2019. The company also had the following debt outstanding throughout 2018:

$2,000,000, 9% long-term note payable
$4,000,000, 6% long-term bonds payable

In November, the company purchased 10 identical pieces of equipment and office furniture and fixtures for a lump-sum price of $600,000. The fair values of the equipment and the furniture and fixtures were $455,000 and $245,000, respectively. In December, San Antonio paid a contractor $285,000 for the construction of parking lots and for landscaping.

Required:

1. Determine the initial values of the various assets that San Antonio acquired or constructed during 2018. The company uses the specific interest method to determine the amount of interest capitalized on the building construction.
2. How much interest expense will San Antonio report in its 2018 income statement?

Broaden Your Perspective

Apply your critical-thinking ability to the knowledge you've gained. These cases will provide you an opportunity to develop your research, analysis, judgment, and communication skills. You also will work with other students, integrate what you've learned, apply it in real-world situations, and consider its global and ethical ramifications. This practice will broaden your knowledge and further develop your decision-making abilities.

Judgment Case 10–1
Acquisition costs
● LO10–1, LO10–3, LO10–6

A company may acquire property, plant, and equipment and intangible assets for cash, in exchange for a deferred payment contract, by exchanging other assets, or by a combination of these methods.

Required:

1. Identify six types of costs that should be capitalized as the cost of a parcel of land. For your answer, assume that the land has an existing building that is to be removed in the immediate future in order that a new building can be constructed on the site.
2. At what amount should a company record an asset acquired in exchange for a deferred payment contract?
3. In general, at what amount should assets received in exchange for other nonmonetary assets be valued? Specifically, at what amount should a company value a new machine acquired by exchanging an older, similar machine and paying cash?

(AICPA adapted)

Research Case 10–2
FASB codification; locate and extract relevant information and cite authoritative support for a financial reporting issue; restoration costs; asset retirement obligation
● LO10–1

Your client, Hazelton Mining, recently entered into an agreement to obtain the rights to operate a coal mine in West Virginia for $15 million. Hazelton incurred development costs of $6 million in preparing the mine for extraction, which began on July 1, 2018. The contract requires Hazelton to restore the land and surrounding area to its original condition after extraction is complete in three years.

The company controller, Alice Cushing, is not sure how to account for the restoration costs and has asked your advice. Alice is aware of an accounting standard addressing this issue, but is not sure of its provisions. She has narrowed down the possible cash outflows for the restoration costs to four possibilities.

Cash Outflow	Probability
$3 million	20%
4 million	30%
5 million	25%
6 million	25%

Alice also informs you that the company's credit-adjusted risk-free interest rate is 9%. Before responding to Alice, you need to research the issue.

Required:

1. Obtain the relevant authoritative literature on accounting for asset retirement obligations using the *FASB Accounting Standards Codification.* You might gain access at the FASB website (www.fasb.org). Explain the basic treatment of asset retirement obligations. What are the specific citations that you would rely on to determine (a) the accounting treatment for an asset retirement obligation and (b) how to measure the obligation?
2. Determine the capitalized cost of the coal mine.
3. Prepare a summary journal entry to record the acquisition costs of the mine.
4. How much accretion expense will the company record in its income statement for the 2018 fiscal year, related to this transaction? What are the specific citations from the *FASB Accounting Standards Codification* that address (a) the calculation of accretion expense and (b) the classification of accretion expense in the income statement?
5. Explain to Alice how Hazelton would account for the restoration if the restoration costs differed from the recorded liability in three years. By way of explanation, prepare the journal entry to record the payment of the retirement obligation in three years assuming that the actual restoration costs were $4.7 million.
6. Describe to Alice the necessary disclosure requirements for the obligation. What is the specific citation from the *FASB Accounting Standards Codification* that contains these disclosure requirements?

Judgment Case 10–3
Self-constructed assets
● LO10–7

Chilton Peripherals manufactures printers, scanners, and other computer peripheral equipment. In the past, the company purchased equipment used in manufacturing from an outside vendor. In March 2018, Chilton decided to design and build equipment to replace some obsolete equipment. A section of the manufacturing plant was set aside to develop and produce the equipment. Additional personnel were hired for the project. The equipment was completed and ready for use in September.

Required:

1. In general, what costs should be capitalized for a self-constructed asset?
2. Discuss two alternatives for the inclusion of overhead costs in the cost of the equipment constructed by Chilton. Which alternative is generally accepted for financial reporting purposes?
3. Under what circumstance(s) would interest be included in the cost of the equipment?

Judgment Case 10–4
Interest capitalization
● LO10–7

GAAP provides guidelines for the inclusion of interest in the initial cost of a self-constructed asset.

Required:

1. What assets qualify for interest capitalization? What assets do not qualify for interest capitalization?
2. Over what period should interest be capitalized?
3. Explain average accumulated expenditures.
4. Explain the two methods that could be used to determine the appropriate interest rate(s) to be used in capitalizing interest.
5. Describe the three steps used to determine the amount of interest capitalized during a reporting period.

Research Case 10–5
Goodwill
● LO10–1

Accounting for acquired goodwill has been a controversial issue for many years. In the United States, the amount of acquired goodwill is capitalized and not amortized. Globally, the treatment of goodwill varies significantly, with some countries not recognizing goodwill as an asset. Professors Johnson and Petrone, in "Is Goodwill an Asset?" discuss this issue.

Required:

1. In your library or from some other source, locate the indicated article in *Accounting Horizons,* September 1998.
2. Does goodwill meet the FASB's definition of an asset?
3. What are the key concerns of those that believe goodwill is not an asset?

Real World Case 10–6
Property, plant, and equipment; Norfolk Southern Corporation
● LO10–1

Real World Financials

Norfolk Southern Corporation, one of the nation's premier transportation companies, reported the following amounts in the asset section of its balance sheets for the years ended December 31, 2015 and 2014:

	($ in millions)	
	December 31, 2015	**December 31, 2014**
Property and equipment, net	$28,992	$27,694

In addition, information from the 2015 statement of cash flows and related notes reported the following items ($ in millions):

Depreciation	$1,059
Additions to property and equipment	2,385
Sales price of property and equipment	63

Required:

For what amount was the sales price above book value of property and equipment sold for the year ended December 31, 2015?

Judgment Case 10–7
Goodwill
● LO10–1

Athena Paper Corporation acquired for cash 100% of the outstanding common stock of Georgia, Inc., a supplier of wood pulp. The $4,500,000 amount paid was significantly higher than the book value of Georgia's net assets (assets less liabilities) of $2,800,000. The Athena controller recorded the difference of $1,700,000 as an asset, goodwill.

Required:

1. Discuss the meaning of the term goodwill.
2. In what situation would the Athena controller be correct in her valuation of goodwill?

Judgment Case 10–8
Research and development
● LO10–8

Prior to 1974, accepted practice was for companies to either expense or capitalize R&D costs. In 1974, the FASB issued a Standard that requires all research and development costs to be charged to expense when incurred. This was a controversial standard, opposed by many companies who preferred delaying the recognition of these expenses until later years when presumably the expenditures bear fruit.

Several research studies have been conducted to determine if the Standard had any impact on the behavior of companies. One interesting finding was that, prior to 1974, companies that expensed R&D costs were significantly larger than those companies that capitalized R&D costs.

Required:

1. Explain the FASB's logic in deciding to require all companies to expense R&D costs in the period incurred.
2. Identify possible reasons to explain why, prior to 1974, companies that expensed R&D costs were significantly larger than those companies that capitalized R&D costs.

Judgment Case 10–9
Research and development
● LO10–8

Clonal, Inc., a biotechnology company, developed and patented a diagnostic product called Trouver. Clonal purchased some research equipment to be used exclusively for Trouver and subsequent research projects. Clonal defeated a legal challenge to its Trouver patent, and began production and marketing operations for the project.

Corporate headquarters' costs were allocated to Clonal's research division as a percentage of the division's salaries.

Required:

1. How should the equipment purchased for Trouver be reported in Clonal's income statements and statements of financial position?
2. a. Describe the accounting treatment of research and development costs.

b. What is the justification for the accounting treatment of research and development costs?
3. How should corporate headquarters' costs allocated to the research division be classified in Clonal's income statements? Why?
4. How should the legal expenses incurred in defending Trouver's patent be reported in Clonal's financial statements?

(AICPA adapted)

Communication Case 10–10
Research and development
● LO10–8

The focus of this case is the situation described in Case 10–9. What is the appropriate accounting for R&D costs? Do you believe that (1) capitalization is the correct treatment of R&D costs, (2) expensing is the correct treatment of R&D costs, or (3) that companies should be allowed to choose between expensing and capitalizing R&D costs?

Required:

1. Develop a list of arguments in support of your view prior to the class session for which the case is assigned. Do not be influenced by the method required by the FASB. Base your opinion on the conceptual merit of the options.
2. In class, your instructor will pair you (and everyone else) with a classmate who also has independently developed a position.
   a. You will be given three minutes to argue your view to your partner. Your partner likewise will be given three minutes to argue his or her view to you. During these three-minute presentations, the listening partner is not permitted to speak.
   b. Then after each person has had a turn attempting to convince his or her partner, the two partners will have a three-minute discussion in which they will decide which alternative is more convincing and arguments will be merged into a single view for each pair.
3. After the allotted time, a spokesperson for each of the three alternatives will be selected by the instructor. Each spokesperson will field arguments from the class as to the appropriate alternative. The class will then discuss the merits of the alternatives and attempt to reach a consensus view, though a consensus is not necessary.

Communication Case 10–11
Research and development
● LO10–8

Thomas Plastics is in the process of developing a revolutionary new plastic valve. A new division of the company was formed to develop, manufacture, and market this new product. As of year-end (December 31, 2018), the new product has not been manufactured for sale; however, prototype units were built and are in operation.

Throughout 2018, the new division incurred a variety of costs. These costs included expenses (including salaries of administrative personnel) and market research costs. In addition, approximately $500,000 in equipment (estimated useful life of 10 years) was purchased for use in developing and manufacturing the new valve. Approximately $200,000 of this equipment was built specifically for developing the design of the new product; the remaining $300,000 of the equipment was used to manufacture the preproduction prototypes and will be used to manufacture the new product once it is in commercial production.

The president of the company, Sally Rogers, has been told that research and development costs must be expensed as incurred, but she does not understand this treatment. She believes the research will lead to a profitable product and to increased future revenues. Also, she wonders how to account for the $500,000 of equipment purchased by the new division. "I thought I understood accounting," she growled. "Explain to me why expenditures that benefit our future revenues are expensed rather than capitalized!"

Required:

Write a one-to two-page report to Sally Rogers explaining the generally accepted accounting principles relevant to this issue. The report also should address the treatment of the equipment purchases.

(AICPA adapted)

Ethics Case 10–12
Research and development
● LO10–8

Mayer Biotechnical, Inc., develops, manufactures, and sells pharmaceuticals. Significant research and development (R&D) expenditures are made for the development of new drugs and the improvement of existing drugs. During 2018, $220 million was spent on R&D. Of this amount, $30 million was spent on the purchase of equipment to be used in a research project involving the development of a new antibiotic.

The controller, Alice Cooper, is considering capitalizing the equipment and depreciating it over the five-year useful life of the equipment at $6 million per year, even though the equipment likely will be used on only one project. The company president has asked Alice to make every effort to increase 2018 earnings because in 2019 the company will be seeking significant new financing from both debt and equity sources. "I guess we might use the equipment in other projects later," Alice wondered to herself.

Required:

1. Assuming that the equipment was purchased at the beginning of 2018, by how much would Alice's treatment of the equipment increase before tax earnings as opposed to expensing the equipment cost?
2. Discuss the ethical dilemma Alice faces in determining the treatment of the $30 million equipment purchase.

IFRS Case 10–13
Research and development; comparison of U.S. GAAP and IFRS; Siemens AG
● LO10–8, LO10–9
IFRS

Siemens AG, a German company, is Europe's largest engineering and electronics company. The company prepares its financial statements according to IFRS.

Required:

1. Use the Internet to locate the most recent financial report for Siemens. The address is www.siemens.com. Locate the significant accounting policies disclosure note.
2. How does the company account for research and development expenditures? Does this policy differ from U.S. GAAP?

Analysis Case 10–14
Fixed-asset turnover ratio; Pier 1 Imports, Inc.
● LO10–5
Real World Financials

Pier 1 Imports, Inc., is a leading retailer of domestic merchandise and home furnishings. The company's 2016 fixed-asset turnover ratio, using the average book value of property, plant, and equipment (PP&E) as the denominator, was approximately 8.97. Additional information taken from the company's 2016 annual report is as follows:

	($ in thousands)
Book value of PP&E—beginning of 2016	$214,048
Purchases of PP&E during 2016	51,813
Depreciation of PP&E for 2016	55,830

Equipment having a book value of $2,398 thousand was sold during 2016.

Required:

1. How is the fixed-asset turnover ratio computed? How would you interpret Pier 1's ratio of 8.97?
2. Use the data to determine Pier 1's net sales for 2016.
3. Obtain annual reports from three corporations in the same primary industry as Pier 1 Imports, Inc. (Bed, Bath & Beyond and Williams-Sonoma, Inc., are two well-known companies in the same industry) and compare the management of each company's investment in property, plant, and equipment.

Note: You can obtain copies of annual reports from your library, from friends who are shareholders, from the investor relations department of the corporations, from a friendly stockbroker, or from EDGAR (Electronic Data Gathering, Analysis, and Retrieval) on the Internet (www.sec.gov).

Judgment Case 10–15
Computer software costs
● LO10–8

The Elegant Software Company recently completed the development and testing of a new software program that provides the ability to transfer data from among a variety of operating systems. The company believes this product will be quite successful and capitalized all of the costs of designing, developing, coding, and testing the software. These costs will be amortized over the expected useful life of the software on a straight-line basis.

Required:

1. Was Elegant correct in its treatment of the software development costs? Why?
2. Explain the appropriate method for determining the amount of periodic amortization for any capitalized software development costs.

Real World Case 10–16
Property, plant, and equipment; Home Depot
● LO10–1, LO10–7
Real World Financials

EDGAR, the Electronic Data Gathering, Analysis, and Retrieval system, performs automated collection, validation, indexing, and forwarding of submissions by companies and others who are required by law to file forms with the U.S. Securities and Exchange Commission (SEC). All publicly traded domestic companies use EDGAR to make the majority of their filings. (Some foreign companies file voluntarily.) Form 10-K, which includes the annual report, is required to be filed on EDGAR. The SEC makes this information available on the Internet.

Required:

1. Access EDGAR on the Internet. The web address is www.sec.gov.
2. Search for Home Depot, Inc. Access the 10-K filing for the most recent fiscal year. Search or scroll to find the financial statements and related notes.
3. Answer the following questions related to the company's property, plant, and equipment:
   a. Name the different types of assets the company lists in its balance sheet under property, plant, and equipment.
   b. How much cash was used for the acquisition of property, plant, and equipment during the year?
   c. What was the amount of interest capitalized during the year?
   d. Compute the fixed-asset turnover ratio for the fiscal year.

Continuing Cases

Target Case

● LO10–1, LO10–5

Target Corporation prepares its financial statements according to U.S. GAAP. Target's financial statements and disclosure notes for the year ended January 30, 2016, are available in Connect. This material is also available under the Investor Relations link at the company's website (www.target.com).

Required:

1. What categories of property, plant, and equipment and intangible assets does Target report in its January 30, 2016 balance sheet?
2. How much cash was used in the fiscal year ended January 30, 2016, to purchase property and equipment? How does this compare with purchases in previous years?
3. Do you think a company like Target would have significant research and development costs or capitalized interest related to self-constructed assets? Explain.
4. What is Target's fixed-asset turnover ratio for the fiscal year ended January 30, 2016? What is the ratio intended to measure?

Air France–KLM Case

● LO10–9

Air France–KLM (AF), a Franco-Dutch company, prepares its financial statements according to International Financial Reporting Standards. AF's financial statements and disclosure notes for the year ended December 31, 2015, are available in Connect. This material is also available under the Finance link at the company's website (www.airfranceklm.com).

Required:

1. What method does Air France-KLM use to amortize the cost of computer software development costs? How does this approach differ from U.S. GAAP?
2. AF does not report any research and development expenditures. If it did, its approach to accounting for research and development would be significantly different from U.S. GAAP. Describe the differences between IFRS and U.S. GAAP in accounting for research and development expenditures.
3. AF does not report the receipt of any governments grants. If it did, its approach to accounting for government grants would be significantly different from U.S. GAAP. Describe the differences between IFRS and U.S. GAAP in accounting for government grants. If AF received a grant for the purchase of assets, what alternative accounting treatments are available under IFRS?

CPA Exam Questions and Simulations

Sample CPA Exam questions from Roger CPA Review are available in Connect as support for the topics in this chapter. These Multiple Choice Questions and Task-Based Simulations include expert-written explanations and solutions, and provide a starting point for students to become familiar with the content and functionality of the actual CPA Exam.

CHAPTER

11 Property, Plant, and Equipment and Intangible Assets: Utilization and Disposition

OVERVIEW

This chapter completes our discussion of accounting for property, plant, and equipment and intangible assets. We address the allocation of the cost of these assets to the periods benefited by their use.

The usefulness of most of these assets is consumed as the assets are applied to the production of goods or services. Cost allocation corresponding to this consumption of usefulness is known as *depreciation* for plant and equipment, *depletion* for natural resources, and *amortization* for intangibles.

We also consider other issues until final disposal such as impairment of these assets and the treatment of expenditures subsequent to acquisition.

LEARNING OBJECTIVES

After studying this chapter, you should be able to:

- **LO11–1** Explain the concept of cost allocation as it pertains to property, plant, and equipment and intangible assets. *(p. 575)*
- **LO11–2** Determine periodic depreciation using both time-based and activity-based methods and account for dispositions. *(p. 578)*
- **LO11–3** Calculate the periodic depletion of a natural resource. *(p. 591)*
- **LO11–4** Calculate the periodic amortization of an intangible asset. *(p. 593)*
- **LO11–5** Explain the appropriate accounting treatment required when a change is made in the service life or residual value of property, plant, and equipment and intangible assets. *(p. 599)*
- **LO11–6** Explain the appropriate accounting treatment required when a change in depreciation, amortization, or depletion method is made. *(p. 600)*
- **LO11–7** Explain the appropriate treatment required when an error in accounting for property, plant, and equipment and intangible assets is discovered. *(p. 601)*
- **LO11–8** Identify situations that involve a significant impairment of the value of property, plant, and equipment and intangible assets and describe the required accounting procedures. *(p. 603)*
- **LO11–9** Discuss the accounting treatment of repairs and maintenance, additions, improvements, and rearrangements to property, plant, and equipment and intangible assets. *(p. 614)*
- **LO11–10** Discuss the primary differences between U.S. GAAP and IFRS with respect to the utilization and impairment of property, plant, and equipment and intangible assets. *(pp. 584, 589, 593, 596, 605, 607, 611, and 617)*

© fStop/Getty Images

FINANCIAL REPORTING CASE

What's in a Name?

"I don't understand this at all," your friend Penny Lane moaned. "Depreciation, depletion, amortization; what's the difference? Aren't they all the same thing?" Penny and you are part of a class team working on a case involving Weyerhaeuser Company, a large forest products company. Part of the project involves comparing reporting methods over a three-year period. "Look at these disclosure notes from last year's annual report. Besides mentioning those three terms, they also talk about asset impairment. How is that different?" Penny showed you the disclosure notes.

Property and Equipment and Timber and Timberlands (in part)

Depreciation is calculated using a straight-line method at rates based on estimated service lives. Logging roads are generally amortized—as timber is harvested—at rates based on the volume of timber estimated to be removed. We carry timber and timberlands at cost less depletion.

Depletion (in part)

To determine depletion rates, we divide the net carrying value by the related volume of timber estimated to be available over the growth cycle.

Impairment of Long-Lived Assets (in part)

We review long-lived assets—including certain identifiable intangibles—for impairment whenever events or changes in circumstances indicate that the carrying amount of the assets may not be recoverable.

QUESTIONS

By the time you finish this chapter, you should be able to respond appropriately to the questions posed in this case. Compare your response to the solution provided at the end of the chapter.

1. Is Penny correct? Do the terms *depreciation, depletion,* and *amortization* all mean the same thing? (*p. 576*)
2. Weyerhaeuser determines depletion based on the "volume of timber estimated to be available." Explain this approach. (*p. 581*)
3. Explain how asset impairment differs from depreciation, depletion, and amortization. How do companies measure impairment losses for property, plant, and equipment and intangible assets with finite useful lives? (*p. 602*)

PART A

Depreciation, Depletion, and Amortization

Cost Allocation—an Overview

LO11–1

Property, plant, and equipment and intangible assets are purchased with the expectation that they will provide future benefits. Specifically, they are acquired to be used as part of the revenue-generating operations, usually for several years. Logically, then, the cost of these acquisitions initially should be recorded as assets (as we saw in Chapter 10), and then these costs should be allocated to expense over the reporting periods benefited by their use. That is, their costs are reported with the revenues they help generate.

Let's suppose that a company purchases a used truck for $8,200 to deliver products to customers. The company estimates that five years from the acquisition date the truck will be sold for $2,200. It is estimated, then, that $6,000 ($8,200 − 2,200) of the truck's purchase cost will be used up (consumed) during a five-year useful life. The situation is portrayed in Illustration 11–1.

Illustration 11–1

Cost Allocation

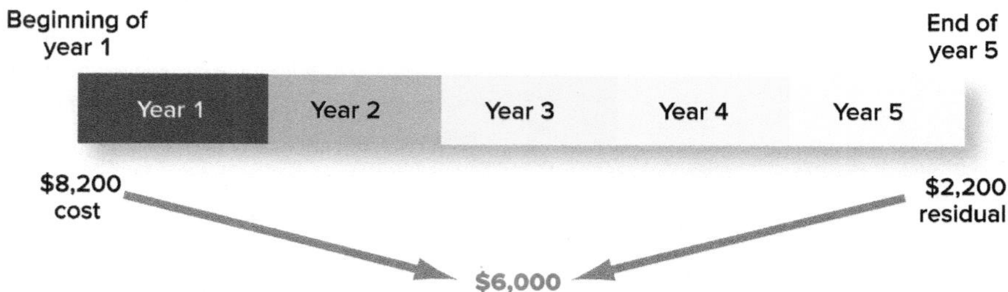

Because the truck will help to produce revenues over the next five years, an asset of $8,200 is recorded at the time of acquisition. Over the subsequent five years, $6,000 of the truck's costs is expected to be consumed and, conceptually, should be allocated to expense in those years in direct proportion to the role the asset played in revenue production. However, very seldom is there a clear-cut relationship between the use of the asset and revenue production. In other words, we can't tell precisely the portion of the total benefits of the asset that was consumed in any particular period. As a consequence, we must resort to arbitrary allocation methods to approximate the portion of the asset's cost used each period. Contrast this situation with the $24,000 prepayment of one year's rent on an office building at $2,000 per month. In that case, we know precisely that the benefits of the asset (prepaid rent) are consumed at a rate of $2,000 per month. That's why we allocate $2,000 of prepaid rent to rent expense for each month that passes.

The process of allocating the cost of plant and equipment over the periods they are used to produce revenues is known as **depreciation**. The process of depreciation often is confused with measuring a decline in fair value of an asset. For example, let's say our delivery truck purchased for $8,200 can be sold for $5,000 at the end of one year but we intend to keep it for the full five-year estimated life. It has experienced a decline in value of $3,200 ($8,200 − 5,000). However, *depreciation is a process of cost allocation, not valuation.* We would not record depreciation expense of $3,200 for year one of the truck's life. Instead, we would distribute the cost of the asset, less any anticipated residual value, over the estimated useful life in a systematic and rational manner that attempts to associate revenues with the *use* of the asset, not the decline in its value. After all, the truck is purchased to be used in operations, not to be sold.

FINANCIAL Reporting Case

Q1, p. 575

Depreciation, depletion, and amortization are processes that allocate an asset's cost to periods of benefit.

For natural resources, we refer to cost allocation as **depletion**, and for intangible assets, we refer to it as **amortization**. While the terms *depreciation*, *depletion*, and *amortization* differ across types of assets, they conceptually refer to the same idea—the process of allocating an asset's cost over the periods it is used to produce revenues.

For assets used in the manufacture of a product, depreciation, depletion, or amortization is considered a product cost to be included as part of the cost of inventory. Eventually, when the product is sold, it becomes part of the cost of goods sold. For assets *not* used in production, primarily plant and equipment and certain intangibles used in the selling and administrative functions of the company, depreciation or amortization is reported as a period expense in the income statement. You might recognize this distinction between a product cost and a period cost. A product cost is reported as an expense (cost of goods sold) when the product is sold; a period cost is reported as an expense in the reporting period in which it is incurred.

Measuring Cost Allocation

The process of cost allocation requires that three factors be established at the time the asset is put into use. These factors are

1. **Service life**—The estimated use that the company expects to receive from the asset.

2. Allocation base—The cost of the asset expected to be consumed during its service life.
3. Allocation method—The pattern in which the allocation base is expected to be consumed.

Let's consider these one at a time.

Service Life

The service life, or useful life, is the amount of use that the company expects to obtain from the asset before disposing of it. This use can be expressed in units of time or in units of activity. For example, the estimated service life of a delivery truck could be expressed in terms of years or in terms of the number of miles that the company expects the truck to be driven before disposition. We use the terms service life and useful life interchangeably throughout the chapter.

The *service life,* or *useful life,* can be expressed in units of time or in units of activity.

Physical life provides the upper bound for service life of tangible, long-lived assets. Physical life will vary according to the purpose for which the asset is acquired and the environment in which it is operated. For example, a diesel powered electric generator may last for many years if it is used only as an emergency backup or for only a few years if it is used regularly.

The service life of a tangible asset may be less than physical life for a variety of reasons. For example, the expected rate of technological change may shorten service life. If suppliers are expected to develop new technologies that are more efficient, the company may keep an asset for a period of time much shorter than physical life. Likewise, if the company sells its product in a market that frequently demands new products, the machinery and equipment used to produce products may be useful only for as long as its output can be sold. Similarly, a mineral deposit might be projected to contain 4 million tons of a mineral, but it may be economically feasible with existing extraction methods to mine only 2 million tons. For intangible assets, legal or contractual life often is a limiting factor. For instance, a patent might be capable of providing enhanced profitability for 50 years, but the legal life of a patent is only 20 years.

Expected obsolescence can shorten service life below physical life.

Management intent also may shorten the period of an asset's usefulness below its physical, legal, or contractual life. For example, a company may have a policy of using its delivery trucks for a three-year period and then trading the trucks for new models.

Companies quite often disclose the range of service lives for different categories of assets. For example, Illustration 11–2 shows how IBM Corporation disclosed its service lives in a note accompanying recent financial statements.

Summary of Significant Accounting Policies (in part)

Depreciation and Amortization

The estimated useful lives of certain depreciable assets are as follows: buildings, 30 to 50 years; building equipment, 10 to 20 years; land improvements, 20 years; plant, laboratory, and office equipment, 2 to 20 years; and computer equipment, 1.5 to 5 years.

Illustration 11–2
Service Life Disclosure—International Business Machines Corporation

Real World Financials

Allocation Base

The amount of cost to be allocated over an asset's service life is called its allocation base. The amount is the difference between the asset's capitalized cost at the date placed in service and the asset's residual value. Residual value (sometimes called *salvage value*) is the amount the company expects to receive for the asset at the end of its service life less any anticipated disposal costs.

Allocation base is the difference between the cost of the asset and its anticipated *residual value*.

For plant and equipment, we commonly refer to the allocation base as the *depreciable base*. In our delivery truck example above, the depreciable base is $6,000 ($8,200 cost less $2,200 anticipated residual value). We will allocate a portion of the $6,000 to each year of the truck's service life. For the depletion of natural resources, we refer to the allocation base as the *depletion base*. For amortization of intangible asset, we refer to the allocation base as the *amortization base*.

In certain situations, residual value can be estimated by referring to a company's prior experience or to publicly available information concerning resale values of various types of assets. For example, if a company intends to trade its delivery truck in three years for the new model, approximations of the three-year residual value for that type of truck can be obtained from used truck values.

However, estimating residual value for many assets can be very difficult due to the uncertainty about the future. For this reason, along with the fact that residual values often are immaterial, many companies simply assume a residual value of zero. Companies usually do not disclose estimated residual values.

Allocation Method

The *allocation method* used should be systematic and rational and correspond to the pattern of asset use.

In determining how much cost to allocate to periods of an asset's use, a method should be selected that corresponds to the pattern of benefits received from the asset's use. Generally accepted accounting principles state that the chosen method should allocate the asset's cost "as equitably as possible to the periods during which services are obtained from [its] use." GAAP further specifies that the method should produce a cost allocation in a "systematic and rational manner."[1] The objective is to try to allocate cost to the period in an amount that is proportional to the amount of benefits generated by the asset during the period relative to the total benefits provided by the asset during its life.

In practice, there are two general approaches that attempt to obtain this systematic and rational allocation. The first approach allocates the cost base according to the *passage of time.* Methods following this approach are referred to as time-based methods. The second approach allocates an asset's cost base using a measure of the asset's *input* or *output.* This is an activity-based method. We compare these approaches first in the context of depreciation. Later we see that depletion of natural resources typically follows an activity-based approach, and the amortization of intangibles typically follows a time-based approach.

Depreciation

LO11–2

To demonstrate and compare the most common depreciation methods, we refer to the situation described in Illustration 11–3.

Illustration 11–3
Depreciation Methods

The Hogan Manufacturing Company purchased a machine for $250,000. The company expects the service life of the machine to be five years. During that time, it is expected that the machine will produce 140,000 units. The estimated residual value is $40,000. The machine was disposed of after five years of use. Actual production during the five years of the asset's life was:

Year	Units Produced
1	20,000
2	32,000
3	44,000
4	28,000
5	26,000
Total	150,000

Time-Based Depreciation Methods

The *straight-line method* depreciates an equal amount of the depreciable base to each year of the asset's service life.

STRAIGHT-LINE METHOD By far the most easily understood and widely used depreciation method is straight line. In this approach, an equal amount of the depreciable base (or allocation base) is allocated to each year of the asset's service life. The depreciable base is simply divided by the number of years in the asset's life to determine annual depreciation.

[1]FASB ASC 360–10–35–4: Property, Plant, and Equipment–Overall–Subsequent Measurement (previously "Restatement and Revision of Accounting Research Bulletins," *Accounting Research Bulletin No. 43* (New York: AICPA, 1953), Ch. 9).

Using the information given in Illustration 11–3, straight-line depreciation expense in each year is $42,000, calculated as follows:

$$\frac{\$250{,}000 - 40{,}000}{5 \text{ years}} = \$42{,}000 \text{ per year}$$

The calculation of depreciation over the entire five-year life is demonstrated in detail in Illustration 11–3A. Notice the last three columns. **Depreciation expense** is the portion of the asset's cost that is allocated to an expense *in the current year.* **Accumulated depreciation** (a contra-asset account) represents the cumulative amount of the asset's cost that has been depreciated *in all prior years including the current year.* This amount represents the reduction in the asset's cost reported in the balance sheet. The asset is reported in the balance sheet at its **book value,** which is the asset's cost minus accumulated depreciation. Book value is sometimes called carrying value or carrying amount. The residual value ($40,000 in this example) does not affect the calculation of book value, but the residual value does set a limit on which book value cannot go below.

Illustration 11–3A Straight-Line Depreciation

Using the information given in Illustration 11–3:

Year	Depreciable Base ($250,000 − 40,000)	×	Depreciation Rate per Year	=	Depreciation Expense	Accumulated Depreciation	Book Value End of Year ($250,000 less Accum. Depreciation)
1	$210,000		⅕*		$ 42,000	$ 42,000	$208,000
2	210,000		⅕		42,000	84,000	166,000
3	210,000		⅕		42,000	126,000	124,000
4	210,000		⅕		42,000	168,000	82,000
5	210,000		⅕		42,000	210,000	40,000
Totals					$210,000		

*The rate equals one divided by the asset's five-year estimated service life (⅕ = 20%).

The entry to record depreciation at the end of each year using the straight-line method would be:

Depreciation expense	42,000*	
Accumulated depreciation		42,000

*$42,000 = ($250,000 − 40,000) ÷ 5 years.

Accelerated depreciation methods report higher depreciation in earlier years.

ACCELERATED METHODS Using the straight-line method implicitly assumes that the benefits derived from the use of the asset are the same each year. In some situations it might be more appropriate to assume that the asset will provide greater benefits in the early years of its life than in the later years. In these cases, a more appropriate matching of depreciation with revenues is achieved with a declining pattern of depreciation, with higher depreciation in the early years of the asset's life and lower depreciation in later years.

An accelerated depreciation method also would be appropriate when benefits derived from the asset are approximately equal over the asset's life, but repair and maintenance costs increase significantly in later years. The early years incur higher depreciation and lower repairs and maintenance expense, while the later years have lower depreciation and higher repairs and maintenance. Two ways to achieve such a declining pattern of depreciation are the sum-of-the-years'-digits method and declining balance methods.

The *SYD method* multiplies depreciable base by a declining fraction.

Sum-of-the-years'-digits method. The sum-of-the-years'-digits (SYD) method has no logical foundation other than the fact that it accomplishes the objective of accelerating depreciation in a systematic manner. This is achieved by multiplying the depreciable base by a fraction that declines each year and results in depreciation that decreases by the same amount each year. The denominator of the fraction remains constant and is the *sum of the digits* from one to *n,* where *n* is the number of years in the asset's service life. For example, if there are five years in the service life, the denominator is the sum of 1, 2, 3, 4, and 5, which equals 15.[2] The numerator decreases each year; it begins with the value of *n* in the first year and decreases by one each year until it equals one in the final year of the asset's estimated service life. The annual fractions for an asset with a five-year life are: 5/15, 4/15, 3/15, 2/15, and 1/15. We calculate depreciation for the five years of the machine's life using the sum-of-the-years'-digits method in Illustration 11–3B.

Illustration 11–3B Sum-of-the-Years'-Digits Depreciation

Using the information given in Illustration 11–3:

Year	Depreciable Base ($250,000 − 40,000)	×	Depreciation Rate per Year	=	Depreciation Expense	Accumulated Depreciation	Book Value End of Year ($250,000 less Accum. Depreciation)
1	$210,000		5/15*		$ 70,000	$ 70,000	$180,000
2	210,000		4/15		56,000	126,000	124,000
3	210,000		3/15		42,000	168,000	82,000
4	210,000		2/15		28,000	196,000	54,000
5	210,000		1/15		14,000	210,000	40,000
Totals			15/15		$210,000		

*$\frac{n(n+1)}{2} = \frac{5(5+1)}{2} = 15$

Notice that total depreciation ($210,000) is the same for an accelerated method like SYD as it is for the straight-line method, as shown in Illustration 11–3A. The difference is the pattern in which this total cost is allocated to each year of the asset's service life.

Declining balance depreciation methods multiply beginning-of-year book value, not depreciable base, by an annual rate that is a multiple of the straight-line rate.

Declining balance methods. As an alternative, an accelerated depreciation pattern can be achieved by a declining balance method. Rather than multiplying a constant balance by a declining fraction as we do in SYD depreciation, we multiply a constant fraction by a declining balance each year. Specifically, we multiply a constant percentage rate times the decreasing book value (cost less accumulated depreciation) of the asset (not depreciable base) at the beginning of the year. Because the rate remains constant while the book value declines, annual depreciation declines each year.

A common declining balance method is known as the **double-declining-balance (DDB) method**. Under this method, we multiply the straight-line rate by 200% (or *double* the straight-line rate). For example, in our illustration, the double-declining-balance rate would be 40% (double the straight-line rate of 20%). Various other multiples are used in practice, such as 125% or 150% of the straight-line rate.

Depreciation using the double-declining-balance method is calculated in Illustration 11–3C for the five years of the machine's life. Notice that book value at the beginning of the year, rather than the depreciable base, is used as the starting point. Further, notice that in year 4 we did not multiply $54,000 by 40%. If we had, annual depreciation would have been $21,600. This amount would have resulted in accumulated depreciation by the end of year 4 of $217,600 and book value of $32,400, which is below the asset's expected residual value of $40,000. Therefore, we instead use a plug amount that reduces book value to the expected residual value (book value beginning of year, $54,000, minus expected residual value, $40,000 = $14,000). This also means there is no depreciation in year 5 since book value has already been reduced to the expected residual value. Declining balance methods often allocate the asset's depreciable base over fewer years than the expected service life.

[2]A formula useful when calculating the denominator is $n\,(n + 1)/2$.

Using the information given in Illustration 11–3:

Year	Book Value Beginning of Year	×	Depreciation Rate per Year	=	Depreciation Expense	Accumulated Depreciation	Book Value End of Year ($250,000 less Accum. Depreciation)
1	$250,000		40%*		$100,000	$100,000	$150,000
2	150,000		40%		60,000	160,000	90,000
3	90,000		40%		36,000	196,000	54,000
4	54,000				14,000†	210,000	40,000
5	40,000				—		40,000
Total					$210,000		

*Double the straight-line rate of 20%. The straight-line rate is one divided by the asset's five-year estimated service life (⅕ = 20%).
†Amount necessary to reduce book value to residual value.

Illustration 11–3C

Double-Declining-Balance Depreciation

SWITCH FROM ACCELERATED TO STRAIGHT LINE. The result of applying the double-declining-balance method in our illustration produces an awkward result in the later years of the asset's life. By using the double-declining-balance method in our illustration, no depreciation is recorded in year 5 even though the asset is still producing benefits. As a planned approach to depreciation, many companies have a formal policy to use accelerated depreciation for approximately the first half of an asset's service life and then switch to the straight-line method for the remaining life of the asset.

It is not uncommon for a company to switch from accelerated to straight line approximately halfway through an asset's useful life as part of the company's planned depreciation approach.

In our illustration, the company would switch to straight line in either year 3 or year 4. Assuming the switch is made at the beginning of year 4, and the book value at the beginning of that year is $54,000, an additional $14,000 ($54,000 − 40,000 in residual value) of depreciation must be recorded over the remaining life of the asset. Applying the straight-line concept, $7,000 ($14,000 divided by two remaining years) in depreciation is recorded in both year 4 and year 5.

It should be noted that this switch to straight line is not a change in depreciation method. The switch is part of the company's planned depreciation approach. However, as you will learn later in the chapter, the accounting treatment is the same as a change in depreciation method.

Activity-Based Depreciation Methods

Activity-based depreciation methods estimate service life in terms of some measure of productivity.

The most logical way to allocate an asset's cost to periods of an asset's use is to measure the usefulness of the asset in terms of its productivity. For example, we could measure the service life of a machine in terms of its *output* (for example, the estimated number of units it will produce) or in terms of its *input* (for example, the number of hours it will operate). We have already mentioned that one way to measure the service life of a vehicle is to estimate the number of miles it will operate. The most common activity-based method is called the **units-of-production method.**

FINANCIAL Reporting Case

Q2, p. 575

The measure of output used is the estimated number of units (pounds, items, barrels, etc.) to be produced by the machine. By the units-of-production method, we first compute the average depreciation rate per unit by dividing the depreciable base by the number of units expected to be produced. This per unit rate is then multiplied by the actual number of units produced each period. In our illustration, the depreciation rate per unit is $1.50, computed as follows:

The *units-of-production method* computes a depreciation rate per measure of activity and then multiplies this rate by actual activity to determine periodic depreciation.

$$\frac{\$250{,}000 - 40{,}000}{140{,}000 \text{ units}} = \$1.50 \text{ per unit}$$

Each unit produced will require $1.50 of depreciation to be recorded. In other words, each unit produced is assigned $1.50 of the asset's cost.

Illustration 11–3D shows that depreciation each year is the actual units produced multiplied by the depreciation rate per unit. This means that the amount of depreciation each year varies proportionately with the number of units being produced, with one exception. Notice that the asset produced 26,000 units in year 5, causing total production over the life of the asset (150,000 units) to exceed its estimated production (140,000 units). In this case, we cannot record depreciation for the final 10,000 units produced. Depreciation in year five is limited to the amount that brings the book value of the asset down to its residual value (book value beginning of year, $64,000, minus expected residual value, $40,000 = $24,000).

Illustration 11–3D

Units-of-Production Depreciation

Using the information given in Illustration 11–3:

Year	Units Produced	×	Depreciation Rate per Unit	=	Depreciation Expense	Accumulated Depreciation	Book Value End of Year ($250,000 less Accum. Depreciation)
1	20,000		$1.50*		$ 30,000	$ 30,000	$220,000
2	32,000		1.50		48,000	78,000	172,000
3	44,000		1.50		66,000	144,000	106,000
4	28,000		1.50		42,000	186,000	64,000
5	26,000				24,000†	210,000	40,000
Totals	150,000				$210,000		

*($250,000 − 40,000) / 140,000 units = $1.50 per unit.
†Amount necessary to reduce book value to residual value.

The machine may produce *fewer than* 140,000 units by the end of its useful life. For example, suppose production in year 5 had been only 6,000 units, bringing total production to 130,000 units, and management has no future plans to use the machine. We would record depreciation in Year 5 for $9,000 (6,000 units × $1.50). If management then develops a formal plan to sell the machine, the machine is classified as "held for sale" (discussed in more detail below) and reported at the lower of its current book value or its fair value less any cost to sell. If management plans to retire the asset without selling it, a loss is recorded for the remaining book value.

Decision Makers' Perspective—Selecting A Depreciation Method

All methods provide the same total depreciation over an asset's life.

Illustration 11–3E compares periodic depreciation calculated using each of the alternatives we discussed and illustrated.

Illustration 11–3E

Comparison of Various Depreciation Methods

Year	Straight Line	Sum-of-the-Years'-Digits	Double-Declining Balance	Units of Production
1	$ 42,000	$ 70,000	$100,000	$ 30,000
2	42,000	56,000	60,000	48,000
3	42,000	42,000	36,000	66,000
4	42,000	28,000	14,000	42,000
5	42,000	14,000	0	24,000
Total	$210,000	$210,000	$210,000	$210,000

Conceptually, using an activity-based depreciation method provides a better matching of the asset's cost to the use of that asset to help produce revenues. Clearly, the productivity of a plant asset is more closely associated with the benefits provided by that asset than the mere passage of time. Also, these methods allow for patterns of depreciation to correspond with the patterns of asset use.

Activity-based methods are conceptually superior to time-based methods but often are impractical to apply in practice.

However, activity-based methods quite often are either infeasible or too costly to use. For example, buildings don't have an identifiable measure of productivity. Even for machinery, there may be an identifiable measure of productivity such as machine hours or units produced, but it frequently is more costly to determine each period than it is to simply measure the passage of time. For these reasons, most companies use time-based depreciation methods.

Illustration 11–4 shows the results of a recent survey of depreciation methods used by large public companies.[3]

Depreciation Method	Number of Companies
Straight line	490
Declining balance	9
Sum-of-the-years'-digits	2
Accelerated method—not specified	9
Units of production	12
Group/composite	17

Illustration 11–4

Use of Various Depreciation Methods

Real World Financials

Why do so many companies use the straight-line method as opposed to other time-based methods? Many companies perhaps consider the benefits derived from the majority of plant assets to be realized approximately evenly over these assets' useful lives. Certainly a contributing factor is that straight-line is the easiest method to understand and apply.

Another motivation is the positive effect on reported income. Straight-line depreciation produces a higher net income than accelerated methods in the early years of an asset's life. In Chapter 8 we pointed out that reported net income can affect bonuses paid to management or debt agreements with lenders.

Conflicting with the desire to report higher profits is the desire to reduce taxes by reducing taxable income. An accelerated method serves this objective by reducing taxable income more in the early years of an asset's life than straight line. You probably recall a similar discussion from Chapter 8 in which the benefits of using the LIFO inventory method during periods of increasing costs were described. However, remember that the LIFO conformity rule requires companies using LIFO for income tax reporting to also use LIFO for financial reporting. *No such conformity rule exists for depreciation methods.* Income tax regulations allow firms to use different approaches to computing depreciation in their tax returns and in their financial statements. The method used for tax purposes is therefore not a constraint in the choice of depreciation methods for financial reporting. As a result, most companies use the straight-line method for financial reporting and the Internal Revenue Service's prescribed accelerated method (discussed in Appendix 11A) for income tax purposes. For example, Illustration 11–5 shows Merck & Co.'s depreciation policy as reported in a disclosure note accompanying recent financial statements.

A company does not have to use the same depreciation method for both financial reporting and income tax purposes.

Summary of Accounting Policies (in part):
Depreciation

Depreciation is provided over the estimated useful lives of the assets, principally using the straight-line method. For tax purposes, accelerated methods are used.

Illustration 11–5

Depreciation Method Disclosure—Merck & Co.

Real World Financials

It is not unusual for a company to use different depreciation methods for different classes of assets. For example, Illustration 11–6 illustrates the International Paper Company depreciation policy disclosure contained in a note accompanying recent financial statements.

[3]*U.S. GAAP Financial Statements–Best Practices in Presentation and Disclosure– 2013* (New York: AICPA, 2013).

Illustration 11–6
Depreciation Method Disclosure—International Paper Company

Real World Financials

Summary of Accounting Policies (in part):
Plants, Properties, and Equipment
Plants, properties, and equipment are stated at cost, less accumulated depreciation. The units-of-production method of depreciation is used for major pulp and paper mills and the straight-line method is used for other plants and equipment.

International Financial Reporting Standards

Depreciation. *IAS No. 16* requires that each component of an item of property, plant, and equipment must be depreciated separately if its cost is significant in relation to the total cost of the item.[4] In the United States, component depreciation is allowed but is not often used in practice.

Consider the following illustration:

LO11–10

Cavandish LTD. purchased a delivery truck for $62,000. The truck is expected to have a service life of six years and a residual value of $12,000. At the end of three years, the oversized tires, which have a cost of $6,000 (included in the $62,000 purchase price), will be replaced.

Under U.S. GAAP, the typical accounting treatment is to depreciate the $50,000 ($62,000 – 12,000) depreciable base of the truck over its six-year useful life. Using IFRS, the depreciable base of the truck is $44,000 ($62,000 – 12,000 – 6,000) and is depreciated over the truck's six-year useful life, and the $6,000 cost of the tires is depreciated separately over a three-year useful life.

U.S. GAAP and IFRS determine depreciable base in the same way, by subtracting estimated residual value from cost. However, IFRS requires a review of residual values at least annually.

Sanofi-Aventis, a French pharmaceutical company, prepares its financial statements using IFRS. In its property, plant, and equipment note, the company discloses its use of the component-based approach to accounting for depreciation.

Property, plant, and equipment (in part)
The component-based approach to accounting for property, plant, and equipment is applied. Under this approach, each component of an item of property, plant, and equipment with a cost which is significant in relation to the total cost of the item and which has a different useful life from the other components must be depreciated separately.

Depreciation Methods. *IAS No. 16* specifically mentions three depreciation methods: straight-line, units-of-production, and the diminishing balance method. The diminishing balance method is similar to the declining balance method sometimes used by U.S. companies. As in the U.S., the straight-line method is used by most companies. A recent survey of large companies that prepare their financial statement according to IFRS reports 93% of the surveyed companies used the straight-line method.[5]

Concept Review Exercise

DEPRECIATION METHODS

The Sprague Company purchased a fabricating machine on January 1, 2018, at a net cost of $130,000. At the end of its four-year useful life, the company estimates that the machine will be worth $30,000. Sprague also estimates that the machine will run for 25,000 hours during its four-year life. The company's fiscal year ends on December 31.

[4] "Property, Plant and Equipment," *International Accounting Standard No. 16* (IASCF), par. 42, as amended effective January 1, 2016.
[5] "*IFRS Accounting Trends and Techniques*" (New York, AICPA, 2011), p. 328.

Required:

Compute depreciation for 2018 through 2021 using each of the following methods:
1. Straight line
2. Sum-of-the-years'-digits
3. Double-declining balance
4. Units of production (using machine hours); actual production was as follows:

Year	Machine Hours
2018	6,000
2019	8,000
2020	5,000
2021	7,000

Solution:

1. Straight line:

$$\frac{\$130,000 - 30,000}{4 \text{ years}} = \$25,000 \text{ per year}$$

2. Sum-of-the-years'-digits:

Year	Depreciable Base	×	Depreciation Rate per Year	=	Depreciation Expense
2018	$100,000		4/10		$ 40,000
2019	100,000		3/10		30,000
2020	100,000		2/10		20,000
2021	100,000		1/10		10,000
Total					$100,000

3. Double-declining balance:

Year	Book Value Beginning of Year	×	Depreciation Rate per Year	=	Depreciation Expense	Book Value End of Year
2018	$130,000		50%*		$ 65,000	$65,000
2019	65,000		50%		32,500	32,500
2020	32,500				2,500†	30,000
2021	30,000				—	30,000
Total					$100,000	

*Double the straight-line rate of 25%. The straight-line rate is one divided by the asset's four-year estimated service life.

†Amount necessary to reduce book value to residual value.

4. Units of production (using machine hours):

Year	Machine Hours	×	Depreciation Rate per Hour	=	Depreciation Expense	Book Value End of Year
2018	6,000		$4*		$ 24,000	$106,000
2019	8,000		4		32,000	74,000
2020	5,000		4		20,000	54,000
2021	7,000				24,000†	30,000
Total					$100,000	

*($130,000 – 30,000)/25,000 hours = $4 per hour.

†Amount necessary to reduce book value to residual value.

Dispositions

After using property, plant, and equipment and intangible assets, companies will sell or retire those assets. When selling property, plant, and equipment and intangible assets for monetary consideration (cash or a receivable), the seller recognizes a **gain** or **loss** for the difference between the consideration received and the book value of the asset sold.

A gain or loss is recognized for the difference between the consideration received and the asset's book value.

Consideration received	$xxx
Less: Book value of asset sold	(xxx)
Gain/loss on sale of asset	$xxx

We'll demonstrate this calculation next in Illustration 11–3F by modifying our earlier example of Hogan Manufacturing Company in Illustration 11–3A. In Illustration 11–3F, Hogan sells a machine before the end of its service life and receives more cash than the asset's book value (cost minus accumulated depreciation) at the time of the sale. This causes a gain to be recognized. We then modify the example to show that when the amount of cash received is less than the asset's book value, a loss is recognized.

Illustration 11–3F

Sale of Property, Plant, and Equipment

On January 1, 2018, Hogan Manufacturing Company purchased a machine for $250,000. The company expects the service life of the machine to be five years. The estimated residual value is $40,000. Hogan uses the straight-line depreciation method.

Suppose Hogan decides not to hold the machine for the expected five years but instead sells it on December 31, 2020 (three years later), for $140,000. We first need to update depreciation to the date of sale. Since depreciation for 2018 and 2019 has already been recorded in those years, we need to update depreciation only for the current year, 2020.

The entry to update depreciation for 2020:

	Debit	Credit
Depreciation expense	42,000*	
Accumulated depreciation		42,000

*$42,000 = ($250,000 − 40,000) ÷ 5 years. See also Illustration 11–3A.

The balance of accumulated depreciation equals depreciation that has already been recorded in 2018 and 2019 ($42,000 + $42,000) plus the depreciation recorded above in 2020 ($42,000).

Accumulated Depreciation

	42,000	2018
	42,000	2019
	42,000	2020
	126,000	

We can now calculate the gain or loss on the sale as the difference between consideration received and the asset's book value. In this example, the amount of cash received is greater than the asset's book value, so a gain is recognized.

Consideration received	$140,000
Less: Book value of asset sold	(124,000)[†]
Gain on sale of machine	$ 16,000

[†]Book value = Cost ($250,000) − Accumulated Depreciation ($126,000)

Finally, the sale of the equipment requires (1) the cash received to be recorded, (2) the machine's account balance as well as its accumulated depreciation balance to be removed from the books, and (3) the gain or loss recognized.

The entry to record the sale on December 31, 2020, for $140,000:

	Debit	Credit
Cash	140,000	
Accumulated depreciation (account balance)	126,000	
Machine (account balance)		250,000
Gain on sale of machine (difference)		16,000

The balances of the machine account and the accumulated depreciation account will be $0 after this entry. The gain on the sale normally is reported in the income statement as a separate component of operating expenses.

Now, assume that Hogan sold the machine on December 31, 2020, for only $110,000. This amount is less than book value by $14,000 and a loss on the sale would be recorded.

Consideration received	$ 110,000
Less: Book value of asset sold	(124,000)
Loss on sale of machine	$ (14,000)

The entry to record the sale on December 31, 2020, for $110,000

Cash	110,000	
Accumulated depreciation (account balance)	126,000	
Loss on sale of machine (difference)	14,000	
Machine (account balance)		250,000

Notice that the amounts of the machine and accumulated depreciation removed from the books upon sale of the asset do not depend on whether a gain or loss is recorded; the asset's book value is written off completely. It's the amount of cash received relative to the asset's book value that determines the amount of the gain or loss.

Decision Makers' Perspective—Understanding gains and losses

It's tempting to think of a "gain" and "loss" on the sale of a depreciable asset as "good" and "bad" news. For example, we commonly use the term "gain" in everyday language to mean we sold something for more than we bought it. Gain could also be misinterpreted to mean the asset was sold for more than its fair value (we got a "good deal"). However, neither of these represents the meaning of a gain on the sale of assets. Refer back to our example in Illustration 11–3F. The sale of the machine resulted in a gain, but the machine was sold for *less than* its original cost, and there is no indication that Hogan sold the machine for more than its fair value.

A gain on the sale of a depreciable asset simply means the asset was sold for more than its book value. In other words, the asset being received and recorded (such as cash) is greater than the recorded book value of the asset being sold and written off. The net increase in the book value of total assets is an accounting gain (not an economic gain).

The same is true for losses. A loss signifies that the cash received is less than the book value of the asset being sold; there is a net decrease in the book value of total assets. ●

ASSETS HELD FOR SALE. Sometimes management plans to sell property, plant, and equipment or an intangible asset but that sale hasn't yet happened. In this case, the asset is classified as "held for sale" in the period in which all of the following criteria are met:[6]

Property, plant, and equipment or an intangible asset to be disposed of by sale is classified as held for sale and measured at the lower of the asset's book value or the asset's fair value less cost to sell.

1. Management commits to a plan to sell the asset.
2. The asset is available for immediate sale in its present condition.
3. An active plan to locate a buyer and sell the asset has been initiated.
4. The completed sale of the asset is probable and typically expected to occur within one year.
5. The asset is being offered for sale at a reasonable price relative to its current fair value.
6. Management's actions indicate the plan is unlikely to change significantly or be withdrawn.

An asset that is classified as held for sale is no longer depreciated or amortized. *An asset classified as held for sale is reported at the lower of its current book value or its fair value less any cost to sell.* If the fair value less cost to sell is below book value, we recognize a loss in the current period. If financial statements are again prepared prior to the sale, we reassess the asset's fair value less selling costs. If a further decline has occurred, we recognize another loss. If the fair value less selling costs has increased since the previous measurement, we recognize a gain, but limited to the cumulative amount of any previous losses.

[6]FASB ASC 360–10–45–9: Property, Plant, and Equipment–Overall–Other Presentation Matters–Impairment or Disposal of Long-Lived Assets.

RETIREMENTS. Sometimes instead of selling a used asset, a company will retire (or abandon) the asset. Retirements are treated similarly to selling for monetary consideration. At the time of retirement, the asset account and the corresponding accumulated deprecation account are removed from the books and a loss equal to the remaining book value of the asset is recorded because there will be no monetary consideration received. When there is a formal plan to retire an asset but before the actual retirement, there may be some revision in depreciation due a change in the estimated service life or residual value.

Group and Composite Depreciation Methods

Group and composite depreciation methods aggregate assets to reduce the recordkeeping costs of determining periodic depreciation.

As you might imagine, depreciation records could become quite cumbersome and costly if a company has hundreds, or maybe thousands, of depreciable assets. However, the burden can be lessened if the company uses the group or composite method to depreciate assets collectively rather than individually. The two methods are the same except for the way the collection of assets is aggregated for depreciation. The **group depreciation method** defines the collection as depreciable assets that share similar service lives and other attributes. For example, group depreciation could be used for fleets of vehicles or collections of machinery. The **composite depreciation method** is used when assets are physically dissimilar but are aggregated anyway to gain the convenience of a collective depreciation calculation. For instance, composite depreciation can be used for all of the depreciable assets in one manufacturing plant, even though individual assets in the composite may have widely diverse service lives.

Both approaches are similar in that they involve applying a single straight-line rate based on the average service lives of the assets in the group or composite.[7] The process is demonstrated using Illustration 11–7.

Illustration 11–7
Group Depreciation

The Express Delivery Company began operations in 2018. It will depreciate its fleet of delivery vehicles using the group method. The cost of vehicles purchased early in 2018, along with residual values, estimated lives, and straight-line depreciation per year by type of vehicle, are as follows:

Asset	Cost	Residual Value	Depreciable Base	Estimated Life (years)	Depreciation per Year (straight line)
Vans	$150,000	$30,000	$120,000	6	$ 20,000
Trucks	120,000	16,000	104,000	5	20,800
Wagons	60,000	12,000	48,000	4	12,000
Totals	$330,000	$58,000	$272,000		$52,800

The *group depreciation* rate is determined by dividing the depreciation per year by the total cost. The group's *average service* life is calculated by dividing the depreciable base by the depreciation per year:

$$\text{Group depreciation rate} = \frac{\$52,800}{\$330,000} = 16\%$$

$$\text{Average service life} = \frac{\$272,000}{\$52,800} = 5.15 \text{ years (rounded)}$$

The depreciation rate is applied to the total cost of the group or composite for the period.

If there are no changes in the assets contained in the group, depreciation of $52,800 per year ($330,000 × 16%) will be recorded for 5.15 years. This means the depreciation in the sixth year will be $7,920 (0.15 of a full year's depreciation = 15% × $52,800), which depreciates the cost of the group down to its estimated residual value. In other words, the group will be depreciated over the average service life of the assets in the group.

[7]A declining balance method could also be used with either the group or composite method by applying a multiple (e.g., 200%) to the straight-line group or composite rate.

In practice, there very likely will be changes in the assets constituting the group as new assets are added and others are retired or sold. Additions are recorded by increasing the group asset account for the cost of the addition. Depreciation is determined by multiplying the group rate by the total cost of assets in the group for that period. Once the group or composite rate and the average service life are determined, they normally are continued despite the addition and disposition of individual assets. This implicitly assumes that the service lives of new assets approximate those of individual assets they replace.

Because depreciation records are not kept on an individual asset basis, dispositions are recorded under the assumption that the book value of the disposed item exactly equals any proceeds received and no gain or loss is recorded. For example, if a delivery truck in the above illustration that cost $15,000 is sold for $3,000 in the year 2021, the following journal entry is recorded:

No gain or loss is recorded when a group or composite asset is retired or sold.

Cash	3,000	
Accumulated depreciation (difference)	12,000	
Vehicles		15,000

Any actual gain or loss is included in the accumulated depreciation account. This practice generally will not distort income as the unrecorded gains tend to offset unrecorded losses.

The group and composite methods simplify the recordkeeping of depreciable assets. This simplification justifies any immaterial errors in income determination. Illustration 11–8 shows a disclosure note accompanying recent financial statements of the El Paso Natural Gas Company (EPNG) describing the use of the group depreciation method for its property that is regulated by federal statutes.

Summary of Significant Accounting Policies (in part)
Property, Plant, and Equipment (in part)

We use the group method to depreciate property, plant, and equipment. Under this method, assets with similar lives and characteristics are grouped and depreciated as one asset. We apply the depreciation rate approved in our rate settlements to the total cost of the group until its net book value equals its salvage value. The majority of our property, plant, and equipment are on our El Paso Natural Gas Company (EPNG) system, which has depreciation rates ranging from one percent to 50 percent.

When we retire property, plant, and equipment, we charge accumulated depreciation and amortization for the original cost of the assets in addition to the cost to remove, sell, or dispose of the assets, less their salvage value. We do not recognize a gain or loss unless we sell an entire operating unit.

Illustration 11–8

Disclosure of Depreciation Method—El Paso Natural Gas Company

Real World Financials

Additional group-based depreciation methods, the retirement and replacement methods, are discussed in Appendix 11B.

International Financial Reporting Standards

● LO11–10

Valuation of Property, Plant, and Equipment. As we've discussed, under U.S. GAAP a company reports property, plant, and equipment (PP&E) in the balance sheet at cost less accumulated depreciation (book value). *IAS No. 16* allows a company to report property, plant, and equipment at that amount or, alternatively, at its fair value (revaluation).[8] If a company chooses revaluation, all assets within a class of PP&E must be revalued on a regular basis. U.S. GAAP prohibits revaluation.

(continued)

[8] "Property, Plant and Equipment," *International Accounting Standard No. 16* (IASCF), as amended effective January 1, 2016.

(concluded)

If the revaluation option is chosen, the way the company reports the difference between fair value and book value depends on which amount is higher:

- If fair value is higher than book value, the difference is reported as *other comprehensive income (OCI)* which then accumulates in a "revaluation surplus" (sometimes called revaluation reserve) account in equity.
- If book value is higher than fair value, the difference is reported as an *expense in the income statement.* An exception is when a revaluation surplus account relating to the same asset has a balance from a previous *increase* in fair value, that balance is eliminated before debiting revaluation expense.

Consider the following illustration:

Candless Corporation prepares its financial statements according to IFRS. At the beginning of its 2018 fiscal year, the company purchased equipment for $100,000. The equipment is expected to have a five-year useful life with no residual value, so depreciation for 2018 is $20,000. At the end of the year, Candless chooses to revalue the equipment as permitted by *IAS No. 16.* Assuming that the fair value of the equipment at year-end is $84,000, Candless records depreciation and the revaluation using the following journal entries:

(a) Depreciation expense ($100,000 ÷ 5 years)	20,000	
Accumulated depreciation		20,000

After this entry, the book value of the equipment is $80,000; the fair value is $84,000. We use the ratio of the two amounts to adjust both the equipment and the accumulated depreciation accounts (and thus the book value) to fair value ($ in thousands):

December 31, 2018	**Before Revaluation**				**After Revaluation**
Equipment	$100	×	84/80	=	$105
Accumulated depreciation	20	×	84/80	=	21
Book value	$ 80	×	84/80	=	$ 84

The entries to revalue the equipment and the accumulated depreciation accounts (and thus the book value) are:

To record the revaluation of equipment to its fair value.

(b) Equipment ($105,000 – 100,000)	5,000	
Accumulated depreciation ($21,000 – 20,000)		1,000
Revaluation surplus—OCI ($84,000 – 80,000)		4,000

The new basis for the equipment is its fair value of $84,000 ($105,000 – 21,000), and the following years' depreciation is based on that amount. Thus, 2019 depreciation would be $84,000 divided by the four remaining years, or $21,000:[9]

(a) Depreciation expense ($84,000 ÷ 4 years)	21,000	
Accumulated depreciation		21,000

After this entry, the accumulated depreciation is $42,000 and the book value of the equipment is $63,000. Let's say the fair value now is $57,000. We use the ratio of the two amounts (fair value of $57,000 divided by book value of $63,000) to adjust both the equipment and the accumulated depreciation accounts (and thus the book value) to fair value ($ in thousands):

December 31, 2019	**Before Revaluation**				**After Revaluation**
Equipment	$105	×	57/63	=	$95
Accumulated depreciation	42	×	57/63	=	38
Book value	$ 63	×	57/63	=	$57

(continued)

[9]*IAS No. 16* allows companies to choose between the method illustrated here and an alternative. The second method eliminates the entire accumulated depreciation account and adjusts the asset account (equipment in this illustration) to fair value. Using either method the revaluation surplus (or expense) would be the same.

(concluded)

The entries to revalue the equipment and the accumulated depreciation accounts (and thus the book value) are:

(b) Revaluation surplus—OCI ($57,000 – 63,000 = $6,000; limit: $4,000 balance)	4,000	
Revaluation expense (to balance)	2,000	
Accumulated depreciation ($38,000 – 42,000)	4,000	
Equipment ($95,000 – 105,000)		10,000

A decrease in fair value, as occurred in 2019, is expensed unless it reverses a revaluation surplus account relating to the same asset, as in this illustration. So, of the $6,000 decrease in value ($63,000 book value less $57,000 fair value), $4,000 is debited to the previously created revaluation surplus and the remaining $2,000 is recorded as revaluation expense in the income statement.

Investcorp, a provider and manager of alternative investment products headquartered in London, prepares its financial statements according to IFRS. The following disclosure note included in a recent annual report discusses the company's method of valuing its building and certain operating assets.

Premises and Equipment (in part)

The Bank carries its building on freehold land and certain operating assets at revalued amounts, being the fair value of the assets at the date of revaluation less any subsequent accumulated depreciation and subsequent accumulated impairment losses. Any revaluation surplus is credited to the asset revaluation reserve included in equity, except to the extent that it reverses a revaluation decrease of the same asset previously recognized in profit and loss, in which case the increase is recognized in profit or loss. A revaluation deficit is recognized directly in profit or loss, except that a deficit directly offsetting a previous surplus on the same asset is directly offset against the surplus in the asset revaluation reserve.

The revaluation alternative is used infrequently. A recent survey of large companies that prepare their financial statements according to IFRS reports that only 10 of the 160 surveyed companies used the revaluation alternative for at least one asset class.[10]

Depletion of Natural Resources

Allocation of the cost of natural resources is called **depletion**. Because the usefulness of natural resources generally is directly related to the amount of the resources extracted, the activity-based units-of-production method is widely used to calculate periodic depletion. Service life is therefore the estimated amount of natural resource to be extracted (for example, tons of mineral or barrels of oil).

Depletion of the cost of natural resources usually is determined using the units-of-production method.

● LO11–3

The depletion base is cost less any anticipated residual value. Residual value could be significant if cost includes land that has a value after the natural resource has been extracted.

The example in Illustration 11–9 was first introduced in Chapter 10 in Illustration 10–6.

Illustration 11–9

Depletion of Natural Resources

In 2018, Jackson Mining Company has the following costs related to 500 acres of land in Pennsylvania.

1.	Payment for the right to explore for a coal deposit	$1,000,000
2.	Actual exploration costs for a coal deposit	800,000
3.	Intangible development costs in digging and constructing the mine shaft.	500,000
4.	Purchase of excavation equipment for the project	600,000
5.	Restoration of the land for recreational use after extraction is completed, as required by contract (determined using the expected cash flow approach)	468,360

The company's geologist estimates that 1,000,000 tons of coal will be extracted over a three-year period. After the coal is removed from the site, the excavation equipment will be sold for an anticipated residual value of $60,000. During 2018, 300,000 tons were extracted.

[10]"*IFRS Accounting Trends and Techniques*" (New York, AICPA, 2011), p. 171.

In Illustration 10–6 we determined that the capitalized cost of the coal mine (natural resource), including the expected restoration costs, is $2,768,360. Since there is no residual value to the land, the depletion base equals cost and the depletion rate per ton is calculated as follows:

$$\text{Depletion per ton} = \frac{\text{Depletion base}}{\text{Estimated extractable tons}}$$

$$\text{Depletion per ton} = \frac{\$2{,}768{,}360}{1{,}000{,}000 \text{ tons}} = \$2.76836 \text{ per ton}$$

For each ton of coal extracted, $2.76836 in depletion is recorded. In 2018, the following journal entry records depletion for the 300,000 tons of coal actually extracted.

Depletion ($2.76836 × 300,000 tons)	830,508	
Coal mine		830,508

Notice that the credit is to the asset, coal mine, rather than to a contra account, accumulated depletion. Although this approach is traditional, the use of a contra account is acceptable.

Depletion is a product cost and is included in the cost of the inventory of coal, just as the depreciation on manufacturing equipment is included in inventory cost. The depletion is then included in cost of goods sold in the income statement when the coal is sold.

What about depreciation on the $600,000 cost of excavation equipment? If the equipment can be moved from the site and used on future projects, the equipment's depreciable base should be allocated over its useful life. If the asset is not movable, as in our illustration, then it should be depreciated over its useful life or the life of the natural resource, whichever is shorter.

The units-of-production method often is used to determine depreciation and amortization on assets used in the extraction of natural resources.

Quite often, companies use the units-of-production method to calculate depreciation and amortization on assets used in the extraction of natural resources. The activity base used is the same as that used to calculate depletion, the estimated recoverable natural resource. In our illustration, the depreciation rate would be $0.54 per ton, calculated as follows.

$$\text{Depreciation per ton} = \frac{\$600{,}000 - 60{,}000}{1{,}000{,}000 \text{ tons}} = \$0.54 \text{ per ton}$$

In 2018, depreciation of $162,000 ($0.54 × 300,000 tons) is recorded and also included as part of the cost of the coal inventory.

The summary of significant accounting policies disclosure accompanying recent financial statements of ConocoPhilips shown in Illustration 11–10 provides a good summary of depletion, amortization, and depreciation for natural resource properties.

Illustration 11–10

Depletion Method Disclosure—ConocoPhilips

Real World Financials

Summary of Significant Accounting Policies (in part)

Depletion and Amortization—Leasehold costs of producing properties are depleted using the units-of-production method based on estimated proved oil and gas reserves. Amortization of intangible development costs is based on the units-of-production method using estimated proved developed oil and gas reserves.

Depreciation and Amortization—Depreciation and amortization of PP&E on producing hydrocarbon properties and certain pipeline assets (those which are expected to have a declining utilization pattern), are determined by the units-of-production method. Depreciation and amortization of all other PP&E are determined by either the individual-unit-straight-line method or the group-straight-line method (for those individual units that are highly integrated with other units).

Additional Consideration

Percentage Depletion

Depletion of cost less residual value required by GAAP should not be confused with percentage depletion (also called *statutory depletion*) allowable for income tax purposes for oil, gas, and most mineral natural resources. Under these tax provisions, a producer is allowed to deduct the greater of cost-based depletion or a fixed percentage of gross income as depletion expense. Over the life of the asset, depletion could exceed the asset's cost. The percentage allowed for percentage-based depletion varies according to the type of natural resource.

Because percentage depletion usually differs from cost depletion, a difference between taxable income and financial reporting income before tax results. Differences between taxable income and financial reporting income are discussed in Chapter 16.

International Financial Reporting Standards

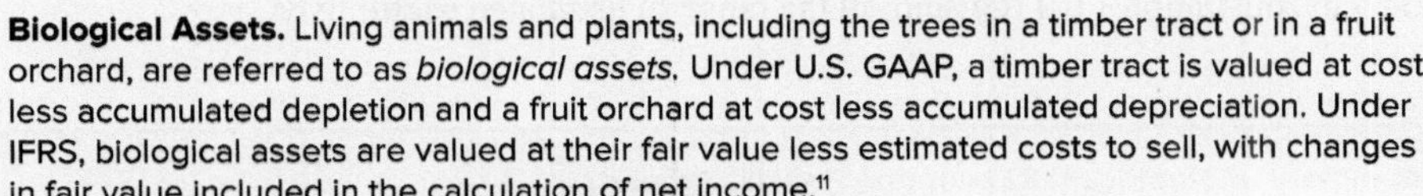

Biological Assets. Living animals and plants, including the trees in a timber tract or in a fruit orchard, are referred to as *biological assets*. Under U.S. GAAP, a timber tract is valued at cost less accumulated depletion and a fruit orchard at cost less accumulated depreciation. Under IFRS, biological assets are valued at their fair value less estimated costs to sell, with changes in fair value included in the calculation of net income.[11]

● LO11–10

Mondi Limited, an international paper and packing group headquartered in Johannesburg, South Africa, prepares its financial statements according to IFRS. The following disclosure note included in a recent annual report discusses the company's policy for valuing its forestry assets.

> **Owned Forestry Assets (in part)**
> Owned forestry assets are measured at fair value, calculated by applying the expected selling price, less costs to harvest and deliver, to the estimated volume of timber on hand at each reporting date.
> Changes in fair value are recognized in the combined and consolidated income statement within other net operating expenses.

Amortization of Intangible Assets

Let's turn now to a third type of long-lived asset—intangible assets. As with other assets we have discussed, we allocate the cost of an intangible asset over its service or useful life. The allocation of intangible asset cost is called **amortization**. Below we distinguish those intangible assets with *finite versus indefinite* useful lives. For the few intangible assets with *indefinite* useful lives, amortization is inappropriate.

● LO11–4

Intangible Assets Subject to Amortization

Most intangible assets have a finite useful life. This means their estimated useful life is limited in nature. We allocate the capitalized cost less any estimated residual value of an intangible asset to the periods in which the asset is expected to contribute to the company's revenue-generating activities. This requires that we determine the asset's useful life, its amortization base (cost less estimated residual value), and the appropriate allocation method, similar to our depreciating tangible assets.

The cost of an intangible asset with a *finite* useful life is *amortized*.

USEFUL LIFE. Legal, regulatory, or contractual provisions often limit the useful life of an intangible asset. On the other hand, useful life might sometimes be less than the asset's legal

[11] "Agriculture," *International Accounting Standard No. 41* (IASCF), as amended effective January 1, 2016.

or contractual life. For example, the useful life of a patent would be considerably less than its legal life of 20 years if obsolescence were expected to limit the longevity of a protected product.

RESIDUAL VALUE. We discussed the cost of intangible assets in Chapter 10. The expected residual value of an intangible asset usually is zero. This might not be the case, though, if at the end of its useful life to the reporting entity the asset will benefit another entity. For example, if Quadra Corp. has a commitment from another company to purchase one of Quadra's patents at the end of its useful life at a determinable price, we use that price as the patent's residual value.

ALLOCATION METHOD. The method of amortization should reflect the pattern of use of the asset in generating benefits. Most companies use the straight-line method. We discussed and illustrated a unique approach to determining the periodic amortization of software development costs in Chapter 10. Recall that the periodic amortization percentage for software development costs is the *greater* of (1) the ratio of current revenues to current and anticipated revenues (percentage of revenue method), or (2) the straight-line percentage over the useful life of the asset.

Intel Corporation reported several intangible assets in a recent balance sheet. A note, shown in Illustration 11–11, disclosed the range of estimated useful lives.

Illustration 11–11

Intangible Asset Useful Life Disclosure—Intel Corporation

Real World Financials

Summary of Significant Accounting Policies (in part)
Identified Intangible Assets (in part)

The estimated useful life ranges for identified intangible assets that are subject to amortization are as follows:

(in years)	**Estimated Useful Life**
Acquisition-related developed technology	3–9
Acquisition-related customer relationships	5–11
Acquisition-related brands	5–8
Licensed technology and patents	2–17

Like depletion, amortization expense traditionally is credited to the asset account itself rather than to accumulated amortization. However, the use of a contra account is acceptable. Let's look at an example in Illustration 11–12.

Illustration 11–12

Amortization of Intangibles

Hollins Corporation began operations in 2018. Early in January, the company purchased a franchise from Ajax Industries for $200,000. The franchise agreement is for a period of 10 years. In addition, Hollins purchased a patent for $50,000. The remaining legal life of the patent is 13 years. However, due to expected technological obsolescence, the company estimates that the useful life of the patent is only 8 years. Hollins uses the straight-line amortization method for all intangible assets. The company's fiscal year-end is December 31.

The journal entries to record a full year of amortization for these intangibles are as follows:

Amortization expense ($200,000 ÷ 10 years)	20,000	
Franchise		20,000
To record amortization of franchise		
Amortization expense ($50,000 ÷ 8 years)	6,250	
Patent		6,250
To record amortization of patent		

(continued)

(concluded)

Assume that Hollins decided to sell the patent on December 31, 2022 (five years after acquisition), for $21,000.

The journal entries to update amortization of the patent in 2022, and to sell the patent are as follows:

Amortization expense ($50,000 ÷ 8 years)	6,250	
Patent		6,250
To record amortization of patent in 2022		
Cash	21,000	
Patent (account balance)*		18,750
Gain on sale of patent (difference)		2,250
To record sale of patent		

*$50,000 − ($6,250 × 5 years)

Similar to depreciation, amortization is either a product cost or a period cost depending on the use of the asset. For intangibles used in the manufacture of a product, amortization is a product cost and is included in the cost of inventory (and doesn't become an expense until the inventory is sold). For intangible assets not used in production, such as the franchise cost in our illustration, periodic amortization is expensed in the period incurred.

Intangible Assets Not Subject to Amortization

Intangible assets with an indefinite useful life are those with no foreseeable limit on the period of time over which the asset is expected to contribute to the cash flows of the entity.[12] In other words, there are no legal, contractual, or economic factors that are expected to limit their useful life to a company. Because of their indefinite lives, these intangible assets are not subject to periodic amortization.

The cost of an intangible asset with an *indefinite* useful life is *not* amortized

For example, suppose Collins Corporation acquired a trademark in conjunction with the acquisition of a tire company. Collins plans to continue to produce the line of tires marketed under the acquired company's trademark. Recall from our discussion in Chapter 10 that trademarks have a legal life of 10 years, but the registration can be renewed for an indefinite number of 10-year periods. Therefore, the life of the purchased trademark is initially considered to be indefinite and the cost of the trademark is not amortized. However, if after several years management decides to phase out production of the tire line over the next three years, Collins would amortize the remaining book value over a three-year period.

Trademarks or tradenames often are considered to have indefinite useful lives.

In 2015, Boeing Company reported indefinite-lived intangible assets (other than goodwill) of $490 million. The company states that, "Indefinite-lived intangibles consist of brand and trade names acquired in business combinations." Illustration 11–13 provides another example in a disclosure made by The Estee Lauder Companies Inc., in a recent annual report.

Other Intangible Assets

Indefinite-lived intangible assets (e.g., trademarks) are not subject to amortization and are assessed at least annually for impairment during the fiscal fourth quarter, or more frequently if certain events or circumstances warrant.

Illustration 11–13

Indefinite-Life Intangibles Disclosure—The Estee Lauder Companies Inc.

Real World Financials

Goodwill is the most common intangible asset with an indefinite useful life. Recall that goodwill is measured as the difference between the purchase price of a company and the fair value of all of the identifiable net assets acquired (tangible and intangible assets minus the fair value of liabilities assumed). Does this mean that goodwill and other intangible assets with indefinite useful lives will remain in a company's balance sheet at their original capitalized values indefinitely? Not necessarily. Like other assets, intangibles are subject to the impairment rules we discuss in a subsequent section of this chapter.

Goodwill is an intangible asset whose cost is *not* expensed through periodic amortization.

[12]FASB ASC 350–30–35–4: Intangibles–Goodwill and Other–General Intangibles Other than Goodwill–Subsequent Measurement (previously "Goodwill and Other Intangible Assets," *Statement of Financial Accounting Standards No. 142* (Norwalk, Conn.: FASB, 2001), par. B45).

International Financial Reporting Standards

• LO11–10

Valuation of Intangible Assets. *IAS No. 38* allows a company to value an intangible asset subsequent to initial valuation at (1) cost less accumulated amortization or (2) fair value, if fair value can be determined by reference to an active market.[13] If revaluation is chosen, all assets within that class of intangibles must be revalued on a regular basis. Goodwill, however, cannot be revalued. U.S. GAAP prohibits revaluation of any intangible asset.

Notice that the revaluation option is possible only if fair value can be determined by reference to an active market, making the option relatively uncommon. However, the option possibly could be used for intangibles such as franchises and certain license agreements.

If the revaluation option is chosen, the accounting treatment is similar to the way we applied the revaluation option for property, plant, and equipment earlier in this chapter. Recall that the way the company reports the difference between fair value and book value depends on which amount is higher. If fair value is higher than book value, the difference is reported as other comprehensive income (OCI) and then accumulates in a revaluation surplus account in equity. On the other hand, if book value is higher than fair value, the difference is expensed after reducing any existing revaluation surplus for that asset.

Consider the following illustration:

Amershan LTD. prepares its financial statements according to IFRS. At the beginning of its 2018 fiscal year, the company purchased a franchise for $500,000. The franchise has a 10-year contractual life and no residual value, so amortization in 2018 is $50,000. The company does not use an accumulated amortization account and credits the franchise account directly when amortization is recorded. At the end of the year, Amershan chooses to revalue the franchise as permitted by *IAS No. 38*. Assuming that the fair value of the franchise at year-end, determined by reference to an active market, is $600,000, Amershan records amortization and the revaluation using the following journal entries:

To record the revaluation of franchise to its fair value.

Amortization expense ($500,000 ÷ 10 years)	50,000	
Franchise		50,000
Franchise ($600,000 – 450,000)	150,000	
Revaluation surplus—OCI		150,000

With the second entry Amershan increases the book value of the franchise from $450,000 ($500,000 – 50,000) to its fair value of $600,000 and records a revaluation surplus for the difference. The new basis for the franchise is its fair value of $600,000, and the following years' amortization is based on that amount. Thus, 2019 amortization would be $600,000 divided by the nine remaining years, or $66,667.

Partial Periods

Only in textbooks are property, plant, and equipment and intangible assets purchased and disposed of at the very beginning or very end of a company's fiscal year. When acquisition and disposal occur at other times, a company theoretically must determine how much depreciation, depletion, and amortization to record for the part of the year that each asset actually is used.

Let's repeat the Hogan Manufacturing Company illustration used earlier in Illustration 11–3 but modify it in Illustration 11–14 to assume that the asset was acquired *during* the company's fiscal year.

Illustration 11–14
Depreciation Methods—Partial Year

On April 1, 2018, the Hogan Manufacturing Company purchased a machine for $250,000. The company expects the service life of the machine to be five years and the anticipated residual value is $40,000. The machine was disposed of after five years of use. The company's fiscal year-end is December 31. Partial-year depreciation is recorded based on the number of months the asset is in service.

[13]"Intangible Assets," *International Accounting Standard No. 38* (IASCF), as amended effective January 1, 2016.

Notice that no information is provided on the estimated output of the machine. Partial-year depreciation presents a problem only when time-based depreciation methods are used. In an activity-based method, the rate per unit of output simply is multiplied by the actual output for the period, regardless of the length of that period.

Depreciation per year of the asset's life calculated earlier in Illustration 11–3A, Illustration 11–3B, and Illustration 11–3C for the various time-based depreciation methods is summarized in Illustration 11–14A.

Illustration 11–14A Yearly Depreciation

Year	Straight Line	Sum-of-the-Years'-Digits	Double-Declining Balance
1	$ 42,000	$ 70,000	$100,000
2	42,000	56,000	60,000
3	42,000	42,000	36,000
4	42,000	28,000	14,000
5	42,000	14,000	0
Total	$210,000	$210,000	$210,000

Illustration 11–14B shows how Hogan would depreciate the machinery by these three methods assuming an April 1 acquisition date.

Illustration 11–14B Partial-Year Depreciation

Year	Straight Line		Sum-of-the-Years'-Digits		Double-Declining Balance	
2018	$42,000 × ¾ =	**$ 31,500**	$70,000 × ¾ =	**$ 52,500**	$100,000 × ¾ =	**$ 75,000**
2019		**$ 42,000**	$70,000 × ¼ =	$ 17,500	$100,000 × ¼ =	$ 25,000
			+56,000 × ¾ =	42,000	+60,000 × ¾ =	45,000
				$ 59,500		**$ 70,000***
2020		**$ 42,000**	$56,000 × ¼ =	$ 14,000	$60,000 × ¼ =	$ 15,000
			+42,000 × ¾ =	31,500	+36,000 × ¾ =	27,000
				$ 45,500		**$ 42,000**
2021		**$ 42,000**	$42,000 × ¼ =	$ 10,500	$36,000 × ¼ =	$ 9,000
			+28,000 × ¾ =	21,000	+14,000 × ¾ =	10,500
				$ 31,500		**$ 19,500**
2022		**$ 42,000**	$28,000 × ¼ =	$ 7,000	$14,000 × ¼ =	**$ 3,500**
			+14,000 × ¾ =	10,500		
				$ 17,500		
2023	$42,000 × ¼ =	**$ 10,500**	$14,000 × ¼ =	**$ 3,500**		
	Totals	**$210,000**		**$210,000**		**$210,000**

*Could also be determined by multiplying the book value at the beginning of the year by twice the straight-line rate: ($250,000 − 75,000) × 40% = $70,000.

Notice that 2018 depreciation is three-fourths of the full year's depreciation for the first year of the asset's life, because the asset was used nine months, or ¾ of the year. The remaining one-fourth of the first year's depreciation is included in 2019's depreciation along with three-fourths of the depreciation for the second year of the asset's life. This calculation is not necessary for the straight-line method because a full year's depreciation is the same for each year of the asset's life.

Usually, the above procedure is impractical or at least cumbersome. As a result, most companies adopt a simplifying assumption, or convention, for computing partial year's depreciation and use it consistently. A common convention is to record one-half of a full year's depreciation in the year of acquisition and another half year in the year of disposal. This is known as the **half-year convention.**[14]

Concept Review Exercise

DEPLETION AND AMORTIZATION

Part A:

On March 29, 2018, the Horizon Energy Corporation purchased the mineral rights to a coal deposit in New Mexico for $2 million. Development costs and the present value of estimated land restoration costs totaled an additional $3.4 million. The company removed 200,000 tons of coal during 2018 and estimated that an additional 1,600,000 tons would be removed over the next 15 months.

Required:

Compute depletion on the mine for 2018.

Solution:

Cost of Coal Mine:	($ in millions)
Purchase price of mineral rights	$2.0
Development and restoration costs	3.4
	$5.4

Depletion:

$$\text{Depletion per ton} = \frac{\$5.4 \text{ million}}{1.8 \text{ million tons*}} = \$3 \text{ per ton}$$

*200,000 + 1,600,000

$$2018 \text{ depletion} = \$3 \times 200{,}000 \text{ tons} = \$600{,}000$$

Part B:

On October 1, 2018, Advanced Micro Circuits, Inc., completed the purchase of Zotec Corporation for $200 million. Included in the allocation of the purchase price were the following identifiable intangible assets ($ in millions), along with the fair values and estimated useful lives:

Intangible Asset	Fair value	Useful Life (in years)
Patent	$10	5
Developed technology	50	4
Customer list	10	2

In addition, the fair value of acquired tangible assets was $100 million. Goodwill was valued at $30 million. Straight-line amortization is used for all purchased intangibles.

During 2018, Advanced finished work on a software development project. Development costs incurred after technological feasibility was achieved and before the product release date totaled $2 million. The software was available for release to the general public on September 29, 2018. During the last three months of the year, revenue from the sale of the software was $4 million. The company estimates that the software will generate an additional $36 million in revenue over the next 45 months.

Required:

Compute amortization for purchased intangibles and software development costs for 2018.

Solution:

Amortization of Purchased Intangibles:	
Patent	$10 million / 5 = $2 million × 3/12 year = $0.5 million
Developed technology	$50 million / 4 = $12.5 million × 3/12 year = $3.125 million
Customer list	$10 million / 2 = $5 million × 3/12 year = $1.25 million
Goodwill	The cost of goodwill is not amortized.

[14]Another common method is the modified half-year convention. This method records a full year's depreciation when the asset is acquired in the first half of the year or sold in the second half. No depreciation is recorded if the asset is acquired in the second half of the year or sold in the first half. These half-year conventions are simple and, in most cases, will not result in material differences from a more precise calculation.

Amortization of Software Development Costs:

(1) Percentage-of-revenue method:

$$\frac{\$4 \text{ million}}{(\$4 \text{ million} + 36 \text{ million})} = 10\% \times \$2 \text{ million} = \$200{,}000$$

(2) Straight-line:

$$\frac{3 \text{ months}}{48 \text{ months}} \text{ or } 6.25\% \times \$2 \text{ million} = \$125{,}000$$

Advanced will use the percentage-of-revenue method since it produces the greater amortization, $200,000.

Additional Issues

PART B

In this part of the chapter, we discuss the following issues related to cost allocation:

1. Change in estimates
2. Change in method
3. Error correction
4. Impairment of value

Change in Estimates

LO11–5

The calculation of depreciation, depletion, or amortization requires estimates of both service life and residual value. It's inevitable that at least some estimates will prove incorrect. Chapter 4 briefly introduced the topic of changes in estimates along with coverage of changes in accounting principles and the correction of errors. Here and in subsequent sections of this chapter, we provide overviews of the accounting treatment and disclosures required for these changes and errors when they involve property, plant, and equipment and intangible assets.

A change in estimate should be reflected in the financial statements of the current period and future periods.

Changes in estimates are accounted for prospectively. When a company revises a previous estimate based on new information, prior financial statements are not restated. Instead, the company merely incorporates the new estimate in any related accounting determinations from then on. So, it usually will affect some aspects of both the balance sheet and the income statement in the current and future periods. Companies typically make these changes at the beginning of the year of the change, but they could be made at other times. A disclosure note should describe the effect of a change in estimate on net income and per share amounts for the current period.

Consider the example in Illustration 11–15.

Illustration 11–15
Change in Accounting Estimate

On January 1, 2016, the Hogan Manufacturing Company purchased a machine for $250,000. The company expects the service life of the machine to be five years and the anticipated residual value to be $40,000. The company's fiscal year-end is December 31 and the straight-line depreciation method is used for all depreciable assets. On January 1, 2018, the company revised its estimate of service life **from five to eight years** and also revised estimated residual value **from $40,000 to $22,000.**

Prior to the revision (2016 and 2017), depreciation was $42,000 per year [($250,000 – 40,000) ÷ 5 years] or $84,000 for the two years. The remaining book value at the beginning of 2018 is $166,000 ($250,000 – 84,000). Depreciation for 2018 and subsequent years is determined by allocating the remaining book value less the revised residual value equally over the remaining service life of six years (8 – 2). Depreciation for 2018 and subsequent years is recorded as follows:

Depreciation expense (below)	24,000	
Accumulated depreciation		24,000

(continued)

(concluded)

	$250,000	Cost
$42,000		Previous annual depreciation ($210,000 ÷ 5 years)
× 2 years	84,000	Depreciation to date (2016–2017)
	166,000	Book value as of January 1, 2018
	22,000	Less revised residual value
	144,000	Revised depreciable base
	÷ 6	Estimated remaining life (8 years – 2 years)
	$ 24,000	New annual depreciation

The asset's book value is depreciated down to the anticipated residual value of $22,000 at the end of the revised eight-year service life. In addition, a note discloses the effect of the change in estimate on income, if material. The before-tax effect is an increase in income of $18,000 (depreciation of $42,000 if the change had not been made, less $24,000 depreciation after the change).

Verizon Communications Inc. recently revised its estimates of the service lives of certain property, plant, and equipment. Illustration 11–16 shows the note that disclosed the change.

Illustration 11–16

Change in Estimate Disclosure—Verizon Communications Inc.

Real World Financials

Plant and Depreciation (in part)

In connection with our ongoing review of the estimated remaining average useful lives of plant, property and equipment, we determined that changes were necessary to the remaining estimated useful lives of certain assets as a result of technology upgrades, enhancements, and planned retirements. These changes resulted in an increase in depreciation expense of $0.4 billion and $0.6 billion in 2015 and 2014, respectively. While the timing and extent of current deployment plans are subject to ongoing analysis and modification, we believe the current estimates of useful lives are reasonable.

Change in Depreciation, Amortization, or Depletion Method

Changes in depreciation, amortization, or depletion methods are accounted for the same way as a change in accounting estimate.

● LO11–6

Generally accepted accounting principles allow a company to change from one depreciation method to another if the company can justify the change. For example, new information might become available to suggest that a different depreciation method would better represent the pattern of the asset's consumption relative to revenue production.

We account for these changes prospectively, exactly as we would any other change in estimate. One difference is that most changes in estimate do not require a company to justify the change. However, this change in estimate is a result of changing an accounting principle and therefore requires a clear justification as to why the new method is preferable. Consider the example in Illustration 11–17.

Illustration 11–17

Change in Depreciation Method

On January 1, 2016, the Hogan Manufacturing Company purchased a machine for $250,000. The company expects the service life of the machine to be five years and its anticipated residual value to be $30,000. The company's fiscal year-end is December 31 and the double-declining-balance (DDB) depreciation method is used. During 2018, the company switched from the DDB to the straight-line method. In 2018, the adjusting entry is:

Depreciation expense (below)	20,000	
Accumulated depreciation		20,000

DDB depreciation:

2016	$100,000	($250,000 × 40%*)
2017	60,000	[($250,000 – 100,000)] × 40%*)]
Total	$160,000	

*Double the straight-line rate for 5 years [(⅕ = 20%)] × 2 = 40%)]

(continued)

(concluded)

$250,000	Cost
160,000	Depreciation to date, DDB (2016–2017)
90,000	Undepreciated cost as of January 1, 2018
30,000	Less residual value
60,000	Depreciable base
÷ 3 yrs.	Remaining life (5 years – 2 years)
$ 20,000	New annual depreciation

A disclosure note reports the effect of the change on net income and earnings per share along with clear justification for changing depreciation methods.

Illustration 11–18 shows a disclosure note describing a recent change in depreciation method made by Agrium Inc.

Illustration 11–18

Change in Depreciation Method—Agrium Inc.

Real World Financials

Accounting standards and policy changes (in part)

We changed the method of depreciation from the straight-line basis to the units of production basis for our potash facility mining and milling assets beginning January 1, 2015, and our nitrogen and phosphate mining and plant assets beginning October 1, 2015. The change in method of depreciation reflects anticipated changes to our production schedule due to facility expansions, volatility in market conditions, and the frequency and duration of plant turnarounds. The current and expected reduction in depreciation expense is 2015 – $30 million and 2016 – $7 million.

Frequently, when a company changes depreciation method, the change will be effective only for assets placed in service after that date. Of course, that means depreciation schedules do not require revision because the change does not affect assets depreciated in prior periods. A disclosure note still is required to provide justification for the change and to report the effect of the change on the current year's income.

Error Correction

● LO11–7

Errors involving property, plant, and equipment and intangible assets include computational errors in the calculation of depreciation, depletion, or amortization and mistakes made in determining whether expenditures should be capitalized or expensed. These errors can affect many years. For example, let's say a major addition to equipment should be capitalized but incorrectly is expensed. Not only is income in the year of the error understated, but subsequent years' income is overstated because depreciation is omitted.

Recall from our discussion of inventory errors in Chapter 9 that if a material error is discovered in an accounting period subsequent to the period in which the error is made, any previous years' financial statements that were incorrect as a result of the error are retrospectively restated to reflect the correction. Any account balances that are incorrect as a result of the error are corrected by journal entry. If retained earnings is one of the incorrect accounts, the correction is reported as a *prior period adjustment* to the beginning balance in the statement of shareholders' equity.[15] In addition, a disclosure note is needed to describe the nature of the error and the impact of its correction on net income and earnings per share.

Here is a summary of the treatment of material errors occurring in a previous year:

- Previous years' financial statements are retrospectively restated.
- Account balances are corrected.

[15]The prior period adjustment is applied to beginning retained earnings for the year following the error, or for the earliest year being reported in the comparative financial statements when the error occurs prior to the earliest year presented. The retained earnings balances in years after the first year also are adjusted to what those balances would be if the error had not occurred, but a company may choose not to explicitly report those adjustments as separate line items.

- If retained earnings requires correction, the correction is reported as a prior period adjustment.
- A note describes the nature of the error and the impact of the correction on income.

Consider Illustration 11–19. The 2016 and 2017 financial statements that were incorrect as a result of the error are *retrospectively restated* to report the addition to the patent and to reflect the correct amount of amortization expense, assuming both statements are reported again for comparative purposes in the 2018 annual report.

Illustration 11–19
Error Correction

Sometimes, the analysis is easier if you re-create the entries actually recorded incorrectly and those that would have been recorded if the error hadn't occurred, and then compare them.

In 2018, the controller of the Hathaway Corporation discovered an error in recording $300,000 in legal fees to successfully defend a patent infringement suit in 2016. The $300,000 was charged to legal fee expense but should have been capitalized and amortized over the five-year remaining life of the patent. Straight-line amortization is used by Hathaway for all intangibles.

Analysis

	Correct (Should Have Been Recorded)			Incorrect (As Recorded)		
2016	Patent	300,000		Expense	300,000	
	Cash		300,000	Cash		300,000
2016	Expense	60,000		Amortization entry omitted		
	Patent		60,000			
2017	Expense	60,000		Amortization entry omitted		
	Patent		60,000			

During the two-year period (2016 and 2017), amortization expense was *understated* by $120,000, but other expenses were *overstated* by $300,000, so net income during the period was *understated* by $180,000 (ignoring income taxes). This means retained earnings is currently *understated* by that amount.

Patent is understated by $180,000.

Patent	180,000	
Retained earnings		180,000
To correct incorrect accounts		

Because retained earnings is one of the accounts incorrect as a result of the error, a correction to that account of $180,000 is reported as a prior period adjustment to the 2018 beginning retained earnings balance in Hathaway's comparative statements of shareholders' equity. Assuming that 2017 is included with 2018 in the comparative statements, a correction would be made to the 2017 beginning retained earnings balance as well. That prior period adjustment, though, would be for the pre-2017 difference: $300,000 − 60,000 = $240,000.

Also, a disclosure note accompanying Hathaway's 2018 financial statements should describe the nature of the error and the impact of its correction on each year's net income (understated by $240,000 in 2016 and overstated by $60,000 in 2017), and earnings per share.

Chapter 20 provides in-depth coverage of changes in estimates and methods, and of accounting errors. We cover the tax effect of these changes and errors in that chapter.

Impairment of Value

FINANCIAL Reporting Case

Q3, p. 575

Depreciation, depletion, and amortization reflect a gradual consumption of the benefits inherent in property, plant, and equipment and intangible assets. An implicit assumption in allocating the cost of an asset over its useful life is that there has been no significant reduction in the anticipated total benefits or service potential of the asset. Situations can arise, however, that cause a significant decline or impairment of those benefits or service potential. An extreme case would be the destruction of a plant asset—say a building destroyed by fire—before the asset is fully depreciated. The remaining book value of the asset in that case should be written off as a loss. Sometimes, though, the impairment of future value is more subtle.

● LO11–8

The way we recognize and measure an impairment loss differs depending on whether the assets are classified as (1) held and used or (2) held for sale. Accounting is different, too, for assets with finite lives and those with indefinite lives. We consider those differences now.

Assets Held and Used

An increasingly common occurrence in practice is the partial write-down of property, plant, and equipment and intangible assets that remain in use. For example, in 2015, Murphy Oil Corporation recorded impairment charges of $2.4 billion. The charges reflect the decline in asset values associated with lower oil and gas prices.

Conceptually, there is considerable merit for a policy requiring the write-down of an asset when there has been a significant decline in value. A write-down can provide important information about the future cash flows that a company can generate from using the asset. However, in practice, this process is very subjective. Even if it appears certain that significant impairment of value has occurred, it often is difficult to measure the amount of the required write-down.

An asset held for use should be written down if there has been a significant impairment of value.

For example, let's say a company purchased $2,000,000 of equipment to be used in the production of a new type of laser printer. Depreciation is determined using the straight-line method over a useful life of six years and the residual value is estimated at $200,000. At the beginning of year 3, the machine's book value has been depreciated to $1,400,000 [$2,000,000 – ($300,000 × 2)]. At that time, new technology is developed causing a significant reduction in the selling price of the new laser printer as well as a reduction in anticipated demand for the product. Management estimates that the equipment will be useful for only two more years and will have no significant residual value.

This situation is not simply a matter of a change in the estimates of useful life and residual value. Management must decide if the events occurring in year 3 warrant a write-down of the asset below $1,400,000. A write-down would be appropriate if the company decided that it would be unable to fully recover this amount through future use.

For assets to be held and used, different guidelines apply to (1) property, plant, and equipment and intangible assets with finite useful lives (subject to depreciation, depletion, or amortization) and (2) intangible assets with indefinite useful lives (not subject to amortization).

PROPERTY, PLANT, AND EQUIPMENT AND FINITE-LIFE INTANGIBLE ASSETS

Generally accepted accounting principles provide guidelines for when to recognize and how to measure impairment losses of long-lived tangible assets and intangible assets with finite useful lives.[16] For purposes of this recognition and measurement, assets are grouped at the lowest level for which identifiable cash flows are largely independent of the cash flows of other assets.

When to Test for Impairment. It would be impractical to test all assets or asset groups for impairment at the end of every reporting period. GAAP requires investigation of possible impairment only if events or changes in circumstances indicate that the book value of the asset or asset group may not be recoverable. This might happen from:

a. A significant decrease in market price
b. A significant adverse change in how the asset is being used or in its physical condition
c. A significant adverse change in legal factors or in the business climate
d. An accumulation of costs significantly higher than the amount originally expected for the acquisition or construction of an asset

Property, plant, and equipment and finite-life intangible assets are tested for impairment only when events or changes in circumstances indicate book value may not be recoverable.

[16] FASB ASC 360–10–35–15 through 20: Property, Plant, and Equipment–Overall–Subsequent Measurement–Impairment or Disposal of Long-Lived Assets (previously "Accounting for the Impairment of Long-Lived Assets and for Long-Lived Assets to Be Disposed Of," *Statement of Financial Accounting Standards No. 144* (Norwalk, Conn.: FASB, 2001)).

e. A current-period loss combined with a history of losses or a projection of continuing losses associated with the asset
f. A realization that the asset will be disposed of significantly before the end of its estimated useful life[17]

Determining whether an impairment loss has occurred and for how much to record the loss is a two-step process.

1. **Recoverability Test**. An impairment occurs when the undiscounted sum of estimated future cash flows from an asset is less than the asset's book value.
2. **Measurement**. If the recoverability test indicates an impairment has occurred, an impairment loss is recorded for the difference between the asset's book value and its fair value.

For Step 2, fair value is the amount at which the asset could be bought or sold in a current transaction between willing parties. Quoted market prices could be used if they're available. If fair value is not determinable, it must be estimated.

If an impairment loss is recognized, the written-down book value becomes the new cost base for future cost allocation. Later recovery of an impairment loss is prohibited.

The process is best described by an example. Consider Illustration 11–20.

Illustration 11–20

Impairment Loss—Property, Plant, and Equipment

The Dakota Corporation operates several factories that manufacture medical equipment. Near the end of the company's 2018 fiscal year, a change in business climate related to a competitor's innovative products indicated to management that the $170 million book value (original cost of $300 million less accumulated depreciation of $130 million) of the assets of one of Dakota's factories may not be recoverable.

Management is able to identify cash flows from this factory and estimates that future cash flows over the remaining useful life of the factory will be $150 million. The fair value of the factory's assets is not readily available but is estimated to be $135 million.

Change in circumstances. A change in the business climate related to a competitor's innovative products requires Dakota to investigate for possible impairment.

Step 1. Recoverability Test. Because the book value of $170 million exceeds the $150 million undiscounted future cash flows, an impairment loss is indicated.

Step 2. Measurement of impairment loss. The impairment loss is $35 million, determined as follows:

Book value	$170 million
Less: Fair value	135 million
Impairment loss	$ 35 million

The entry to record the loss is ($ in millions):

Loss on impairment (above)	35	
Accumulated depreciation (reduce to zero)	130	
Factory assets (decrease to fair value)		165

The loss normally is reported in the income statement as a separate component of operating expenses.

In the entry in Illustration 11–20, we reduce accumulated depreciation to zero and decrease the cost base of the assets to their fair value of $135 million ($300 – 165). The new book value of $135 serves as the revised basis for subsequent depreciation over the remaining useful life of the assets, just as if the assets had been acquired on the impairment date for their fair values.

[17]FASB ASC 360–10–35–21: Property, Plant, and Equipment–Overall–Subsequent Measurement–Impairment or Disposal of Long-Lived Assets (previously "Accounting for the Impairment of Long-Lived Assets and for Long-Lived Assets to Be Disposed Of," *Statement of Financial Accounting Standards No. 144* (Norwalk, Conn.: FASB, 2001), par.8).

Because the fair value of the factory assets was not readily available to Dakota in Illustration 11–20, the $135 million had to be estimated. One method that can be used to estimate fair value is to compute the discounted present value of future cash flows expected from the asset. Keep in mind that we use *undiscounted* estimates of cash flows in Step 1 to determine whether an impairment loss is indicated, but *discounted* estimates of cash flows in Step 2 to determine the amount of the loss. In calculating present value, either a traditional approach or an expected cash flow approach can be used. The traditional approach is to incorporate risk and uncertainty into the discount rate. Recall from discussions in previous chapters that the expected cash flow approach incorporates risk and uncertainty instead into a determination of a probability-weighted cash flow expectation, and then discounts this expected cash flow using a risk-free interest rate. We discussed and illustrated the expected cash flow approach in previous chapters.

The present value of future cash flows often is used as a measure of fair value.

A disclosure note is needed to describe the impairment loss. The note should include a description of the impaired asset or asset group, the facts and circumstances leading to the impairment, the amount of the loss if not separately disclosed on the face of the income statement, and the method used to determine fair value.

Macy's, Inc., is a department store chain providing brand-name clothing, accessories, home furnishings, and housewares. Illustration 11–21 shows the company's disclosure notes describing recent impairment losses. The notes also provide a summary of the process used to identify and measure impairment losses for property, plant, and equipment and finite-life intangible assets.

Illustration 11–21

Asset Impairment Disclosure—Macy's, Inc.

Real World Financials

Property and Equipment (in part)

The carrying values of long-lived assets are periodically reviewed by the Company whenever events or changes in circumstances indicate that the carrying value may not be recoverable, such as historical operating losses or plans to close stores before the end of their previously estimated useful lives. Additionally, on an annual basis, the recoverability of the carrying values of individual stores are evaluated. A potential impairment has occurred if projected future undiscounted cash flows are less than the carrying value of the assets. The estimate of cash flows includes management's assumptions of cash inflows and outflows directly resulting from the use of those assets in operations. When a potential impairment has occurred, an impairment write-down is recorded if the carrying value of the long-lived asset exceeds its fair value.

Impairments, Store Closing and Other Costs (in part)

As a result of the Company's projected undiscounted future cash flows related to certain store locations and other assets being less than their carrying value, the Company recorded impairment charges, including properties that were the subject of announced store closings. The fair values of these assets were calculated based on the projected cash flows and an estimated risk-adjusted rate of return that would be used by market participants in valuing these assets or based on prices of similar assets. During 2015, long-lived assets held and used with a carrying value of $201 million were written down to their fair value of $53 million, resulting in asset impairment charges of $148 million.

International Financial Reporting Standards

Impairment of Value: Property, Plant, and Equipment and Finite-Life Intangible Assets. Highlighted below are some important differences in accounting for impairment of value for property, plant, and equipment and finite-life intangible assets between U.S. GAAP and *IAS No. 36.*[18]

● LO11–10

(continued)

[18] "Impairment of Assets," *International Accounting Standard No. 36* (IASCF), as amended effective January 1, 2016.

(concluded)

	U.S. GAAP	IFRS
When to Test	When events or changes in circumstances indicate that book value may not be recoverable.	Assets must be assessed for indicators of impairment at the end of each reporting period. Indicators of impairment are similar to U.S. GAAP.
Recoverability	An impairment loss is required when an asset's book value exceeds the undiscounted sum of the asset's estimated future cash flows.	There is no equivalent recoverability test. An impairment loss is required when an asset's book value exceeds the higher of the asset's value-in-use (present value of estimated future cash flows) and fair value less costs to sell.
Measurement	The impairment loss is the difference between book value and fair value.	The impairment loss is the difference between book value and the "recoverable amount" (the higher of the asset's value-in-use and fair value less costs to sell).
Subsequent Reversal of Loss	Prohibited.	Required if the circumstances that caused the impairment are resolved.

Let's look at an illustration highlighting the important differences described above. The Jasmine Tea Company has a factory that has significantly decreased in value due to technological innovations in the industry. Below are data related to the factory's assets:

	($ in millions)
Book value	$18.5
Undiscounted sum of estimated future cash flows	19.0
Present value of future cash flows	16.0
Fair value less cost to sell (determined by appraisal)	15.5

What amount of impairment loss should Jasmine Tea recognize, if any, under U.S. GAAP? Under IFRS?

U.S. GAAP There is no impairment loss. The sum of undiscounted estimated future cash flows exceeds the book value.

IFRS Jasmine should recognize an impairment loss of $2.5 million. Indicators of impairment are present and book value exceeds both value-in-use (present value of cash flows) and fair value less costs to sell. The recoverable amount is $16 million, the higher of value-in-use ($16 million) and fair value less costs to sell ($15.5 million). The impairment loss is the difference between book value of $18.5 million and the $16 million recoverable amount.

Nokia, a Finnish company, prepares its financial statements according to IFRS. The following disclosure note describes the company's impairment policy:

Assessment of the Recoverability of Long-Lived Assets, Intangible Assets, and Goodwill (in part)

The carrying value of identifiable intangible assets and long-lived assets is assessed if events or changes in circumstances indicate that such carrying value may not be recoverable. Factors that trigger an impairment review include, but are not limited to, underperformance relative to historical or projected future results, significant changes in the manner of the use of the acquired assets or the strategy for the overall business and significant negative industry or economic trends.

Nokia conducts its impairment testing by determining the recoverable amount for the asset. The recoverable amount of an asset is the higher of its fair value less costs to sell and its value-in-use. The recoverable amount is then compared to the asset's carrying amount and an impairment loss is recognized if the recoverable amount is less than the carrying amount. Impairment losses are recognized immediately in the income statement.

INDEFINITE-LIFE INTANGIBLE ASSETS OTHER THAN GOODWILL. Intangible assets with indefinite useful lives, other than goodwill, should be tested for impairment annually and more frequently if events or changes in circumstances indicate that it is more likely than not that the asset is impaired.

A company has the option of first undertaking a qualitative assessment. Companies selecting this option will evaluate relevant events and circumstances to determine whether it is "more likely than not" (a likelihood of more than 50 percent) that the fair value of the asset is less than its book value. Only if that's determined to be the case will the company perform the quantitative impairment test described in the next paragraph.

The measurement of an impairment loss for indefinite-life intangible assets other than goodwill is a one-step process. We compare the fair value of the asset with its book value. If book value exceeds fair value, an impairment loss is recognized for the difference. Notice that we omit the recoverability test with these assets. Because we anticipate cash flows to continue indefinitely, recoverability is not a good indicator of impairment.

If book value exceeds fair value, an impairment loss is recognized for the difference.

Similar to property, plant, and equipment and finite-life intangible assets, if an impairment loss is recognized, the written-down book value becomes the new cost base for future cost allocation. Recovery of the impairment loss is prohibited. Disclosure requirements also are similar.

International Financial Reporting Standards

Impairment of Value: Indefinite-Life Intangible Assets Other than Goodwill. Similar to U.S. GAAP, IFRS requires indefinite-life intangible assets other than goodwill to be tested for impairment at least annually. However, under U.S. GAAP, a company has the option to avoid annual testing by making qualitative evaluations of the likelihood of asset impairment. Also, under U.S. GAAP, the impairment loss is measured as the difference between book value and fair value, while under IFRS the impairment loss is the difference between book value and the recoverable amount. The recoverable amount is the higher of the asset's value-in-use (present value of estimated future cash flows) and fair value less costs to sell.

IFRS requires the reversal of an impairment loss if the circumstances that caused the impairment are resolved. Reversals are prohibited under U.S. GAAP.

Also, indefinite-life intangible assets may not be combined with other indefinite-life intangible assets for the required annual impairment test. Under U.S. GAAP, though, if certain criteria are met, indefinite-life intangible assets should be combined for the required annual impairment test.

● LO11–10

GOODWILL. Recall that goodwill is a unique intangible asset. Unlike other assets, its cost (a) can't be directly associated with any specific identifiable right and (b) is not separable from the company as a whole. Because of these unique characteristics, we don't measure the impairment of goodwill the same way as we do other assets. GAAP provides guidelines for impairment, which, while similar to general impairment guidelines, are specific to goodwill.[19] Let's compare the two-step process for measuring goodwill impairment with the two-step process for measuring impairment for property, plant, and equipment and finite-life intangible assets.

In Step 1, for all classifications of assets, we decide whether a write-down due to impairment is required by determining whether the value of an asset has fallen below its book value. However, in this comparison, the value of assets for property, plant, and equipment and finite-life intangible assets is considered to be value-in-use as measured by the sum of undiscounted cash flows expected from the asset. But due to its unique characteristics, the value of goodwill is not associated with any specific cash flows and must be measured in a unique way. By its very nature, goodwill is inseparable from a particular *reporting unit.* A reporting unit is an operating segment of a company or a component of an operating segment for which discrete financial information is available and segment management

STEP 1—A goodwill impairment loss is indicated when the fair value of the reporting unit is less than its book value.

[19]FASB ASC 350–20–35: Intangibles–Goodwill and Other–Goodwill–Subsequent Measurement (previously "Goodwill and Other Intangible Assets," *Statement of Financial Accounting Standards No. 142* (Norwalk, Conn.: FASB, 2001)).

regularly reviews the operating results of that component. So, for Step 1, we compare the value of the reporting unit itself with its book value. If the fair value of the reporting unit is less than its book value, an impairment loss is indicated.

STEP 2—A goodwill impairment loss is measured as the excess of the book value of the goodwill over its "implied" fair value.

In Step 2, for all classifications of property, plant, and equipment and intangible assets, if impairment is indicated from Step 1, we measure the amount of impairment as the excess of the book value of the asset over its fair value. However, unlike for most other assets, the fair value of goodwill cannot be measured directly (market value, present value of associated cash flows, etc.) and so must be "implied" from the fair value of the reporting unit that acquired the goodwill.

The implied fair value of goodwill is calculated in the same way that goodwill is determined in a business combination. That is, it's a residual amount measured by subtracting the fair value of all identifiable net assets from the purchase price using the unit's previously determined fair value as the purchase price.[20]

If goodwill is tested for impairment at the same time as other assets of the reporting unit, the other assets must be tested first and any impairment loss and asset write-down is recorded prior to testing goodwill. Subsequent reversal (recovery) of a previous goodwill impairment loss is not allowed.

When to test for impairment. Prior to 2012, companies were required to perform *Step 1* of the two-step test for goodwill impairment at least once a year, as well as in between annual test dates if something occurred that would indicate that the fair value of the reporting unit was below its book value. Then, if the first step indicated that the fair value of the reporting unit was indeed below book value, the company would perform *Step 2* to measure the amount of goodwill impairment.

In response to concerns about the cost and complexity of performing Step 1 every year, the FASB now allows companies the option to decide whether Step 1 is necessary.[21] Companies selecting this option will perform a qualitative assessment by evaluating relevant events and circumstances to determine whether it is "more likely than not" (a likelihood of more than 50 percent) that the fair value of a reporting unit is now less than its book value. Only if that's determined to be the case will the company perform the first step of the two-step goodwill impairment test. A list of possible events and circumstances that a company should consider in this qualitative assessment is provided in ASC 350–20–35-3C.

A goodwill impairment example is provided in Illustration 11–22.

Illustration 11–22

Impairment Loss—Goodwill

The "implied" fair value of goodwill is a residual amount measured by subtracting the fair value of all identifiable net assets from the unit's fair value.

In 2017, the Upjane Corporation acquired Pharmacopia Corporation for $500 million. Upjane recorded $100 million in goodwill related to this acquisition because the fair value of the net assets of Pharmacopia was $400 million. After the acquisition, Pharmacopia continues to operate as a separate company and is considered a reporting unit.

At the end of 2018, events and circumstances indicated that it is more likely than not that the fair value of Pharmacopia is less than its book value requiring Upjane to perform Step 1 of the goodwill impairment test. The book value of Pharmacopia's net assets at the end of 2018 is $440 million, including the $100 million in goodwill. On that date, the fair value of Pharmacopia is estimated to be $360 million and the fair value of all of its identifiable tangible and intangible assets, excluding goodwill, is estimated to be $335 million.

Step 1. Recoverability Test. Because the book value of the net assets of $440 million exceeds the $360 million fair value of the reporting unit, an impairment loss is indicated.

Step 2. Measurement of impairment loss. The impairment loss is $75 million, determined as follows:

Determination of the implied fair value of goodwill:

Fair value of Pharmacopia	$360 million
Fair value of Pharmacopia's net assets (excluding goodwill)	335 million
Implied fair value of goodwill	$ 25 million

(continued)

[20]The impairment loss recognized can't exceed the book value of goodwill.

[21]FASB ASC 350–20–35-3: Intangibles–Goodwill and Other–Goodwill–Subsequent Measurement (previously "Goodwill and Other Intangible Assets," *Statement of Financial Accounting Standards No. 142* (Norwalk, Conn.: FASB, 2001)).

(concluded)

Measurement of the impairment loss:

Book value of goodwill	$ 100 million
Implied fair value of goodwill	25 million
Impairment loss	$ 75 million

The entry to record the loss is ($ in millions):

Loss on impairment of goodwill	75	
Goodwill		75

The loss normally is reported in the income statement as a separate component of operating expenses.

Where We're Headed 

In May 2016, the Financial Accounting Standards Board (FASB) issued a proposed Accounting Standards Update (ASU) that would simplify the accounting for goodwill impairment. The proposed ASU is Phase 1 of a two-phase project. The proposal is to eliminate Step 2 in the goodwill impairment test. As a result, companies would no longer be required to measure the goodwill impairment loss for a reporting unit as the excess of the book value of the goodwill over its "implied" fair value as we did in Illustration 11–22. Instead, using only the measurements from Step 1, **the impairment loss would be the book value of the reporting unit minus its fair value (not to exceed the book value of goodwill).** Here is the difference in the current and proposed approach to measuring the loss:

Current measurement:

Goodwill impairment loss = Book value of goodwill − Implied fair value of goodwill

Proposed measurement:

Goodwill impairment loss = Book value of reporting unit − Fair value of reporting unit

By proposing to remove Step 2, the FASB intends to reduce the cost and complexity of evaluating goodwill for impairment. However, at the time this book was published, the FASB had not yet decided whether to adopt the proposed ASU. To demonstrate how the proposed measurement would look if adopted, let's reexamine the example in Illustration 11–22.

Upjane Corporation believes that it is more likely than not that the fair value of Pharmacopia Corporation (a reporting unit) is less than its book value. In this case, Upjane determines that the book value of the net assets of $440 million exceeds the $360 million fair value of Pharmacopia. The difference of $80 million is the impairment loss.

Measurement of the impairment loss:

Book value of the net assets of Pharmacopia	$440 million
Fair value of Pharmacopia	360 million
Impairment loss	$ 80 million

The entry to record the loss is ($ in millions):

Loss on impairment of goodwill	80	
Goodwill		80

Recall that Upjane recorded $100 million in goodwill related to the initial acquisition of Pharmacopia. After the impairment loss of $80 million is recorded, the balance of goodwill is reduced to $20 million. If Pharmacopia's book value had exceeded its fair value by more than $100 million, then the goodwill impairment loss would have been limited to only $100 million to reduce the balance of goodwill to zero.

In Phase 2 of the project (which is not part of the proposed ASU discussed above), the FASB will consider permitting or requiring companies to amortize goodwill, and also consider making other changes in the impairment testing methodology.

Some examples of multibillion dollar goodwill impairment losses in recent years are shown in Illustration 11–23.

Illustration 11–23
Goodwill Impairment Losses

Real World Financials

Company	Goodwill Impairment Loss
General Motors	$27.1 billion
Hewlett-Packard	13.7 billion
Microsoft	6.2 billion
Yahoo	4.5 billion
Boston Scientific	4.4 billion

Yahoo's disclosure of its goodwill impairment loss is shown in Illustration 11–24.

Illustration 11–24
Goodwill Impairment Disclosure—Yahoo Inc.

Real World Financials

Goodwill Impairment Charge (in part)

During 2015, we recorded a $4,461 million goodwill impairment charge. The impairments were a result of a combination of factors, including a sustained decrease in our market capitalization in the fourth quarter of 2015 and lower estimated projected revenue and profitability in the near term. We concluded that the carrying value of our U.S. & Canada, Europe, Tumblr, and Latin America reporting units exceeded their respective estimated fair values and recorded a goodwill impairment charge of approximately $3,692 million, $531 million, $230 million, and $8 million, respectively.

Additional Consideration

Private Company GAAP—Accounting for Goodwill. The Private Company Council (PCC) sought feedback from private company stakeholders on the issue of goodwill accounting and found that most users of private company financial statements disregard goodwill and goodwill impairment losses. As a result, the PCC concluded that the cost and complexity of goodwill accounting outweigh the benefits for private companies.

In response to the PCC's conclusion, the FASB issued an Accounting Standards Update in 2014 that allows an accounting alternative for the subsequent measurement of goodwill for private companies that calls for goodwill to be amortized and also simplifies the goodwill impairment test.[22]

The main provisions of the alternative are:

1. Amortizing goodwill on a straight-line basis over a maximum of 10 years
2. Testing goodwill for impairment at either the company level or the reporting unit level
3. Testing goodwill for impairment only when a triggering event occurs indicating that goodwill may be impaired
4. The option of determining whether a quantitative impairment test is necessary when a triggering event occurs
5. If a quantitative test is necessary, measuring the goodwill impairment loss as the excess of the book value of the company (or reporting unit) over its fair value, not to exceed the book value of goodwill

The fifth provision is now being proposed for public companies. We discussed this above in the previous "Where We're Headed" box.

Assets Held for Sale

For assets held for sale, if book value exceeds fair value less cost to sell, an impairment loss is recognized for the difference.

We have been discussing the recognition and measurement for the impairment of value of assets to be held and used. We also test for impairment of assets held for sale. These are assets management has actively committed to immediately sell in their present condition and for which sale is probable.

[22]*Accounting Standards Update No. 2014–02*, "Intangibles-Goodwill and Other (Topic 350): Accounting for Goodwill," (Norwalk, Conn.: FASB, January 2014).

International Financial Reporting Standards

● LO11–10

Impairment of Value—Goodwill. Highlighted below are some important differences in accounting for the impairment of goodwill between U.S. GAAP and *IAS No. 36.*

	U.S. GAAP	IFRS
Level of Testing	*Reporting unit*—a segment or a component of an operating segment for which discrete financial information is available.	*Cash-generating unit (CGU)*—the lowest level at which goodwill is monitored by management. A CGU can't be lower than a segment.
Measurement	*A two-step process:* 1. Compare the fair value of the reporting unit with its book value. A loss is indicated if fair value is less than book value. 2. The impairment loss is the excess of book value over implied fair value.	*A one-step process:* Compare the recoverable amount of the CGU to book value. If the recoverable amount is less, reduce goodwill first, then other assets. The recoverable amount is the higher of fair value less costs to sell and value-in-use (present value of estimated future cash flows).

IAS No. 36 requires goodwill to be tested for impairment at least annually. U.S. GAAP allows a company to avoid annual testing by making qualitative evaluations of the likelihood of goodwill impairment to determine if step one is necessary. Both U.S. GAAP and *IAS No. 36* prohibit the reversal of goodwill impairment losses.

Let's look at an illustration highlighting these differences.

Canterbury LTD. has $38 million of goodwill in its balance sheet from the 2016 acquisition of Denton, Inc. At the end of 2018, Canterbury's management provided the following information for the year-end goodwill impairment test ($ in millions):

Fair value of Denton (determined by appraisal)	$132
Fair value of Denton's net assets (excluding goodwill)	120
Book value of Denton's net assets (including goodwill)	150
Present value of Denton's estimated future cash flows	135

Assume that Denton is considered a reporting unit under U.S. GAAP and a cash-generating unit under IFRS, and that its fair value approximates fair value less costs to sell. What is the amount of goodwill impairment loss that Canterbury should recognize, if any, under U.S. GAAP? Under IFRS?

U.S. GAAP	Fair value of Denton	$132
	Fair value of Denton's net assets (excluding goodwill)	120
	Implied fair value of goodwill	$ 12
	Book value of goodwill	$ 38
	Implied fair value of goodwill	12
	Impairment loss	$ 26
IFRS	The recoverable amount is $135 million, the higher of the $135 million value-in-use (present value of estimated future cash flows) and the $132 million fair value less costs to sell.	
	Denton's book value	$150
	Recoverable amount	135
	Impairment loss	$ 15

Deutsche Bank is the largest bank in Germany and one of the largest financial institutions in Europe and the world. The company prepares its financial statements according to IFRS. The following disclosures describe the company's goodwill impairment policy as well as goodwill impairment loss.

(continued)

(concluded)

Impairment of Goodwill (in part)
Goodwill is tested for impairment annually in the fourth quarter by comparing the recoverable amount of each goodwill-carrying cash-generating unit (CGU) with its carrying amount. In addition, in accordance with IAS 36, the Group tests goodwill whenever a triggering event is identified. The recoverable amount is the higher of a CGU's fair value less costs of disposal and its value in use.

Impairment charge during the period (in part)
The goodwill impairment test in the third quarter 2015 resulted in goodwill impairments totaling € 4,933 million, consisting of € 2,168 million and € 2,765 million in the CGUs CB&S, and PBC, respectively. The impairment in CB&S was mainly driven by changes to the business mix in light of expected higher regulatory capital requirements, leading to a recoverable amount of approximately € 26.1 billion. The impairment in PBC was, in addition to the changed capital requirements, mainly driven by current disposal expectations regarding Hua Xia Bank Co. Ltd. and Postbank, which resulted in a recoverable amount of approximately € 12.3 billion for the CGU.

An asset or group of assets classified as held for sale is measured at the lower of its book value, or fair value less cost to sell. An impairment loss is recognized for any write-down to fair value less cost to sell.[23] Except for including the cost to sell, notice the similarity to impairment of assets to be held and used. We don't depreciate or amortize these assets while classified as held for sale and we report them separately in the balance sheet. Recall from our discussion of discontinued operations in Chapter 4 that similar rules apply for a component of an entity that is classified as held for sale.

Illustration 11–25 summarizes the guidelines for the recognition and measurement of impairment losses.

Illustration 11–25
Summary of Asset Impairment Guidelines

Asset Classification	When to Test for Impairment	Impairment Test
Held and Used		
Property, plant, and equipment and finite-life intangible assets	When events or circumstances indicate book value may not be recoverable.	Step 1—An impairment loss is required only when book value is not recoverable (undiscounted sum of estimated future cash flows less than book value). Step 2—The impairment loss is the excess of book value over fair value.
Indefinite-life intangible assets (other than goodwill)	At least annually, and more frequently if indicated. Option to avoid annual testing by making qualitative evaluations of the likelihood of asset impairment.	If book value exceeds fair value, an impairment loss is recognized for the difference.
Goodwill	At least annually, and more frequently if indicated. Option to avoid annual testing by making qualitative evaluations of the likelihood of goodwill impairment to determine if Step 1 is necessary.	Step 1—A loss is indicated when the fair value of the reporting unit is less than its book value. Step 2—An impairment loss is measured as the excess of book value over implied fair value.
Held for Sale	At the time of classification as held for sale and thereafter.	If book value exceeds fair value less cost to sell, an impairment loss is recognized for the difference.

[23]If the asset is unsold at the end of a subsequent reporting period, a gain is recognized for any increase in fair value less cost to sell, but not in excess of the loss previously recognized.

Impairment Losses and Earnings Quality

What do losses from the write-down of inventory and restructuring costs have in common? The presence of these items in a corporate income statement presents a challenge to an analyst trying to determine a company's permanent earnings—those likely to continue in the future. We discussed these issues in prior chapters.

We now can add asset impairment losses to the list of "big bath" accounting techniques some companies use to manipulate earnings. By writing off large amounts of assets, companies significantly reduce earnings in the year of the write-off but are able to increase future earnings by lowering future depreciation, depletion, or amortization. Here's how. We measure the impairment loss as the difference between an asset's book value and its fair value. However, in most cases, fair value must be estimated, and the estimation process usually involves a forecast of future net cash flows the company expects to generate from the asset's use. If a company underestimates future net cash flows, fair value is understated. This has two effects: (1) current year's income is unrealistically low due to the impairment loss being overstated and (2) future income is unrealistically high because depreciation, depletion, and amortization are based on understated asset values.

An analyst must decide whether to consider asset impairment losses as temporary in nature or as a part of permanent earnings.

Concept Review Exercise

IMPAIRMENT

Part A:

Illumination Inc. owns a factory in Wisconsin that makes light bulbs. During 2018, due to increased competition from LED light bulb manufacturers, the company determined that an impairment test was appropriate. Management has prepared the following information for the assets of the factory ($ in millions):

Cost	$345
Accumulated depreciation	85
Estimated future undiscounted cash flows to be generated by the factory	230
Estimated fair value of the factory assets	170

Required:

1. Determine the amount of impairment loss Illumination should recognize, if any.
2. If a loss is indicated, prepare the journal entry to record the loss.
3. Repeat requirement 1 assuming that the estimated undiscounted future cash flows are $270 million instead of $230 million.

Solution:

1. Determine the amount of impairment loss Illumination should recognize, if any.

   Recoverability Test: Because the book value of $260 ($345 – 85) million exceeds the $230 million undiscounted future cash flows, an impairment loss is indicated.

   Measurement: The impairment loss is $90 million, determined as follows:

	($ in millions)
Book value	$260
Less: Fair value	170
Impairment loss	$ 90

2. If a loss is indicated, prepare the journal entry to record the loss.

	($ in millions)	
Loss on impairment (determined above)	90	
Accumulated depreciation (balance)	85	
Factory assets ($345 – 170)		175

3. Repeat requirement 1 assuming that the estimated undiscounted future cash flows are $270 million instead of $230 million.

Because the undiscounted sum of future cash flows of $270 million exceeds book value of $260 million, the recoverability test indicates that there is no impairment, so no impairment loss is recorded.

Part B:

In 2016, Illumination Inc. acquired Zapo Lighting Company for $620 million, of which $80 million was allocated to goodwill. After the acquisition, Zapo continues to operate a separate company and is considered a reporting unit. At the end of 2018, management provided the following information for a required goodwill impairment test ($ in millions):

Fair value of Zapo Lighting	$540
Fair value of Zapo's net assets (excluding goodwill)	510
Book value of Zapo's net assets (including goodwill)	600

Required:

Determine the amount of goodwill impairment loss that Illumination should recognize at the end of 2018, if any.

Solution:

Recoverability Test: Because the book value of the net assets of $600 million exceeds the $540 million fair value of the reporting unit, an impairment loss is indicated.

Measurement: The impairment loss is $50 million, determined as follows:

Determination of implied fair value of goodwill:	($ in millions)
Fair value of Zapo	$540
Fair value of Zapo's net assets (excluding goodwill)	510
Implied fair value of goodwill	$ 30
Measurement of impairment loss:	
Book value of goodwill	$ 80
Implied fair value of goodwill	30
Impairment loss	$ 50

PART C

Subsequent Expenditures

Now that we have acquired and measured assets, we can address accounting issues incurred subsequent to their acquisition. This part of the chapter deals with the treatment of expenditures made over the life of these assets to maintain and/or improve them.

Expenditures Subsequent to Acquisition

Many long-lived assets require expenditures to repair, maintain, or improve them after their acquisition. These expenditures can present accounting problems if they are material. In general, a choice must be made between capitalizing the expenditures by either increasing the asset's book value or creating a new asset, or expensing them in the period in which they are incurred. Typically, we capitalize expenditures that are expected to produce benefits beyond the current fiscal year. In contrast, expenditures that simply maintain a given level of benefits are expensed in the period they are incurred.

LO11–9

Expenditures related to assets can increase future benefits in the following ways:

1. An extension of the *useful life* of the asset
2. An increase in the *operating efficiency* of the asset resulting in either an increase in the quantity of goods or services produced or a decrease in future operating costs
3. An increase in the *quality* of the goods or services produced by the asset

Expenditures that cause any of these results should be capitalized initially and then expensed in future periods through depreciation, depletion, or amortization. Of course, materiality is an important factor in the practical application of this approach.

For convenience, many companies set materiality thresholds for the capitalization of any expenditure. For example, a company might decide to expense all expenditures under $1,000 regardless of whether or not future benefits are increased. Judgment is required to determine the appropriate materiality threshold as well as the appropriate treatment of expenditures over $1,000. There often are practical problems in capitalizing these expenditures. For example, even if future benefits are increased by the expenditure, it may be difficult to determine how long the benefits will last. It's important for a company to establish a policy for treating these expenditures and apply it consistently.

Many companies do not capitalize any expenditure unless it exceeds a predetermined amount that is considered material.

We classify subsequent expenditures as (1) repairs and maintenance, (2) additions, (3) improvements, or (4) rearrangements.

Repairs and Maintenance

These expenditures are made to *maintain* a given level of benefits provided by the asset and do not *increase* future benefits. For example, the cost of an engine tune-up or the repair of an engine part for a delivery truck allows the truck to continue its productive activity. If the maintenance is not performed, the truck will not provide the benefits originally anticipated. In that sense, future benefits are provided; without the repair, the truck will no longer operate. The key, though, is that future benefits are not provided *beyond those originally anticipated.* Expenditures for these activities should be expensed in the period incurred.

Expenditures for *repairs and maintenance* generally are expensed when incurred.

Additional Consideration

If repairs and maintenance costs are seasonal, interim financial statements may be misstated. For example, suppose annual maintenance is performed on a company's fleet of delivery trucks. The annual income statement correctly includes one year's maintenance expense. However, for interim reporting purposes, if the entire expenditure is made in one quarter, should that quarter's income statement include as expense the entire cost of the annual maintenance? If these expenditures can be anticipated, they should be accrued evenly throughout the year by crediting an allowance account. The allowance account is then debited when the maintenance is performed.

Additions

As the term implies, **additions** involve adding a new major component to an existing asset and should be capitalized because future benefits are increased. For example, adding a refrigeration unit to a delivery truck increases the capability of the truck, thus increasing its future benefits. Other examples include the construction of a new wing on a building and the addition of a security system to an existing building.

The capitalized cost includes all necessary expenditures to bring the addition to a condition and location for use. For a building addition, this might include the costs of tearing down and removing a wall of the existing building. The capitalized cost of additions is depreciated over the remaining useful life of the original asset or its own useful life, whichever is shorter.

The costs of *additions* usually are capitalized.

Improvements

Expenditures classified as **improvements** involve the replacement of a major component of an asset. The replacement can be a new component with the same characteristics as the old component or a new component with enhanced operating capabilities. For example, an existing refrigeration unit in a delivery truck could be replaced with a new but similar unit or with a new and improved refrigeration unit. In either case, the cost of the improvement usually increases future benefits and should be capitalized by increasing the book value of the related asset (the delivery truck) and depreciated over the useful life of the improved asset. There are three methods used to record the cost of improvements.

The costs of *improvements* usually are capitalized.

1. *Substitution.* The improvement can be recorded as both (1) a disposition of the old component and (2) the acquisition of the new component. This approach is conceptually appealing but it is practical only if the original cost and accumulated depreciation of the old component can be separately identified.
2. *Capitalization of new cost.* Another way to record an improvement is to include the cost of the improvement (net of any consideration received from the disposition of the old component) as a debit to the related asset account, without removing the original cost and accumulated depreciation of the original component. This approach is acceptable only if the book value of the original component has been reduced to an immaterial amount through prior depreciation.
3. *Reduction of accumulated depreciation.* Another way to increase an asset's book value is to leave the asset account unaltered but decrease its related accumulated depreciation. The argument for this method is that many improvements extend the useful life of an asset and are equivalent to a partial recovery of previously recorded depreciation. This approach produces the same book value as the capitalization of cost to the asset account. However, cost and accumulated depreciation amounts will differ under the two methods.

The three methods are compared in Illustration 11–26.

Illustration 11–26
Improvements

The Palmer Corporation replaced the air conditioning system in one of its office buildings that it leases to tenants. The cost of the old air conditioning system, $200,000, is included in the cost of the building. However, the company has separately depreciated the air conditioning system. Depreciation recorded up to the date of replacement totaled $160,000. The old system was removed and the new system installed at a cost of $230,000, which was paid in cash. Parts from the old system were sold for $12,000.

Accounting for the improvement differs depending on the alternative chosen.

	Alternative 1—Substitution		
1. Substitution (a) Disposition of old component	Cash	12,000	
	Accumulated depreciation—buildings (remove old)	160,000	
	Loss on disposal (difference)	28,000	
	Buildings (remove old)		200,000
(b) Acquisition of new component.	Buildings (add new)	230,000	
	Cash		230,000
	Alternative 2—Capitalization of new cost		
2. Capitalization of new cost.	Buildings	218,000	
	Cash ($230,000 − 12,000)		218,000
	Alternative 3—Reduction of accumulated depreciation		
3. Reduction of accumulated depreciation.	Accumulated depreciation—buildings	218,000	
	Cash ($230,000 − 12,000)		218,000

Rearrangements

The costs of material *rearrangements* should be capitalized if they clearly increase future benefits.

Expenditures made to restructure an asset without addition, replacement, or improvement are termed **rearrangements**. The objective is to create a new capability for the asset and not necessarily to extend its useful life. Examples include the rearrangement of machinery on the production line to increase operational efficiency and the relocation of a company's operating plant or office building. If these expenditures are material and they clearly increase future benefits, they should be capitalized and expensed in the future periods benefited. If the expenditures are not material or if it's not certain that future benefits have increased, they should be expensed in the period incurred.

Illustration 11–27 provides a summary of the accounting treatment for the various types of expenditures related to property, plant, and equipment.

Type of Expenditure	Definition	Usual Accounting Treatment
Repairs and maintenance	Expenditures to maintain a given level of benefits	Expense in the period incurred
Additions	The addition of a new major component to an existing asset	Capitalize and depreciate over the remaining useful life of the *original asset or its own useful* life, whichever is shorter
Improvements	The replacement of a major component	Capitalize and depreciate over the useful life of the improved asset
Rearrangements	Expenditures to restructure an asset without addition, replacement, or improvement	If expenditures are material and clearly increase future benefits, capitalize and depreciate over the future periods benefited

Illustration 11–27

Expenditures Subsequent to Acquisition

Costs of Defending Intangible Rights

Repairs, additions, improvements, and rearrangements generally relate to property, plant, and equipment. A possible significant expenditure incurred subsequent to the acquisition of intangible assets is the cost of defending the right that gives the intangible asset its value. If an intangible right is *successfully* defended, the litigation costs should be capitalized and amortized over the remaining useful life of the related intangible. This is the appropriate treatment of these expenditures even if the intangible asset was originally developed internally rather than purchased.

The costs incurred to *successfully* defend an intangible right should be capitalized.

If the defense of an intangible right is *unsuccessful,* then the intangible asset has no future value. In this case, the litigation costs provide no future benefit and should be expensed immediately. In addition, the book value of the intangible asset should be reduced to realizable value. For example, if a company is unsuccessful in defending a patent infringement suit, the patent's value may be eliminated and a loss recorded.

The costs incurred to *unsuccessfully* defend an intangible right should be expensed.

International Financial Reporting Standards

Costs of Defending Intangible Rights. Under U.S. GAAP, litigation costs to successfully defend an intangible right are capitalized and amortized over the remaining useful life of the related intangible. Under IFRS, these costs are expensed, except in rare situations when an expenditure increases future benefits.[24]

● LO11–10

Financial Reporting Case Solution

© fStop/Getty Images

1. **Is Penny correct? Do the terms *depreciation, depletion,* and *amortization* all mean the same thing?** *(p. 576)* Penny is correct. Each of these terms refers to the cost allocation of assets over their service lives. The term *depreciation* is used for plant and equipment, *depletion* for natural resources, and *amortization* for intangible assets.
2. **Weyerhaeuser determines depletion based on the "volume of timber estimated to be available." Explain this approach.** *(p. 581)* Weyerhaeuser is using the units-of-production method to determine depletion. The units-of-production method is an activity-based method that computes a depletion (or depreciation or amortization) rate per measure of activity and then multiplies this rate by actual activity to determine periodic cost allocation. The method is used by Weyerhaeuser to measure depletion of the cost of timber harvested and the amortization of logging roads. Logging roads are intangible assets because the company does not own the roads.

[24]"Intangible Assets," *International Accounting Standard No. 38* (IASCF), par. 20, as amended effective January 1, 2016.

3. Explain how asset impairment differs from depreciation, depletion, and amortization. How do companies measure impairment losses for property, plant, and equipment and intangible assets with finite useful lives? *(p. 602)* Depreciation, depletion, and amortization reflect a gradual consumption of the benefits inherent in a long-lived asset. An implicit assumption in allocating the cost of an asset over its useful life is that there has been no significant reduction in the anticipated total benefits or service potential of the asset. Situations can arise, however, that cause a significant decline or *impairment* of those benefits or service potentials. Determining whether to record an impairment loss for an asset and actually recording the loss is a two-step process. The first step is a recoverability test—an impairment loss is required only when the undiscounted sum of estimated future cash flows from an asset is less than the asset's book value. The measurement of impairment loss—Step 2—is the difference between the asset's book value and its fair value. If an impairment loss is recognized, the written-down book value becomes the new cost base for future cost allocation. ●

The Bottom Line

- **LO11–1** The use of property, plant, and equipment and intangible assets represents a consumption of benefits, or service potentials, inherent in the assets. The cost of these inherent benefits or service potentials should be recognized as an expense over the periods they help to produce revenues. As there very seldom is a direct relationship between the use of assets and revenue production, accounting resorts to arbitrary methods to allocate these costs over the periods of their use. (*p. 575*)
- **LO11–2** The allocation process for plant and equipment is called *depreciation.* Time-based depreciation methods estimate service life in years and then allocate depreciable base, cost less estimated residual value, using either a straight-line or accelerated pattern. Activity-based depreciation methods allocate the depreciable base by estimating service life according to some measure of productivity. When an item of property, plant, and equipment or an intangible asset is sold, a gain or loss is recognized for the difference between the consideration received and the asset's book value. (*p. 578*)
- **LO11–3** The allocation process for natural resources is called *depletion.* The activity-based method called units-of-production usually is employed to determine periodic depletion. (*p. 591*)
- **LO11–4** The allocation process for intangible assets is called *amortization.* For an intangible asset with a finite useful life, the capitalized cost less any estimated residual value must be allocated to periods in which the asset is expected to contribute to the company's revenue-generating activities. An intangible asset that is determined to have an indefinite useful life is not subject to periodic amortization. Goodwill is perhaps the most typical intangible asset with an indefinite useful life. (*p. 593*)
- **LO11–5** A change in either the service life or residual value of property, plant, and equipment and intangible assets should be reflected in the financial statements of the current period and future periods by recalculating periodic depreciation, depletion, or amortization. (*p. 599*)
- **LO11–6** A change in depreciation, depletion, or amortization method is considered a change in accounting estimate that is achieved by a change in accounting principle. We account for these changes prospectively, exactly as we would any other change in estimate. One difference is that most changes in estimate do not require a company to justify the change. However, this change in estimate is a result of changing an accounting principle and therefore requires a clear justification as to why the new method is preferable. (*p. 600*)
- **LO11–7** A material error in accounting for property, plant, and equipment and intangible assets that is discovered in a year subsequent to the year of the error requires that previous years' financial statements that were incorrect as a result of the error are retrospectively restated to reflect the correction. Any account balances that are incorrect as a result of the error are corrected by journal entry. If retained earnings is one of the incorrect accounts, the correction is reported as a prior period adjustment to the beginning balance in the statement of shareholders' equity. In addition, a disclosure note is needed to describe the nature of the error and the impact of its correction on income. (*p. 601*)
- **LO11–8** Conceptually, there is considerable merit for a policy requiring the write-down of an asset when there has been a *significant* decline in value below book value. The write-down provides important information

about the future cash flows to be generated from the use of the asset. However, in practice this policy is very subjective. GAAP [FASB ASC 360] establishes guidance for when to recognize and how to measure impairment losses of property, plant, and equipment and intangible assets that have finite useful lives. GAAP [FASB ASC 350] also provides guidance for the recognition and measurement of impairment for indefinite-life intangibles and goodwill. *(p. 603)*

● LO11–9 Expenditures for repairs and maintenance generally are expensed when incurred. The costs of additions and improvements usually are capitalized. The costs of material rearrangements should be capitalized if they clearly increase future benefits. *(p. 614)*

● LO11–10 Among the several differences between U.S. GAAP and IFRS with respect to the utilization and impairment of property, plant, and equipment and intangible assets pertains to reporting assets in the balance sheet. IFRS allows a company to value property, plant, and equipment (PP&E) and intangible assets subsequent to initial valuation at (1) cost less accumulated depreciation/amortization or (2) fair value (revaluation). U.S. GAAP prohibits revaluation. There also are significant differences in accounting for the impairment of property, plant, and equipment and intangible assets. *(pp. 584, 589, 593, 596, 605, 607, 611,* and *617)* ●

APPENDIX 11A

Comparison with MACRS (Tax Depreciation)

Depreciation for financial reporting purposes is an attempt to distribute the cost of the asset, less any anticipated residual value, over the estimated useful life in a systematic and rational manner that attempts to match revenues with the use of the asset. Depreciation for income tax purposes is influenced by the revenue needs of government as well as the desire to influence economic behavior. For example, accelerated depreciation schedules currently allowed are intended to provide incentive for companies to expand and modernize their facilities thus stimulating economic growth.

The federal income tax code allows taxpayers to compute depreciation for their tax returns on assets acquired after 1986 using the **modified accelerated cost recovery system (MACRS)**.[25] Key differences between the calculation of depreciation for financial reporting and the calculation using MACRS are:

1. Estimated useful lives and residual values are not used in MACRS.
2. Firms can't choose among various accelerated methods under MACRS.
3. A half-year convention is used in determining the MACRS depreciation amounts.

Under MACRS, each asset generally is placed within a recovery period category. The six categories for personal property are 3, 5, 7, 10, 15, and 20 years. For example, the 5-year category includes automobiles, light trucks, and computers.

Depending on the category, fixed percentage rates are applied to the original cost of the asset. The rates for the 5-year asset category are as follows:

Year	Rate
1	20.00%
2	32.00
3	19.20
4	11.52
5	11.52
6	5.76
Total	100.00%

These rates are equivalent to applying the double-declining-balance method with a switch to straight-line in the year straight-line yields an equal or higher deduction than DDB. In most cases, the half-year convention is used regardless of when the asset is placed in service.[26] The first-year rate of 20% for the five-year category is one-half of the DDB rate for an asset with a five-year life (2 × 20%). The sixth year rate of 5.76% is one-half of

[25]For assets acquired between 1981 and 1986, tax depreciation is calculated using the accelerated cost recovery system (ACRS), which is similar to MACRS. For assets acquired before 1981, tax depreciation can be calculated using any of the depreciation methods discussed in the chapter. Residual values are used in the calculation of depreciation for pre-1981 assets.

[26]In certain situations, mid-quarter and mid-month conventions are used.

the straight-line rate established in year 4, the year straight-line depreciation exceeds DDB depreciation.

Companies have the option to use the straight-line method for the entire tax life of the asset, applying the half-year convention, rather than using MACRS depreciation schedules. Because of the differences discussed above, tax depreciation for a given year will likely be different from GAAP depreciation. ●

APPENDIX 11B Retirement and Replacement Methods of Depreciation

Retirement and replacement depreciation methods occasionally are used to depreciate relatively low-valued assets with short service lives. Under either approach, an aggregate asset account that represents a group of similar assets is increased at the time the initial collection is acquired.

Retirement Method

The *retirement depreciation method records* depreciation when assets are disposed of and measures depreciation as the difference between the proceeds received and cost.

Using the retirement depreciation method, the asset account also is increased for the cost of subsequent expenditures. When an item is disposed of, the asset account is credited for its cost, and depreciation expense is recorded for the difference between cost and proceeds received, if any. No other entries are made for depreciation. As a consequence, one or more periods may pass without any expense recorded. For example, the following entry records the purchase of 100 handheld calculators at $50 acquisition cost each:

Calculators (100 × $50)	5,000	
Cash		5,000
To record the acquisition of calculators		

If 20 new calculators are acquired at $45 each, the asset account is increased.

Calculators (20 × $45)	900	
Cash		900
To record additional calculator acquisitions		

Thirty calculators are disposed of (retired) by selling them secondhand to a bookkeeping firm for $5 each. The following entry reflects the retirement method:

Cash (30 × $5)	150	
Depreciation expense (difference)	1,350	
Calculators (30 × $50)		1,500
To record the sale/depreciation of calculators		

Notice that the retirement system assumes a FIFO cost flow approach in determining the cost of assets, $50 each, that were disposed.

Replacement Method

By the *replacement method, depreciation* is recorded when assets are replaced.

By the replacement depreciation method, the initial acquisition of assets is recorded the same way as by the retirement method; that is, the aggregate cost is increased. However, depreciation expense is the amount paid for new or replacement assets. Any proceeds received from asset dispositions reduces depreciation expense. For our example, the acquisition of 20 new calculators at $45 each is recorded as depreciation as follows:

Depreciation expense (20 × $45)	900	
Cash		900
To record the replacement/depreciation of calculators		

The sale of the old calculators is recorded as a reduction of depreciation:

Cash (30 × $5)	150	
Depreciation expense		150
To record the sale of calculators		

The asset account balance remains the same throughout the life of the aggregate collection of assets.

Because these methods are likely to produce aggregate expense measurements that differ from individual calculations, retirement and replacement methods are acceptable only in situations where the distortion in depreciation expense does not have a material effect on income. These methods occasionally are encountered in regulated industries such as utilities.

Questions For Review of Key Topics

Q 11–1 Explain the similarities in and differences among depreciation, depletion, and amortization.

Q 11–2 Depreciation is a process of cost allocation, not valuation. Explain this statement.

Q 11–3 Identify and define the three characteristics of an asset that must be established to determine periodic depreciation, depletion, or amortization.

Q 11–4 Discuss the factors that influence the estimation of service life for a depreciable asset.

Q 11–5 What is meant by depreciable base? How is it determined?

Q 11–6 Briefly differentiate between activity-based and time-based allocation methods.

Q 11–7 Briefly differentiate between the straight-line depreciation method and accelerated depreciation methods.

Q 11–8 Why are time-based depreciation methods used more frequently than activity-based methods?

Q 11–9 What are some factors that could explain the predominant use of the straight-line depreciation method?

Q 11–10 When an item of property, plant, and equipment is disposed of, how is gain or loss on disposal computed?

Q 11–11 Briefly explain the differences and similarities between the group approach and composite approach to depreciating aggregate assets.

Q 11–12 Define depletion and compare it with depreciation.

Q 11–13 Compare and contrast amortization of intangible assets with depreciation and depletion.

Q 11–14 What are some of the simplifying conventions a company can use to calculate depreciation for partial years?

Q 11–15 Explain the accounting treatment required when a change is made to the estimated service life of a machine.

Q 11–16 Explain the accounting treatment and disclosures required when a change is made in depreciation method.

Q 11–17 Explain the steps required to correct an error in accounting for property, plant, and equipment and intangible assets that is discovered in a year subsequent to the year the error was made.

Q 11–18 Explain what is meant by the impairment of the value of property, plant, and equipment and intangible assets. How should these impairments be accounted for?

Q 11–19 Explain the differences in the accounting treatment of repairs and maintenance, additions, improvements, and rearrangements.

IFRS **Q 11–20** Identify any differences between U.S. GAAP and International Financial Reporting Standards in the subsequent valuation of property, plant, and equipment and intangible assets.

IFRS **Q 11–21** Briefly explain the difference between U.S. GAAP and IFRS in the *measurement* of an impairment loss for property, plant, and equipment and finite-life intangible assets.

IFRS **Q 11–22** Briefly explain the differences between U.S. GAAP and IFRS in the measurement of an impairment loss for goodwill.

IFRS **Q 11–23** Under U.S. GAAP, litigation costs to successfully defend an intangible right are capitalized and amortized over the remaining useful life of the related intangible. How are these costs typically accounted for under IFRS?

Brief Exercises

BE 11–1
Cost allocation
● LO11–1

At the beginning of its fiscal year, Koeplin Corporation purchased a machine for $50,000. At the end of the year, the machine had a fair value of $32,000. Koeplin's controller recorded depreciation of $18,000 for the year, the decline in the machine's value. Why is this an incorrect approach to measuring periodic depreciation?

BE 11–2
Depreciation methods
● LO11–2

On January 1, 2018, Canseco Plumbing Fixtures purchased equipment for $30,000. Residual value at the end of an estimated four-year service life is expected to be $2,000. The company expects the machine to operate for 10,000 hours. Calculate depreciation expense for 2018 and 2019 using each of the following depreciation methods: (a) straight line, (b) sum-of-the-years'-digits, (c) double-declining balance, and (d) units-of-production using machine hours. The machine operated for 2,200 and 3,000 hours in 2018 and 2019, respectively.

BE 11–3
Depreciation methods; partial periods
● LO11–2

Refer to the situation described in BE 11–2. Assume the machine was purchased on March 31, 2018, instead of January 1. Calculate depreciation expense for 2018 and 2019 using each of the following depreciation methods: (a) straight line, (b) sum-of-the-years'-digits, and (c) double-declining balance.

BE 11–4
Disposal of property, plant, and equipment
● LO11–2

Lawler Clothing sold manufacturing equipment for $16,000. Lawler originally purchased the equipment for $80,000, and depreciation through the date of sale totaled $71,000. What was the gain or loss on the sale of the equipment?

BE 11–5
Disposal of property, plant, and equipment
● LO11–2

Funseth Farms Inc. purchased a tractor in 2015 at a cost of $30,000. The tractor was sold for $3,000 in 2018. Depreciation recorded through the disposal date totaled $26,000. Prepare the journal entry to record the sale. Now assume the tractor was sold for $10,000; prepare the journal entry to record the sale.

BE 11–6
Disposal of property, plant, and equipment and intangible assets
● LO11–2

On July 15, 2018, Cottonwood Industries sold a patent and equipment to Roquemore Corporation for $750,000 and $325,000, respectively. The book value of the patent and equipment on the date of sale were $120,000 and $400,000 (cost of $550,000 less accumulated depreciation of $150,000), respectively. Prepare the journal entries to record the sales of the patent and equipment.

BE 11–7
Group depreciation; disposal
● LO11–2

Mondale Winery depreciates its equipment using the group method. The cost of equipment purchased in 2018 totaled $425,000. The estimated residual value of the equipment was $40,000 and the group depreciation rate was determined to be 18%. What is the annual depreciation for the group? If equipment that cost $42,000 is sold in 2019 for $35,000, what amount of gain or loss will the company recognize for the sale?

BE 11–8
Depletion
● LO11–3

Fitzgerald Oil and Gas incurred costs of $8.25 million for the acquisition and development of a natural gas deposit. The company expects to extract 3 million cubic feet of natural gas during a four-year period. Natural gas extracted during years 1 and 2 were 700,000 and 800,000 cubic feet, respectively. What was the depletion for year 1 and year 2?

BE 11–9
Amortization; Partial periods
● LO11–4

On June 28 Lexicon Corporation acquired 100% of the common stock of Gulf & Eastern. The purchase price allocation included the following items: $4 million, patent; $3 million, developed technology; $2 million, in-process research and development; $5 million, goodwill. Lexicon's policy is to amortize intangible assets using the straight-line method, no residual value, and a five-year useful life. What is the total amount of expenses (ignoring taxes) that would appear in Lexicon's income statement for the year ended December 31 related to these items?

BE 11–10
Change in estimate; useful life of equipment
● LO11–5

At the beginning of 2016, Robotics Inc. acquired a manufacturing facility for $12 million. $9 million of the purchase price was allocated to the building. Depreciation for 2016 and 2017 was calculated using the straight-line method, a 25-year useful life, and a $1 million residual value. In 2018, the estimates of useful life and residual value were changed to 20 years and $500,000, respectively. What is depreciation on the building for 2018?

BE 11–11
Change in principle; change in depreciation method
● LO11–6

Refer to the situation described in BE 11–10. Assume that instead of changing the useful life and residual value, in 2018 the company switched to the double-declining-balance depreciation method. How should Robotics account for the change? What is depreciation on the building for 2018?

BE 11–12
Error correction
● LO11–7

Refer to the situation described in BE 11–10. Assume that 2016 depreciation was incorrectly recorded as $32,000. This error was discovered in 2018. How should Robotics account for the error? What is depreciation on the building for 2018 assuming no change in estimate of useful life or residual value?

BE 11–13
Impairment; property, plant, and equipment
● LO11–8

Collison and Ryder Company (C&R) has been experiencing declining market conditions for its sportswear division. Management decided to test the assets of the division for possible impairment. The test revealed the following: book value of division's assets, $26.5 million; fair value of division's assets, $21 million; sum of estimated future cash flows generated from the division's assets, $28 million. What amount of impairment loss should C&R recognize?

BE 11–14
Impairment; property, plant, and equipment
● LO11–8

Refer to the situation described in BE 11–13. Assume that the sum of estimated future cash flows is $24 million instead of $28 million. What amount of impairment loss should C&R recognize?

BE 11–15
IFRS; impairment; property, plant, and equipment
● LO11–8, LO11–10

IFRS

Refer to the situation described in BE 11–13. Assume that the present value of the estimated future cash flows generated from the division's assets is $22 million and that their fair value approximates fair value less costs to sell. What amount of impairment loss should C&R recognize if the company prepares its financial statements according to IFRS?

BE 11–16
Impairment; goodwill
● LO11–8

WebHelper Inc. acquired 100% of the outstanding stock of Silicon Chips Corporation (SCC) for $45 million, of which $15 million was allocated to goodwill. At the end of the current fiscal year, an impairment test revealed the following: fair value of SCC, $40 million; fair value of SCC's net assets (excluding goodwill), $31 million; book value of SCC's net assets (including goodwill), $42 million. What amount of impairment loss should WebHelper recognize?

BE 11–17
Impairment; goodwill
● LO11–8

Refer to the situation described in BE 11–16. Assume that the fair value of SCC is $44 million instead of $40 million. What amount of impairment loss should WebHelper recognize?

BE 11–18
IFRS; impairment; goodwill
● LO11–10

IFRS

Refer to the situation described in BE 11–16. Assume that SCC's fair value of $40 million approximates fair value less costs to sell and that the present value of SCC's estimated future cash flows is $41 million. If WebHelper prepares its financial statements according to IFRS and SCC is considered a cash-generating unit, what amount of impairment loss, if any, should WebHelper recognize?

BE 11–19
Subsequent expenditures
● LO11–9

Demmert Manufacturing incurred the following expenditures during the current fiscal year: annual maintenance on its machinery, $5,400; remodeling of offices, $22,000; rearrangement of the shipping and receiving area resulting in an increase in productivity, $35,000; addition of a security system to the manufacturing facility, $25,000. How should Demmert account for each of these expenditures?

Exercises

E 11–1
Depreciation methods
● LO11–2

On January 1, 2018, the Excel Delivery Company purchased a delivery van for $33,000. At the end of its five-year service life, it is estimated that the van will be worth $3,000. During the five-year period, the company expects to drive the van 100,000 miles.

Required:

Calculate annual depreciation for the five-year life of the van using each of the following methods. Round all computations to the nearest dollar.

1. Straight line
2. Sum-of-the-years'-digits
3. Double-declining balance
4. Units of production using miles driven as a measure of output, and the following actual mileage:

Year	Miles
2018	22,000
2019	24,000
2020	15,000
2021	20,000
2022	21,000

E 11–2
Depreciation methods
● LO11–2

On January 1, 2018, the Allegheny Corporation purchased machinery for $115,000. The estimated service life of the machinery is 10 years and the estimated residual value is $5,000. The machine is expected to produce 220,000 units during its life.

Required:
Calculate depreciation for 2018 and 2019 using each of the following methods. Round all computations to the nearest dollar.
1. Straight line
2. Sum-of-the-years'-digits
3. Double-declining balance
4. One hundred fifty percent declining balance
5. Units of production (units produced in 2018, 30,000; units produced in 2019, 25,000)

E 11–3
Depreciation methods; partial periods
● LO11–2

[This is a variation of Exercise 11–2 modified to focus on depreciation for partial years.]

On October 1, 2018, the Allegheny Corporation purchased machinery for $115,000. The estimated service life of the machinery is 10 years and the estimated residual value is $5,000. The machine is expected to produce 220,000 units during its life.

Required:
Calculate depreciation for 2018 and 2019 using each of the following methods. Partial-year depreciation is calculated based on the number of months the asset is in service. Round all computations to the nearest dollar.
1. Straight line
2. Sum-of-the-years'-digits
3. Double-declining balance
4. One hundred fifty percent declining balance
5. Units of production (units produced in 2018, 10,000; units produced in 2019, 25,000)

E 11–4
Depreciation methods; asset addition; partial period
● LO11–2, LO11–9

Tristen Company purchased a five-story office building on January 1, 2016, at a cost of $5,000,000. The building has a residual value of $200,000 and a 30-year life. The straight-line depreciation method is used. On June 30, 2018, construction of a sixth floor was completed at a cost of $1,650,000.

Required:
Calculate the depreciation on the building and building addition for 2018 and 2019 assuming that the addition did not change the life or residual value of the building.

E 11–5
Depreciation methods; solving for unknowns
● LO11–2

For each of the following depreciable assets, determine the missing amount (?). Abbreviations for depreciation methods are SL for straight line, SYD for sum-of-the-years'-digits, and DDB for double-declining balance.

Asset	Cost	Residual Value	Service Life (Years)	Depreciation Method	Depreciation (Year 2)
A	?	$20,000	5	DDB	$24,000
B	$ 40,000	?	8	SYD	7,000
C	65,000	5,000	?	SL	6,000
D	230,000	10,000	10	?	22,000
E	200,000	20,000	8	150%DB	?

E 11–6
Depreciation methods; partial periods
● LO11–2

On April 30, 2018, Quality Appliances purchased equipment for $260,000. The estimated service life of the equipment is six years and the estimated residual value is $20,000. Quality's fiscal year ends on December 31.

Required:
Calculate depreciation for 2018 and 2019 using each of the three methods listed. Quality calculates partial year depreciation based on the number of months the asset is in service. Round all computations to the nearest dollar.
1. Straight-line
2. Sum-of-the-years'-digits
3. Double-declining balance

E 11–7
Depreciation methods; partial periods
● LO11–2

On March 31, 2018, Susquehanna Insurance purchased an office building for $12,000,000. Based on their relative fair values, one-third of the purchase price was allocated to the land and two-thirds to the building. Furniture and fixtures were purchased separately from office equipment on the same date for $1,200,000 and $700,000, respectively. The company uses the straight-line method to depreciate its buildings and the double-declining-balance method to depreciate all other depreciable assets. The estimated useful lives and residual values of these assets are as follows:

	Service Life	Residual Value
Building	30	10% of cost
Furniture and fixtures	10	10% of cost
Office equipment	5	$30,000

Required:
Calculate depreciation for 2018 and 2019.

E 11–8
IFRS; depreciation; partial periods
● LO11–2, LO11–10
IFRS

On June 30, 2018, Rosetta Granite purchased a machine for $120,000. The estimated useful life of the machine is eight years and no residual value is anticipated. An important component of the machine is a specialized high-speed drill that will need to be replaced in four years. The $20,000 cost of the drill is included in the $120,000 cost of the machine. Rosetta uses the straight-line depreciation method for all machinery.

Required:
1. Calculate depreciation for 2018 and 2019 applying the typical U.S. GAAP treatment.
2. Repeat requirement 1 applying IFRS.

E 11–9
IFRS; revaluation of machinery; depreciation; partial periods
● LO11–10
IFRS

Dower Corporation prepares its financial statements according to IFRS. On March 31, 2018, the company purchased equipment for $240,000. The equipment is expected to have a six-year useful life with no residual value. Dower uses the straight-line depreciation method for all equipment. On December 31, 2018, the end of the company's fiscal year, Dower chooses to revalue the equipment to its fair value of $220,000.

Required:
1. Calculate depreciation for 2018.
2. Prepare the journal entry to record the revaluation of the equipment. Round calculations to the nearest thousand.
3. Calculate depreciation for 2019.
4. Repeat requirement 2 assuming that the fair value of the equipment at the end of 2018 is $195,000.

E 11–10
Disposal of property, plant, and equipment
● LO11–2

Mercury Inc. purchased equipment in 2016 at a cost of $400,000. The equipment was expected to produce 700,000 units over the next five years and have a residual value of $50,000. The equipment was sold for $210,000 part way through 2018. Actual production in each year was: 2016 = 100,000 units; 2017 = 160,000 units; 2018 = 80,000 units. Mercury uses units-of-production depreciation, and all depreciation has been recorded through the disposal date.

Required:
1. Prepare the journal entry to record the sale.
2. Assuming that the equipment was sold for $245,000, prepare the journal entry to record the sale.

E 11–11
Disposal of property, plant, and equipment; partial periods
● LO11–2

On July 1, 2013, Farm Fresh Industries purchased a specialized delivery truck for $126,000. At the time, Farm Fresh estimated the truck to have a useful life of eight years and a residual value of $30,000. On March 1, 2018, the truck was sold for $58,000. Farm Fresh uses the straight-line depreciation method for all of its plant and equipment. Partial-year depreciation is calculated based on the number of months the asset is in service.

Required:
1. Prepare the journal entry to update depreciation in 2018.
2. Prepare the journal entry to record the sale of the truck.
3. Assuming that the truck was sold for $80,000, prepare the journal entry to record the sale.

E 11–12
Depreciation methods; disposal; partial periods
● LO11–2

Howarth Manufacturing Company purchased a lathe on June 30, 2014, at a cost of $80,000. The residual value of the lathe was estimated to be $5,000 at the end of a five-year life. The lathe was sold on March 31, 2018, for $17,000. Howarth uses the straight-line depreciation method for all of its plant and equipment. Partial-year depreciation is calculated based on the number of months the asset is in service.

Required:
1. Prepare a schedule to calculate the gain or loss on the sale.
2. Prepare the journal entry to record the sale.

3. Assuming that Howarth had instead used the sum-of-the-years'-digits depreciation method, prepare the journal entry to record the sale.

E 11–13
Group depreciation
● LO11–2

Highsmith Rental Company purchased an apartment building early in 2018. There are 20 apartments in the building and each is furnished with major kitchen appliances. The company has decided to use the group depreciation method for the appliances. The following data are available:

Appliance	Cost	Residual Value	Service Life (in years)
Stoves	$15,000	$3,000	6
Refrigerators	10,000	1,000	5
Dishwashers	8,000	500	4

In 2021, three new refrigerators costing $2,700 were purchased for cash. The old refrigerators, which originally cost $1,500, were sold for $200.

Required:
1. Calculate the group depreciation rate, group life, and depreciation for 2018.
2. Prepare the journal entries to record the purchase of the new refrigerators and the sale of the old refrigerators.

E 11–14
Double-declining-balance method; switch to straight line
● LO11–2, LO11–6

On January 2, 2018, the Jackson Company purchased equipment to be used in its manufacturing process. The equipment has an estimated life of eight years and an estimated residual value of $30,625. The expenditures made to acquire the asset were as follows:

Purchase price	$154,000
Freight charges	2,000
Installation charges	4,000

Jackson's policy is to use the double-declining-balance (DDB) method of depreciation in the early years of the equipment's life and then switch to straight line halfway through the equipment's life.

Required:
1. Calculate depreciation for each year of the asset's eight-year life.
2. Discuss the accounting treatment of the depreciation on the equipment.

E 11–15
Depletion
● LO11–3

On April 17, 2018, the Loadstone Mining Company purchased the rights to a coal mine. The purchase price plus additional costs necessary to prepare the mine for extraction of the coal totaled $4,500,000. The company expects to extract 900,000 tons of coal during a four-year period. During 2018, 240,000 tons were extracted and sold immediately.

Required:
1. Calculate depletion for 2018.
2. Discuss the accounting treatment of the depletion calculated in requirement 1.

E 11–16
Depreciation and depletion
● LO11–2, LO11–3

At the beginning of 2018, Terra Lumber Company purchased a timber tract from Boise Cantor for $3,200,000. After the timber is cleared, the land will have a residual value of $600,000. Roads to enable logging operations were constructed and completed on March 30, 2018. The cost of the roads, which have no residual value and no alternative use after the tract is cleared, was $240,000. During 2018, Terra logged 500,000 of the estimated five million board feet of timber.

Required:
Calculate the 2018 depletion of the timber tract and depreciation of the logging roads assuming the units-of-production method is used for both assets.

E 11–17
Cost of a natural resource; depletion and depreciation; Chapters 10 and 11
● LO11–2, LO11–3

[This exercise is a continuation of Exercise 10–4 in Chapter 10 focusing on depletion and depreciation.]

Jackpot Mining Company operates a copper mine in central Montana. The company paid $1,000,000 in 2018 for the mining site and spent an additional $600,000 to prepare the mine for extraction of the copper. After the copper is extracted in approximately four years, the company is required to restore the land to its original condition, including repaving of roads and replacing a greenbelt. The company has provided the following three cash flow possibilities for the restoration costs:

	Cash Outflow	Probability
1	$300,000	25%
2	400,000	40%
3	600,000	35%

To aid extraction, Jackpot purchased some new equipment on July 1, 2018, for $120,000. After the copper is removed from this mine, the equipment will be sold for an estimated residual amount of $20,000. There will be no residual value for the copper mine. The credit-adjusted risk-free rate of interest is 10%.

The company expects to extract 10 million pounds of copper from the mine. Actual production was 1.6 million pounds in 2018 and 3 million pounds in 2019.

Required:

1. Compute depletion and depreciation on the mine and mining equipment for 2018 and 2019. The units-of-production method is used to calculate depreciation.
2. Discuss the accounting treatment of the depletion and depreciation on the mine and mining equipment.

E 11–18
Amortization
● LO11–4, LO11–5

Janes Company provided the following information on intangible assets:

a. A patent was purchased from the Lou Company for $700,000 on January 1, 2016. Janes estimated the remaining useful life of the patent to be 10 years. The patent was carried on Lou's accounting records at a net book value of $350,000 when Lou sold it to Janes.
b. During 2018, a franchise was purchased from the Rink Company for $500,000. The contractual life of the franchise is 10 years and Janes records a full year of amortization in the year of purchase.
c. Janes incurred research and development costs in 2018 as follows:

Materials and supplies	$140,000
Personnel	180,000
Indirect costs	60,000
Total	$380,000

d. Effective January 1, 2018, based on new events that have occurred, Janes estimates that the remaining life of the patent purchased from Lou is only five more years.

Required:

1. Prepare the entries necessary for years 2016 through 2018 to reflect the above information.
2. Prepare a schedule showing the intangible asset section of Janes's December 31, 2018, balance sheet.

E 11–19
Patent amortization; patent defense
● LO11–4, LO11–9

On January 2, 2018, David Corporation purchased a patent for $500,000. The remaining legal life is 12 years, but the company estimated that the patent will be useful only for eight years. In January 2020, the company incurred legal fees of $45,000 in successfully defending a patent infringement suit. The successful defense did not change the company's estimate of useful life.

Required:

Prepare journal entries related to the patent for 2018, 2019, and 2020.

E 11–20
Change in estimate; useful life of patent
● LO11–4, LO11–5

Van Frank Telecommunications has a patent on a cellular transmission process. The company has amortized the patent on a straight-line basis since 2014, when it was acquired at a cost of $9 million at the beginning of that year. Due to rapid technological advances in the industry, management decided that the patent would benefit the company over a total of six years rather than the nine-year life being used to amortize its cost. The decision was made at the beginning of 2018.

Required:

Prepare the year-end journal entry for patent amortization in 2018. No amortization was recorded during the year.

E 11–21
IFRS; revaluation of patent; amortization
● LO11–10

IFRS

Saint John Corporation prepares its financial statements according to IFRS. On June 30, 2018, the company purchased a franchise for $1,200,000. The franchise is expected to have a 10-year useful life with no residual value. Saint John uses the straight-line amortization method for all intangible assets. On December 31, 2018, the end of the company's fiscal year, Saint John chooses to revalue the franchise. There is an active market for this particular franchise and its fair value on December 31, 2018, is $1,180,000.

Required:

1. Calculate amortization for 2018.
2. Prepare the journal entry to record the revaluation of the patent.
3. Calculate amortization for 2019.

E 11–22
Change in estimate; useful life and residual value of equipment
● LO11–2, LO11–5

Wardell Company purchased a minicomputer on January 1, 2016, at a cost of $40,000. The computer was depreciated using the straight-line method over an estimated five-year life with an estimated residual value of $4,000. On January 1, 2018, the estimate of useful life was changed to a total of 10 years, and the estimate of residual value was changed to $900.

Required:

1. Prepare the year-end journal entry for depreciation in 2018. No depreciation was recorded during the year.
2. Repeat requirement 1 assuming that the company uses the sum-of-the-years'-digits method instead of the straight-line method.

E 11–23
Change in principle; change in depreciation methods
● LO11–2, LO11–6

Alteran Corporation purchased office equipment for $1.5 million in 2015. The equipment is being depreciated over a 10-year life using the sum-of-the-years'-digits method. The residual value is expected to be $300,000. At the beginning of 2018, Alteran decided to change to the straight-line depreciation method for this equipment.

Required:

Prepare the journal entry to record depreciation for 2018.

E 11–24
Change in principle; change in depreciation methods
● LO11–2, LO11–6

For financial reporting, Clinton Poultry Farms has used the declining-balance method of depreciation for conveyor equipment acquired at the beginning of 2015 for $2,560,000. Its useful life was estimated to be six years, with a $160,000 residual value. At the beginning of 2018, Clinton decides to change to the straight-line method. The effect of this change on depreciation for each year is as follows:

	($ in thousands)		
Year	Straight Line	Declining Balance	Difference
2015	$ 400	$ 853	$453
2016	400	569	169
2017	400	379	(21)
	$1,200	$1,801	$601

Required:

1. Briefly describe the way Clinton should report this accounting change in the 2016–2018 comparative financial statements.
2. Prepare any 2018 journal entry related to the change.

E 11–25
Error correction
● LO11–2, LO11–7

In 2018, internal auditors discovered that PKE Displays, Inc. had debited an expense account for the $350,000 cost of equipment purchased on January 1, 2015. The equipment's life was expected to be five years with no residual value. Straight-line depreciation is used by PKE.

Required:

1. Prepare the correcting entry assuming the error was discovered in 2018 before the adjusting and closing entries. (Ignore income taxes.)
2. Assume the error was discovered in 2020 after the 2019 financial statements are issued. Prepare the correcting entry.

E 11–26
Impairment; property, plant, and equipment
● LO11–8

Chadwick Enterprises, Inc. operates several restaurants throughout the Midwest. Three of its restaurants located in the center of a large urban area have experienced declining profits due to declining population. The company's management has decided to test the assets of the restaurants for possible impairment. The relevant information for these assets is presented below.

Book value	$6.5 million
Estimated undiscounted sum of future cash flows	4.0 million
Fair value	3.5 million

Required:

1. Determine the amount of the impairment loss, if any.
2. Repeat requirement 1 assuming that the estimated undiscounted sum of future cash flows is $6.8 million and fair value is $5 million.

E 11–27
IFRS; impairment; property, plant, and equipment
● LO11–10

IFRS

Refer to the situation described in Exercise 11–26.

Required:

How might your solution differ if Chadwick Enterprises, Inc. prepares its financial statements according to International Financial Reporting Standards? Assume that the fair value amount given in the exercise equals both (a) the fair value less costs to sell and (b) the present value of estimated future cash flows.

E 11–28
IFRS; Impairment; property, plant, and equipment
● LO11–8, LO11–10

IFRS

Collinsworth LTD., a U.K. company, prepares its financial statements according to International Financial Reporting Standards. Late in its 2018 fiscal year, a significant adverse change in business climate indicated to management that the assets of its appliance division may be impaired. The following data relate to the division's assets:

	(£ in millions)
Book value	£220
Undiscounted sum of estimated future cash flows	210
Present value of future cash flows	150
Fair value less cost to sell (determined by appraisal)	145

Required:

1. What amount of impairment loss, if any, should Collinsworth recognize?
2. Assume that Collinsworth prepares its financial statements according to U.S. GAAP and that fair value less cost to sell approximates fair value. What amount of impairment loss, if any, should Collinsworth recognize?

E 11–29
Impairment; property, plant, and equipment
● LO11–8

General Optic Corporation operates a manufacturing plant in Arizona. Due to a significant decline in demand for the product manufactured at the Arizona site, an impairment test is deemed appropriate. Management has acquired the following information for the assets at the plant:

Cost	$ 32,500,000
Accumulated depreciation	14,200,000
General's estimate of the total cash flows to be generated by selling the products manufactured at its Arizona plant, not discounted to present value	15,000,000

The fair value of the Arizona plant is estimated to be $11,000,000.

Required:

1. Determine the amount of impairment loss, if any.
2. If a loss is indicated, where would it appear in General Optic's multiple-step income statement?
3. If a loss is indicated, prepare the entry to record the loss.
4. Repeat requirement 1 assuming that the estimated undiscounted sum of future cash flows is $12,000,000 instead of $15,000,000.
5. Repeat requirement 1 assuming that the estimated undiscounted sum of future cash flows is $19,000,000 instead of $15,000,000

E 11–30
Impairment; goodwill
● LO11–8

In 2016, Alliant Corporation acquired Centerpoint, Inc. for $300 million, of which $50 million was allocated to goodwill. At the end of 2018, management has provided the following information for a required goodwill impairment test:

Fair value of Centerpoint, Inc.	$220 million
Fair value of Centerpoint's net assets (excluding goodwill)	200 million
Book value of Centerpoint's net assets (including goodwill)	250 million

Required:

1. Determine the amount of the impairment loss.
2. Repeat requirement 1 assuming that the fair value of Centerpoint is $270 million.

E 11–31
IFRS; impairment; goodwill
● LO11–10

IFRS

Refer to the situation described in E 11–30, requirement 1. Alliant prepares its financial statements according to IFRS, and Centerpoint is considered a cash-generating unit. Assume that Centerpoint's fair value of $220 million approximates fair value less costs to sell and that the present value of Centerpoint's estimated future cash flows is $225 million.

Required:

Determine the amount of goodwill impairment loss Alliant should recognize.

E 11–32
Goodwill valuation and impairment; Chapters 10 and 11
● LO11–8

On May 28, 2018, Pesky Corporation acquired all of the outstanding common stock of Harman, Inc. for $420 million. The fair value of Harman's identifiable tangible and intangible assets totaled $512 million, and the fair value of liabilities assumed by Pesky was $150 million.

Pesky performed a goodwill impairment test at the end of its fiscal year ended December 31, 2018. Management has provided the following information:

Fair value of Harman, Inc.	$400 million
Fair value of Harman's net assets (excluding goodwill)	370 million
Book value of Harman's net assets (including goodwill)	410 million

Required:

1. Determine the amount of goodwill that resulted from the Harman acquisition.
2. Determine the amount of goodwill impairment loss that Pesky should recognize at the end of 2018, if any.
3. If an impairment loss is required, prepare the journal entry to record the loss.

E 11–33
FASB codification research
● LO11–8

The *FASB Accounting Standards Codification* represents the single source of authoritative U.S. generally accepted accounting principles.

Required:

1. Obtain the relevant authoritative literature on the impairment or disposal of long-lived assets using the *FASB Accounting Standards Codification* at the FASB website (www.fasb.org). Indicate the Codification topic number that provides guidance on accounting for the impairment of long-lived assets.
2. What is the specific citation that discusses the disclosures required in the notes to the financial statements for the impairment of long-lived assets classified as held and used?
3. Describe the disclosure requirements.

E 11–34
FASB codification research
● LO11–2, LO11–1, LO11–6, LO11–8

Access the *FASB Accounting Standards Codification* at the FASB website (www.fasb.org). Determine the specific citation for each of the following items:

1. Depreciation involves a systematic and rational allocation of cost rather than a process of valuation
2. The calculation of an impairment loss for property, plant, and equipment
3. Accounting for a change in depreciation method
4. Goodwill should not be amortized

E 11–35
Subsequent expenditures
● LO11–9

Belltone Company made the following expenditures related to its 10-year-old manufacturing facility:

1. The heating system was replaced at a cost of $250,000. The cost of the old system was not known. The company accounts for improvements as reductions of accumulated depreciation.
2. A new wing was added at a cost of $750,000. The new wing substantially increases the productive capacity of the plant.
3. Annual building maintenance was performed at a cost of $14,000.
4. All of the equipment on the assembly line in the plant was rearranged at a cost of $50,000. The rearrangement clearly increases the productive capacity of the plant.

Required:

Prepare journal entries to record each of the above expenditures.

E 11–36
IFRS; amortization; cost to defend a patent
● LO11–4, LO11–9, LO11–10
IFRS

On September 30, 2016, Leeds LTD. acquired a patent in conjunction with the purchase of another company. The patent, valued at $6 million, was estimated to have a 10-year life and no residual value. Leeds uses the straight-line method of amortization for intangible assets. At the beginning of January 2018, Leeds successfully defended its patent against infringement. Litigation costs totaled $500,000.

Required:

1. Calculate amortization of the patent for 2016 and 2017.
2. Prepare the journal entry to record the 2018 litigation costs.
3. Calculate amortization for 2018.
4. Repeat requirements 2 and 3 assuming that Leeds prepares its financial statements according to IFRS.

E 11–37
Concepts; terminology
● LO11–1 through LO11–6, LO11–8

Listed below are several items and phrases associated with depreciation, depletion, and amortization. Pair each item from List A with the item from List B (by letter) that is most appropriately associated with it.

List A	List B
_____ 1. Depreciation	a. Cost allocation for natural resource
_____ 2. Service life	b. Accounted for prospectively
_____ 3. Depreciable base	c. When there has been a significant decline in value
_____ 4. Activity-based methods	d. The amount of use expected from plant and equipment and finite-life intangible assets
_____ 5. Time-based methods	e. Estimates service life in units of output
_____ 6. Double-declining balance	f. Cost less residual value
_____ 7. Group method	g. Cost allocation for plant and equipment
_____ 8. Composite method	h. Does not subtract residual value from cost
_____ 9. Depletion	i. Accounted for in the same way as a change in estimate
_____ 10. Amortization	j. Aggregates assets that are similar
_____ 11. Change in useful life	k. Aggregates assets that are physically unified
_____ 12. Change in depreciation method	l. Cost allocation for an intangible asset
_____ 13. Write-down of asset	m. Estimates service life in years

E 11–38
Retirement and replacement depreciation
● Appendix B

Cadillac Construction Company uses the retirement method to determine depreciation on its small tools. During 2016, the first year of the company's operations, tools were purchased at a cost of $8,000. In 2018, tools originally costing $2,000 were sold for $250 and replaced with new tools costing $2,500.

Required:

1. Prepare journal entries to record each of the above transactions.
2. Repeat requirement 1 assuming that the company uses the replacement depreciation method instead of the retirement method.

Problems

P 11–1
Depreciation methods; change in methods
● LO11–2, LO11–6

The fact that generally accepted accounting principles allow companies flexibility in choosing between certain allocation methods can make it difficult for a financial analyst to compare periodic performance from firm to firm.

Suppose you were a financial analyst trying to compare the performance of two companies. Company A uses the double-declining-balance depreciation method. Company B uses the straight-line method. You have the following information taken from the 12/31/2018 year-end financial statements for Company B:

Income Statement	
Depreciation expense	$ 10,000
Balance Sheet	
Assets:	
Plant and equipment, at cost	$200,000
Less: Accumulated depreciation	(40,000)
Net	$160,000

You also determine that all of the assets constituting the plant and equipment of Company B were acquired at the same time, and that all of the $200,000 represents depreciable assets. Also, all of the depreciable assets have the same useful life and residual values are zero.

Required:

1. In order to compare performance with Company A, estimate what B's depreciation expense would have been for 2018 if the double-declining-balance depreciation method had been used by Company B since acquisition of the depreciable assets.
2. If Company B decided to switch depreciation methods in 2018 from the straight line to the double-declining-balance method, prepare the 2018 journal entry to record depreciation for the year, assuming no journal entry for depreciation in 2018 has yet been recorded.

P 11–2
Comprehensive problem; Chapters 10 and 11
● LO11–2, LO11–4

At December 31, 2017, Cord Company's plant asset and accumulated depreciation and amortization accounts had balances as follows:

Category	Plant Asset	Accumulated Depreciation and Amortization
Land	$ 175,000	$ —
Buildings	1,500,000	328,900
Machinery and equipment	1,125,000	317,500
Automobiles and trucks	172,000	100,325
Leasehold improvements	216,000	108,000
Land improvements	—	—

Depreciation methods and useful lives:
Buildings—150% declining balance; 25 years.
Machinery and equipment—Straight line; 10 years.
Automobiles and trucks—150% declining balance; 5 years, all acquired after 2014.
Leasehold improvements—Straight line.
Land improvements—Straight line.

Depreciation is computed to the nearest month and residual values are immaterial. Transactions during 2018 and other information:

a. On January 6, 2018, a plant facility consisting of land and building was acquired from King Corp. in exchange for 25,000 shares of Cord's common stock. On this date, Cord's stock had a fair value of $50 a share. Current assessed values of land and building for property tax purposes are $187,500 and $562,500, respectively.
b. On March 25, 2018, new parking lots, streets, and sidewalks at the acquired plant facility were completed at a total cost of $192,000. These expenditures had an estimated useful life of 12 years.

c. The leasehold improvements were completed on December 31, 2014, and had an estimated useful life of eight years. The related lease, which would terminate on December 31, 2020, was renewable for an additional four-year term. On April 30, 2018, Cord exercised the renewal option.
d. On July 1, 2018, machinery and equipment were purchased at a total invoice cost of $325,000. Additional costs of $10,000 for delivery and $50,000 for installation were incurred.
e. On August 30, 2018, Cord purchased a new automobile for $12,500.
f. On September 30, 2018, a truck with a cost of $24,000 and a book value of $9,100 on date of sale was sold for $11,500. Depreciation for the nine months ended September 30, 2018, was $2,650.
g. On December 20, 2018, a machine with a cost of $17,000 and a book value of $2,975 at date of disposition was scrapped without cash recovery.

Required:
1. Prepare a schedule analyzing the changes in each of the plant asset accounts during 2018. This schedule should include columns for beginning balance, increase, decrease, and ending balance for each of the plant asset accounts. Do not analyze changes in accumulated depreciation and amortization.
2. For each asset category, prepare a schedule showing depreciation or amortization expense for the year ended December 31, 2018. Round computations to the nearest whole dollar.

(AICPA adapted)

P 11–3
Depreciation methods; partial periods Chapters 10 and 11
● LO11–2

[This problem is a continuation of Problem 10–3 in Chapter 10 focusing on depreciation.]

Required:
For each asset classification, prepare a schedule showing depreciation for the year ended December 31, 2018, using the following depreciation methods and useful lives:

Land improvements—Straight line; 15 years
Building—150% declining balance; 20 years
Machinery and equipment—Straight line; 10 years
Automobiles—150% declining balance; 3 years

Depreciation is computed to the nearest month and no residual values are used.

(AICPA adapted)

P 11–4
Partial-year depreciation; asset addition; increase in useful life
● LO11–2, LO11–5, LO11–9

On April 1, 2016, the KB Toy Company purchased equipment to be used in its manufacturing process. The equipment cost $48,000, has an eight-year useful life, and has no residual value. The company uses the straight-line depreciation method for all manufacturing equipment.

On January 4, 2018, $12,350 was spent to repair the equipment and to add a feature that increased its operating efficiency. Of the total expenditure, $2,000 represented ordinary repairs and annual maintenance and $10,350 represented the cost of the new feature. In addition to increasing operating efficiency, the total useful life of the equipment was extended to 10 years.

Required:
Prepare journal entries for the following:
1. Depreciation for 2016 and 2017
2. The 2018 expenditure
3. Depreciation for 2018

P 11–5
Property, plant, and equipment and intangible assets; comprehensive
● LO11–2

The Thompson Corporation, a manufacturer of steel products, began operations on October 1, 2016. The accounting department of Thompson has started the fixed-asset and depreciation schedule presented below. You have been asked to assist in completing this schedule. In addition to ascertaining that the data already on the schedule are correct, you have obtained the following information from the company's records and personnel:
a. Depreciation is computed from the first of the month of acquisition to the first of the month of disposition.
b. Land A and Building A were acquired from a predecessor corporation. Thompson paid $812,500 for the land and building together. At the time of acquisition, the land had a fair value of $72,000 and the building had a fair value of $828,000.
c. Land B was acquired on October 2, 2016, in exchange for 3,000 newly issued shares of Thompson's common stock. At the date of acquisition, the stock had a par value of $5 per share and a fair value of $25 per share. During October 2016, Thompson paid $10,400 to demolish an existing building on this land so it could construct a new building.
d. Construction of Building B on the newly acquired land began on October 1, 2017. By September 30, 2018, Thompson had paid $210,000 of the estimated total construction costs of $300,000. Estimated completion and occupancy are July 2019.

e. Certain equipment was donated to the corporation by the city. An independent appraisal of the equipment when donated placed the fair value at $16,000 and the residual value at $2,000.

f. Machine A's total cost of $110,000 includes installation charges of $550 and normal repairs and maintenance of $11,000. Residual value is estimated at $5,500. Machine A was sold on February 1, 2018.

g. On October 1, 2017, Machine B was acquired with a down payment of $4,000 and the remaining payments to be made in 10 annual installments of $4,000 each beginning October 1, 2018. The prevailing interest rate was 8%.

THOMPSON CORPORATION
Fixed Asset and Depreciation Schedule
For Fiscal Years Ended September 30, 2017, and September 30, 2018

Assets	Acquisition Date	Cost	Residual	Depreciation Method	Estimated Life (in years)	Depreciation for Year Ended 9/30 2017	Depreciation for Year Ended 9/30 2018
Land A	10/1/16	$(1)	N/A	N/A	N/A	N/A	N/A
Building A	10/1/16	(2)	$47,500	SL	(3)	$14,000	$(4)
Land B	10/2/16	(5)	N/A	N/A	N/A	N/A	N/A
Building B	Under construction	210,000 to date	—	SL	30	—	(6)
Donated Equipment	10/2/16	(7)	2,000	150% Declining balance	10	(8)	(9)
Machine A	10/2/16	(10)	5,500	Sum-of-the-years'-digits	10	(11)	(12)
Machine B	10/1/17	(13)	—	SL	15	—	(14)

N/A = not applicable

Required:

Supply the correct amount for each numbered item on the schedule. Round each answer to the nearest dollar.

(AICPA adapted)

P 11–6
Depreciation methods; partial-year depreciation; sale of assets
● LO11–2

On March 31, 2018, the Herzog Company purchased a factory complete with machinery and equipment. The allocation of the total purchase price of $1,000,000 to the various types of assets along with estimated useful lives and residual values are as follows:

Asset	Cost	Estimated Residual Value	Estimated Useful Life (in years)
Land	$ 100,000	N/A	N/A
Building	500,000	none	25
Machinery	240,000	10% of cost	8
Equipment	160,000	$13,000	6
Total	$1,000,000		

On June 29, 2019, machinery included in the March 31, 2018, purchase that cost $100,000 was sold for $80,000. Herzog uses the straight-line depreciation method for buildings and machinery and the sum-of-the-years'-digits method for equipment. Partial-year depreciation is calculated based on the number of months an asset is in service.

Required:

1. Compute depreciation expense on the building, machinery, and equipment for 2018.
2. Prepare the journal entries to record (1) depreciation on the machinery sold on June 29, 2019, and (2) the sale of machinery.
3. Compute depreciation expense on the building, remaining machinery, and equipment for 2019.

P 11–7
Depletion; change in estimate
● LO11–3, LO11–5

In 2018, the Marion Company purchased land containing a mineral mine for $1,600,000. Additional costs of $600,000 were incurred to develop the mine. Geologists estimated that 400,000 tons of ore would be extracted. After the ore is removed, the land will have a resale value of $100,000.

To aid in the extraction, Marion built various structures and small storage buildings on the site at a cost of $150,000. These structures have a useful life of 10 years. The structures cannot be moved after the ore has been removed and will be left at the site. In addition, new equipment costing $80,000 was purchased and installed at the site. Marion does not plan to move the equipment to another site, but estimates that it can be sold at auction for $4,000 after the mining project is completed.

In 2018, 50,000 tons of ore were extracted and sold. In 2019, the estimate of total tons of ore in the mine was revised from 400,000 to 487,500. During 2019, 80,000 tons were extracted, of which 60,000 tons were sold.

Required:

1. Compute depletion and depreciation of the mine and the mining facilities and equipment for 2018 and 2019. Marion uses the units-of-production method to determine depreciation on mining facilities and equipment.
2. Compute the book value of the mineral mine, structures, and equipment as of December 31, 2019.
3. Discuss the accounting treatment of the depletion and depreciation on the mine and mining facilities and equipment.

P 11–8
Amortization; partial period
● LO11–4

The following information concerns the intangible assets of Epstein Corporation:

a. On June 30, 2018, Epstein completed the acquisition of the Johnstone Corporation for $2,000,000 in cash. The fair value of the net identifiable assets of Johnstone was $1,700,000.
b. Included in the assets purchased from Johnstone was a patent that was valued at $80,000. The remaining legal life of the patent was 13 years, but Epstein believes that the patent will only be useful for another eight years.
c. Epstein acquired a franchise on October 1, 2018, by paying an initial franchise fee of $200,000. The contractual life of the franchise is 10 years.

Required:

1. Prepare year-end adjusting journal entries to record amortization expense on the intangibles at December 31, 2018.
2. Prepare the intangible asset section of the December 31, 2018, balance sheet.

P 11–9
Straight-line depreciation; disposal; partial period; change in estimate
● LO11–2, LO11–5

The property, plant, and equipment section of the Jasper Company's December 31, 2017, balance sheet contained the following:

Property, plant, and equipment:		
Land		$120,000
Building	$ 840,000	
Less: Accumulated depreciation	(200,000)	640,000
Equipment	180,000	
Less: Accumulated depreciation	?	?
Total property, plant, and equipment		?

The land and building were purchased at the beginning of 2013. Straight-line depreciation is used and a residual value of $40,000 for the building is anticipated.

The equipment is comprised of the following three machines:

Machine	Cost	Date Acquired	Residual Value	Life (in years)
101	$70,000	1/1/15	$7,000	10
102	80,000	6/30/16	8,000	8
103	30,000	9/1/17	3,000	9

The straight-line method is used to determine depreciation on the equipment. On March 31, 2018, Machine 102 was sold for $52,500. Early in 2018, the useful life of machine 101 was revised to seven years in total, and the residual value was revised to zero.

Required:

1. Calculate the accumulated depreciation on the equipment at December 31, 2017.
2. Prepare the journal entry to record 2018 depreciation on machine 102 up to the date of sale.
3. Prepare a schedule to calculate the gain or loss on the sale of machine 102.
4. Prepare the journal entry for the sale of machine 102.
5. Prepare the 2018 year-end journal entries to record depreciation on the building and equipment.

P 11–10
Accounting changes; three accounting situations
● LO11–2, LO11–5, LO11–6

Described below are three independent and unrelated situations involving accounting changes. Each change occurs during 2018 before any adjusting entries or closing entries are prepared.

a. On December 30, 2014, Rival Industries acquired its office building at a cost of $10,000,000. It has been depreciated on a straight-line basis assuming a useful life of 40 years and no residual value. Early in 2018, the estimate of useful life was revised to 28 years in total with no change in residual value.
b. At the beginning of 2014, the Hoffman Group purchased office equipment at a cost of $330,000. Its useful life was estimated to be 10 years with no residual value. The equipment has been depreciated by the sum-of-the-years'-digits method. On January 1, 2018, the company changed to the straight-line method.
c. At the beginning of 2018, Jantzen Specialties, which uses the sum-of-the-years'-digits method, changed to the straight-line method for newly acquired buildings and equipment. The change increased current year net income by $445,000.

Required:

For each situation:

1. Identify the type of change.
2. Prepare any journal entry necessary as a direct result of the change as well as any adjusting entry for 2018 related to the situation described. (Ignore income tax effects.)
3. Briefly describe any other steps that should be taken to appropriately report the situation.

P 11–11
Error correction; change in depreciation method
● LO11–2, LO11–6, LO11–7

Collins Corporation purchased office equipment at the beginning of 2016 and capitalized a cost of $2,000,000. This cost figure included the following expenditures:

Purchase price	$1,850,000
Freight charges	30,000
Installation charges	20,000
Annual maintenance charge	100,000
Total	$2,000,000

The company estimated an eight-year useful life for the equipment. No residual value is anticipated. The double-declining-balance method was used to determine depreciation expense for 2016 and 2017.

In 2018, after the 2017 financial statements were issued, the company decided to switch to the straight-line depreciation method for this equipment. At that time, the company's controller discovered that the original cost of the equipment incorrectly included one year of annual maintenance charges for the equipment.

Required:

1. Ignoring income taxes, prepare the appropriate correcting entry for the equipment capitalization error discovered in 2018.
2. Ignoring income taxes, prepare any 2018 journal entry(s) related to the change in depreciation methods.

P 11–12
Depreciation and amortization; impairment
● LO11–2, LO11–4, LO11–8

At the beginning of 2016, Metatec Inc. acquired Ellison Technology Corporation for $600 million. In addition to cash, receivables, and inventory, the following assets and their fair values were also acquired:

Plant and equipment (depreciable assets)	$150 million
Patent	40 million
Goodwill	100 million

The plant and equipment are depreciated over a 10-year useful life on a straight-line basis. There is no estimated residual value. The patent is estimated to have a 5-year useful life, no residual value, and is amortized using the straight-line method.

At the end of 2018, a change in business climate indicated to management that the assets of Ellison might be impaired. The following amounts have been determined:

Plant and equipment:	
Undiscounted sum of future cash flows	$ 80 million
Fair value	60 million
Patent:	
Undiscounted sum of future cash flows	$ 20 million
Fair value	13 million
Goodwill:	
Fair value of Ellison Technology Corporation	$450 million
Fair value of Ellison's net assets (excluding goodwill)	390 million
Book value of Ellison's net assets (including goodwill)	470 million*

*After first recording any impairment losses on plant and equipment and the patent.

Required:

1. Compute the book value of the plant and equipment and patent at the end of 2018.
2. When should the plant and equipment and the patent be tested for impairment?
3. When should goodwill be tested for impairment?
4. Determine the amount of any impairment loss to be recorded, if any, for the three assets.

P 11–13
Depreciation and depletion; change in useful life; asset retirement obligation; Chapters 10 and 11
● LO11–2, LO11–3, LO11–5

On May 1, 2018, Hecala Mining entered into an agreement with the state of New Mexico to obtain the rights to operate a mineral mine in New Mexico for $10 million. Additional costs and purchases included the following:

Development costs in preparing the mine	$3,200,000
Mining equipment	140,000
Construction of various structures on site	68,000

After the minerals are removed from the mine, the equipment will be sold for an estimated residual value of $10,000. The structures will be torn down.

Geologists estimate that 800,000 tons of ore can be extracted from the mine. After the ore is removed the land will revert back to the state of New Mexico.

The contract with the state requires Hecala to restore the land to its original condition after mining operations are completed in approximately four years. Management has provided the following possible outflows for the restoration costs:

Cash Outflow	Probability
$600,000	30%
700,000	30%
800,000	40%

Hecala's credit-adjusted risk-free interest rate is 8%. During 2018, Hecala extracted 120,000 tons of ore from the mine. The company's fiscal year ends on December 31.

Required:

1. Determine the amount at which Hecala will record the mine.
2. Calculate the depletion of the mine and the depreciation of the mining facilities and equipment for 2018, assuming that Hecala uses the units-of-production method for both depreciation and depletion. Round depletion and depreciation rates to four decimals.
3. How much accretion expense will the company record in its income statement for the 2018 fiscal year?
4. Are depletion of the mine and depreciation of the mining facilities and equipment reported as separate expenses in the income statement? Discuss the accounting treatment of these items in the income statement and balance sheet.
5. During 2019, Hecala changed its estimate of the total amount of ore originally in the mine from 800,000 to 1,000,000 tons. Briefly describe the accounting treatment the company will employ to account for the change *and* calculate the depletion of the mine and depreciation of the mining facilities and equipment for 2019 assuming Hecala extracted 150,000 tons of ore in 2019.

Broaden Your Perspective

Apply your critical-thinking ability to the knowledge you've gained. These cases will provide you an opportunity to develop your research, analysis, judgment, and communication skills. You also will work with other students, integrate what you've learned, apply it in real-world situations, and consider its global and ethical ramifications. This practice will broaden your knowledge and further develop your decision-making abilities.

Analysis Case 11–1
Depreciation, depletion, and amortization
● LO11–1

The terms depreciation, depletion, and amortization all refer to the process of allocating the cost of an asset to the periods the asset is used.

Required:

Discuss the differences between depreciation, depletion, and amortization as the terms are used in accounting for property, plant, and equipment and intangible assets.

Communication Case 11–2
Depreciation
● LO11–1

At a recent luncheon, you were seated next to Mr. Hopkins, the president of a local company that manufactures bicycle parts. He heard that you were a CPA and made the following comments to you:

> Why is it that I am forced to recognize depreciation expense in my company's income statement when I know that I could sell many of my assets for more than I paid for them? I thought that the purpose of the balance sheet was to reflect the value of my business and that the purpose of the income statement was to report the net change in value or wealth of a company. It just doesn't make sense to penalize my profits when there hasn't been any loss in value from using the assets.

At the conclusion of the luncheon, you promised to send him a short explanation of the rationale for current depreciation practices.

Required:

Prepare a letter to Mr. Hopkins. Explain the accounting concept of depreciation and include a brief example in your explanation showing that over the life of the asset the change in value approach to depreciation and the allocation of cost approach will result in the same total effect on income.

Judgment Case 11–3
Straight-line method; composite depreciation
● LO11–1, LO11–2

Portland Co. uses the straight-line depreciation method for depreciable assets. All assets are depreciated individually except manufacturing machinery, which is depreciated by the composite method.

Required:

1. What factors should have influenced Portland's selection of the straight-line depreciation method?
2. a. What benefits should derive from using the composite method rather than the individual basis for manufacturing machinery?
   b. How should Portland have calculated the manufacturing machinery's annual depreciation in its first year of operation?

(AICPA adapted)

Judgment Case 11–4
Depreciation
● LO11–1, LO11–2

At the beginning of the year, Patrick Company acquired a computer to be used in its operations. The computer was delivered by the supplier, installed by Patrick, and placed into operation. The estimated useful life of the computer is five years, and its estimated residual value is significant.

Required:

1. a. What costs should Patrick capitalize for the computer?
   b. What is the objective of depreciation accounting?
2. What is the rationale for using accelerated depreciation methods?

(AICPA adapted)

Judgment Case 11–5
Capitalize or expense; materiality
● LO11–9

Redline Publishers, Inc. produces various manuals ranging from computer software instructional booklets to manuals explaining the installation and use of large pieces of industrial equipment. At the end of 2018, the company's balance sheet reported total assets of $62 million and total liabilities of $40 million. The income statement for 2018 reported net income of $1.1 million, which represents an approximate 3% increase from the prior year. The company's effective income tax rate is 30%.

Near the end of 2018, a variety of expenditures were made to overhaul the company's manufacturing equipment. None of these expenditures exceeded $750, the materiality threshold the company has set for the capitalization of any such expenditure. Even though the overhauls extended the service life of the equipment, the expenditures were expensed, not capitalized.

John Henderson, the company's controller, is worried about the treatment of the overhaul expenditures. Even though no individual expenditure exceeded the $750 materiality threshold, total expenditures were $70,000.

Required:

Should the overhaul expenditures be capitalized or expensed?

Communication Case 11–6
Capitalize or expense; materiality
● LO11–9

The focus of the case is the situation described in Judgment Case 11–5. Your instructor will divide the class into two to six groups depending on the size of the class. The mission of your group is to determine the treatment of the overhaul expenditures.

Required:

1. Each group member should deliberate the situation independently and draft a tentative argument prior to the class session for which the case is assigned.
2. In class, each group will meet for 10 to 15 minutes in different areas of the classroom. During the meeting, group members will take turns sharing their suggestions for the purpose of arriving at a single group treatment.
3. After the allotted time, a spokesperson for each group (selected during the group meetings) will share the group's solution with the class. The goal of the class is to incorporate the views of each group into a consensus approach to the situation.

Integrating Case 11–7
Errors; change in estimate; change in principle; inventory, patent, and equipment
● LO11–5 through LO11–7

Whaley Distributors is a wholesale distributor of electronic components. Financial statements for the year ended December 31, 2018, reported the following amounts and subtotals ($ in millions):

	Assets	Liabilities	Shareholders' Equity	Net Income	Expenses
2017	$640	$330	$310	$210	$150
2018	$820	$400	$420	$230	$175

In 2019 the following situations occurred or came to light:

a. Internal auditors discovered that ending inventories reported in the financial statements the two previous years were misstated due to faulty internal controls. The errors were in the following amounts:

2017 inventory	Overstated by $12 million
2018 inventory	Understated by $10 million

b. A patent costing $18 million at the beginning of 2017, expected to benefit operations for a total of six years, has not been amortized since acquired.

c. Whaley's conveyer equipment has been depreciated by the sum-of-the-years'-digits (SYD) method since constructed at the beginning of 2017 at a cost of $30 million. It has an expected useful life of five years and no expected residual value. At the beginning of 2019, Whaley decided to switch to straight-line depreciation.

Required:

For each situation:

1. Prepare any journal entry necessary as a direct result of the change or error correction as well as any adjusting entry for 2019 related to the situation described. (Ignore tax effects.)
2. Determine the amounts to be reported for each of the items shown above from the 2017 and 2018 financial statements when those amounts are reported again in the 2019, 2018, and 2017 comparative financial statements.

Judgment Case 11–8
Accounting changes
● LO11–5, LO11–6

There are various types of accounting changes, each of which is required to be reported differently.

Required:

1. What type of accounting change is a change from the sum-of-the-years'-digits method of depreciation to the straight-line method for previously recorded assets as a result of new information related to production patterns? Under what circumstances does this type of accounting change occur?
2. What type of accounting change is a change in the expected service life of an asset arising because of more experience with the asset? Under what circumstances does this type of accounting change occur?

(AICPA adapted)

Research Case 11–9
FASB codification; locate and extract relevant information and cite authoritative support for a financial reporting issue; impairment of property, plant, and equipment and intangible assets
● LO11–8

The company controller, Barry Melrose, has asked for your help in interpreting the authoritative accounting literature that addresses the recognition and measurement of impairment losses for property, plant, and equipment and intangible assets. "We have a significant amount of goodwill on our books from last year's acquisition of Churchill Corporation. Also, I think we may have a problem with the assets of some of our factories out West. And one of our divisions is currently considering disposing of a large group of depreciable assets."

Your task as assistant controller is to research the issue.

Required:

1. Obtain the relevant authoritative literature on accounting for the impairment of property, plant, and equipment and intangible assets using the *FASB Accounting Standards Codification*. You might gain access at the FASB website (www.fasb.org). Cite the reference locations regarding impairment of property, plant, and equipment and intangible assets.
2. When should property, plant, and equipment and finite-life intangible assets be tested for impairment?
3. Explain the process for measuring an impairment loss for property, plant, and equipment and finite-life intangible assets to be held and used.
4. What are the specific criteria that must be met for an asset or asset group to be classified as held-for-sale? What is the specific citation reference from the *FASB Accounting Standards Codification* that contains these criteria?
5. Explain the process for measuring an impairment loss for property, plant, and equipment and finite-life intangible assets classified as held-for-sale.

Ethics Case 11–10
Asset impairment
● LO11–8

At the beginning of 2016, the Healthy Life Food Company purchased equipment for $42 million to be used in the manufacture of a new line of gourmet frozen foods. The equipment was estimated to have a 10-year service life and no residual value. The straight-line depreciation method was used to measure depreciation for 2016 and 2017.

Late in 2018, it became apparent that sales of the new frozen food line were significantly below expectations. The company decided to continue production for two more years (2019 and 2020) and then discontinue the line. At that time, the equipment will be sold for minimal scrap values.

The controller, Heather Meyer, was asked by Harvey Dent, the company's chief executive officer (CEO), to determine the appropriate treatment of the change in service life of the equipment. Heather determined that there has been an impairment of value requiring an immediate write-down of the equipment of $12,900,000. The remaining book value would then be depreciated over the equipment's revised service life.

The CEO does not like Heather's conclusion because of the effect it would have on 2018 income. "Looks like a simple revision in service life from 10 years to 5 years to me," Dent concluded. "Let's go with it that way, Heather."

Required:

1. What is the difference in before-tax income between the CEO's and Heather's treatment of the situation?
2. Discuss Heather Meyer's ethical dilemma.

Judgment Case 11–11
Earnings management and accounting changes; impairment
● LO11–5, LO11–6, LO11–8

Companies often are under pressure to meet or beat Wall Street earnings projections in order to increase stock prices and also to increase the value of stock options. Some resort to earnings management practices to artificially create desired results.

Required:

1. How can a company manage earnings by changing its depreciation method? Is this an effective technique to manage earnings?
2. How can a company manage earnings by changing the estimated useful lives of depreciable assets? Is this an effective technique to manage earnings?
3. Using a fictitious example and numbers you make up, describe in your own words how asset impairment losses could be used to manage earnings. How might that benefit the company?

Trueblood Accounting Case 11–12
Accounting for impairment losses; property, plant, and equipment
● LO11–8

The following Trueblood case is recommended for use with this chapter. The case provides an excellent opportunity for class discussion, group projects, and writing assignments. The case, along with Professor's Discussion Material, can be obtained from the Deloitte Foundation at its website www.deloitte.com/us/truebloodcases.

Case 12–9: Rough Waters Ahead
This case concerns the impairment test for a cruise ship.

Judgment Case 11–13
Subsequent expenditures
● LO11–9

The Cummings Company charged various expenditures made during 2018 to an account called repairs and maintenance expense. You have been asked by your supervisor in the company's internal audit department to review the expenditures to determine if they were appropriately recorded. The amount of each of the transactions included in the account is considered material.

1. Engine tune-up and oil change on the company's 12 delivery trucks—$1,300.
2. Rearrangement of machinery on the main production line—$5,500. It is not evident that the rearrangement will increase operational efficiency.
3. Installation of aluminum siding on the manufacturing plant—$32,000.
4. Replacement of the old air conditioning system in the manufacturing plant with a new system—$120,000.
5. Replacement of broken parts on three machines—$1,500.
6. Annual painting of the manufacturing plant—$11,000.
7. Purchase of new forklift to move finished product to the loading dock—$6,000.
8. Patching leaks in the roof of the manufacturing plant—$6,500. The repair work did not extend the useful life of the roof.

Required:

For each of the transactions listed above, indicate whether the expenditure is appropriately charged to the repair and maintenance expense account, and if not, indicate the proper account to be charged.

Real World Case 11–14
Disposition and depreciation; Chapters 10 and 11; D.R. Horton
● LO11–1

Real World Financials

D.R. Horton, Inc., is the largest homebuilding company by volume in the United States. D.R. Horton reported the following in a disclosure note accompanying its 2015 financial statements ($ in millions):

	2015	2014
Property and equipment	$ 313.8	$ 334.8
Less: Accumulated depreciation	(166.9)	(141.1)
Property, plant, and equipment - Net	$ 146.9	$ 193.7

Also, the company disclosed that the total cost of property and equipment included $26.7 and $66.9 (dollars in millions) in land at the end of 2015 and 2014, respectively. In addition, the statement of cash flows for the year ended December 31, 2015, reported the following as cash flows from investing activities:

	($ in millions)
Purchases of property and equipment	$(56.1)
Proceeds from the sale of property and equipment	56.0

The statement of cash flows also reported 2015 depreciation and amortization of $54.1 million (depreciation of $50.3 and amortization of $3.8).

Required:

1. Assume that all property and equipment acquired during 2015 were purchased for cash. Determine the amount of gain or loss from sale of property and equipment that D.R. Horton recognized during 2015.
2. Assume that D.R. Horton uses the straight-line method to depreciate property and equipment (excluding land). What is the approximate average service life of depreciable assets?

Real World Case 11–15
Depreciation and depletion method; asset impairment; subsequent expenditures; Chevron
● LO11–2, LO11–3, LO11–8, LO11–9

Real World Financials

EDGAR, the Electronic Data Gathering, Analysis, and Retrieval system, performs automated collection, validation, indexing, and forwarding of submissions by companies and others who are required by law to file forms with the U.S. Securities and Exchange Commission (SEC). All publicly traded domestic companies use EDGAR to make the majority of their filings. (Some foreign companies file voluntarily.) Form 10-K, which includes the annual report, is required to be filed on EDGAR. The SEC makes this information available on the Internet.

Required:

1. Access EDGAR on the Internet. The web address is www.sec.gov.
2. Search for Chevron Corporation. Access the 10-K filing for most recent fiscal year. Search or scroll to find the financial statements and related notes.
3. Answer the following questions related to the company's property, plant, and equipment and intangible assets:
   a. Describe the company's depreciation and depletion policies.
   b. Describe the company's policy for subsequent expenditures made for plant and equipment.

IFRS Case 11–16
Subsequent valuation of property, plant, and equipment; comparison of U.S. GAAP and IFRS; GlaxoSmithKline
● LO11–10

Real World Financials

IFRS

GlaxoSmithKline is a global pharmaceutical and consumer health-related products company located in the United Kingdom. The company prepares its financial statements in accordance with International Financial Reporting Standards.

Required:

1. Use the Internet to locate GlaxoSmithKline's most recent annual report. The address is www.gsk.com/en-gb/investors/. Locate the significant accounting policies disclosure note.
2. How does the company value its property, plant, and equipment? Does the company have any other options under IFRS for valuing these assets? How do these options differ from U.S. GAAP?
3. What are the company's policies for possible reversals of impairment losses for goodwill and for other non-current assets? How do these policies differ from U.S. GAAP?

Continuing Cases

Target Case
● LO11–2, LO11–8, LO11–9

Target Corporation prepares its financial statements according to U.S. GAAP. Target's financial statements and disclosure notes for the year ended January 30, 2016, are available in Connect. This material is also available under the Investor Relations link at the company's website (www.target.com).

Required:

1. Compare the property and equipment listed in the balance sheet with the list in Note 14. What are the estimated useful lives for recording depreciation? Why is land not listed in Note 14?
2. Which depreciation method does Target use for property and equipment for financial reporting? Which depreciation method is used for tax purposes? Why might these methods be chosen?
3. How does Target record repairs and maintenance expense?
4. How does Target account for impairment of property and equipment? Were any impairments recorded for the year ended January 30, 2016? If so, what was the amount and what were the reasons for the impairments?
5. From Notes 15 and 16, what was the amount of intangible assets for the year ended January 30, 2016? Were any impairments related to intangible assets recorded for the year ended January 30, 2016? If so, what was the amount and what were the reasons for the impairments?

Air France–KLM Case

● LO11–10

Air France–KLM (AF), a Franco-Dutch company, prepares its financial statements according to International Financial Reporting Standards. AF's financial statements and disclosure notes for the year ended December 31, 2015, are available in Connect. This material is also available under the Finance link at the company's website (www.airfranceklm.com).

Required:

1. AF's property, plant, and equipment is reported at cost. The company has a policy of not revaluing property, plant, and equipment. Suppose AF decided to revalue its flight equipment on December 31, 2015, and that the fair value of the equipment on that date was €10,000 million. Prepare the journal entry to record the revaluation assuming that the journal entry to record annual depreciation had already been recorded. (*Hint:* you will need to locate the original cost and accumulated depreciation of the equipment at the end of the year in the appropriate disclosure note.)
2. Under U.S. GAAP, what alternatives do companies have to value their property, plant, and equipment?
3. AF calculates depreciation of plant and equipment on a straight-line basis, over the useful life of the asset. Describe any differences between IFRS and U.S. GAAP in the calculation of depreciation.
4. When does AF test for the possible impairment of fixed assets? How does this approach differ from U.S. GAAP?
5. Describe the approach AF uses to determine fixed asset impairment losses. (*Hint:* see Note 4.14) How does this approach differ from U.S. GAAP?
6. The following is included in AF's disclosure note 4.13: "Intangible assets are recorded at initial cost less accumulated amortization and any accumulated impairment losses." Assume that on December 31, 2015, AF decided to revalue its Other intangible assets (see Note 18) and that the fair value on that date was determined to be €500 million. Amortization expense for the year already has been recorded. Prepare the journal entry to record the revaluation.

CPA Exam Questions and Simulations

Sample CPA Exam questions from Roger CPA Review are available in Connect as support for the topics in this chapter. These Multiple Choice Questions and Task-Based Simulations include expert-written explanations and solutions, and provide a starting point for students to become familiar with the content and functionality of the actual CPA Exam.

CHAPTER

12 Investments

OVERVIEW

In this chapter, you will learn about various approaches we use to account for investments that companies make in the debt and equity securities of other companies. An investing company always has the option to account for these investments at fair value, with changes in fair values reported in the income statement. However, depending on the nature of a *debt* investment, investors use accounting approaches that either ignore most fair value changes (*held-to-maturity* investments) or that include fair value changes only in other comprehensive income (*available-for-sale* investments) until the debt investment is sold. For an *equity* investment, when an investor owns enough stock to "significantly influence" an investee but does not control it, the investor uses the *equity method* of accounting, which ignores fair value changes but includes a portion of the investee's income in the investor's income. In appendices to this chapter, we discuss other types of investments as well as how to deal with an investment whose value has been "other-than-temporarily impaired."

LEARNING OBJECTIVES

After studying this chapter, you should be able to:

- **LO12–1** Describe the key characteristics of a debt investment and demonstrate how to account for a purchase and for interest revenue. (*p. 644*)
- **LO12–2** Demonstrate how to identify and account for debt investments classified for reporting purposes as held-to-maturity. (*p. 648*)
- **LO12–3** Demonstrate how to identify and account for debt investments classified for reporting purposes as trading securities. (*p. 649*)
- **LO12–4** Demonstrate how to identify and account for debt investments classified for reporting purposes as available-for-sale securities. (*p. 653*)
- **LO12–5** Demonstrate how to identify and account for equity investments classified for reporting purposes as fair value through net income. (*p. 667*)
- **LO12–6** Demonstrate how to identify and account for equity investments accounted for under the equity method. (*p. 672*)
- **LO12–7** Explain the adjustments made in the equity method when the fair value of the net assets underlying an investment exceeds their book value at acquisition. (*pp. 661 and 674*)
- **LO12–8** Explain how electing the fair value option and how impairment recognition affect accounting for investments. (*p. 661* and *679*)
- **LO12–9** Discuss the primary differences between U.S. GAAP and IFRS with respect to investments. (*pp. 660–663, 671, 680,* and *690*)

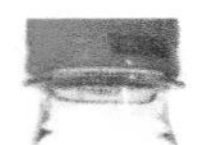

© McGraw-Hill Education/Mark Dierker, photographer

FINANCIAL REPORTING CASE

A Case of Coke

You are the lone accounting major in your five-member group in your Business Policy class. A part of the case your group is working on is the analysis of the financial statements of The Coca-Cola Company.

The marketing major in the group is confused by the following disclosure note included in Coca-Cola's 2015 annual report:

NOTE 3: INVESTMENTS (in part)

Investments in debt securities that the Company has the positive intent and ability to hold to maturity are carried at amortized cost and classified as held-to-maturity. Investments in debt securities that are not classified as held-to-maturity are carried at fair value and classified as either trading or available-for-sale. Realized and unrealized gains and losses on trading securities and realized gains and losses on available-for-sale securities are included in net income. Unrealized gains and losses, net of deferred taxes, on available-for-sale securities are included in our consolidated balance sheets as a component of AOCI . . .

"So they have held-to-maturity securities, trading securities, and available-for-sale securities. What's the difference? And they say that unrealized gains and losses on available-for-sale securities are reported as part of AOCI. What's that? I don't see these gains and losses in the income statement," he complained. "And what about equity method investments? On the balance sheet they have over $12 *billion* of investments accounted for under the equity method! They made almost $500 million on those investments in 2015. Is that cash they can use?"

QUESTIONS

By the time you finish this chapter, you should be able to respond appropriately to the questions posed in this case. Compare your response to the solution provided at the end of the chapter.

1. Why are held-to-maturity securities treated differently from other investment securities? (*p. 648*)
2. Why are unrealized gains and losses on trading securities reported in the income statement? (*p. 650*)
3. Why are unrealized gains and losses on available-for-sale securities not reported in the income statement, but instead are reported in other comprehensive income, and then shown in accumulated other comprehensive income (AOCI) in the balance sheet? (*p. 655*)
4. Explain why Coke accounts for some of its investments by the equity method and what that means. (*p. 672*)

Corporations raise funds to finance their operations by selling equity securities (common and preferred stock) and debt securities (bonds and notes). These securities, also called financial instruments, are purchased as investments by individual investors, mutual funds, and also by other corporations. In later chapters we discuss equity and debt securities from the perspective of the issuing company. Our focus in this chapter is on the corporations that invest in debt and equity securities issued by other corporations as well as in debt securities issued by governmental units (bonds, Treasury bills, and Treasury bonds).

Most companies invest in financial instruments issued by other companies. For some investors, these investments represent ongoing affiliations with the companies whose securities are acquired. Recent examples of those sorts of investments include Microsoft's acquisition of LinkedIn for over $25 billion and Anheuser-Busch InBev's acquisition of SABMiller for over $100 billion. Some investments, though, are not made to obtain a favorable business relationship with another firm. Instead, companies seek only to earn a return from the dividends or interest the securities pay or from increases in the market prices of the securities—the same reasons that might motivate you to buy stocks, bonds, or other investment securities.

With such diversity in investment objectives, it's not surprising that there is diversity in the approaches used to account for investments. As you'll discover when reading this chapter, investments are accounted for in several different ways, depending on whether the investment is in a debt or equity security, the investor's purpose for holding the investment, and the nature of the investment relationship. In Part A, we discuss accounting for debt investments. In Part B, we discuss accounting for equity investments.

PART A

Accounting for Debt Investments

Example of a Debt Investment

LO12–1

Have you ever bought a CD (Certificate of Deposit) at a bank? If so, you've invested in a debt instrument. Let's say you buy a $500, 2-year, 4% CD. What's happened is that you are lending the bank $500 for 2 years, and the bank is promising to pay you 4% interest each year before returning your $500 after two years. The bank's debt (the $500 borrowed from you) is represented by a debt instrument (the CD), which specifies the maturity date (2 years), the principal (or face amount, $500), and the annual rate of interest (4%).

Companies invest in debt too. Like a CD, a bond or other debt security has a specified date when it matures, and on that maturity date, the *principal* (also called the *face amount*) is paid to investors. In the meantime, interest equal to some *stated interest rate* multiplied by the principal is paid to investors on specified interest dates (usually twice a year). Think of the principal and interest payments of the bond as a stream of cash flows that an investor will receive in the future in exchange for purchasing the bond today. The investor values that stream of future cash flows based on the prevailing *market interest rate* for debt of similar risk and maturity at the time the investor purchases the bond.

For an example of how an investor would determine how much to pay for a bond, see Illustration 12–1.

Illustration 12–1

Example of a Debt Investment: Bonds Purchased at a Discount

Because interest is paid semiannually, the present value calculations use:

a. one-half the stated rate (6%),
b. one-half the market rate (7%), and
c. 6 (= 3 × 2) semiannual periods.

On July 1, 2018, Masterwear Industries issued $700,000 of 12% bonds, dated July 1. Interest of $42,000 is payable semiannually on June 30 and December 31. The bonds mature in three years, on June 30, 2021. The market interest rate for bonds of similar risk and maturity is 14%. The entire bond issue was purchased by United Intergroup, Inc.*

Calculation of the Price of the Bonds		**Present Values**
Interest	$ 42,000 × 4.76654**	= $200,195
Principal (face amount)	$700,000 × 0.66634†	= 466,438
Present value (price) of the bonds		$666,633

*The numbers in this illustration are the same as those in Illustration 14–3 in Chapter 14 (except for some differences in dates between the two chapters). This helps us to better appreciate in Chapter 14 how Masterwear's accounting for its bond liability to United compares to United's accounting for its investment in Masterwear bonds. You can find further explanation of why we calculate the bond price this way in Chapter 14.
**Present value of an ordinary annuity of $1: $n = 6, i = 7\%$ (Table 4).
†Present value of $1: $n = 6, i = 7\%$ (Table 2).
Note: Present value tables are provided at the end of this textbook. If you need to review the concept of the time value of money, refer to the discussions in Chapter 6.

Illustration 12–1 shows that United will pay Masterwear $666,633 on July 1, 2018. In return, United expects to receive from Masterwear $42,000 every six months for the next three years plus the face amount of $700,000 when the bonds mature on June 30, 2021. Of course, if United sells the bonds to another investor, that investor will receive the remaining payments of interest and principal.

Notice that United paid $666,633 to purchase the $700,000 bonds. Why the difference? To determine the issue price of the bonds, it's important to understand how investors compare the bond's stated rate with the market rate. If the interest rate paid by the bond (the stated rate) is higher than the market rate, investors are willing to purchase the bond for more than its maturity value (so it's sold at a *premium*). If the bond's stated rate is lower than the market rate, then investors are willing to purchase the bond only at an amount less than its maturity value (so it's sold at a *discount*). Masterwear was offering its bonds for 12%, but investors could have obtained bonds of similar risk and maturity at a more favorable, higher rate of 14%. To attract investors, Masterwear had to sell its bonds at a discount.

The Masterwear bonds have the key characteristics of all debt investments. Over the three-year life of the bonds, United has to determine how it will account for four events:

1. Purchasing the debt investment.
2. Receiving interest every six months.
3. Holding the bonds during periods in which the bonds' fair value changes (and thus incurring *unrealized holding gains and losses,* since the bonds have not been sold).
4. Either selling the bonds before maturity or receiving the principal payment at their maturity date.

As we discuss below, companies classify debt investments as one of three types: held-to-maturity, trading, or available-for-sale. Accounting for the first two events—the purchase of a bond and the receipt of interest payments—is handled the same way regardless of how the debt investment is classified. We'll look at those events first. Then we'll look at the second two events, which are accounted for differently depending on how the debt investment is classified.

Recording the Purchase of a Debt Investment

When debt investments are purchased, they are recorded at cost—that is, the total amount paid for the investment, including any brokerage fees. Referring back to Illustration 12–1, we see that United paid $666,633 to purchase Masterwear's $700,000 bonds. United would record the purchase as:

All investment securities are initially recorded at cost.

July 1, 2018		
Investment in bonds (face amount)	700,000	
Discount on bond investment (difference)		33,367
Cash (price paid for the bonds)		666,633

Because United purchased the bonds for an amount that's less than their face amount, it credits *Discount on bond investment* for the difference. Discount on bond investment is a contra-asset to the investment account that serves to reduce the carrying value of the investment to its cost at the date of purchase. If United instead had purchased the bonds for an amount (say, $725,000) that is higher than the face amount of the bond ($700,000), it would instead debit *Premium on bond investment* (for $25,000) to record the investment at its cost at the date of purchase.[1]

Recording Interest Revenue

United will record interest revenue using the **effective interest method**. Here's how it works.

Masterwear's bonds have a *stated rate* of 12%, payable semiannually. This means that every six months, United will receive exactly $42,000 in cash from Masterwear:

[1]This is called the gross method. An alternative would be to record the cost ($666,633 or $725,000) directly in the investment account, called the net method.

$700,000	×	(12% ÷ 2)	=	**$42,000**
Face amount		Stated rate		Interest received

However, recall that United purchased the $700,000 bonds at a discounted amount of $666,633. Why could United pay less than the $700,000 face value for the bonds (and why was Masterwear willing to sell the bonds for less than $700,000)? At the time United purchased the bonds, the *market rate* of interest for bonds of similar risk was 14%. So, United would only be willing to invest in these bonds if it could earn the 14% it could get elsewhere (not the 12% stated rate). To earn this higher rate, United needed to pay only $666,633. Paying the lower amount means United lowered its investment cost and effectively increased its rate of return to 14% (refer back to Illustration 12–1 to see the details of this calculation). While United will receive $42,000 (6%) in interest from Masterwear in the first six months, it will effectively earn interest revenue of $46,664 (7%) on its investment.

$666,633	×	(14% ÷ 2)	=	$46,664
Outstanding balance		Market rate		Interest revenue

Under the *effective interest method,* interest for a period equals the market rate of interest when the debt was purchased multiplied by the outstanding balance of the debt at the beginning of the period.

The amount by which interest revenue exceeds interest received ($46,664 − $42,000 = $4,664 in the first six months) represents a piece of the cost savings from purchasing the investment at a discount. This piece of the cost savings increases United's investment return from the rate the bond pays (12%) to the higher rate (14%) that investors could have earned on other similar bonds at the time they purchased the bond. In fact, this approach is called the *effective interest method* because interest revenue is based on the effective interest rate that the investment earns over its lifetime.

The journal entry to record the interest received for the first six months as investment revenue is:

December 31, 2018		
Cash (stated rate × face amount)	**42,000**	
Discount on bond investment (difference)	4,664	
Interest revenue (market rate × outstanding balance)		**46,664**

This entry reduces the discount by $4,664 (from $33,367 to $28,703). Because the discount gets smaller, the "amortized cost" of the investment (equal to $700,000 less discount) gets larger by the same amount (from $666,633 to $671,297).

Illustration 12–2 demonstrates interest revenue being recorded at the effective rate over the life of this investment. As you can see, amortization of the discount gradually increases the amortized cost of the investment, until the investment reaches its face amount of $700,000, which is the amount to be received when the debt matures.

Illustration 12–2

Amortization Schedule—Discount

If a bond is purchased at a discount, less cash is received each period than the effective interest earned by the investor, so the unpaid difference increases the outstanding balance of the investment.

Date	Cash Interest	Effective Interest (Interest Revenue)	Amortization of Discount	Discount Balance	Amortized Cost
	(6% × Face amount)	(7% × Outstanding balance)	(Difference)		(Face amount less discount)
7/1/2018				33,367	666,633
12/31/2018	42,000	0.07(666,633) = 46,664	4,664	28,703	671,297
6/30/2019	42,000	0.07(671,297) = 46,991	4,991	23,712	676,288
12/31/2019	42,000	0.07(676,288) = 47,340	5,340	18,372	681,628
6/30/2020	42,000	0.07(681,628) = 47,714	5,714	12,658	687,342
12/31/2020	42,000	0.07(687,342) = 48,114	6,114	6,544	693,456
6/30/2021	42,000	0.07(693,456) = 48,544*	6,544	0	700,000
	252,000	285,367	33,367		

*Rounded

If the bonds were instead purchased at a premium, a similar amortization schedule would *reduce* the premium over time until the bond's amortized cost reached the face amount of $700,000, which is the amount to be received when the debt matures.

Three Classifications of Debt Investments

The amortization schedule shown in Illustration 12–2 is based on the market interest rate (14%) that prevailed at the time United purchased the Masterwear bonds. United will use that amortization schedule for the life of the investment, and *won't change it* in response to changes in prevailing interest rates. However, the prevailing market rate may not always be 14%. The fair value of the bonds will change with changes in the prevailing market interest rate, because market participants will use the prevailing rate to compute the present value of the cash flows provided by the bond. United will incur unrealized holding gains and losses as a result of holding the bond during periods in which its fair value changes.

If the market rate of interest *rises* after a bond is purchased, the market will compute the present value of the cash flows provided by the bond using that higher discount rate, so the fair value of the bond falls. In that case, the person holding the bond suffers an *unrealized holding loss.* The fair value of the bond has decreased, but that loss hasn't been realized, because the investment has not been sold.

The fair value of a fixed-rate investment moves in the opposite direction of market interest rates.

Conversely, if the market rate of interest *falls* after a bond is purchased, the market will calculate the present value of the cash flows provided by the bond using that lower rate, so the fair value of the bond rises. In that case, the investor holding the bond enjoys an *unrealized holding gain.* The fair value of the bond has increased but that gain hasn't yet been realized, because the investment hasn't been sold.

Changes in fair value give rise to unrealized holding gains and losses.

Accounting for changes in fair value depends on the classification of the debt investment. As shown in Illustration 12–3, debt investments are classified in one of three categories: held-to-maturity (HTM) securities, trading securities (TS), or available-for-sale (AFS) securities.

Illustration 12–3
Accounting for Unrealized Holding Gains and Losses on Debt Investments

Reporting Approach	Treatment of Unrealized Holding Gains and Losses	Carried in Balance Sheet at
Held-to-maturity (HTM): used for debt for which the investor has the "positive intent and ability" to hold to maturity.	Not recognized*	Amortized Cost
Trading (TS): used for debt that is held in an active trading account for immediate resale.	Recognized in net income, and therefore in retained earnings as part of shareholders' equity.	Fair Value
Available-for-sale (AFS): used for debt that does not qualify as held-to-maturity or trading.	Recognized in other comprehensive income, and therefore in accumulated other comprehensive income in shareholders' equity*.	Fair Value

*If the investor elects the *fair value option (FVO)*, this type of investment also can be accounted for using the same approach that's used for trading securities, with the investment reported at fair value and unrealized holding gains and losses included in net income.

Illustration 12–4 provides a description from a recent annual report of how the Bank of America accounts for its debt investments in each of the three reporting categories.

Illustration 12–4
Disclosure about Investments—Bank of America

Real World Financials

Note 1 (in part): Securities

Debt securities which management has the intent and ability to hold to maturity are classified as held-to-maturity (HTM) and reported at amortized cost. Debt securities that are bought and held principally for the purpose of resale in the near term are classified as trading and are carried at fair value with unrealized gains and losses included in trading account profits (losses). Other debt securities are classified as AFS and carried at fair value with net unrealized gains and losses included in accumulated OCI on an after-tax basis.

FINANCIAL Reporting Case

Q1, p. 643

Why treat unrealized holding gains and losses differently depending on the type of investment? As you know, the primary purpose of accounting is to provide information useful for making decisions. What's most relevant for that purpose is not necessarily the same for each investment a company might make. For example, a company might invest in corporate bonds to provide a steady return until the bonds mature, in which case day-to-day changes in fair value may not be viewed as very relevant, so the held-to-maturity approach is preferable. On the other hand, a company might invest in the same bonds because it plans to sell them at a profit in the near future, in which case the day-to-day changes in fair value could be viewed as very relevant, and the trading security or available-for-sale approach is preferable.

We'll discuss each reporting approach in turn, including how that approach accounts for unrealized holding gains and losses.

Debt Investments to Be Held to Maturity (HTM)

Unrealized Holding Gains and Losses Are Not Recognized for HTM Investments

Held to maturity (HTM) investments require the "positive intent and ability" to hold the investments to maturity.

Unrealized holding gains and losses are less important if sale before maturity isn't an alternative, because those gains and losses will never be realized by sale. For this reason, if an investor has the "positive intent and ability" to hold the securities to maturity, investments in debt securities typically are classified as held-to-maturity (HTM) and reported at their *amortized cost* in the balance sheet.[2] A debt security cannot be classified as held-to-maturity if the investor might sell it before maturity in response to changes in market prices or interest rates, to meet the investor's liquidity needs, or similar factors.

● LO12–2

Held to maturity (HTM) investments are reported at amortized cost in the balance sheet.

To consider accounting for unrealized gains and losses, suppose that on December 31, 2018, the market interest rate for securities similar to the Masterwear bonds has fallen to 11%. An investor valuing the Masterwear bonds at that time would do so considering the current market interest rate (11%) because that's the rate of return available for similar bonds. Calculating the present value of the bonds using a lower discount rate results in a higher present value (price).

Let's say that checking market prices in *The Wall Street Journal* indicates that the fair value of the Masterwear bonds on December 31, 2018, is $714,943. As shown in Illustration 12–2, those same bonds have an amortized cost of $671,297. This means there is an unrealized gain of $43,646 for the difference. How will United account for this increase in the fair value of its debt investment? If United views the bonds as HTM investments, that change in fair value will be *ignored* so long as it is viewed as temporary.[3] The investment simply will be shown in the balance sheet at amortized cost of $671,297. United will *disclose* the fair value of its HTM investments in a note to the financial statements, but will not recognize any fair value changes in the income statement or balance sheet.[4]

Sale of HTM Investments

Typically, held-to-maturity investments are—you guessed it—held to maturity. However, suppose that due to unforeseen circumstances the company decided to sell its debt investment for $725,000 on January 5, 2019.[5] United would record the sale as follows (for simplicity we ignore interest earned during the first five days of 2019):[6]

[2]FASB ASC 320–10–25–1: Investments–Debt Securities–Overall–Recognition (previously "Accounting for Certain Investments in Debt and Equity Securities," *Statement of Financial Accounting Standards No. 115* (Norwalk, Conn.: FASB, 1993)).

[3]If an unrealized loss from holding an HTM investment is not viewed as temporary, an "other-than-temporary impairment" (OTT impairment) may have to be recorded. We discuss OTT impairments in more detail in Appendix 12B.

[4]If United had chosen the fair value option for this investment, it would classify the investment as a trading security rather than as an HTM security. We'll illustrate the fair value option when we discuss trading securities.

[5]GAAP [FASB ASC 320–10–25–6: Investments–Debt Securities–Overall–Recognition, previously *Statement of Financial Accounting Standards No. 115*] lists major unforeseen events that could justify sale of an HTM investment. Sale for other reasons could call into question whether the company actually had the intent and ability to hold the investment to maturity. In that case, the company's HTM classification is viewed as "tainted," and the company can be required to reclassify *all* of its HTM investments as AFS investments and avoid using the HTM classification for two years. Similar provisions exist under IFRS for public companies.

[6]For purposes of this example, we ignore any interest accrued for the first five days of 2019. In practice, United would accrue five days of interest revenue and record five days of amortization of the discount, which would produce a revised amortized cost of the bonds that would be used to calculate any gain or loss on sale.

January 5, 2019		
Cash	725,000	
Discount on bond investment (account balance)	28,703	
Investment in Masterwear bonds (account balance)		700,000
Gain on sale of investments (to balance)		53,703

In other words, United would record this sale just like any other asset sale, with a realized gain or loss determined by comparing the cash received with the carrying value (in this case, the amortized cost) of the asset sold.

Additional Consideration

Recall from Chapter 1 that GAAP identifies different ways a firm can determine fair value. If the Masterwear bonds are publicly traded, United can find the fair value by looking up the current market price (this way of obtaining fair value is consistent with "level 1" of the fair value hierarchy). On the other hand, if the bonds are not publicly traded, United can calculate the fair value by using the present value techniques shown in Illustration 12–1 (this way of obtaining fair value is consistent with "level 2" of the fair value hierarchy). With five interest periods remaining, and a current market rate of 11% (5.5% semiannually), the present value would be $714,943.

			Present Values
Interest	$ 42,000 × 4.27028*	=	$179,352
Principal	$700,000 × 0.76513†	=	535,591
Present value of the bonds			$714,943

*Present value of an ordinary annuity of $1: $n = 5, i = 5.5\%$. (Table 4)
†Present value of $1: $n = 5, i = 5.5\%$. (Table 2)

Using Excel, enter:
=PV(.055,5, −42000, −700000)
Output: 714,946

Using a calculator:
enter: N 5 I 5.5 PMT −42000 FM −700000
Output: = PV 714,946

Financial Statement Presentation

HTM securities appear in the financial statements as follows:

- **Income Statement and Statement of Comprehensive Income:** *Realized* gains and losses are shown in net income in the period in which securities are sold. *Unrealized* holding gains and losses are disclosed in the notes to financial statements. Investments in HTM securities do not affect other comprehensive income.
- **Balance Sheet:** Investments in HTM securities are reported at amortized cost. Fair values of those investments are disclosed in the notes to financial statements.
- **Cash Flow Statement:** Cash flows from buying and selling HTM securities typically are classified as investing activities.

Assuming United sold its investment on January 5, 2019, United's 2018 and 2019 financial statements will include the amounts shown in Illustration 12–5.

Debt Investments Classified as Trading Securities

Trading securities are actively managed in a trading account for the purpose of profiting from short-term price changes.

● LO12–3

Some companies—primarily financial institutions—actively and frequently buy and sell securities, expecting to earn profits on short-term price fluctuations. Investments in debt acquired principally for the purpose of selling them in the near term are classified as trading securities. The holding period for trading securities generally is measured in hours and days rather than months or years. These investments typically are reported among the investor's current assets. Usually only banks and other financial operations invest in securities in the manner and for the purpose necessary to be categorized as trading securities.

Just like HTM investments, trading securities are recorded at cost when they are purchased, and any discount or premium is amortized to interest revenue over time as periodic

Illustration 12–5
Reporting Held-to-Maturity Investments

(Ignoring income taxes)	2018	2019
Statement of Comprehensive Income		
Revenues	$ ◆	$ ◆
Expenses	◆	◆
Other income (expense):		
Interest revenue	46,664	–0–
Realized gain on sale of investments	–0–	53,703
Net income	46,664	53,703
Other comprehensive income (OCI)	–0–	–0–
Comprehensive income (Net income + OCI)	46,664	53,703
Balance Sheet		
Assets:		
HTM investments	671,297	–0–
Shareholders' equity:		
Retained Earnings	46,664	100,367*
Statement of Cash Flows (direct method)		
Operating Activities:		
Cash from interest received	42,000	–0–
Investing Activities:		
Purchase of HTM securities	(666,633)	–0–
Sale of HTM securities	–0–	725,000

*Net income of $46,664 (2018) + $53,703 (2019) = $100,367 accumulates in retained earnings by the end of 2019.

Only *realized* gains and losses are included in net income.

HTM securities are reported at amortized cost.

Cash flows from buying and selling HTM securities are classified as investing activities.

interest payments are received. However, in subsequent periods, there are two important differences between trading securities and HTM investments.

1. Trading securities are written up or down to their fair value, or "marked to market", in the balance sheet. (HTM securities are kept at amortized cost.)
2. Corresponding unrealized holding gains and losses on trading securities are included in net income in the income statement. (HTM securities do not include unrealized holdings gains and losses in net income.)

Be sure to notice that reporting trading securities at their fair value is a departure from amortized cost, which is the way many assets are reported in the balance sheet. Why the difference? For trading securities, fair value information is more relevant than for other assets intended primarily to be used in company operations, like buildings, land and equipment, or for debt investments intended to be held to maturity. Changes in fair values provide an indication of management's success in deciding when to acquire the investment, when to sell it, whether to invest in fixed-rate or variable-rate securities, and whether to invest in long-term or short-term securities. For that reason, it makes sense to report unrealized holding gains and losses on trading securities in net income during a period that fair values change, even though those gains and losses haven't yet been realized through the sale of the securities.

FINANCIAL Reporting Case

Q2, p. 643

To see how we account for trading securities, let's return to our Masterwear bond example, but assume that those debt investments are held in an active trading portfolio. As of December 31, 2018, United has recorded the purchase of the bonds as well as receipt of the first semiannual interest payment, so the bonds have an amortized cost of $671,297 (refer back to Illustration 12–2).

Adjust Trading Security Investments to Fair Value (2018)

Trading securities are adjusted to their fair value in each reporting period.

Unlike HTM securities, trading securities are carried at fair value in the balance sheet, so their carrying value must be adjusted to fair value by the end of every reporting period. In fact, many companies adjust trading securities to fair value at the end of every day. Rather than increasing or decreasing the investment account itself, we use a valuation allowance, *fair value adjustment,* to increase or decrease the carrying value of the investment. At the same time, we record an unrealized holding gain or loss that is included in net income in the period in which fair value changes (remember, the gain or loss is *unrealized* because the securities haven't been sold).

Assuming the Masterwear bonds have a fair value of $714,943 as of December 31, 2018, the next table shows the calculation of the balance in the fair value adjustment account that is required on that date.

December 31, 2018

Security	Amortized Cost	Fair Value	Necessary Fair Value Adjustment Balance
Masterwear	$671,297	$714,943	$43,646

The bonds need to be reported at their fair value of $714,943. Because the bonds currently are recorded at their amortized cost of $671,297, the fair value adjustment account needs a debit balance of $43,646. United will recognize whatever unrealized holding gain or loss is necessary to move the fair value adjustment from its current balance of $0 (at purchase date) to $43,646 (on December 31, 2018). In this case, the calculation is simple:

	Fair Value Adjustment
Beginning balance on 7/1/2018	$ 0
± Adjustment needed to update fair value	?
Balance needed on 12/31/2018	$43,646

Fair Value Adjustment	
0	
43,646	
43,646	

The journal entry to record the $43,646 change in United's fair value adjustment and the corresponding unrealized holding gain is:

December 31, 2018		
Fair value adjustment (calculated above)*	43,646	
Unrealized holding gain on trading securities—NI†		43,646

*Sometimes companies don't bother with a separate fair value adjustment account and simply adjust the investment account to fair value.

†We title this account "Unrealized. . .—NI" to highlight that, for trading securities, unrealized holding gains and losses are included in the income statement in the period in which they occur.

Each period United owns the Masterwear bonds, it will recognize whatever unrealized holding gain or loss is necessary to move the fair value adjustment to the value it needs to have at the end of the accounting period. Increases in the fair value adjustment produce gains on trading securities that increase net income; decreases produce losses that decrease net income.

Unrealized holding gains and losses for trading securities are included in net income in the period in which fair value changes.

Additional Consideration

Accounting for Portfolios

We have focused on accounting for an individual security, but United would use the same approach to account for a *portfolio* of trading securities. For example, assume that United has the following portfolio of trading securities as of December 31, 2018, as shown below:

Security	Amortized Cost	Fair Value	Necessary Fair Value Adjustment Balance
Miley Inc.	$ 800,000	$ 875,000	$ 75,000
Perry Corp.	950,000	790,000	(160,000)
Total	$1,750,000	$1,665,000	$ (85,000)

(continued)

(concluded)

As of December 31, 2019, the portfolio's status is as follows:

Security	Amortized Cost	Fair Value	Necessary Fair Value Adjustment Balance
Miley Inc.	$ 600,000	$575,000	$ (25,000)
Swift Co.	450,000	325,000	(125,000)
Total	$1,050,000	$900,000	$(150,000)

Fair Value Adjustment

	85,000
	65,000
	150,000

On December 31, 2019, the balance of the fair value adjustment needs to change from a credit of $85,000 to a credit of $150,000, requiring an additional credit of $65,000 and recognition of a corresponding loss in net income.

To make that happen, United records the following journal entry:

Unrealized holding loss on trading securities—NI	65,000	
Fair value adjustment		65,000

Sale of Trading Security Investments

Now assume that United sells the bonds for $725,000 on January 5, 2019. To account for the sale, United needs to do two things. First, United needs to update the carrying value of the bonds to fair value and record in net income any unrealized holding gains and losses that occurred during 2019 up to the date of sale. Second, on the date of sale, United needs to record the receipt of cash and remove the amounts associated with the investment from the relevant balance sheet accounts. Let's record each of these entries. (As in our example for HTM investments, for simplicity we ignore interest earned during the first five days of 2019.)

For trading securities, unrealized holding gains and losses from fair value changes are recorded up to the date an investment is sold.

1. Adjust Trading Securities to Fair Value (2019). We first need to update the fair value adjustment and recognize any unrealized holding gains or losses that have occurred during the current reporting period prior to the date of sale. We already have accounted for fair value changes that occurred during 2018. Now we need to record the additional fair value changes and their related unrealized holding gains and losses that have occurred each day in 2019 up to the moment of sale. Companies might record these changes in fair value at the end of each day, but we use a single summary entry that captures those changes in fair value up to the moment of sale.

Remember that on December 31, 2018, the amortized cost of the Masterwear bonds was $671,297, and the fair value was $714,943. We recorded a fair value adjustment of $43,646 for this unrealized holding gain. Now, on January 5, 2019, the fair value has increased further to $725,000, so we need to update the fair value adjustment for the additional $10,057 increase in fair value.

December 31, 2018

Security	Amortized Cost	Fair Value	Necessary Fair Value Adjustment Balance
Masterwear	$671,297	$725,000	$53,703

Fair Value Adjustment

43,646	
10,057	
53,703	

	Fair Value Adjustment
Beginning balance on 12/31/2018	$43,646
± Adjustment needed to update fair value	?
Balance needed as of date of sale	$53,703

United needs to record an increase in the fair value adjustment and an additional unrealized holding gain of $10,057 that occurred during the first week of 2019. The journal entry is:

January 5, 2019

Fair value adjustment	10,057	
Unrealized holding gain on trading securities—NI (to balance)		10,057

2. Record the Sale Transaction. After making the previous journal entry, the investment is carried at its fair value as of the date it is being sold, and already has included in net income any gain or loss arising from the difference between amortized cost and fair value as of the date of sale. All that remains is for United to record receipt of cash and remove the investment-related accounts from the balance sheet (again, for simplicity we ignore interest earned during the first five days of 2019).

When a trading security is sold, all of the gain or loss already has been included in net income, so no additional gain or loss is recognized.

January 5, 2019		
Cash	725,000	
Discount on bond investment (account balance)	28,703	
Investment in Masterwear bonds (account balance)		700,000
Fair value adjustment (account balance)		53,703

As with the sale of the HTM investment, we record the receipt of $725,000 cash and remove all the balance sheet accounts associated with the investment. However, unlike the HTM investment, our TS investment has an additional balance sheet account, the fair value adjustment, that needs to be removed when we record the sale. Another difference between the HTM and TS approach is that, because we carry trading securities at fair value as of the date of sale and already have included in net income the entire gain associated with changes in the fair value of the investment, there is no gain or loss to recognize on the date of sale.[7] However, over the life of the investments, United recognized the same amount of gain under the TS approach ($43,646 + 10,057 = $53,703) as it recognized upon sale under the HTM approach ($53,703). The only difference is timing, with trading securities recognizing unrealized holding gains and losses from fair value changes as they occur but the HTM approach recognizing gains or losses only when they are realized upon sale.

Financial Statement Presentation

Trading securities appear in the financial statements as follows:

- **Income Statement and Statement of Comprehensive Income:** For trading securities, gains and losses are included in the income statement in the periods in which fair value changes, *regardless of whether they are realized or unrealized.* Investments in trading securities do not affect other comprehensive income.
- **Balance Sheet:** Investments in trading securities are reported at fair value, typically as current assets.
- **Cash Flow Statement:** Cash flows from buying and selling trading securities typically are classified as operating activities, because the financial institutions that routinely hold trading securities consider them as part of their normal operations.

Assuming United sold its investment on January 5, 2019, United's 2018 and 2019 financial statements will include the amounts shown in Illustration 12–6.

Debt Investments Classified as Available-for-Sale Securities

● LO12–4

The HTM treatment assumes we hold the bonds for their entire life. The trading securities treatment assumes we are planning to sell the bonds in the very near future. Our third treatment, available-for-sale (AFS) securities, falls in the middle. We aren't planning to trade

AFS investments aren't held for trading or designated as held to maturity.

[7]As noted in FASB ASC 320-10-40: Investments–Debt Securities–Overall–Derecognition, for expediency companies may not update the fair value adjustment to the fair value as of the date of sale before recording the sale. In that case, the investment is carried at fair value as of the last balance sheet date, and this second entry would include a gain or loss based on the difference between the cash received and the carrying value of the investment. In our example, the fair value adjustment balance was $43,646 on December 31, 2018, and United would record the following sale entry on January 5, 2019:

Cash	725,000	
Discount on bond investment (account balance)	28,703	
Investment in Masterwear bonds (account balance)		700,000
Fair value adjustment (account balance)		43,646
Gain on trading securities - NI (to balance)		10,057

Illustration 12–6
Reporting Trading Securities

For trading securities, fair value changes affect net income in the period in which they occur.

Trading securities are reported at fair value in the balance sheet.

Cash flows from buying and selling trading securities are classified as operating activities.

(Ignoring income taxes) **Statement of Comprehensive Income**	**2018**	**2019**
Revenues	$ ◆	$ ◆
Expenses	◆	◆
Other income (expense):		
Interest revenue	46,664	–0–
Gains and losses on trading securities	43,646	10,057
Net income	90,310	10,057
Other comprehensive income (OCI)	–0–	–0–
Comprehensive income (Net income + OCI)	$ 90,310	$ 10,057
Balance Sheet		
Assets:		
Trading securities	714,943	–0–
Shareholders' equity:		
Retained Earnings	90,310	100,367*
Statement of Cash Flows (direct method)		
Operating Activities:		
Cash from interest received	42,000	–0–
Purchase of trading securities	(666,633)	–0–
Sale of trading securities	–0–	725,000

*Net income of $90,310 (2018) + $10,057 (2019) = $100,367 accumulates in retained earnings by the end of 2019.

AFS investments are reported at their fair values.

the debt investment actively, but the investment is available to sell if, for example, cash needs arise or the market is particularly favorable. In that case, the company classifies its debt investment as AFS. Like trading securities, we report AFS securities in the balance sheet at fair value. Unlike trading securities, though, unrealized holding gains and losses on AFS securities are *not* included in net income. Instead, they are reported in the statement of comprehensive income as other comprehensive income (OCI).

Additional Consideration

Don't Shoot the Messenger. Or, as written in *The Economist*, "Messenger, Shot: Accounting rules are under attack. Standard-setters should defend them. Politicians and banks should back off."[8] Using fair values that are hard to estimate is controversial. For example, during the financial crisis of 2008/2009 many financial-services companies had to recognize huge unrealized losses associated with their investments. Some blamed their losses on GAAP for requiring estimates of fair value that were driven by depressed current market prices, argued that those losses worsened the financial crisis, and lobbied for a move away from fair-value accounting. Others countered that these companies were using GAAP's requirement for fair value accounting as a "scapegoat" for their bad investment decisions. "Fair value accounting . . . does not create losses but rather reflects a firm's present condition," says Georgene Palacky, director of the CFA's financial reporting group."[9]

Comprehensive Income

Recall from Chapter 4 that comprehensive income is a more all-encompassing view of operations than net income. It includes not only net income but also all other changes in equity that do not arise from transactions with owners.[10] Comprehensive income therefore includes net

[8]Transactions with owners primarily include dividends and the sale or purchase of shares of the company's stock.
[9]"Messenger, Shot," *The Economist*, April 8, 2009.
[10]Sarah Johnson, "The Fair Value Blame Game," CFO.com, March 19, 2008.

income as well as *other comprehensive income (OCI).* You know that net income is closed to retained earnings at the end of each accounting period, and therefore accumulates in retained earnings over time in the shareholders' equity section of the balance sheet. Similarly, OCI is closed to *accumulated other comprehensive income (AOCI)* at the end of each accounting period, and therefore accumulates in AOCI in the shareholders' equity section of the balance sheet. OCI relates to AOCI the same way that net income relates to retained earnings.

Rationale for AFS Treatment of Unrealized Holding Gains and Losses

Why use an approach for accounting for AFS securities that differs from that used for trading securities? Because AFS securities are likely to be held for multiple reporting periods, one could argue that there is sufficient time for unrealized holding gains in some periods to balance out with unrealized holding losses in other periods, so including unrealized holding gains and losses in income each period would confuse investors by making income appear more volatile than it really is over the long run.[11] But how can we show AFS investments at fair value in the balance sheet without recording in net income the unrealized gains and losses associated with changes in fair value? The solution is to show those unrealized gains and losses in OCI as they occur and then only include realized gains and losses in net income in the period in which an investment is actually sold.

FINANCIAL Reporting Case

Q3, p. 643

Adjust AFS Investments to Fair Value (2018)

To see how we adjust AFS investments to their fair value, let's assume the Masterwear bond investment is classified as AFS. As of December 31, 2018, United has recorded the purchase of the bonds on July 1, 2018, as well as receipt of the first semiannual interest payment, so the bonds have an amortized cost of $671,297 (refer back to Illustration 12–2). The fair value of the bonds on December 31, 2018, is $714,943. The next table shows the calculation of the balance in the fair value adjustment account that is required on that date.

December 31, 2018

Security	Amortized Cost	Fair Value	Necessary Fair Value Adjustment Balance
Masterwear	$671,297	$714,943	$43,646

United needs to adjust the balance of the fair value adjustment account from its current balance of $0 (at purchase date) to a debit balance of $43,646 (on December 31, 2018).

	Fair Value Adjustment
Beginning balance on 7/1/2018	$ 0
± Adjustment needed to update fair value	?
Balance needed on 12/31/2018	$43,646

Fair Value Adjustment

Debit	Credit
0	
43,646	
43,646	

The journal entry to record the $43,646 change in United's fair value adjustment and the corresponding unrealized holding gain is:

December 31, 2018		
Fair value adjustment*	43,646	
Unrealized holding gain on AFS investments—OCI†		43,646

*Sometimes companies don't bother with a separate fair value adjustment account and simply adjust the investment account to fair value.
†We title this account "Unrealized . . .—OCI" to highlight that, for available-for-sale securities, unrealized holding gains and losses are included in other comprehensive income (OCI) in the period in which they occur.

For AFS securities, unrealized holding gains and losses from fair value changes are not included in net income, but instead are reported as OCI.

Notice that the amount of unrealized holding gain is the same for these AFS securities as it was for the trading securities in the previous section. What differs is that the

[11]Of course, one could counter-argue that these unrealized holding gains and losses still are relevant, given that each period an investor has discretion over whether or not to continue holding the security or sell that security to realize a gain or loss. For that reason, many accountants would prefer that the FASB do away with the AFS approach and just treat these investments as trading securities.

unrealized holding gain is included in OCI for AFS securities instead of net income as it is for trading securities. At the end of the reporting period, the unrealized holding gain is closed to a shareholders' equity account for both approaches. What differs is that net income gets closed to retained earnings, and OCI gets closed to Accumulated Other Comprehensive Income (AOCI). As with trading securities, the fair value adjustment will be adjusted up or down each period, either for individual securities or for a portfolio of securities, and a corresponding unrealized holding gain or loss reported in OCI. Net income normally is not affected by AFS investments until the period an AFS investment is sold, as we'll discuss next.

Sale of AFS Investments

Let's once again assume that United sells its Masterwear bonds for $725,000 on January 5, 2019 (as with our HTM and TS examples, for simplicity we ignore any interest earned during 2019). For AFS securities, United needs to record three journal entries.[12]

For AFS investments, unrealized holding gains and losses from fair value changes are recorded up to the date an investment is sold.

1. **Adjust AFS Investments to Fair Value (2019).** As with trading securities, we first need to update the fair value adjustment and recognize any unrealized holding gains or losses that have occurred during the current reporting period prior to the date of sale. Remember that on December 31, 2018, the amortized cost of the Masterwear bonds was $671,297, and the fair value was $714,943. We recorded a fair value adjustment of $43,646 for this unrealized holding gain. Now, on January 5, 2019, the fair value has increased further to $725,000, so we need to update the fair value adjustment for the additional $10,057 increase in fair value.

January 5, 2019

Security	Amortized Cost	Fair Value	Necessary Fair Value Adjustment Balance
Masterwear	$671,297	$725,000	$53,703

Fair Value Adjustment

43,646	
10,057	
53,703	

	Fair Value Adjustment
Balance as of 12/31/2018	$43,646
± Adjustment needed to update fair value	?
Balance needed as of date of sale	$53,703

United needs to record an increase in the fair value adjustment and an additional unrealized holding gain of $10,057 that occurred during the first week of 2019. The journal entry to record the gain is:

January 5, 2019		
Fair value adjustment	10,057	
Unrealized holding gain on AFS investments—OCI		10,057

At this point, the investment is carried in the balance sheet at its fair value as of the date it is being sold, and all unrealized gains and losses associated with the investment have been included in OCI. Because OCI gets closed to AOCI, the unrealized gains and losses accumulate in AOCI, which acts as a sort of "holding tank" in the shareholders' equity section of the balance sheet. Unrealized holding gains in some years offset unrealized losses in other years as they accumulate in the tank.

When an AFS investment is sold, accumulated unrealized gains and losses are removed from AOCI using a reclassification entry.

2. **Reverse Previous Fair Value Adjustments.** United has been recording changes in fair value over the life of the investment. If United now sells that investment, the effects of those fair value changes must be reversed. United reverses previous unrealized holding gains included in OCI by debiting a reclassification adjustment to OCI for the same amount. Similarly, the account balance of the fair value adjustment is eliminated.

[12]This description of accounting for sales of AFS investments is adapted from the example of journal entries and financial statement presentation shown by FASB ASC 220-10-55 (para. 24-27): Comprehensive Income—Overall—Implementation Guidance and Illustrations—Case B: Available-for-Sale Debt Securities. The three journal entries we describe could be combined into one or two entries in practice.

January 5, 2019		
Reclassification adjustment—OCI	53,703	
Fair value adjustment (account balance)		53,703

Fair Value Adjustment

43,646	
10,057	53,703
0	

AOCI (after closing)

	43,646
53,703	10,057
	0

After this journal entry is recorded, the fair value adjustment account has a zero balance. Also, after the reclassification adjustment is closed to AOCI, all of the unrealized gains that are associated with the investment have been removed from the AOCI holding tank in shareholders' equity.[13] It's as if no accounting for unrealized gains and losses had ever taken place.[14] That's important, because in the next entry United recognizes in net income a gain or loss on sale . If United didn't use the reclassification entry to back out the unrealized gains and losses from AOCI, it would end up having double counted them in comprehensive income and shareholders equity after it records the sale in the next entry.

3. **Record the Sale Transaction.** Now that all of the unrealized holding gains and losses and the fair value adjustment have been cleared away, the final step is to "plug" for the realized gain or loss (a gain in this case).

January 5, 2019		
Cash	725,000	
Discount on bond investment (account balance)	28,703	
Investment in Masterwear bonds (account balance)		700,000
Gain on AFS investments—NI (to balance)		53,703

This entry is identical to the entry United made to record sale of the investment under the HTM approach. As with the HTM investments, no gain or loss is recognized in net income over the life of the investment. Instead, the entire gain or loss is recognized in net income at the time of the sale. So, with this entry and the one preceding it, United has reclassified its $53,703 gain from OCI to net income. That's why the process is called reclassification.

When an AFS investment is sold, realized gains and losses are included in net income.

Additional Consideration

More About Reclassification

Look back through the three entries that are shown for recording a sale of an AFS investment. Think about what has happened. First, United recorded unrealized holding gains in OCI each period as fair value changed over time, and at the end of each period it closed OCI to AOCI in shareholders' equity. Then, once the investment was sold, United backed those unrealized gains out of OCI (and thus out of AOCI) and included them in net income (which is closed to retained earnings in shareholders' equity). From the perspective of shareholders' equity, the unrealized gains were first accumulated in AOCI and then were reclassified from AOCI to retained earnings in the period of sale.

We can rearrange the second and third journal entries to highlight this reclassification process:

Reclassification adjustment—OCI	**53,703**	
Gain on AFS investments—NI (to balance)		**53,703**
Cash	725,000	
Discount on bond investment (account balance)	28,703	
Investment in Masterwear bonds (account balance)		700,000
Fair value adjustment (account balance)		53,703

Once the investment is sold, all the balance sheet accounts are removed and the unrealized holding gains and losses that have been accumulating in AOCI are transferred out of AOCI (via the reclassification entry) and included in net income.

[13]As noted in FASB ASC 320-10-40: Investments—Debt Securities—Overall—Derecognition, for expediency companies might not update the fair value adjustment to fair value before recording the sale. In that case, this second entry would be based on the fair value adjustment as of the last balance sheet date. In our example, the fair value adjustment balance would be $43,646, so that is the amount by which it would be reduced and that is the amount of reclassification adjustment that would be recorded in OCI.

[14]Companies may choose to make this journal entry at the end of the reporting period when they update their fair value adjustment. The order doesn't matter, so long as the journal entry is recorded in the correct reporting period.

It may seem odd that we bother to put all of the unrealized holding gains and losses into OCI and then take them out again, but that approach makes it very clear when gains and losses are moving in and out of AOCI and getting recognized in net income. Here's what happens in the financial statements.

Financial Statement Presentation

AFS securities appear in the financial statements as follows:

- **Income Statement and Statement of Comprehensive Income:** Gains and losses are shown in OCI in the periods in which changes in fair value occur. Those amounts are reclassified out of OCI and recognized in net income in the periods in which securities are sold.
- **Balance Sheet:** Investments in AFS securities are reported at fair value. *Unrealized* holding gains and losses become part of AOCI in shareholders' equity, and are reclassified out of AOCI in the periods in which securities are sold.
- **Cash Flow Statement:** Cash flows from buying and selling AFS securities typically are classified as investing activities.

Assuming United sold its investment on January 5, 2019, United's 2018 and 2019 financial statements will include the amounts shown in Illustration 12–7.

Illustration 12–7
Reporting Available-for-Sale Securities

Only *realized* gains and losses are included in net income.

Other comprehensive income includes *unrealized* holding gains and losses *that occur during the reporting period.*

AFS securities are reported at fair value.

AOCI (in shareholders' equity) includes net unrealized holding gains or losses *accumulated over the current and prior periods.*

Cash flows from buying and selling AFS securities usually are classified as investing activities.

(Ignoring income taxes) **Statement of Comprehensive Income**	**2018**	**2019**
Revenues	$ ◆	$ ◆
Expenses	◆	◆
Other income (expense):		
Interest revenue	46,664	–0–
Realized gain on sale of investments	–0–	53,703
Net income	46,664	53,703
Other comprehensive income (loss) items (OCI):*		
Unrealized holding gains (losses) on investments	43,646	10,057
Reclassification adjustment for net gains and losses included in net income	–0–	(53,703)
Total OCI	43,646	(43,646)
Comprehensive income (Net income + OCI)	$ 90,310	$ 10,057
Balance Sheet		
Assets:		
Available-for-sale securities	$714,943	$ –0–
Shareholders' equity:		
Accumulated other comprehensive income (AOCI)	43,646	–0–
Retained Earnings	46,664	100,367[†]
Statement of Cash Flows (direct method)		
Operating activities:		
Cash from interest received	42,000	–0–
Investing activities:		
Purchase of available-for-sale securities	(666,633)	–0–
Sale of available-for-sale securities	–0–	725,000

*As we discuss in more detail in Chapter 18, the statement of comprehensive income can be presented as a continuation of the income statement as shown here, or in a separate statement that immediately follows the income statement.
[†]Net income of $46,664 (2018) + $53,703 (2019) = $100,367 accumulates in retained earnings by the end of 2019.

Individual securities available for sale are classified as either current or noncurrent assets, depending on how long they're likely to be held. An example from the 2015 annual report of Cisco Systems is shown in Illustration 12–8.

Illustration 12–8

Investments in Securities Available-for-Sale—Cisco Systems

Real World Financials

Item 1A: Risk Factors (in part)

We maintain an investment portfolio of various holdings, types, and maturities. These securities are generally classified as available-for-sale and, consequently, are recorded on our Consolidated Balance Sheets at fair value with unrealized gains or losses reported as a component of accumulated other comprehensive income.

Note 8: Investments (in part)

The following tables summarize the Company's available-for-sale investments ($ in millions):

July 25, 2015	Amortized Cost	Gross Unrealized Gains	Gross Unrealized Losses	Fair Value
Fixed income securities:				
U.S. Government	$29,904	$41	$ (6)	$29,939
U.S. Government agency	3,662	2	(1)	3,663
Non-U.S. Gov't agency	1,128	1	(1)	1,128
Corporate debt securities	15,802	34	(53)	15,783
U.S. agency mortgage-backed	1,456	8	(3)	1,461
Total fixed income securities	51,952	86	(64)	51,974

Comparison of HTM, TS, and AFS Approaches

Illustration 12–9 compares accounting for the Masterwear bonds under the three different approaches.

Illustration 12–9 Comparison of HTM, TS, and AFS Approaches

	Held-to-Maturity (HTM)			Trading (TS)			Available-for-Sale (AFS)		
Purchase bonds at a discount	Investments	700,000		Same as HTM			Same as HTM		
	Discount		33,367						
	Cash		666,633						
Record interest revenue	Cash	42,000		Same as HTM			Same as HTM		
	Discount	4,664							
	Interest rev.		46,664						
Adjust to fair value, 2018	No entry			FV adjustment	43,646		FV adjustment	43,646	
				Holding gain—NI		43,646	Holding gain—OCI		43,646
Sell bonds in 2019									
1. Adjust to fair value, 2019	No entry			FV adjustment	10,057		FV adjustment	10,057	
				Holding gain—NI		10,057	Holding gain—OCI		10,057
2. Reclassify unrealized holding gains/losses	No entry			No entry			Reclassification—OCI	53,703	
							FV adjustment		53,703
3. Record sale of bonds	Cash	725,000		Cash	725,000		Cash	725,000	
	Discount	28,703		Discount	28,703		Discount	28,703	
	Investments		700,000	Investments		700,000	Investments		700,000
	Gain—NI		53,703	FV Adjustment		53,703	Gain—NI		53,703
	Note: Total gain of $53,703 is recognized in net income in the period of the sale.			Note: Total gain of $53,703 is recognized in net income over the periods in which the investment is held (43,646 + 10,057).			Note: Reclassification backs out unrealized gains from OCI (and therefore from AOCI), so total gain of $53,703 is recognized in net income in the period of the sale.		

AOCI

Debit	Credit
	43,646
	10,057
53,703	
	0

This side-by-side comparison highlights several aspects of these accounting approaches:

- To record the purchase of an investment and the receipt of interest revenue, we use identical entries in all three approaches.
- To record changes in fair value, the entries we use for TS and AFS securities have the same effect on the investment (via the fair value adjustment valuation allowance) and the same eventual effect on total shareholders' equity. What differs is whether the unrealized holding gain or loss is recognized in net income and then in retained earnings (TS) or recognized in OCI and then in AOCI (AFS). No fair value adjustment is reported for HTM securities.
- Regardless of approach, the cash flows are the same, and the same total amount of gain or loss is recognized in the income statement (TS: $43,646 in 2018 + $10,057 in 2019 = $53,703 total; AFS and HTM: $53,703 in 2019). The question is not *how much* total net income is recognized, but *when* the amounts are recognized in net income.

Additional Consideration

Available-for-Sale Investments and Income Taxes. When comparing accounting for TS and AFS securities, we saw that total shareholders' equity ends up being the same amount, regardless of whether unrealized gains and losses are included in net income and closed to retained earnings in shareholders' equity (for TS) or included only in OCI and shown in AOCI in shareholders' equity (for AFS securities). But what about taxes? Tax expense affects net income, so retained earnings includes after-tax amounts. For AOCI to be equivalent to retained earnings, it also should include only after-tax amounts. Therefore, adjustments must be made to OCI and AOCI to account for tax effects. Typically these adjustments also give rise to deferred tax assets and liabilities, as unrealized holding gains and losses rarely affect the current period's taxes payable. Deferred tax assets and liabilities are discussed in Chapter 16.

International Financial Reporting Standards

Accounting for Debt Investments. Until recently, *IAS No. 39* was the standard that specified appropriate accounting for all investments under IFRS.[15] The primary categories in *IAS No. 39* are similar to those in U.S. GAAP, consisting of Fair Value through Profit & Loss (FVPL), similar to TS, HTM, and AFS.

IFRS No. 9, amended on July 24, 2014, will be required after January 1, 2018, and earlier adoption is permitted, so until 2018 either *IAS No. 39* or *IFRS No. 9* might be in effect for a particular company.[16] *IFRS No. 9* eliminates the HTM and AFS classifications, replaced by new classifications that are more restrictive. Specifically, under *IFRS No. 9*, investments in debt securities are classified either as amortized cost (accounted for like HTM investments in U.S. GAAP), fair value through other comprehensive income ("FVOCI," accounted for like AFS investments, except for different impairment recognition criteria) or fair value through profit or loss ("FVPL," accounted for like trading securities). Classification depends on two criteria: (1) whether the investment's contractual cash flows consist solely of payments of principal and interest (SPPI), and (2) whether the business purpose of the investment is to hold it for purposes of collecting contractual cash flows, sell the investment at a profit, or both. If the investment qualifies as SPPI and is held only to collect cash flows, it is classified as amortized cost. If it qualifies as SPPI and is held both to collect cash flows and potentially be sold, it is classified as FVOCI. Otherwise it is classified as FVPL.

One other difference between U.S. GAAP and IFRS is worth noting. U.S. GAAP allows specialized accounting (beyond the scope of this textbook) for particular industries like securities brokers/dealers, investment companies, and insurance companies. IFRS does not.

[15] "Financial Instruments: Recognition and Measurement," *International Accounting Standard No. 39* (IASCF), as amended effective January 1, 2009.

[16] "Financial Instruments," *International Financial Reporting Standard No. 9* (IASCF), November 12, 2009, as amended effective January 1, 2016.

Transfers between Reporting Categories

At each reporting date, the appropriateness of the classification of a debt investment is reassessed. For instance, if the investor no longer has the ability to hold certain securities to maturity and will now hold them for resale, those securities would be reclassified from HTM to AFS. When a security is reclassified between two reporting categories, the security is transferred at its fair value on the date of transfer. Any unrealized holding gain or loss at reclassification should be accounted for *in a manner consistent with the classification into which the security is being transferred.* A summary is provided in Illustration 12–10.

A transfer of a security between reporting categories is accounted for at fair value and in accordance with *the new reporting classification.*

Illustration 12–10

Transfer between Investment Categories

Transfer from:	**To:**	**Unrealized Gain or Loss from Transfer at Fair Value**
Either HTM or AFS	Trading	Include in current net income the total unrealized gain or loss, as if it all occurred in the current period.
Trading	Either HTM or AFS	Include in current net income any unrealized gain or loss that occurred in the current period prior to the transfer. (Unrealized gains and losses that occurred in prior periods already were included in net income in those periods.)
Held-to-maturity	Available-for-sale	No current income effect. Report total unrealized gain or loss as a separate component of shareholders' equity (in AOCI).
Available-for-sale	Held-to-maturity	No current income effect. Don't write off any existing unrealized holding gain or loss in AOCI, but amortize it to net income over the remaining life of the security (fair value amount becomes the security's amortized cost basis).

Reclassifications are quite unusual, so when they occur, disclosure notes should describe the circumstances that resulted in the transfers. Other disclosure notes are described in a later section.

International Financial Reporting Standards

Transfers Between Investment Categories. *IAS No. 39* allows transfers of debt investments out of the FVPL category into AFS or HTM in "rare circumstances." Under *IFRS No. 9*, transfers of debt investments between the amortized cost, FVOCI, and FVPL categories occurs if and only if the company changes its business model with respect to the debt investment.

● LO12–9

Fair Value Option

You may recall from Chapter 1 that GAAP allows a **fair value option** (FVO) that permits companies to elect to account for most financial assets and liabilities at fair value. Under the FVO, HTM and AFS investments are shown in the balance sheet at their fair values, and unrealized gains and losses are recognized in net income in the period in which they occur. That accounting approach should sound familiar—it's the same approach we use to account for trading securities. However, unlike trading securities, purchases and sales of investments accounted for under the FVO are likely to be classified as investing activities in the statement of cash flows, because those investments are not held for sale in the near term and therefore are not operational in nature.

Choosing the *fair value option* for HTM and AFS investments means accounting for them like trading securities.

● LO12–8

The company decides whether to elect the FVO on the date the company purchases the investment. The company can elect the FVO for some securities and not for identical others—it's entirely up to the company, but the company has to explain in the notes why it made a partial election. The election is *irrevocable.* So, for example, if a company elects the FVO and later believes that the fair value of an investment is likely to decline, it can't change the election and discontinue use of fair value accounting to avoid recognizing a loss.

Why allow the FVO? As described in Appendix A of this book, companies sometimes enter into *hedging arrangements* that are intended to reduce earnings volatility by offsetting changes in the fair value of assets with changes in the fair value of liabilities. Complex rules apply to many hedging arrangements. The FVO simplifies this process by allowing companies to choose whether to use fair value for most types of financial assets and liabilities. Thus, when a company enters into a hedging arrangement, it just has to make sure to elect the FVO for each asset and liability in the hedging arrangement, and fair value changes of those assets and liabilities will be included in earnings.

International Financial Reporting Standards

LO12–9

Fair Value Option. International accounting standards are more restrictive than U.S. standards for determining when firms are allowed to elect the FVO. Under both *IAS No. 39* and *IFRS No. 9,* companies can elect the FVO only in specific circumstances. For example, a firm could elect the FVO for an asset or liability in order to avoid the "accounting mismatch" that occurs when some parts of a fair value risk-hedging arrangement are accounted for at fair value and others are not. Although U.S. GAAP indicates that the intent of the FVO is to address these sorts of circumstances, it does not require that those circumstances exist.

Impairment of Debt Investments

An "other-than-temporary" impairment loss is recognized in net income even though the security hasn't been sold.

In this chapter we've seen that declines (as well as increases) in the fair value of some investments are reported in earnings. For instance, if the fair value of an investment in trading securities declines, we reduce the reported amount of that investment in the balance sheet and include the loss from the fair value decline in the income statement. Likewise, if the investor has elected the FVO for HTM or AFS investments, those investments are accounted for as trading securities, so fair value changes always are recognized in earnings. Otherwise, fair value changes for HTM and AFS investments typically are not recognized in earnings.

However, there is an exception. If the fair value of an HTM or AFS investment declines below the amortized cost of the investment, and that decline is deemed to be *other-than-temporary (OTT),* the company recognizes an OTT impairment loss in earnings. Accounting for OTT impairments is complicated, both with respect to determining whether an impairment is OTT and in determining the amount of the impairment to include in earnings. After an OTT impairment is recognized, the ordinary treatment of unrealized gains and losses is resumed; that is, further changes in fair value are reported in OCI for AFS investments and not recognized for HTM investments.

CURRENT EXPECTED CREDIT LOSS (CECL) MODEL FOR DEBT INVESTMENTS. Guidance in this area is changing. Starting in 2020, companies will be required to use the CECL ("Current Expected Credit Loss") model to account for impairments of HTM and AFS investments, and companies can choose to use that approach starting in 2019.[17] The CECL model uses the allowance method to account for impairments that you learned to use to account for bad debts in Chapter 7. It requires recognizing impairments of HTM and AFS investments regardless of whether they are judged to be other than temporary. Therefore impairments of debt investments are likely to be recognized sooner under the CECL model than under the current approach.

An in-depth discussion of accounting for impairments of debt investments is provided in Appendix 12B.

[17]"Financial Instruments--Credit Losses (Topic 326)" *Accounting Standards Update 2016-13* (Norwalk, Conn: FASB, 2016).

International Financial Reporting Standards

Impairments. *IFRS No. 9,* amended on July 24, 2014, will be required after January 1, 2018, and earlier adoption is permitted.[18] *IFRS No. 9* calculates impairment of debt investments measured at amortized cost or FVOCI using the *expected credit loss (ECL)* model, which is somewhat similar to the CECL model that will be required soon in U.S. GAAP. Both the U.S. CECL model, and the IFRS ECL model calculate expected credit losses over the remaining life of the investment if there has been a significant increase in credit risk. The U.S. CECL model also does that if there has not been a significant increase in credit risk. In contrast, under the IFRS ECL model, if the credit risk of a debt investment has not increased, the estimate of credit losses only has to include credit losses that result from default events that are possible within the *next 12 months.* For many debt investments, this approach accrues very little credit loss, because the credit risk of the investment hasn't changed and default within the next twelve months is very unlikely. Companies can elect to always recognize lifetime credit losses, but it is unlikely that many will choose to do so. That means that U.S. GAAP will tend to recognize impairment losses earlier, and in higher amounts, than are recognized under IFRS. Further convergence in this area is unlikely in the near future.

● LO12–9

Concept Review Exercise

VARIOUS INVESTMENT SECURITIES

Diversified Services, Inc. offers a variety of business services, including financial services through its escrow division. Diversified's fiscal year ends on December 31. Diversified entered into the following investment activities during the last month of 2018 and the first week of 2019:

2018

Dec. 1	**Purchased $30 million of 12% bonds of Vince-Gill Amusement Corporation and $24 million of 10% bonds of Eastern Waste Disposal Corporation, both at face value. The Vince-Gill bonds are to be held until they mature. The Eastern Waste bonds are to be held but might be sold if cash needs require it. Interest on each bond issue is payable semiannually on November 30 and May 31.**
30	**Purchased U.S. Treasury bonds for $5.8 million as trading securities hoping to earn profits on short-term differences in prices.**
31	**Recorded the necessary adjusting entries relating to the investments.**

As of December 31, 2018, the fair value of the Vince-Gill bonds was $32 million, the fair value of the Eastern Waste bonds was $25 million, and the fair value of the Treasury bonds was $5.7 million.

2019

Jan. 7	**Sold the Eastern Waste bonds for $22 million and sold the U.S Treasury bonds for $6 million.**

Required:

1. Prepare the appropriate journal entry for each transaction or event and show the amounts that would be reported in the company's 2018 income statement relative to these investments. Record interest accruing in 2018, but ignore any interest accruing in 2019.
2. Determine the effects of the Eastern Waste investment on net income, other comprehensive income, and comprehensive income for 2018, 2019, and combined over both years. Ignore interest revenue.

[18] "Financial Instruments," *International Financial Reporting Standard No. 9* (IASCF), November 12, 2009, as amended effective January 1, 2016.

1. Journal entries:

2018

Dec. 1 **Purchased $30 million of 12% bonds of Vince-Gill Amusement Corporation and $24 million of 10% bonds of Eastern Waste Disposal Corporation, both at face value. The Vince-Gill bonds are to be held until they mature, but the Eastern Waste bonds are to be held but might be sold if cash needs require it. Interest on each bond issue is payable semiannually on November 30 and May 31.**

	($ in millions)	
Investment in HTM securities (Vince-Gill)	30	
Investment in AFS securities (Eastern Waste)	24	
Cash		54

Dec. 30 **Purchased U.S. Treasury bonds for $5.8 million as trading securities, hoping to earn profits on short-term differences in prices.**

	($ in millions)	
Investment in trading securities (U.S. Treasury bonds)	5.8	
Cash		5.8

Dec. 31 **Recorded the necessary adjusting entries relating to the investments.**

Accrued Interest (one month)	($ in millions)	
Interest receivable—Vince-Gill ($30 million × 12% × 1/12)	0.3	
Interest receivable—Eastern Waste ($24 million × 10% × 1/12)	0.2	
Interest revenue		0.5
Fair Value Adjustments		
Unrealized holding loss—NI ($5.7 − 5.8)	0.1	
Fair value adjustment, TS investments		0.1
Fair value adjustment, AFS investments ($25 million cost − 24 million fair value)	1	
Unrealized holding gain—OCI		1

Note: Securities held-to-maturity are not adjusted to fair value.

Reported in the 2018 Income Statement	($ in millions)
Interest revenue ($0.5 interest)	$0.5
Loss on investments (trading securities)	(0.1)

Note: The $1 million unrealized holding gain for the Eastern Waste bonds is not included in net income because it pertains to available-for-sale securities rather than trading securities, and so is reflected in OCI.

2019

Jan. 7 **Sold the Eastern Waste bonds for $22 million and sold the U.S Treasury bonds for $6 million.**

First consider the AFS investment (Eastern Waste). The fair value of the Eastern Waste bonds at the time of sale is $22 million. Those bonds were carried at a fair value of $25 million as of December 31, 2018, so have suffered an unrealized loss of $3 million during the first part of 2019.

	($ in millions)	
Unrealized holding loss—OCI ($25 − 22)	3	
Fair value adjustment, AFS investments		3

Second, given that the fair value adjustment for the Eastern Waste bonds now has a $2 million credit balance, we need to remove that amount and record the corresponding reclassification entry for OCI:

FV Adjustment, AFS Investments

Debit	Credit	
1		2018 unrealized gain
	3	2019 unrealized loss
	2	Preadjustment balance
2		Reclassification entry
	0	

	($ in millions)	
Fair value adjustment, AFS investments (account balance)	2	
Reclassification adjustment—OCI		2

Third, we need to record the receipt of cash and the loss realized upon sale of the investment:

	($ in millions)	
Cash	22	
Loss—NI (to balance)	2	
Investment in AFS securities (Eastern Waste)		24

Next consider the investment in trading securities (U.S. Treasuries). The fair value of the U.S. Treasury bonds at the time of sale is $6 million. Those bonds were carried at a fair value of $5.7 million as of December 31, 2018, so have enjoyed an unrealized holding gain of $0.3 million during the first part of 2019.

	($ in millions)	
Fair value adjustment, trading securities	0.3	
Unrealized holding gain—NI		0.3

FV Adjustment, U.S. Treasuries

Debit	Credit	
	0.1	2018 unrealized loss
0.3		2019 unrealized gain
0.2		Preadjustment balance
	0.2	Sale entry
0		

On the date of sale, we also need to record the receipt of cash and remove the accounts associated with the trading security from the balance sheet:

	($ in millions)	
Cash	6	
Fair value adjustment, trading securities (account balance)		0.2
Investment in trading securities (U.S. Treasury bonds)		5.8

2. Effects of the Eastern Waste investments on net income, other comprehensive income, and comprehensive income for 2018, 2019, and combined over both years. Ignore interest revenue.

	2018	2019	Cumulatively
Net Income	$0	($2)	($2)
OCI	$1	($3) + 2 = ($1)	$0
Comprehensive Income	$1	($3)	($2)

Financial Statement Presentation and Disclosure

Trading securities, held-to-maturity securities and available-for-sale securities are either current or noncurrent depending on when they are expected to mature or to be sold. However, it's not necessary that a company report individual amounts for the three categories of investments—held-to-maturity, available-for-sale, or trading—on the face of the balance sheet as long as that information is presented in the disclosure notes.[19]

Investors should disclose the following in the disclosure notes for each year presented:

- Aggregate fair value
- Gross realized and unrealized holding gains
- Gross realized and unrealized holding losses
- Change in net unrealized holding gains and losses
- Amortized cost basis by major security type

The notes also include disclosures designed to help financial statement users understand the quality of the inputs companies use when determining fair values and to identify parts of the financial statements that are affected by those fair value estimates. For example, the notes should include the level of the fair value hierarchy (levels 1, 2, or 3) in which all fair value measurements fall. For level 2 or 3 fair values, the notes to the financial statements must include a description of the valuation technique(s) and the inputs used in the fair value measurement process. For level 3 fair values, the notes must indicate the significant inputs used in the fair value measurement, the sensitivity of fair values to significant changes in those inputs, and information about the effect of fair value measurements on earnings, including a reconciliation of beginning and ending balances of the investment that identifies the following:

- Total gains or losses for the period (realized and unrealized), unrealized gains and losses associated with assets and liabilities still held at the reporting date, and where those amounts are included in earnings or shareholders' equity
- Purchases, sales, issuances, and settlements
- Transfers in and out of the level 3 category

All of this disclosure is designed to provide financial statement users with information about those fair values that are most vulnerable to bias or error in the estimation process. For example, as shown in Illustration 12–11, note 2 of HP Inc.'s 2015 annual report includes the following discussion of fair values.

Illustration 12–11

Fair Value Disclosures of Investment Securities—HP Incorporated

Real World Financials

Fair Value (partial)

	As of October 31, 2015			
	Fair Value Measured Using			
($ in millions)	Level 1	Level 2	Level 3	Total
Assets:				
Cash equivalents and Investments:				
Time deposits	$ –	$3,584	$ –	$ 3,584
Money market funds	8,895	–	–	8,895
Mutual funds	–	246	–	246
Marketable equity securities	52	10	–	62
Foreign bonds	8	347	–	355
Other debt securities	–	2	40	42
Derivative Instruments:				
Interest rate contracts	–	38	–	38
Foreign exchange contracts	–	1,029	2	1,031
Other derivatives	–	8	–	8
Total assets	$8,955	$5,264	$42	$14,261

[19]FASB ASC 320–10–45–13: Investments–Debt Securities–Overall–Other Presentation Matters (previously *Statement of Financial Accounting Standards No. 115*, "Accounting for Certain Investments in Debt and Equity Securities" (Norwalk, Conn.: FASB, 1993), par. 18).

We can see from these disclosures that HP has relatively few level 3 investments (which are those with the most subjectively estimated fair values). That fact should give financial statement users more faith in the reliability of HP's fair value estimates.

Accounting for Equity Investments

PART B

The critical events over the life of an investment in the equity of another company, such as shares of common stock, include the following:

1. Purchasing the equity security
2. Receiving dividends (for some equity securities)
3. Holding the investment during periods in which the investment's fair value changes (and thus incurring *unrealized holding* gains and losses, since the security has not yet been sold)
4. Selling the investment (and thus incurring *realized* gains and losses, since the security has been sold and the gains or losses actually incurred)

Also, equity investors typically get to vote on key decisions made by the company, such as who will serve on the company's board of directors. Each share of common stock gets a vote, so if an equity investor owns enough shares, the investor has enough votes to influence the operations of the company whose shares it owns. Therefore, accounting for equity investments also considers the extent to which the investor can influence the activities of the investee. As shown in Illustration 12–12, we use three different approaches to account for equity investments.

Illustration 12–12
Reporting Categories for Equity Investments

Characteristics of the Equity Investment	Reporting Method Used by the Investor
The investor ***lacks significant influence*** over the operating and financial policies of the investee (typically owns less than 20% of voting stock):	**Fair Value Through Net Income**—similar to the trading-securities approach used for debt; investment reported at fair value (with unrealized holding gains and losses included in net income), unless fair value is not readily determinable*
The investor ***has significant influence*** over the operating and financial policies of the investee (typically owns between 20% and 50% of the voting stock):	**Equity method**—investment reported at cost adjusted for investor's share of subsequent earnings and dividends of the investee**
The investor ***controls*** the investee (typically owns more than 50% of voting stock):	**Consolidation**—the financial statements of the investor and investee are combined as if they are a single company

*Later in this chapter we discuss in an Additional Consideration box the alternative approach that is used if fair value is not readily determinable.
**If the investor elects the *fair value option*, this type of investment also can be accounted for using the fair-value-through-net-income approach.

We'll first discuss the *fair value through net income* approach that is used when the investor lacks significant influence over the investee. Then we'll cover the *equity method* that's used when the investor does have significant influence. We won't cover *consolidation accounting,* which is used when the investor controls the investee, as that topic is beyond the scope of this book. However, we will discuss consolidations briefly when we discuss the equity method, as the two approaches are related.

When the Investor Lacks Significant Influence: Fair Value through Net Income

If an investor owns less than 20% of the voting shares of an investee, the investor is typically assumed to lack significant influence over the investee. In other words, the investor is in the same position you would be in if you bought a share of the company's stock—the investor

LO12–5

hopes to receive dividends and that the value of the shares appreciate over time, but can't really tell the company what to do.

Until very recently, those sorts of equity investments were accounted for as either trading securities or available-for-sale investments, just like we would treat debt investments that weren't intended to be held to maturity. However, starting in 2018, investors are not allowed to use the AFS approach for equity investments. Instead, all equity investments are accounted for like trading securities, using a classification commonly referred to as *fair value through net income*. That means that equity investments for which the investor lacks significant influence are reported the same way we report debt investments that are classified as trading securities (Part A of this chapter). The equity investments are carried at fair value in the balance sheet, with unrealized holding gains and losses recognized in net income in whatever period they occur.[20] Illustration 12–13 provides a simple example of an equity investment that we'll use throughout this section. Let's walk through the key events in the life of United's Arjent investment to see how the fair value through net income approach works for an equity investment.

Illustration 12–13

Example of an Equity Investment Accounted for as Fair Value Through Net Income

The following events during 2018 and 2019 pertain to United Intergroup's investment in the common stock of Arjent, Inc.

July 1, 2018	**Purchase** Arjent, Inc., common stock for $1,500,000
December 31, 2018	**Recognize investment revenue** for a $75,000 cash dividend received from Arjent.
December 31, 2018	**Record a fair value adjustment** to recognize a decline in the value of the Arjent stock investment to $1,450,000.
January 5, 2019	**Sell** the Arjent stock for $1,446,000.

Purchase Investments

All equity investments are recorded initially at cost.

The journal entry to record the purchase of an equity investment is simple, just exchanging one asset (cash) for another (investment):

July 1, 2018		
Investment in Arjent stock	1,500,000	
Cash		1,500,000

Recognize Investment Revenue

Dividends received for equity investments are included in income.

The journal entry to record the receipt of dividends related to the Arjent equity investment also is straightforward.

December 31, 2018		
Cash	75,000	
Dividend revenue		75,000

Adjust Equity Investments to Fair Value (2018)

Equity investments are adjusted to their fair value at each reporting date.

The carrying value of equity investments must be adjusted to fair value at the end of every reporting period. As with trading securities, we use a valuation allowance, *fair value adjustment*, to increase or decrease the carrying value of the investment, and we simultaneously record an unrealized holding gain or loss that is included in net income in the period in which fair value changes. The next table shows the calculation of the balance in the fair value adjustment that is required on December 31, 2018.

December 31, 2018

Security	Cost	Fair Value	Necessary Fair Value Adjustment Balance
Arjent	$1,500,000	$1,450,000	$(50,000)

[20]FASB ASC 321–10–35–1: Investments–Equity Securities–Overall–General (previously *Accounting Standards Update No. 2016-1*, "Recognition and Measurement of Financial Assets and Financial Liabilities" (Norwalk, Conn.: FASB, 2016)).

United needs to move the fair value adjustment from a balance of $0 (at purchase date) to a credit balance of $50,000:

	Fair Value Adjustment
Beginning balance	$ 0
± Adjustment needed to update fair value	?
Balance needed on 12/31/2018	$(50,000)

Fair Value Adjustment	
0	
	50,000
	50,000

The journal entry to record United's unrealized holding loss of $50,000 and the corresponding decrease in United's fair value adjustment account is:

December 31, 2018		
Unrealized holding loss—NI*	50,000	
Fair value adjustment†		50,000

*We title this account "Unrealized . . .—NI" to highlight that, for equity investments accounted for as fair value through net income, unrealized holding gains and losses are included in net income in the period in which they occur.
†Sometimes companies don't bother with a separate fair value adjustment account and simply adjust the investment account to fair value.

What if Arjent's investment instead had a fair value of, say, $1,550,000 as of December 31, 2018? In that case, United would have an unrealized holding *gain* of $50,000, which would require a *debit* to the fair value adjustment account to *increase* the carrying value of the equity to fair value.

Sell the Equity Investment

Now assume United sells the Arjent stock for $1,446,000 on January 5, 2019. According to the FASB, "because all changes in an equity security's fair value are reported in earnings as they occur, the sale of an equity security does not necessarily give rise to a gain or loss. Generally, a debit to cash . . . is recorded for the sales proceeds, and a credit is recorded to remove the security at its fair value (or sales price)."[21] Thus, as with trading securities, United must make two journal entries. United first records in net income any unrealized holding gains and losses that occurred during 2019 prior to the date of sale. Then, on the date of sale, United records the receipt of cash and removes the amounts associated with the investment from the relevant balance sheet accounts.

1. **Adjust Securities to Fair Value (2019).** We first need to update the fair value adjustment and recognize any unrealized holding gains or losses that have occurred during the current reporting period prior to the date of sale.

January 5, 2019

Security	Cost	Fair Value	Necessary Fair Value Adjustment Balance
Arjent	$1,500,000	$1,446,000	$(54,000)

United needs to move the fair value adjustment from a credit balance of $50,000 to a credit balance of $54,000, which requires a credit of $4,000 to this asset valuation account:

	Fair Value Adjustment
Beginning balance on 1/1/2019	$ (50,000)
± Adjustment needed to update fair value	?
Balance needed as of date of sale	$(54,000)

Fair Value Adjustment	
0	50,000
	4,000
	54,000

The journal entry to record the investment's decrease in fair value is:

[21]FASB ASC 321-10-40: Investments–Equity Securities–Overall–Derecognition, (previously *Accounting Standards Update No. 2016-1,* "Recognition and Measurement of Financial Assets and Financial Liabilities" (Norwalk, Conn.: FASB, 2016)).

January 5, 2019		
Unrealized holding loss—NI	4,000	
Fair value adjustment		4,000

2. **Record the Sale.** After making the previous journal entry, the investment is carried at its fair value as of the date it is being sold, and all unrealized holding gains and losses associated with the investment have been included in net income. All that remains is for United to record receipt of cash and remove the investment-related accounts from the balance sheet:

January 5, 2019		
Cash	1,446,000	
Fair value adjustment (account balance)	54,000	
Investment in Arjent stock (account balance)		1,500,000

If all of the unrealized holding gains or losses have been included in net income, no additional gain or loss is recognized.

A *realized* gain or loss for the difference between carrying value and the cash received from selling an equity investment is included in net income.

Because United carries the investment at fair value as of the date of sale, and already included in net income the entire loss associated with the investment, there is no realized gain or loss to recognize on the date of sale.[22] Over the life of the investment, United has recognized a total loss of $54,000, but that loss is spread over the life of the investment, recognized as the fair value of the investment changes:

2018 loss recognized in NI:	$(50,000)
2019 loss recognized in NI:	(4,000)
Total over 2018 and 2019:	$(54,000)

Adjust Equity Investments to Fair Value (2019)

If United hadn't sold the Arjent investment during 2019, it would just keep recording whatever fair value adjustment would be necessary to carry the investment at fair value in the balance sheet. For example, if the Arjent investment had a fair value of $1,300,000 at December 31, 2019, United would face the following situation:

December 31, 2019

Security	Cost	Fair Value	Necessary Fair Value Adjustment Balance
Arjent	$1,500,000	$1,300,000	$(200,000)

United would need to credit the fair value adjustment account by another $150,000 to account for the large drop in fair value that occurred during 2019.

Fair Value Adjustment

	50,000
	150,000
	200,000

	Fair Value Adjustment
12/31/2018 balance	$ (50,000)
± Adjustment needed to update fair value	?
12/31/2019 balance	$(200,000)

[22]As noted in FASB ASC 321-10-40: Investments–Equity Securities–Overall–Derecognition, for expediency companies may not update the fair value adjustment to the fair value that exists on the date of sale before recording the sale. In that case, this second entry would include a realized gain or loss based on the difference between the cash received and the fair value of the investment recorded on the last balance sheet date. In our example, the fair value adjustment balance was $50,000 as of December 31, 2018, and United would record the following sale entry on January 5, 2019:

Cash	1,446,000	
Fair value adjustment (account balance)	50,000	
Realized loss—NI	4,000	
Investment in Arjent		1,500,000

The necessary journal entry is shown below:

December 31, 2019		
Unrealized holding loss—NI	150,000	
Fair value adjustment (calculated above)		150,000

Additional Consideration

What If Fair Value Is Not Readily Determinable?. Equity investments are accounted for using the *fair value through net income* approach when the fair value of shares is *readily determinable* by referencing prices on a security exchange or over-the-counter market. But what if fair value isn't readily determinable? In that case, investors can elect to base measurement of fair value on an adjusted cost of the security. Specifically, the investor estimates fair value as cost, minus any impairments that have been recognized previously, and plus or minus adjustments indicated by changes in the prices of similar equity issued by the same investee. Every accounting period, the investor needs to reevaluate whether fair value still is not readily determinable, and also needs to assess whether the investment has been impaired. The investor considers various qualitative factors to assess whether an investment is impaired, such as whether the earnings, cash flows, or business prospects of the investee have deteriorated. If the investor concludes the investment is impaired, it recognizes in net income whatever amount of impairment loss is necessary to reduce the carrying value of the investment to fair value.

International Financial Reporting Standards

● LO12–8

Accounting for Equity Investments When the Investor Lacks Significant Influence. As indicated previously, until recently *IAS No. 39* was the standard that specified appropriate accounting for all investments under IFRS.[23] The primary categories in *IAS No. 39* are similar to those used for debt investments in U.S. GAAP, consisting of Fair Value through Profit & Loss (FVPL), similar to TS, HTM, and AFS. *IFRS No. 9,* amended on July 24, 2014, will be required after January 1, 2018, and earlier adoption is permitted, so until 2018 either *IAS No. 39* or *IFRS No. 9* might be in effect for a particular company.[24] Under *IFRS No. 9,* investments in equity securities are classified as either FVPL or FVOCI (Fair Value through Other Comprehensive Income). If the equity is held for trading, it must be classified as FVPL, but otherwise the company can irrevocably elect to classify it as FVOCI. FVOCI is similar to the AFS treatment used for debt investments in U.S. GAAP, but there is an important difference. Unlike AFS, realized gains and losses are not reclassified out of OCI and into net income when the investment is later sold. Rather, the accumulated unrealized gain or loss associated with a sold investment is just transferred from AOCI to retained earnings (both shareholders' equity accounts), without passing through the income statement.

Financial Statement Presentation

We present investments in equity securities in the financial statements the same way we present debt investments classified as trading securities, but they are shown on their own separate line. Equity investments that are held for trading should be classified as current assets in the balance sheet, with cash flows treated as operating activities on the statement of cash flows. On the other hand, equity investments that are held for more long-term purposes should be classified as noncurrent assets in the balance sheet, with cash flows typically treated as investing activities in the statement of cash flows. Notes to the financial

[23]"Financial Instruments: Recognition and Measurement," *International Accounting Standard No. 39* (IASCF), as amended effective January 1, 2009.

[24]"Financial Instruments," *International Financial Reporting Standard No. 9* (IASCF), November 12, 2009, as amended effective January 1, 2016.

statements should disclose the portion of unrealized holding gains and losses for the period that relate to any equity securities still held by the company at the end of the reporting period. Notes also should provide information about how the carrying value was calculated for equity investments for which fair value is not readily determinable.

Additional Consideration

Transition from Prior GAAP. Our discussion of investments in equity securities is based on *ASU 2016-01*, which becomes effective for fiscal years beginning after December 15, 2017.[25] Prior to that ASU, equity investments could be treated as trading securities or AFS investments, similar to debt investments. When companies adopt *ASU 2016-01*, they will make a cumulative-effect adjustment to the balance sheet as of the beginning of the period of adoption, adjusting equity AFS investments to fair value on that date and adjusting retained earnings to appear as if those investments had been accounted for at fair value through net income all along.

When the Investor Has Significant Influence: The Equity Method

● LO12–6

Control and Significant Influence

Usually an investor can *control* the investee if it owns more than 50% of the investees voting shares.

Consolidated financial statements combine the individual elements of the parent and subsidiary statements.

If a company acquires more than 50% of the voting stock of another company, it's said to have **control**, because by voting those shares, the investor actually can control the company acquired. The investor is called the *parent;* the investee is called the *subsidiary.* Both companies continue to operate as separate legal entities, and the subsidiary reports separate financial statements. However, because of the controlling interest, the parent company reports **consolidated financial statements** which treat the parent and the subsidiary as if there were only one company. This entails an item-by-item combination of the parent and subsidiary statements (after first eliminating any amounts that are shared by the separate financial statements).[26] For instance, if the parent has $8 million cash and the subsidiary has $3 million cash, the consolidated balance sheet would report $11 million cash.

Usually an investor can exercise *significant influence* over the investee when it owns at least 20% of the investee's voting shares.

Even if effective control is absent, the investor still may be able to exercise **significant influence** over the operating and financial policies of the investee. This would be the case if the investor owns a large percentage of the outstanding shares relative to other shareholders. By voting those shares as a block, decisions often can be swayed in the direction the investor desires. It is presumed, in the absence of evidence to the contrary, that the investor exercises significant influence over the investee when it owns at least 20% of the investee's voting shares.[27]

The equity method is used when an investor can't control, but can significantly influence, the investee.

When significant influence exists but the investor does not have effective control, the investment should be accounted for by the **equity method**. Under the equity method, the investment is initially recorded at cost. After that, the investment balance is:

Under the *equity method,* the investor recognizes on its own income statement its proportionate share of the investee's income.

- Increased by the investor's percentage share of the investee's net income (or decreased by its share of a loss).
- Decreased by the investor's percentage share of the investee's dividends paid.
- Potentially adjusted for other items (discussed next).

[25]FASB ASC 321–10–35–1: Investments–Equity Securities–Overall–General (previously *Accounting Standards Update No. 2016-1,* "Recognition and Measurement of Financial Assets and Financial Liabilities" (Norwalk, Conn.: FASB, 2016)).

[26]This avoids double counting those amounts in the consolidated statements. For example, amounts owed by one company to the other are represented by accounts payable in one set of financial statements and accounts receivable in the other. These amounts are not included in the statements of the consolidated entity because a company can't "owe itself."

[27]Shareholders are the owners of the corporation. By voting their shares, it is they who determine the makeup of the board of directors—who, in turn, appoint officers—who, in turn, manage the company. Common stock usually is the class of shares that has voting privileges. However, a corporation can create classes of preferred shares that also have voting rights. This is discussed at greater length in Chapter 18.

Additional Consideration

It's possible that a company owns more than 20% of the voting shares but still cannot exercise significant influence over the investee. If, for instance, another company or a small group of shareholders owns 51% or more of the shares, they control the investee regardless of how other investors vote their shares. GAAP provides this and other examples of indications that an investor may be unable to exercise significant influence.

- The investee challenges the investor's ability to exercise significant influence (through litigation or complaints to regulators).
- The investor surrenders significant shareholder rights in a signed agreement.
- The investor is unable to acquire sufficient information about the investee to apply the equity method.
- The investor tries and fails to obtain representation on the board of directors of the investee.[28]

Conversely, it's also possible that a company owns less than 20% of the voting shares but is able to exercise significant influence over the investee. Ability to exercise significant influence with less than 20% ownership might be indicated, for example, by having an officer of the investor corporation on the board of directors of the investee corporation or by having, say, 18% of the voting shares while no other single investor owns more than 50%. In such cases the equity method would be appropriate.

FINANCIAL Reporting Case

Q4, p. 643

The rationale for this approach is the presumption that the fortunes of the investor and investee are so intertwined that, as the investee prospers, the investor prospers proportionately. Stated differently, as the investee earns additional net assets (income), the investor's share of those net assets increases. When the investee pays out assets (dividends), the investor's share of the remaining net assets decreases.

To see how the equity method works, let's turn to Illustration 12–14. In that illustration, we assume that United Intergroup purchased **30%** of Arjent, Inc.'s, common stock for $1,500,000 cash on January 2, 2018. Let's start by thinking about Arjent overall, and then we'll account for United's 30% investment.

Illustration 12–14

Information for Arjent, Inc., at the time United Intergroup purchased 30% for $1,500,000.

	Book Value on Arjent's Financial Statements	Fair Value at Time of United's Investment	
Total fair value of Arjent (1/2/2018)			$5,000,000*
Buildings**	$1,000,000	$2,000,000	
Land	500,000	1,000,000	
Other net assets†	600,000	600,000	
Net assets	$2,100,000		3,600,000
Goodwill			$1,400,000
Other information (12/31/2018):			
Arjent's 2018 net income:	$ 500,000		
Arjent's 2018 dividends:	$ 250,000		

*$5,000,000 × 30% purchased = **$1,500,000 purchase price.**
**10-year remaining useful life, no salvage value.
†Other net assets = other assets – total liabilities.

As shown in Illustration 12–14, buying 30% of Arjent for $1,500,000 implies that the full (100%) *fair value* of Arjent's assets and liabilities is $5,000,000 (because $5,000,000 × 30% purchased = $1,500,000 purchase price). However, notice that the *book value* of Arjent's net assets is only $2,100,000. Why do fair value and book value differ? Part of the difference in total fair value and book value represents assets (in this case, buildings and

[28]FASB ASC 323–10–15–10: Investments–Equity Method and Joint Ventures–Overall–Scope and Scope Exceptions (previously "Criteria for Applying the Equity Method of Accounting for Investments in Common Stock," FASB Interpretation No. 35 (Stamford, Conn.: FASB, 1981)).

land) that have fair values greater than their book values. Arjent recorded those assets at historical cost and recognized depreciation of the buildings over time, so the book values of those assets don't reflect their fair values. The remaining difference is previously unrecognized goodwill (e.g., because of loyal customers, well-trained workers, etc.) that GAAP doesn't capture as separate assets but nevertheless represents value for which United was willing to pay. We will see that, under the equity method, all of these amounts are shown in a single investment account, but we still need to track their individual information to account for them correctly.

Purchase of Investment

Recording United's purchase of 30% of Arjent is straightforward. The investment is recorded at cost:

Investment in Arjent stock	1,500,000	
Cash		1,500,000

Recording Investment Revenue

As the investee earns additional net assets, the investor's investment in those net assets increases.

Under the equity method, the investor includes in net income its proportionate share of the investee's net income. The reasoning is that, as the investee earns additional net assets, the value of the investor's share of those net assets also increases, so the investor increases its investment by the amount of income recognized. United's entry would be:

Investment in Arjent stock	150,000	
Investment revenue (30% × $500,000)		150,000

Of course, if Argent had recorded a net loss rather than net income, United would *reduce* its investment in Arjent and recognize a *loss* on investment for its share of the loss. You won't always see these amounts called "investment revenue" or "investment loss." Rather, United might call this line "equity in earnings (losses) of affiliate" or some other title that suggests it is using the equity method.

Receiving Dividends

As the investee distributes net assets as dividends, the investor does not recognize revenue. Rather, the investor's investment in the investee's net assets is reduced.

Because we recognize investment revenue as it is earned by the investee, it would be inappropriate to recognize revenue again when earnings are distributed as dividends. That would be double counting. Instead, we view the dividend distribution as reducing the investee's net assets. The rationale is that the investee is returning assets to its investors in the form of a cash payment, so each investor's equity interest in the remaining net assets declines proportionately.

Cash	75,000	
Investment in Arjent stock (30% × $250,000)		75,000

Further Adjustments

LO12–7

When the investor's expenditure to acquire an equity-method investment exceeds the book value of the underlying net assets acquired, additional adjustments to both the investment account and investment revenue might be needed. The purpose is to approximate the effects of consolidation, without actually consolidating financial statements. More specifically, both the investment account and investment revenue are adjusted for differences between net income reported by the investee and what that amount would have been if consolidation procedures had been followed. This process is often referred to as "amortizing the differential," because it mimics the process of expensing some of the difference between the price paid for the investment and the book value of the investment. Let's look closer at what that means.

Consolidated financial statements report (a) the acquired company's assets at their fair values on the date of acquisition rather than their book values on the investee's balance sheet, and (b) goodwill for the excess of the acquisition price over the fair value of the identifiable net assets acquired. This matters because increasing asset balances to their fair values can result in higher expenses in the future. If it's land or goodwill that's increased, there is no income effect because we don't depreciate or amortize those assets over time.[29] On the other hand, if buildings, equipment, or other depreciable assets are recorded at higher values, depreciation expense will be higher during their remaining useful lives. Likewise, if the recorded amount of inventory is increased, cost of goods sold will be higher when the inventory is sold. When expenses rise, income falls. It is this negative effect on income that the equity method seeks to imitate.

In our example, United needs to make adjustments for the fact that, at the time it purchased its investment in Arjent, the fair values of Arjent's assets and liabilities were higher than the book values of those assets and liabilities in Arjent's balance sheet (refer back to Illustration 12–14). Illustration 12–15 shows United's 30% proportionate share of the amounts shown in Illustration 12–14:

Illustration 12–15

Explanation for Differences Between the Investment and the Book Value of Net Assets Acquired

	Investee Net Assets		Net Assets Purchased		
Purchase price	$5,000,000	× 30% =	$1,500,000		
Fair value (identifiable)	3,600,000	× 30% =	1,080,000		
Difference	$1,400,000	× 30% =	$ 420,000	Goodwill	
Fair value (identifiable)	$3,600,000	× 30% =	$1,080,000		
Book value (identifiable)	2,100,000	× 30% =	630,000		
Difference	$1,500,000	× 30% =	$ 450,000	{ Buildings	$300,000
				Land	$150,000

Notice in Illustration 12–15 that United paid $1,500,000 for 30% of the identifiable net assets that, sold separately, would have a fair value of $1,080,000. The $420,000 difference between the price paid and the fair value of United's share of Arjent's identifiable net assets is attributable to goodwill. The 30% of identifiable net assets with a fair value of $1,080,000 have a book value on Arjent's balance sheet of only $630,000. The $450,000 difference is attributable to undervalued buildings ($300,000) and land ($150,000). Now let's see what adjustments, if any, United needs to make for these differences.

Adjustments for Additional Depreciation

When Arjent determines its net income, it bases depreciation expense on the book value of its buildings on its own balance sheet. United, however, needs to depreciate its share of the *fair value* of those buildings at the time it made its investment. To account for this higher amount of depreciation expense, United reduces investment revenue as if Arjent had included the additional expense in its earnings.

The investor adjusts its share of the investee's net income to reflect revenues and expenses associated with differences between the fair value and book value of the investee's assets and liabilities that existed at the time the investment was made.

As shown in Illustration 12–14, the book value of Argent's buildings is $1,000,000 and the fair value is $2,000,000, which creates a difference of $1,000,000. United will need to recognize its 30% share of additional depreciation expense for this difference, totaling $300,000 over the remaining life of the buildings. Assuming a 10-year life of the buildings and straight-line depreciation, United must recognize $30,000 of additional depreciation each year for ten years. Had Arjent recorded that additional depreciation in its income statement, United's portion of Arjent's net income would have been lower by $30,000 (ignoring taxes). So, to act as if Arjent had recorded the additional depreciation, United reduces investment revenue and reduces its investment in Arjent stock by $30,000.

---

[29]Goodwill is not amortized periodically to expense. Only if the asset's value is subsequently judged to be impaired will all or a portion of the recorded amount charged against earnings. FASB ASC 350–20–35: Intangibles–Goodwill and Other–Goodwill–Subsequent Measurement (previously "Goodwill and Other Intangible Assets," *Statement of Financial Accounting Standards No. 141* (Norwalk, Conn.: FASB, 2001)). For review, see Chapter 11.

Investment revenue	30,000	
Investment in Arjent stock [30% × ($2,000,000 – 1,000,000) ÷ 10 years]		30,000

No Adjustments for Land or Goodwill

United makes no adjustments for land or goodwill. Land is not an asset we depreciate. As a result, the difference between the fair value and book value of the land would not cause higher expenses, and we have no need to adjust investment revenue or the investment in Arjent stock for the land.

Recall from Chapter 11 that goodwill, unlike most other intangible assets, is not amortized. In that sense, goodwill resembles land. Thus, acquiring goodwill will not cause higher expenses, so we have no need to adjust investment revenue or the investment in Arjent stock for goodwill.

Adjustments for Other Assets and Liabilities

If the fair value of purchased inventory exceeds its book value, we usually assume the inventory is sold in the next year and reduce investment revenue in the next year by the entire difference.

Also, because in our example there is no difference between the book value and fair value of the remaining net assets, we don't need an adjustment for them either. However, that often will not be the case. For example, Arjent's inventory could have had a fair value that exceeded its book value at the time United purchased its Arjent investment. To recognize expense associated with that higher fair value, United would need to identify the period in which that inventory is sold (usually the next year) and, in that period, reduce its investment revenue and its investment in Arjent stock by its 30% share of the difference between the fair value and book value of the inventory. If, for instance, the $1,000,000 difference between fair value and book value had been attributable to inventory rather than buildings, and that inventory was sold by Arjent in the year following United's investment, United would reduce investment revenue by its 30% share of the difference ($300,000) in the year following the investment. More generally, an equity method investor needs to make these sorts of adjustments whenever there are revenues or expenses associated with an asset or liability that had a difference between book value and fair value at the time the investment was made.

Additional Consideration

Effect on Deferred Income Taxes. Investment revenue is recorded by the equity method when income is earned by the investee, but that revenue is not taxed until it's actually received as cash dividends. This creates a temporary difference between book income and taxable income. You will learn in Chapter 16 that the investor must report a deferred tax liability for the income tax that ultimately will be paid when the income eventually is received as dividends.

Reporting the Investment

The carrying amount of the investment is its initial cost plus the investor's equity in the undistributed earnings of the investee.

The fair value of the investment shares at the end of the reporting period is not reported when using the equity method. The investment account is reported at its original cost, increased by the investor's share of the investee's net income (adjusted for additional expenses like depreciation), and decreased by the portion of those earnings actually received as dividends.

The balance of United's 30% investment in Arjent at December 31, 2018, would be calculated as follows:

Investment in Arjent Stock

Purchase price	1,500,000		
Share of income	150,000		
		75,000	Dividends
		30,000	Depreciation adjustment
	1,545,000		

In the statement of cash flows, we report the purchase and sale of the investment as outflows and inflows of cash in the investing activities section, and the receipt of dividends is reported as an inflow of cash in the operating activities section.[30]

Additional Consideration

Much like consolidation, the equity method views the investor and investee collectively as a special type of single entity (as if the two companies were one company). However, the equity method doesn't require the investor to record separate financial statement items of the investee on an item-by-item basis as in consolidation. Instead, the investor reports its equity interest in the investee as a single investment account. Also, the adjustments that investors make when applying the equity method are designed to mimic what would happen if an investment were consolidated. For those reasons, the equity method sometimes is referred to as a "one-line consolidation," because it essentially collapses the consolidation approach into single lines in the balance sheet and income statement, while having the same effect on total income and shareholders' equity.

When the Investment is Acquired in Mid-Year

Obviously, we've simplified the illustration by assuming the investment was acquired at the beginning of 2018, entailing a full year's income, dividends, and adjustments to account for the income effects of any differences between book value and fair value on the date the investment was acquired. In the more likely event that an investment is acquired sometime after the beginning of the year, applying the equity method is easily modified to include the appropriate fraction of each of those amounts. For example, if United's purchase of 30% of Arjent had occurred on October 1 rather than January 2, we would simply record income, dividends, and adjustments for three months (3/12) of the year. This would result in the following entries to the investment account:

Investment in Arjent Stock

Cost	1,500,000		
Share of income (3/12 × $150,000)	37,500		
		7,500	Depreciation adjustment (3/12 × $30,000)
		18,750	Dividends (3/12 × $75,000)
	1,511,250		

Changes in the investment account the first year are adjusted for the fraction of the year the investor has owned the investment.

AT&T reported its 2015 investments in affiliated companies for which it exercised significant influence using the equity method as shown in Illustration 12–16.

When the Investee Reports a Net Loss

Our illustration assumed the investee earned net income. If the investee reports a *net loss* instead, the investment account would be *decreased* by the investor's share of the investee's net loss (adjusted for additional expenses).

What If Conditions Change?

A CHANGE FROM THE EQUITY METHOD TO ANOTHER METHOD. When the investor's level of influence changes, it may be necessary to change from the equity method

[30]Most companies prepare a statement of cash flows using the indirect method of reporting operating activities. In that case, the operating section begins with net income and adjustments are made to back out the effects of accrual accounting and calculate cash from operations. For companies with equity method investments, net income will include investment revenue and gains or losses associated with sold investments, but cash from operations should include only cash dividends. As an example, because United's 2018 net income includes $120,000 of investment revenue from Arjent ($150,000 portion of income - $30,000 depreciation adjustment), but United received only $75,000 of dividends from Arjent, an indirect method statement of cash flows would include an adjustment, often titled "undistributed earnings of investee," that reduces net income by $45,000 ($75,000 - $120,000) when determining cash from operations.

Illustration 12–16
Equity Method Investments in the Balance Sheet—AT&T

Real World Financials

	Dec 31, 2015	Dec 31, 2014
Total current assets	$ 35,992	$ 33,606
Property, plant, and equipment—Net	124,450	112,898
Goodwill	104,568	69,692
Licenses	93,093	60,824
Customer lists and relationships—Net	18,208	812
Other intangible assets—net	9,409	5,327
Investments in equity affiliates	1,606	250
Other assets	15,346	13,425
Total assets	$402,672	$296,834

Additional Consideration

It's possible that the investor's proportionate share of investee losses could exceed the carrying amount of the investment. If this happens, the investor should discontinue applying the equity method until the investor's share of subsequent investee earnings has equaled losses not recognized during the time the equity method was discontinued. This avoids reducing the investment account below zero.

to another method. For example, when Air-France/KLM's ownership interest in WAM (Amadeus) declined from 22% to 15% during the 2011 fiscal year, it had to stop using the equity method to account for its investment.

When this situation happens, *no adjustment* is made to the remaining carrying amount of the investment. Instead, the equity method is simply discontinued and the new method applied from then on. The balance in the investment account when the equity method is discontinued would serve as the new cost basis for writing the investment up or down to fair value on the next set of financial statements.

A CHANGE FROM ANOTHER METHOD TO THE EQUITY METHOD. Sometimes companies change from another method to the equity method. For example, when the Mitsubishi UFJ Financial Group converted its investment in the convertible preferred stock of Morgan Stanley into common stock, its ownership interest was large enough to qualify for accounting for the investment under the equity method. When a change *to* the equity method is appropriate, the previous method is discontinued and the balance in the investment account at the date of the change (including any unrealized holding gains or losses that occurred prior to the date the investment qualifies for the equity method) is used as the starting balance for applying the equity method. Any cost of acquiring additional shares is added to that balance, and going forward that balance is adjusted for the investor's portion of investee earnings and dividends. A disclosure note also should describe the change.[31]

IF AN EQUITY METHOD INVESTMENT IS SOLD. When an investment reported by the equity method is sold, we recognize a gain or loss if the selling price is more or less than the carrying amount (book value) of the investment. For example, let's continue our illustration and assume United sells its investment in Arjent on January 1, 2019, for $1,446,000. A journal entry would record a loss as follows:

When an equity method investment is sold, a gain or loss is recognized for the difference between its selling price and its carrying amount.

Cash	1,446,000	
Loss on sale of investments (to balance)	99,000	
Investment in Arjent stock (account balance)		1,545,000

[31]Retroactive restatement used to be required when a company changed to the equity method, but as of 2017 that is no longer necessary, per FASB ASC 323–10–35–33: Investments–Equity Method and Joint Ventures–Overall–Increase in Level of Ownership or Degree of Influence (previously "Investments—Equity Method and Joint Ventures (Topic 323): Simplifying the Transition to the Equity Method of Accounting," *Accounting Standards Update No. 2016-07* (Norwalk, Conn.: FASB, 2016)).

COMPARISON OF FAIR VALUE AND THE EQUITY METHOD. Illustration 12–17 compares accounting for the Arjent investment at fair value through net income and under the equity method:

Illustration 12–17 Comparison of Fair Value and Equity Methods

	Fair Value Through Net Income			Equity Method		
Purchase equity investment	Investment in Arjent	1,500,000		Investment in Arjent	1,500,000	
	Cash		1,500,000	Cash		1,500,000
Recognize proportionate share of investee's net income and any related adjustments	No entry			Investment in Arjent	150,000	
				Investment revenue		150,000
				Investment revenue	30,000	
				Investment in Arjent		30,000
Adjust to fair value, 2018	Holding loss—NI	50,000		No entry		
	FV adjustment		50,000			
Receive dividend	Cash	75,000		Cash	75,000	
	Dividend revenue		75,000	Investment in Arjent		75,000
Sell equity investment						
1. Adjust to fair value, 2019	Holding loss—NI	4,000		No entry		
	FV adjustment		4,000			
2. Record sale	Cash	1,446,000		Cash	1,446,000	
	FV adjustment	54,000		Loss—IN (to balance)	99,000	
	Investment in Arjent		1,500,000	Investment in Arjent		1,545,000

This side-by-side comparison highlights several aspects of these accounting approaches.

- To record the purchase of an investment, we use identical entries for both approaches.
- The two approaches differ in whether we record investment revenue when dividends are received and whether we recognize unrealized holding gains and losses associated with changes in the fair value of the investment.
- The differences in how the two approaches account for unrealized holding gains and losses result in different carrying values for the investment at the time the investment is sold, and therefore result in different realized gains or losses when the investment is sold.
- Regardless of approach, the same cash flows occur, and the same total amount of net income is recognized over the life of the investment. In the case of Arjent:
  - **Fair value through net income:** A total of $21,000 of net income is recognized over the life of the investment, equal to $75,000 of dividend revenue minus $54,000 ($50,000 + $4,000) loss on the investment.
  - **Equity method:** A total of $21,000 of net income is recognized over the life of the investment, equal to $150,000 of United's portion of Arjent's net income minus $30,000 depreciation adjustment and minus $99,000 loss realized on sale of investment.
  - Thus, the question is not how much total net income is recognized, but *when* that net income is recognized.

Fair Value Option

● LO12–8

If the fair value option is chosen for investments otherwise accounted for by the equity method, the amount that is reported at fair value is clearly indicated.

Companies can choose the fair value option (FVO) for "significant influence" investments that otherwise would be accounted for under the equity method. The company makes an irrevocable decision about whether to elect the FVO, and can make that election for some investments and not for others. As shown in Illustration 12–17, the company carries the investment at fair value in the balance sheet and includes unrealized gains and losses in earnings. These investments are shown on their own line in the balance sheet or are combined with equity method investments with the amount at fair value shown parenthetically. Also, all of the disclosures that are required when reporting fair values as well as some of those that would be required under the equity method still must be provided.[32]

Exactly how a company does the bookkeeping necessary to comply with these broad requirements is up to the company. One alternative is to account for the investment using the entries that would be used if the investor lacked significant influence and accounted for it at fair value through net income. A second alternative is to record all of the accounting entries during the period under the equity method, and then record a fair value adjustment at the end of the period. Regardless of which alternative the company uses, though, the same fair value is reported in the balance sheet at the end of the period, and the same total amount is shown in the income statement (the fair value adjustment amount plus the investment revenue recorded).

International Financial Reporting Standards

LO12–9

Equity Method. Like U.S. GAAP, international accounting standards require the equity method for use with significant influence investees (which they call "associates"), but there are a few important differences. First, *IAS No. 28* governs application of the equity method and requires that the accounting policies of investees be adjusted to correspond to those of the investor when applying the equity method.[33] U.S. GAAP has no such requirement.

Second, IFRS does not provide the fair value option for most investments that qualify for the equity method. U.S. GAAP provides the fair value option for all investments that qualify for the equity method.

Concept Review Exercise

THE EQUITY METHOD

Delta Apparatus bought 40% of Clay Crating Corp.'s outstanding common shares on January 2, 2018, for $540 million. The carrying amount of Clay Crating's net assets (shareholders' equity) at the purchase date totaled $900 million. Book values and fair values were the same for all financial statement items except for inventory and buildings, for which fair values exceeded book values by $25 million and $225 million, respectively. All inventory on hand at the acquisition date was sold during 2018. The buildings have average remaining useful lives of 18 years. During 2018, Clay Crating reported net income of $220 million and paid an $80 million cash dividend.

Required:

1. Prepare the appropriate journal entries during 2018 for the investment.
2. Determine the amounts relating to the investment that Delta Apparatus should report in the 2018 financial statements
   a. as an investment in the balance sheet
   b. as an investment revenue in the income statement
   c. as investing and/or operating activities in the statement of cash flows (direct method)

Solution

1. Prepare the appropriate journal entries during 2018 for the investment.

[32]FASB ASC 825–10–50–28: Financial Instruments–Overall–Disclosure–Fair Value Option (previously "The Fair Value Option for Financial Assets and Financial Liabilities," *Statement of Financial Accounting Standards No. 159* (Norwalk, Conn.: FASB, 2007), para.18.f).

[33]"Investments in Associates," *International Accounting Standard 28* (London, UK: IASCF, 2003), as amended, effective January 1, 2016.

	($ in millions)	
Purchase		
Investment in Clay Crating shares	540	
Cash		540
Net income		
Investment in Clay Crating shares (40% × $220 million)	88	
Investment revenue		88
Dividends		
Cash (40% × $80 million)	32	
Investment in Clay Crating shares		32
Inventory		
Investment revenue (as if 2018 cost of goods sold is higher because beginning inventory was adjusted to fair value)	10	
Investment in Clay Crating shares (40% × $25 million)		10
Buildings		
Investment revenue [($225 million × 40%) ÷ 18 years]	5	
Investment in Clay Crating shares		5

	Investee Net Assets		Net Assets Purchased
Fair value (identifiable)	$1,150*	× 40% =	$460
Book value (identifiable)	900	× 40% =	360
Difference	$ 250	× 40% =	$100

*($900 + 25 + 225)

2. Determine the amounts that Delta Apparatus should report in the 2018 financial statements.

a. As an investment in the balance sheet:

Investment in Clay Crating
($ in millions)

Purchase price	540		
40% of Clay Crating net income	88		
		32	Dividends
		10	Cost of goods sold adjustment for inventory (all sold in 2018)
		5	Depreciation adjustment for buildings ($90,000 ÷ 18)
Balance	581		

b. As investment revenue in the income statement:

$88 million (share of income) − ($10 + 5) million (adjustments) = $73 million

c. In the statement of cash flows (direct method):

- Investing activities: $540 million cash outflow
- Operating activities: $32 million cash inflow

Decision Makers' Perspective

The various approaches used to account for investments can have very different effects on an investor's income statement and balance sheet. Consequently, it's critical that both managers and external decision makers clearly understand those effects and make decisions accordingly.

To highlight key considerations, suppose that, on January 1, 2018, BigCo spent $5,000,000 to purchase 20% of TechStart, a small start-up company that is developing products that apply an exciting new technology. The purchase price included $500,000 for BigCo's share of the difference between the fair value and book value of TechStart's inventory, all of which was then sold in 2018. TechStart paid a small dividend of $100,000 in 2018, so BigCo received 20% of it, or $20,000. TechStart incurs and expenses large amounts of research and development costs as it develops new technology, so it had a net loss in 2018 of $1,000,000. Yet, the future income-generating potential of the products that TechStart is developing has made TechStart a hot stock, and the fair value of BigCo's 20% investment increased to $5,500,000 by the end of 2018. Illustration 12–18 shows how BigCo's investment would be accounted for under two alternative approaches.

Illustration 12–18

Comparison of Methods Used to Account for Investments

	Fair Value Through Net Income	Equity Method
Share of investee net income (loss)*	$ –0–	$ (700,000)
Dividend income**	20,000	–0–
Increase in investee's fair value†	500,000	–0–
Total 2018 effect on net income (loss)	$ 520,000	$ (700,000)
December 31, 2018 investment book value††	$5,500,000	$4,280,000

*Not recognized if account for the investment at fair value through net income. Under the equity method, investment revenue (loss) is 20% × ($1,000,000 loss) + ($500,000) additional expense for fair value inventory adjustment = ($700,000).
**Not recognized for equity method investments. Instead, dividends reduce book value of the investment.
†Recognized in net income if accounted for at fair value through net income. Not recognized under the equity method.
††Equals fair value if accounted for at fair value through net income. Equals initial cost plus income (or minus loss) and minus dividends for equity method.

The way an investment is accounted for affects net income, investment book value, and the amount of gain or loss recognized when the investment is sold.

The accounting method does not affect cash flows, but it has a big effect on net income in current and future periods. Also, because the accounting method affects the book value of the investment, it affects gain or loss on sale of that investment. In our example, if BigCo sold its TechStart investment at the beginning of 2019 for $5,000,000, it would recognize a $720,000 gain on sale if the investment was accounted for under the equity method, but a $500,000 loss if it was accounted for at fair value through net income. All of these income effects are predictable, but only if a user understands the relevant accounting methods and the fact that those methods all end up recognizing the same amount of total gain or loss over the life of an investment. Nevertheless, sometimes even experienced analysts get confused.[34]

Managers may structure equity investments to qualify for their preferred accounting approach.

A benefit of fair value accounting is that it prevents managers from timing the sale of investments to recognize gains or losses in particular accounting periods.

One strength of the equity method is that it prevents the income manipulation that would be possible if a company recognized income when it received dividends and could significantly influence an investee to pay dividends whenever the company needed an income boost. Remember, under the equity method dividends aren't income, but rather reduce the book value of the investment. Nevertheless, users still need to realize that managers may choose and apply methods in ways that make their company appear most attractive. For example, research suggests that investments sometimes are structured to avoid crossing the 20 to 25 percent threshold that typically requires using the equity method, presumably to avoid the negative effect on earnings that comes from having to recognize the investor's share of investee losses and other income adjustments.[35] Also, a company might smooth income by timing the sale of equity method investments to realize gains in otherwise poor periods and realize losses in otherwise good periods. While consistent with GAAP, mixing these sorts of one-time gains and losses with operating income could encourage users to think that operating income is less volatile than it really is.

[34]For example, in 2000, analysts were accustomed to including Intel's investment gains as ordinary income, because those amounts were not particularly large and could be viewed as part of Intel's business. However, in the 2nd quarter of 2000, Intel recorded a net $2.1 billion gain from selling securities in its available-for-sale portfolio. Analysts were surprised and confused, with some eliminating the gain from their earnings estimates but others including them ("Intel Says Net Jumped 79%; Analysts Upset," *The Wall Street Journal*, July 19, 2000, p. A3).

[35]E. E. Comiskey and C. W. Mulford, "Investment Decisions and the Equity Accounting Standard," *The Accounting Review* 61, no. 3 (July 1986), pp. 519–525.

Regarding the fair value through net income approach, of particular concern is the potential for inaccurate fair value estimates. Even if management is trying to provide the most accurate fair value estimate possible, there is much potential for error, particularly when making estimates at level 3 of the fair value hierarchy. Also, a company conceivably could use the discretion inherent in fair value estimation to manage earnings with respect to trading securities or other investments for which they have elected the fair value option. Given this potential for error and bias, it's not surprising that investors are nervous about the accuracy of fair value estimates. To address these sorts of concerns, the FASB has required extensive note disclosure about the quality of inputs associated with estimates of fair value, but financial statement users need to know to look for those disclosures and still must understand that they cannot assess fully the accuracy of fair value estimates. ●

A concern with fair value accounting is that management has much discretion over fair values, and may not be able to estimate fair values accurately.

FINANCIAL INSTRUMENTS AND INVESTMENT DERIVATIVES A financial instrument is defined as one of the following:

1. Cash
2. Evidence of an *ownership interest* in an entity[36]
3. A contract that (a) imposes on one entity an obligation to *deliver* cash (say accounts payable) or another financial instrument and (b) conveys to the second entity a right to *receive* cash (say accounts receivable) or another financial instrument
4. A contract that (a) imposes on one entity an obligation to *exchange* financial instruments on potentially unfavorable terms (say the issuer of a stock option) and (b) conveys to a second entity a right to *exchange* other financial instruments on potentially favorable terms (say the holder of a stock option)[37]

A complex class of financial instruments exists in financial markets in response to the desire of firms to manage risks. In fact, these financial instruments would not exist in their own right, but have been created solely to hedge against risks created by other financial instruments or by transactions that have yet to occur but are anticipated. Financial futures, interest rate swaps, forward contracts, and options have become commonplace.[38] These financial instruments often are called derivatives because they "derive" their values or contractually required cash flows from some other security or index. For instance, an option to buy an asset in the future at a preset price has a value that is dependent on, or derived from, the value of the underlying asset. Their rapid acceptance as indispensable components of the corporate capital structure has left the accounting profession scrambling to keep pace.

Derivatives are financial instruments that "derive" their values from some other security or index.

The urgency to establish accounting standards for financial instruments has been accelerated by headline stories in the financial press reporting multimillion-dollar losses on exotic derivatives by Enron Corporation, Procter & Gamble, Orange County (California), Piper Jaffrey, and Gibson Greetings, to mention a few. The headlines have tended to focus attention on the misuse of these financial instruments rather than their legitimate use in managing risk.

The FASB has been involved for many years in a project to provide a consistent framework for resolving financial instrument accounting issues, including those related to derivatives and other "off-balance-sheet" instruments. The financial instruments project has three separate but related parts: disclosure, recognition and measurement, and distinguishing between liabilities and equities. Unfortunately, issues to be resolved are extremely complex and will likely require several more years to resolve. To help fill the disclosure gap in the meantime, the FASB has offered a series of temporary, "patchwork" solutions. These are primarily in the form of additional disclosures for financial instruments. More recently, the FASB has tackled the issues of recognition and measurement of derivatives. We discuss these requirements in Appendix A to this book.

The FASB's ongoing financial instruments project is expected to lead to a consistent framework for accounting for all financial instruments.

[36]This category includes not just shares of stock, but also partnership agreements and stock options.

[37]FASB ASC Master Glossary: Financial Instrument (previously "Disclosure of Information about Financial Instruments with Off-Balance-Sheet Risk and Financial Instruments with Concentrations of Credit Risk," *Statement of Financial Accounting Standards No. 105* (Stamford, Conn.: FASB, 1990), par. 6).

[38]Interest rate futures were traded for the first time in 1975 on the Chicago Board of Trade. Interest rate swaps were invented in the early 1980s. They now comprise over 70% of derivatives in use.

Financial Reporting Case Solution

© McGraw-Hill Education/
Mark Dierker, photographer

1. **How should you respond? Why are held-to-maturity securities treated differently from other investment securities?** *(p. 648)* You should explain that if an investor has the positive intent and ability to hold the securities to maturity, investments in debt securities are classified as held-to-maturity and reported at amortized cost in the balance sheet. Increases and decreases in fair value are not reported in the financial statements. The reasoning is that the changes are not as relevant to an investor who will hold a security to its maturity regardless of those changes. Changes in the fair value between the time a debt security is acquired and the day it matures to a prearranged maturity value aren't as important if sale before maturity isn't an alternative.
2. **Why are unrealized gains and losses on trading securities reported in the income statement?** *(p. 650)* Trading securities are acquired for the purpose of profiting from short-term market price changes, so gains and losses from holding these securities while prices change are often viewed as relevant performance measures that should be included in net income.
3. **Why are unrealized gains and losses on available-for-sale securities not reported in the income statement, but instead are in other comprehensive income, and then shown in accumulated other comprehensive income (AOCI) in the balance sheet?** *(p. 655)* Available-for-sale securities are not acquired for the purpose of profiting from short-term market price changes, so gains and losses from holding these securities while prices change are viewed as insufficiently relevant performance measures to be included in net income. Instead, those amounts are shown in other comprehensive income (OCI) and accumulated in an owners' equity account (AOCI). It's likely that holding gains in some periods will be offset by holding losses in other periods. When the investment is sold, the net amount of gain or loss is removed from AOCI and recognized in net income.
4. **Explain why Coca-Cola accounts for some of its investments by the equity method and what that means.** *(p. 672)* When an investor does not have "control," but still is able to exercise *significant influence* over the operating and financial policies of the investee, the investment should be accounted for by the equity method. Apparently Coke owns between 20% and 50% of the voting shares of some of the companies it invests in. By the equity method, Coke recognizes investment income in an amount equal to its percentage share of the net income earned by those companies, instead of the amount of that net income it receives as cash dividends. The rationale is that as the investee earns additional net assets, Coke's share of those net assets increases. ●

The Bottom Line

- **LO12-1** Key events in the life of a debt investment are purchase, recording interest revenue, incurring unrealized holding gains and losses due to fair value changes, and recording sale or maturity. *(p. 644)*
- **LO12-2** If an investor has the positive intent and ability to hold the securities to maturity, investments in debt securities are classified as HTM and reported at amortized cost in the balance sheet. These investments are recorded at cost, and holding gains or losses from fair value changes are ignored. *(p. 648)*
- **LO12-3** Investments in debt securities acquired principally for the purpose of selling them in the near term are classified as trading securities. They are reported at their fair values. Holding gains and losses for trading securities are included in earnings. *(p. 649)*
- **LO12-4** Investments in debt securities that don't fit the definitions of the other reporting categories are classified as available-for-sale. They are reported at their fair values. Holding gains and losses from retaining securities during periods of price change are not included in the determination of income for the period; they are reported as a separate component of other comprehensive income in shareholders' equity. *(p. 653)*
- **LO12-5** Investments in equity securities for which the investor lacks the ability to exercise significant influence over the investee are accounted for using a fair value through net income approach. They are reported at their fair values. Holding gains and losses are included in earnings. *(p. 667)*

- **LO12-6** The equity method requires the investor to recognize investment income equal to its percentage share (based on share ownership) of the net income earned by the investee, rather than the amount received as cash dividends. The investment account is adjusted for the investor's percentage share of net income or loss reported by the investee. When the investor actually receives dividends, the investment account is reduced accordingly. (*p. 672*)
- **LO12-7** When the fair value of identifiable net assets acquired exceeds the book value of the underlying net assets acquired in the purchase of an equity investment, both the investment account and investment revenue are adjusted for differences between net income reported by the investee and what that amount would have been if consolidation procedures had been followed. (*pp. 661* and *674*)
- **LO12-8** Impairment recognition requires that, even if a debt investment is accounted for as HTM or AFS, unrealized holding losses are included in net income when the impairment is judged to be other than temporary. The fair value option allows companies to account for most financial assets and liabilities in the same way they account for trading securities, with unrealized holding gains and losses included in net income and the investment carried at fair value in the balance sheet. For equity method investments, this requires clearly identifying the portion of those investments classified in the significant-influence category that is being accounted for at fair value. (*p. 661* and *679*)
- **LO12-9** U.S. GAAP and IFRS are similar in most respects concerning how they account for investments, but accounting in this area is being overhauled by both the IASB and the FASB, and IFRS companies may report under two different standards (either *IAS No. 39* or *IFRS No. 9*) until 2018. IFRS allows proportionate consolidation as well as the equity method to account for joint ventures, although the option to use proportionate consolidation may be eliminated soon. IFRS is more restrictive in terms of the circumstances in which the fair-value option can be used. Finally, as discussed in Appendix 12B, IFRS recognizes different amounts of OTT impairment for HTM and AFS debt investments, and allows recovery of OTT impairments for debt investments (but not equity investments). (*pp. 660–663, 671, 680,* and *690*)

Other Investments (Special Purpose Funds, Investments In Life Insurance Policies)

APPENDIX 12A

Special Purpose Funds

It's often convenient for companies to set aside money to be used for specific purposes. You learned about one such special purpose fund in Chapter 7 when we discussed petty cash funds. Recall that a petty cash fund is money set aside to conveniently make small expenditures using currency rather than having to follow the time-consuming, formal procedures normally used to process checks. Similar funds sometimes are used to pay interest, payroll, or other short-term needs. Like petty cash, these short-term special purpose funds are reported as current assets.

Some special purpose funds—like petty cash—are current assets.

Special purpose funds also are sometimes established to serve longer-term needs. It's common, for instance, to periodically set aside cash into a fund designated to repay bonds and other long-term debt. Such funds usually accumulate cash over the debt's term to maturity and are composed of the company's periodic contributions plus interest or dividends from investing the money in various return-generating investments. In fact, some debt contracts require the borrower to establish such a fund to repay the debt. In similar fashion, management might voluntarily choose to establish a fund to accumulate money to expand facilities, provide for unexpected losses, buy back shares of stock, or any other special purpose that might benefit from an accumulation of funds. Of course, funds that won't be used within the upcoming operating cycle are noncurrent assets. They typically are reported as part of investments. The same criteria for classifying securities into reporting categories that we discussed previously should be used to classify securities in which funds are invested. Any investment revenue from these funds is reported as such in the income statement.

A special purpose fund can be established for *virtually any purpose.*

Noncurrent special purpose funds are reported within the category *investments and funds.*

Investments in Life Insurance Policies

Certain life insurance policies can be surrendered while the *insured is still alive* in exchange for its *cash surrender value.*

Companies frequently buy life insurance policies on the lives of their key officers. Under normal circumstances, the company pays the premium for the policy and, as beneficiary, receives the proceeds when the officer dies. Of course, the objective is to compensate the company for the untimely loss of a valuable resource in the event the officer dies. However, some types of life insurance policies can be surrendered while the insured is still alive in exchange for a determinable amount of money, called the **cash surrender value**. In effect, a portion of each premium payment is not used by the insurance company to pay for life insurance coverage, but instead is invested on behalf of the insured company in a fixed-income investment. Accordingly, the cash surrender value increases each year by the portion of premiums invested plus interest on the previous amount invested. This is simply a characteristic of whole life insurance, unlike term insurance that has lower premiums and provides death benefits only.

Part of each insurance premium represents an increase in the cash surrender value.

From an accounting standpoint, the periodic insurance premium should not be expensed in its entirety. Rather, part of each premium payment, the investment portion, is recorded as an asset. Illustration 12A–1 provides an example.

Illustration 12A–1
Cash Surrender Value

Several years ago, American Capital acquired a $1 million insurance policy on the life of its chief executive officer, naming American Capital as beneficiary. Annual premiums are $18,000, payable at the beginning of each year. In 2018, the cash surrender value of the policy increased according to the contract from $5,000 to $7,000. The CEO died at the end of 2018.

Part of the annual premium represents a build-up in the cash surrender value.

Insurance expense (difference)	16,000	
Cash surrender value of life insurance ($7,000 – 5,000)	2,000	
Cash (2018 premium)		18,000

To record insurance expense and the increase in the investment.

The cash surrender value is considered to be a noncurrent investment and would be reported in the investments and funds section of the balance sheet. Of course when the insured officer dies, the corporation receives the death benefit of the insurance policy, and the cash surrender value ceases to exist because canceling the policy no longer is an option. The corporation recognizes a gain for the amount of the death benefit less the cash surrender value.

When the death benefit is paid, the cash surrender value becomes null and void.

Cash (death benefit)	1,000,000	
Cash surrender value of life insurance (balance)		7,000
Gain on life insurance settlement (difference)		993,000

To record the proceeds at death.

APPENDIX 12B Impairment of Debt Investments

An "other-than-temporary" impairment loss is recognized in net income even though the security hasn't been sold.

We saw in Chapter 11 that intangible assets and property, plant, and equipment are subject to impairment losses that reduce earnings if a decline in fair value indicates that the assets' value has been impaired. The same is true for investments. As indicated in Chapter 12, if the fair value of an investment declines to a level below cost, and that decline is not viewed as temporary, companies typically have to recognize an other-than-temporary (OTT) impairment loss in earnings. We don't need to worry about OTT impairments for trading securities, equity investments for which the investor lacks significant influence, or other investments for which a company has chosen the fair value option, because all changes in the fair values of those investments (whether temporary or OTT) always are recognized in earnings. However, that is not the case for held-to-maturity (HTM) and available-for-sale (AFS) debt investments. Declines in fair value typically are ignored for HTM investments and recorded in OCI for AFS investments. Therefore, companies need to evaluate HTM and AFS investments to determine whether an OTT impairment loss has occurred.

We use a three-step process to determine whether an OTT impairment loss must be recognized and how that loss is to be measured and recorded: (1) determine if the investment is impaired, (2) determine whether any impairment is OTT, and (3) determine where to report the OTT impairment.[39] Illustration 12B–1 summarizes those steps.

Is the investment impaired?	Yes, if the fair value is less than the investment's amortized cost.
Is any of the impairment *other-than-temporary (OTT)?*	Yes, if the investor (a) intends to sell the investment, (b) believes it is "more likely than not" that the investor will be required to sell the investment prior to recovering the amortized cost of the investment, less any current-period credit loss, or (c) has incurred credit losses.
Where is the OTT impairment reported?	In net income, if the investor intends to sell the security or is "more likely than not" to be required to sell it before recovery of its amortized cost. Otherwise: • Credit loss portion in net income (Credit loss = amortized cost − PV of expected cash flows) • Noncredit loss portion in OCI (Noncredit loss portion = total impairment − credit loss)

Illustration 12B–1

Other-Than-Temporary Impairment of Debt Investments

A three-step process is used to determine whether an impairment loss on debt investments must be recognized and how that loss is to be measured and recorded.[40] We'll start with the assumption that the investment is AFS, and then indicate what is different if it is HTM.

Debt impairments can be divided into credit losses and noncredit losses.

Credit losses are due to anticipated reductions in cash flows from the debt investment; all others are *noncredit losses.*

1. **Is the investment impaired?** Impairment of a debt investment occurs when fair value has declined to a level below amortized cost. It also may be necessary to split the total amount of impairment into credit losses and noncredit losses. *Credit losses* reflect expected reductions in future cash flows from anticipated defaults on interest or principal payments. We calculate credit losses as the difference between the amortized cost of the debt and the *present value of the cash flows* expected to be collected, using a discount rate equal to the effective interest rate that existed at the date the investment was acquired. *Noncredit losses* capture other reductions in fair value such as those due to changes in general economic conditions.

Debt impairments are OTT if the investor:
a. intends to sell the investment, or
b. believes it is more likely than not that they will sell the investment prior to fair value recovery, or
c. has suffered a credit loss.

2. **Is any impairment other-than-temporary (OTT)?** We view a debt impairment as OTT if one of three conditions holds:
   a. The investor intends to sell the investment,
   b. The investor believes it is "more likely than not" that the investor will be required to sell the investment prior to recovering the amortized cost of the investment less any current-period credit losses, or
   c. The investor determines that a credit loss exists on the investment.

The rationale for 2a and 2b is that an impairment is OTT if the investor is likely to sell the investment before fair value can recover. The rationale for 2c is that an impairment is OTT if the company believes the cash flows provided by the investment won't be enough to allow it to recover the amortized cost of the investment over the life of the investment.

3. **Where is the OTT impairment reported?** If the debt impairment is considered OTT, the investor always writes the investment down to fair value in the balance sheet, but the

[39]FASB ASC 320–10–35: Investments–Debt Securities–Overall–Subsequent Measurement (originally "The Meaning of Other-Than-Temporary Impairment and Its Application to Certain Investments," *FASB Staff Position No. 115-1 and 124-1* (Norwalk, Conn.: FASB, November 5, 2005)).

[40]FASB ASC 320–10–35: Investments–Debt Securities–Overall–Subsequent Measurement (previously "Recognition and Presentation of Other-Than-Temporary Impairments," *FASB Staff Position No. 115-2 and 124-2* (Norwalk, Conn.: FASB, April 9, 2009)).

amount included in net income or other comprehensive income depends on the reason the impairment is considered OTT:

- If the impairment is considered OTT due to reasons 2a or 2b above, the entire impairment loss is included in net income, because it is likely the company will incur a loss equal to the entire difference between fair value and amortized cost.
- If the impairment is considered OTT due to reason 2c above, *only the credit loss* component is included in net income, as that amount of amortized cost is unlikely to be recovered. Any noncredit loss component reduces OCI, similar to how we normally account for unrealized gains and losses on AFS investments.

If a debt impairment is OTT:

- Investment is written down to fair value.
- If OTT because of 2a or 2b, all of the OTT impairment loss is recognized in net income.
- If OTT because of 2c, only the credit loss is recognized in net income; noncredit loss in OCI.

Also, if the debt investment is classified as AFS, recognizing an OTT impairment may involve reclassifying amounts out of OCI that were recorded previously as unrealized gains or losses.

Illustration 12B–2 provides a description of the OTT debt impairment process from Bank of America's recent annual report.

Illustration 12B–2

Disclosure about OTT Impairments of Debt Investments—Bank of America

Real World Financials

Note 1 (in part): Securities

The Corporation regularly evaluates each AFS and HTM debt security where the value has declined below amortized cost to assess whether the decline in fair value is other-than-temporary. In determining whether an impairment is other-than-temporary, the Corporation considers the severity and duration of the decline in fair value, the length of time expected for recovery, the financial condition of the issuer, and other qualitative factors, as well as whether the Corporation either plans to sell the security or it is more likely than not that it will be required to sell the security before recovery of its amortized cost. Beginning in 2009, under new accounting guidance for impairments of debt securities that are deemed to be other-than-temporary, the credit component of an other-than-temporary impairment (OTTI) loss is recognized in earnings and the noncredit component is recognized in accumulated OCI in situations where the Corporation does not intend to sell the security and it is not more-likely-than-not that the Corporation will be required to sell the security prior to recovery. If there is an OTTI on any individual security classified as HTM, the Corporation writes down the security to fair value with a corresponding charge to other income (loss).

For an example of an OTT impairment for an AFS debt investment, see Illustration 12B–3.

In both Cases 1 and 2 of Illustration 12B–3, the amortized cost of the investment is reduced by the amount of OTT impairment that is recognized in earnings ($50,000 for Case 1, $30,000 for Case 2). United achieves this by crediting a contra-asset, discount on bond investment, which United amortizes over the remaining life of the debt the same way it would if it had initially purchased the debt at that discounted amount. In Case 2, the carrying value of the investment also is decreased by the *noncredit loss* component of the impairment ($20,000). United achieves this by crediting a second contra-asset account, fair value adjustment—noncredit loss, with the offsetting loss recognized in OCI, the same way it would be if it were viewed as an unrealized loss under normal accounting for fair value declines of AFS investments.

Note that in both cases the carrying value of the debt becomes $950,000, reduced by the entire amount of the OTT impairment. In Case 1 this occurs via the $50,000 discount, and in Case 2 via the combination of the $30,000 discount and $20,000 fair value adjustment. Also, in both cases all of the OTT impairment is reflected in comprehensive income. The question is how much is reflected in net income as opposed to OCI. To clarify this distinction, GAAP requires that the entire OTT impairment be shown in the income statement, and then the portion attributed to noncredit losses backed out, such that only the credit loss portion reduces net income. That way, financial statement users are aware of the total amount as

Illustration 12B–3
Other-than-temporary Impairment of Debt Investment

United Intergroup, Inc., buys and sells debt securities of other companies as investments, and classifies these investments as AFS. United's fiscal year-end is December 31. The following events occurred during 2018.

Purchase Investment

July 1, 2018 — Purchased $1,000,000 of Bendac bonds, maturing on December 31, 2019.

Adjust Investment to Fair Value

December 31, 2018 — Valued the Bendac bonds at $950,000. Of the $50,000 impairment, $30,000 is credit loss and $20,000 is noncredit loss.

We'll consider two cases:

- Case 1: United either plans to sell the investment or believes it is more likely than not that it will have to sell the investment before fair value recovers (such that the impairment is viewed as OTT under 2a or 2b above).
- Case 2: United does *not* intend to sell the investment and does *not* believe it is more likely than not that it will have to sell the Bendac investment before fair value recovers, but estimates that $30,000 of credit losses have occurred (such that the impairment is viewed as OTT under 2c above).

	Case 1		Case 2	
December 31, 2018				
OTT impairment loss—NI	50,000		30,000	
Discount on bond investment		50,000		30,000
OTT impairment loss—OCI			20,000	
Fair value adjustment—Noncredit loss				20,000

Note: If United had included unrealized gains or losses for this investment in OCI in a prior period, it also would have to make a reclassification entry, as demonstrated for an equity OTT impairment in Illustration 12B–3.

well as the amount included in net income. Continuing Illustration 12B–3, income statement presentation of the two cases would be as follows:

Income Statement Presentation, December 31, 2018	Case 1	Case 2
OTT impairment of AFS investments:		
Total OTT impairment loss	$50,000	$50,000
Less: portion recognized in OCI	-0-	20,000
Net impairment loss recognized in net income	$50,000	$30,000

What if a debt investment is classified as HTM rather than AFS? Most of the accounting is the same, but an important difference relates to the recognition of *noncredit* losses in OCI. HTM investments normally don't include unrealized gains and losses in OCI, so these won't routinely be adjusted up or down over time. Therefore, for HTM investments, GAAP requires that companies gradually reverse any amounts included in OCI over the remaining life of the investment, debiting the fair value adjustment and crediting OCI each period.

After an OTT impairment is recorded, the usual treatment of unrealized gains or losses is resumed. Changes in fair value are reported in OCI for AFS investments, and are ignored for HTM investments. Any impairment loss recognized in earnings is not eligible for reversal should fair value recover.

CURRENT EXPECTED CREDIT LOSS (CECL) MODEL FOR DEBT INVESTMENTS As indicated earlier in this chapter and in Chapter 7, guidance is changing with respect to accounting for impairments. These changes will be mandatory starting in 2020, and companies can choose to adopt them starting in 2019.[41]

[41]"Financial Instruments--Credit Losses (Topic 326)" *Accounting Standards Update 2016-13* (Norwalk, Conn: FASB, 2016).

For HTM investments, companies will be required to use the **CECL ("Current Expected Credit Loss") model** to account for impairments. That means that companies will recognize bad debts for HTM investments the same way they recognize bad debts for any other note receivable. They will use a contra-asset account, the allowance for credit losses, to reduce the carrying value of HTM investments to the net amount expected to be collected, and each period will record whatever credit loss (bad debt expense) or recovery of credit loss is necessary to adjust that allowance to its appropriate balance. Unlike current practice for OTT impairments, reversal of impairments will be allowed if the fair value of the HTM investment recovers. Estimates of the allowance for credit losses will incorporate historical and current data as well as reasonable and supportable forecasts about the future.

For AFS investments, companies won't apply the CECL model. Instead, they'll apply a new AFS Credit Loss model that is very similar to what companies currently use for OTT impairments. It still will be the case that, if companies plan to sell the investment or think it is more likely than not that they will have to sell the investment before fair value recovers, they will recognize in net income an amount of impairment loss equal to the entire difference between amortized cost and fair value. Also, it still will be the case that, in the remaining circumstance in which companies don't think they will have to sell the investment before fair value recovers, companies will recognize credit losses in net income and noncredit losses in OCI. The main difference is that, when companies recognize credit losses in net income using the new AFS Credit Loss model, they will credit an allowance for credit losses (an allowance for bad debts), rather than reducing the amortized cost of the investment directly by crediting a discount on investment account. Similar to HTM investments, the allowance for credit losses will be adjusted upward or downward as necessary to reflect credit losses, with the offsetting expense or recovery of expense shown in net income. However, the allowance for credit losses is not permitted to exceed the difference between amortized cost and fair value of the investment (because the company can always sell the investment at fair value to avoid additional credit losses).

International Financial Reporting Standards

LO12–8

Accounting for Impairments. Our coverage of impairments focuses on *IFRS No. 9*, which is required after 2018 and can be used in practice in periods before then. Under *IFRS No. 9*, companies recognize impairments for debt investments that are accounted for at amortized cost (rather than fair value through net income) or at fair value through other comprehensive income (FVOCI). There is no distinction made for OTT status. The impairment is calculated using the ECL model discussed previously, and is measured either as the 12-month expected credit loss (if the credit risk on the investment has increased significantly) or the lifetime expected credit loss (if the credit risk on the investment has not increased significantly. The entire impairment is recognized in earnings (there is no equivalent to recognizing in OCI any noncredit losses on debt investments), with an offsetting allowance reducing the carrying value of the investment to the appropriate amount.

IFRS allows recoveries of impairments of debt investments to be recognized in earnings. This is a difference from current U.S. GAAP, which does not allow recoveries of any OTT impairment, but not the CECL model that will be required in U.S. GAAP, which allows recoveries.

To illustrate, let's modify our Bendac debt example from Illustration 12B–3 to assume amortized cost of €1,000,000, €30,000 of 12-month expected credit losses and €20,000 of additional credit losses expected for default events occurring after 12 months. Assuming there has not been a significant increase in credit risk, Bendac would recognize an impairment of €30,000:

Impairment loss—NI	30,000	
Allowance for credit losses		30,000

Assuming instead that there has been a significant increase in credit risk, Bendac would recognize an impairment of €50,000:

Impairment loss—NI	50,000	
Allowance for credit losses		50,000

(continued)

(concluded)

If in a subsequent period the fair value of the debt investment improved by €15,000, IFRS would allow *reversal* of that amount of impairment charge.

Allowance for credit losses	15,000	
Reversal of impairment loss—NI		15,000

Companies can elect to always recognize lifetime credit losses, but only have to do so when a significant increase in credit loss has occurred.

Questions For Review of Key Topics

Q 12–1 All investments in *debt* securities are classified for reporting purposes in one of three categories, and can be accounted for differently depending on the classification. What are these three categories?

Q 12–2 When market rates of interest *rise* after a fixed-rate security is purchased, the value of the now-below-market, fixed-interest payments declines, so the market value of the investment falls. On the other hand, if market rates of interest *fall* after a fixed-rate security is purchased, the fixed-interest payments become relatively attractive, and the market value of the investment rises. Assuming these price changes are not viewed as giving rise to an other-than-temporary impairment, how are they reflected in the investment account for a security classified as held-to-maturity?

Q 12–3 Does GAAP distinguish between fair values that are readily determinable from current market prices versus those needing to be calculated based on the company's own assumptions? Explain how a user will know about the reliability of the inputs used to determine fair value.

Q 12–4 When a debt investment is acquired to be held for an unspecified period of time as opposed to being held to maturity, it is reported at the fair value of the investment securities on the reporting date. Why?

Q 12–5 Reporting an investment at its fair value means adjusting its carrying amount for changes in fair value after its acquisition (or since the last reporting date if it was held at that time). Such changes are called unrealized holding gains and losses because they haven't yet been realized through the sale of the security. If the security is classified as available-for-sale, how are unrealized holding gains and losses typically reported?

Q 12–6 What is "comprehensive income"? Its composition varies from company to company but may include which items related to available-for-sale investments that are not included in net income?

Q 12–7 Why are holding gains and losses treated differently for trading securities and securities available-for-sale?

Q 12–8 Western Die-Casting Company holds an investment in unsecured bonds of LGB Heating Equipment, Inc. When the investment was acquired, management's intention was to hold the bonds for resale. Now management has the positive intent and ability to hold the bonds to maturity. How should Western account for the reclassification of the investment?

Q 12–9 Is it necessary for an investor to report individual amounts for the three categories of investments—held-to-maturity, available-for-sale, or trading—in the financial statements? What information should be disclosed about these investments?

IFRS **Q 12–10** Under *IFRS No. 9,* what reporting categories are used to account for debt investments? What about for equity investments when the investor lacks the ability to significantly influence the operations of the investee?

IFRS **Q 12–11** Under *IFRS No. 9,* which reporting categories are used to account for equity investments when the investor lacks the ability to significantly influence the operations of the investee?

Q 12–12 What is the effect of a company electing the fair value option with respect to a held-to-maturity investment or an available-for-sale investment?

IFRS **Q 12–13** Do U.S. GAAP and IFRS differ in the amount of flexibility that companies have in electing the fair value option? Explain.

Q 12–14 Under what circumstances is the equity method used to account for an investment in stock?

Q 12–15 The equity method has been referred to as a *one-line consolidation.* What might prompt this description?

Q 12–16 In the application of the equity method, how should dividends from the investee be accounted for? Why?

Q 12–17 The fair value of depreciable assets of Penner Packaging Company exceeds their book value by $12 million. The assets' average remaining useful life is 10 years. They are being depreciated by the straight-line method. Finest Foods Industries buys 40% of Penner's common shares. When adjusting investment revenue and the investment by the equity method, how will the situation described affect those two accounts?

Q 12–18 Superior Company owns 40% of the outstanding stock of Bernard Company. During 2018, Bernard paid a $100,000 cash dividend on its common shares. What effect did this dividend have on Superior's 2018 financial statements?

Q 12–19 Sometimes an investor's level of influence changes, making it necessary to change from the equity method to another method. How should the investor account for this change in accounting method?

IFRS **Q 12–20** How does IFRS differ from U.S. GAAP with respect to using the equity method?

Q 12–21 What is the effect of a company electing the fair value option with respect to an investment that otherwise would be accounted for using the equity method?

Q 12–22 Define a financial instrument. Provide three examples of current liabilities that represent financial instruments.

Q 12–23 Some financial instruments are called derivatives. Why?

Q 12–24 (Based on Appendix 12A) Northwest Carburetor Company established a fund in 2015 to accumulate money for a new plant scheduled for construction in 2018. How should this special purpose fund be reported in Northwest's balance sheet?

Q 12–25 (Based on Appendix 12A) Whole-life insurance policies typically can be surrendered while the insured is still alive in exchange for a determinable amount of money called the *cash surrender value.* When a company buys a life insurance policy on the life of a key officer to protect the company against the untimely loss of a valuable resource in the event the officer dies, how should the company account for the cash surrender value?

Q 12–26 (Based on Appendix 12B) When market rates of interest *rise* after a fixed-rate security is purchased, the value of the now-below-market, fixed-interest payments declines, so the market value of the investment falls. If that drop in fair value is viewed as giving rise to an other-than-temporary impairment, how would it be reflected in the investment account for a security classified as held-to-maturity?

Q 12–27 (Based on Appendix 12B) Reporting an investment at its fair value requires adjusting its carrying amount for changes in fair value after its acquisition (or since the last reporting date if it was held at that time). Such changes are called unrealized holding gains and losses because they haven't yet been realized through the sale of the security. If a security is classified as available-for-sale, and an unrealized holding loss is viewed as giving rise to an other-than-temporary (OTT) impairment, how is it reported in the financial statements?

Q 12–28 (Based on Appendix 12B) The market value of Helig Forestry and Mining Corporation bonds dropped 6⅛ points when the federal government passed new legislation banning one of the company's primary techniques for extracting ore. Harris Corporation owns Helig bonds and classifies its investment as securities available-for-sale. How should the decline in market value be handled by Harris?

Q 12–29 Explain how the CECL model (introduced in *ASU No. 2016-13* and required in 2020) differs from current GAAP in its calculation of impairment losses.

IFRS **Q 12–30** (Based on Appendix 12B) How does IFRS differ from current U.S. GAAP in accounting for other-than-temporary impairments?

Brief Exercises

connect

BE 12–1
Securities held-to-maturity; bond investment; effective interest
● LO12-1

Lance Brothers Enterprises acquired $720,000 of 3% bonds, dated July 1, on July 1, 2018, as a long-term investment. Management has the positive intent and ability to hold the bonds until maturity. The market interest rate (yield) was 4% for bonds of similar risk and maturity. Lance Brothers paid $600,000 for the investment in bonds and will receive interest semiannually on June 30 and December 31. Prepare the journal entries (a) to record Lance Brothers' investment in the bonds on July 1, 2018, and (b) to record interest on December 31, 2018, at the effective (market) rate.

BE 12–2
Trading securities
● LO12-3

S&L Financial buys and sells securities expecting to earn profits on short-term differences in price. On December 27, 2018, S&L purchased Coca-Cola bonds at par for $875,000 and sold the bonds on January 3, 2019, for $880,000. At December 31, the bonds had a fair value of $873,000. What pretax amounts did S&L include in its 2018 and 2019 net income as a result of this investment (ignoring interest)?

BE 12–3
Trading securities
● LO12-3

For the Coca-Cola bonds described in BE 12-2, prepare journal entries to record (a) any unrealized gains or losses occurring in 2018 and (b) the sale of the bonds in 2019.

BE 12–4
Available-for-sale securities
● LO12-4

S&L Financial buys and sells securities which it classifies as available-for-sale. On December 27, 2018, S&L purchased Coca-Cola bonds at par for $875,000 and sold the bonds on January 3, 2019, for $880,000. At December 31, the bonds had a fair value of $873,000, and S&L has the intent and ability to hold the investment until fair value recovers. What pretax amounts did S&L include in its 2018 and 2019 net income as a result of this investment?

BE 12–5
Available-for-sale securities
● LO12-4

For the Coca-Cola bonds described in BE 12-4, prepare journal entries to record (a) any unrealized gains or losses occurring in 2018 and (b) the sale of the bonds in 2019, including recognition of any unrealized gains in 2019 prior to sale and reclassification of amounts out of OCI.

BE 12–6
Fair value option; available-for-sale securities
● LO12-8

S&L Financial buys and sells securities that it typically classifies as available-for-sale. On December 27, 2018, S&L purchased Coca-Cola bonds at par for $875,000 and sold the bonds on January 3, 2019, for $880,000. At December 31, the bonds had a fair value of $873,000. When it purchased the Coca-Cola bonds, S&L Financial decided to elect the fair value option for this investment. What pretax amounts did S&L include in its 2018 and 2019 net income as a result of this investment (ignoring interest)?

BE 12–7
Available-for-sale securities
● LO12-4

For several years Fister Links Products has held Microsoft bonds, considered by the company to be securities available-for-sale. The bonds were acquired at a cost of $500,000. At the end of 2018, their fair value was $610,000 and their amortized cost was $510,000. At the end of 2019, their fair value was $600,000 and their amortized cost was $520,000. At what amount will the investment be reported in the December 31, 2019, balance sheet? What adjusting entry is required to accomplish this objective (ignore interest)?

BE 12–8
Debt investments under IFRS
● LO12-4, LO12-9
IFRS

Fowler Inc. purchased $75,000 of bonds on January 1, 2018. The bonds pay interest semiannually and mature in 20 years, at which time the $75,000 principal will be paid. The bonds do not pay any amounts other than interest and principal. Fowler's intention is to collect contractual cash flows and eventually sell the bonds within the next couple of years if the price is right. During 2018, the fair value of the bonds increased to $80,000. Fowler reports investments under *IFRS No. 9*. How much unrealized gain or loss will Fowler include in 2018 net income with respect to the bonds?

BE 12–9
Debt investments under IFRS
● LO12-2, LO12-9
IFRS

Assume the same facts as in BE 12–8, but that Fowler intends to hold the bonds until maturity. How much unrealized gain or loss would Fowler include in 2018 net income with respect to the bonds?

BE 12–10
Equity securities
● LO12-5

Adams Industries holds 40,000 shares of FedEx common stock, which is not a large enough ownership interest to allow Adams to exercise significant influence over FedEx. On December 31, 2018, and December 31, 2019, the market value of the stock is $95 and $100 per share, respectively. What is the appropriate reporting category for this investment and at what amount will it be reported in the 2019 balance sheet?

BE 12–11
Equity investments and dividends
● LO12-5

Turner Company owns 10% of the outstanding stock of ICA Company. During the current year, ICA paid a $5 million cash dividend on its common shares. What effect did this dividend have on Turner's 2018 financial statements? Explain the reasoning for this effect.

BE 12–12
Equity method and dividends
● LO12-6

Turner Company owns 40% of the outstanding stock of ICA Company. During the current year, ICA paid a $5 million cash dividend on its common shares. What effect did this dividend have on Turner's 2018 financial statements? Explain the reasoning for this effect.

BE 12–13
Equity method
● LO12-6, LO12-7

The fair value of Wallis, Inc.'s depreciable assets exceeds their book value by $50 million. The assets have an average remaining useful life of 15 years and are being depreciated by the straight-line method. Park Industries buys 30% of Wallis's common shares. When Park adjusts its investment revenue and the investment by the equity method, how will the situation described affect those two accounts?

BE 12–14
Equity method investments
● LO12-6, LO12-9
IFRS

Kim Company bought 30% of the shares of Phelps, Inc., at the start of 2018. Kim paid $10 million for the shares. Thirty percent of the book value of Phelps's net assets is $8 million, and the difference of $2 million is due to land that Phelps owns that has appreciated in value. During 2018, Phelps reported net income of $1 million and paid a cash dividend of $0.5 million. At what amount does Kim carry the Phelps investment on its balance sheet as of December 31, 2018?

BE 12–15
Change in principle; change to the equity method
● LO12-7

At the beginning of 2018, Pioneer Products' ownership interest in the common stock of LLB Co. increased to the point that it became appropriate to begin using the equity method of accounting for the investment. The balance in the investment account was $44 million at the time of the change but would have been $56 million if Pioneer had used the equity method since first investing in LLB. How should Pioneer report the change? Would your answer be the same if Pioneer is changing *from* the equity method rather than *to* the equity method?

BE 12–16
Fair value option; equity method investments
● LO12-8

Turner Company purchased 40% of the outstanding stock of ICA Company for $10,000,000 on January 2, 2018. Turner elects the fair value option to account for the investment. During 2018, ICA earns $750,000 of income and on December 30 pays a dividend of $500,000. On December 31, 2018, the fair value of Turner's investment has increased to $11,500,000. What journal entries would Turner make to account for this investment during 2018, assuming Turner will account for the investment similar to how it would account for a trading security?

BE 12–17
Available-for-sale securities and impairment (Appendix 12B)
● LO12-4, LO12-8

LED Corporation owns $1,000,000 of Branch Pharmaceuticals bonds and classifies its investment as securities available-for-sale. The market price of Branch's bonds fell by $450,000, due to concerns about one of the company's principal drugs. The concerns were justified when the FDA banned the drug. $100,000 of that decline in value already had been included in OCI as a temporary unrealized loss in a prior period. LED views $200,000 of the $450,000 loss as related to *credit* losses, and the other $250,000 as *noncredit* losses. LED thinks it is more likely than not that it will have to sell the investment before fair value recovers. What journal entries should LED record to account for the decline in market value in the current period? How should the decline affect net income and comprehensive income?

BE 12–18
Impairments (AFS Credit Loss Model) (Appendix 12B)
● LO12-4, LO12-8

Answer BE 12-17 under the assumption that LED Corporation used the AFS Credit Loss Model introduced in *ASU 2016-13* and required after 2020.

BE 12–19
Available-for-sale securities and impairment (Appendix 12B)
● LO12-4, LO12-8

LED Corporation owns $1,000,000 of Branch Pharmaceuticals bonds and classifies its investment as securities available-for-sale. The market price of Branch's bonds fell by $450,000, due to concerns about one of the company's principal drugs. The concerns were justified when the FDA banned the drug. $100,000 of that decline in value already had been included in OCI as a temporary unrealized loss in a prior period. LED views $200,000 of the $450,000 loss as related to *credit* losses, and the other $250,000 as *noncredit* losses. LED does not plan to sell the investment and does not think it is more likely than not that it will have to sell the investment before fair value recovers. What journal entries should LED record to account for the decline in market value in the current period? How should the decline affect net income and comprehensive income?

BE 12–20
Recovery of impairments under IFRS (Appendix 12B)
● LO12-3, LO12-8, LO12-9

Wickum Corporation reports under IFRS, and recognized a $500,000 other-than-temporary impairment of an HTM debt investment in Right Corporation. Subsequently, the fair value of Wickum's investment in Right increased by $300,000. How would Wickum account for that increase in fair value?

Exercises

E 12–1
Securities held-to-maturity; bond investment; effective interest, discount
● LO12-1

Tanner-UNF Corporation acquired as a long-term investment $240 million of 6% bonds, dated July 1, on July 1, 2018. Company management has the positive intent and ability to hold the bonds until maturity. The market interest rate (yield) was 8% for bonds of similar risk and maturity. Tanner-UNF paid $200 million for the bonds. The company will receive interest semiannually on June 30 and December 31. As a result of changing market conditions, the fair value of the bonds at December 31, 2018, was $210 million.

Required:

1. Prepare the journal entry to record Tanner-UNF's investment in the bonds on July 1, 2018.
2. Prepare the journal entries by Tanner-UNF to record interest on December 31, 2018, at the effective (market) rate.
3. At what amount will Tanner-UNF report its investment in the December 31, 2018, balance sheet? Why?
4. Suppose Moody's bond rating agency downgraded the risk rating of the bonds motivating Tanner-UNF to sell the investment on January 2, 2019, for $190 million. Prepare the journal entry to record the sale.

E 12–2
Securities held-to-maturity; bond investment; effective interest, premium
● LO12-1

Mills Corporation acquired as a long-term investment $240 million of 6% bonds, dated July 1, on July 1, 2018. Company management has the positive intent and ability to hold the bonds until maturity. The market interest rate (yield) was 4% for bonds of similar risk and maturity. Mills paid $280 million for the bonds. The company will receive interest semiannually on June 30 and December 31. As a result of changing market conditions, the fair value of the bonds at December 31, 2018, was $270 million.

Required:

1. Prepare the journal entry to record Mills' investment in the bonds on July 1, 2018.
2. Prepare the journal entries by Mills to record interest on December 31, 2018, at the effective (market) rate.
3. At what amount will Mills report its investment in the December 31, 2018, balance sheet? Why?
4. Suppose Moody's bond rating agency upgraded the risk rating of the bonds, and Mills decided to sell the investment on January 2, 2019, for $290 million. Prepare the journal entry to record the sale.

E 12–3
Securities held-to-maturity
● LO12-1

FF&T Corporation is a confectionery wholesaler that frequently buys and sells securities to meet various investment objectives. The following selected transactions relate to FF&T's investment activities during the last two months of 2018. At November 1, FF&T held $48 million of 20-year, 10% bonds of Convenience, Inc., purchased May 1, 2018, at face value. Management has the positive intent and ability to hold the bonds until maturity. FF&T's fiscal year ends on December 31.

Nov. 1	Received semiannual interest of $2.4 million from the Convenience, Inc., bonds.
Dec. 1	Purchased 12% bonds of Facsimile Enterprises at their $30 million face value, to be held until they mature in 2024. Semiannual interest is payable May 31 and November 30.
31	Purchased U.S. Treasury bills to be held until they mature in two months for $8.9 million.
31	Recorded any necessary adjusting entry(s) relating to the investments.

The fair values of the investments at December 31 were:

Convenience bonds	$44.7 million
Facsimile Enterprises bonds	30.9 million
U.S. Treasury bills	8.9 million

Required:

Prepare the appropriate journal entry for each transaction or event.

E 12–4
FASB codification research
● LO12-2

The *FASB Accounting Standards Codification* represents the single source of authoritative U.S. generally accepted accounting principles.

Required:

1. Obtain the relevant authoritative literature on accounting for investments in held-to-maturity securities using the FASB's Codification Research System at the FASB website www.fasb.org.
2. What is the specific citation that describes examples of circumstances under which an investment in debt is available to be sold and therefore should not be classified as held-to-maturity?
3. List the circumstances and conditions.

E 12–5
Trading securities
● LO12-2

[This is a variation of E 12–1 focusing on trading securities.]
Tanner-UNF Corporation acquired as a long-term investment $240 million of 6% bonds, dated July 1, on July 1, 2018. The market interest rate (yield) was 8% for bonds of similar risk and maturity. Tanner-UNF paid $200 million for the bonds. The company will receive interest semiannually on June 30 and December 31. Company management is holding the bonds in its trading portfolio. As a result of changing market conditions, the fair value of the bonds at December 31, 2018, was $210 million.

Required:

1. Prepare the journal entry to record Tanner-UNF's investment in the bonds on July 1, 2018.
2. Prepare the journal entries by Tanner-UNF to record interest on December 31, 2018, at the effective (market) rate.
3. Prepare any additional journal entry necessary for Tanner-UNF to report its investment in the December 31, 2018, balance sheet.
4. Suppose Moody's bond rating agency downgraded the risk rating of the bonds motivating Tanner-UNF to sell the investment on January 2, 2019, for $190 million. Prepare the journal entry to record the sale.

E 12–6
Trading securities
● LO12-1

[This is a variation of E 12–2 focusing on trading securities.]
Mills Corporation acquired as a long-term investment $240 million of 6% bonds, dated July 1, on July 1, 2018. Company management is holding the bonds in its trading portfolio. The market interest rate (yield) was 4% for bonds of similar risk and maturity. Mills paid $280 million for the bonds. The company will receive interest semiannually on June 30 and December 31. As a result of changing market conditions, the fair value of the bonds at December 31, 2018, was $270 million.

Required:

1. Prepare the journal entry to record Mills' investment in the bonds on July 1, 2018.
2. Prepare the journal entries by Mills to record interest on December 31, 2018, at the effective (market) rate.

3. At what amount will Mills report its investment in the December 31, 2018, balance sheet? Why?
4. Suppose Moody's bond rating agency upgraded the risk rating of the bonds, and Mills decided to sell the investment on January 2, 2019, for $290 million. Prepare the journal entry to record the sale.

E 12–7
Various transactions relating to trading securities
● LO12-1, LO12-3

Rantzow-Lear Company buys and sells debt securities expecting to earn profits on short-term differences in price. The company's fiscal year ends on December 31. The following selected transactions relating to Rantzow-Lear's trading account occurred during December 2018 and the first week of 2019.

2018	
Dec. 17	Purchased 100 Grocers' Supply Corporation bonds at par for $350,000.
28	Received interest of $2,000 from the Grocers' Supply Corporation bonds.
31	Recorded any necessary adjusting entry relating to the Grocers' Supply Corporation bonds. The market price of the stock was $4,000 per bond.
2019	
Jan. 5	Sold the Grocers' Supply Corporation bonds for $395,000.

Required:
1. Prepare the appropriate journal entry for each transaction.
2. Indicate any amounts that Rantzow-Lear Company would report in its 2018 balance sheet and income statement as a result of this investment.

E 12–8
FASB codification research
● LO12-3, LO12-4, LO12-6, LO12-7

Access the *FASB's Codification Research System* at the FASB website www.fasb.org.

Required:
Determine the specific citation for accounting for each of the following items:
1. Unrealized holding gains for trading securities should be included in earnings.
2. Under the equity method, the investor accounts for its share of the earnings or losses of the investee in the periods they are reported by the investee in its financial statements.
3. Transfers of securities between categories are accounted for at fair value.
4. Disclosures for available-for-sale securities should include total losses for securities that have net losses included in accumulated other comprehensive income.

E 12–9
Securities available-for-sale; adjusting entries
● LO12-4

Loreal-American Corporation purchased several marketable securities during 2018. At December 31, 2018, the company had the investments in bonds listed below. None was held at the last reporting date, December 31, 2017, and all are considered securities available-for-sale.

	Cost	Fair Value	Unrealized Holding Gain (Loss)
Short term:			
Blair, Inc.	$ 480,000	$ 405,000	$(75,000)
ANC Corporation	450,000	480,000	30,000
Totals	$ 930,000	$ 885,000	$(45,000)
Long term:			
Drake Corporation	$ 480,000	$ 560,000	$ 80,000
Aaron Industries	720,000	660,000	(60,000)
Totals	$1,200,000	$1,220,000	$ 20,000

Required:
1. Prepare appropriate adjusting entries at December 31, 2018.
2. What amounts would be reported in the income statement at December 31, 2018, as a result of these adjusting entries?

E 12–10
Available-for-sale securities
● LO12-1, LO12-4

[This is a variation of E 12–1 focusing on available-for-sale securities.]
Tanner-UNF Corporation acquired as a long-term investment $240 million of 6% bonds, dated July 1, on July 1, 2018. The market interest rate (yield) was 8% for bonds of similar risk and maturity. Tanner-UNF paid $200 million for the bonds. The company will receive interest semiannually on June 30 and December 31. Company management has classified the bonds as available-for-sale investments. As a result of changing market conditions, the fair value of the bonds at December 31, 2018, was $210 million.

Required:
1. Prepare the journal entry to record Tanner-UNF's investment in the bonds on July 1, 2018.
2. Prepare the journal entries by Tanner-UNF to record interest on December 31, 2018, at the effective (market) rate.

3. Prepare any additional journal entry necessary for Tanner-UNF to report its investment in the December 31, 2018, balance sheet.
4. Suppose Moody's bond rating agency downgraded the risk rating of the bonds motivating Tanner-UNF to sell the investment on January 2, 2019, for $190 million. Prepare the journal entries necessary to record the sale, including updating the fair-value adjustment, recording any reclassification adjustment, and recording the sale.

E 12–11
Available-for-sale securities
● LO12-1, LO12-4

[This is a variation of E 12–2 focusing on available-for-sale securities.]
Mills Corporation acquired as a long-term investment $240 million of 6% bonds, dated July 1, on July 1, 2018. Company management Mills determined that it should account for the bonds as an available-for-sale investment. The market interest rate (yield) was 4% for bonds of similar risk and maturity. Mills paid $280 million for the bonds. The company will receive interest semiannually on June 30 and December 31. As a result of changing market conditions, the fair value of the bonds at December 31, 2018, was $270 million.

Required:
1. Prepare the journal entry to record Mills' investment in the bonds on July 1, 2018.
2. Prepare the journal entries by Mills to record interest on December 31, 2018, at the effective (market) rate.
3. At what amount will Mills report its investment in the December 31, 2018, balance sheet? Why?
4. Suppose Moody's bond rating agency upgraded the risk rating of the bonds, and Mills decided to sell the investment on January 2, 2019, for $290 million. Prepare the journal entry to record the sale.

E 12–12
Available-for-sale securities
● LO12-1, LO12-4

Colah Company purchased $1 million of Jackson, Inc., 5% bonds at par on July 1, 2018, with interest paid semi-annually. Colah determined that it should account for the bonds as an available-for-sale investment. At December 31, 2018, the Jackson bonds had a fair value of $1.2 million. Colah sold the Jackson bonds on July 1, 2019 for $900,000.

Required:
1. Prepare Colah's journal entries to record:
   a. The purchase of the Jackson bonds on July 1
   b. Interest revenue for the last half of 2018
   c. Any year-end 2018 adjusting entries
   d. Interest revenue for the first half of 2019
   e. Any entries necessary upon sale of the Jackson bonds on July 1, 2019, including updating the fair-value adjustment, recording any reclassification adjustment, and recording the sale
2. Fill out the following table to show the effect of the Jackson bonds on Colah's net income, other comprehensive income, and comprehensive income for 2018, 2019, and cumulatively over 2018 and 2019.

	2018	2019	Total
Net Income			
OCI			
Comprehensive Income			

E 12–13
Classification of securities; adjusting entries
● LO12-4

On February 18, 2018, Union Corporation purchased 10,000 shares of IBM bonds as a long-term investment for $600,000. Union will hold the bonds indefinitely, and may sell them if their price increases sufficiently. On December 31, 2018, and December 31, 2019, the market value of the bonds was $580,000 and $610,000, respectively.

Required:
1. What is the appropriate reporting category for this investment? Why?
2. Prepare the adjusting entry for December 31, 2018.
3. Prepare the adjusting entry for December 31, 2019.

E 12–14
Various investment securities
● LO12-3, LO12-4

At December 31, 2018, Hull-Meyers Corp. had the following investments that were purchased during 2018, its first year of operations:

	Cost	Fair Value
Trading Securities:		
Security A	$ 900,000	$ 910,000
Security B	105,000	100,000
Totals	$1,005,000	$1,010,000

(continued)

(concluded)

Securities Available-for-Sale:		
Security C	$ 700,000	$ 780,000
Security D	900,000	915,000
Totals	$1,600,000	$1,695,000
Securities to Be Held-to-Maturity:		
Security E	$ 490,000	$ 500,000
Security F	615,000	610,000
Totals	$1,105,000	$1,110,000

No investments were sold during 2018. All securities except Security D and Security F are considered short-term investments. None of the fair value changes is considered permanent.

Required:

Determine the following amounts at December 31, 2018.

1. Investments reported as current assets
2. Investments reported as noncurrent assets
3. Unrealized gain (or loss) component of income before taxes
4. Unrealized gain (or loss) component of accumulated other comprehensive income in shareholders' equity

E 12–15
Equity investments; fair value through net income
● LO12-4

On March 31, 2018, Chow Brothers, Inc., bought 10% of KT Manufacturing's capital stock for $50 million. KT's net income for the year ended December 31, 2018, was $80 million. The fair value of the shares held by Chow was $35 million at December 31, 2018. KT did not declare or pay a dividend during 2018.

Required:

1. Prepare all appropriate journal entries related to the investment during 2018.
2. Assume that Chow sold the stock on January 20, 2019 for $30 million. Prepare the journal entry Sanborn would use to record the sale.

E 12–16
Equity investments; fair value through net income
● LO12-4

On January 2, 2018, Sanborn Tobacco Inc. bought 5% of Jackson Industry's capital stock for $90 million. Jackson Industry's net income for the year ended December 31, 2018, was $120 million. The fair value of the shares held by Sanborn was $98 million at December 31, 2018. During 2018, Jackson declared a dividend of $60 million.

Required:

1. Prepare all appropriate journal entries related to the investment during 2018.
2. Assume that Sanborn sold the stock on January 2, 2019 for $110 million. Prepare the journal entry Sanborn would use to record the sale.

E 12–17
Equity investments; fair value through net income
● LO12-4

The accounting records of Jamaican Importers, Inc., at January 1, 2018, included the following:

Assets:	
Investment in IBM common shares	$1,345,000
Less: Fair value adjustment	(145,000)
	$1,200,000
Shareholders' Equity:	
Accumulated unrealized holding gains and losses	$ 145,000

No changes occurred during 2018 in the investment portfolio.

Required:

Prepare appropriate adjusting entry(s) at December 31, 2018, assuming the fair value of the IBM common shares was:

1. $1,175,000
2. $1,275,000
3. $1,375,000

E 12–18
Equity investments; fair value through net income
● LO12-4

The investments of Harlon Enterprises included the following cost and fair value amounts ($ in millions):

		Fair Value, Dec. 31	
Equity Investments	**Cost**	**2018**	**2019**
A Corporation shares	$ 20	$14	na
B Corporation bonds	35	35	$ 37
C Corporation shares	15	na	14
D Industries shares	45	46	50
Totals	$115	$95	$101

Harlon accounts for its equity investment portfolio at fair value through net income. Harlon sold its holdings of A Corporation shares on June 1, 2019, for $15 million. On September 12, it purchased the C Corporation shares.

Required:

1. What is the effect of the sale of the A Corporation shares and the purchase of the C Corporation shares on Harlon's 2019 pretax earnings?
2. At what amount should Harlon's securities equity investment portfolio be reported in its 2019 balance sheet?

E 12–19
Investment securities and equity method investments compared
● LO12-5, LO12-6

As a long-term investment, Painters' Equipment Company purchased 20% of AMC Supplies Inc.'s 400,000 shares for $480,000 at the beginning of the fiscal year of both companies. On the purchase date, the fair value and book value of AMC's net assets were equal. During the year, AMC earned net income of $250,000 and distributed cash dividends of 25 cents per share. At year-end, the fair value of the shares is $505,000.

Required:

1. Assume no significant influence was acquired. Prepare the appropriate journal entries from the purchase through the end of the year.
2. Assume significant influence was acquired. Prepare the appropriate journal entries from the purchase through the end of the year.

E 12–20
Equity method; purchase; investee income; dividends
● LO12-6

As a long-term investment at the beginning of the 2018 fiscal year, Florists International purchased 30% of Nursery Supplies Inc.'s 8 million shares for $56 million. The fair value and book value of the shares were the same at that time. During the year, Nursery Supplies earned net income of $40 million and distributed cash dividends of $1.25 per share. At the end of the year, the fair value of the shares is $52 million.

Required:

Prepare the appropriate journal entries from the purchase through the end of the year.

E 12–21
Error corrections; equity method investment
● LO12-6, LO12-7

On December 12, 2018, an equity investment costing $80,000 was sold for $100,000. The investment was carried in the balance sheet at $75,000, and was accounted for under the equity method. An error was made in which the total of the sale proceeds was credited to the investment account.

Required:

1. Prepare the journal entry to correct the error assuming it is discovered before the books are adjusted or closed in 2018. (Ignore income taxes.)
2. Prepare the journal entry to correct the error assuming it is not discovered until early 2019. (Ignore income taxes.)

E 12–22
Equity method; adjustment for depreciation
● LO12-6, LO12-7

Fizer Pharmaceutical paid $68 million on January 2, 2018, for 4 million shares of Carne Cosmetics common stock. The investment represents a 25% interest in the net assets of Carne and gave Fizer the ability to exercise significant influence over Carne's operations. Fizer received dividends of $1 per share on December 21, 2018, and Carne reported net income of $40 million for the year ended December 31, 2018. The fair value of Carne's common stock at December 31, 2018, was $18.50 per share.

- The book value of Carne's net assets was $192 million.
- The fair value of Carne's depreciable assets exceeded their book value by $32 million. These assets had an average remaining useful life of eight years.
- The remainder of the excess of the cost of the investment over the book value of net assets purchased was attributable to goodwill.

Required:

Prepare all appropriate journal entries related to the investment during 2018.

E 12–23
Equity method
● LO12-6, LO12-7

On January 1, 2018, Cameron Inc. bought 20% of the outstanding common stock of Lake Construction Company for $300 million cash. At the date of acquisition of the stock, Lake's net assets had a fair value of $900 million. Their book value was $800 million. The difference was attributable to the fair value of Lake's buildings and its land exceeding book value, each accounting for one-half of the difference. Lake's net income for the year ended December 31, 2018, was $150 million. During 2018, Lake declared and paid cash dividends of $30 million. The buildings have a remaining life of 10 years.

Required:

1. Prepare all appropriate journal entries related to the investment during 2018, assuming Cameron accounts for this investment by the equity method.
2. Determine the amounts to be reported by Cameron:
   a. As an investment in Cameron's 2018 balance sheet

b. As investment revenue in the income statement
c. Among investing activities in the statement of cash flows

E 12–24
Equity method, partial year
● LO12-6, LO12-7

On July 1, 2018, Gupta Corporation bought 25% of the outstanding common stock of VB Company for $100 million cash. At the date of acquisition of the stock, VB's net assets had a total fair value of $350 million and a book value of $220 million. Of the $130 million difference, $20 million was attributable to the appreciated value of inventory that was sold during the last half of 2018, $80 million was attributable to buildings that had a remaining depreciable life of 10 years, and $30 million related to equipment that had a remaining depreciable life of 5 years. Between July 1, 2018, and December 31, 2018, VB earned net income of $32 million and declared and paid cash dividends of $24 million.

Required:

1. Prepare all appropriate journal entries related to the investment during 2018, assuming Gupta accounts for this investment by the equity method.
2. Determine the amounts to be reported by Gupta:
   a. As an investment in Gupta's December 31, 2018, balance sheet
   b. As investment revenue or loss in Gupta's 2018 income statement
   c. Among investing activities in Gupta's 2018 statement of cash flows

E 12–25
Fair value option; held-to-maturity investments
● LO12-1, LO12-2, LO12-3, LO12-8

[This is a variation of E12–1 focusing on the fair value option.]
Tanner-UNF Corporation acquired as a long-term investment $240 million of 6% bonds, dated July 1, on July 1, 2018. Company management has the positive intent and ability to hold the bonds until maturity, but when the bonds were acquired Tanner-UNF decided to elect the fair value option for accounting for its investment. The market interest rate (yield) was 8% for bonds of similar risk and maturity. Tanner-UNF paid $200 million for the bonds. The company will receive interest semiannually on June 30 and December 31. As a result of changing market conditions, the fair value of the bonds at December 31, 2018, was $210 million.

Required:

1. Would this investment be classified on Tanner-UNF's balance sheet as held-to-maturity securities, trading securities, available-for-sale securities, significant-influence investments, or other? Explain.
2. Prepare the journal entry to record Tanner-UNF's investment in the bonds on July 1, 2018.
3. Prepare the journal entries by Tanner-UNF to record interest on December 31, 2018, at the effective (market) rate.
4. Prepare any journal entry necessary to recognize fair value changes as of December 31, 2018.
5. At what amount will Tanner-UNF report its investment in the December 31, 2018, balance sheet? Why?
6. Suppose Moody's bond rating agency downgraded the risk rating of the bonds motivating Tanner-UNF to sell the investment on January 2, 2019, for $190 million. Prepare the journal entry to record the sale.

E 12–26
Fair value option; available-for-sale investments
● LO12-2, LO12-3, LO12-8

[This is a variation of E12–12 focusing on the fair value option.]
Colah Company purchased $1 million of Jackson, Inc. 5% bonds at par on July 1, 2018, with interest paid semi-annually. When the bonds were acquired Colah decided to elect the fair value option for accounting for its investment. At December 31, 2018, the Jackson bonds had a fair value of $1.2 million. Colah sold the Jackson bonds on July 1, 2019 for $900,000.

Required:

3. Prepare Colah's journal entries to record:
   a. The purchase of the Jackson bonds on July 1
   b. Interest revenue for the last half of 2018
   c. Any year-end 2018 adjusting entries
   d. Interest revenue for the first half of 2019
   e. Any entry or entries necessary upon sale of the Jackson bonds on July 1, 2019
4. Fill out the following table to show the effect of the Jackson bonds on Colah's net income, other comprehensive income, and comprehensive income for 2018, 2019, and cumulatively over 2018 and 2019.

	2018	2019	Total
Net Income			
OCI			
Comprehensive Income			

E 12–27
Fair value option; equity method investments
● **LO12-6, LO12-8**

[This is a variation of E 12–20 focusing on the fair value option.]

As a long-term investment at the beginning of the 2018 fiscal year, Florists International purchased 30% of Nursery Supplies Inc.'s 8 million shares for $56 million. The fair value and book value of the shares were the same at that time. The company realizes that this investment typically would be accounted for under the equity method, but instead chooses the fair value option. During the year, Nursery Supplies earned net income of $40 million and distributed cash dividends of $1.25 per share. At the end of the year, the fair value of the shares is $52 million.

Required:

1. Would this investment be classified on Florists' balance sheet as held-to-maturity securities, trading securities, available-for-sale securities, significant-influence investments, or other? Explain.
2. Prepare all appropriate journal entries related to the investment during 2018.
3. Indicate the effect of this investment on 2018 income before taxes.

E 12–28
Life insurance policy (Appendix 12A)

Edible Chemicals Corporation owns a $4 million whole life insurance policy on the life of its CEO, naming Edible Chemicals as beneficiary. The annual premiums are $70,000 and are payable at the beginning of each year. The cash surrender value of the policy was $21,000 at the beginning of 2018.

Required:

1. Prepare the appropriate 2018 journal entry to record insurance expense and the increase in the investment assuming the cash surrender value of the policy increased according to the contract to $27,000.
2. The CEO died at the end of 2018. Prepare the appropriate journal entry.

E 12–29
Life insurance policy (Appendix 12A)

Below are two unrelated situations relating to life insurance.

Required:

Prepare the appropriate journal entry for each situation.

1. Ford Corporation owns a whole life insurance policy on the life of its president. Ford Corporation is the beneficiary. The insurance premium is $25,000. The cash surrender value increased during the year from $2,500 to $4,600.
2. Petroleum Corporation received a $250,000 life insurance settlement when its CEO died. At that time, the cash surrender value was $16,000.

E 12–30
Held-to-maturity securities; impairments (Appendix 12B)
● **LO12-2, LO12-8**

Bloom Corporation purchased $1,000,000 of Taylor Company 5% bonds at par with the intent and ability to hold the bonds until they matured in 2025, so Bloom classifies their investment as HTM. Unfortunately, a combination of problems at Taylor Company and in the debt market caused the fair value of the Taylor investment to decline to $600,000 during 2018.

Required:

For each of the following scenarios, prepare appropriate entry(s) at December 31, 2018, and indicate how the scenario will affect the 2018 income statement (ignoring income taxes).

1. Bloom now believes it is more likely than not that it will have to sell the Taylor bonds before the bonds have a chance to recover their fair value. Of the $400,000 decline in fair value, Bloom attributes $250,000 to credit losses, and $150,000 to noncredit losses.
2. Bloom does not plan to sell the Taylor bonds prior to maturity, and does not believe it is more likely than not that it will have to sell the Taylor bonds before the bonds have a chance to recover their fair value. Of the $400,000 decline in fair value, Bloom attributes $250,000 to credit losses, and $150,000 to noncredit losses.

E 12–31
Available-for-sale debt securities; impairments (Appendix 12B)
● **LO12-4, LO12-8**

[Note: This exercise is a variation of E 12–30, modified to categorize the investment as securities available-for-sale.] Assume all of the same facts and scenarios as E 12–30, except that Bloom Corporation classifies their Taylor investment as AFS.

Required:

1. For each of the scenarios shown in E 12–30, prepare the appropriate entry(s) at December 31, 2018. Indicate how the scenario will affect the 2018 income statement, OCI, and comprehensive income.
2. Repeat requirement 1, but now assume that, at the end of 2017, Bloom had recorded a temporary unrealized loss (not an OTT impairment) of $100,000 on the Taylor investment.

E 12–32
Impairments (AFS Credit Loss Model) (Appendix 12B)
● **LO12-4, LO12-8**

Answer E 12-31 under the assumption that Bloom Corporation used the AFS Credit Loss Model introduced in *ASU 2016-13* and required after 2020.

Required:

Prepare appropriate entry(s) at December 31, 2018, and for each year indicate how the scenario will affect net income, OCI, and comprehensive income.

E 12–33
Accounting for impairments under IFRS (Appendix 12B)
● LO12-2, LO12-8, LO12-9

Rell Corporation reports under IFRS No. 9. Rell has an investment in Tirish, Inc. bonds that Rell accounts for at amortized cost, given that the bonds pay only interest and principal and Rell's business purpose is to hold the bonds to maturity. Rell purchased the bonds for €10,000,000. As of December 31, 2018, Rell calculates €750,000 of credit losses expected for default events occurring during 2019 and €450,000 of credit losses expected for default events occurring after 2019.

Required:

1. Assume the Tirish bonds have not had a significant increase in credit risk. Prepare the journal entry to record any impairment loss as of December 31, 2018.
2. Assume the Tirish bonds have had a significant increase in credit risk. Prepare the journal entry to record any impairment loss as of December 31, 2018.
3. Assume the Tirish bonds have not had a significant increase in credit risk, and that as of December 31, 2019, Rell calculates €650,000 of credit losses expected for default events occurring during 2020 and €350,000 of credit losses expected for default events occurring after 2020. Prepare the journal entry Rell would make with respect to any impairment loss as of December 31, 2019.

Problems

P 12–1
Securities held-to-maturity; bond investment; effective interest
● LO12-1, LO12-2

Fuzzy Monkey Technologies, Inc., purchased as a long-term investment $80 million of 8% bonds, dated January 1, on January 1, 2018. Management has the positive intent and ability to hold the bonds until maturity. For bonds of similar risk and maturity the market yield was 10%. The price paid for the bonds was $66 million. Interest is received semiannually on June 30 and December 31. Due to changing market conditions, the fair value of the bonds at December 31, 2018, was $70 million.

Required:

1. Prepare the journal entry to record Fuzzy Monkey's investment on January 1, 2018.
2. Prepare the journal entry by Fuzzy Monkey to record interest on June 30, 2018 (at the effective rate).
3. Prepare the journal entries by Fuzzy Monkey to record interest on December 31, 2018 (at the effective rate).
4. At what amount will Fuzzy Monkey report its investment in the December 31, 2018, balance sheet? Why?
5. How would Fuzzy Monkey's 2018 statement of cash flows be affected by this investment?

P 12–2
Trading securities; bond investment; effective interest
● LO12-1, LO12-3

[This problem is a variation of P12–1, modified to categorize the investment as trading securities.]

Fuzzy Monkey Technologies, Inc., purchased as a short-term investment $80 million of 8% bonds, dated January 1, on January 1, 2018. Management intends to include the investment in a short-term, active trading portfolio. For bonds of similar risk and maturity the market yield was 10%. The price paid for the bonds was $66 million. Interest is received semiannually on June 30 and December 31. Due to changing market conditions, the fair value of the bonds at December 31, 2018, was $70 million.

Required:

1. Prepare the journal entry to record Fuzzy Monkey's investment on January 1, 2018.
2. Prepare the journal entry by Fuzzy Monkey to record interest on June 30, 2018 (at the effective rate).
3. Prepare the journal entries by Fuzzy Monkey to record interest on December 31, 2018 (at the effective rate).
4. At what amount will Fuzzy Monkey report its investment in the December 31, 2018, balance sheet? Why? Prepare any entry necessary to achieve this reporting objective.
5. How would Fuzzy Monkey's 2018 statement of cash flows be affected by this investment?

P 12–3
Securities available-for-sale; bond investment; effective interest
● LO 12-1, LO12-4

(Note: This problem is a variation of P12–1, modified to categorize the investment as securities available-for-sale.)

Fuzzy Monkey Technologies, Inc., purchased as a long-term investment $80 million of 8% bonds, dated January 1, on January 1, 2018. Management intends to have the investment available for sale when circumstances warrant. For bonds of similar risk and maturity the market yield was 10%. The price paid for the bonds was $66 million. Interest is received semiannually on June 30 and December 31. Due to changing market conditions, the fair value of the bonds at December 31, 2018, was $70 million.

Required:

1. Prepare the journal entry to record Fuzzy Monkey's investment on January 1, 2018.
2. Prepare the journal entry by Fuzzy Monkey to record interest on June 30, 2018 (at the effective rate).
3. Prepare the journal entries by Fuzzy Monkey to record interest on December 31, 2018 (at the effective rate).
4. At what amount will Fuzzy Monkey report its investment in the December 31, 2018, balance sheet? Why? Prepare any entry necessary to achieve this reporting objective.
5. How would Fuzzy Monkey's 2018 statement of cash flows be affected by this investment?

P 12–4
Fair value option; bond investment; effective interest
● LO12-1, LO12-2, LO12-3, LO12-4, LO12-8

[This problem is a variation of P 12–3, modified to cause the investment to be accounted for under the fair value option.]

Fuzzy Monkey Technologies, Inc., purchased as a long-term investment $80 million of 8% bonds, dated January 1, on January 1, 2018. Management intends to have the investment available for sale when circumstances warrant. When the company purchased the bonds, management elected to account for them under the fair value option. For bonds of similar risk and maturity the market yield was 10%. The price paid for the bonds was $66 million. Interest is received semiannually on June 30 and December 31. Due to changing market conditions, the fair value of the bonds at December 31, 2018, was $70 million.

Required:

1. Prepare the journal entry to record Fuzzy Monkey's investment on January 1, 2018.
2. Prepare the journal entry by Fuzzy Monkey to record interest on June 30, 2018 (at the effective rate).
3. Prepare the journal entries by Fuzzy Monkey to record interest on December 31, 2018 (at the effective rate).
4. At what amount will Fuzzy Monkey report its investment in the December 31, 2018, balance sheet? Why? Prepare any entry necessary to achieve this reporting objective.
5. How would Fuzzy Monkey's 2018 statement of cash flows be affected by this investment?
6. How would your answers to requirements 1–5 differ if management had the intent and ability to hold the investments until maturity?

P 12–5
Various transactions related to trading securities
● LO12-1, LO12-3

The following selected transactions relate to investment activities of Ornamental Insulation Corporation during 2018. The company buys debt securities, intending to profit from short-term differences in price and maintaining them in an active trading portfolio. Ornamental's fiscal year ends on December 31. No investments were held by Ornamental on December 31, 2017.

Mar. 31	Acquired 8% Distribution Transformers Corporation bonds costing $400,000 at face value.
Sep. 1	Acquired $900,000 of American Instruments' 10% bonds at face value.
Sep. 30	Received semiannual interest payment on the Distribution Transformers bonds.
Oct. 2	Sold the Distribution Transformers bonds for $425,000.
Nov. 1	Purchased $1,400,000 of M&D Corporation 6% bonds at face value.
Dec. 31	Recorded any necessary adjusting entry(s) relating to the investments. The market prices of the investments are:

American Instruments bonds	$ 850,000
M&D Corporation bonds	$1,460,000
(Hint: Interest must be accrued.)	

Required:

1. Prepare the appropriate journal entry for each transaction or event during 2018, as well as any adjusting entries necessary at year end.
2. Indicate any amounts that Ornamental Insulation would report in its 2018 income statement, 2018 statement of comprehensive income, and 12/31/2018 balance sheet as a result of these investments.

P 12–6
Various transactions related to securities available-for-sale
● LO12-1, LO12-4

(Note: This problem is a variation of P 12–5, modified to categorize the investments as securities available-for-sale.)

The following selected transactions relate to investment activities of Ornamental Insulation Corporation during 2018. The company buys debt securities, *not* intending to profit from short-term differences in price and *not* necessarily to hold debt securities to maturity, but to have them available for sale when circumstances warrant. Ornamental's fiscal year ends on December 31. No investments were held by Ornamental on December 31, 2017.

Mar. 31	Acquired 8% Distribution Transformers Corporation bonds costing $400,000 at face value.
Sep. 1	Acquired $900,000 of American Instruments' 10% bonds at face value.
Sep. 30	Received semiannual interest payment on the Distribution Transformers bonds.
Oct. 2	Sold the Distribution Transformers bonds for $425,000.
Nov. 1	Purchased $1,400,000 of M&D Corporation 6% bonds costing at face value.
Dec. 31	Recorded any necessary adjusting entry(s) relating to the investments. The market prices of the investments are:

American Instruments bonds	$ 850,000
M&D Corporation bonds	$1,460,000
(Hint: Interest must be accrued.)	

Required:

1. Prepare the appropriate journal entry for each transaction or event during 2018, as well as any adjusting entries necessary at year end. For any sales, prepare entries to update the fair-value adjustment, record any reclassification adjustment, and record the sale.
2. Indicate any amounts that Ornamental Insulation would report in its 2018 income statement, 2018 statement of comprehensive income, and 12/31/2018 balance sheet as a result of these investments.

P 12–7
Various transactions related to equity investments: fair value through net income
● LO12-5

(Note: This problem is a variation of P12–5, modified to consider equity investments.)

The following selected transactions relate to investment activities of Ornamental Insulation Corporation during 2018. The company buys equity securities as investments. None of Ornamental's investments are large enough to exert significant influence on the investee. Ornamental's fiscal year ends on December 31. No investments were held by Ornamental on December 31, 2017.

Mar. 31	Acquired Distribution Transformers Corporation common stock for $400,000.
Sep. 1	Acquired $900,000 of American Instruments' common stock.
Sep. 30	Received a $16,000 dividend on the Distribution Transformers common stock.
Oct. 2	Sold the Distribution Transformers common stock for $425,000.
Nov. 1	Purchased $1,400,000 of M&D Corporation common stock.
Dec. 31	Recorded any necessary adjusting entry(s) relating to the investments. The market prices of the investments are:

American Instruments common stock	$ 850,000
M&D Corporation common stock	$1,460,000

Required:

1. Prepare the appropriate journal entry for each transaction or event during 2018, as well as any adjusting entries necessary at year end.
2. Indicate any amounts that Ornamental Insulation would report in its 2018 income statement, 2018 statement of comprehensive income, and 12/31/2018 balance sheet as a result of these investments.

P 12–8
Various transactions relating to trading securities and equity investments
● LO12-1, LO12-3, LO12-5

American Surety and Fidelity buys and sells securities expecting to earn profits on short-term differences in price. For the first 11 months of 2018, gains from selling trading securities totaled $8 million, losses were $11 million, and the company had earned $5 million in investment revenue. The following selected transactions relate to American's trading account and equity securities investment account during December 2018, and the first week of 2019. The company's fiscal year ends on December 31. No trading securities were held by American on December 1, 2018.

2018	
Dec. 12	Purchased FF&G Corporation bonds for $12 million.
13	Purchased 2 million Ferry Intercommunications common shares for $22 million.
15	Sold the FF&G Corporation bonds for $12.1 million.
22	Purchased U.S. Treasury bills for $56 million and Treasury bonds for $65 million.
23	Sold half the Ferry Intercommunications common shares for $10 million.
26	Sold the U.S. Treasury bills for $57 million.
27	Sold the Treasury bonds for $63 million.
28	Received cash dividends of $200,000 from the Ferry Intercommunications common shares.
31	Recorded any necessary adjusting entry(s) and closing entries relating to the investments. The market price of the Ferry Intercommunications stock was $10 per share.
2019	
Jan. 2	Sold the remaining Ferry Intercommunications common shares for $10.2 million.
5	Purchased Warehouse Designs Corporation bonds for $34 million.

Required:

1. Prepare the appropriate journal entry for each transaction or event during 2018.
2. Indicate any amounts that American would report in its 2018 balance sheet and income statement as a result of these investments.
3. Prepare the appropriate journal entry for each transaction or event during 2019.

P 12–9
Securities held-to-maturity; securities available for sale; trading securities and equity investments
● LO12-1, LO12-2, LO12-3, LO12-4, LO12-5

Amalgamated General Corporation is a consulting firm that also offers financial services through its credit division. From time to time the company buys and sells securities. The following selected transactions relate to Amalgamated's investment activities during the last quarter of 2018 and the first month of 2019. The only securities held by Amalgamated at October 1 were $30 million of 10% bonds of Kansas Abstractors, Inc., purchased on May 1 at face value and held in Amalgamated's trading portfolio. The company's fiscal year ends on December 31.

2018	
Oct. 18	Purchased 2 million preferred shares of Millwork Ventures Company for $58 million.
31	Received semiannual interest of $1.5 million from the Kansas Abstractors bonds.
Nov. 1	Purchased 10% bonds of Holistic Entertainment Enterprises at their $18 million face value, to be held until they mature in 2025. Semiannual interest is payable April 30 and October 31.

(continued)

(concluded)

1	Sold the Kansas Abstractors bonds for $28 million because rising interest rates are expected to cause their fair value to continue to fall. No unrealized gains and losses had been recorded on these bonds previously.
Dec. 1	Purchased 12% bonds of Household Plastics Corporation at their $60 million face value, to be held until they mature in 2028. Semiannual interest is payable May 31 and November 30.
20	Purchased U. S. Treasury bonds for $5.6 million as trading securities, hoping to earn profits on short-term differences in prices.
21	Purchased 4 million common shares of NXS Corporation for $44 million, planning to earn profits from dividends or gains if prevailing market conditions encourage sale.
23	Sold the Treasury bonds for $5.7 million.
29	Received cash dividends of $3 million from the Millwork Ventures Company preferred shares.
31	Recorded any necessary adjusting entry(s) and closing entries relating to the investments. The market price of the Millwork Ventures Company preferred stock was $27.50 per share and $11.50 per share for the NXS Corporation common. The fair values of the bond investments were $58.7 million for Household Plastics Corporation and $16.7 million for Holistic Entertainment Enterprises.
2019	
Jan. 7	Sold the NXS Corporation common shares for $43 million.

Required:
Prepare the appropriate journal entry for each transaction or event.

P 12–10
Investment securities and equity method investments compared
● LO12-6, LO12-7

On January 4, 2018, Runyan Bakery paid $324 million for 10 million shares of Lavery Labeling Company common stock. The investment represents a 30% interest in the net assets of Lavery and gave Runyan the ability to exercise significant influence over Lavery's operations. Runyan received dividends of $2.00 per share on December 15, 2018, and Lavery reported net income of $160 million for the year ended December 31, 2018. The market value of Lavery's common stock at December 31, 2018, was $31 per share. On the purchase date, the book value of Lavery's net assets was $800 million and:

a. The fair value of Lavery's depreciable assets, with an average remaining useful life of six years, exceeded their book value by $80 million.
b. The remainder of the excess of the cost of the investment over the book value of net assets purchased was attributable to goodwill.

Required:
1. Prepare all appropriate journal entries related to the investment during 2018, assuming Runyan accounts for this investment by the equity method.
2. Prepare the journal entries required by Runyan, assuming that the 10 million shares represent a 10% interest in the net assets of Lavery rather than a 30% interest.

P 12–11
Fair value option; equity method investments
● LO12-5, LO12-8

[This problem is a variation of P 12–10 focusing on the fair value option.]

On January 4, 2018, Runyan Bakery paid $324 million for 10 million shares of Lavery Labeling Company common stock. The investment represents a 30% interest in the net assets of Lavery and gave Runyan the ability to exercise significant influence over Lavery's operations. Runyan chose the fair value option to account for this investment. Runyan received dividends of $2.00 per share on December 15, 2018, and Lavery reported net income of $160 million for the year ended December 31, 2018. The market value of Lavery's common stock at December 31, 2018, was $31 per share. On the purchase date, the book value of Lavery's net assets was $800 million and:

a. The fair value of Lavery's depreciable assets, with an average remaining useful life of six years, exceeded their book value by $80 million.
b. The remainder of the excess of the cost of the investment over the book value of net assets purchased was attributable to goodwill.

Required:
Assuming Runyan accounts for this investment under the fair value option, prepare all appropriate journal entries in a manner similar to accounting for securities for which there is not significant influence.

P 12–12
Fair value option; equity method investments
● LO12-5, LO12-6, LO12-7, LO12-8

[This problem is an expanded version of P 12–11 that considers alternative ways in which a firm might apply the fair value option to account for significant-influence investments that would normally be accounted for under the equity method.]

Companies can choose the fair value option for investments that otherwise would be accounted for under the equity method. If the fair value option is chosen, the investment is shown at fair value in the balance sheet, and unrealized holding gains and losses are recognized in the income statement. However, exactly how a company complies with those broad requirements is up to the company. This problem requires you to consider alternative

ways in which a company might apply the fair value option for investments that otherwise would be accounted for under the equity method.

On January 4, 2018, Runyan Bakery paid $324 million for 10 million shares of Lavery Labeling Company common stock. The investment represents a 30% interest in the net assets of Lavery and gave Runyan the ability to exercise significant influence over Lavery's operations. Runyan chose the fair value option to account for this investment. Runyan received dividends of $2.00 per share on December 15, 2018, and Lavery reported net income of $160 million for the year ended December 31, 2018. The market value of Lavery's common stock at December 31, 2018, was $31 per share. On the purchase date, the book value of Lavery's net assets was $800 million and:

a. The fair value of Lavery's depreciable assets, with an average remaining useful life of six years, exceeded their book value by $80 million.
b. The remainder of the excess of the cost of the investment over the book value of net assets purchased was attributable to goodwill.

Required:

1. Prepare all appropriate journal entries related to the investment during 2018, assuming Runyan accounts for this investment under the fair value option, and accounts for the Lavery investment in a manner similar to what it would use for securities for which there is not significant influence. Indicate the effect of these journal entries on 2018 net income, and indicate the amount at which the investment is carried in the December 31, 2018, balance sheet.
2. Prepare all appropriate journal entries related to the investment during 2018, assuming Runyan accounts for this investment under the fair value option, but uses equity method accounting to account for Lavery's income and dividends, and then records a fair value adjustment at the end of the year that allows it to comply with GAAP. Indicate the effect of these journal entries on 2018 net income, and indicate the amount at which the investment is carried in the December 31, 2018, balance sheet. (Note: You should end up with the same total 2018 income effect and same carrying value on the balance sheet for requirements 1 and 2.)

P 12–13
Equity method
● LO12-6, LO12-7

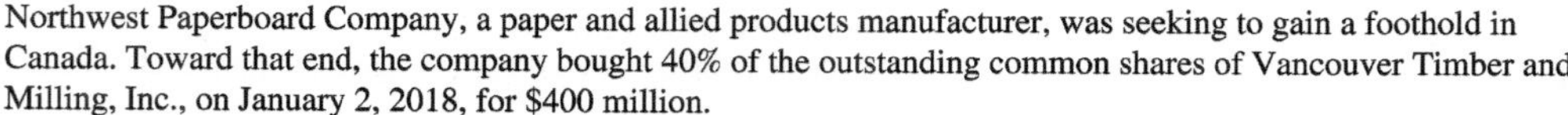

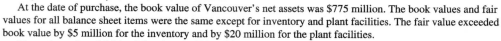

Northwest Paperboard Company, a paper and allied products manufacturer, was seeking to gain a foothold in Canada. Toward that end, the company bought 40% of the outstanding common shares of Vancouver Timber and Milling, Inc., on January 2, 2018, for $400 million.

At the date of purchase, the book value of Vancouver's net assets was $775 million. The book values and fair values for all balance sheet items were the same except for inventory and plant facilities. The fair value exceeded book value by $5 million for the inventory and by $20 million for the plant facilities.

The estimated useful life of the plant facilities is 16 years. All inventory acquired was sold during 2018.

Vancouver reported net income of $140 million for the year ended December 31, 2018. Vancouver paid a cash dividend of $30 million.

Required:

1. Prepare all appropriate journal entries related to the investment during 2018.
2. What amount should Northwest report as its income from its investment in Vancouver for the year ended December 31, 2018?
3. What amount should Northwest report in its balance sheet as its investment in Vancouver?
4. What should Northwest report in its statement of cash flows regarding its investment in Vancouver?

P 12–14
Equity method
● LO12-6, LO12-7

On January 2, 2018, Miller Properties paid $19 million for 1 million shares of Marlon Company's 6 million outstanding common shares. Miller's CEO became a member of Marlon's board of directors during the first quarter of 2018.

The carrying amount of Marlon's net assets was $66 million. Miller estimated the fair value of those net assets to be the same except for a patent valued at $24 million above cost. The remaining amortization period for the patent is 10 years.

Marlon reported earnings of $12 million and paid dividends of $6 million during 2018. On December 31, 2018, Marlon's common stock was trading on the NYSE at $18.50 per share.

Required:

1. When considering whether to account for its investment in Marlon under the equity method, what criteria should Miller's management apply?
2. Assume Miller accounts for its investment in Marlon using the equity method. Ignoring income taxes, determine the amounts related to the investment to be reported in its 2018:
   a. Income statement
   b. Balance sheet
   c. Statement of cash flows

P 12–15
Classifying investments
● LO12-2 through LO12-6

Indicate (by letter) the way each of the investments listed below most likely should be accounted for based on the information provided.

Item	Reporting Category
____ 1. 35% of the nonvoting preferred stock of American Aircraft Company	T. Trading securities
____ 2. Treasury bills to be held to maturity	M. Securities held-to-maturity
____ 3. Two-year note receivable from affiliate	A. Securities available-for-sale
____ 4. Accounts receivable	F. Fair value through net income
____ 5. Treasury bond maturing in one week	E. Equity method
____ 6. Common stock held in an investment account for immediate resale	C. Consolidation
____ 7. Bonds acquired to profit from short-term differences in price	N. None of these
____ 8. 35% of the voting common stock of Computer Storage Devices Company	
____ 9. 90% of the voting common stock of Affiliated Peripherals, Inc	
____ 10. Corporate bonds of Primary Smelting Company to be sold if interest rates fall ½%	
____ 11. 25% of the voting common stock of Smith Foundries Corporation (51% family-owned by Smith family; fair value readily determinable)	
____ 12. 17% of the voting common stock of Shipping Barrels Corporation (Investor's CEO on the board of directors of Shipping Barrels Corporation)	

P 12–16
Fair value option; held-to-maturity investments
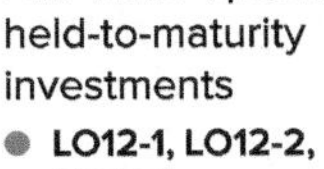
● LO12-1, LO12-2, LO12-8

On January 1, 2018, Ithaca Corp. purchases Cortland Inc. bonds that have a face value of $150,000. The Cortland bonds have a stated interest rate of 6%. Interest is paid semiannually on June 30 and December 31, and the bonds mature in 10 years. For bonds of similar risk and maturity, the market yield on particular dates is as follows:

January 1, 2018	7.0%
June 30, 2018	8.0%
December 31, 2018	9.0%

Required:

1. Calculate the price Ithaca would have paid for the Cortland bonds on January 1, 2018 (ignoring brokerage fees), and prepare a journal entry to record the purchase.
2. Prepare all appropriate journal entries related to the bond investment during 2018, assuming Ithaca accounts for the bonds as a held-to-maturity investment. Ithaca calculates interest revenue at the effective interest rate as of the date it purchased the bonds.
3. Prepare all appropriate journal entries related to the bond investment during 2018, assuming that Ithaca chose the fair value option when the bonds were purchased, and that Ithaca determines fair value of the bonds semiannually. Ithaca calculates interest revenue at the effective interest rate as of the date it purchased the bonds.

P 12–17
Accounting for debt and equity investments
● LO12-1, LO12-4, LO12-5, LO12-9

Feherty, Inc., accounts for its investments under *IFRS No. 9* and purchased the following investments during December 2018:

1. Fifty of Donald Company's $1,000 bonds. The bonds pay semiannual interest, return principal in eight years, and include no other cash flows or other features. Feherty plans to hold 10 of the bonds to collect contractual cash flows over the life of the investment and to hold 40, both to collect contractual cash flows but also to sell them if their price appreciates sufficiently. Subsequent to Feherty's purchase of the bonds, but prior to December 31, the fair value of the bonds increased to $1,040 per bond, and Feherty sold 10 of the 40 bonds. Feherty also sold 5 of the 10 bonds it had planned to hold to collect contractual cash flows over the life of the investment. The fair value of the bonds remained at $1,040 as of December 31, 2018.
2. $25,000 of Watson Company common stock. Feherty does not have the ability to significantly influence the operations of Watson. Feherty elected to account for this equity investment at fair value through OCI (FVOCI). Subsequent to Feherty's purchase of the stock, the fair value of the stock investment increased to $30,000 as of December 31, 2018.

Required:

1. Indicate how Feherty would account for its investments when it acquired the Donald bonds and Watson stock.
2. Calculate the effect of realized and unrealized gains and losses associated with the Donald bonds and the Watson stock on Feherty's net income, other comprehensive income, and comprehensive income for the year ended December 31, 2018. Ignore interest revenue and taxes.

P 12–18
Accounting for other-than-temporary impairments (Appendix 12B)
● LO12-2, LO12-3, LO12-4, LO12-8

Stewart Enterprises has the following investments, all purchased prior to 2018:

1. Bee Company 5% bonds, purchased at face value, with an amortized cost of $4,000,000, and classified as held to maturity. At December 31, 2018, the Bee investment had a fair value of $3,500,000, and Stewart calculated that $240,000 of the fair value decline is a credit loss and $260,000 is a noncredit loss. At December 31, 2019, the Bee investment had a fair value of $3,700,000, and Stewart calculated that $140,000 of the difference between fair value and amortized cost was a credit loss and $160,000 was a noncredit loss.

2. Oliver Corporation 4% bonds, purchased at face value, with an amortized cost of $2,500,000, classified as a trading security. Because of unrealized losses prior to 2018, the Oliver bonds have a fair value adjustment account with a credit balance of $200,000, such that the carrying value of the Oliver investment is $2,300,000 prior to making any adjusting entries in 2018. At December 31, 2018, the Oliver investment had a fair value of $2,200,000, and Stewart calculated that $120,000 of the difference between amortized cost and fair value is a credit loss and $180,000 is a noncredit loss. At December 31, 2019, the Oliver investment had a fair value of $2,700,000.
3. Jones Inc. 6% bonds, purchased at face value, with an amortized cost of $3,500,000, and classified as an available-for-sale investment. Because of unrealized losses prior to 2018, the Jones bonds have a fair value adjustment account with a credit balance of $400,000, such that the carrying value of the Jones investment is $3,100,000 prior to making any adjusting entries in 2018. At December 31, 2018, the Jones investment had a fair value of $2,700,000, and Stewart calculated that $225,000 of the difference between amortized cost and fair value is a credit loss and $575,000 is a noncredit loss. At December 31, 2019, the Jones investment had a fair value of $2,900,000, and Stewart calculated that $125,000 of the difference between amortized cost and fair value is a credit loss and $475,000 is a noncredit loss.

Stewart does not intend to sell any of these investments and does not believe it is more likely than not that it will have to sell any of the bond investments before fair value recovers.

Required:

Prepare the appropriate adjusting journal entries to account for fair value changes during 2018 and 2019, assuming that each investment is viewed as qualifying as an other-than-temporary (OTT) impairment as of December 31, 2018, and then is accounted for normally during 2019 (with no additional OTT impairment in 2019).

Broaden Your Perspective

Apply your critical-thinking ability to the knowledge you've gained. These cases will provide you an opportunity to develop your research, analysis, judgment, and communication skills. You also will work with other students, integrate what you've learned, apply it in real world situations, and consider its global and ethical ramifications. This practice will broaden your knowledge and further develop your decision-making abilities.

Real World Case 12–1
Intel's investments
● LO12-4

The following disclosure note appeared in the December 26, 2015, annual report of the Intel Corporation.

Note 5: Cash and Investments (partial)

Available-for-sale investments as of December 26, 2015, and December 27, 2014, were as follows:

	December 26, 2015				December 27, 2014			
($ in millions)	Adjusted Cost	Gross Unrealized Gains	Gross Unrealized Losses	Fair Value	Adjusted Cost	Gross Unrealized Gains	Gross Unrealized Losses	Fair Value
Asset-backed securities	$ 5	$ —	$ (1)	$ 4	$ 8	$ —	$(2)	$ 6
Corporate debt	4,164	3	(10)	4,157	2,040	13	(5)	2,048
Financial institution instruments	11,140	1	(2)	11,139	3,146	2	(1)	3,147
Government debt	748	—	(1)	747	741	—	(1)	740
Marketable equity securities	3,254	2,706	—	5,960	3,318	3,779	—	7,097
Total available-for-sale investments	$19,311	$2,710	$(14)	$22,007	$9,253	$3,794	$(9)	$13,038

Intel also indicates the following: "During 2015, we sold available-for-sale investments for proceeds of $2.2 billion . . . The gross realized gains on sales of available-for-sale investments were $133 million in 2015. Intel's Note 24 (Other Comprehensive Income) indicates unrealized holding losses of $999 million during 2015, and a reclassification adjustment of $93 for gains that had previously been included in OCI and recorded in the fair value adjustment but which were now being included in net income after being realized upon sale. Note: Intel's 2015 financial statements were issued prior to the effective date of *ASU 2016-01*, so Intel includes equity investments among its available-for-sale investments. That difference from current GAAP will not affect your answer to the case questions.

Required:

1. Draw a T-account that shows the change between the December 27, 2014, and December 26, 2015, balances for the fair value adjustment associated with Intel's AFS investments for 2015. By how much did the fair value adjustment change during 2015?
2. Prepare a journal entry that records any unrealized holding gains and losses that occurred during 2015. Ignore income taxes.
3. Prepare a journal entry that records any reclassification adjustment for available-for-sale investments sold during 2015. Ignore income taxes.
4. Using your journal entries from requirements 2 and 3, adjust your T-account from requirement 1. Have you accounted for the entire change in the fair value adjustment that occurred during 2015? Speculate as to the cause of any difference.

Real World Case 12–2
Reporting securities available-for-sale; obtain and critically evaluate an annual report
● LO12-4

All publicly traded domestic companies use EDGAR, the Electronic Data Gathering, Analysis, and Retrieval system, to make the majority of their filings with the SEC. You can access EDGAR at www.sec.gov.

Required:

1. Locate a recent annual report of a public company that includes a footnote that describes an investment in securities available-for-sale. You can use EDGAR at www.sec.gov.
2. Under what caption are the investments reported in the comparative balance sheets? Are they reported as current or noncurrent assets?
3. Are realized gains or losses reported in the comparative income statements?
4. Are unrealized gains or losses reported in the comparative statements and shareholders' equity?
5. Are accumulated unrealized gains or losses identifiable in the comparative balance sheets? If so, under what caption? Why are unrealized gains or losses reported here rather in the income statement?
6. Are cash flow effects of these investments reflected in the company's comparative statements of cash flows? If so, what information is provided by this disclosure?

International Case 12–3
Comparison of equity method between IFRS and U.S. GAAP
● LO12-5, LO12-6, LO12-7, LO12-9

IFRS

The following are excerpts from the 2015 financial statements of Renault, a large French automobile manufacturer.

14 – INVESTMENT IN NISSAN

A – Nissan consolidation method

Renault's percentage interest in Nissan is 43.7% and Renault holds 43.4% of voting rights in Nissan. Renault and Nissan have chosen to develop a unique type of alliance between two distinct companies with common interests, uniting forces to achieve optimum performance. The Alliance is organized so as to preserve individual brand identities and respect each company's corporate culture.

Consequently:

- Renault is not assured of holding the majority of voting rights in Nissan's Shareholders' Meeting.
- The terms of the Renault-Nissan agreement do not entitle Renault to appoint the majority of Nissan directors, nor to hold the majority of voting rights at meetings of Nissan's Board of Directors; Renault cannot unilaterally appoint the President of Nissan; on December 31, 2015, Renault occupied two of the nine seats on Nissan's Board of Directors (unchanged since December 31, 2014).
- Renault-Nissan B.V., owned 50% by Renault and 50% by Nissan, is the Alliance's joint decision-making body for strategic issues concerning either group individually. Its decisions are applicable to both Renault and Nissan. This decision-making power was conferred on Renault-Nissan B.V. to generate synergies and bring both automakers worldwide economies of scale. This entity does not enable Renault to direct Nissan's financial and operating strategies, which are governed by Nissan's Board of Directors and cannot therefore be considered to represent contractual control by Renault over Nissan. The matters examined by Renault-Nissan B.V. since it was formed have remained strictly within this contractual framework, and are not an indication that Renault exercises control over Nissan.
- Renault can neither use nor influence the use of Nissan's assets in the same way as its own assets.
- Renault provides no guarantees in respect of Nissan's debt.

In view of this situation, Renault is considered to exercise significant influence over Nissan, and therefore uses the equity method to include its investment in Nissan in the consolidation.

Renault's Note D lists various restatements that Renault makes when accounting for its Nissan investment under the equity method. Some of those changes harmonize Nissan's accounting (under Japanese accounting standards). Others reflect adjustments to fair value of assets and liabilities applied by Renault at the time of acquisitions in 1999 and 2002.

Required:

1. Go to Deloitte's IAS Plus website and examine the summary of the IASB's *IAS No. 28* (http://www.iasplus.com/standard/ias28.htm), which governs application of the equity method. Focus on two areas: Identification of Associates and Applying the Equity Method of Accounting.

2. Evaluate Renault's decision to use the equity method to account for its investment in Nissan. Does Renault have insignificant influence, significant influence, or control?
3. Evaluate the fact that, when accounting for its investment in Nissan under the equity method, Renault makes adjustments that take into account the fair value of assets and liabilities at the time Renault invested in Nissan. Give an example of the sorts of adjustments that might be made. Are such adjustments consistent with IFRS? With U.S. GAAP? Explain.
4. Evaluate the fact that, when accounting for its investment in Nissan under the equity method, Renault makes adjustments for harmonization of accounting standards. Are such adjustments consistent with IFRS? With U.S. GAAP? Explain.

International Case 12–4
Comparison of equity method and proportionate consolidation under IFRS
● LO12-6, LO12-9

Obtain the 2015 annual report of FCA Group (www.fcagroup.com), which manufactures Fiat-brand automobiles as well as other products.

Required:

Find FCA's discussion of "Interests in other companies" in the "Significant Accounting Policies" note that follows the financial statements. Is FCA accounting for its equity investments in a way that is consistent with U.S. GAAP? Explain.

Research Case 12–5
Researching the way investments are reported; retrieving information from the Internet
● LO12-2, LO12-3, LO12-4, LO12-5, LO12-6

All publicly traded domestic companies use EDGAR, the Electronic Data Gathering, Analysis, and Retrieval system, to make the majority of their filings with the SEC. You can access EDGAR at www.sec.gov.

Required:

1. Search for a public company with which you are familiar. Access its most recent 10-K filing. Search or scroll to find financial statements and related notes.
2. Answer the following questions. (If the chosen company does not report investments in the securities of other companies, choose another company.)
   a. What is the amount and classification of any investment securities reported in the balance sheet? Are unrealized gains or losses reported in the shareholders' equity section?
   b. Are any investments reported by the equity method?
   c. What amounts from these investments are reported in the comparative income statements? Has that income increased or decreased over the years reported?
   d. Are any acquisitions or disposals of investments reported in the statement of cash flows?

Real World Case 12–6
Merck's investments
● LO12-4, LO12-5, LO12-6

Corporations frequently invest in securities issued by other corporations. Some investments are acquired to secure a favorable business relationship with another company. On the other hand, others are intended only to earn an investment return from the dividends or interest the securities pay or from increases in the market prices of the securities—the same motivations that might cause you to invest in stocks, bonds, or other securities. This diversity in investment objectives means no single accounting method is adequate to report every investment.

Merck & Co., Inc., invests in securities of other companies. Access Merck's 2015 10-K (which includes financial statements) using EDGAR at www.sec.gov. Note: Merck's 2015 financial statements were issued prior to the effective date of *ASU 2016-01*, so do not be surprised by the fact that Merck includes equity investments among its available-for-sale investments.

Required:

1. What is the amount and classification of any investment securities reported on the balance sheet? In which current and noncurrent asset categories are investments reported by Merck? What criteria are used to determine the classifications?
2. How are unrealized gains or losses reported? Realized gains and losses?
3. Are any investments reported by the equity method?
4. What amounts from equity method investments are reported in the comparative income statements?
5. Are cash flow effects of these investments reflected in the company's comparative statements of cash flows? If so, what information is provided by this disclosure?

Real World Case 12–7
Comprehensive income—Microsoft
● LO12-4

Microsoft's 2015 10-K includes the following information in Note 20—Accumulated Other Comprehensive Income relevant to its available-for-sale investments:

($ in millions)	Year Ended June 30, 2015	2014	2013
Investments			
Accumulated other comprehensive income balance, beginning of period	$3,531	$1,794	$1,431
Unrealized gains, net of tax effects of $59, $1,067 and $244	110	2,053	453
Reclassification adjustments for gains included in other income (expense), net	(728)	(447)	(139)
Tax expense included in provision for income taxes	256	131	49
Amounts reclassified from accumulated other comprehensive income	(472)	(316)	(90)
Net current period other comprehensive income (loss)	(362)	1,737	363
Accumulated other comprehensive income balance, end of period	$3,169	$3,531	$1,794

Required:

1. Prepare a journal entry to record unrealized gains for 2015. (*Hint*: $110 is net tax effects, so you will need to add back tax effects to show the amount of unrealized gain gross taxes.)
2. Prepare a journal entry to record Microsoft's reclassification adjustment for 2015.

Trueblood Accounting Case 12–8
Impairments (Appendix 12B)
● LO12-4

The following Trueblood case is recommended for use with this chapter. The case provides an excellent opportunity for class discussion, group projects, and writing assignments. The case, along with Professor's Discussion Material, can be obtained from the Deloitte Foundation at its website: www.deloitte.com/us/truebloodcases.

Case: 14-9: O.T.T. Incorporated
This case gives students an opportunity to discuss accounting for other-than-temporary impairments.

Research Case 12–9
Changes in accounting for other-than-temporary impairments (Appendix 12B)
● LO12-2, LO12-4, LO12-8

In Appendix 12B, you learned that accounting for other-than-temporary impairments has changed recently. You also learned that these changes were controversial. In fact, two of the five members of the FASB voted against the changes and provided an explanation for their position when the standard that defined the changes was issued. That information isn't included in the FASB's Accounting Standards Codification, but you can find it in the original standard, "Recognition and Presentation of Other-Than-Temporary Impairments," FASB Staff Position (FSP) No. 115-2 and 124-2 (Norwalk, Conn.: FASB, April 9, 2009), which is available under the "Reference Library" and "Superseded Standards" link at www.fasb.org.

Required:

Access the FSP, turn to page 17, and read why FASB members Linsmeier and Siegel dissented. What were their major concerns with the new approach for accounting for OTT impairments? Do you find those concerns compelling?

Continuing Cases

Target Case
● LO12-4, LO12-6

Target Corporation prepares its financial statements according to U.S. GAAP. Target's financial statements and disclosure notes for the year ended January 30, 2016, are available Connect. This material also is available under the Investor Relations link at the company's website (www.target.com). Target does not have investments in stock or bonds. However, CVS Health Corp., which purchased Target's pharmacy and clinical business during 2015, does have some investments. Access CVS's 2015 10K (issued on February 9, 2016) at investors.cvshealth.com to answer the following questions,

Required:

1. CVS indicates in Note 1 that it has some short-term investments that consist of certificates of deposit (CDs).
   a. How has CVS classified those CDs for accounting purposes?
   b. Per CVS's balance sheet, what was the balance in CVS's short-term investments as of December 31, 2015 and December 31, 2014?
   c. Per CVS's statement of cash flows, what cash transactions affected short-term investments during 2015?
   d. Prepare a T-account that summarizes transactions affecting CVS's short-term investments during 2015. Speculate as to the explanation for any "plug" figure necessary to make the T-account balance.

2. Per Note 1, CVS has equity-method investments in SureScripts, LLC and in Heartland Healthcare Services. CVS indicates that those investments are immaterial for the year ended December 31, 2015. Assuming that the Heartland investment is material,
   a. How would Heartland's earnings affect CVS's income statement?
   b. How would Heartland's earnings affect CVS's balance sheet?

Air France–KLM Case

Air France-KLM (AF), a Franco-Dutch company, prepares its financial statements according to International Financial Reporting Standards. AF's financial statements and disclosure notes for the year ended December 31, 2015, are available in Connect. This material is also available under the Finance link at the company's website (www.airfranceklm.com).

Required:

1. Read Notes 24 and 36.4. Focusing on investments accounted for at fair value through profit and loss (FVTPL):
   a. As of December 31, 2015, what is the total balance of those investments in the balance sheet?
   b. How much of that balance is classified as current and how much as noncurrent?
   c. How much of the fair value of those investments is accounted for using level 1, level 2, and level 3 inputs of the fair value hierarchy? Given that information, assess the reliability (representational faithfulness) of this fair value estimate.
2. Complete Requirement 1 again, but for investments accounted for as available for sale.
3. Read Notes 4.3 and 22.
   a. When AF can exercise significant influence over an investee, what accounting approach does it use to account for the investment? How does AF determine if it can exercise significant influence?
   b. If AF is involved in a joint venture, what accounting approach does it use to account for the investment?
   c. What is the carrying value of AF's equity-method investments in its December 31, 2015 balance sheet?
   d. How did AF's equity-method investments affect AF's 2015 net income from continuing operations?

CPA Exam Questions and Simulations

Sample CPA Exam questions from Roger CPA Review are available in Connect as support for the topics in this chapter. These Multiple Choice Questions and Task-Based Simulations include expert-written explanations and solutions, and provide a starting point for students to become familiar with the content and functionality of the actual CPA Exam.

APPENDIX A

Derivatives

". . . derivatives are financial weapons of mass destruction . . ."

— Warren Buffett, Berkshire Hathaway CEO

". . . the growing use of complex financial instruments known as derivatives does not pose a threat to the country's financial system . . ."

— Alan Greenspan, Federal Reserve Chairman

"Total world derivatives are $1000 trillion or 19 times the total world GDP of $54 trillion."

— Chuck Burr, *Culture Change*

In today's global economy and evolving financial markets, businesses are increasingly exposed to a variety of risks, which, unmanaged, can have major impacts on earnings or even threaten a company's very existence. Risk management, then, has become critical. Derivative financial instruments have become the key tools of risk management.[1]

Derivatives are financial instruments that "derive" their values from some other security or *index.*

Derivatives are financial instruments that "derive" their values or contractually required cash flows from some other security or index. For instance, a contract allowing a company to buy a particular asset (say steel, gold, or flour) at a designated future date at a predetermined price is a financial instrument that derives its value from expected and actual changes in the price of the underlying asset. Financial futures, forward contracts, options, and interest rate swaps are the most frequently used derivatives. Derivatives are valued as tools to manage or hedge companies' increasing exposures to risk, including interest rate risk, price risk, and foreign exchange risk. The variety, complexity, and magnitude of derivatives have grown rapidly in recent years. Accounting standard-setters have scrambled to keep pace.

Derivatives serve as a form of "insurance" against risk.

A persistent stream of headline stories has alerted us to multimillion-dollar losses by many companies and the financial collapse of Bear Stearns and AIG.[2] Focusing on these headlines, it would be tempting to conclude that derivatives are risky business indeed. Certainly they can be quite risky if misused, but the fact is, these financial instruments exist to lessen, not increase, risk. Properly used, they serve as a form of "insurance" against risk. In fact, if a company is exposed to a substantial risk and does not hedge that risk, it is taking a gamble. On the other hand, if a derivative is used improperly, it can be a huge gamble itself.

The notional amount of the derivatives market vastly exceeds the total value of the assets they are intended to mimic or mirror. This implies that firms are using derivatives for purposes other than risk management. Many observers are fearful that the size of the derivatives market poses significant risk to the economy. Some caution that the vast derivatives market could even cause the entire global financial system to crash. Why? If interest rates rise, then many speculative interest rate swaps would incur losses. But it's the size of the interest rate swap market, and thus the size of the resultant losses, that prompts the anxiety. At the start of 2014, the over-the-counter derivatives market was $702 trillion. Yes, that's 702 with twelve zeroes ($702,000,000,000,000). And, that's over 30 times the U.S. Gross Domestic Product. Eighty-two percent of those derivatives ($584 trillion) are interest rate swaps.[3] Our focus here, though, is not on the risk posed by the speculative use of derivatives, but instead on the use of derivatives to reduce company risk.

[1]Almost all financial institutions and over half of all nonfinancial companies use derivatives.

[2]Bear Sterns has since been sold at a bargain basement price to JP Morgan, and AIG has since recovered from its difficulties.

[3]Bank for International Settlements, *BIS Quarterly Review,* June 2014.

Derivatives Used to Hedge Risk

Hedging means taking a risk position that is opposite to an actual position that is exposed to risk.

Hedging means taking an action that is expected to produce exposure to a particular type of risk that is precisely the *opposite* of an actual risk to which the company already is exposed. For instance, the volatility of interest rates creates exposure to interest-rate risk for companies that issue debt—which, of course, includes most companies. So, a company that frequently arranges short-term loans from its bank under a floating (variable) interest rate agreement is exposed to the risk that interest rates might increase and adversely affect borrowing costs. Similarly, a company that regularly reissues commercial paper as it matures faces the possibility that new rates will be higher and cut into forecasted income. When borrowings are large, the potential cost can be substantial. So, the firm might choose to hedge its position by entering into a transaction that would produce a *gain* of roughly the same amount as the potential loss if interest rates do, in fact, increase.

Hedging is used to deal with three areas of risk exposure: fair value risk, cash flow risk, and foreign currency risk. Let's look at some of the more common derivatives.

A *futures contract* allows a firm to sell (or buy) a financial instrument at a designated future date, at today's price.

FINANCIAL FUTURES A futures contract is an agreement between a seller and a buyer that requires the seller to deliver a particular commodity (say corn, gold, or pork bellies) at a designated future date, at a *predetermined* price. These contracts are actively traded on regulated futures exchanges. When the "commodity" is a *financial instrument,* such as a Treasury bond, Treasury bill, commercial paper, or a certificate of deposit, the agreement is referred to as a *financial futures contract.*[4]

To appreciate the way these hedges work, you need to remember that when interest rates rise, the market price of interest-bearing securities goes down. For instance, if you have an investment in a 10% bond and market interest rates go up to, say, 12%, your 10% bond is less valuable relative to other bonds paying the higher rate. Conversely, when interest rates decline, the market price of interest-bearing securities goes up. This risk that the investment's value might change is referred to as *fair value risk.* The company that issued the securities is faced with fair value risk also. If interest rates decline, the fair value of that company's debt would rise, a risk the borrower may want to hedge against. Later in this section, we'll look at an illustration of how the borrower would account for and report such a hedge.

The seller in a financial futures contract realizes a gain (loss) when interest rates rise (decline).

Now let's look at the effect on a contract to sell or buy securities (or any asset for that matter) at preset prices. One who is contracted to *sell* securities at a *preset* price after their market price has fallen benefits from the rise in interest rates. Consequently, the value of the contract that gives one the right to sell securities at a preset price goes up as the market price declines. The seller in a futures contract derives a gain (loss) when interest rates rise (decline).[5] Conversely, the one obligated to buy securities at a preset price experiences a loss. This risk of having to pay more cash or receive less cash is referred to as *cash flow risk.*

Another example of cash flow risk would be borrowing money by issuing a variable (floating) rate note. If market interest rates rise, the borrower would have to pay more interest. Similarly, the lender (investor) in the variable (floating) rate note transaction would face cash flow risk that interest rates would decline, resulting in lower cash interest receipts.

Let's look closer at how a futures contract can mitigate cash flow risk. Consider a company in April that will replace its $10 million of 8.5% bank notes with a bond issue when the notes mature in June. The company is exposed to the risk that interest rates in June will have risen, increasing borrowing costs. To counteract that possibility, the firm might enter a contract in April to deliver (sell) bonds in June at their *current* price. Since there are no corporate bond futures contracts, the company buys Treasury bond futures, which will accomplish essentially the same purpose. In essence, the firm agrees to sell Treasury bonds in June at a price established now (April). Let's say it's April 6 and the price of Treasury bond futures on the International Monetary Market of the Chicago Mercantile Exchange is quoted as 95.24.[6] Since the trading unit of Treasury bond futures is a 15-year, $100,000, 8% Treasury bond,

[4]Note that a financial futures contract meets the definition of a financial instrument because it entails the exchange of financial instruments (cash for Treasury bonds, for instance). But, a futures contract for the sale or purchase of a nonfinancial commodity like corn or gold does not meet the definition because one of the items to be exchanged is not a financial instrument.

[5]The seller of a futures contract is obligated to sell the bonds at a future date. The buyer of a futures contract is obligated to buy the bonds at a future date. The company in our example, then, is the seller of the futures contract.

[6]Price quotes are expressed as a percentage of par.

the company might sell 105 Treasury bond futures to hedge the June issuance of debt. This would effectively provide a hedge of 105 × \$100,000 × 95.24% = \$10,000,200.[7]

Here's what happens then. If interest rates rise, borrowing costs will go up for our example company because it will have to sell debt securities at a higher interest cost (or lower price). But that loss will be offset (approximately) by the gain produced by being in the opposite position on Treasury bond futures. Take note, though, this works both ways. If interest rates go down causing debt security prices to rise, the potential benefit of being able to issue debt at that lower interest rate (higher price) will be offset by a loss on the futures position.

A very important point about futures contracts is that the seller does not need to have actual possession of the commodity (the Treasury bonds, in this case), nor is the purchaser of the contract required to take possession of the commodity. In fact, virtually all financial futures contracts are "netted out" before the actual transaction is to take place. This is simply a matter of reversing the original position. A seller closes out his transaction with a purchase. Likewise, a purchaser would close out her transaction with a sale. After all, the objective is not to actually buy or sell Treasury bonds (or whatever the commodity might be), but to incur the financial impact of movements in interest rates as reflected in changes in Treasury bond prices. Specifically, it will buy at the lower price (to reverse the original seller position) at the same time it's selling its new bond issue at that same lower price. The financial futures market is an "artificial" exchange in that its reason for existing is to provide a mechanism to transfer risk from those exposed to it to those willing to accept the risk, not to actually buy and sell the underlying financial instruments.

If the impending debt issue being hedged is a short-term issue, the company may attain a more effective hedge by selling Treasury *bill* futures since Treasury bills are 90-day securities, or maybe certificate of deposit (CD) futures that also are traded in futures markets. The object is to get the closest association between the financial effects of interest rate movements on the actual transaction and the effects on the financial instrument used as a hedge.

The effectiveness of a hedge is influenced by the closeness of the match between the item being hedged and the financial instrument chosen as a hedge.

FINANCIAL FORWARD CONTRACTS A forward contract is similar to a futures contract but differs in three ways:

1. A forward contract calls for delivery on a specific date, whereas a futures contract permits the seller to decide later which specific day within the specified month will be the delivery date (if it gets as far as actual delivery before it is closed out).
2. Unlike a futures contract, a forward contract usually is not traded on a market exchange.
3. Unlike a futures contract, a forward contract does not call for a daily cash settlement for price changes in the underlying contract. Gains and losses on forward contracts are paid only when they are closed out.

OPTIONS Options frequently are purchased to hedge exposure to the effects of changing interest rates. Options serve the same purpose as futures in that respect but are fundamentally different. An option on a financial instrument—say a Treasury bill—gives its holder the right either to buy or to sell the Treasury bill at a specified price and within a given time period. Importantly, though, the option holder has no obligation to exercise the option. On the other hand, the holder of a futures contract must buy or sell within a specified period unless the contract is closed out before delivery comes due.

FOREIGN CURRENCY FUTURES Foreign loans frequently are denominated in the currency of the lender (Japanese yen, Swiss franc, Euro, and so on). When loans must be repaid in foreign currencies, a new element of risk is introduced. This is because if exchange rates change, the dollar equivalent of the foreign currency that must be repaid differs from the dollar equivalent of the foreign currency borrowed.

To hedge against "foreign exchange risk" exposure, some firms buy or sell foreign currency futures contracts. These are similar to financial futures except specific foreign

Foreign exchange risk often is hedged in the same manner as interest rate risk.

[7]This is a simplification of the more sophisticated way financial managers determine the optimal number of futures.

currencies are specified in the futures contracts rather than specific debt instruments. They work the same way to protect against foreign exchange risk as financial futures protect against fair value or cash flow risk.

Interest rate swaps exchange fixed interest payments for floating rate payments, or vice versa, without exchanging the underlying notional amounts.

INTEREST RATE SWAPS Over 82% of derivatives are interest rate contracts, of which 75% are **interest rate swaps**. These contracts exchange fixed interest payments for floating rate payments, or vice versa, without exchanging the underlying principal amounts. For example, suppose you owe $100,000 on a 10% fixed rate home loan. You envy your neighbor who also is paying 10% on her $100,000 mortgage, but hers is a floating rate loan, so if market rates fall, so will her loan rate. To the contrary, she is envious of your fixed rate, fearful that rates will rise, increasing her payments. A solution would be for the two of you to effectively swap interest payments using an interest rate swap agreement. The way a swap works, you both would continue to actually make your own interest payments, but you would exchange the net cash difference between payments at specified intervals. So, in this case, if market rates (and thus floating payments) increase, you would pay your neighbor; if rates fall, she pays you. The net effect is to exchange the consequences of rate changes. In other words, you have effectively converted your fixed-rate debt to floating-rate debt; your neighbor has done the opposite.

Of course, this technique is not dependent on happening into such a fortuitous pairing of two borrowers with opposite philosophies on interest rate risk. Instead, banks or other intermediaries offer, for a fee, one-sided swap agreements to companies desiring to be either fixed-rate payers or variable-rate payers. Intermediaries usually strive to maintain a balanced portfolio of matched, offsetting swap agreements.

Theoretically, the two parties to such a transaction exchange principal amounts, say the $100,000 amount above, in addition to the interest on those amounts. It makes no practical sense, though, for the companies to send each other $100,000. So, instead, the principal amount is not actually exchanged, but serves merely as the computational base for interest calculations and is called the *notional amount.* Similarly, the fixed-rate payer doesn't usually send the entire fixed interest amount (say 10% × $100,000 = $10,000) and receive the entire variable interest amount (say 9% × $100,000 = $9,000). Generally, only the net amount ($1,000 in this case) is exchanged. This is illustrated in Illustration A–1.

Illustration A–1
Interest Rate Swap—Shortcut Method

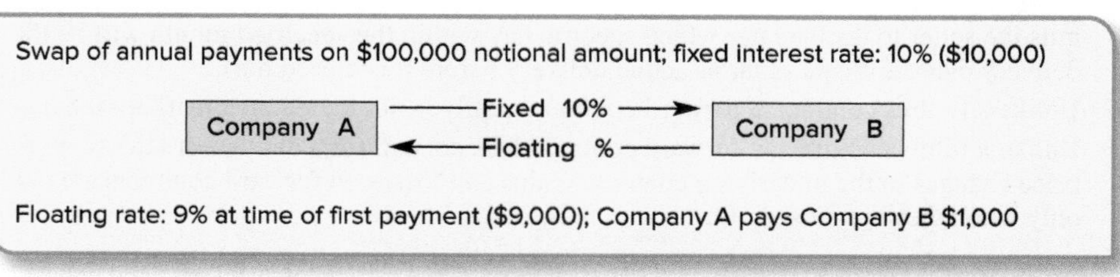
Swap of annual payments on $100,000 notional amount; fixed interest rate: 10% ($10,000)
Company A
Fixed 10%
Floating %
Company B
Floating rate: 9% at time of first payment ($9,000); Company A pays Company B $1,000

From an accounting standpoint, the central issue is not the operational differences among various hedge instruments, but their similarities in functioning as hedges against risk.

Accounting for Derivatives

A key to accounting for derivatives is knowing the purpose for which a company holds them and whether the company is effective in serving that purpose. Derivatives, for instance, may be held for risk management (hedging activities). The desired effect, and often the real effect, is a reduction in risk. On the other hand, derivatives sometimes are held for speculative position taking, hoping for large profits. The effect of this activity usually is to *increase* risk. Perhaps more important, derivatives acquired as hedges and intended to reduce risk may, in fact, unintentionally increase risk instead.

Derivatives not serving as hedges are extremely speculative due to the high leverage inherent in such investments.

It's important to understand that, serving as investments rather than as hedges, derivatives are extremely speculative. This is due to the high leverage inherent in derivatives. Here's why. The investment outlay usually is negligible, but the potential gain or loss on the investment usually is quite high. A small change in interest rates or another underlying event can trigger a large change in the fair value of the derivative. Because the initial investment was minimal, the change in value relative to the investment itself represents a huge percentage gain or loss. Their extraordinarily risky nature prompted Warren Buffett, one of the country's most celebrated financiers, to refer to derivatives as "financial weapons of mass destruction." Accounting for derivatives is designed to treat differently (a) derivatives designated as hedges and those not designated as hedges as well as (b) the effective portion and the ineffective portion of gains and losses from intended hedges.

The basic approach to accounting for derivatives is fairly straightforward, although implementation can be quite cumbersome. All derivatives, no exceptions, are carried on the balance sheet as either assets or liabilities at fair (or market) value.[8] The reasoning is that (a) derivatives create either rights or obligations that meet the definition of assets or liabilities, and (b) fair value is the most meaningful measurement.

Each derivative contract has a "fair value," which is an amount that one side owes the other at a particular moment.

Accounting for the gain or loss on a derivative depends on how it is used. Specifically, if the derivative is not designated as a hedging instrument or doesn't qualify as one, any gain or loss from fair value changes is recognized immediately in earnings. On the other hand, if a derivative is used to hedge against exposure to risk, any gain or loss from fair value changes is either (a) recognized immediately in earnings along with an offsetting loss or gain on the item being hedged or (b) deferred in comprehensive income until it can be recognized in earnings at the same time as earnings are affected by a hedged transaction. Which way depends on whether the derivative is designated as a (a) fair value hedge, (b) cash flow hedge, or (c) foreign currency hedge. Let's look now at each of the three hedge designations.

FAIR VALUE HEDGES A company can be adversely affected when a change in either prices or interest rates causes a change in the fair value of one of its assets, its liabilities, or a commitment to buy or sell assets or liabilities. If a derivative is used to hedge against the exposure to changes in the fair value of an asset, liability, or a firm commitment, it can be designated as a **fair value hedge**. In that case, when the derivative is adjusted to reflect changes in fair value, the other side of the entry recognizes a gain or loss to be included *currently* in earnings. At the same time, though, the loss or gain from changes in the fair value (due to the risk being hedged)[9] of the item being hedged also is included currently in earnings. This means that, to the extent the hedge is effective in serving its purpose, the gain or loss on the derivative will be offset by the loss or gain on the item being hedged. In fact, this is precisely the concept behind the procedure.

A gain or loss from a *fair value hedge* is recognized immediately in earnings, along with the loss or gain from the item being hedged.

The reasoning is that as interest rates or other underlying events change, a hedge instrument will produce a gain approximately equal to a loss on the item being hedged (or vice versa). These income effects are interrelated and offsetting, so it would be improper to report the income effects in different periods. More critically, the intent and effect of having the hedge instrument is to *lessen* risk. And yet, recognizing gains in one period and counterbalancing losses in another period would tend to cause fluctuations in income that convey an *increase* in risk. However, to the extent that a hedge is ineffective and produces gains or losses different from the losses or gains being hedged, the ineffective portion is recognized in earnings immediately.

The income effects of the hedge instrument and the income effects of the item being hedged should affect earnings at the same time.

Some of the more common fair value hedges use as follows:

- An interest rate swap to synthetically convert fixed-rate debt (for which interest rate changes could change the fair value of the debt) into floating-rate debt
- A futures contract to hedge changes in the fair value (due to price changes) of aluminum, sugar, or some other type of inventory
- A futures contract to hedge the fair value (due to price changes) of a firm commitment to sell natural gas or some other asset

ILLUSTRATION Because interest rate swaps comprise the majority of derivatives in use, we will use swaps to illustrate accounting for derivatives. Let's look at the example in Illustration A–2.

[8]FASB ASC 815–10: Derivatives and Hedging–Overall (previously "Accounting for Derivative Instruments and Hedging Activities," *Statement of Financial Accounting Standards No. 133* (Norwalk, Conn.: FASB, 1998)).

[9]The fair value of a hedged item might also change for reasons other than from effects of the risk being hedged. For instance, the hedged risk may be that a change in interest rates will cause the fair value of a bond to change. The bond price might also change, though, if the market perceives that the bond's default risk has changed.

Illustration A–2

Interest Rate Swap—Shortcut Method

Wintel Semiconductors issued $1 million of 18-month, 10% bank notes on January 1, 2018. Wintel is exposed to the risk that general interest rates will decline, causing the fair value of its debt to rise. (If the fair value of Wintel's debt increases, its effective borrowing cost is higher relative to the market.) To hedge against this fair value risk, the firm entered into an 18-month interest rate swap agreement on January 1 and designated the swap as a hedge against changes in the fair value of the note. The swap calls for the company to receive payment based on a 10% fixed interest rate on a notional amount of $1 million and to make payment based on a floating interest rate tied to changes in general rates.* As the Illustration will show, this effectively converts Wintel's fixed-rate debt to floating-rate debt. Cash settlement of the net interest amount is made semiannually at June 30 and December 31 of each year, with the net interest being the difference between the $50,000 fixed interest [$1 million × (10% × ½)] and the floating interest rate, times $1 million at those dates.

Floating (market) settlement rates were 9% at June 30, 2018, 8% at December 31, 2018, and 9% at June 30, 2019. Net interest receipts can be calculated as shown below. Fair values of both the derivative and the note resulting from those market rate changes are assumed to be quotes obtained from securities dealers.

	1/1/18	6/30/18	12/31/18	6/30/19
Fixed rate	10%	10%	10%	10%
Floating rate	10%	9%	8%	9%
Fixed payments [$1 million × (10% × ½)]		$ 50,000	$ 50,000	$ 50,000
Floating payments ($1 million × ½ floating rate)		45,000	40,000	45,000
Net interest receipts		$ 5,000	$ 10,000	$ 5,000
Fair value of interest rate swap	0	$ 9,363	$ 9,615	0
Fair value of note payable	$1,000,000	$1,009,363	$1,009,615	$1,000,000

*A common measure for benchmarking variable interest rates is LIBOR, the London Interbank Offered Rate, a base rate at which large international banks lend funds to each other.

When the floating rate declined from 10% to 9%, the fair values of both the derivative (swap) and the note increased. This created an offsetting gain on the derivative and a holding loss on the note. Both are recognized in earnings at the same time (at June 30, 2018).

The interest rate swap is designated as a fair value hedge on this note at issuance.

The swap settlement is the difference between the fixed interest (5%) and variable interest (4.5%).

The fair value of derivatives is recognized in the balance sheet.

The hedged liability (or asset) is adjusted to fair value as well.

	Debit	Credit
January 1, 2018		
Cash	1,000,000	
Notes payable		1,000,000
To record the issuance of the note.		
June 30, 2018		
Interest expense (10% × ½ × $1 million)	50,000	
Cash		50,000
To record interest.		
Cash [$50,000 − (9% × ½ × $1 million)]	5,000	
Interest expense		5,000
To record the net cash settlement.		
Interest rate swap* ($9,363 − 0)	9,363	
Holding gain—interest rate swap		9,363
To record change in fair value of the derivative.		
Holding loss—hedged note	9,363	
Note payable ($1,009,363 − 1,000,000)		9,363
To record change in fair value of the note due to interest rate changes.		

*This would be a liability rather than an investment (asset) if the fair value had declined.

The net interest settlement on June 30, 2018, is $5,000 because the fixed rate is 5% (half of the 10% annual rate) and the floating rate is 4.5% (half of the 9% annual rate).

December 31, 2018		
Interest expense	50,000	
Cash (10% × ½ × $1,000,000)		50,000
To record interest.		
Cash [$50,000 – (8% × ½ × $1 million)]	10,000	
Interest expense		10,000
To record the net cash settlement.		
Interest rate swap ($9,615 – 9,363)	252	
Holding gain—interest rate swap		252
To record the change in fair value of the derivative.		
Holding loss—hedged note	252	
Note payable ($1,009,615 – 1,009,363)		252
To record the change in fair value of the note due to interest rate changes.		

As with any debt, interest expense is the effective rate times the outstanding balance.

The settlement is the difference between the fixed interest (5%) and variable interest (4%).

The derivative is increased by the change in fair value. The note is increased by the change in fair value.

The fair value of the swap increased by $252 (from $9,363 to $9,615). Similarly, we adjust the note's book value by the amount necessary to increase it to fair value. This produces a holding loss on the note that exactly offsets the gain on the swap. This result is the hedging effect that motivated Wintel to enter the fair value hedging arrangement in the first place.

At June 30, 2019, Wintel repeats the process of adjusting to fair value both the derivative investment and the note being hedged.

June 30, 2019		
Interest expense	50,000	
Cash (10% × ½ × $1,000,000)		50,000
To record interest.		
Cash [$50,000 – (9% × ½ × $1 million)]	5,000	
Interest expense		5,000
To record the net cash settlement.		
Holding loss—interest rate swap	9,615	
Interest rate swap ($0 – 9,615)		9,615
To record the change in fair value of the derivative.		
Note payable ($1,000,000 – 1,009,615)	9,615	
Holding gain—hedged note		9,615
To record the change in fair value of the note due to interest rate changes.		
Note payable	1,000,000	
Cash		1,000,000
To repay the loan.		

The net interest received is the difference between the fixed interest (5%) and floating interest (4.5%).

The swap's fair value now is zero.

The net interest received is the difference between the fixed rate (5%) and floating rate (4.5%) times $1 million. The fair value of the swap decreased by $9,615 (from $9,615 to zero).[10] That decline represents a holding *loss* that we recognize in earnings. Similarly, we record an offsetting holding gain on the note for the change in its fair value.

Now let's see how the book values changed for the swap account and the note:

	Swap		Note	
Jan. 1, 2018				1,000,000
June 30, 2018	9,363			9,363
Dec. 31, 2018	252			252
June 30, 2019		9,615	9,615	
			1,000,000	
	0			0

[10]Because there are no future cash receipts from the swap arrangement at this point, the fair value of the swap is zero.

The income statement is affected as follows:

	Income Statement + (−)	
June 30, 2018	(50,000)	Interest expense—fixed payment
	5,000	Interest expense—net cash settlement
	9,363	Holding gain—interest rate swap
	(9,363)	Holding loss—hedged note
	(45,000)	Net effect—same as floating interest payment
Dec. 31, 2018	(50,000)	Interest expense—fixed payment
	10,000	Interest expense—net cash settlement
	252	Holding gain—interest rate swap
	(252)	Holding loss—hedged note
	(40,000)	Net effect—same as floating interest payment
June 30, 2019	(50,000)	Interest expense—fixed payment
	5,000	Interest expense—net cash settlement
	9,615	Holding gain—interest rate swap
	(9,615)	Holding loss—hedged note
	(45,000)	Net effect—same as floating interest payment

As this demonstrates, the swap effectively converts fixed-interest debt to floating-interest debt.

Additional Consideration

Fair Value of the Swap

The fair value of a derivative typically is based on a quote obtained from a derivatives dealer. That fair value will approximate the present value of the expected net interest settlement receipts for the remaining term of the swap. In fact, we can actually calculate the fair value of the swap that we accepted as given in our illustration.

Since the June 30, 2018, floating rate of 9% caused the cash settlement on that date to be $5,000, it's reasonable to look at 9% as the best estimate of future floating rates and therefore assume the remaining two cash settlements also will be $5,000 each. We can then calculate at June 30, 2018, the present value of those expected net interest settlement receipts for the remaining term of the swap.

Fixed interest	10% × ½ × $1 million	$ 50,000
Expected floating interest	9% × ½ × $1 million	45,000
Expected cash receipts for both Dec. 31, 2018 and June 30, 2019		$ 5,000
		× 1.87267*
Present value		$ 9,363

*Present value of an ordinary annuity of $1: $n = 2$, $i = 4.5\%$ (½ of 9%) (from Table 4)

Fair Value of the Notes

The fair value of the note payable will be the present value of principal and remaining interest payments discounted at the market rate. The market rate will vary with the designated floating rate but might differ due to changes in default (credit) risk and the term structure of interest rates. Assuming it's 9% at June 30, 2018, we can calculate the fair value (present value) of the notes.

Interest	$50,000* × 1.87267† =	$ 93,633
Principal	$1,000,000 × 0.91573‡ =	915,730
		$1,009,363

*½ of 10% × $1,000,000
†Present value of an ordinary annuity of $1: $n = 2$, $i = 4.5\%$ (from Table 4)
‡Present value of $1: $n = 2$, $i = 4.5\%$ (from Table 2)

(continued)

(concluded)

Note: Often the cash settlement rate is "reset" as of each cash settlement date. Thus, the floating rate actually used at the end of each period to determine the payment is the floating market rate as of the beginning of the same period. In our illustration, for instance, there would have been no cash settlement at June 30, 2018, since we would use the beginning floating rate of 10% to determine payment. Similarly, we would have used the 9% floating rate at June 30, 2018, to determine the cash settlement six months later at December 31. In effect, each cash settlement would be delayed six months. Had this arrangement been in effect in the current illustration, there would have been one fewer cash settlement payment (two rather than three), but would not have affected the fair value calculations above because, either way, our expectation would be cash receipts of $5,000 for both Dec. 31, 2018, and June 30, 2019.

CASH FLOW HEDGES The risk in some transactions or events is the risk of a change in cash flows, rather than a change in fair values. We noted earlier, for instance, that *fixed-rate* debt subjects a company to the risk that interest rate changes could change the fair value of the debt. On the other hand, if the obligation is *floating-rate* debt, the fair value of the debt will not change when interest rates do, but cash flows will. If a derivative is used to hedge against the exposure to changes in cash inflows or cash outflows of an asset or liability or a forecasted transaction (like a future purchase or sale), it can be designated as a cash flow hedge. In that case, when the derivative is adjusted to reflect changes in fair value, the other side of the entry is a gain or loss to be deferred as a component of other comprehensive income and included in earnings later, at the same time as earnings are affected by the hedged transaction. Once again, the effect is matching the earnings effect of the derivative with the earnings effect of the item being hedged, precisely the concept behind hedge accounting.

A gain or loss from a *cash flow hedge* is deferred as other comprehensive income until it can be recognized in earnings along with the earnings effect of the item being hedged.

To understand the deferral of the gain or loss, we need to revisit the concept of comprehensive income. Comprehensive income, as you may recall from Chapters 4, 12, 17, and 18, is a more expansive view of the change in shareholders' equity than traditional net income. In fact, it encompasses all changes in equity other than from transactions with owners.[11] So, in addition to net income itself, comprehensive income includes up to four other changes in equity that don't (yet) belong in net income, namely, net holding gains (losses) on investments in debt securities (Chapter 12), gains (losses) from and amendments to postretirement benefit plans (Chapter 17), gains (losses) from foreign currency translation, and deferred gains (losses) from derivatives designated as cash flow hedges.[12]

Some of the more commonly used cash flow hedges are:

- An interest rate swap to synthetically convert floating rate debt (for which interest rate changes could change the cash interest payments) into fixed rate debt.
- A futures contract to hedge a forecasted sale (for which price changes could change the cash receipts) of natural gas, crude oil, or some other asset.

FOREIGN CURRENCY HEDGES Today's economy is increasingly a global one. The majority of large "U.S." companies are, in truth, multinational companies that may receive only a fraction of their revenues from U.S. operations. Many operations of those companies are located abroad. Foreign operations often are denominated in the currency of the foreign country (the Euro, Japanese yen, Russian rubles, and so on). Even companies without foreign operations sometimes hold investments, issue debt, or conduct other transactions denominated in foreign currencies. As exchange rates change, the dollar equivalent of the

The possibility that foreign currency exchange rates might change exposes many companies to foreign currency risk.

[11]Transactions with owners primarily include dividends and the sale or purchase of shares of the company's stock.

[12]FASB ASC 220–10–55–2: Comprehensive Income–Overall–Implementation Guidance and Illustrations (previously "Reporting Comprehensive Income," *Statement of Financial Accounting Standards No. 130* (Norwalk, Conn.: FASB, 1997)).

foreign currency changes. The possibility of currency rate changes exposes these companies to the risk that some transactions require settlement in a currency other than the entities' functional currency or that foreign operations will require translation adjustments to reported amounts.

A **foreign currency hedge** can be a hedge of foreign currency exposure of the following:

- A firm commitment—treated as a fair value hedge
- An available-for-sale security—treated as a fair value hedge
- A forecasted transaction—treated as a cash flow hedge
- A company's net investment in a foreign operation—the gain or loss is reported in *other comprehensive income* as part of unrealized gains and losses from foreign currency translation[13]

To qualify as a hedge, the hedging relationship must be highly effective in achieving offsetting changes in fair values or cash flows.

HEDGE EFFECTIVENESS When a company elects to apply hedge accounting, it must establish at the inception of the hedge the method it will use to assess the effectiveness of the hedging derivative, as well as the measurement approach it will use to determine the ineffective portion of the hedge.[14] The key criterion for qualifying as a hedge is that the hedging relationship must be "highly effective" in achieving offsetting changes in fair values or cash flows based on the hedging company's specified risk management objective and strategy.

An assessment of this effectiveness must be made at least every three months and whenever financial statements are issued. There are no precise guidelines for assessing effectiveness, but it generally means a high correlation between changes in the fair value or cash flows of the derivative and of the item being hedged, not necessarily a specific reduction in risk. Hedge accounting must be terminated for hedging relationships that no longer are highly effective.

Imperfect hedges result in part of the derivative gain or loss being included in current earnings.

HEDGE INEFFECTIVENESS In Illustration A–2, the loss on the hedged note exactly offset the gain on the swap. This is because the swap in this instance was highly effective in hedging the risk due to interest rate changes. However, the loss and gain would not have exactly offset each other if the hedging arrangement had been ineffective. For instance, suppose the swap's term had been different from that of the note (say a three-year swap term compared with the 18-month term of the note) or if the notional amount of the swap differed from that of the note (say $500,000 rather than $1 million). In that case, changes in the fair value of the swap and changes in the fair value of the note would not be the same. The result would be a greater (or lesser) amount recognized in earnings for the swap than for the note. Because there would not be an exact offset, earnings would be affected, an effect resulting from hedge ineffectiveness. That is a desired effect of hedge accounting; to the extent that a hedge is effective, the earnings effect of a derivative cancels out the earnings effect of the item being hedged. However, even if a hedge is highly effective, all ineffectiveness is recognized currently in earnings.

FAIR VALUE CHANGES UNRELATED TO THE RISK BEING HEDGED In Illustration A–2, the fair value of the hedged note and the fair value of the swap changed by the same amounts each year because we assumed the fair values changed only due to interest rate changes. It's also possible, though, that the note's fair value would change by an amount different from that of the swap for reasons unrelated to interest rates. Remember from our earlier discussion that the market's perception of a company's creditworthiness,

[13]This is the same treatment previously prescribed for these translation adjustments by FASB ASC 830: Foreign Currency Matters (previously *Statement of Financial Accounting Standards No. 52*).

[14]Remember, if a derivative is not designated as a hedge, any gains or losses from changes in its fair value are recognized immediately in earnings.

and thus its ability to pay interest and principal when due, also can affect the value of debt, whether interest rates change or not. In hedge accounting, we ignore those changes. We recognize only the fair value changes in the hedged item that we can attribute to the risk being hedged (interest rate risk in this case). For example, if a changing perception of default risk had caused the note's fair value to increase by an additional, say $5,000, our journal entries in Illustration A–2 would have been unaffected. Notice, then, that although we always mark a *derivative* to fair value, the reported amount of the *item being hedged* may not be its fair value. We mark a hedged item to fair value only to the extent that its fair value changed due to the risk being hedged.

Fair value changes unrelated to the risk being hedged are ignored.

Disclosure of Derivatives and Risk

To be adequately informed about the effectiveness of a company's risk management, investors and creditors need information about strategies for holding derivatives and specific hedging activities. Toward that end, extensive disclosure requirements provide information that includes the following:

- Objectives and strategies for holding and issuing derivatives
- A description of the items for which risks are being hedged
- For forecasted transactions: a description, time before the transaction is expected to occur, the gains and losses accumulated in other comprehensive income, and the events that will trigger their recognition in earnings
- Beginning balance of, changes in, and ending balance of the derivative component of other comprehensive income
- The net amount of gain or loss reported in earnings (representing aggregate hedge ineffectiveness)
- Qualitative and quantitative information about failed hedges: canceled commitments or previously hedged forecasted transactions no longer expected to occur

The intent is to provide information about the company's success in reducing risks and, consequently, about risks not managed successfully. Remember, too, that when derivatives are employed ineffectively, risks can escalate. Ample disclosures about derivatives are essential to maintain awareness of potential opportunities and problems with risk management.

In addition, GAAP requires companies to provide enhanced disclosures indicating (a) how and why the company uses derivative instruments, (b) how the company accounts for derivative instruments and related hedged items, and (c) how derivative instruments and related hedged items affect the company's balance sheet, income statement, and cash flows.[15] The required disclosures include two tables, one that highlights the location and fair values of derivative instruments in the balance sheet, and another that indicates the location and amounts of gains and losses on derivative instruments in the income statement. The two tables distinguish between derivative instruments that are designated as hedging instruments and those that are not. The tables also categorize derivative instruments by each major type—interest rate contracts, foreign exchange contracts, equity contracts, commodity contracts, credit contracts, and other types of contracts.

Even for some traditional liabilities, the amounts reported on the face of the financial statements provide inadequate disclosure about the degree to which a company is exposed to risk of loss. To provide adequate disclosure about a company's exposure to risk, additional information must be provided about (a) concentrations of credit risk and (b) the fair value of all financial instruments.[16]

[15]FASB ASC 815: Derivatives and Hedging (previously "Disclosures about Derivative Instruments and Hedging Activities—an amendment of FASB Statement No. 133," *Statement of Financial Accounting Standards No. 161* (Stamford, Conn.: FASB, 2008)).

[16]FASB ASC 825–10–50–1: Financial Instruments–Overall–Disclosure (previously "Disclosures About Fair Values of Financial Instruments," *Statement of Financial Accounting Standards No. 107* (Norwalk, Conn.: FASB, 1991), as amended by *Statement of Financial Accounting Standards No. 133,* "Accounting for Derivative Instruments and Hedging Activities" (Norwalk, Conn.: FASB, 1998)).

Extended Method for Interest Rate Swap Accounting

A shortcut method for accounting for an interest rate swap is permitted when a hedge meets certain criteria. In general, the criteria are designed to see if the hedge supports the assumption of "no ineffectiveness." Illustration A–2 of a fair value hedge met those criteria, in particular, (a) the swap's notional amount matches the note's principal amount, (b) the swap's expiration date matches the note's maturity date, (c) the fair value of the swap is zero at inception, and (d) the floating payment is at the market rate.[17] Because Wintel can conclude that the swap will be highly effective in offsetting changes in the fair value of the debt, it can use the changes in the fair value of the swap to measure the offsetting changes in the fair value of the debt. That's the essence of the shortcut method used in Illustration A–2. The extended method required when the criteria are *not* met for the short-cut method is described in this section (Illustration A–3 begins by describing the same scenario as in Illustration A–2). It produces the same effect on earnings and in the balance sheet as does the procedure shown in Illustration A–2.

Illustration A–3
Interest Rate Swap—Extended Method

Wintel Semiconductors issued $1 million of 18-month, 10% bank notes on January 1, 2018. Wintel is exposed to the risk that general interest rates will decline, causing the fair value of its debt to rise. (If the fair value of Wintel's debt increases, its effective borrowing cost is higher relative to the market.) To hedge against this fair value risk, the firm entered into an 18-month interest rate swap agreement on January 1 and designated the swap as a hedge against changes in the fair value of the note. The swap calls for the company to receive payment based on a 10% fixed interest rate on a notional amount of $1 million and to make payment based on a floating interest rate tied to changes in general rates. Cash settlement of the net interest amount is made semiannually at June 30 and December 31 of each year, with the net interest being the difference between the $50,000 fixed interest [$1 million × (10% × ½)] and the floating interest rate, times $1 million at those dates.

Floating (market) settlement rates were 9% at June 30, 2018, 8% at December 31, 2018, and 8% at June 30, 2019. Net interest receipts can be calculated as shown below. Fair values of both the derivative and the note resulting from those market rate changes are assumed to be quotes obtained from securities dealers.

	1/1/18	6/30/18	12/31/18	6/30/19
Fixed rate	10%	10%	10%	10%
Floating rate	10%	9%	8%	9%
Fixed payments				
[$1 million × (10% × ½)]		$ 50,000	$ 50,000	$ 50,000
Floating payments				
($1 million × ½ floating rate)		45,000	40,000	45,000
Net interest receipts		$ 5,000	$ 10,000	$ 5,000
Fair value of interest rate swap	0	$ 9,363	$ 9,615	0
Fair value of note payable	$1,000,000	$1,009,363	$1,009,615	$1,000,000

When the floating rate declined in Illustration A–3 from 10% to 9%, the fair values of both the derivative (swap) and the note increased. This created an offsetting gain on the derivative and holding loss on the note. Both are recognized in earnings the same period (June 30, 2018).

The interest rate swap is designated as a fair value hedge on this note at issuance.

January 1, 2018		
Cash	1,000,000	
Notes payable		1,000,000
To record the issuance of the note.		

[17]There is no precise minimum interval, though it generally is three to six months or less. Other criteria are specified by FASB ASC 815–20–25–104: Derivatives and Hedging–Hedging-General–Recognition–Shortcut Method, *SFAS No. 133* (para. 68), in addition to the key conditions listed here.

June 30, 2018		
Interest expense (10% × ½ × $1 million)	50,000	
Cash		50,000
To record interest.		
Cash [$50,000 − (9% × ½ × $1 million)]	5,000	
Interest rate swap ($9,363 − 0)	9,363	
Interest revenue (10% × ½ × $0)		0
Holding gain—interest rate swap (to balance)		14,363
To record the net cash settlement, accrued interest on the swap, and change in the fair value of the derivative.		
Holding loss—hedged note	9,363	
Notes payable ($1,009,363 − 1,000,000)		9,363
To record change in fair value of the note due to interest rate changes.		

The swap settlement is the difference between the fixed interest (5%) and variable interest (4.5%).

The fair value of derivatives is recognized in the balance sheet.

The hedged liability (or asset) is adjusted to fair value as well.

The net interest settlement on June 30, 2018, is $5,000 because the fixed rate is 5% (half of the 10% annual rate) and the floating rate is 4.5% (half of the 9% annual rate). A holding gain ($14,363) is produced by holding the derivative security during a time when an interest rate decline caused an increase in the value of that asset. A portion ($5,000) of the gain was received in cash, and another portion ($9,363) is reflected as an increase in the value of the asset.

We also have a holding loss of the same amount. This is because we also held a liability during the same time period, and the interest rate change caused its fair value to increase as well.

December 31, 2018		
Interest expense (9% × ½ × $1,009,363)	45,421	
Notes payable (difference)*	4,579	
Cash (10% × ½ × $1,000,000)		50,000
To record interest.		
Cash [$50,000 − (8% × ½ × $1 million)]	10,000	
Interest rate swap ($9,615 − 9,363)	252	
Interest revenue (9% × ½ × $9,363)		421
Holding gain—interest rate swap (to balance)		9,831
To record the net cash settlement, accrued interest on the swap, and change in the fair value of the derivative.		
Holding loss—hedged note	4,831	
Notes payable ($1,009,615 − 1,009,363 + 4,579)		4,831
To record the change in fair value of the note due to interest rate changes.		

*We could use a premium on the note to adjust its book value.

As with any debt, interest expense is the effective rate times the outstanding balance.

The cash settlement is the difference between the fixed interest (5%) and variable interest (4%).

Interest ($421) accrues on the asset.

The note is increased by the change in fair value.

We determine interest on the note the same way we do for any liability, as you learned earlier—at the effective rate (9% × ½) times the outstanding balance ($1,009,363). This results in reducing the note's book value for the cash interest paid in excess of the interest expense.

The fair value of the swap increased due to the interest rate decline by $252 (from $9,363 to $9,615). The holding gain we recognize in earnings consists of that increase (a) plus the $10,000 cash settlement also created by the interest rate decline and (b) minus the $421 increase that results not from the interest rate decline, but from interest accruing on the asset.[18] Similarly, we adjust the note's book value by the amount necessary to increase it to fair value, allowing for the $4,579 reduction in the note in the earlier entry to record interest.

At June 30, 2019, Wintel repeats the process of adjusting to fair value both the derivative investment and the note being hedged.

[18]The investment in the interest rate swap represents the present value of expected future net interest receipts. As with other such assets, interest accrues at the effective rate times the outstanding balance. You also can think of the accrued interest mathematically as the increase in present value of the future cash flows as we get one period nearer to the dates when the cash will be received.

Interest expense is the effective rate times the outstanding balance.

The net interest received is the difference between the fixed interest (5%) and floating interest (4.5%).

The swap's fair value now is zero.

June 30, 2019		
Interest expense (8% × ½ × $1,009,615)	40,385	
Notes payable (difference)	9,615	
Cash (10% × ½ × $1,000,000)		50,000
To record interest.		
Cash [$50,000 − (9% × ½ × $1 million)]	5,000	
Holding loss—interest rate swap (to balance)	5,000	
Interest rate swap ($0 − $9,615)		9,615
Interest revenue (8% × ½ × $9,615)		385
To record the net cash settlement, accrued interest on the swap, and change in the fair value of the derivative.		
Notes payable ($1,000,000 − 1,009,615 + 9,615)	0	
Holding gain—hedged note		0
To record the change in fair value of the note due to interest rate changes.		
Note payable	1,000,000	
Cash		1,000,000
To repay the loan.		

The net interest received is the difference between the fixed rate (5%) and floating rate (4.5%), times $1 million. The fair value of the swap decreased by $9,615 (from $9,615 to zero).[19] The holding loss we recognize in earnings consists of that decline (a) minus the $5,000 portion of the decline resulting from it being realized in cash settlement and (b) plus the $385 increase that results not from the interest rate change, but from interest accruing on the asset.

Now let's see how the book values changed for the swap account and the note.

	Swap (Dr.)	Swap (Cr.)	Note (Dr.)	Note (Cr.)
Jan. 1, 2018				1,000,000
June 30, 2018	9,363			9,363
Dec. 31, 2018	252		4,579	4,831
June 30, 2019		9,615	9,615	
			1,000,000	
	0			0

The income statement is affected as follows:

Income Statement + (—)		
June 30, 2018	(50,000)	Interest expense
	0	Interest revenue (no time has passed)
	14,363	Holding gain interest rate swap
	(9,363)	Holding loss—hedged note
	(45,000)	Net effect—same as floating interest payment
Dec. 31, 2018	(45,421)	Interest expense
	421	Interest revenue
	9,831	Holding gain—interest rate swap
	(4,831)	Holding loss—hedged note
	(40,000)	Net effect—same as floating interest payment
June 30, 2019	(40,385)	Interest expense
	385	Interest revenue
	(5,000)	Holding gain—interest rate swap
	0	Holding loss—hedged note
	(45,000)	Net effect—same as floating interest payment

As this demonstrates, the swap effectively converts Wintel's fixed-interest debt to floating interest debt.

[19]Because there are no future cash receipts or payments from the swap arrangement at this point, the fair value of the swap is zero.

Additional Consideration

Private Company GAAP – Derivatives and Hedging. The Private Company Council (PCC) sought feedback from private company stakeholders and found that most users of private company financial statements find it difficult to obtain fixed-rate borrowing and often enter into an interest rate swap to economically convert their variable-rate borrowing into a fixed-rate borrowing, which under GAAP caused significant variability in the income statements. As a result, the PCC concluded that the cost and complexity of hedge accounting outweigh the benefits for private companies.

In response to the PCC's conclusion, the FASB issued an Accounting Standards Update in 2014 that allows an accounting alternative to make it easier for certain interest rate swaps to qualify for hedge accounting for private companies that is quite different from what is required for public companies.[20] This alternative allows a nonpublic company (that's not a financial institution) to apply hedge accounting to its interest rate swaps as long as the terms of the swap and the related debt are aligned. If the conditions are met, the company can assume the cash flow hedge is fully effective. Those applying the simplified hedge accounting approach will be able to recognize the swap at its settlement value, instead of at its fair value.

This alternative should significantly reduce the cost and complexity of accounting for derivatives and hedging transactions of private companies.

Where We're Headed 

One phase of the FASB's *Financial Instruments* project aspires to improve, simplify, and converge the financial reporting requirements for hedging activities. In May 2010, the FASB proposed revisions of standards for hedge accounting in its proposed Accounting Standards Update, *Accounting for Financial Instruments and Revisions to the Accounting for Derivative Instruments and Hedging Activities—Financial Instruments (Topic 825) and Derivatives and Hedging (Topic 815).*

In July 2014, the International Accounting Standards Board (IASB) issued a revision of IFRS 9 *Financial Instruments.* This guidance differs significantly from the FASB's proposal.

At the time this textbook was written, the FASB was actively developing a proposed new standard intended to make hedge accounting easier for companies to apply and for users of the financial statements to understand. The FASB had reached several tentative decisions that included:

- Helping companies take advantage of the favorable accounting treatment that reduces income-statement volatility.
- Changing language that currently can result in restating financial statements.
- Allowing companies to defer the recognition of ineffectiveness for cash flow hedges until the hedged item affects earnings.
- Allowing companies to hedge contractually specified components of nonfinancial items.
- Expanding the types of interest rates that could be designated as the hedged risk in cash flow and fair value hedges.
- Relaxing certain hedge effectiveness assessment requirements.
- Eliminating the burden to complete ongoing analysis associated with the long-haul method (when the short-cut method is not allowed) for fair value hedges of financial items.

[20] *Accounting Standards Update No. 2014-03,* "Derivatives and Hedging (Topic 815): Accounting for Certain Receive-Variable, Pay-Fixed Interest Rate Swaps—Simplified Hedge Accounting Approach (a consensus of the Private Comapny Council)," (Norwalk, Conn.: FASB, January 2014).

The Bottom Line

- **LOA–1** All derivatives are reported in the balance sheet at fair value.
- **LOA–2** *Hedging* means taking a risk position that is opposite to an actual position that is exposed to risk. For a derivative used to hedge against exposure to risk, treatment of any gain or loss from fair value changes depends on whether the derivative is designated as (a) a fair value hedge, (b) a cash flow hedge, or (c) a foreign currency hedge.
- **LOA–3** We recognize a gain or loss from a *fair value hedge* immediately in earnings along with the loss or gain from the item being hedged. This is so the income effects of the hedge instrument and the income effects of the item being hedged will affect earnings at the same time.
- **LOA–4** We defer a gain or loss from a *cash flow hedge* as part of other comprehensive income until it can be recognized in earnings along with the earnings effect of the item being hedged.
- **LOA–5** Imperfect hedges result in part of the derivative gain or loss being included in current earnings. We ignore market value changes unrelated to the risk being hedged.
- **LOA–6** Extensive disclosure requirements about derivatives are designed to provide investors and creditors information about the adequacy of a company's risk management and the company's success in reducing risks, including risks not managed successfully.

Questions For Review of Key Topics

Q A–1 Some financial instruments are called derivatives. Why?

Q A–2 Should gains and losses on a fair value hedge be recorded as they occur, or should they be recorded to coincide with losses and gains on the item being hedged?

Q A–3 Hines Moving Company held a fixed-rate debt of $2 million. The company wanted to hedge its fair value exposure with an interest rate swap. However, the only notional available at the time, on the type of swap it desired, was $2.5 million. What will be the effect of any gain or loss on the $500,000 notional difference?

Q A–4 What is a futures contract?

Q A–5 What is the effect on interest of an interest rate swap?

Q A–6 How are derivatives reported on the balance sheet? Why?

Q A–7 When is a gain or a loss from a cash flow hedge reported in earnings?

Exercises

E A–1
Derivatives; hedge classification

Indicate (by abbreviation) the type of hedge each activity described below would represent.

Hedge Type

FV	Fair value hedge
CF	Cash flow hedge
FC	Foreign currency hedge
N	Would not qualify as a hedge

Activity

____ 1. An options contract to hedge possible future price changes of inventory

____ 2. A futures contract to hedge exposure to interest rate changes prior to replacing bank notes when they mature

____ 3. An interest rate swap to synthetically convert floating rate debt into fixed rate debt

____ 4. An interest rate swap to synthetically convert fixed rate debt into floating rate debt

____ 5. A futures contract to hedge possible future price changes of timber covered by a firm commitment to sell

____ 6. A futures contract to hedge possible future price changes of a forecasted sale of tin

____ 7. ExxonMobil's net investment in a Kuwait oil field

____ 8. An interest rate swap to synthetically convert floating rate interest on a stock investment into fixed rate interest

____ 9. An interest rate swap to synthetically convert fixed rate interest on a held-to-maturity debt investment into floating rate interest

(continued)

(concluded)

_____ 10. **An interest rate swap to synthetically convert floating rate interest on a held-to-maturity debt investment into fixed rate interest**

_____ 11. **An interest rate swap to synthetically convert fixed rate interest on a stock investment into floating rate interest**

E A–2
Derivatives; interest rate swap; fixed rate debt

On January 1, 2018, LLB Industries borrowed $200,000 from Trust Bank by issuing a two-year, 10% note, with interest payable quarterly. LLB entered into a two-year interest rate swap agreement on January 1, 2018, and designated the swap as a fair value hedge. Its intent was to hedge the risk that general interest rates will decline, causing the fair value of its debt to increase. The agreement called for the company to receive payment based on a 10% fixed interest rate on a notional amount of $200,000 and to pay interest based on a floating interest rate. The contract called for cash settlement of the net interest amount quarterly.

Floating (LIBOR) settlement rates were 10% at January 1, 8% at March 31, and 6% June 30, 2018. The fair values of the swap are quotes obtained from a derivatives dealer. Those quotes and the fair values of the note are as indicated below.

	January 1	March 31	June 30
Fair value of interest rate swap	0	$ 6,472	$ 11,394
Fair value of note payable	$200,000	$206,472	$211,394

Required:

1. Calculate the net cash settlement at March 31 and June 30, 2018.
2. Prepare the journal entries through June 30, 2018, to record the issuance of the note, interest, and necessary adjustments for changes in fair value.

E A–3
Derivatives; interest rate swap; fixed rate investment

(This is a variation of E A–2, modified to consider an investment in debt securities.)

On January 1, 2018, S&S Corporation invested in LLB Industries' negotiable two-year, 10% notes, with interest receivable quarterly. The company classified the investment as available-for-sale. S&S entered into a two-year interest rate swap agreement on January 1, 2018, and designated the swap as a fair value hedge. Its intent was to hedge the risk that general interest rates will decline, causing the fair value of its investment to increase. The agreement called for the company to make payment based on a 10% fixed interest rate on a notional amount of $200,000 and to receive interest based on a floating interest rate. The contract called for cash settlement of the net interest amount quarterly.

Floating (LIBOR) settlement rates were 10% at January 1, 8% at March 31, and 6% June 30, 2018. The fair values of the swap are quotes obtained from a derivatives dealer. Those quotes and the fair values of the investment in notes are as follows:

	January 1	March 31	June 30
Fair value of interest rate swap	0	$ 6,472	$ 11,394
Fair value of the investment in notes	$200,000	$206,472	$211,394

Required:

1. Calculate the net cash settlement at March 31 and June 30, 2018.
2. Prepare the journal entries through June 30, 2018, to record the investment in notes, interest, and necessary adjustments for changes in fair value.

E A–4
Derivatives; interest rate swap; fixed rate debt; fair value change unrelated to hedged risk

(This is a variation of E A–2, modified to consider fair value change unrelated to hedged risk.)

LLB Industries borrowed $200,000 from Trust Bank by issuing a two-year, 10% note, with interest payable quarterly. LLB entered into a two-year interest rate swap agreement on January 1, 2018, and designated the swap as a fair value hedge. Its intent was to hedge the risk that general interest rates will decline, causing the fair value of its debt to increase. The agreement called for the company to receive payment based on a 10% fixed interest rate on a notional amount of $200,000 and to pay interest based on a floating interest rate.

Floating (LIBOR) settlement rates were 10% at January 1, 8% at March 31, and 6% at June 30, 2018. The fair values of the swap are quotes obtained from a derivatives dealer. Those quotes and the fair values of the note are as indicated below. The additional rise in the fair value of the note (higher than that of the swap) on June 30 was due to investors' perceptions that the creditworthiness of LLB was improving.

	January 1	March 31	June 30
Fair value of interest rate swap	0	$ 6,472	$ 11,394
Fair value of note payable	$200,000	$206,472	$220,000

Required:

1. Calculate the net cash settlement at June 30, 2018.
2. Prepare the journal entries on June 30, 2018, to record the interest and necessary adjustments for changes in fair value.

E A–5
Derivatives; interest rate swap; fixed rate debt; extended method

(This is a variation of Exercise A–2, modified to consider the extended method.)

On January 1, 2018, LLB Industries borrowed $200,000 from Trust Bank by issuing a two-year, 10% note, with interest payable quarterly. LLB entered into a two-year interest rate swap agreement on January 1, 2018, and designated the swap as a fair value hedge. Its intent was to hedge the risk that general interest rates will decline, causing the fair value of its debt to increase. The agreement called for the company to receive payment based on a 10% fixed interest rate on a notional amount of $200,000 and to pay interest based on a floating interest rate. The contract called for cash settlement of the net interest amount quarterly.

Floating (LIBOR) settlement rates were 10% at January 1, 8% at March 31, and 6% at June 30, 2018. The fair values of the swap are quotes obtained from a derivatives dealer. Those quotes and the fair values of the note are as follows:

	January 1	March 31	June 30
Fair value of interest rate swap	0	$ 6,472	$ 11,394
Fair value of note payable	$200,000	$206,472	$211,394

Required:

Prepare the journal entries through June 30, 2018, to record the issuance of the note, interest, and necessary adjustments for changes in fair value. Use the extended method demonstrated in Illustration A–3.

E A–6
Derivatives; interest rate swap; fixed-rate debt; fair value change unrelated to hedged

(Note: This is a variation of Exercise A–5, modified to consider fair value change unrelated to hedged risk.)

On January 1, 2018, LLB Industries borrowed $200,000 from Trust Bank by issuing a two-year, 10% note, with interest payable quarterly. LLB entered into a two-year interest rate swap agreement on January 1, 2018, and designated the swap as a fair value hedge. Its intent was to hedge the risk that general interest rates will decline, causing the fair value of its debt to increase. The agreement called for the company to receive payment based on a 10% fixed interest rate on a notional amount of $200,000 and to pay interest based on a floating interest rate. The contract called for cash settlement of the net interest amount quarterly.

Floating (LIBOR) settlement rates were 10% at January 1, 8% at March 31, and 6% June 30, 2018. The fair values of the swap are quotes obtained from a derivatives dealer. Those quotes and the fair values of the note are as indicated below. The additional rise in the fair value of the note (higher than that of the swap) on June 30 was due to investors' perceptions that the creditworthiness of LLB was improving.

	January 1	March 31	June 30
Fair value of interest rate swap	0	$ 6,472	$ 11,394
Fair value of note payable	$200,000	206,472	220,000

Required:

1. Calculate the net cash settlement at June 30, 2018.
2. Prepare the journal entries on June 30, 2018, to record the interest and necessary adjustments for changes in fair value. Use the extended method demonstrated in Illustration A–3.

Problems

P A–1
Derivatives; interest rate swap

On January 1, 2018, Labtech Circuits borrowed $100,000 from First Bank by issuing a three-year, 8% note, payable on December 31, 2020. Labtech wanted to hedge the risk that general interest rates will decline, causing the fair value of its debt to increase. Therefore, Labtech entered into a three-year interest rate swap agreement on January 1, 2018, and designated the swap as a fair value hedge. The agreement called for the company to receive payment based on an 8% fixed interest rate on a notional amount of $100,000 and to pay interest based on a floating interest rate tied to LIBOR. The contract called for cash settlement of the net interest amount on December 31 of each year.

Floating (LIBOR) settlement rates were 8% at inception and 9%, 7%, and 7% at the end of 2018, 2019, and 2020, respectively. The fair values of the swap are quotes obtained from a derivatives dealer. These quotes and the fair values of the note are as follows:

	January 1		December 31	
	2018	2018	2019	2020
Fair value of interest rate swap	0	$ (1,759)	$ 935	0
Fair value of note payable	$100,000	$98,241	$100,935	$100,000

Required:

1. Calculate the net cash settlement at the end of 2018, 2019, and 2020.
2. Prepare the journal entries during 2018 to record the issuance of the note, interest, and necessary adjustments for changes in fair value.
3. Prepare the journal entries during 2019 to record interest, net cash interest settlement for the interest rate swap, and necessary adjustments for changes in fair value.
4. Prepare the journal entries during 2020 to record interest, net cash interest settlement for the interest rate swap, necessary adjustments for changes in fair value, and repayment of the debt.
5. Calculate the book values of both the swap account and the note in each of the three years.
6. Calculate the net effect on earnings of the hedging arrangement in each of the three years. (Ignore income taxes.)
7. Suppose the fair value of the note at December 31, 2018, had been $97,000 rather than $98,241, with the additional decline in fair value due to investors' perceptions that the creditworthiness of Labtech was worsening. How would that affect your entries to record changes in the fair values?

P A–2
Derivatives; interest rate swap; comprehensive

CMOS Chips is hedging a 20-year, $10 million, 7% bond payable with a 20-year interest rate swap and has designated the swap as a fair value hedge. The agreement called for CMOS to receive payment based on a 7% fixed interest rate on a notional amount of $10 million and to pay interest based on a floating interest rate tied to LIBOR. The contract calls for cash settlement of the net interest amount on December 31 of each year.

At December 31, 2018, the fair value of the derivative and of the hedged bonds has increased by $100,000 because interest rates declined during the reporting period.

Required:

1. Does CMOS have an unrealized gain or loss on the derivative for the period? On the bonds? Will earnings increase or decrease due to the hedging arrangement? Why?
2. Suppose interest rates increased, rather than decreased, causing the fair value of both the derivative and of the hedged bonds to decrease by $100,000. Would CMOS have an unrealized gain or loss on the derivative for the period? On the bonds? Would earnings increase or decrease due to the hedging arrangement? Why?
3. Suppose the fair value of the bonds at December 31, 2018, had increased by $110,000 rather than $100,000, with the additional increase in fair value due to investors' perceptions that the creditworthiness of CMOS was improving. Would CMOS have an unrealized gain or loss on the derivative for the period? On the bonds? Would earnings increase or decrease due to the hedging arrangement? Why?
4. Suppose the notional amount of the swap had been $12 million, rather than the $10 million principal amount of the bonds. As a result, at December 31, 2018, the swap's fair value had increased by $120,000 rather than $100,000. Would CMOS have an unrealized gain or loss on the derivative for the period? On the bonds? Would earnings increase or decrease due to the hedging arrangement? Why?
5. Suppose BIOS Corporation is an investor, having purchased all $10 million of the bonds issued by CMOS as described in the original situation above. BIOS is hedging its investment, classified as available-for-sale, with a 20-year interest rate swap and has designated the swap as a fair value hedge. The agreement called for BIOS to make *payment* based on a 7% fixed interest rate on a notional amount of $10 million and to *receive* interest based on a floating interest rate tied to LIBOR. Would BIOS have an unrealized gain or loss on the derivative for the period due to interest rates having declined? On the bonds? Would earnings increase or decrease due to the hedging arrangement? Why?

P A–3
Derivatives; interest rate swap; fixed rate debt; extended method

(Note: This is a variation of P A–1, modified to consider the extended method demonstrated in Illustration A–3.)

On January 1, 2018, Labtech Circuits borrowed $100,000 from First Bank by issuing a three-year, 8% note, payable on December 31, 2020. Labtech wanted to hedge the risk that general interest rates will decline, causing the fair value of its debt to increase. Therefore, Labtech entered into a three-year interest rate swap agreement on January 1, 2018, and designated the swap as a fair value hedge. The agreement called for the company to receive payment based on an 8% fixed interest rate on a notional amount of $100,000 and to pay interest based on a floating interest rate tied to LIBOR. The contract called for cash settlement of the net interest amount on December 31 of each year.

Floating (LIBOR) settlement rates were 8% at inception and 9%, 7%, and 7% at the end of 2018, 2019, and 2020, respectively. The fair values of the swap are quotes obtained from a derivatives dealer. Those quotes and the fair values of the note are as follows:

	January 1	December 31		
	2018	2018	2019	2020
Fair value of interest rate swap	0	$ (1,759)	$ 935	0
Fair value of note payable	$100,000	$ 98,241	100,935	$100,000

Required:

Use the extended method demonstrated in Illustration A–3.

1. Calculate the net cash settlement at the end of 2018, 2019, and 2020.
2. Prepare the journal entries during 2018 to record the issuance of the note, interest, and necessary adjustments for changes in fair value.
3. Prepare the journal entries during 2019 to record interest, net cash interest settlement for the interest rate swap, and necessary adjustments for changes in fair value.
4. Prepare the journal entries during 2020 to record interest, net cash interest settlement for the interest rate swap, necessary adjustments for changes in fair value, and repayment of the debt.
5. Calculate the book values of both the swap account and the note in each of the three years.
6. Calculate the net effect on earnings of the hedging arrangement in each of the three years. (Ignore income taxes.)
7. Suppose the fair value of the note at December 31, 2018, had been $97,000 rather than $98,241, with the additional decline in fair value due to investors' perceptions that the creditworthiness of Labtech was worsening. How would that affect your entries to record changes in the fair values?

Broaden Your Perspective

Apply your critical-thinking ability to the knowledge you've gained. These cases will provide you an opportunity to develop your research, analysis, judgment, and communication skills. You also will work with other students, integrate what you've learned, apply it in real-world situations, and consider its global and ethical ramifications. This practice will broaden your knowledge and further develop your decision-making abilities.

Real World Case A–1
Derivative losses; recognition in earnings

The following is an excerpt from a disclosure note of Johnson & Johnson:

---

6. Fair Value Measurements (in part)

As of January 3, 2016, the balance of deferred net losses on derivatives included in accumulated other comprehensive income was $36 million after-tax. The Company expects that substantially all of the amounts related to forward foreign exchange contracts will be reclassified into earnings over the next 12 months as a result of transactions that are expected to occur over that period.

Required:

1. Johnson & Johnson indicates that it expects that substantially all of the balance of deferred net losses on derivatives will be reclassified into earnings over the next 12 months as a result of transactions that are expected to occur over that period. What is meant by "reclassified into earnings"?
2. What type(s) of hedging transaction might be accounted for in this way?

Communication Case A–2
Derivatives; hedge accounting

A conceptual question in accounting for derivatives is this: Should gains and losses on a hedge instrument be recorded as they occur, or should they be recorded to coincide (match) with income effects of the item being hedged?

ABI Wholesalers plans to issue long-term notes in May that will replace its $20 million of 9.5% bonds when they mature in July. ABI is exposed to the risk that interest rates in July will have risen, increasing borrowing costs (reducing the selling price of its notes). To hedge that possibility, ABI entered a (Treasury bond) futures contract in May to deliver (sell) bonds in July at their *current* price.

As a result, if interest rates rise, borrowing costs will go up for ABI because it will sell notes at a higher interest cost (or lower price). But that loss will be offset (approximately) by the gain produced by being in the opposite position on Treasury bond futures.

Two opposing viewpoints are:

View 1: Gains and losses on instruments designed to hedge anticipated transactions should be recorded as they occur.

View 2: Gains and losses on instruments designed to hedge anticipated transactions should be recorded to coincide (match) with income effects of the item being hedged.

In considering this question, focus on conceptual issues regarding the practicable and theoretically appropriate treatment, unconstrained by GAAP. Your instructor will divide the class into two to six groups, depending on the size of the class. The mission of your group is to reach consensus on the appropriate accounting for the gains and losses on instruments designed to hedge anticipated transactions.

Required:

1. Each group member should deliberate the situation independently and draft a tentative argument prior to the class session for which the case is assigned.
2. In class, each group will meet for 10 to 15 minutes in different areas of the classroom. During that meeting, group members will take turns sharing their suggestions for the purpose of arriving at a single group treatment.
3. After the allotted time, a spokesperson for each group (selected during the group meetings) will share the group's solution with the class. The goal of the class is to incorporate the views of each group into a consensus approach to the situation.

Real World Case A–3
Researching the way interest rate futures prices are quoted on the Chicago Mercantile Exchange; retrieving information from the Internet

The Chicago Mercantile Exchange, or Merc, at 30 S. Wacker Drive in Chicago, is the world's largest financial exchange, an international marketplace enabling institutions and businesses to trade futures and options contracts including currencies, interest rates, stock indexes, and agricultural commodities.

Required:

1. Access the Merc on the Internet. The web address is www.cmegroup.com.
2. Access the daily settlements within the site. In the Search box, enter "U.S. Treasury Bond." Choose U.S. Treasury Bond.
3. What are the settlement prices for September futures contracts?

Research Case A–4
Issue related to the derivatives standard; research an article

In an effort to keep up with the rapidly changing global financial markets, the FASB issued standards on accounting for and disclosure of derivative financial instruments. A *Journal of Accountancy* article that discusses this standard is "The Decision on Derivatives," by Arlette C. Wilson, Gary Waters, and Barry J. Bryan, November 1998.

Required:

On the Internet, go to the AICPA site at www.aicpa.org and find the article mentioned.

1. What are the primary problems or issues the FASB attempts to address regarding accounting for derivative financial instruments?
2. In considering the issues, the FASB made four fundamental decisions that became the cornerstones of the statement issued in 1998. What are those fundamental decisions? Which do you think is most critical to fair financial reporting?

APPENDIX

B GAAP Comprehensive Case

Target Corporation prepares its financial statements according to U.S. GAAP. Target's financial statements and disclosure notes for the year ended January 30, 2016, are available in Connect. This material is also available under the Investor Relations link at the company's website (www.target.com). This case addresses a variety of characteristics of financial statements prepared using U.S. GAAP. Questions are grouped in parts according to various sections of the textbook.

Part A: Financial Statements, Income Measurement, and Current Assets

A1. By what name does Target label its balance sheet?

A2. What amounts did Target report for the following items on January 30, 2016?
  a. Current assets
  b. Long-term assets
  c. Total assets
  d. Current liabilities
  e. Long-term liabilities
  f. Total liabilities
  g. Total shareholders' equity

A3. What was Target's largest current asset? What was its largest current liability?

A4. Compute Target's current ratio and debt to equity ratio in 2016?

A5. Assuming Target's industry had an average current ratio of 1.0 and an average debt to equity ratio of 2.5, comment on Target's liquidity and long-term solvency.

A6. Why do you think Target has chosen to have its fiscal year end on January 30, as opposed to December 31?

A7. Regarding Target's audit report:
  a. Who is Target's auditor?
  b. Did Target receive a "clean" (unmodified) audit opinion?

A8. By what name does Target label its income statement?

A9. What amounts did Target report for the following items for the year ended January 30, 2016?
  a. Sales
  b. Gross margin
  c. Earnings from continuing operations before income taxes
  d. Net earnings from continuing operations
  e. Net earnings

A10. What was Target's basic earnings per share for the year ended January 30, 2016?

A11. What additional items, if any, does Target report as part of its comprehensive income?

A12. Does Target prepare the statement of cash flows using the direct method or the indirect method?

A13. Which is higher, net earnings or operating cash flows? Which line item is the biggest reason for this difference? Explain why.

A14. Note 13 provides information on Target's current assets. Assume all prepaid expenses are for prepaid insurance and that insurance expense comprises $50 million of the $14,665 million of Selling, general and administrative expenses reported in the income statement for the year ended January 30, 2016. How much cash did Target pay for insurance coverage during the year? Prepare the adjusting entry Target would make to record all insurance expense for the year. What would be the effect on the income statement and balance sheet if Target didn't record an adjusting entry for prepaid expenses?

A15. What are the largest investing cash flow and the largest financing cash flow reported by the company for the year ended January 30, 2016?

A16. On what line of Target's income statement is revenue reported? What was the amount of revenue Target reported for the fiscal year ended January 30, 2016?

A17. Disclosure Note 2 indicates that Target generally records revenue in retail stores at the point of sale. Does that suggest that Target generally records revenue at a point in time or over a period of time? Explain.

A18. Disclosure Note 2 indicates that customers ("guests") can return some merchandise within 90 days of purchase and can return other merchandise within a year of purchase. How are Target's revenue and net income affected by returns, given that it does not know at the time a sale is made which items will be returned?

A19. Disclosure Note 2 indicates that "Commissions earned on sales generated by leased departments are included within sales and were $37 million . . . in 2015. . ." Do you think it likely that Target is accounting for those sales as a principal or an agent? Explain.

A20. Disclosure Note 2 discusses Target's accounting for gift card sales. Does Target recognize revenue when it sells a gift card to a customer? If not, when does it recognize revenue? Explain.

A21. Disclosure Note 4 discussed how Target accounts for consideration received from vendors, which they call "vendor income." Does that consideration produce revenue for Target? Does that consideration produce revenue for Target's vendors? Explain.

A22. What is Target's policy for designating investments as cash equivalents?

A23. What is Target's balance of cash equivalents for the fiscal year ended January 30, 2016?

A24. What is Target's policy with respect to accounting for merchandise returns?

A25. Does Target have accounts receivable? Speculate as to why it has the balance that it has. (Hint, see Disclosure Notes 9, 11 and 13.)

A26. What inventory method(s) does Target use to value its inventories?

A27. In addition to the purchase price, what additional expenditures does the company include in the initial cost of merchandise?

A28. Calculate the gross profit ratio and the inventory turnover ratio for the fiscal year ended January 30, 2016. Compare Target's ratios with the industry averages of 24.5% and 7.1 times.

A29. What indexes does Target use to measure the LIFO provision?

A30. Why does Target feel that the retail inventory method will result in inventory being valued at the lower of cost or market?

A31. How does Target account for inventory when arrangements are made with vendors whereby Target does not purchase or pay for merchandise until the merchandise is ultimately sold to a customer?

Part B: Property, Plant, and Equipment and Intangible Assets

B1. What categories of property, plant, equipment, and intangible assets does Target report in its January 30, 2016, balance sheet?

B2. How much cash was used in the fiscal year ended January 30, 2016, to purchase property and equipment? How does this compare with purchases in previous years?

B3. Do you think a company like Target would have significant research and development costs or capitalized interest related to self-constructed assets? Explain.

B4. What is Target's fixed-asset turnover ratio for the fiscal year ended January 30, 2016? What is the ratio intended to measure?

B5. Compare the property and equipment listed in the balance sheet with the list in Note 14. What are the estimated useful lives for recording depreciation? Why is land not listed in Note 14?

B6. Which depreciation method does Target use for property and equipment for financial reporting? Which depreciation method is used for tax purposes? Why might these methods be chosen?

B7. How does Target record repairs and maintenance expense?

B8. How does Target account for impairment of property and equipment? Were any impairments recorded for the year ended January 30, 2016? If so, what was the amount, and what were the reasons for the impairments?

B9. From Notes 15 and 16, what was the amount of intangible assets for the year ended January 30, 2016? Were any impairments related to intangible assets recorded for the year ended January 30, 2016? If so, what was the amount and, what were the reasons for the impairments?

Part C: Investments

Target does not have investments in stock or bonds. However, CVS Health Corp., which purchased Target's pharmacy and clinical business during 2015, does have some investments. Access CVS's 2015 10K (issued on February 9, 2016) at investors.cvshealth.com to answer the following questions:

C1. CVS indicates in Note 1 that it has some short-term investments that consist of certificates of deposit (CDs).

a. How has CVS classified those CDs for accounting purposes?

b. Per CVS's balance sheet, what was the balance in CVS's short-term investments as of December 31, 2015 and December 31, 2014?

c. Per CVS's statement of cash flows, what cash transactions affected short-term investments during 2015?

d. Prepare a T-account that summarizes transactions affecting CVS's short-term investments during 2015. Speculate as to the explanation for any "plug" figure necessary to make the T-account balance.

C2. Per Note 1, CVS has equity-method investments in SureScripts, LLC and in Heartland Healthcare Services. CVS indicates that those investments are immaterial for the year ended December 31, 2015. Assuming that the Heartland investment is material:

a. How would Heartland's earnings affect CVS's income statement?

b. How would Heartland's earnings affect CVS's balance sheet?

Part D: Liabilities

D1. Target's Consolidated Statement of Financial Position (its balance sheet) discloses its current assets and current liabilities.

a. What are the four components of Target's current liabilities?

b. Are current assets sufficient to cover current liabilities? What is the current ratio for the year ended January 30, 2016? How does the ratio compare with the prior year?

c. Why might a company want to avoid having its current ratio be too low? Too high?

D2. Disclosure Note 2 discusses Target's accounting for gift card sales. Disclosure Note 18 indicates the amount of gift card liability that is recognized in Target's balance sheet.

a. By how much did Target's gift card liability change between January 30, 2016 and January 31, 2015?

b. How would the following affect Target's gift card liability (indicate "increase," "decrease," or "no change" for each):
   i. Sale of a gift card
   ii. Redemption of a gift card (the holder using it to acquire goods or services)
   iii. Increase in breakage estimated for gift cards already sold

D3. Disclosure Note 19 discusses Target's accounting for a data breach in 2013, when "an intruder stole certain payment card and other guest information from our network."
   a. What is Target's approach for accruing losses for litigation claims associated with the data breach? Is their approach appropriate?
   b. Prepare a journal entry to record Target's recognition of new expenses associated with the data breach litigation for the fiscal year ended January 30, 2016.
   c. Prepare a journal entry to record Target's reduction of its liability associated with the data breach litigation for the fiscal year ended January 30, 2016.

D4. Calculate the debt to equity ratio for Target at January 30, 2016. The average ratio for companies in the General Retailers industry sector in a comparable time period was 1.6. What information does your calculation provide an investor?

D5. Calculate Target's times interest earned ratio for the year ended January 30, 2016. The coverage for companies in the General Retailers industry sector in a comparable time period was 10.6. What does your calculation indicate about Target's risk?

Part E: Leases, Income Taxes, and Pensions

E1. Refer to Disclosure Note 22 following Target's financial statements. What is the amount reported for "capital" leases (shown as the present value of minimum lease payments)? What is the total of those lease payments? What accounts for the difference between the two amounts?

E2. What is the total of the operating lease payments? New lease accounting guidance (discussed in Chapter 15) will require companies to report operating leases at present value, as well as capital leases (now called finance leases). If Target had used the new lease accounting guidance in its 2016 financial statements, what would be the amount reported for operating leases? Hint: Assume the payments "after 2020" are to be paid evenly over a 16 years period and all payments are at the end of years indicated. Target indicates elsewhere in its financial statements that 6% is an appropriate discount rate for its leases.

E3. In its Analysis of "Financial Condition: New Accounting Pronouncements," Target's financial statements for the year ended January 30, 2016, the company indicates that:

> In February 2016, the FASB issued ASU No. 2016-02, Leases, to require organizations that lease assets to recognize the rights and obligations created by those leases on the balance sheet. The new standard is effective in 2019, with early adoption permitted. We are currently evaluating the effect the new standard will have on our financial statements.

Refer to Note 22: Leases. When Target applies the new standard, what will be the primary effect on its financial statements? Explain.

E4. From the income statement, determine the income tax expense for the most recent year. Tie that number to the second table in Disclosure Note 23, "Provision for Income Taxes," and prepare a summary journal entry that records Target's tax expense from continuing operations for the year ended January 30, 2016.

E5. Focusing on the third table in Disclosure Note 23, "Net Deferred Tax Asset/ (Liability)," calculate the change in net deferred tax assets or liability. By how much did that amount change? To what extent did you account for that change in the journal entry you wrote for the first requirement of this case? List possible causes of any difference.

E6. Target's Note 23 indicates that "We have not recorded deferred taxes when earnings from foreign operations are considered to be indefinitely invested outside the U.S. These accumulated net earnings relate to certain ongoing operations and were

$685 million at January 30, 2016 and $328 million at January 31, 2015." Are these amounts treated as temporary or permanent differences by Target? If Target decides to repatriate earnings in the future, what will be the effect on net income in the year of the repatriation?

E7. What is Target's liability for unrecognized tax benefits as of January 30, 2016? If Target were to prevail in court and realize $50 million more in tax savings than it thought more likely than not to occur, what would be the effect on the liability for unrecognized tax benefits and on net income?

E8. What were the changes in Target's Projected Benefits Obligation in the fiscal years ended January 30, 2016 (fiscal 2015) and January 31, 2015 (fiscal 2014), for its qualified pension plans?

E9. What were the changes in Target's Pension Plan Assets in the fiscal years ended January 30, 2016 and January 31, 2015, for its qualified pension plans?

E10. Were these pension plans overfunded or underfunded for the fiscal years ended January 30, 2016 and January 31, 2015?

E11. What were the components of Target's Pension Expense in the fiscal years ended January 30, 2016, January 31, 2015, and February 1, 2014?

Part F: Shareholders' Equity and Additional Financial Reporting Issues

F1. Refer to Target's Consolidated Statements of Shareholders' Investment. What are the five types of events and transactions that affected one or more of the Shareholders' Investment accounts in the year ended January 30, 2016?

F2. Note 25, "Share Repurchase," provides the information we need to reconstruct the journal entry that summarizes Target's share repurchases in the year ended January 30, 2016. Provide that entry. Does Target account for share repurchases as treasury stock or retired shares? Explain.

F3. Over how many years is the compensation associated with Target's share-based awards expensed?

F4. Based on the fair value of the awards, what was Target's primary form of share-based compensation for the year ended January 30, 2016?

F5. If projecting Target's earnings per share based solely on EPS reported over the most recent three years, would you project increasing or decreasing EPS?

F6. How many shares were included in diluted earnings per share, but not basic earnings per share, due to share-based compensation awards?

F7. Refer to Target's financial statements for the year ended January 30, 2016. Note 12 provides information on Target's inventories. What method does Target use to report most of its inventories? If Target changed that method to another method, what are the steps Target would take to account for and report the change?

F8. Suppose that Target uses FIFO costing method but decided to change to the LIFO method. What are the steps Target would take to account for and report the change?

F9. Target's cash flows from its operations over the previous three years have significantly exceeded its net income. Without regard to Target specifically, explain the difference between net income and the cash flows from operating activities.

F10. Why did Target add $2.213 million in the determination of cash flows from operating activities for depreciation and amortization for the year ended January 30, 2016?

F11. A contributor to the difference in Target's net income and cash flows from operating activities and net income in each of the three years presented is a sizable increase in the amount Target owes its suppliers. If Target had used the direct rather than the indirect method of reporting operating activities, how would this reduction in accounts payable have affected cash from operating activities?

F12 Cash outflows for financing activities during each of the three years presented exceeded cash inflows from financing activities. In fact, investing activities also produced net cash outflows in two of the three years. How is that possible? What is the major contributor from year to year in the amount of cash used in financing activities? What are the next two highest contributors to that difference?

F13. Some transactions that don't increase or decrease cash must be reported in conjunction with a statement of cash flows. What activity of this type did Target report during each of the three years presented? What are two other such activities that some companies might report?

APPENDIX

C IFRS Comprehensive Case

Air France–KLM (AF), a Franco-Dutch company, prepares its financial statements according to International Financial Reporting Standards. AF's financial statements and disclosure notes for the year ended December 31, 2015, are available in Connect. This material is also available under the Finance link at the company's website (www.airfranceklm.com). This case addresses a variety of characteristics of financial statements prepared using IFRS, often comparing and contrasting those attributes of statements prepared under U.S. GAAP. Questions are grouped in parts according to various sections of the textbook.

Part A: Financial Statements, Income Measurement, and Current Assets

A1. What amounts did AF report for the following items for the fiscal year ended December 31, 2015?

a. Total revenues
b. Income from current operations
c. Net income or net loss (AF equity holders)
d. Total assets
e. Total equity

A2. What was AF's basic earnings or loss per share for the year ended December 31, 2015?

A3. Examine Note 4.1 of AF's annual report. What accounting principles were used to prepare AF's financial statements? Under those accounting principles, could AF's financial information differ from that of a company that exactly followed IFRS as published by the IASB? Explain.

A4. Refer to AF's balance sheet and compare it to the balance sheet presentation in Illustration 2–14. What differences do you see in the format of the two balance sheets?

A5. What differences do you see in the terminology used in the two balance sheets?

A6. How does AF classify operating expenses in its income statement? How are these expenses typically classified in a U.S. company's income statement?

A7. How does AF classify interest paid, interest received, and dividends received in its statement of cash flows? What other alternatives, if any, does the company have for the classification of these items? How are these items classified under U.S. GAAP?

A8. In Note 4.6, AF indicates that "Sales related to air transportation are recognized when the transportation service is provided so passenger and freight tickets are consequently recorded as 'Deferred revenue upon issuance.'"

a. Examine AF's balance sheet. What is the total amount of deferred revenue on ticket sales as of December 31, 2015?
b. When transportation services are provided with respect to the deferred revenue on ticket sales, what journal entry would AF make to reduce deferred revenue?
c. Does AF's treatment of deferred revenue under IFRS appear consistent with how these transactions would be handled under U.S. GAAP? Explain.

A9. AF has a frequent flyer program, "Flying Blue," which allows members to acquire "miles" as they fly on Air France or partner airlines that are redeemable for free flights or other benefits.

a. How does AF account for these miles?

b. Does AF report any liability associated with these miles as of December 31, 2015?
c. Although AF's 2015 annual report was issued prior to the effective date of ASU No. 2014-09, consider whether the manner in which AF accounts for its frequent flier program appears consistent with the revenue recognition guidelines included in the ASU.

A10. In Note 4.11, AF describes how it values trade receivables. How does the approach used by AF compare to U.S. GAAP?

A11. In Note 26, AF reconciles the beginning and ending balances of its valuation allowance for trade accounts receivable. Prepare a T-account for the valuation allowance and include entries for the beginning and ending balances and any reconciling items that affected the account during 2015.

A12. Examine Note 28. Does AF have any bank overdrafts? If so, are the overdrafts shown in the balance sheet the same way they would be shown under U.S. GAAP?

A13. What method does the company use to value its inventory? What other alternatives are available under IFRS? Under U.S. GAAP?

A14. AF's inventories are valued at the lower of cost or net realizable value. Does this approach differ from U.S. GAAP?

Part B: Property, Plant, and Equipment and Intangible Assets

B1. AF's property, plant, and equipment is reported at cost. The company has a policy of not revaluing property, plant, and equipment. Suppose AF decided to revalue its flight equipment on December 31, 2015, and that the fair value of the equipment on that date was €10,000 million. Prepare the journal entry to record the revaluation, assuming that the journal entry to record annual depreciation had already been recorded. (Hint: you will need to locate the original cost and accumulated depreciation of the equipment at the end of the year in the appropriate disclosure note.)

B2. Under U.S. GAAP, what alternatives do companies have to value their property, plant, and equipment?

B3. AF calculates depreciation of plant and equipment on a straight-line basis, over the useful life of the asset. Describe any differences between IFRS and U.S. GAAP in the calculation of depreciation.

B4. When does AF test for the possible impairment of fixed assets? How does this approach differ from U.S. GAAP?

B5. Describe the approach AF uses to determine fixed asset impairment losses. (Hint: see Note 4.14.) How does this approach differ from U.S. GAAP?

B6. The following is included in AF's Disclosure Note 4.13: "Intangible assets are recorded at initial cost less accumulated amortization and any accumulated impairment losses." Assume that on December 31, 2015, AF decided to revalue its Other intangible assets (see Note 18), and that the fair value on that date was determined to be €500 million. Amortization expense for the year already has been recorded. Prepare the journal entry to record the revaluation.

Part C: Investments

C1. Read Notes 24 and 36.4. Focusing on investments accounted for at fair value through profit and loss (FVTPL):
a. As of December 31, 2015, what is the total balance of those investments in the balance sheet?
b. How much of that balance is classified as current and how much as noncurrent?
c. How much of the fair value of those investments is accounted for using level 1, level 2, and level 3 inputs of the fair value hierarchy? Given that information, assess the reliability (representational faithfulness) of this fair value estimate.

C2. Complete C1 again, but for investments accounted for as available for sale.

C3. Read Notes 4.3. and 22.
   a. When AF can exercise significant influence over an investee, what accounting approach does it use to account for the investment? How does AF determine if it can exercise significant influence?
   b. If AF is involved in a joint venture, what accounting approach does it use to account for the investment?
   c. What is the carrying value of AF's equity-method investments in its December 31, 2015, balance sheet?
   d. How did AF's equity-method investments affect AF's 2015 net income from continuing operations?

Part D: Liabilities

D1. Read Notes 4.6 and 35. What do you think gave rise to total deferred income of €249 as of the end of fiscal 2015? Would transactions of this type be handled similarly under U.S. GAAP?

D2. Is the threshold for recognizing a provision under IFRS different than it is under U.S. GAAP? Explain.

D3. Note 32 lists "other provisions."
   a. Do the beginning and ending balances of total provisions and retirement benefits shown in Note 32 for fiscal 2015 tie to the balance sheet? By how much has the total amount of AF's "other provisions" increased or decreased during fiscal 2015?
   b. Write journal entries for the following changes in the litigation provision that occurred during fiscal 2015, assuming any amounts recorded on the income statement are recorded as "provision expense" and any use of provisions is paid for in cash. In each case, provide a brief explanation of the event your journal entry is capturing.
      i. New provision.
      ii. Use of provision.
   c. Is AF's treatment of litigation provision under IFRS similar to how it would be treated under U.S. GAAP?

D4. Note 32.2 lists a number of contingent liabilities. Are amounts for those items recognized as a liability on AF's balance sheet? Explain.

D5. Examine the long-term borrowings in AF's balance sheet and the related note (33.2.2). Note that AF has convertible bonds outstanding that it issued in 2013. Prepare the journal entry AF would use to record the issue of convertible bonds. Prepare the journal entry AF would use to record the issue of the convertible bonds if AF used U.S. GAAP.

D6. AF does not elect the fair value option (FVO) to report its financial liabilities. Examine Note 36.3, "Market value of financial instruments." If the company had elected the FVO for all of its debt measured at amortized cost, what would be the balance at December 31, 2015, in the fair value adjustment account?

Part E: Leases, Income Taxes, and Pensions

E1. In Note 4, "Summary of accounting policies," part 4.14, "Leases," AF states that "leases are classified as finance leases when the lease arrangement transfers substantially all the risks and rewards of ownership to the lessee." Is this the policy companies using U.S. GAAP follow?

E2. Is this the policy AF will follow when it begins applying the new lease guidance in the 2015 update to *IFRS 17*? Explain.

E3. Where in its December 31, 2015, balance sheet does AF report deferred taxes? How does this approach differ from the way deferred taxes are reported using U.S. GAAP? Using the Internet, determine how deferred taxes would be reported using IFRS at the time of your research. Explain why that approach might differ from the way AF reported deferred taxes at December 31, 2015.

E4. Here's an excerpt from one of AF's notes to its financial statements:

> **Deferred taxes (in part)**
> The Group records deferred taxes using the balance sheet liability method, providing for any temporary differences between the carrying amounts of assets and liabilities for financial reporting purposes and the amounts used for taxation purposes, except for exceptions described in IAS 12 "Income taxes." The tax rates used are those enacted or substantively enacted at the balance sheet date.

Is this policy consistent with U.S. GAAP? Explain.

E5. Below is an excerpt from one of AF's notes to its financial statements:

> **Deferred taxes (in part)**
> Deferred tax assets related to temporary differences and tax losses carried forward are recognized only to the extent it is probable that a future taxable profit will be available against which the asset can be utilized at the tax entity level.

Is this policy consistent with U.S. GAAP? Explain.

E6. Look at Note 31.2, "Retirement Benefits." AF incorporates estimates regarding staff turnover, life expectancy, salary increase, retirement age, and discount rates. How did AF report changes in these assumptions? Is that reporting method the same or different from the way we report changes under U.S. GAAP?

E7. AF does not report remeasurement gains and losses in its income statement. Where did AF report these amounts? Is that reporting method the same or different from the way we report pension expense under U.S. GAAP?

E8. See Note 23. Did AF report Net interest cost or Net interest income in 2015? How is that amount determined?

Part F: Shareholders' Equity and Additional Financial Reporting Issues

F1. AF lists four items in the shareholders' equity section of its balance sheet. If AF used U.S. GAAP, what would be the likely account titles for the first and fourth of those components?

F2. Locate Note 29.5 in AF's financial statements. What items comprise "Reserves and retained earnings," as reported in the balance sheet? If Air France-KLM used U.S. GAAP, what would be different for the reporting of these items?

F3. Describe the apparent differences in the order of presentation of the components of liabilities and shareholders' equity between IFRS as applied by AF and a typical balance sheet prepared in accordance with U.S. GAAP.

F4. AF provides share-based compensation in the form of PPSs, Phantom Performance Shares. Recipients receive compensation in what form? How are such plans reported in the balance sheet? 2015? [Hint: See Note 30, "Share-Based Compensation."] Are AF's share PPSs cliff vesting or graded vesting? How does accounting differ between U.S. GAAP and IFRS for graded-vesting plans?

F5. What amount(s) of earnings per share did AF report in its income statement for the year ended December 31, 2015? If AF used U.S. GAAP, would it have reported EPS using the same classification?

F6. Refer to AF's disclosure notes, in particular Note 2, "Restatement of Accounts 2014." For the three changes in accounting principle reported in the note, does AF account for the changes prospectively or retrospectively? Is this the same approach AF would follow if using U.S. GAAP?

F7. For the change described in 2.1, which, if any, account balances required adjustment?

F8. What are the primary classifications into which AF's cash inflows and cash outflows are separated? Is this classification the same as or different from cash flow statements prepared in accordance with U.S. GAAP?

F9. How are cash inflows from dividends and interest and cash outflows for dividends and interest classified in AF's cash flow statements? Is this classification the same as or different from cash flow statements prepared in accordance with U.S. GAAP?

Glossary

Accounting equation the process used to capture the effect of economic events; Assets = Liabilities + Owner's Equity.

Accounting Principles Board (APB) the second private sector body delegated the task of setting accounting standards.

Accounts storage areas used to keep track of increases and decreases in financial position elements.

Accounts payable obligations to suppliers of merchandise or of services purchased on open account.

Accounts receivable aging schedule calculating the necessary allowance for uncollectible accounts by applying different percentages to accounts receivable balances depending on the length of time outstanding.

Accounts receivable receivables resulting from the sale of goods or services on account.

Accretion expense the increase in an asset retirement obligation that accrues as an operating expense.

Accrual accounting measurement of the entity's accomplishments and resource sacrifices during the period, regardless of when cash is received or paid.

Accruals when the cash flow comes after either expense or revenue recognition.

Accrued interest interest that has accrued since the last interest date.

Accrued liabilities expenses already incurred but not yet paid (accrued expenses).

Accrued receivables recognition of revenue earned before cash is received.

Accumulated benefit obligation (ABO) the discounted present value of estimated retirement benefits earned so far by employees, applying the plan's pension formula using existing compensation levels.

Accumulated other comprehensive income amount of other comprehensive income (nonowner changes in equity other than net income) accumulated over the current and prior periods.

Acid-test ratio current assets, excluding inventories and prepaid items, divided by current liabilities.

Acquisition costs the amounts paid to acquire the rights to explore for undiscovered natural resources or to extract proven natural resources.

Activity-based method allocation of an asset's cost base using a measure of the asset's input or output.

Actuary a professional trained in a particular branch of statistics and mathematics to assess the various uncertainties and to estimate the company's obligation to employees in connection with its pension plan.

Additions the adding of a new major component to an existing asset.

Adjusted trial balance trial balance after adjusting entries have been recorded.

Adjusting entries internal transactions recorded at the end of any period when financial statements are prepared.

Advance payment payment made at the beginning of the lease that represents prepaid rent

Agent facilitates transfers of goods and services between sellers and customers.

Allocation method the pattern in which the allocation base is expected to be consumed.

Allowance for sales returns contra account to accounts receivable that reduces the receivables balance for estimated future returns.

Allowance for uncollectible accounts contra account that reduces accounts receivable to the net amount expected to be collected. Also called the allowance for bad debts, the allowance for doubtful accounts, or the allowance for credit losses.

Allowance method recording bad debt expense and reducing accounts receivable indirectly by crediting a contra account (allowance for uncollectible accounts) to accounts receivable for an estimate of the amount that eventually will prove uncollectible.

American Institute of Accountants (AIA) national organization of professional public accountants.

American Institute of Certified Public Accountants (AICPA) national organization of professional public accountants.

Amortization cost allocation for intangibles.

Annual bonuses one-time payments in addition to normal salary, typically tied to performance of the individual or company during a period

Annuity cash flows received or paid in the same amount each period.

Annuity due cash flows occurring at the beginning of each period.

Antidilutive securities the effect of the conversion or exercise of potential common shares would be to increase, rather than decrease, EPS.

Articles of incorporation statement of the nature of the firm's business activities, the shares to be issued, and the composition of the initial board of directors.

Asset retirement obligations (AROs) obligations associated with the disposition of an operational asset.

Asset turnover ratio measure of a company's efficiency in using assets to generate revenue.

Asset/liability approach recognition and measurement of assets and liabilities drives revenue and expense recognition.

Assigning using receivables as collateral for loans; nonpayment of a debt will require the proceeds from collecting the assigned receivables to go directly toward repayment of the debt.

Auditors independent intermediaries who help ensure that management has appropriately applied GAAP in preparing the company's financial statements.

Auditor's report report issued by CPAs who audit the financial statements that informs users of the audit findings.

Average collection period indication of the average age of accounts receivable.

Average cost method assumes cost of goods sold and ending inventory consist of a mixture of all the goods available for sale.

Average days in inventory indicates the average number of days it normally takes to sell inventory.

Balance sheet a position statement that presents an organized list of assets, liabilities, and equity at a particular point in time.

Balance sheet approach determining bad debt expense by estimating the appropriate carrying value of accounts receivable to be reported in the balance sheet and then adjusting the allowance for uncollectible accounts as necessary to reach that carrying value.

Bank reconciliation comparison of the bank balance with the balance in the company's own records.

Basic EPS computed by dividing income available to common stockholders (net income less any preferred stock dividends) by the weighted-average number of common shares outstanding for the period.

Bill-and-hold A *bill-and-hold* arrangement occurs when a customer purchases goods but requests that the seller retain physical possession of the goods until a later date.

Billings on construction contract contra account to the asset construction in progress recognizing that a customer has been billed for work performed; subtracted from construction in progress to determine balance sheet presentation.

Board of directors establishes corporate policies and appoints officers who manage the corporation.

Bond indenture document that describes specific promises made to bondholders.

Bonds a form of debt consisting of separable units (bonds) that obligates the issuing corporation to repay a stated amount at a specified maturity date and to pay interest to bondholders between the issue date and maturity.

Book value assets minus liabilities as shown in the balance sheet.

Callable allows the issuing company to buy back, or call, outstanding bonds from the bondholders before their scheduled maturity date.

Capital budgeting the process of evaluating the purchase of operational assets.

Capital leases installment purchases/sales that are formulated outwardly as leases.

Capital markets mechanisms that foster the allocation of resources efficiently.

Cash currency and coins, balances in checking accounts, and items acceptable for deposit in these accounts, such as checks and money orders received from customers.

Cash basis accounting/net operating cash flow difference between cash receipts and cash disbursements during a reporting period from transactions related to providing goods and services to customers.

Cash disbursements journal record of cash disbursements.

Cash discounts sales discounts; represent reductions not in the selling price of a good or service but in the amount to be paid by a credit customer if paid within a specific period of time.

Cash equivalents short-term, highly liquid investments that can be readily converted to cash with little risk of loss.

Cash flows from financing activities both inflows and outflows of cash resulting from the external financing of a business.

Cash flows from investing activities both outflows and inflows of cash caused by the acquisition and disposition of assets.

Cash flows from operating activities both inflows and outflows of cash that result from activities reported on the income statement.

Cash receipts journal record of cash receipts.

Certified Public Accountants (CPAs) licensed individuals who can represent that the financial statements have been audited in accordance with generally accepted auditing standards.

Change in accounting estimate a change in an estimate when new information comes to light.

Change in accounting principle switch by a company from one accounting method to another.

Change in reporting entity presentation of consolidated financial statements in place of statements of individual companies, or a change in the specific companies that constitute the group for which consolidated or combined statements are prepared.

Closing process the temporary accounts are reduced to zero balances, and these temporary account balances are closed (transferred) to retained earnings to reflect the changes that have occurred in that account during the period.

Commercial paper unsecured notes sold in minimum denominations of $25,000, with maturities ranging from 30 to 270 days.

Committee on Accounting Procedure (CAP) first private sector body that was delegated the task of setting accounting standards.

Comparability the ability to help users see similarities and differences among events and conditions.

Comparative financial statements corresponding financial statements from the previous years accompanying the issued financial statements.

Compensating balance specified balance (usually some percentage of the committee amount) a borrower of a loan is asked to maintain in a low-interest or noninterest-bearing account at the bank.

Complete depiction is complete if it includes all information necessary for faithful representation.

Complex capital structure potential common shares are outstanding.

Composite depreciation method physically dissimilar assets are aggregated to gain the convenience of group depreciation.

Compound interest interest computed not only on the initial investment but also on the accumulated interest in previous periods.

Comprehensive income traditional net income plus other nonowner changes in equity.

Conceptual framework deals with theoretical and conceptual issues and provides an underlying structure for current and future accounting and reporting standards.

Confirmatory value confirmation of investor expectations about future cash-generating ability.

Conservatism practice followed in an attempt to ensure that uncertainties and risks inherent in business situations are adequately considered.

Consignment the consignor physically transfers the goods to the other company (the consignee), but the consignor retains legal title.

Consistency permits valid comparisons between different periods.

Consolidated financial statements combination of the separate financial statements of the parent and subsidiary each period into a single aggregate set of financial statements, as if there were only one company.

Construction in progress asset account equivalent to the asset work-in-progress inventory in a manufacturing company.

Contingently issuable shares additional shares of common stock to be issued, contingent on the occurrence of some future circumstance.

Contract an agreement that creates legally enforceable rights and obligations; can be explicit or implicit.

Contract asset asset recognizing that a seller has a conditional right to receive payment after satisfying a performance obligation.

Contract liability a label given to deferred revenue or unearned revenue accounts.

Control usually an investor can control the investee if it owns more than 50% of the investee's voting shares.

Conventional retail method applying the retail inventory method in such a way that LCM is approximated.

Convertible bonds bonds for which bondholders have the option to convert the bonds into shares of stock.

Copyright exclusive right of protection given to a creator of a published work, such as a song, painting, photograph, or book.

Corporation dominant form of business organization that acquires capital from investors in exchange for ownership interest and from creditors by borrowing.

Correction of an error an adjustment a company makes due to an error made.

Cost effectiveness the perceived benefit of increased decision usefulness exceeds the anticipated cost of providing that information.

Cost of goods sold cost of the inventory sold during the period.

Cost recovery method deferral of all gross profit recognition until the cost of the item sold has been recovered.

Cost-to-retail percentage ratio found by dividing goods available for sale at cost by goods available for sale at retail.

Coupon bonds name of the owner was not registered; the holder actually clipped an attached coupon and redeemed it in accordance with instructions on the indenture.

Credit losses losses due to failure by customers to pay amounts owed for purchase of goods or services; also called bad debts, impairments of receivables, and uncollectible accounts.

Credits represent the right side of the account.

Cumulative if the specified dividend is not paid in a given year, the unpaid dividends accumulate and must be made up in a later dividend year before any dividends are paid on common shares.

Current assets includes assets that are cash, will be converted into cash, or will be used up within one year or the operating cycle, whichever is longer.

Current costs the costs that would be incurred to purchase or reproduce an asset.

Current expected credit loss (CECL) model a model used to estimate credit losses (bad debts) for receivables and for debt investments that are accounted for as held to maturity or available for sale.

Current liabilities expected to require the use of current assets for payment, and usually are payable within one year.

Current maturities of long-term debt current installment due on long-term debt, reported as a current liability.

Current ratio current assets divided by current liabilities.

Date of record specific date stated as to when the determination will be made of the recipient of the dividend.

Debenture bond secured only by the "full faith and credit" of the issuing corporation.

Debits represent the left side of the account.

Debt issue costs costs of issuing debt securities are called "debt issue costs" and are accounted for the same way as bond discount.

Debt to equity ratio compares resources provided by creditors with resources provided by owners.

Decision usefulness the quality of being useful to decision making.

Default risk a company's ability to pay its obligations when they come due.

Deferred annuity first cash flow occurs more than the one period after the date the agreement begins.

Deferred revenues cash received from a customer for goods or services to be provided in a future period.

Deferred tax asset taxes to be saved in the future when future deductible amounts reduce taxable income (when the temporary differences reverse).

Deferred tax liability taxes to be paid in the future when future taxable amounts become taxable (when the temporary differences reverse).

Deficit debit balance in retained earnings.

Defined benefit pension plans fixed retirement benefits defined by a designated formula, based on employees' years of service and annual compensation.

Defined contribution pension plans fixed annual contributions to a pension fund; employees choose where funds are invested—usually stocks or fixed-income securities.

Depletion allocation of the cost of natural resources.

Depreciable base cost of the asset expected to be consumed during its service life.

Depreciation cost allocation for plant and equipment.

Derivatives financial instruments usually created to hedge against risks created by other financial instruments or by transactions that have yet to occur but are anticipated and that "derive" their values or contractually required cash flows from some other security or index.

Detachable stock purchase warrants the investor has the option to purchase a stated number of shares of common stock at a specified option price, within a given period of time.

Development costs for natural resources, costs incurred after the resource has been discovered but before production begins.

Diluted EPS incorporates the dilutive effect of all potential common shares in the calculation of EPS.

Direct financing lease lease in which the lessor finances the asset for the lessee and earns interest revenue over the lease term.

Direct method cash effect of each operating activity (i.e., income statement item) is reported directly on the statement of cash flows.

Direct write-off method an allowance for uncollectible accounts is not used; instead, bad debts that do arise are written off as bad debt expense.

Disclosure including pertinent information in the financial statements and accompanying notes.

Disclosure notes additional insights about company operations, accounting principles, contractual agreements, and pending litigation written in notes that accompany the financial statements.

Discontinued operations the discontinuance of a component of an entity whose operations and cash flows can be clearly distinguished from the rest of the entity.

Discount arises when bonds are sold for less than face amount.

Discounting the transfer of a note receivable to a financial institution.

Distinct a good or service is *distinct* if it is both *capable of being distinct* (the customer could use the good or service on its own or in combination with other goods and services it could obtain elsewhere), and *separately identifiable from other goods or services in the contract* (the good or service is distinct in the context of the contract because it is not highly interrelated with other goods and services in the contract). Distinct goods and services are accounted for as separate performance obligations.

Dividend distribution to shareholders of a portion of assets earned.

Dollar-value LIFO (DVL) inventory is viewed as a quantity of value instead of a physical quantity of goods. Instead of layers of units from different purchases, the DVL inventory pool is viewed as comprising layers of dollar value from different years.

Dollar-value LIFO retail method LIFO retail method combined with dollar-value LIFO.

Double-declining-balance (DDB) method 200% of the straight-line rate is multiplied by book value.

Double-entry system dual effect that each transaction has on the accounting equation when recorded.

DuPont framework depict return on equity as determined by profit margin (representing profitability), asset turnover (representing efficiency), and the equity multiplier (representing leverage).

Early extinguishment of debt debt is retired prior to its scheduled maturity date.

Earnings per share (EPS) the amount of income earned by a company expressed on a per share basis.

Earnings quality refers to the ability of reported earnings (income) to predict a company's future earnings.

Economic entity assumption presumes that economic events can be identified specifically with an economic entity.

Economic entity assumption The economic entity assumption presumes that economic events can be identified with a particular economic entity.

Economic event any event that directly affects the financial position of the company.

Effective interest method calculates interest revenue as the market rate of interest multiplied by the outstanding balance of the investment.

Effective rate the actual rate at which money grows per year.

Effective tax rate equals tax expense divided by pretax accounting income.

Emerging Issues Task Force (EITF) responsible for providing more timely responses to emerging financial reporting issues.

Employee share purchase plans permit all employees to buy shares directly from their company, often at favorable terms.

Equity method used when an investor can't control, but can significantly influence, the investee. Under the equity method, the investor recognizes on its own income statement its proportionate share of the investee's income.

Estimates prediction of future events.

Ethics a code or moral system that provides criteria for evaluating right and wrong.

Ex-dividend date date usually two business days before the date of the record and is the first day the stock trades without the right to receive the declared dividend.

Executory costs maintenance, insurance, taxes, and any other costs usually associated with ownership.

Expected cash flow approach adjusts the cash flows, not the discount rate, for the uncertainty or risk of those cash flows.

Expected return on plan assets estimated long-term return on invested assets.

Expenses outflows or other using up of assets or incurrences of liabilities during a period from delivering or producing goods, rendering services, or other activities that constitute the entity's ongoing major, or central, operations.

Exploration costs for natural resources, expenditures such as drilling a well, excavating a mine, or any other costs of searching for natural resources.

Extended warranties additional, extended service that covers new problems arising after the buyer takes control of the product.

External events exchange between the company and a separate economic entity.

F.O.B. (free on board) destination the seller is responsible for shipping and the legal title does not pass until the goods arrive at their destination.

F.O.B. (free on board) shipping point legal title to the goods changes hands at the point of shipment when the seller delivers the goods to the common carrier, and the purchaser is responsible for shipping costs and transit insurance.

Factor financial institution that buys receivables for cash, handles the billing and collection of the receivables, and charges a fee for this service.

Fair value bases measurements on the price that would be received to sell assets or transfer liabilities in an orderly market transaction.

Fair value hedge a derivative is used to hedge against the exposure to changes in the fair value of an asset or liability or a firm commitment.

Fair value option allows companies to report specified financial assets and liabilities at fair value.

Faithful representation exists when there is agreement between a measure or description and the phenomenon it purports to represent.

Finance leases lessee has, in substance, purchased the lease asset; assumed when one of five classification criteria is met.

Financial Accounting Foundation (FAF) responsible for selecting the members of the FASB and its Advisory Council, ensuring adequate funding of FASB activities, and exercising general oversight of the FASB's activities.

Financial Accounting Standards Board (FASB) the current private sector body that has been delegated the task of setting accounting standards.

Financial accounting provides relevant financial information to various external users.

Financial instrument cash; evidence of an ownership interest in an entity; a contract that imposes on one entity an obligation to deliver cash or another financial instrument, and conveys to the second entity a right to receive cash or another financial instrument; and a contract that imposes on one entity an obligation to exchange financial instruments on potentially unfavorable terms and conveys to a second entity a right to exchange other financial instruments on potentially favorable terms.

Financial leverage by earning a return on borrowed funds that exceeds the cost of borrowing the funds, a company can provide its shareholders with a total return higher than it could achieve by employing equity funds alone.

Financial reporting process of providing financial statement information to external users.

Financial statements primary means of communicating financial information to external parties.

Finished goods costs that have accumulated in work-in-process are transferred to finished goods once the manufacturing process is completed.

First-in, first-out (FIFO) method assumes that items sold are those that were acquired first.

Fixed-asset turnover ratio used to measure how effectively managers used PP&E.

$$\text{Fixed-asset turnover ratio} = \frac{\text{Net sales}}{\text{Average-fixed assets}}$$

Foreign currency futures contract agreement that requires the seller to deliver a specific foreign currency at a designated future date at a specific price.

Foreign currency hedge if a derivative is used to hedge the risk that some transactions require settlement in a currency other than the entities' functional currency or that foreign operations will require translation adjustments to reported amounts.

Forward contract calls for delivery on a specific date; is not traded on a market exchange; does not call for a daily cash settlement for price changes in the underlying contract.

Franchise contractual arrangement under which the franchisor grants the franchisee the exclusive right to use the franchisor's trademark or tradename within a geographical area, usually for specified period of time.

Franchisee individual or corporation given the right to operate a business involving the franchisor's products or services and use its name and other symbols for a specific period of time.

Franchisor grants to the franchisee the right to operate a business involving the franchisor's products or services and use its name and other symbols for a specific period of time.

Fraud an intentional act by one or more individuals among management, those charged with governance, employees, or third parties, involving the use of deception that results in a misstatement in the financial statements that are the subject of an audit.

Free from error information is free from error if it contains no errors or omissions.

Freight-in transportation-in; in a periodic system, freight costs generally are added to this temporary account, which is added to purchases in determining net purchases.

Full-cost method allows costs incurred in searching for oil and gas within a large geographical area to be capitalized as assets and expensed in the future as oil and gas from the successful wells are removed from that area.

Full-disclosure principle financial reports should include any information that could affect the decisions made by external users.

Functional intellectual property property, like software, drug formulas, and completed media content, that performs a function or task, or can be played or aired, so it transfers a right of use for which the seller typically recognizes revenue at the point in time the customer can start using the intellectual property.

Future deductible amounts the future tax consequence of a temporary difference will be to decrease taxable income relative to accounting income.

Future taxable amounts the future tax consequence of temporary difference will be to increase taxable income relative to accounting income.

Future value amount of money that a dollar will grow to at some point in the future.

Gains increases in equity from peripheral, or incidental, transactions of an entity.

General journal used to record any type of transaction.

General ledger collection of accounts.

Generally Accepted Accounting Principles (GAAP) set of both broad and specific guidelines that companies should follow when measuring and reporting the information in their financial statements and related notes.

Gift card transferable prepayments for a specified dollar value of goods or services to be delivered at a future date; gift cards give rise to deferred revenue liabilities until they are redeemed or viewed as not going to be redeemed (broken).

Going concern assumption in the absence of information to the contrary, it is anticipated that a business entity will continue to operate indefinitely.

Governmental Accounting Standards Board (GASB) responsible for developing accounting standards for governmental units such as states and cities.

Gross method for the buyer, views a discount not taken as part of the cost of inventory; for the seller, views a discount not taken by the customer as part of sales of revenue.

Gross profit method (gross margin method) estimates cost of goods sold, which is then subtracted from cost of goods available for sale to estimate ending inventory.

Gross profit/ratio highlights the important relationship between net sales revenue and cost of goods sold.

$$\text{Gross profit ratio} = \frac{\text{Gross profit}}{\text{Net sales}}$$

Group depreciation method collection of assets defined as depreciable assets that share similar service lives and other attributes.

Half-year convention record one-half of a full year's depreciation in the year of acquisition and another half year in the year of disposal.

Hedging taking an action that is expected to produce exposure to a particular type of risk that is precisely the opposite of an actual risk to which the company already is exposed.

Historical costs original transaction value.

Horizontal analysis comparison by expressing each item as a percentage of that same item in the financial statements of another year (base amount) in order to more easily see year-to-year changes.

Illegal acts violations of the law, such as bribes, kickbacks, and illegal contributions to political candidates.

Implicit rate of interest rate implicit in the agreement.

Improvements replacement of a major component of an operational asset.

Income from continuing operations revenues, expenses (including income taxes), gain, and losses, excluding those related to discontinued operations and extraordinary items.

Income statement statement of operations or statement of earnings that is used to summarize the profit-generating activities that occurred during a particular reporting period.

Income statement approach estimating bad debt expense as a percentage of each period's net credit sales; usually determined by reviewing the company's recent history of the relationship between credit sales and actual bad debts.

Income summary account that is a bookkeeping convenience used in the closing process that provides a check that all temporary accounts have been properly closed.

Indirect method the net cash increase or decrease from operating activities is derived indirectly by starting with reported net income and working backwards to convert that amount to a cash basis.

Initial direct costs costs incurred by the lessor that are associated directly with originating a lease and are essential to acquire the lease.

Initial market transactions provide for new cash by the issuance of stocks and bonds by the corporation.

Installment sales method recognizes revenue and costs only when cash payments are received.

Institute of Internal Auditors national organization of accountants providing internal auditing services for their own organizations.

Institute of Management Accountants (IMA) primary national organization of accountants working in industry and government.

Intangible assets operational assets that lack physical substance; examples include patents, copyrights, franchises, and goodwill.

Interest "rent" paid for the use of money for some period of time.

Interest cost interest accrued on the projected benefit obligation calculated as the discount rate multiplied by the projected benefit obligation at the beginning of the year.

Interest rate swap agreement to exchange fixed interest payments for floating rate payments, or vice versa, without exchanging the underlying principal amounts.

Interest-bearing note receivable notes that state a principal and interest rate to be paid by a debtor to a creditor.

Internal control a company's plan to encourage adherence to company policies and procedures, promote operational efficiency, minimize errors and theft, and enhance the reliability and accuracy of accounting data.

Internal events events that directly affect the financial position of the company but don't involve an exchange transaction with another entity.

International Accounting Standards Board (IASB) objectives are to develop a single set of high-quality, understandable global accounting standards, to promote the use of those standards, and to bring about the convergence of national accounting standards and International Accounting Standards.

International Accounting Standards Committee (IASC) umbrella organization formed to develop global accounting standards.

International Financial Reporting Standards (IFRS) developed by the IASB and used by more than 100 countries.

Intrinsic value difference between the market price of the shares and the option price at which they can be acquired.

Inventories goods awaiting sale (finished goods), goods in the course of production (work in process), and goods to be consumed directly or indirectly in production (raw materials).

Inventory goods acquired, manufactured, or in the process of being manufactured for sale.

Inventory turnover ratio measures a company's efficiency in managing its investment in inventory.

Investing activities involve the acquisition and sale of long-term assets used in the business and non-operating investment assets.

Journal a chronological record of all economic events affecting financial position.

Journal entry captures the effect of a transaction on financial position in debit/credit form.

Just-in-time (JIT) system a system used by a manufacturer to coordinate production with suppliers so that raw materials or components arrive just as they are needed in the production process.

Land improvements the cost of parking lots, driveways, and private roads and the costs of fences and lawn and garden sprinkler systems.

Last-in, first-out (LIFO) method assumes units sold are the most recent units purchased.

Lease payments payments the lessee is required to make in connection with the lease.

Leasehold improvement account title when a lessee makes improvements to leased property that reverts back to the lessor at the end of the lease.

Lessee user of a leased asset.

Lessor owner of a leased asset.

Liabilities probable future sacrifices of economic benefits arising from present obligations of a particular entity to transfer assets or provide services to other entities in the future as a result of past transactions or events.

Licenses allow the customer to use the seller's intellectual property.

LIFO conformity rule if a company uses LIFO to measure taxable income, the company also must use LIFO for external financial reporting.

LIFO inventory pools simplifies recordkeeping and reduces the risk of LIFO liquidation by grouping inventory units into pools based on physical similarities of the individual units.

LIFO liquidation the decline in inventory quantity during the period.

LIFO reserve contra account to inventory used to record the difference between the internal method and LIFO.

Limited liability company (LLC) owners are not liable for the debts of the business, except to the extent of their investment; all members can be involved with managing the business without losing liability protection; no limitations on the number of owners.

Limited liability partnership similar to a limited liability company, except it doesn't offer all the liability protection available in the limited liability company structure.

Line of credit allows a company to borrow cash without having to follow formal loan procedures and paperwork.

Liquidating dividend when a dividend exceeds the balance in retained earnings and returns invested capital to owners

Liquidity period of time before an asset is converted to cash or until a liability is paid.

Long-term solvency the riskiness of a company with regard to the amount of liabilities in its capital structure.

Loss contingency existing, uncertain situation involving potential loss depending on whether some future event occurs.

Losses decreases in equity from peripheral, or incidental, transactions of the entity.

Lower of cost or market subsequent measurement of inventory applied by companies that use LIFO or the retail inventory method. This approach requires companies to report ending inventory at the lower of cost or market.

Lower of cost or net realizable value (LCNRV) subsequent measurement of inventory applied by companies that use FIFO, average cost, or any other method besides LIFO or the retail inventory method. This approach requires companies to report ending inventory at the lower of cost or net realizable value.

Management discussion and analysis (MDA) provides a biased but informed perspective of a company's operations, liquidity, and capital resources.

Material has qualitative or quantitative characteristics that make it matter for decision making.

Measurement process of associating numerical amounts to the elements.

Model Business Corporation Act designed to serve as a guide to states in the development of their corporation statutes.

Modified accelerated cost recovery system (MACRS) federal income tax code allows taxpayers to compute depreciation for their tax returns using this method.

Modified retrospective approach accounting change is applied only to the adoption period with adjustment of the balance of retained earnings at the beginning of the adoption period to capture the cumulative effects of prior periods.

Monetary assets money and claims to receive money, the amount of which is fixed or determinable.

Monetary liabilities obligations to pay amounts of cash, the amount of which is fixed or determinable.

Monetary unit assumption states that financial statement elements should be measured in a particular monetary unit (in the United States, the U.S. dollar).

Mortgage bond backed by a lien on specified real estate owned by the issuer.

Multiple-step income statement format that includes a number of intermediate subtotals before arriving at income from continuing operations.

Natural resources oil and gas deposits, timber tracts, and mineral deposits.

Net income income statement bottom line.

Net markdown net effect of the change in selling price (increase, decrease, increase).

Net markup net effect of the change in selling price (increase, increase, decrease).

Net method For the buyer, considers the cost of inventory to include the net, after-discount amount, and any discounts not taken are reported as interest expense. For the seller, considers sales revenue to be the net amount, after discount, and any discounts not taken by the customer as interest revenue.

Net operating loss negative taxable income because tax-deductible expenses exceed taxable revenues.

Net operating loss carryforward offsets future taxable income with an NOL to provide a reduction of taxes payable in that future period; therefore, gives rise to a deferred tax asset because it is a future deductible amount.

Net realizable value the amount of cash the company expects to actually collect from customers.

Neutral implies freedom from bias.

Non-GAAP earnings actual (GAAP) earnings reduced by any expenses the reporting company feels are unusual and should be excluded.

Noncash investing and financing activities transactions that do not increase or decrease cash but that result in significant investing and financing activities.

Noncumulative if the specified dividend is not declared in any given year, it need never be paid.

Noninterest-bearing note notes for which the interest is deducted from the face amount of the note to determine the cash proceeds made available to the borrower at the outset.

Nonoperating income includes gains, losses, revenues, and expenses related to peripheral or incidental activities of the company.

Nonparticipating preferred shareholder dividends are limited to the stated amount.

Notes payable promissory notes (essentially an IOU) that obligate the issuing corporation to repay a stated amount at or by a specified maturity date and to pay interest to the lender between the issue date and maturity.

Notes receivable receivables supported by a formal agreement or note that specifies payment terms.

Objectives-oriented/principles-based accounting standards approach to standard setting stresses professional judgment, as opposed to following a list of rules.

Operating activities inflows and outflows of cash related to transactions entering into the determination of net income.

Operating cycle period of time necessary to convert cash to raw materials, raw materials to finished product, the finished product to receivables, and then finally receivables back to cash.

Operating income includes revenues and expenses directly related to the principal revenue-generating activities of the company.

Operating leases fundamental rights and responsibilities of ownership are retained by the lessor and the lessee merely is using the asset temporarily.

Operating segment a component of an enterprise that engages in business activities from which it may earn revenues and incur expenses (including revenues and expenses relating to transactions with other companies of the same enterprise); whose operating results are regularly reviewed by the enterprise's chief operating decision maker to make decisions about resources to be allocated to the segment and assess its performance; for which discrete financial information is available.

Operational risk how adept a company is at withstanding various events and circumstances that might impair its ability to earn profits.

Option gives the holder the right either to buy or sell a financial instrument at a specified price.

Option pricing models statistical models that incorporate information about a company's stock and the terms of the stock option to estimate the option's fair value.

Ordinary annuity cash flows occur at the end of each period.

Other comprehensive income certain gains and losses that are excluded from the calculation of net income, but included in the calculation of comprehensive income.

Paid-in capital invested capital consisting primarily of amounts invested by shareholders when they purchase shares of stock from the corporation.

Parenthetical comments/modifying comments supplemental information disclosed on the face of financial statements.

Participating preferred shareholders are allowed to receive additional dividends beyond the stated amount.

Patent exclusive right to manufacture a product or to use a process.

Pension plan assets employer contributions and accumulated earnings on the investment of those contributions to be used to pay retirement benefits to retired employees.

Performance obligations promises to transfer goods and services to a customer; satisfied when the seller transfers *control* of goods or services to the customer.

Periodic inventory system the merchandise inventory account balance is not adjusted as purchases and sales are made but only periodically at the end of a reporting period when a physical count of the period's ending inventory is made and costs are assigned to the quantities determined.

Periodicity assumption allows the life of a company to be divided into artificial time periods to provide timely information.

Permanent accounts represent assets, liabilities, and shareholders' equity at a point in time.

Permanent difference difference between pretax accounting income and taxable income and, consequently, between the reported amount of an asset or liability in the financial statements and its tax basis that will not "reverse," resulting from transactions and events that under existing tax law will never affect taxable income or taxes payable.

Perpetual inventory system account inventory is continually adjusted for each change in inventory, whether it's caused by a purchase, a sale, or a return of merchandise by the company to its supplier.

Pledging trade receivables in general rather than specific receivables are pledged as collateral; the responsibility for collection of the receivables remains solely with the company.

Post-closing trial balance verifies that the closing entries were prepared and posted correctly and that the accounts are now ready for next year's transactions.

Posting transferring debits and credits recorded in individual journal entries to the specific accounts affected.

Potential common shares securities that, while not being common stock, may become common stock through their exercise, conversion, or issuance and therefore dilute (reduce) earnings per share.

Predictive value confirmation of investor expectations about future cash-generating ability.

Preferred stock typically has a preference (a) to a specified amount of dividends (stated dollar amount per share or percentage of par value per share) and (b) to distribution of assets in the event the corporation is dissolved.

Premium arises when bonds are sold for more than face amount.

Prepaid expense represents an asset recorded when an expense is paid in advance, creating benefits beyond the current period.

Prepayments/deferrals the cash flow precedes either expense or revenue recognition.

Present value today's equivalent to a particular amount in the future, after backing out the time value of money.

Principal controls goods or services and is responsible for providing them to the customer.

Prior period adjustment addition to or reduction in the beginning retained earnings balance in a statement of shareholders' equity due to a correction of an error.

Prior service cost the cost of credit given for an amendment to a pension plan to employee service rendered in prior years.

Product costs costs associated with products and expensed as cost of goods sold only when the related products are sold.

Profit margin on sales net income divided by net sales; measures the amount of net income achieved per sales dollar.

Projected benefit obligation (PBO) the discounted present value of estimated retirement benefits earned so far by employees, applying the plan's pension formula using projected future compensation levels.

Property dividend when a noncash asset is distributed.

Property, plant, and equipment land, buildings, equipment, machinery, autos, and trucks.

Proxy statement contains disclosures on compensation to directors and executives; sent to all shareholders each year.

Purchase commitments contracts that obligate a company to purchase a specified amount of merchandise or raw materials at specified prices on or before specified dates.

Purchase discounts reductions in the amount to be paid if remittance is made within a designated period of time.

Purchase option a provision of some lease contracts that gives the lessee the option of purchasing the leased property during, or at the end of, the lease term at a specified price.

Purchase return a reduction in both inventory and accounts payable (if the account has not yet been paid) at the time of the return.

Purchases journal records the purchase of merchandise on account.

Quality-assurance warranty obligation by the seller to make repairs or replace products that are later demonstrated to be defective for some period of time after the sale.

Quasi reorganization a firm undergoing financial difficulties, but with favorable future prospects, may use a quasi reorganization to write down inflated asset values and eliminate an accumulated deficit.

Rate of return on stock investment

$$\frac{\text{Dividends} + \text{Share price appreciation}}{\text{Initial investment}}$$

Ratio analysis comparison of accounting numbers to evaluate the performance and risk of a firm.

Raw materials cost of components purchased from suppliers that will become part of the finished product.

Realization principle revenue recognition on completion of the earnings process and reasonable certainty about collectibility.

Rearrangements expenditures made to restructure an asset without addition, replacement, or improvement.

Receivables a company's claims to the future collection of cash, other assets, or services.

Receivables turnover ratio indicates how quickly a company is able to collect its accounts receivable.

Recognition process of admitting information into the basic financial statements.

Redemption privilege might allow preferred shareholders the option, under specified conditions, to return their shares for a predetermined redemption price.

Related-party transactions transactions with owners, management, families of owners or management, affiliated companies, and other parties that can significantly influence or be influenced by the company.

Relevance one of the primary decision-specific qualities that make accounting information useful; made up of predictive value and/or feedback value and timeliness.

Replacement depreciation method depreciation is recorded when assets are replaced.

Residual asset carrying amount of a leased asset not transferred to the lessee.

Residual value or salvage value, the amount the company expects to receive for the asset at the end of its service life, less any anticipated disposal costs.

Restoration costs costs to restore land or other property to its original condition after extraction of the natural resource ends.

Restricted stock shares issued in the name of the employee, subject to forfeiture by the employee if employment is terminated within some specified number of years from the date of grant.

Restricted stock units right to receive shares, subject to forfeiture by the employee if employment is terminated within some specified number of years from the date of grant.

Restructuring costs costs associated with plans by management to materially change either the scope or manner in which its company's operations are conducted.

Retained earnings amounts earned by the corporation on behalf of its shareholders and not (yet) distributed to them as dividends.

Retired stock shares repurchased and not designated as treasury stock.

Retirement depreciation method records depreciation when assets are disposed of and measures depreciation as the difference between the proceeds received and cost.

Retrospective approach financial statements issued in previous years are revised to reflect the impact of an accounting change whenever those statements are presented again for comparative purpose.

Return on assets (ROA) indicates a company's overall profitability.

Return on shareholders' equity (ROE) amount of profit management can generate from the assets that owners provide.

Revenue/expense approach recognition and measurement of revenues and expenses are emphasized.

Revenues inflows or other enhancements of assets of an entity or settlements of its liabilities (or a combination of both) from delivering or producing goods, rendering services, or other activities that constitute the entity's ongoing major or central operations.

Reverse stock split when a company decreases, rather than increases, its outstanding shares.

Reversing entries optional entries that remove the effects of some of the adjusting entries made at the end of the previous reporting period for the sole purpose of simplifying journal entries made during the new period.

Right of conversion shareholders' right to exchange shares of preferred stock for common stock at specified conversion ratio.

Right of return customers' right to return merchandise to retailers if they are not satisfied.

Rules-based accounting standards a list of rules for choosing the appropriate accounting treatment for a transaction.

S corporation characteristics of both regular corporations and partnerships.

SAB No. 101 *Staff Accounting Bulletin 101* summarizes SEC's views on revenue recognition.

Sale-leaseback transaction the owner of an asset sells it and immediately leases it back from the new owner.

Sales journal records credit sales.

Sales return the return of merchandise for a refund or for credit to be applied to other purchases.

Sales-type lease lessor transfers control of lease asset to lessee, with or without a selling profit on the sale of the asset.

Secondary market transactions provide for the transfer of stocks and bonds among individuals and institutions.

Securities and Exchange Commission (SEC) responsible for setting accounting and reporting standards for companies whose securities are publicly traded.

Securities available-for-sale debt securities the investor acquires for purposes other than active trading or to be held to maturity.

Securities to be held-to-maturity debt securities for which the investor has the "positive intent and ability" to hold the securities to maturity.

Securitization the company creates a special purpose entity (SPE), usually a trust or a subsidiary; the SPE buys a pool of trade receivables, credit card receivables, or loans from the company and then sells related securities.

Selling profit when the fair value of the asset (usually the present value of the lease payments, or "selling price") exceeds the cost or carrying value of the asset sold.

Separation of duties an internal control technique in which various functions are distributed amongst employees to provide cross-checking that encourages accuracy and discourages fraud.

Serial bonds more structured (and less popular) way to retire bonds on a piecemeal basis.

Service cost increase in the projected benefit obligation attributable to employee service performed during the period.

Service life (useful life) the estimated use that the company expects to receive from the asset.

Service method allocation approach that reflects the declining service pattern of the prior service cost.

Short-term investments investments not classified as cash equivalents that will be liquidated in the coming year or operating cycle, whichever is longer.

Significant influence effective control is absent but the investor is able to affect the operating and financial policies of the investee (usually is the case when investor holds between 20% and 50% of the investee's voting shares).

Simple capital structure a firm that has no potential common shares (outstanding securities that could potentially dilute earnings per share).

Simple interest computed by multiplying an initial investment times both the applicable interest rate and the period of time for which the money is used.

Single-step income statement format that groups all revenues and gains together and all expenses and losses together.

Sinking fund debentures bonds that must be redeemed on a prespecified year-by-year basis; administered by a trustee who repurchases bonds in the open market.

Source documents relay essential information about each transaction to the accountant, e.g., sales invoices, bills from suppliers, cash register tapes.

Special journal record of a repetitive type of transaction, e.g., a sales journal.

Specific identification method each unit sold during the period or each unit on hand at the end of the period to be matched with its actual cost.

Specific interest method for interest capitalization, rates from specific construction loans, to the extent of specific borrowings are used before using the average rate of other debt.

Stand-alone selling price the amount at which the good or service is sold separately under similar circumstances.

Start-up costs whenever a company introduces a new product or service, or commences business in a new territory or with a new customer, it incurs one-time costs that are expensed in the period incurred.

Statement of cash flows change statement summarizing the transactions that caused cash to change during the period.

Statement of shareholders' equity statement disclosing the source of changes in the shareholders' equity accounts.

Stock appreciation rights (SARs) awards that enable an employee to benefit by the amount that the market price of the company's stock rises above a specified amount, without having to buy shares.

Stock dividend distribution of additional shares of stock to current shareholders of the corporation.

Stock options employees aren't actually awarded shares, but rather are given the option to buy shares at a specified exercise price within some specified number of years from the date of grant.

Stock split stock distribution of 25% or higher, sometimes called a *large* stock dividend.

Straight line an equal amount of depreciable base is allocated to each year of the asset's service life.

Straight-line method recording interest each period at the same dollar amount.

Subordinated debenture the holder is not entitled to receive any liquidation payments until the claims of other specified debt issues are satisfied.

Subsequent event a significant development that takes place after the company's fiscal year-end but before the financial statements are issued.

Subsidiary ledger record of a group of subsidiary accounts associated with a particular general ledger control account.

Successful efforts method requires that exploration costs that are known not to have resulted in the discovery of oil or gas be included as expense in the period the expenditures are made.

Sum-of-the-years'-digits (SYD) method systematic acceleration of depreciation by multiplying the depreciable base by a fraction that declines each year.

Supplemental schedules and tables reports containing more detailed information than is shown in the primary financial statements.

Symbolic intellectual property property, like trademarks, logos, brand names and franchise rights, has usefulness to the customer that depends on the seller's ongoing activities, so it transfers a right of access for which the seller recognizes revenue over the period of time the customer accesses the IP.

T-account account with space at the top for the account title and two sides for recording increases and decreases.

Tax basis of an asset or liability is its original value for tax purposes reduced by any amounts included to date on tax returns.

Technological feasibility established when the enterprise has completed all planning, designing, coding, and testing activities that are necessary to establish that the product can be produced to meet its design specifications, including functions, features, and technical performance requirements.

Temporary accounts represent changes in the retained earnings component of shareholders' equity for a corporation caused by revenue, expense, gain, and loss transactions.

Temporary difference difference between pretax accounting income and taxable income and, consequently, between the reported amount of an asset or liability in the financial statements and its tax basis, which will "reverse" in later years.

Time value of money money can be invested today to earn interest and grow to a larger dollar amount in the future.

Time-based methods allocates the cost base according to the passage of time.

Timeliness information that is available to users early enough to allow its use in the decision process.

Times interest earned ratio a way to gauge the ability of a company to satisfy its fixed debt obligations by comparing interest charges with the income available to pay those charges.

Trade discounts percentage reduction from the list price.

Trade notes payable formally recognized by a written promissory note.

Trademark (tradename) exclusive right to display a word, a slogan, a symbol, or an emblem that distinctively identifies a company, a product, or a service.

Trading securities equity or debt securities the investor (usually a financial institution) acquires principally for the purpose of selling in the near term.

Transaction analysis process of reviewing the source documents to determine the dual effect on the accounting equation and the specific elements involved.

Transaction price the amount the seller expects to be entitled to receive from the customer in exchange for providing goods and services.

Transactions economic events.

Treasury stock shares repurchased and not retired.

Troubled debt restructuring the original terms of a debt agreement are changed as a result of financial difficulties experienced by the debtor (borrower).

Trustee person who accepts employer contributions, invests the contributions, accumulates the earnings on the investments, and pays benefits from the plan assets to retired employees or their beneficiaries.

Unadjusted trial balance a list of the general ledger accounts and their balances at a particular date.

Understandability users must understand the information within the context of the decision being made.

Units-of-production method computes a depreciation rate per measure of activity and then multiplies this rate by actual activity to determine periodic depreciation.

Unrealized holding gains and losses gains and losses that arise from holding an investment during a period in which its fair value changes.

Valuation allowance indirect reduction (contra account) in a deferred tax asset when it is more likely than not that some portion or all of the deferred tax asset will not be realized.

Variable consideration transaction price is uncertain because it includes an amount that varies depending on the occurrence or nonoccurrence of a future event.

Verifiability implies a consensus among different measurers.

Vertical analysis expression of each item in the financial statements as a percentage of an appropriate corresponding total, or base amount, but within the same year.

Vested benefits benefits that employees have the right to receive even if their employment were to cease today.

Weighted-average interest method for interest capitalization, weighted-average rate on all interest-bearing debt, including all construction loans, is used.

With recourse the seller retains the risk of uncollectibility.

Without recourse the buyer assumes the risk of bad debts.

Work-in-process inventory products that are not yet complete in the manufacturing process.

Working capital differences between current assets and current liabilities.

Worksheet used to organize the accounting information needed to prepare adjusting and closing entries and the financial statements.

Subject Index

Notes: Page numbers followed by *n* indicate material in footnotes. General information about standards and standard-setting organizations may be found in this index. Specific standards and pronouncements are listed in the Accounting Standards Index.

J

O

P

U

Accounting Standards Index

Notes: Page numbers followed by *n* indicate material in footnotes. Specific standards and pronouncements are found in this index; general information about standards and standard-setting organizations is found in the Subject Index. Unless otherwise noted, standards will be found under the name of the issuing organization.

Present and Future Value Tables

This table shows the future value of $1 at various interest rates (i) and time periods (n). It is used to calculate the future value of any single amount.

TABLE 1 Future Value of $1

$FV = \$1(1+i)^n$

n/i	1.0%	1.5%	2.0%	2.5%	3.0%	3.5%	4.0%	4.5%	5.0%	5.5%	6.0%	7.0%	8.0%	9.0%	10.0%	11.0%	12.0%	20.0%
1	1.01000	1.01500	1.02000	1.02500	1.03000	1.03500	1.04000	1.04500	1.05000	1.05500	1.06000	1.07000	1.08000	1.09000	1.10000	1.11000	1.12000	1.20000
2	1.02010	1.03022	1.04040	1.05063	1.06090	1.07123	1.08160	1.09203	1.10250	1.11303	1.12360	1.14490	1.16640	1.18810	1.21000	1.23210	1.25440	1.44000
3	1.03030	1.04568	1.06121	1.07689	1.09273	1.10872	1.12486	1.14117	1.15763	1.17424	1.19102	1.22504	1.25971	1.29503	1.33100	1.36763	1.40493	1.72800
4	1.04060	1.06136	1.08243	1.10381	1.12551	1.14752	1.16986	1.19252	1.21551	1.23882	1.26248	1.31080	1.36049	1.41158	1.46410	1.51807	1.57352	2.07360
5	1.05101	1.07728	1.10408	1.13141	1.15927	1.18769	1.21665	1.24618	1.27628	1.30696	1.33823	1.40255	1.46933	1.53862	1.61051	1.68506	1.76234	2.48832
6	1.06152	1.09344	1.12616	1.15969	1.19405	1.22926	1.26532	1.30226	1.34010	1.37884	1.41852	1.50073	1.58687	1.67710	1.77156	1.87041	1.97382	2.98598
7	1.07214	1.10984	1.14869	1.18869	1.22987	1.27228	1.31593	1.36086	1.40710	1.45468	1.50363	1.60578	1.71382	1.82804	1.94872	2.07616	2.21068	3.58318
8	1.08286	1.12649	1.17166	1.21840	1.26677	1.31681	1.36857	1.42210	1.47746	1.53469	1.59385	1.71819	1.85093	1.99256	2.14359	2.30454	2.47596	4.29982
9	1.09369	1.14339	1.19509	1.24886	1.30477	1.36290	1.42331	1.48610	1.55133	1.61909	1.68948	1.83846	1.99900	2.17189	2.35795	2.55804	2.77308	5.15978
10	1.10462	1.16054	1.21899	1.28008	1.34392	1.41060	1.48024	1.55297	1.62889	1.70814	1.79085	1.96715	2.15892	2.36736	2.59374	2.83942	3.10585	6.19174
11	1.11567	1.17795	1.24337	1.31209	1.38423	1.45997	1.53945	1.62285	1.71034	1.80209	1.89830	2.10485	2.33164	2.58043	2.85312	3.15176	3.47855	7.43008
12	1.12683	1.19562	1.26824	1.34489	1.42576	1.51107	1.60103	1.69588	1.79586	1.90121	2.01220	2.25219	2.51817	2.81266	3.13843	3.49845	3.89598	8.91610
13	1.13809	1.21355	1.29361	1.37851	1.46853	1.56396	1.66507	1.77220	1.88565	2.00577	2.13293	2.40985	2.71962	3.06580	3.45227	3.88328	4.36349	10.69932
14	1.14947	1.23176	1.31948	1.41297	1.51259	1.61869	1.73168	1.85194	1.97993	2.11609	2.26090	2.57853	2.93719	3.34173	3.79750	4.31044	4.88711	12.83918
15	1.16097	1.25023	1.34587	1.44830	1.55797	1.67535	1.80094	1.93528	2.07893	2.23248	2.39656	2.75903	3.17217	3.64248	4.17725	4.78459	5.47357	15.40702
16	1.17258	1.26899	1.37279	1.48451	1.60471	1.73399	1.87298	2.02237	2.18287	2.35526	2.54035	2.95216	3.42594	3.97031	4.59497	5.31089	6.13039	18.48843
17	1.18430	1.28802	1.40024	1.52162	1.65285	1.79468	1.94790	2.11338	2.29202	2.48480	2.69277	3.15882	3.70002	4.32763	5.05447	5.89509	6.86604	22.18611
18	1.19615	1.30734	1.42825	1.55966	1.70243	1.85749	2.02582	2.20848	2.40662	2.62147	2.85434	3.37993	3.99602	4.71712	5.55992	6.54355	7.68997	26.62333
19	1.20811	1.32695	1.45681	1.59865	1.75351	1.92250	2.10685	2.30786	2.52695	2.76565	3.02560	3.61653	4.31570	5.14166	6.11591	7.26334	8.61276	31.94800
20	1.22019	1.34686	1.48595	1.63862	1.80611	1.98979	2.19112	2.41171	2.65330	2.91776	3.20714	3.86968	4.66096	5.60441	6.72750	8.06231	9.64629	38.33760
21	1.23239	1.36706	1.51567	1.67958	1.86029	2.05943	2.27877	2.52024	2.78596	3.07823	3.39956	4.14056	5.03383	6.10881	7.40025	8.94917	10.80385	46.00512
25	1.28243	1.45095	1.64061	1.85394	2.09378	2.36324	2.66584	3.00543	3.38635	3.81339	4.29187	5.42743	6.84848	8.62308	10.83471	13.58546	17.00006	95.39622
30	1.34785	1.56308	1.81136	2.09757	2.42726	2.80679	3.24340	3.74532	4.32194	4.98395	5.74349	7.61226	10.06266	13.26768	17.44940	22.89230	29.95992	237.37631
40	1.48886	1.81402	2.20804	2.68506	3.26204	3.95926	4.80102	5.81636	7.03999	8.51331	10.28572	14.97446	21.72452	31.40942	45.25926	65.00087	93.05097	1469.77160

This table shows the present value of $1 at various interest rates (i) and time periods (n). It is used to calculate the present value of any single amount.

TABLE 2 Present Value of $1

$$PV = \frac{\$1}{(1+i)^n}$$

n/i	1.0%	1.5%	2.0%	2.5%	3.0%	3.5%	4.0%	4.5%	5.0%	5.5%	6.0%	7.0%	8.0%	9.0%	10.0%	11.0%	12.0%	20.0%
1	0.99010	0.98522	0.98039	0.97561	0.97087	0.96618	0.96154	0.95694	0.95238	0.94787	0.94340	0.93458	0.92593	0.91743	0.90909	0.90090	0.89286	0.83333
2	0.98030	0.97066	0.96117	0.95181	0.94260	0.93351	0.92456	0.91573	0.90703	0.89845	0.89000	0.87344	0.85734	0.84168	0.82645	0.81162	0.79719	0.69444
3	0.97059	0.95632	0.94232	0.92860	0.91514	0.90194	0.88900	0.87630	0.86384	0.85161	0.83962	0.81630	0.79383	0.77218	0.75131	0.73119	0.71178	0.57870
4	0.96098	0.94218	0.92385	0.90595	0.88849	0.87144	0.85480	0.83856	0.82270	0.80722	0.79209	0.76290	0.73503	0.70843	0.68301	0.65873	0.63552	0.48225
5	0.95147	0.92826	0.90573	0.88385	0.86261	0.84197	0.82193	0.80245	0.78353	0.76513	0.74726	0.71299	0.68058	0.64993	0.62092	0.59345	0.56743	0.40188
6	**0.94205**	**0.91454**	**0.88797**	**0.86230**	**0.83748**	**0.81350**	**0.79031**	**0.76790**	**0.74622**	**0.72525**	**0.70496**	**0.66634**	**0.63017**	**0.59627**	**0.56447**	**0.53464**	**0.50663**	**0.33490**
7	0.93272	0.90103	0.87056	0.84127	0.81309	0.78599	0.75992	0.73483	0.71068	0.68744	0.66506	0.62275	0.58349	0.54703	0.51316	0.48166	0.45235	0.27908
8	0.92348	0.88771	0.85349	0.82075	0.78941	0.75941	0.73069	0.70319	0.67684	0.65160	0.62741	0.58201	0.54027	0.50187	0.46651	0.43393	0.40388	0.23257
9	0.91434	0.87459	0.83676	0.80073	0.76642	0.73373	0.70259	0.67290	0.64461	0.61763	0.59190	0.54393	0.50025	0.46043	0.42410	0.39092	0.36061	0.19381
10	0.90529	0.86167	0.82035	0.78120	0.74409	0.70892	0.67556	0.64393	0.61391	0.58543	0.55839	0.50835	0.46319	0.42241	0.38554	0.35218	0.32197	0.16151
11	**0.89632**	**0.84893**	**0.80426**	**0.76214**	**0.72242**	**0.68495**	**0.64958**	**0.61620**	**0.58468**	**0.55491**	**0.52679**	**0.47509**	**0.42888**	**0.38753**	**0.35049**	**0.31728**	**0.28748**	**0.13459**
12	0.88745	0.83639	0.78849	0.74356	0.70138	0.66178	0.62460	0.58966	0.55684	0.52598	0.49697	0.44401	0.39711	0.35553	0.31863	0.28584	0.25668	0.11216
13	0.87866	0.82403	0.77303	0.72542	0.68095	0.63940	0.60057	0.56427	0.53032	0.49856	0.46884	0.41496	0.36770	0.32618	0.28966	0.25751	0.22917	0.09346
14	0.86996	0.81185	0.75788	0.70773	0.66112	0.61778	0.57748	0.53997	0.50507	0.47257	0.44230	0.38782	0.34046	0.29925	0.26333	0.23199	0.20462	0.07789
15	0.86135	0.79985	0.74301	0.69047	0.64186	0.59689	0.55526	0.51672	0.48102	0.44793	0.41727	0.36245	0.31524	0.27454	0.23939	0.20900	0.18270	0.06491
16	**0.85282**	**0.78803**	**0.72845**	**0.67362**	**0.62317**	**0.57671**	**0.53391**	**0.49447**	**0.45811**	**0.42458**	**0.39365**	**0.33873**	**0.29189**	**0.25187**	**0.21763**	**0.18829**	**0.16312**	**0.05409**
17	0.84438	0.77639	0.71416	0.65720	0.60502	0.55720	0.51337	0.47318	0.43630	0.40245	0.37136	0.31657	0.27027	0.23107	0.19784	0.16963	0.14564	0.04507
18	0.83602	0.76491	0.70016	0.64117	0.58739	0.53836	0.49363	0.45280	0.41552	0.38147	0.35034	0.29586	0.25025	0.21199	0.17986	0.15282	0.13004	0.03756
19	0.82774	0.75361	0.68643	0.62553	0.57029	0.52016	0.47464	0.43330	0.39573	0.36158	0.33051	0.27651	0.23171	0.19449	0.16351	0.13768	0.11611	0.03130
20	0.81954	0.74247	0.67297	0.61027	0.55368	0.50257	0.45639	0.41464	0.37689	0.34273	0.31180	0.25842	0.21455	0.17843	0.14864	0.12403	0.10367	0.02608
21	**0.81143**	**0.73150**	**0.65978**	**0.59539**	**0.53755**	**0.48557**	**0.43883**	**0.39679**	**0.35894**	**0.32486**	**0.29416**	**0.24151**	**0.19866**	**0.16370**	**0.13513**	**0.11174**	**0.09256**	**0.02174**
24	0.78757	0.69954	0.62172	0.55288	0.49193	0.43796	0.39012	0.34770	0.31007	0.27666	0.24698	0.19715	0.15770	0.12640	0.10153	0.08170	0.06588	0.01258
25	0.77977	0.68921	0.60953	0.53939	0.47761	0.42315	0.37512	0.33273	0.29530	0.26223	0.23300	0.18425	0.14602	0.11597	0.09230	0.07361	0.05882	0.01048
28	0.75684	0.65910	0.57437	0.50088	0.43708	0.38165	0.33348	0.29157	0.25509	0.22332	0.19563	0.15040	0.11591	0.08955	0.06934	0.05382	0.04187	0.00607
29	0.74934	0.64936	0.56311	0.48866	0.42435	0.36875	0.32065	0.27902	0.24295	0.21168	0.18456	0.14056	0.10733	0.08215	0.06304	0.04849	0.03738	0.00506
30	**0.74192**	**0.63976**	**0.55207**	**0.47674**	**0.41199**	**0.35628**	**0.30832**	**0.26700**	**0.23138**	**0.20064**	**0.17411**	**0.13137**	**0.09938**	**0.07537**	**0.05731**	**0.04368**	**0.03338**	**0.00421**
31	0.73458	0.63031	0.54125	0.46511	0.39999	0.34423	0.29646	0.25550	0.22036	0.19018	0.16425	0.12277	0.09202	0.06915	0.05210	0.03935	0.02980	0.00351
40	0.67165	0.55126	0.45289	0.37243	0.30656	0.25257	0.20829	0.17193	0.14205	0.11746	0.09722	0.06678	0.04603	0.03184	0.02209	0.01538	0.01075	0.00068

This table shows the future value of an ordinary annuity of $1 at various interest rates (i) and time periods (n). It is used to calculate the future value of any series of equal payments made at the *end* of each compounding period.

TABLE 3 Future Value of an Ordinary Annuity of $1

$$FVA = \frac{(1+i)^n - 1}{i}$$

n/i	1.0%	1.5%	2.0%	2.5%	3.0%	3.5%	4.0%	4.5%	5.0%	5.5%	6.0%	7.0%	8.0%	9.0%	10.0%	11.0%	12.0%	20.0%
1	1.0000	1.0000	1.0000	1.0000	1.0000	1.0000	1.0000	1.0000	1.0000	1.0000	1.0000	1.0000	1.0000	1.0000	1.0000	1.0000	1.0000	1.0000
2	2.0100	2.0150	2.0200	2.0250	2.0300	2.0350	2.0400	2.0450	2.0500	2.0550	2.0600	2.0700	2.0800	2.0900	2.1000	2.1100	2.1200	2.2000
3	3.0301	3.0452	3.0604	3.0756	3.0909	3.1062	3.1216	3.1370	3.1525	3.1680	3.1836	3.2149	3.2464	3.2781	3.3100	3.3421	3.3744	3.6400
4	4.0604	4.0909	4.1216	4.1525	4.1836	4.2149	4.2465	4.2782	4.3101	4.3423	4.3746	4.4399	4.5061	4.5731	4.6410	4.7097	4.7793	5.3680
5	5.1010	5.1523	5.2040	5.2563	5.3091	5.3625	5.4163	5.4707	5.5256	5.5811	5.6371	5.7507	5.8666	5.9847	6.1051	6.2278	6.3528	7.4416
6	**6.1520**	**6.2296**	**6.3081**	**6.3877**	**6.4684**	**6.5502**	**6.6330**	**6.7169**	**6.8019**	**6.8881**	**6.9753**	**7.1533**	**7.3359**	**7.5233**	**7.7156**	**7.9129**	**8.1152**	**9.9299**
7	7.2135	7.3230	7.4343	7.5474	7.6625	7.7794	7.8983	8.0192	8.1420	8.2669	8.3938	8.6540	8.9228	9.2004	9.4872	9.7833	10.0890	12.9159
8	8.2857	8.4328	8.5830	8.7361	8.8923	9.0517	9.2142	9.3800	9.5491	9.7216	9.8975	10.2598	10.6366	11.0285	11.4359	11.8594	12.2997	16.4991
9	9.3685	9.5593	9.7546	9.9545	10.1591	10.3685	10.5828	10.8021	11.0266	11.2563	11.4913	11.9780	12.4876	13.0210	13.5795	14.1640	14.7757	20.7989
10	10.4622	10.7027	10.9497	11.2034	11.4639	11.7314	12.0061	12.2882	12.5779	12.8754	13.1808	13.8164	14.4866	15.1929	15.9374	16.7220	17.5487	25.9587
11	**11.5668**	**11.8633**	**12.1687**	**12.4835**	**12.8078**	**13.1420**	**13.4864**	**13.8412**	**14.2068**	**14.5835**	**14.9716**	**15.7836**	**16.6455**	**17.5603**	**18.5312**	**19.5614**	**20.6546**	**32.1504**
12	12.6825	13.0412	13.4121	13.7956	14.1920	14.6020	15.0258	15.4640	15.9171	16.3856	16.8699	17.8885	18.9771	20.1407	21.3843	22.7132	24.1331	39.5805
13	13.8093	14.2368	14.6803	15.1404	15.6178	16.1130	16.6268	17.1599	17.7130	18.2868	18.8821	20.1406	21.4953	22.9534	24.5227	26.2116	28.0291	48.4966
14	14.9474	15.4504	15.9739	16.5190	17.0863	17.6770	18.2919	18.9321	19.5986	20.2926	21.0151	22.5505	24.2149	26.0192	27.9750	30.0949	32.3926	59.1959
15	16.0969	16.6821	17.2934	17.9319	18.5989	19.2957	20.0236	20.7841	21.5786	22.4087	23.2760	25.1290	27.1521	29.3609	31.7725	34.4054	37.2797	72.0351
16	**17.2579**	**17.9324**	**18.6393**	**19.3802**	**20.1569**	**20.9710**	**21.8245**	**22.7193**	**23.6575**	**24.6411**	**25.6725**	**27.8881**	**30.3243**	**33.0034**	**35.9497**	**39.1899**	**42.7533**	**87.4421**
17	18.4304	19.2014	20.0121	20.8647	21.7616	22.7050	23.6975	24.7417	25.8404	26.9964	28.2129	30.8402	33.7502	36.9737	40.5447	44.5008	48.8837	105.9306
18	19.6147	20.4894	21.4123	22.3863	23.4144	24.4997	25.6454	26.8551	28.1324	29.4812	30.9057	33.9990	37.4502	41.3013	45.5992	50.3959	55.7497	128.1167
19	20.8109	21.7967	22.8406	23.9460	25.1169	26.3572	27.6712	29.0636	30.5390	32.1027	33.7600	37.3790	41.4463	46.0185	51.1591	56.9395	63.4397	154.7400
20	22.0190	23.1237	24.2974	25.5447	26.8704	28.2797	29.7781	31.3714	33.0660	34.8683	36.7856	40.9955	45.7620	51.1601	57.2750	64.2028	72.0524	186.6880
21	**23.2392**	**24.4705**	**25.7833**	**27.1833**	**28.6765**	**30.2695**	**31.9692**	**33.7831**	**35.7193**	**37.7861**	**39.9927**	**44.8652**	**50.4229**	**56.7645**	**64.0025**	**72.2651**	**81.6987**	**225.0256**
30	34.7849	37.5387	40.5681	43.9027	47.5754	51.6227	56.0849	61.0071	66.4388	72.4355	79.0582	94.4608	113.2832	136.3075	164.4940	199.0209	241.3327	1181.8816
40	48.8864	54.2679	60.4020	67.4026	75.4013	84.5503	95.0255	107.0303	120.7998	136.6056	154.7620	199.6351	259.0565	337.8824	442.5926	581.8261	767.0914	7343.8578

This table shows the future value of an annuity due of $1 at various interest rates (i) and time periods (n). It is used to calculate the future value of any series of equal payments made at the *beginning* of each compounding period.

TABLE 4 Present Value of an Ordinary Annuity of $1

$$PVA = \frac{1 - \frac{1}{(1+i)^n}}{i}$$

n/i	1.0%	1.5%	2.0%	2.5%	3.0%	3.5%	4.0%	4.5%	5.0%	5.5%	6.0%	7.0%	8.0%	9.0%	10.0%	11.0%	12.0%	20.0%
1	0.99010	0.98522	0.98039	0.97561	0.97087	0.96618	0.96154	0.95694	0.95238	0.94787	0.94340	0.93458	0.92593	0.91743	0.90909	0.90090	0.89286	0.83333
2	1.97040	1.95588	1.94156	1.92742	1.91347	1.89969	1.88609	1.87267	1.85941	1.84632	1.83339	1.80802	1.78326	1.75911	1.73554	1.71252	1.69005	1.52778
3	2.94099	2.91220	2.88388	2.85602	2.82861	2.80164	2.77509	2.74896	2.72325	2.69793	2.67301	2.62432	2.57710	2.53129	2.48685	2.44371	2.40183	2.10648
4	3.90197	3.85438	3.80773	3.76197	3.71710	3.67308	3.62990	3.58753	3.54595	3.50515	3.46511	3.38721	3.31213	3.23972	3.16987	3.10245	3.03735	2.58873
5	4.85343	4.78264	4.71346	4.64583	4.57971	4.51505	4.45182	4.38998	4.32948	4.27028	4.21236	4.10020	3.99271	3.88965	3.79079	3.69590	3.60478	2.99061
6	5.79548	5.69719	5.60143	5.50813	5.41719	5.32855	5.24214	5.15787	5.07569	4.99553	4.91732	4.76654	4.62288	4.48592	4.35526	4.23054	4.11141	3.32551
7	6.72819	6.59821	6.47199	6.34939	6.23028	6.11454	6.00205	5.89270	5.78637	5.68297	5.58238	5.38929	5.20637	5.03295	4.86842	4.71220	4.56376	3.60459
8	7.65168	7.48593	7.32548	7.17014	7.01969	6.87396	6.73274	6.59589	6.46321	6.33457	6.20979	5.97130	5.74664	5.53482	5.33493	5.14612	4.96764	3.83716
9	8.56602	8.36052	8.16224	7.97087	7.78611	7.60769	7.43533	7.26879	7.10782	6.95220	6.80169	6.51523	6.24689	5.99525	5.75902	5.53705	5.32825	4.03097
10	9.47130	9.22218	8.98259	8.75206	8.53020	8.31661	8.11090	7.91272	7.72173	7.53763	7.36009	7.02358	6.71008	6.41766	6.14457	5.88923	5.65022	4.19247
11	10.36763	10.07112	9.78685	9.51421	9.25262	9.00155	8.76048	8.52892	8.30641	8.09254	7.88687	7.49867	7.13896	6.80519	6.49506	6.20652	5.93770	4.32706
12	11.25508	10.90751	10.57534	10.25776	9.95400	9.66333	9.38507	9.11858	8.86325	8.61852	8.38384	7.94269	7.53608	7.16073	6.81369	6.49236	6.19437	4.43922
13	12.13374	11.73153	11.34837	10.98319	10.63496	10.30274	9.98565	9.68285	9.39357	9.11708	8.85268	8.35765	7.90378	7.48690	7.10336	6.74987	6.42355	4.53268
14	13.00370	12.54338	12.10625	11.69091	11.29607	10.92052	10.56312	10.22283	9.89864	9.58965	9.29498	8.74547	8.24424	7.78615	7.36669	6.98187	6.62817	4.61057
15	13.86505	13.34323	12.84926	12.38138	11.93794	11.51741	11.11839	10.73955	10.37966	10.03758	9.71225	9.10791	8.55948	8.06069	7.60608	7.19087	6.81086	4.67547
16	14.71787	14.13126	13.57771	13.05500	12.56110	12.09412	11.65230	11.23402	10.83777	10.46216	10.10590	9.44665	8.85137	8.31256	7.82371	7.37916	6.97399	4.72956
17	15.56225	14.90765	14.29187	13.71220	13.16612	12.65132	12.16567	11.70719	11.27407	10.86461	10.47726	9.76322	9.12164	8.54363	8.02155	7.54879	7.11963	4.77463
18	16.39827	15.67256	14.99203	14.35336	13.75351	13.18968	12.65930	12.15999	11.68959	11.24607	10.82760	10.05909	9.37189	8.75563	8.20141	7.70162	7.24967	4.81219
19	17.22601	16.42617	15.67846	14.97889	14.32380	13.70984	13.13394	12.59329	12.08532	11.60765	11.15812	10.33560	9.60360	8.95011	8.36492	7.83929	7.36578	4.84350
20	18.04555	17.16864	16.35143	15.58916	14.87747	14.21240	13.59033	13.00794	12.46221	11.95038	11.46992	10.59401	9.81815	9.12855	8.51356	7.96333	7.46944	4.86958
21	18.85698	17.90014	17.01121	16.18455	15.41502	14.69797	14.02916	13.40472	12.82115	12.27524	11.76408	10.83553	10.01680	9.29224	8.64869	8.07507	7.56200	4.89132
25	22.02316	20.71961	19.52346	18.42438	17.41315	16.48151	15.62208	14.82821	14.09394	13.41393	12.78336	11.65358	10.67478	9.82258	9.07704	8.42174	7.84314	4.94759
30	25.80771	24.01584	22.39646	20.93029	19.60044	18.39205	17.29203	16.28889	15.37245	14.53375	13.76483	12.40904	11.25778	10.27365	9.42691	8.69379	8.05518	4.97894
40	32.83469	29.91585	27.35548	25.10278	23.11477	21.35507	19.79277	18.40158	17.15909	16.04612	15.04630	13.33171	11.92461	10.75736	9.77905	8.95105	8.24378	4.99660

This table shows the future value of an annuity due of $1 at various interest rates (i) and time periods (n). It is used to calculate the future value of any series of equal payments made at the *beginning* of each compounding period.

TABLE 5 Future Value of an Annuity Due of $1

$$FVAD = \left[\frac{(1+i)^n - 1}{i}\right] \times (1+i)$$

n/i	1.0%	1.5%	2.0%	2.5%	3.0%	3.5%	4.0%	4.5%	5.0%	5.5%	6.0%	7.0%	8.0%	9.0%	10.0%	11.0%	12.0%	20.0%
1	1.0100	1.0150	1.0200	1.0250	1.0300	1.0350	1.0400	1.0450	1.0500	1.0550	1.0600	1.0700	1.0800	1.0900	1.1000	1.1100	1.1200	1.2000
2	2.0301	2.0452	2.0604	2.0756	2.0909	2.1062	2.1216	2.1370	2.1525	2.1680	2.1836	2.2149	2.2464	2.2781	2.3100	2.3421	2.3744	2.6400
3	3.0604	3.0909	3.1216	3.1525	3.1836	3.2149	3.2465	3.2782	3.3101	3.3423	3.3746	3.4399	3.5061	3.5731	3.6410	3.7097	3.7793	4.3680
4	4.1010	4.1523	4.2040	4.2563	4.3091	4.3625	4.4163	4.4707	4.5256	4.5811	4.6371	4.7507	4.8666	4.9847	5.1051	5.2278	5.3528	6.4416
5	5.1520	5.2296	5.3081	5.3877	5.4684	5.5502	5.6330	5.7169	5.8019	5.8881	5.9753	6.1533	6.3359	6.5233	6.7156	6.9129	7.1152	8.9299
6	6.2135	6.3230	6.4343	6.5474	6.6625	6.7794	6.8983	7.0192	7.1420	7.2669	7.3938	7.6540	7.9228	8.2004	8.4872	8.7833	9.0890	11.9159
7	7.2857	7.4328	7.5830	7.7361	7.8923	8.0517	8.2142	8.3800	8.5491	8.7216	8.8975	9.2598	9.6366	10.0285	10.4359	10.8594	11.2997	15.4991
8	8.3685	8.5593	8.7546	8.9545	9.1591	9.3685	9.5828	9.8021	10.0266	10.2563	10.4913	10.9780	11.4876	12.0210	12.5795	13.1640	13.7757	19.7989
9	9.4622	9.7027	9.9497	10.2034	10.4639	10.7314	11.0061	11.2882	11.5779	11.8754	12.1808	12.8164	13.4866	14.1929	14.9374	15.7220	16.5487	24.9587
10	10.5668	10.8633	11.1687	11.4835	11.8078	12.1420	12.4864	12.8412	13.2068	13.5835	13.9716	14.7836	15.6455	16.5603	17.5312	18.5614	19.6546	31.1504
11	11.6825	12.0412	12.4121	12.7956	13.1920	13.6020	14.0258	14.4640	14.9171	15.3856	15.8699	16.8885	17.9771	19.1407	20.3843	21.7132	23.1331	38.5805
12	12.8093	13.2368	13.6803	14.1404	14.6178	15.1130	15.6268	16.1599	16.7130	17.2868	17.8821	19.1406	20.4953	21.9534	23.5227	25.2116	27.0291	47.4966
13	13.9474	14.4504	14.9739	15.5190	16.0863	16.6770	17.2919	17.9321	18.5986	19.2926	20.0151	21.5505	23.2149	25.0192	26.9750	29.0949	31.3926	58.1959
14	15.0969	15.6821	16.2934	16.9319	17.5989	18.2957	19.0236	19.7841	20.5786	21.4087	22.2760	24.1290	26.1521	28.3609	30.7725	33.4054	36.2797	71.0351
15	16.2579	16.9324	17.6393	18.3802	19.1569	19.9710	20.8245	21.7193	22.6575	23.6411	24.6725	26.8881	29.3243	32.0034	34.9497	38.1899	41.7533	86.4421
16	17.4304	18.2014	19.0121	19.8647	20.7616	21.7050	22.6975	23.7417	24.8404	25.9964	27.2129	29.8402	32.7502	35.9737	39.5447	43.5008	47.8837	104.9306
17	18.6147	19.4894	20.4123	21.3863	22.4144	23.4997	24.6454	25.8551	27.1324	28.4812	29.9057	32.9990	36.4502	40.3013	44.5992	49.3959	54.7497	127.1167
18	19.8109	20.7967	21.8406	22.9460	24.1169	25.3572	26.6712	28.0636	29.5390	31.1027	32.7600	36.3790	40.4463	45.0185	50.1591	55.9395	62.4397	153.7400
19	21.0190	22.1237	23.2974	24.5447	25.8704	27.2797	28.7781	30.3714	32.0660	33.8683	35.7856	39.9955	44.7620	50.1601	56.2750	63.2028	71.0524	185.6880
20	22.2392	23.4705	24.7833	26.1833	27.6765	29.2695	30.9692	32.7831	34.7193	36.7861	38.9927	43.8652	49.4229	55.7645	63.0025	71.2651	80.6987	224.0256
21	23.4716	24.8376	26.2990	27.8629	29.5368	31.3289	33.2480	35.3034	37.5052	39.8643	42.3923	48.0057	54.4568	61.8733	70.4027	80.2143	91.5026	270.0307
25	28.5256	30.5140	32.6709	35.0117	37.5530	40.3131	43.3117	46.5706	50.1135	53.9660	58.1564	67.6765	78.9544	92.3240	108.1818	126.9988	149.3339	566.3773
30	35.1327	38.1018	41.3794	45.0003	49.0027	53.4295	58.3283	63.7524	69.7608	76.4194	83.8017	101.0730	122.3459	148.5752	180.9434	220.9132	270.2926	1418.2579
40	49.3752	55.0819	61.6100	69.0876	77.6633	87.5095	98.8265	111.8467	126.8398	144.1189	164.0477	213.6096	279.7810	368.2919	486.8518	645.8269	859.1424	8812.6294

This table shows the present value of an annuity due of $1 at various interest rates (i) and time periods (n). It is used to calculate the present value of any series of equal payments made at the *beginning* of each compounding period.

TABLE 6 Present Value of an Annuity Due of $1

$$PVAD = \left[\frac{1 - \frac{1}{(1+i)^n}}{i}\right] \times (1+i)$$

n/i	1.0%	1.5%	2.0%	2.5%	3.0%	3.5%	4.0%	4.5%	5.0%	5.5%	6.0%	7.0%	8.0%	9.0%	10.0%	11.0%	12.0%	20.0%
1	1.00000	1.00000	1.00000	1.00000	1.00000	1.00000	1.00000	1.00000	1.00000	1.00000	1.00000	1.00000	1.00000	1.00000	1.00000	1.00000	1.00000	1.00000
2	1.99010	1.98522	1.98039	1.97561	1.97087	1.96618	1.96154	1.95694	1.95238	1.94787	1.94340	1.93458	1.92593	1.91743	1.90909	1.90090	1.89286	1.83333
3	2.97040	2.95588	2.94156	2.92742	2.91347	2.89969	2.88609	2.87267	2.85941	2.84632	2.83339	2.80802	2.78326	2.75911	2.73554	2.71252	2.69005	2.52778
4	3.94099	3.91220	3.88388	3.85602	3.82861	3.80164	3.77509	3.74896	3.72325	3.69793	3.67301	3.62432	3.57710	3.53129	3.48685	3.44371	3.40183	3.10648
5	4.90197	4.85438	4.80773	4.76197	4.71710	4.67308	4.62990	4.58753	4.54595	4.50515	4.46511	4.38721	4.31213	4.23972	4.16987	4.10245	4.03735	3.58873
6	5.85343	5.78264	5.71346	5.64583	5.57971	5.51505	5.45182	5.38998	5.32948	5.27028	5.21236	5.10020	4.99271	4.88965	4.79079	4.69590	4.60478	3.99061
7	6.79548	6.69719	6.60143	6.50813	6.41719	6.32855	6.24214	6.15787	6.07569	5.99553	5.91732	5.76654	5.62288	5.48592	5.35526	5.23054	5.11141	4.32551
8	7.72819	7.59821	7.47199	7.34939	7.23028	7.11454	7.00205	6.89270	6.78637	6.68297	6.58238	6.38929	6.20637	6.03295	5.86842	5.71220	5.56376	4.60459
9	8.65168	8.48593	8.32548	8.17014	8.01969	7.87396	7.73274	7.59589	7.46321	7.33457	7.20979	6.97130	6.74664	6.53482	6.33493	6.14612	5.96764	4.83716
10	9.56602	9.36052	9.16224	8.97087	8.78611	8.60769	8.43533	8.26879	8.10782	7.95220	7.80169	7.51523	7.24689	6.99525	6.75902	6.53705	6.32825	5.03097
11	10.47130	10.22218	9.98259	9.75206	9.53020	9.31661	9.11090	8.91272	8.72173	8.53763	8.36009	8.02358	7.71008	7.41766	7.14457	6.88923	6.65022	5.19247
12	11.36763	11.07112	10.78685	10.51421	10.25262	10.00155	9.76048	9.52892	9.30641	9.09254	8.88687	8.49867	8.13896	7.80519	7.49506	7.20652	6.93770	5.32706
13	12.25508	11.90751	11.57534	11.25776	10.95400	10.66333	10.38507	10.11858	9.86325	9.61852	9.38384	8.94269	8.53608	8.16073	7.81369	7.49236	7.19437	5.43922
14	13.13374	12.73153	12.34837	11.98318	11.63496	11.30274	10.98565	10.68285	10.39357	10.11708	9.85268	9.35765	8.90378	8.48690	8.10336	7.74987	7.42355	5.53268
15	14.00370	13.54338	13.10625	12.69091	12.29607	11.92052	11.56312	11.22283	10.89864	10.58965	10.29498	9.74547	9.24424	8.78615	8.36669	7.98187	7.62817	5.61057
16	14.86505	14.34323	13.84926	13.38138	12.93794	12.51741	12.11839	11.73955	11.37966	11.03758	10.71225	10.10791	9.55948	9.06069	8.60608	8.19087	7.81086	5.67547
17	15.71787	15.13126	14.57771	14.05500	13.56110	13.09412	12.65230	12.23402	11.83777	11.46216	11.10590	10.44665	9.85137	9.31256	8.82371	8.37916	7.97399	5.72956
18	16.56225	15.90765	15.29187	14.71220	14.16612	13.65132	13.16567	12.70719	12.27407	11.86461	11.47726	10.76322	10.12164	9.54363	9.02155	8.54879	8.11963	5.77463
19	17.39827	16.67256	15.99203	15.35336	14.75351	14.18968	13.65930	13.15999	12.68959	12.24607	11.82760	11.05909	10.37189	9.75563	9.20141	8.70162	8.24967	5.81219
20	18.22601	17.42617	16.67846	15.97889	15.32380	14.70984	14.13394	13.59329	13.08532	12.60765	12.15812	11.33560	10.60360	9.95011	9.36492	8.83929	8.36578	5.84350
21	19.04555	18.16864	17.35143	16.58916	15.87747	15.21240	14.59033	14.00794	13.46221	12.95038	12.46992	11.59401	10.81815	10.12855	9.51356	8.96333	8.46944	5.86958
25	22.24339	21.03041	19.91393	18.88499	17.93554	17.05837	16.24696	15.49548	14.79864	14.15170	13.55036	12.46933	11.52876	10.70661	9.98474	9.34814	8.78432	5.93710
30	26.06579	24.37608	22.84438	21.45355	20.18845	19.03577	17.98371	17.02189	16.14107	15.33310	14.59072	13.27767	12.15841	11.19828	10.36961	9.65011	9.02181	5.97472
40	33.16303	30.36458	27.90259	25.73034	23.80822	22.10250	20.58448	19.22966	18.01704	16.92866	15.94907	14.26493	12.87858	11.72552	10.75696	9.93567	9.23303	5.99592

Online Supplements

Connect Online Access for Intermediate Accounting, Ninth Edition

McGraw-Hill Connect is a digital teaching and learning environment that improves performance over a variety of critical outcomes. With Connect, instructors can deliver assignments, quizzes and tests easily online. Students can practice important skills at their own pace and on their own schedule.

HOW TO REGISTER

Using a Print Book?
To register and activate your Connect account, simply follow these easy steps:

1. **Go to the Connect course web address provided by your instructor or visit the Connect link set up on your instructor's course within your campus learning management system.**
2. **Click on the link to register.**
3. **When prompted, enter the Connect code found on the inside back cover of your book and click Submit. Complete the brief registration form that follows to begin using Connect.**

Using an eBook?
To register and activate your Connect account, simply follow these easy steps:

1. **Upon purchase of your eBook, you will be granted automatic access to Connect.**
2. **Go to the Connect course web address provided by your instructor or visit the Connect link set up on your instructor's course within your campus learning management system.**
3. **Sign in using the same email address and password you used to register on the eBookstore. Complete your registration and begin using Connect.**

**Note: Access Code is for one use only. If you did not purchase this book new, the access code included in this book is no longer valid.*

Need help? Visit mhhe.com/support